HBO's
Guide to
MOVIES
on
VIDEO-CASSETTE
and
CABLE TV
1990

PERENNIAL LIBRARY

Harper & Row, Publishers, New York
Grand Rapids, Philadelphia, St. Louis, San Francisco
London, Singapore, Sydney, Tokyo, Toronto

HOME BOX OFFICE

Editors
Daniel Eagan
Olga Humphrey
Douglas Lee
Linda Sunshine

Contributing Editors
Robert Potter
Ted Winterer

Administrative Editor
Joanne Grazi

Research Assistants
Mary Ellen Donohue
Amy Strong

HBO'S GUIDE TO MOVIES ON VIDEOCASSETTE AND CABLE TV 1990. Copyright © 1989 by Home Box Office. All rights reserved. Printed in the United States of America. No part of this book may be used or reproduced in any manner whatsoever without written permission except in the case of brief quotations embodied in critical articles and reviews. For information address Harper & Row, Publishers, Inc., 10 East 53rd Street, New York, NY 10022.

FIRST EDITION

Designed by Karen Savary

Library of Congress Cataloging-in-Publication Data

HBO's guide to movies on videocassette and cable TV 1990 / editors, Daniel
    Eagan . . . [et al.]. — 1st ed.
        p.   cm.
    ISBN 0-06-096356-5
    1. Video recordings—Catalogs.   2. Videocassettes—Catalogs.   3. Motion
pictures—Catalogs.   I. Eagan, Daniel.   II. Harper & Row, Publishers.   III.
Title: Cable TV 1990
PN1992.95.H3   1989
016.79143'75—dc20   89-19861

89 90 91 92 93 CC/FG 10 9 8 7 6 5 4 3 2 1

Working from a sixteen-year tradition of quality entertainment as America's premier pay-TV service, HBO has amassed a wealth of material on thousands of films on videocassette and shown on cable TV—information not readily available to the viewing public. After numerous requests from our subscribers for an unbiased, comprehensive guide to these films, we set out to write a book that would combine the best aspects of film reference guides with the unique information we've gathered here at HBO. The result is **HBO's Guide to Movies on Videocassette and Cable TV,** a book that includes the details we know interest viewers the most about a wide range of popular feature films: accurate synopses, impartial ratings based on the opinions of HBO viewers, full credits, cautions about potentially offensive material, running times, important awards, and much more.

Over 5,000 Listings

We began this project by assembling a list of some 5,000 films, selecting the titles we felt would be most popular and therefore most likely to be rented by our readers. Our selection covers every type of film, from romance to Western, thriller to biography, documentary to musical.

Our first criterion was that the film be available on videocassette, as all our more than 5,000 titles are. The vast majority of these titles have also played or will play on cable TV as well. After we were satisfied with our film choices, our team of researchers carefully checked title variations, credits, and running times. For films that underwent title changes, we've listed them under their most frequently used names while mentioning alternative titles in the synopsis. For example, the British film *Tight Little Island* is found under its American name, *Whisky Galore!,* while a film that was called variously *Shivers* and *The Parasite Murders* appears under its most common title, *They Came From Within.* Exceptions are foreign films that are usually known by their original titles (e.g., *La Dolce*

Vita, Mon Oncle d'Amerique, etc.). We've also reverted to original titles for films that were rereleased under different names (e.g., *Rose Marie,* not *Indian Love Call; Honeysuckle Rose,* not *On the Road Again*).

All films are arranged alphabetically for quick reference. Our method was to list each title in strict alphabetical order, ignoring both initial articles "the," "an," and "a" and punctuation within a title. Numbers are treated as if they were spelled out. The only exceptions are films within a series, which are listed chronologically (e.g., *Rocky II* follows *Rocky*).

The information included for each film is also arranged for easy use. The categories are largely self-evident, but some warrant additional clarification.

Subscribers Rate the Films, Not Critics

Star recommendations are one of the most important features of the book and were carefully developed. After every screening of a film on the HBO services, researchers poll randomly selected viewers to record their impressions. The findings are entered into a computer program that ranks films according to viewer "satisfaction." The entries in this book received star recommendations as described below:

★ ★ ★ ★ ★	Excellent
★ ★ ★ ★	Very good
★ ★ ★	Good
★ ★	Fair
★	Poor
☆	Not recommended

It's worth repeating that these recommendations are derived *solely from our viewers' preferences,* not individual opinions of the HBO staff. This ensures that the stars accurately reflect the mainstream audience and not one critic's particular—and perhaps biased—opinion. Some critically praised films targeted toward smaller, more demanding audiences; older black-and-white films; foreign films; and documentaries are not as popular with our viewers, but the synopsis will generally reflect how successfully the film accomplishes its goals. We hope that by using our star rating system, you'll be able to discover a number of underappreciated gems that have been either overlooked or dismissed by critics. Our star rating system shows you the movies our subscribers really enjoy.

Ratings are assigned for the purpose of alerting viewers that material contained within a movie may be deemed inappropriate for young viewers. We consulted the Motion Picture Association of America

(MPAA) for their official ratings, the same ratings used when movies are released theatrically. MPAA classifications are

G	"General Audiences. All ages admitted."
PG	"Parental Guidance Suggested. Some material may not be suitable for children."
PG-13	"Parents Strongly Cautioned. Some material may be inappropriate for children under 13."
R	"Restricted. Under 17 requires accompanying parent or adult guardian." (Please note: age may vary in different jurisdictions.)
X	"No one under 17 admitted." (Again, age may vary.)
NR	"No Rating."

Unless distributors resubmitted titles for new ratings, most theatrical films made before 1968 and all made-for-TV films receive an NR, or no rating. Exceptions apply here as well. Most Walt Disney Studio movies, for example, have been recently resubmitted to achieve a G rating. In some instances, distributors have added material to home cassette releases that invalidate the MPAA ratings; e.g., cassette versions of *Angel Heart* and *Warrior Queen* contain additional erotic material and no longer qualify as R films. Instances like these have been noted in the synopses.

Cautions Help Families Plan Their Viewing

Cautions are a second unique feature of our book. Every movie shown on HBO has been carefully screened by our staff of professional evaluators to note the presence of material that could prove offensive to some viewers. Evaluators note, in order of importance to our viewers, whether the movie contains any of the following situations:

Rape	Explicit language
Nudity	Graphic violence
Brief nudity	Violence
Strong sexual content	Mild violence
Adult situations	Adult humor

These ten categories are largely self-explanatory. "Adult situations" refers to material of a violent or sexual nature that parents may not want younger viewers to see. While some older (pre-1960) films contain scenes or themes best appreciated by mature viewers, in general, Hollywood studios treated them in a discreet manner that does not offend contemporary audiences.

Genre classifications are included for every film. We provided these categories as a loose umbrella to help guide you in your choice of films. Our genres include Action-Adventure, Animation, Biography, Comedy, Crime, Dance, Documentary, Drama, Espionage, Family (i.e., recommended for family viewing, not necessarily about the family), Fantasy, Horror, MFTV (made for TV), Martial Arts, Music, Musical, Mystery-Suspense, Romance, Sci-Fi, Sex, Sports, War, and Western.

In some instances, a film proves hard to classify because it crosses over two categories, such as a drama that includes a lot of comedy; in these cases, both genres will be listed. Some viewers may quibble with a film listed as "Horror" instead of "Sci-Fi," but on the whole, the categories make a useful guideline.

Release dates can vary widely, particularly for a film that received little or no theatrical exposure. We've generally included the year the film received theatrical release in America; in lieu of that, we've chosen the date the film was copyrighted.

Country of origin refers not only to where the film was released, but also to where it was produced. For example, although the 1950 version of *Treasure Island* was filmed in Great Britain with English actors, it is considered an American film because it was produced by Walt Disney Studio. Similarly, *Paris, Texas* is classified as French/German because its production companies were based in those countries. For foreign films, we've noted when the English version is dubbed or subtitled.

Running times proved particularly difficult to verify, especially in those cases where studios added or deleted footage for videocassette release. The running times in this book conform as nearly as possible to the times on videocassette, and should prove reliable in those instances where various versions of a particular film exist.

Synopses provided for each film emphasize plot over critical opinion. Even among our staff of writers, opinions vary greatly over each film. For this reason, we tried to be objective and, as much as possible, restrict our writing to story lines and character descriptions. For your reference, we also list the director and up to six actors and actresses (in order of their star billing) for each film.

Closed captioned versions of numerous films exist for the convenience of the hearing-impaired. If a title has been closed-captioned, the symbol **(CC)** follows the synopsis.

Subtitled foreign films are preferred to dubbed versions of the same movies by many viewers. The symbol $\boxed{S}$ signifies availability of a subtitled version on videocassette.

Comprehensive Indexes

At the back of the book, we have included an index in each of three categories, providing listings arranged by genre, director, and cast to enable you to easily find the films that will be of most interest to you.

Summing up, our purpose in creating **HBO's Guide to Movies on Videocassette and Cable TV** was to help introduce you to the best films currently on home video and cable TV.

Last, but not least, we'd like to acknowledge the many people at HBO who contributed to this project. Michael Fuchs, Chairman of HBO, was enthusiastic and supportive throughout our work. Larry Carlson guided the book from its opening stages. Doug Lee, who conceived the project, and Art Bell, who saw it through to completion, deserve special thanks. Film evaluators Roger Blunck, Ty Burr, Jim Byerley, Camilla Carpenter, Howard Cohen, Harriet Greisser, David Himelfarb, Susan McGuirk, Steve Molton, Rob Odell, and Mary Suarez provided valuable information. We are indebted to the assistance received from computer experts Bruce Probst, Rose Han, Tim Daly, Roslyn Gottlieb, Stephen Flax, and Larry Jacobson. Finally, Carol Cohen, Susan Randol, Helen Moore, and Eric Wirth at Harper & Row were crucial in assuring the publication of this book.

Happy viewing!

ABBOTT AND COSTELLO MEET FRANKENSTEIN 1948
★★★ NR Comedy 1:23 B&W
Dir: Charles Barton *Cast:* Bud Abbott, Lou Costello, Lon Chaney, Jr., Bela Lugosi, Glenn Strange, Jane Randolph
▶ One of Bud and Lou's most popular films is a surprisingly effective mix of laughs and chills. Plot has the boys getting involved with Dracula (Lugosi), Frankenstein (Strange), the Wolfman (Chaney, Jr.), and a scheme to transplant Costello's brain inside the monster's body.

ABE LINCOLN IN ILLINOIS 1940
★★★ NR Biography 1:50 B&W
Dir: John Cromwell *Cast:* Raymond Massey, Gene Lockhart, Ruth Gordon, Mary Howard, Dorothy Tree, Harvey Stephens
▶ Earnest, believable biography of Lincoln shows a broader picture of his life—including tragic first love Ann Rutledge (Howard), law practice, debates with Stephen Douglas (Lockhart), and Presidential election—than its competitor, *Young Abe Lincoln*. Massey won an Oscar nomination for his historically accurate portrayal of Lincoln. Adapted by Robert Sherwood from his Pulitzer prize-winning play.

ABOUT LAST NIGHT 1986
★★★★ R Drama 1:53
☑ Nudity, adult situations, explicit language
Dir: Edward Zwick *Cast:* Rob Lowe, Demi Moore, James Belushi, Elizabeth Perkins, George DiCenzo
▶ Glossy romance set in Chicago examines the stormy relationship between Lowe and Moore as they experiment with living together. Sanitized version of playwright David Mamet's *Sexual Perversity in Chicago* scores points with the supporting work by Belushi and Perkins.

ABOVE THE LAW 1988
★★★ R Action-Adventure 1:44
☑ Explicit language, violence
Dir: Andrew Davis *Cast:* Steven Seagal, Pam Grier, Sharon Stone, Daniel Faraldo, Henry Silva, Ronnie Barron
▶ Ex-CIA agent Seagal is suspended from Chicago police after he tries to shut down government-sponsored drug ring. When his family is attacked, he introduces his own version of the law to the Windy City villains. Crude but effective thriller marred by muddy politics. Film debut for former bodyguard Seagal (who also produced and co-wrote the story). (CC)

ABSENCE OF MALICE 1981
★★★★★ PG Drama 1:56
☑ Adult situations, explicit language, mild violence
Dir: Sydney Pollack *Cast:* Paul Newman, Sally Field, Melinda Dillon, Luther Adler, Bob Balaban
▶ Ex-newspaperman Kurt Luedtke wrote the screenplay for this engrossing drama of overzealous journalism and its human toll. Newman stars as a legitimate businessman unjustly implicated in a labor boss murder by journalist Field. Newman manages to clear his name, get his revenge, and engage in a romance with the conscience-stricken Field. Oscar-nominated performances by Newman, Field, and Dillon.

ABSENT MINDED PROFESSOR, THE 1961
★★★★ NR Comedy 1:37 B&W
Dir: Robert Stevenson *Cast:* Fred MacMurray, Nancy Olson, Keenan Wynn, Tommy Kirk, Leon Ames, Ed Wynn
▶ Delightful screwball comedy with MacMurray as a professor who invents "flubber," an antigravity potion that gives magical flying powers to ordinary rubber. Keenan Wynn plays an industrial spy determined to steal the formula; his father Ed has a cameo as the fire chief. Above-par Disney film was followed by *Son of Flubber*. Available in a colorized version.

ABSOLUTE BEGINNERS 1986 British
★ PG-13 Musical 1:48
☑ Adult situations, explicit language, violence
Dir: Julien Temple *Cast:* Eddie O'Connell, Patsy Kensit, Ray Davies, David Bowie, Sade Adu
▶ A young photographer pursues a beautiful model amid London's swinging sixties fashion scene. Expensive adaptation of a cult novel by Colin MacInnes features elaborate musical productions, amusing cameos by rock stars Bowie, Davies, and Sade, and hyperkinetic direction by rock video master Julien Temple.

ACCIDENT 1966 British
★ NR Drama 1:45
Dir: Joseph Losey *Cast:* Dirk Bogarde, Stanley Baker, Jacqueline Sassard, Delphine Seyrig, Alexander Knox, Michael York
▶ Oxford undergraduate's death in a car

crash brings into focus competition between teachers Bogarde and Baker, both obsessed with victim's girlfriend Sassard. Intricate flashback structure and cryptic dialogue by playwright Harold Pinter form an intriguing intellectual puzzle about the English class system.

ACCIDENTAL TOURIST, THE 1988
★★★ PG Drama 2:02
☑ Adult situations
Dir: Lawrence Kasdan   *Cast:* William Hurt, Kathleen Turner, Geena Davis, Amy Wright, Bill Pullman, Ed Begley, Jr.
▶ Travel writer Hurt becomes increasingly set in his eccentric ways after his son dies and wife Turner leaves. It takes a relationship with kooky dog trainer Davis to bring him out of his shell. Wonderful adaptation of the Anne Tyler best-seller is alternately funny (Wright shines in scenes of Hurt's bizarre family; don't overlook Hurt's dog) and tender (Hurt telling Davis about his son, Hurt teaching Davis's son to fix sink). Marvelously restrained Hurt registers maximum emotion with the subtlest facial gestures, while delightful, Oscar-winning Davis wins his heart and yours. Nominations for Best Picture, Screenplay Adaptation, and Original Score.

ACCUSED, THE 1988
★★★★ R Drama 1:55
☑ Rape, nudity, strong sexual content, explicit language, violence
Dir: Jonathan Kaplan   *Cast:* Kelly McGillis, Jodie Foster, Bernie Coulson, Leo Rossi, Ann Hearn, Carmen Argenziano
▶ Provocative drama examines the legal difficulties in prosecuting men who gang-raped waitress Foster in a seedy bar. Attorney McGillis reluctantly settles for lesser charge of reckless endangerment; egged on by Foster, she then prosecutes the onlookers who cheered on the rapists. Apart from powerful climax and Foster's bravura, Oscar-winning performance, a routine examination of a potentially devastating subject.

ACROSS 110TH STREET 1972
★★★★ R Action-Adventure 1:42
☑ Graphic violence
Dir: Barry Shear   *Cast:* Anthony Quinn, Yaphet Kotto, Anthony Franciosa, Paul Benjamin
▶ Hard-hitting, slam-bang crime melodrama features Quinn and Kotto as cops caught in the middle of a gang war when three blacks steal $30,000 from a Mafia numbers bank. A suspenseful but quite brutal film that should please action fans (although it didn't please the Legion of Decency, which condemned it).

ACROSS THE PACIFIC 1942
★★★ NR Action-Adventure 1:37 B&W
Dir: John Huston   *Cast:* Humphrey Bogart, Mary Astor, Sydney Greenstreet, Victor Sen Yung, Keye Luke
▶ Wartime thriller reunites the stars and director of *The Maltese Falcon*. Not in the same league as that classic, but still quick-moving espionage fun as secret agent Bogart takes on Greenstreet, a professor with ties to the Japanese, with mysterious Astor caught in the middle. Available in a colorized version.

ACTION IN THE NORTH ATLANTIC 1943
★★★ NR Action-Adventure 2:07 B&W
Dir: Lloyd Bacon   *Cast:* Humphrey Bogart, Raymond Massey, Alan Hale, Julie Bishop, Ruth Gordon, Dane Clark
▶ Brisk salute to the Merchant Marine during World War II follows the crew of a freighter dodging deadly U-boats while delivering supplies to Murmansk, Russia. Vivid characterizations of idealistic captain Massey, loyal first mate Bogart, and temperamental Polish seaman Clark buttress the exciting scenes of wartime heroics. Available in a colorized version.

ACTION JACKSON 1988
★★★ R Action-Adventure 1:36
☑ Nudity, explicit language, graphic violence
Dir: Craig Baxley   *Cast:* Carl Weathers, Vanity, Craig T. Nelson, Sharon Stone, Sonny Landham
▶ Weathers (Apollo Creed in the *Rocky* movies) is Jackson, a Harvard Law School grad and Detroit supercop trying to win back his stripes after a run-in with corrupt union official/karate expert Nelson. Routine formula picture enlivened by terrific stunts, nonstop (and violent) action, and the presence of sultry rock star Vanity. (CC)

ACT OF VENGEANCE 1986
★★★★ NR Biography/MFTV 1:36
☑ Adult situations, explicit language, violence
Dir: John Mackenzie   *Cast:* Charles Bronson, Ellen Burstyn, Wilford Brimley, Ellen Barkin
▶ Bronson excels in a change-of-pace role as United Mine Workers official Jo-

seph "Jock" Yablonski, who was eventually murdered for his reformist plans. A compelling true-life drama with a solid cast that includes Burstyn as Yablonski's wife and Brimley as Tony Boyle, the corrupt official convicted of the murder.

ADAM 1983
★★★★ NR Drama/MFTV 1:40
Dir: Michael Tuchner   *Cast:* Daniel J. Travanti, JoBeth Williams, Martha Scott, Richard Masur, Paul Regina
▶ Superior telemovie about John Walsh (Travanti) and wife Williams's living hell after their child Adam mysteriously disappears. Unhappy true story (Adam was never found) led to missing children's legislation. Wrenching drama with superb performances. In real life, Walsh went on to host Fox-TV's *Most Wanted*. **(CC)**

ADAM'S RIB 1949
★★★★ NR Comedy 1:41 B&W
Dir: George Cukor   *Cast:* Katharine Hepburn, Spencer Tracy, Judy Holliday, Tom Ewell, Jean Hagen
▶ Sixth teaming of Hepburn and Tracy is a classic battle-of-the-sexes comedy. She's a lawyer defending Holliday in a shooting case; he's her husband as well as the opposing attorney. The stars have never been more delightful, and they're supported by an expert cast. Brilliant script by Ruth Gordon and Garson Kanin and smooth direction by Cukor made this one of the most popular of the duo's comedies.

ADVENTURE OF SHERLOCK HOLMES' SMARTER BROTHER, THE 1975
★★★ PG Comedy 1:31
☑ Adult situations
Dir: Gene Wilder   *Cast:* Gene Wilder, Madeline Kahn, Marty Feldman, Dom DeLuise, Leo McKern, Thorley Walters
▶ Sherlock Holmes satire stars Wilder (who also wrote and directed) as Sigerson Holmes, obsessively jealous of his more famous brother but brilliant in his own right, tackling the evil Professor Moriarty (McKern). Feldman provides Watsonesque support as Sigerson's associate. In the broad tradition of Mel Brooks but somewhat sweeter in tone. Comic highlight: a musical number, "The Kangaroo Hop."

ADVENTURES IN BABYSITTING 1987
★★★★ PG-13 Comedy 1:39
☑ Explicit language, mild violence
Dir: Chris Columbus   *Cast:* Elisabeth Shue, Maia Brewton, Anthony Rapp, Keith Coogan, Calvin Levels
▶ A broad comedy of errors in which suburban babysitter Shue and her two young charges are chased through inner-city Chicago by car thieves, street gangs, mobsters, and even blues singers. Debut film from Spielberg protégé Columbus has a naive point of view but is fast-paced entertainment. **(CC)**

ADVENTURES OF BUCKAROO BANZAI, THE: ACROSS THE 8TH DIMENSION 1984
★★ PG Sci-Fi 1:42
☑ Adult situations, explicit language, mild violence
Dir: W. D. Richter   *Cast:* John Lithgow, Peter Weller, Ellen Barkin, Christopher Lloyd, Jeff Goldblum
▶ Wild sci-fi farce with neurosurgeon/ rock star/race-car driver Banzai (Weller) out to save the Earth from mad scientists, aliens, and World War III. He's aided by the Hong Kong Cavaliers, electroids from Planet 10, and Penny Priddy (Barkin), his dead wife's twin sister. Dense plotting, breathless pacing, and an over-the-top performance from Lithgow have made this a cult item, but the film's tongue-in-cheek style and deliberately obscure story line are not for all tastes.

ADVENTURES OF BULLWHIP GRIFFIN, THE 1967
★★★★ NR Action-Adventure 1:50
Dir: James Neilson   *Cast:* Roddy McDowall, Suzanne Pleshette, Karl Malden, Harry Guardino, Brian Russell, Mike Mazurki
▶ Young Russell, accompanied by proper family butler McDowall, leaves Boston to make his fortune in the San Francisco Gold Rush. Delightful Disney adventure highlighted by a slapstick fistfight between McDowall and Mountain Ox (Mazurki). Barbershop quartet numbers and title cards in the silent film style are amusing touches.

ADVENTURES OF DON JUAN 1949
★★★ NR Action-Adventure 1:50
Dir: Vincent Sherman   *Cast:* Errol Flynn, Viveca Lindfors, Robert Douglas, Alan Hale, Romney Brent, Robert Warwick
▶ As a seventeenth-century roué, Flynn forsakes romance to save his queen Lindfors from the machinations of evil duke Douglas. Lavish, action-filled swashbuckler poked fun at Flynn's reputation as a

great lover and won a Costume Design Oscar.

ADVENTURES OF HERCULES 1985
Italian
★ **PG Action-Adventure 1:30**
☑ Violence
Dir: Lewis Coates (Luigi Cozzi) *Cast:* Lou Ferrigno, Milly Carlucci, Sonia Viviani, William Berger, Carlotta Green
▶ Hercules has to recover Zeus's seven thunderbolts by murdering a Fire Monster, the Spider Queen of the Amazons, and assorted other villains. Ferrigno is the muscle-bound hero in this Italian sequel to 1983's *Hercules*. Both films were shot at the same time with Italian unknowns, and feature bad dubbing, cheesy special effects, and ridiculous dialogue. Even kids may be disappointed. **(CC)**

ADVENTURES OF HUCKLEBERRY FINN, THE 1960
★★★ **NR Action-Adventure 1:47**
Dir: Michael Curtiz *Cast:* Tony Randall, Eddie Hodges, Archie Moore, Patty McCormick, Neville Brand, Buster Keaton
▶ Huckleberry Finn (Hodges) and escaped slave Jim (Moore) travel down the Mississippi via raft and get into all sorts of adventures, such as encountering con man Randall. Entertaining adaptation of the Mark Twain classic; former boxing champ Moore is the standout in a fine cast.

ADVENTURES OF HUCKLEBERRY FINN, THE 1985
★★★★ **NR Family 2:01**
Dir: Peter H. Hunt *Cast:* Patrick Day, Samm-Art Williams, Jim Dale, Frederic Forrest, Lillian Gish, Barnard Hughes
▶ Mark Twain's classic adventure receives a flavorful treatment in this first-rate adaptation. Day is disarming as the shrewd rascal Huck; Williams brings depth and dignity to his role as escaped slave Jim. Peppered with wonderful supporting actors, including Richard Kiley, Geraldine Page, and Butterfly McQueen.

ADVENTURES OF MARK TWAIN, THE 1944
★★★ **NR Biography 2:10 B&W**
Dir: Irving Rapper *Cast:* Fredric March, Alexis Smith, Donald Crisp, Alan Hale, C. Aubrey Smith, John Carradine
▶ Respectful biography of the great humorist, capably played by March, follows his picaresque career as a steamboat navigator on the Mississippi, editor in the

Wild West, and world-famous lecturer. Not always factual, but shows the inspiration for many of Twain's best stories. Carradine stands out in a large cast as fellow writer Bret Harte.

ADVENTURES OF ROBIN HOOD, THE 1938
★★★★ **NR Action-Adventure 1:42**
Dir: Michael Curtiz, William Keighley *Cast:* Errol Flynn, Olivia de Havilland, Basil Rathbone, Claude Rains, Patric Knowles
▶ Perhaps the most famous of all swashbuckling movies, this classic adventure is first-rate on all levels. Flynn is perfect as the charming bandit who steals from the rich and gives to the poor. He's assisted by superb performances by Eugene Pallette, Alan Hale, and other famous character actors, with Rathbone especially memorable as the evil Sir Guy. Sumptuous production values, Oscar-winning score by Erich Korngold, and sparkling Technicolor are big bonuses. An enduring favorite for all ages.

ADVENTURES OF ROBINSON CRUSOE 1954 Mexican
★★ **NR Action-Adventure 1:30**
Dir: Luis Buñuel *Cast:* Dan O'Herlihy, Jaime Fernandez, Felipe De Alba, Chel Lopez
▶ Straightforward adaptation of the classic Defoe tale about a seventeenth-century shipwrecked mariner aptly played by O'Herlihy. Screenplay remains faithful to the novel, concentrating on realistic details that capture Crusoe's humanity during his twenty-eight years on a desert island. Stunning photography, a moving score by Anthony Collins, and assured direction add up to a film everyone can enjoy. O'Herlihy was nominated for Best Actor.

ADVENTURES OF SHERLOCK HOLMES, THE 1939
★★★★ **NR Mystery-Suspense 1:22 B&W**
Dir: Alfred Werker *Cast:* Basil Rathbone, Nigel Bruce, Ida Lupino, Alan Marshal, Terry Kilburn, George Zucco
▶ Sequel to *The Hound of the Baskervilles*, which introduced the inspired casting of Rathbone as Holmes and Bruce as his bumbling sidekick Dr. Watson. Moriarty (Zucco), the detective's perennial nemesis, plans to steal the crown jewels while throwing Rathbone off the trail with a series of murders in foggy Victorian En-

gland. Gripping, atmospheric fun for all ages; followed by long-running series setting Holmes in modern era, starting with *Sherlock Holmes and the Voice of Terror.* **(CC)**

ADVENTURES OF THE WILDERNESS FAMILY, THE 1976
★★★★★ **G Family 1:39**
Dir: Stewart Raffill *Cast:* Robert Logan, Susan Damante Shaw, Heather Rattray, George "Buck" Flower
▶ A construction worker moves his family from Los Angeles to a log cabin in Utah so his daughter can recover her health. Adjusting to life in the mountains, they learn to cope with bears, wolves, and other wild animals. The first of many popular family-oriented features in this series benefits from breathtaking photography and a wholesome point of view.

ADVENTURES OF TOM SAWYER, THE 1938
★★★ **NR Action-Adventure 1:17**
Dir: Norman Taurog *Cast:* Tommy Kelly, Jackie Moran, Ann Gillis, May Robson, Walter Brennan, Victor Jory
▶ Charming adaptation of the Mark Twain classic about the irrepressible Tom Sawyer (Kelly) and his friend Huck Finn (Moran). The novel's best scenes—Tom conning two boys into whitewashing Aunt Polly's (Robson) fence, attending his own funeral, etc.—are reproduced with loving care. Jory—a memorably evil Injun Joe in the film's best sequence, a frightening chase through a mammoth cave. **(CC)**

ADVISE AND CONSENT 1962
★★★★ **NR Drama 2:19 B&W**
Dir: Otto Preminger *Cast:* Henry Fonda, Charles Laughton, Gene Tierney, Walter Pidgeon, Peter Lawford, Franchot Tone
▶ Ailing President Tone nominates a liberal for Secretary of State. As the Senate debates his choice, politicians resort to blackmail to sway the final vote. Sprawling adaptation of Allen Drury's Pulitzer prize-winning novel is dominated by strong performances by Fonda as the liberal candidate and Laughton as an unscrupulous Southern senator. Tame by today's standards, although still smooth entertainment in the Preminger style.

AFFAIR TO REMEMBER, AN 1957
★★★★ **NR Romance 1:54**
Dir: Leo McCarey *Cast:* Cary Grant,

Deborah Kerr, Cathleen Nesbitt, Neva Patterson, Richard Denning
▶ Leo McCarey's own remake of his classic *Love Affair.* Old-fashioned star power (Irene Dunne, Charles Boyer) made it work the first time around. Grant and Kerr continue the hallowed tradition as the shipboard lovers who decide to meet after an interval to make sure their feelings are for real.

AFRICAN QUEEN, THE 1951
★★★★★ **NR Action-Adventure 1:43**
Dir: John Huston *Cast:* Katharine Hepburn, Humphrey Bogart, Robert Morley, Peter Bull, Theodore Bikel
▶ In World War I Africa, spinsterish missionary Hepburn and hard-drinking boatman Bogart journey through German-occupied waters in the ramshackle craft *The African Queen.* Bickering and fighting, the unlikely duo fall in love and demolish the Germans' big guns in John Huston's classic adventure tale from the C. S. Forester novel. Marvelous chemistry between the two stars. Bogart's Oscar performance.

AFTER HOURS 1985
★ **R Comedy 1:37**
☑ Nudity, adult situations, explicit language, violence
Dir: Martin Scorsese *Cast:* Griffin Dunne, Rosanna Arquette, Teri Garr, John Heard, Linda Fiorentino
▶ Dunne plays an uptight word-processing trainer whose blind date with Arquette turns into a comic nightmare. After losing his bearings in arty downtown New York, his problems escalate when Arquette commits suicide and vigilantes mistake him for a burglar. Offbeat, sophisticated urban comedy has a strong cast, assured direction, and an unpredictable plot. **(CC)**

AFTER THE FALL OF NEW YORK 1985
Italian/French
★ **R Action-Adventure 1:35**
☑ Explicit language, violence
Dir: Martin Dolman (Sergio Martino)
Cast: Michael Sopkiw, Anna Kanakis, Valentine Monnier, Roman Geer, Vincent Scalondro
▶ Twenty years after a devastating nuclear war, a rough-hewn hero named Parsifal leads his gang of misfits into New York to rescue the world's last fertile woman from a hulk known as Big Ape. Lots of mindless action, bad dubbing, cheap sets and special effects, and a

plot borrowed from *Escape from New York.*

AFTER THE FOX 1966 U.S./British/Italian
★★ NR Comedy 1:42
Dir: Vittorio De Sica *Cast:* Peter Sellers, Victor Mature, Britt Ekland, Martin Balsam
▶ Neil Simon co-wrote the screenplay for this nutty farce about Italian con man Sellers who impersonates a famous film director to pull off a heist. Virtuoso comic performance by Sellers, who indulges his penchant for outlandish disguises. Even the theme song (written by Burt Bacharach and performed by Sellers and the Hollies) is funny.

AFTER THE THIN MAN 1936
★★★ NR Mystery-Suspense 1:50 B&W
Dir: W. S. Van Dyke II *Cast:* William Powell, Myrna Loy, James Stewart, Elissa Landi, Joseph Calleia
▶ The second entry in the Thin Man series, with Powell and Loy as those wisecracking married detectives, Nick and Nora Charles. In San Francisco, the Charleses (as always, accompanied by their faithful dog Asta) get involved in the case of the missing husband of Nora's cousin. Snappy dialogue, mystery, and comedy mix once more in the typical fashion of the series.

AGAINST ALL FLAGS 1952
★★★ NR Action-Adventure 1:23
Dir: George Sherman *Cast:* Errol Flynn, Maureen O'Hara, Anthony Quinn, Mildred Natwick, Alice Kelley, Robert Warwick
▶ English officer Flynn poses as pirate to get the goods on buccaneer Quinn and his swashbuckling cutthroats. Flynn rescues captured princess Kelley, wins the heart of female pirate O'Hara, and eventually battles Quinn to the death. Pirate yarn delivered with verve and excitement.

AGAINST ALL ODDS 1984
★★★ R Mystery-Suspense 2:01
☑ Nudity, adult situations, explicit language, graphic violence
Dir: Taylor Hackford *Cast:* Rachel Ward, Jeff Bridges, James Woods, Richard Widmark, Alex Karras, Swoosie Kurtz
▶ Ex-football player Bridges is hired by sleazy nightclub owner Woods to locate his runaway girlfriend Ward in this sexy, steamy remake of the 1947 *Out of the Past.* Bridges and Ward become lovers and an intricate web of corruption, jealousy, and murder ensues. Stylishly directed by Hackford, this thriller makes up for some confused plotting with plenty of action and sex. Haunting title song by Phil Collins. **(CC)**

AGATHA 1979
★★★ PG Drama 1:38
☑ Adult situations, explicit language
Dir: Michael Apted *Cast:* Dustin Hoffman, Vanessa Redgrave, Timothy Dalton, Helen Morse, Celia Gregory
▶ Fictional explanation of events during Agatha Christie's famous two-week disappearance in 1926 has the acclaimed mystery writer hatching a real-life murder plot of her own. Redgrave stars as Agatha, the creator of Hercule Poirot and Jane Marple and wife of the philandering Dalton whom she finds at a seaside resort with his secretary. Hoffman plays an earnest journalist who uncovers the real story and falls in love.

AGENCY 1981 Canadian
★★ R Mystery-Suspense 1:33
☑ Adult situations, explicit language, violence
Dir: George Kaczender *Cast:* Robert Mitchum, Lee Majors, Valerie Perrine, Saul Rubinek
▶ Majors stars as a New York ad agency creative director who uncovers a plot to affect the presidential election via subliminal advertising. The trail leads to big boss Mitchum but Majors eventually makes the world safe for democracy in this rather routine thriller that fails to adequately exploit the talents of a good cast.

AGNES OF GOD 1985
★★★★ PG-13 Drama 1:39
☑ Adult situations, explicit language
Dir: Norman Jewison *Cast:* Anne Bancroft, Jane Fonda, Meg Tilly, Anne Pitoniak, Winston Rekert
▶ Did Sister Agnes (Tilly) murder her baby or is there a more mystical explanation for this scandal behind convent walls? It's up to court-appointed shrink Fonda to find out in this talky but engrossing adaptation of John Pielmeier's Broadway hit. Worth seeing for Fonda's sparring with Mother Superior Anne Bancroft (Oscar-nominated, as was Tilly). **(CC)**

AGONY AND THE ECSTASY, THE 1965
★★★ NR Biography 2:20
Dir: Carol Reed *Cast:* Charlton Heston, Rex Harrison, Diane Cilento, Harry Andrews, Alberto Lupo, Adolfo Celi

► Earnest but overlong account of the painting of the ceiling frescoes in the Vatican's Sistine Chapel describes Michelangelo's (Heston) inspiration in terms of a bitter feud with his patron, Pope Julius II (Harrison). Production details are impressive, but plodding pacing and historical inaccuracies are drawbacks. Based on Irving Stone's best-seller.

AIR FORCE 1943
★★★★ **NR War 2:04 B&W**
Dir: Howard Hawks *Cast:* John Garfield, Gig Young, Arthur Kennedy, Charles Drake, Harry Carey, John Ridgely
► Exciting tribute to the crew of the *Mary Ann*, a B-17 Flying Fortress in action over Pearl Harbor, Manila, and the Coral Sea during World War II. Sober, realistic screenplay by Dudley Nichols adds depth to authentic dogfight sequences. Despite anti-Japanese racism, film holds up quite well. Oscar-nominated for writing and photography. **(CC)**

AIRPLANE! 1980
★★★★ **PG Comedy 1:28**
☑ Brief nudity, adult situations, violence, adult humor
Dir: Jim Abrahams, Jerry Zucker, David Zucker *Cast:* Robert Hays, Lloyd Bridges, Julie Hagerty, Robert Stack, Peter Graves
► In this wild parody of the *Airport* disaster series, Hays stars as a washed-up, lovelorn pilot flying a planeful of mixed nuts suffering from food poisoning. Directors Abrahams, Zucker, and Zucker imbue the film with an everything-but-the-kitchen-sink sense of humor that propelled it into a runaway hit. A diverse supporting cast features basketball star Kareem Abdul Jabbar and Graves as the co-pilot/gladiator movie enthusiast.

AIRPLANE II: THE SEQUEL 1982
★★ **PG Comedy 1:24**
☑ Brief nudity, adult situations, adult humor
Dir: Ken Finkelman *Cast:* Robert Hays, Julie Hagerty, Lloyd Bridges, William Shatner, Raymond Burr
► In this genial follow-up to the hugely successful *Airplane!*, pilot Hays escapes from an insane asylum to save the space shuttle from destruction. Wide-eyed Hagerty, Hays's former love, is also back from the first film and "Captain Kirk" Shatner has been added to the cast of zanies. Although not quite as inventive as the first

movie, the broad visual humor still brings quite a few laughs.

AIRPORT 1970
★★★★★ **G Action-Adventure 2:15**
Dir: George Seaton *Cast:* Burt Lancaster, Dean Martin, George Kennedy, Helen Hayes, Jean Seberg
► In this granddaddy of the disaster genre, a mad bomber blows up half an airliner in midflight which must then land at a totally snowbound airport. Adapted from Arthur Hailey's best-seller, the movie's all-star cast features Lancaster as the airport manager, Martin as the pilot, Van Heflin as the bomber, and Hayes in an Oscar-winning performance as the little old lady who stows away. Taut, suspenseful, and easily the best of the genre.

AIRPORT 1975 1975
★★★★ **PG Action-Adventure 1:46**
☑ Adult situations
Dir: Jack Smight *Cast:* Charlton Heston, Karen Black, George Kennedy, Efrem Zimbalist, Jr., Susan Clark
► "The stewardess is flying the plane!" a passenger shouts as Black attempts to land a wounded airliner, assisted by Heston's radioed instructions, after a midair collision wipes out the flight crew. Serves up all the genre's key elements—contrived but suspenseful situations, corny dialogue, and an all-star cast (featuring Helen Reddy as a singing nun, Linda Blair as a kidney transplant patient, and Gloria Swanson). An entertaining concoction.

AIRPORT '77 1977
★★★★★ **PG Action-Adventure 1:53**
☑ Adult situations
Dir: Jerry Jameson *Cast:* Jack Lemmon, Lee Grant, Brenda Vaccaro, Darren McGavin, Christopher Lee, James Stewart
► Millionaire Stewart invites a planeful of people to the opening of his museum, only to have the plane hijacked by art thieves who proceed to crash it into the Bermuda Triangle. Third in the popular *Airport* series.

ALAMO, THE 1960
★★★ **NR Western 2:41**
Dir: John Wayne *Cast:* John Wayne, Richard Widmark, Laurence Harvey, Patrick Wayne, Linda Cristal, Frankie Avalon
► Inspiring re-creation of the famous 1836 siege in Texas, brought to the

screen with care and imagination by Wayne, directing for the only time in his career. The Duke gives a tough, sharp performance as Davy Crockett, and he's ably matched by Widmark as a flinty Jim Bowie and Richard Boone as Sam Houston. Superb score by Dmitri Tiomkin.

ALAMO BAY 1985
★★ R Drama 1:39
☑ Brief nudity, adult situations, violence
Dir: Louis Malle *Cast:* Amy Madigan, Ed Harris, Ho Nguyen, Donald Moffat, Truyen V. Tran
▶ Harris and Madigan (husband and wife in real life) find themselves on opposite sides of a conflict between Texas fishermen and the Vietnamese refugees who become their competition. Madigan shines as the feisty Glory, who alienates boyfriend Harris when she sides with Vietnamese Nguyen. Harris responds by joining the KKK, leading to an explosive climax in Malle's sensitive fact-based drama. **(CC)**

AL CAPONE 1959
★★ NR Biography/Crime 1:45 B&W
Dir: Richard Wilson *Cast:* Rod Steiger, Fay Spain, James Gregory, Martin Balsam, Nehemiah Persoff, Murvyn Vye
▶ Energetic, semidocumentary approach to the infamous Chicago gangster presents an unvarnished look at his career, from his rise as a hit man for Johnny Torrio (Persoff) to his ultimate arrest for income tax evasion. Steiger gives a larger-than-life portrait of Capone; good supporting work by Vye as Bugs Moran and Gregory as an uncompromising cop.

ALCHEMIST, THE 1985
☆ R Horror 1:24
☑ Explicit language, violence
Dir: James Armante *Cast:* Robert Ginty, Lucinda Dooling, John Sanderford, Viola Kate Stimpson, Robert Glaudini
▶ An 1871 alchemist's curse transforms glassmaker Aaron McCallum (Ginty) into an immortal murderous beast. Then the action cuts to 1955 as the reincarnation of Aaron's wife fights for his soul. Low-budget horror tale for hard-core genre fans.

ALEXANDER THE GREAT 1956
★★ NR Biography 2:21
Dir: Robert Rossen *Cast:* Richard Burton, Fredric March, Claire Bloom, Danielle Darrieux, Harry Andrews, Stanley Baker

▶ Burton is magnetic as the Greek leader who conquered all of the known world in the fourth century B.C.; March provides powerful counterpoint as his insatiable father Philip. Stirring battle scenes and Burton's tender love affair with Barsine (Bloom) almost salvage film's interminable philosophical debates.

ALEX IN WONDERLAND 1970
☆ R Comedy/Drama 1:49
☑ Nudity, adult situations, explicit language
Dir: Paul Mazursky *Cast:* Donald Sutherland, Ellen Burstyn, Federico Fellini, Jeanne Moreau
▶ Unfocused and disappointing effort from Mazursky, essentially an attempt to redo Fellini's *8½* in American terms. Filmmaker Sutherland struggles to come up with an idea for his next movie, a quandary inspired by Mazursky's own creative dilemma after his successful debut with *Bob and Carol and Ted and Alice.*

ALFIE 1966 British
★★★ PG Drama 1:53
☑ Adult situations
Dir: Lewis Gilbert *Cast:* Michael Caine, Shelley Winters, Julia Foster, Millicent Martin, Shirley Anne Field, Vivien Merchant
▶ Hard-hitting story of a hedonistic Cockney womanizer catapulted Caine to international stardom and his first Oscar nomination. As Alfie, a self-proclaimed "bird-watcher," Caine flits through a series of relationships: from Winters, a brassy, well-heeled extrovert in love with another man, to Merchant, a dutiful married woman pregnant by Alfie. For all its humor, startlingly no-nonsense. Nominated for five Academy Awards.

ALICE ADAMS 1935
★★★★ NR Drama 1:40 B&W
Dir: George Stevens *Cast:* Katharine Hepburn, Fred MacMurray, Fred Stone, Evelyn Venable, Frank Alberston, Hedda Hopper
▶ Hepburn, a small-town girl from the wrong side of the tracks, desperately tries to snag eligible upper-class bachelor MacMurray in spite of her family's gauche background. Sensitive, low-key adaptation of the Booth Tarkington bestseller has a beautifully bittersweet mood, with Hepburn astonishing as the aggressive but still appealing heroine. Both she and the picture won Oscar nominations.

ALICE DOESN'T LIVE HERE ANYMORE
1975
★★★★ PG Drama 1:52
☑ Adult situations, explicit language
Dir: Martin Scorsese *Cast:* Ellen Burstyn, Kris Kristofferson, Jodie Foster, Alfred Lutter, Harry Dean Stanton
▶ Burstyn is absolutely superb in her Oscar-winning turn as Alice Hyatt, a woman left on her own with an eleven-year-old son when her husband is killed in a crash. As Alice rebuilds her life, she finds new work as a singer and waitress, a new man in Kristofferson, and most importantly, new strength in herself. Inspired the popular TV series "Alice."

ALICE IN WONDERLAND 1933
★★ NR Fantasy 1:17 B&W
Dir: Norman Z. McLeod *Cast:* Charlotte Henry, Richard Arlen, Gary Cooper, W. C. Fields, Cary Grant, Sterling Holloway
▶ As young Alice, Henry falls into a rabbit hole, embarking on a series of often frightening adventures. Relatively faithful adaptation of Lewis Carroll's classic is a glum, slow-moving comedy notable only for its all-star cast, most of whom are hidden under masks and makeup. Best performers: Edward Everett Horton as the Mad Hatter, Fields as Humpty Dumpty, Edna May Oliver as the Red Queen, and May Robson as the Queen of Hearts. (CC)

ALICE IN WONDERLAND 1951
★★★★ G Animation 1:15
Dir: Clyde Geronimi, Hamilton Luske, Wilfred Jaxon *Cast:* Voices of Kathryn Beaumont, Ed Wynn, Sterling Holloway, Richard Haydn, Jerry Colonna
▶ Delightful Disney version of Lewis Carroll's novels boasts superb animation, tuneful score, and excellent characterizations, particularly Holloway's amusing Cheshire Cat. Script sacrifices some of Carroll's intellectual humor, concentrating instead on the humor and suspense of young Alice's amazing adventures. Oliver Wallace's orchestrations received an Oscar nomination.

ALICE'S RESTAURANT 1969
★★ PG Musical 1:50
☑ Adult situations, explicit language
Dir: Arthur Penn *Cast:* Arlo Guthrie, Pat Quinn, James Broderick, Michael McClanathan
▶ Folk singer Guthrie plays himself in this adaptation of his famous talking blues record "Alice's Restaurant," the story of an arrest for garbage dumping that left Guthrie happily unfit for military service in the Vietnam era. Anyone nostalgic for the days of draft physicals, hippies, and flower children will be in heaven here. The film's natural, easygoing tone is embodied by the star's performance.

ALIEN 1979
★★★ R Sci-Fi 1:57
☑ Explicit language, graphic violence
Dir: Ridley Scott *Cast:* Tom Skerritt, Sigourney Weaver, John Hurt, Ian Holm, Harry Dean Stanton
▶ A spaceship crew battles a most unpleasant stowaway—an alien creature determined to destroy all life on ship—in Scott's literally gut-wrenching sci-fi thriller. Terrific visual effects combine with Scott's virtuoso style to create nonstop suspense. Weaver is plenty tough as the one person on board who can outwit the alien. Spawned a sequel and many imitators.

ALIEN NATION 1988
★★★★ R Sci-Fi 1:34
☑ Explicit language, graphic violence
Dir: Graham Baker *Cast:* James Caan, Mandy Patinkin, Terence Stamp, Kevyn Major Howard, Leslie Bevis, Peter Jason
▶ Dome-topped aliens emigrate to tomorrow's Los Angeles, where they fit into society with surprising ease. Patinkin, the first alien promoted to police officer, is paired with Caan, who hates the "newcomers," in a case involving murder and drug smuggling. Dynamite premise and oustanding opening unfortunately give way to routine buddy-cop plotting.

ALIEN PREDATOR 1987
★★ R Sci-Fi 1:30
☑ Adult situations, explicit language, graphic violence
Dir: Deran Sarafian *Cast:* Dennis Christopher, Martin Hewitt, Lynn-Holly Johnson, Luis Prendes, J. O. Bosso, Yousaf Bokhari
▶ Extraterrestrial microbes attached to downed NASA satellite infect inhabitants of Spanish village, endangering American tourist Christopher and his two pals. Scientist Prendes orders authorities to destroy village before plague spreads as Christopher plots escape plan. Inept adventure, filmed in 1984, features disappointing special effects.

ALIENS 1986
★★★★★ R Sci-Fi 2:17

☑ Explicit language, graphic violence
Dir: James Cameron *Cast:* Sigourney Weaver, Carrie Henn, Michael Biehn, Paul Reiser, Lance Henriksen
▶ Astronaut Weaver awakes from fifty-seven years in suspended animation and returns to the original planet from the first *Alien*. With a Marine unit led by Biehn, Weaver takes on a whole army of alien monsters. Director Cameron keeps the action and violence whizzing by in this edge-of-your-seat sci-fi thriller that may even surpass its predecessor. **(CC)**

ALL ABOUT EVE 1950
★★★★ NR Drama 2:18 B&W
Dir: Joseph L. Mankiewicz *Cast:* Bette Davis, Anne Baxter, George Sanders, Marilyn Monroe, Celeste Holm
▶ Writer/director Joseph L. Mankiewicz's masterpiece gave Bette Davis the role of a lifetime as Margo Channing, an aging Broadway star suddenly upstaged by young, sweet-faced, ruthlessly ambitious Eve Harrington (Baxter). Witty one-liners fly as the caustic, cantankerous Margo takes on the predatory Eve and the rest of a superb cast. Nominated for fourteen Oscars, winner of six (including Best Picture); a must-see Hollywood classic.

ALLAN QUARTERMAIN AND THE LOST CITY OF GOLD 1987
★★ PG Action-Adventure 1:43
☑ Explicit language, violence
Dir: Gary Nelson *Cast:* Richard Chamberlain, Sharon Stone, James Earl Jones, Henry Silva, Robert Donner
▶ Chamberlain returns as the dashing adventurer Allan Quartermain in this sequel to *King Solomon's Mines*. Quartermain and his girlfriend Stone battle nasty slave trader Silva while they search for the lost city of the title. A campy effort with tacky production values that nevertheless offers plenty of action.

ALLEGHENY UPRISING 1939
★★ NR Action-Adventure 1:21 B&W
Dir: William A. Seiter *Cast:* John Wayne, Claire Trevor, George Sanders, Brian Donlevy, Moroni Olsen, Chill Wills
▶ Pre-Revolutionary America provides the setting for Wayne's frontier heroics against Donlevy, an evil gunrunner supplying liquor to the Indians, and Sanders, a British captain determined to control the colony by force. Feisty girlfriend Trevor, a crack shot, helps the Duke during a rigged trial. Modest action vehicle reteamed Wayne and Trevor after their

success in *Stagecoach*. Available in a colorized version.

ALLIGATOR 1980
★★ R Horror 1:31
☑ Explicit language, violence
Dir: Lewis Teague *Cast:* Robert Forster, Robin Riker, Henry Silva, Dean Jagger
▶ An alligator flushed down the toilet twelve years earlier runs amok through Chicago's sewers before surfacing to terrorize innocent bystanders. Police detective Forster can't convince his superiors that anything's wrong, and goes after the gator himself with the help of reptile expert Riker. Modest but enjoyable picture benefits from a tongue-in-cheek screenplay by John Sayles.

ALL IN A NIGHT'S WORK 1961
★★ NR Comedy 1:34
Dir: Joseph Anthony *Cast:* Dean Martin, Shirley MacLaine, Charles Ruggles, Cliff Robertson, Norma Crane, Gale Gordon
▶ Rich publisher dies after spending the night with a woman; Martin, his successor, thinks that dizzy MacLaine planned the death and is after Dean's life as well. She goes into hiding, aided by a cast of veteran character actors. Sidney Sheldon was one of the writers on this slight but fast-paced comedy.

ALL MY SONS 1948
★★★ NR Drama 1:34 B&W
Dir: Irving Reis *Cast:* Edward G. Robinson, Burt Lancaster, Mady Christians, Louisa Horton, Howard Duff, Arlene Francis
▶ Lancaster and Horton, the fiancée of his late brother killed in World War II, fall in love. The relationship leads to revelations about Lancaster's dad Robinson, a munitions manufacturer who sold defective parts during the war. Sterling adaptation of Arthur Miller's play features shattering performances by Robinson and Lancaster.

ALLNIGHTER, THE 1987
★ PG-13 Drama 1:35
☑ Adult situations, explicit language
Dir: Tamar Simon Hoffs *Cast:* Susanna Hoffs, Dedee Pfeiffer, Joan Cusack, Michael Ontkean, Pam Grier
▶ The misadventures of three roommates on the night before graduation from a party college. Music, dancing, surfing, romance, and prerequisite heartbreak add up to another formula beach movie. Nonstop soundtrack (Mike + the Me-

chanics, Timbuk 3, etc.) and performance of Hoffs (lead singer of the Bangles rock group) should please fans. Hoffs's mother directed, produced, and co-wrote film.

ALL NIGHT LONG 1981
★ R Comedy 1:28
☑ Adult situations, explicit language
Dir: Jean-Claude Tramont   *Cast:* Gene Hackman, Barbra Streisand, Dennis Quaid, Diane Ladd
▶ After losing his job, executive Hackman is hired as manager of an all-night drug store. He discovers son Quaid's affair with his fourth cousin Streisand and is soon involved with Streisand himself. Hackman's mid-life crisis is the focus here but Streisand fans might enjoy seeing her in this offbeat mix of comedy and romance.

ALL OF ME 1984
★★★★ PG Comedy 1:32
☑ Adult situations, explicit language, adult humor
Dir: Carl Reiner   *Cast:* Steve Martin, Lily Tomlin, Victoria Tennant, Jason Bernard, Madolyn Smith
▶ A guru's goof-up leaves half of Martin's body possessed by eccentric rich woman Tomlin in this hilarious body switch comedy from director Reiner. The simplest bodily function takes on new meaning as these mismatched psyches battle it out. Martin's truly original physical clowning steals the show in this poignant and funny movie.

ALL QUIET ON THE WESTERN FRONT 1930
★★★★ NR War 2:10 B&W
Dir: Lewis Milestone   *Cast:* Lew Ayres, Louis Wolheim, John Wray, Beryl Mercer, Ben Alexander
▶ In 1914, young student Ayres enlists in the German army. He and his classmates are sent to the front, where they confront the horrors of war. Although dated in some technical aspects, this enduring classic was one of the first and most effective antiwar movies. Filled with emotionally harrowing vignettes and shocking scenes of fighting, it won Oscars for Best Picture and Direction. Adapted from the novel by Erich Maria Remarque.

ALL THAT HEAVEN ALLOWS 1956
★★★★ NR Drama 1:29
Dir: Douglas Sirk   *Cast:* Jane Wyman, Rock Hudson, Agnes Moorehead, Conrad Nagel, Virginia Grey
▶ Suburban widow Wyman loses her heart to a younger man, gardener Hudson. The lovers try to ignore the differences in social class and age but the disapproval of Wyman's grown children and neighbors wear her down. She breaks off the relationship but love triumphs in the end. Intelligent, sincere melodrama makes you care about these chararacters.

ALL THAT JAZZ 1979
★★ R Drama/Musical 2:03
☑ Nudity, adult situations, explicit language
Dir: Bob Fosse   *Cast:* Roy Scheider, Jessica Lange, Ann Reinking, Leland Palmer, Ben Vereen, John Lithgow
▶ Nine Oscar nominations went to Fosse's dazzling autobiographical musical about choreographer Joe Gideon (Scheider) who juggles ex-wife, mistress, and daughter while simultaneously working on a Broadway musical and a film. A heart attack and a visit from the Angel of Death ensue in this flashy musical for adults, highlighted by Scheider's terrific performance and some wonderful music and dancing. The squeamish should be warned about the quite graphic open-heart surgery scene. (CC)

ALL THE KING'S MEN 1949
★★★★ NR Biography 1:49 B&W
Dir: Robert Rossen   *Cast:* Broderick Crawford, John Ireland, Mercedes McCambridge, John Derek, Joanne Dru
▶ Crawford dominates this hard-hitting drama adapted from Robert Penn Warren's Pulitzer prize–winning novel about an ambitious Southern politician. Based on the life of Louisiana's Huey Long, the film shows how a poor farmer uses graft and corruption to become a near-dictator. Superior writing and action highlight a controversial story whose themes are still relevant today. Received seven Oscar nominations, winning Best Picture, Actor (Crawford), and Supporting Actress (McCambridge).

. . . ALL THE MARBLES 1981
★★★ R Drama 1:53
☑ Nudity, adult situations, explicit language, mild violence
Dir: Robert Aldrich   *Cast:* Peter Falk, Vicki Frederick, Laurene Landon, Burt Young, Tracy Reed
▶ Mild comedy about a small-time manager who pins his hopes for big money on

two comely female wrestlers. They make the rounds through small-town Middle America hoping for a shot at a title match in Reno. Considering its subject matter, a surprisingly tame and warm-hearted film that relies heavily on Falk's charm for its humor.

ALL THE PRESIDENT'S MEN 1976
★★★★★ PG Drama 2:18
☑ Adult situations, explicit language
Dir: Alan J. Pakula *Cast:* Robert Redford, Dustin Hoffman, Jason Robards, Jack Warden, Martin Balsam
▶ Landmark film about the investigation by reporters Bob Woodward and Carl Bernstein into the Watergate conspiracy won four Oscars, including Supporting Actor for Robards as editor Ben Bradlee. A concise script by William Goldman and uniformly strong action helped explain complex issues to a wide audience in gripping, believable terms. Highly influential documentary approach was imitated in a number of subsequent films. Eight Oscar nominations overall for what has become a modern classic.

ALL THE RIGHT MOVES 1983
★★★★ R Drama 1:26
☑ Nudity, adult situations, explicit language, mild violence, adult humor
Dir: Michael Chapman *Cast:* Tom Cruise, Craig T. Nelson, Lea Thompson, Charles Cioffi
▶ Popular sports drama was one of Cruise's early hits. He plays an ambitious teen who needs to win a college football scholarship to escape his depressed mining town. When he clashes with coach Nelson after losing an important game, his future looks bleak—until fetching Thompson steps in to help. But the two discover that they still face difficult choices. **(CC)**

ALL THE RIVERS RUN 1983 Australian
★★★★★ NR Romance/MFTV 8:00
Dir: George Miller, Pino Amenta *Cast:* Sigrid Thornton, John Waters, Charles Tingwell, William Upjohn, Diane Craig
▶ Orphan Philadelphia Gordon (Thornton) struggles to assert her independence in nineteenth-century Melbourne's male-dominated society. After a stint as an artist, she falls for the dashing Brenton Edwards (Waters), an adventurer trying to establish a boating company. Gordon goes on to become Australia's first female riverboat pilot in

this diverting miniseries adapted from Nancy Cato's novel.

ALL THIS AND HEAVEN TOO 1940
★★★ NR Romance 2:23 B&W
Dir: Anatole Litvak *Cast:* Bette Davis, Charles Boyer, Jeffrey Lynn, Barbara O'Neil, Virginia Weidler, June Lockhart
▶ Nineteenth-century France: nanny Davis tends to nobleman Boyer's kids and wins his heart. Although Boyer loves Davis chastely, jealous wife O'Neil suspects an affair. When O'Neil is murdered, Davis is wrongly accused. A multi-Kleenex movie that deserves a bigger reputation; shattering ending and fine performances.

ALL THROUGH THE NIGHT 1942
★★★ NR Comedy 1:47 B&W
Dir: Vincent Sherman *Cast:* Humphrey Bogart, Conrad Veidt, Kaaren Verne, Jane Darwell, Frank McHugh, Peter Lorre
▶ Fast-paced, action-packed World War II espionage film with a generous dose of humor. Bogart plays a gambler who uncovers a German conspiracy to blow up New York harbor. Veidt, Lorre, and Judith Anderson are suitably villainous, but character actors William Demarest, Jackie Gleason, Phil Silvers, and others make the story shine. Bogart and Demarest share a hilarious double-talk scene in front of the Nazis.

ALMOST ANGELS 1962
★★★ NR Drama 1:25
Dir: Steven Previn *Cast:* Peter Weck, Vincent Winter, Sean Scully, Hans Holt, Fritz Echardt, Bruni Lobel
▶ Appealing Disney drama about the Vienna Boys Choir takes a tour-guide approach to the world-famous group. Training and rehearsal sessions in beautiful settings provide most of the action; negligible subplot about two friends who love practical jokes barely detracts from outstanding versions of music by Brahms, Strauss, etc.

ALMOST PERFECT AFFAIR, AN 1979
★★ PG Romance 1:32
☑ Brief nudity, adult situations, explicit language
Dir: Michael Ritchie *Cast:* Keith Carradine, Monica Vitti, Raf Vallone, Christian De Sica
▶ Carradine plays an aspiring director trying to sell his first feature at the Cannes Film Festival. He loses his film to a censor, and turns to producer's wife Vitti for help. Although wildy incompatible, they fall in

love. Luscious settings and some fleeting industry satire have more impact than the rather tame love interest.

ALMOST YOU 1985
★ **R Comedy 1:37**
☐ Adult situations, explicit language
Dir: Adam Brooks *Cast:* Brooke Adams, Griffin Dunne, Karen Young, Marty Watt, Christine Estabrook
▶ Dunne is a bored husand who falls in love with Young, the nurse he hired to look after his injured wife Adams. Will he return to his senses? Dunne helped finance this personal project shot in Manhattan. Billed as a "traumatic comedy," its style and tone may be too narrow for most viewers. **(CC)**

ALOHA, BOBBY AND ROSE 1975
★★★ **PG Drama 1:29**
Dir: Floyd Mutrux *Cast:* Paul LeMat, Dianne Hull, Tim McIntire, Leigh French, Robert Carradine
▶ Modest crime melodrama with a familiar theme: LeMat is a Los Angeles auto mechanic mistakenly involved in a robbery. With the cops hot on his trail, he takes off for Mexico with pretty car wash worker Hull. Good actors are hampered by predictable plotting.

ALOHA SUMMER 1988
★★★ **PG Drama 1:37**
☑ Brief nudity, adult situations, explicit language
Dir: Tommy Lee Wallace *Cast:* Chris Makepeace, Don Michael Paul, Tia Carrere, Yuji Okumoto, Lorie Griffin
▶ Coming-of-age story set on Hawaii in 1959 follows budding surfer Makepeace as he makes friends, falls in love, and becomes a man. Beautiful scenery, some pointed racial subplots, and top-notch oldies soundtrack add depth to a routine tale.

ALONG CAME JONES 1945
★★ **NR Western/Comedy 1:30 B&W**
Dir: Stuart Heisler *Cast:* Gary Cooper, Loretta Young, William Demarest, Dan Duryea, Frank Sully
▶ Entertaining satire of Westerns with Cooper spoofing his typical tight-lipped hero roles by playing Jones, an easygoing, gun-shy drifter mistaken for notorious outlaw Duryea. At first Jones enjoys his newfound celebrity, but he has second thoughts when Duryea challenges him to a showdown. Cooper, who also produced the film, has rarely been as charming.

ALONG THE GREAT DIVIDE 1951
★★ **NR Western 1:28 B&W**
Dir: Raoul Walsh *Cast:* Kirk Douglas, Virginia Mayo, John Agar, Walter Brennan, Ray Teal, Hugh Sanders
▶ Principled marshal Douglas (in his first Western) refuses to budge when a lynch mob condemns Brennan to death. Despite a dangerous desert sandstorm, the lawman and his prisoner set out for a fair trial in the next town. Brennan's daughter Mayo provides the love interest in this well-mounted adventure.

ALPHABET CITY 1984
★★ **R Drama 1:25**
☑ Nudity, adult situations, explicit language, graphic violence
Dir: Amos Poe *Cast:* Vincent Spano, Michael Winslow, Kate Vernon, Jami Gertz
▶ Spano, who collects payments for a heroin ring, is ordered to burn down the tenement where his mother and sister live. If he doesn't, he has only one night to escape from Alphabet City, New York's East Village slums. Overwrought direction by underground favorite Poe can't elevate this above B-movie status.

ALTERED STATES 1980
★★ **R Sci-Fi 1:42**
☑ Nudity, adult situations, explicit language, graphic violence
Dir: Ken Russell *Cast:* William Hurt, Blair Brown, Bob Balaban, Charles Haid, Thaao Penghilis
▶ Hurt gives a terrific performance as obsessed scientist Eddie Jessup, whose experiments on himself to achieve genetic memory bring about some alarming physical transformations. Russell's bravura direction is visually powerful and the hallucination sequences are dazzling and original. A verbose but provocative movie from a script by Paddy Chayefsky (who used the pseudonym "Sidney Aaron" after feuding with Russell).

ALVAREZ KELLY 1966
★★★ **NR Western 1:56 B&W**
Dir: Edward Dmytryk *Cast:* William Holden, Richard Widmark, Janice Rule, Patrick O'Neal, Victoria Shaw
▶ Offbeat Civil War saga tests Holden's neutral politics when he's kidnapped by Confederate colonel Widmark to steal cattle from the North. Holden doesn't realize that as soon as they reach safety,

Widmark will kill him for sleeping with Rule.

ALWAYS 1985
★ **R Comedy 1:46**
☑ Nudity, adult situations, explicit language
Dir: Henry Jaglom *Cast:* Henry Jaglom, Patrice Townsend, Melissa Leo, Jonathan Kaufer, Joanna Frank, Alan Rachins
▶ An about-to-be-divorced couple hosts two other couples for a Fourth of July weekend. They discuss love and romance and occasionally fall into each other's beds. Low-budget talkfest short on technical polish but long on funny dialogue and warm yet realistic characterizations. Jaglom and Townsend were married and divorced in real life. **(CC)**

AMADEUS 1984
★★★★ **PG Drama 2:38**
☑ Brief nudity, adult situations, explicit language, violence
Dir: Milos Forman *Cast:* Tom Hulce, F. Murray Abraham, Elizabeth Berridge, Simon Callow, Jeffrey Jones
▶ Peter Shaffer's play comes to the screen under Forman's meticulous guidance. Abraham won an Oscar as Salieri, the successful but mediocre composer spurred by jealousy to declare psychological war on the prodigy, Mozart (Hulce). Superb production, performances, and period detail. Forman's greatest triumph may be in making classical music accessible to the mass audience. Oscars for Best Picture and Director.

AMARCORD 1974
★ **R Comedy/Drama 2:07**
☑ Brief nudity, adult situations, explicit language
Dir: Federico Fellini *Cast:* Magali Noel, Bruno Zanin, Pupella Maggio, Armando Brancia
▶ The great Fellini's autobiographical account of life in an Italian town, circa 1930, focusing on Zanin as the director's childhood alter ego. Emphasis is less on plot than on creating a mosaic of atmosphere, childhood discoveries, and rites of passage. Oscar for Best Foreign Film.

AMATEUR, THE 1982
★★★ **R Mystery-Suspense 1:51**
☑ Brief nudity, explicit language, violence
Dir: Charles Jarrott *Cast:* John Savage, Marthe Keller, Christopher Plummer, Arthur Hill, Ed Lauter
▶ CIA codecracker Savage is out for revenge after his girlfriend is killed by a terrorist group in Germany. When his bosses are reluctant to approve the mission, he resorts to blackmail and then finds himself facing both the CIA (who have decided to terminate him) and the terrorists. Interesting premise.

AMAZING DOBERMANS, THE 1976
★★★ **PG Family 1:34**
Dir: Byron Chudnow *Cast:* Fred Astaire, James Franciscus, Barbara Eden, Jack Carter, Billy Barty
▶ Five Doberman dogs, trained by excon man Astaire, help Justice Department agent Franciscus thwart a racketeer in this third installment of the Doberman series. Astaire is charming, the dogs are appealing, and the film provides nonviolent family entertainment.

AMAZING GRACE AND CHUCK 1987
★★★★ **PG Drama 1:55**
☑ Explicit language
Dir: Mike Newell *Cast:* Jamie Lee Curtis, Alex English, Gregory Peck, William L. Petersen, Joshua Welch Zuehlke
▶ Little League pitcher Zuehlke decides to give up baseball until nuclear weapons are abolished. Basketball star Amazing Grace Smith (Denver Nuggets all-star English) joins him and a worldwide peace movement grows. Peck plays the concerned U.S. President in this sincere, sweet movie about fighting for what you believe in.

AMAZON WOMEN ON THE MOON 1987
★ **R Comedy 1:24**
☑ Nudity, adult situations, explicit language, adult humor
Dir: John Landis, Joe Dante, Peter Horton, Carl Gottlieb, Robert Weiss *Cast:* Rosanna Arquette, Ralph Bellamy, Steve Guttenberg, Carrie Fisher, Robert Loggia, Sybil Danning
▶ Compilation film uses a couch potato sucked into his cable system as an anchor for twenty parody sketches such as "Blacks Without Soul," "Son of the Invisible Man," "Reckless Youth," and the title piece, a satire on inept 1950s sci-fi. Irreverent, often vulgar humor and slapdash production values similar to Landis's earlier *Kentucky Fried Movie*.

AMBASSADOR, THE 1985
★★★ **R Mystery-Suspense 1:30**

☑ Adult situations, explicit language
Dir: J. Lee Thompson *Cast:* Ellen Burstyn, Robert Mitchum, Rock Hudson, Fabio Testi, Donald Pleasence
▶ Strong cast featured in a rather weak tale of political intrigue in the Middle East. Mitchum plays the ambassador who is being blackmailed with footage of his wife Burstyn's affair with PLO bigwig Testi. Nice performances but technically shoddy with a farfetched story. Plot was inspired by Elmore Leonard's novel *52 Pick-Up*, later made into a better movie starring Roy Scheider.

AMBUSHERS, THE 1967
★★ NR Espionage/Action-Adventure 2:00
Dir: Henry Levin *Cast:* Dean Martin, Senta Berger, Janice Rule, James Gregory, Albert Salmi, Kurt Kasznar
▶ Third in series featuring Martin as Donald Hamilton's superspy Matt Helm. Space program intrigue provides background as Martin battles villainous Salmi; thin plot works mainly as a vehicle for Martin's boozy joking.

AMERICAN ANTHEM 1986
★★★★ PG-13 Drama/Sports 1:42
☑ Explicit language, violence
Dir: Albert Magnoli *Cast:* Mitch Gaylord, Janet Jones, Michelle Phillips, Andrew White, John Aprea
▶ Olympic Gold Medal winner (Los Angeles, 1984) Gaylord makes his screen debut in this story of a gymnast with problems both on and off the mat. Jones (Mrs. Wayne Gretzky) co-stars as the female gymnast who wins his heart. Slick production works best for the gymnastic sequences and for spotlighting the physiques of the leads. Gaylord does okay for a nonactor.

AMERICAN CHRISTMAS CAROL, AN 1979
★★★★ NR Family/MFTV 1:40
Dir: Eric Till *Cast:* Henry Winkler, David Wayne, Chris Wiggins, R. H. Thomson, Ken Pogue
▶ Mean-spirited businessman Winkler is visited by ghosts who lead him on a journey back through his life, which changes him forever. Adaptation of Dickens's "A Christmas Carol," set in Depression-era America, provides holiday entertainment. Winkler tries hard in his Scrooge-like role.

AMERICAN DREAMER 1984
★★★★ PG Action-Adventure 1:45

☑ Explicit language, mild violence
Dir: Rick Rosenthal *Cast:* JoBeth Williams, Tom Conti, Giancarlo Giannini, Coral Browne, James Staley
▶ Housewife Williams wins a writing contest and a trip to Paris, where a bump on the head causes her to think she's daring fictional heroine Rebecca Ryan. Embroiled in an espionage plot, she steals the heart of Conti, although he believes she's quite mad. Williams is very appealing and the French locations are lovely in this glossy entertaining fluff. **(CC)**

AMERICAN FLYERS 1985
★★★★ PG-13 Drama 1:52
☑ Brief nudity, adult situations, explicit language
Dir: John Badham *Cast:* David Marshall Grant, Kevin Costner, Rae Dawn Chong, Alexandra Paul, Janice Rule
▶ Formula bike-racing movie—quite entertaining if you overlook the contrivances. Brothers Grant and Costner enter the big race, the twist being that one of them is dying. Upbeat screenplay by Steve Tesich (who won an Oscar for his previous bike movie *Breaking Away*) combines with terrific racing footage and beautiful Colorado Rockies scenery to create a movie that will leave you feeling good, if not totally convinced. **(CC)**

AMERICAN FRIEND, THE 1977
German/French
★★ NR Drama 2:07
☑ Adult situations, explicit language, violence
Dir: Wim Wenders *Cast:* Bruno Ganz, Dennis Hopper, Samuel Fuller, Nicholas Ray, Liza Kreuzer
▶ Ganz plays a picture framer with an incurable blood disease who's blackmailed by Hopper into murdering a gangster. The two are drawn into a peculiar relationship when Hopper assists Ganz in further killings. Cult film noir based on *Ripley's Game* by Patricia Highsmith has excellent acting and photography, but its abstract plotting may disappoint action fans. Ⓢ

AMERICAN GIGOLO 1980
★★★ R Mystery-Suspense 1:57
☑ Nudity, strong sexual content, adult situations, explicit language
Dir: Paul Schrader *Cast:* Richard Gere, Lauren Hutton, Hector Elizondo, Nina Van Pallandt, Bill Duke
▶ Handsome gigolo Gere is framed for murder. Will Hutton, the politician's wife

who loves him, provide his alibi? Unusual thriller that combines dazzling visuals and steamy love scenes with a basic sincerity and seriousness. Good music score by Giorgio Moroder includes the hit song "Call Me." Gere is fine in a role that requires him to literally show his all.

AMERICAN GOTHIC 1988
★ R Horror 1:30
☑ Explicit language, violence
Dir: John Hough *Cast:* Rod Steiger, Yvonne De Carlo, Michael J. Pollard, Fiona Hutchinson, Sarah Torgov, William Hootkins
▶ Mentally unstable Torgov seeks peace with husband and friends on island off Seattle, only to encounter bizarre older couple, Steiger and De Carlo, with middle-aged children Pollard, Hutchinson, and Hootkins still bedecked in kids' clothes. At first Torgov and her group are welcomed with apple pie and Bible readings, but soon mayhem erupts. Alternately campy and horrifying, unsurprising slasher movie won't satisfy fans of either genre.

AMERICAN GRAFFITI 1973
★★★★ PG Drama 1:55
☑ Explicit language
Dir: George Lucas *Cast:* Richard Dreyfuss, Ron Howard, Cindy Williams, Mackenzie Phillips, Candy Clark, Paul LeMat
▶ Nostalgic and moving story of one memorable night for a group of graduating high school seniors in a small northern California town, circa 1962, a time when kids cruised in their cars to the strains of "Rock Around the Clock" and other hits. Wonderfully directed by a pre–*Star Wars* Lucas. Look for future stars like Harrison Ford and Suzanne Somers in small parts.

AMERICAN HOT WAX 1978
★★★★ PG Biography/Music 1:31
☑ Explicit language
Dir: Floyd Mutrux *Cast:* Tim McIntire, Laraine Newman, Jay Leno, Chuck Berry, Fran Drescher
▶ Story of the life and times of disc jockey Alan Freed (McIntire), the man who hosted radio's first show devoted to rock 'n' roll, culminates in a near riot at Brooklyn's Paramount Theater when the cops try to close a rock show. This enjoyable salute to the oldies but goodies era features Berry, Jerry Lee Lewis, and Screamin' Jay Hawkins performing their own hits.

Jay Leno provides comic relief as Freed's driver.

AMERICAN IN PARIS, AN 1951
★★★★ NR Musical 1:53
Dir: Vincente Minnelli *Cast:* Gene Kelly, Leslie Caron, Oscar Levant, Nina Foch, Georges Guetary
▶ In Paris, ex-GI-turned-starving-artist Kelly falls for dancer Caron who's engaged to Guetary. Love, a grand Gershwin score, and MGM musical know-how triumph in this romantic, spectacular production that won seven Oscars (including Best Picture, plus a special award to Kelly). Highlights range from the intimate (Caron and Kelly dancing "Our Love Is Here to Stay" by the Seine; "I Got Rhythm") to the opulent ("I'll Build a Stairway to Paradise" and the famed ballet sequence). Kelly discovered Paris ballet dancer Caron and immediately cast her in her debut film role.

AMERICANIZATION OF EMILY, THE 1964
★★★★ NR Comedy 1:55 B&W
Dir: Arthur Hiller *Cast:* James Garner, Julie Andrews, Melvyn Douglas, James Coburn, Joyce Grenfell
▶ Daring comedy by Paddy Chayefsky takes a bleak look at wartime heroism. Garner plays a Navy officer who preaches pacifism; Andrews is a motorpool driver who thinks he's a coward. Their relationship is severely tested when Garner is ordered to be the first casualty on Omaha Beach. A witty, racy story with surprisingly serious undertones.

AMERICAN JUSTICE 1986
★★ R Action-Adventure 1:35
☑ Explicit language, graphic violence
Dir: Gary Grillo *Cast:* Jack Lucarelli, Gerald McRaney, Jameson Parker, Jeannie Wilson, Wilford Brimley
▶ Vacationing ex-cop Lucarelli witnesses a murder and teams with pal Parker to investigate. They uncover an illegal alien trafficking ring run by corrupt cop McRaney. Sturdy action achieves fair amount of tension with *Simon and Simon* co-stars McRaney and Parker on opposite sides of the law. Also known as *Jackals.*

AMERICAN NINJA 1985
★★★ R Martial Arts 1:35
☑ Explicit language, graphic violence
Dir: Sam Firstenberg *Cast:* Michael Dudikoff, John LaMotta, Guich Koock, Steve James, Don Stewart

► Fourth entry in this martial arts series follows a predictable formula: Dudikoff has amnesia and doesn't know that he's a Ninja master, but he discovers his powers when he sets out to rescue his kidnapped girlfriend from an evil Ninja army. Dudikoff was a last-minute fill-in for Chuck Norris.

AMERICAN NINJA 2: THE CONFRONTATION 1987
★★★ **R Martial Arts 1:30**
☑ Explicit language, graphic violence
Dir: Sam Firstenberg *Cast:* Michael Dudikoff, Steve James, Larry Poindexter, Gary Conway, Jeff Weston, Michelle Botes
► Army rangers Dudikoff and James are sent to Caribbean island to investigate disappearance of Marines guarding U.S. Embassy. They discover plot by druglord Conway to clone an army of ninja killers in a genetic experiment. Superior sequel to *American Ninja,* filled with action and humor, is stolen by James's energetic performance.

AMERICAN POP 1981
★★ **R Animation/Adult 1:36**
☑ Adult situations, explicit language
Dir: Ralph Bakshi *Cast:* Voices of Ron Thompson, Lisa Jane Persky, Roz Kelly
► Ambitious but downbeat cartoon traces the history of American music through four generations of a musical family. Fifty tunes are crammed into a story that spans everything from Russian pogroms to coked-out punks. Dazzling artwork, brilliant use of songs and newsreel footage, and a refreshingly adult approach to animation, but definitely not for all tastes.

AMERICAN SUCCESS COMPANY, THE 1979
★★ **PG Comedy 1:34**
☺ Brief nudity, adult situations, explicit language
Dir: William Richert *Cast:* Jeff Bridges, Belinda Bauer, Ned Beatty, Steven Keats, Bianca Jagger, John Glover
► Ineffectual Bridges is pushed around by wife Bauer and wealthy father-in-law/boss Beatty. In an effort to become more forceful, Bridges dons disguise, gets lovemaking tips from prostitute Jagger, and pulls a scam against the family. Inventive plot and good-humored cast generate laughs.

AMERICAN TAIL, AN 1986
★★★★★ **G Animation/Musical 1:25**

Dir: Don Bluth *Cast:* Voices of Dom DeLuise, Madeline Kahn, Christopher Plummer
► Old-fashioned cartoon describes the Russian immigrant experience from the point of view of Fievel, a young mouse separated from his family in a harsh turn-of-the-century New York. Typically lavish Steven Spielberg production: richly detailed animation, lush soundtrack (including Oscar-nominated "Somewhere Out There"), and lovable characters. Grim plot may frighten younger viewers. (CC)

AMERICAN WEREWOLF IN LONDON, AN 1981
★★★ **R Horror 1:37**
☑ Nudity, explicit language, graphic violence
Dir: John Landis *Cast:* David Naughton, Jenny Agutter, John Woodvine, Griffin Dunne
► American students Naughton and Dunne are attacked by a werewolf while backpacking on the English moors. Dunne is killed (although he has an annoying habit of returning from the dead) and Naughton turns into a werewolf. The transformation scenes are truly horrifying, thanks to excellent special effects by Rick Baker. Director Landis mixes comedy and horror most effectively, although he loses his touch with the gruesome car crash finale.

AMITYVILLE HORROR, THE 1979
★★★★ **R Horror 1:58**
☑ Adult situations, explicit language, violence
Dir: Stuart Rosenberg *Cast:* James Brolin, Margot Kidder, Rod Steiger, Don Stroud, Murray Hamilton
► The Lutzes (Brolin and Kidder) move into an old Long Island mansion that's possessed by the Devil. Priests are unable to protect them from ensuing malevolent events. Popular horror film based on Jay Anson's best-seller about a real Long Island family contained enough scary tricks to spawn two further films.

AMITYVILLE II: THE POSSESSION 1982
★★★ **R Horror 1:44**
☑ Rape, nudity, strong sexual content, explicit language, graphic violence
Dir: Damiano Damiani *Cast:* Burt Young, Rutanya Alda, James Olson, Jack Magner, Diane Franklin
► Prequel to *The Amityville Horror* sends child-abuser Young and his family of five

into Long Island's most famous haunted house, where the Devil causes rape, incest, and murder before possessing a priest. Unsavory characters and gruesome special effects should appeal to hard-core horror fans.

AMITYVILLE 3-D 1983
★★ PG Horror 1:33
☑ Adult situations, explicit language, violence
Dir: Richard Fleischer *Cast:* Tony Roberts, Tess Harper, Robert Joy, Candy Clark, John Beal
▶ Cocky reporter Roberts, skeptical about the famous Amityville house of horrors, buys the place over the objections of colleague Clark and estranged wife Harper and soon finds himself besieged by paranormal phenomena (like man-eating flies who munch the real estate broker). Originally released in 3-D, this third Amityville flick has some decent effects but suffers from lame scripting and production.

AMSTERDAM KILL, THE 1978 Hong Kong
★★★ R Action-Adventure 1:38
☑ Explicit language, violence
Dir: Robert Clouse *Cast:* Robert Mitchum, Bradford Dillman, Richard Egan, Leslie Nielsen, Keye Luke
▶ A narcotics agent who's addicted to heroin is hired by a drug czar to expose rival gangs to the police, but the plan backfires when someone starts tipping off the pushers. Hong Kong production has good scenery and a solid performance from Mitchum.

AMY 1981
★★★★ G Drama 1:40
Dir: Vincent McEveety *Cast:* Jenny Agutter, Barry Newman, Kathleen Nolan, Chris Robinson, Margaret O'Brien, Nanette Fabray
▶ Warm-hearted turn-of-the-century drama about Agutter, a spirited wife who leaves her rich husband to work at a school for handicapped children. With the help of school doctor Newman, she teaches the kids to play football. Excellent Disney film should please parents as well as children.

ANATOMY OF A MURDER 1959
★★★★ NR Drama 2:40 B&W
Dir: Otto Preminger *Cast:* James Stewart, Ben Gazzara, Lee Remick, Arthur O'Connell, Eve Arden, George C. Scott
▶ Defense attorney Stewart defends Army man Gazzara, who killed his wife Remick's rapist. Stewart is then challenged by clever prosecutor Scott. Unforgettable adult drama from director Otto Preminger contains some riveting courtroom theatrics. Top-notch performances all around.

ANCHORS AWEIGH 1945
★★★★ NR Musical 2:23
Dir: George Sidney *Cast:* Gene Kelly, Frank Sinatra, Kathryn Grayson, Jose Iturbi, Dean Stockwell
▶ Sinatra and Kelly are sailors on a Hollywood spree, finding love and romance in Tinseltown. MGM musical is not the studio's finest hour, but features some outstanding musical numbers, especially Kelly's famous dance with the animated mouse Jerry (of "Tom and Jerry" fame) and Sinatra singing first-rate Sammy Cahn/Jule Styne tunes. **(CC)**

ANDERSON TAPES, THE 1971
★★★ PG Mystery-Suspense 1:38
☑ Mild violence
Dir: Sidney Lumet *Cast:* Sean Connery, Dyan Cannon, Martin Balsam, Ralph Meeker, Alan King
▶ New York–based thriller with a cynical kick. Convict Connery emerges from prison and masterminds a heist, unaware that law enforcement officials are watching and taping his every move. Unusually strong cast for the genre features Connery's dependable presence, Cannon as his sexy girlfriend, Balsam as a homosexual, King as a mobster, and a young Christopher Walken as "The Kid."

. . . AND GOD CREATED WOMAN 1957 French
☆ PG Drama 1:33
☑ Adult situations
Dir: Roger Vadim *Cast:* Brigitte Bardot, Curt Jurgens, Jean-Louis Trintignant, Christian Marquand
▶ Bardot's breakthrough film ran into censorship problems when it was released, but is pretty tame by today's standards. She plays a voluptuous orphan who seduces two of four sons in a straitlaced family. Saint-Tropez locations give Bardot plenty of opportunities to display her body. Vadim used the title thirty years later for a completely different film.

AND GOD CREATED WOMAN 1988
★★ R Drama 1:40
☑ Nudity, adult situations, explicit language

Dir: Roger Vadim **Cast:** Rebecca De Mornay, Vincent Spano, Frank Langella, Donovan Leitch, Judith Chapman
▶ De Mornay's a convict who proposes to carpenter Spano for parole purposes, but she's really in love with politician Langella. Can she clear up her love life in time to form a rock 'n' roll band? Painless remake of Vadim's notorious 1957 film has some very hot sex scenes, particularly in the opening.

. . . AND JUSTICE FOR ALL 1979
★ ★ ★ ★ ★ **R Drama 2:00**
☑ Nudity, adult situations, explicit language
Dir: Norman Jewison **Cast:** Al Pacino, Jack Warden, John Forsythe, Lee Strasberg, Jeffrey Tambor, Christine Lahti
▶ Comedy and drama are mixed to good advantage by director Jewison in this irreverent and often outrageous look at our legal system. Pacino gives a passionate performance as the lawyer fighting to free a wrongly imprisoned client. His refusal to help corrupt judge Forsythe leads to a climactic courtroom speech that will leave you cheering.

AND NOW FOR SOMETHING COMPLETELY DIFFERENT 1972 British
★ ★ **PG Comedy 1:29**
☑ Adult humor
Dir: Ian McNaughton **Cast:** Graham Chapman, John Cleese, Eric Idle, Terry Gilliam, Terry Jones, Michael Palin
▶ Hilarious collection of comic sketches from England's "Monty Python's Flying Circus." Gilliam's brilliant animated sequences connect the skits, which include the classic "Lumberjack Song," the "Upper Class Twit of the Year" contest, and Cleese's turn as a Hungarian tourist with a most inappropriate phrase book. A wild assortment of the troupe's surreal off-the-wall humor.

ANDROCLES AND THE LION 1952
★ ★ **NR Comedy 1:38**
Dir: Chester Erskine **Cast:** Jean Simmons, Alan Young, Victor Mature, Robert Newton, Maurice Evans, Elsa Lanchester
▶ Bland adaptation of George Bernard Shaw's satirical play retains enough of his sparkling dialogue to remain intriguing. Young plays a tailor who removes a thorn from a lion's paw, an act of kindness repaid in a Roman arena. Troubled romance between Simmons and Mature adds plot complications. Young was

Howard Hughes's replacement for Harpo Marx, originally signed to the Androcles role.

ANDROID 1984
★ **PG Sci-Fi 1:20**
☑ Brief nudity, adult situations, explicit language, violence
Dir: Aaron Kipstadt **Cast:** Klaus Kinski, Don Opper, Brie Howard, Norbert Weisser, Crofton Hardester, Kendra Kirschner
▶ Naive, obsolete android Opper lives on a space station with mad scientist Kinski. Faced with termination, he goes on a rampage with three escaped convicts. Ultra-low-budget film (shot on sets left over from *Battle Beyond the Stars*) has a charming sense of humor and some touching passages to compensate for weak plot.

ANDROMEDA STRAIN, THE 1971
★ ★ ★ **G Sci-Fi 2:07**
Dir: Robert Wise **Cast:** Arthur Hill, David Wayne, James Olson, Kate Reid, Paula Kelly
▶ Mutant strain of bacteria comes to Earth via crashed satellite, threatening all life. At an underground complex, a team of scientists searches for a solution. Race-against-time thriller builds maximum tension and suspense. No-nonsense cast of veteran character actors exemplifies Wise's craftsmanlike, low-key approach to Michael Crichton's bestseller.

AND SOON THE DARKNESS 1970 British
★ ★ **PG Mystery-Suspense 1:38**
☑ Adult situations, violence
Dir: Robert Fuest **Cast:** Pamela Franklin, Michele Dotrice, Sandor Eles, John Nettleton, Clare Kelly
▶ English nurses Franklin and Dotrice bicycle through the French countryside, but their vacation is disrupted when a sex killer stalks them. Dotrice disappears, and the locals are of little help. Moody and ominous thriller is worth a look.

AND THEN THERE WERE NONE 1945
★ ★ ★ ★ **NR Mystery-Suspense 1:38 B&W**
Dir: René Clair **Cast:** Barry Fitzgerald, Walter Huston, Louis Hayward, Roland Young, June Duprez, C. Aubrey Smith
▶ Ten guests, each hiding past crimes, are summoned to remote English island for a party. As an unknown killer murders them one by one, they realize they've been trapped in a grotesque plot. Supe-

rior whodunit based on Agatha Christie's classic *Ten Little Indians* features tricky script, gripping direction, and uniformly strong performances. Remade in 1966 and 1975.

AND THE SHIP SAILS ON 1984 Italian
★ **PG Drama 2:10**
☑ Explicit language
Dir: Federico Fellini   *Cast:* Freddie Jones, Barbara Jefford, Victor Poletti, Peter Cellier, Elisa Mainardi, Norma West
▶ Journalist Jones serves as host on an ocean liner setting sail from Naples, Italy, to scatter the ashes of a recently deceased opera singer. On board are a bevy of operatic oddballs, an Austro-Hungarian archduke and his entourage, and a lovesick rhinoceros. Class tensions arise when the ship picks up Serbian refugees. Visually striking, stately drama about colorful characters is mainly for Fellini fans.   ⑤

ANDY WARHOL'S BAD 1977 Italian
☆ **R Comedy 1:45**
☑ Nudity, adult situations, explicit language, violence
Dir: Jed Johnson   *Cast:* Carroll Baker, Perry King, Susan Tyrrell, Stefania Cassini, Cyrinda Foxe, Mary Boylan
▶ Queens housewife Baker, owner of an electrolysis business, supplements her income running Murder, Inc., dispatching her workers to do away with her clients' unwanted pets and relatives. Poor taste of audacious black comedy will offend many. Last and most expensive of Warhol's Factory films is primarily for devotees.

ANDY WARHOL'S DRACULA 1974 Italian/French
☆ **R Horror/Comedy 1:46**
☑ Nudity, adult situations, explicit language, graphic violence
Dir: Paul Morrissey   *Cast:* Joe Dallesandro, Udo Kier, Arno Juerging, Vittorio De Sica, Roman Polanski, Maxime McKendry
▶ Sex, camp humor, and lots of blood mark this reworking of the Dracula legend, as vampire Kier meets his match in lusty gardener Dallesandro. For the adventurous only. Originally X-rated; also known as *Blood of Dracula*.

ANDY WARHOL'S FRANKENSTEIN 1974 Italian/German/French
☆ **R Horror/Comedy 1:34**
☑ Nudity, adult situations, explicit language, graphic violence

Dir: Paul Morrissey   *Cast:* Joe Dallesandro, Monique Van Vooren, Udo Kier, Srdjan Zelenovic, Dalila Di Lazzaro
▶ Crazed scientist Kier creates strikingly attractive humanoids out of disinterred body parts. Outrageous version of Mary Shelley's classic horror yarn has plenty of gore and some of the more gruesome sex scenes in movie history. Originally X-rated; also released as *The Frankenstein Experiment* and *Flesh for Frankenstein*.

ANGEL 1984
★★★ **R Drama 1:32**
☑ Nudity, strong sexual content, adult situations, explicit language, violence
Dir: Robert Vincent O'Neil   *Cast:* Cliff Gorman, Dick Shawn, Donna Wilkes, Rory Calhoun, Susan Tyrrell
▶ Wilkes plays Angel, a teenager who pays her private high school tuition by turning tricks at night. When a psycho starts murdering her friends, she offers herself as a decoy. Low-grade exploitation that became a surprise success due to its memorable ad campaign ("Honor student by day, Hollywood hooker by night"), but film doesn't really deliver on its more lurid themes. Sequel: *Avenging Angel*.

ANGEL AND THE BADMAN 1947
★★★★★ **NR Western 1:40 B&W**
Dir: James Edward Grant   *Cast:* John Wayne, Gail Russell, Harry Carey, Bruce Cabot, Irene Rich, Lee Dixon
▶ Wayne is Quirt Evans, a wounded outlaw nursed back to health by a pacifist Quaker family. He falls in love with daughter Russell, who begs him not to seek out his enemy Cabot. Predictable but sincere story expertly handled by veteran Western actors. Thanks to its intelligent, satisfying script, Wayne's first production stands up better than some of his more action-oriented films. Available in a colorized version.

ANGEL HEART 1987
★★ **R Mystery-Suspense 1:53**
☑ Nudity, adult situations, explicit language, violence
Dir: Alan Parker   *Cast:* Mickey Rourke, Robert De Niro, Charlotte Rampling, Lisa Bonet, Stocker Fontelieu
▶ In 1955 New York City, Harry Angel (Rourke) is hired by the mysterious Louis Cyphre (De Niro) to look for a missing singer. The trail leads him to New Orleans, voodoo cults, and murder. Parker's con-

troversial movie is atmospheric and visually fascinating but the plot is tangled and confused. Originally rated X, the unrated video version has six extra seconds of steamy sex.

ANGEL OF H.E.A.T. 1982
★ R Sex 1:33
☑ Nudity, strong sexual content, explicit language
Dir: Myrl A. Schriebman *Cast:* Marilyn Chambers, Stephen Johnson
▶ Angel Harmony (Chambers), the top secret agent of a vigilante organization, poses as a mud wrestler so she can spy on a kingpin. Soft-core erotica. Badly acted and cheap production values but plenty of nudity and general sleaziness from wholesome-looking porno queen Chambers.

ANGELO, MY LOVE 1983
☆ R Drama 1:54
☑ Adult situations, explicit language, violence
Dir: Robert Duvall *Cast:* Angelo Evans, Michael Evans, Ruthie Evans, Steve "Patalay" Tsigonoff
▶ Intriguing film uses real-life gypsies in a slight story about a stolen ring worth $10,000. Director Duvall's long friendship with the pint-sized Angelo was the main inspiration behind the project, and his performance is remarkable. So are the glimpses into gypsy life, but the dialogue (often improvised and subtitled) and plot are confusing at times.

ANGEL ON MY SHOULDER 1946
★★★ NR Fantasy/Comedy 1:41 B&W
Dir: Archie Mayo *Cast:* Paul Muni, Anne Baxter, Claude Rains, Onslow Stevens, George Cleveland
▶ In order to get revenge on his killer, dead gangster Muni makes pact with Devil Rains to come back to Earth as a judge. Muni becomes involved with his alter ego's girlfriend Baxter and, much to Rains's chagrin, becomes a do-gooder in his new persona. Heavenly fun with winning performances by Muni and Rains.

ANGELS OVER BROADWAY 1940
★★ NR Drama 1:20 B&W
Dir: Ben Hecht, Lee Garmes *Cast:* Douglas Fairbanks, Jr., Rita Hayworth, Thomas Mitchell, John Qualen, George Watts
▶ Alcoholic writer Mitchell rescues meek embezzler Qualen from suicide, then suggests entering high stakes poker game to pay back Qualen's stolen loot.

Con man Fairbanks and moll Hayworth are only too happy to take advantage of them. Eccentric, sardonic drama set in Manhattan's sleazy underworld builds to unpredictable climax. Co-director Hecht's biting script received an Oscar nomination.

ANGELS WITH DIRTY FACES 1938
★★★ NR Drama 1:37 B&W
Dir: Michael Curtiz *Cast:* James Cagney, Pat O'Brien, Humphrey Bogart, Ann Sheridan, George Bancroft, Dead End Kids
▶ Friends grow up together on the wrong side of the tracks but their paths diverge; Cagney becomes a gangster, O'Brien a priest. Dead End Kids idolize Cagney, setting up the famous climax where O'Brien convinces Cagney, on his way to the gas chamber, to go out like a coward to disillusion boys from life of crime. Powerful classic from Warner Brothers' socially conscious period still packs a wallop.

ANGEL III: THE FINAL CHAPTER 1988
★★ R Action-Adventure 1:39
☑ Nudity, adult situations, explicit language, violence
Dir: Tom DeSimone *Cast:* Maud Adams, Mitzi Kapture, Mark Blankfield, Kin Shriner, Emile Beaucard, Richard Roundtree
▶ Sequel to *Avenging Angel* finds student hooker grown up as New York photographer Kapture. Reunion with her mother in Los Angeles reveals existence of stepsister held slave in Adams's bordello. Kapture dons prostitute disguise to battle Adams in this tired but still lurid melodrama.

ANGRY RED PLANET, THE 1959
☆ NR Sci-Fi 1:23
Dir: Ib Melchior *Cast:* Gerald Mohr, Nora Hayden, Les Tremayne, Jack Kruschen, Paul Hahn
▶ Expedition to Mars faces variety of horrors including giant carnivorous plant, humongous amoeba, and a rodent/crab monster. Upon returning to Earth, scientist Hayden must invent a serum to save the life of the only other survivor. Rather dated special effects, with Martian scenes given special tint through process called Cinemagic.

ANGUISH 1988
★★ R Horror 1:29
☑ Explicit language, graphic violence
Dir: Bigas Luna *Cast:* Michael Lerner,

Zelda Rubinstein, Talia Paul, Clara Pastor
▶ A genuinely weird little horror movie that cleverly mixes fantasy and reality. Lerner is an orderly who loses his job due to diabetes-induced blindness. Rubinstein is the domineering mother who encourages Lerner to take grisly revenge against his enemies by plucking their eyes out. Quite gory and sometimes confusing but generally effective. **(CC)**

ANIMAL CRACKERS 1930
★★★★ **G Comedy 1:38**
Dir: Victor Heerman *Cast:* The Marx Brothers, Margaret Dumont, Lillian Roth, Louis Sorin, Hal Thompson
▶ Second and least-known Marx Brothers film (legal problems kept it out of circulation for years), based on their Broadway hit by Morrie Ryskind and George S. Kaufman, has some dull passages when the brothers aren't on the screen but also boasts some of their best work. Ignore the uninspired musical comedy plot (about a painting stolen from a Long Island mansion) and concentrate on the wonderful high points: Groucho singing "Hurray for Captain Spaulding," Chico and Harpo playing a vicious game of bridge, etc.

ANIMAL HOUSE 1978
★★★★ **R Comedy 1:48**
☑ Nudity, adult situations, explicit language
Dir: John Landis *Cast:* John Belushi, Tim Matheson, Peter Riegert, Karen Allen, Tom Hulce, Stephen Furst
▶ Much imitated, but seldom surpassed, campus comedy about Delta House, the wild, party-loving fraternity that's the bane of Dean Wormer's (John Vernon) existence. The craziest of the Deltas is Belushi's Bluto, a party animal so indestructible that he can smash beer cans on his head without flinching. Film's sense of humor is often tasteless and gross but, just as often, laugh-out-loud funny.

ANIMALS ARE BEAUTIFUL PEOPLE 1975
★★★★★ **G Documentary 1:32**
Dir: Jamie Uys *Cast:* Narrated by Paddy O'Byrne
▶ A decade before he made *The Gods Must Be Crazy*, South African director Uys made this documentary about African wildlife. Four years in the making, this film covers all creatures great and small, from elephants to insects, and the footage is often astonishing.

ANIMALYMPICS 1979
★★★★ **NR Animation 1:18**
Dir: Steven Lisberger *Cast:* Voices of Gilda Radner, Billy Crystal, Harry Shearer, Michael Fremer
▶ Winter and Summer Olympics are combined in this animated animal competition hosted by an ostrich resembling Barbara Walters (Radner doing "Baba WaWa"). Commentators also include a turkey and a turtle (Crystal as Howard Cosell and Henry Kissinger). Glossy, inventive, quality animation; a real treat.

ANNA 1987
★★ **PG-13 Drama 1:35**
☑ Nudity, adult situations, explicit language
Dir: Yurek Bogayevicz *Cast:* Sally Kirkland, Paulina Porizkova, Robert Fields, Gibby Brand, John Robert Tillotson, Joe Aufiery
▶ Expatriate Czech movie star Kirkland, a struggling actress in New York, welcomes stunning Czech refugee Porizkova into her home. Their friendship deteriorates when Porizkova naively swipes Kirkland's writer/boyfriend Fields and achieves overnight stardom. Low-budget drama, with roots in *All About Eve*, features charming screen debut for model Porizkova and brilliant, Oscar-nominated performance from Kirkland. **(CC)**

ANNA AND THE KING OF SIAM 1946
★★★★ **NR Drama 2:08 B&W**
Dir: John Cromwell *Cast:* Irene Dunne, Rex Harrison, Linda Darnell, Lee J. Cobb, Gale Sondergaard
▶ Nonmusical precursor to the great Rodgers and Hammerstein musical *The King and I*. English governess Dunne goes to work for iron-fisted Thai monarch Harrison; he begins to soften under her guidance. Well-acted, well-made movie; entertaining even without music. Based on real-life governess Margaret Langdon's experiences and book.

ANNA CHRISTIE 1930
★★ **NR Drama 1:26 B&W**
Dir: Clarence Brown *Cast:* Greta Garbo, Marie Dressler, Charles Bickford, Lee Phelps, George F. Marion
▶ Somewhat creaky early talkie, adapted from a play by America's greatest playwright, Eugene O'Neill, as a vehicle for one of Hollywood's greatest actresses, Garbo. Holds interest for her performance as the ex-hooker who finds true love with seaman Bickford and as

the movie in which Garbo made a successful transition to the sound era. Advertised at the time with the slogan "Garbo Talks."

ANNA KARENINA 1935
★★★ NR Drama 1:35 B&W
Dir: Clarence Brown *Cast:* Greta Garbo, Fredric March, Freddie Bartholomew, Maureen O'Sullivan, May Robson, Basil Rathbone
▶ Anna Karenina (Garbo), unhappily married to politician Rathbone in nineteenth-century Russia, falls in love with handsome Count Vronsky (March) but the affair ends in tragedy. The *Anna Christie* team (MGM, director Brown, star Garbo) reunited for this high-quality literary adaptation of Leo Tolstoy's classic. Garbo is superb, as always.

ANNA TO THE INFINITE POWER 1983
★★ NR Sci-Fi 1:45
Dir: Robert Weimer *Cast:* Dina Merrill, Martha Byrne, Jack Gilford, Mark Patton, Donna Mitchell
▶ Bright young Byrne, haunted by disaster-filled nightmares, learns she has ESP when her mother Merrill reveals she's the result of a cloning study. Byrne then searches for her telepathic comrades, scattered after the conclusion of the experiment. Tame sci-fi drama will appeal mainly to younger viewers.

ANNE OF GREEN GABLES 1934
★★ NR Drama 1:20
Dir: George Nicholls *Cast:* Anne Shirley, Tom Brown, O. P. Heggie, Helen Westley, Sara Haden, Murray Kinnell
▶ Moving account of bachelor farmer (Heggie) and his sister (Westley) who adopt charming pig-tailed orphan (Shirley). She wins the hearts of everyone she meets, especially handsome Gilbert Blythe (Brown). Canadian locations help this heartfelt adaptation of Lucy Maud Montgomery's classic novel. Shirley, previously Dawn O'Day, took her screen name from this character. Remade as a Canadian miniseries in 1985.

ANNE OF GREEN GABLES 1985
Canadian
★★★ NR Drama/MFTV 3:19
Dir: Kevin Sullivan *Cast:* Megan Follows, Colleen Dewhurst, Patricia Hamilton, Marilyn Lightstone, Charmion King, Richard Farnsworth
▶ Inspired adaptation of L. H. Montgomery's classic novels follows adventures of young orphan Follows in Canadian wilderness community. Sweet, simple story line is touching and uplifting. Double cassette combines two episodes of miniseries, *A New Home* and *A Bend in the Road*. Sequel, *Anne of Avonlea*, appeared in 1987.

ANNE OF THE THOUSAND DAYS 1969
British
★★★★ PG Drama 2:25
☑ Adult situations
Dir: Charles Jarrott *Cast:* Richard Burton, Genevieve Bujold, Irene Papas, Anthony Quayle, Michael Hordern, John Colicos
▶ In sixteenth-century England, King Henry VIII (Burton) chooses Anne Boleyn (Bujold) over current wife Katherine (Papas) and marries her, but the union proves ill-fated when Bujold fails to deliver a son. Beautifully mounted and fascinating; Burton and Bujold (both Oscar-nominated) are incredible. Best Picture nominee; won for Costume Design. From Maxwell Anderson's historical play.

ANNIE 1982
★★★★★ PG Musical 2:08
☑ Explicit language
Dir: John Huston *Cast:* Albert Finney, Carol Burnett, Aileen Quinn, Bernadette Peters, Tim Curry, Geoffrey Holder
▶ Quinn is America's favorite orphan Annie, singing and dancing her way into the heart of billionaire Daddy Warbucks (Finney). Burnett has a comic field day as Miss Hannigan, the drunken orphanage supervisor plotting to reclaim Annie and get her hands on Warbucks's loot. Lavish version of the Broadway musical is overproduced (to the rumored tune of $50 million or so) but still makes fine family fare. Finney is warm and winning and sings surprisingly well. Score includes the hit song "Tomorrow." **(CC)**

ANNIE GET YOUR GUN 1950
★★★★ NR Musical 1:47
Dir: George Sidney *Cast:* Betty Hutton, Howard Keel, Louis Calhern, J. Carrol Naish, Edward Arnold, Keenan Wynn
▶ Brassy, extravagant version of Irving Berlin's Broadway hit based very loosely on the life of sharpshooter Annie Oakley (Hutton). The plot—about her competitive romance with marksman Frank Butler (Keel) in Buffalo Bill's Wild West Show—takes a back seat to the songs, most of them wonderful pop standards: "Doin' What Comes Natur'lly," "Anything You

Can Do," "There's No Business Like Show Business," etc. Won an Oscar for score.

ANNIE HALL 1977
★★★ **PG Comedy 1:34**
☑ Adult humor
Dir: Woody Allen *Cast:* Woody Allen, Diane Keaton, Tony Roberts, Carol Kane, Paul Simon, Shelley Duvall
▶ Oscars for Best Picture, Best Director, and Best Actress (Keaton) went to Allen's wise and wonderful look at modern relationships. Woody plays neurotic Jewish comic Alvy Singer, recalling his long love affair with Keaton's equally neurotic but WASPy Annie. The crazy humor of Woody's early films is here but, for the first time, tempered with a new sophistication and maturity. Poignant, funny, and memorable.

ANNIE OAKLEY 1935
★★★ **NR Western 1:30 B&W**
Dir: George Stevens *Cast:* Barbara Stanwyck, Preston Foster, Melvyn Douglas, Moroni Olsen, Andy Clyde, Chief Thundercloud
▶ Stanwyck is charming in her first Western as the rambunctious shooting star of Buffalo Bill's Wild West Show. Entertaining film provides a fairly honest account of her rise from an uncultured Ozarks background to fame and glamour. Foster and Douglas play rivals for her affections, with Chief Thundercloud providing comic relief as Sitting Bull, Annie's mentor.

ANNIHILATORS, THE 1985
★★★ **R Action-Adventure 1:25**
☑ Nudity, explicit language, graphic violence
Dir: Charles E. Sellier *Cast:* Christopher Stone, Andy Wood, Lawrence Hilton-Jacobs, Gerrit Graham, Dennis Redfield
▶ In Atlanta, Vietnam vets band together to wipe out three evil gangs. They break up a drug ring, rescue a hijacked school bus, and gain the grudging respect of cops and the homeless. Violent, unpleasant exploitation fare has cheap production values and often unintelligible dialogue.

ANOTHER COUNTRY 1984 British
★ **PG Drama 1:31**
☑ Adult situations, explicit language
Dir: Marek Kanievska *Cast:* Rupert Everett, Colin Firth, Michael Jenn, Robert Addie, Rupert Wainwright, Cary Elwes
▶ Intelligent small-scaled drama of a 1930s homosexual love affair at a British school. Guy Bennett (Everett) rebels against the system by indulging in Marxist politics (under the influence of best pal Firth) and having an affair with Elwes. Guy is expelled when his affair is discovered. Based on the life of Guy Burgess, the Englishman who spied for, and eventually defected to, the Soviet Union.

ANOTHER MAN, ANOTHER CHANCE 1977 U.S./French
★★ **PG Drama 2:08**
☑ Rape, explicit language
Dir: Claude Lelouch *Cast:* James Caan, Genevieve Bujold, Francis Huster, Jennifer Warren, Susan Tyrrell
▶ A romantic drama, set in the 1870s American West, featuring Lelouch's customary lyricism. Two widowed people, French immigrant Bujold and American veterinarian Caan, get a second chance at happiness with one another. Appealing characters and excellent photography but overlong and languidly paced.

ANOTHER THIN MAN 1939
★★ **NR Mystery-Suspense 1:45 B&W**
Dir: W. S. Van Dyke II *Cast:* William Powell, Myrna Loy, Virginia Grey, Otto Kruger, C. Aubrey Smith, Ruth Hussey
▶ Third entry in the popular Thin Man series takes Nick and Nora to Long Island to protect millionaire Smith from murder. Not as distinguished as some of its companion films, but Powell and Loy are as charming and sophisticated as ever, their dog Asta performs his old tricks, and their son Nicky Jr. makes his first appearance. **(CC)**

ANOTHER WOMAN 1988
★ **PG Drama 1:24**
☑ Explicit language
Dir: Woody Allen *Cast:* Gena Rowlands, Mia Farrow, Ian Holm, Blythe Danner, Gene Hackman, Betty Buckley
▶ Philosophy professor Rowlands, having just turned fifty, examines her life; she discovers she's relied on control to avoid emotion, in the process hurting many around her. Well-made character study with top-flight cast explores the human condition through inner turmoil of gifted New Yorkers. Stark drama marks another of Allen's attempts to deal with more serious subject matter.

ANTARCTICA 1984 Japanese
★★★ **G Action-Adventure 1:50**
Dir: Koreyoshi Kurahara *Cast:* Ken Takakura, Tsunehiko Watase
▶ Real-life Japanese drama about accidentally abandoned sled dogs fighting

for survival through a brutal Antarctic winter. The most successful Japanese film ever released in Japan includes breathtaking South Pole footage. Sense of genuine disaster may be too intense for younger viewers. **(CC)** Ⓢ

ANTHONY ADVERSE 1936
★★★ **NR Drama 2:21 B&W**
Dir: Mervyn LeRoy *Cast:* Fredric March, Olivia de Havilland, Edmund Gwenn, Claude Rains, Anita Louise, Gale Sondergaard
▶ Massive, sprawling soap opera from Hervey Allen's best-seller follows the adventures in nineteenth-century Europe and America of the ambitious but illegitimate Adverse (March). His tragic love affair with opera star de Havilland and rivalry with evil business partners Rains and Sondergaard provide the core of the story. Sondergaard, composer Erich Korngold, and cinematographer Tony Gaudio all won Oscars.

ANTONY AND CLEOPATRA 1973 British
★ **NR Drama 2:40**
Dir: Charlton Heston *Cast:* Charlton Heston, Hildegard Neil, Eric Porter, John Castle, Fernando Rey, Juan Luis Galiardo
▶ Faithful adaptation of the Shakespeare play with writer/director Heston as Antony, lover of Egyptian queen Cleopatra (Neil) and political rival of Octavius Caesar (Castle). Stagey, low-budget result has some fine moments by Heston and impressive work by Porter as Heston's treacherous aide.

ANY WEDNESDAY 1966
★★★ **NR Comedy 1:49**
Dir: Robert Ellis Miller *Cast:* Jane Fonda, Jason Robards, Dean Jones, Rosemary Murphy, Ann Prentiss
▶ Wednesday is the day married man Robards cheats on his wife Murphy with luscious but dim-witted Fonda. The status quo is threatened when salesman Jones learns of the arrangement. Jovial farce from the Muriel Resnik play features fine comic performances from the four leads.

ANY WHICH WAY YOU CAN 1980
★★★★ **PG Comedy 1:56**
☑ Adult situations, explicit language, violence, adult humor
Dir: Buddy Van Horn *Cast:* Clint Eastwood, Sondra Locke, Geoffrey Lewis, William Smith, Harry Guardino, Ruth Gordon
▶ Critics scratched their heads when

Every Which Way But Loose made more money than any previous Eastwood effort, but even they enjoyed this lighthearted sequel. Original's winning formula remains, with a welcome touch of sensitivity added to the characters. Eastwood repeats his role as a brawling mechanic, this time forced by the mob to face King of the Streetfighters Smith in a no-holds-barred battle in Jackson Hole, Wyoming. Clyde the orangutan is also back, stealing the film with his raunchy gags. Music includes songs by Fats Domino and Glen Campbell.

ANZIO 1968
★★★★ **PG War 2:00**
☑ Violence
Dir: Edward Dmytryk *Cast:* Robert Mitchum, Peter Falk, Arthur Kennedy, Robert Ryan
▶ The Allies invade Italy in the bloody battle of Anzio in World War II; war reporter Mitchum covers the story. Interesting subject with notable cast, but lackluster script is unlikely to please genre fans.

APACHE 1954
★★ **NR Western 1:31**
Dir: Robert Aldrich *Cast:* Burt Lancaster, Jean Peters, John McIntire, Charles Buchinski, John Dehner, Paul Guilfoyle
▶ After Geronimo's surrender, Massai (Lancaster), the last unconquered Apache chief, conducts a guerrilla war against the Army. McIntire plays a cavalry guide sympathetic to Massai's plight; Peters, the chief's beautiful companion. Film's unusual perspective is supportive of Indian rights. Charles Bronson (using his real name Buchinski) has a minor role as a soldier.

APARTMENT, THE 1960
★★★★ **NR Comedy 2:05 B&W**
Dir: Billy Wilder *Cast:* Jack Lemmon, Shirley MacLaine, Fred MacMurray, Ray Walston, Jack Kruschen
▶ Ambitious corporate employee Lemmon tries to work his way up by lending his apartment key to philandering boss MacMurray for assignations with girlfriend MacLaine. Lemmon then falls in love with her himself. Billy Wilder masterfully mixes comedy and drama. Superb acting, especially Lemmon in his archetypal role of the schnook who develops a conscience. Multi-Oscar winner, including Best Picture.

APOCALYPSE NOW 1979
★ ★ ★ R Action-Adventure 2:33
☑ Adult situations, violence
Dir: Francis Coppola *Cast:* Martin
Sheen, Marlon Brando, Robert Duvall,
Frederic Forrest, Sam Bottoms
▶ Coppola's visionary Vietnam film was
inspired by Joseph Conrad's novel *Heart
of Darkness.* Sheen is the U.S. soldier assigned to "terminate with extreme prejudice" Brando's renegade Colonel Kurtz,
but first he must journey upriver. His voyage brings home the horrors of war. Excellent performances (especially by Duvall as the gung-ho officer who loves "the
smell of napalm in the morning") and
stunning visuals. Oscar-winning cinematography by Vittorio Storaro.

APOLOGY 1986
★ ★ ★ ★ NR Mystery-Suspense/MFTV
1:38
☑ Brief nudity, adult situations, explicit
language, violence
Dir: Robert Bierman *Cast:* Lesley Ann
Warren, Peter Weller, John Glover,
Jimmie Ray Weeks, George Loros,
Harvey Fierstein
▶ Conceptual artist Warren solicits anony-
mous confessions from phone callers in
New York City, only to become the target
for a serial killer. Weller is the cop who
tries to help her in this slick and stylish
mystery from the pen of Mark Medoff.

APPALOOSA, THE 1966
★ ★ ★ NR Western 1:38
Dir: Sidney J. Furie *Cast:* Marlon
Brando, Anjanette Comer, John Saxon,
Emilio Fernandez, Alex Montoya, Rafael
Campos
▶ Buffalo hunter Brando's prized Ap-
paloosa horse is stolen by Mexican ban-
dit Saxon. Brando is wounded by Saxon's
gang when he tries to recover the horse.
He recuperates with the aid of Saxon's
ex-lover Comer; they fall in love as Saxon
chases them. Off-beat Western features
one of Brando's lesser performances.

APPLE DUMPLING GANG, THE 1975
★ ★ ★ ★ G Comedy 1:40
Dir: Norman Tokar *Cast:* Bill Bixby,
Susan Clark, Don Knotts, Tim Conway,
David Wayne
▶ Lively, wholesome family Western from
Walt Disney Studios. Bixby is a gambler
who finds himself saddled with three chil-
dren in this jolly tale of bank robbers and
gold mines in the Old West. Most of the
comedy is provided by Conway and

Knotts as a team of incompetent desper-
adoes.

**APPLE DUMPLING GANG RIDES
AGAIN, THE** 1979
★ ★ ★ ★ G Comedy 1:29
Dir: Vincent McEveety *Cast:* Tim Conway, Don Knotts, Tim Matheson,
Kenneth Mars, Elyssa Davalos
▶ Good old-fashioned Disney fun in this
sequel to *The Apple Dumpling Gang.* Former bad guys Conway and Knotts vow to
reform, but despite their good intentions
the local sheriff mistakes them for banditos. The bumbling duo redeem themselves by foiling an attempted train robbery.

APPOINTMENT WITH DEATH 1988
★ ★ ★ PG Mystery-Suspense 1:42
☑ Violence
Dir: Michael Winner *Cast:* Peter Ustinov, Lauren Bacall, John Gielgud,
Carrie Fisher, Piper Laurie
▶ Ustinov returns as Agatha Christie's famous detective Hercule Poirot, whose
travels take him to the Holy Land circa
1937. His vacation is interrupted by the
murder of wealthy grand dame Laurie.
The usual cast of all-star suspects is on
hand. Slow and talky at times but spectacular scenery and a sassy Bacall make
this painless entertainment. (CC)

**APPRENTICESHIP OF DUDDY KRAVITZ,
THE** 1974 Canadian
★ ★ ★ PG Comedy 2:01
☑ Brief nudity, adult situations, explicit
language
Dir: Ted Kotcheff *Cast:* Richard Dreyfuss, Randy Quaid, Jack Warden, Denholm Elliott
▶ Wicked comedy about a success-
driven schemer in 1940s Montreal gave
Dreyfuss his first leading role. He hustles
everything from heroin to pinball machines in scenes that are often biting as
well as manic. Although uneven, the
highlights (including an outrageous bar
mitzvah home movie directed by Elliott)
are hilarious. Mordecai Richler was
Oscar-nominated for adapting his novel.

APPRENTICE TO MURDER 1988
★ ★ PG-13 Drama 1:34
☑ Brief nudity, adult situations, vio-
lence
Dir: Ralph L. Thomas *Cast:* Donald
Sutherland, Chad Lowe, Mia Sara, Knut
Husebo, Rutanya Alda
▶ Young millworker Lowe falls under the
spell of faith healer Sutherland, who may

have ties to the Devil. Testing his protégé's loyalty, the "Pow Pow" doctor sets out to murder an evil hermit. Atmospheric horror film shot in Norway was based on a purportedly true incident in Pennsylvania, 1927. **(CC)**

APRIL FOOLS, THE 1969
★★★★ **PG Comedy 1:35**
☑ Adult situations
Dir: Stuart Rosenberg *Cast:* Jack Lemmon, Catherine Deneuve, Peter Lawford, Sally Kellerman
▶ Surburbanite Lemmon, trapped in a bad marriage to Kellerman, falls in love with Deneuve, the wife of his boss Lawford. These kinds of Hollywood movie romances usually end on a bittersweet note, but here Lemmon and Deneuve actually run away together to Paris. Solid cast makes it work. Dionne Warwick sings the hit Bacharach/David title song.

APRIL FOOL'S DAY 1986
★★ **R Horror 1:30**
☑ Adult situations, explicit language, violence
Dir: Fred Walton *Cast:* Griffin O'Neal, Deborah Foreman, Tom Wilson, Amy Steel, Jay Baker
▶ Spoiled teen Muffy (Foreman) throws a party for her friends on a remote island. Is her insane twin Buffy behind the subsequent murders? Gimmick film from the *Friday the 13th* gang has an attractive cast and good production values, but resorts to familiar slasher stunts. Trick ending will disappoint most viewers. **(CC)**

ARABESQUE 1966
★★★ **NR Mystery-Suspense 1:06**
Dir: Stanley Donen *Cast:* Gregory Peck, Sophia Loren, Alan Badel, Kieron Moore, Carl Duering, George Coulouris
▶ Glossy, diverting espionage caper with Peck as an Oxford professor and code expert asked to spy on Middle Eastern oil tycoon Badel. When his cover is blown, Peck kidnaps Badel's mistress Loren and embarks on a wild flight to safety. Donen's follow-up to *Charade* was equally romantic and elegant, with Loren particularly fetching in Dior costumes.

ARCH OF TRIUMPH 1948
★★★ **NR Drama 2:00 B&W**
Dir: Lewis Milestone *Cast:* Ingrid Bergman, Charles Boyer, Charles Laughton, Louis Calhern, Ruth Warrick
▶ In World War II Paris, doctor Boyer befriends troubled singer Bergman and they fall in love. But Boyer is deported; when he returns, Bergman has a new lover, and Boyer becomes embroiled in plot for revenge against Nazi Laughton. Highly emotional drama with good performances by Boyer and Bergman. Based on the novel by Erich Maria Remarque.

ARIA 1988 British
☆ **R Musical 1:38**
☑ Nudity, adult situations, violence
Dir: Derek Jarman, Nicolas Roeg, Robert Altman, Bill Bryden, Bruce Beresford, Julien Temple, Jean-Luc Godard, Charles Sturridge, Franc Roddam, Ken Russell *Cast:* Theresa Russell, Nicola Swain, Buck Henry, Anita Morris, Genevieve Page
▶ Ten of the world's top directors reinterpret famous operatic arias in rock-video-style vignettes. Some striking sequences (like Roddam's young suicide variation on *Tristan und Isolde*, featuring Bridget Fonda, daughter of Peter) but overall this rather mixed bag is inaccessible.

ARMED AND DANGEROUS 1986
★★★ **PG-13 Comedy 1:28**
☑ Brief nudity, adult situations, explicit language, mild violence
Dir: Mark L. Lester *Cast:* John Candy, Eugene Levy, Robert Loggia, Meg Ryan, Kenneth McMillan, Steve Railsback
▶ Cop Candy, who loses his job after a frame-up, and inept lawyer Levy become partners at the Guard Dog School. Together they break up a crime ring by crashing Mafia parties. Broad comedy coasts on stars' talents (Candy's impersonation of Divine is priceless). **(CC)**

ARMED RESPONSE 1986
★★ **R Action-Adventure 1:26**
☑ Nudity, explicit language, graphic violence
Dir: Fred Olen Ray *Cast:* David Carradine, Lee Van Cleef, Mako, Lois Hamilton, Ross Hagen, Dick Miller
▶ Carradine, a Vietnam vet plagued by flashbacks, is out to avenge the death of his brother, killed by Japanese gangsters over a stolen jade statue. When his family is kidnapped, he's joined by his ex-cop father Van Cleef in a brutal manhunt. Lots of action and veteran B-characters perk up familiar plot.

ARNOLD 1973
★★ **PG Comedy 1:40**
☑ Explicit language, violence

Dir: Georg Fenady   *Cast:* Stella Stevens, Roddy McDowall, Farley Granger, Elsa Lanchester, Victor Buono, Shani Wallis
▶ Stevens marries a corpse in order to inherit his estate and then gets worried when the wedding guests are bumped off one by one. Silly comedy from Bing Crosby Productions features imaginative murders and a cast of veteran actors.

AROUND THE WORLD IN 80 DAYS
1956
★ ★ ★ ★ G Action-Adventure 2:55
Dir: Michael Anderson   *Cast:* David Niven, Shirley MacLaine, Cantinflas, John Gielgud, Marlene Dietrich, Robert Newton
▶ Large-scale adaptation of the famous Jules Verne story about the efforts of Phileas Fogg (Niven) and his valet Passepartout (Cantinflas) to circle the globe. Producer Michael Todd spared no expense for this blockbuster, which won five Oscars: Best Picture, Screenplay (S. J. Perelman, John Farrow, James Poe), Cinematography, Editing, and Score (Victor Young). Forty-four stars ranging from Frank Sinatra to Jose Greco have cameo parts. Wide-screen process will suffer somewhat on TV.

AROUND THE WORLD UNDER THE SEA
1966
★ NR Action-Adventure 1:57
Dir: Andrew Marton   *Cast:* Lloyd Bridges, Shirley Eaton, Brian Kelly, David McCallum, Keenan Wynn, Gary Merrill
▶ Six scientists, all expert divers, set out in an experimental submarine on a dangerous mission to monitor underwater volcanoes. Eaton, the only female on board, causes some tension, but expedition leader Bridges keeps his men firmly in line. Dated science fiction from the makers of TV's "Sea Hunt."

AROUSERS, THE 1973
★ R Mystery-Suspense 1:27
☑ Nudity, adult situations, explicit language, violence
Dir: Curtis Hanson   *Cast:* Tab Hunter, Sherry Latimer, Nadyne Turney, Isabel Jewell
▶ Phys ed teacher Hunter kills a young girl to disguise his impotence. Further killings result when the girl's roommate searches for her friend. Low-budget thriller from Roger Corman has become a cult favorite for its case-study approach.

ARRANGEMENT, THE 1969
★ ★ R Drama 2:06
☑ Adult situations, explicit language, violence
Dir: Elia Kazan   *Cast:* Kirk Douglas, Faye Dunaway, Deborah Kerr, Richard Boone, Hume Cronyn
▶ Suffering a mid-life crisis, successful Madison Avenue ad executive Douglas has a serious car crash. He reexamines his life while convalescing, then goes on a rampage that leaves his wife Kerr and mistress Dunaway in tears. Kazan wrote, produced, and directed this feverish soap opera based on his own novel.

ARSENIC AND OLD LACE 1944
★ ★ ★ NR Comedy 1:58 B&W
Dir: Frank Capra   *Cast:* Cary Grant, Priscilla Lane, Raymond Massey, Peter Lorre, Josephine Hull, Jean Adair
▶ Fast-paced, often hilarious black farce about two sweet old ladies, Hull and Adair, who murder unsuspecting bachelors with homemade elderberry wine. Nephew Grant frantically tries to protect them from the police and two homicidal psychopaths who have unexpectedly dropped in. Adaptation of the hit Joseph Kesselring play was a pet project for Capra, who produced and shot the film in four weeks before entering the Army in 1941.

ARTHUR 1981
★ ★ ★ ★ ★ PG Comedy 1:37
☑ Adult situations, explicit language
Dir: Steve Gordon   *Cast:* Dudley Moore, Liza Minnelli, John Gielgud, Geraldine Fitzgerald, Jill Eikenberry
▶ Winning screwball comedy about drunken heir Moore who falls for Queens waitress Minnelli instead of the debutante Eikenberry he's supposed to marry. Moore (nominated for best actor) fits his part perfectly. Gielgud won an Oscar for his role as a caustic valet, as did "Arthur's Theme" for best song. Debut director Gordon was also nominated for his screenplay, but tragically died before completing another film. Followed by *Arthur 2 On the Rocks.*

ARTHUR 2 ON THE ROCKS 1988
★ ★ ★ PG Comedy 1:52
☑ Explicit language
Dir: Bud Yorkin   *Cast:* Dudley Moore, Liza Minnelli, Stephen Elliott, Cynthia Sikes, John Gielgud, Geraldine Fitzgerald
▶ In sequel to immensely popular *Arthur,*

lovable billionaire drunk Moore and new bride Minnelli fall upon hard times as vengeful Elliott, his daughter Sikes spurned by Moore in the original film, conspires to render the newlyweds penniless and homeless. Elliott demands Moore divorce Minnelli and marry Sikes or spend his life on the other side of the tracks. More of Moore's engaging mugging and clowning, but spin-off isn't up to source and employs Gielgud all too briefly. **(CC)**

ASHANTI 1979 Swiss
★★★ **R Action-Adventure 1:57**
☑ Nudity, explicit language, violence
Dir: Richard Fleischer **Cast:** Michael Caine, Peter Ustinov, Beverly Johnson, Omar Sharif, Rex Harrison, William Holden
▶ Johnson, the black wife of missionary Caine, is kidnapped by African slave trader Ustinov. Authorities are powerless to help, so Caine hires mercenaries to rescue her. The trail leads from the desert to the yacht of a Middle Eastern prince. Cast (mostly limited to cameos) is the best aspect of this formula adventure.

ASPHALT JUNGLE, THE 1950
★★★ **NR Crime/Drama 1:52 B&W**
Dir: John Huston **Cast:** Sterling Hayden, Sam Jaffe, Louis Calhern, Jean Hagen, James Whitmore, Marilyn Monroe
▶ Taut, realistic account of a criminal gang planning a perfect robbery with their mastermind Jaffe. Superb performances (including Monroe's best early role), exciting action, and a provocative view of the underworld. Highly influential film received four Oscar nominations and was the unacknowledged inspiration for countless caper movies. Based on a novel by W. R. Burnett.

ASSASSINATION 1987
★★★ **PG-13 Action-Adventure 1:28**
☑ Adult situations, explicit language, violence
Dir: Peter Hunt **Cast:** Charles Bronson, Jill Ireland, Stephen Elliott, Jan Gan Boyd, Eric Stern
▶ Bronson plays a Secret Service agent guarding feisty First Lady Ireland (code-named "One Mama") from a band of assassins. Cross-country chases stick to tried-and-true action sequences, and the relationship between real-life couple Bronson and Ireland is curiously flat. **(CC)**

ASSAULT, THE 1986 Dutch
☆ **PG Drama 2:29**
☑ Violence
Dir: Fons Rademakers **Cast:** Derek de Lint, Marc van Uchelen, Monique van de Ven, John Kraaykamp, Huub van der Lubbe
▶ During World War II, a young Dutch boy watches the Nazis execute his family. Forty years later he still struggles to understand why the incident occurred. Earnest but slow-paced story based on a respected novel by Harry Mulisch won Oscar for Best Foreign Film. **S**

ASSAULT OF THE KILLER BIMBOS 1988
★★ **R Comedy 1:21**
☑ Nudity, adult situations, explicit language, mild violence
Dir: Anita Rosenberg **Cast:** Christina Whitaker, Elizabeth Kaiton, Tammara Souza, Patti Astor, Nick Cassavetes, Griffin O'Neal
▶ Tongue-in-cheek comedy about two go-go dancers and a waitress framed for murder. The girls pick up three "bimboys" and head for Mexico, where they run into the real criminals. Very low-budget (and low-brow) satire merits some praise for its sympathetic treatment of the heroines.

ASSAULT ON PRECINCT 13 1976
★★★ **R Action-Adventure 1:31**
☑ Explicit language, graphic violence
Dir: John Carpenter **Cast:** Austin Stoker, Darwin Joston, Laurie Zimmer, Nancy Loomis, Kim Richards
▶ A lone cop, several innocent bystanders, and some death-row prisoners are trapped inside an about-to-be-abandoned police station when a revenge-seeking gang lays siege to it. Explosive, hard-hitting urban crime drama is tremendously suspenseful, thanks to realistic performances by its unknown cast and slam-bang direction from Carpenter. Story was inspired by Howard Hawks's classic western *Rio Bravo.*

ASSISI UNDERGROUND, THE 1985
★★★★ **PG Drama 1:54**
☑ Violence
Dir: Alexander Ramati **Cast:** Ben Cross, James Mason, Maximilian Schell, Irene Papas, Karl-Heinz Hackl
▶ In war-torn Assisi, young priest Cross is ordered to hide sixteen Jews from the Germans. Using convents and monasteries, he sets up a forgery ring to outfox the Nazis. Based on a true story, earnest but plodding film features one of Mason's

last roles as a bishop determined to help the Jews. A three-hour miniseries version also exists.

AS SUMMERS DIE 1986
★ ★ ★ **NR Drama/MFTV 1:27**
Dir: Jean-Claude Tramont   *Cast:* Scott Glenn, Jamie Lee Curtis, Bette Davis, Ron O'Neal, Beah Richards
▶ Glenn, a struggling small-town Southern lawyer in the late 1950s, finds himself defending a poor black woman against the seizure of her oil-rich land by the town's reigning white family. Curtis, as a rebellious Southern belle who wins Glenn's heart, and screen legend Davis co-star as the only family members sympathetic to Glenn's cause. Quality melodrama of little guy who takes on the establishment is enhanced by first-rate cast and splendid Southern atmosphere.

AS YOU LIKE IT 1936 British
★ **NR Comedy 1:36 B&W**
Dir: Paul Czinner   *Cast:* Elisabeth Bergner, Laurence Olivier, Sophie Stewart, Henry Ainley
▶ Way before *Tootsie, Yentl*, and other role reversal stories there was William Shakespeare's comedy of wooing and romance. Rosalind (Bergner), a noblewoman exiled to the forests of Arden, falls for nobleman Orlando (a young Olivier) and disguises herself as a boy to teach him a few lessons in love. Adaptation co-written by J. M. Barrie.

AT CLOSE RANGE 1986
★ ★ ★ **R Drama 1:55**
☑ Brief nudity, adult situations, explicit language, violence
Dir: James Foley   *Cast:* Sean Penn, Christopher Walken, Mary Stuart Masterson, Christopher Penn, Millie Perkins, Candy Clark
▶ Moody, frightening thriller with a strong performance from Walken as a father who returns to his family after many years and lures his sons (Sean and Christopher Penn) into crime. When the police close in on Walken, he decides that his sons have to die. Vivid evocation of gritty Pennsylvania underclass and often shocking violence. Based on a true story. Madonna sings her hit "Live to Tell." (CC)

ATLANTIC CITY 1981
★ ★ **R Drama 1:44**
☑ Nudity, adult situations, explicit language
Dir: Louis Malle   *Cast:* Burt Lancaster,

Susan Sarandon, Kate Reid, Michel Piccoli, Hollis McLaren, Robert Joy
▶ Old-time gangster Lancaster and aspiring croupier Sarandon team up to outsmart the Mafia over a dope deal in this very unusual offbeat film for sophisticated audiences. The plot is full of melodramatic conventions but they are given a new look and feel by director Malle. The script by playwright John Guare has a genuine feel for these down-and-out dreamers, and the city, in all its seedy grandeur, provides a meaningful backdrop to the action. Nominated for five Oscars, including Best Picture. Singer Robert Goulet appears as himself.

ATOMIC CAFE, THE 1982
★ ★ **NR Documentary 1:32 C/B&W**
Dir: Kevin Rafferty, Jayne Loader, Pierce Rafferty
▶ Nostalgia with an ironic apocalyptic twist. The filmmakers juxtapose archival footage to demonstrate the government's manipulation of American public opinion about The Bomb. Documentary and newsreel footage of real figures—Nixon, Krushchev, Truman, the Rosenbergs—evokes the Cold War era. Most disturbing are the "happy talk" propaganda films, such as Bert the Turtle's "Duck and Cover" cartoon warning to children. Repetitive but powerful.

ATOR, THE FIGHTING EAGLE 1983 Italian
☆ **PG Action-Adventure 1:40**
☑ Adult situations, explicit language, violence
Dir: David Hills   *Cast:* Miles O'Keeffe, Sabrina Siani, Ritza Brown, Edmund Purdom, Laura Gemser
▶ Low-budget imitation of *Conan the Barbarian* features muscular O'Keeffe in pursuit of his bride Brown, abducted by spider-worshipping sect. Amazonian robber/warrior Siani aids him in his endeavor. Mainly for hard-core sword-and-sorcery fans. Best line: "The Earth trembled like a virgin drawn to the nuptial bed." Followed by sequel *The Blade Master*.

ATTACK AT DAWN 1976 Israeli
★ ★ ★ ★ **PG-13 Action-Adventure 1:45**
☑ Explicit language, violence
Dir: Menahem Golan   *Cast:* Rick Jason, Peter Brown, Joseph Shiloa
▶ Simplistic action fare teams escaped Israeli POW Jason and American reporter Brown on a mission to free soldiers from an Arab prison. Bad dubbing and by-the-

numbers plotting, but enough action for undemanding fans.

ATTACK FORCE Z 1981
Australian/Taiwanese
★★★ NR War 1:24
☑ Explicit language, violence
Dir: Tim Burstall *Cast:* John Phillip Law, Sam Neill, Mel Gibson, Chris Haywood
► During World War II, five Australian commandos are dropped behind enemy lines to bring back an important defector. Surrounded by Japanese soldiers, they must decide between killing the defector or exposing their resistance network. Credible suspense and good acting despite bleak, downbeat tone.

ATTACK OF THE KILLER TOMATOES 1978
★ PG Comedy 1:28
☑ Explicit language
Dir: John De Bello *Cast:* David Miller, George Wilson, Sharon Taylor, Jack Riley, Rock Peace, John De Bello
► Title and credits are the best things about this cheapie sci-fi parody. Nonsensical plot (beautiful investigative reporter uncovers rampage of homicidal plants) is simply an excuse for corny jokes and double entendres. Film has a reputation as one of the world's worst, but camp fans can find much funnier examples.

ATTACK OF THE 50-FOOT WOMAN 1958
★★ NR Sci-Fi 1:06 B&W
Dir: Nathan Hertz *Cast:* Allison Hayes, William Hudson, Yvette Vickers, Roy Gordon, George Douglas, Ken Terrell
► Housewife Hayes, obsessed with her husband Hudson's affairs, is lured into a flying saucer and transformed overnight into a gigantic killer. One of the true low points in cinema, with spectacularly bad acting and dismal special effects. Kitsch fans consider this a classic.

AT THE CIRCUS 1939
★★ NR Comedy 1:27 B&W
Dir: Edward Buzzell *Cast:* The Marx Brothers, Kenny Baker, Eve Arden, Margaret Dumont, Nat Pendleton
► Chico sends for lawyer J. Cheever Loophole (Groucho) to help struggling circus owner Baker save his show. Funniest moments in an uneven vehicle: Groucho singing "Lydia, the Tattooed Lady," his drinking a zillion cups of coffee to buy time for his friends, and the big circus finale.

AUDREY ROSE 1977
★★★★ PG Horror 1:53
Dir: Robert Wise *Cast:* Marsha Mason, Anthony Hopkins, John Beck, Susan Swift
► Ten years after the car crash death of his daughter Audrey Rose, Hopkins becomes convinced she's been reincarnated as the daughter of Mason and Beck. Very few scary moments as the emphasis is on domestic relations over horror and the ending is a real letdown. Frank De Felitta adapted this supernatural tale from his own best-seller.

AUNTIE MAME 1958
★★★★ NR Comedy 2:26
Dir: Morton Da Costa *Cast:* Rosalind Russell, Forrest Tucker, Roger Smith, Peggy Cass, Patric Knowles
► In the 1920s, an orphaned boy is adopted by extravagant aunt Russell whose motto is: "Live, live, live. Life's a banquet and most poor suckers are starving!" Featuring Russell's kaleidoscopic star turn and a standout performance by Cass as the very pregnant, unwed Agnes Gooch. Adapted from the best-selling book by Patrick Dennis and later reincarnated as the musical *Mame*, this genuine comedy classic, nominated for six Oscars, was the top-grossing film of 1959.

AU REVOIR, LES ENFANTS 1988 French
★★ PG Drama 1:43
☑ Explicit language
Dir: Louis Malle *Cast:* Gaspard Manesse, Raphael Fejto, Francine Racette, Stanislas Carre de Malberg, Phillipe Morier-Genoud, François Berleand
► At a French boarding school during World War II, Manesse, a Catholic, and Fetjo, a Jew trying to avoid capture under a phony name, develop a close relationship that is cut short by the Nazis. Beautifully acted drama, although slowly paced, works up emotional steam. Oscar-nominated for Best Foreign Film. Also known under its English title, *Goodbye, Children.* ⑤

AURORA ENCOUNTER, THE 1986
★★ PG Sci-Fi 1:30
☑ Adult situations, explicit language, mild violence
Dir: Jim McCullough *Cast:* Jack Elam, Peter Brown, Carol Bagdasarian, Spanky McFarland, Dottie West
► In 1897, an alien lands his spaceship outside the small town of Aurora, Texas.

Only schoolchildren can see the visitor at first, and can't convince their parents that he needs help. Cheap special effects and mediocre acting dampen what is otherwise warm family entertainment.

AUTHOR! AUTHOR! 1982
★★★★ **PG Comedy 1:50**
☑ Adult situations, explicit language
Dir: Arthur Hiller   *Cast:* Al Pacino, Tuesday Weld, Dyan Cannon, Alan King, Bob Dishy, Bob (Elliott) & Ray (Goulding)
► In a rare comedic role, Pacino portrays a neurotic New York playwright saddled with an impeding opening night, adulterous wife Weld, anxiety-ridden friends, and a disintegrating family of five adorable kids, only one of which is his. Diverting domestic comedy delivers a prerequisite happy ending. Written by playwright Israel Horovitz.

AUTOBIOGRAPHY OF MISS JANE PITTMAN, THE 1974
★★★★★ **NR Biography/MFTV 1:50**
Dir: John Korty   *Cast:* Cicely Tyson, Thalmus Rasulala, Richard Dysart, Michael Murphy, Katherine Helmond, Barbara Chaney
► Tyson plays a former slave who ages from 19 to 110 to live through the Civil War and become part of the 1960s civil rights movement. Her bravura performance raises this made-for-television movie way above standard fare. Tyson won one of nine Emmys, as did director Korty, screenwriter Tracy Keenan Wynn, and Rick Baker and Stan Wilson for their extraordinary and totally convincing aging makeup work. Adapted from Ernest J. Gaines's epic novel.

AUTUMN LEAVES 1956
★★ **NR Drama 1:48 B&W**
Dir: Robert Aldrich   *Cast:* Joan Crawford, Cliff Robertson, Vera Miles, Lorne Greene, Ruth Donnelly, Shepperd Strudwick
► Crawford gives an assured performance as a lonely spinster who marries younger Robertson after a whirlwind romance. What starts as an undemanding soap opera turns into a tense psychodrama as Crawford discovers Robertson is already married and mentally deranged as well. Interesting direction and capable supporting cast enhance unpredictable plot.

AUTUMN SONATA 1978 Swedish
★ **PG Drama 1:37**
☑ Adult situations
Dir: Ingmar Bergman   *Cast:* Liv Ullmann, Ingrid Bergman, Lena Nyman, Halvar Bjork, Gunnar Bjornstrand
► After a seven-year separation, concert pianist Bergman visits daughter Ullmann, a parson's wife, to find that a second daughter, wasting away from an undisclosed disease, has been brought out of a state hospital for seemingly charitable reasons. Emotionally charged, this explosive mother-daughter confrontation was the first collaboration between Bergman and Bergman, as well as Ingrid's last Swedish-speaking film. ⑤

AVALANCHE 1978
★★ **PG Action-Adventure 1:31**
☑ Explicit language, mild violence
Dir: Corey Allen   *Cast:* Rock Hudson, Mia Farrow, Robert Forester, Jeanette Nolan
► Ski lodge operator Hudson defies environmentalists and nature by cutting down a slew of trees uphill from his resort, ensuring the unthinkable—an avalanche that succeeds in burying the entire lodge, including Hudson's ex-wife Farrow and mother Nolan. Swift pacing, archival footage of an actual massive avalanche, and some exciting trapped-beneath-the-snow sequences raise this formula movie slightly above the average—but only slightly.

AVALANCHE EXPRESS, THE 1979
★★★ **PG Action-Adventure 1:28**
☑ Explicit language, violence
Dir: Mark Robson   *Cast:* Lee Marvin, Robert Shaw, Linda Evans, Maximilian Schell, Joe Namath, Mike Connors
► Handsome action adventure concerns renegade Soviet KGB spy Shaw, ready to defect, and American agents Marvin, Evans, and Connors who engineer his safe passage to the USA amid boat chases, avalanches, and terrorist train attacks. All-star cast performs admirably, especially Shaw.

AVANTI! 1972
★★★★ **R Comedy 2:24**
☑ Nudity, explicit language
Dir: Billy Wilder   *Cast:* Jack Lemmon, Juliet Mills, Clive Revill, Edward Andrews
► American businessman Lemmon goes to Italy to claim his wealthy father's body and discovers dad had an English mis-

tress. Lemmon falls in love with mistress's daughter Mills. A little heavy-handed and some slow spots but good rapport between the leads in this generally amusing mid-life crisis comedy from Wilder.

AVENGING ANGEL 1985
★★ R Action-Adventure 1:33
☑ Nudity, adult situations, explicit language, violence
Dir: Robert Vincent O'Neil *Cast:* Rory Calhoun, Betsy Russell, Susan Tyrrell, Ossie Davis, Robert F. Lyons
▶ America's favorite "straight A student by day/hustler by night" is back in this sequel to the 1983 *Angel.* Teen tramp Molly/Angel (Russell) has cleaned up her act, gone to college, and is now ready for law school, but her plans change when cop guardian Lyons is killed. Russell then hits the streets to find the murderer. Dumb script and lackadaisical direction but plenty of sleazy atmosphere and tons of revealing outfits for the sexy Miss Russell. (CC)

AVENGING FORCE 1986
★★★ R Action-Adventure 1:43
☑ Adult situations, explicit language, violence
Dir: Sam Firstenberg *Cast:* Michael Dudikoff, Steve James, James Booth, John P. Ryan, Bill Wallace, Karl Johnson
▶ Retired CIA agent/martial arts expert Dudikoff seeks peace on Louisiana homestead. But when liberal black buddy James, a Senate candidate, becomes the target of lunatic-fringe, right-wing terrorist outfit run by psychotic professor Ryan, Dudikoff reprises his one-man army routine. Fine fare for genre fans, with Ryan noteworthy as villain. Dudikoff and James also teamed for *American Ninja* and *American Ninja II.* (CC)

AVIATOR, THE 1985
★★★ PG Action-Adventure 1:36
☑ Explicit language, violence
Dir: George Miller *Cast:* Christopher Reeve, Rosanna Arquette, Tyne Daly, Jack Warden, Sam Wanamaker
▶ In 1928, mail pilot Reeve and his rich bratty passenger Arquette crash in an isolated mountain region. Antagonists at first, the two grow closer as they fight to survive wolves and other dangers. Adapted from Ernest K. Gann's bestseller, there's plenty of pretty scenery, decent period details, and solid acting, yet the end result lacks spark between the leads.

AWAKENING, THE 1980
★★ R Horror 1:40
☑ Adult situations, graphic violence
Dir: Mike Newell *Cast:* Charlton Heston, Susannah York, Jill Townsend, Stephanie Zimbalist, Patrick Drury
▶ Archaeologist Heston discovers the long-lost tomb of an ancient Egyptian princess, whose spirit subsequently possesses Heston's daughter Zimbalist. Unusual story line unravels effectively as moody direction by Newell provides some genuine chills.

AWFUL TRUTH, THE 1937
★★★★★ NR Comedy 1:31 B&W
Dir: Leo McCarey *Cast:* Cary Grant, Irene Dunne, Ralph Bellamy, Cecil Cunningham, Skippy the Terrier
▶ The awful truth is that recently divorced Grant and Dunne can't stay away from each other. They bicker, fight over custody of the dog (Skippy, the canine who played Asta in the Thin Man series), and break up each other's respective new romances. Lively, quintessentially crazy screwball comedy. Witty performances from leads with Bellamy providing his classic hapless foil. Five Oscar nominations, winning for Best Director.

BABES IN ARMS 1939
★★★ NR Musical 1:37 B&W
Dir: Busby Berkeley *Cast:* Judy Garland, Mickey Rooney, Charles Winninger, Guy Kibbee, June Preisser, Grace Hayes
▶ First musical teaming of Garland and Rooney follows the archetypal "let's put on a show" formula. Rooney (who won an Oscar nomination) writes and directs a hit for his schoolmates, but spoiled teen star Preisser threatens to steal the lead from Garland. Loosely based on a Rodgers and Hart play, and featuring "You Are My Lucky Star," "Where or When," and "The Lady Is a Tramp."

BABES IN TOYLAND 1934
★★★★★ NR Family/Fantasy 1:13 B&W
Dir: Gus Meins, Charles Rogers *Cast:* Stan Laurel, Oliver Hardy, Charlotte Henry, Henry Kleinbach, Felix Knight, Florence Roberts
▶ When evil Kleinbach forces the sweetheart of Little Bo Peep (Henry) into exile and tries to take over Toyland, toymaker's

bumbling assistants Laurel and Hardy send an army of six-foot wooden soldiers to thwart him. Delightful holiday classic; Laurel and Hardy are wonderful as always, and the climactic march of the soldiers will thrill small children. Based on Victor Herbert's operetta; also known as *March of the Wooden Soldiers*.

BABETTE'S FEAST 1987 Danish
★ **G Drama 1:42**
Dir: Gabriel Axel   *Cast:* Stephane Audran, Birgitte Federspiel, Bodil Kjer, Vibeke Hastrup, Hanne Stensgard, Jarl Kulle
▶ In nineteenth-century Denmark, spinster sisters Federspiel and Kjer, leaders of a spartan Protestant sect, take in French refugee Audran as their unpaid housekeeper. After many years, Audran wins the lottery and uses her previously hidden culinary skills to teach the sisters and their flock about earthly passions and pleasures. Adaptation of an Isak Dinesen story won Best Foreign Film Oscar. Audan is warm and witty, but stately drama is for discriminating tastes.
S

BABY BOOM 1987
★★★★ **PG Comedy 1:43**
☑ Adult situations, explicit language
Dir: Charles Shyer   *Cast:* Diane Keaton, Sam Shepard, Harold Ramis, Mary Kay Place, James Spader
▶ Keaton is steely New York City management consultant J. C. Wiatt, who finds her fast-track yuppie lifestyle turned upside down when she inherits a baby from a recently deceased, long-lost cousin. Eventually, she chucks corporate life for a rural Vermont existence and finds happiness in the arms of small-town veterinarian Shepard. Broad sit-com fun with an adorable kid played by twins Kristina and Michelle Kennedy and a smashing star performance by Keaton. **(CC)**

BABY DOLL 1956
★★ **R Drama 1:54 B&W**
☑ Adult situations, explicit language
Dir: Elia Kazan   *Cast:* Carroll Baker, Karl Malden, Eli Wallach, Mildred Dunnock, Lonny Chapman
▶ Tennessee Williams wrote the screenplay for this odd Southern drama, which caused a furor when first released and was condemned by the Catholic Legion of Decency for its then shocking child-bride theme. Baker is young Baby Doll, who sleeps in a crib and won't let husband Malden touch her. Wallach is the local cotton-gin king who pursues Baker. Now more dated than outrageous but the performances and Southern atmosphere hold up.

BABY, IT'S YOU 1983
★★ **R Romance 1:45**
☑ Brief nudity, adult situations, explicit language, violence
Dir: John Sayles   *Cast:* Rosanna Arquette, Vincent Spano, Joanna Merlin, Jack Davidson
▶ Period high school romance features Arquette as perky, popular Jill, pursued by "the Sheik" (Spano), a greaser from the wrong side of the tracks with a surprisingly tender side. Class differences doom their poignant relationship. Affecting, if predictable; Arquette is sexy and smart and Spano is appealing. Rich in period detail with plenty of 1960s hits on the soundtrack.

BABY . . . SECRET OF THE LOST LEGEND 1985
★★★ **PG Action-Adventure 1:35**
☑ Nudity, adult situations, violence
Dir: B.W.L. Norton   *Cast:* William Katt, Sean Young, Patrick McGoohan, Julian Fellowes, Kyalo Mativo
▶ Zoologist Young and her sportswriter husband Katt discover family of brontosaurus in modern-day Africa, and then must save them from ruthless scientist McGoohan. Nice premise routinely scripted. The dinosaurs are cute and their scenes will be irresistible to anyone with a weakness for babies or pets. Family entertainment, although parents should note a slight excess of gunplay.

BABY, THE RAIN MUST FALL 1965
★★★ **NR Drama 1:39 B&W**
Dir: Robert Mulligan   *Cast:* Steve McQueen, Lee Remick, Don Murray, Paul Fix, Josephine Hutchinson
▶ Downbeat drama featuring worthy star performances. McQueen is guitar-playing ex-con Henry, starting a new life after prison with wife Remick and their four-year-old daughter, but he can't overcome his violent ways. Horton Foote adapted his own play *The Traveling Lady*. Title song was a 1965 hit.

BACHELOR AND THE BOBBYSOXER, THE 1947
★★★ **NR Comedy 1:34 B&W**
Dir: Irving Reis   *Cast:* Cary Grant, Myrna Loy, Shirley Temple, Rudy Vallee, Johnny Sands

▶ After being arrested in a nightclub slugfest, dashing artist Grant comes before judge Loy. When Loy's teenage sister Temple falls for Grant, she sentences him to escort the girl until she gets over the crush. Airy, amusing comedy sustained by Cary's trademark charm and Loy's tart wit. Hugely popular in its time, won 1947 Oscar for Best Original Screenplay by Sidney Sheldon.

BACHELOR MOTHER 1939
★★★★★ **NR Comedy 1:22 B&W**
Dir: Garson Kanin *Cast:* Ginger Rogers, David Niven, Charles Coburn, Frank Albertson, Ernest Truex
▶ Salesgirl Rogers's life is turned upside down when she takes in an abandoned baby. Taking an interest in mother and child, department-store heir Niven falls in love. Sweet, charming, swiftly paced romantic comedy still seems fresh today, thanks to great work from Rogers, Niven, Coburn, and an absolutely adorable baby who steals every scene.

BACHELOR PARTY, THE 1957
★★ **NR Drama 1:33 B&W**
Dir: Delbert Mann *Cast:* Don Murray, E. G. Marshall, Jack Warden, Philip Abbott, Larry Blyden, Carolyn Jones
▶ New York bookkeepers throw a party for their nervous colleague Murray before his wedding; alcohol and the arrival of a shrewd but heartless woman (Jones, in an Oscar-nominated performance) bring out the tensions underneath their quietly desperate lives. Incisive Paddy Chayefsky script probes into the characters with precision and compassion.

BACHELOR PARTY 1984
★★★★ **R Comedy 1:51**
☑ Nudity, adult situations, explicit language, mild violence, adult humor
Dir: Neil Israel *Cast:* Tom Hanks, Tawny Kitaen, Adrian Zmed, Barry Diamond, Bronson Pinchot
▶ Bawdy comedy about a bachelor party that gets amusingly out of hand. Carefree bachelor Hanks is about to marry Kitaen while her uppity father Grizzard and ex-boyfriend plot to break up the engagement. Plenty of low-rent humor (including a mule snorting cocaine). Although silly at times, Hanks's brash humor carries the day. (CC)

BACKFIRE 1988
★★★ **R Mystery-Suspense 1:31**
Dir: Gilbert Cates *Cast:* Karen Allen, Keith Carradine, Jeff Fahey, Dinah Manoff, Dean Paul Martin
▶ Intrigue and double-crossing between Vietnam vet Fahey haunted by war-related nightmares, his scheming wife Allen, her ex-boyfriend Martin, and her new lover Carradine. Loses momentum about midway through, but overall a professional production with a nice nasty edge.

BACK ROADS 1981
★★★ **R Comedy 1:34**
☑ Explicit language, violence
Dir: Martin Ritt *Cast:* Sally Field, Tommy Lee Jones, David Keith, Miriam Colon, Michael V. Gazzo
▶ Hooker Field and out-of-work boxer Jones go on the lam when they get into trouble with the law. It's far from love at first sight but they eventually fall in love on the road. Escapist comedy is short on plot but the film achieves a pleasant lightweight tone. The leads do what they can with clichéd characters.

BACK STREET 1961
★★★ **NR Drama 1:47**
Dir: David Miller *Cast:* Susan Hayward, John Gavin, Vera Miles, Charles Drake, Virginia Grey, Reginald Gardiner
▶ Older but glamorous Hayward falls in love with prominent businessman Gavin, whose alcoholic wife Miles won't give him a divorce. Third sound version of Fannie Hurst's best-selling novel is a glossy but superficial soap opera with an emphasis on haute couture.

BACK TO BATAAN 1945
★★★★ **NR War 1:35 B&W**
Dir: Edward Dmytryk *Cast:* John Wayne, Anthony Quinn, Beulah Bondi, Fely Franquelli, Richard Loo, Philip Ahn
▶ Action-packed World War II drama about the fall of the Philippines to the Japanese. Wayne is a heroic colonel called back from devastating front-line fighting to help defend Bataan; he arrives too late and witnesses the horrific Death March. Quinn, a Filipino rebel, escapes with the help of guerrillas and rejoins Wayne as the Allied powers finally defeat the enemy. Marred somewhat by flag-waving speeches, but overall a riveting war picture.

BACK TO SCHOOL 1986
★★★★ **PG-13 Comedy 1:36**
☑ Brief nudity, explicit language, adult humor
Dir: Alan Metter *Cast:* Rodney Dan-

gerfield, Sally Kellerman, Ned Beatty, Burt Young, Keith Gordon, Robert Downey, Jr.

▶ Dangerfield is lovably uncouth Thornton Melon, who made his fortune with a chain of "Tall and Fat" clothing stores. He enrolls in college to help his unhappy son Gordon in this very funny and surprisingly charming comedy. Slob Rodney earns respect and a diploma; his usual one-liners are combined with some real sweetness. Able support from Beatty as "Dean" Martin, Downey as Gordon's eccentric roommate, comic Sam Kinison as a professor who can't forget Nam, and Kellerman as the literature professor who falls for Rodney. **(CC)**

BACK TO THE BEACH 1987
★ **PG Musical/Comedy 1:32**
☑ Adult situations
Dir: Lyndall Hobbs *Cast:* Annette Funicello, Frankie Avalon, Connie Stevens, Lori Loughlin, Tommy Hinkley, Demian Slade

▶ Two decades after their string of beach movies captivated teens in the early sixties, the "Big Kahuna" Avalon and his wife Funicello have settled into boring domesticity in Ohio. On vacation to visit daughter Loughlin and her beach-bum boyfriend Hinkley in Southern Cal, Avalon and Funicello reprise many of their youthful high jinks, including his attraction to bad-girl bar owner Stevens. Cameos by Bob Denver, Don Adams, Jerry Mathers, Tony Dow, and David Bowie. **(CC)**

BACK TO THE FUTURE 1985
★★★★★ **PG Sci-Fi/Comedy 1:56**
☑ Adult situations, explicit language, mild violence
Dir: Robert Zemeckis *Cast:* Michael J. Fox, Lea Thompson, Christopher Lloyd, Crispin Glover, Tom Wilson

▶ Enormously popular time-travel fantasy from producer Spielberg and Zemeckis. Typical 1980s teenager Fox is catapulted back to the 1950s by nutty inventor Lloyd's time machine. There Fox meets the teenage versions of his future parents, Thompson and Glover, and must play Cupid to save his own life. One complication—Thompson prefers Fox to the wimpy Glover. An intricate, intelligent plot comes to a quite satisfying conclusion. Terrific performances (especially Glover) in a joyous movie that deftly combines comedy, fantasy, sci-fi, and Freud. **(CC)**

BAD AND THE BEAUTIFUL, THE 1952
★★ **NR Drama 1:58 B&W**
Dir: Vincente Minnelli *Cast:* Lana Turner, Kirk Douglas, Dick Powell, Gloria Grahame, Walter Pidgeon

▶ Five Oscars, including Best Supporting Actress (Grahame), went to this well-acted, well-written exposé of the movie business and its treacheries. Douglas is terrific as Jonathan Shields, a ruthless movie producer on the skids who attempts to use the people he stepped on to make a comeback. Turner is also fine as an alcoholic actress. **(CC)**

BAD BOYS 1983
★★★★ **R Drama 2:03**
☑ Rape, adult situations, explicit language, violence
Dir: Rick Rosenthal *Cast:* Sean Penn, Ally Sheedy, Reni Santoni, Esai Morales

▶ Grim but riveting prison film. Penn is outstanding as Mick O'Brien, a tough Chicago street kid sent to a juvenile correctional facility after a shootout. On the inside, he is confronted by Morales, the rival gang leader who blames Mick for his brother's death. Realistic and powerful.

BAD COMPANY 1972
★★ **PG Western 1:33**
☑ Adult situations, explicit language, violence
Dir: Robert Benton *Cast:* Jeff Bridges, Barry Brown, John Savage, Jim Davis, David Huddleston, Jerry Houser

▶ During the Civil War, teenage draft dodgers Bridges and Brown form an outlaw gang of runaways. Director Benton's unjustly neglected antiwar Western combines raunchy humor, gritty action, and appealing performances from a wonderful cast of young actors.

BAD DAY AT BLACK ROCK 1955
★★★★ **NR Drama 1:21**
Dir: John Sturges *Cast:* Spencer Tracy, Robert Ryan, Anne Francis, Dean Jagger, Walter Brennan, Lee Marvin

▶ In this tense contemporary Western, Tracy plays a one-armed stranger who stops at Black Rock looking for a Japanese farmer. Despite threats from hostile townspeople, he uncovers a terrible conspiracy. Powerful, disturbing moral drama is still relevant today, thanks to a tough script, fine ensemble acting, and innovative use of CinemaScope. Received Oscar nominations for Screenplay and Direction.

BAD DREAMS 1988
★★ R Horror 1:24
☑ Adult situations, explicit language, graphic violence
Dir: Andrew Fleming *Cast:* Jennifer Rubin, Bruce Abbott, Richard Lynch, Dean Cameron, Harris Yulin
▶ Rubin, the sole survivor of a mass suicide pact led by cult leader Lynch, awakes from a thirteen-year coma and joins a group run by Abbott. Participants in the therapy session start getting killed. Is Lynch back from the dead to wreck the living? Nicely executed debut flick from young NYU grad Fleming and producer Gale Ann Hurd, although derivative plot is reminiscent of the Nightmare on Elm Street movies. **(CC)**

BADGE 373 1973
★★ R Drama 1:56
☑ Adult situations, explicit language, violence
Dir: Howard W. Koch *Cast:* Robert Duvall, Verna Bloom, Henry Darrow, Eddie Egan
▶ Duvall is a super-tough maverick cop who, after being unfairly suspended from the force, tracks down the killer of his partner and girlfriend. The real-life French Connection cop, Egan, makes a cameo appearance as Duvall's hardboiled superior caught in the hot spot between friendship and the law. Sturdy, well-acted genre effort.

BADLANDS 1974
★★★ PG Drama 1:35
☑ Violence
Dir: Terrence Malick *Cast:* Martin Sheen, Sissy Spacek, Warren Oates, Ramon Bieri, Alan Vint
▶ Based on the true story of Charles Starkweather's murderous binge that left ten people dead, this beautifully photographed and hauntingly scored film contains memorable performances by Sheen and Spacek as two young adults on an all-American joyride/killing spree across the Middle West. When first released, audiences were shocked by this portrait of two cool, detached criminals mostly bored by their crimes. Today, many consider the film a modern classic.

BAD MANNERS 1984
★★ R Comedy 1:22
☑ Brief nudity, adult situations, explicit language, violence, adult humor
Dir: Robert Houston *Cast:* Karen Black, Martin Mull, Murphy Dunne, Anne De Salvo
▶ Mildly offensive comedy about life in a Catholic orphanage. De Salvo is Sister Serena, who runs the place with prison-like discipline, while Mull and Black play a ditsy affluent couple who get more than they bargained for when they adopt a rebellious foundling.

BAD MEDICINE 1985
★★ PG-13 Comedy 1:36
☑ Adult situations, explicit language, adult humor
Dir: Harvey Miller *Cast:* Steve Guttenberg, Alan Arkin, Julie Hagerty, Bill Macy
▶ Bad grades force med student Guttenberg south of the border for his degree, where he enrolls in a run-down institution headed by Arkin (whose Spanish accent out-Fernandos Billy Crystal). After a caustic and funny first half, the film loses the courage of its cynicism and turns into a mushy drama of students helping out an impoverished village. **(CC)**

BAD NEWS BEARS, THE 1976
★★★★★ PG Comedy/Family 1:42
☑ Explicit language
Dir: Michael Ritchie *Cast:* Walter Matthau, Tatum O'Neal, Vic Morrow, Joyce Van Patten, Jackie Earle Haley
▶ Matthau, an alcoholic pool-cleaner and ex-minor leaguer, is recruited to coach an inept Little League team. With the help of pitcher O'Neal, he turns the Bears into winners. Consistently funny baseball comedy with likable characters will appeal to anybody who's ever worn a baseball glove. Nifty direction by Ritchie. Parents should note that the kids' language is a bit spicy.

BAD NEWS BEARS GO TO JAPAN, THE 1978
★★ PG Comedy/Family 1:32
☑ Explicit language
Dir: John Berry *Cast:* Tony Curtis, Jackie Earle Haley, Matthew D. Anton, Erin Blunt, George Gonzales
▶ Seedy huckster Curtis cons the Little Leaguer Bears into a Japanese tour, but by the end the foulmouthed tykes persuade him to go straight. Broad comedy, baseball action, plus some exotic Japanese locations add up to lightweight, easygoing family fare. Amusing cameo by ABC sports commentator Dick Button.

BAD NEWS BEARS IN BREAKING TRAINING, THE 1977
★★★★ PG Comedy/Family 1:39
☑ Explicit language
Dir: Michael Pressman   *Cast:* William Devane, Clifton James, Jackie Earle Haley, Jimmy Baio, Chris Barnes
▶ Little Leaguers from the popular *Bad News Bears* are back in this first of two sequels. This time out, team leader Haley must recruit his estranged dad Devane to be the coach before the kids can play in the Houston Astrodome. Very good-natured and amusing.

BAD SEED, THE 1956
★★ NR Drama 2:09 B&W
Dir: Mervyn LeRoy   *Cast:* Nancy Kelly, Patty McCormack, Henry Jones, Eileen Heckart, Evelyn Varden, Jesse White
▶ Child McCormack murders classmate for penmanship medal, then commits other killings. Only horrified mom Kelly suspects the truth. An unnerving experience. Oscar-nominated McCormack delivers perhaps the most chilling child performance ever; Kelly and Heckart were also nominated. Based on the Maxwell Anderson play.

BAD TIMING: A SENSUAL OBSESSION 1980 British
☆ R Drama 2:01
☑ Nudity, strong sexual content, adult situations, explicit language
Dir: Nicolas Roeg   *Cast:* Theresa Russell, Art Garfunkel, Harvey Keitel, Denholm Elliott
▶ In Vienna, research psychologist Garfunkel meets Russell and they become involved in a stormy, passionate sexual relationship which ends in her near suicide and a police investigation headed by suspicious detective Keitel. Typical Roeg touches—abrupt time shifts and deliberately paced timing—may confuse some viewers. Graphic and controversial sexual content.

BAGDAD CAFE 1988 West German
★ PG Comedy 1:31
☑ Nudity, explicit language
Dir: Percy Adlon   *Cast:* Marianne Sägebrecht, Jack Palance, CCH Pounder, Christine Kaufmann, Monica Calhoun, George Aguilar
▶ Stranded by her husband in the Mojave Desert, German tourist Sägebrecht seeks refuge in a seedy cafe/motel. Her presence brings new life to angry owner Pounder and clientele of irregulars like mute tattoo artist Kaufmann and retired Hollywood set painter Palance. Offbeat comedy recommended to those looking for something different. (CC)

BAJA OKLAHOMA 1988
★★★ NR Drama/MFTV 1:45
☑ Nudity, adult situations
Dir: Bobby Roth   *Cast:* Lesley Ann Warren, Peter Coyote, Swoosie Kurtz, William Forsythe
▶ Bored barmaid Warren longs to escape her job, her rocky marriage, and runaway daughter. Her prayers are answered by the reappearance of ex-boyfriend Coyote, who arranges for her to sing with Willie Nelson. Based on Dan Jenkins's best-selling novel, this amiable country-western fairy tale features an original soundtrack with eight new songs by Willie Nelson, Emmylou Harris, and others.

BALLAD OF CABLE HOGUE, THE 1970
★★★★ R Western/Comedy 2:01
☑ Brief nudity, adult situations, explicit language, violence
Dir: Sam Peckinpah   *Cast:* Jason Robards, Stella Stevens, David Warner, Strother Martin, Slim Pickens
▶ Charming desert-rat Robards, left to die by his villainous partners, discovers water and prospers as rest-stop proprietor on stage route. Stevens, the cow-town harlot, romances and then abandons Robards for a rich man in Frisco. Warner plays an amiable wandering preacher. Although highly praised by the critics, Peckinpah fans expecting another *Wild Bunch* may be disappointed in this character-rich but slow action change-of-pace oater.

BALLAD OF GREGORIO CORTEZ, THE 1983
★★ PG Western 1:39
☑ Explicit language, graphic violence
Dir: Robert M. Young   *Cast:* Edward James Olmos, James Gammon, Tom Bower, Bruce McGill, Alan Vint
▶ Based on a true 1901 incident. Olmos plays a Mexican cowhand unjustly accused of horse theft and pursued by 600 Texas Rangers in the biggest manhunt in the state's history. Artfully re-creating Texas bordertowns and their inhabitants, this action-packed Western was developed by Robert Redford's Sundance Institute and praised for its fresh and origi-

nal vision, climactic courtroom scene, and naturalistic style.

BALL OF FIRE 1941
★ ★ ★ ★ NR Comedy 1:52 B&W
Dir: Howard Hawks *Cast:* Gary Cooper, Barbara Stanwyck, Dana Andrews, Oscar Homolka, Henry Travers, Dan Duryea
▶ Stanwyck is Sugarpuss O'Shea, a nightclub singer on the lam, who holes up with eight professors working on a dictionary of American slang, led by gangly Cooper. Coop and Babs fall in love in this engaging and tremendously entertaining comedy. Stanwyck has never been sexier, especially in the classic scene where she teaches Cooper the meaning of "yum yum."

BALTIMORE BULLET, THE 1980
★ ★ ★ ★ PG Drama/Sports 1:43
☑ Brief nudity, adult situations, explicit language
Dir: Robert Ellis Miller *Cast:* James Coburn, Omar Sharif, Bruce Boxleitner, Ronee Blakley, Jack O'Halloran
▶ Slick, fast-talking pool hustler Coburn and young partner Boxleitner must raise big money to play a high-stakes rematch with their nemesis Sharif. Simple story and average production values, but good location shooting provides grit and reality. Some remarkable billiards action includes guest appearances by well-known pool sharks.

BANANAS 1971
★ ★ PG Comedy 1:22
☑ Adult situations, adult humor
Dir: Woody Allen *Cast:* Woody Allen, Louise Lasser, Carlos Montalban, Howard Cosell
▶ Allen is Fielding Mellish, a sex-starved gadget-tester who falls hopelessly in love with Lasser (the real-life former Mrs. Allen), a young political activist. He follows her to the banana republic of San Marcos where he inadvertently manages to unseat the country's dictator and become president. Howard Cosell makes an appearance to host both San Marcos's Assassination of the Week and, later, the on-camera consummation of Allen's marriage. Pure vintage Allen.

BAND OF THE HAND 1986
★ ★ ★ ★ R Action-Adventure 1:49
☑ Adult situations, explicit language, violence
Dir: Paul Michael Glaser *Cast:* Stephen Lang, Michael Carmine, Lauren Holly, John Cameron Mitchell, Danielle Quinn
▶ Crusading Vietnam vet Lang takes five juvenile delinquents into the Florida swamps and trains them to be crimefighters. Once reformed, the fearsome fivesome return to the city to take on a drug lord. Slick, well-made action flick.

BANDOLERO! 1968
★ ★ ★ PG Western 1:47
☑ Mild violence
Dir: Andrew V. McLaglen *Cast:* James Stewart, Dean Martin, Raquel Welch, George Kennedy, Andrew Prine
▶ Outlaw brothers Stewart and Martin kidnap beautiful widow Welch while fleeing the forces of the law led by sheriff Kennedy. Tough Western adds nothing new to the genre but is generally above average. Stewart stands out among the cast. (CC)

BAND WAGON, THE 1953
★ ★ ★ ★ NR Musical 1:51
Dir: Vincente Minnelli *Cast:* Fred Astaire, Cyd Charisse, Oscar Levant, Nanette Fabray, Jack Buchanan
▶ Down-on-his-luck Hollywood star Astaire makes a stab at a Broadway comeback in this classic MGM musical. Wonderful score by Howard Dietz and Arthur Schwartz includes the romantic dance duet "Dancing in the Dark," "A Shine on Your Shoes," "That's Entertainment." Astaire, Fabray, and Buchanan have a great time as little brats in the famous "Triplets" number.

BANG THE DRUM SLOWLY 1973
★ ★ ★ ★ PG Drama/Sports 1:38
☑ Brief nudity, adult situations, explicit language
Dir: John Hancock *Cast:* Robert De Niro, Michael Moriarty, Vincent Gardenia, Heather MacRae, Ann Wedgeworth, Danny Aiello
▶ Touching drama of the friendship between baseball players Moriarty and De Niro, who is dying of Hodgkin's Disease. Moriarty is the good-looking "golden boy" pitcher who stands by dim-witted loser De Niro even when his teammates (unaware of De Niro's condition) rag him about the relationship. Sensitively directed by Hancock and adapted by Mark Harris from his novel.

BANK DICK, THE 1940
★ ★ ★ NR Comedy 1:19 B&W
Dir: Edward Cline *Cast:* W. C. Fields,

Cora Witherspoon, Una Merkel, Franklin Pangborn, Shemp Howard
▶ Quintessential vehicle for the bulbous-nosed Fields playing the aptly named Egbert Souse, who prefers drinking at his favorite bar (where the bartender is Howard of the Three Stooges) to hard work. Souse parlays accidental heroism into gigs as a bank guard and film director. Written by Fields under the pseudonym Mahatma Kane Jeeves.

BANK SHOT 1974
★ ★ **PG Comedy/Crime 1:23**
☑ Adult situations, explicit language
Dir: Gower Champion   *Cast:* George C. Scott, Joanna Cassidy, Sorrell Booke, Bob Balaban, G. Wood, Clifton James
▶ Crook Scott and his gang set sights on unique bank heist: they plot to steal the entire building by towing it away. Cute caper from a novel by Donald Westlake; Scott and Cassidy are pleasant company.

BARABBAS 1962
★ ★ ★ ★ **NR Drama 2:15**
Dir: Richard Fleischer   *Cast:* Anthony Quinn, Silvana Mangano, Arthur Kennedy, Katy Jurado, Harry Andrews, Vittorio Gassman
▶ Biblical epic about the condemned murderer who was freed in place of Christ is long but consistently engrossing. Quinn gives a determined performance as Barabbas, a nonbeliever who spends years as a slave and gladiator struggling to understand the meaning of Christ's life. Adaptation of a novel by Nobel laureate Par Lagerkvist is filled with spectacle and action. Enormous cast also includes Jack Palance and Ernest Borgnine.

BARBARELLA 1968 French/Italian
★ **PG Sci-Fi 1:38**
☑ Brief nudity, adult situations, explicit language
Dir: Roger Vadim   *Cast:* Jane Fonda, Milo O'Shea, John Phillip Law, David Hemmings
▶ Sexy comic strip adaptation directed by Fonda's then husband Roger Vadim was controversial in its initial release but seems relatively tame now. Fonda is the sci-fi heroine of the future who takes on an evil villainess in a world where sex has been reduced to a handshake and a pill. Made in the actress's pre-political period, Fonda performs a free-floating strip-tease and wears various scanty costumes. Campy fun.

BARBARIAN AND THE GEISHA, THE 1958
★ ★ **NR Biography 1:45**
Dir: John Huston   *Cast:* John Wayne, Eiko Ando, Sam Jaffe, So Yamamura, Norman Thomson, James Robbins
▶ Appointed ambassador to Japan in the mid-nineteenth century, Townsend Harris (Wayne) finds his peaceful goals blocked by suspicious natives until a servant (Ando) sent to spy on him falls in love. Wayne is miscast in this slow-moving, heavily fictionalized biography. (CC)

BARBARIANS, THE 1987
★ **R Action-Adventure 1:27**
☑ Nudity, adult situations, explicit language, graphic violence
Dir: Ruggero Deodato   *Cast:* Peter Paul, David Paul, Richard Lynch, Eva La Rue, Virginia Bryant, Sheeba Alahani
▶ The Paul brothers play twins condemned as children to slave labor by evil overlord Lynch and now grown into superstrong, untamed young men. Aided by cute, wise-cracking young La Rue, they seek revenge against Lynch while rescuing beautiful queen Bryant. Body-building fans will enjoy the Pauls' bulging muscles, but others will be left cold by adventure set in "some other time and place."

BARBAROSA 1982
★ ★ ★ **PG Western 1:30**
☑ Explicit language, violence
Dir: Fred Schepisi   *Cast:* Willie Nelson, Gary Busey, Gilbert Roland, Isela Vega
▶ Critically praised Western shows how legendary outlaw Nelson teaches protégé Busey to survive in the wilderness. Pursued by bounty hunters and killers, they take refuge in a small Mexican village. Stunning photography and Nelson's commanding presence triumph over a sometimes rambling plot. Screen veteran Roland contributes a memorable cameo.

BARBARY COAST 1935
★ ★ **NR Drama 1:37 B&W**
Dir: Howard Hawks   *Cast:* Miriam Hopkins, Edward G. Robinson, Joel McCrea, Walter Brennan, Brian Donlevy, Harry Carey
▶ Fast-paced, rollicking adventure set in 1849 San Francisco with Hopkins as a genteel Easterner pursued by gangster

Robinson and honest gold prospector McCrea. Screenplay by Ben Hecht and Charles MacArthur spices up the romantic triangle with bawdy jokes and innuendoes; action and sets are superb.

BAREFOOT CONTESSA, THE 1954
★★★ NR Drama 2:08
Dir: Joseph L. Mankiewicz *Cast:* Humphrey Bogart, Ava Gardner, Edmond O'Brien, Marius Goring, Rossano Brazzi, Valentina Cortese
▶ Dancer Gardner is plucked from obscurity to stardom by director Bogart. However, success has its bitter side: she gets involved with wealthy tycoon Goring and then marries nobleman Brazzi, whose impotence sets up an unhappy conclusion. Somewhat overdone but also quite entertaining; O'Brien does an Oscar-winning, scene-stealing turn as the press agent.

BAREFOOT IN THE PARK 1967
★★★★ G Comedy 1:45
Dir: Gene Saks *Cast:* Robert Redford, Jane Fonda, Charles Boyer, Mildred Natwick, Herb Edelman
▶ Newlyweds, lawyer Redford and free-spirited wife Fonda, move into a run-down Greenwich Village apartment. They fight over his stuffiness, as symbolized by his refusal to go "barefoot in the park," while Fonda's mom Natwick is wooed by old charmer Boyer. Youthful, romantic fun from Neil Simon.

BARFLY 1987
★★ R Drama 1:39
☑ Nudity, adult situations, explicit language, violence
Dir: Barbet Schroeder *Cast:* Mickey Rourke, Faye Dunaway, Alice Krige, Jack Nance, J. C. Quinn, Frank Stallone
▶ Convincing but downbeat depiction of life on the scuzzy side of Los Angeles. Rourke is Henry, an alcoholic writer (the character is based on the life of the film's screenwriter, poet Charles Bukowski) who prefers drinking to the typewriter, Dunaway the fellow alcoholic who shares his bottle and bed. Meandering story line but fine performances from the two leads. Rourke seems born to play this part while Dunaway, eschewing her usual glamour, is surprisingly effective. **(CC)**

BARKLEYS OF BROADWAY, THE 1949
★★★ NR Musical 1:49
Dir: Charles Walters *Cast:* Fred Astaire, Ginger Rogers, Oscar Levant, Billie Burke, Gale Robbins

▶ Last Astaire-Rogers film, their only one in color, is a modest story about a famous musical team that breaks up when Rogers pursues a serious acting career. An elegant "They Can't Take That Away from Me" and Astaire's witty special effects solo "Shoes with Wings On" are the highlights.

BARON BLOOD 1972 Italian
☆ PG Horror 1:30
☑ Adult situations, violence
Dir: Mario Bava *Cast:* Joseph Cotten, Elke Sommer, Massimo Girotti, Rada Rassimov, Antonio Canafora
▶ Italian horror master Bava brings style and wit to predictable tale about heir to spooky castle who is persuaded by Sommer to turn it into a hotel. He accidentally brings his evil ancestor Cotten back to life. Resulting murders are shown in a series of tense sequences.

BARRACUDA 1978
★★ PG Horror 1:30
☑ Explicit language, violence
Dir: Harry Kerwin *Cast:* Wayne-David Crawford, Jason Evers, Bert Freed, Roberta Leighton
▶ Marine biology students are arrested after breaking into a chemical plant to take samples of water they believe has been polluted. When fishermen start disappearing, the police turn to the students for help with the case. Typical drive-in fare with a cast of unknowns.

BARRY LYNDON 1975 British
★★★ PG Drama 3:04
☑ Violence
Dir: Stanley Kubrick *Cast:* Ryan O'Neal, Marisa Berenson, Patrick Magee, Hardy Kruger, Steven Berkoff
▶ Master filmmaker Kubrick sumptuously re-creates the eighteenth century in this adaptation of William Makepeace Thackeray's novel of the rise and eventual ruin of naive but ambitious Irishman O'Neal in English society. Natural lighting and painterly visuals enhance this physically beautiful film. The pace is somewhat slow but the story is engrossing. Oscars for Costume Design, Cinematography, Musical Score, and Art Direction.

BASIC TRAINING 1985
★ R Comedy 1:25
☑ Nudity, strong sexual content, explicit language
Dir: Andrew Sugarman *Cast:* Ann Dus-

enberry, Rhonda Shear, Marty Brill, Angela Aames, Walter Gotell
▶ Glossy professional-looking sex comedy containing all the genre conventions—gratuitous sex, bathroom jokes, and adolescent tone. Dusenberry comes to Washington, D.C., to start a career in government, only to find her bosses more interested in her body than in her work. Subsequently, and to no one's surprise, she uses her female wiles to ascend the Washington ladder.

BASKET CASE 1982
☆ R Horror 1:23
☑ Nudity, adult situations, explicit language, graphic violence
Dir: Frank Henenlotter *Cast:* Kevin Van Hentryck, Terri Susan Smith, Beverly Bonner, Lloyd Pace
▶ Low-budget splatter film about young Van Hentryck, who carries his detached Siamese twin around in a wicker basket. They travel to New York to kill the doctors responsible for separating them. Lowbrow humor, genuinely weird characters, and copious bloodletting made this a cult favorite at midnight screenings. A much more graphic X-rated version is also available.

BATAAN 1943
★★★ NR War 1:54 B&W
Dir: Tay Garnett *Cast:* Robert Taylor, George Murphy, Thomas Mitchell, Lloyd Nolan, Lee Bowman, Robert Walker
▶ Grim, realistic World War II drama focusing on heroic defense of the Philippines by vastly outnumbered American and native troops. Sturdy cast (including Walker in his film debut as a naive recruit) retains their high spirits despite steadily advancing Japanese. Taylor is particularly convincing in his last film before entering Navy as fighter pilot.

BATMAN 1966
★ NR Action-Adventure 1:45
Dir: Leslie H. Martinson *Cast:* Adam West, Burt Ward, Burgess Meredith, Cesar Romero, Lee Meriwether, Frank Gorshin
▶ The ABC-TV series was so popular that it spawned a feature film at the height of its success. West and Ward as the Caped Crusader and Robin the Boy Wonder are besieged by archenemies Joker (Romero), Penguin (Meredith), Catwoman (Meriwether), and Riddler (Gorshin). Tongue-in-cheek comic-book fun. Followed by a big-budget version starring Michael Keaton and Jack Nicholson, made twenty-three years later. **(CC)**

BAT PEOPLE, THE 1974
☆ PG Horror 1:35
☑ Explicit language, violence
Dir: Jerry Jameson *Cast:* Stewart Moss, Marianne McAndrew, Michael Pataki, Paul Carr, Arthur Space
▶ On their honeymoon at a ski resort, physician Moss and his wife McAndrew take a side trip to some caverns where he's bitten by a bat. Hallucinations and nightmares about bats ensue, so Moss is hospitalized, but modern medicine can't cure his ailment, and in fact his woes have just begun. Low-budget creature feature mainly for die-hards. Also known as *Angel of Fear*.

BATTERIES NOT INCLUDED 1987
★★★★ PG Sci-Fi 1:46
☑ Explicit language, violence
Dir: Matthew Robbins *Cast:* Hume Cronyn, Jessica Tandy, Frank McRae, Elizabeth Peña, Michael Carmine
▶ Real estate developers harass elderly couple Cronyn and Tandy and other inhabitants of a New York tenement until midget alien spaceships miraculously appear to aid the beleaguered tenants. Special effects hardware tends to outshine the human characters, but basically a heartwarming, wholesome fantasy from producer Steven Spielberg.

BATTLE BEYOND THE STARS 1980
★★ PG Sci-Fi 1:43
☑ Adult situations, adult humor
Dir: Jimmy T. Murakami *Cast:* Richard Thomas, Robert Vaughn, George Peppard, John Saxon, Sam Jaffe, Sybil Danning
▶ When the planet Akir faces destruction at the hands of evil villains, Thomas rounds up interplanetary mercenaries to aid his people. Modest but amusing lowbudget sci-fi designed by Roger Corman to capitalize on the *Star Wars* phenomenon (he reused the sets in numerous other films). John Sayles based his screenplay on *The Seven Samurai*.

BATTLE CRY 1955
★★★ NR War 2:28
Dir: Raoul Walsh *Cast:* Van Heflin, Aldo Ray, Mona Freeman, Nancy Olson, James Whitmore, Raymond Massey
▶ Elaborate but unfocused adaptation of a Leon Uris best-seller follows the romances of a group of Marines training for

battle in the Pacific during World War II. Heflin convincingly portrays the hardened major in charge of the recruits; Ray and Olson conduct a steamy affair. Large cast is filled with familiar faces: Tab Hunter, Dorothy Malone, Anne Francis, Fess Parker, and Justus McQueen (who adopted his character's name L. Q. Jones in real life). Score by Max Steiner received an Oscar nomination.

BATTLE FOR THE PLANET OF THE APES 1973
★★★ G Sci-Fi 1:26
Dir: J. Lee Thompson *Cast:* Roddy McDowall, Claude Akins, John Huston, Natalie Trundy, Lew Ayres, Paul Williams
▶ Can apes and humans live in peace or are they doomed to fight out the cycle of war enacted in the first four films? Forward-thinking chimpanzee McDowall opts for peace but militaristic gorilla Akins opposes him. Last installment in the series ends on an upbeat note. (CC)

BATTLE OF ALGIERS, THE 1966
Italian/Algerian
★ PG Drama 2:05 B&W
☑ Graphic violence
Dir: Gillo Pontecorvo *Cast:* Jean Martin, Yacef Saadi, Brahim Haggiag, Tommaso Neri, Fawzia El Kader
▶ Acclaimed docudrama about Algeria's struggle for independence from France uses graphic, hard-hitting camerawork to show the revolution in human terms. Film's heavy anti-French bias and pseudodocumentary tone raised considerable controversy on release, but it's still an undeniably powerful indictment. Ⓢ

BATTLE OF BRITAIN 1969 British
★★★ G War 2:12
Dir: Guy Hamilton *Cast:* Harry Andrews, Michael Caine, Trevor Howard, Curt Jurgens, Ian McShane, Laurence Olivier
▶ Big-budget drama about the defense of England against the Nazi Luftwaffe soars during brilliant dogfight sequences; earthbound scenes sink into clichés. Olivier gives a crafty performance as Air Chief Marshal Hugh Dowding, but most roles are as small as cameos. All-star cast also includes Christopher Plummer, Michael Redgrave, Ralph Richardson, Robert Shaw, Susannah York, and Edward Fox. William Walton contributed to the score.

BATTLE OF THE BULGE 1965
★★ NR War 2:42
Dir: Ken Annakin *Cast:* Henry Fonda, Robert Shaw, Robert Ryan, Dana Andrews, George Montgomery, Pier Angeli
▶ Disappointing account of crucial World War II battle sacrifices realism for Hollywood heroics. Shaw is convincing as the German colonel who masterminds the surprise Nazi tank attack in the Ardennes, but Fonda and Ryan are saddled with thankless roles as American officers ill-prepared to meet the onslaught. Expensive, large-scale drama is filled with historical blunders.

BATTLESHIP POTEMKIN 1925 Russian
★ NR Drama 1:05 B&W
Dir: Sergei Eisenstein *Cast:* Alexander Antonov, Vladmir Barsky, Grigory Alexandrov, Mikhail Gomorov, Levchenko, Repnikova
▶ Silent film depicts the ill-fated 1905 uprising against the Russian czar by focusing on the mutiny aboard a warship in the Odessa harbor. Writer/director Eisenstein's innovative use of editing and composition to build emotion and drama made this one of the most influential films in history. Famous "Odessa Steps" sequence has been affectionately imitated in such films as Woody Allen's *Bananas,* Terry Gilliam's *Brazil,* and Brian De Palma's *The Untouchables.* A must for students of the medium.

BATTLESTAR GALACTICA 1979
★★★ PG Sci-Fi 2:05
☑ Adult situations
Dir: Richard A. Colla *Cast:* Richard Hatch, Dirk Benedict, Lorne Greene, Ray Milland, Jane Seymour
▶ Greene commands a fleet of spaceships fleeing the Cylons, insect-shaped villains out to eradicate mankind. On the planet Carillon, Greene orders son Hatch and other fighter pilots to battle the aliens. Story and special effects by John Dykstra owe a lot to *Star Wars.* Stitched together from the first and fifth episodes of the failed TV series.

BAT 21 1988
★★★★ R War 1:45
☑ Explicit language, graphic violence
Dir: Peter Markle *Cast:* Gene Hackman, Danny Glover, Jerry Reed, David Marshall Grant, Clayton Rohner, Erich Anderson
▶ Hackman, Air Force colonel and intelli-

gence expert, is shot down behind enemy lines during the Vietnam War. Spotter pilot Glover uses radio contact to help maneuver him back through region too dangerous for a rescue mission. Hackman gets a close-up look at the war he'd previously observed only from 30,000 feet. Officer and "grunt" form bond in suspenseful, well-acted war drama based on a true story. **(CC)**

BAWDY ADVENTURES OF TOM JONES, THE 1975 British
★★★ R Comedy 1:28
☑ Nudity, strong sexual content
Dir: Cliff Owen **Cast:** Nicky Henson, Trevor Howard, Joan Collins, Terry-Thomas, Arthur Lowe
▶ Henry Fielding's famous bastard, Tom Jones, is back for the first time since the 1963 Albert Finney version. In this good-natured romp, Tom wants to marry the squire's daughter even though he's not in her social class. Good production values and period settings. The story, with many ironic and sexy twists, is true to the spirit of the original. Contains some musical numbers and extensive nudity.

BAY BOY, THE 1985
★★ R Drama 1:44
☑ Nudity, adult situations, adult humor
Dir: Daniel Petrie **Cast:** Liv Ullmann, Kiefer Sutherland, Peter Donat, Mathieu Carriere, Alan Scarfe
▶ Sensitive coming-of-age drama set in 1937 Nova Scotia. Sutherland plays a teenager coping with a sickly brother, mother Ullmann, who still grieves over the death of a daughter, and the pangs of first love. As if life weren't complex enough, he also witnesses a murder. Plot clumsily mixes teen sex comedy with more serious elements, but nice period details and breathtaking locations.

BEACHBALLS 1988
☆ R Comedy 1:18
☑ Nudity, adult situations, explicit language
Dir: Joe Ritter **Cast:** Phillip Paley, Heidi Helmer, Amanda Goodwin, Steven Rash
▶ Teen lust and assorted beach games in Southern California. With their parents out of town, an aspiring musician pursues a gorgeous blond while his sister goes after a handsome lifeguard. Obvious humor but an attractive cast and plenty of beach lingo ("radical," "bitchin'," "dudes," etc.).

BEACH BLANKET BINGO 1965
★★ NR Comedy 1:38
Dir: William Asher **Cast:** Frankie Avalon, Annette Funicello, Paul Lynde, Harvey Lembeck, Don Rickles, Buster Keaton
▶ The *Beach Party* gang mix it up with skydivers, pop stars, motorcycle gangs, and mermaids in this brainless but fun comedy. First-rate nostalgia piece is considered the best in the series. Linda Evans is delightful as Sugar Kane, a singer who allows herself to be kidnapped to help her career. Strong comic support from Lynde, Rickles, and Keaton.

BEACHES 1988
★★★★ PG-13 Comedy/Drama 2:00
☑ Adult situations, explicit language
Dir: Garry Marshall **Cast:** Bette Midler, Barbara Hershey, John Heard, Spalding Gray, Lainie Kazan, James Read
▶ Two very different women meet as kids on an Atlantic City beach and form a lifelong friendship. New Yorker Midler is poor, outspoken, Jewish, and homely; Hershey is rich, reserved, WASPy, and beautiful. Film traces their lives as roommates in New York, romantic rift over stage director Heard, Midler's success as an entertainer and Hershey's sacrifice of her legal career to marriage. Two drift apart as they grow older, but tragedy brings them together again.

BEACH GIRLS 1982
★★ R Comedy 1:31
☑ Nudity, strong sexual content, explicit language
Dir: Pat Townsend **Cast:** Debra Blee, Val Kline, Jeana Tomasina, James Daughton
▶ Beach blanket comedy features acres of teen flesh as two bikini bunnies vacation at a beach house belonging to a friend's absent uncle. Not much plot but low-budget high jinks include seductions, a Peeping Tom's series of accidents, drug smuggling, and the climactic mud wrestling scene.

BEACH PARTY 1963
★★ NR Musical 1:41
Dir: William Asher **Cast:** Frankie Avalon, Annette Funicello, Bob Cummings, Dorothy Malone, Harvey Lembeck, Jody McCrea
▶ First of a string of successful teen musicals has dated poorly, but still offers fun escapist entertainment. Anthropologist Cummings picks Malibu as the site of his

investigations into teenage sex habits, provoking jealous arguments among the kids. Notable for Lembeck's broad parody of a biker, a role he would repeat in *Bikini Beach*, and romantic pairing of Frankie and Annette. Sequel: *Muscle Beach Party*.

BEAR, THE 1984
★★★ **PG Biography/Sports 1:52**
☑ Explicit language
Dir: Richard Sarafian   *Cast:* Gary Busey, Cynthia Leake, Harry Dean Stanton, D'Urville Martin, Jon-Erik Hexum
▶ Inspirational football drama features Busey as the legendary college football coach Paul "Bear" Bryant, who got his nickname wrestling a live bear in his Arkansas hometown. At the University of Alabama, Bear coaches Joe Namath, recruits the school's first black player, survives charges of game fixing, and wins a slew of big games. Busey is outstanding in his return to the biography genre where he previously earned an Oscar nomination playing Buddy Holly.

BEAR ISLAND 1980 British/Canadian
★★★ **PG Action-Adventure 1:58**
☑ Explicit language, mild violence
Dir: Don Sharp   *Cast:* Donald Sutherland, Vanessa Redgrave, Richard Widmark, Christopher Lee, Barbara Parkins
▶ Members of a UN science expedition in Norway stumble across abandoned Nazi U-boats filled with gold. As the scientists are killed off one by one, it's up to Sutherland to stop the murders. Large-scale Arctic adventure based on Alistair MacLean's best-seller may please fans of his work, but apart from one snowmobile chase there's very little action.

BEAST, THE 1988
★★★★ **R War 1:49**
☑ Explicit language, graphic violence
Dir: Kevin Reynolds   *Cast:* George Dzundza, Jason Patric, Steven Bauer, Don Harvey, Stephen Baldwin
▶ During the war in Afghanistan, crazed Soviet Dzundza brutally commands the tank known as "the Beast." Rebellious Russian Patric teams up with Afghan resistance leader Bauer to topple the tank. Muscular action and impressive technology laced with message of brotherhood. High violence level not for the weak of stomach.

BEASTMASTER, THE 1982
★★★★ **PG Fantasy 1:58**
☑ Brief nudity, violence

Dir: Don Coscarelli   *Cast:* Marc Singer, Tanya Roberts, Rip Torn, John Amos
▶ In a magical feudal world, young warrior Singer uses his telepathy with animals to battle Torn, an evil magician who's enslaved the beautiful virgin Roberts. Derivative sword-and-sorcery epic has enough special effects battles and animal tricks to please younger viewers, although the violence is often excessive.

BEAST WITHIN, THE 1982
★★ **R Horror 1:38**
☑ Rape, nudity, explicit language, graphic violence
Dir: Philippe Mora   *Cast:* Ronny Cox, Bibi Besch, Paul Clemens, Don Gordon, R. G. Armstrong
▶ In Mississippi, honeymooning Besch is raped by a mysterious swamp creature. Seventeen years later, her teenage son Clemens, the product of that rape, falls seriously ill. With Dad Cox, they return to Mississippi to gather clues about the son's condition. Apparently possessed by the spirit of his dead father, the son turns into a beast and goes on a murderous rampage.

BEATLEMANIA 1981
★ **PG Musical 1:36**
☑ Brief nudity
Dir: Joseph Manduke   *Cast:* Mitch Weissman, David Leon, Tom Tooley, Ralph Castelli
▶ Adaptation of popular Broadway play features four look-alikes performing thirty Beatles hits. Divided into eight chronological segments consisting mostly of concert footage, although some newsreels and cartoons are included. The songs are great, but film can't hide the fact that these are impersonations, not the real thing.

BEAT STREET 1984
★★★ **PG Musical 1:46**
☑ Explicit language, mild violence
Dir: Stan Lathan   *Cast:* Rae Dawn Chong, Guy Davis, Jon Chardiet, Leon Grant
▶ Upbeat teen musical follows old formula of young kids trying to break into show business, this time through break dancing, rapping, and graffiti. Energetic performers, realistic view of racial issues, and authentic South Bronx feel should satisfy hip-hop fans. The real achievement here is the soundtrack (co-produced by Harry Belafonte and re-mix whiz Arthur Baker) featuring Grandmas-

ter Melle Mel, Afrika Bambaataa, Rock Steady, etc.

BEAT THE DEVIL 1954
★★ NR Comedy 1:29 B&W
Dir: John Huston *Cast:* Humphrey Bogart, Gina Lollobrigida, Jennifer Jones, Robert Morley, Peter Lorre, Edward Underdown
▶ Low-key satire of caper movies has an extremely unlikely plot: Bogart leads four crooks to Africa on a uranium scam, but the arrival of blond femme fatale Jones and an unexpected shipwreck force a change in plans. Nonsensical script (by Huston and Truman Capote) is played straight-faced by the extraordinary cast. A failure on release, film is now a cult favorite.

BEAU GESTE 1939
★★★ NR Action-Adventure 1:54 B&W
Dir: William Wellman *Cast:* Gary Cooper, Ray Milland, Robert Preston, Brian Donlevy, Susan Hayward, J. Carrol Naish
▶ When their brother Beau (Cooper) joins the Foreign Legion after admitting to a jewel theft, Milland and Preston follow to redeem the family name. They are drawn into rebellion against malicious sergeant Donlevy while battling native attacks. Smashing Sahara adventure won Donlevy an Oscar nomination for his genuinely frightening performance. Donald O'Connor plays Beau as a child. Remade in 1966.

BEAU PERE 1981 French
★ NR Drama 2:00
☑ Nudity, adult situations, explicit language
Dir: Bertrand Blier *Cast:* Patrick Dewaere, Ariel Besse, Maurice Ronet, Nicole Garcia, Nathalie Baye
▶ Musician Dewaere lives with a woman and her teenage daughter Besse. When the woman is killed in a car accident, the girl insists on staying with the musician. She falls for him and he eventually succumbs to her persistent advances. Despite the somewhat controversial subject matter, the film is sensitively handled and at times humorous.

BEAUTY AND THE BEAST 1946 French
★★ NR Fantasy 1:30 B&W
Dir: Jean Cocteau *Cast:* Jean Marais, Josette Day, Marcel André, Mila Parely, Nane Germon, Michel Auclair
▶ Exquisitely filmed version of the classic fairy tale is one of the landmarks of surrealism. Director Cocteau concentrated on bizarre props and symbolism in telling the story of merchant's daughter Day, who sacrifices herself to a hideous but kind-hearted beast (Marais) to save her father. Evocative but slowly paced, with outstanding photography by Henri Alekan. ⑤

BECKET 1964
★★★★ NR Drama 2:32
Dir: Peter Glenville *Cast:* Richard Burton, Peter O'Toole, John Gielgud, Donald Wolfit, Martita Hunt
▶ Rich costume drama, set in twelfth-century England, chronicles the friendship between Henry II (O'Toole), ruler of Saxony, and Thomas à Becket (Burton), Archbishop of Canterbury, which dissolved into a bitter conflict over issues of Church and Crown. Highly reputed classic makes impressive use of three formidable stars and an ambitious, historically credible, Oscar-winning screenplay. Also nominated for Best Picture and Director.

BEDAZZLED 1968 British
★★ NR Comedy 1:47
Dir: Stanley Donen *Cast:* Peter Cook, Dudley Moore, Eleanor Bron, Raquel Welch, Alba, Robert Russell
▶ Suicidal short-order cook (Moore) signs pact with the Devil (Cook) to win the heart of sexy waitress (Bron). But the plan goes disastrously awry as the Devil introduces Moore to the seven deadly sins instead. Uneven comic updating of *Faust* has priceless, irreverent, bawdy moments, notably Welch as a steamy Lillian Lust. Written by Cook and Moore (Moore also wrote the music).

BEDFORD INCIDENT, THE 1965
★★★ NR Drama 1:42 B&W
Dir: James B. Harris *Cast:* Richard Widmark, Sidney Poitier, James MacArthur, Martin Balsam, Wally Cox
▶ Tough American destroyer commander Widmark stalks Russian sub off the coast of Greenland. His crew begins to crack under the strain, leading to a shocking conclusion. Tense nuclear-age drama is well plotted and well acted by Widmark and Poitier as a journalist on board.

BEDKNOBS AND BROOMSTICKS 1971
★★★★ G Family 1:57
Dir: Robert Stevenson *Cast:* Angela Lansbury, David Tomlinson, Roddy McDowall, Sam Jaffe, Roy Snart
▶ A solid Disney classic, based on the

story by Mary Norton and set in London during the Blitzkrieg. As the nanny of three orphans Lansbury is hell-bent on helping Churchill stave off the Nazis. With the aid of the Correspondence College of Witchcraft, she takes the children to the cartoon land of Naboombu, in search of the ultimate magic spell. A treat for kids and adults.

BEDLAM 1946
★★ **NR Horror 1:19 B&W**
Dir: Mark Robson *Cast:* Boris Karloff, Anna Lee, Billy House, Glen Vernon, Jason Robards, Sr., Joan Newton
▶ Karloff delivers one of his best performances as the brutal head of an eighteenth-century mental asylum; actress Lee attempts to expose his wrongdoings and ends up an inmate herself. Chilling horror tale produced by Val Lewton was based on actual events at London's Hospital of St. Mary of Bethlehem.

BEDROOM WINDOW, THE 1987
★★★★ **R Mystery-Suspense 1:52**
☑ Nudity, adult situations, explicit language, violence
Dir: Curtis Hanson *Cast:* Steve Guttenberg, Elizabeth McGovern, Isabelle Huppert, Paul Shenar, Frederick Coffin
▶ Likable Baltimore executive Guttenberg is having an affair with Huppert, his boss's wife, when during a tryst in his apartment, she sees a woman being assaulted outside the bedroom window. To protect her, Guttenberg tells the police he saw the attack and, in true Hitchcock fashion, soon becomes the chief suspect in a rash of killings and has to prove his innocence while running from the law. Competent execution of standard thriller fare raised above average by good cast and twisty plot. **(CC)**

BEDTIME FOR BONZO 1951
★★ **NR Comedy 1:23 B&W**
Dir: Frederick De Cordova *Cast:* Ronald Reagan, Diana Lynn, Walter Slezak, Jesse White, Lucille Barkley
▶ Trying to prove environment rather than heredity is the main factor in how kids turn out, professor Reagan takes a chimp into his home. Jokes about the future careers of those involved aside (we all know that De Cordova became "The Tonight Show" producer, right?), this is actually a pleasant little diversion.

BEER 1985
★ **R Comedy 1:22**

☑ Adult situations, explicit language, adult humor
Dir: Patrick Kelly *Cast:* Loretta Swit, Kenneth Mars, Rip Torn, Dick Shawn, William Russ, David Alan Grier
▶ Swit is B. D., advertising executive on the Norbecker beer account, desperately in need of a new campaign. After witnessing three guys thwart a robbery, she signs them as beer spokesmen. Naturally, sales skyrocket with the sexist "whip out your Norbecker" slogan. This Madison Avenue satire, full of shtick and sight gags, has some vaudevillian star turns from Mars, Shawn, and Torn but overall is mostly foam. **(CC)**

BEER DRINKER'S GUIDE TO FITNESS AND FILM MAKING, THE 1988
★★ **PG Documentary/Comedy 1:24**
☑ Explicit language, adult humor
Dir: Fred G. Sullivan *Cast:* Fred G. Sullivan, Polly Sullivan, Tate Sullivan, Katie Sullivan, Kirk Sullivan, Jan Jalenek
▶ In New York's Adirondack Mountains, filmmaker Sullivan struggles to balance the call of his dreams with the need for diaper money. Interviews with friends and neighbors, flashbacks to Sullivan's childhood and career struggles, and phone calls from bill collectors reveal the perils of being a rural filmmaker raising a family. Heartwarming, free-form home movie avoids self-indulgence. Young Tate Sullivan has the best line: "My daddy says if you don't come see this movie, we'll all starve."

BEES, THE 1978
★★ **PG Horror 1:23**
☑ Violence
Dir: Alfredo Zacharias *Cast:* John Saxon, Angel Tompkins, John Carradine, Claudio Brook, Alicia Encinias
▶ Deadly killer bees, furious at the ecological damage caused by pollution, band together to attack humanity. Hero Saxon joins scientists Carradine and Brook to stop them. Uninspired low-budget variation on *The Swarm* lacks sting.

BEETLEJUICE 1988
★★★ **PG Fantasy/Comedy 1:30**
☑ Adult situations, explicit language, violence
Dir: Tim Burton *Cast:* Michael Keaton, Alec Baldwin, Geena Davis, Jeffrey Jones, Catherine O'Hara, Winona Ryder
▶ A delightfully deranged and endlessly inventive grand-scale funhouse from director Burton. Keaton is Beetlejuice, a

renegade freelance ghost hired by recently deceased newlyweds Davis and Baldwin to evict a real-life family from their home. Jam-packed with ghoulish sight gags and special effects. Younger audiences will appreciate Keaton's hilariously obnoxious performance. (CC)

BEGINNER'S LUCK 1986
★ R Comedy 1:25
☑ Nudity, adult situations, explicit language
Dir: Frank Mouris *Cast:* Sam Rush, Riley Steiner, Charles Humet, Kate Talbot, Mickey Coburn
▶ Modest, shaggy-dog romantic comedy with a rather skimpy plot. An about-to-be-married couple bring their lonely neighbor into their home for a ménage à trois, although there's no sex involved. The leads are pleasant enough but everyone tries a bit too hard to be cute.

BEGUILED, THE 1971
★★ R Drama 1:49
☑ Brief nudity, adult situations, explicit language, violence
Dir: Don Siegel *Cast:* Clint Eastwood, Geraldine Page, Elizabeth Hartman, Jo Ann Harris, Darleen Carr, Mae Mercer
▶ Oddly compelling psychological thriller with Eastwood in an uncharacteristic role as a wounded Union soldier held prisoner in a Confederate girls' boarding school. Sexual tensions lead to gruesome complications as the students and teachers vie for his affections. Interesting but slow paced, and often quite gory.

BEHOLD A PALE HORSE 1964
★★ NR Drama 1:58 B&W
Dir: Fred Zinnemann *Cast:* Gregory Peck, Anthony Quinn, Omar Sharif, Mildred Dunnock, Raymond Pellegrin, Paolo Stoppa
▶ Spanish insurgent Peck, refusing to admit defeat after the 1937 Civil War, conducts guerrilla raids from French outpost. Nemesis Quinn, a police captain, arranges a trap for Peck involving his ailing mother Dunnock. Subtle but talky battle of wits based on Emeric Pressburger's novel *Killing a Mouse on Sunday*.

BEING, THE 1983
★ R Horror 1:22
☑ Explicit language, violence
Dir: Jackie Kong *Cast:* Martin Landau, Jose Ferrer, Dorothy Malone, Ruth Buzzi, Kinky Friedman
▶ The population of Pottsville, Idaho

("spud capital of the universe"), drops alarmingly when a nuclear waste mutant starts sliming people to death, but mayor Ferrer and toxic-dump owner Landau won't admit the monster exists. Zero-budget horror spoof has some nice comic touches and good political points, but don't expect much action.

BEING THERE 1979
★★★ PG Comedy 2:07
☑ Adult situations, explicit language, adult humor
Dir: Hal Ashby *Cast:* Peter Sellers, Shirley MacLaine, Melvyn Douglas, Jack Warden, Richard Dysart
▶ Sellers gives a brilliant performance as Chance, a gardener whose only knowledge of the world comes from TV. People mistake his naiveté for wisdom, and soon he's advising the President. Literate, incisive screenplay by Jerzy Kosinski actually improves on his novel. Ashby brings a delightfully serene tone to this sophisticated black comedy. Douglas won a supporting actor Oscar for his role as an ailing millionaire.

BELIEVERS, THE 1987
★★★ R Horror 1:40
☑ Nudity, adult situations, explicit language, violence
Dir: John Schlesinger *Cast:* Martin Sheen, Helen Shaver, Harley Cross, Robert Loggia, Richard Masur, Elizabeth Wilson
▶ New York psychiatrist Sheen treats a cop suffering from nightmares about a secret voodoo cult. When the cop commits suicide, Sheen realizes his son may be the cult's next victim. Manipulative but effective horror film has some truly frightening and grotesque sequences.

BELIZAIRE THE CAJUN 1985
★★ PG Drama 1:35
☑ Explicit language, violence
Dir: Glen Pitre *Cast:* Armand Assante, Gail Youngs, Michael Schoeffling, Stephen McHattie, Will Patton
▶ Moody period drama about Assante, an 1850s Cajun faith healer who becomes the victim of racial prejudice. After falling in love with a white man's wife, he is falsely accused of murder. Sincere but uneven screenplay by Pitre, a Cajun himself, was developed at Robert Redford's Sundance Institute. Robert Duvall has a brief cameo. (CC)

BELL, BOOK AND CANDLE 1959
★★★ NR Comedy 1:43

Dir: Richard Quine *Cast:* James Stewart, Kim Novak, Jack Lemmon, Ernie Kovacs, Hermione Gingold, Elsa Lanchester
► Novak, a beautiful modern-day witch, casts a spell on staid publisher Stewart on the eve of his wedding. Her warlock brother Lemmon and parapsychology expert Kovacs bring Stewart to rival witch Gingold to break the spell. Expert cast breezes through this pleasant adaptation of the John Van Druten play.

BELLBOY, THE 1960
★★★ NR Comedy 1:12 B&W
Dir: Jerry Lewis *Cast:* Jerry Lewis, Alex Gerry, Bob Clayton, Sonnie Sands, Bill Richmond
► Miami Beach's Fontainebleau Hotel provides the backdrop for series of non-stop sight gags and slapstick jokes linked together by Stanley (Lewis), an inept bellboy who never speaks. Lewis's directing debut is also one of his better solo vehicles. Includes cameos by Maxie Rosenblum, Milton Berle, and Joe E. Ross.

BELLE DE JOUR 1967 French/Italian
★ R Drama 1:40
☑ Rape, strong sexual content, explicit language, violence
Dir: Luis Buñuel *Cast:* Catherine Deneuve, Jean Sorel, Michel Piccoli, Genevieve Page, Francisco Rabal
► Brilliant, disturbing black comedy stars Deneuve as a virginal wife who spends her afternoons working in a bordello. Unique blend of fantasy, satire, and savage realism is considered a masterpiece by critics, although many viewers may be offended by its unsettling approach to prostitution. Deneuve is remarkable in one of her best performances. [S]

BELLE OF NEW YORK, THE 1952
★★ NR Musical 1:22
Dir: Charles Walters *Cast:* Fred Astaire, Vera-Ellen, Marjorie Main, Keenan Wynn, Alice Pearce, Gale Robbins
► In Gay Nineties New York, dashing playboy Astaire pursues chaste social worker Vera-Ellen, but she won't accept him until he gets a respectable job. Lesser Astaire vehicle based on an old vaudeville play features "I Wanna Be a Dancin' Man" and "Let a Little Love Come In."

BELLES OF ST. TRINIAN'S, THE 1955 British
★★ NR Comedy 1:26 B&W
Dir: Frank Launder *Cast:* Alastair Sim, Joyce Grenfell, George Cole, Vivienne Martin, Eric Pohlmann, Lorna Henderson
► Fast-paced, frequently hilarious farce about seedy British girls' school, notorious for its bootleg gin, that becomes hiding place for kidnapped thoroughbred. Based on Ronald Searle's cartoons, and highlighted by Sim in a dual role as a dotty headmistress and her malevolent brother. Hermione Baddeley and Beryl Reid are marvelous as incompetent faculty members. *Blue Murder at St. Trinian's* was the first of three sequels.

BELL FOR ADANO, A 1945
★★★★ NR War 1:44 B&W
Dir: Henry King *Cast:* John Hodiak, Gene Tierney, William Bendix, Glenn Langan, Richard Conte, Stanley Prager
► At the end of World War II, American occupation forces led by Hodiak and his orderly Bendix are faced with rebuilding the devastated Italian village of Adano. Hodiak wins over the hearts of the villagers through his compassionate leadership in this warm, sentimental adaptation of John Hersey's famous novel.

BELL JAR, THE 1979
★★ R Drama 1:53
☑ Nudity, adult situations, explicit language
Dir: Larry Peerce *Cast:* Marilyn Hassett, Julie Harris, Anne Jackson, Barbara Barrie, Robert Klein
► In the 1950s, an ambitious, gifted college woman travels to New York to become a poet. Unable to cope with the real world, she undergoes shock therapy at a mental institution. Sensitive adaptation of Sylvia Plath's autobiographical novel has superior performances from the talented supporting cast. Extremely depressing despite attempts to lighten the novel's tone.

BELLMAN AND TRUE 1988 British
★★ R Drama 1:58
☑ Adult situations, explicit language, violence
Dir: Richard Loncraine *Cast:* Bernard Hill, Kieran O'Brien, Richard Hope, Frances Tomelty, Derek Newark
► Computer expert Hill and his son are kidnapped by gangsters planning a difficult bank robbery. Hill breaks the bank's alarm system, but can't free his son unless he takes on the crooks. Complex caper film concentrates on realistic personalities involved in compelling conflicts. Still

has more than enough gripping moments. Produced by George Harrison.

BELLS ARE RINGING 1960
★ ★ ★ ★ NR Musical 2:06
Dir: Vincente Minnelli *Cast:* Judy Holliday, Dean Martin, Fred Clark, Eddie Foy, Jr., Jean Stapleton, Frank Gorshin
▶ A shy telephone answering service operator, Holliday forms warm friendships with her clients and helps them with their problems, especially struggling playwright Martin, with whom she falls in love. Last screen appearance for Holliday, who delightfully re-creates her Tony-winning Broadway triumph in this first-class MGM musical. Songs include "Just in Time."

BELLS OF ST. MARY'S, THE 1945
★ ★ ★ ★ NR Drama 2:06 B&W
Dir: Leo McCarey *Cast:* Bing Crosby, Ingrid Bergman, Henry Travers, Ruth Donnelly, Joan Carroll, Martha Sleeper
▶ Moving sequel to *Going My Way* sends unorthodox Father Chuck O'Malley (Crosby) to help impoverished parish run by Bergman, a beautiful Sister Superior. She objects to his relaxed ways until recognizing his influence on her schoolchildren. Wistfully sentimental tearjerker received eight Oscar nominations, winning for Best Sound. Highlighted by Crosby's "Aren't You Glad You're You" and Bergman's attempt to teach a youth how to box.

BELOW THE BELT 1979
★ R Drama/Sports 1:31
☑ Adult situations, explicit language, violence
Dir: Robert Fowler *Cast:* Regina Baff, Mildred Burke, John C. Becher, Annie McGreevey, Jane O'Brien
▶ After witnessing waitress Baff knock out a lecherous customer, a promoter recruits her into the world of women's wrestling. Using the name "Rosa Carlo, the Mexican Spitfire," Baff works her way up to a title match. Despite the seedy settings, a surprisingly affectionate and realistic look at wrestling. Film suffers from shoestring budget.

BEN 1972
★ ★ PG Horror 1:35
Dir: Phil Karlson *Cast:* Lee Harcourt Montgomery, Joseph Campanella, Arthur O'Connell, Rosemary Murphy, Meredith Baxter
▶ Sequel to the horror hit *Willard*. The terror begins when Ben, supersmart leader of the first flick's evil rat pack, befriends troubled Montgomery. Creepy stuff; rodent fearers beware! Hit title tune sung by a young Michael Jackson, first love song about a rat ever to top the charts.

BEND OF THE RIVER 1952
★ ★ ★ NR Western 1:31
Dir: Anthony Mann *Cast:* James Stewart, Arthur Kennedy, Julie Adams, Rock Hudson, Lori Nelson, Jay C. Flippen
▶ Tough Missouri border raider Stewart guides a group of settlers to a remote Oregon river valley. When their supplies fail to arrive, he rides to Portland to retrieve them from the unscrupulous trader who's hoarding them for gold miners. Sturdy, unsentimental Western has excellent action sequences and another of Stewart's intriguing, fully rounded characterizations.

BENEATH THE PLANET OF THE APES 1970
★ ★ ★ G Sci-Fi 1:35
Dir: Ted Post *Cast:* James Franciscus, Kim Hunter, Charlton Heston, Maurice Evans, Linda Harrison
▶ First of four sequels to *Planet of the Apes*. Astronaut Franciscus arrives on the ape-ruled orb to search for the missing Heston and finds himself caught in a war between the primates and an underground mutant race. Not as imaginative as its predecessor but still features striking visual design and ape makeup. Best moments revolve around discovery of buried New York subway system. **(CC)**

BEN HUR 1959
★ ★ ★ ★ ★ NR Action-Adventure 3:32
Dir: William Wyler *Cast:* Charlton Heston, Jack Hawkins, Stephen Boyd, Haya Harareet, Cathy O'Donnell, Martha Scott
▶ During the rule of Caesar, wealthy Jew Heston refuses to turn in rebels, including Jesus of Nazareth, to Roman commander Boyd. Heston is sentenced to be a galley slave while his mother Scott and sister O'Donnell are imprisoned. When Heston saves the life of Roman admiral Hawkins, he's granted his freedom and the chance to seek revenge in rousing chariot race against Boyd. Classic sword-and-sandals spectacle won a record eleven Academy Awards, including Best Picture, Director, and Actor (Heston). (CC)

BENIKER GANG, THE 1985
★ ★ ★ ★ G Family 1:27

Dir: Ken Kwapis   *Cast:* Andrew McCarthy, Jennifer Dundas, Danny Pintauro

▶ McCarthy stars as Arthur Beniker, a parentless eighteen-year-old who supports four younger orphans by writing an advice column. When their unorthodox family is threatened with adoption, the fivesome run away. Heartwarming sleeper with a cast of fresh young faces.

BENJI 1975
★★★★★ G Family 1:25
Dir: Joe Camp   *Cast:* Peter Breck, Cynthia Smith, Christopher Connelly, Patsy Garrett, Mark Slade

▶ Man's best four-legged friend, Benji, outwits two-legged kidnappers in this delightful family flick. The lovable mutt saves two kids and is adopted by their grateful family. Director Camp heightens our identification with the furry hero by telling the story from Benji's point of view, including a slow-motion love scene with a Pekingese! Country star Charlie Rich sings the Oscar-nominated theme song, "I Feel Love."

BENJI THE HUNTED 1987
★★★★★ G Family 1:33
Dir: Joe Camp   *Cast:* Benji, Red Stegall, Joe Camp, Steve Zanolini, Karen Thorndike

▶ The most popular canine hero since Lassie is back in a warmhearted family film. Kids will have no trouble following the plot: Benji adopts four orphaned cougar cubs whose mother has been killed by a hunter and protects them from bears, wolves, foxes, and eagles. The cuddly cubs prove as adept at stealing scenes as Benji.

BENNY GOODMAN STORY, THE 1955
★★ G Biography/Musical 1:56
Dir: Valentine Davies   *Cast:* Steve Allen, Donna Reed, Berta Gersten, Herbert Anderson, Robert F. Simon, Sammy Davis, Sr.

▶ Allen is surprisingly good in his acting debut as the famed clarinetist, and the first-rate music makes up for routine story about his rise from poverty to fame. Goodman dubbed in his own playing, working with the cream of jazz musicians: Harry James, Teddy Wilson, Gene Krupa, Lionel Hampton, etc. That's Sammy Davis's father as Fletcher Henderson.

BERLIN ALEXANDERPLATZ 1983 West German
☆ NR Drama/MFTV 15:51

☑ Adult situations, explicit language, violence
Dir: Rainer Werner Fassbinder   *Cast:* Gunter Lamprecht, Hanna Schygulla, Barbara Sukowa, Gottfried John, Brigitte Mara

▶ German director Fassbinder's masterpiece, originally made as thirteen episodes for German television. Lamprecht stars as Franz Biberkopf, a dough-faced ex-con attempting an ultimately doomed effort to start a new life in post–World War I Berlin. Serious, powerful themes are handled in a much more accessible style than usual for this noted director. ⑤

BERLIN EXPRESS 1948
★★ NR Drama 1:26 B&W
Dir: Jacques Tourneur   *Cast:* Merle Oberon, Robert Ryan, Charles Korvin, Paul Lukas, Robert Coote

▶ In postwar Germany, Ryan joins three other Allied police officers in guarding liberal politician Lukas from assassination at the hands of neo-Nazis. Location shooting in the ruins of Frankfurt and Berlin add authenticity to this tightly plotted suspenser.

BERSERK 1967 British
★★ NR Horror 1:36
Dir: Jim O'Connolly   *Cast:* Joan Crawford, Ty Hardin, Diana Dors, Michael Gough, Judy Geeson

▶ Tawdry melodrama about circus owner Crawford exploiting an accidental death for publicity purposes. When new high-wire daredevil Hardin dies, she's suspected of murder. Further killings occur when Geeson, her deranged daughter, arrives. Crawford's next-to-last film.

BEST BOY 1979
★★ NR Documentary 1:44
Dir: Ira Wohl   *Cast:* Phillip Wohl

▶ Uplifting Oscar-winning documentary about "Philly" Wohl, a fifty-two-year-old retarded man living with his parents. Concerned with the fate of Philly's future once his parents die, his cousin Ira helps him become more independent. Philly's enthusiasm for his expanding horizons is contagious; viewers will really get to know him and his family. Deliberately paced but quite moving. Brief appearance by Zero Mostel.

BEST DEFENSE 1984
★★ R Comedy 1:34

☑ Brief nudity, adult situations, explicit language, adult humor
Dir: Willard Huyck *Cast:* Dudley Moore, Eddie Murphy, Kate Capshaw, Helen Shaver, George Dzundza, David Rasche
▶ Loud, brassy military comedy actually has two plots. In one, Moore, an inept scientist, uses stolen KGB plans for a "dip-gyro" weapon to further his career. In the second, "Strategic Guest Star" Murphy is stuck in a Middle Eastern war with a dip-gyro that doesn't work. Film's big problem is that the two stars never appear together. Written by Huyck and his wife Gloria Katz. **(CC)**

BEST FOOT FORWARD 1943
★★★ **NR Musical 1:35**
Dir: Edward Buzzell *Cast:* Lucille Ball, William Gaxton, Virginia Weidler, Tommy Dix, Nancy Walker, Gloria De Haven
▶ Publicity-seeking movie star Ball, playing herself, allows a small-town military academy to name her their prom queen. Chaos results in this amusing, high-spirited romp (with Walker supplying most of the laughs). Includes "Buckle Down Winsocki" and a first-rate "Two O'Clock Jump" by Harry James and his Orchestra.

BEST FRIENDS 1982
★★ **PG Comedy 1:56**
☑ Brief nudity, adult situations, explicit language
Dir: Norman Jewison *Cast:* Burt Reynolds, Goldie Hawn, Jessica Tandy, Barnard Hughes, Audra Lindley, Ron Silver
▶ Burt and Goldie are live-together L.A. screenwriters who decide to get married. A cross-country honeymoon to meet their respective parents puts strains on their relationship until they realize it's possible to remain best friends. Sophisticated romantic comedy with the stars in top form and a funny supporting turn by Silver as an obnoxious Hollywood producer. Well-observed script by Valerie Curtin and Barry Levinson, who were married at the time and obviously knew the territory.

BEST LITTLE WHOREHOUSE IN TEXAS, THE 1982
★★★★ **R Musical 1:54**
☑ Nudity, adult situations, explicit language
Dir: Colin Higgins *Cast:* Burt Reynolds, Dolly Parton, Dom DeLuise, Charles Durning, Jim Nabors, Lois Nettleton
▶ Gaudy, expensive adaptation of the hit Broadway play about the efforts of TV envangelist DeLuise to close down the most popular "chicken ranch" in Texas. Parton is in rare form as the madam of the bordello, and adds two of her own songs to the soundtrack. Although game, Reynolds proves once again that he's not a singer. Durning steals the film with the show's best tune, "Sidestep."

BEST MAN, THE 1964
★★★ **NR Drama 1:42 B&W**
Dir: Franklin J. Schaffner *Cast:* Henry Fonda, Cliff Robertson, Lee Tracy, Edie Adams, Margaret Leighton, Ann Sothern
▶ Backstage machinations at a political convention as Adlai Stevensonesque liberal Fonda and his more ruthless foe Robertson vie for the favor of the dying President, played by Oscar-nominated Tracy. Dirt from both candidates' past comes into play. In light of the Gary Hart/Donna Rice affair and other recent scandals, this incisive look at the nominating process is more topical than ever. From Gore Vidal's Broadway play.

BEST OF TIMES, THE 1986
★★★ **PG-13 Comedy 1:44**
☑ Adult situations, explicit language
Dir: Roger Spottiswoode *Cast:* Robin Williams, Kurt Russell, Pamela Reed, Holly Palance, Donovan Scott
▶ For thirteen years, Williams has been haunted by the memory of the dropped pass that would've won the big high school football game. Finally, he stages a rematch. Underrated small-town comedy from screenwriter Ron Shelton nicely mixes irony and a sense of rueful mid-life regret. Williams is manic and funny, Russell is perfect as his best pal and former star quarterback, and Palance and Reed almost steal the movie as their long-suffering wives. Muddy big-game climax will leave you cheering. **(CC)**

BEST REVENGE 1984
★ **R Action-Adventure 1:27**
☑ Adult situations, explicit language, violence
Dir: John Trent *Cast:* John Heard, Levon Helm, Alberta Watson, John Rhys-Davies
▶ Heard, a drug smuggler blackmailed into a deal in Morocco, asks for help from best friend Helm. Arrested in a double-cross, they must fight both the police and mobsters to return to Spain. Typical mod-

ern-day film noir has a strong perform-ance from former Band drummer Helm.

BEST SELLER 1987
★★★★ R Drama 1:50
☑ Brief nudity, explicit language, vio-lence
Dir: John Flynn *Cast:* James Woods, Brian Dennehy, Victoria Tennant, Paul Shenar, Allison Balson
▶ Suffering from writer's block, top crime novelist Dennehy agrees to co-author a book on professional hit man Woods's career. But Woods's boss Shenar will stop at nothing to see that the book is never completed. Larry Cohen's screenplay works best when examining the intriguing relationship between the two leads.

BEST YEARS OF OUR LIVES, THE 1946
★★★★ NR Drama 2:54 B&W
Dir: William Wyler *Cast:* Fredric March, Myrna Loy, Dana Andrews, Teresa Wright, Virginia Mayo, Hoagy Carmi-chael
▶ Classic study of three World War II vet-erans readjusting their lives is still riveting today. Heartbreaking and funny by turns, with memorable supporting work by Loy and Wright. Andrews is excellent as a bit-ter Air Force captain; March won Best Actor as a sergeant who isn't happy working for a bank; but real-life amputee Harold Russell (who won both Supporting Actor and a Special Oscar for inspiring other veterans) is the surprise here. Film won eight Oscars overall, including Best Picture, Direction, Screenplay (Robert E. Sherwood), Editing, and Score.

BETRAYAL 1983 British
★ R Drama 1:35
☑ Adult situations, explicit language
Dir: David Jones *Cast:* Ben Kingsley, Jeremy Irons, Patricia Hodge
▶ Playwright Harold Pinter's unconven-tional look at a long-term extramarital affair receives penetrating screen treat-ment by three distinguished actors. The story of Hodge's affair with husband Kingsley's best friend Irons unfolds in re-verse chronological order. Wonderful trio of performances and witty dialogue, but the arty technique gives this somewhat limited appeal.

BETRAYED 1988
★★★★ R Drama 2:03
☑ Adult situations, explicit language, violence
Dir: Costa-Gavras *Cast:* Tom Berenger, Debra Winger, John Heard, Betsy Blair, John Mahoney, Richard Libertini
▶ When left-wing talk show host Libertini is murdered by right-wing extremists, FBI honcho Heard dispatches agent Winger on undercover mission into the Iowa heartland. Winger falls in love with chief suspect, warm single father/farmer Be-renger. As romance deepens, he reveals his secret world of paranoia and hatred, setting up a conflict for Winger between love and morality. Topical thriller with shock power and strong leads.

BETSY, THE 1978
★★★★ R Drama 2:05
☑ Nudity, explicit language
Dir: Daniel Petrie *Cast:* Laurence Olivier, Robert Duvall, Katharine Ross, Tommy Lee Jones, Jane Alexander, Lesley-Anne Down
▶ Amusing adaptation of Harold Rob-bins's best-seller describes three genera-tions of auto tycoons in terms of incest, homosexuality, and more conventional couplings in Grosse Pointe, Michigan. Labyrinthine plot moves a bit slowly, but not every soap opera boasts Lord Olivier.

BETTE MIDLER: DIVINE MADNESS 1980
★★ R Documentary/Music 1:33
☑ Explicit language, adult humor
Dir: Michael Ritchie *Cast:* Bette Midler
▶ Concert keepsake of the Divine Miss M, filmed in Pasadena, mixes her trademark blend of campy comedy and belted bal-lads. Technically assured direction by Rit-chie with several strong numbers includ-ing "The Rose" and "Leader of the Pack." A sure Bette for her fans.

BETTER LATE THAN NEVER 1982
★★★ PG Comedy 1:31
☑ Adult situations, explicit language
Dir: Bryan Forbes *Cast:* David Niven, Maggie Smith, Art Carney, Kimberly Partridge, Catherine Hicks
▶ Niven and Carney, two elderly gentle-men who shared a girlfriend years ago in Paris, vie for the affection (and the for-tune) of young Partridge, who could be either's granddaughter. Cute diversion with gorgeous Riviera scenery and a wonderful performance by Smith as the child's nanny.

BETTER OFF DEAD 1985
★★★ PG Comedy 1:37
☑ Explicit language, adult humor
Dir: Savage Steve Holland *Cast:* John Cusack, David Ogden Stiers, Kim Darby, Diane Franklin, Amanda Wyss

▶ Hapless high school student Cusack loses the girl of his dreams to a jock and figures he'd be better off dead. However, he eventually finds happiness with a pretty French exchange student and bests the jock in a ski race. Some overly broad and gross moments but young Holland provides some truly original and outrageous bits. **(CC)**

BETTY BLUE 1986 French
☆ **NR Drama 2:00**
☑ Nudity, strong sexual content, adult situations, explicit language, violence
Dir: Jean-Jacques Beineix *Cast:* Beatrice Dalle, Jean-Hugues Anglade, Consuelo de Havilland, Gerard Darmon, Clementine Celarie
▶ Flashy, erotic psychodrama about affair between a schizophrenic free spirit Dalle (in an impressive debut) and aspiring writer Anglade. Episodic plot eventually concentrates on Dalle's descent into madness. Director Beineix pumps up the far-fetched story with exotic colors and graphic sex scenes. Has a cult following, and was selected for Best Foreign Film consideration. **(CC)** ⑤

BETWEEN FRIENDS 1983
★★★★ **NR Drama/MFTV 1:40**
☑ Adult situations, explicit language
Dir: Lou Antonio *Cast:* Elizabeth Taylor, Carol Burnett, Henry Ramer, Barbara Bush, Stephen Young
▶ Female friendship sustains two recent divorcées through the difficulties of middle-aged single life. Taylor plays a sharp-tongued woman who keeps company with an aging tycoon because she can't imagine life without a man. Burnett is a real estate agent who pursues a series of casual affairs while trying to maintain a relationship with her daughter. Fine performances by two superstars, together for the first time.

BETWEEN THE LINES 1977
★ **R Comedy 1:41**
☑ Brief nudity, explicit language
Dir: Joan Micklin Silver *Cast:* John Heard, Lindsay Crouse, Jeff Goldblum, Jill Eikenberry, Gwen Welles, Stephen Collins
▶ The staff of a countercultural Boston newspaper undergoes a collective identity crisis after a conglomerate takeover. Crouse and Goldblum are standouts among the attractive young cast of 1960s survivors facing a new lifestyle. A

gentle, humanistic comedy from director Silver.

BEVERLY HILLS COP 1984
★★★★★ **R Action-Adventure 1:45**
☑ Explicit language, violence
Dir: Martin Brest *Cast:* Eddie Murphy, Judge Reinhold, Lisa Eilbacher, John Ashton, Steven Berkoff, James Russo
▶ Street-smart Detroit cop Axel Foley (Murphy) travels to Los Angeles to find his friend's killer. Ignoring the L.A. police, Foley pushes his way into upper-crust society to uncover a stolen art ring. Expert blend of comedy and action with Murphy in top form was a huge commercial success. Bronson Pinchot's career took off after his cameo as an art salesman. Followed by a sequel. **(CC)**

BEVERLY HILLS COP II 1987
★★★★ **R Comedy 1:42**
☑ Brief nudity, explicit language, violence, adult humor
Dir: Tony Scott *Cast:* Eddie Murphy, Judge Reinhold, Jurgen Prochnow, Ronny Cox, John Ashton, Brigitte Nielsen
▶ In this sequel to the 1984 megahit, Detroit cop Axel Foley (Murphy) returns to L.A. to investigate the shooting of pal Cox and comes up against hit woman Nielsen and her gang. Eddie's fans won't be disappointed as he once again gives the verbal shaft to snobs and authority figures at every comic turn. Gilbert Gottfried contributes a hysterical bit as a flaky financial advisor. In all, *Cop II* manages to duplicate the original's formula on a more lavish scale.

BEYOND THE FOREST 1949
★★★ **NR Drama 1:36 B&W**
Dir: King Vidor *Cast:* Bette Davis, Joseph Cotten, Ruth Roman, David Brian, Minor Watson, Dona Drake
▶ "What a dump!" says Davis, unhappy wife of doctor Cotten, as she surveys her small-town surroundings. Davis becomes involved with wealthy Chicagoan Brian, but pregnancy and blackmailer Watson complicate her plan to leave Cotten. Extremely trashy, but Davis is as watchable as always.

BEYOND THE LIMIT 1983
★★ **R Drama 1:43**
☑ Nudity, explicit language, violence
Dir: John Mackenzie *Cast:* Richard Gere, Michael Caine, Bob Hoskins, Elpidia Carrillo
▶ Unsatisfying if well-mounted adapta-

tion of Graham Greene's best-seller *The Honorary Consul.* Gere, a doctor, gets inadvertently involved when dissidents kidnap British Consul Caine, whose wife is also Gere's lover. Plenty of atmosphere, colorful locations, and good acting, especially from Hoskins as a police chief, but overall rather less than passionate, and disappointing.

BEYOND THE POSEIDON ADVENTURE 1979
★★ PG Action-Adventure 2:02
☑ Explicit language, mild violence
Dir: Irwin Allen *Cast:* Michael Caine, Sally Field, Telly Savalas, Peter Boyle, Jack Warden
▶ Sequel to the immensely popular *The Poseidon Adventure* involves two groups of scavengers. Caine leads the good ones and Savalas is in charge of the bad; they attempt to salvage the ship and some of the survivors we didn't meet the first time around. Large-scale action-adventure resembles its illustrious predecessor so closely, it almost qualifies as a remake.

BEYOND THERAPY 1987
☆ R Comedy 1:33
☑ Brief nudity, adult situations, explicit language, adult humor
Dir: Robert Altman *Cast:* Glenda Jackson, Tom Conti, Jeff Goldblum, Christopher Guest, Julie Hagerty
▶ Sexual farce about neurotic Hagerty and bisexual Goldblum who meet through a personal ad, their respective incompetent shrinks Conti and Jackson, and Goldblum's jealous male lover Guest. Off-the-padded-wall performances and humor from director Robert Altman and screenwriter Christopher Durang fall flat in this disappointing adaptation of Durang's Broadway play. (CC)

BEYOND THE VALLEY OF THE DOLLS 1970
★ X Drama 1:49
☑ Nudity, adult situations, explicit language, violence
Dir: Russ Meyer *Cast:* Dolly Read, Cynthia Myers, Marcia McBroom, John LaZar, Michael Blodgett, Edy Williams
▶ Campy "insider's" look at fast track lives of Hollywood's filthy rich focuses on efforts by pop singers Read, Myers, and McBroom to break into show biz. Their experiences involve requisite corrupt actors, homosexual jet-setters, and climac-

tic killing spree. Co-written by film critic Roger Ebert.

BIBLE, THE 1966
★★★★ NR Drama 2:54
Dir: John Huston *Cast:* George C. Scott, Peter O'Toole, Ava Gardner, Richard Harris, Franco Nero, Michael Parks
▶ Colorful, and sometimes quite beautiful, cinematic rendering of the first twenty-two chapters of Genesis, covering the creation of the world, Adam (Parks) and Eve (Ulla Bergryd), Cain (Harris) and Abel (Nero), Noah's Ark, the Towel of Babel, Sodom and Gomorrah, and the plight of Abraham and Sarah (Scott and Gardner). Director Huston plays Noah and also narrates the voice of God.

BICYCLE THIEF, THE 1949 Italian
★★★ NR Drama 1:30 B&W
Dir: Vittorio De Sica *Cast:* Lamberto Maggiorani, Enzo Staiola, Lianella Carell, Elena Altieri
▶ In unemployment-plagued Italy, thief steals the bike a poor man needs for work. The man and his son search for the culprit. Postwar classic is still penetrating and real forty years after initial release. Tightly woven story; acting and starkly shaded photography couldn't be better. ⑤

BIG 1988
★★★★★ PG Comedy 1:42
☑ Adult situations, explicit language
Dir: Penny Marshall *Cast:* Tom Hanks, Elizabeth Perkins, Robert Loggia, John Heard, Jared Rushton, David Moscow
▶ After being rejected by a fifteen-year-old beauty, thirteen-year-old Moscow asks a mysterious carnival machine to make him big. The next morning he awakens to find his wish come true: he's now adult Hanks! Chased out of his home as an intruder, he moves to New York City with help of shrewd teen pal Rushton. Hanks's childlike perspective and enthusiasm win him a job with toy bigwig Loggia and romance with colleague Perkins. Runaway hit carried by Hanks's sweetly touching little big man, a role that won him his first Oscar nomination.

BIG BAD MAMA 1974
★★ R Action-Adventure 1:24
☑ Nudity, adult situations, explicit language
Dir: Steve Carver *Cast:* Angie Dickinson, William Shatner, Tom Skerritt, Susan Sennett, Robbie Lee

▶ Dickinson, a widow in depression-era Texas, resorts to bootlegging and bank robbing to keep her family together. Highly diverting *Bonnie and Clyde* clone delivers plenty of action (often bloody), comedy, and steamy sex. Angie's nude scenes made this low-budget Roger Corman production such a cult favorite that a sequel was shot fourteen years later.

BIG BAD MAMA II 1987
★ R Action-Adventure 1:24
☑ Nudity, adult situations, explicit language, violence
Dir: Jim Wynorski   *Cast:* Angie Dickinson, Robert Culp, Danielle Brisebois, Julie McCullough, Bruce Glover
▶ Widowed after a shootout over her foreclosed farm, Dickinson hits the road with buxom daughters Brisebois and McCullough for a bank-robbing spree in Depression Texas. Lusty tongue-in-cheek sequel provides plenty of shootouts and skin; ageless Angie still looks great.

BIG BIRD CAGE, THE 1972
★ R Action-Adventure 1:33
☑ Nudity, adult situations, violence
Dir: Jack Hill   *Cast:* Pam Grier, Candice Roman, Anitra Ford, Carol Speed
▶ After being mistakenly implicated in a nightclub robbery, attractive seductress Grier is imprisoned in a brutal work camp. Sprung by revolutionaries, she then competes for the affections of the rebel leader. Philippines-set action vehicle for black star Grier.

BIG BLUE, THE 1988 French
★★ PG Action-Adventure 1:58
☑ Adult situations, explicit language
Dir: Luc Besson   *Cast:* Jean-Marc Barr, Jean Reno, Rosanna Arquette, Paul Shenar, Sergio Castellito, Jean Bouise
▶ Frenchman Barr and Sicilian Reno, longtime friends, compete against each other in the sport of free-diving, setting new records for depths reached without oxygen tanks. American insurance agent Arquette falls for Barr, but he's more interested in trying to talk to dolphins. Meanwhile Barr and Reno free-dive deeper, pushing the limits of the human body. Gorgeous underwater photography wasted on waterlogged yarn.

BIG BRAWL, THE 1980
★★ R Martial Arts 1:35
☑ Adult situations, explicit language, graphic violence
Dir: Robert Clouse   *Cast:* Jackie Chan,

Jose Ferrer, Kristine DeBell, Mako, Ron Max
▶ American debut of Asian superstar Chan starts out as a parody of 1930s gangster films and ends up in a wild free-for-all at the famous Texas Battle Creek Brawl. Producers hoped this good-hearted comedy would position Chan (whose martial arts skills are dazzling) as a successor to Bruce Lee, but he didn't catch on with audiences.

BIG BUS, THE 1976
★ PG Comedy 1:28
☑ Explicit language
Dir: James Frawley   *Cast:* Joseph Bologna, Stockard Channing, Ruth Gordon, John Beck, Ned Beatty
▶ Uneven spoof of disaster movies takes place on the first nuclear-powered bus making premier nonstop trip from New York to Denver. Some funny moments (but also some dull stretches) in a genre parody; entertaining on a TV sitcom level.

BIG BUSINESS 1988
★★★★★ PG Comedy 1:31
☑ Adult situations, explicit language
Dir: Jim Abrahams   *Cast:* Bette Midler, Lily Tomlin, Fred Ward, Edward Herrmann, Michele Placido, Michael Gross
▶ Two pairs of identical twins are mixed up at birth, sending each set of parents home with mismatched baby girls. Years later Midler is a ruthless New York corporate executive planning to strip-mine small town of Jupiter Hollow with the help of her meek sister Tomlin. Coincidentally, Jupiter Hollow sends the other two sisters to New York to protest: strong-willed, do-gooder Tomlin and yodeling hick Midler. Confusion of identities and biting one-liners yield many laughs in this breezy farce.

BIG CARNIVAL, THE 1951
★★★ NR Drama 1:51 B&W
Dir: Billy Wilder   *Cast:* Kirk Douglas, Jan Sterling, Robert Arthur, Porter Hall
▶ Bitterly powerful drama from director Wilder. When New Mexico man is trapped in a mine shaft cave-in, reporter Douglas exploits the story for all it's worth, endangering the victim further in order to sell papers. Unflattering portrait of the power of the press with a first-rate Douglas. Also known as *Ace in the Hole*.

BIG CHILL, THE 1983
★★★★ R Drama 1:43
☑ Brief nudity, adult situations, explicit language

Dir: Lawrence Kasdan *Cast:* William Hurt, JoBeth Williams, Glenn Close, Jeff Goldblum, Mary Kay Place, Kevin Kline
▶ When a young man commits suicide, his college friends gather for a weekend of self-scrutiny and renewal of old ties in this sharp, literate drama that struck a chord with those who came of age in the 1960s. Outstanding ensemble acting by a dream cast features Hurt as a burned-out Vietnam vet and Place as a lawyer looking for someone to father her baby before her biological clock stops ticking. Hit soundtrack contains lots of Motown classics. **(CC)**

BIG CLOCK, THE 1948
★★★ NR Mystery-Suspense 1:35 B&W
Dir: John Farrow *Cast:* Ray Milland, Charles Laughton, Maureen O'Sullivan, George Macready, Rita Johnson, Elsa Lanchester
▶ Suspenseful drama about Milland, a crime magazine editor falsely implicated in a murder and forced by tyrannical publisher Laughton to conduct a search for the killer. Adaptation of Kenneth Fearing's novel features a marvelously twisty plot and first-rate performance by Laughton's real-life wife Lanchester as an abstract artist. Loosely remade in 1987 as *No Way Out*.

BIG COMBO, THE 1955
★★ NR Drama 1:29 B&W
Dir: Joseph H. Lewis *Cast:* Cornel Wilde, Richard Conte, Brian Donlevy, Jean Wallace, Robert Middleton, Lee Van Cleef
▶ Determined cop Wilde attacks mobster Conte's gang despite sadistic beatings by his thugs; Conte's spurned wife provides info that helps topple his crime empire. Fast-paced, influential film noir won critical acclaim for its realism and uncompromising violence.

BIG COUNTRY, THE 1958
★★★★ NR Western 2:45
Dir: William Wyler *Cast:* Gregory Peck, Jean Simmons, Charlton Heston, Carroll Baker, Burl Ives, Charles Bickford
▶ Ex-seaman Peck, engaged to rancher Bickford's daughter Baker, pursues teacher Simmons instead and gets involved in Bickford/Ives feud over water supply. Heston, Bickford's foreman, provokes more trouble when Simmons is kidnapped. Larger-than-life and quite rousing Western won Best Supporting Actor Oscar for Ives.

BIG DEAL ON MADONNA STREET 1956
Italian
★ NR Comedy 1:31 B&W
Dir: Mario Monicelli *Cast:* Marcello Mastroianni, Vittorio Gassman, Renato Salvatori, Claudia Cardinale, Rossana Rory, Toto
▶ Clumsy crook Gassman plots heist of Madonna Street store and enlists equally unskilled helpers, including Mastroianni, for the gig. The robbery predictably and amusingly goes awry. Caper classic evokes virtually nonstop laughter and is vastly superior to its 1984 American remake, *Crackers*. ⑤

BIG DOLL HOUSE, THE 1971
★ R Action-Adventure 1:33
☑ Nudity, adult situations, explicit language, violence
Dir: Jack Hill *Cast:* Judy Brown, Roberta Collins, Pam Grier, Brooke Mills, Pat Woodell, Sid Haig
▶ Brown, Grier, and other inmates are the victims of sadistic wardens and guards in a brutal women's prison. Their escape attempt leads to an extremely violent climax. Highly influential exploitation film started a cycle of sexy, tongue-in-cheek prison films. Followed by *The Big Bird Cage*.

BIG EASY, THE 1987
★★★★ R Mystery-Suspense 1:41
☑ Nudity, adult situations, explicit language, violence
Dir: Jim McBride *Cast:* Dennis Quaid, Ellen Barkin, Ned Beatty, John Goodman, Ebbe Roe Smith, Charles Ludlam
▶ Brash cop Quaid teaches uptight Assistant D.A. Barkin to mix pleasure with business in this snappy, sassy thriller of New Orleans police corruption. Professional antagonists at first, they investigate underworld killings; as the bodies pile up, the solution hits closer to home than Quaid anticipated. Lots of Cajun atmosphere, excellent camerawork and music, and tons of superspicy sexual electricity between Barkin and Quaid.

BIG FIX, THE 1978
★★★★ PG Mystery-Suspense 1:48
☑ Adult situations, explicit language, violence
Dir: Jeremy Paul Kagan *Cast:* Richard Dreyfuss, Susan Anspach, Bonnie Bedelia, John Lithgow, F. Murray Abraham
▶ Berkeley-based private eye Moses Wine (Dreyfuss) is hired by ex-sweetheart

Anspach to find the culprit who's smearing the political candidate she works for. Is missing ex-sixties radical Abraham involved? Comedy/mystery has an intricate plot, plenty of sixties nostalgia, and works best as a vehicle for Dreyfuss's wisecracking heroics. Adapted by Roger L. Simon from his novel.

BIG HEAT, THE 1953
★★ NR Mystery-Suspense 1:29 B&W
Dir: Fritz Lang   *Cast:* Glenn Ford, Gloria Grahame, Jocelyn Brando, Lee Marvin, Carolyn Jones
▶ Classic thriller from director Lang, almost unparalleled for sheer intensity. Ford is the honest cop who obsessively takes on a crime ring after the bad guys kill his wife. Gangster's moll Grahame pays a heavy price for helping Ford—the menacing Marvin throws scalding coffee in her face in just one of several surreal scenes.

BIG JAKE 1971
★★★★★ PG Western 1:50
☑ Explicit language, violence
Dir: George Sherman   *Cast:* John Wayne, Richard Boone, Maureen O'Hara, Patrick Wayne, Chris Mitchum, Bobby Vinton
▶ As Big Jake, Wayne takes a million dollars to villain Boone to ransom his kidnapped grandson (played by his real-life son John Ethan). Jake tries a double-cross that puts the entire scheme in jeopardy. Some awkward comic touches, but good Mexican scenery, plenty of violence, and a cast of familiar faces (Wayne's fifth film with O'Hara). **(CC)**

BIG MO 1973
★★★★ G Drama 1:53
Dir: Daniel Mann   *Cast:* Bernie Casey, Bo Svenson, Janet MacLachlan, Stephanie Edwards, Pauline Myers
▶ Cincinnati Royals basketball star Maurice Stokes (Casey) suffers a paralyzing stroke. His teammate Jack Twyman (Svenson) devotes his life to raising money for Mo's rehabilitation. Sentimental treatment of a true story works on a soap-opera level. Released in theaters as *Maurie*.

BIG MOUTH, THE 1967
★★★ NR Comedy 1:47
Dir: Jerry Lewis   *Cast:* Jerry Lewis, Harold J. Stone, Susan Bay, Buddy Lester, Del Moore
▶ Fisherman Lewis hooks the big one; no, not a marlin but a treasure-seeking diver.

Bad guys also want the hidden trove and Lewis is in trouble when he gets the map. Zany antics in patented Lewis style.

BIG PICTURE, THE 1988
★★★ NR Comedy 1:39
☑ Adult situations, explicit language
Dir: Christopher Guest   *Cast:* Kevin Bacon, Emily Longstreth, J. T. Walsh, Jennifer Jason Leigh, Martin Short, Michael McKean
▶ Student filmmaker Bacon wins award and plenty of attention in Hollywood from agent Short, studio boss Tracy Brooks Swope, and others, but finds the road to Tinseltown success rather rocky. Actor Guest's directorial debut is never less than genial and often clever; however, inside jabs at movieland may puzzle the uninitiated. Amusing performance by Short.

BIG RED 1962
★★★★ NR Family 1:29
Dir: Norman Tokar   *Cast:* Walter Pidgeon, Gilles Payant, Emile Genest, Janette Bertrand, George Bouvier, Doris Lussier
▶ Winsome Disney drama set in Canada shows how wealthy businessman and amateur dog breeder Pidgeon's outlook on life is changed by young Payant's attachment to a champion Irish setter. Moving plot and beautiful locations make this perfect viewing for youngsters. Based on a novel by Jim Kjelgaard.

BIG RED ONE, THE 1980
★★★★ PG War 1:53
☑ Explicit language, violence
Dir: Samuel Fuller   *Cast:* Lee Marvin, Mark Hamill, Robert Carradine, Bobby DiCicco, Stephane Audran
▶ Autobiographical adventure based on director Fuller's war experiences in the First Infantry Division (the "Big Red One") focuses on veteran sergeant Marvin and his young, untried special infantry squad. Old-fashioned war film is crammed with thrilling action and vivid, firsthand account of fighting. Cult director Fuller spent thirty-five years trying to get this movie made.

BIG SCORE, THE 1983
★★ R Action-Adventure 1:25
☑ Nudity, adult situations, explicit language, violence
Dir: Fred Williamson   *Cast:* Fred Williamson, Nancy Wilson, Richard Roundtree, John Saxon
▶ Williamson stars as a Dirty Harryish narc

who runs afoul of cops and crooks when he's suspected of confiscating a fortune in a large-scale drug bust. Plenty of blood, mayhem, and well-staged action to entertain genre fans yet generally a cut above the usual blaxploitation fare. Singer Wilson provides the love interest.

BIG SHOTS 1987
★★★ PG-13 Action-Adventure 1:30
☑ Explicit language, violence
Dir: Robert Mandel *Cast:* Ricky Busker, Darius McCrary, Robert Joy, Robert Prosky, Jerzy Skolimowski
▶ Distraught after the death of his father, eleven-year-old suburban white kid Obie (Busker) wanders into a ghetto. He's mugged, then befriended by a smooth-talking black kid (McCrary). The two unlikely pals embark on a wild Chicago-to-Louisiana journey when they come into possession of a hoodlum's car. Free-wheeling adventure with an appealing central duo and an upbeat finale, nicely directed by Mandel. **(CC)**

BIG SKY, THE 1952
★★ NR Western 2:20 B&W
Dir: Howard Hawks *Cast:* Kirk Douglas, Dewey Martin, Elizabeth Threatt, Arthur Hunnicutt, Buddy Baer, Steven Geray
▶ In 1830, unruly fur trapper Douglas and grizzled frontiersman Hunnicutt join Geray's expedition up the Missouri River into Blackfoot country. As they haul their boats by hand against the swift current, Crow Indians mount an attack. Long but action-packed Western, based on an A. B. Guthrie novel, is filled with colorful incidents. Hunnicutt won an Oscar nomination for his scene-stealing performance.

BIG SLEEP, THE 1946
★★★★ NR Mystery-Suspense 1:54 B&W
Dir: Howard Hawks *Cast:* Humphrey Bogart, Lauren Bacall, John Ridgely, Martha Vickers, Dorothy Malone, Elisha Cook, Jr.
▶ Outstanding adaptation of Raymond Chandler's novel is one of the most stylish and satisfying mysteries of the 1940s. Bogart is the definitive Philip Marlowe, a laconic private eye drawn into a web of blackmail and murder when he tries to protect Vickers, a millionaire's spoiled daughter. The plot thickens when Marlowe falls for her older sister Bacall. Vivid atmosphere, sparkling dialogue, and great suspense, although the plot is so convoluted that the writers (William

Faulkner, Jules Furthman, and Leigh Brackett) turned to Chandler to figure out one of the murders.

BIG SLEEP, THE 1978 British
★★★ R Mystery-Suspense 1:40
☑ Nudity, explicit language, violence
Dir: Michael Winner *Cast:* Robert Mitchum, Sarah Miles, Candy Clark, Oliver Reed, Joan Collins, Richard Boone
▶ Remake of 1946 film has Mitchum reprising his *Farewell, My Lovely* role as detective Philip Marlowe. Faithful adaptation of the Raymond Chandler novel, updated and set in London, with strong production values and a stellar cast. James Stewart has a cameo as General Sternwood, an ailing millionaire who sets Marlowe off on a complex case involving blackmail and murder.

BIG STEAL, THE 1949
★★ NR Mystery-Suspense 1:11 B&W
Dir: Don Siegel *Cast:* Robert Mitchum, Jane Greer, William Bendix, Patric Knowles
▶ Mitchum and Greer, so memorably teamed in the classic 1947 film noir *Out of the Past*, give the genre another shot in this short but potent thriller from director Siegel. Plot involves stolen army loot; Knowles has it, Greer and Mitchum pursue him south of the border to get it back.

BIG STORE, THE 1941
★★ NR Comedy 1:23 B&W
Dir: Charles Riesner *Cast:* Groucho Marx, Harpo Marx, Chico Marx, Tony Martin, Virginia Grey, Margaret Dumont
▶ The brothers Marx will always provide a few laughs even in a vehicle that's far from their strongest. Plot involves store detective Wolf J. Flywheel (Groucho) who helps department store owner Martin foil the store's villainous manager. The musical interludes (especially Martin singing "Tenement Symphony") are overlong but there are some funny moments.

BIG STREET, THE 1942
★★★★ NR Drama 1:29 B&W
Dir: Irving Reis *Cast:* Lucille Ball, Henry Fonda, Agnes Moorehead, Sam Levene, Barton MacLane, Eugene Pallette
▶ Lowly busboy Little Pinks (Fonda) worships selfish nightclub singer Ball and devotes his life to her, even after she is crippled. Perhaps Lucy's best dramatic performance and Fonda matches her as the naive busboy. Based on a story by

Damon Runyon with some of the same characters as *Guys and Dolls.*

BIG TOP PEE-WEE 1988
★★ **PG Comedy 1:22**
☑ Adult situations
Dir: Randal Kleiser *Cast:* Pee-wee Herman, Kris Kristofferson, Valeria Golino, Penelope Ann Miller, Susan Tyrrell, Albert Henderson
▶ After a storm, farmer Herman emerges from his cellar to discover Kristofferson's circus pitched on his property. Herman falls for trapeze artist Golino, much to the dismay of girlfriend Miller. He decides to join the troupe but must first create an act. Meanwhile the townsfolk want the circus to hit the road. Not up to *Pee-wee's Big Adventure.* **(CC)**

BIG TOWN, THE 1987
★★★ **R Drama 1:50**
☑ Nudity, adult situations, explicit language
Dir: Ben Bolt *Cast:* Matt Dillon, Diane Lane, Tommy Lee Jones, Bruce Dern, Lee Grant, Tom Skerritt
▶ Dillon, a small-town boy with a talent for craps, heads for Chicago to make his fortune. Although attracted to a single mother, he's seduced by stripper Lane who's married to the dangerous Jones. Stylish but underdeveloped drama set in 1957 is highlighted by Jones's swaggering villain and Lane's steamy fan dance.

BIG TROUBLE 1986
★★ **R Comedy 1:33**
☑ Explicit language, mild violence, adult humor
Dir: John Cassavetes *Cast:* Alan Arkin, Peter Falk, Beverly D'Angelo, Charles Durning, Paul Dooley, Robert Stack
▶ Curious comedy about insurance salesman Arkin duped into murdering D'Angelo's husband Falk for his $5 million insurance policy. A double-cross leads to trouble with kidnappers and terrorists. This attempt to recapture the lunacy of the leads' *In-Laws* was plagued with production problems (Andrew Bergman dropped out as director and took his name off the screenplay). Barely released to theaters, although there are some funny moments.

BIG TROUBLE IN LITTLE CHINA 1986
★★★ **PG-13 Action-Adventure 1:40**
☑ Explicit language, violence
Dir: John Carpenter *Cast:* Kurt Russell, Kim Cattrall, Dennis Dun, James Hong, Kate Burton, Suzee Pai
▶ Bizarre action–comedy–kung-fu–science fiction film about macho truck driver Russell and Chinese waiter Dun battling the 2,000-year-old Godfather of Chinatown. Heavy-handed at times, but the stunts and special effects are delightful. Russell does a credible tongue-in-cheek John Wayne impersonation. **(CC)**

BIG WEDNESDAY 1978
★★ **PG Drama 2:05**
☑ Explicit language, adult humor
Dir: John Milius *Cast:* Jan-Michael Vincent, Gary Busey, William Katt, Lee Purcell, Patti D'Arbanville
▶ Male-bonding film about three young men, friends since high school, drawn together by a common love of surfing. Their friendship survives two decades; one gets married and two go off to Vietnam. Spectacular surfing footage, including a twenty-minute "big swell" (when waves can reach 15 feet).

BIKINI BEACH 1964
★★ **NR Comedy 1:40**
Dir: William Asher *Cast:* Frankie Avalon, Annette Funicello, Martha Hyer, Don Rickles, Harvey Lembeck, Keenan Wynn
▶ Surf bums and bunnies face disaster when millionaire Wynn threatens to buy their beach; on top of that, Frankie might lose Annette to British rock star Potato Bug (Avalon, playing dual roles). Mindless escapism features a performance by "Little" Stevie Wonder. Third entry in the Beach Party series, followed by *Pajama Party.*

BILL 1981
★★★★★ **NR Biography/MFTV 1:37**
Dir: Anthony Page *Cast:* Mickey Rooney, Dennis Quaid, Largo Woodruff, Harry Goz, Anna Maria Horsford
▶ True story of mentally retarded Bill Sackter (Rooney), who slowly adjusts to life in the outside world after forty-six years in an institution. Young filmmaker Quaid helps him. Beautiful made-for-TV film about true meaning of friendship. Unforgettable Emmy-winning performance by Rooney and excellent support from Quaid.

BILL & TED'S EXCELLENT ADVENTURE 1989
★★★ **PG Comedy 1:30**
☑ Explicit language
Dir: Stephen Herek *Cast:* Keanu Reeves, Alex Winter, Bernie Casey,

George Carlin, Terry Camilleri, Jane Wiedlin
▶ California high school students Reeves and Winter are failing history class. Futuristic hipster Carlin appears with his magical telephone booth to transport the hapless dudes through the past so historical figures, like Napoleon and Julius Caesar, can help them pass. Scattered laughs in freewheeling plot. Funniest line: the boys' description of Joan of Arc.

BILL COSBY—"HIMSELF" 1983
★★★★★ PG Documentary/Comedy 1:44
☑ Explicit language, adult humor
Dir: Bill Cosby *Cast:* Bill Cosby
▶ No-frills concert footage of Cosby doing what he does best: complaining about his family, dentists, old age, etc. Patched together from four 1981 performances in Hamilton, Ontario, and featuring some of Cosby's home movies. Sure to please his many fans. **(CC)**

BILLION DOLLAR BRAIN 1967 British
★★★ NR Espionage 1:48
Dir: Ken Russell *Cast:* Michael Caine, Karl Malden, Ed Begley, Oscar Homolka, Françoise Dorleac
▶ Caine's third go-round as the low-key, bespectacled secret agent Harry Palmer finds him dealing with ex-CIA agent Malden, anti-Communist Begley, and Helsinki intrigue. Russell's rare stab at a straight genre film; not up to the standard set by *The Ipcress File* and *Funeral in Berlin.*

BILLION DOLLAR HOBO, THE 1978
★★★★ G Comedy/Family 1:36
Dir: Stuart E. McGowan *Cast:* Tim Conway, Will Geer, Eric Weston, Sydney Lassick, John Myhers
▶ Conway, a hopeless klutz, will inherit a fortune if he can make the long trip to Seattle as a hobo. He sets off with his amazing (and funny) wonder dog Bo, only to run afoul of bad guys who have kidnapped a rare Chinese dog. Amiable family-oriented comedy is uninspired but consistently entertaining.

BILL ON HIS OWN 1983
★★★★ NR Biography/MFTV 1:40
Dir: Anthony Page *Cast:* Mickey Rooney, Helen Hunt, Teresa Wright, Dennis Quaid, Largo Woodruff, Paul Leiber
▶ Sequel to immensely popular TV movie *Bill* about mentally retarded adult coping with life in the outside world after forty-six years in an institution. Rooney reprises his Emmy-winning turn as Bill Sackter, overcoming another hurdle as friend Quaid and his wife Woodruff move away, learning to read with the help of Wright, and struggling when a fire destroys his small business. Rooney's heartwarming performances as the childlike but determined Sackter revitalized his career.

BILLY BUDD 1962
★★ NR Drama 2:03 B&W
Dir: Peter Ustinov *Cast:* Robert Ryan, Peter Ustinov, Melvyn Douglas, Terence Stamp, John Neville
▶ Saintly, innocent young sailor Billy Budd (Stamp) is opposed by iron-handed officer Ryan and weak-willed captain Ustinov is caught in between. Stamp accidentally kills Ryan and Ustinov reluctantly presides at his court-martial. Literary adaptation of Herman Melville's novella really works, thanks to terrific cast and director/star/co-screenwriter Ustinov's craftsmanship. **(CC)**

BILLY GALVIN 1987
★★★ PG Drama 1:35
☑ Explicit language
Dir: John Gray *Cast:* Karl Malden, Lenny Von Dohlen, Joyce Van Patten, Toni Kalem, Keith Szarabajka
▶ Earnest but predictable melodrama about the conflict between construction worker Malden, who wants his children to have a better life, and his son Billy (Von Dohlen), who wants nothing more than to follow in his father's footsteps. Sincere performances and gritty blue-collar Boston settings add to the film's realism.

BILLY JACK 1971
★★★★ PG Action-Adventure 1:54
☑ Rape, nudity, adult situations, violence
Dir: T. C. Frank (Tom Laughlin) *Cast:* Tom Laughlin, Delores Taylor, Clark Howat, Julie Webb, Kenneth Tobey
▶ Half-Indian ex–Green Beret Billy Jack lives on a reservation that's unpopular with the bigoted townsfolk. When the son of the local kingpin rapes the schoolmarm and kills an Indian boy, Billy Jack murders the boy's killer, takes a bullet in the gut, and then gives himself up so that he can go on to star in the first of two extremely popular sequels, *The Trial of Billy Jack.* Surprise 1970s megahit was written, directed, and produced (under pseudonym T. C. Frank) by and stars Laughlin and wife, Delores Taylor.

BILLY LIAR 1963 British
★ **NR Comedy 1:36 B&W**
Dir: John Schlesinger *Cast:* Tom Courtenay, Julie Christie, Mona Washbourne, Finlay Currie, Wilfred Pickles
▶ Courtenay excels as the title character, a young man who deals with mundane day-to-day reality by daydreaming, telling lies, and romancing women, including Christie. Memorable characterization will appeal to anyone whose mind ever wandered between nine and five. Schlesinger beautifully directs the Keith Waterhouse/Willis Hall adaptation of their play.

BILLY ROSE'S JUMBO 1962
★★ **NR Musical 2:05**
Dir: Charles Walters *Cast:* Doris Day, Stephen Boyd, Jimmy Durante, Martha Raye, Dean Jagger, Billy Barty
▶ Durante and his daughter Day struggle to keep their Wonder Circus afloat, unaware that rival Jagger has sent his son Boyd, supposedly a roustabout, to sabotage their efforts. Passable romance enlivened by beautiful Rodgers and Hart score ("This Can't Be Love," "The Most Beautiful Girl in the World"), Busby Berkeley choreography, and energetic clowning by Durante and Raye. Adapted by Sidney Sheldon from a Ben Hecht/Charles MacArthur play.

BILOXI BLUES 1988
★★★★ **PG-13 Comedy 1:44**
☑ Adult situations, explicit language
Dir: Mike Nichols *Cast:* Matthew Broderick, Christopher Walken, Corey Parker, Matt Mulhern, Markus Flanagan, Penelope Ann Miller
▶ In 1945, Brooklyn Jewish youth Broderick has three goals in life: win the Pulitzer prize, lose his virginity, and fall in love with his dream girl. During Army basic training in Biloxi, Mississippi, he achieves two of the three, despite harassment of foul-tempered drill sergeant Walken and antics of his bunkmates. Fine coming-of-age tale with plenty of laughs. Based on the Broadway smash; Broderick character is writer Neil Simon's alter ego. Preceded by *Brighton Beach Memoirs*.

BINGO LONG TRAVELING ALL-STARS AND MOTOR KINGS, THE 1976
★★★★ **PG Drama 1:50**
☑ Explicit language
Dir: John Badham *Cast:* Billy Dee Williams, James Earl Jones, Richard Pryor, Ted Ross

▶ Badham made his film debut with this high-spirited tale of a barnstorming Negro League baseball team in the days when blacks were barred from the majors. Beautifully shot with an evocative period feel. Nice work from Williams as the team leader, Jones as a burly catcher, and Pryor as a light-skinned black hoping to pass for Hispanic.

BIRCH INTERVAL 1976
★★ **PG Drama 1:45**
☑ Adult situations
Dir: Delbert Mann *Cast:* Eddie Albert, Rip Torn, Ann Wedgeworth, Susan McClung, Anne Revere
▶ In 1947, delicate eleven-year-old McClung is sent to Amish Pennsylvania to live with grandfather Albert. She learns about love and understanding from retarded uncle Torn, only to watch him victimized by local bigots. Sensitive coming-of-age story from Joanna Crawford's novel has beautiful photography and outstanding performances from Albert and Torn.

BIRD 1988
★★ **R Biography/Music 2:43**
☑ Adult situations, explicit language
Dir: Clint Eastwood *Cast:* Forest Whitaker, Diane Venora, Michael Zelniker, Samuel E. Wright, Keith David, Michael McGuire
▶ Whitaker plays Charlie Parker, legendary saxophone player who changed the nature of jazz during the bebop era. Not always appreciated during his time, Parker struggled with booze and drugs despite the help of faithful wife Venora. Exultant and sorrowful tale of musical mastery and personal disintegration directed by jazz fan Eastwood will please music lovers; its dark look and frequent flashbacks/forwards may leave others restless. Received Oscar for Best Sound.

BIRDMAN OF ALCATRAZ 1962
★★★ **NR Biography 2:23 B&W**
Dir: John Frankenheimer *Cast:* Burt Lancaster, Karl Malden, Thelma Ritter, Neville Brand, Edmond O'Brien, Hugh Marlowe
▶ True story of prison lifer Robert Stroud (Lancaster), who became an outstanding ornithologist after nursing back to health a sick bird that flew into his cell. Stroud got along better with birds than humans, leading to conflict with tough warden Malden. Wonderful Oscar-nomi-

nated performance by Lancaster highlights this long but engrossing film.

BIRDS, THE 1963
★★★★ PG-13 Mystery-Suspense 2:00
☑ Violence
Dir: Alfred Hitchcock *Cast:* Rod Taylor, Tippi Hedren, Jessica Tandy, Suzanne Pleshette, Veronica Cartwright
▶ In a small Northern California town, wealthy young Hedren and lawyer Taylor are among those menaced when birds suddenly and mysteriously start attacking people. Hitchcock's technical mastery has never been more apparent than in this classic thriller of nature against man. Eerie visuals plus Bernard Herrmann's synthesized soundtrack (using no actual music) create a constant sense of unease.

BIRDY 1984
★★ R Drama 2:00
☑ Nudity, explicit language, violence
Dir: Alan Parker *Cast:* Nicolas Cage, Matthew Modine, John Harkins, Sandy Baron, Karen Young
▶ Offbeat character drama directed with care and sensitivity by Alan Parker. Cage and pigeon-obsessed Birdy (Modine), childhood pals from Philly, are sent to Vietnam. When the war drives Birdy completely off the deep end and into an institution, Cage tries to reach out to him. Terrific performances, especially by Modine, and amazing footage re-creating Birdy's fantasies of flight. Not for all tastes but nonetheless powerful and thought provoking. Adapted from William Wharton's acclaimed novel. **(CC)**

BIRTH OF THE BEATLES 1979
★★★ NR Biography/MFTV 1:36
Dir: Richard Marquand *Cast:* Stephen Mackenna, Rod Culbertson, John Altman, Ray Ashcroft, Ryan Mitchell, David Wilkinson
▶ The rise of the Fab Four from the slums of Liverpool to their final American tour. Story chronicles early struggles and personnel changes, including death of their first bassist and replacement of drummer Pete Best with Ringo Starr. Not bad performances, particularly Mackenna as John Lennon, but rather uninspired narrative fails to flesh out bones of the story.

BISHOP'S WIFE, THE 1947
★★★★ NR Fantasy 1:49 B&W
Dir: Henry Koster *Cast:* Cary Grant, Loretta Young, David Niven, Monty Woolley, James Gleason, Elsa Lanchester
▶ As an Angel, Grant comes to Earth to help harried bishop Niven, who neglects wife Young and daughter due to career demands. Classic Christmas story is truly timeless and so filled with charm and sweetness that few will be able to resist. Young is delicate and lovely, Grant his dependably dashing self, Niven convincingly cast against type. A Best Picture Oscar nominee. Available in a colorized version.

BITCH, THE 1979 British
★ R Drama 1:30
☑ Nudity, strong sexual content, adult situations
Dir: Gerry O'Hara *Cast:* Joan Collins, Kenneth Haigh, Michael Coby, Ian Hendry, Carolyn Seymour
▶ Follow-up to *The Stud* has disco owner Collins involved in diamond smuggling and fixing horse races to save her failing club. Based on a story by Joan's sister, Jackie, the plot is simply an excuse for frequent sex in beds, pools, showers, sauna, etc. Exploitation fare should please Collins fans.

BITE THE BULLET 1975
★★★★ PG Western 2:11
☑ Explicit language, mild violence
Dir: Richard Brooks *Cast:* Gene Hackman, Candice Bergen, James Coburn, Ben Johnson, Jan-Michael Vincent, Dabney Coleman
▶ Large-scale Western about wildly different characters involved in a grueling 700-mile endurance race across mountains, deserts, woodlands, and mesas. Old-fashioned entertainment (based on an actual 1908 race sponsored by the *Denver Post*) helped by beautiful photography and strong performances.

BITTERSWEET LOVE 1976
★★ PG Drama 1:30
☑ Adult situations
Dir: David Miller *Cast:* Lana Turner, Robert Lansing, Celeste Holm, Robert Alda, Meredith Baxter Birney, Scott Hylands
▶ Birney and Hylands are about to have a baby when they discover they're brother and sister. Should they continue their marriage? "Problem" drama with an intriguing cast (Turner's role as the mother was her first after a long absence from the screen) treats its delicate theme in a romantic, glossy style.

BITTER VICTORY 1958 French
★★★ NR War 1:42 B&W
Dir: Nicholas Ray   *Cast:* Richard Burton, Curt Jurgens, Ruth Roman, Raymond Pellegrin, Christopher Lee
▶ World War II action drama of British commando officers on a grueling escape through the trackless Sahara Desert. Burton and Jurgens give riveting performances as rival soldiers in this study of courage and cowardice. Roman adds intrigue as Jurgens's wife, who has had an affair with officer Burton.

BLACK AND WHITE IN COLOR 1976 French
★ PG Comedy 1:40
☑ Explicit language, violence
Dir: Jean-Jacques Annaud   *Cast:* Jean Carmet, Jacques Dufilho, Catherine Rouvel, Jacques Spiesser
▶ French and German settlers in Africa, having lived without conflict for years, fight one another when World War I breaks out in Europe. Biting antiwar satire from director Annaud beat out more heralded *Cousine, Cousine* and Lina Wertmuller's *Seven Beauties* for Best Foreign Film Oscar.   ⑤

BLACKBEARD'S GHOST 1968
★★★ G Fantasy/Comedy 1:47
Dir: Robert Stevenson   *Cast:* Peter Ustinov, Dean Jones, Suzanne Pleshette, Elsa Lanchester, Joby Baker, Richard Deacon
▶ Lighthearted Disney antic stars Ustinov as the ghost of legendary pirate Blackbeard, summoned back to life by Jones when gangsters target his home for conversion to a casino. Merry mixture of delightful Ustinov and top-notch special effects.

BLACK BEAUTY 1971 British
★★★★ G Family 1:14
Dir: James Hill   *Cast:* Mark Lester, Walter Slezak, Peter Lee Lawrence, Ursula Glas
▶ Young Lester loses his beloved horse Black Beauty when his father is forced to sell his farm. Black Beauty undergoes many adventures in the hands of different owners while Lester tries to get her back. Scrupulous adaptation of Anna Sewell's classic is perfect viewing for children. Also filmed in 1946.

BLACK BELT JONES 1974
☆ R Martial Arts 1:25
☑ Violence
Dir: Robert Clouse   *Cast:* Jim Kelly,

Gloria Hendry, Scatman Crothers, Alan Weeks, Eric Laneuville
▶ Bodies go flying as karate king Black Belt Jones (Kelly) takes on bad guys who covet the dojo belonging to the Scatman and his sultry daughter Hendry. American blaxploitation-meets-kung-fu flick reunites real-life martial arts champ Kelly and his *Enter the Dragon* director Clouse.

BLACK BIRD, THE 1975
★★★ PG Comedy 2:02
☑ Explicit language, mild violence
Dir: David Giler   *Cast:* George Segal, Stephane Audran, Lionel Stander, Lee Patrick, Elisha Cook, Jr.
▶ Comedy that is both a parody of and a sequel to the 1941 Bogart classic *The Maltese Falcon*. Story takes place in San Francisco thirty years later, as the priceless statue appears once again and Sam Spade, Jr. (Segal) finds himself involved in the resulting intrigue. Patrick as the secretary Effie and Cook as gunman Wilmer reprise their roles from the original.

BLACKBOARD JUNGLE, THE 1955
★★★★ NR Drama 1:41 B&W
Dir: Richard Brooks   *Cast:* Glenn Ford, Anne Francis, Vic Morrow, Louis Calhern, Sidney Poitier, Paul Mazursky
▶ Earnest English teacher Ford takes job at tough New York City vocational school and deals with problems of juvenile delinquents—rape, physical beatings, and blackmail. Eventually he wins the respect of the students. Tough, realistic melodrama presenting a frightening picture of inner-city education caused quite a sensation in its day. A bit dated but still holds up. Song "Rock Around the Clock" represents first Hollywood use of rock music.

BLACK CAT, THE 1934
★★ NR Horror 1:05 B&W
Dir: Edgar G. Ulmer   *Cast:* Boris Karloff, Bela Lugosi, David Manners, Jacqueline Wells, Lucille Lund, Henry Armetta
▶ Bizarre horror film pits Lugosi, a doctor determined to avenge his country's honor, against evil architect/devil worshipper Karloff, who he feels betrayed Austria during World War I. Eye-opening sets and intentionally outlandish touches (including hints of necrophilia, sadism, and fish worship) highlight this first of many Karloff-Lugosi teamings. Title was used for completely different films in 1941 and 1984.

BLACK CAULDRON, THE 1985
★★★★ PG Animation 1:21
☑ Mild violence
Dir: Ted Berman, Richard Rich **Cast:**
Voices of Grant Bardsley, Susan Sheridan, Freddie Jones, Nigel Hawthorne, John Byner
▶ Taran, a young lad who hopes to become a warrior, battles the evil Horned King for possession of a magic cauldron that could determine the fate of the world. Aided by Princess Eilonwy and the bumbling Gurgi, Taran breaks into the king's sinister castle. Captivating Disney sword-and-sorcery fantasy features superb animation and a narration by John Huston.

BLACK EMANUELLE 1976
★★ R Sex 1:28
☑ Nudity, strong sexual content
Dir: Albert Thomas **Cast:** Karin Schubert, Isabelle Marchald, Angelo Intute, Laura Gemser
▶ Black American photographer Gemser goes to Africa for a story and finds a nest of debauched white colonials. She gets involved sexually with both host and hostess and later finds satisfaction with a field hockey team. Visual splendor provided by the lovely and frequently unclothed Ms. Gemser and the African backdrops.

BLACK FURY 1935
★★★ NR Drama 1:32 B&W
Dir: Michael Curtiz **Cast:** Paul Muni, Karen Morley, William Gargan, Barton MacLane, John Qualen, J. Carrol Naish
▶ Muni delivers a sterling performance as a furious, nearly illiterate coal miner whose attempt to form a new union is undermined by corrupt bosses. Hospitalized by company goons, he resorts to violence against strikebreakers. Assured direction enhances this message drama based on a real incident in 1929 Pennsylvania.

BLACK HOLE, THE 1979
★★ PG Sci-Fi 1:37
☑ Mild violence
Dir: Gary Nelson **Cast:** Maximilian Schell, Anthony Perkins, Robert Forster, Joseph Bottoms, Yvette Mimieux, Ernest Borgnine
▶ A space expedition led by Forster is trapped by Schell, a mad scientist intent on dragging them into a dangerous black hole. Disney's first PG film has magnificent special effects and two standout nonhuman characters: Vincent, a free-floating minicomputer, and Max, a sinister robot.

BLACK LEGION 1937
★★ NR Drama 1:23 B&W
Dir: Archie Mayo **Cast:** Humphrey Bogart, Dick Foran, Erin O'Brien-Moore, Robert Barrat, Helen Flint, Joseph Sawyer
▶ When a foreigner receives the promotion he coveted, Detroit auto worker Bogart joins secret "racial purity" group and becomes one of its leading enforcers. His strong-arm tactics lead to breakup of his marriage and death of his best friend Foran. Strong performance by Bogey boosts this well-made drama. Robert Lord's story (based on an actual Black Legion) received an Oscar nomination.

BLACK LIKE ME 1964
★★ NR Drama 1:47 B&W
Dir: Carl Lerner **Cast:** James Whitmore, Roscoe Lee Browne, Sorrell Booke, Will Geer, Dan Priest
▶ Well-meaning exploration of racial problems. Trying to understand what it's like to be black, white writer Whitmore darkens his skin with chemicals and sets out in the world. A true story, from the best-selling book by John Howard Griffin.

BLACK MAGIC 1949
★★ NR Drama 1:45 B&W
Dir: Gregory Ratoff **Cast:** Orson Welles, Nancy Guild, Akim Tamiroff, Raymond Burr, Frank Latimore, Valentina Cortese
▶ In the eighteenth century, villainous Welles uses hypnotism on the rich and powerful in an attempt to control the destiny of Europe. Based on Alexandre Dumas's account of real-life charlatan Cagliostro, historical drama is undermined by Welles's heavy-handed aping of the broad acting styles of the era.

BLACK MAMA, WHITE MAMA 1973
U.S./Filipino
☆ R Action-Adventure 1:27
☑ Nudity, adult situations, explicit language, graphic violence
Dir: Eddie Romero **Cast:** Pam Grier, Margaret Markow, Sid Haig, Lynn Borden, Zaldy Zshomack, Laurie Burton
▶ Gimmick exploitation film chains black prostitute Grier to white revolutionary Markow in a sordid Filipino prison ruled by lesbian guards. Mamas manage to escape and join guerrilla group in an attack on the jail. Crude low-budget drama filmed in the Philippines.

BLACK MARBLE, THE 1980
★★ **PG Drama 1:53**
☑ Adult situations, explicit language, violence
Dir: Harold Becker *Cast:* Robert Foxworth, Paula Prentiss, Harry Dean Stanton, Barbara Babcock, James Woods
▶ Second collaboration between Becker and Joseph Wambaugh (*The Onion Field*) is an accurate, insightful look at depressed cop Foxworth slowly killing himself with alcohol. Saddled with Prentiss, a sexy new partner who thinks he's obsolete, Foxworth takes on an unimportant dognapping case to prove his moral values are still valid. Stanton excels in another offbeat villain role.

BLACK MOON RISING 1986
★★★ **R Action-Adventure 1:40**
☑ Brief nudity, adult situations, explicit language, violence
Dir: Harley Cokliss *Cast:* Tommy Lee Jones, Linda Hamilton, Robert Vaughn, Richard Jaeckel, Lee Ving, Bubba Smith
▶ Thieves led by industrialist Vaughn steal the Black Moon, a high-tech race car that has secret government evidence hidden inside. Free-lance thief Jones joins up with another free-lancer (Hamilton) to steal the car back from Vaughn's heavily guarded headquarters. Fast and eventful, with a full-throttle finale. (CC)

BLACK NARCISSUS 1946 British
★★★ **NR Drama 1:41**
Dir: Michael Powell, Emeric Pressburger *Cast:* Deborah Kerr, Sabu, David Farrar, Flora Robson, Jean Simmons, Kathleen Byron
▶ Kerr and Byron lead a group of Anglican nuns seeking to maintain a school and hospital in the remote Himalayas. Farrar is the British agent who proves a thorn in their sides; Sabu is the Indian general using the Black Narcissus perfume to woo nubile local Simmons. Conflicts break out among the nuns, a result of mounting pressures and their growing isolation from the world. Wonderfully photographed, unusual but winning drama won Oscars for Cinematography and Set Decoration.

BLACK ORPHEUS 1959 French
★★ **NR Drama 1:38**
Dir: Marcel Camus *Cast:* Breno Mello, Marpessa Dawn, Lourdes de Oliveira, Lea Garcia, Adhemar da Silva, Alexandro Constantino
▶ Rio de Janeiro carnival is the exotic visual backdrop for a modernized version of the Orpheus and Eurydice legend set to a samba score. Dawn and Mello fall in love but she is killed by her angry ex-boyfriend. Mello attempts to resurrect Dawn. Won Best Foreign Film Oscar. Dubbed.

BLACKOUT 1978
★★ **R Action-Adventure 1:30**
☑ Explicit language, violence
Dir: Eddy Matalon *Cast:* Jim Mitchum, Belinda Montgomery, Robert Carradine, June Allyson, Ray Milland, Jean-Pierre Aumont
▶ Cop Mitchum takes on four psychopaths, led by Carradine, who take advantage of a blackout to menace residents in an apartment building. Thriller inspired by the massive Manhattan blackout of July 13, 1977 (although film was shot in Canada), combines action and an interesting cast of Hollywood vets as the beleaguered tenants.

BLACK ROOM, THE 1935
★★ **NR Horror 1:10 B&W**
Dir: Roy William Neill *Cast:* Boris Karloff, Marian Marsh, Robert Allen, Thurston Hall, Katherine De Mille
▶ In the nineteenth century, evil baron Karloff presides cruelly over a Czech village. His good twin, also played by Karloff, takes over and gladdens the hearts of the townspeople. The bad twin plots against his brother. Well done; Karloff shines in his dual role.

BLACK ROSE, THE 1950
★★ **NR Action-Adventure 2:00**
Dir: Henry Hathaway *Cast:* Tyrone Power, Orson Welles, Cecile Aubry, Jack Hawkins, Michael Rennie, Herbert Lom
▶ In the thirteenth century, Saxon noble Power and archer Hawkins flee England after participating in rebellion against Norman king Rennie. They go to China, are imprisoned by their hosts, and attempt to escape with gorgeous Aubry. Rousing costume adventure from the Thomas Costain novel.

BLACK SABBATH 1964 Italian
★★ **NR Horror 1:39**
Dir: Mario Bava *Cast:* Boris Karloff, Susy Anderson, Mark Damon, Jacqueline Pierreux, Milli Monti, Michele Mercier
▶ Intriguing three-part horror anthology narrated by Karloff. In the first episode,

based on Chekov's "The Drop of Water," nurse Pierreux makes a bad mistake when she robs a medium's corpse; "The Telephone" is an eerie exercise in suspense as prostitute Mercier is haunted by jailed killer; "The Wurdalak," based on a Tolstoy short story, stars Karloff as a vampire who preys on his own family. Karloff's turn is the standout here, although all three episodes receive stylish direction.

BLACK STALLION, THE 1979
★★★★★ G Family 1:56
Dir: Carroll Ballard *Cast:* Kelly Reno, Mickey Rooney, Teri Garr, Clarence Muse, Hoyt Axton
▶ Walter Farley's adventure about young Reno shipwrecked on a desert island with an Arabian thoroughbred receives a lavish production in this beautiful family film. Story follows Reno's reunion with mother Garr and horse-racing adventures with trainer Rooney. Outstanding photography by Caleb Deschanel and intriguing use of wildlife. Film received a special Oscar for sound editing, and was followed four years later by *The Black Stallion Returns*.

BLACK STALLION RETURNS, THE 1983
★★★★ PG Family 1:43
☑ Explicit language, mild violence
Dir: Robert Dalva *Cast:* Kelly Reno, Mickey Rooney, Vincent Spano, Allen (Goorwitz) Garfield, Teri Garr, Jodi Thelen
▶ Teenager Reno searches the Sahara for the Black, his beloved horse, kidnapped by an evil Arab. Lacks the magical feel of the original movie but may be more accessible to younger tots. Provides plenty of action, adventure, production values, and Middle Eastern atmosphere. Rousing big race climax will entertain the whole family.

BLACK SUNDAY 1961 Italian
★★ NR Horror 1:23 B&W
Dir: Mario Bava *Cast:* Barbara Steele, John Richardson, Ivo Garrani, Andrea Cecchi, Arturo Dominici, Enrico Olivieri
▶ Steele, a witch brought back to life two hundred years after her original execution, wreaks revenge on the Moldavian descendents of the brother who betrayed her. Director Bava's swooping camera and acute sense of the grisly have won this chilling horror drama cult status over the years.

BLACK SUNDAY 1977
★★★★ R Mystery-Suspense 2:23
☑ Explicit language, violence
Dir: John Frankenheimer *Cast:* Robert Shaw, Bruce Dern, Marthe Keller, Fritz Weaver, Steven Keats
▶ Terrorist leader Keller teams up with brainwashed, shellshocked Vietnam vet Dern to explode the Goodyear Blimp over the crowded Super Bowl. Shaw saves the day as a heroic Israeli agent. Somewhat overlong but suspenseful, topical thriller from director Frankenheimer. The climax generates real terror and excitement. Adapted from the Thomas Harris best-seller.

BLACK WIDOW 1987
★★★★ R Mystery-Suspense 1:42
☑ Nudity, adult situations, explicit language, violence
Dir: Bob Rafelson *Cast:* Debra Winger, Theresa Russell, Nicol Williamson, Sami Frey, Dennis Hopper, Terry O'Quinn
▶ Winger, a Justice Department investigator, wonders if Russell, a frequent widow, may be murdering her wealthy husbands. Winger becomes so obsessed with the case that she forms a friendship with Russell in order to spy on her. The leads are convincing, as well as beautiful, in this absorbing thriller. Eye-catching locations range from the Pacific Northwest to Hawaii. **(CC)**

BLACK WINDMILL, THE 1974
★★★ PG Espionage 1:46
☑ Violence
Dir: Don Siegel *Cast:* Michael Caine, Joseph O'Conor, Donald Pleasence, John Vernon, Janet Suzman, Delphine Seyrig
▶ British spy Caine learns that his agency has kidnapped his son; with the help of his estranged wife Suzman, he races against time to rescue the boy. Strong opening leads to disappointing climax in this middling spy thriller. Pleasence overacts as the creepy chief villain.

BLACULA 1972
☆ PG Horror 1:32
☑ Violence
Dir: William Crain *Cast:* William Marshall, Denise Nicholas, Vonetta McGee, Thalmus Rasulala, Ketty Lester, Elisha Cook, Jr.
▶ Marshall, an African prince turned into a vampire by Dracula in 1815, searches for new victims in modern-day Los Angeles. Stylish, violent, and often amusing picture billed as the first black horror film. Features a surprisingly dignified perform-

ance from Marshall. Followed by *Scream, Blacula, Scream*.

BLADE MASTER, THE 1984 Italian
★ PG Action-Adventure 1:32
☑ Adult situations, explicit language, violence
Dir: David Hills   *Cast:* Miles O'Keeffe, Lisa Foster, Charles Borromel, David Cain Haughton, Chen Wong
▶ Sequel to *Ator, the Fighting Eagle*. In prehistoric times, muscular warrior O'-Keeffe leads a small band of men to the "Castle of Knowledge" to prevent the ultimate weapon, known as the Geometric Nucleus, from being used to destroy the world. Live action comic book was originally titled *Ator, the Invincible*.

BLADE RUNNER 1982
★★ R Sci-Fi 2:01
☑ Brief nudity, explicit language, violence
Dir: Ridley Scott   *Cast:* Harrison Ford, Rutger Hauer, Sean Young, Daryl Hannah, Edward James Olmos, Joanna Cassidy
▶ Ford plays a twenty-first-century cop forced out of retirement to track down a rebellious gang of Replicants, androids indistinguishable from humans. During a deadly cat-and-mouse chase through Los Angeles, Ford falls in love with a woman who may be one of the killers. Postmodern film noir highlighted by dazzling production design. Based on *Do Androids Dream of Electric Sheep?* by Philip K. Dick. Videocassette version contains five minutes of additional footage.

BLAME IT ON RIO 1984
★★★ R Comedy 1:40
☑ Nudity, adult situations, explicit language, adult humor
Dir: Stanley Donen   *Cast:* Michael Caine, Joseph Bologna, Michelle Johnson, Demi Moore, Valerie Harper
▶ Remake of French farce *One Wild Moment* has Caine and Bologna as best friends who take their teenaged daughters, Moore and Johnson, on a Rio vacation. To his dismay, Caine finds himself seduced by Johnson. Suggestive material handled adroitly by the leads. Beautiful Rio de Janeiro locations.

BLAME IT ON THE NIGHT 1984
★★★ PG-13 Drama 1:25
☑ Adult situations, explicit language
Dir: Gene Taft   *Cast:* Nick Mancuso, Byron Thames, Leslie Ackerman, Dick Bakalyan, Merry Clayton

▶ After his wife dies, rock 'n' roll star Mancuso gets custody of son Thames, a military academy student who doesn't take easily to the music world. Some moving moments as father and son iron out their differences. Based on an idea by Mick Jagger. Plenty of music from Merry Clayton, Billy Preston, and Ollie E. Brown appearing as themselves.

BLAST OFF 1967
★★ NR Sci-Fi/Comedy 1:35
Dir: Don Sharp   *Cast:* Burl Ives, Troy Donahue, Gert Frobe, Terry-Thomas, Hermione Gingold, Jimmy Clitheroe
▶ In Victorian England, American promoter P. T. Barnum (Ives) announces his plan to send Tom Thumb (Clitheroe) on a one-way rocket trip to the moon. Foreign spies seek to steal the spaceship's design, while rocketeer Donahue suggests that his craft is superior and can make the round trip. Film's uninspired high jinks, loosely based on a Jules Verne story, are adequate for kids. Also titled *Those Fantastic Flying Fools*.

BLAZING SADDLES 1974
★★★★ R Comedy 1:33
☑ Explicit language, violence, adult humor
Dir: Mel Brooks   *Cast:* Mel Brooks, Gene Wilder, Cleavon Little, Harvey Korman, Madeline Kahn, Alex Karras
▶ Mel Brooks's wild send-up of the wild West. Little stars as Bart, the black sheriff challenged by the corrupt villain Hedley Lamarr (Korman). Hugely popular and unabashedly vulgar comedy with many memorable moments including Kahn's uproarious Marlene Dietrich parody, Brooks as a Yiddish-speaking Indian chief, and the notorious eating-beans-around-the-campfire scene.

BLESS THE BEASTS AND CHILDREN 1971
★★ PG Drama 1:49
☑ Explicit language, violence
Dir: Stanley Kramer   *Cast:* Billy Mumy, Barry Robins, Miles Chapin, Darel Glaser, Jesse White, Ken Swofford
▶ Six private-school outcasts, including Mumy and Chapin, are upset when they witness the killing of buffalo. They decide to free a herd slated for slaughter. Sincere adaptation of the Glendon Swarthout novel. Oscar-nominated title song performed by the Carpenters.

BLIND ALLEY 1984
★★ R Mystery-Suspense 1:31

☑ Nudity, adult situations, explicit language, violence
Dir: Larry Cohen *Cast:* Anne Carlisle, Brad Rijn, John Woehrle, Matthew Stockley, Stephen Lack
▶ After toddler Stockley witnesses a Mafia slaying, hit man Rijn befriends the kid's mom (Carlisle) to learn if Stockley can identify him. Nice use of Greenwich Village locations in this moderately interesting, if not always believable, thriller from the prolific B-movie king Cohen.

BLIND DATE 1984
★ ★ R Mystery-Suspense 1:39
☑ Nudity, adult situations, explicit language, violence
Dir: Nico Mastorakis *Cast:* Joseph Bottoms, Kirstie Alley, Keir Dullea, James Daughton
▶ Slick formula thriller with some fresh twists. American account executive Bottoms, living in Athens, is blinded in a fall while chasing a serial murder suspect. Medical researcher Dullea outfits Bottoms with experimental artificial vision, which enables him to find the killer. Meandering story line but stylishly shot.

BLIND DATE 1987
★ ★ ★ PG-13 Comedy 1:35
☑ Explicit language
Dir: Blake Edwards *Cast:* Bruce Willis, Kim Basinger, John Larroquette, Joyce Van Patten, Mark Blum
▶ "Just don't get her drunk," is the warning to yuppie Willis about beautiful blind date Basinger. Willis ignores the advice and Basinger proceeds to go "ca-razy," leading him on the wildest night of his life. Charming performances by the likable leads amidst plenty of slapstick gags from director Edwards in this lightweight romantic comedy.

BLIND RAGE 1983 Filipino
★ ★ ★ R Action-Adventure 1:20
☑ Explicit language, violence
Dir: Efren C. Pinion *Cast:* D'Urville Martin, Leo Fong, Fred Williamson, Tony Ferrer
▶ International cast in a Filipino thriller. Five blind men pull off a $15 million bank heist but are killed in the getaway. Williamson is the mercenary hired by the CIA to track down the surviving mastermind. Cheap-looking production and bad dubbing but some action and fiery explosions for genre addicts.

BLINDSIDE 1988
★ ★ R Mystery-Suspense 1:42

☑ Nudity, adult situations, explicit language, violence
Dir: Paul Lynch *Cast:* Harvey Keitel, Lori Hallier, Lolita David, Michael Rudder
▶ Creepy hotel owner Keitel is immersed in deception and double-crosses when a drug kingpin strongarms him into keeping tabs on one of the guests. A cross between Coppola's *The Conversation* and Hitchcock's *Psycho*, the story can be confusing at times but improves as it goes along. Stylish direction from Lynch.

BLITHE SPIRIT 1945 British
★ ★ ★ ★ NR Comedy 1:36
Dir: David Lean *Cast:* Rex Harrison, Constance Cummings, Kay Hammond, Margaret Rutherford, Hugh Wakefield, Joyce Carey
▶ Hammond, first wife of novelist Harrison, comes back as a ghost and wreaks havoc on his marriage to Cummings. Grandly produced Noel Coward comedy/fantasy with four fine performances, especially Rutherford's classic character acting as the psychic Madame Arcati. Director Lean's skillful use of color nicely complements Coward's witty dialogue.

BLOB, THE 1958
★ ★ NR Sci-Fi 1:22
Dir: Irvin S. Yeaworth, Jr. *Cast:* Steve McQueen, Aneta Corseaut, Earl Rowe, Olin Howlin
▶ The original sticky-creature-from-outer-space flick lacks the budget and slick effects of the 1988 remake but it does have a young McQueen as the hero and a certain primitively campy charm all its own. Hilarious theme song (with lyrics like "Beware the blob, it leaps, and creeps, and leaps") by Burt Bacharach and Hal David.

BLOB, THE 1988
★ ★ R Sci-Fi 1:30
☑ Explicit language, violence
Dir: Chuck Russell *Cast:* Kevin Dillon, Shawnee Smith, Joe Seneca, Donovan Leitch, Candy Clark
▶ A meteor brings a pink gelatinous mass to menace a small town in this upscale remake of the 1958 Steve McQueen low-budget classic. Only local bad boy Dillon and feisty cheerleader Smith have the moxie to defeat the sticky monster-mass. Good special effects and old-fashioned suspense. Genre fans should lap this up like Jell-O.

BLOCKHEADS 1938
★★ NR Comedy 0:58 B&W
Dir: John G. Blystone *Cast:* Stan Laurel, Oliver Hardy, Patricia Ellis, Minna Gombell, Billy Gilbert, James Finlayson
► Laurel's been guarding the same trench for twenty years, unaware that World War I is over; Hardy finally brings him home to England with chaotic results. Short but marvelous comedy features some of Stan and Ollie's greatest routines.

BLONDE VENUS 1932
★★ NR Drama 1:37 B&W
Dir: Josef von Sternberg *Cast:* Marlene Dietrich, Cary Grant, Herbert Marshall, Sidney Toler, Dickie Moore
► When her scientist husband Marshall falls ill, performer Dietrich struggles to support her family and gets involved with Grant. Bizarrely stylized Dietrich/von Sternberg collaboration with a wild plot line: Dietrich degenerates into prostitution and even dons an ape suit in one scene before a final reconciliation with her hubby.

BLOOD AND SAND 1941
★★★ NR Drama 2:03
Dir: Rouben Mamoulian *Cast:* Tyrone Power, Linda Darnell, Rita Hayworth, Alla Nazimova, Anthony Quinn
► Bullfighter Power is the toast of the town until he hooks up with beautiful bad girl Hayworth, who lures him away from his wife Darnell and guides him down the road to ruin. Remake of the Rudolph Valentino silent is a classic in its own right, thanks to lush direction from Mamoulian, plush early Technicolor, and Power's charisma.

BLOOD BATH AT THE HOUSE OF DEATH 1985 British
☆ NR Horror/Comedy 1:30
☑ Rape, brief nudity, explicit language, violence
Dir: Ray Cameron *Cast:* Kenny Everett, Pamela Stephenson, Vincent Price
► The body count piles up in this British genre send-up. Eighteen people are found dead at Headstone Manor and no explanation for the killings is uncovered. Everett leads a group of high-strung parapsychologists who attempt to disprove the place's "haunted house" reputation. Funniest moment is a lampoon of John Hurt's death scene in *Alien.*

BLOOD BEACH 1981
★★ R Horror 1:32
☑ Nudity, adult situations, explicit language, graphic violence
Dir: Jeffrey Bloom *Cast:* John Saxon, Burt Young, David Huffman, Marianna Hill, Otis Young, Stefan Gierasch
► Various mutilations and deaths are occurring beneath the sands of a Santa Monica beach, but no remains can be found. Led by Saxon, police try to locate the mysterious creature responsible for the mayhem while keeping skeptical sun worshippers away from the sea. Average horror has few surprises.

BLOODBROTHERS 1978
★★★ R Drama 1:56
☑ Adult situations, explicit language
Dir: Robert Mulligan *Cast:* Richard Gere, Paul Sorvino, Tony Lo Bianco, Lelia Goldoni, Kenneth McMillan, Marilu Henner
► Young Stony DeCoco (Gere) prefers working in a children's hospital to the construction work employing his macho dad (Lo Bianco) and uncle (Sorvino). Domestic strife escalates as the relatives fight over Stony's future. Old-fashioned drama of Brooklyn Italian family was unjustly ignored in its theatrical run. Many moving moments and strong performances. Based on the novel by Richard Price.

BLOOD FEUD 1980 Italian
☆ R Drama 1:39
☑ Adult situations, explicit language, violence
Dir: Lina Wertmuller *Cast:* Sophia Loren, Marcello Mastroianni, Giancarlo Giannini, Tuli Ferro
► Widow Loren vows revenge after her husband is killed by the Sicilian Mafia in the 1920s. She's helped by socialist lawyer Mastroianni and hit man Giannini, both of whom fall in love with her. Powerhouse performances by the three leads in this gritty antifascist drama from Wertmuller, one of the most important Italian directors of the 1970s.

BLOODLINE 1979
★★★ R Mystery-Suspense 1:57
☑ Nudity, adult situations, explicit language
Dir: Terence Young *Cast:* Audrey Hepburn, Ben Gazzara, James Mason, Michelle Phillips, Omar Sharif
► After the death of her father, Hepburn struggles for control of his pharmaceutical empire. Plenty of jet-set flash and glamour, intrafamily viciousness, colorful

locations (Sardinia, Paris, Rome, New York), intrigue, and mystery in this glossy adaptation of Sidney Sheldon's best-seller.

BLOOD LINK 1986
★ **R Mystery-Suspense 1:30**
☑ Nudity, adult situations, explicit language, violence
Dir: Alberto DeMartino *Cast:* Michael Moriarty, Penelope Milford, Geraldine Fitzgerald, Cameron Mitchell, Sarah Langenfeld
► Dr. Craig Mannings (Moriarty), separated at birth from his Siamese twin Keith (also Moriarty), discovers that his brother has become a lady killer (literally). Good twin tries to thwart bad twin in this far-fetched but decently made thriller. Uneven performance by Moriarty in his dual role, but a few genuinely tense moments.

BLOOD OF OTHERS, THE 1984
★ ★ **NR Drama/MFTV 2:56**
☑ Adult situations, explicit language, mild violence
Dir: Claude Chabrol *Cast:* Jodie Foster, Michael Ontkean, Sam Neill, Stephane Audran, Lambert Wilson, Jean-Pierre Aumont
► Romantic saga of star-crossed lovers Ontkean, an antifascist activist from a wealthy background, and Foster, a seamstress and part-time model from a poor upbringing. Vividly played out against the social and policial upheaval of the years preceding World War II through the German occupation of France. Adapted from the novel by Simone de Beauvoir.

BLOOD ON THE MOON 1948
★ ★ **NR Western 1:28 B&W**
Dir: Robert Wise *Cast:* Robert Mitchum, Barbara Bel Geddes, Robert Preston, Walter Brennan, Phyllis Thaxter, Frank Faylen
► Gunfighter Mitchum takes advantage of feud between beautiful rancher Bel Geddes and rival Brennan, helping outlaw Preston in the process. Romance leads to a change of heart and deadly showdown. Brooding, atmospheric Western with unusually rich characterizations.

BLOOD SIMPLE 1985
★ ★ **R Mystery-Suspense 1:36**
☑ Adult situations, explicit language, graphic violence
Dir: Joel Coen *Cast:* John Getz, Frances McDormand, Dan Hedaya, Samm-Art Williams, M. Emmet Walsh
► In rural Texas, bar-owner Hedaya hires detective Walsh to kill unfaithful wife McDormand and lover Getz. The plot that follows has to be seen to be believed—as murdered bodies don't quite stay dead and nothing is what it seems—in this visually stylish, ingenious thriller from writer/director Joel Coen and his producer/co-writer brother Ethan.

BLOODSPORT 1988
★ ★ ★ **R Martial Arts 1:37**
☑ Explicit language, violence
Dir: Newt Arnold *Cast:* Jean-Claude Van Damme, Donald Gibb, Leah Ayres, Roy Chiao, Bolo Yeung, Norman Burton
► Slipping out of Defense Intelligence Agency training camp, martial arts expert Van Damme journeys to Hong Kong to compete in the Kumite, a secret full-contact kick-boxing tournament. While romancing journalist Ayres and befriending wild-eyed competitor Gibb, Van Damme establishes himself as the likely contender to dethrone reigning champ Yeung. Based on the true story of the first Westerner to win the Kumite. **(CC)**

BLOODY MAMA 1970
★ ★ **R Action-Adventure 1:30**
☑ Strong sexual content, adult situations, violence
Dir: Roger Corman *Cast:* Shelley Winters, Don Stroud, Pat Hingle, Robert De Niro, Bruce Dern, Robert Walden
► Ma Barker (Winters) teaches sons Walden, De Niro, and Stroud the tricks of the family trade: bank robbery. They prove to be good learners, much to the dismay of the law. B-movie action from the prolific Corman features prestardom performances by De Niro and Dern.

BLOW OUT 1981
★ ★ ★ **R Mystery-Suspense 1:48**
☑ Adult situations, explicit language, violence
Dir: Brian De Palma *Cast:* John Travolta, Nancy Allen, John Lithgow, Dennis Franz, Peter Boyden
► Travolta, a sound-effects expert for a fly-by-night film company, records evidence that a politician may have been murdered, but the only person who believes him is prostitute Allen, who's also a target of the conspiracy. Shooting in his Philadelphia hometown, De Palma and a superb crew push suspense to the limit. Buffs will spot many in-jokes and references to other films.

BLOW-UP 1966 British/Italian
★★ **NR Mystery-Suspense 1:51**
☑ Nudity, adult situations, explicit language
Dir: Michelangelo Antonioni *Cast:* David Hemmings, Vanessa Redgrave, Sarah Miles, Jill Kennington, Verushka
▶ Alienated London photographer Hemmings photographs couple in park, then enlarges pics when he suspects he's stumbled on a murder. Elegant murder mystery (whose plot influenced *The Conversation* and *Blow Out*, among others) may seem too oblique and arty to some but is still Antonioni's most accessible film. Technically superb, although director's wide-screen compositions may suffer on video. Sexy portrait of swinging London would be R-rated by today's standards.

BLUE ANGEL, THE 1930 German
★★ **NR Drama 1:43 B&W**
Dir: Josef von Sternberg *Cast:* Emil Jannings, Marlene Dietrich, Kurt Gerron, Rosa Valette, Hans Albers, Eduard von Winterstein
▶ Conservative teacher Jannings falls hopelessly in love with tawdry but irresistible cabaret singer Dietrich, sacrificing his career for her casual favors. Morbid, painfully incisive study of human degradation has lost none of its power over the years. Dietrich's Lola-Lola became an international icon as she sang "Falling in Love Again." ⑤

BLUEBEARD 1972 French/Italian/German
★ **R Drama 2:04**
☑ Nudity, adult situations
Dir: Edward Dmytryk *Cast:* Richard Burton, Raquel Welch, Virna Lisi, Joey Heatherton, Nathalie Delon, Karin Schubert
▶ On her honeymoon, American bride Heatherton learns that aristocratic husband Burton has murdered his seven previous brides. Through flashbacks, he explains how their frozen corpses ended up in his basement. Offbeat drama has an impressive cast in unusual roles (Welch plays a nun; Burton, a Nazi).

BLUEBERRY HILL 1988
★★ **R Drama 1:29**
☑ Brief nudity, adult situations, explicit language
Dir: Strathford Hamilton *Cast:* Margaret Avery, Carrie Snodgress, Matt Lattanzi, Jennifer Rubin

▶ Coming-of-age story features Lattanzi as an aimless aspiring mechanic and Rubin as his girlfriend, a young woman suffering a troubled relationship with her widowed mother Snodgress. Avery is a piano teacher who befriends Rubin in this slowly paced but competently handled melodrama with a good soundtrack of fifties tunes.

BLUE BIRD, THE 1976 U.S./Russian
★★ **G Fantasy 1:37**
Dir: George Cukor *Cast:* Elizabeth Taylor, Cicely Tyson, Jane Fonda, Ava Gardner, Todd Lookinland, Patsy Kensit
▶ Children Lookinland and Kensit search for the mythical bluebird of happiness, encountering Taylor (in four roles), Fonda (as Night), Tyson (Cat), and Gardner (Luxury) along the way. Expensive third film version of the Maurice Maeterlinck children's story is notable as the first U.S./Russian co-production.

BLUE CITY 1986
★ **R Mystery-Suspense 1:23**
☑ Nudity, adult situations, explicit language, violence
Dir: Michelle Manning *Cast:* Judd Nelson, Ally Sheedy, Paul Winfield, Scott Wilson, David Caruso
▶ Brat Pack homage to 1940s film noir mysteries may appeal to teens. Rebellious Nelson returns to his sleazy hometown to discover his dad has been murdered and no one is anxious to nail the culprit. He investigates with help from kid sister Sheedy, who goes undercover as a go-go dancer. Based on a novel by Ross MacDonald.

BLUE COLLAR 1978
★★★ **R Drama 1:53**
☑ Explicit language
Dir: Paul Schrader *Cast:* Richard Pryor, Harvey Keitel, Yaphet Kotto, Ed Begley, Jr., Harry Bellaver
▶ Hard-hitting, realistic thriller about three assembly-line auto workers whose friendship falls apart when they find evidence that their union is corrupt. Schrader's directing debut (he also wrote the screenplay with his brother Leonard) is a graphic, unsettling film with unexpected comic touches. Convincing acting from all three leads.

BLUE HAWAII 1961
★★★★ **NR Musical 1:41**
Dir: Norman Taurog *Cast:* Elvis Presley, Joan Blackman, Nancy Walters, Angela Lansbury, Roland Winters, Iris Adrian

▶ Presley, the heir to a pineapple fortune, shocks parents Winters and Lansbury when he turns his back on wealth to work in a tourist bureau. Above-average Presley vehicle has beautiful locations, plenty of romance, and a fine acting job by Lansbury. Elvis sings one of his biggest hits, "Can't Help Falling in Love."

BLUE IGUANA, THE 1988
★★ R Comedy 1:30
☑ Adult situations, explicit language, violence
Dir: John Lafia *Cast:* Dylan McDermott, Jessica Harper, James Russo, Pamela Gidley, Dean Stockwell, Tovah Feldshuh
▶ Down-and-out bounty hunter McDermott is hired by the IRS to retrieve contraband loot. South of the border, he finds himself in the middle of a war between mobster Russo and greedy bank owner Harper. Pungent film noir spoof lays on the murky plot details and loco characterizations with an unashamedly heavy hand. (CC)

BLUE LAGOON, THE 1980
★★★ R Drama 1:45
☑ Nudity, adult situations
Dir: Randal Kleiser *Cast:* Brooke Shields, Christopher Atkins, Leo McKern, William Daniels, Elva Josephson, Glenn Kohan
▶ Victorian-era teenagers Shields and Atkins are shipwrecked on a deserted Pacific island. Survival in this tropical paradise proves easy for a number of years; then, as developing adolescents, they struggle with their new sexual attraction for one another. Gorgeous photography by Nestor Almendros.

BLUE MAX, THE 1966
★★★ NR War 2:35
☑ Brief nudity, adult situations, violence
Dir: John Guillermin *Cast:* George Peppard, James Mason, Ursula Andress, Jeremy Kemp, Carl Schell, Anton Diffring
▶ In World War I, upstart German infantry soldier Peppard transfers to the air force and ruthlessly manipulates his fellow pilots to win the Blue Max, Germany's highest medal. Thrilling dogfight sequences and Peppard's steamy love scenes with Andress as Mason's unfaithful wife perk up the uneven plotting.

BLUE MONKEY 1987
★★ R Horror 1:38

☑ Adult situations, explicit language, violence
Dir: William Fruet *Cast:* Steve Railsback, Susan Anspach, Gwynyth Walsh, John Vernon, Joe Flaherty
▶ Deadpan, low-budget horror flick should entertain genre fans. Plot is sort of an earthbound, hospital version of *Alien*, as a monstrous creature (more like a bug than a monkey) menaces doctors and patients. Nothing new but a decent cast and spooky atmosphere enliven a familiar script.

BLUES BROTHERS, THE 1980
★★★★ R Comedy 2:13
☑ Explicit language
Dir: John Landis *Cast:* John Belushi, Dan Aykroyd, James Brown, Cab Calloway, Ray Charles, Carrie Fisher
▶ Jake Blues (Belushi) gets out of prison and teams with brother Elwood (Aykroyd) for "a mission from God"—to reassemble their old band and raise money for the orphanage where they grew up. Blockbuster combo of music (great numbers by Calloway, Charles, and Aretha Franklin), comedy in the "Saturday Night Live" style, and mayhem (plenty of car chases and crashes).

BLUE SKIES 1946
★★★ NR Musical 1:44
Dir: Stuart Heisler *Cast:* Bing Crosby, Fred Astaire, Joan Caulfield, Billy de Wolfe, Olga San Juan
▶ Flashbacks reveal the rivalry between nightclub owner Crosby and dancer Astaire over beautiful Caulfield. Plot barely gets in the way of a first-rate Irving Berlin score, with thirty complete songs and snatches of twelve others. "You Keep Coming Back Like a Song" was Oscar-nominated, but the standouts here are Fred and Bing's duo to "A Couple of Song and Dance Men," de Wolfe's "Mrs. Murgatroyd," and Fred's incredible solo of "Puttin' on the Ritz."

BLUE SKIES AGAIN 1983
★★★ PG Comedy 1:36
☑ Adult situations, explicit language
Dir: Richard Michaels *Cast:* Harry Hamlin, Robyn Barto, Mimi Rogers, Kenneth McMillan, Dana Elcar
▶ Charming, fun performance by Barto as a woman struggling to become the first female minor league baseball player. This easy-to-root-for underdog must overcome harassment from the other players, prejudice, and the resistance of team

owner (Hamlin) before she gets her chance to win the big game in the movie's final inning.

BLUE SUNSHINE 1978
★★★ R Horror 1:37
☑ Explicit language, violence
Dir: Jeff Lieberman *Cast:* Zalman King, Deborah Winters, Robert Walden, Alice Ghostley, Ray Young
▶ Students who took "Blue Sunshine," a certain brand of acid, at Stanford ten years ago begin to experience shocking and violent aftereffects—they become crazed killers. Some plot holes but this eerie, fairly plausible suspense drama delivers an ample number of thrills and chills.

BLUE THUNDER 1983
★★★★ R Action-Adventure 1:50
☑ Nudity, adult situations, explicit language, violence
Dir: John Badham *Cast:* Roy Scheider, Candy Clark, Malcolm McDowell, Warren Oates, Daniel Stern
▶ High-flying, breathlessly paced action-adventure from director Badham. Scheider, a Vietnam vet flying choppers for the L.A.P.D., uncovers an evil government conspiracy involving a high-tech "Blue Thunder" helicopter. He steals the craft, thus setting the stage for an exciting, climactic battle with archenemy McDowell. Plot implausibilities easily outweighed by action, drive, and suspense. (CC)

BLUE VELVET 1986
★★ R Mystery-Suspense 2:00
☑ Rape, nudity, adult situations, explicit language, graphic violence
Dir: David Lynch *Cast:* Isabella Rossellini, Kyle MacLachlan, Laura Dern, Hope Lange, Dennis Hopper, Dean Stockwell
▶ Young college student MacLachlan returns to his Norman Rockwellish hometown and discovers a web of corruption involving Rossellini, a chanteuse being tortured by psychopath Hopper. Weird stuff is undeniably gripping, thanks to surreal, brilliantly nightmarish direction from Lynch. Hopper is mesmerizing. The graphic sex and violence makes this experience not for everyone, but it is hard to forget. (CC)

BLUME IN LOVE 1973
★★ R Comedy 1:57
☑ Adult situations, explicit language
Dir: Paul Mazursky *Cast:* George

Segal, Susan Anspach, Kris Kristofferson, Marsha Mason, Shelley Winters
▶ Philandering divorce attorney Blume (Segal) is literally caught with his pants down by wife Anspach, so she divorces him and takes up with hippie Kristofferson. However, Blume still loves his wife and pursues her obsessively. Compassionate and satirical.

BOARDING SCHOOL 1977 German
★ R Sex/Comedy 1:38
☑ Nudity, strong sexual content, adult situations, explicit language
Dir: Andre Farwagi *Cast:* Nastassia Kinski, Gerry Sundquist, Stephane D'Amato, Gabrielle Blum, Marion Kracht, Nigel Greaves
▶ At a Swiss boarding school for girls in 1956, precocious students, more interested in learning facts of life than calculus, enlist aid of experienced Kinski in effort to lose virginity. They offer to sell their services to the boys' school across the lake, but the play-for-pay setup goes comically awry. Undraped Kinski in early stages of her career.

BOATNIKS, THE 1970
★★★ G Comedy/Family 1:40
Dir: Norman Tokar *Cast:* Robert Morse, Stefanie Powers, Phil Silvers, Norman Fell, Mickey Shaughnessy, Wally Cox
▶ Inept jewel thieves Silvers, Fell, and Shaughnessy lose their loot in a harbor overseen by naive Coast Guard ensign Morse. Their outlandish schemes to recover the gems provide plenty of brisk slapstick in this strong Disney comedy.

BOB AND CAROL AND TED AND ALICE 1969
★★ R Comedy 1:44
☑ Adult situations, explicit language
Dir: Paul Mazursky *Cast:* Natalie Wood, Robert Culp, Dyan Cannon, Elliott Gould, Horst Ebersberg
▶ Hip couple Culp and Wood and their square counterparts Gould and Cannon flirt with the notion of wife-swapping in this landmark comedy, which was somewhat of a sexual breakthrough in 1960s Hollywood. May seem a bit dated today, but Mazursky's satiric wit and the fine performances still hold up nicely.

BOBBIE JO AND THE OUTLAW 1976
★★ R Action-Adventure 1:29
☑ Nudity, adult situations, explicit language, violence
Dir: Mark L. Lester *Cast:* Marjoe Gort-

ner, Lynda Carter, Jesse Vint, Merrie Lynn Ross, Belinda Belaski
▶ Outlaw Gortner gets his kicks stealing cars and winning shooting contests. He falls for waitress Carter and they shoot their way across New Mexico. Bloody bank robbery leads to heavy pursuit by the law, climaxing in a violent shootout. Sexy action-adventure with a country-western flavor.

BOBBY DEERFIELD 1977
★ ★ PG Drama 2:04
☑ Brief nudity, explicit language
Dir: Sydney Pollack *Cast:* Al Pacino, Marthe Keller, Anny Duperey, Walter McGinn, Romolo Valli
▶ Grand Prix racer Bobby Deerfield (Pacino) survives his dangerous sport by cutting himself off from human emotion, but he changes when he falls in love with Keller, a free-spirited but terminally ill woman. Old-fashioned love story based on a novel by Erich Maria Remarque.

BOB LE FLAMBEUR 1957 French
★ PG Drama 1:42 B&W
Dir: Jean-Pierre Melville *Cast:* Isabel Corey, Roger Duchesne, Andre Garet, Daniel Cauchy, Guy Decomble
▶ Funny, jaunty film amazingly fresh after 30 years. Bob Le Flambeur (Duchesne), a former bank robber now living in Paris in semiretirement, spends his time gambling and losing. To recoup his fortune, Bob plans one last heist at the casino at Deauville. Ⓢ

BOBO, THE 1967 British
★ ★ NR Comedy 1:43
Dir: Robert Parrish *Cast:* Peter Sellers, Britt Ekland, Rossano Brazzi, Adolfo Celi, Hattie Jacques
▶ Spanish matador Sellers dreams of becoming a singer. He can get a gig at Celi's club by winning Ekland's heart, but it turns out to be mission impossible for the bungling bullfighter. Sellers evokes a few chuckles, but overall not one of his stronger vehicles.

BODY AND SOUL 1947
★ ★ ★ NR Drama/Sports 1:44 B&W
Dir: Robert Rossen *Cast:* John Garfield, Lilli Palmer, Hazel Brooks, Anne Revere, William Conrad, Canada Lee
▶ Dynamic boxing drama with Garfield in one of his best roles as a champion fighter corrupted by gangsters. Ordered to throw his next bout, he returns to his mother Revere and girlfriend Palmer for advice. Oscar-winning editing brings extraordinary tension to boxing scenes.

BODY AND SOUL 1981
★ ★ ★ R Drama/Sports 1:49
☑ Nudity, adult situations, explicit language, violence
Dir: George Bowers *Cast:* Leon Isaac Kennedy, Jayne Kennedy, Muhammad Ali, Peter Lawford, Perry Lang, Michael V. Gazzo
▶ Aspiring medical student and amateur fighter Leon Kennedy, determined to win the welterweight title, learns his little sister suffers from sickle cell anemia. While falling in love with sportswriter Jayne Kennedy, the fighter contends with mob hood Lawford and trains under watchful eye of Gazzo, with brief assist from Ali as himself. Passable remake of 1947 version from then-husband-wife Kennedy team.

BODY DOUBLE 1984
★ ★ ★ R Mystery-Suspense 1:50
☑ Nudity, strong sexual content, adult situations, explicit language, graphic violence
Dir: Brian De Palma *Cast:* Craig Wasson, Melanie Griffith, Gregg Henry, Deborah Shelton, Guy Boyd
▶ L.A. actor Wasson is set up as a murder witness. Obsessively investigating the crime himself, he hooks up with porno queen Griffith, who may provide the key to the killing. Typical De Palma mixture of Hitchcockian plotting, voyeurism, violence, stylish camerawork, and suspense. Definitely not for the squeamish. (CC)

BODY HEAT 1981
★ ★ ★ R Mystery-Suspense 1:53
☑ Nudity, adult situations, explicit language, violence
Dir: Lawrence Kasdan *Cast:* William Hurt, Kathleen Turner, Richard Crenna, Ted Danson, Mickey Rourke, J. A. Preston
▶ Luckless lawyer Hurt gets involved with sultry Turner, who's rich, beautiful—and married to Crenna. The lovers plot Crenna's murder with hapless Hurt unaware that Turner's hiding several double crosses up her sexy sleeve. Torrid, steamy thriller successfully updates 1940s-style film noir to the 1980s. Terrific hard-boiled dialogue, stylish visuals from writer/director Kasdan, sizzling chemistry between Hurt and Turner, and noteworthy supporting turns from Danson, Crenna, Preston, and Rourke (in his first major film role).

BODY ROCK 1984
★★ **PG-13 Musical 1:34**
☑ Brief nudity, adult situations, explicit language
Dir: Marcelo Epstein *Cast:* Lorenzo Lamas, Michelle Nicastro, Ray Sharkey, Vicki Frederick, Joseph Whipp
▶ Pushy Brooklyn kid Lamas attempts to make it in the world of breakdancing. On his way to the top, will he forget his old friends from the neighborhood? Lots of music, dancing, and an unrelenting beat in this glitzy look at the New York counterculture scene. Energetic soundtrack assembled by music industry vet Phil Ramone.

BODY SLAM 1987
★★ **PG Comedy 1:29**
☑ Explicit language
Dir: Hal Needham *Cast:* Dirk Benedict, Tanya Roberts, Roddy Piper, Captain Lou Albano, Barry Gordon
▶ The fortunes of down-on-his-luck promoter Benedict improve when he takes on a new client, former pro wrestler Piper, and combines rock 'n' wrestling in arena shows. But then former manager Albano and his goons mess up the works. Mixture of rock music, comedy, and wrestling has some sexist and racist humor but might amuse those looking for an easy laugh.

BODY SNATCHER, THE 1945
★★ **NR Horror 1:17 B&W**
Dir: Robert Wise *Cast:* Boris Karloff, Bela Lugosi, Henry Daniell, Edith Atwater, Russell Wade, Rita Corday
▶ Daniell, a Scottish doctor requiring cadavers for his experiments, turns to Karloff, a menacing cabbie with a disconcerting supply of fresh bodies. Thoughtful Val Lewton version of a Robert Louis Stevenson story features evocatively gloomy atmosphere and restrained performances. Karloff and Lugosi have one scene together, a powerful confrontation.

BOLERO 1984
★ **R Drama 1:44**
☑ Nudity, adult situations, explicit language
Dir: John Derek *Cast:* Bo Derek, Andrea Occhipinti, George Kennedy, Ana Obregon, Olivia d'Abo
▶ After graduation, sheltered schoolgirl Derek sets out to lose her virginity with an Arab sheik, then falls in love with a bullfighter. Suggestive plot (played mostly for laughs) gives Bo plenty of opportunities to display her assets. Written, shot, edited, and directed by husband John.

BONJOUR TRISTESSE 1958
★★ **NR Drama 1:33**
Dir: Otto Preminger *Cast:* Jean Seberg, Deborah Kerr, David Niven, Mylene Demongeot, Geoffrey Horne, Juliette Greco
▶ Through flashbacks, Seberg tells of her last summer on the Riviera with father Niven, a rake whose endless pursuit of women leads to tragedy when he tries to seduce shy Kerr. Superficial soap opera based on Françoise Sagan's novel features beautiful scenery and touching performance by Kerr.

BONNIE AND CLYDE 1967
★★★★ **NR Biography/Crime 1:51**
☑ Adult situations, explicit language, graphic violence, adult humor
Dir: Arthur Penn *Cast:* Warren Beatty, Faye Dunaway, Michael J. Pollard, Gene Hackman, Estelle Parsons
▶ Legendary Depression-era bank robbers Bonnie Parker (Dunaway) and Clyde Barrow (Beatty) were transformed into glamorous antiheroes by director Penn and producer/star Beatty in one of the great films of the 1960s. Story traces the larcenous couple from their first "meet cute" (Clyde tries to steal Bonnie's mom's car) through their life on the lam to their tragic deaths; deftly mixing violence, comedy, and moments of great tenderness. Oscar nominations went to all five leading players and Best Picture, but only Parsons and the cinematography won.

BONNIE SCOTLAND 1935
★★ **NR Comedy 1:20 B&W**
Dir: James W. Horne *Cast:* Stan Laurel, Oliver Hardy, Anne Grey, David Torrence, June Lang, James Finlayson
▶ Penniless, Laurel and Hardy take a cattle boat to Scotland in a quest for an uncle's inheritance. Bequeathed only bagpipes and a snuff box, they head for India to join the British Lancers. Slow-moving comedy is one of the duo's lesser efforts.

BON VOYAGE, CHARLIE BROWN (AND DON'T COME BACK!) 1980
★★★★ **G Animation 1:15**
Dir: Bill Melendez *Cast:* Voices of Daniel Anderson, Debbie Muller, Scott Beach, Casey Carlson
▶ Charles Schulz's "Peanuts" gang is back as Charlie Brown and company spend two weeks as exchange students

in France, where they run afoul of a local baron until Linus and his blanket save the day. Simple animation, characteristic of this series, is charming and colorful.

BOOGENS, THE 1981
★★ **R Horror 1:35**
☑ Nudity, adult situations, explicit language, graphic violence
Dir: James L. Conway *Cast:* Rebecca Balding, Fred McCarren, Anne-Marie Martin, Jeff Harlan
▶ An abandoned mine, home to vicious little creatures known as "boogens," is reopened after many years by unsuspecting young miners. The newly freed monsters go on the attack in this low-budget but well-made horror flick that will effectively scare undemanding fans.

BOOK OF NUMBERS 1973
★ **R Action-Adventure 1:20**
☑ Brief nudity, explicit language, violence
Dir: Raymond St. Jacques *Cast:* Raymond St. Jacques, Phillip Michael Thomas, Freda Payne, Hope Clarke, D'Urville Martin
▶ St. Jacques and Thomas play black Northerners who set up a numbers racket in a small Louisiana town despite opposition by the mob and the Ku Klux Klan. Better-than-average exploitation fare has a good feel for its Depression-era settings and some gospel tunes from pop star Freda Payne.

BOOM! 1968 U.S./British
★ **PG Drama 1:52**
☑ Adult situations
Dir: Joseph Losey *Cast:* Elizabeth Taylor, Richard Burton, Noel Coward, Joanna Shimkus, Michael Dunn, Romolo Valli
▶ Terminally ill millionaire Taylor entertains itinerant poet/philosopher Burton in a Sardinian palace staffed by bohemian oddballs. Lots of pretentious talk about Big Issues made this star vehicle one of the bigger bombs in Hollywood history, although Coward excels in a brief turn as a homosexual gossip. Based on Tennessee Williams's Broadway flop *The Milk Train Doesn't Stop Here Anymore*.

BOOMERANG 1947
★★ **NR Drama 1:28 B&W**
Dir: Elia Kazan *Cast:* Dana Andrews, Jane Wyatt, Lee J. Cobb, Arthur Kennedy, Cara Williams, Sam Levene
▶ In 1924, drifter Kennedy is arrested for the murder of a priest in Bridgeport, Con-

necticut. Prosecutor Andrews must risk his career and forego an easy conviction to prove the man is innocent. Director Kazan used actual locations and a documentary style in a compelling drama based on real events. Result spawned a new wave of American realism and established Kazan as a topflight director.

BOOST, THE 1988
★★ **R Drama 1:35**
☑ Brief nudity, adult situations, explicit language, mild violence
Dir: Harold Becker *Cast:* James Woods, Sean Young, John Kapelos, Steven Hill, Kelle Kerr
▶ Ambitious real estate salesman Woods and wife Young become cocaine addicts after business reversals. As life goes increasingly downhill, Woods abuses Young but can't kick the habit. Dated morality tale suffers from unrelentingly depressing tone but provides emotional tour de force for the always fascinating Woods.

BORDER, THE 1982
★★★ **R Drama 1:47**
☑ Nudity, adult situations, explicit language, violence
Dir: Tony Richardson *Cast:* Jack Nicholson, Valerie Perrine, Harvey Keitel, Warren Oates, Elpidia Carrillo
▶ Nicholson, a U.S. border patrolman, battles corruption within the ranks when he helps Mexican Carrillo recover her baby from an adoption ring. Gritty, topical, emotionally charged drama with strong supporting performances and haunting music by Ry Cooder. Nicholson's towering work as the conscience-stricken Charlie is the real focal point.

BORDERLINE 1980
★★★★ **PG Action-Adventure 1:43**
☑ Explicit language, violence
Dir: Jerrold Freedman *Cast:* Charles Bronson, Bruno Kirby, Ed Harris, Wilford Brimley, Michael Lerner
▶ Bronson is solid as a Border Patrol cop searching for his partner's killers. The Feds think drug smugglers are responsible, but Bronson goes after the leader of an illegal alien ring instead. Topical subject matter and strong supporting performances (notably Harris in his debut role) make this one of Bronson's better vehicles. (CC)

BORN AMERICAN 1986
★★ **R Action-Adventure 1:36**

☑ Nudity, explicit language, graphic violence
Dir: Renny Harlin   *Cast:* Mike Norris, Steve Durham, David Coburn, Thalmus Rasulala, Albert Salmi
▶ While exploring Lapland, three young Americans cross the Russian border on a whim. Caught by Russian soldiers and tortured in a gulag, their only hope is to escape across the hostile Arctic. Norris (Chuck's son) displays some karate tricks during a training sequence. Ultrapatriotic fantasy was filmed in (and banned from) Finland.

BORN FREE 1966 British
★★★★★ NR Drama/Family 1:35
Dir: James Hill   *Cast:* Virginia McKenna, Bill Travers, Geoffrey Keen, Peter Lukoye
▶ Game warden George Adamson and his wife Joy (McKenna) raise Elsa, a lion cub, in captivity. When Elsa matures, they teach her how to survive in the wilderness. Based on a true story and shot on location in Kenya, this heartwarming adaptation of Joy Adamson's best-selling book will please everyone in the family. Title song and soundtrack both won Oscars. Sequel: *Living Free.*

BORN IN EAST L.A. 1987
★★ R Comedy 1:24
☑ Adult situations, explicit language, mild violence
Dir: Cheech Marin   *Cast:* Cheech Marin, Paul Rodriguez, David Stern, Kamala Lopez, Jan-Michael Vincent
▶ Marin, an auto mechanic from East Los Angeles, is accidentally nabbed in a roundup of illegal aliens. Stuck in Mexico with no money or papers, he has to rely on shady nightclub owner Stern to get home. Based on his rock video parody of Bruce Springsteen's "Born in the USA," Marin's post–Cheech and Chong debut is a surprisingly good-natured comedy about a touchy subject. (CC)

BORN LOSERS 1967
★★★ PG Action-Adventure 1:52
☑ Adult situations, violence
Dir: T. C. Frank (Tom Laughlin)   *Cast:* Tom Laughlin, Elizabeth James, Jeremy Slate, William Wellman, Jr.
▶ Vicious bikers terrorize a small town and threaten to gang-rape beautiful hippie James. But brave half-breed Laughlin fights fire with fire to rescue her. Violent motorcycle film is notable chiefly for the introduction of Laughlin's "Billy Jack" character, the hero of three subse-

quent films. Jane Russell has a cameo as James's mother.

BORN TO KILL 1974
★★ R Drama 1:24
☑ Adult situations, explicit language, violence
Dir: Monte Hellman   *Cast:* Warren Oates, Richard B. Shull, Harry Dean Stanton, Troy Donahue, Millie Perkins, Laurie Bird
▶ Offbeat but engrossing story of a maniacal breeder of fighting cocks (Oates), who takes a vow of silence until he wins a championship. Voice-overs explaining the action grow tedious, although supporting characters are quirkily amusing and photography by Nestor Almendros is excellent. Filmed in Georgia under the titles *Wild Drifters* and *Gamblin' Man,* and also available as *Cockfighter.*

BORN TO RACE 1988
★★ R Drama/Sports 1:38
☑ Brief nudity, explicit language, mild violence
Dir: James Fargo   *Cast:* Joseph Bottoms, Antonio Sabato, George Kennedy, Marla Heasley, Marc Singer
▶ In North Carolina's Charlotte Speedway, greedy sponsor Kennedy enlists top driver Singer to kidnap sexy Italian engineer Heasley who has important state-of-the-art jalopy blueprints. Good-guy driver Bottoms loses his heart to Heasley and comes to her rescue. Sexual chemistry between the leads and authentic locations enliven this racetrack yarn.

BORN YESTERDAY 1950
★★★★★ NR Comedy 1:42 B&W
Dir: George Cukor   *Cast:* Judy Holliday, William Holden, Broderick Crawford, Howard St. John, Frank Otto
▶ Junk dealer millionaire Crawford, upset with crass girlfriend Billie Dawn's (Holliday) lack of social graces, hires newspaperman Holden to coach her. The plan backfires as the not-so-dumb Billie outwits Crawford and falls in love with Holden. Classic screen comedy with Judy's hilarious yet vulnerable characterization winning a well-deserved Oscar. Garson Kanin's Broadway hit also received Best Picture nomination.

BOSS'S WIFE, THE 1986
★ R Comedy 1:23
☑ Nudity, adult situations, explicit language, adult humor
Dir: Ziggy Steinberg   *Cast:* Daniel Stern, Arielle Dombasle, Christopher

Plummer, Fisher Stevens, Melanie Mayron, Martin Mull
▶ Stern, a mild-mannered stockbroker, fears for his career and his marriage when, on a company weekend, boss Plummer's gorgeous wife Dombasle pursues him. Extremely broad sex farce with plenty of sight gags.   (CC)

BOSTONIANS, THE 1984
★ NR Drama 2:00
☑ Adult situations
Dir: James Ivory   *Cast:* Christopher Reeve, Vanessa Redgrave, Madeleine Potter, Jessica Tandy, Nancy Marchand
▶ In nineteenth-century Boston, young suffragette orator Potter becomes the object of a battle of wills between Redgrave, a spinster tutoring her in feminism, and Reeve, a handsome antifeminist Southern lawyer attempting to woo her away. Slow-moving but first-rate work from Reeve and Redgrave. Picture postcard re-creation of the Henry James novel from the team that later created *A Room with a View.*

BOSTON STRANGLER, THE 1968
★★ R Crime 2:00
☑ Violence
Dir: Richard Fleischer   *Cast:* Tony Curtis, Henry Fonda, George Kennedy, Mike Kellin, Hurd Hatfield, Murray Hamilton
▶ Deliberate, unsensational account of real-life killer Albert DeSalvo (Curtis), seemingly ordinary family man who was actually serial killer of women. Criminologist Fonda investigates and eventually brings Curtis to justice. Superb performances from Curtis and Fonda.   (CC)

BOULEVARD NIGHTS 1979
★★ R Action-Adventure 1:42
☑ Adult situations, explicit language, violence
Dir: Michael Pressman   *Cast:* Richard Yniguez, Danny De La Paz, Marta Du Bois, Betty Carvalho, Carmen Zapata
▶ Affecting melodrama about Yniguez and De La Paz, brothers trapped by poverty and gang warfare in the barrios of East Los Angeles. Yniguez dreams of taking his wife out of the slums, but honor forces him to avenge his mother's murder. Authentic locations and details distinguish this from other gang films.

BOUND FOR GLORY 1977
★★★★ PG Biography 2:27
☑ Adult situations
Dir: Hal Ashby   *Cast:* David Carradine,

Ronny Cox, Melinda Dillon, Gail Strickland, Randy Quaid
▶ The autobiography of folk singer Woody Guthrie is transformed into a moving, heartfelt account of Dustbowl America during the Depression. Vignettes of Okies, miners, migrant farmers, and unionizers reveal the inspiration behind Guthrie's songs. Superb photography by Haskell Wexler won an Oscar, as did Leonard Rosenman's scoring of Guthrie's music. Carradine is quite convincing in the lead role.

BOUNTY, THE 1984
★★★★ PG Drama 2:12
☑ Nudity, adult situations, explicit language, violence
Dir: Roger Donaldson   *Cast:* Mel Gibson, Anthony Hopkins, Laurence Olivier, Edward Fox, Daniel Day-Lewis, Bernard Hill
▶ Third big-screen version of *Mutiny on the Bounty* offers revisionist portraits of the infamous Captain Bligh (Hopkins) and his enemy, Fletcher Christian (Gibson, in a charged, erotic performance). Bligh's bravery as he crosses the ocean in a small boat contrasts well with Christian's adventures on exotic Tahiti, whose breathtaking scenery provides a memorable backdrop to the large-scale action scenes. Robert Bolt's screenplay concentrates on revealing personal details glossed over in the earlier films.

BOXCAR BERTHA 1972
★★ R Drama 1:28
☑ Nudity, strong sexual content, adult situations, explicit language, violence
Dir: Martin Scorsese   *Cast:* Barbara Hershey, David Carradine, Barry Primus, Bernie Casey, John Carradine
▶ Competent low-budget variation on *Bonnie and Clyde* with Hershey turning to crime after the death of her father. Forming a gang with union organizer Carradine, she crosses Depression-era Arkansas robbing banks and kidnapping evil millionaires. Scorsese's studio debut is a fairly typical Roger Corman quickie production.

BOY AND HIS DOG, A 1975
★★ R Sci-Fi 1:27
☑ Strong sexual content, explicit language, violence
Dir: L. Q. Jones   *Cast:* Don Johnson, Jason Robards, Suzanne Benton, Charles McGraw, Alvy Moore

▶ A pre-"Miami Vice" Johnson stars as Vic, a young man attempting to survive in post-atomic-war America (circa 2024) with the help of his faithful companion, a telepathic talking dog named Blood (voice of Tim McIntire). Blackly comic adaptation of Harlan Ellison's award-winning novella has developed a cult following over the years. Outrageous twist ending, in which Johnson must choose between the dog or Benton, might offend feminists.

BOY FRIEND, THE 1971 British
★★★ G Musical 1:50 B&W
Dir: Ken Russell **Cast:** Twiggy, Christopher Gable, Max Adrian, Tommy Tune, Glenda Jackson
▶ Affectionate send-up of Busby Berkeley musicals uses a time-honored plot (aspiring actress gets her big break when the star is injured) as a framework for lavish, glittering production numbers. Former model Twiggy gives a steady performance, and she's backed by top-notch hoofers. Fourteen songs in all (although the British version includes two extra tunes).

BOY IN BLUE, THE 1986
★★★ R Drama 1:38
☑ Nudity, adult situations, explicit language
Dir: Charles Jarrott **Cast:** Nicolas Cage, David Naughton, Christopher Plummer, Cynthia Dale, Melody Anderson
▶ Canadian variation on the *Rocky* theme based on the life of nineteenth-century rower Ned Hanlan (Cage). Story traces Ned's rise from the working class to the top of his sport, his conflict with villainous sponsor Plummer who tries to get him to throw the big race, and his romance with the sponsor's daughter Dale. Straightforward formula plot delivers the underdog's climactic victory. **(CC)**

BOY NAMED CHARLIE BROWN, A 1970
★★★★ G Animation 1:25
Dir: Bill Melendez **Cast:** Voices of Peter Robbins, Pamelyn Ferdin, B. Melendez, Glenn Gilger
▶ First animated feature film about the Peanuts gang brings the precocious bunch to life. The usually hapless Charlie Brown finally finds something he can do well as he wins the school spelling bee and goes on to the national contest. Pleasant, good-humored family entertainment. Music by Rod McKuen. **(CC)**

BOY ON A DOLPHIN 1957
★★ NR Drama 1:51
Dir: Jean Negulesco **Cast:** Alan Ladd, Sophia Loren, Clifton Webb, Jorge Mistral, Laurence Naismith
▶ Sponge diver Loren (in her U.S. film debut) finds ancient sunken wreck filled with priceless treasure; American archaeologist Ladd and unscrupulous millionaire Webb race each other to salvage the fortune. Lushly photographed in Greece, lively drama is marred only by weak love subplot.

BOYS FROM BRAZIL, THE 1978
★★★★ R Mystery-Suspense 2:03
☑ Brief nudity, explicit language, violence
Dir: Franklin J. Schaffner **Cast:** Gregory Peck, Laurence Olivier, James Mason, Lilli Palmer, Uta Hagen
▶ Intriguing suspense thriller highlighted by the legendary leads. Peck, getting a rare chance to play a villain, has an evil field day as Dr. Josef Mengele, the mad Nazi doctor plotting a Fourth Reich via ninety-four clones of Adolf Hitler (the "boys" of the title). Olivier is Nazi hunter Lieberman (a characterization obviously inspired by real-life Nazi hunter Simon Wiesenthal), who tries to stop him. From the best-selling novel by Ira Levin.

BOYS IN COMPANY C, THE 1978
★★★★ R War 2:06
☑ Adult situations, explicit language, violence
Dir: Sidney J. Furie **Cast:** Stan Shaw, Andrew Stevens, James Canning, Michael Lembeck, Craig Wasson
▶ Five young Marine recruits become friends in boot camp before being sent to Vietnam, where they confront the real horrors of war. Sturdy war drama overcomes formula plotting with gritty, authentic action, salty humor (especially in the opening boot-camp sequence), and fine acting, particularly by Shaw.

BOYS IN THE BAND, THE 1970
★ R Drama 2:00
☑ Adult situations, explicit language
Dir: William Friedkin **Cast:** Frederick Combs, Leonard Frey, Cliff Gorman, Reuben Greene, Robert La Tourneaux, Laurence Luckinbill
▶ Playwright Matt Crowley adopted his own off-Broadway hit in this landmark (for Hollywood) sympathetic treatment of gays. A group of gays gather for a birthday party that quickly degenerates into

a hornet's nest of confrontations and revelations. Nicely directed by Friedkin and well acted by all.

BOYS NEXT DOOR, THE 1985
★ **R Drama 1:31**
☐ Brief nudity, adult situations, explicit language, violence
Dir: Penelope Spheeris *Cast:* Maxwell Caulfield, Charlie Sheen, Christopher McDonald, Hank Garrett, Patti D'Arbanville
► Unpopular high school students Caulfield and Sheen, victims of rough upbringings and facing a bleak future as factory workers, vent their rage in a violent spree. Director Spheeris presents a gruesome vision of people who appear innocent but are capable of horrendous crimes. Not pleasant but well made.

BOYS TOWN 1938
★★★★ **NR Drama 1:36 B&W**
Dir: Norman Taurog *Cast:* Spencer Tracy, Mickey Rooney, Henry Hull, Leslie Fenton, Addison Richards
► "There's no such thing as a bad boy," theorizes Father Flanagan (Tracy), real-life figure who opens Nebraska home for juvenile delinquents. Tracy proves his axiom by reforming bad-boy Rooney and others. Old-fashioned sentiment is still enormously appealing. Oscars for Best Actor (Tracy) and Original Story.

BOY WHO COULD FLY, THE 1986
★★★★ **PG Fantasy 1:54**
☑ Explicit language
Dir: Nick Castle *Cast:* Jay Underwood, Lucy Deakins, Bonnie Bedelia, Fred Savage, Colleen Dewhurst
► Recently widowed Bedelia and her children Deakins and Savage move into a new neighborhood and endure all sorts of personal problems. Deakins befriends Underwood, the autistic boy next door, whose belief that he can fly leads to the uplifting climax. Sweet, mild-mannered drama tugs honestly at the heartstrings and is perfect small-screen family viewing. **(CC)**

BOY WITH GREEN HAIR, THE 1948
★★ **NR Drama 1:22**
Dir: Joseph Losey *Cast:* Dean Stockwell, Robert Ryan, Pat O'Brien, Barbara Hale, Richard Lyon, Walter Catlett
► Stockwell awakes one morning to find he has mysteriously become a boy with green hair. The condition leads to ostracism and harassment from his classmates and neighbors. Child actor Stockwell is

quite affecting in this haunting allegory about prejudice. Most disturbing image: the shaved head.

BRADDOCK: MISSING IN ACTION III 1988
★★★★ **R Action-Adventure 1:41**
☑ Explicit language, graphic violence
Dir: Aaron Norris *Cast:* Chuck Norris, Roland Harrah III, Aki Aleong, Miki Kim, Yehuda Efroni
► U.S. Army Colonel James Braddock (Norris) returns to Vietnam to liberate his wife and son and a group of Amerasian foundlings. Martial artist supreme, Norris uses every part of his anatomy to destroy the Red villains, but he also gets to show a more sensitive side, even shedding a tear when he embraces his newfound son. Action-packed.

BRADY'S ESCAPE 1984
★★★ **NR Action-Adventure 1:36**
☑ Violence
Dir: Pal Gabor *Cast:* John Savage, Kelly Reno, Ildiko Bansagi, Laszlo Mensaros, Dzsoko Bacs
► During World War II, Hungarian cowboys, known as Csikos, help downed U.S. aviator Savage escape the Nazis. Reno plays a local kid who befriends Savage and dreams of returning with him to "Vyoming." Low-key, modest action-adventure tale is somber but likable.

BRAIN, THE 1988 Canadian
★ **R Horror 1:30**
☑ Nudity, explicit language, violence
Dir: Edward Hunt *Cast:* Tom Breznahan, Cyndy Preston, David Gale, George Buza, Brett Pearson
► Teen Breznahan, a disciplinary problem at school, is ordered to see shrink/TV personality Gale. He discovers Gale has been turning townspeople violent with his giant experimental brain and tries to stop him. Way-out plot provides wild chases, fierce battles, narrow escapes, and a few scattered chuckles.

BRAINSTORM 1983
★★ **PG Sci-Fi 1:46**
☑ Brief nudity, adult situations, explicit language, violence
Dir: Douglas Trumbull *Cast:* Christopher Walken, Natalie Wood, Louise Fletcher, Cliff Robertson, Joe Dorsey
► Scientist Walken and wife Wood try to prevent the government from misusing his incredible discovery: a system that transfers perceptual experience from one mind to another. Provocative sci-fi

has some murky plotting (Wood's death left some scenes unshot and caused a dispute between the studio and Trumbull) compensated by fine performances (especially Fletcher), thrilling special effects, and exciting subjective camerawork.

BRAIN THAT WOULDN'T DIE, THE 1959
★ NR Sci-Fi 1:21 B&W
Dir: Joseph Green *Cast:* Herb Evers, Virginia Leith, Adele Lamont, Paul Maurice
▶ Campy sci-fi horror B-movie has a plot so wild, it must be seen to be believed. Scientist Evers has problems: he's got a monster in the basement and, when girlfriend Leith is decapitated in a car crash, he keeps the head alive in a solution on his lab table. The bodiless lass spends the rest of the movie begging to be put out of her misery.

BRAINWAVES 1982
★ ★ PG Mystery-Suspense 1:21
☑ Brief nudity, adult situations, explicit language, violence
Dir: Uli Lommel *Cast:* Keir Dullea, Suzanna Love, Tony Curtis, Vera Miles
▶ Young Love falls into a coma after a car accident. Her recovery turns into a nightmare after mad doctor Curtis tampers with her brain. Dullea, her concerned husband, tries to uncover the reason for her psychosis. A good cast and stylish camerawork enliven this pulpy story.

BRANNIGAN 1975 British
★ ★ ★ PG Action-Adventure 1:51
☑ Adult situations, explicit language, violence
Dir: Douglas Hickox *Cast:* John Wayne, Richard Attenborough, Judy Geeson, Mel Ferrer, Del Henney, Lesley-Anne Down
▶ Wayne, a tough Chicago cop, tracks criminal to England, where strict Scotland Yard detective Attenborough proves as much an obstacle as the crook's sneaky lawyer Ferrer. Predictable Wayne vehicle, typical of his later efforts, features strong car chases and fistfights.

BRASS TARGET 1978
★ ★ ★ PG Mystery-Suspense 1:51
☑ Explicit language, violence
Dir: John Hough *Cast:* Sophia Loren, John Cassavetes, George Kennedy, Robert Vaughn, Patrick McGoohan, Max Von Sydow
▶ Intriguing plot based on historical speculation that General George Patton (Kennedy) was murdered to cover up a gold heist conspiracy involving U.S. Army officers in post–World War II Germany. Cassavetes is the OSS man who investigates, Von Sydow the assassin working for the bad guys, and Loren is the woman involved with both men.

BRAVADOS, THE 1958
★ ★ ★ NR Western 1:38
Dir: Henry King *Cast:* Gregory Peck, Joan Collins, Stephen Boyd, Albert Salmi, Henry Silva, Kathleen Gallant
▶ Peck, a rancher whose wife has been raped and murdered, pursues four criminals to Mexican frontier town where they face hanging. When they escape, he exacts vengeance on them one by one. Stark, thoughtful Western features a brooding performance by Peck as a vigilante who becomes as evil as his prey.

BRAZIL 1985 British
★ R Sci-Fi 2:11
☑ Adult situations, explicit language, violence
Dir: Terry Gilliam *Cast:* Jonathan Pryce, Robert De Niro, Michael Palin, Kim Geist, Katherine Helmond, Ian Richardson
▶ Controversial black comedy about naive bureaucrat Pryce trapped in an Orwellian nightmare by a computer mixup is a wildly inventive but bleak vision of the future as seen by Monty Python member Gilliam. Stunning art direction was nominated for an Oscar, as was the sophisticated screenplay (by Gilliam, Tom Stoppard, and Charles McKeown). Uniformly good cast includes Bob Hoskins in an amusing cameo as a sanitation engineer. (CC)

BREAD AND CHOCOLATE 1978 Italian
★ NR Comedy 1:51
☑ Adult situations, explicit language
Dir: Franco Brusati *Cast:* Nino Manfredi, Anna Karina, Johnny Dorell, Paolo Turco
▶ Italian immigrant Manfredi goes to work in Switzerland to support his family back home. Struggling to survive in a country that considers him inferior in every respect, his compassion for others and sense of humor ultimately sees him through. Manfredi gives an almost Chaplinesque performance.

BREAKER! BREAKER! 1977
★ ★ PG Action-Adventure 1:26
☑ Violence

Dir: Don Hulette *Cast:* Chuck Norris, George Murdock, Terry O'Connor, Don Gentry, Michael Augenstein
▶ Kung-fu combines with citizens' band radio in this Chuck Norris vehicle. Norris plays a karate-chopping trucker rescuing younger brother Augenstein, the prisoner of some evil small-town types. Norris provides the action/mayhem mix we've come to expect.

BREAKER MORANT 1980 Australian
★★★★ PG Drama 1:47
☑ Explicit language, violence
Dir: Bruce Beresford *Cast:* Edward Woodward, Jack Thompson, Bryan Brown, John Waters, Lewis Fitz-Gerald
▶ During the Boer War in South Africa circa 1901, Australian soldiers Woodward, Brown, and Fitz-Gerald are made scapegoats for war crimes by their guilt-ridden British allies. Inexperienced attorney Thompson stoutly defends them in the controversial court-martial. Beautifully crafted, absolutely gripping fact-based Australian antiwar drama. Terrific ensemble acting really brings us close to these characters and we become completely involved in their tragic fate. Well worth a look.

BREAKFAST AT TIFFANY'S 1961
★★★★ NR Romance 1:55
Dir: Blake Edwards *Cast:* Audrey Hepburn, George Peppard, Patricia Neal, Buddy Ebsen, Mickey Rooney, Martin Balsam
▶ Sparkling adaptation of Truman Capote's novella stars Hepburn in a lovely performance as the free-spirited but vulnerable Holly Golightly. Struggling New York writer Peppard, the kept man of wealthy woman Neal, falls for Holly. Director Edwards weaves together an adult film of contrasting yet cohesive moods, from haunting loneliness to broad comedy. Oscar for Best Song, "Moon River."

BREAKFAST CLUB, THE 1985
★★★★ R Drama 1:37
☑ Explicit language, adult humor
Dir: John Hughes *Cast:* Molly Ringwald, Ally Sheedy, Emilio Estevez, Anthony Michael Hall, Judd Nelson
▶ Five high school students face eight hours of detention on a Saturday. Nerd Hall, delinquent Nelson, jock Estevez, prom queen Ringwald, and kooky introvert Sheedy use the time to discuss their innermost secrets and really get to know

one another. An ambitious and very funny comedy-drama from director Hughes. The excellent young cast keeps all the talk interesting. **(CC)**

BREAKHEART PASS 1976
★★★★ PG Western 1:32
☑ Adult situations, explicit language, violence
Dir: Tom Gries *Cast:* Charles Bronson, Ben Johnson, Richard Crenna, Jill Ireland, Charles Durning, Ed Lauter
▶ Crackling Western adventure with Bronson a secret agent on the trail of a gang of killers. Set primarily aboard a luxury steam train, and featuring a full complement of extraordinary stunts: runaway cars, rooftop fistfights, Indian ambushes, etc. Supporting villains include rodeo star Casey Tibbs, boxer Archie Moore, and pro quarterback Joe Kapp. **(CC)**

BREAKIN' 1984
★★★ PG Musical 1:27
☑ Adult situations, explicit language, mild violence
Dir: Joel Silberg *Cast:* Lucinda Dickey, Adolfo "Shabba-Doo" Quinones, Michael "Boogaloo Shrimp" Chambers, Ben Lokey, Christopher McDonald
▶ First feature film devoted entirely to the breakdancing craze. Dickey is a serious dance student turned on to breakin' by her new friends Quinones and Chambers. The dancing establishment refuses to acknowledge the style but the kids prove them wrong by winning parts in a Broadway musical. Plenty of music, dance, energy, and movement. The three leads are quite likable and one scene with three pint-sized breakdancers is absolutely magical.

BREAKING ALL THE RULES 1985
★★ R Comedy 1:31
☑ Nudity, adult situations, explicit language
Dir: James Orr *Cast:* Carl Marotte, Thor Bishopria, Carolyn Dunn, Rachel Hayward
▶ Comedy and romantic entanglements highlight lightweight teen fare for the youth audience. Teenagers Marotte, a security guard, and Bishopria spend a day at the amusement park. They woo two pretty girls and become the target of inept hoods who have hidden a valuable diamond in a stuffed toy won by Marotte in a park game.

BREAKING AWAY 1979
★★★★ PG Comedy 1:40

☑ Explicit language
Dir: Peter Yates *Cast:* Dennis Christopher, Dennis Quaid, Barbara Barrie, Paul Dooley, Jackie Earle Haley, Robyn Douglass
▶ Simply wonderful coming-of-age comedy set in Indiana. Christopher is a young man so obsessed with being an Italian bike racing champ that he pedals the day away and speaks with an Italian accent, upsetting salt-of-the-earth dad Dooley and delighting coed Douglass, who mistakes him for the real article. The local college boys look down on Christopher and his townie friends; their conflict is resolved in a thrilling bike-race climax. Tender, funny, insightful Oscar-winning script from Steve Tesich. A Best Picture nominee.

BREAKING GLASS 1980 British
☆ **PG Musical 1:34**
☑ Adult situations, explicit language
Dir: Brian Gibson *Cast:* Hazel O'Connor, Phil Daniels, Jon Finch, Jonathan Pryce, Peter-Hugo Daly
▶ British New Wave music provides the background for a story in the show biz/ heartbreak tradition of *The Rose* and *A Star is Born.* O'Connor plays angry punker Kate, whose rock star dreams dissolve because of music industry pressures, drugs, and egotism. O'Connor, alternately tough and vulnerable, gives a warts-and-all performance.

BREAKIN' 2: ELECTRIC BOOGALOO 1984
★★★ **PG Musical 1:34**
☑ Explicit language
Dir: Sam Firstenberg *Cast:* Adolfo "Shabba-Doo" Quinones, Lucinda Dickey, Michael "Boogaloo Shrimp" Chambers, Susie Bono, Harry Caesar
▶ Breakdancing trio from the original *Breakin'* returns, this time to save a local community center from the greedy hands of evil developers. In the best Judy Garland/Mickey Rooney tradition, they decide to put on a show. Simple, rather predictable plot provides the anchor for lots of music and plenty of acrobatic dancing.

BREAK OF HEARTS 1935
★ **NR Drama 1:20 B&W**
Dir: Phillip Moeller *Cast:* Katharine Hepburn, Charles Boyer, John Beal, Jean Hersholt, Sam Hardy, Inez Courtney
▶ Struggling composer Hepburn falls for

world-famous conductor Boyer, but leaves him when she learns of his many affairs. Boyer sinks into alcoholism until Hepburn returns to redeem him. Weepy melodrama is dull and often improbable, despite stars' accomplished performances.

BREAKOUT 1975
★★ **PG Action-Adventure 1:36**
☑ Explicit language, violence
Dir: Tom Gries *Cast:* Charles Bronson, Jill Ireland, Robert Duvall, Randy Quaid, John Huston
▶ Texas bush pilot Bronson is hired by Ireland to liberate her husband Duvall, who has been unjustly imprisoned in a Mexican jail. Huston plays Duvall's evil grandfather, who is behind the frame-up. Hardhitting, realistic escape melodrama for fans of Bronson and action.

BREAKTHROUGH 1979 West German
★★★ **PG War 1:51**
☑ Adult situations, explicit language, violence
Dir: Andrew V. McLaglen *Cast:* Richard Burton, Robert Mitchum, Rod Steiger, Helmut Griem, Curt Jurgens, Michael Parks
▶ Despondent German officer Burton becomes entangled in a plot to assassinate Hitler, maintaining his command long enough to ensure the American seizure of a town pivotal to the Allied victory. Not the usual one-sided pro-American drama, a humane look at individuals on both sides with plenty of action. Sequel to *Cross of Iron.*

BREATHLESS 1961 French
★★ **NR Drama 1:30 B&W**
Dir: Jean-Luc Godard *Cast:* Jean-Paul Belmondo, Jean Seberg, Daniel Boulanger, Jean-Pierre Melville, Liliane Robin, Henri-Jacques Huet
▶ Small-time hood Belmondo, on the run from the law, hooks up with bohemian American Seberg in Paris. Highly influential cult film, a textbook of jump cuts, offbeat camera angles, and improvised acting, legitimized French New Wave directors for an international audience. Story by François Truffaut. Filmed again in 1983 with Richard Gere. French title: *A Bout de Souffle.* ⑤

BREATHLESS 1983
★★ **R Drama 1:40**
☑ Nudity, adult situations, explicit language, violence
Dir: Jim McBride *Cast:* Richard Gere,

Valerie Kaprisky, Art Metrano, John P. Ryan, William Tepper
▶ Updated remake of the 1959 French classic switches the setting to Los Angeles, but retains the basic plot. Gere plays a small-time hood on the run from the cops; Kaprisky is a French college student who can't fight her attraction to him. As the cops close in, she realizes she may have to betray him. Highly stylized, with a bold color scheme and pounding rock soundtrack.

BREED APART, A 1986
★ ★ ★ ★ R Action-Adventure 1:41
☑ Nudity, adult situations, explicit language, violence
Dir: Philippe Mora *Cast:* Rutger Hauer, Powers Boothe, Kathleen Turner, Donald Pleasence, John Dennis Johnston
▶ Vet-turned-conservationist Hauer battles famous mountain climber Boothe over a nest of rare bald eagle eggs. Turner plays a local merchant who has to choose between them. Beautiful mountain scenery (shot on location in North Carolina) provides an attractive background to this offbeat adventure.

BREWSTER McCLOUD 1970
☆ R Comedy 1:44
☑ Nudity, adult situations, explicit language
Dir: Robert Altman *Cast:* Bud Cort, Sally Kellerman, Michael Murphy, William Windom, Shelley Duvall
▶ Odd young Cort lives in the Houston Astrodome while developing a pair of wings to support his fantasy of flight. Eventually he's linked to a series of murders in which the victims are covered with bird droppings. Altman's surreal, satiric fantasy has garnered a cult following and is reportedly the director's favorite among his films.

BREWSTER'S MILLIONS 1945
★ ★ NR Comedy 1:19 B&W
Dir: Allan Dwan *Cast:* Dennis O'Keefe, Helen Walker, Eddie "Rochester" Anderson, June Havoc, Gail Patrick, Mischa Auer
▶ Soldier O'Keefe returns home and discovers he stands to inherit a multimillion-dollar windfall if he can spend $1 million within two months. Oft-filmed property (most recently with Richard Pryor in 1985) gets pretty funny treatment here.

BREWSTER'S MILLIONS 1985
★ ★ ★ ★ PG Comedy 1:41
☑ Violence

Dir: Walter Hill *Cast:* Richard Pryor, John Candy, Lonette McKee, Stephen Collins, Jerry Orbach, Hume Cronyn
▶ Frantic, large-scale updating of the venerable play has Pryor as a minor league pitcher who must spend $30 million in a month to inherit a vast fortune. Lawyers try to cheat him out of the money, but they haven't counted on his pals: beautiful accountant McKee and chubby teammate Candy (an excellent foil for Pryor). Although first staged in 1907, the premise is still delightful. (CC)

BRIAN'S SONG 1970
★ ★ ★ ★ ★ G Biography/MFTV 1:13
Dir: Buzz Kulik *Cast:* James Caan, Billy Dee Williams, Jack Warden, Bud Furillo, Shelley Fabares
▶ Heartbreaking true-life story of the friendship between Chicago Bears football stars Brian Piccolo (Caan) and Gale Sayers (Williams) was one of the most popular of all made-for-TV movies. Dealing honestly with Piccolo's fatal cancer, the story is a rich, rewarding experience full of life and hope. Based on Sayers's *I Am Third*. Winner of many awards, with a sensitive screenplay by William Blinn and beautiful Michel Legrand score. (CC)

BRIDE, THE 1985
★ PG-13 Horror 1:58
☑ Nudity, violence
Dir: Franc Roddam *Cast:* Sting, Jennifer Beals, Geraldine Page, Clancy Brown, David Rappaport, Phil Daniels
▶ Dr. Frankenstein (Sting) creates wife (Beals) for his monster Victor (Brown), but ends up falling in love with the creature himself. Victor escapes and joins a circus with dwarf Rappaport, but after a tragic murder he returns to claim his bride. Intriguing remake of 1935 film presents a more faithful interpretation of Mary Shelley's characters. Rock star Sting turns in a magnetic performance, but Brown and Rappaport have the best moments. (CC)

BRIDE OF FRANKENSTEIN, THE 1935
★ ★ ★ NR Horror 1:15 B&W
Dir: James Whale *Cast:* Boris Karloff, Elsa Lanchester, Colin Clive, Ernest Thesiger, Valerie Hobson, Dwight Frye
▶ Superior sequel to the 1931 *Frankenstein* focuses on mad doctor Clive's disastrous attempt to create a bride (Lanchester) for unhappy monster (Karloff). In this horror classic, director Whale

mixes macabre black comedy with poignancy, especially in the famous scene where the blind hermit befriends the monster. Thesiger, as Clive's eerie rival, is nearly as scary as the great Karloff.

BRIDGE OF SAN LUIS REY, THE 1944
★ NR Drama 1:29 B&W
Dir: Rowland V. Lee *Cast:* Lynn Bari, Akim Tamiroff, Francis Lederer, Alla Nazimova, Louis Calhern, Blanche Yurka
▶ Faithful adaptation of Thornton Wilder's novel examines the reactions of superstitious eighteenth-century Peruvians to the collapse of a mountain bridge that kills five villagers. Slowly paced drama about an intriguing subject is notable for its accomplished cast and unusual production design. Score by Dimitri Tiomkin received an Oscar nomination.

BRIDGE ON THE RIVER KWAI, THE
1957 British
★★★★★ NR War/Drama 2:44
Dir: David Lean *Cast:* Alec Guinness, William Holden, Jack Hawkins, Sessue Hayakawa, Geoffrey Horne
▶ Superlative World War II adventure about Allied POWs forced to build a strategic bridge for the Japanese in the jungles of Thailand. Guinness won the Best Actor Oscar as the proud colonel determined to complete the bridge despite British saboteurs. Beautifully realized production also won Oscars for Best Picture, Direction, Cinematography, Score, Editing, and Screenplay (Carl Foreman and Michael Wilson were both blacklisted at the time, so the award was given to Pierre Boulle, author of the original novel).

BRIDGE TOO FAR, A 1977 British
★★★★★ PG War 3:03
☑ Explicit language, mild violence
Dir: Richard Attenborough *Cast:* Dirk Bogarde, James Caan, Michael Caine, Sean Connery, Edward Fox, Gene Hackman
▶ Multimillion-dollar version of Cornelius Ryan's best-seller. Gripping tale of Operation Market Garden, the Allied Force's attempt to cross the Rhine into Germany—resulting in history's largest airborne assault. Star studded and action packed, with terrific battle scenes, strong dramatic sequences and excellent photography of Dutch locations. Despite three-hour length and disconsolate mood, an epic of great proportions.

BRIEF ENCOUNTER 1945 British
★★★ NR Romance 1:26 B&W
Dir: David Lean *Cast:* Celia Johnson, Trevor Howard, Stanley Holloway, Joyce Carey, Cyril Raymond
▶ Chance train station meeting between married doctor Howard and housewife Johnson leads to an ultimately doomed romance. Adaptation of Noel Coward play is a beautiful and poignant classic, thanks to the superb leads and director Lean, whose intimate touch here will be a revelation to those only familiar with his later spectacles: *A Passage to India* and *Lawrence of Arabia*. Celebrated score features Rachmaninoff's *Second Piano Concerto*.

BRIGADOON 1954
★★★★ G Musical 1:48
Dir: Vincente Minnelli *Cast:* Gene Kelly, Cyd Charisse, Van Johnson, Elaine Stewart, Barry Jones
▶ Americans Kelly and Johnson happen upon a mythical Scottish kingdom that comes to life only once every 100 years. Kelly falls in love with Charisse and must choose between her world and his. Screen adaptation of one of the best-loved Lerner and Loewe musicals features songs like "The Heather on the Hill" and "It's Almost Like Being in Love."

BRIGHT LIGHTS, BIG CITY 1988
★★★ R Drama 1:34
☑ Adult situations, explicit language
Dir: James Bridges *Cast:* Michael J. Fox, Kiefer Sutherland, Dianne Wiest, Phoebe Cates, Swoosie Kurtz, Frances Sternhagen
▶ From the best-selling book about Manhattan life in the too-fast lane. Starring Fox as a yuppie magazine fact-checker at the end of his rope: mother Wiest has recently died of cancer, bitchy wife Cates has left him, and he's snorting cocaine to oblivion. Smirking Sutherland is Ted Allagash, his partner in disco and drug excess. Tracy Pollan (real-life Mrs. Michael J. Fox) appears as Ted's cousin. Fine camerawork, soundtrack, and supporting actors still add up to bright lights, big deal. (CC)

BRIGHTON BEACH MEMOIRS 1986
★★★ PG-13 Comedy 1:50
☑ Adult situations, explicit language
Dir: Gene Saks *Cast:* Blythe Danner, Bob Dishy, Stacey Glick, Judith Ivey, Jonathan Silverman
▶ Semiautobiographical comedy based

on Neil Simon's hit Broadway play. Eugene (Silverman) is a 1930s teen growing up in Brooklyn in a house so small that no one is afforded any privacy. While grappling with raging hormones, Eugene comes to the realization that he'll never pitch for the Yankees. Warmly nostalgic period piece. **(CC)**

BRIMSTONE AND TREACLE 1982 British
★ R Drama 1:25
☑ Nudity, adult situations, explicit language, violence
Dir: Richard Loncraine *Cast:* Denholm Elliott, Joan Plowright, Sting, Suzanna Hamilton
▶ Offbeat psychological thriller featuring rock 'n' roll singer Sting in his first starring role. He invades the drab lives of married couple Elliot and Plowright, who are devoted to their daughter, paralyzed by a hit-and-run accident. The mother welcomes his attention; the father fears he has an evil purpose in mind, which of course he does. Sting himself provides the musical score, along with the Police and the Go-Gos. Screenplay by Dennis Potter, based on the British teleplay.

BRINGING UP BABY 1938
★★★★ NR Comedy 1:42 B&W
Dir: Howard Hawks *Cast:* Katharine Hepburn, Cary Grant, Charles Ruggles, Barry Fitzgerald, May Robson, Walter Catlett
▶ Hysterically funny screwball comedy virtually defines the genre. Shy, bespectacled paleontologist Grant needs just one bone to complete his prized dinosaur skeleton—the same bone snatched by dizzy heiress Hepburn's dog (Asta of the Thin Man movies). A whirlwind plot follows as hurricane Hepburn wins the reluctant Grant's heart. Breathless direction by Hawks and two terrific comic performances by the stars.

BRING ME THE HEAD OF ALFREDO GARCIA 1974
★★ R Action-Adventure 1:52
☑ Brief nudity, adult situations, explicit language, graphic violence
Dir: Sam Peckinpah *Cast:* Warren Oates, Isela Vega, Gig Young, Robert Webber, Helmut Dantine, Kris Kristofferson
▶ Mexican millionaire hires seedy bar owner Oates to kill Garcia, the man who seduced his daughter. Discovering that Garcia is already dead, Oates chops off his head to receive his fee, and then

fights off hitmen, bikers, and other thugs who also want the money. Jarring, bloody adventure has plenty of Peckinpah's trademark violence.

BRING ON THE NIGHT 1985 British
★★★ PG-13 Documentary/Music 1:37
☑ Adult situations, explicit language
Dir: Michael Apted *Cast:* Sting, Omar Hakim, Darryl Jones, Kenny Kirkland, Branford Marsalis
▶ Rockumentary traces the founding of a new jazz-oriented band by Sting, former lead singer of the Police, from rehearsals in the lush French countryside to a premiere Paris concert. Devotees of the star will thrill to behind-the-scenes footage. Concert includes such Sting favorites as "Roxanne," "If You Love Somebody Set Them Free," and "Message in a Bottle." **(CC)**

BRINK'S JOB, THE 1978
★★★★ PG Comedy 1:58
☑ Explicit language, mild violence
Dir: William Friedkin *Cast:* Peter Falk, Peter Boyle, Allen Goorwitz (Garfield), Warren Oates, Gena Rowlands, Paul Sorvino
▶ Suspense and laughs as ringleader Falk and a gang of petty crooks attempt the crime of the century by robbing $2.7 million from Boston's Brink's vault. Eventually costing the government ten times that amount, they're caught less than a week before the statute of limitations runs out. Vivid re-creation of the famous 1950 heist, blessed with a light touch and sturdy cast.

BRITANNIA HOSPITAL 1983 British
☆ R Comedy 1:56
☑ Nudity, explicit language
Dir: Lindsay Anderson *Cast:* Leonard Rossiter, Graham Crowden, Malcolm McDowell, Joan Plowright, Jill Bennett
▶ Chaos reigns at London's venerable Britannia Hospital as the administration copes with riots, strikes, and mass disorder prior to a visit from the Royal Family. Humor is very British, and combined with black comedy elements may not be everyone's cup of tea. McDowell reprises his *O Lucky Man!* role.

BROADCAST NEWS 1987
★★★★ R Comedy/Drama 2:13
☑ Brief nudity, adult situations, explicit language
Dir: James L. Brooks *Cast:* William Hurt,

Albert Brooks, Holly Hunter, Robert Prosky, Lois Chiles, Jack Nicholson
► Brooks's clever, poignant look at three TV newspeople struggling with the problems of love and work in the eighties. Highly principled producer Jane Craig (Hunter) is attracted to charismatic anchorman Tom Grunick (Hurt), even though he represents everything she despises professionally. Her best friend Aaron Altman (Brooks), a brainy journalist who lacks the slickness to make it on TV, is hopelessly in love with her. Terrific dialogue, wonderful performances; fully rounded, very human characterizations. Oscar nominations for Picture, Director, and the three leads. **(CC)**

BROADWAY DANNY ROSE 1984
★★ **PG Comedy 1:24 B&W**
☑ Adult situations, explicit language, mild violence, adult humor
Dir: Woody Allen *Cast:* Woody Allen, Mia Farrow, Nick Apollo Forte, Sandy Baron, Corbett Monica, Jackie Gayle
► Danny Rose (Allen), a Broadway agent with a good heart and a bad eye for talent (clients include a blind xylophone player), finds himself on the lam from Mafia hitmen along with gangster's widow Tina (Farrow), the girlfriend of Rose's one hot client, Italian crooner Forte. Farrow eschews her usual delicate persona and does wonders as the gum-chewing, bleached-blond Tina. Sharp dialogue and excellent black-and-white photography in this enchanting comic fable.

BROADWAY MELODY OF 1938 1937
★★★ **NR Musical 1:50 B&W**
Dir: Roy Del Ruth *Cast:* Robert Taylor, Eleanor Powell, George Murphy, Binnie Barnes, Buddy Ebsen, Sophie Tucker
► Broadway producer Taylor can't finance his next show unless Powell's horse wins at Saratoga. Plot is little more than a thin frame for nine songs, including "Everybody Sing" and "Follow in My Footsteps." Powell's tap solos are superb; Tucker reprises her vaudeville routines; but the real highlight is a young Judy Garland on the verge of stardom singing "Dear Mr. Gable." **(CC)**

BROADWAY MELODY OF 1940 1940
★★★ **NR Musical 1:42 B&W**
Dir: Norman Taurog *Cast:* Fred Astaire, Eleanor Powell, George Murphy, Frank Morgan, Ian Hunter
► Astaire and Murphy's dancing team

splits up when Murphy lands a solo spot in a show. While Fred woos Powell, Murphy becomes an insufferable star—until he realizes he still needs Fred's help. The stars breeze through this light, glossy MGM comedy. Fourth and final entry in the Melody series has a wonderful Cole Porter score ("I Concentrate on You") and a knock-out duet to "Begin the Beguine."

BROKEN ARROW 1950
★★★ **NR Western 1:32**
Dir: Delmer Daves *Cast:* James Stewart, Jeff Chandler, Debra Paget, Will Geer, Jay Silverheels
► In Civil War Arizona, ex–Union soldier Stewart marries Apache Paget, befriends the warrior Cochise (Chandler), and teams with him to settle battles between whites and Indians. Terrific adventure delivers action, romance, scenery, fine performances, and even a rare (for Hollywood) pro-Indian message. **(CC)**

BROKEN LANCE 1954
★★★ **NR Western 1:36**
Dir: Edward Dmytryk *Cast:* Spencer Tracy, Robert Wagner, Jean Peters, Richard Widmark, Katy Jurado, Hugh O'Brian
► Ruthless cattle baron Tracy suffers a stroke struggling to keep his empire intact. Faithful son Wagner is forced into a deadly feud with his scheming brothers (including Widmark in a typically nasty role). Solid, intelligent Western, with Oscar-nominated Jurado particularly impressive as Tracy's wife. Philip Yordan won an Oscar for Original Story (loosely based on *King Lear*).

BROKEN RAINBOW 1985
★★ **NR Documentary 1:09 C/B&W**
Dir: Victoria Mudd *Cast:* Narrated by Martin Sheen, Burgess Meredith, Buffy Sainte-Marie
► Academy Award–winning documentary dramatizes the continuing exploitation of Indians from a native American point of view. Director Mudd traces the Navajo tribe from 1868, when they were forced off their lands, to the present, when they begin protesting the wholesale ecological destruction of their territory.

BRONCO BILLY 1980
★★★ **PG Comedy 1:56**
☑ Adult situations, explicit language
Dir: Clint Eastwood *Cast:* Clint East-

wood, Sondra Locke, Geoffrey Lewis, Scatman Crothers, Bill McKinney
▶ Engaging low-key comedy about the love-hate relationship between Eastwood, owner of a flea-bitten Wild West show, and his real-life girlfriend Locke, who plays a spoiled heiress. Warm, gentle story was a real change of pace for Eastwood, who acts and directs with winning simplicity. He even sings with Merle Haggard (who also performs two solo country-western hits).

BROOD, THE 1979 Canadian
★★ R Horror 1:31
☑ Explicit language, graphic violence
Dir: David Cronenberg *Cast:* Oliver Reed, Samantha Eggar, Art Hindle, Cindy Hines, Nuala FitzGerald
▶ Disturbing, extremely gruesome shocker about mad scientist Reed, whose genetic experiments go disastrously awry, spreading a lethal plague on an unsuspecting city. Mentally disturbed mother Eggar's children may hold the key to understanding the virus—if a bizarre mutant doesn't kill them first. Fans of cult director Cronenberg champion the script's allegorical touches.

BROTHER, CAN YOU SPARE A DIME? 1975
★★★ PG Documentary 1:45 B&W
Dir: Philippe Mora
▶ In his portrait of the 1930s Depression era, director Mora uses fascinating, previously unseen footage. Compilation documentary intercuts newsreel film of real-life figures with clips from Hollywood classics. Inventive editing, effective use of music. Prime example of its kind.

BROTHER FROM ANOTHER PLANET, THE 1984
★ NR Sci-Fi/Comedy 1:49
☑ Adult situations, explicit language, violence, adult humor
Dir: John Sayles *Cast:* Joe Morton, Darryl Edwards, Steve James, Leonard Jackson, Bill Cobbs
▶ Morton, a mute black alien, escapes from slavery on another planet and arrives in Harlem via Ellis Island. Wise, winsome comedy-allegory from writer/director Sayles gently mixes satire with social comment. Wonderful work from Morton as he adjusts to a strange new world. Sayles appears as an alien bounty hunter tracking Morton. (CC)

BROTHERHOOD, THE 1968
★★★ NR Drama 1:38

Dir: Martin Ritt *Cast:* Kirk Douglas, Alex Cord, Irene Papas, Luther Adler, Susan Strasberg, Eduardo Ciannelli
▶ Douglas produced and stars as mafioso who gets involved in power struggle with younger brother Cord. After Douglas kills Cord's father-in-law Adler, Cord accepts the task of murdering Douglas. Well-done mob tale features fine work from Douglas and Cord.

BROTHERHOOD OF SATAN, THE 1971
★ PG Horror 1:32
☑ Violence
Dir: Bernard McEveety *Cast:* Strother Martin, L. Q. Jones, Charles Bateman, Ahna Capri, Charles Robinson
▶ Producer Jones plays the sheriff of an isolated small town who can't explain why twenty-six citizens have been butchered in four days. Survivors spread the rumor that witches are responsible. Low-budget thriller effectively exploits mob hysteria.

BROTHER JOHN 1971
★★ PG Comedy/Drama 1:34
☑ Adult situations, violence
Dir: James Goldstone *Cast:* Sidney Poitier, Will Geer, Bradford Dillman, Paul Winfield, Beverly Todd
▶ Mysterious Poitier returns to small Southern town when his mother becomes fatally ill. Sheriff Dillman fears Poitier will stir up local blacks, as there are hints that he may be the messiah. Dated, inadequately constructed screenplay begins with interesting clues but never brings tale to climax. Geer outshines Poitier, whose performance is lackluster.

BROTHERS KARAMAZOV, THE 1958
★★★★ NR Drama 2:30
Dir: Richard Brooks *Cast:* Maria Schell, Yul Brynner, Lee J. Cobb, William Shatner, Claire Bloom
▶ Sin, salvation, greed, and depravity are examined in this sophisticated story of a lecherous father, his four sons (one illegitimate), their loves and tragedies. Good-looking all-star cast; based on Dostoyevsky's classic Russian novel.

BROTHER SUN, SISTER MOON 1973 British/Italian
★★★ PG Drama 2:01
☑ Adult situations
Dir: Franco Zeffirelli *Cast:* Graham Faulkner, Judi Bowker, Alec Guinness, Leigh Lawson, Kenneth Cranham
▶ Lyrical version of the life of St. Francis of Assisi with Faulkner as the young soldier

who renounces wealth to found a religious order. Beautiful images overwhelm the plot, which assumes a mystical, wide-eyed approach to Francis's achievements. Guinness has a small role as the Pope who supports Francis. Folk-singer Donovan wrote the soundtrack.

BROWNING VERSION, THE 1951 British
★★★ NR Drama 1:29 B&W
Dir: Anthony Asquith *Cast:* Michael Redgrave, Jean Kent, Nigel Patrick, Wilfrid Hyde-White, Ronald Howard
▶ About-to-retire prep-school teacher Redgrave with unfaithful wife Kent reminisces about his career and realizes he has lost touch with his ideals. Intimate portrayal of an unlikely character: rigid and reserved on the outside, complex and human inside. Redgrave is magnificent and few eyes will remain dry at his closing speech, in which he apologizes for his failures as a man and teacher.

BRUBAKER 1980
★★★★★ R Drama 2:12
☑ Brief nudity, explicit language, violence
Dir: Stuart Rosenberg *Cast:* Robert Redford, Yaphet Kotto, Jane Alexander, Murray Hamilton, David Keith, Morgan Freeman
▶ Reform-minded warden Redford disguises himself as a prisoner to investigate a notoriously harsh prison. He uncovers evidence that prisoners are being systematically murdered, then has to confront corrupt prison officials who want to cover up the conspiracy. Earnest drama was based on a true story. Screenplay by W. D. Richter was nominated for an Oscar.

BRUTE FORCE 1947
★★★ NR Action-Adventure 1:36 B&W
Dir: Jules Dassin *Cast:* Burt Lancaster, Hume Cronyn, Charles Bickford, Yvonne De Carlo, Ann Blyth, Ella Raines
▶ Hard-boiled prisoner Lancaster clashes with sadistic guard Cronyn. Lancaster enlists fellow inmates in a plan to bust out of the joint; Cronyn tries to bust up the break. Gripping and tense prison drama features one of Cronyn's best screen performances.

BUCCANEER, THE 1938
★★ NR Action-Adventure 2:04 B&W
Dir: Cecil B. DeMille *Cast:* Fredric March, Franciska Gaal, Akim Tamiroff, Margot Grahame, Walter Brennan, Ian Keith

▶ March stars as the real-life nineteenth-century pirate Jean Lafitte. Story traces his transition from looter to war hero as he aids U.S. forces against the British in the War of 1812's Battle of New Orleans. DeMille brings his patented epic touch to this stylish swashbuckler.

BUCCANEER, THE 1959
★★ NR Action-Adventure 2:01
Dir: Anthony Quinn *Cast:* Yul Brynner, Charlton Heston, Claire Bloom, Charles Boyer, Inger Stevens, Lorne Greene
▶ During the Battle of New Orleans, pirate Jean Lafitte (Brynner) allies himself with American general Andrew Jackson (Heston) to defeat the British and end the War of 1812. Producer Cecil B. DeMille's remake of his own 1938 film is better cast than the original but somehow not a better film.

BUCK AND THE PREACHER 1972
★★ PG Western 1:42
☑ Explicit language
Dir: Sidney Poitier *Cast:* Sidney Poitier, Harry Belafonte, Ruby Dee, Cameron Mitchell, Denny Miller, Nita Talbot
▶ Two blacks, bunco artist/preacher Belafonte and good guy Poitier, team up to outwit evil whites, including Mitchell, a greedy bounty hunter trying to catch runaway slaves in the old West. Thin story enlivened by the charm and charisma of Poitier and Belafonte. Poitier's directorial debut.

BUCK PRIVATES 1941
★★ NR Comedy 1:24 B&W
Dir: Arthur Lubin *Cast:* Bud Abbott, Lou Costello, The Andrews Sisters, Lee Bowman, Nat Pendleton
▶ Early Bud and Lou vehicle is one of their best efforts. Army comedy high jinks as the boys go to boot camp during the early days of World War II. Also on hand: the Andrews Sisters (who sing "Boogie Woogie Bugle Boy from Company B" and several others) and Stooge Shemp Howard in a bit part. Spawned a 1947 sequel.

BUDDY BUDDY 1981
★★★ R Comedy 1:36
☑ Brief nudity, explicit language, mild violence
Dir: Billy Wilder *Cast:* Jack Lemmon, Walter Matthau, Paula Prentiss, Klaus Kinski, Dana Elcar, Miles Chapin
▶ Mob hitman Matthau rents a hotel room to rub out a government witness but a suicidal Lemmon, in despair over wife Prentiss's affair with sex doctor Kinski,

occupies the room next door and keeps foiling Matthau. Fourth teaming of these two stars has an off-the-wall plot taken from the French film *A Pain in the A.* The last film to date of director Wilder.

BUDDY HOLLY STORY, THE 1978
★★★★ PG Biography/Music 1:39
☑ Explicit language
Dir: Steve Rash *Cast:* Gary Busey, Don Stroud, Charles Martin Smith, Maria Richwine, Conrad Janis, Amy Johnston
▶ Honest, enjoyable biography of rock 'n' roll star Buddy Holly. Bravura performance by Busey, Oscar-nominated for his uncanny impersonation of the Lubbock, Texas, musician who achieved early fame before his tragic death. Use of live music (which won the Oscar for Song Adaptation) and accurate period detail brought the late 1950s back to life. Broad sampling of Holly's music: "That'll Be the Day," "Maybe Baby," "Peggy Sue," "Oh Boy," "Every Day," etc.

BUDDY SYSTEM, THE 1984
★★★★ PG Comedy 1:50
☑ Adult situations, explicit language
Dir: Glenn Jordan *Cast:* Richard Dreyfuss, Susan Sarandon, Nancy Allen, Jean Stapleton, Wil Wheaton
▶ Security guard and aspiring writer Dreyfuss befriends single mother Sarandon. Her young son wants a father, but Dreyfuss is too busy coping with dizzy girlfriend Allen to realize what he's missing. Likable stars bring warmth to this pleasant romantic trifle. (CC)

BUFFALO BILL AND THE INDIANS, OR SITTING BULL'S HISTORY LESSON 1976
☆ PG Western 2:00
☑ Adult situations, explicit language
Dir: Robert Altman *Cast:* Paul Newman, Joel Grey, Kevin McCarthy, Harvey Keitel, Geraldine Chaplin, Will Sampson
▶ Altman's follow-up to *Nashville* is a sprawling, revisionist look at how Buffalo Bill (Newman) exploited the press to become the nation's first Wild West star. Offbeat, convoluted screenplay (by Altman and Alan Rudolph, based on Arthur Kopit's play *Indians*) gives a weird, hallucinatory cast to the proceedings. Burt Lancaster has a sharp cameo as Ned Buntline, the writer who actually invented most of Bill's adventures.

BUG 1975
★ PG Horror 1:40
☑ Violence

Dir: Jeannot Szwarc *Cast:* Bradford Dillman, Joanna Miles, Richard Gilliland, Jamie Smith Jackson, Alan Fudge
▶ An earthquake in California unleashes a plague of prehistoric beetles who set their victims on fire. Attempts by scientists to eradicate the insects end in failure. Often nasty film with obvious special effects. B-movie master William Castle's last production (he also had a hand in the screenplay).

BUGS BUNNY/ROAD RUNNER MOVIE, THE 1979
★★★★★ G Animation 1:23
Dir: Chuck Jones *Cast:* Voice of Mel Blanc
▶ Animated anthology marks the return of the world's most popular rabbit. (Sorry, Peter.) Released in honor of Bugs Bunny's fortieth anniversary. Bugs narrates, joined by zany cohorts Daffy Duck, Yosemite Sam, and Road Runner. Funny opening parodies *Star Wars* and *Superman.*

BUGS BUNNY'S 3RD MOVIE: 1001 RABBIT TALES 1982
★★★★★ G Animation 1:14
Dir: David Detiege, Art Davis, Bill Perez *Cast:* Voice of Mel Blanc
▶ Bugs and Daffy are competing book salesmen for "Rambling House Publications" in Friz Freleng's blend of classic cartoons and new footage of the famous rabbit and his pals. Vocals provided by Mel Blanc, Man of 1000 Voices.

BUGSY MALONE 1976 British
★★★ G Comedy 1:33
Dir: Alan Parker *Cast:* Scott Baio, Jodie Foster, Florrie Dugger, John Cassisi, Martin Lev
▶ Unusual musical spoof of gangster films: the tough-guy clichés are left intact, but they're performed by an all-kid cast whose guns shoot whipped cream instead of bullets. Plot about a feud between rival mobs relies heavily on slapstick chases. Delightful, sometimes coy story should please adults as well as children. Paul Williams did the score.

BULL DURHAM 1988
★★★★ R Comedy/Sports 1:55
☑ Nudity, adult situations, explicit language
Dir: Ron Shelton *Cast:* Kevin Costner, Susan Sarandon, Tim Robbins, Trey Wilson, Robert Wuhl, Jenny Robertson
▶ Every year Southern belle/baseball groupie Sarandon dedicates herself to a

new player on the minor league Durham Bulls. This season's candidates are bonus-baby Robbins, a pitcher with a million-dollar arm and two-cent brain, and veteran Costner, a shrewd catcher with the job of prepping Robbins for the major leagues. Romantic triangle yields comical squeeze play. Saucy, witty, and authentic screenplay from writer/director Shelton, former bush leaguer, hits homer.

BULLETPROOF 1988
★★★ R Action-Adventure 1:34
☑ Rape, brief nudity, adult situations, explicit language, violence
Dir: Steve Carver *Cast:* Gary Busey, Darlanne Fluegel, Henry Silva, Rene Enriquez, L. Q. Jones
▶ As the credits announce, "Gary Busey *is* Bulletproof," a renegade cop sent to Central America to recover Thunderblast, a top-secret tank that's fallen into the hands of the Communists. The bad guys have also kidnapped Fluegel, Bulletproof's lover, so he's fighting mad. Busey and Fluegel make a great team in this fast-paced B-movie.

BULLFIGHTER AND THE LADY 1951
★ NR Drama 1:27 B&W
Dir: Budd Boetticher *Cast:* Robert Stack, Gilbert Roland, Katy Jurado, Joy Page, Virginia Grey, John Hubbard
▶ American Stack gets bullfighting lessons from Mexican pro Roland but causes his mentor's death in the ring. Stack gets a chance at redemption in this authentic drama from director Boetticher, a bullfighting buff best known for his Randolph Scott Westerns, and producer John Wayne (best known for his own Westerns).

BULLFIGHTERS, THE 1945
★★ NR Comedy 1:01 B&W
Dir: Malcolm St. Clair *Cast:* Stan Laurel, Oliver Hardy, Margo Woode, Richard Lane, Carol Andrews
▶ Inept private dicks Laurel and Hardy travel south of the border on a case, and Stan's resemblance to a star toreador causes comic complications. Made toward the end of the duo's illustrious career and not top-notch stuff, but some amusing bits.

BULLITT 1968
★★★★ PG Action-Adventure 1:53
☑ Mild violence
Dir: Peter Yates *Cast:* Steve McQueen, Robert Vaughn, Jacqueline Bisset, Robert Duvall, Simon Oakland

▶ Suspenseful, influential cop thriller with McQueen creating an indelible image as the tough-guy prototype Bullitt, pursuing the killers of a government witness. Great action scenes, including an incredibly exciting car chase through the streets of San Francisco and a slam-bang airport finale.

BULLSHOT 1985 British
★★ PG Comedy 1:26
☑ Adult situations, explicit language
Dir: Dick Clement *Cast:* Alan Shearman, Diz White, Ron House, Frances Tomelty, Ron Pember, Mel Smith
▶ Shearman (who, with White and House, adapted his British stage hit) stars as Bullshot Crummond, a parody of English hero Bulldog Drummond, who comes to aid of dizzy White when German count kidnaps her scientist father. Preposterous plot full of slapstick silliness; endearing cast, especially White, but British wit is a matter of taste.

BUNNY LAKE IS MISSING 1965
★★ NR Mystery-Suspense 1:47 B&W
Dir: Otto Preminger *Cast:* Laurence Olivier, Carol Lynley, Keir Dullea, Noel Coward, Martita Hunt
▶ In London, American expatriate Lynley's daughter vanishes without a trace. English detective Olivier investigates and begins to wonder if Lynley is fabricating everything, including a daughter who doesn't exist. Intriguing puzzler from director Preminger.

BUNNY O'HARE 1972
☆ PG Comedy 1:32
☑ Explicit language
Dir: Gerd Oswald *Cast:* Bette Davis, Ernest Borgnine, Jack Cassidy, Joan Delaney, John Astin
▶ Senior-citizen Davis, evicted by a cruel banker, teams up with plumbing supply salesman Borgnine to get revenge. Disguised as hippies, they embark on a successful crime wave. Soon other robbers are imitating their disguises. Bizarre comedy will leave most viewers speechless. Davis sued the producers to prevent the film's release.

'BURBS, THE 1989
★★★ PG Comedy 1:42
☑ Explicit language, mild violence
Dir: Joe Dante *Cast:* Tom Hanks, Bruce Dern, Carrie Fisher, Rick Ducommun, Corey Feldman, Henry Gibson
▶ Suburbanites Hanks, Dern, and Ducommun are nonplussed by their new

neighbors, the sinister Klopeks, and use guerrilla tactics to learn the secret behind their nocturnal activities. Large-scale comedy concentrates on slapstick and satirical jabs at suburbia, but failed to win over audiences.

BURGLAR 1987
★★★★ **R Action-Adventure 1:40**
☑ Brief nudity, adult situations, explicit language, mild violence
Dir: Hugh Wilson   *Cast:* Whoopi Goldberg, Bob Goldthwait, Lesley Ann Warren, G. W. Bailey, James Hardy
► Ex-con Goldberg, blackmailed into committing one last burglary by retired cop Bailey, must prove her innocence when blamed for a murder. Comedy/thriller from director Wilson features plenty of shtick from Goldberg, and from Goldthwait as her wacked-out best friend. **(CC)**

BURN! 1970 Italian/French
★★ **PG Drama 1:52**
☑ Nudity, violence
Dir: Gillo Pontecorvo   *Cast:* Marlon Brando, Ernesto Marquez, Renato Salvatori, Norman Hill, Tom Lyons
► British agent Brando incites Black revolution on a Portugese-controlled Caribbean island, then betrays the revolt's leader when the rebellion succeeds. Overly complex, convoluted political story is emotionally distant if topical and provocative. Brando is fine playing a difficult and unattractive character.

BURNING, THE 1981
★★ **R Horror 1:30**
☑ Adult situations, graphic violence
Dir: Tony Maylam   *Cast:* Brian Mathews, Leah Ayres, Brian Backer, Larry Joshua, Jason Alexander, Fisher Stevens
► Drunken camp handyman is badly disfigured when kids set him afire in practical joke. Five years later, the handyman returns to menace the campers with garden shears. Formula story is professionally filmed but overly familiar; delivers requisite number of chills, but characters fail to generate much empathy.

BURNING BED, THE 1984
★★★★ **NR Drama/MFTV 1:36**
☑ Violence
Dir: Robert Greenwald   *Cast:* Farrah Fawcett, Paul LeMat, Richard Masur, Grace Zabriskie, Penelope Milford
► Fawcett, abused by husband LeMat, eventually fights back, killing him by setting their bed on fire while he's still in it.

LeMat's brutality becomes an issue in Fawcett's trial. Shattering true story sustained by Emmy-nominated Fawcett's breakthrough performance; she proves her merits as a serious actress. **(CC)**

BURNING SECRET 1988
U.S/British/German
★★ **PG-13 Drama 1:47**
☑ Adult situations
Dir: Andrew Birkin   *Cast:* Faye Dunaway, Klaus Maria Brandauer, David Eberts, Ian Richardson, John Nettleton, Martin Obernigg
► In 1920s Austria, Dunaway is a young mother who takes her asthmatic son (Eberts) to an Alpine sanatorium. There they meet war-scarred baron Brandauer, who fulfills Eberts's need for male guidance until he turns his attentions to Dunaway, causing Eberts to flee in a jealous rage. Old World romantic drama at times is too stately and refined for its own good.

BURNT OFFERINGS 1976
★★★ **PG Horror 1:55**
☑ Violence
Dir: Dan Curtis   *Cast:* Karen Black, Oliver Reed, Burgess Meredith, Eileen Heckart, Bette Davis
► A clean-cut family rents an ancient mansion from two invalids. The house's evil spirit gradually possesses the family, leading to terror and violence. Moody atmosphere and a fascinating setting (Oakland's Dunsmuir House) account for film's small cult following.

BUSHIDO BLADE, THE 1980 British
★★★ **R Martial Arts 1:34**
☑ Brief nudity, adult situations, explicit language, graphic violence
Dir: Tom Kotani   *Cast:* Richard Boone, Frank Converse, James Earl Jones, Toshiro Mifune, Mako, Sonny Chiba
► Period kung-fu drama set in 1854 describes the efforts of American soldiers to recover a sacred sword needed for a treaty-signing ceremony with Japan. Boone (in his last role) plays Commodore Perry; Mifune repeats his role from the *Shogun* miniseries. Jones and Chiba are limited to cameos. Shot on location in Japan. Also known as *The Bloody Bushido Blade*.

BUSINESS AS USUAL 1988 British
★★ **PG Drama 1:28**
☑ Explicit language
Dir: Lezli-An Barrett   *Cast:* Glenda Jackson, John Thaw, Cathy Tyson, Mark

McGann, Eamon Boland, James Hazeldine

▶ British boutique manager Jackson gets sacked for confronting boss Boland about sexual harassment of employee Tyson. Encouraged by her son McGann and father Keegan, both union activists, Jackson files suit against the boutique's owners, despite the objections of househusband Thaw. Based on a true incident.

BUS RILEY'S BACK IN TOWN 1965
★★ NR Drama 1:33
Dir: Harvey Hart *Cast:* Ann-Margret, Michael Parks, Janet Margolin, Brad Dexter, Jocelyn Brando, Larry Storch
▶ Directionless young Parks leaves Navy, returns to his hometown, and gets involved with two women: nice girl Margolin and trashy sexpot Ann-Margret. Based on a story by playwright William Inge, this has the flavor, but not the quality, of superior Inge work like *Bus Stop*.

BUS STOP 1956
★★★★ NR Romance/Comedy 1:31
Dir: Joshua Logan *Cast:* Marilyn Monroe, Don Murray, Arthur O'Connell, Betty Field, Eileen Heckart, Hope Lange
▶ In Phoenix, voluptuous cafe singer Monroe is pursued by high-spirited rodeo cowboy Murray. She resists but he is persistent; eventually, true love finds its way. Monroe is both sexy and innocent; Oscar-nominated Murray is marvelous. Based on the William Inge Broadway hit.

BUSTED UP 1986
☆ R Action-Adventure 1:32
☑ Explicit language, violence
Dir: Conrad E. Palmisano *Cast:* Paul Coufos, Irene Cara, Stan Shaw, Tony Rosato
▶ Boxer Coufos is in trouble: thugs are threatening to take over his gym, his singer girlfriend Cara wants to leave him, and he's going blind in one eye. He stages a winner-takes-all brawl in a last-ditch effort to pull his life together. Lots of fights, and Cara gets to sing four songs. (CC)

BUSTER AND BILLIE 1974
★★ R Romance 1:30
☑ Rape, adult situations, explicit language, violence
Dir: Daniel Petrie *Cast:* Jan-Michael Vincent, Joan Goodfellow, Pamela Sue Martin, Clifton James, Robert Englund
▶ "The guys all know about Billie," high school heartthrob Vincent is told by buddies in reference to good-time girl Goodfellow. Vincent discovers Goodfellow's more sensitive side, falls in love, but faces violent opposition from local toughs. Pungent period settings in post–World War II Georgia provide backdrop for truly affecting love story.

BUSTIN' LOOSE 1981
★★★★ R Comedy 1:34
☑ Adult situations, explicit language, violence
Dir: Oz Scott *Cast:* Richard Pryor, Cicely Tyson, Alphonso Alexander, Robert Christian, George Coe
▶ Rather than return to jail, parolee Pryor agrees to drive a busload of reform-school kids across country to a Washington farm. Along the way he battles breakdowns, bigots, and antagonistic teacher Tyson who gradually falls in love with him. Despite the rough language, a warm, positive comedy. Pryor's encounter with the KKK is hilarious.

BUTCH AND SUNDANCE: THE EARLY DAYS 1979
★★★ PG Western 1:50
☑ Explicit language, mild violence
Dir: Richard Lester *Cast:* William Katt, Tom Berenger, Jill Eikenberry, Jeff Corey, Arthur Hill
▶ Prequel to *Butch Cassidy and the Sundance Kid* traces the first meeting and subsequent adventures of the legendary partners in crime. Although overshadowed by its hugely popular predecessor, this is an easy-to-take Western on its own terms, as director Lester inventively mixes comedy and action. Katt and Berenger are a likable duo, resembling Redford and Newman physically without mimicking their earlier performances.

BUTCH CASSIDY AND THE SUNDANCE KID 1969
★★★★★ PG Western 1:52
☑ Adult situations, explicit language, violence
Dir: George Roy Hill *Cast:* Robert Redford, Paul Newman, Katharine Ross, Strother Martin, Henry Jones
▶ Immensely entertaining Western classic starring Newman and Redford as the infamous, affable outlaws on the run. Ross is the proper, pristine schoolmarm infatuated with both of them. Stunt-packed and slickly packaged, this box-office smash won four Oscars, including Best Screenplay (William Goldman) and Song ("Raindrops Keep Fallin' on My

Head" by Burt Bacharach and Hal David).

BUTTERFIELD 8 1960
★★★ NR Drama 1:49
Dir: Daniel Mann **Cast:** Elizabeth Taylor, Laurence Harvey, Eddie Fisher, Dina Merrill, Betty Field
▶ Model/prostitute Taylor falls for married Harvey and can't come to grips with her illusions when he refuses to leave his wife. Daring (for its day) look at sex and love worth seeing for Taylor's Oscar-winning performance. Based on a John O'Hara novel.

BUTTERFLIES ARE FREE 1972
★★★★★ PG Comedy/Drama 1:49
Dir: Milton Katselas **Cast:** Goldie Hawn, Edward Albert, Eileen Heckart, Mike Warren
▶ Hawn falls for blind Albert in the film version of a favorite Broadway play. He breaks free of an overprotective mother (Oscar-winner Heckart) and Goldie matures because of their feisty and funny relationship. Nominated for three Academy Awards.

BUTTERFLY 1982
☆ R Drama 1:47
☑ Nudity, strong sexual content, explicit language, mild violence
Dir: Matt Cimber **Cast:** Stacy Keach, Pia Zadora, Orson Welles, Lois Nettleton, Edward Albert, Ed McMahon
▶ Sexy nymphet Zadora is reunited with long-lost father Keach, now the guard of an abandoned silver mine. Their passionate affair brings them before Welles, a nasty judge determined to stamp out incest. Low-budget adaptation of a James M. Cain novel is considered a classic by Zadora's fans.

BUY AND CELL 1988
★ NR Comedy 1:31
☑ Nudity, adult situations, explicit language, mild violence
Dir: Robert Boris **Cast:** Robert Carradine, Malcolm McDowell, Imogene Coca, Ben Vereen, Randall "Tex" Cobb
▶ Framed yuppie stockbroker Carradine makes prison pay in this wacky but implausible comedy. Not ready for life in prison, Carradine, with the help of a motley group of murderers and career criminals, resorts to insider trading to improve conditions. Genuinely funny at times, but the zany sight gags tend to fall flat.

BY DESIGN 1982 Canadian
☆ R Drama 1:30
☑ Nudity, adult situations, explicit language
Dir: Claude Jutra **Cast:** Patty Duke Astin, Sara Botsford, Saul Rubinek, Sonia Zimmer
▶ Lesbians Astin and Botsford are happy and successful fashion designers but want to have a baby. When an adoption agency rejects them because of their lifestyle, they search for a man. Slim plot, but Astin rises above it.

BYE BYE BIRDIE 1963
★★★ NR Musical 1:52
Dir: George Sidney **Cast:** Janet Leigh, Dick Van Dyke, Ann-Margret, Bobby Rydell, Maureen Stapleton, Jesse Pearson
▶ Conrad Birdie, a rock 'n' roll sensation with swinging hips, is subject to immediate Army call, but not before he appears on Ed Sullivan's show to kiss a local fan, Ann-Margret. Her hometown of Sweet Apple, Ohio, is thrown into a frenzy, particularly her easily agitated dad Lynde. From the hit Broadway musical; Oscar-nominated for Best Sound, Musical Scoring.

CABARET 1972
★★★ PG Musical 2:03
☑ Adult situations, violence
Dir: Bob Fosse **Cast:** Liza Minnelli, Joel Grey, Michael York, Helmut Griem, Fritz Weber
▶ Eight-Oscar winner, set in early 1930s Germany when Nazism was on the rise, is based on the hit Broadway musical. Minnelli, in her Best Actress–winning role, is an aspiring cabaret singer/dancer who falls in love with both York and Griem. Her dreams of stardom are dashed by the shadow of Hitler. Grey is eerily, joyfully decadent in his Best Supporting Actor performance. Stunning music by Kander and Ebb and smashing choreography make this one of the most memorable movie musicals of all time, winning Best Screenplay, Scoring, Director, and more. **(CC)**

CABIN IN THE SKY 1943
★★ NR Musical 1:38 B&W
Dir: Vincente Minnelli **Cast:** Ethel Waters, Eddie "Rochester" Anderson, Lena Horne, Louis Armstrong, Rex Ingram, Kenneth Spencer
▶ Delightful all-black musical turns Anderson's indecision between the charms of wife Waters and those of seductive

Horne into an allegorical battle between agents from heaven and hell. Excellent score features "Happiness Is Just a Thing Called Joe" and "Taking a Chance on Love." Among the many guest stars are Duke Ellington, Butterfly McQueen, John "Bubbles" Sublett, and Ford "Buck" Washington.

CABOBLANCO 1980
★★ R Drama 1:32
☑ Nudity, adult situations, mild violence
Dir: J. Lee Thompson *Cast:* Charles Bronson, Jason Robards, Dominique Sanda, Fernando Rey, Camilla Sparv
▶ Sleepy story of macho hotel owner Bronson, beautiful widow Sanda, and millions in sunken Nazi gold set in postwar coastal Peru. Robards appears as a standard fugitive war criminal. Lush visual appeal is the film's real plus.

CACTUS FLOWER 1969
★★★★ PG Comedy 1:44
☑ Adult situations
Dir: Gene Saks *Cast:* Walter Matthau, Ingrid Bergman, Goldie Hawn, Jack Weston, Rick Lenz
▶ Frothy adaptation of the Broadway smash. Bergman stars as a dowdy assistant to bachelor/dentist Matthau, who asks her to cover as his "wife" so he won't have to marry girlfriend, Hawn. When she agrees, Matthau falls for her and gets caught in a love triangle. Hawn snagged an Oscar for her role as the spurned girlfriend saved by next-door-neighbor Lenz.

CADDIE 1981 Australian
★ NR Drama 1:46
☑ Explicit language
Dir: Donald Crombie *Cast:* Helen Morse, Takis Emmanuel, Jack Thompson, Jacki Weaver, Melissa Jaffer, Ron Blanchard
▶ In 1920s Australia, Morse, the mother of two small children, walks out on her unfaithful husband and tries to support the kids by working as a barmaid. She endures hard times and gets involved with married Greek Emmanuel. Beautifully rendered period details enhance a sympathetic true story, although pacing is a bit too leisurely.

CADDY, THE 1953
★★ NR Comedy 1:35 B&W
Dir: Norman Taurog *Cast:* Dean Martin, Jerry Lewis, Donna Reed, Barbara Bates, Frank Calleia, Fred Clark
▶ Martin is a golfer trying to break into the professional circuit; Lewis is his zany

caddy-manager. Predictable blend of slapstick and light romance, with cameos from famous pros (Ben Hogan, Sam Snead, Julius Boros, etc.) and an improbable Martin-Lewis duet to "That's Amore."

CADDYSHACK 1980
★★★★ R Comedy 1:38
☑ Brief nudity, explicit language, adult humor
Dir: Harold Ramis *Cast:* Chevy Chase, Rodney Dangerfield, Ted Knight, Michael O'Keefe, Bill Murray
▶ Megahit comedy about caddy O'Keefe's efforts to win a college scholarship. *Animal House* approach to country clubs works best when pros Murray (as a demented greenskeeper pursuing a gopher), Dangerfield (an unforgettably obnoxious real estate developer), and Chase (in a daffy WASP impersonation) deliver their material. Followed by *Caddyshack II.*

CADDYSHACK II 1988
★★ PG Comedy 1:36
☑ Brief nudity, explicit language, adult humor
Dir: Allan Arkush *Cast:* Jackie Mason, Robert Stack, Dyan Cannon, Dina Merrill, Jessica Lundy, Brian McNamara
▶ Sequel to immensely popular *Caddyshack* pits loud shirt Mason against stuffed shirt Stack. Since his daughter Lundy longs for preppy country club member McNamara, wealthy-but-ethnic Mason applies to join, antagonizing president Stack and snobby wife Merrill. Winner-take-all golf match climax, with sexy divorcée Cannon rooting for Mason. Despite cameo appearances of Chevy Chase and Dan Aykroyd, spin-off isn't on par with original.

CAESAR AND CLEOPATRA 1946 British
★★ NR Drama 2:18
Dir: Gabriel Pascal *Cast:* Vivien Leigh, Claude Rains, Stewart Granger, Flora Robson, Francis L. Sullivan
▶ George Bernard Shaw co-wrote the screenplay for this adaptation of his modern classic play. Playwright's typically intelligent and witty dialogue tells of the relationship between an elderly Caesar (Rains) and a bewitching young Cleopatra (Leigh). Elaborate sets, costumes, and production values.

CAGED HEAT 1974
★ R Action-Adventure 1:24
☑ Nudity, explicit language, violence

Dir: Jonathan Demme *Cast:* Juanita Brown, Roberta Collins, Erica Gavin, Ella Reid, Rainbeaux Smith, Barbara Steele
▶ An innocent Gavin is unjustly sentenced to a hellish prison run by crippled, sexually repressed warden Steele. Gavin breaks out with two friends, but returns to free the other inmates from the clutches of a maniacal doctor. Oddball humor tempers Demme's directing debut.

CAHILL—U.S. MARSHALL 1973
★★★★ PG Western 1:43
☑ Violence
Dir: Andrew V. McLaglen *Cast:* John Wayne, George Kennedy, Gary Grimes, Neville Brand, Marie Windsor, Clay O'Brien
▶ Cahill (Wayne) spends so much time chasing badmen that he neglects young sons Grimes and O'Brien. Pa faces a real dilemma when the boys—blackmailed by vicious crook Kennedy—start robbing banks. Action is quite violent at times.

CAINE MUTINY, THE 1954
★★★★★ NR Drama 2:05
Dir: Edward Dmytryk *Cast:* Humphrey Bogart, Van Johnson, Jose Ferrer, Fred MacMurray, Robert Francis, E. G. Marshall
▶ First-rate adaptation of Herman Wouk's Pulitzer prize–winning novel and Broadway hit, with Bogart in one of his most memorable roles as Queeg, the neurotic captain of a Pacific minesweeper. Johnson plays a lieutenant who questions Queeg's command during a typhoon; Ferrer, the attorney who defends him in a court-martial. Excellent supporting cast includes Lee Marvin and Claude Akins in small roles. Classic study of military loyalty won seven Oscar nominations, including Best Picture and Actor. (CC)

CAL 1984 Irish
★ R Drama 1:42
☑ Nudity, adult situations, explicit language, graphic violence
Dir: Pat O'Connor *Cast:* Helen Mirren, John Lynch, Donal McCann, John Kavanagh, Ray McAnally
▶ Moving drama set in Northern Ireland describes the rocky love affair between IRA member Lynch and Mirren, the widow of an assassinated policeman. Told with style and insight, film provides a compelling portrait of Belfast but may be too downbeat for many. Moody score by Mark Knopfler.

CALAMITY JANE 1953
★★★★ NR Musical 1:41
Dir: David Butler *Cast:* Doris Day, Howard Keel, Allyn Ann McLerie, Phil Carey, Gale Robbins, Dick Wesson
▶ Rambunctious tomboy Day charms Western legend Wild Bill Hickok (Keel) with her sharpshooting and singing. Mild comedy patterned after *Annie Get Your Gun* introduced the Oscar-winning "Secret Love," one of Day's biggest hits.

CALIFORNIA DREAMING 1976
★★ R Comedy 1:32
☑ Brief nudity, adult situations, explicit language
Dir: John Hancock *Cast:* Glynnis O'Connor, Seymour Cassel, Dorothy Tristan, Dennis Christopher, Tanya Roberts, Jimmy Van Patten
▶ Christopher, a nerd from Chicago, moves to California, where he falls for beautiful virginal O'Connor. Will he succumb to the empty morals of surfers and bikini girls, or impress O'Connor with higher goals? Unpretentious beach comedy with a heavy emphasis on sex and a bouncy soundtrack.

CALIFORNIA SPLIT 1974
★★ R Comedy/Drama 1:51
☑ Adult situations, explicit language, mild violence
Dir: Robert Altman *Cast:* George Segal, Elliott Gould, Ann Prentiss, Gwen Welles, Joseph Walsh, Bert Remsen
▶ Altman's look at the world of gambling features Segal and Gould as two small-timers on a spree. Loosely structured adventures as the pair win and lose a few times before hitting the big score. As with many Altman films of this period, emphasis is more on atmosphere and throwaway comic bits than on plot.

CALIFORNIA SUITE 1978
★★★★ PG Comedy 1:42
☑ Adult situations, explicit language
Dir: Herbert Ross *Cast:* Michael Caine, Maggie Smith, Jane Fonda, Alan Alda, Bill Cosby, Richard Pryor
▶ Writer Neil Simon intercuts four stories set in the Beverly Hills Hotel: divorced couple Fonda and Alda fight over their teenaged daughter; sexually mismatched English couple Smith and Caine arrive for the Oscar ceremonies; husband Walter Matthau tries to hide a hooker from wife, Elaine May; and pals Cosby and Pryor vacation with their wives and find their friendship tested by a series

of mishaps. Slick and clever, with superb work by Caine and Smith (Oscar, Best Supporting Actress).

CALIGULA 1980
☆ **X Drama/Sex 2:36**
☑ Rape, nudity, strong sexual content, explicit language, graphic violence
Dir: Tinto Brass *Cast:* Malcolm McDowell, Teresa Ann Savoy, Helen Mirren, Peter O'Toole, John Gielgud
► Big-budget erotica produced by *Penthouse* magazine gained some notoriety for its six minutes of hard-core footage, but for the most part it's a slow, extravagant look at the orgies of two Roman emperors: syphilitic Tiberius (O'Toole) and epileptic Caligula (McDowell). Screenwriter Gore Vidal had his name removed from the credits.

CALL ME 1988
★ **R Mystery-Suspense 1:37**
☑ Strong sexual content, adult situations, explicit language, violence
Dir: Sollace Mitchell *Cast:* Patricia Charbonneau, Patti D'Arbanville, Stephen McHattie, Boyd Gaines, Steve Buscemi, Sam Freed
► Lured by an obscene phone call she mistakenly believes is from her beau Freed, hip writer Charbonneau goes to a bar where she's hit on by McHattie. She witnesses the drug-related murder of a transvestite and is terrorized by increasingly threatening calls she assumes come from McHattie, unaware that she's the target of a killer. Sleek, erotic look at trendy downtown New York lacks substance.

CALL OF THE WILD, THE 1935
★★★★ **NR Action-Adventure 1:21 B&W**
Dir: William Wellman *Cast:* Clark Gable, Loretta Young, Jack Oakie, Reginald Owen, Frank Conroy, Buck the Dog
► Jack London's thrilling Yukon-adventure-turned-film-classic stars Gable as the virile gold prospector Jack Thornton taking on bad guys and bad dogs. With his faithful canine friend, he prospects gold in the treacherous Arctic wilderness, which is no place for a woman—until Young arrives. Grand story and great acting; memorable adventure for everyone.

CAMELOT 1967
★★★★ **G Musical 2:58**
Dir: Joshua Logan *Cast:* Richard Harris, Vanessa Redgrave, Franco Nero, David Hemmings, Lionel Jeffries
► In the mystical kingdom of Camelot, King Arthur (Harris) invites Lancelot (Nero) to join his Knights of the Round Table. Guenevere (Redgrave), Arthur's queen, starts a tragic romance with Lancelot. Large-scale adaptation of the Lerner-Loewe hit musical has beautiful production values and an exciting, Oscar-winning score including "If Ever I Would Leave You." Also won Oscars for Set Direction and Costumes.

CAMILLE 1936
★★★★ **NR Drama 1:48 B&W**
Dir: George Cukor *Cast:* Greta Garbo, Robert Taylor, Lionel Barrymore, Henry Daniell, Elizabeth Allan
► Cukor's meticulous adaptation of Alexandre Dumas's novel and play is justly remembered as a vehicle for Garbo's magnificent yet delicately nuanced performance as the ill-fated Paris courtesan who sacrifices herself for Taylor, the man she loves. The tragic ending has been breaking hearts and bringing tears for over fifty years.

CAMPUS MAN 1987
★★ **PG Comedy 1:34**
☑ Brief nudity, adult situations, explicit language
Dir: Ron Casden *Cast:* John Dye, Steve Lyon, Kathleen Wilhoite, Kim Delaney, Miles O'Keeffe, Morgan Fairchild
► Unable to pay his tuition, Arizona State University student Dye convinces diving champ roommate Lyon to pose for beefcake calendar. The calendar is a sensation, but Dye soon runs afoul of loan shark O'Keeffe and campus newspaper editor Wilhoite. Amusing adolescent comedy based on a true incident has an amiable tone and good songs by Robert Cray, Corey Hart, E-I-E-I-O, and others.

CAN-CAN 1960
★★★★ **NR Musical 2:11**
Dir: Walter Lang *Cast:* Frank Sinatra, Shirley MacLaine, Maurice Chevalier, Louis Jourdan, Juliet Prowse, Marcel Dalio
► Nightclub owner MacLaine is sued when she tries to introduce the naughty can-can dance to 1890s Paris. Attorney Sinatra reluctantly agrees to defend her, upsetting his girlfriend. Glossy comedy benefits from an outstanding Cole Porter score ("I Love Paris," "Let's Do It," "Just One of Those Things," etc.). **(CC)**

CANDIDATE, THE 1972
★★★ PG Drama 1:50
☑ Explicit language
Dir: Michael Ritchie *Cast:* Robert Redford, Peter Boyle, Don Porter, Allen Garfield, Melvyn Douglas
▶ Idealistic attorney Redford agrees to enter a Senate campaign if he can run on his own terms. But he quickly learns he can't win without giving in to powerful interests. Sharp, convincing look at the political scene with uniformly strong performances, particularly by Boyle as the campaign manager and Douglas as Redford's father; incisive, Oscar-winning screenplay by Jeremy Larner.

CANDLESHOE 1977
★★★★ G Drama 1:41
Dir: Norman Tokar *Cast:* David Niven, Helen Hayes, Jodie Foster, Leo McKern, Veronica Quilligan
▶ Con man McKern tries to pass off Foster as the long-lost heiress to Hayes's English estate. Butler Niven uses amusing disguises to hide the fact that Hayes is actually penniless. Clever Disney film has a fun plot filled with twists and double-crosses. Wholesome entertainment for children and adults alike.

CANDY 1968 U.S./Italian/French
☆ R Comedy 1:59
☑ Nudity, strong sexual content, violence
Dir: Christian Marquand *Cast:* Ewa Aulin, Marlon Brando, Richard Burton, Walter Matthau, Ringo Starr, James Coburn
▶ Aulin, an innocent high school girl, is seduced by an odd assortment of crazies in this freewheeling sex comedy from the Terry Southern/Mason Hoffenberg bestseller. Inane plotting and dated sixties satire but still fun watching Brando, Burton, Matthau, and Coburn goof on their own images. Soundtrack features the Byrds.

CANNERY ROW 1982
★★★★ PG Drama 2:00
☑ Brief nudity, adult situations, explicit language
Dir: David S. Ward *Cast:* Nick Nolte, Debra Winger, Audra Lindley, Frank McRae, M. Emmet Walsh
▶ Flavorful, highly romanticized period drama about the picaresque denizens of Monterey in the 1940s. Nolte plays a marine biologist and former baseball star who falls in love with pretty, wisecracking prostitute Winger. Based on two John Steinbeck stories, with a narration by John Huston.

CANNONBALL 1976
★★ PG Action-Adventure 1:33
☑ Explicit language
Dir: Paul Bartel *Cast:* David Carradine, Bill McKinney, Veronica Hamel, Gerrit Graham
▶ Not to be confused with the Burt Reynolds flicks, this free-wheeling action-comedy stars Carradine as Cannonball Buckman, a racer intent on winning the "most dangerous race in America" and the $100,000 prize. Features cameos by Martin Scorsese, Sylvester Stallone, Joe Dante, and producer Roger Corman. Lovers of car chases will be in four-wheel heaven.

CANNONBALL RUN, THE 1981
★★★★ PG Action-Adventure/Comedy 1:36
☑ Nudity, explicit language, adult humor
Dir: Hal Needham *Cast:* Burt Reynolds, Roger Moore, Farrah Fawcett, Dom DeLuise, Dean Martin
▶ Reynolds and guest star buddies DeLuise, Martin, and Moore enter a cross-country race in which there are no rules, no speed limits, no strategies—except avoid the police and get to California first. Though predictable, this action-packed good ol' boy picture was a major hit, inspiring a sequel. Great for those in the mood for a smash-'em-up.

CANNONBALL RUN II 1984
★★★ PG Action-Adventure/Comedy 1:48
☑ Nudity, explicit language, adult humor
Dir: Hal Needham *Cast:* Burt Reynolds, Dom DeLuise, Marilu Henner, Frank Sinatra, Dean Martin, Sammy Davis, Jr.
▶ Reynolds and DeLuise are two wild and crazy cannonballers competing in a cross-country race for a million-dollar prize offered by Arab sheik Jamie Farr. The contestants include two showgirls masquerading as nuns, two bums masquerading as cops, an orangutan masquerading as a chauffeur, and two long-legged bimbos masquerading as themselves. Lots of mayhem and mangled cars before the winner crosses the finish line. (CC)

CAN SHE BAKE A CHERRY PIE? 1983
★★ R Comedy 1:30

☑ Brief nudity, adult situations, explicit language, adult humor
Dir: Henry Jaglom *Cast:* Karen Black, Michael Emil, Michael Margotta, Frances Fisher, Paul Williams
▶ Abandoned by her husband, Black cautiously starts an affair with divorced hypochondriac Emil. Loose, largely improvised comedy may seem aimless at first, but the film's quirky humor and accomplished performances have their own charm. Shot on New York's Upper West Side.

CAN'T BUY ME LOVE 1987
★★★ PG-13 Comedy 1:34
☑ Adult situations, explicit language
Dir: Steve Rash *Cast:* Patrick Dempsey, Amanda Peterson, Courtney Gains, Seth Green, Devin De Vasquez
▶ Nerdy Dempsey wants to be accepted by the popular crowd in high school so he hires beautiful Peterson to be his girlfriend. What starts out as a bogus courtship turns into the real thing in this pert teen comedy that actually has something to say about the price of popularity. Even grown-ups might enjoy this fresh-faced, likable romp. **(CC)**

CAN'T STOP THE MUSIC 1980
★★ PG Musical 1:57
☑ Brief nudity, adult situations, explicit language
Dir: Nancy Walker *Cast:* Valerie Perrine, Bruce Jenner, Village People, Steve Guttenberg, Paul Sand
▶ Aspiring songwriter Guttenberg and ex-model Perrine gather some "Village" types and form the disco group Village People, in this lavish, colorful musical with a pounding dance beat. Olympic decathalon champ Jenner makes his film debut as the square lawyer who falls for Perrine but is nonplussed by her choice of friends. Harmless and genially campy fluff. Songs include the hit "YMCA."

CAPE FEAR 1962
★★★ NR Drama 1:46 B&W
Dir: J. Lee Thompson *Cast:* Gregory Peck, Robert Mitchum, Polly Bergen, Lori Martin, Martin Balsam, Telly Savalas
▶ Rapist Mitchum finds Peck, the lawyer responsible for his jail sentence, in a small North Carolina town. He starts a campaign of terror against Peck's family which the police are powerless to stop. Unbearably tense drama improves on John D. MacDonald's novel thanks to

Mitchum's riveting portrayal of a shrewd psychopath.

CAPONE 1975
★★ R Biography/Crime 1:41
☑ Brief nudity, adult situations, explicit language, violence
Dir: Steve Carver *Cast:* Ben Gazzara, Susan Blakely, Harry Guardino, John Cassavetes, Sylvester Stallone
▶ Biography of the legendary gangster Al Capone (Gazzara) from his bloody reign to his downfall, income tax evasion conviction, and syphilis-induced madness. Ben tries hard and Sly provides effectively low-key support, but the film rambles.

CAPRICORN ONE 1978
★★★★ PG Sci-Fi 2:07
☑ Explicit language, mild violence
Dir: Peter Hyams *Cast:* Elliott Gould, James Brolin, Karen Black, Telly Savalas, Sam Waterston, O. J. Simpson
▶ NASA executive Holbrook fakes a Mars mission in a TV studio rather than risk a failure that would jeopardize funding. Nosy reporter Gould investigates the conspiracy and astronauts Brolin, Simpson, and Waterston find themselves running for their lives when the scheme goes awry. Slick, fast-paced thriller has terrific chase scenes and an intricate, interesting "it could happen" plot.

CAPTAIN BLOOD 1935
★★★★ NR Action-Adventure 1:39 B&W
Dir: Michael Curtiz *Cast:* Errol Flynn, Olivia de Havilland, Lionel Atwill, Basil Rathbone, Guy Kibbee, Ross Alexander
▶ Seventeenth-century English doctor Flynn is sold into Caribbean slavery when a rebellion is crushed. He revolts against his captors, turns pirate, fights colonial governor Atwill, and, in one of cinema's great swordfights, battles fellow pirate Rathbone for de Havilland. Grand classic fueled by Flynn's high spirit. Adaptation of Rafael Sabatini novel; available in a colorized version.

CAPTAIN FROM CASTILE 1948
★★★★ NR Action-Adventure 2:21
Dir: Henry King *Cast:* Tyrone Power, Jean Peters, Cesar Romero, Lee J. Cobb, John Sutton
▶ Power stars in one of his most spectacular and popular films as dashing Spanish swashbuckler Pedro de Vargas. When he incurs the wrath of the Inquisition, he leaves Spain for Mexico to offer his ser-

vices to Cortez (Romero). In her film debut, Peters gives a sultry performance as the peasant girl madly in love with the cavalier. Academy Award nomination for Best Musical Scoring.

CAPTAIN HORATIO HORNBLOWER
1951 British
★ ★ ★ ★ NR Action-Adventure 1:57
Dir: Raoul Walsh *Cast:* Gregory Peck, Virginia Mayo, Robert Beatty, James Robertson Justice, Denis O'Dea, Terence Morgan
▶ Peck is dashing as the heroic Hornblower, an eighteenth-century British captain fighting villains in Central America and France while romancing Duke of Wellington's beautiful sister (Mayo). Boisterous swashbuckler based on C. S. Forester's best-seller has beautiful production values and plenty of action.

CAPTAIN NEWMAN, M.D. 1963
★ ★ ★ ★ NR Comedy/Drama 2:06
Dir: David Miller *Cast:* Gregory Peck, Tony Curtis, Bobby Darin, Eddie Albert, Angie Dickinson, Jane Withers
▶ Offbeat combination of drama and comedy set in a mental institution at the close of World War II, focusing on psychiatrist Peck's work with Darin, a war hero suffering from fears of cowardice, and Albert, a colonel guilty over the losses in his command. Curtis supplies the laughs as a slick corporal. Cast includes Robert Duvall, Larry Storch, Dick Sargent, and Ted Bessell. Received Oscar nominations for Darin's affecting performance and screenplay adapted from Leo Rosten's novel.

CAPTAINS COURAGEOUS 1937
★ ★ ★ ★ NR Drama/Family 1:56 B&W
Dir: Victor Fleming *Cast:* Freddie Bartholomew, Spencer Tracy, Melvyn Douglas, Lionel Barrymore, Mickey Rooney, John Carradine
▶ Child star Bartholomew plays a spoiled heir who falls off an ocean liner and is rescued by Tracy, a gruff Portuguese fisherman. His pleas to be sent home are ignored until the fishermen finish their three-month voyage. Although ungrateful at first, with Tracy's help he learns the value of love and trust. Beautiful adaptation of Rudyard Kipling's novel is outstanding on all levels, with a deeply affecting performance by Tracy that won him a richly deserved Oscar. Available in a computer colorized version.

CAPTAIN'S PARADISE, THE 1953 British
★ ★ NR Comedy 1:29 B&W
Dir: Anthony Kimmins *Cast:* Alec Guinness, Yvonne De Carlo, Celia Johnson, Charles Goldner, Bill Fraser, Sebastian Cabot
▶ Ship captain Guinness's idea of paradise is bigamy; homey Gibraltar bride Johnson and gorgeous North African wife De Carlo are unaware of each other's existence. Although the wives get the last laugh in the end, before that the audience is kept in stitches by the delicious antics.

CAPTIVE 1986 British
★ ★ R Drama 1:43
☑ Nudity, adult situations, explicit language
Dir: Paul Mayersberg *Cast:* Irina Brook, Oliver Reed, Hiro Arai, Xavier Deluc, Corinne Dacla
▶ Gang kidnaps pretty heiress Brook who lives in a castle with rich father Reed. Drugged, locked up and brainwashed, she reflects on her less-than-loving relationship with daddy and grows closer to her captors. Thinly disguised version of Patty Hearst's life is stylish-looking but lacks depth.

CAPTIVE HEARTS 1987
★ ★ ★ PG Drama/Romance 1:41
☑ Adult situations, explicit language, violence
Dir: Paul Almond *Cast:* Noriyuki "Pat" Morita, Michael Sarrazin, Chris Makepeace, Mari Sato, Seth Sakai
▶ Tough-talking U.S. airman Sarrazin and baby-faced cohort Makepeace are shot down over Japan during World War II and parachute into an isolated town. Village elder Morita intervenes to save the Americans from execution and puts them to work. Makepeace soon falls in love with Sato, Morita's widowed daughter-in-law, and the star-crossed lovers must contend with the harsh realities of war.

CAR, THE 1977
★ ★ ★ PG Horror 1:35
Dir: Elliot Silverstein *Cast:* James Brolin, Ronny Cox, Kathleen Lloyd, John Marley
▶ An ominous, mysterious—and driverless—car terrorizes and kills the residents of a small Southwestern town. Police chief Brolin and his men finally lure the car into the mountains and bury it under tons of dynamited rock. Takes off at a fast

pace but loses speed in the home stretch.

CARBINE WILLIAMS 1952
★ ★ ★ NR Biography 1:31 B&W
Dir: Richard Thorpe *Cast:* James Stewart, Jean Hagen, Wendell Corey, Carl Benton Reid, Paul Stewart
▶ Straightforward biography of Marsh Williams (Stewart), a North Carolina moonshiner jailed for thirty years after a Federal raid. Bucking warden Corey, Williams lands in solitary, where he invents a radical new gun design that becomes World War II's M-1 carbine.

CARBON COPY 1981
★ ★ ★ ★ PG Comedy 1:31
☑ Adult situations, adult humor
Dir: Michael Schultz *Cast:* George Segal, Susan Saint James, Denzel Washington, Jack Warden, Dick Martin
▶ White corporate executive Segal, married to Saint James, the daughter of his boss Warden, discovers he has black son Washington by a previous lover. His career and marriage are jeopardized as wife and employer prove less than understanding. Simple, broadly drawn farce pleasantly mixes social comment and comedy. Some clever moments (the son turns out to be the one black kid inept at basketball) and appealing performances by Segal and Washington.

CARDINAL, THE 1963
★ ★ ★ ★ NR Drama 2:55
Dir: Otto Preminger *Cast:* Tom Tryon, Carol Lynley, Romy Schneider, John Huston, Burgess Meredith
▶ Three decades in the life of Roman Catholic priest Stephen Fermoyle (Tryon), who matures from religious rigidity to idealism as a fighter against bigotry and Hitler. Long but compelling saga from director Preminger cunningly mixes religion and soap opera for good old-fashioned grand-scale entertainment. Stunning camera work and costumes, fine acting (Huston is a charmer as a curmudgeonly cleric), sweeping musical score, and an inspirational ending.

CARE BEARS MOVIE, THE 1985
★ ★ ★ ★ ★ G Animation 1:15
Dir: Arna Selznick *Cast:* Voices of Mickey Rooney, Georgia Engel, Harry Dean Stanton
▶ Cuddly Care Bears to the rescue when a misguided magician's assistant comes under the control of an evil spirit plotting to remove all feelings from the world.

Small children seem to love these furry do-gooders and parents will appreciate their message of friendship, caring, and feeling. Catchy title tune by Carole King and a bouncy John Sebastian score merrily move things along. **(CC)**

CARE BEARS MOVIE II: A NEW GENERATION 1986
★ ★ ★ ★ ★ G Animation 1:17
Dir: Dale Schott *Cast:* Voices of Kay Hadley, Chris Wiggins, Cree Summer Francks, Alyson Court, Michael Fantini
▶ Prequel to the original *Care Bears Movie* traces how the compassionate bears became the guardians of love in the world. The animals help a little girl named Christy, who trades her soul to the evil Dark Heart in return for summer camp success. All ends happily in this vehicle for small children. **(CC)**

CARE BEARS ADVENTURE IN WONDERLAND, THE 1987
★ ★ ★ ★ ★ G Animation 1:15
Dir: Raymond Jafelice *Cast:* Voice of Colin Fox
▶ Third in the series is variation on Lewis Carroll's *Alice in Wonderland* as furry heroes accompany Alice through the looking glass to stop evil wizard who has kidnapped princess. Wizard scoffs at bears as "puffballs" but they save the day. Should enthrall tykes between ages three and seven. Sprightly John Sebastian score includes "Welcome Back to Wonderland."

CAREFREE 1938
★ ★ ★ NR Musical 1:20 B&W
Dir: Mark Sandrich *Cast:* Fred Astaire, Ginger Rogers, Ralph Bellamy, Jack Carson, Franklin Pangborn, Hattie McDaniel
▶ Lesser Astaire/Rodgers vehicle is a light-hearted send-up of psychology. Singing star Rogers won't accept marriage proposal from stuffy lawyer Bellamy, so he hires psychiatrist Astaire to hypnotize her into submission. Duo's eighth teaming has more comedy than music, but the dances and Irving Berlin score (including "Change Partners" and "I Used to Be Color Blind") are still unbeatable.

CAREFUL, HE MIGHT HEAR YOU 1984
Australian
★ ★ ★ ★ PG Drama 1:53
☑ Adult situations, explicit language
Dir: Carl Schultz *Cast:* Nicholas Gled-

hill, Wendy Hughes, Robyn Nevin, John Hargreaves, Peter Whitford
▶ In 1930s Sydney, two aunts—working class housewife Nevin and sophisticated but neurotic and rich Hughes—fight for custody over P.S. (Gledhill), their deceased sister's son. Australian *Kramer Vs. Kramer* is slowly paced but well acted. Gledhill is a remarkably subtle child actor and Hughes won an Australian Film Institute Award (one of eight the film received, including Best Picture). **(CC)**

CARLTON-BROWNE OF THE F.O. 1958 British
★ **NR Comedy 1:31 B&W**
Dir: Jeffrey Dell, Roy Boulting *Cast:* Terry-Thomas, Peter Sellers, Luciana Paluzzi, Thorley Walters, Ian Bannen
▶ Extremely British farce about the obscure island of Gallardia, caught in a political tug-of-war over valuable mineral deposits. Thomas stars as Carlton Browne, dim-witted "Chief of Miscellaneous Territories," who gums up Britain's plan to recapture the former colony. With Sellers as the isle's corrupt Prime Minister.

CARMEN 1983 Spanish
☆ **R Dance 1:39**
Dir: Carlos Saura *Cast:* Antonio Gades, Laura Del Sol, Paco de Lucia, Christina Hoyos, Sebastian Moreno
▶ A choreographer rehearses a flamenco version of Bizet's opera and falls in love with his leading lady, an obsession that turns into tragedy because of the dancer's drug-dealer husband. The drama of love and jealousy verges on the banal but the dancing, enhanced by some fine camerawork, is dramatic and thrilling. ⑤

CARMEN 1984 French/Italian
★★★★ **PG Music 2:32**
☑ Adult situations, violence
Dir: Francesco Rosi *Cast:* Julia Migenes-Johnson, Placido Domingo, Ruggero Raimondi, Faith Esham, Jean-Philippe Lafont
▶ Oft-filmed story about an aristocratic Spanish soldier who loses his heart to a faithless gypsy receives a full operatic treatment here. Distinguished tenor Domingo tops an accomplished cast in a faithful version of Bizet's original score. Beautiful Spanish settings and exotic local color. Also known as *Bizet's Carmen*. ⑤

CARMEN JONES 1954
★★ **NR Musical 1:45**

Dir: Otto Preminger *Cast:* Dorothy Dandridge, Harry Belafonte, Olga James, Pearl Bailey, Diahann Carroll, Roy Glenn
▶ Ambitious updating of Bizet's famous opera, with new lyrics by Oscar Hammerstein II. Set in a World War II parachute factory, story describes tragic affair of beautiful flirt Dandridge (who received an Oscar nomination) and hot-headed soldier Belafonte. Dandridge's singing dubbed by Marilyn Horne.

CARNAL KNOWLEDGE 1971
★★ **R Drama 1:38**
☑ Nudity, adult situations, explicit language
Dir: Mike Nichols *Cast:* Jack Nicholson, Candice Bergen, Art Garfunkel, Ann-Margret, Rita Moreno, Carol Kane
▶ Caustic drama traces the sexual attitudes of friends Nicholson and Garfunkel from college through middle age. The women in their lives include Smith college student Bergen, voluptuous model Ann-Margret (in an Oscar-nominated performance), prostitute Moreno, and young hippie Kane. Provocative script by cartoonist Jules Feiffer was expertly directed by Nichols.

CARNY 1980
★★ **R Drama 1:47**
☑ Nudity, adult situations, explicit language
Dir: Robert Kaylor *Cast:* Jodie Foster, Gary Busey, Robbie Robertson, Meg Foster, Kenneth McMillan, Elisha Cook, Jr.
▶ Eccentric but appealing drama about Foster, a young runaway who comes between friends Busey and rock star Robertson (in his first dramatic role) when she joins a seedy carnival. Effective use of sideshow atmosphere adds depth to the predictable plot. Foster is excellent in her first "adult" role.

CAROUSEL 1956
★★★★ **NR Musical 2:09**
Dir: Henry King *Cast:* Gordon MacRae, Shirley Jones, Cameron Mitchell, Barbara Ruick, Claramae Turner, Gene Lockhart
▶ Carnival barker MacRae is killed when committing a robbery to support wife Jones and unborn child. In heaven, he gets another chance to return to earth and redeem himself. Sentimental musical fantasy has rather stagebound production but leads' lovely voices do jus-

tice to a familiar, much-loved Rodgers and Hammerstein score which includes "If I Loved You," "June is Busting Out All Over," and "You'll Never Walk Alone."

CARPETBAGGERS, THE 1964
★★★ **PG Drama 2:30**
Dir: Edward Dmytryk *Cast:* George Peppard, Alan Ladd, Carroll Baker, Bob Cummings, Martha Hyer, Elizabeth Ashley
▶ In the early 1930s, playboy Peppard inherits millions, buys a movie studio, turns father's widow Baker into a star, then dumps her for prostitute Hyer. His friend Nevada Smith (Ladd, in his last film) is the only one who can bring him to his senses. Adaptation of Harold Robbins's bestseller was loosely based on the life of Howard Hughes. Steve McQueen played Ladd's character in a prequel, *Nevada Smith.*

CARRIE 1976
★★★★★ **R Horror 1:37**
☑ Nudity, adult situations, explicit language, graphic violence
Dir: Brian De Palma *Cast:* Sissy Spacek, Piper Laurie, William Katt, John Travolta, Nancy Allen, Amy Irving
▶ Stephen King's novel about repressed high school girl with telekinetic powers became an absorbing, frightening hit thanks to director De Palma's clever tricks. Carrie (Spacek) is tormented at home by religious zealot mother Laurie and at school by cruel students, including Allen and Travolta in his film debut. She unleashes her powers after a particularly mean practical joke on prom night. Widely imitated film won Oscar nominations for both Spacek and Laurie.

CARSON CITY 1952
★★ **NR Western 1:27**
Dir: Andre de Toth *Cast:* Randolph Scott, Lucille Norman, Raymond Massey, Don Beddoe, Richard Webb
▶ Energetic Western with Scott as an engineer hired to bring the railroad to Nevada. Landslides and Indians are the least of his worries: Massey, the owner of a gold mine, is out to frame him for a brutal murder. Norman is attractive as a reporter's daughter who falls for Scott.

CARS THAT ATE PARIS, THE 1974
Australian
☆ **PG Comedy 1:31**
☑ Adult situations, explicit language, violence
Dir: Peter Weir *Cast:* Terry Camilleri,

John Meillon, Melissa Jaffa, Kevin Miles, Max Gillies, Bruce Spence
▶ Citizens of Paris, Australia, lure unsuspecting motorists into traffic accidents; unscrupulous doctor performs medical experiments on the victims while looters and mechanics reap a fortune from the wrecks. Extremely black comedy with a minor cult reputation suffers from hit-or-miss gags.

CAR WASH 1976
★★★ **PG Comedy 1:37**
☑ Explicit language, adult humor
Dir: Michael Schultz *Cast:* Richard Pryor, Franklyn Ajaye, Sully Boyar, George Carlin, Irwin Corey, Melanie Mayron
▶ Fast, rowdy look at the workers and customers at an inner-city L.A. car wash is basically a series of skits tied together by a pounding rock score. Pryor steals the film as Daddy Rich, a wealthy evangelist who shows up in a gold limo to do a song with the Pointer Sisters, but everyone in the large cast gets some bright lines.

CASABLANCA 1943
★★★★★ **NR Drama 1:42 B&W**
Dir: Michael Curtiz *Cast:* Humphrey Bogart, Ingrid Bergman, Paul Henreid, Claude Rains, Conrad Veidt, Peter Lorre
▶ "Of all the gin joints in all the world, she walks into mine," says cafe owner Rick (Bogart) when old love Bergman arrives in World War II Casablanca with freedom fighter hubby Henreid. Will Rick stay neutral or overcome his bitterness and help Bergman and Henreid in the cause? Cynical French captain Rains and Nazi leader Veidt want to know. Immortal Hollywood classic, full of memorable moments, romance, intrigue, and perhaps the most quoted dialogue of any film. When they say they don't make 'em like they used to, this is what they mean. Oscar for Best Picture. **(CC)**

CASANOVA'S BIG NIGHT 1954
★★★ **NR Comedy 1:26**
Dir: Norman Z. McLeod *Cast:* Bob Hope, Joan Fontaine, Audrey Dalton, Basil Rathbone, Hugh Marlowe, Vincent Price
▶ Hope's uncanny resemblance to the notorious lover prompts duchess to hire him to test motives of son's fiancée Fontaine. Memorable villains Rathbone, John Carradine, Lon Chaney, Jr., and Raymond Burr mistake Hope for the real

thing, leading to frequent slapstick chases in this amiable period comedy. Price has an amusing cameo as the "real" Casanova.

CASEY'S SHADOW 1978
★★★★ PG Family 1:56
☑ Adult situations, explicit language
Dir: Martin Ritt *Cast:* Walter Matthau, Alexis Smith, Robert Webber, Murray Hamilton, Andrew S. Rubin
▶ Cajun horse trainer Matthau and his three sons groom their quarterhorse, Casey's Shadow, for an important race at New Mexico's Ruidoso Downs—even though the owner plans to sell the horse. A well-made, old-fashioned family film; emotionally honest as well as touching. Matthau, playing a good-natured slob, is wonderful, and he receives excellent support from Smith as a wealthy horse breeder.

CASINO ROYALE 1967 British
★★ NR Comedy 2:11
Dir: John Huston, Ken Hughes, Robert Parrish, Joseph McGrath, Val Guest
Cast: Peter Sellers, Ursula Andress, David Niven, Orson Welles, Woody Allen
▶ Overblown spoof of the 007 series, with a huge all-star cast. The aging Sir James Bond (Niven) is recruited to crush the evil organization SMERSH, but lots of other Bond impersonators have been recruited as well (including Allen as nephew Jimmy Bond) to confuse the enemy.

CASSANDRA CROSSING, THE 1977 British
★★★★★ R Action-Adventure 2:08
☑ Adult situations, violence
Dir: George Pan Cosmatos *Cast:* Sophia Loren, Richard Harris, Ava Gardner, Burt Lancaster, Martin Sheen, O. J. Simpson
▶ A terrorist infected with a deadly virus boards the Stockholm Express, forcing Army general Lancaster to seal the train and send it to its doom across the shaky Cassandra Bridge. An all-star cast (including Loren as a novelist, Harris as her scientist-husband, and Simpson as a gun-toting priest) tries to halt the speeding locomotive in time. Impressive stunts and special effects highlight this adventure.

CAST A GIANT SHADOW 1966
★★ NR Biography 2:18
Dir: Melville Shavelson *Cast:* Kirk Douglas, Senta Berger, Angie Dickin-

son, Yul Brynner, John Wayne, Frank Sinatra
▶ True story of Colonel Mickey Marcus (Douglas), an American Jew who guided the Israeli Army to victories over Arab enemies in the 1949 war. Along the way, Douglas, although married to Dickinson, finds time for romance with freedom fighter Berger. All-star cast adds punch to fascinating tale. **(CC)**

CASTAWAY 1987 British
★ R Drama 1:57
☑ Nudity, adult situations, explicit language
Dir: Nicolas Roeg *Cast:* Oliver Reed, Amanda Donohoe, Georgina Hale, Frances Barber, Tony Richards
▶ The Seychelles Islands provide an exotic tropical backdrop to an intriguing psychological drama based on a true story. Reed signs a book contract to spend a year on a desert island, and selects Donohoe through a personal ad to share the experience. Cut off from civilization, the two prey on each other's weaknesses.

CASTAWAY COWBOY, THE 1974
★★★ G Comedy 1:31
Dir: Vincent McEveety *Cast:* James Garner, Vera Miles, Robert Culp, Eric Shea, Elizabeth Smith, Manu Tupou
▶ Texas sailor Garner, shipwrecked on Hawaii in 1850, protects widow Miles from villain Culp, who wants her potato ranch. Likable stars boost the familiar Western-style plot in this enjoyable Disney comedy.

CASUAL SEX? 1988
★★★ R Comedy 1:30
☑ Nudity, strong sexual content, explicit language
Dir: Genevieve Robert *Cast:* Lea Thompson, Victoria Jackson, Stephen Shellen, Jerry Levine, Andrew Dice Clay, Mary Gross
▶ Thompson and Jackson, two of Los Angeles' most eligible beauties, are intimidated by the AIDS crisis and their single status. Looking for Mr. Rights, they venture to a health resort. Thompson fends off crude Clay while batting eyes at a musician; Jackson may have found her man in chiropractor Levine. Amusing look at modern dating woes.

CAT AND MOUSE 1978 French
★ PG Mystery-Suspense 1:47
☑ Adult situations
Dir: Claude Lelouch *Cast:* Michele

Morgan, Serge Reggiani, Phillipe Leotard, Jean-Pierre Aumont
► Wealthy art collector Aumont is murdered. Police inspector Reggiani suspects the widow Morgan but then begins to fall in love with her. Complex mystery plot combines romance, comedy (especially in scenes with the inspector's dog Sam), and wryly amusing performances.

CAT AND THE CANARY, THE 1939
★ ★ ★ NR Mystery-Suspense/Comedy
1:12 B&W
Dir: Elliott Nugent *Cast:* Bob Hope, Paulette Goddard, Gale Sondergaard, John Beal, Douglass Montgomery, George Zucco
► Goddard inherits a haunted house in a swamp, but according to the will, she loses the estate if she goes insane. When corpses start appearing behind hidden doors, her hapless boyfriend Hope must solve the mystery. Delightful combination of chills and laughs gave Goddard her first leading role and Hope his first big success in films. Stars were reteamed the next year for *The Ghost Breakers*. An inferior British remake came out in 1979.

CATASTROPHE 1977
★ ★ ★ ★ PG Documentary 1:31 C/B&W
☑ Graphic violence
Dir: Larry Savadore *Cast:* Narrated by William Conrad
► Extraordinary compilation of natural and man-made disasters from around the world features horrifying newsreel footage of a skyscraper fire in São Paulo, the destructive fury of Hurricane Camille, car crashes at the Indy 500, a killer tornado in Ohio, etc. A number of black-and-white sections contain famous older tragedies (the Hindenburg disaster, the wreck of the *Andrea Doria*, etc.).

CAT BALLOU 1965
★ ★ ★ ★ NR Western/Comedy 1:36
Dir: Elliot Silverstein *Cast:* Jane Fonda, Lee Marvin, Michael Callan, Dwayne Hickman, Nat "King" Cole, Stubby Kaye
► Young Wild West schoolteacher Fonda is forced into a life of crime by a crooked land baron. Threatened by hired killers, she teams up with cattle rustler Callan, con man Hickman, and notorious gunslinger Marvin. Popular spoof of Westerns won Marvin an Oscar for his dual role as the drunken has-been Kid Shelleen and his deadly twin, Silvernose. Wandering minstrels Kaye and Cole provide an amusing commentary on the action as

they sing the Oscar-nominated title song.

CATCH-22 1970
★ ★ R War/Comedy 1:59
Dir: Mike Nichols *Cast:* Alan Arkin, Richard Benjamin, Art Garfunkel, Martin Balsam, Jack Gilford, Bob Newhart
► An all-star cast brings to life Joseph Heller's classic antiwar novel. As Captain Yossarian, Arkin represents every war-weary soldier. He tries to plead insanity to escape flight duty but, according to catch-22, if he says he's crazy, he can't be crazy. Nichols's black comedy also features: Buck Henry, Orson Welles, Jon Voight, Charles Grodin, Anthony Perkins, Bob Balaban, and Paula Prentiss.

CAT FROM OUTER SPACE, THE 1978
★ ★ ★ ★ G Comedy 1:43
Dir: Norman Tokar *Cast:* Ken Berry, Sandy Duncan, Harry Morgan, Roddy McDowall, McLean Stevenson
► Jake, an extraterrestrial feline, crash-lands on Earth and enlists goofy physicist Berry to repair his spaceship. It's a race against time because the Pentagon wants Jake's magic crystal collar. Likable stars, crazy shenanigans, and the typical Disney gloss make this perfect viewing for children.

CATHERINE & CO. 1976 French/Italian
★ R Sex 1:24
☑ Nudity, adult situations, explicit language
Dir: Michel Boisrond *Cast:* Jane Birkin, Patrick Dewaere, Jean-Claude Brialy, Vittorio Capriolo, Jean-Pierre Aumont
► Typical French sex farce about Birkin, a British dropout who takes a novel approach to prostitution: she incorporates herself and sells out time to five different investors. Complications result when one of the men falls in love with her. Distinguished French cast adds some depth to the proceedings.

CAT ON A HOT TIN ROOF 1958
★ ★ ★ NR Drama 1:48
Dir: Richard Brooks *Cast:* Elizabeth Taylor, Paul Newman, Burl Ives, Jack Carson, Judith Anderson
► Dying Big Daddy (Ives) wants an heir. Daughter-in-law Maggie (Taylor) would love to provide one (and get her hands on the family fortune) but hubby Brick (Newman) has psychological problems that preclude this goal. Playwright Tennessee Williams's homosexual subtext was muted here but much of the steamy power of the original play comes

through, thanks to some terrific acting. Six Oscar nominations including Best Picture, (Actor) Newman and Actress (Taylor).

CAT PEOPLE 1942
★★ NR Horror 1:13 B&W
Dir: Jacques Tourneur *Cast:* Simone Simon, Kent Smith, Tom Conway, Jane Randolph, Jack Holt
▶ Smith falls for Simon. Problem: she may have nasty habit of turning into a killer beast. Producer Val Lewton is the real genius behind this minor classic of the horror genre. Lewton's pictures avoided the gore of today's movies and achieved their scares with provocative ideas and stylized visuals (in contrast especially to the interesting but bloody 1982 remake).

CAT PEOPLE 1982
★★ R Horror 1:58
☑ Nudity, strong sexual content, adult situations, explicit language
Dir: Paul Schrader *Cast:* Nastassia Kinski, Malcolm McDowell, John Heard, Annette O'Toole, Ruby Dee
▶ When McDowell visits his sister Kinski in New Orleans, he reveals their family's mysterious heritage. Can Kinski consummate her love for zookeeper Heard without turning into a killer feline? Unusual fantasy, not for every taste, creates plenty of spooky atmosphere. Remake is much more graphic (both in sex and in violence) than the 1942 original. Hit theme song by David Bowie.

CAT'S EYE 1985
★★★★ PG-13 Horror 1:30
☑ Explicit language, violence
Dir: Lewis Teague *Cast:* Drew Barrymore, James Woods, Robert Hays, Alan King, Kenneth McMillan, Candy Clark
▶ Three tales of terror from genre master Stephen King: chain smoker Woods suffers through clinic head Alan King's shocking cure, tennis pro Hays accepts gambler McMillan's bet that he can't walk around building ledge and live, and stray cat protects little Barrymore against deadly troll (a remarkable creation from *E.T.* designer Carlo Rambaldi). Strong stuff with touches of tongue-in-cheek humor.

CATTLE ANNIE AND LITTLE BRITCHES 1981
★★★ PG Western 1:37
☑ Adult situations, explicit language
Dir: Lamont Johnson *Cast:* Burt Lancaster, John Savage, Rod Steiger,

Diane Lane, Amanda Plummer, Scott Glenn
▶ In 1893, footloose teens Lane and Plummer from "back east" hook up with the infamous Doolin-Dalton gang (led by Lancaster) and prove their mettle in some tight scrapes with the law. Lighthearted comic western with fresh-faced Lane and Plummer (who is especially good) serving as effective foils for the he-man stars.

CATTLE QUEEN OF MONTANA 1954
★★ NR Western 1:28
Dir: Allan Dwan *Cast:* Barbara Stanwyck, Ronald Reagan, Gene Evans, Lance Fuller, Anthony Caruso, Jack Elam
▶ Despite her father's murder, beautiful rancher Stanwyck vows to build an empire equal to villain Evans's spread. Reagan plays a federal agent who exposes Evans's ties to murdering Indians. Stanwyck, who did her own stunts, impressed the local Blackfeet so much that they made her their blood sister. Shot in Montana's Glacier National Park.

CAVEMAN 1981
★★ PG Comedy 1:31
☑ Adult humor
Dir: Carl Gottlieb *Cast:* Ringo Starr, Barbara Bach, Dennis Quaid, Shelley Long, Jack Gilford, John Matuszak
▶ Kicked out of his tribe after making eyes at the chief's woman, caveman Starr bands together with other outcasts. With his new friends he discovers fire, music, the wheel, and the love of sincere cavegirl Long. Broad prehistoric spoof has plenty of slapstick, with dialogue mostly of grunts and funny special-effects dinosaurs. Film led to wedding bells for Ringo and Bach.

C.C. AND COMPANY 1970
★ PG Action-Adventure 1:34
☑ Explicit language, violence
Dir: Seymour Robbie *Cast:* Joe Namath, Ann-Margret, William Smith, Jennifer Billingsley, Don Chastain
▶ Dramatic debut for former quarterback Namath is an inept, unintentionally funny biker drama about vicious goons led by Smith who attempt to gang-rape beautiful hitchhiker Ann-Margret. Namath not only rescues Ann-Margret, earning her love, but also wins control of Smith's gang.

CEASE FIRE 1985
★★★★ R Drama 1:37

☑ Explicit language, violence
Dir: David Nutter *Cast:* Don Johnson, Lisa Blount, Robert F. Lyons, Richard Chaves, Rick Richards
▶ Vietnam vet Johnson's war flashbacks threaten to destroy his marriage until fellow vet Lyons introduces him to Veterans Center group therapy sessions. Wife Blount helps him on the long road to recovery. Sensitive treatment of a timely subject is slow-paced but emotionally rewarding.

CELLAR DWELLER 1988
★ NR Horror 1:17
☑ Nudity, adult situations, explicit language, violence
Dir: John Buechler *Cast:* Debrah Mulrowney, Brian Robbins, Vince Edwards, Cheryl-Ann Wilson, Jeffrey Combs, Yvonne De Carlo
▶ Aspiring cartoonist Mulrowney joins De Carlo's art institute to work on "Cellar Dweller" comic strip. When she visits studio basement, she unwittingly releases same monster who appears in her strip. Predictable horror formula receives uninspired treatment.

CERTAIN FURY 1985
★★ R Action-Adventure 1:27
☑ Rape, nudity, adult situations, explicit language, violence
Dir: Steven Gyllenhaal *Cast:* Tatum O'Neal, Irene Cara, Nicholas Campbell, Moses Gunn, Peter Fonda
▶ Street-smart tough O'Neal and rich kid Cara are mistakenly implicated in a courtroom shootout. Although enemies, they are forced on the lam together. After encounters with drug dealer Campbell and pimp Fonda, the girls become friends. Sordid exploitation fare handled with flair by the leads.

CHAINED HEAT 1983
★★ R Action-Adventure 1:35
☑ Rape, nudity, adult situations, explicit language, violence
Dir: Paul Nichols *Cast:* Linda Blair, John Vernon, Sybil Danning, Tamara Dobson, Stella Stevens, Henry Silva
▶ Convicted of manslaughter, naive Blair ends up in a hellish prison run by warden Vernon (with a hot tub in his office) and his partner Stevens, who also heads a drug and prostitution ring. Blair gets caught in the middle of a feud between black and white inmates, then leads a riot against her corrupt guards. Follow-up

to *The Concrete Jungle* has a heavy emphasis on rape and nudity.

CHALK GARDEN, THE 1964 British
★★ NR Drama 1:46
Dir: Ronald Neame *Cast:* Deborah Kerr, Hayley Mills, John Mills, Edith Evans, Felix Aylmer
▶ When her mother remarries, Laurel (Hayley Mills) is sent to her grandmother Evans's house. Feeling rejected, she becomes a disruptive force until Kerr, a governess with a shady past, teaches her the value of love. Delicate adaptation of an Enid Bagnold play also features Hayley's father John as the grandmother's butler.

CHALLENGE, THE 1982
★★★ R Action-Adventure 1:46
☑ Nudity, adult situations, explicit language, graphic violence
Dir: John Frankenheimer *Cast:* Scott Glenn, Toshiro Mifune, Donna Kei Benz, Atsuo Nakamura, Calvin Young
▶ When American boxer Glenn is hired to transport an antique sword back to Japan, he unknowingly steps into a vicious feud between traditional warrior Mifune and his industrialist brother Nakamura. Intriguing look at ancient rituals in modern-day Japan was co-written by John Sayles. An intense training sequence and violent climax are not for the squeamish.

CHALLENGE TO BE FREE 1975
★★★ G Action-Adventure 1:27
Dir: Tay Garnett *Cast:* Mike Mazurki, Jimmy Kane, Vic Christy, Fritz Ford, Tay Garnett
▶ Burly loner Mazurki frees an injured wolf from a trap set by a no-good Frenchman out to sell animals to profiteers. The authorities come for him and by accident he kills one of them. A manhunt ensues and Mazurki heads for the mountains to avoid the posse. Solid family fare with lots of animal footage and beautiful Alaskan scenery.

CHAMP, THE 1979
★★★★★ PG Drama 2:01
☑ Explicit language
Dir: Franco Zeffirelli *Cast:* Jon Voight, Faye Dunaway, Ricky Schroder, Jack Warden, Arthur Hill
▶ Alcoholic former boxing champion Voight, desperate to keep young son Schroder from glamorous ex-wife Dunaway, decides to make a comeback despite doctor's advice. Touching Voight/

Schroder relationship, lushly filmed, is sentimental remake of the 1931 King Vidor classic. Goes unashamedly for the tear ducts. Pro boxer Randall "Tex" Cobb is Voight's foe in the final tragic fight.

CHAMPION 1949
★★★ NR Drama/Sports 1:39 B&W
Dir: Mark Robson *Cast:* Kirk Douglas, Marilyn Maxwell, Arthur Kennedy, Paul Stewart, Ruth Roman, John Day
▶ Uncompromising portrait of boxer Douglas's rise to fame and corruption by gangsters ranks among the best sports dramas. Highlighted by brisk direction and uniformly strong acting, particularly Roman's spurned wife and Maxwell's ruthless mistress. Oscar-winning editing boosts fighting sequences; Kennedy received a nomination as Douglas's crippled brother, as did Carl Foreman for adapting Ring Lardner's story.

CHAMPIONS 1984 British
★★★★ PG Biography/Sports 1:54
☑ Adult situations, explicit language
Dir: John Irvin *Cast:* John Hurt, Edward Woodward, Ben Johnson, Jan Francis, Ann Bell
▶ True sports drama of two incredible comebacks. England's top steeplechase jockey Bob Champion (Hurt) is stricken with cancer at age 31 while his horse Aldaniti is crippled in a race. Both man and beast triumph over their afflictions and win the 1981 Grand National Steeplechase. Inspirational tale suffers from slow pacing but Hurt is excellent. **(CC)**

CHANCES ARE 1988
★★★★ PG Comedy 1:48
☑ Adult situations, explicit language
Dir: Emile Ardolino *Cast:* Cybill Shepherd, Robert Downey, Jr., Ryan O'Neal, Mary Stuart Masterson, Christopher McDonald
▶ When her husband is killed in a car accident, Shepherd mourns for twenty-three years while ignoring O'Neal's advances. Her daughter Masterson falls for Downey, who discovers to his dismay that he's the reincarnation of Shepherd's husband. Romantic comedy earns some genuine chuckles with its elaborate mistaken identity complications.

CHANEL SOLITAIRE 1981
★★ R Biography 2:04
☑ Adult situations, explicit language
Dir: George Kaczender *Cast:* Marie-France Pisier, Timothy Dalton, Rutger Hauer, Karen Black, Brigitte Fossey
▶ Glossy rags-to-riches biography of fashion designer Coco Chanel (Pisier), an orphan who rises from seamstress to the leader of Parisian haute couture. Along the way, she falls in love with handsome Brit Dalton but tragedy strikes when he dies in a car accident. Languidly paced but nice-looking soap opera with lovely costumes.

CHANGELING, THE 1980 Canadian
★★★★ R Horror 1:47
☑ Adult situations, explicit language, violence
Dir: Peter Medak *Cast:* George C. Scott, Trish Van Devere, Melvyn Douglas, John Colicos, Jean Marsh
▶ Music professor Scott loses his family in a tragic accident and rents an old house to recuperate. The place turns out to be haunted because title-holder Douglas, a Senator from a prestigious family, had committed an evil act some time back. Real estate agent Van Devere helps Scott crack the secrets of the house. Chilling tale with an intense performance from Scott.

CHANGE OF HABIT 1969
★★ G Drama 1:33
Dir: William Graham *Cast:* Elvis Presley, Mary Tyler Moore, Barbara McNair, Jane Elliot, Leora Dana
▶ Teaming of Presley and Moore is not either's finest moment. Moore plays a nun who helps doctor Presley run a clinic in a bad New York neighborhood. Fans of the two stars may enjoy seeing them so oddly cast but be warned, Presley barely gets to sing here.

CHANGE OF SEASONS, A 1980
★★★ R Comedy 1:42
☑ Nudity, adult situations, explicit language
Dir: Richard Lang *Cast:* Shirley MacLaine, Bo Derek, Anthony Hopkins, Michael Brandon, Mary Beth Hurt
▶ Middle-aged college professor Hopkins is having an affair with Derek, one of his students. Wife MacLaine finds out and responds in kind with young carpenter Brandon. Agreeable romantic comedy with old pros MacLaine and Hopkins providing the acting expertise and Derek giving her all to the hot tub scene.

CHAN IS MISSING 1982
★ NR Drama 1:20 B&W
☑ Adult situations, explicit language, violence
Dir: Wayne Wang *Cast:* Wood Moy,

Marc Hayashi, Laureen Chew, Judy Nihei, Peter Wang
▶ Critically acclaimed independent film from Chinese-American filmmaker Wang is quality delivered on a home-movie budget ($20,000). Mystery plot, concerning the search of two Chinese cabbies, older man Moy and his young nephew Hayashi, for a missing immigrant in San Francisco's Chinatown, explores the Chinese lifestyle in America.

CHAPTER TWO 1979
★★★★★ **PG Comedy/Drama 2:04**
☑ Adult situations, explicit language
Dir: Robert Moore *Cast:* Marsha Mason, James Caan, Valerie Harper, Joseph Bologna
▶ Playwright Neil Simon adapted his autobiographical Broadway hit, taken from his own painful experiences after the death of his first wife. Caan plays a writer/widower racked with guilt when he falls in love with divorcée Mason. Oscar-nominated turn by Mason, who shines in a role based on her life (she was the second Mrs. Neil Simon). Her "I'm nuts about me" speech provides the film's emotional climax and has become a favored monologue used by acting students. **(CC)**

CHARADE 1963
★★★★ **NR Mystery-Suspense 1:53**
Dir: Stanley Donen *Cast:* Cary Grant, Audrey Hepburn, Walter Matthau, James Coburn, George Kennedy
▶ In Paris, Hepburn finds herself caught up in intrigue when her husband is murdered. Can she trust the handsome but mysterious Grant who comes to her aid? Stylish and sparkling, with sleek direction by Donen, great Henry Mancini score, and plenty of romantic chemistry from the leads.

CHARGE OF THE LIGHT BRIGADE, THE 1936
★★★ **NR Action-Adventure 1:56 B&W**
Dir: Michael Curtiz *Cast:* Errol Flynn, Olivia de Havilland, Patric Knowles, Donald Crisp, Henry Stephenson, Nigel Bruce
▶ In 1850s India, British major Flynn saves the life of an evil khan. When the khan orders the massacre of a British outpost, Flynn seeks revenge by leading his troops in a heroic but costly assault on the khan's men. Sweeping, action-packed adventure, loosely based on the Tennyson poem, is justly famed for its thundering climax. Max Steiner's rousing score

was nominated for an Oscar. Available in a colorized version. **(CC)**

CHARIOTS OF FIRE 1981 British
★★★★ **PG Drama/Sports 2:03**
☑ Adult situations, explicit language
Dir: Hugh Hudson *Cast:* Ben Cross, Ian Charleson, Ian Holm, John Gielgud, Alice Krige
▶ The true story of two British runners in the 1924 Olympics who were of disparate backgrounds but united in their desire to win—Harold Abrahams (Cross), a Jew driven by anti-Semitism, and Eric Liddell (Charleson), a Christian missionary who felt God's presence when he ran. Genuinely stirring, superbly filmed drama exquisitely re-creates the period. Oscars for Best Picture, Original Screenplay, Costume Design, and for Vangelis's stunning musical score.

CHARLEY AND THE ANGEL 1973
★★★ **G Comedy 1:33**
Dir: Vincent McEveety *Cast:* Fred MacMurray, Cloris Leachman, Harry Morgan, Kurt Russell, Kathleen Cody, Vincent Van Patten
▶ Pleasant Disney fantasy about Depression-era shopkeeper MacMurray, who neglects his family until angel Morgan warns him that his time on earth has expired. MacMurray's new devotion to home alarms his family, especially a son who's mixed up with the mob.

CHARLEY VARRICK 1973
★★★ **PG Action-Adventure 1:51**
☑ Adult situations, explicit language, violence
Dir: Don Siegel *Cast:* Walter Matthau, Joe Don Baker, Felicia Farr, Andy Robinson, John Vernon, Sheree North
▶ Small-time con Matthau and his partner Robinson mistakenly steal $750,000 from the Mafia; Matthau must find a way to return the money before sadistic hitman Baker finds him. Ingenious, hard-edged caper film has crisp pacing, brutal action sequences, and a wily performance from Matthau. Good example of director Siegel's flair with action pictures.

CHARLIE CHAN AND THE CURSE OF THE DRAGON QUEEN 1981
★★ **PG Comedy 1:32**
☑ Adult situations, explicit language
Dir: Clive Donner *Cast:* Peter Ustinov, Lee Grant, Angie Dickinson, Richard Hatch, Brian Keith
▶ Veteran crime solver Charlie Chan (Ustinov) is called out of retirement to help

the San Francisco police solve a mysterious series of murders. Accompanied by bumbling grandson Hatch, Chan encounters his old nemesis, the Dragon Queen (Dickinson). Comic mystery has nutty characters, broad performances, and nonstop slapstick.

CHARLIE, THE LONESOME COUGAR 1968
★★★★ NR Family 1:15
Dir: Winston Hibler *Cast:* Ron Brown, Brian Russell, Linda Wallace, Jim Wilson
▶ A lumberjack in the Pacific Northwest adopts Charlie, an orphaned cougar cub who stirs up so much trouble around the logging camp that he's caged. The lumberjack realizes Charlie belongs in the wild, and takes him on a long journey into the wilderness. Another fine Disney animal adventure with good photography and a remarkable performance by Charlie. Narrated by Rex Allen.

CHARLOTTE'S WEB 1973
★★★★★ G Animation 1:34
Dir: Charles A. Nichols, Iwao Takamoto
Cast: Voices of Debbie Reynolds, Paul Lynde, Henry Gibson, Charles Nelson Reilly
▶ Wilbur is a runt pig slated for the slaughterhouse until his spider friend Charlotte weaves words into her web to convince a superstitious farmer that Wilbur is a miraculous hog. Charming animated musical from E. B. White's beloved children's classic. Bouncy score by Robert B. Sherman and Richard M. Sherman.

CHARLY 1968
★★★★ PG Drama 1:43
Dir: Ralph Nelson *Cast:* Cliff Robertson, Claire Bloom, Lilia Skala, Leon Janney, Dick Van Patten
▶ Retarded Robertson is turned into a genius by a scientific experiment. He knows a brief period of happiness with teacher Bloom before the process begins to reverse. Some story contrivances and overly busy camerawork but Robertson is moving and poignant in his Oscar-winning role. Based on *Flowers for Algernon* by Daniel Keyes.

CHASE, THE 1966
★★ NR Drama 2:15
Dir: Arthur Penn *Cast:* Marlon Brando, Jane Fonda, Robert Redford, E. G. Marshall, Angie Dickinson, Janice Rule
▶ Overblown melodrama examines the reactions of small-town citizens to the jailbreak of Redford, a local boy imprisoned on false charges. As he tries to join girlfriend Fonda, corrupt banker Marshall encourages a drunken posse to kill him. Upright sheriff Brando is the only man on Redford's side. Lillian Hellman's adaptation of a Horton Foote novel was disowned by director Penn. Cast also includes Miriam Hopkins, Martha Hyer, and Robert Duvall.

CHATTANOOGA CHOO CHOO 1984
★★★ PG Comedy 1:42
☑ Adult situations, explicit language
Dir: Bruce Bilson *Cast:* George Kennedy, Barbara Eden, Joe Namath, Tony Azito, Melissa Sue Anderson, Clu Gulager
▶ Football team owner Kennedy can inherit one million tax free dollars from his father-in-law if he restores the old man's favorite train and makes a 24-hour Chattanooga-to-New York run. Cheerleaders, players, coach Namath, and Kennedy's chief rival Gulager are along for the ride in this cornball comedy in the tradition of *Harper Valley PTA.*

CHEAP DETECTIVE, THE 1978
★★★ PG Comedy 1:32
☑ Explicit language
Dir: Robert Moore *Cast:* Peter Falk, Ann-Margret, Madeline Kahn, Marsha Mason, Eileen Brennan, Louise Fletcher
▶ Neil Simon's follow-up to *Murder By Death.* Falk reprises his Bogart-like character in a parody plot that involves a *Maltese Falcon*–like search for a dozen diamond eggs and a *Casablanca*-like love triangle. High-spirited fun will please film buffs and Simon fans alike. Fletcher and Fernando Lamas (in the Ingrid Bergman and Paul Henried parts) are standouts in an all-star comic cast.

CHEAPER TO KEEP HER 1980
★★★ R Comedy 1:31
☑ Strong sexual content, explicit language
Dir: Ken Annakin *Cast:* Mac Davis, Tovah Feldshuh, Rose Marie, Jack Gilford, Priscilla Lopez, Ian McShane
▶ Sex comedy about recently divorced detective Davis who is hired by tough attorney Feldshuh to track down men who've lapsed in their alimony payments. Davis's on-the-job adventures include wooing Feldshuh's secretary Lopez and investigating her ex-husband McShane before he ends up with the lady lawyer. Basically a raunchy sitcom.

CHECK IS IN THE MAIL, THE 1986
★★ R Comedy 1:23
☑ Brief nudity, adult situations, explicit language
Dir: Joan Darling *Cast:* Brian Dennehy, Anne Archer, Hallie Todd, Chris Hebert, Michael Bowen
▶ Pharmacist Dennehy, having trouble making ends meet for wife Archer and their three kids, declares war on the system. He rips up his credit cards, cancels his automobile insurance, and converts his family to *Whole Earth Catalog*-style living, even to the point of raising chickens to provide eggs. Sitcom-type humor.

CHEECH & CHONG'S NEXT MOVIE 1980
★★★ R Comedy 1:35
☑ Nudity, explicit language, adult humor
Dir: Thomas Chong *Cast:* Cheech Marin, Thomas Chong, Evelyn Guerrero, Betty Kennedy, Sy Dramer
▶ Usual dose of silly routines and irreverent "dope humor" for the Chino-Latino duo's many fans. They roll a lot of illegal herb and wind up at a massage parlor. Predictable but fun.

CHEECH & CHONG'S NICE DREAMS 1981
★★ R Comedy 1:27
☑ Nudity, explicit language, adult humor
Dir: Thomas Chong *Cast:* Cheech Marin, Thomas Chong, Evelyn Guerrero, Stacy Keach, Timothy Leary
▶ Their third film has "Los Guys" amassing a stash of dinero by dealing drugs out of an ice cream truck. Keach keeps a watchful eye over them as their narcotics agent/boss hooked on the weed. Leary appears as himself, dispensing little pills at an insane asylum. Fans should have a snorting good time.

CHEECH & CHONG'S THE CORSICAN BROTHERS 1984
★ PG Comedy 1:30
☑ Explicit language, violence, adult humor
Dir: Thomas Chong *Cast:* Cheech Marin, Thomas Chong, Roy Dotrice, Shelby Fiddis, Rikki Marin
▶ Cheech and Chong are a couple of American musicians paid *not* to play on the streets of Paris in this takeoff of the Dumas tale about twins separated at birth but spiritually linked. Not one reference to marijuana, but plenty of other jokes about women, bodily functions, and minorities.

CHEERS FOR MISS BISHOP 1941
★★ NR Drama 1:35 B&W
Dir: Tay Garnett *Cast:* Martha Scott, William Gargan, Sterling Holloway, Edmund Gwenn, Sidney Blackmer, Mary Anderson
▶ Well-turned tale of fifty years in life of nineteenth-century midwestern schoolteacher Scott. Two frustrated romances leave her unmarried, so she devotes herself with a passion to educating young minds. Female equivalent to *Goodbye, Mr. Chips.*

CHERRY 2000 1987
★★ PG-13 Fantasy 1:38
☑ Brief nudity, adult situations, explicit language, violence
Dir: Steve DeJarnatt *Cast:* Melanie Griffith, David Andrews, Ben Johnson, Tim Thomerson, Pamela Gidley
▶ Futuristic fable of young Andrews in love with a sexy robot-girl until he discovers that he truly desires the flesh and blood of the real thing. Griffith is great as the daredevil heroine who refuses to wear a crash helmet because it messes up her hair. Mock-sexist and slyly funny fantasy comic strip is a hoot. (CC)

CHEYENNE AUTUMN 1964
★★★ NR Western 2:25
Dir: John Ford *Cast:* Richard Widmark, Carroll Baker, James Stewart, Edward G. Robinson, Karl Malden, Ricardo Montalban
▶ The Cheyenne Indians make a journey to protest their treatment by the white man, only to be pursued by the U.S. cavalry (led by Widmark). Sincere revisionism from, of all people, John Ford. Indians, often the bad guys in his classic Wayne westerns, are here treated with the utmost sympathy and respect.

CHILDREN, THE 1980
★ R Horror 1:31
☑ Adult situations, explicit language, violence
Dir: Max Kalmanowicz *Cast:* Martin Shakar, Gil Rogers, Gale Garnett, Jesse Abrams
▶ Little darlings become deadly brats after their schoolbus is contaminated by radiation. The kids go on the rampage, menacing their parents, the townspeople, and anyone else who gets in their way. Genre fans may dig the display of severed limbs.

CHILDREN OF A LESSER GOD 1986
★★★★ R Drama 1:56
☑ Nudity, adult situations, explicit language
Dir: Randa Haines *Cast:* William Hurt, Marlee Matlin, Piper Laurie, Philip Bosco, Allison Gompf
▶ Tender, beautifully crafted drama of the romance between Hurt, a teacher at a school for the deaf, and Matlin, a rebellious deaf student who refuses to learn how to speak. Completely convincing and moving without being excessively sentimental. Wonderfully acted by the Oscar-nominated Hurt. Matlin, deaf in real life, deservedly won the Oscar for her complex, poignant, and charismatic performance. Also nominated for Best Picture. From Mark Medoff's Tony-winning play. **(CC)**

CHILDREN OF PARADISE 1945 French
★★ NR Drama 3:08 B&W
Dir: Marcel Carne *Cast:* Arletty, Jean-Louis Barrault, Pierre Brasseur, Marcel Harrand, Pierre Renoir, Maria Casares
▶ In nineteenth-century Paris, mime Barrault and his comedian friend Brasseur both fall for Arletty, the theater's leading actress, but she chooses wealth over love by becoming a count's mistress. Monumental drama of doomed romance has exquisite acting, shimmering photography, and heartbreaking script by Jacques Prévert. Shot under extraordinary circumstances during the Nazi occupation, and often acclaimed as the greatest French film ever made. ⑤

CHILDREN OF THE CORN 1984
★★ R Horror 1:33
☑ Explicit language, graphic violence
Dir: Fritz Kiersch *Cast:* Peter Horton, Linda Hamilton, R. G. Armstrong, John Franklin, Courtney Gains, Robby Kiger
▶ Cross-country travelers Horton and Hamilton find themselves menaced in Nebraska town where child Franklin leads killer-kid cult bent on slaughtering adults. Hamilton is kidnapped and Horton must rescue her. Taut, bloodthirsty shocker is based on the short story by Stephen King.

CHILDREN OF THE DAMNED 1964
British
★★ NR Horror 1:21 B&W
Dir: Anton M. Leader *Cast:* Ian Hendry, Alan Badel, Barbara Ferris, Alfred Burke, Sheila Allen, Frank Summerscales
▶ Rival scientists Hendry and Badel are baffled by six uncannily intelligent children with deadly laser eyes, but their experiments result in tragedy when the youngsters escape from a heavily guarded research compound. Loose adapatation of John Wyndham's *The Midwich Cuckoos* is a sequel of sorts to the vastly superior *Village of the Damned.*

CHILD'S PLAY 1988
★★★ R Horror 1:28
☑ Explicit language, violence
Dir: Tom Holland *Cast:* Catherine Hicks, Chris Sarandon, Brad Dourif, Alex Vincent, Dinah Manoff, Tommy Swerdlow
▶ Widowed working mom Hicks gives six-year-old son Vincent a "Good Guy" doll for his birthday, unaware that the doll possesses the soul of deceased murderer Dourif. When Vincent's new pal "Chucky" runs amok, no one except the kid believes the demon doll is responsible until it's too late. Sarandon plays the homicide detective who finds himself in pursuit of a toy in this well-crafted spine-tingler.

CHILLY SCENES OF WINTER 1979
★★ PG Drama 1:37
☑ Adult situations, explicit language
Dir: Joan Micklin Silver *Cast:* John Heard, Mary Beth Hurt, Peter Riegert, Kenneth McMillan, Gloria Grahame
▶ Heard, a Salt Lake City civil servant, falls in love with Hurt, just separated from her husband. His passion is so overwhelming that she returns to her family—but Heard still won't give up. Quirky, low-key comedy/drama has a brilliant cameo by Grahame (as Heard's suicidal mother). Adapted from the novel by Ann Beattie, and originally released as *Head Over Heels.*

CHINA GIRL 1987
★★ R Drama 1:28
☑ Adult situations, explicit language, violence
Dir: Abel Ferrara *Cast:* James Russo, Sari Chang, Richard Panebianco, David Caruso, Russell Wong
▶ Love affair between young pizza shop worker Panebianco and Chang, a beautiful Chinese teenager, leads to war between Italian and Chinese gangs. The tragedy is played out on the nightclub dance floors and alleyways of New York's Little Italy and Chinatown. Russo is convincing as the hero's older brother, and director Ferrara brings a gritty realism to

this modern-day *Romeo and Juliet*. Soundtrack includes Run-D.M.C. and David Johansen.

CHINA SEAS 1935
★ ★ ★ NR Drama 1:30 B&W
Dir: Tay Garnett   *Cast:* Clark Gable, Jean Harlow, Wallace Beery, Lewis Stone, Rosalind Russell, Robert Benchley
▶ Contrived but highly enjoyable adventure aboard a liner between Shanghai and Singapore, with Gable as a valiant captain battling pirates led by Beery and choosing between English aristocrat Russell and spunky dance-hall girl Harlow. Slick, action-filled story may not make much sense, but the stars are wonderful.

CHINA SYNDROME, THE 1979
★ ★ ★ ★ ★ PG Drama 2:02
☑ Explicit language
Dir: James Bridges   *Cast:* Jane Fonda, Jack Lemmon, Michael Douglas, Scott Brady, James Hampton, Wilford Brimley
▶ Thrilling account of neophyte TV reporter Fonda, who digs up evidence that a nuclear power plant may have structural flaws. When the plant owners start a cover-up, she has to convince conscientious engineer Lemmon to break ranks and speak out about the danger. Realistic, hard-hitting drama scores points against TV news as well as nuclear power. Lemmon and Fonda both won Oscar nominations, as did the screenplay. (CC)

CHINATOWN 1974
★ ★ ★ ★ R Drama 2:11
☑ Adult situations, explicit language, violence
Dir: Roman Polanski   *Cast:* Jack Nicholson, Faye Dunaway, John Huston, Perry Lopez, John Hillerman, Diane Ladd
▶ Haunting, beautifully realized mystery set in 1930s Los Angeles. Nicholson is superb as J. J. Gittes, a private eye drawn into a case much larger than he can handle. He finds himself protecting Dunaway, an enigmatic widow who may be responsible for a murder. In an excellent cast, Huston stands out as a genial millionaire who hires Gittes to find his granddaughter. Director Polanski has a memorable cameo as a vicious thug. Influential film received eleven Oscar nominations, winning for Robert Towne's screenplay.

CHINESE CONNECTION, THE 1973
Chinese
★ ★ R Martial Arts 1:47
☑ Explicit language, violence
Dir: Lo Wei   *Cast:* Bruce Lee, Miao Ker Hsio, James Tien, Robert Baker
▶ When his martial arts teacher is murdered, Lee searches through turn-of-the-century Shanghai for the killers. At the same time he faces challenge from Japanese fighters who claim they're superior to Chinese martial arts experts. Apart from obvious dubbing, an excellent showcase for the charismatic Lee.

CHINO 1973 Italian
★ ★ PG Western 1:38
☑ Adult situatins, explicit language, violence
Dir: John Sturges   *Cast:* Charles Bronson, Jill Ireland, Vincent Van Patten, Marcel Bozzuffi, Melissa Chimenti, Fausto Tozzi
▶ Downbeat Western about poor New Mexican horse breeder Bronson, who falls in love with Ireland, the sister of wealthy rancher Bozzuffi. Van Patten is a teenage runaway befriended by Bronson. Uncharacteristic role for Bronson, who rejects revenge for peace. His scenes with wife Ireland are subtly erotic.

CHISUM 1970
★ ★ ★ ★ G Western 1:51
Dir: Andrew V. McLaglen   *Cast:* John Wayne, Forrest Tucker, Christopher George, Ben Johnson, Glenn Corbett, Geoffrey Deuel
▶ Quality Western, loosely based on the 1878 Lincoln County land wars, with Wayne playing real-life cattle baron John Chisum. The Duke locks horns with Tucker, a wealthy crook stealing land from farmers. Wayne gets steady support from Johnson as his foreman, but the younger stars (Corbett as Pat Garrett, Deuel as Billy the Kid, George as bounty hunter Dan Nodeen) take up most of the story. Country-and-western star Merle Haggard sings two ballads.

CHITTY CHITTY BANG BANG 1968
★ ★ ★ ★ G Musical/Family 2:36
Dir: Ken Hughes   *Cast:* Dick Van Dyke, Sally Ann Howes, Lionel Jeffries, Gert Frobe, Benny Hill
▶ Lavish children's musical based on the novel by Ian Fleming. Van Dyke is a tinkerer and widowed father of two who invents a magical flying car coveted by evil king Gert Frobe. Songs by Richard M.

Sherman and Robert B. Sherman include the title tune, "Truly Scrumptious," and "Hushabye Mountain."

CHLOE IN THE AFTERNOON 1972 French
☆ **R Comedy 1:37**
Dir: Eric Rohmer *Cast:* Bernard Verley, Zouzou, Francoise Verley, Daniel Ceccaldi
▶ Happily married Verley gets involved with bohemian Zouzou. The films of Rohmer are not for everyone, certainly, but patient adult viewers will be rewarded with insight into human nature and relationships. Deceptively simple camerawork, well-crafted dialogue, and small-scale story add up to the cinematic equivalent of a fine miniature. Ⓢ

CHOCOLATE WAR, THE 1989
★★ **R Drama 1:40**
☑ Adult situations, explicit language, violence
Dir: Keith Gordon *Cast:* John Glover, Ilan Mitchell-Smith, Wally Ward, Doug Hutchinson, Adam Baldwin, Brent Fraser
▶ At rigid Catholic boys' high school, freshman Mitchell-Smith is tyrannized by dictatorial teachers and bullied by a secret club of students led by Ward. Ambitious teacher Glover, hoping for promotion to headmaster, seeks to double the quota of chocolates sold by each boy during the annual fund-raiser; Ward and his clique compel Mitchell-Smith to refuse Glover's demands. Well-crafted but bleak adaptation of Robert Cormier novel. Writing/directing debut for actor Gordon.

CHOICE OF ARMS 1983 French
★★ **NR Action-Adventure 1:57**
☑ Explicit language, graphic violence
Dir: Alain Corneau *Cast:* Yves Montand, Gerard Depardieu, Catherine Deneuve, Michel Galabru
▶ Tense crime thriller about retired gangster Montand, whose rural life is upset by young psychopath Depardieu. Unable to turn to the police, Montand must reenter the underworld and kill Depardieu to protect wife Deneuve. Rich characterizations, with Depardieu especially striking as a mad-dog killer. Ⓢ

CHOIRBOYS, THE 1977
★★★★ **R Action-Adventure 1:59**
☑ Brief nudity, adult situations, explicit language
Dir: Robert Aldrich *Cast:* Charles Durning, Louis Gossett, Jr., Perry King, Clyde Kasatsu, Stephen Macht, Tim McIntire
▶ Raunchy comedy/drama about L.A. cops who relieve tension by holding wild "choir practice" sex-and-booze parties in MacArthur Park. Story follows ten different choirboys on and off duty. Burt Young (as a grubby vice squad sergeant) stands out in an enormous cast that also includes Randy Quaid, Don Stroud, James Woods, Blair Brown, Vic Tayback, etc. Based on Joseph Waumbaugh's best-seller.

CHOKE CANYON 1986
★★★ **PG Action-Adventure 1:34**
☑ Explicit language, violence
Dir: Chuck Bail *Cast:* Stephen Collins, Janet Julian, Lance Henriksen, Bo Svenson, Victoria Racimo
▶ Physicist Collins, developing a new form of clean energy in Choke Canyon, learns that an evil conglomerate is dumping nuclear waste on the site of his experiments. When he threatens to expose the crime, ruthless hitman Svenson is hired to silence him. Fast-paced genre picture features an exciting dogfight between a plane and a futuristic helicopter.

C.H.O.M.P.S. 1979
★★★★ **G Comedy 1:29**
Dir: Don Chaffey *Cast:* Wesley Eure, Valerie Bertinelli, Conrad Bain, Chuck McCann, Red Buttons, Jim Backus
▶ Eure plays a young inventor whose latest project, C.H.O.M.P.S. (the Canine Home Protection System, a Benji-like mechanical guard dog), is the target of bumbling crooks McCann and Buttons. The robot dog saves the day and smoothes the way for a romance between Eure and Bertinelli, his boss's daughter. Younger viewers should love the adorable dog star.

CHOOSE ME 1984
★ **R Drama 1:46**
☑ Adult situations, explicit language
Dir: Alan Rudolph *Cast:* Genevieve Bujold, Keith Carradine, Lesley Ann Warren, Patrick Bauchau, Rae Dawn Chong, John Larroquette
▶ Offbeat mixture of comedy and drama takes a romantic, stylized look at the love affairs of three unusual loners: radio talk show sex therapist Bujold, womanizing mental patient Carradine, and vulnerable bar owner Warren. Top-notch ensemble acting, wonderful Teddy Pendergrass score, and unpredictable plotting and

directing make this a treat for sophisticated viewers.

CHOPPING MALL 1986
☆ R Horror 1:16
☑ Nudity, adult situations, explicit language, graphic violence
Dir: Jim Wynorski *Cast:* Kelli Maroney, Tony O'Dell, John Terlesky, Russell Todd, Paul Bartel, Mary Woronov
▶ Eight teenagers are trapped overnight in a Los Angeles shopping mall guarded by demented, murderous robots. Can they fight their way out? Campy slasher film played for laughs is filled with in-jokes and references to other films (Bartel and Woronov repeat their *Eating Raoul* roles).

CHORUS LINE, A 1985
★★★ PG-13 Musical 1:53
☑ Explicit language
Dir: Richard Attenborough *Cast:* Michael Douglas, Terrence Mann, Alyson Reed, Vicki Frederick, Nicole Fosse, Matt West
▶ Big-budget adaptation of Broadway's longest-running musical examines aspiring dancers auditioning for demanding choreographer Douglas. Through songs and soliloquies the anonymous "gypsies" reveal their secret hopes and fears. The Pulitzer prize–winning play is essentially transferred intact, although composers Marvin Hamlisch and Edward Kleban added Oscar-nominated "Surprise, Surprise" to the score. Inherently theatrical experience was a major box office disappointment on film. **(CC)**

CHOSEN, THE 1978 Italian/British
★★★★ R Horror 1:45
☑ Brief nudity, graphic violence
Dir: Alberto De Martino *Cast:* Kirk Douglas, Simon Ward, Agostina Belli, Anthony Quayle, Virginia McKenna, Alexander Knox
▶ While financing a chain of nuclear fission reactors, industrialist Douglas discovers that son Ward has designed structural flaws into the plants—turning them into atom bombs. When Douglas tries to stop the project, he learns he's dealing with the Antichrist. Violent, derivative horror story was based on the Book of Revelations.

CHOSEN, THE 1982
★★★ PG Drama 1:48
☑ Adult situations, mild violence
Dir: Jeremy Paul Kagan *Cast:* Maximilian Schell, Rod Steiger, Robby Benson, Barry Miller, Hildy Brooks, Ron Rifkin

▶ Warm, moving adaptation of Chaim Potok's novel has a simple story line: 1940s Jewish-American boys—Hasidic Benson and liberal Miller—become friends in Brooklyn. Miller is amazed at Benson's strict Hasidic life; Benson's father Steiger, a rabbi, worries that his son may be corrupted by nonsectarians. Religious themes are handled with sincerity and taste, and insights into friendship and father-son relationships have universal appeal.

CHRISTINE 1983
★★ R Horror 1:50
☑ Adult situations, explicit language, violence
Dir: John Carpenter *Cast:* Keith Gordon, John Stockwell, Alexandra Paul, Robert Prosky, Harry Dean Stanton
▶ Gordon, a social outcast at school, devotes all his time to renovating a 1958 Plymouth Fury named Christine. Best friend Stockwell tries to warn him that something's wrong with the car, but the evil spirit possessing the Fury is more dangerous than they anticipated. Slick adaptation of the Stephen King best-seller has a good soundtrack showcasing Christine's favorite 1950s rock 'n' roll hits. **(CC)**

CHRISTMAS CAROL, A 1951 British
★★★★ NR Drama/Family 1:26 B&W
Dir: Brian Desmond Hurst *Cast:* Alastair Sim, Kathleen Harrison, Jack Warner, Michael Hordern, Mervyn Johns, Hermione Baddeley
▶ Marvelous version of the Charles Dickens tale features Sim in one of his best roles as the tightfisted Scrooge. Encounters with three ghosts on Christmas Eve lead him to confront his own mortality. Strong supporting cast and good use of period detail add to the film's charm. Perennial Christmas favorite lives up to its reputation as a classic. **(CC)**

CHRISTMAS IN CONNECTICUT 1945
★★★ NR Comedy 1:41 B&W
Dir: Peter Godfrey *Cast:* Barbara Stanwyck, Dennis Morgan, Sydney Greenstreet, Reginald Gardiner, S. Z. Sakall
▶ Stanwyck, a magazine housekeeping expert, is coerced by editor Greenstreet into bringing war hero Morgan home to her family for the holidays. Unfortunately, Stanwyck doesn't have a home, or a family, and she doesn't know the first thing about housekeeping—but she learns plenty before Greenstreet arrives

for dinner. Bright farce has plenty of slapstick to top off its warm holiday mood.

CHRISTMAS IN JULY 1940
★★★ NR Comedy 1:07 B&W
Dir: Preston Sturges *Cast:* Dick Powell, Ellen Drew, William Demarest, Franklin Pangborn, Raymond Walburn, Ernest Truex
▶ Powell, a struggling but ambitious clerk, enters a coffee slogan contest with a slogan that even fiancée Drew doesn't understand ("If you can't sleep at night, it isn't the coffee, it's the bunk"). When co-workers fool him into thinking he's won, he goes on a spending spree. Merry take on the American Dream from writer/ director Sturges.

CHRISTMAS STORY, A 1983
★★★★ PG Comedy 1:33
☑ Explicit language
Dir: Bob Clark *Cast:* Melinda Dillon, Peter Billingsley, Darren McGavin, Ian Petrella, Scott Schwartz
▶ Imaginative, nostalgic look at Christmas in the 1940s has the feel of a future classic. Adaptation of Jean Shepherd's humorous recollections of the Midwest is primarily about a young boy's obsession for a Red Ryder BB gun, but the film's real successes are its sharply observed vignettes about small-town family life. Nightmarish visit to a department store Santa Claus is one of many highlights.

CHRISTMAS THAT ALMOST WASN'T, THE 1966
★★★★ G Musical/Family 1:34
Dir: Rossano Brazzi *Cast:* Rossano Brazzi, Paul Tripp, Sonny Fox, Mischa Auer, Lydia Brazzi
▶ Mean millionaire Brazzi buys the North Pole and threatens to evict Santa and Mrs. Claus unless they come up with back rent by Christmas Eve. Children learn of Santa's plight and help him save Christmas. Classic holiday tale delightfully combines animation, live action, and musical numbers including "Why Can't Every Day Be Christmas?"

CHRISTMAS TO REMEMBER, A 1978
★★★★ NR Family/MFTV 2:00
Dir: George Englund *Cast:* Jason Robards, Jr., Eva Marie Saint, Joanne Woodward, George Parry, Bryan Englund, Louise Hockmeyer
▶ TV movie depicts elderly farm couple Robards and Saint, who take in their city-bred grandson Parry for the holidays during the Depression. Robards, still grieving over the death of only son in World War I, reluctantly warms to Parry. Woodward makes cameo appearance as Parry's mom. Splendid cast assures adaptation of Glendon Swarthout's *The Melodeon* never gets mired in sentimentality.

CHU CHU AND THE PHILLY FLASH 1981
★ PG Comedy 1:40
☑ Explicit language
Dir: David Lowell Rich *Cast:* Alan Arkin, Carol Burnett, Jack Warden, Danny Aiello, Danny Glover, Ruth Buzzi
▶ Former baseball player Arkin and dance instructor Burnett pounce on a briefcase filled with stolen government papers. Although enemies, they work together on a complicated scheme to ransom the goods. Shrill slapstick comedy was written by Arkin's wife, Barbara Dana.

C.H.U.D. 1984
★★ R Horror 1:28
☑ Adult situations, explicit language, graphic violence
Dir: Douglas Creek *Cast:* John Heard, Kim Greist, Daniel Stern, Christopher Curry, George Martin
▶ A government plot to dump nuclear waste under Manhattan turns unsuspecting bag people into C.H.U.D.'s: Cannibalistic Humanoid Underground Dwellers. Since the cops won't help, it's up to bored fashion photographer Heard, his favorite model Greist, and hippie Stern to defeat the monsters. Low-budget exploitation fare has some humor and ecological points to accompany the requisite gore.

C.H.U.D. II 1988
★★ R Horror/Comedy 1:25
☑ Explicit language, violence
Dir: David Irving *Cast:* Brian Robbins, Bill Calvert, Tricia Leigh Fisher, Gerrit Graham, Robert Vaughn, Bianca Jagger
▶ Graham is the last zombie left from government C.H.U.D. program headed by Vaughn. High school teens Calvert and Robbins, having lost their cadaver for a biology project, steal Graham's corpse and accidentally bring him back to life. Graham goes on a killing spree, turning victims into fellow zombies, and soon his small town is crawling with the creatures. Horror sequel to C.H.U.D. plays mostly for laughs, but has more than enough gore for genre buffs.

CINCINNATI KID, THE 1965
★★★ NR Drama 1:45
Dir: Norman Jewison   *Cast:* Steve McQueen, Edward G. Robinson, Ann-Margret, Karl Malden, Tuesday Weld, Joan Blondell
▶ McQueen, a New Orleans gambler known as the "Cincinnati Kid," takes on long-time champion Robinson, known as "The Man," in a high stakes game of stud poker. Engrossing story builds slowly (with time out for romantic interludes with Weld and Ann-Margret) but segues into a tense finish. McQueen is fine in one of his best roles but acting honors are stolen by Blondell as the dealer, "Ladyfingers."

CINDERELLA 1950
★★★★★ G Animation 1:14
Dir: Wilfred Jackson, Hamilton Luske, Clyde Geronimi   *Cast:* Voices of Ilene Woods, William Phipps, Eleanor Audley, Verna Felton, James MacDonald
▶ Smooth, sentimental version of Perrault's fairy tale adds large cast of animals—comical mice Jacques and Gus-Gus, sinister cat, energetic bluebirds—to classic story of abused stepdaughter who captures dashing prince's heart. Typically strong Disney animation enhanced by tuneful score, including Oscar-nominated "Bibbidy-Bobbidi-Boo." Highlighted by inspired rendition of Cinderella's transformation into princess. (CC)

CINDERELLA LIBERTY 1973
★★ R Drama/Romance 1:57
☑ Adult situations, explicit language
Dir: Mark Rydell   *Cast:* James Caan, Marsha Mason, Kirk Calloway, Eli Wallach, Burt Young, Dabney Coleman
▶ While on a pass, sailor Caan meets prostitute Mason, the mother of mulatto son Calloway. Caan falls for her and becomes close to the kid but complications, such as Mason's pregnancy, arise in the relationship. Warm and winning; Mason's Oscar-nominated performance is solidly supported by Caan.

CIRCLE OF IRON 1979
★★ R Martial Arts 1:42
☑ Adult situations, explicit language, graphic violence
Dir: Richard Moore   *Cast:* David Carradine, Jeff Cooper, Roddy McDowall, Eli Wallach, Christopher Lee
▶ Atypical kung-fu adventure set in a bizarre fantasy land mixes Zen philosophy with well-staged martial arts mayhem. A blind teacher guides young pupil Cooper through battles with monkey people, demons, and bandits to enlightenment at the hands of Zetan the Great (Lee). Carradine, replacing Bruce Lee after his untimely death, plays four roles. Lee wrote the story with James Coburn and Stirling Silliphant.

CIRCLE OF POWER 1984
★ R Drama 1:37
☑ Nudity, adult situations, explicit language, violence
Dir: Bobby Roth   *Cast:* Yvette Mimieux, Christopher Allport, Cindy Pickett, John Considine, Scott Marlowe, Walter Olkewicz
▶ Businessmen and their wives attend an Executive Development Training session, expecting director Mimieux to help them cope with a variety of problems. Instead, she instigates a series of ghastly rituals to degrade and humiliate her clients. Off-beat psychodrama is often uncomfortable to watch. Also known as *Mystique* and *Naked Weekend*.

CIRCLE OF TWO 1980 Canadian
★★★ PG Drama 1:39
☑ Nudity
Dir: Jules Dassin   *Cast:* Richard Burton, Tatum O'Neal, Nuala FitzGerald, Patricia Collins, Kate Reid
▶ Tedious account of the platonic affair between Burton, a creatively blocked artist, and O'Neal, a teenager who inspires him to paint again. A touchy subject is handled with delicacy, and Burton gives one of his better later performances. Ryan O'Neal (Tatum's father) appears as an extra in the porno theater where the friends meet.

CIRCUS OF HORRORS 1960 British
★★ NR Horror 1:28
☑ Violence
Dir: Sidney Hayers   *Cast:* Anton Diffring, Erika Remberg, Yvonne Monlaur, Donald Pleasence, Kenneth Griffith
▶ Grisly horror film about plastic surgeon Diffring, who uses a small circus to pursue illegal experiments. His altered patients are forced to perform in dangerous circus acts; if they complain, they meet with gruesome "accidents." Alternately ghastly and comic, with heavy overtones of sex and sadism.

CIRCUS WORLD 1964
★★★ NR Drama 2:15
Dir: Henry Hathaway   *Cast:* John Wayne, Claudia Cardinale, Rita Hay-

worth, Lloyd Nolan, Richard Conte, Kay Walsh

▶ Wayne, owner of a nineteenth-century circus and Wild West show, plans a tour of Europe to search for the mother of foster daughter Cardinale. Shipwreck threatens show's survival, but Wayne's horse stunts and Cardinale's budding trapeze talents save the day. She's also reunited with her mother, Hayworth. Large-scale, eye-pleasing drama features exciting acts by Austria's Franz Althoff Circus.

CITADEL, THE 1938 British
★★ NR Drama 1:52 B&W
Dir: King Vidor *Cast:* Robert Donat, Rosalind Russell, Ralph Richardson, Rex Harrison, Emlyn Williams, Penelope Dudley Ward

▶ Faithful adaptation of A. J. Cronin's best-selling novel describes the choice idealistic doctor Donat must make between caring for impoverished Welsh village or taking lucrative London practice. Russell offers stirring support as his devoted wife. Earnest but slowly paced picture received four Oscar nominations.

CITIZEN KANE 1941
★★★★ NR Drama 1:59 B&W
Dir: Orson Welles *Cast:* Orson Welles, Joseph Cotten, Ruth Warrick, Agnes Moorehead, Everett Sloane

▶ Welles's film masterpiece about the scandalous public and private life of newspaper publisher Charles Foster Kane (Welles), who dies murmuring "Rosebud" and sets off a nationwide search for the meaning of the word. Sure and penetrating performances by the entire cast, magnificent production values that set a new standard in cinematic craftsmanship, and a stunning musical score by Bernard Herrmann. Nominated for nine Oscars, winning for the screenplay by Welles and Herman Mankiewicz. Indisputably one of the great American classics.

CITY GIRL, THE 1985
★ NR Drama 1:25
☑ Adult situations, explicit language, violence
Dir: Martha Coolidge *Cast:* Laura Harrington, Joe Mastroianni, Carole McGill, Peter Riegert, Jim Carrington, Lawrence Phillips

▶ Photographer Harrington tries to find a balance between career and romance and winds up with no real satisfaction. Shaking free of conventional boyfriend Mastroianni, she experiments with sexual abandon and struggles with professional setbacks. Often funny and sometimes unsympathetic, hard-nosed drama examines a young woman's attempt to garner self-esteem.

CITY HEAT 1984
★★★ PG Action-Adventure 1:37
☑ Adult situations, explicit language, violence
Dir: Richard Benjamin *Cast:* Clint Eastwood, Burt Reynolds, Jane Alexander, Madeline Kahn, Irene Cara, Rip Torn

▶ Tongue-in-cheek 1930s mystery with private eye Reynolds pursuing two mob gangs who killed his lowlife colleague; Eastwood, spoofing his Dirty Harry role, doubts his former partner's motives. Good showcase for the leads, appearing together for the first time. Eastwood, tight-lipped as ever, is especially funny. (CC)

CITY LIGHTS 1931
★★★★ G Comedy 1:26 B&W
Dir: Charlie Chaplin *Cast:* Charlie Chaplin, Virginia Cherrill, Florence Lee, Harry Myers, Hank Mann

▶ Chaplin's masterpiece is funny, poignant, sentimental, and heartbreaking all at once. The Little Tramp falls in love with a blind flower seller and is befriended by an alcoholic millionaire who likes him when he's drunk but doesn't recognize him while sober. The Tramp's efforts to finance his love's eye operation bring about a delicately understated but incredibly moving finale. Silent, with a musical score by Chaplin.

CITY LIMITS 1985
★★ PG-13 Sci-Fi 1:25
☑ Brief nudity, adult situations, violence
Dir: Aaron Lipstadt *Cast:* Darrell Larson, John Stockwell, Kim Cattrall, Rae Dawn Chong, John Diehl, Don Opper

▶ In a postapocalyptic wasteland, teenager Stockwell is caught in a gang war between vicious punks and deadly bikers. Chong and Cattrall play the beautiful women who lead the hero to safety. Robby Benson and James Earl Jones have bit parts.

CITY ON FIRE 1979 Canadian
★★★ R Action-Adventure 1:44
☑ Explicit language, violence
Dir: Alvin Rakoff *Cast:* Barry Newman, Henry Fonda, Ava Gardner, Shelley Winters, Susan Clark

▶ After a lunatic sets off an explosion in a

chemical refinery, fire engulfs the nearby drought-ridden town, trapping an all-star cast in a hospital. Fonda is the fire chief coping bravely with the disaster; Gardner, an alcoholic TV reporter covering the story; and Newman, a hospital director responsible for the safety of his patients.

CLAIRE'S KNEE 1971 French
☆ **PG Comedy 1:43**
☑ Adult situations
Dir: Eric Rohmer   *Cast:* Jean-Claude Brialy, Aurora Cornu, Beatrice Romand, Laurence De Monaghan
▶ While on vacation, Brialy becomes obsessed with a much younger teenage De Monaghan; specifically he yearns to touch her knee. Dry, civilized adult entertainment in the director's patented mode, emphasizing talk and character development. Fifth in Rohmer's "Six Moral Tales" collection.

CLAIRVOYANT, THE 1983
★★★ **R Mystery-Suspense 1:37**
☑ Rape, nudity, adult situations, graphic violence
Dir: Armand Mastroianni   *Cast:* Perry King, Elizabeth Kemp, Norman Parker, Kenneth McMillan
▶ Talk show host King exploits a series of brutal murders to improve his ratings. At first he's helped by Parker, a cop moonlighting as a stand-up comic, but as the murders continue the police grow increasingly suspicious of King. The plot is further complicated by clairvoyant artist Kemp, whose drawings of the killer place her in danger. Extremely graphic at times, particularly during a gruesome nightmare sequence.

CLAMBAKE 1967
★★ **NR Musical 1:39**
Dir: Arthur H. Nadel   *Cast:* Elvis Presley, Shelley Fabares, Will Hutchins, Bill Bixby, Gary Merrill, Angelique Pettyjohn
▶ Texas oil heir Presley trades places with a poor Miami ski instructor to see if he can win women without money. He falls for Fabares, his first student, and steals her away from playboy boyfriend Bixby by entering a big boat race. Lower-grade Presley vehicle includes the title song, "Hey, Hey, Hey," "Who Needs Money," and three other tunes.

CLAN OF THE CAVE BEAR, THE 1986
★★ **R Action-Adventure 1:38**
☑ Rape, brief nudity, violence
Dir: Michael Chapman   *Cast:* Daryl

Hannah, Pamela Reed, James Remar, Thomas G. Waites, John Doolittle
▶ Respectful adaptation of Jean M. Auel's best-seller about the transition 35,-000 years ago from the Neanderthal age to the Cro-Magnon era. Hannah is Ayla, a beautiful blond woman resented by the swarthy members of her adopted tribe. Mastering weapons reserved for males, she earns respect and becomes a medicine woman. **(CC)**

CLARA'S HEART 1988
★★★★ **PG-13 Comedy/Drama 1:43**
☑ Adult situations, explicit language
Dir: Robert Mulligan   *Cast:* Whoopi Goldberg, Michael Ontkean, Kathleen Quinlan, Neal Patrick Harris, Spalding Gray, Beverly Todd
▶ Troubled suburban couple Ontkean and Quinlan hire Jamaican housekeeper Goldberg. Obnoxious son Harris resents Goldberg's presence and gives her grief, but unflappable maid has a witty rejoinder for every smart-aleck remark. When parents separate, Harris surrenders to Goldberg's innate warmth. Unapologetically sentimental drama carried by true performance from Goldberg.

CLASH BY NIGHT 1952
★★★ **NR Drama 1:45 B&W**
Dir: Fritz Lang   *Cast:* Barbara Stanwyck, Paul Douglas, Robert Ryan, Marilyn Monroe, Keith Andes
▶ A disillusioned Stanwyck comes home to Monterey and accepts a marriage of convenience to big-hearted fisherman Douglas. Still unhappy, she starts an affair with cynical projectionist Ryan that leads to tragedy. Somber, downbeat version of a Clifford Odets play is notable for its strong acting, expert direction, and vivid atmosphere. Monroe performs capably as a young woman who wants to follow in Stanwyck's footsteps.

CLASH OF THE TITANS 1981
★★★★ **PG Fantasy 1:58**
☑ Brief nudity, violence
Dir: Desmond Davis   *Cast:* Laurence Olivier, Harry Hamlin, Claire Bloom, Judi Bowker, Maggie Smith, Burgess Meredith
▶ Perseus (Hamlin) battles fearsome obstacles to save the kidnapped Andromeda (Bowker). Although mortal, he receives guidance and protection from the gods (including Olivier as Zeus and Bloom as Hera). Special effects by Ray Harryhausen are often outstanding in this

loose adaptation of Greek mythology. Children will be entranced by Pegasus, a flying horse, and the snake-haired Medusa.

CLASS 1983
★★★ R Comedy/Drama 1:38
☑ Nudity, adult situations, explicit language
Dir: Lewis John Carlino *Cast:* Rob Lowe, Jacqueline Bisset, Andrew McCarthy, Stuart Margolin, Cliff Robertson, John Cusack
▶ During a wild weekend in Chicago, naive boarding school student McCarthy has a fling with older woman Bisset, who he later learns is roommate Lowe's mother. Bisset's portrayal of a troubled character brings serious overtones to this preppie comedy.

CLASS OF '44 1973
★★★ PG Drama 1:35
☑ Adult situations, explicit language
Dir: Paul Bogart *Cast:* Gary Grimes, Jerry Houser, Oliver Conant, William Atherton, Sam Bottoms, Deborah Winters
▶ Sequel to *Summer of '42* focuses on Hermie (Grimes, repeating his earlier role) after he graduates from his Brooklyn high school. Friend Conant enlists in the Marines, but Hermie and Oscy (Houser) enter college instead, where Hermie has a troubling affair with young Winters. Effective period details add to film's nostalgic tone.

CLASS OF 1984 1982
★★★ R Action-Adventure 1:36
☑ Nudity, explicit language, graphic violence
Dir: Mark L. Lester *Cast:* Perry King, Timothy Van Patten, Merrie Lynn Ross, Roddy McDowall
▶ Graphic, hard-hitting exposé of shocking conditions in an inner-city high school where rebellious teenagers conduct a guerrilla war against beleaguered teachers King and McDowall. When the punks, led by Van Patten, kidnap and rape King's wife Ross, he goes on the warpath. The violence is often excessive.

CLASS OF NUKE 'EM HIGH 1986
★ R Horror 1:21
☑ Nudity, adult situations, explicit language, graphic violence
Dir: Richard W. Haines, Samuel Weil
Cast: Janelle Brady, Gilbert Brenton, Robert Prichard, R. L. Ryan, James Nugent Vernon
▶ Leak from a nuclear power plant seeps into the water supply at Tromaville, "The Toxic Waste Capital of the World." The first victims are the high school's Honor Society, clean-cut preppies who are turned overnight into violent mutants. Follow-up to *Toxic Avenger* has the same amusingly disgusting special effects and slapstick humor.

CLAUDINE 1974
★★★ PG Drama 1:32
☑ Adult situations, explicit language
Dir: John Berry *Cast:* Diahann Carroll, James Earl Jones, Lawrence Hilton-Jacobs, Tamu, Adam Wade, David Kruger
▶ Ghetto mom Carroll, struggling to raise six children, falls in love with garbage collector Jones. He provides a needed father figure but fears his job makes him unworthy of Carroll. Engaging and wholesome although marred somewhat by preachy climax. Music by Gladys Knight and the Pips and Curtis Mayfield.

CLEAN AND SOBER 1988
★★★★ R Drama 2:04
☑ Adult situations, explicit language
Dir: Glenn Gordon Caron *Cast:* Michael Keaton, Kathy Baker, Morgan Freeman, M. Emmet Walsh, Tate Donovan, Brian Benben
▶ Yuppie cocaine and alcohol addict Keaton has some serious problems: he's embezzled funds from his company and given drugs to a woman who subsequently died. Hiding out in a detox clinic, he spars with counselor Freeman and fellow patient Baker. Once he's out of the hospital, Keaton finds new take on life doesn't necessarily yield easy answers. Convincing, thought-provoking drama generates power from solid supporting cast and impressive first foray into drama by Keaton.

CLEOPATRA 1963
★★★ G Drama 4:03
Dir: Joseph L. Mankiewicz *Cast:* Elizabeth Taylor, Richard Burton, Rex Harrison, Roddy McDowall, Martin Landau, Pamela Brown
▶ Egyptian queen Cleopatra's (Taylor) affair with Julius Caesar (Harrison) is cut short by his assassination; she then takes up with Roman senator Mark Antony (Burton) for ill-fated romance/political alliance. Lavish epic won notoriety for huge budget and Taylor/Burton affair; Oscar-nominated Harrison outshines his more

publicized co-stars. Best Picture nominee nabbed Oscars for Cinematography, Costume Design, Special Effects, Art Direction/Set Decoration.

CLEOPATRA JONES 1973
★★ PG Action-Adventure 1:29
☑ Violence
Dir: Jack Starrett *Cast:* Tamara Dobson, Shelley Winters, Bernie Casey, Brenda Sykes, Antonio Fargas
▶ The 6'2" Tamara Dobson is Cleopatra Jones, a black CIA narcotics agent who takes on Winters, a lesbian underworld antagonist running an international dope ring. A James Bond-type adventure in black drag with a story line straight out of comic books. Fans can check out sequel *Cleopatra Jones and the Casino of Gold.*

CLEOPATRA JONES AND THE CASINO OF GOLD 1975
★★ R Action-Adventure 1:36
☑ Nudity, explicit language, violence
Dir: Chuck Bail *Cast:* Tamara Dobson, Stella Stevens, Tanny, Norman Fell, Albert Popwell
▶ Sassy black superagent Cleopatra Jones (Dobson) returns to battle larger-than-life drug queen villainess Stevens in this action-packed adventure sequel. Filmed on location in Hong Kong. Good support from Fell and oriental martial arts beauty Tanny.

CLOAK & DAGGER 1984
★★★★ PG Action-Adventure 1:41
☑ Explicit language, violence
Dir: Richard Franklin *Cast:* Henry Thomas, Dabney Coleman, Michael Murphy, Christina Nigra, John McIntire
▶ Thomas is an overly imaginative Cloak & Dagger computer game whiz-kid who becomes entangled in a real-life spy caper involving government secrets and enemy agents. Coleman doubles as Thomas's dad and make-believe superhero pal. Appealing adventure with a child hero that's not for kids only. **(CC)**

CLOCKWISE 1986 British
★★ PG Comedy 1:32
☑ Adult humor
Dir: Christopher Morhan *Cast:* John Cleese, Alison Steadman, Sharon Maiden, Penelope Wilton, Stephen Moore
▶ Monty Python's Cleese is the most pompous, punctilious headmaster in England. Through a series of silly mishaps, he's late for the most important speech

of his life. For those who appreciate British humor.

CLOCKWORK ORANGE, A 1971
★★ R Drama 2:17
☑ Nudity, adult situations, explicit language, graphic violence
Dir: Stanley Kubrick *Cast:* Malcolm McDowell, Patrick Magee, Adrienne Corri, Aubrey Morris, James Marcus
▶ Sadistic young McDowell of the near future is "rehabilitated" by a special conditioning treatment. "Cured" of his savage excesses and love for Beethoven, he's a misfit in a still violent society. Brilliantly directed by Kubrick, this magically violent film (though tame by today's standards) was nominated for four Academy Awards and is considered a classic by many critics.

CLOSE ENCOUNTERS OF THE THIRD KIND 1977
★★★★ PG Sci-Fi 2:15
☑ Adult situations, explicit language
Dir: Steven Spielberg *Cast:* Richard Dreyfuss, François Truffaut, Teri Garr, Melinda Dillon, Cary Guffey, Bob Balaban
▶ Dreyfuss, a power company worker, encounters UFOs and searches for the truth behind his vision. Also on the aliens' trail: scientist Truffaut, leader of an international research team, and Dillon, who's searching for her missing son. Spielberg's stunning, joyous portrait of a quite benign alien invasion culminates in a joining of man and spaceman at Wyoming's Devil's Tower. Technical wizardry combines music, visuals, and great special effects. Reissued in 1980 with new footage as *Close Encounters of the Third Kind: The Special Edition.* **(CC)**

CLOSELY WATCHED TRAINS 1966 Czech
★ NR Comedy 1:29 B&W
Dir: Jiri Menzel *Cast:* Vaclav Neckar, Jitka Bendova, Josef Somr, Vladimir Valenta, Jiri Menzel
▶ In World War II German-occupied Czechoslovakia, railroad employee Neckar attempts to lose his virginity and turns his attention to a more serious matter: blowing up Nazi train. Alternately amusing and moving mix of moods. Oscar winner for Best Foreign Film. ⑤

CLOSE TO MY HEART 1951
★★★ NR Drama 1:31 B&W
Dir: William Keighley *Cast:* Ray Mil-

land, Gene Tierney, Fay Bainter, Howard St. John, Mary Beth Hughes
▶ Sturdy soap opera featuring Milland and Tierney as a loving couple in conflict over their adopted child's true heritage. Touching and nicely handled without being maudlin, but composer Max Steiner goes for the heart with an all-out weepy score.

CLOUD DANCER 1979
★★ PG Drama 1:48
☑ Explicit language, violence
Dir: Barry Brown *Cast:* David Carradine, Jennifer O'Neill, Joseph Bottoms, Colleen Camp, Albert Salmi, Nina Van Pallandt
▶ Old-fashioned adventure about stunt pilot Carradine whose daring exploits in a flying circus upset his friends. O'Neill is a photographer who causes Carradine to rethink his priorities when she reveals he's a father; Bottoms, a fellow pilot who falls victim to drugs. Good aerial sequences overcome a mechanical plot.

CLOUDS OVER EUROPE 1939 British
★★★ NR Action-Adventure 1:22 B&W
Dir: Tim Whelan *Cast:* Laurence Olivier, Valerie Hobson, Ralph Richardson, George Curzon, George Merritt
▶ English newspaper reporter Hobson alerts brother Richardson, a Scotland Yard detective, about a secret German ray that can disable British planes. With Olivier's help, he pursues the ship carrying the weapon. Droll sense of humor and outstanding stars spark this early anti-Nazi effort.

CLOWN, THE 1953
★ NR Drama 1:32 B&W
Dir: Robert Z. Leonard *Cast:* Red Skelton, Tim Considine, Jane Greer, Loring Smith, Philip Ober, Walter Reed
▶ Maudlin show-biz remake of *The Champ* features Skelton in a rare dramatic role as a down-on-his-luck vaudeville star who battles alcoholism with the help of his devoted son Considine. Through perseverance and grit, he wins the lead in a new TV show. Charles Bronson and Roger Moore have bit parts.

CLOWNHOUSE 1988
★ NR Horror 1:21
☑ Explicit language, violence
Dir: Victor Salva *Cast:* Nathan Forrest Winters, Brian McHugh, Sam Rockwell, Tree, Byron Weible, David C. Reinecker
▶ Despite young Winters's terror of clowns, his bullying older brother Rock-

well forces him to attend a performance of Jolly Brothers Circus. Unfortunately, escaped mental patients have invaded the show disguised as clowns and pursue the boys back to their deserted Victorian house. Low-budget horror downplays gore while emphasizing suspense.

CLUB PARADISE 1986
★★ PG-13 Comedy 1:44
☑ Explicit language
Dir: Harold Ramis *Cast:* Robin Williams, Rick Moranis, Peter O'Toole, Adolph Caesar, Twiggy, Andrea Martin
▶ Williams is a burned-out fireman trying to turn a ramshackle Caribbean resort into a tropical paradise. Subplots include nerds trying to pick up women, guests lost in the jungle, and a local revolution. Williams sparkles, despite heat stroke material. Reggae star Jimmy Cliff's bouncy tunes give the film a lift. **(CC)**

CLUE 1985
★★ PG Mystery-Suspense/Comedy 1:27
☑ Explicit language, violence
Dir: Jonathan Lynn *Cast:* Eileen Brennan, Tim Curry, Madeline Kahn, Christopher Lloyd, Michael McKean
▶ Plastic game pieces come to life and you guess who killed whom and with what. Host Mr. Boddy and Yvette, his bosomy French maid, greet guests Mrs. White, Mrs. Peacock, Mr. Green, Miss Scarlet and Colonel Mustard before the lights go out and Boddy is killed. Or is he? Theaters offered one of three endings; all appear on videotape. Especially good performances from Kahn and McKean. **(CC)**

CLUNY BROWN 1946
★★★★ NR Comedy 1:40 B&W
Dir: Ernst Lubitsch *Cast:* Charles Boyer, Jennifer Jones, Peter Lawford, Helen Walker, Reginald Gardiner
▶ Jones gives one of her best performances as a maid with plumbing expertise stuck in a pre–World War II English household of snobbish, brainless twits. She falls in love with Czech refugee Boyer, who exposes his hosts' empty lives. Satire on Britain's stuffy upper classes is directed with polish and subtlety.

COAL MINER'S DAUGHTER 1980
★★★★★ PG Biography/Music 2:05
☑ Adult situations, explicit language, mild violence
Dir: Michael Apted *Cast:* Sissy Spacek,

Tommy Lee Jones, Beverly D'Angelo, Levon Helm, Phyllis Boyens, Ernest Tubb ► Heartwarming story of country-western legend Loretta Lynn. Perceptive script and sympathetic direction resulted in compelling portraits of the people in her life: dirt-poor father Helm, husband Mooney (Jones), and best friend Patsy Cline (D'Angelo). Location shooting captured the Appalachian essence of Tennessee and Kentucky. Spacek, who sang the songs herself, won an Oscar for her uncanny imitation of the singer. The film also received five other nominations (including Best Picture and Screenplay).

COAST TO COAST 1980
★★★ PG Comedy 1:34
☑ Adult situations, explicit language
Dir: Joseph Sargent *Cast:* Dyan Cannon, Robert Blake, Quinn Redeker, Michael Lerner, Maxine Stuart
► Semi-loony but very rich Cannon escapes from a New York hospital and hitches a ride to California with debt-ridden truck driver Blake. The unlikely pair fall in love while fleeing an assortment of villains. Smash finale includes a ten-wheeler driven into a Beverly Hills living room.

COBRA 1986
★★★ R Action-Adventure 1:27
☑ Explicit language, graphic violence
Dir: George Pan Cosmatos *Cast:* Sylvester Stallone, Brigitte Nielsen, Reni Santoni, Andrew Robinson, Art La Fleur
► Unconventional L.A. cop Marion "Cobra" Cobretti (Stallone) takes on a neo-fascist gang of killers in this efficient, action-packed thriller reuniting Sly with his *Rambo: First Blood Part II* director. Stallone's then-wife Nielsen portrays the murder witness who's on the gang's hit list. Macho heaven for Stallone fans as their man successfully invades *Dirty Harry* territory. (CC)

COCA-COLA KID, THE 1985 Australian
★ R Comedy 1:34
☑ Nudity, explicit language
Dir: Dusan Makavejev *Cast:* Eric Roberts, Greta Scacchi, Bill Kerr, Chris Haywood, Max Gillies
► Roberts is an American hotshot Coca-Cola executive who tries to discover why Australia's Anderson Valley is the one spot in the whole country where Coke isn't sold. May not be for mainstream audiences but will reward the patient viewer with its original moments. Arrest-ing visuals and a sympathetic performance by Scacchi as a troubled secretary. (CC)

COCAINE WARS 1986
★★ R Action-Adventure 1:22
☑ Nudity, adult situations, explicit language, violence
Dir: Hector Olivera *Cast:* John Schneider, Kathryn Witt, Federico Luppi, Royal Dano, Rodolfo Ranni
► DEA agent Schneider gathers evidence on South American drug kingpin Luppi, but his cover is blown by his old girlfriend, reporter Witt. When Luppi kidnaps Witt, Schneider arms himself for a one-man assault on his headquarters. Diverting exploitation fare for action fans.

COCKTAIL 1988
★★★★ R Drama 1:40
☑ Adult situations, explicit language
Dir: Roger Donaldson *Cast:* Tom Cruise, Bryan Brown, Elisabeth Shue, Lisa Banes, Laurence Luckinbill, Kelly Lynch
► Cocky young Cruise rises to the top of New York bartending trade under corrupt tutelage of Brown. In Jamaica, Cruise has romance with wealthy Shue. Will her love redeem him? Shallow but brassy and energetic. Cruise, Shue, and Jamaica look terrific; Brown plays his role to the hilt, spouting the wisdom he calls "Coughlin's Law." Most outlandish scene: Cruise reciting poetry in bar. Hard-rocking soundtrack includes Bobby McFerrin's "Don't Worry, Be Happy," Beach Boys' "Kokomo," and John Cougar Mellencamp's version of Buddy Holly's "Rave On."

COCOANUTS 1929
★★ NR Comedy 1:36 B&W
Dir: Robert Florey, Joseph Santley
Cast: The Marx Brothers, Mary Eaton, Margaret Dumont, Kay Francis, Oscar Shaw
► First Marx Brothers film is a straight transfer of their Broadway hit by George S. Kaufman and Irving Berlin. Primitive sound and camerawork make it extremely difficult to watch, but fans will want to see some of the brothers' best routines: a hilarious rigged auction, the "viaduct" skit, and all of Groucho's scenes with Dumont. Berlin score includes "Monkey-Doodle-Doo" and "When My Dreams Come True."

COCOON 1985
★★★★★ PG-13 Fantasy 1:57

☑ Brief nudity, adult situations, explicit language
Dir: Ron Howard *Cast:* Don Ameche, Wilford Brimley, Steve Guttenberg, Hume Cronyn, Brian Dennehy, Jessica Tandy
▶ Old codgers Ameche, Brimley and Cronyn are suddenly rejuvenated when they find a swimming pool filled with mysterious cocoons; a fountain of youth provided by benevolent aliens led by Dennehy. Magical, upbeat comedy/fantasy with a touching script and wonderful ensemble acting. Ameche, whose breakdancing scene brings down the house, won the Oscar for Best Supporting Actor. Spawned sequel. **(CC)**

COCOON: THE RETURN 1988
★★★★ PG Fantasy 1:56
☑ Explicit language
Dir: Daniel Petrie *Cast:* Don Ameche, Wilford Brimley, Hume Cronyn, Jack Gilford, Steve Guttenberg, Maureen Stapleton
▶ Undersea earthquake endangers alien cocoons, so Ameche, Brimley, and Cronyn return to Earth to help recover them. They cheer up old buddy Gilford and rescue a spacedweller from marine biologists. Slick sequel benefits greatly from the charm of its geriatric cast members (led by Ameche re-creating his Oscar-winning role), but lacks the magic of the original.

CODE NAME: EMERALD 1985
★★★★ PG Action-Adventure 1:35
Dir: Jonathan Sanger *Cast:* Ed Harris, Max Von Sydow, Eric Stoltz, Helmut Berger, Horst Buchholz
▶ Tense espionage thriller features Harris as a World War II double agent fighting to keep the Nazis from discovering the time and place of D-Day. Good-looking spy drama with believable performances; a nail-biter. **(CC)**

CODENAME: WILDGEESE 1986
German/Italian
★★★ R Action-Adventure 1:42
☑ Explicit language, violence
Dir: Anthony M. Dawson (Antonio Margheriti) *Cast:* Ernest Borgnine, Lewis Collins, Lee Van Cleef, Mimsy Farmer, Klaus Kinski
▶ A team of mercenaries (led by Collins) is hired to destroy a Communist-run drug ring in the jungles of Thailand. The mission is accomplished, with the help of intrepid chopper pilot Van Cleef, in quite violent

fashion. Plenty of explosions, dismembered limbs, and general brutality in a film longer on action than plot logic.

CODE OF SILENCE 1985
★★★★ R Action-Adventure 1:40
☑ Explicit language, graphic violence
Dir: Andrew Davis *Cast:* Chuck Norris, Henry Silva, Bert Remsen, Mike Genovese, Nathan Davis
▶ Chicago cop Norris defies the "code of silence" by testifying against a policeman who wrongly shot a teenager. The decision does not make him popular with his peers and thus he must stand alone against two warring drug gangs. First-rate Norris vehicle combines the anticipated action with more depth in its plotting and characterization. Chuck's best performance to date.

COFFY 1973
☆ R Action-Adventure 1:31
☑ Nudity, adult situations, explicit language, violence
Dir: Jack Hill *Cast:* Pam Grier, Booker Bradshaw, Robert DoQui, William Elliott, Allan Arbus
▶ High-grade exploitation fare gave Grier one of her best roles as a tough nurse whose sister is turned into a junkie by greasy dealers. Grier uses her wit, beautiful body, and shotgun to eliminate the villians. Fast-paced, sexy, and extremely violent.

COLD FEET 1984
☆ PG Comedy 1:36
☑ Adult situations, explicit language
Dir: Bruce van Dusen *Cast:* Griffin Dunne, Blanche Baker, Marrissa Chibas, Mark Cronogue, Kurt Knudson
▶ Dunne, a TV writer/director who just broke up with wife Baker, becomes friendly with research scientist Chibas who just broke up with boyfriend Cronogue. After bad dates with other people and some wrangling with their respective ex's, Dunne and Chibas find their relationship turning into a romance in this New York–based comedy. Music by Todd Rundgren. **(CC)**

COLDITZ STORY, THE 1955 British
★★★ NR Drama 1:37 B&W
Dir: Guy Hamilton *Cast:* John Mills, Eric Portman, Christopher Rhodes, Lionel Jeffries, Bryan Forbes, Theodore Bikel
▶ Tense World War II drama about POWs determined to break out of the Colditz Castle, an "escape-proof" Nazi prison. When attempts by Polish and French in-

mates fail, Pat Reid (Mills) concocts a daring plan that requires bravery and split-second timing. Authentic and exciting film was based on a true story.

COLD RIVER 1982
★★★ PG Action-Adventure 1:32
☑ Adult situations, explicit language, mild violence
Dir: Fred G. Sullivan *Cast:* Suzanne Weber, Pat Petersen, Brad Sullivan, Richard Jaeckel, Robert Earl Jones
▶ Children Weber and Petersen are stranded in the Adirondacks when father Jaeckel has a fatal heart attack. The pair brave the winter elements under the protection of old trapper Jones but they must deal with an escaped con by themselves. Meatier, somewhat more mature fare than others in the wilderness genre. Independent filmmaker Sullivan's experiences with making this movie are humorously detailed in his *Beerdrinker's Guide to Fitness and Film Making.*

COLD ROOM, THE 1983
★★ NR Mystery-Suspense/MFTV 1:35
☑ Rape, adult situations, explicit language, violence
Dir: James Dearden *Cast:* George Segal, Amanda Pays, Renee Soutendijk, Warren Clarke, Anthony Higgins
▶ Engrossing psychological thriller about father Segal and daughter Pays who visit East Berlin and find themselves supernaturally drawn into a forty-year-old intrigue. Atmosphere enhanced by location shooting, including Checkpoint Charlie, the actual crossing point between West and East Berlin. Written and directed by Dearden from the novel by Jeffrey Caine.

COLD STEEL 1987
★★ R Action-Adventure 1:30
☑ Nudity, adult situations, explicit language, violence
Dir: Dorothy Ann Puzo *Cast:* Brad Davis, Sharon Stone, Jonathan Banks, Adam Ant, Jay Acovone
▶ Davis, a tough cop who doesn't play by the rules, investigates his father's brutal murder. The trail leads to old friend Banks and vicious British punk Ant. Competently filmed if predictable cop film with its fair share of car chases, violence, and shootouts.

COLD SWEAT 1974 Italian/French
★ PG Action-Adventure 1:34
☑ Violence
Dir: Terence Young *Cast:* Charles

Bronson, Liv Ullmann, James Mason, Jill Ireland, Jean Topart, Yannick Delulle
▶ Bronson, a former drug dealer, retires to France with wife Ullmann and daughter Delulle, but his past comes back to haunt him when Southern smuggler Mason sets up one more drug run. After his family is kidnapped, Bronson goes on a rampage, taking hostage Mason's mistress Ireland. Adapted from Richard Matheson's *Ride the Nightmare.*

COLLECTOR, THE 1965
★★★ NR Mystery-Suspense 1:59
Dir: William Wyler *Cast:* Terence Stamp, Samantha Eggar, Mona Washbourne, Maurice Dallimore
▶ Young, neurotic Stamp collects butterflies and decides to take on another hobby: "collecting" a fiancée for himself. He kidnaps beautiful student Eggar and tries to force her into falling in love with him. Powerful suspense drama, both disturbing and highly entertaining. Compelling performances by Stamp and Eggar in what is essentially a two-character movie; claustrophobic tension created by the great Wyler. From the John Fowles best-seller.

COLLISION COURSE 1987
★★★ PG Action-Adventure 1:45
☑ Explicit language, violence
Dir: Lewis Teague *Cast:* Jay Leno, Noriyuki "Pat" Morita, Chris Sarandon, Tom Noonan, Ernie Hudson
▶ Japanese cop Morita teams up with Detroit policeman Leno to investigate car industry–related murders. Formula mismatched partners tale enlivened by action, stunts, violence, and a wild car chase finale through the streets of Detroit. Humor is a little heavy on the racial slurs but Morita adds a touch of class and comedian/talk show host Leno does a nice job in his first major movie role.

COLOR OF MONEY, THE 1986
★★★★ R Drama 1:57
☑ Nudity, adult situations, explicit language, mild violence
Dir: Martin Scorsese *Cast:* Paul Newman, Tom Cruise, Mary Elizabeth Mastrantonio, Helen Shaver, John Turturro
▶ In this follow-up to 1961's *The Hustler,* Newman won his long-awaited Oscar as "Fast Eddie" Felson, instructing rebellious but talented protégé Cruise in the ways of the hustle. Teacher and pupil separate but meet again for a climactic game. Bravura direction by Scorsese, flavorful di-

alogue from screenwriter Richard Price, terrific performances from Newman, Cruise, and Mastrantonio (as Cruise's hard-boiled girlfriend).

COLOR PURPLE, THE 1985
★ ★ ★ ★ ★ **PG-13 Drama 2:32**
☑ Adult situations, explicit language, violence
Dir: Steven Spielberg *Cast:* Danny Glover, Whoopi Goldberg, Margaret Avery, Willard E. Pugh, Oprah Winfrey, Adolph Caesar
▶ Spielberg abandoned the world of aliens and adventurers for this controversial but visually beautiful adaptation of Alice Walker's best-seller which traces the struggle and eventual triumph of Celie (Goldberg), a poor black woman under the brutal thumb of husband Glover in 1909–47 rural South. Some criticized Spielberg's approach as sugarcoated but the performances are excellent (especially TV talk show hostess Oprah in her first dramatic role) and the story is overflowing with powerful emotions. Nominated for eleven Oscars, including Best Picture. **(CC)**

COLORS 1988
★ ★ ★ **R Action-Adventure 2:00**
☑ Nudity, adult situations, explicit language, graphic violence
Dir: Dennis Hopper *Cast:* Sean Penn, Robert Duvall, Maria Conchita Alonso, Randy Brooks, Brand Bush, Don Cheadle
▶ Hotheaded rookie cop Penn and streetwise veteran Duvall are partnered to patrol tough Los Angeles neighborhood plagued by warfare between rival gangs, the Bloods and the Crips. Penn romances barrio girl Alonso, but his aggressive approach to street punks alienates and infuriates her, Duvall, and the gangs. Realistic, hard-hitting look at cop/gang battle for control of the streets is not for the squeamish. **(CC)**

COMA 1978
★ ★ ★ ★ **PG Mystery-Suspense 1:52**
☑ Adult situations, explicit language, violence
Dir: Michael Crichton *Cast:* Genevieve Bujold, Michael Douglas, Elizabeth Ashley, Richard Widmark, Rip Torn, Tom Selleck
▶ When a close friend goes into a permanent coma during an otherwise routine operation, intrepid doctor Bujold begins investigating similar incidents. She uncovers a sinister medical conspiracy, even though boyfriend Douglas is doubtful. Taut, quickly paced hospital thriller from the best-selling novel by Robin Cook. Bujold gives an intelligent, immensely sympathetic performance as the beleaguered heroine.

COMANCHEROS, THE 1961
★ ★ ★ ★ **NR Western 1:47**
Dir: Michael Curtiz *Cast:* John Wayne, Stuart Whitman, Ina Balin, Lee Marvin, Patrick Wayne
▶ Texas Rangers Wayne and Whitman battle the Comancheros, an outlaw band supplying guns and liquor to the dreaded Commanche Indians. Solid western, neither Wayne's best nor worst, with the Duke well suited to his tough, sarcastic role. Whitman, gunslinger Marvin, Wayne's son Pat, and a rousing Elmer Bernstein score add extra zing. **(CC)**

COME AND GET IT 1936
★ ★ ★ **NR Drama 1:39 B&W**
Dir: Howard Hawks, William Wyler
Cast: Edward Arnold, Joel McCrea, Frances Farmer, Walter Brennan, Andrea Leeds, Frank Shields
▶ Sprawling epic of the Pacific Northwest and larger-than-life timberman Arnold, who sacrifices love for wealth. Farmer, playing both the woman Arnold rejects and her daughter, whom he tries to wed, considered this her best film. Based on Edna Ferber novel. Contains some fascinating lumbering sequences. Brennan, as Arnold's pal, won the first of three Supporting Oscars.

COME BACK, LITTLE SHEBA 1952
★ ★ ★ **NR Drama 1:36 B&W**
Dir: Daniel Mann *Cast:* Shirley Booth, Burt Lancaster, Terry Moore, Richard Jaeckel, Philip Ober
▶ Booth deservedly won a Best Actress Oscar for her bravura performance as a desperately unhappy housewife married to alcoholic Lancaster (also fine in a change-of-pace performance). Their relationship is reexamined when lively art student Moore moves in with them. From William Inge's Broadway drama.

COME BACK TO THE FIVE AND DIME, JIMMY DEAN, JIMMY DEAN 1982
★ **PG Drama 1:49**
☑ Adult situations, explicit language, adult humor
Dir: Robert Altman *Cast:* Cher, Karen Black, Sandy Dennis, Sudie Bond, Kathy Bates

▶ Six women in the James Dean fan club reunite in a run-down Texas five and dime near where the actor shot *Giant*. Revelations start pouring out in Ed Graczyk's heavy-handed adaptation of his own play, which is transformed into affecting drama by the fine performances of the three leads and Altman's artful direction.

COMEDY OF TERRORS, THE 1964
★★ NR Horror/Comedy 1:28
Dir: Jacques Tourneur *Cast:* Vincent Price, Peter Lorre, Boris Karloff, Basil Rathbone, Joe E. Brown, Joyce Jameson
▶ In turn-of-the-century New England, business is slow for undertakers Price and Karloff, so Price and gnomish aide Lorre turn to murder to bring in new customers. Mean-spirited landlord Rathbone is the victim who won't stay dead. Broad spoof succeeds due to all-star cast of horror heavies.

COMES A HORSEMAN 1978
★★★★ PG Western/Drama 1:58
☑ Explicit language, mild violence
Dir: Alan J. Pakula *Cast:* Jane Fonda, James Caan, Jason Robards, George Grizzard, Richard Farnsworth, Mark Harmon
▶ In the 1940s, independent ranchers—tomboyish spinster Fonda and World War II vet Caan—join forces to battle Robards, a land baron intent on amassing an empire. Austere, slowly paced Western filmed in Colorado's majestic Wet Mountain Valley convincingly updates a traditional theme. Farnsworth won a Supporting Actor nomination for his role as Fonda's aging hired hand.

COMFORT AND JOY 1984 Scottish
★ PG Comedy 1:45
☑ Adult situations, violence
Dir: Bill Forsyth *Cast:* Bill Paterson, Eleanor David, C. P. Grogan, Alex Norton, Patrick Malahide, Rikki Fulton
▶ A mild-mannered Scottish radio disc jockey (Paterson), saddened when his girlfriend leaves him, throws himself into a mission to reconcile two Mafia families warring over local ice cream racket. Good-natured, subtle bit of Scottish drollery from Forsyth, who invests the slim story with his trademark whimsy and dry humor. Best appreciated by sophisticated viewers.

COMIC, THE 1969
★★ PG Comedy 1:35
☑ Explicit language

Dir: Carl Reiner *Cast:* Dick Van Dyke, Michele Lee, Mickey Rooney, Cornel Wilde, Nina Wayne, Steve Allen
▶ Silent film star Van Dyke destroys his career through egotism and alcoholism, then rejects friends who try to help him. Sincere but heavy-handed study of a doomed figure (a composite of several screen clowns) is ultimately mawkish and unrevealing.

COMING HOME 1978
★★★★★ R Drama 2:07
☑ Nudity, adult situations, explicit language
Dir: Hal Ashby *Cast:* Jane Fonda, Jon Voight, Bruce Dern, Penelope Milford, Robert Ginty, Robert Carradine
▶ Fonda, the proper, repressed wife of Vietnam Marine captain Dern, does volunteer work at a local veteran's hospital, where she falls in love with paraplegic vet Voight. The husband, freaked out by the war, returns to find his wife radically changed and independent. One of Hollywood's first attempts to explore Vietnam, but the political slant takes a back seat to the touching and emotionally charged love story. Outstanding Oscar-winning performances by Voight and Fonda. Score of classic sixties music adds to the period feel.

COMING SOON 1983
★★★★ NR Horror 0:55
☑ Violence
Dir: Allen Smithee *Cast:* Jamie Lee Curtis
▶ Aptly titled compilation of horror film trailer/coming attraction shorts featuring the cream of Universal Studios' best and worst—from *The Invisible Man* to *Psycho* to *E.T.*. Curtis hosts this clever package of entertainment, history and retrospective tribute.

COMING TO AMERICA 1988
★★★★ R Comedy 1:55
☑ Nudity, adult situations, explicit language, adult humor
Dir: John Landis *Cast:* Eddie Murphy, James Earl Jones, Arsenio Hall, John Amos, Madge Sinclair, Shari Headley
▶ Pressured into an arranged marriage by his father Jones, pampered African prince Murphy travels to America with sidekick Hall in search of true love. Murphy meets beautiful Headley in Queens, New York, and to be near her gets a job in the burger joint owned by her dad, Amos. Romantic prospects look bright

until Jones interferes. Despite critical condemnation, fans flocked to Murphy vehicle; part of the fun comes from identifying Murphy and Hall in disguised multiple roles.

COMMANDO 1985
★ ★ ★ ★ R Action-Adventure 1:30
☑ Brief nudity, explicit language, graphic violence
Dir: Mark L. Lester *Cast:* Arnold Schwarzenegger, Rae Dawn Chong, Dan Hedaya, Vernon Wells, James Olson, Alyssa Milano
▶ Retired commando Schwarzenegger returns to action when daughter Milano is kidnapped. Not much in the way of plot, but plenty of energetic, powerhouse action scenes. Chong, as a stewardess along for Arnie's violent ride, is appealing and the big man evinces a nice sense of humor. "I like you, Sully, you're a funny guy," he tells one thug. "That's why I'll kill you last." **(CC)**

COMMANDOS STRIKE AT DAWN, THE 1942
★ ★ ★ NR War 1:39 B&W
Dir: John Farrow *Cast:* Paul Muni, Anna Lee, Lillian Gish, Cedric Hardwicke, Alexander Knox
▶ Nazis invade a small Norwegian fishing community and take Muni's daughter captive. He escapes to England, where admiral Hardwicke convinces him to lead a raid on a Nazi airfield. Interesting Irwin Shaw screenplay concentrates on the personal impact of the war.

COMPANY OF WOLVES, THE 1985
British
★ R Horror 1:35
☑ Adult situations, violence
Dir: Neil Jordan *Cast:* Angela Lansbury, David Warner, Stephen Rea, Tusse Silberg, Sarah Patterson
▶ Young Patterson, visiting grandmother Lansbury, has a series of peculiar dreams about wolves. Eccentric, unpredictable, and extremely adult approach to "Little Red Riding Hood" overflowing with Freudian symbols. Alternately comic and horrifying, with an amusing cameo by Terence Stamp as the Devil. **(CC)**

COMPETITION, THE 1980
★ ★ ★ ★ PG Drama 2:09
☑ Adult situations, explicit language
Dir: Joel Oliansky *Cast:* Richard Dreyfuss, Amy Irving, Lee Remick, Sam Wanamaker, Joseph Cali
▶ A romantic exploration of talented pianists Dreyfuss and Irving, competing for first prize in a contest despite their growing love for one another. Well-acted if somewhat overlong drama with effective Dreyfuss in a complex if not always sympathetic role. Irving is fine but Remick, as her bitchy mentor, almost steals the movie.

COMPLEAT BEATLES, THE 1984
★ ★ ★ ★ NR Documentary/Music 2:00
☑ Adult situations
Dir: Patrick Montgomery *Cast:* Paul McCartney, John Lennon, Ringo Starr, George Harrison, Brian Epstein, George Martin
▶ Exhaustive documentary on the Beatles uses interviews, newsreel footage, and concert excerpts to describe every facet of their career. Although their personal lives aren't ignored, the film concentrates squarely on the music, from their start as the Quarrymen to their breakup after "Let It Be." Narration (by Malcolm McDowell) will inform and entertain even the most knowledgeable fans.

COMPROMISING POSITIONS 1985
★ ★ R Mystery-Suspense 1:38
☑ Brief nudity, adult situations, explicit language, mild violence
Dir: Frank Perry *Cast:* Susan Sarandon, Raul Julia, Edward Herrmann, Judith Ivey, Mary Beth Hurt, Joe Mantegna
▶ A quiet Long Island community goes into shock when philandering gum surgeon Mantegna (in a funny cameo) is murdered. Local homemaker Sarandon turns sleuth to investigate the case, much to the chagrin of stuffy hubby Herrmann. Murder suburban style is handled with humor, nifty dialogue, and a little romance (between Sarandon and cop Julia). Susan Isaacs adapted from her best-seller. **(CC)**

COMPULSION 1959
★ ★ NR Drama 1:43 B&W
Dir: Richard Fleischer *Cast:* Orson Welles, Diane Varsi, Dean Stockwell, Bradford Dillman, E. G. Marshall, Martin Milner
▶ Chicago 1920s: disturbed rich kids Stockwell and Dillman plot and carry out a murder. Clarence Darrow–like lawyer Welles defends them in court by challenging capital punishment. Welles's climactic courtroom speech is the highlight of this absorbing drama. From the Meyer

Levin best-seller inspired by the Leopold and Loeb murder case.

COMPUTER WORE TENNIS SHOES, THE
1970
★★★★ G Comedy 1:30
Dir: Robert Butler *Cast:* Kurt Russell, Cesar Romero, Joe Flynn, William Schallert, Alan Hewitt
▶ Above-average Disney comedy about not-too-bright college student Russell, transformed into a genius after he's accidentally zapped with a supercomputer's data bank. Unfortunately, gangster Romero's records are transferred into Russell as well, leading to a series of well-executed chases. Russell repeated his successful role in sequels: *Now Your See Him, Now You Don't* and *The Strongest Man in the World*.

CONAN THE BARBARIAN 1982
★★ R Action-Adventure 1:55
☑ Nudity, adult situations, graphic violence
Dir: John Milius *Cast:* Arnold Schwarzenegger, Sandahl Bergman, James Earl Jones, Max Von Sydow, Ben Davidson
▶ Robert E. Howard's pulp hero Conan comes to the screen in the muscular, hulking presence of Schwarzenegger. Violent saga traces the rise of Conan from enslaved orphaned boy to revenge-seeking barbarian who goes after his parents' killer, the evil Thulsa Doom (Jones). Macho tale is full of blood, gore, rippling biceps, and beautiful women.

CONAN THE DESTROYER 1984
★★★ PG Action-Adventure 1:43
☑ Violence
Dir: Richard Fleischer *Cast:* Arnold Schwarzenegger, Grace Jones, Wilt Chamberlain, Mako, Sarah Douglas, Olivia d'Abo
▶ Schwarzenegger's sequel to *Conan the Barbarian.* Conan is recruited by scheming queen Douglas to accompany virginal princess d'Abo to a castle containing a magical gem. Along the way, Schwarzenegger hooks up with hoop legend Chamberlain and disco queen Jones. An improvement over the first movie: less violence, more laughs, and certainly more suitable for the family. (CC)

CONCERT FOR BANGLADESH, THE
1972
★★★★★ G Documentary/Music 1:39

Dir: Saul Swimmer *Cast:* George Harrison, Bob Dylan, Eric Clapton, Ringo Starr, Leon Russell, Ravi Shankar
▶ Decent recording of former Beatle Harrison's 1971 benefit for the starving masses of Bangladesh. Extended opening Ravi Shankar set is tough to watch for non-sitar buffs but film picks up considerably when Harrison, Dylan, Clapton, and Starr rock out.

CONCORDE, THE—AIRPORT '79 1979
★★★ PG Action-Adventure 2:03
☑ Adult situations, violence
Dir: David Lowell Rich *Cast:* Alain Delon, Susan Blakely, Robert Wagner, Sylvia Kristel, George Kennedy, Eddie Albert
▶ Fourth episode in the *Airport* series throws an all-star cast into extreme jeopardy aboard a Concorde flight to the Moscow Olympics. Evil tycoon Wagner sabotages the plane over the Alps, forcing the resourceful crew and passengers to fight for their lives. Large cast also includes Charo, John Davidson, Andrea Marcovicci, Cicely Tyson, Jimmie Walker, and Sybil Danning.

CONCRETE JUNGLE, THE 1982
★★★ R Action-Adventure 1:39
☑ Rape, nudity, adult situations, explicit language
Dir: Tom DeSimone *Cast:* Jill St. John, Tracy Bregman, Barbara Luna, June Barrett
▶ Framed in a drug bust, young WASP Bregman winds up in a women's prison ruled by corrupt warden St. John. She becomes the pawn of lesbian heroin dealer Luna who dominates the other inmates. Exploitation fare includes all the expected elements: beatings in the showers, cat fights in the cafeteria, etc.

CONDORMAN 1981
★ PG Comedy 1:30
☑ Explicit language
Dir: Charles Jarrott *Cast:* Michael Crawford, Oliver Reed, Barbara Carrera, James Hampton, Dana Elcar, Jean-Pierre Kalfon
▶ Superhero spoof stars Crawford as comic strip artist who gets involved in CIA/KGB intrigue and assumes the identity of winged hero. Carrera provides the romantic interest as the Russian operative who wins Crawford's heart. Lighthearted Disney fare.

CONFORMIST, THE 1970
Italian/French/German
☆ **R Drama 1:55**
☑ Nudity, adult situations, explicit language
Dir: Bernardo Bertolucci **Cast:** Jean-Louis Trintignant, Stefania Sandrelli, Dominique Sanda, Pierre Clementi
▶ Psychological portrait of weak-willed Trintignant, who joins the Italian Fascist party in 1938 to further his radio career. His beliefs are tested when he's ordered to kill his college professor. Powerful, intellectually astute film has stunning photography and a beautiful score by Georges Delerue, but it may not be for everyone. Ⓢ

CONNECTICUT YANKEE IN KING ARTHUR'S COURT, A 1949
★★★ **NR Fantasy 1:46**
Dir: Tay Garnett **Cast:** Bing Crosby, William Bendix, Cedric Hardwicke, Rhonda Fleming, Virginia Field
▶ Crosby, a nineteenth-century Yankee blacksmith, is magically transported back in time to Camelot, where he astounds King Arthur (Hardwicke) with his "magic" compass and kitchen matches. Dubbed "Sir Boss," he pursues a romance with Fleming. Premise is all that remains of Mark Twain's grimly humorous novel, but Crosby's easygoing performance and tunes like "Busy Doing Nothing" are delightful. Pointlessly remade in 1979 as *The Unidentified Flying Oddball.*

CONQUEROR, THE 1956
★★★ **G Action-Adventure 1:51**
Dir: Dick Powell **Cast:** John Wayne, Susan Hayward, Pedro Armendariz, Agnes Moorehead, Thomas Gomez, Lee Van Cleef
▶ Mongol leader Wayne kidnaps Tartar bride-to-be Hayward, the daughter of his father's killer, and then falls in love with her. Exotic action adventure has a silly story and miscast leads (although Wayne is fun to watch), but plenty of action and spectacle in the "cast of thousands" battle scenes. Excellent music score by Victor Young.

CONQUEST OF THE PLANET OF THE APES 1972
★★★ **PG Sci-Fi 1:27**
☑ Explicit language, violence
Dir: J. Lee Thompson **Cast:** Roddy McDowall, Don Murray, Ricardo Montalban, Natalie Trundy, Hari Rhodes
▶ After dogs and cats are killed by a virus in the near future, apes are trained to do menial labor and other unpleasant tasks. They live under the iron hand of stern human governor Murray until intelligent talking ape McDowall leads a revolt. Fourth in the Apes series is a surprisingly taut and suspenseful effort. **(CC)**

CONRACK 1974
★★★★★ **PG Drama 1:46**
☑ Explicit language
Dir: Martin Ritt **Cast:** Jon Voight, Hume Cronyn, Paul Winfield, Madge Sinclair, Tina Andrews
▶ Moving, tremendously affecting story of young white schoolteacher Voight helping a group of culturally deprived black youngsters on a remote island off the South Carolina coast. Voight gives an extremely appealing and tender performance and the kids are wonderful. Based on the book *The Water Is Wide* by best-selling author Pat Conroy. **(CC)**

CONSPIRACY: THE TRIAL OF THE CHICAGO 8 1987
★★★★ **NR Drama/MFTV 1:58**
☑ Explicit language
Dir: Jeremy Kagan **Cast:** Peter Boyle, Robert Carradine, Elliott Gould, Robert Loggia, Michael Lembeck, David Opatoshu
▶ Made-for-cable dramatization of the trial of the "Chicago 8," the antiwar activists accused of inciting the riots that disrupted the 1968 Democratic national convention. Newsreel footage, interviews with the real defendants as they are today, and dialogue based on the court transcripts combine to re-create the circuslike atmosphere of the trial.

CONSUMING PASSIONS 1988
U.S./British
★ **R Comedy 1:40**
☑ Adult situations, explicit language
Dir: Giles Foster **Cast:** Vanessa Redgrave, Jonathan Pryce, Tyler Butterworth, Freddie Jones, Sammi Davis, Prunella Scales
▶ Three workmen meet a sticky end when chocolate factory management trainee Butterworth accidentally pushes them into a vat. Amazingly, the public responds to this "new ingredient" and the company searches for fresh meat to add to the candies. Offbeat black comedy bon bon from Britain for those with unusual tastes. Based on a play by Monty Python graduates Michael Palin and Terry Jones.

CONTEMPT 1963 French/Italian
★ ★ NR Drama 1:43
☑ Nudity, adult situations, explicit language
Dir: Jean-Luc Godard **Cast:** Brigitte Bardot, Jack Palance, Michel Piccoli, Fritz Lang, Giorgia Moll, Jean-Luc Godard
▶ Idealistic playwright Piccoli is lured into writing a screenplay of *The Odyssey* to please extravagant wife Bardot; she derides him for selling out and starts an affair with producer Palance. Challenging but perceptive look at the process of writing for the screen was director Godard's subtle dig at his own producer, Joseph E. Levine. ⑤

CONTINENTAL DIVIDE 1981
★ ★ ★ ★ PG Romance 1:43
☑ Brief nudity, adult situations, explicit language
Dir: Michael Apted **Cast:** John Belushi, Blair Brown, Allen Goorwitz, Carlin Glynn, Tony Ganios
▶ Crack Chicago reporter Belushi is assigned to a story about reclusive ornithologist Brown who is doing research in the Rockies. They fall in love but must work out a solution to their separate careers in this modern variation on the Tracy/Hepburn formula. Agreeable, pleasant romantic comedy with a charming Brown and a nice, surprisingly low-key Belushi.

CONTROL 1987
★ ★ ★ NR Drama/MFTV 1:22
Dir: Giuliano Montaldo **Cast:** Burt Lancaster, Kate Nelligan, Ben Gazzara, Kate Reid, Erland Josephson, Ingrid Thulin
▶ Fifteen volunteers from around the world agree to test a state-of-the-art nuclear bomb shelter for twenty days. Malfunction in the ventilating system increases tensions, but the participants quickly learn of an even greater threat. Timely message drama with an all-star cast, including Gazzara as a reporter, Nelligan as a peace activist, and Lancaster as supervisor of the experiment.

CONVERSATION, THE 1974
★ ★ PG Drama 1:53
☑ Adult situations, explicit language
Dir: Francis Ford Coppola **Cast:** Gene Hackman, John Cazale, Allen Garfield, Frederic Forrest, Cindy Williams, Teri Garr
▶ Expert wire-tapper Hackman is hired to spy on Forrest and Williams. Reviewing his tapes, Hackman realizes someone is planning a murder, but professional pride prevents him from telling his employers (Robert Duvall and Harrison Ford). On all levels a stunning, deeply disturbing film. Nominated for Best Picture, Screenplay (Coppola), and Sound (Walter Murch).

CONVERSATION PIECE 1977 Italian
☆ R Drama 1:52
☑ Nudity, adult situations, explicit language, violence
Dir: Luchino Visconti **Cast:** Burt Lancaster, Silvana Mangano, Helmut Berger, Claudia Marsani, Stefano Patrizi, Claudia Cardinale
▶ Aging American professor Lancaster lives in a Roman house filled with paintings called "conversation pieces." When decadent Mangano, lover Berger, and daughter Marsani move into the upstairs apartment, sexual intrigue and death intrude upon Lancaster's well-ordered life. Static, talky drama of corruption was filmed in English.

CONVOY 1978
★ ★ ★ ★ PG Action-Adventure 1:51
☑ Explicit language
Dir: Sam Peckinpah **Cast:** Kris Kristofferson, Ali MacGraw, Ernest Borgnine, Burt Young, Madge Sinclair
▶ Good-natured trucker movie based on the hit song by C. W. McCall describes the feud between Rubber Duck (Kristofferson) and Borgnine, a hotheaded speed-trap cop. Borgnine sets up a roadblock to arrest the Duck, who turns to his CB buddies for help. MacGraw is a photojournalist along for the ride. Above-average truck stunts and scenery add to the excitement.

COOGAN'S BLUFF 1968
★ ★ ★ R Action-Adventure 1:34
☑ Nudity, adult situations, explicit language, violence
Dir: Don Siegel **Cast:** Clint Eastwood, Lee J. Cobb, Susan Clark, Tisha Sterling, Don Stroud, Betty Field
▶ Arizona deputy Eastwood is fish out of water when he comes to New York City to fetch criminal Stroud, who is being held by NYPD. Stroud escapes, but he's no match for Clint's Wild West techniques. Initial Eastwood/Siegel (*Dirty Harry*) teaming is satisfying, if not as exciting as later efforts. Inspiration for TV series "McCloud" makes effective use of New York locale.

COOLEY HIGH 1975
★★ PG Comedy 1:47
☑ Adult situations, explicit language
Dir: Michael Schultz *Cast:* Glynn Turman, Lawrence Hilton-Jacobs, Garrett Morris, Cynthia Davis, Corin Rogers, Maurice Leon Havis
▶ Inner-city Chicago high schoolers Turman and Jacobs contend with girls, teachers, and the law in a hybrid of broad comedy and sociological drama. Result is relatively effective, with plenty of warmth and humor. Later made into TV series "What's Happening!!"

COOL HAND LUKE 1967
★★★★★ PG Drama 2:06
☑ Adult situations, explicit language
Dir: Stuart Rosenberg *Cast:* Paul Newman, George Kennedy, Strother Martin, J. D. Cannon, Jo Van Fleet, Clifton James
▶ Enormously popular prison story features a sterling performance by Newman as a petty thief who refuses to submit to authority on a Southern chain gang. Although brutal at times, film's many vignettes are surprisingly funny and upbeat. As the warden, Martin delivers the memorable line, "What we have here is a failure to communicate." Newman and screenwriters Donn Pearce and Frank R. Pierson were nominated for Oscars; Kennedy, as a harsh gang foreman, won Best Supporting Actor. Dennis Hopper, Wayne Rogers, Harry Dean Stanton, and Joe Don Baker can be seen among the inmates.

COP 1988
★★★ R Mystery-Suspense 1:45
☑ Nudity, adult situations, explicit language, graphic violence
Dir: James B. Harris *Cast:* James Woods, Lesley Ann Warren, Charles Durning, Charles Haid, Randi Brooks
▶ Maverick cop Woods tackles the police department and his inner demons while obsessively investigating a series of grisly slayings. Chilling, gritty murder mystery with a twisty plot, sleazy but smart dialogue, and an edgy, compelling performance by the unique Woods as a cop so tough he's almost unhinged. Fine support from Durning as Woods's born-again superior.

CORNBREAD, EARL AND ME 1975
★★ PG Drama 1:34
☑ Adult situations, explicit language
Dir: Joseph Manduke *Cast:* Moses Gunn, Rosalind Cash, Madge Sinclair, Keith Wilkes, Tierre Turner, Larry Fishburne
▶ High school basketball star Cornbread (pro hoops star Wilkes), idolized by ghetto youths Turner and Fishburne, is mistaken for a rapist by two cops and then fatally shot. The cops try to intimidate potential witnesses when Cornbread's family fights to clear his name. Well-intentioned, modest black family drama.

CORN IS GREEN, THE 1945
★★★ NR Drama 1:54 B&W
Dir: Irving Rapper *Cast:* Bette Davis, John Dall, Nigel Bruce, Joan Lorring, Rhys Williams
▶ In Wales circa 1895, middle-aged schoolteacher Davis goes to work in a backward mining town and takes a brilliant but untutored young Dall under her wing. The relationship that develops between student and pupil is quite moving. Excellent work from both Davis and Dall. Based on the play by Emlyn Williams.

CORRUPT 1984
★ R Drama 1:39
☑ Adult situations, explicit language, graphic violence
Dir: Roberto Faenza *Cast:* Harvey Keitel, John Lydon, Sylvia Sidney, Nicole Garcia, Leonard Mann
▶ Exploration of strange sadomasochistic relationship between Keitel, a corrupt New York City policeman, and confessed cop-killer Lydon (a.k.a. Johnny Rotten). Story starts with a bang but goes downhill. Street grit with psychological pretensions plays like a weird hybrid of *Mean Streets* and *The Night Porter*.

CORSICAN BROTHERS, THE 1941
★★★★ NR Action-Adventure 1:51 B&W
Dir: Gregory Ratoff *Cast:* Douglas Fairbanks, Jr., Ruth Warrick, Akim Tamiroff, H. B. Warner, J. Carrol Naish
▶ Separated twin brothers avenge the death of their parents (caused by a family feud on Corsica), while vying for the hand of the same woman. Light, tongue-in-cheek version of the Dumas classic, full of sword fights, battles, and heroic deeds, features silver-screen idol Fairbanks at his swashbuckling best.

CORVETTE SUMMER 1978
★★ PG Action-Adventure 1:36
☑ Brief nudity, explicit language
Dir: Matthew Robbins *Cast:* Mark Ha-

mill, Annie Potts, Eugene Roche, Kim Milford, Richard McKenzie
▶ High school student Hamill obsessively searches for stolen Corvette. The trail leads him to Las Vegas, where hooker Potts helps him. Attractive, amiable youth adventure/comedy with nicely staged action and genuine chemistry between the appealing Hamill and Potts, whose wacky comic style is original and refreshing.

COTTON CLUB, THE 1984
★ ★ R Drama 2:01
☑ Adult situations, explicit language, violence
Dir: Francis Coppola   *Cast:* Richard Gere, Gregory Hines, Diane Lane, Lonette McKee, Bob Hoskins
▶ Against the background of Harlem's legendary Cotton Club, struggling musician Gere has a dangerous affair with gangster's moll Lane. His best pal, tap dancer Hines, gets involved with McKee, a black singer trying to pass for white. Flashy gangster epic is long on atmosphere, dancing, music, and technique but somewhat short on plot and likable characters.   (CC)

COTTON COMES TO HARLEM 1970
★ R Action-Adventure 1:37
☑ Brief nudity, adult situations, explicit language, violence
Dir: Ossie Davis   *Cast:* Raymond St. Jacques, Godfrey Cambridge, Calvin Lockhart, Judy Pace, Redd Foxx, John Anderson
▶ Coffin Ed Johnson (St. Jacques) and Grave Digger Jones (Cambridge), Harlem's toughest cops, tackle Lockhart, a corrupt minister whose "Back to Africa" campaign may be a con. Top-notch action film, based on a Chester Himes novel, mixes in plenty of comedy with the violence. Filmed on location in Harlem.

COUCH TRIP, THE 1988
★ ★ R Comedy 1:38
☑ Adult situations, explicit language
Dir: Michael Ritchie   *Cast:* Dan Aykroyd, Charles Grodin, Donna Dixon, Walter Matthau, Richard Romanus, Mary Gross
▶ Swindler Aykroyd, confined to a mental institution, escapes and then successfully poses as a Beverly Hills radio sex therapist. Psychiatry and L.A. lifestyle are satirized in this vehicle for Aykroyd's motormouthed comic style. Grodin steals scenes as the unhinged shrink replaced by Aykroyd.   (CC)

COUNTDOWN 1968
★ ★ ★ NR Sci-Fi 1:41
Dir: Robert Altman   *Cast:* James Caan, Joanna Moore, Robert Duvall, Barbara Baxley, Michael Murphy, Ted Knight
▶ NASA officials forsake safety precautions in a race against the Russians to the moon. At the same time, dedicated astronaut Duvall is replaced by civilian scientist Caan, a move which seriously affects their private lives. Once-provocative film has dated badly (particularly its technology); still an honest effort to portray the space program realistically.

COUNT OF MONTE CRISTO, THE 1934
★ ★ ★ NR Action-Adventure 1:56 B&W
Dir: Rowland V. Lee   *Cast:* Robert Donat, Elissa Landi, Louis Calhern, Sidney Blackmer, Raymond Walburn
▶ Superb adaptation of Alexander Dumas's classic tale of Edmond Dantes, a man unjustly imprisoned twenty years for treason—and his revenge. Rousing combination of adventure, romance, and intrigue receives a first-rate production; Donat is convincing in a difficult role.

COUNTRY 1984
★ ★ ★ ★ PG Drama 1:48
☑ Explicit language, violence
Dir: Richard Pearce   *Cast:* Jessica Lange, Sam Shepard, Wilford Brimley, Matt Clark, Therese Graham, Levi L. Knebel
▶ An Iowa farm family faces foreclosure unless they can repay a Federal loan. When a tornado destroys their equipment, husband Shepard loses faith and turns to alcohol. Determined to keep the farm, wife Lange organizes a support group with her neighbors. Down-to-earth slice of Americana provides a compelling look at modern-day problems. Lange won a Best Actress nomination.

COUNTRY GIRL, THE 1954
★ ★ ★ NR Drama 1:44 B&W
Dir: George Seaton   *Cast:* Bing Crosby, Grace Kelly, William Holden, Anthony Ross, Gene Reynolds, Jacqueline Fontaine
▶ Alcoholic actor Crosby returns to stage in director Holden's play. As he struggles to stay sober, Crosby's wife Kelly gets into disputes with Holden about the situation; later, more loving feelings grow between these two. Towering trio of performances

highlight adaptation of Clifford Odets play; Kelly and the screenplay won Oscars.

COUNT YORGA, VAMPIRE 1970
★★ **PG Horror 1:31**
☑ Adult situations, explicit language, violence
Dir: Bob Kelljan *Cast:* Robert Quarry, Roger Perry, Donna Anders, Michael Murphy, Michael Macready
▶ Sunny Southern California is the new home base for Count Yorga (Quarry), a peculiar medium who lures unsuspecting young couples to seances. When Anders wakes up one morning missing several pints of blood, husband Murphy sets out to kill the Count. Amusing, effective updating of the Dracula story is played more for laughs than chills.

COUP DE TETE 1980 French
★ **R Comedy 1:28**
☑ Nudity, explicit language
Dir: Jean-Jacques Annaud *Cast:* Patrick Dewaere, France Dougnac, Jean Bouise, Michel Aumont, Paul Le Person
▶ Dewaere, a soccer player, is dropped from his small-town team when he injures the team's star. Then he's wrongly jailed on a rape charge but gains his freedom and his vengeance when the team needs him again. Lightweight comedy from France features adept performance by Dewaere.

COUP DE TORCHON 1981 French
★ **NR Comedy/Drama 2:08**
☑ Nudity, explicit language, violence
Dir: Bertrand Tavernier *Cast:* Philippe Noiret, Isabelle Huppert, Stephane Audran, Jean-Pierre Marielle, Eddy Mitchell
▶ In West Africa circa 1938, French police official Noiret, fed up with being harassed by community members, decides to kill his tormentors. Exotic background provides a nice contrast to theme of absurdities of civilization but the black comic tone is hard to handle. Somewhat overlong but definitely original. French director Tavernier adapted from American pulp novelist Jim Thompson's *Pop. 1280*.

COURT JESTER, THE 1956
★★★★ **NR Comedy 1:41**
Dir: Norman Panama, Melvin Frank
Cast: Danny Kaye, Glynis Johns, Basil Rathbone, Angela Lansbury, Mildred Natwick, Cecil Parker
▶ Forest outlaw Kaye becomes involved in scheme to restore rightful heir to the throne of England. In order to infiltrate the castle, Kaye impersonates the court jester. One of Kaye's funniest vehicles features good score, excellent supporting cast, and the comic's famous routine ("The pellet with the poison's in the vessel with the pestle").

COUSIN, COUSINE 1976 French
★★ **R Romance/Comedy 1:35**
☑ Nudity, adult situations
Dir: Jean-Charles Tacchella *Cast:* Marie-Christine Barrault, Victor Lanoux, Marie-France Pisier, Guy Marchand
▶ Barrault and Lanoux, whose unfaithful spouses Marchand and Pisier have a brief affair with one another, become friends and then lovers. Exhilarating French comedy that deals delightfully with middle-class values. Although the attitude toward sex and relationships is very adult and very French, the movie is quite accessible to American audiences. Oscar-nominated for Best Foreign Film, Original Screenplay, and Actress (Barrault). American remake in 1989: *Cousins*. [S]

COUSINS 1989
★★★★ **PG-13 Romance/Comedy 1:51**
☑ Brief nudity, adult situations, explicit language
Dir: Joel Schumacher *Cast:* Ted Danson, Isabella Rossellini, Sean Young, William L. Petersen, Lloyd Bridges, Norma Aleandro
▶ Danson and Rossellini play cousins by marriage who, after discovering affair between their respective spouses Young and Petersen, become friends and eventually lovers. Sunny remake of the 1975 French *Cousin, Cousine* is vibrantly shot, brightly cast (especially the winningly vulnerable Rossellini), and laced with humor and good cheer.

COVERGIRL 1984 Canadian
★ **R Drama 1:33**
☑ Nudity, strong sexual content, explicit language
Dir: Jean-Claude Lord *Cast:* Jeff Conaway, Irena Ferris, Cathie Shiriff, Roberta Leighton, Deborah Wakeman, Kenneth Welsh
▶ Beautiful young Ferris and fashion mogul Conaway meet in a traffic accident and fall in love. He turns her into a top model and, when threatened by a corporate takeover, she teams with other models to save the day. Sleek behind-

the-scenes look at modeling has attractive actors and fair amount of nudity and debauchery.

COWBOYS, THE 1972
★★★★ PG Western 2:08
☑ Adult situations, explicit language, violence
Dir: Mark Rydell **Cast:** John Wayne, Roscoe Lee Browne, Bruce Dern, Colleen Dewhurst, Slim Pickens, Lonny Chapman
▶ When his ranch hands abandon cattle drive for gold rush, Wayne turns to eleven youngsters to help guide his steers four hundred miles across the wilderness. Maniacal killer Dern dogs their steps, leading to a violent confrontation. Slow-paced Western's disturbing themes made this a rare box-office failure for Wayne, but he turns in an exemplary performance as a two-fisted teacher who turns his young charges into men.

CRACKERS 1984
★ PG Comedy 1:32
☑ Adult situations, explicit language, adult humor
Dir: Louis Malle **Cast:** Donald Sutherland, Sean Penn, Jack Warden, Wallace Shawn, Larry Riley
▶ Ringleader Sutherland and his inept gang of amateur thieves bungle a pawnshop heist in San Francisco's seedy Mission District in this droll comic caper. A good cast does its best with some broad comic stereotypes. Remake of the 1960 Italian *Big Deal on Madonna Street*.

CRACKING UP 1985
★★ PG Comedy 1:26
☑ Explicit language, adult humor
Dir: Jerry Lewis **Cast:** Jerry Lewis, Sammy Davis, Jr., Milton Berle, Herb Edelman, Foster Brooks
▶ Lewis is a nerd who tries to ice-skate at a roller rink and fails even at suicide. After a series of zany vignettes, psychiatrist Edelman dubs him a hopeless case. Not vintage Lewis; even die-hard fans might be disappointed.

CRAIG'S WIFE 1936
★★ NR Drama 1:14 B&W
Dir: Dorothy Arzner **Cast:** Rosalind Russell, John Boles, Billie Burke, Dorothy Wilson, Jane Darwell
▶ In her first starring role, Russell plays a self-absorbed woman who loves her house and possessions more than her husband. Surprisingly good melodrama was based on a Pulitzer prize–winning

play and directed by the only American woman director of the 1930s.

CRAWLSPACE 1986
☆ R Horror 1:20
☑ Nudity, adult situations, explicit language, graphic violence
Dir: David Schmoeller **Cast:** Klaus Kinski, Tahne Caine, Talia Balsam, Carol Francis, David Abbott
▶ Creepy Kinski plays the son of a Nazi war criminal who runs a boarding house for pretty women only. New tenant Balsam gets suspicious and fears the walls hide more than rats. Well made for a B-grade movie but for horror fans only.

CRAZY MAMA 1975
★★ PG Action-Adventure 1:21
☑ Adult situations, explicit language
Dir: Jonathan Demme **Cast:** Cloris Leachman, Stuart Whitman, Ann Sothern, Jim Backus, Linda Purl
▶ Leachman plays a crazy widow wanted for bigamy, robbery, kidnapping, assaulting an officer and numerous traffic violations. She resorts to crime to win back the family farm lost during the Depression. Early effort by director Demme provides lots of laughs and adventure. With Sothern and Purl as Leachman's mother and daughter.

CRAZY MOON 1986 Canadian
★★★ PG-13 Drama 1:29
☑ Adult situations, explicit language
Dir: Allan Eastman **Cast:** Kiefer Sutherland, Vanessa Vaughan, Peter Spence, Ken Pogue, Eve Napier
▶ Sutherland is a poor little rich boy withdrawn from life, passing time listening to 1930s music, dressing a female mannequin, and photographing dog droppings. He comes out of his eccentric shell when he falls for Anne, a deaf girl (real-life deaf actress Vaughan), who teaches him to swim. She's absolutely wonderful; so what's she doing with him? Goofy and warm. **(CC)**

CREATOR 1985
★★★ R Comedy 1:47
☑ Nudity, adult situations, explicit language
Dir: Ivan Passer **Cast:** Peter O'Toole, Mariel Hemingway, Vincent Spano, David Ogden Stiers, Virginia Madsen
▶ Student Spano works for unorthodox scientist O'Toole, who's trying to clone his long-dead wife from an egg donated by friendly nymphomaniac Hemingway. A crisis occurs when Spano's girlfriend

Madsen falls into a coma. Plot wanders in many directions and the movie mixes many different moods, but the actors are quite charming and elicit a surprising amount of genuine emotion.

CREATURE 1985
★ R Sci-Fi 1:35
☑ Nudity, adult situations, explicit language, violence
Dir: Gordon Hessler *Cast:* Klaus Kinski, Stan Ivar, Robert Jaffe, Annette McCarthy, John Stinson
▶ On one of Saturn's cobwebby moons, snaggle-toothed, saliva-dripping monsters are on the loose to eat a team of American researchers. Low-budget thriller is tasty fare for sci-fi lovers and horror fans. With Kinski in one of his mad-scientist-lecher roles. **(CC)**

CREATURE FROM THE BLACK LAGOON 1954
★★ NR Horror 1:18 B&W
Dir: Jack Arnold *Cast:* Richard Carlson, Julie Adams, Richard Denning, Antonio Moreno, Whit Bissell
▶ Scientists on Amazon expedition battle monstrous creature from murky depths. Sci-fi classic from the director of *Incredible Shrinking Man* and *It Came From Outer Space.* Beautifully shot and quite chilling. Originally in 3-D.

CREEPERS 1985 Italian
★★ R Horror 1:23
☑ Explicit language, graphic violence
Dir: Dario Argento *Cast:* Jennifer Connelly, Donald Pleasence, Dalila Di Lazzaro, Daria Nicolodi, Patrick Bauchau
▶ Connelly, a young American student, stops a killer by using her ability to telepathically communicate with insects. Slick direction from cult favorite Argento and some real shocks, but gross-out ratio is pretty high: lots of rotting body parts and close-ups of maggots. For die-hard horror addicts.

CREEPING FLESH, THE 1972 British
★ PG Horror 1:33
☑ Violence
Dir: Freddie Francis *Cast:* Christopher Lee, Peter Cushing, Lorna Heilbron, George Benson, Kenneth J. Warren
▶ Scientist Cushing experiments on ancient skeleton that grows flesh when touched with water, injecting his daughter Heilbron with resulting serum. His brother Lee, head of an insane asylum, plots to steal skeleton and discover se-

cret of evil. Good cast strengthens intriguing monster plot.

CREEPSHOW 1982
★★ R Horror 1:57
☑ Explicit language, graphic violence
Dir: George A. Romero *Cast:* Hal Holbrook, Adrienne Barbeau, Fritz Weaver, Leslie Nielsen, Carrie Nye
▶ Five horror vignettes written by Stephen King based on the infamous E. C. *Creepshow* comic books. Great for genre junkies with short attention spans, stories range from a return of the undead to angry roaches on the rampage. With King's son Joe as the boy reading the comics. Spawned a sequel.

CREEPSHOW 2 1987
★★ R Horror 1:29
☑ Adult situations, explicit language, graphic violence
Dir: Michael Gornick *Cast:* Lois Chiles, George Kennedy, Dorothy Lamour, David Holbrook, Tom Savini
▶ *Creepshow* sequel serves up three stories for another horror anthology connected by animation. From a wooden Indian that comes to life to an oil slick that devours teens, the tales are quick and to the gruesome point, but will leave horror fans wanting more. Low-budget technical aspects translate well to the small screen. **(CC)**

CRIES AND WHISPERS 1972 Swedish
★★ R Drama 1:34
☑ Nudity, adult situations
Dir: Ingmar Bergman *Cast:* Liv Ullmann, Ingrid Thulin, Harriet Andersson, Erland Josephson, Kari Sylwan, George Arlin
▶ Sisters Thulin and Ullmann, visiting dying sister Andersson, are haunted by their own unhappy pasts; servant Sylwan has a more positive outlook to share with Andersson. Powerful and magnificently crafted. Oscar nominations for Best Picture, Director, Screenplay, Costume Design; won for Cinematography. Ⓢ

CRIME AND PASSION 1976
★ R Comedy 1:32
☑ Adult situations, explicit language, violence
Dir: Ivan Passer *Cast:* Omar Sharif, Karen Black, Joseph Bottoms, Bernhard Wicki, Heinz Ehrenfreund, Elma Karlowa
▶ When his stock gambles fail, financial advisor Sharif finds himself pursued by assassins hired by angry industrialist Wicki.

Sharif persuades his girlfriend Black to marry Wicki, but the killers refuse to back off. Sharif's dignified performance and beautiful Alpine locations are the only assets of this mediocre comedy.

CRIMES OF PASSION 1984
★★ R Drama 1:42
☑ Nudity, strong sexual content, adult situations, explicit language, violence
Dir: Ken Russell *Cast:* Kathleen Turner, Anthony Perkins, John Laughlin, Annie Potts, Bruce Davison
▶ Unhappy suburban husband Laughlin gets involved with Turner, who lives a double life: designer by day, streetwalker by night. Meanwhile, someone's stalking Turner; perhaps bizarre street preacher Perkins? Russell's often outrageous movie goes over the top with blatantly wild dialogue and plot twists in a disturbing look at adult sexuality in America. Explicit sex and nudity; available in an unrated video version. **(CC)**

CRIMES OF THE HEART 1986
★★★ PG-13 Comedy/Drama 1:45
☑ Adult situations, adult humor
Dir: Bruce Beresford *Cast:* Diane Keaton, Jessica Lange, Sissy Spacek, Sam Shepard, Tess Harper, Hurd Hatfield
▶ Entertaining adaptation of Beth Henley's Pulitzer prize–winning play focuses on three sisters who have a reunion in their small Southern hometown. Keaton is upset over her thirtieth birthday; Spacek just shot her husband because of his "stinking looks"; and Lange has given up her singing career for a job with a dog food company. Alternately zany and heartwarming, with accomplished direction providing an excellent showcase for the leads. Spacek, Harper and Beth Henley were all nominated for Oscars. **(CC)**

CRIMEWAVE 1986
★ PG-13 Comedy 1:22
☑ Explicit language, violence
Dir: Sam Raimi *Cast:* Louise Lasser, Paul L. Smith, Brion James, Bruce Campbell, Reed Birney
▶ Rodent exterminators run riot in this farce spoofing gangster films of the thirties. Through a series of mishaps, small businessman Birney finds himself awaiting execution for murders he didn't commit. Off-the-wall comedy written by Joel and Ethan Coen. **(CC)**

CRIMINAL LAW 1989
★★★ R Mystery-Suspense 1:57
☑ Nudity, adult situations, explicit language, violence
Dir: Martin Campbell *Cast:* Gary Oldman, Kevin Bacon, Tess Harper, Karen Young, Joe Don Baker
▶ Oldman, a young Boston defense attorney, wins an acquittal for wealthy young client Bacon, who turns out to be a psychotic killer. When Bacon goes on a murderous rampage, the lawyer risks his career and life to trap him. Straightforward thriller gets bogged down in ethical issues but does provide food for thought. Reverse casting works beautifully: handsome Bacon makes a great psycho while English actor Oldman is fine in his first American role.

CRIMSON CULT, THE 1970 British
★ PG Horror 1:27
☑ Violence
Dir: Vernon Sewell *Cast:* Boris Karloff, Christopher Lee, Mark Eden, Barbara Steele, Virginia Wetherell, Michael Gough
▶ Searching for his missing brother, Eden enters sinister Lee's mansion, where the lovely Wetherell persuades him to stay for a while. Soon Eden is haunted by Steele, a witch burned at the stake years before, and must enlist the aid of supernatural expert Karloff. Noteworthy mainly for eighty-year-old horror veteran Karloff in one of his last roles.

CRIMSON PIRATE, THE 1952
★★★ NR Action-Adventure 1:44
Dir: Robert Siodmak *Cast:* Burt Lancaster, Nick Cravat, Eva Bartok, Torin Thatcher, James Hayter, Christopher Lee
▶ Pirate Lancaster intends to exploit battle between Caribbean rebels and Spanish rulers for his own profitable purposes, but when he meets gorgeous freedom fighter Bartok, it's viva la revolution! Enormously exuberant entertainment sparked by Lancaster's high spirits and Hayter's turn as an inventor.

CRISS CROSS 1949
★★ NR Crime 1:27 B&W
Dir: Robert Siodmak *Cast:* Burt Lancaster, Yvonne De Carlo, Dan Duryea, Stephen McNally, Richard Long, Tony Curtis
▶ Lancaster plays an armored car driver who gets involved with gorgeous De Carlo. De Carlo's criminal husband Du-

ryea ropes Lancaster into a robbery plan; Lancaster plots to run away with De Carlo but a series of double crosses ensues. Hard-hitting crime drama.

CRITICAL CONDITION 1987
★★ R Comedy 1:40
☑ Adult situations, explicit language
Dir: Michael Apted *Cast:* Richard Pryor, Rachel Ticotin, Ruben Blades, Joe Dallesandro, Sylvia Miles
► During a hospital blackout, fast-talking con man Pryor impersonates a doctor and takes charge of the ordeal, heightened by a crazed killer, a fire, and other assorted crises. Not Pryor's best vehicle but he gets his share of laughs out of the hospital high jinks. **(CC)**

CRITTERS 1986
★★★ PG-13 Horror 1:26
☑ Explicit language, graphic violence
Dir: Stephen Herek *Cast:* Dee Wallace Stone, M. Emmet Walsh, Billy Green Bush, Scott Grimes, Nadine Van Der Velde, Don Opper
► Krites—vicious alien furballs—escape from space prison and land in Kansas, where they terrorize an isolated farm family. While Mom Stone fights off the monsters, son Grimes races into town for help. He finds two alien bounty hunters who mount an attack on the Krites. Low-budget mixture of comedy and science fiction has some particularly nasty violence. Followed by *Critters 2*.

CRITTERS 2: THE MAIN COURSE 1988
★★ PG-13 Horror 1:26
☑ Nudity, explicit language, violence
Dir: Mick Garris *Cast:* Scott Grimes, Liane Curtis, Don Opper, Barry Corbin
► Grimes returns to quiet little Grovers Bend to visit grandma and soon encounters ravenous outer space critters. Sheriff Corbin provides little help but alien bounty hunters help save the day. Never takes itself too seriously and moves along nicely; cute touches take edge off the violence and Corbin is very funny. However, monsters are rather cheap-looking. **(CC)**

CROCODILE 1979 Thai
☆ R Horror 1:35
☑ Adult situations, explicit language, graphic violence
Dir: Herman Cohen *Cast:* Nat Puvanai, Tany Tim, Angela Wells, Kirk Warren
► Combination of atomic test gone awry and malignant Nature spawns gigantic crocodile that attacks residents of Thai

beach resort. Scientists and hunters are unable to cope with fearsome creature. Low-budget exploitation is bloody and predictable.

CROCODILE DUNDEE 1986 Australian
★★★★★ PG-13 Action-Adventure 1:34
☑ Adult situations, explicit language
Dir: Peter Faiman *Cast:* Paul Hogan, Linda Kozlowski, Mark Blum, David Gulpilil, Michael Lombard
► Down Under darling Paul "Throw another shrimp on the barbie" Hogan stars in this half-adventure, half-romance as Mick "Crocodile" Dundee, who saves sexy American reporter Kozlowski from an Outback crocodile attack. She, in turn, invites him to her jungle, Manhattan, where they fall in love and he faces new perils: room service, assorted muggers, transvestites, and Kozlowski's boyfriend Blum. Hogan, making his film debut, also co-wrote the screenplay to this surprise, worldwide blockbuster hit. Followed by sequel. **(CC)**

CROCODILE DUNDEE II 1988
U.S./Australian
★★★★ PG Action-Adventure 1:50
☑ Explicit language, violence
Dir: John Cornell *Cast:* Paul Hogan, Linda Kozlowski, John Meillon, Ernie Dingo, Hechter Ubarry
► G'day, amigo—Mick "Crocodile" Dundee (Hogan) is back and living in New York City with movie #1 flame Sue (Kozlowski). When her ex-husband is murdered after taking photos of Colombian cocaine dealers, the thugs chase Sue and Mick to Australia. On his own turf, no one can compete with the affable Aussie knife-thrower/alligator wrestler.

CROMWELL 1970 British
★★ G Biography 2:21
Dir: Ken Hughes *Cast:* Richard Harris, Alec Guinness, Robert Morley, Dorothy Tutin, Frank Finlay, Timothy Dalton
► Dull account of the seventeenth-century duel between Cromwell (Harris), a Puritan bent on reforming the English court, and Charles I (Guinness), an ineffectual ruler devoted to his Catholic queen (Tutin). Lackluster history lesson won an Oscar for Costume Design.

CROSS COUNTRY 1983
★★ R Drama 1:32
☑ Nudity, strong sexual content, adult situations, explicit language, graphic violence

Dir: Paul Lynch *Cast:* Richard Beymer, Nina Axelrod, Michael Ironside, Brent Carver, Michael Kane
▶ Call girl is brutally murdered and police suspect Beymer, a TV advertising exec who was involved with her. Detective Ironside pursues him across Canada. Gritty, gross, and unsavory, but the twisty plot effectively exploits elements of suspense and action.

CROSS CREEK 1983
★★★★ PG Biography 2:00
☑ Explicit language, violence
Dir: Martin Ritt *Cast:* Mary Steenburgen, Rip Torn, Malcolm McDowell, Alfre Woodard, Dana Hill, Peter Coyote
▶ In 1928, after her marriage crumbles, author Marjorie Kinnan Rawlings (Steenburgen) relocates from New York to the swamps of Florida, where the locals inspire her to write the children's classic *The Yearling.* Sweet, old-fashioned movie is slowly paced but excellently crafted and filled with real emotion. Steenburgen gives a warm and sensitive performance with fine support from Woodward and Torn, both nominated for Best Supporting Oscars. Also nominated for Original Score and Costume Design.

CROSSED SWORDS 1978
★★★ PG Action-Adventure 1:53
☑ Mild violence
Dir: Richard Fleischer *Cast:* Oliver Reed, Raquel Welch, Mark Lester, Ernest Borgnine, George C. Scott, Rex Harrison
▶ Opulent version of Mark Twain's *The Prince and the Pauper,* with Lester in dual role as heir to the throne who switches places with earthy ragamuffin on a lark that backfires. Reed is his swashbuckling rescuer; con man Scott and aristocrat Harrison strike strongest dramatic sparks. Large cast includes Charlton Heston, David Hemmings, and Sybil Danning. Screenplay by George MacDonald Fraser. Also known as *The Prince and the Pauper.*

CROSSFIRE 1947
★★ NR Crime 1:26 B&W
Dir: Edward Dmytryk *Cast:* Robert Young, Robert Mitchum, Robert Ryan, Gloria Grahame, Sam Levene, Paul Kelly
▶ Bigoted soldier Ryan murders Jewish Levene. Cop Young and army man Mitchum team up to investigate and bring the killer to justice. Groundbreaking

look at anti-Semitism creates much tension while hitting home a powerful message; outstanding performances by Mitchum, Young, and Ryan.

CROSSING DELANCEY 1988
★★★★ PG Romance/Comedy 1:37
☑ Adult situations
Dir: Joan Micklin Silver *Cast:* Amy Irving, Peter Riegert, Jeroen Krabbe, Reizl Bozyk, Sylvia Miles, George Martin
▶ Irving is a thirty-four-year-old New Yorker with a rent-controlled apartment and a fine job managing a book store; but she's very single, much to the dismay of her grandmother Bozyk. Matchmaker Miles introduces Irving to pickle merchant Riegert, but she prefers the more upscale company of womanizing writer Krabbe. Modern fairy tale romance uses rich neighborhood atmosphere, understated Riegert, and charming Irving for fine result.

CROSS MY HEART 1987
★ R Comedy 1:31
☑ Nudity, adult situations, explicit language
Dir: Armyan Bernstein *Cast:* Martin Short, Annette O'Toole, Paul Reiser, Joanna Kerns, Jessica Puscas
▶ Short and O'Toole nervously embark on their third date. Sex and even commitment could be in the offing but the secrets they've kept from each other (she chain-smokes and has a young daughter; he's lost his job but pretends he's been promoted) could sabotage the romance. Thin plot sustained by sitcom story twists but likable leads and some insight into 1980s dating mores.

CROSS OF IRON 1977 British/West German
★★★★ R Action-Adventure 2:00
☑ Violence
Dir: Sam Peckinpah *Cast:* James Coburn, Maximilian Schell, James Mason, David Warner, Senta Berger
▶ Solid World War II adventure told from the German point of view. Opportunistic captain Schell, out to win a medal, comes into conflict with Coburn, a battle-scarred sergeant trying to protect his young troops from the advancing Russians. Harrowing battle sequences highlight this realistic look at the war. Followed by a sequel, *Breakthrough.*

CROSSOVER 1980 Canadian
★★ R Drama 1:37

☑ Nudity, adult situations, explicit language
Dir: John Guillermin *Cast:* James Coburn, Kate Nelligan, Fionnula Flanagan, Les Carlson, Candy Kane
▶ Colburn is Mr. Patman, an Irish orderly who works the night shift in a hospital psychiatric ward. Patman befriends the insane, gradually loses his mind and becomes a patient himself. Intense film-noir portrait of a man's deterioration. Filmed in Vancouver. Also known as *Mr. Patman.*

CROSSOVER DREAMS 1985
★ NR Drama 1:25
☑ Adult situations, explicit language
Dir: Leon Ichaso *Cast:* Ruben Blades, Shawn Elliot, Tom Signorelli, Elizabeth Peña, Frank Robles
▶ Spanish Harlem barrio crooner Rudy (real-life salsa star Blades) longs to "cross over" to the Anglo charts and make it as a mainstream pop singer. With Robles as sleazeball manager/furniture salesman who pitches lines like "Plastic is forever." Low-budget but heartfelt.

CROSSROADS 1986
★★★★ R Drama 1:39
☑ Adult situations, explicit language
Dir: Walter Hill *Cast:* Ralph Macchio, Joe Seneca, Jami Gertz, Joe Morton, Robert Judd
▶ Juilliard classical guitar student Macchio and Willie Brown (Seneca), an aging Mississippi blues musician, travel to the heart of the Delta. Once there, they recapture the crossroads of Willie's memory and release him from a contract made with the devil years ago. Leisurely paced character study with a strong blues soundtrack by Ry Cooder and first-rate performance by Seneca. **(CC)**

CRUEL SEA, THE 1953 British
★★★★ NR War 2:04 B&W
Dir: Charles Frend *Cast:* Jack Hawkins, Donald Sinden, Denholm Elliott, John Stratton, Stanley Baker
▶ Realistic World War II drama examines the crew of a typical corvette during its hazardous convoy runs across the Atlantic. Hawkins is outstanding as a dedicated skipper torn between protecting his men and battling the Nazis. Often brutal plot is handled in a convincing documentary fashion. Screenwriter Eric Ambler won an Oscar nomination for his adaptation of Nicholas Monssarrat's best-seller.

CRUISING 1980
★★ R Drama 1:46
☑ Strong sexual content, adult situations, explicit language, graphic violence
Dir: William Friedkin *Cast:* Al Pacino, Paul Sorvino, Karen Allen, Richard Cox, Don Scardino
▶ Innocent New York cop Pacino goes undercover to ferret out a dangerous killer menacing the lower strata of the gay world. More of an exploration of the sadomasochistic lifestyle than murder mystery, this controversial film was criticized for its one-sided, sensationalistic depiction of homosexuals.

CRY FREEDOM 1987 British
★★★★ PG Biography/Drama 2:37
☑ Explicit language, violence
Dir: Richard Attenborough *Cast:* Kevin Kline, Denzel Washington, Penelope Wilton, Kevin McNally, John Thaw, Timothy West
▶ Black activist Steven Biko (Washington) fights against South African apartheid and raises the consciousness of white liberal editor Donald Woods (Kline). When Biko is martyred in prison, Woods attempts to escape the country to tell the world his story. Forthright, deeply felt, and engrossing, true story features rich camerawork, strong production values, and excellent performances. Washington was Oscar-nominated.

CRY IN THE DARK, A 1988
★★★ PG-13 Biography/Drama 2:01
☑ Explicit language
Dir: Fred Schepisi *Cast:* Meryl Streep, Sam Neill, Bruce Myles, Charles Tingwell, Nick Tate, Neil Fitzpatrick
▶ True story of Lindy Chamberlain (Streep), an Australian woman who found herself charged with murder after a wild dog stole her baby. Public opinion and a media circus prejudiced the case against Lindy. Husband Michael (Neill) stood by her side even after the stress threatened their marriage. Interesting indictment of judicial system. Trial sequence a bit long, but Streep, with perfect Australian accent, creates a fully rounded, hard-edged protagonist.

CRY OF THE BANSHEE 1970 British
☆ PG Horror 1:27
☑ Brief nudity, adult situations, violence
Dir: Gordon Hessler *Cast:* Vincent Price, Elisabeth Bergner, Essy Persson,

Hugh Griffith, Patrick Mower, Hilary Dwyer

▶ In the sixteenth century, witch Bergner puts a curse on Price when he slays her children. Evil spirit Mower then terrorizes Price and his family. Average B-grade witch-busting fare, with lines like "Take care of your tongue, woman!" and "You're much too pretty to be a witch."

CRYSTAL HEART 1987
★★★ R Drama 1:43
☑ Nudity, adult situations, explicit language
Dir: Gil Bettman *Cast:* Tawny Kitaen, Lee Curreri, May Heatherly, Lloyd Bochner, Simon Andrea
▶ Born without immune defenses and confined to a glass laboratory in his parents' L.A. mansion, Curreri falls in love with free-spirited rock star Kitaen. When she has to leave to tour, he forsakes his hermetically sealed environment for a final fling. Good-looking leads and heartfelt script.

CRY, THE BELOVED COUNTRY 1952
British
★★ NR Drama 1:51 B&W
Dir: Zoltan Korda *Cast:* Canada Lee, Charles Carson, Sidney Poitier, Joyce Carey, Edric Connor, Geoffrey Keen
▶ Searching for his errant son, country preacher Lee travels to Johannesburg, where he learns his daughter has been forced into prostitution and his son into a life of crime. Straightforward, unsentimental, and emotionally powerful drama is an early indictment of apartheid. Written by Alan Paton from his classic novel (also the inspiration for the Kurt Weill/Maxwell Anderson musical *Lost in the Stars*).

CUBA 1979
★★ R Drama 2:02
☑ Nudity, explicit language, violence
Dir: Richard Lester *Cast:* Sean Connery, Brooke Adams, Jack Weston, Hector Elizondo, Denholm Elliott, Lonette McKee
▶ Working for the British government, mercenary Connery rekindles his affair with tobacco plantation owner Adams, who's now married to a spineless playboy. He must convince her to leave Cuba before Castro comes to power. Strong supporting cast and good period detail provide an intriguing look at Havana in 1958.

CUJO 1983
★★★ R Horror 1:29
☑ Adult situations, explicit language, graphic violence
Dir: Lewis Teague *Cast:* Dee Wallace, Danny Pintauro, Daniel Hugh-Kelly, Christopher Stone, Ed Lauter
▶ Horror master Stephen King deviates from his usual supernatural bent to tell the terrifying story of mother Wallace and son Pintauro, trapped in their stalled car for days by a mammoth St. Bernard. Stalwart genre fans will love this simply crafted chiller.

CULPEPPER CATTLE COMPANY, THE 1972
★★★ PG Western 1:32
☑ Violence
Dir: Dick Richards *Cast:* Gary Grimes, Billy "Green" Bush, Luke Askew, Bo Hopkins, Geoffrey Lewis
▶ Sixteen-year-old Grimes joins a Texas cattle drive and is exposed to the harsh, unforgiving Wild West of the post–Civil War era. Meticulously authentic production will please Western fans, but violent plot is very downbeat.

CURLY TOP 1935
★★★ NR Musical/Family 1:15 B&W
Dir: Irving Cummings *Cast:* Shirley Temple, John Boles, Rochelle Hudson, Jane Darwell, Esther Dale, Arthur Treacher
▶ Orphan Temple wins the heart of millionaire Boles, then encourages his romance with her older sister Hudson. Above-average Temple vehicle features the songs "When I Grow Up," "The Simple Things in Life," and "Animal Crackers in My Soup." Treacher provides comic relief as Boles's butler. **(CC)**

CURSE, THE 1987
★ R Horror 1:30
☑ Adult situations, explicit language, violence
Dir: David Keith *Cast:* Wil Wheaton, Claude Akins, Malcolm Danare, Cooper Huckabee, John Schneider, Amy Wheaton
▶ Meteorite lands on Tennessee farm and contaminates the water supply. Youths Wil and Amy Wheaton (real-life siblings) watch in horror as toxin turns stepfather Akins and others into disfigured psychotics; state official Schneider comes to the rescue. Directorial debut for actor Keith is loosely based on H. P. Love-

craft yarn "The Colour Out of Space." (CC)

CURSE OF FRANKENSTEIN, THE 1957 British
★★ NR Horror 1:23
Dir: Terence Fisher *Cast:* Peter Cushing, Christopher Lee, Hazel Court, Robert Urquhart, Valerie Gaunt
▶ Efficient version of Mary Shelley's classic tells in flashbacks the story of Baron Victor Frankenstein's (Cushing) experiments in creating human life. Lee takes a realistic approach in portraying the creature. Popular Hammer Studios picture revitalized the horror genre and led to six further entries in the series. Sequel: *Revenge of Frankenstein.*

CURSE OF THE CAT PEOPLE, THE 1944
★★ NR Horror 1:10 B&W
Dir: Gunther von Fritsch, Robert Wise *Cast:* Simone Simon, Kent Smith, Jane Randolph, Ann Carter, Elizabeth Russell, Julia Dean
▶ Wise made his directorial debut in this follow-up to producer Val Lewton's 1942 *Cat People.* Simon, the panther-possessed heroine of the first movie, returns as imaginary playmate of her husband's (Smith) little daughter, Carter. Focus is not on terror but on psychological portrait of the child and family.

CURSE OF THE DEMON 1958 British
★★★ NR Horror 1:22 B&W
Dir: Jacques Tourneur *Cast:* Dana Andrews, Peggy Cummins, Niall MacGinnis, Maurice Denham
▶ Psychologist Andrews investigates murder and refuses to believe supernatural explanations until it's almost too late, as satanic cultist MacGinnis conjures creature to kill him. Moody and chilling; atmospheric direction by Tourneur creates a sense of consistent menace.

CURSE OF THE PINK PANTHER 1983
★★ PG Comedy 1:50
☑ Brief nudity, explicit language, mild violence, adult humor
Dir: Blake Edwards *Cast:* Ted Wass, David Niven, Robert Wagner, Capucine, Joanna Lumley, Herbert Lom
▶ Inspector Clouseau is missing in this post–Peter Sellers reprise of the "Panther" series. Wass plays Clifton Sleigh, a bumbling New York cop legendary for his ineptitude, hired to find Clouseau and the missing "Panther Diamond." Niven plays a charming jewel thief. Glossy and ade-

quately cast, but pale in comparison to past Panther plots.

CURTAINS 1983 Canadian
★★ R Horror 1:29
☑ Rape, nudity, adult situations, explicit language, graphic violence
Dir: Jonathan Stryker (Richard Ciupka) *Cast:* John Vernon, Samantha Eggar, Linda Thorson, Anne Ditchburn
▶ Actress Samantha Sherwood (Eggar) commits herself to a mental institution to research a "mad woman" movie role. Shocked to discover director Vernon is interviewing other actresses for her part, she escapes and shows up at his mansion where five other contenders, all dying for the role, assemble for auditions. Muddled exploitation was plagued by production problems.

CUTTER'S WAY 1981
★★ R Mystery-Suspense 1:49
☑ Nudity, adult situations, explicit language, violence
Dir: Ivan Passer *Cast:* Jeff Bridges, John Heard, Lisa Eichhorn, Ann Dusenberry, Stephen Elliot
▶ Santa Barbara hustler Bridges witnesses a murderer dumping a body. His best pal, embittered and crippled Vietnam vet Heard, becomes obsessed with proving a powerful businessman is the killer. Dark, moody, underrated thriller with brilliant cinematography that makes you feel the corruption in the air. Convincingly sordid milieu and ambiguous ending are not for everyone, but the three leads are terrific, especially Heard's snarling, larger-than-life portrayal. Originally released as *Cutter and Bone.*

CYCLONE 1987
★★ R Action-Adventure 1:26
☑ Brief nudity, explicit language, violence
Dir: Fred Olen Ray *Cast:* Heather Thomas, Jeffrey Combs, Ashley Ferrare, Dan Robinson
▶ Motorcycle enthusiasts Thomas and Combs go dancing at a rock club where Combs is murdered with an icepick. Thomas discovers her dead boyfriend's secret project, a transformer for a hydrogen-powered motorcycle wanted by both the CIA and KGB, which she must return to friendly hands.

CYRANO DE BERGERAC 1950
★★★ NR Drama 1:52 B&W
Dir: Michael Gordon *Cast:* Jose Ferrer,

Mala Powers, William Prince, Morris Carnovsky, Ralph Clanton

► Adaptation of Edmond Rostand's classic romantic tragedy. Soldier/poet Cyrano (Ferrer) loves the fair Roxanne (Powers) but is too ashamed of his repulsive nose to woo her. He puts his great wit at the service of handsome Christian (Prince), who also loves Roxanne but is too tongue-tied to tell her. Brilliant Oscar-winning performance by Ferrer. Story later adapted by Steve Martin into a comedy *Roxanne*.

DA 1988
★★★ PG Drama 1:42
☑ Explicit language
Dir: Matt Clark *Cast:* Martin Sheen, Barnard Hughes, William Hickey, Karl Hayden, Doreen Hepburn

► Sheen returns to Ireland for the funeral of adoptive father Hughes and has a confrontation with his Da's ghost. Reminiscences of times past include a painful incident when Da tried to drown the family dog and his interference with Sheen's attempt at losing his virginity. Talky and seemingly stagebound at times but touching nonetheless. Hughes re-creates his stage role from Hugh Leonard's Tony Award–winning play. **(CC)**

DADDY LONG LEGS 1955
★★★ NR Musical 2:06
Dir: Jean Negulesco *Cast:* Fred Astaire, Leslie Caron, Terry Moore, Thelma Ritter, Fred Clark, Charlotte Austin

► Effective but slow-moving May-December romance about playboy Astaire who supports beautiful French orphan Caron. They fall in love to a tuneful Johnny Mercer score (including the Oscar-nominated "Something's Got to Give"). Highlighted by Astaire's drum specialty number.

DAFFY DUCK'S MOVIE: FANTASTIC ISLAND 1983
★★★★ G Animation 1:18
Dir: Friz Freleng *Cast:* Voices of Mel Blanc, Les Tremayne

► Classic Looney Tuners Porky Pig, Tweety Pie and Sylvester, Pepe Le Pew and more team up in this spoof of TV's "Fantasy Island." Daffy Duck is the Ricardo Montalban–type host and Speedy Gonzales is hilarious in a brief Herve Villechaize parody.

DAISY MILLER 1974
★ G Drama 1:31
Dir: Peter Bogdanovich *Cast:* Cybill

Shepherd, Barry Brown, Cloris Leachman, Mildred Natwick, Eileen Brennan

► Spoiled American Shepherd tours Europe with mother Leachman and bratty little brother, shocking nineteenth-century polite society with her flirting and directness before tragedy strikes. Beautifully detailed period piece with lavish costumes and sumptuous settings. From the Henry James novel.

DALEKS—INVASION EARTH 2150 A.D.
1966 British
★ NR Sci-Fi 1:24
Dir: Gordon Flemyng *Cast:* Peter Cushing, Bernard Cribbins, Ray Brooks, Jill Curzon, Andrew Keir, Roberta Tovey

► Cushing stars as Dr. Who, a brilliant scientist accidentally propelled into a future where Daleks, evil creatures from outer space, have taken over London. Cushing, with a little help from his friends, manages to overcome the invaders. Second feature inspired by the BBC television series; first was 1965's *Dr. Who and the Daleks*.

DAM BUSTERS, THE 1954 British
★★★ NR War 1:59 B&W
Dir: Michael Anderson *Cast:* Richard Todd, Michael Redgrave, Ursula Jeans, Basil Sydney, Derek Farr, Patrick Barr

► During World War II, scientist Redgrave invents a new bomb to destroy Nazis' strategic and previously impregnable dams; wing commander Todd trains his pilots for the almost impossible mission. Based on actual incidents, this first-rate war drama maintains tension by sticking to the facts. Thrilling climax received an Oscar nomination for special effects.

DAMES 1934
★★ NR Musical 1:30 B&W
Dir: Ray Enright *Cast:* Joan Blondell, Dick Powell, Ruby Keeler, ZaSu Pitts, Hugh Herbert, Guy Kibbee

► Bumbling millionaire Herbert wants to spend a fortune to close "scandalous" Broadway musicals; instead, his partner Kibbee is blackmailed by chorus girl Blondell into investing in Powell's latest show. Silly plot takes back seat to eye-opening Busby Berkeley versions of "I Only Have Eyes for You," "Try to See It My Way," and other tunes.

DAMIEN—OMEN II 1978
★★★ R Horror 1:47
☑ Explicit language, graphic violence
Dir: Don Taylor *Cast:* William Holden,

Lee Grant, Lew Ayres, Sylvia Sidney, Robert Foxworth, Jonathan Scott-Taylor
▶ Damien (Scott-Taylor), Satan's spawn from the 1976 original, has grown into a spoiled, obnoxious teenager. Reading the Book of Revelations at military school, the little Antichrist learns his true identity—and kills his second set of relatives. Holden plays the business tycoon father who thinks Damien is an angel. For more carnage, see *The Final Conflict*, the third title in this popular supernatural horror trilogy.

DAMNATION ALLEY 1977
★★ PG Sci-Fi 1:27
☑ Violence
Dir: Jack Smight *Cast:* Jan-Michael Vincent, George Peppard, Dominique Sanda, Paul Winfield, Jackie Earle Haley
▶ After a nuclear holocaust, a small band of survivors cross America to the last outpost of humanity in upstate New York. Along the dangerous route, they encounter tornadoes, giant cockroaches, and murderous hillbillies. Comic-book screenplay enlivened by good special effects and well-paced action.

DAMNED, THE 1969 Italian/German
★ R Drama 2:41
☑ Nudity, adult situations, violence
Dir: Luchino Visconti *Cast:* Dirk Bogarde, Ingrid Thulin, Helmut Griem, Helmut Berger, Charlotte Rampling
▶ Challenging study of a rich, amoral family of German industrialists that divides and disintegrates under Nazi influence. Incest, adultery, homosexuality, and mass murder abound as family members struggle among themselves for dominance and power. Academy Award nominations for Best Story and Screenplay.

DAMN THE DEFIANT! 1962 British
★★★ NR War 1:41
Dir: Lewis Gilbert *Cast:* Alec Guinness, Dirk Bogarde, Maurice Denham, Nigel Stock, Anthony Quayle, Peter Gill
▶ Late eighteenth-century: aboard a British warship, captain Guinness finds himself caught between his evil lieutenant Bogarde and the crew ready to mutiny against Bogarde's iron fist. Fighting among themselves, the British must also battle the French. Handsome production featuring first-rate Guinness and Bogarde.

DAMN YANKEES 1958
★★★ NR Musical 1:50
Dir: George Abbott, Stanley Donen
Cast: Tab Hunter, Gwen Verdon, Ray Walston, Shannon Bolin, Nathaniel Frey
▶ Middle-aged Hunter makes deal with the Devil (Walston) to live out his dream of being a youthful baseball star. Entertaining version of the Broadway musical hit with Verdon nicely re-creating her stage role as Lola, the devil's sexy helper. Bob Fosse (who choreographed) appears briefly. Oscar-nominated Adler/Ross score includes "Whatever Lola Wants," "Two Lost Souls," "Heart."

DAMSEL IN DISTRESS, A 1937
★★★ NR Musical 1:40 B&W
Dir: George Stevens *Cast:* Fred Astaire, George Burns, Gracie Allen, Joan Fontaine, Reginald Gardiner, Ray Noble
▶ American dancing star Astaire romances English aristocrat Fontaine, helped by his pals Burns and Allen. Breezy musical based on a P. G. Wodehouse novel and play has a wonderful Gershwin score, including "A Foggy Day in London Town," "Nice Work If You Can Get It," and "I Can't Be Bothered Now." Choreographer Hermes Pan won an Oscar for his work on the delightful "Fun House" sequence.

DANCERS 1987
★★★ PG Drama/Dance 1:39
☑ Adult situations, explicit language
Dir: Herbert Ross *Cast:* Mikhail Baryshnikov, Allesandra Ferri, Leslie Browne, Thomas Rall, Lynn Seymour, Julie Kent
▶ While supervising production of *Giselle* in Italy, world's best dancer and notorious womanizer Baryshnikov romances young ballerina Kent, despite warnings from his jaded former lovers Ferri and Browne. Soon the backstage romance mirrors the tragic tale of the ballet being rehearsed. Baryshnikov, Browne, and director Ross reprise their successful teaming from *The Turning Point.* (CC)

DANCE WITH A STRANGER 1985 British
★★ R Drama 1:42
☑ Adult situations, explicit language, violence
Dir: Mike Newell *Cast:* Miranda Richardson, Rupert Everett, Ian Holm, Matthew Carroll, Tom Chadbon
▶ Powerful if downbeat true story of Ruth Ellis (Richardson), the nightclub hostess who killed wealthy beau Everett and

then, in 1955, became the last woman executed in England. Low-key, realistic drama refuses to pander to our emotions, but the amazing Richardson makes Ruth a woman to remember. **(CC)**

DANCING LADY 1933
★★ NR Musical 1:34 B&W
Dir: Robert Z. Leonard *Cast:* Joan Crawford, Clark Gable, Franchot Tone, Fred Astaire, Nelson Eddy, May Robson
▶ Crawford is a poor but spunky dancer; Tone, a wealthy playboy sponsoring her in a Broadway play; and Gable, the director who resents Tone's interference. Glossy romance includes "Everything I Have Is Yours" and "Hold Your Man," but it's notable chiefly for Astaire's film debut in a short duet with Crawford. The Three Stooges and Robert Benchley supply comic relief.

DANGEROUS 1935
★★ NR Drama 1:18 B&W
Dir: Alfred E. Green *Cast:* Bette Davis, Franchot Tone, Margaret Lindsay, Alison Skipworth, John Eldredge, Dick Foran
▶ Davis, an alcoholic actress, has sunk to the bottom when millionaire Tone decides to rehabilitate her. Their romance is threatened by Davis's wastrel husband Eldredge and Tone's fiancée Lindsay. Turgid soap opera is notable for Davis's larger-than-life, Oscar-winning performance.

DANGEROUS LIAISONS 1988
★★★ R Drama 2:00
☑ Nudity, strong sexual content, adult situations, explicit language, violence
Dir: Stephen Frears *Cast:* Glenn Close, John Malkovich, Michelle Pfeiffer, Keanu Reeves, Swoosie Kurtz, Uma Thurman
▶ Adaptation by Christopher Hampton of his London and Broadway hit, *Les Liaisons Dangereuses*, pits eighteenth-century French nobles and former lovers Close and Malkovich in a battle of sexual intrigue. Malkovich seeks to seduce virginal convent girl Thurman to further Close's revenge against Thurman's fiancé; he soon finds a greater challenge in devout and self-righteous Pfeiffer. Meanwhile, Close educates the teenage Reeves in the ways of love. Hampton's screenplay and the sumptuous costumes won Oscars.

DANGEROUSLY CLOSE 1986
★★ R Drama 1:35

☑ Brief nudity, adult situations, explicit language, violence
Dir: Albert Pyun *Cast:* John Stockwell, J. Eddie Peck, Carey Lowell, Bradford Bancroft
▶ Fast times at Vista Verde High. An activist pack of good-looking, ultra-privileged do-gooders keep class delinquents in check, sometimes overstepping disciplinary boundaries. The "wrong element" is suddenly dropping dead. Stockwell plays ringleader Randy; Lowell, his naive girlfriend Julie. Slick MTV-type editing will please teens and vigilantes. **(CC)**

DANGEROUS MOVES 1984 Swiss
★★★ NR Drama 1:40
☑ Explicit language
Dir: Richard Dembo *Cast:* Michel Piccoli, Leslie Caron, Liv Ullmann, Alexandre Arbatt, Bernhard Wicki, Wojtek Pszoniak
▶ Aging Russian grandmaster Piccoli takes on upstart defector Arbatt in a championship chess match. Tense psychological battle heats up as Piccoli contends with a failing heart and Arbatt's brash conduct while the younger man struggles with a faltering marriage to Ullmann and his increasing paranoia. Winner of Oscar for Best Foreign Film.
Ⓢ

DANGEROUS WHEN WET 1953
★★★ NR Musical 1:35
Dir: Charles Walters *Cast:* Esther Williams, Fernando Lamas, Jack Carson, Charlotte Greenwood, William Demarest
▶ Sneaky entrepreneur Carson sponsors young Arkansas girl Williams in her attempt to swim the English Channel. Along the way she's wooed by champagne salesman Lamas. Lush production values and an animated sequence with Tom and Jerry highlight this MGM musical. Lamas and Williams later became husband and wife.

DANIEL 1983
★★ R Drama 2:09
☑ Adult situations, explicit language, violence
Dir: Sidney Lumet *Cast:* Timothy Hutton, Mandy Patinkin, Lindsay Crouse, Edward Asner, Amanda Plummer, Ellen Barkin
▶ Fictionalized account of the famous Rosenberg espionage trial from the point of view of the doomed couple's children.

Story cuts back and forth in time as Daniel (Hutton), the angry son of socialists Patinkin and Crouse executed for giving away atomic secrets, investigates his past. Strongest scene: Patinkin using a cereal box to explain capitalism to his young son. Ambitious drama with political overtones adapted from E. L. Doctorow's novel *The Book of Daniel.*

DANTON 1983 French/Polish
★★ PG Drama 2:16
☑ Brief nudity, violence
Dir: Andrzej Wajda *Cast:* Gerard Depardieu, Wojtek Pszoniak, Anne Alvaro, Roland Blanche, Patrice Chereau
▶ Depardieu is magnetic as Danton, an idealistic radical seeking an end to the Reign of Terror in 1793. He is opposed by Robespierre (Pszoniak), a strict lawyer who uses the Revolution for personal goals. Working with French and Polish actors, director Wajda took an intellectual approach to the French Revolution, pointing out its parallels with contemporary Poland. ⑤

DARBY O'GILL AND THE LITTLE PEOPLE 1959
★★★★ NR Fantasy/Family 1:59
Dir: Robert Stevenson *Cast:* Albert Sharpe, Sean Connery, Janet Munro, Jimmy O'Dea, Kieron Moore
▶ Evil spells abound when an about-to-retire Irish caretaker, Darby O'Gill (Sharpe), falls down a well and runs afoul of local leprechaun king O'Dea. Darby manages to outwit the wee folk and orchestrate the marriage of daughter Munro to his handsome young successor Connery. Magical bit of blarney from Walt Disney Studios.

DARING DOBERMANS, THE 1973
★★★ G Action-Adventure 1:30
Dir: Byron Chudnow *Cast:* Charles Knox Robinson, Tim Considine, David Moses, Claudio Martinez, Joan Caulfield
▶ Fun sequel to *The Doberman Gang.* The larcenous dogs are taken over by a new gang of crooks for a daring heist too dangerous for humans to perform, but an Indian lad throws a monkey wrench into their plans. Best for children and dog lovers. (CC)

DARK CORNER, THE 1946
★★★ NR Mystery-Suspense 1:39 B&W
Dir: Henry Hathaway *Cast:* Mark Stevens, Lucille Ball, Clifton Webb, William Bendix, Kurt Kreuger

▶ Tough, exciting mystery about private eye Stevens framed for murder. Chased by both the crooks and the cops, he turns to secretary Ball (in a rare dramatic role) for help. Highly enjoyable example of film noir is notable for its terse dialogue, twisty plot, and moody atmosphere. Bendix is especially effective as a sadistic killer.

DARK CRYSTAL, THE 1982 British
★★★★ PG Fantasy 1:30
☑ Mild violence
Dir: Jim Henson, Frank Oz *Cast:* Voices of Stephen Garlick, Lisa Maxwell, Billie Whitelaw, Perry Edwards
▶ Good versus evil in a fantasy setting where vulturish Skeksis have rid the universe of all but two Gelflings (tiny humanoids). The brave duo, aided by some ancient mystics, attempts to save the world from destruction by finding a missing shard from the Dark Crystal that supplies the evil beings with their power. Solemn, reverential kids' fantasy with amazing puppetry by Muppet master Henson.

DARK EYES 1987 Italian/Russian
★ NR Comedy/Drama 1:58
☑ Nudity, adult situations
Dir: Nikita Mikhalkov *Cast:* Marcello Mastroianni, Silvana Mangano, Marthe Keller, Elena Sofonova, Pina Cei
▶ Wealthy idler Mastroianni visits a ritzy spa and is rejuvenated by a romance with beautiful young (but unhappily married) Russian Sofonova. Sumptuous turn-of-the-century decor often upstages the plot (based on several Chekhov short stories). Poignant, Oscar-nominated performance by Mastroianni as the born-again romantic.

DARK MIRROR, THE 1946
★★ NR Drama 1:25 B&W
Dir: Robert Siodmak *Cast:* Olivia de Havilland, Lew Ayres, Thomas Mitchell, Richard Long, Charles Evans
▶ Acting field day for de Havilland playing both a good sister and her evil twin. Both become murder suspects; shrink Ayres is the man who investigates the case and wins both women's hearts. Quite involving; technical effects are pretty good for pre-*Dead Ringers* era.

DARK OF THE NIGHT 1985 New Zealand
★ NR Horror 1:28
☑ Adult situations, explicit language, violence
Dir: Gaylene Preston *Cast:* Heather

Bolton, David Letch, Margaret Umbers, Suzanne Lee, Gary Stalker, Perry Piercy
▶ Bolton buys a used Jaguar as a symbol of her independence but gradually learns the car is haunted by Piercy, victim of a murderous hitchhiker. Bolton also finds herself pursued by three menacing men in this slowly paced horror fantasy. Originally released as *Mr. Wrong.*

DARK PASSAGE 1947
★★★ NR Mystery-Suspense 1:46 B&W
Dir: Delmer Daves *Cast:* Humphrey Bogart, Lauren Bacall, Bruce Bennett, Agnes Moorehead, Tom D'Andrea
▶ Unjustly accused Bogart escapes prison, changes his identity via plastic surgery, and goes after the real killer. First-rate Warner Brothers thriller with interesting use of subjective camera, San Francisco locations, and Bogart/Bacall chemistry (their third teaming).

DARK PAST, THE 1948
★★★ NR Drama 1:14 B&W
Dir: Rudolph Maté *Cast:* William Holden, Lee J. Cobb, Nina Foch, Adele Jergens, Stephen Dunne
▶ Holden, a vicious young killer, is as afraid of his own dreams as he is of the law until shrewd psychiatrist Cobb helps him understand why he kills. With Foch as the gorgeous moll. Notable as one of Hollywood's first attempts to illustrate psychological ideas. Remake of *Blind Alley.*

DARK PLACES 1974 British
★★ PG Horror 1:15
☑ Explicit language, violence
Dir: Don Sharp *Cast:* Christopher Lee, Joan Collins, Herbert Lom, Robert Hardy, Jane Birkin
▶ Mental hospital administrator Hardy inherits an estate from a dying man and searches for the money supposedly stashed there. The place is haunted, causing the administrator to go beserk and embark on a murderous rampage. Straightforward suspenser has good production values and Collins skillfully plays a scheming bitch.

DARK STAR 1974
★ G Sci-Fi 1:30
☑ Explicit language
Dir: John Carpenter *Cast:* Brian Narelle, Andreijah Pahich, Cal Kuniholm, Dan O'Bannon, Joe Sanders
▶ Four astronauts, trapped in outer space with little chance for reentry, battle an alien and continue their mission to destroy unstable planets. Early low-bud-

get effort of director Carpenter with campy acting but inventive touches and offbeat humor.

DARK VICTORY 1939
★★★★ NR Drama 1:46 B&W
Dir: Edmund Goulding *Cast:* Bette Davis, George Brent, Geraldine Fitzgerald, Humphrey Bogart, Ronald Reagan
▶ Not-a-dry-eye-in-the-house department. Young Davis learns she's contracted a fatal disease and tries to make the rest of her days meaningful. Classy Warners tearjerker with bravura performance by the great Bette (Oscar-nominated, as was the movie), ably supported by Brent as the doctor who loves her and Bogart as her stable master. Available in a colorized version. **(CC)**

DARLING 1965 British
★★★ NR Drama 2:02 B&W
Dir: John Schlesinger *Cast:* Julie Christie, Dirk Bogarde, Laurence Harvey, Roland Curram, José Luis de Villalonga, Alex Scott
▶ Psychological study of amoral model Christie, who casually uses and discards men. Slick, cynical look at the Swinging Sixties has dated poorly, although its treatment of abortion and orgies was once controversial. Bogarde registers strongly as a TV newsman who abandons his family for Christie. Nominated for five Oscars, winning for Best Actress (Christie), Screenplay (by Frederic Raphael), and Costume Design.

DARLING LILI 1970
★★★★ G Musical 2:16
☑ Adult situations, mild violence
Dir: Blake Edwards *Cast:* Julie Andrews, Rock Hudson, Jeremy Kemp, Lance Percival, Jacques Marin
▶ Popular English music hall star Lili Smith (Andrews) is actually a spy for the Germans during World War I. She romances flyer Hudson to get information but then falls in love with him. Overlong, large-budgeted musical/spy spoof has some fun moments and good productions values. Best when Andrews is singing, particularly the Oscar-nominated "Whistling Away the Dark."

D.A.R.Y.L. 1985
★★★★ PG Sci-Fi 1:39
☑ Explicit language, mild violence
Dir: Simon Wincer *Cast:* Mary Beth Hurt, Michael McKean, Kathryn Walker, Colleen Camp, Barrett Oliver

▶ Suburbanites Hurt and McKean adopt amnesiac ten-year-old Daryl (Oliver), who turns out to be a robot on the lam from a government project (his name stands for Data Analysing Robot Youth Lifeform). The boy develops human feelings but the government baddies try to reclaim him anyway. Sweet-natured family adventure with an upbeat ending. **(CC)**

DAS BOOT (THE BOAT) 1982 German
★★★★ R War/Drama 2:30
☑ Explicit language, violence
Dir: Wolfgang Petersen *Cast:* Jurgen Prochnow, Herbert Gronemeyer, Klaus Wenneman, Hubertus Bengsch, Martin Semmelrogge
▶ During World War II, world-weary U-boat commander Prochnow navigates his desperate crew through numerous close encounters with the British and masterminds the raising of the damaged ship when it sinks to the ocean floor. Technically superb German antiwar drama combines claustrophobic feel within the ship with exciting battle sequences outside. Nominated for six Oscars. Dubbed version features original cast members doing their own voices.

DATE WITH AN ANGEL 1987
★★★ PG Fantasy 1:45
☑ Explicit language
Dir: Tom McLoughlin *Cast:* Michael Knight, Emmanuelle Beart, Phoebe Cates, David Dukes, Phil Brock
▶ Young Knight, unsure about his engagement to wealthy Cates, falls in love with an angel (the absolutely beautiful French actress Beart) who crash-lands in his swimming pool. Comedy/fantasy/romance in the *Splash* vein lacks the directoral magic to really fly but has an appealing cast and generally charming lightweight tone.

DAVID AND LISA 1962
★★ NR Drama 1:29 B&W
☑ Adult situations
Dir: Frank Perry *Cast:* Keir Dullea, Janet Margolin, Howard da Silva, Neva Patterson, Clifton James
▶ Disturbed adolescent Dullea, placed in a mental home, begins to blossom because of his relationship with young schizophrenic Margolin. Independently made tale of love conquering madness is a minor classic. Sincere, well-intentioned direction by Perry overcomes the

modest budget. Nicely acted by Dullea and Margolin.

DAVID COPPERFIELD 1935
★★★★ NR Drama 2:13 B&W
Dir: George Cukor *Cast:* Freddie Bartholomew, Frank Lawton, W. C. Fields, Madge Evans, Maureen O'Sullivan, Edna May Oliver
▶ Orphaned as a child, young Copperfield (Bartholomew) faces a bleak future in his stepfather's sweatshop, but through pluck and the help of friends he achieves success. Masterful adaptation of Charles Dickens's beloved classic captures the author's spirit and humor without sacrificing pacing. Superb direction and a perfect cast: Fields (Mr. Micawber), Roland Young (Uriah Heep), and Basil Rathbone (the villainous Murdstone) are particularly impressive. **(CC)**

DAWN OF THE DEAD 1979
★ NR Horror 2:05
☑ Explicit language, graphic violence
Dir: George A. Romero *Cast:* David Emge, Ken Foree, Scott Reiniger, Gaylen Ross, David Crawford
▶ Two military men, a TV reporter, and a lovely blond are trapped in a shopping center filled with menacing zombies in director Romero's follow-up to his 1968 cult classic *Night of the Living Dead*. Very bloody and gory; violence level may offend a good number of people. However, horror fans will be in hellish heaven with the extremely effective, if revolting, special effects. Original R rating was revoked when producers inserted additional graphic violence.

DAWN OF THE MUMMY 1981
★ NR Horror 1:33
☑ Graphic violence
Dir: Armand Weston *Cast:* Brenda King, George Peck, Barry Sateels
▶ A mummy is awakened from nearly five thousand years of sleep when four gorgeous models and their photographers invade his tomb. The hapless women are then pursued by the bandaged monster. Silly screenplay is enlivened by occasionally scary moments.

DAWN PATROL, THE 1938
★★★ NR War 1:43 B&W
Dir: Edmund Goulding *Cast:* Errol Flynn, David Niven, Basil Rathbone, Donald Crisp, Melville Cooper, Barry Fitzgerald
▶ British Royal Flying Corps pilots rely on boyish bravado to counter the deadly

toll of daily missions behind enemy lines. Flynn is outstanding as an ace wracked with guilt when he's promoted to squadron leader. Sentimental World War I drama is famous for its thrilling dogfight sequences.

DAY AFTER, THE 1983
★★★★ NR Drama/MFTV 2:00
Dir: Nicholas Meyer   *Cast:* Jason Robards, JoBeth Williams, John Lithgow, John Cullum, Steven Guttenberg, Amy Madigan
▶ Controversial made-for-television movie details the beginning and aftermath of a nuclear war. Shattering scenes of radiation's effects on a midwestern American community are directed with a heavy hand. Much more effective is the earlier scene in which missiles zooming out of their silos suddenly disrupt the quiet of an ordinary day.

DAY AT THE RACES, A 1937
★★★ NR Comedy 1:51 B&W
Dir: Sam Wood   *Cast:* The Marx Brothers, Allan Jones, Maureen O'Sullivan, Margaret Dumont, Douglas Dumbrille
▶ Delicious Marx Brothers shenanigans in a racetrack and a sanitarium as horse doctor Dr. Hackenbush (Groucho) treats wealthy hypochondriac Dumont for "double blood pressure." Hilarious scenes include Harpo and Chico saving Groucho from a scheming vixen by wallpapering her out of Dumont's sight and Chico's famous "Tootsie fruitsie" ice cream sale of a racetrack tip to Groucho. Does have a dated scene of black stereotypes who mistake Harpo for an angel.

DAY FOR NIGHT 1973 French
★ PG Comedy/Drama 1:56
☑ Adult situations, explicit language
Dir: François Truffaut   *Cast:* Jacqueline Bisset, Jean-Pierre Aumont, François Truffaut, Valentina Cortese, Alexandra Stewart
▶ Delightful inside look at moviemaking with director Truffaut playing shrink, social director, and confidant to his cast and crew as the behind-the-scenes love stories become more complicated than the movie being filmed. Won New York Film Critics Circle Award for Best Film, an Oscar for Best Foreign Film, and an Oscar nomination for Best Supporting Actress for Cortese, who is so good that Ingrid Bergman apologized when she beat Cortese for the award.

DAY OF THE ANIMALS 1977
★★ PG Horror 1:37
☑ Violence
Dir: William Girdler   *Cast:* Christopher George, Leslie Nielsen, Michael Ansara, Lynda Day George, Richard Jaeckel
▶ Animals run amok due to the destruction of earth's ozone layer in this thriller from the makers of *Grizzly*. Forest guide George tries to protect city slickers from killer beasts, including bears, cougars, wolves, hawks, vultures, and snakes. Tense thriller enhanced by Lalo Schifrin score.

DAY OF THE DEAD 1985
★★ R Horror 1:42
☑ Explicit language, graphic violence
Dir: George A. Romero   *Cast:* Lori Cardille, Terry Alexander, Joseph Pilato, Jarlath Conroy, Antone DiLeo, Jr.
▶ The last few humans alive hole up in an underground compound in Florida in the third part of Romero's zombie trilogy. Production values and budget seem higher than earlier entries but the familiar formula remains the same: plenty of blood and guts, well-done gore effects, and marauding zombies. Will gross out some, scare the rest.

DAY OF THE DOLPHIN, THE 1973
★★★★ PG Action-Adventure 1:44
Dir: Mike Nichols   *Cast:* George C. Scott, Trish Van Devere, Paul Sorvino, Fritz Weaver, Edward Herrmann
▶ Scientist Scott teaches two dolphins to talk but evil conspirators try to use the mammals in an assassination scheme. Criticized as simplistic upon initial release but holds up as sweet and enchanting adventure fare, ideal for younger moviegoers. Lyrical direction from Nichols, charming dolphins, and a heartbreaking ending.

DAY OF THE JACKAL, THE 1973 British/French
★★★★ PG Action-Adventure 2:20
Dir: Fred Zinnemann   *Cast:* Edward Fox, Alan Badel, Tony Britton, Cyril Cusack, Michael Lonsdale, Derek Jacobi
▶ In 1962, a terrorist organization hires the Jackal (Fox), the world's best professional hitman, to assassinate French President Charles de Gaulle. French policeman Lonsdale learns of the plot, but the Jackal uses baffling disguises to stay one step ahead of the cops. Methodical semidocumentary approach to Frederick

Forsyth's best-seller is short on characterizations but builds incredible tension.

DAY OF THE LOCUST, THE 1975
★★ R Drama 2:24
☑ Nudity, adult situations, explicit language, violence
Dir: John Schlesinger *Cast:* Donald Sutherland, Karen Black, William Atherton, Burgess Meredith, Geraldine Page
▶ Ambitious look at the dark underside of 1930s Hollywood, as personified by lonely accountant Sutherland, young studio artist Atherton, and loose woman Black with whom they are involved. Meredith shines as Black's alcoholic father. Schlesinger's hellish vision culminates in a nightmarish riot at a movieland premiere. From Nathanael West's classic novel.

DAYS OF HEAVEN 1978
★★ PG Drama 1:35
☑ Brief nudity, explicit language, mild violence
Dir: Terrence Malick *Cast:* Richard Gere, Brooke Adams, Sam Shepard, Linda Manz, Robert Wilke
▶ Factory worker Gere leaves Chicago for the Texas Panhandle with girlfriend Adams and sister Manz. They find work with Shepard, a wealthy farmer who starts a tragic affair with Adams. Technically breathtaking period drama has some of the most beautiful images ever captured on film. Nestor Almendros (assisted by Haskell Wexler) won an Oscar for his photography. Shepard's acting debut.

DAYS OF WINE AND ROSES 1962
★★★★ NR Drama 1:57 B&W
Dir: Blake Edwards *Cast:* Jack Lemmon, Lee Remick, Charles Bickford, Jack Klugman, Alan Hewitt, Jack Albertson
▶ Newlyweds Lemmon and Remick fall into alcoholism as he brings job pressures home with him. Alcoholics Anonymous provides a cure for Lemmon but Remick finds beating the bottle not so easy. Superb Oscar-nominated performances by Lemmon and Remick highlight this adaptation of J. P. Miller's television play. Henry Mancini/Johnny Mercer title tune won Oscar.

DAY THE EARTH CAUGHT FIRE, THE
1962 British
★★★ NR Sci-Fi 1:39 B&W
Dir: Val Guest *Cast:* Edward Judd,
Janet Munro, Leo McKern, Michael Goodliffe, Bernard Braden
▶ Cynical reporter Judd covers what is literally the hottest story of all time: when the Americans and Russians conduct nuclear tests on the same day, the Earth is thrown off its orbit and starts moving dangerously closer to the sun. Realistic treatment emphasizes character over special effects, resulting in blistering tension.

DAY THE EARTH STOOD STILL, THE
1951
★★★★ NR Sci-Fi 1:28 B&W
Dir: Robert Wise *Cast:* Michael Rennie, Patricia Neal, Hugh Marlowe, Bobby Gray, Sam Jaffe
▶ Benevolent alien Rennie, accompanied by a huge robot, lands his flying saucer in Washington, D.C., to bring a message of peace to violence-prone humans. Widow Neal aids him but humanity is suspicious. Powerful, still topical fifties sci-fi classic generates plenty of suspense and food for thought. Rennie is a fine alien and there's a haunting Bernard Herrmann score.

D.C. CAB 1983
★★★ R Comedy 1:39
☑ Nudity, adult situations, explicit language, mild violence
Dir: Joel Schumacher *Cast:* Adam Baldwin, Charlie Barnett, Irene Cara, Max Gail, Mr. T, Gary Busey
▶ Low-key Southerner Baldwin joins Washington's worst taxi company, where his rowdy new colleagues are soon involved in a kidnapping. Good-natured nonsense is consistently funky, fast-paced, and funny. As enormous redneck twins, David and Peter Barbarian stand out in the talented cast. Giorgio Moroder adds a hot soundtrack. **(CC)**

DEAD, THE 1987
★★ PG Drama 1:23
Dir: John Huston *Cast:* Anjelica Huston, Donal McCann, Rachel Dowling, Cathleen Delany, Helena Carroll, Dan O'Herlihy
▶ During a Dublin Christmas party in 1904, husband McCann realizes he knows very little about wife Huston. Low-key, scrupulous adaptation of the James Joyce story features superb ensemble acting from an all-Irish cast and marvelous attention to period detail. The stunning climax is a fitting coda to John Huston's illustrious career. Oscar nominations for Best Adapted Screenplay (by son

Tony Huston) and for Costume Design. (CC)

DEAD AND BURIED 1981
★★ R Horror 1:34
☑ Explicit language, graphic violence
Dir: Gary A. Sherman   *Cast:* James Farentino, Melody Anderson, Jack Albertson, Dennis Redfield, Nancy Locke Hauser
▶ Mad mortician/plastic surgeon Albertson gives new meaning to "life after death" as residents of Potter's Bluff mysteriously become zombies. Grim and grisly crimes start happening all over town. First-rate makeup with a gallery of decomposing faces.

DEAD END 1937
★★★ NR Drama 1:33 B&W
Dir: William Wyler   *Cast:* Sylvia Sidney, Joel McCrea, Humphrey Bogart, Claire Trevor, Marjorie Main, Ward Bond
▶ Sidney Kingsley's powerful play about the slums of New York received a first-rate interpretation from director Wyler, screenwriter Lillian Hellman, and an exceptional cast. Episodic plot weaves a broad spectrum of characters—criminal on the run Bogart, struggling architect McCrea, working girl Sidney watching her brother turn to crime, etc.—into a raw, uncompromising examination of poverty. Film introduced the Dead End Kids (Billy Halop, Leo Gorcey, Huntz Hall, etc.), who went on to star in *Angels With Dirty Faces* and the Bowery Boys series.

DEAD-END DRIVE-IN 1986 Australian
☆ R Action-Adventure 1:27
☑ Nudity, adult situations, explicit language, violence
Dir: Brian Trenchard-Smith   *Cast:* Ned Manning, Natalie McCurry, Peter Whitford, Wilbur Wilde, Brett Climo
▶ In near-future New South Wales, fascist government locks up unruly kids and their revved-up jalopies in a drive-in prison. Cocky Crabs (Manning) plots to escape, which he accomplishes by literally driving through the roof in a wild finale. Imaginative, funny, action-packed Aussie fare has appeal similar to the *Mad Max* trilogy. (CC)

DEAD HEAT 1988
★★ R Action-Adventure/Comedy 1:27
☑ Explicit language, graphic violence
Dir: Mark Goldblatt   *Cast:* Treat Williams, Joe Piscopo, Lindsay Frost, Darren McGavin, Vincent Price, Clare Kirkconnell
▶ Los Angeles cops Williams and Piscopo following a trail of jewel heists learn thieves are zombies reanimated by coroner McGavin. Duo try to crack the undead ring, but Williams gets killed in the action. Can he be brought back to life as a zombie crime-stopper? Unusual premise in light-hearted actioner. (CC)

DEADLINE 1987 German
★ R Drama 1:39
☑ Explicit language, violence
Dir: Nathaniel Gutman   *Cast:* Christopher Walken, Marita Marschall, Hywel Bennett, Arnon Zadok, Amos Lavie, Ette Ankri
▶ Walken is a world-weary TV journalist dispatched to war-torn Lebanon in 1983. An exclusive interview with a PLO bigshot turns out to be a fraud and soon Walken has angered the warring factions. Political drama convinces with footage shot in Jaffa, Israel, but story is often tiring and passionless.

DEADLINE U.S.A. 1952
★★ NR Drama 1:27 B&W
Dir: Richard Brooks   *Cast:* Humphrey Bogart, Ethel Barrymore, Kim Hunter, Ed Begley, Paul Stewart, Warren Stevens
▶ Hard-hitting newspaper drama, with Bogart an embattled editor protecting his paper from hostile new investors as he pulls together an exposé on the local rackets. Strong support from Stewart and Begley as reporters, and Barrymore as the paper's elderly owner.

DEADLY AFFAIR, THE 1967
★★★ NR Drama 1:47
Dir: Sidney Lumet   *Cast:* James Mason, Simone Signoret, Maximilian Schell, Harriet Andersson, Harry Andrews, Lynn Redgrave
▶ Mason, a British agent investigating a Foreign Office suicide, uncovers a spy ring but must sacrifice his marriage and career to defeat the enemy. Grim, sober adaptation of John le Carré's *Call for the Dead* is an accomplished, intellectually demanding thriller.

DEADLY BLESSING 1981
★★ R Horror 1:42
☑ Nudity, adult situations, explicit language, graphic violence
Dir: Wes Craven   *Cast:* Maren Jensen, Susan Buckner, Sharon Stone, Lisa Hartman, Lois Nettleton, Ernest Borgnine
▶ Effective low-budget chiller about sexy

widow Jensen terrorized by the Hittites, a repressive Texas religious sect. Leader Borgnine banishes the widow and her friends, leading to gruesome, lethal confrontations. Unusual feminist subtext and a quirky sense of morality set this a notch above other films in the genre.

DEADLY EYES 1983
★ **R Horror 1:27**
☑ Nudity, explicit language, graphic violence
Dir: Robert Clouse   *Cast:* Sam Groom, Sara Botsford, Scatman Crothers, Lisa Langlois, Cec Linder
▶ Old fashioned "monster on the loose" story about a colony of giant rats plaguing a big-city subway system. High school teacher Groom and health inspector Botsford fall in love while tackling the overgrown rodents. Highlights include nighttime attacks on a movie theater and bowling alley.

DEADLY FORCE 1983
★★★ **R Action-Adventure 1:35**
☑ Nudity, adult situations, explicit language, graphic violence
Dir: Paul Aaron   *Cast:* Wings Hauser, Joyce Ingalls, Paul Shenar, Al Ruscio, Arlen Dean Snyder
▶ Racing against the L.A. police, tough ex-cop-turned-bounty-hunter Hauser tracks down a homicidal psychopath. The cops close the case after a murder, but Hauser, joining forces with ex-wife Ingalls, won't let up until his revenge is complete.

DEADLY FRIEND 1986
★★ **R Horror 1:32**
☑ Explicit language, graphic violence
Dir: Wes Craven   *Cast:* Matthew Laborteaux, Kristy Swanson, Michael Sharrett, Anne Twomey, Anne Ramsey, Richard Marcus
▶ Offbeat horror film about young inventor Laborteaux whose robot "BB" protects his friends from bullies. When girl next door Swanson is murdered by her father, Laborteaux implants BB's memory chip into her brain, bringing her back to life as a vengeful automaton. Surprisingly lighthearted, with Ramsey turning in a funny performance as the neighborhood busybody. **(CC)**

DEADLY ILLUSION 1987
★★ **R Mystery-Suspense 1:30**
☑ Adult situations, explicit language, violence
Dir: Larry Cohen, William Tannen   *Cast:*

Billy Dee Williams, Morgan Fairchild, Vanity, John Beck, Joe Cortese
▶ Hired by a businessman to kill his wife, unlicensed private dick Williams tries to warn her instead and is framed for murder. Entertaining B-movie with likable Williams, clever dialogue, and engaging tongue-in-cheek tone. Nice use of New York City locations, including a fight scene staged in the Rockefeller Center Christmas tree.

DEADLY INTRUDER, THE 1985
★ **NR Horror 1:24**
☑ Nudity, adult situations, explicit language, violence
Dir: John McCauley   *Cast:* Chris Holder, Molly Cheek, Tony Crupi, Danny Bonaduce, Stuart Whitman, Laura Melton
▶ Psychotic killer escapes from institution and terrorizes rural town, baffling policeman Whitman. Meanwhile, drifter Crupi kidnaps young Cheek, who suspects Crupi may be the missing lunatic. Mediocre horror film suffers from lackluster acting and tired plot.

DEADLY STRANGERS 1974 British
★★ **NR Mystery-Suspense 1:33**
☑ Brief nudity, adult situations, explicit language, violence
Dir: Sidney Hayers   *Cast:* Hayley Mills, Simon Ward, Sterling Hayden, Ken Hutchison, Peter Jeffrey
▶ Violent patient escapes from mental institution in the British countryside. Later, Mills, haunted by unhappy love affair, gets a lift from Ward. Is he the killer? Decent performances by Mills and Ward, although those who remember Mills from her child star days may be shocked to see her topless here. Mild tension with surprise ending.

DEAD MEN DON'T WEAR PLAID 1982
★★ **PG Comedy 1:29 B&W**
☑ Explicit language, adult humor
Dir: Carl Reiner   *Cast:* Steve Martin, Rachel Ward, Carl Reiner, Reni Santoni, George Gaynes
▶ Private-eye parody with Martin as a 1940s detective hired by beautiful Ward to solve the murder of her noted cheesemaker/scientist father. Consistently amusing deadpan comedy based on a unique and clever gimmick: clips of old movies are seamlessly woven into the narrative so that Martin gets to interact with Barbara Stanwyck, Humphrey Bogart, Ingrid Bergman, Fred MacMurray,

and other stars of that era. Superlative editing, lighting, sets, and black-and-white cinematography make the device work perfectly.

DEAD OF NIGHT 1945 British
★★★ NR Horror 1:44 B&W
Dir: Cavalcanti, Charles Crichton, Basil Dearden, Robert Hamer *Cast:* Mervyn Johns, Roland Culver, Googie Withers, Michael Redgrave, Basil Radford, Naunton Wayne
▶ Landmark omnibus horror film uses architect Johns's nightmare as a linking device for five separate ghost stories: "The Hearse Driver," "The Christmas Story," "The Haunted Mirror," "The Golfing Story," and "The Ventriloquist's Dummy." Eerie, macabre film suffers from varying quality, but the frightening final sequence—in which ventriloquist Redgrave's dummy slowly drives him insane—was so successful it was expanded into the feature-length *Magic*.

DEAD OF WINTER 1987
★★★ R Mystery-Suspense 1:40
☑ Violence
Dir: Arthur Penn *Cast:* Mary Steenburgen, Roddy McDowall, Jan Rubes, William Ruff, Mark Malone
▶ Struggling actress Steenburgen is lured to an isolated, snowbound house with the promise of a part and soon finds herself an unwilling accomplice to scheme of blackmailers Rubes and McDowall. Old-fashioned suspense thriller with an intricate, surprising plot. Creepy atmosphere, several real scares, and nifty work from Steenburgen in three roles. (CC)

DEAD POOL, THE 1988
★★★★ R Action-Adventure 1:31
☑ Explicit language, violence
Dir: Buddy Van Horn *Cast:* Clint Eastwood, Patricia Clarkson, Evan C. Kim, Liam Neeson, David Hunt, Michael Currie
▶ After jailing a Mafia kingpin, San Francisco cop Harry Callahan (Eastwood) finds himself the center of unwanted publicity, in particular a betting pool predicting celebrities' deaths. Fifth entry in the *Dirty Harry* series maintains formula's high body count while emphasizing humor. Manic car chase highlights sturdy Eastwood vehicle.

DEAD RECKONING 1947
★★★★ NR Mystery-Suspense 1:40 B&W
Dir: John Cromwell *Cast:* Humphrey

Bogart, Lizabeth Scott, Morris Carnovsky, William Prince, Wallace Ford
▶ Steamy whodunit features Bogart as a man determined to solve his army buddy's mysterious disappearance and death—until he learns his friend was a convicted murderer. Sultry Scott plays Bogey's love interest. Underrated film holds up extremely well.

DEAD RINGERS 1988 Canadian
★★ R Drama 1:15
☑ Nudity, adult situations, explicit language, violence
Dir: David Cronenberg *Cast:* Jeremy Irons, Genevieve Bujold, Heidi Von Palleske, Barbara Gordon, Shirley Douglas, Stephen Lack
▶ Irons is eerily convincing in a dual role as identical twin gynecologists who sink into drug addiction and insanity after deceiving actress Bujold in romance. Director Cronenberg fashioned a true incident into a macabre, perversely fascinating fantasy that is unnerving without being overly graphic. Howard Shore's rich score adds to film's compelling style. (CC)

DEADTIME STORIES 1987
★ R Horror 1:23
☑ Explicit language, violence
Dir: Jeffrey Delman *Cast:* Michael Mesmer, Brian DePersia, Scott Valentine, Phyllis Craig, Anne Redfern
▶ Once upon a time . . . little Brian (DePersia) asked for a bedtime story from his Uncle Mike (Mesmer) and got Lizzie Borden and the Three Bears, variations on the Brothers Grimm and more. Cute idea, but not scary enough to give anyone bad dreams.

DEAD ZONE, THE 1983
★★★★ R Mystery-Suspense 1:43
☑ Brief nudity, explicit language, violence
Dir: David Cronenberg *Cast:* Christopher Walken, Brooke Adams, Tom Skerritt, Herbert Lom, Martin Sheen
▶ Schoolteacher Walken awakens from a five-year coma with the eerie power to predict the future. Besieged by pleas for help from anguished people, he retreats into anonymity—until he realizes that a politician may lead the country into war. Restrained adaptation of the Stephen King novel has a few gory moments, but is primarily an absorbing psychological thriller. (CC)

DEAL OF THE CENTURY 1983
★★ PG Comedy 1:38

☑ Adult situations, explicit language, violence, adult humor
Dir: William Friedkin   *Cast:* Chevy Chase, Sigourney Weaver, Gregory Hines, Vince Edwards, Wallace Shawn
▶ Struggling arms dealer Chase gets mixed up with Latin American fascists and beautiful widow Weaver while selling faulty aircraft to unsuspecting Third Worlders. However, the "deal of the century" is sabotaged by Chase's born-again partner Hines, who begins to question his career choice. Irreverent arms-race satire from the director of *The Exorcist* and the screenwriter of *Risky Business.*

DEAR AMERICA: LETTERS HOME FROM VIETNAM 1987
★ ★ ★ ★ **PG-13 Documentary/MFTV 1:27 C/B&W**
☑ Explicit language, violence
Dir: Bill Couturie
▶ Award-winning documentary examines the Vietnam War from viewpoint of soldiers' first-hand accounts of the fighting. Accompanied by masterful use of NBC stock footage, outtakes, and Super-8 home movies, the soldiers' letters are moving, illuminating, and often unbearably painful. Actors contributing to the voice-overs include Tom Berenger, Robert De Niro, Sean Penn, Randy Quaid, Martin Sheen, and Kathleen Turner. Produced by HBO, film received such high praise that it was subsequently released in theaters.

DEAR BRIGITTE 1965
★ ★ **NR Comedy 1:40**
Dir: Henry Koster   *Cast:* James Stewart, Fabian, Glynis Johns, Billy Mumy, John Williams, Brigitte Bardot
▶ Popular family-oriented comedy about young math whiz Mumy, who won't help father Stewart handicap horse races until Dad introduces him to Bardot. Since Stewart needs the money to finance a humanities foundation, he flies to Paris with Mumy to see the great star. Whimsical piece of contemporary Americana also features Ed Wynn as a ferryboat captain. **(CC)**

DEATH BEFORE DISHONOR 1987
★ ★ ★ **R Action-Adventure 1:35**
☑ Explicit language, violence
Dir: Terry Leonard   *Cast:* Fred Dryer, Brian Keith, Joanna Pacula, Paul Winfield, Kasey Walker
▶ It's hardheaded Marine gunnery Sgt.

Jack Burns (Dryer) to the rescue when Arab terrorists kidnap Colonel Keith and the U.S. government refuses to negotiate. The impregnable terrorist hideout is no match for the fists and grenades of Burns in this *Rambo*esque yarn that encourages you to cheer the Marines and hiss the Arabs. **(CC)**

DEATH DRIVER 1978
★ ★ **NR Action-Adventure 1:33**
☑ Adult situations, violence
Dir: Jimmy Huston   *Cast:* Earl Owensby, Mike Allen, Patty Shaw, Mary Ann Hearn
▶ Once the World Motor Rodeo Champion, Owensby leaves his unfaithful wife and seeks to regain his title ten years later. After much womanizing and car crashing with buddy Allen, Owensby must attempt the stunt in which he was critically injured a decade earlier. Low-budget drive-in offering tells story of real-life stunt driver Rex Randolph.

DEATH HUNT 1981
★ ★ ★ ★ **R Action-Adventure 1:37**
☑ Explicit language, graphic violence
Dir: Peter Hunt   *Cast:* Charles Bronson, Lee Marvin, Andrew Stevens, Angie Dickinson, Carl Weathers, Ed Lauter
▶ Bronson plays real-life fugitive Albert Johnson, wrongly accused of murder in 1930s Yukon. Mountie Marvin reluctantly leaves lady love Dickinson to track the "Mad Trapper" in the biggest manhunt in Canadian history. Knockout combination of male stars.

DEATH IN VENICE 1971 Italian/French
★ **PG Drama 2:10**
☑ Adult situations
Dir: Luchino Visconti   *Cast:* Dirk Bogarde, Marisa Berenson, Bjorn Andresen, Silvana Mangano, Mark Burns, Romolo Valli
▶ On the verge of a nervous breakdown in Venice, aging German composer Bogarde finds his dormant emotions reawakened by pretty young boy Andresen. Bogarde follows his obsession around the decaying city without making contact, even as his health rapidly deteriorates. Adaptation of the Thomas Mann novella is beautifully shot and makes powerful use of Mahler's Third and Fifth symphonies, but result is not for all tastes.

DEATH OF A CENTERFOLD: THE DOROTHY STRATTEN STORY 1981
★ ★ ★ **NR Biography/MFTV 1:40**

Dir: Gabrielle Beaumont *Cast:* Jamie Lee Curtis, Bruce Weitz, Robert Reed, Mitchell Ryan, Tracy Reed
▶ TV docudrama about Dorothy Stratten (Curtis), the actress and *Playboy* centerfold, focuses on her relationship with Paul Snider (Weitz), the husband/manager who eventually killed her and then committed suicide in a jealous rage. Good performance by Curtis. Same story was covered (more graphically and perhaps more pretentiously) in Bob Fosse's *Star 80*.

DEATH OF AN ANGEL 1986
★ PG Drama 1:32
☑ Explicit language, violence
Dir: Petru Popescu *Cast:* Bonnie Bedelia, Nick Mancuso, Pamela Ludwig, Alex Colon, Abel Franco
▶ Ludwig, the crippled daughter of widowed Episcopal priest Bedelia, runs away to seek cure from faith healer Mancuso. Bedelia follows and gets involved in Mancuso's quest to find a miraculous cross. Well-intentioned but plodding and obscure.

DEATH OF A SALESMAN 1951
★ NR Drama 1:55 B&W
Dir: Laslo Benedek *Cast:* Fredric March, Mildred Dunnock, Kevin McCarthy, Cameron Mitchell, Howard Smith
▶ Screen version of Arthur Miller play about Willy Loman (March), the salesman whose tragic pursuit of the American Dream poisoned his relationship with his sons. Innovative cinematic techniques by director Benedek and solid acting by March, but the 1985 Dustin Hoffman version has more dramatic intensity.

DEATH OF A SALESMAN 1985
★★★ NR Drama/MFTV 2:14
Dir: Volker Schlondorff *Cast:* Dustin Hoffman, Kate Reid, John Malkovich, Stephen Lang, Charles Durning
▶ Hoffman won both Emmy and Golden Globe awards for his titanic performance as Willy Loman, the sixty-year-old salesman who dreams of being "well liked." Skillful rendition of Arthur Miller's Pulitzer prize–winning play from the Broadway revival cast. Biff, the good kid crushed by his overbearing father, is brilliantly played by Malkovich. **(CC)**

DEATH OF A SOLDIER 1986 Australian
★★ R Drama 1:36
☑ Nudity, explicit language, violence
Dir: Philippe Mora *Cast:* James Coburn, Reb Brown, Maurie Fields, Max Fairchild, Bill Hunter
▶ True story of American soldier Edward J. Leonski (Brown), who was court-martialed and hanged for strangling women in World War II Australia. Military lawyer Coburn tries to win a stay of execution for the unbalanced soldier. Interesting story, credible work from Coburn and Brown, but the last third of film gets static, talky, and preachy. **(CC)**

DEATH ON THE NILE 1978 British
★★★★ PG Mystery-Suspense 2:20
☑ Violence
Dir: John Guillermin *Cast:* Peter Ustinov, David Niven, Mia Farrow, Bette Davis, Maggie Smith, Angela Lansbury
▶ Belgian detective Hercule Poiret (Ustinov) settles in for a cruise down the Nile, which is rudely disrupted by several murders. Follow-up to *Murder on the Orient Express* is leisurely paced but scenic fun with terrific cast of suspects. As Poiret, Ustinov brings a genial grace to the role.

DEATH RACE 2000 1975
★ R Action-Adventure 1:20
☑ Explicit language, graphic violence, adult humor
Dir: Paul Bartel *Cast:* David Carradine, Sylvester Stallone, Simone Griffeth, Louisa Moritz, Mary Woronov
▶ In the year 2000, hit-and-run driving is no longer a felony; it's the national sport and five male/female teams compete in a futuristic road race where running down a woman is worth 10 points, an elderly person, 100. Carradine is Frankenstein, the half-man, half-machine leader of one team; Griffeth, a political rebel, is assigned to eliminate him; and megastar Stallone is competitor. Early action film has cult following.

DEATH SHIP 1980 Canadian
★ R Horror 1:27
☑ Nudity, explicit language, graphic violence
Dir: Alvin Rakoff *Cast:* George Kennedy, Nick Mancuso, Richard Crenna, Sally Ann Howes, Kate Reid
▶ Eight survivors of a sunken cruise ship board a haunted cargo boat navigated by Nazi ghosts. Possessed by the former Nazi captain, Kennedy goes insane; Crenna's believable performance as a frightened man determined to save his family keeps the film afloat.

DEATHSPORT 1978
★ R Sci-Fi 1:23

☑ Nudity, violence
Dir: Henry Suso, Allan Arkush *Cast:* David Carradine, Claudia Jennings, Richard Lynch, William Smithers
▶ The year is 3000 and good guys like Carradine still battle bad guys in this sci-fi gladiator picture. Saber-wielding Ranger Guides ride horses and fight evil cannibal mutants who drive motorcycles known as "Death Machines." Crash scenes light up the screen every few minutes. Sequel of sorts to *Death Race 2000*.

DEATHSTALKER 1983
★ R Action-Adventure 1:20
☑ Rape, nudity, adult situations, explicit language, graphic violence
Dir: John Watson *Cast:* Richard Hill, Barbi Benton, Richard Brooker, Lana Clarkson, Bernard Erhard
▶ Low-budget sword-and-sorcery semi-spoof in which a king loses his empire and daughter Benton (the former Play-mate) to cruel magician Erhard, who rules with the aid of mutant guards. Muscleman Deathstalker (Hill) possesses the "sword of justice" and flexes his pecs to fight ill will. A little sex, lots of t&a and an endless barrage of bloodletting hold the works together.

DEATH TAKES A HOLIDAY 1934
★★★ NR Fantasy 1:18 B&W
Dir: Mitchell Leisen *Cast:* Fredric March, Evelyn Venable, Guy Standing, Katherine Alexander, Gail Patrick, Helen Westley
▶ March delivers another distinguished performance as Death, who disguises himself as an Italian prince to learn why humans fear him. While visiting with no-bleman Standing, Death finds himself drawn to the beautiful but ethereal Venable. Slowly paced and predictable romance has an oddly compelling tone and touching sentiments.

DEATHTRAP 1982
★★★ PG Mystery-Suspense 1:56
☑ Adult situations, explicit language, violence
Dir: Sidney Lumet *Cast:* Michael Caine, Christopher Reeve, Dyan Cannon, Irene Worth, Henry Jones
▶ Caine plays a famous but fading Broadway playwright whose faltering career prompts him to plot several "murders" in the hope of stealing the younger Reeve's superior play. Well acted, funny mindteaser with enough twists and turns

to bait any mystery fan. Based on Ira Levin's Broadway play.

DEATH VALLEY 1982
★★ R Mystery-Suspense 1:28
☑ Nudity, graphic violence
Dir: Dick Richards *Cast:* Paul LeMat, Catherine Hicks, Stephen McHattie, Wilford Brimley, Peter Billingsley
▶ Billingsley vacations in Death Valley with mom Hicks and her new boyfriend LeMat. He accidentally learns the identity of killer McHattie who in turn pursues Billingsley across the desert. A bit more exciting than a mouthful of sand—but not by much.

DEATHWATCH 1966
☆ NR Drama 1:30 B&W
Dir: Vic Morrow *Cast:* Leonard Nimoy, Robert Ellenstein, Paul Mazursky, Michael Forest, Gavin MacLeod
▶ Three men share a cell in one of France's most notorious prisons, in Jean Genet's erotically charged and existentially claustrophobic stage-play-turned-film. Jules (Nimoy) has committed armed robbery and Maurice (Mazursky) is a manipulative homosexual in love with the third inmate, Green Eyes (Forest), a tall, burly murderer. Intrinsically arty and intellectual; unusually casted.

DEATH WISH 1974
★★★★ R Action-Adventure 1:29
☑ Adult situations, explicit language, violence
Dir: Michael Winner *Cast:* Charles Bronson, Hope Lange, Vincent Gardenia, Steven Keats, William Redfield
▶ After muggers murder his wife and cripple his daughter, mild-mannered businessman Bronson takes the law into his own hands. Stalking would-be attackers on the streets of New York, he metes out his own brand of justice. Highly graphic film was a commercial success and spawned many sequels and numerous imitators, even though its premise of vigilante law disturbed many critics.

DEATH WISH II 1982
★★★★ R Action-Adventure 1:28
☑ Rape, nudity, explicit language, graphic violence
Dir: Michael Winner *Cast:* Charles Bronson, Jill Ireland, Vincent Gardenia, J. D. Cannon, Anthony Franciosa, Robin Sherwood
▶ Vigilante architect Bronson finds Los Angeles no more peaceful than New York: a gang of thugs steals his wallet,

attacks his maid, and kidnaps and rapes his daughter. After his daughter dies trying to escape, Bronson hunts the culprits. Hard-hitting and convincing; predictable plot repeats original formula but Bronson evokes audience empathy.

DEATH WISH 3 1985
★ ★ ★ **R Action-Adventure 1:30**
☑ Rape, nudity, adult situations, explicit language, graphic violence
Dir: Michael Winner *Cast:* Charles Bronson, Deborah Raffin, Ed Lauter, Martin Balsam, Gavan O'Herlihy
▶ Further adventures of vigilante Paul Kersey (Bronson). Here he avenges an army pal's death brought on by a punky street gang. Violent excesses; Bronson blows away scores of people, single-handedly, without changing facial expression.

DEATH WISH 4: THE CRACKDOWN 1987
★ ★ ★ ★ **R Action-Adventure 1:32**
☑ Rape, explicit language, graphic violence
Dir: J. Lee Thompson *Cast:* Charles Bronson, Kay Lenz, George Dickerson, Soon-Teck Oh, Perry Lopez
▶ Citizen's arrest, Bronson style. When girlfriend Lenz's teen daughter overdoses on cocaine, architect/vigilante Paul Kersey (Bronson) wipes out the top hoods in L.A.'s drug trade, maintaining his right to remain violent. Ultimate shootout in skating rink parking lot. **(CC)**

DECEIVERS, THE 1988
★ ★ ★ **PG-13 Action-Adventure 1:52**
☑ Violence
Dir: Nicholas Meyer *Cast:* Pierce Brosnan, Saeed Jaffrey, Shashi Kapoor, Helena Michell, Keith Michell
▶ In nineteenth-century India, English officer Brosnan disguises himself as an Indian to infiltrate killer cult and becomes caught up in their murderous ways. Handsomely mounted period piece with a provocative premise falls short due to confused, ambiguous screenplay and slack pacing. Brosnan gamely struggles with his difficult role but the lively Kapoor outshines him.

DECEPTION 1946
★ ★ **NR Drama 1:52 B&W**
Dir: Irving Rapper *Cast:* Bette Davis, Claude Rains, Paul Henreid, John Abbott, Benson Fong
▶ Teacher Davis loves musician Henreid but her conductor ex-beau Rains disrupts

her chance at happiness. Soap operaish Warner Brothers drama is actually great fun, mainly because Rains has a great time playing the wicked interloper.

DECLINE OF THE AMERICAN EMPIRE, THE 1986 French Canadian
☆ **R Comedy/Drama 1:41**
☑ Nudity, adult situations, explicit language
Dir: Denys Arcand *Cast:* Dominque Michel, Dorothee Berryman, Louise Portal, Genevieve Rioux, Pierre Curzi, Remy Girard
▶ Super-literate comedy of modern manners where sophisticated friends gather for dinner and discuss their sexual histories. Smug Girard is a womanizer, Curzi is divorced, Michel has written a book about the decay of society and Jacques, a homosexual, talks of the thrill of indiscriminate sex. Incisive observations and caustic wit; not for all tastes.
S

DECLINE OF WESTERN CIVILIZATION, THE 1981
☆ **NR Documentary/Music 1:40**
☑ Explicit language, violence
Dir: Penelope Spheeris *Cast:* Circle Jerks, Alice Bag Band, Fear, Germs, X, Black Flag
▶ Startling documentary about the late 1970s Los Angeles punk rock scene is a definitive portrait of a disturbing subculture. Concert footage of raw, violent music is interspersed with chilling interviews of the musicians and their fans. Some of the bands achieved legendary status, but sadly many of the performers are now dead. Followed in 1988 by a sequel on heavy metal music.

DECLINE OF WESTERN CIVILIZATION PART II, THE: THE METAL YEARS 1988
★ **R Documentary/Music 1:30**
☑ Explicit language, violence
Dir: Penelope Spheeris *Cast:* Joe Perry, Steven Tyler, Alice Cooper, Gene Simmons, Paul Stanley, Lemmy
▶ Sequel to documentary on punk rockers follows similar formula while focusing on heavy metal music. Interviews with members of Aerosmith, Kiss, Motorhead, Poison, Megadeath, Faster Pussycat, and other groups alternate with brief concert footage to provide an eye-opening look at performers and groupies. Highlighted by chilling talk with Chris Holmes of W.A.S.P., filmed drinking vodka in his swimming pool.

DEEP, THE 1977
★★★★ PG Action-Adventure 2:03
☑ Brief nudity, violence
Dir: Peter Yates *Cast:* Robert Shaw, Jacqueline Bisset, Nick Nolte, Louis Gossett, Jr., Eli Wallach
▶ While skin diving off Bermuda, young Americans Nolte and Bisset discover a World War II ship with a fortune in morphine aboard. Drug dealer and voodoo expert Gossett has designs on the treasure, but crusty recluse Shaw comes to the Americans' aid. Amazing underwater photography and Bisset's eye-catching outfits provide most of the excitement in this adaptation of Peter Benchley's bestseller.

DEEP IN MY HEART 1954
★★★★ NR Biography/Musical 2:12
Dir: Stanley Donen *Cast:* Jose Ferrer, Merle Oberon, Helen Traubel, Doe Avedon, Walter Pidgeon, Paul Henreid
▶ Star-studded biography of composer Sigmund Romberg (ably played by Ferrer) and his rise to fame with the help of writer Dorothy Donnelly (Oberon) and showman Florenz Ziegfeld (Henreid). Hits such as "The Desert Song," "Lover Come Back to Me," and "Softly, As in a Morning Sunrise" are performed by a long list of guest stars including Rosemary Clooney, Jane Powell, Vic Damone, Ann Miller, Cyd Charisse, Howard Keel, Tony Martin, and Gene Kelly in his only film performance with brother Fred.

DEEP IN THE HEART 1984 British
★★ R Action-Adventure 1:39
☑ Rape, nudity, adult situations, explicit language, graphic violence
Dir: Tony Garnett *Cast:* Karen Young, Clayton Day, Suzie Humphreys, Helena Humann, Ben Jones
▶ Pretty Dallas schoolteacher Young is raped on a date with gun-collecting attorney Day. When the cops refuse to do anything about the crime, she becomes a sharpshooter to get revenge. Antihandgun and feminist themes add some spark to this low-budget action picture. Also known as *Handgun*.

DEEP RED 1975 Italian
☆ R Horror 1:38
☑ Graphic violence
Dir: Dario Argento *Cast:* David Hemmings, Daria Nicolodi, Gabriele Lavia, Clara Calamai, Macha Meril
▶ In Rome, Englishman Hemmings sees a psychiatrist fall victim to a serial killer. He

investigates and is stalked by the murderer. Directed by Argento in his trademark fashion in which bravura visuals overwhelm a muddled plot. Also known as *Hatchet Murders*.

DEEPSTAR SIX 1988
★★★ R Horror 1:40
☑ Explicit language, violence
Dir: Sean S. Cunningham *Cast:* Greg Evigan, Nancy Everhard, Taurean Blacque, Miguel Ferrer, Cindy Pickett
▶ Captain Blacque, right-hand man Evigan, and Evigan's pregnant lover Everhard are members of an undersea research crew menaced by a monster crustacean. Generates some scares as attractive stars run for their collective lives, but special effects and formula screenplay are merely okay.

DEER HUNTER, THE 1978
★★★★ R Drama 3:03
☑ Adult situations, explicit language, graphic violence
Dir: Michael Cimino *Cast:* Robert De Niro, John Cazale, John Savage, Christopher Walken, Meryl Streep
▶ Ambitious epic about the effect of the Vietnam War on the blue-collar inhabitants of a Pennsylvania steel town. Filled with magnificent performances—including De Niro as an embittered POW, Streep as an abandoned wife, Cazale (in his last role) as a neurotic alcoholic, and Savage as a maimed vet—and beautiful production values. A milestone for its sympathetic treatment of veterans, film was awarded nine Oscar nominations, winning for Picture, Director, Supporting Actor (Walken), Sound, and Editing.

DEF-CON 4 1985
★★ R Sci-Fi 1:28
☑ Explicit language, graphic violence
Dir: Paul Donovan *Cast:* Lenore Zahn, Maury Chaykin, Kate Lynch, Kevin King, John Walsch, Tim Choate
▶ Three astronauts return to Earth after World War III and find Nova Scotia overrun by sadistic thugs. When their partner is killed, Choate and his lover Zahn begin the arduous journey to safety in Central America. Grim post-apocalyptic fable suffers from a low budget and cast of unknowns.

DEFENCE OF THE REALM 1986 British
★★ PG Mystery-Suspense 1:36
☑ Brief nudity, mild violence
Dir: David Drury *Cast:* Gabriel Byrne,

Greta Scacchi, Denholm Elliott, Ian Bannen, Bill Paterson

▶ Jumbled thriller about investigative reporter Byrne, whose articles destroy politician Bannen's career. When colleague Elliott is murdered, Byrne learns he's been set up by the government. Aided by secretary Scacchi, Byrne sets out to expose the villains. Film raises intriguing themes: terrorism, nuclear politics, press responsibilities, etc. **(CC)**

DEFIANCE 1980
★ ★ ★ ★ **PG Action-Adventure 1:42**
☑ Adult situations, explicit language, graphic violence
Dir: John Flynn *Cast:* Jan-Michael Vincent, Theresa Saldana, Fernando Lopez, Danny Aiello, Art Carney
▶ Between voyages, merchant seaman Vincent finds his New York neighborhood besieged by vicious young punks. When kindly shopkeeper Carney is beaten, Vincent rallies his old friends to defeat the gang. Gritty vigilante drama is restrained and realistic.

DEFIANT ONES, THE 1958
★ ★ ★ ★ **NR Action-Adventure 1:37**
B&W
Dir: Stanley Kramer *Cast:* Tony Curtis, Sidney Poitier, Theodore Bikel, Charles McGraw, Lon Chaney, Jr., Cara Williams
▶ Black convict Poitier and prejudiced white Curtis escape chain gang while still handcuffed together. The pair overcome initial differences to insure mutual survival. Tremendous excitement with something to say; Poitier and Curtis are excellent. Oscars for Best Cinematography and Screenplay; nominated for Picture, Actor (Curtis, Poitier), Supporting Actor (Bikel), Supporting Actress (Williams), Director.

DEJA VU 1985
★ ★ **R Drama 1:34**
☑ Adult situations, mild violence
Dir: Anthony Richmond *Cast:* Jaclyn Smith, Shelley Winters, Claire Bloom, Nigel Terry
▶ Screenwriter Terry notices the uncanny resemblance between his fiancée and famous 1930s dancer Smith (in a dual role) who died in a suspicious fire. Bizarre coincidences lead him to believe that the dancer has possessed his fiancée. Smith's husband shot and directed this handsome fantasy.

DELIVERANCE 1972
★ ★ ★ ★ **R Action-Adventure 1:49**
☑ Rape, explicit language, violence
Dir: John Boorman *Cast:* Jon Voight, Burt Reynolds, Ned Beatty, Ronny Cox, Bill McKinney, Herbert "Cowboy" Coward
▶ Brutal, riveting adventure about backwoods novices Voight, Beatty, and Cox who join macho guide Reynolds on a white-water rafting trip in Georgia. Classic man-against-the-elements premise is taken one step further by the introduction of terrifying hillbillies intent on rape and murder. Stark photography and haunting bluegrass score (including the pop hit "Dueling Banjos") helped make this an enormous success. Nominated for Best Picture and Directing. Based on the novel by James Dickey (who has a cameo as the sheriff).

DELIVERY BOYS 1986
★ **R Comedy 1:32**
☑ Nudity, adult situations, explicit language
Dir: Ken Handler *Cast:* Joss Marcano, Tom Sierchio, Jim Soriero, Mario Van Peebles, Kelly Nichols
▶ Comic misadventures of three breakdancers who earn money delivering pizza. Van Peebles conspires to keep them out of a big contest. Marcano is seduced by porn star Nichols; Sierchio is trapped in an art gallery; and Soriero becomes a guinea pig for an experimental drug. Late addition to the breakdancing genre.

DELTA FORCE, THE 1986
★ ★ ★ ★ **R Action-Adventure 2:09**
☑ Explicit language, violence
Dir: Menahem Golan *Cast:* Lee Marvin, Chuck Norris, Martin Balsam, Shelley Winters, Joey Bishop, George Kennedy
▶ When Palestinian terrorists hijack a TWA flight in Athens and take a group of hostages to Beirut, Marvin and his crack commando unit Delta Force are summoned to help. Lone wolf Norris rejoins his old comrades for Israel-based rescue mission. Actioner revises facts of 1985 hijacking to give Yanks revenge on terrorists, but genre fans won't quibble with such details as Norris and company bust up the bad guys with great gusto. **(CC)**

DEMON, THE 1981
★ ★ **NR Horror 1:33**

☑ Nudity, adult situations, explicit language, graphic violence
Dir: Percival Rubens *Cast:* Jennifer Holmes, Cameron Mitchell, Craig Gardner, Zoli Markey, Mark Tannous
▶ Vicious alien monster attacks women with a steel claw, saving their body parts in plastic bags. Authorities are baffled by the mounting murders. Unremarkable horror exploitation filmed in South Africa.

DEMON SEED 1977
★★ R Sci-Fi 1:34
☑ Nudity, adult situations, violence
Dir: Donald Cammell *Cast:* Julie Christie, Fritz Weaver, Gerrit Graham, Berry Kroeger
▶ Weaver invents Proteus IV, an organic supercomputer with the ability to reproduce. Proteus traps Weaver's wife Christie in a computer-controlled apartment, then proceeds to impregnate her. Bizarre science-fiction story has interesting special effects and stylish direction. Robert Vaughn supplies the computer's voice.

DEMONS OF THE MIND 1972 British
★ R Horror 1:25
☑ Adult situations, explicit language, violence
Dir: Peter Sykes *Cast:* Paul Jones, Patrick Magee, Yvonne Mitchell, Robert Hardy, Gillian Hills, Michael Hordern
▶ Nineteenth-century doctor Magee confronts baron Jones, who believes his children are possessed by demons and has been locking them up in his castle. Uninspired psychological drama with a dollop of horror.

DERSU UZALA 1975 Japanese/Russian
★★ G Drama 2:17
Dir: Akira Kurosawa *Cast:* Maxim Munzuk, Yuri Solomine
▶ In 1902, Mongolian guide Dersu Uzala (Munzuk) teaches Russian surveyor Solomine how to survive the Siberian wilderness. Their friendship deepens over the years as Dersu reveals the wonders and dangers of nature to the surveyor. Deliberate pacing and exotic locations enhance this simple, poignant film. Based on a true story, and winner of the Best Foreign Picture Oscar. Ⓢ

DESERT BLOOM 1986
★★ PG Drama 1:46
☑ Adult situations, explicit language, mild violence
Dir: Eugene Corr *Cast:* Jon Voight, JoBeth Williams, Ellen Barkin, Allen Garfield, Annabeth Gish

▶ Modest, touching coming-of-age story set in 1950 Las Vegas focuses on awkward teenager Gish and her eccentric family. Aunt Sara (Barkin) moves in while awaiting her divorce, sparking a confrontation between father Voight, a troubled veteran who runs a gas station, and mother Williams. Good sense of period detail (including a funny account of A-bomb tests) and sensitive performances.

DESERT FOX, THE 1951
★★★ NR Biography/War 1:28 B&W
Dir: Henry Hathaway *Cast:* James Mason, Cedric Hardwicke, Jessica Tandy, Luther Adler, Everett Sloane, Richard Boone
▶ True story of the brilliant World War II German commander Erwin Rommel (Mason) traces his North African campaign against the British. Later, Rommel turns against Hitler and participates in an ill-fated plot against the Führer's life. Sympathetic account dominated by Mason's characterization; he played Rommel again two years later in *The Desert Rats.*

DESERT HEARTS 1986
★★ R Drama 1:27
☑ Nudity, adult situations, explicit language
Dir: Donna Deitch *Cast:* Helen Shaver, Patricia Charbonneau, Audra Lindley, Andra Akers, Dean Butler
▶ In the 1950s, repressed professor Shaver visits Nevada dude ranch to obtain divorce and is pursued by younger Charbonneau. They fall in love; Shaver deals with society pressure and her own misgivings. Passionate lesbian love story with intelligent direction by Deitch and strong, committed performances by the leads. Steamy love scene is pretty explicit.

DESIGN FOR LIVING 1933
★★★ NR Comedy 1:30 B&W
Dir: Ernst Lubitsch *Cast:* Fredric March, Gary Cooper, Miriam Hopkins, Edward Everett Horton, Franklin Pangborn, Isabel Jewell
▶ Elegant but risqué comedy of manners about commercial artist Hopkins who sets up a ménage à trois in Paris with playwright March and painter Cooper. Although rivals, March and Cooper join together to break up Hopkins's marriage of convenience to stuffy millionaire Horton. Surprisingly adult farce about sexual politics was adapted by Ben Hecht from a Noel Coward play.

DESIGNING WOMAN 1957
★★★★ NR Comedy 1:58
Dir: Vincente Minnelli *Cast:* Gregory Peck, Lauren Bacall, Dolores Gray, Sam Levene, Mickey Shaughnessy, Chuck Connors
► Amiable farce about rough-hewn sportswriter Peck who marries glamorous fashion designer Bacall, then finds it impossible to adapt to her high society life. Romantic as well as amusing, with Gray especially good as a jilted girlfriend. Screenplay by George Wells won an Oscar.

DESIRE 1936
★★ NR Comedy 1:36 B&W
Dir: Frank Borzage *Cast:* Marlene Dietrich, Gary Cooper, John Halliday, William Frawley, Akim Tamiroff
► Dietrich has one of her most alluring roles as a Parisian jewel thief who drags American engineer Cooper into her scheme to cross the Spanish border. Polished, extremely witty romantic comedy made Dietrich a star in America. She also gets to sing "Awake in a Dream."

DESIREE 1954
★★ NR Drama 1:50
Dir: Henry Koster *Cast:* Marlon Brando, Jean Simmons, Merle Oberon, Michael Rennie, Cameron Mitchell, Cathleen Nesbitt
► Young and penniless Napoleon Bonaparte (Brando) wants to marry beautiful Desiree (Simmons) but her dad bars the match. Bonaparte rises to power and marries Josephine (Oberon); Desiree weds nobleman Rennie but still carries a torch for her lost love. An oddly cast Brando still shines. **(CC)**

DESIRE UNDER THE ELMS 1958
★ NR Drama 1:51 B&W
Dir: Delbert Mann *Cast:* Sophia Loren, Anthony Perkins, Burl Ives, Frank Overton, Pernell Roberts
► Story of seduction and murder set against the stark backdrop of 1840 New England. Elderly farmer Ives weds young Italian immigrant Loren; she seduces Ives's son Perkins in order to produce an heir. The affair ends in tragedy. Sparks fly between Loren and Perkins in this adaptation of the Eugene O'Neill play. Oscar-nominated cinematography and top Elmer Bernstein score.

DESK SET 1957
★★★★ NR Comedy 1:43
Dir: Walter Lang *Cast:* Spencer Tracy, Katharine Hepburn, Gig Young, Joan Blondell, Dina Merrill
► Sparks fly when the unbeatable team of Tracy and Hepburn mix business with pleasure at a broadcast network. Hepburn is especially delightful as an intellectual researcher capable of throwing fear and trepidation into the coils of efficiency expert Tracy's computer in this comedy-romance about the onslaught of office automation.

DESPAIR 1979 German
☆ NR Drama 1:59
☑ Brief nudity, adult situations, explicit language
Dir: Rainer Werner Fassbinder *Cast:* Dirk Bogarde, Andrea Ferreol, Volker Spengler, Klaus Lowitsch, Bernhard Wicki, Alexander Allerson
► In 1930s Berlin, Bogarde, the neurotic owner of a chocolate factory, tries to switch identities with drifter Lowitsch to collect on an insurance policy. Surreal psychodrama with bleak comic overtones was adapted by playwright Tom Stoppard from Vladimir Nabokov's novel.

DESPERATE HOURS, THE 1955
★★★ NR Mystery-Suspense 1:52 B&W
Dir: William Wyler *Cast:* Humphrey Bogart, Fredric March, Arthur Kennedy, Martha Scott, Gig Young, Dewey Martin
► Escaped prisoner Bogart and two accomplices break into March's home and hold family hostage. Ordinary guy March cooperates with his captors but then manages to outwit them. Nail-biting adaptation of the Joseph Hayes play and novel; well acted by all with razor-sharp direction by Wyler.

DESPERATELY SEEKING SUSAN 1985
★★ PG-13 Comedy 1:43
☑ Brief nudity, adult situations, explicit language
Dir: Susan Seidelman *Cast:* Rosanna Arquette, Madonna, Aidan Quinn, Robert Joy, Mark Blum
► Bump on the noggin gives bored New Jersey hausfrau Arquette amnesia and makes her think she's wild young Madonna. Arquette finds herself in the middle of caper plot and falls for film projectionist Quinn. Sly, hip direction by Seidelman creates a funky New York City fantasyland that accounts for this comedy's shaggy, offbeat charm. The ladies, solidly supported by Quinn, are fine.

DESTINATION MOON 1950
★★ NR Sci-Fi 1:31
Dir: Irving Pichel *Cast:* Warner Anderson, John Archer, Tom Powers, Dick Wesson, Erin O'Brien-Moore, Ted Warde
▶ Four astronauts make the hazardous journey to the moon, then learn they don't have enough fuel to return to Earth. Although dated, this landmark science fiction film, based on Robert Heinlein's *Rocketship Galileo*, was one of the first to take a realistic approach to space travel. Producer George Pal won an Oscar for Special Effects.

DESTINATION TOKYO 1944
★★★ NR War 2:15 B&W
Dir: Delmer Daves *Cast:* Cary Grant, John Garfield, Alan Hale, John Ridgely, Dane Clark, Faye Emerson
▶ Rousing World War II drama follows the crew of the *Copperfin* submarine on a perilous mission to Tokyo Bay. The wonderful cast features a rugged Grant as the commander and Garfield in one of his best performances as a skirt-chasing sailor. Deliberately claustrophobic set design makes the many highlights (including an improvised appendectomy and a nerve-wracking depth charge sequence) feel even more authentic. Available in a colorized version.

DESTRUCTORS, THE 1974 British
★★★ PG Drama 1:29
☑ Adult situations, violence
Dir: Robert Parrish *Cast:* Michael Caine, Anthony Quinn, James Mason, Maureen Kerwin, Marcel Bozzuffi, Catherine Rouvel
▶ Narcotics agent Quinn hires hitman Caine to eliminate well-protected druglord Mason. Caine worms his way into Mason's drug ring, but his cover is blown when Quinn suddenly changes plans. Interesting cast and French locations add spark to this crime thriller. Also known as *The Marseilles Contract*.

DESTRY RIDES AGAIN 1939
★★★★ NR Western 1:34 B&W
Dir: George Marshall *Cast:* Marlene Dietrich, James Stewart, Mischa Auer, Charles Winninger, Brian Donlevy, Una Merkel
▶ Classic Western comedy from the Max Brand novel about soft-spoken, milk-drinking sheriff Stewart who cleans up a corrupt frontier town without resorting to violence. Dietrich's Frenchy, a saloon singer with a heart of gold, was a turning point in her career. She sings "See What the Boys in the Back Room Will Have," and gets into one of the wildest catfights in filmdom with Merkel. Top-notch supporting work from veteran character actors Auer, Winninger, Allen Jenkins, and Samuel S. Hinds.

DETECTIVE, THE 1968
★★ NR Mystery-Suspense 1:54
Dir: Gordon Douglas *Cast:* Frank Sinatra, Lee Remick, Ralph Meeker, Jack Klugman, William Windom, Jacqueline Bisset
▶ Sinatra, a hard-bitten New York cop investigating the murder of a homosexual, uncovers evidence of widespread police corruption. Twisty, fast-paced mystery based on the Roderick Thorp novel features a credible performance by Sinatra. Look for Robert Duvall and Sugar Ray Robinson in small roles.

DETECTIVE SCHOOL DROPOUTS 1986
★★ PG Comedy 1:30
☑ Adult situations, explicit language
Dir: Filippo Ottoni *Cast:* David Landsberg, Lorin Dreyfuss, Christian De Sica, Valeria Golino, Rick Battaglia, Francesco Cinieri
▶ Pint-sized Landsberg, obsessed with detective stories, becomes student to Dreyfuss, an incompetent private eye who's only interested in Landsberg's money. Pursuing a murder/kidnapping case, the duo find themselves stranded in Italy with no passports or money. Pleasant comedy written by Landsberg and Dreyfuss (Richard's brother) has an unexpectedly innocent tone and smart sight gags.

DETECTIVE STORY 1951
★★★ NR Drama 1:43 B&W
Dir: William Wyler *Cast:* Kirk Douglas, Eleanor Parker, William Bendix, Cathy O'Donnell, George Macready, Gladys George
▶ Searing drama about driven detective Douglas trying to cope with wife Parker's infidelity while struggling against crime in a grimy New York precinct room was a strong influence on countless subsequent cop stories. Once-daring themes have dated somewhat in this hard-hitting adaptation of a Sidney Kingsley play, but strong cast is still impressive. Film debuts for Joseph Wiseman and Lee Grant, who received an Oscar nomination for her role as a troubled shoplifter.

DETOUR 1945
★★ NR Drama 1:07 B&W
Dir: Edgar G. Ulmer *Cast:* Tom Neal, Ann Savage, Claudia Drake, Edmund MacDonald, Tim Ryan
▶ Nihilistic film noir about Neal, a hitch-hiker inexorably drawn into a maze of blackmail and murder, has become a cult favorite over the years. Savage is memorable as a heartless vixen who pawns Neal off as the long-lost heir to a fortune in a scheme to defraud a widow. Shot in six days on a shoestring budget.

DETROIT 9000 1973
★★ R Action-Adventure 1:46
☑ Brief nudity, adult situations, explicit language, violence
Dir: Arthur Marks *Cast:* Alex Rocco, Hari Rhodes, Vonetta McGee, Ella Edwards, Scatman Crothers
▶ When masked gunmen rob the mostly black guests at a posh political fund-raiser, white cop Rocco and black cop Rhodes are paired on the case. The two can barely stand each other but turn color-blind when the going gets rough. Dated blaxploitation buddy pic suffers from passage of time.

DEVIL AND DANIEL WEBSTER, THE 1941
★★★★ NR Fantasy 1:49 B&W
Dir: William Dieterle *Cast:* Edward Arnold, Walter Huston, James Craig, Simone Simon, Anne Shirley, Gene Lockhart
▶ Nineteenth-century New England farmer Craig unwittingly sells his soul to Mr. Scratch (Huston); it's up to lawyer Daniel Webster (Arnold) to rescue him. Wonderful Americana, faithfully adapted from Stephen Vincent Benét's short story, is a delightful showcase for Huston and Arnold. Bernard Herrmann's score won an Oscar.

DEVIL AND MAX DEVLIN, THE 1981
★★★★ PG Comedy 1:36
☑ Explicit language
Dir: Steven Hilliard Stern *Cast:* Elliott Gould, Bill Cosby, Susan Anspach, Adam Rich, Julie Budd, David Knell
▶ Mean landlord Gould killed by a bus winds up in Hell, where Devil Cosby offers him freedom in return for three "unsul-lied" souls. Although he hates children, Gould sets out to befriend, and betray, three innocent kids. Some mild and inoffensive profanity; otherwise, a typical Disney light comedy.

DEVIL AND MISS JONES, THE 1941
★★★ NR Comedy 1:32 B&W
Dir: Sam Wood *Cast:* Jean Arthur, Robert Cummings, Charles Coburn, Edmund Gwenn, Spring Byington, William Demarest
▶ Stuffy multimillionaire Coburn, alarmed at unionizing efforts in one of his department stores, disguises himself as a sales clerk to check conditions first-hand. Arthur, salesperson in shoe department, takes Coburn under her wing. Marvelous comedy raises points still relevant today. Coburn and screenwriter Norman Krasna received Oscar nominations.

DEVIL AT 4 O'CLOCK, THE 1961
★★ NR Action-Adventure 2:06
Dir: Mervyn LeRoy *Cast:* Spencer Tracy, Frank Sinatra, Kerwin Mathews, Jean-Pierre Aumont, Gregoire Aslan, Barbara Luna
▶ Sinatra is one of three prisoners rebuilding a leper colony chapel on a South Seas island. When a volcano explodes, Tracy, an embittered, alcoholic priest, enlists the prisoners' help in guiding the colony children through the jungle to safety. Large-scale adventure dampened somewhat by downbeat tone.

DEVIL DOLL, THE 1936
★★ NR Horror 1:19 B&W
Dir: Tod Browning *Cast:* Lionel Barrymore, Maureen O'Sullivan, Frank Lawton, Robert Greig, Lucy Beaumont
▶ Truly bizarre horror film about escaped convict Barrymore who avenges himself on the people who framed him by shrinking them down to doll-size. Great sets and special effects add to the film's grotesque humor. Barrymore, posing as the owner of a doll store, plays most of the second half in drag. Noted director Erich von Stroheim contributed to the screenplay.

DEVIL IN THE FLESH 1987 Italian/French
☆ X Drama 1:50
☑ Nudity, strong sexual content, adult situations, explicit language
Dir: Marco Bellocchio *Cast:* Maruschka Detmers, Federico Pitzalis, Anita Laurenzi, Riccardo De Torrebruna, Alberto Di Stasio, Anna Orso
▶ Detmers, possibly schizophrenic and engaged to a terrorist sentenced to prison, starts an affair with teenager Pitzalis. Extremely loose contemporary adaptation of Raymond Radiguet's classic novel (filmed before in 1946) gained no-

toriety as the first mainstream release to include an explicit, unsimulated sex act. Dedicated to director Bellocchio's psychiatrist Massimo Faggioli. Ⓢ

DEVILS, THE 1971 British
★ R Drama 1:48
☑ Nudity, adult situations, graphic violence
Dir: Ken Russell *Cast:* Vanessa Redgrave, Oliver Reed, Dudley Sutton, Max Adrian, Gemma Jones
▶ Reed plays an unpopular priest accused of witchcraft by a band of hysterical nuns in this controversial adaptation of Aldous Huxley's *The Devils of Loudun* and the John Whiting play. Set in seventeenth-century France, with powerful images and impressive art direction. Closeups of leprosy and exorcistic torture may offend some viewers.

DEVIL'S PLAYGROUND, THE 1976 Australian
★ NR Drama 1:47
☑ Nudity, explicit language
Dir: Fred Schepisi *Cast:* Arthur Dignam, Nick Tate, Simon Burke, Charles McCallum, John Frawley, Jonathon Hardy
▶ Thoughtful examination of the repressive atmosphere at an Australian Catholic seminary in the early 1950s, contrasting the students' growing physicality with their teachers' morbid fear of sex. Subdued but assured direction from Schepisi, who also wrote the script.

D.I., THE 1957
★★ NR Crime 1:46 B&W
Dir: Jack Webb *Cast:* Jack Webb, Don Dubbins, Monica Lewis, Jackie Loughery, Lin McCarthy
▶ No-nonsense Parris Island drill instructor Webb turns boot camp into living hell for his greenhorn recruits, in particular weak-willed mama's boy Dubbins, who's trying to uphold a family tradition of strong soldiers. Webb (who also produced and directed) dominates the story.

DIABOLIQUE 1955 French
★★ NR Mystery-Suspense 1:47 B&W
Dir: Henri-Georges Clouzot *Cast:* Simone Signoret, Vera Clouzot, Paul Meurisse, Charles Vanel, Jean Brochard
▶ At a boarding school, a brutal man's unhappy mistress (Signoret) and his equally troubled wife (Clouzot) plot his death. They pull off the murder—or do they? The wife keeps thinking she's seen the dead man in this shocking, incredibly

suspenseful chiller that has influenced many subsequent movies.

DIAL M FOR MURDER 1954
★★★ PG Mystery-Suspense 1:45
Dir: Alfred Hitchcock *Cast:* Ray Milland, Grace Kelly, Robert Cummings, John Williams, Anthony Dawson
▶ Husband Milland plots to get rid of wife Kelly, who is having affair with Cummings, by blackmailing killer Dawson into attacking her. Plan goes awry when she kills her assailant. Hitchcock thriller (from Frederick Knott's stage play) generates good deal of tension (especially in Kelly's life-and-death struggle with Dawson over a pair of scissors). Originally shot in 3-D.

DIAMOND HEAD 1962
★★★ NR Drama 1:47
Dir: Guy Green *Cast:* Charlton Heston, Yvette Mimieux, George Chakiris, James Darren, France Nuyen
▶ Heston stars as the domineering family head of a pineapple empire who opposes his sister's love for a full-blooded Hawaiian, even though he himself keeps a native mistress. Based on the popular novel of bigotry and family squabbles by Peter Gilman. Colorful Hawaiian backdrop.

DIAMOND HORSESHOE 1945
★★★★ NR Musical 1:44
Dir: George Seaton *Cast:* Betty Grable, Dick Haymes, William Gaxton, Phil Silvers, Margaret Dumont
▶ Lighthearted musical set in the famous New York nightclub. Pin-Up Queen Grable falls for amateur singer Haymes, but convinces him to return to his medical studies when his family objects to their affair. Songs include, "The More I See You," and "You'll Never Know." Also known as *Billy Rose's Diamond Horseshoe*.

DIAMONDS 1975 Israeli
★★★★ PG Action-Adventure 1:48
☑ Brief nudity
Dir: Menahem Golan *Cast:* Robert Shaw, Richard Roundtree, Barbara Seagull, Shelley Winters, Shai K. Ophir, Gadi Yageel
▶ Diverting caper film set in Jerusalem, with Shaw playing a dual role as wildly opposite twins: one designs security systems, the other breaks into them. The evil brother hires Roundtree and Seagull, who stage a fake robbery to divert attention from his assault on millions of dollars

in diamonds locked in an impregnable vault.

DIAMONDS ARE FOREVER 1971 British
★★★★ PG
Espionage/Action-Adventure 1:59
☑ Adult situations, violence
Dir: Guy Hamilton   *Cast:* Sean Connery, Jill St. John, Charles Gray, Lana Wood, Jimmy Dean
▶ Las Vegas is the backdrop as super spy James Bond (Connery) battles the villainous Blofeld (Gray), who organizes diamond smuggling operation to equip his deadly space satellite. Connery returned to the role after temporarily quitting (George Lazenby starred in 1969's *On Her Majesty's Secret Service*) and his class and panache make him the ultimate Bond. Not the best in the series but still tons of fun gadgets, action, and pretty girls (St. John and Natalie's sister Lana Wood as the aptly named "Plenty O'Toole").

DIANE 1956
★★★★ NR **Romance 1:50**
Dir: David Miller   *Cast:* Lana Turner, Roger Moore, Marisa Pavan, Cedric Hardwicke, Pedro Armendariz
▶ In sixteenth-century France, Diane de Poitiers (Turner) becomes teacher to Prince Henri (Moore) to prepare him for his marriage to Catherine de Medici (Pavan). Henri and Diane fall in love. When he ascends the throne, the affair continues, creating a power struggle between wife and mistress. Lavish production of conventional period piece.

DIARY OF A MAD HOUSEWIFE 1970
★ R **Drama 1:34**
☑ Nudity, adult situations, explicit language
Dir: Frank Perry   *Cast:* Carrie Snodgress, Richard Benjamin, Frank Langella, Lorraine Cullen, Peter Boyle
▶ Stuck in an unhappy marriage to lawyer Benjamin, Manhattan housewife Snodgress turns to selfish writer Langella for sex and solace. Feminist social satire still packs a punch, thanks to compelling performance from Snodgress (Oscar-nominated) and nicely nasty support from Langella.

DIARY OF ANNE FRANK, THE 1959
★★★★ NR **Biography 2:50 B&W**
Dir: George Stevens   *Cast:* Millie Perkins, Joseph Schildkraut, Shelley Winters, Richard Beymer, Lou Jacobi
▶ Perkins gives a remarkably moving performance as the Jewish girl hiding with her family in an Amsterdam attic for two years before being discovered by the Nazis. Actors are well cast; Winters won Supporting Actress Oscar for her role as Mrs. Van Daan. Based on the award-winning play inspired by Anne's diary, the film captures the horror of the Holocaust but also the hope and courage of the people under its threat. Winner of three Academy Awards and remade as a TV movie.

DIE, DIE MY DARLING 1965 British
★★ NR **Horror 1:37**
Dir: Silvio Narizzano   *Cast:* Tallulah Bankhead, Stefanie Powers, Peter Vaughn, Donald Sutherland, Yootha Joyce
▶ Religious zealot Bankhead kidnaps dead son's fiancée Powers and locks her in a basement to purify her soul. Creepy shocker in the *Whatever Happened to Baby Jane?* vein is notable primarily for a campy performance by Bankhead (in her last role). Sutherland has an amusing bit as an illiterate handyman.

DIE HARD 1988
★★★★ R **Action-Adventure 2:11**
☑ Adult situations, explicit language, violence
Dir: John McTiernan   *Cast:* Bruce Willis, Alan Rickman, Bonnie Bedelia, Alexander Godunov, Reginal Veljohnson, Paul Gleason
▶ Terrorists "hijack" Century City skyscraper, holding employees at a Christmas party hostage while they crack the computer code to a fortune in bonds. Only hitch: New York cop Willis, who upsets each step of oily villain Rickman's perfectly timed plan. Powerhouse thriller features amazing stunts, relentless pacing, and agreeable tongue-in-cheek humor. Beefed-up Willis is impressive in one of the year's top hits.

DIE LAUGHING 1980
★★ PG **Comedy 1:47**
☑ Adult situations, explicit language, violence
Dir: Jeff Werner   *Cast:* Robby Benson, Charles Durning, Linda Grovenor, Elsa Lanchester, Bud Cort
▶ Singing cabdriver Benson stumbles into a spy conspiracy when a passenger is murdered in his taxi. He dodges killers while protecting a chimp who holds a secret formula that could destroy the world. A must for Robby's fans: he pro-

duced and wrote, and sings five of his songs.

DIE, MONSTER, DIE! 1965
★ NR Horror 1:18
Dir: Daniel Haller *Cast:* Boris Karloff, Nick Adams, Freda Jackson, Suzan Farmer, Terence de Marney, Patrick Magee
► American scientist Adams visits his fiancée Farmer's parents in England. Invalid mother Jackson begs Adams to take Farmer away, but he wants to solve the puzzle behind father Karloff's mutant houseplants first. Middling horror picture based on an H. P. Lovecraft story with Karloff suitably menacing as the wheelchair-bound villain.

DIFFERENT STORY, A 1978
★★★★ PG Drama 1:48
☑ Adult situations, explicit language
Dir: Paul Aaron *Cast:* Perry King, Meg Foster, Valerie Curtin, Peter Donat
► Gay King and lesbian Foster form a close relationship that turns into love and marriage. Foster and King bring depth and conviction to this uneven but sensitive love story.

DILLINGER 1973
★★ R Biography/Crime 1:36
☑ Adult situations, explicit language, graphic violence
Dir: John Milius *Cast:* Warren Oates, Ben Johnson, Michelle Phillips, Cloris Leachman, Harry Dean Stanton, Geoffrey Lewis
► Oates is suitably hard-bitten as Dillinger, Public Enemy Number One until his confrontation with G-man Melvin Purvis (Johnson) outside Chicago's Biograph Theatre in 1934. Violent film plays loose with the facts, but contains absolutely mesmerizing gun battles. Richard Dreyfuss has a small role as Baby Face Nelson.

DIMPLES 1936
★★ NR Musical/Family 1:18 B&W
Dir: William A. Seiter *Cast:* Shirley Temple, Frank Morgan, Helen Westley, Robert Kent, Stepin Fetchit
► Above-average Temple vehicle set in nineteenth-century New York. A sidewalk dancer adopted by society matron Westley, Shirley prefers to stay with lovable grandfather Morgan, a harmless pickpocket. Songs (choreographed by Bill Robinson) include "Hey, What Did the Bluebird Say?" and "Oh Mister Man Up in the Moon." **(CC)**

DIM SUM: A LITTLE BIT OF HEART 1985
★ PG Comedy 1:28
☑ Adult situations
Dir: Wayne Wang *Cast:* Laureen Chew, Kim Chew, Victor Wong, Ida F. O. Chung, Cora Miao
► Portraying a Chinese-American family living in San Francisco, real-life mother (Laureen Chew) and daughter (Kim Chew) explore the complexities of human relationships. Series of sweet-humored vignettes and lovely images concentrate on the widowed mother's desire to see her last daughter married complicated by her fear of living alone. As a free-spirited uncle, Wong bears witness that the way of Confucius may no longer be appropriate for contemporary Chinese. **S**

DINER 1982
★★ R Comedy/Drama 1:50
☑ Adult situations, explicit language
Dir: Barry Levinson *Cast:* Steve Guttenberg, Daniel Stern, Mickey Rourke, Kevin Bacon, Ellen Barkin, Paul Reiser
► Nostalgic look at buddies in 1959 Baltimore who rely on friendship to cope with life after high school. Married Stern, engaged Guttenberg, trying-to-be-engaged Daly, and playing-the-field Rourke all hang out at the local diner to swap stories about music and sex. Warmly written and engaging, this small film was an unexpected hit, especially for director Levinson who returned to his hometown locale for *Tin Man*.

DINNER AT EIGHT 1933
★★★ NR Comedy 1:53 B&W
Dir: George Cukor *Cast:* Marie Dressler, John Barrymore, Wallace Beery, Jean Harlow, Lionel Barrymore, Billie Burke
► Dizzy socialite Burke plans an exclusive dinner for visiting royalty, but her guests have varying reactions to the invitation. All-star cast shines in this sophisticated version of the long-running Broadway hit by George S. Kaufman and Edna Ferber. Harlow and Beery get the best laughs as a brawling couple; Barrymore is at his most romantic as a doomed matinee idol; but dowager Dressler steals the show.

DIRT BIKE KID, THE 1986
★★★ PG Comedy 1:30
☑ Explicit language
Dir: Hoite Caston *Cast:* Peter Billings-

ley, Stuart Pankin, Anne Bloom, Patrick Collins, Danny Breen
▶ Billingsley plays a pint-size Evel Knievel in this family comedy. As little Jack, he helps save the local hot-dog stand from being mowed down for a new bank site with his magic motorcycle that really takes off—right into the sky. Impressive stuntwork and comic timing. **(CC)**

DIRTY DANCING 1987
★★★★★ PG-13 Romance/Dance 1:41
☑ Adult situations, explicit language
Dir: Emile Ardolino *Cast:* Patrick Swayze, Jennifer Grey, Jerry Orbach, Jack Weston, Cynthia Rhodes
▶ Gigantic box-office hit set in the summer of '63. While vacationing at a Catskills resort with her parents, seventeen-year-old Grey falls for Swayze, a sexy dance instructor from the wrong side of the dining hall. Packed with exciting dance sequences, glossy production values, and a nostalgic music score. "I've Had the Time of My Life" won the 1987 Oscar for Best Song.

DIRTY DOZEN, THE 1967
★★★★ NR War 2:30
☑ Adult situations, mild violence
Dir: Robert Aldrich *Cast:* Lee Marvin, Ernest Borgnine, Charles Bronson, Jim Brown, John Cassavetes, Richard Jaeckel
▶ Tough, unorthodox major Marvin trains twelve hardened convicts for a suicide commando mission behind German lines in World War II. Highly entertaining war adventure expertly combines action, humor, and tension. Outstanding cast also includes George Kennedy, Trini Lopez, Robert Ryan, Telly Savalas, and Donald Sutherland. Cassevetes won a Supporting Oscar nomination for his role as a foulmouthed psychotic. **(CC)**

DIRTY HARRY 1971
★★★★★ R Action-Adventure 1:42
☑ Violence
Dir: Don Siegel *Cast:* Clint Eastwood, Reni Santoni, Harry Guardino, Andy Robinson, John Vernon, John Larch
▶ Psychotic killer Robinson demands $200,000 ransom for his young hostage. The San Francisco police agree to the deal—except for detective Harry Callahan (Eastwood), who ignores the rules to track down the murderer. First and best of the *Dirty Harry* series is a swift, cunning thriller filled with memorable dialogue

and taut action. Followed by *Magnum Force.*

DIRTY MARY, CRAZY LARRY 1974
★★ PG Action-Adventure 1:33
☑ Explicit language, violence
Dir: John Hough *Cast:* Peter Fonda, Susan George, Adam Roarke, Vic Morrow, Fred Daniels, Roddy McDowall
▶ Daredevil racer Fonda and pal Roarke extort $150,000 from supermarket manager McDowall. With the police in hot pursuit, they take off across California in their new top-of-the-line stock car. George plays a groupie they pick up along the way. Nonstop chase has above-average stunts and car wrecks.

DIRTY ROTTEN SCOUNDRELS 1988
★★★★ PG Comedy 1:42
☑ Explicit language, adult humor
Dir: Frank Oz *Cast:* Steve Martin, Michael Caine, Glenne Headly, Barbara Harris, Anton Rodgers, Ian McDiarmid
▶ Suave con man Caine has cushy Riviera scam going until crass American Martin invades his territory. Martin blackmails Caine into reluctant partnership, then becomes his rival in a bet to see who can win the heart and wallet of heiress Headly. Remake of the 1964 *Bedtime Story* hilariously combines broad comic antics with sharp plot twists. Top-notch Martin/Caine teamwork is abetted nicely by Headly. Funniest scene: Martin's impersonation of Caine's lunatic brother.

DIRTY TRICKS 1981 Canadian
★★ PG Comedy 1:31
☑ Adult situations, explicit language, violence
Dir: Alvin Rakoff *Cast:* Elliott Gould, Kate Jackson, Arthur Hill, Rich Little, Nicholas Campbell, Angus MacInnes
▶ When his student is murdered after uncovering a startling George Washington letter, Harvard professor Gould is the target of two different sets of hitmen. Jackson is an investigative reporter who falls for Gould while covering the case. Light-hearted comedy dampened by overly realistic violence.

DISCREET CHARM OF THE BOURGEOISIE, THE 1972 French
★★ PG Comedy 1:40
☑ Adult situations
Dir: Luis Buñuel *Cast:* Fernando Rey, Delphine Seyrig, Stephane Audran, Bulle Ogier, Jean-Pierre Cassel, Julian Bertheau
▶ Deliberately confusing but still exhila-

rating film is actually an elaborate practical joke: six wealthy friends are continually interrupted as they sit down to dinner. Subtle blend of illusion and reality creates the feel of an incomprehensible dream, but adventurous viewers will be rewarded by brilliant acting and often hilarious writing by Buñuel and Jean-Claude Carriere. Oscar-nominated for the screenplay, and winner of the Best Foreign Film Oscar. Also available in a dubbed version. ⑤

DISORDERLIES 1987
★★★ PG Comedy 1:26
☑ Brief nudity, explicit language
Dir: Michael Schultz *Cast:* Ralph Bellamy, Damon Wimbley, Darren Robinson, Mark Morales, Tony Plana, Anthony Geary
► Debt-ridden Geary plots the death of wealthy uncle Bellamy by hiring the Fat Boys rap group (Wimbley, Robinson and Morales) as his nurses. But the rappers turn the tables on Geary and his Mafia hitmen and restore Bellamy's spirits in broad slapstick reminiscent of the Three Stooges. Highlight is the film's only rap number, "Baby You're a Rich Man." (CC)

DISORDERLY ORDERLY, THE 1964
★★ NR Comedy 1:30
Dir: Frank Tashlin *Cast:* Jerry Lewis, Glenda Farrell, Susan Oliver, Everett Sloane, Karen Sharpe, Jack E. Leonard
► Lewis saves for medical school by working as a hospital orderly. Unfortunately, he's afflicted with "identification empathy," causing him to suffer the same pains as his patients. Typically broad Lewis slapstick highlighted by a climactic ambulance chase. Sharpe as a nurse and Oliver as a suicidal patient are rivals for Jerry's affections.

DISTANT THUNDER 1988
★★★ R Drama 1:54
☑ Adult situations, explicit language, violence
Dir: Rick Rosenthal *Cast:* John Lithgow, Ralph Macchio, Kerrie Keane, Jamey Sheridan, Reb Brown, Denis Arndt
► High schooler Macchio journeys to Pacific Northwest for reunion with father Lithgow, a shell-shocked Vietnam vet he hasn't seen in a decade. Unable to cope with society, Lithgow retreats to the wilderness with other displaced vets. There he finally confronts the memories of his war experiences. Earnest but low-keyed drama is glum and often maudlin.

DIVA 1982 French
★★ R Mystery-Suspense 1:58
Dir: Jean-Jacques Beineix *Cast:* Wilhelminia Wiggins Fernandez, Frederic Andrei, Richard Bohringer, Thuy An Luu, Jacques Fabbri
► Messenger Andrei tapes opera star idol Fernandez and gets involved in a complex maze of intrigue. Thriller plot is an excuse to display the dazzling talents of director Beineix, who creates a New Wave Paris full of hip visual references and throws in some jazzy action and chases to boot.

DIVORCE OF LADY X, THE 1938 British
★★ NR Comedy 1:32
Dir: Tim Whelan *Cast:* Merle Oberon, Laurence Olivier, Binnie Barnes, Ralph Richardson
► Frothy drawing-room farce about London divorce attorney Olivier forced to share his hotel room during a storm with pretty debutante Oberon, who Olivier assumes is his client Richardson's wife. Slight plot is buoyed by the charming stars and elegant early use of Technicolor.

D.O.A. 1949
★★★ NR Mystery-Suspense 1:23 B&W
Dir: Rudolph Maté *Cast:* Edmond O'Brien, Pamela Britton, Luther Adler, Neville Brand, Henry Hart
► Strong film noir has a fascinating premise: accountant O'Brien, vacationing in San Francisco, learns he's been given a lethal poison. He searches desperately for his murderer before the poison takes effect. Terse dialogue and accomplished direction have made this a cult favorite. Available in a colorized version; remade in 1988.

D.O.A. 1988
★★★ R Mystery-Suspense 1:40
☑ Explicit language, violence
Dir: Rocky Morton, Annabel Jankel *Cast:* Dennis Quaid, Meg Ryan, Charlotte Rampling, Daniel Stern, Jay Patterson, Jane Kaczmarek
► Berkeley professor Quaid, poisoned by a slow-acting but fatal serum, has twenty-four hours to find his killers. With Ryan's help, he confronts an antagonistic group of suspects, including academic rival Patterson, jealous best friend Stern, and villainous benefactor Rampling. Up-

dated remake of the 1949 film noir classic maintains the original's intriguing premise, but sacrifices plotting for baroque visuals and flashy camera tricks. **(CC)**

DOBERMAN GANG, THE 1972
★★★ G Drama/Family 1:27
Dir: Byron Chudnow *Cast:* Byron Mabe, Hal Reed, Julie Parrish, Simmy Bow, Jojo D'Amore, John Tull
▶ Con man Mabe doesn't trust his bumbling cronies to pull off a difficult bank heist, so he kidnaps six Dobermans and dog trainer Reed to perform the robbery without human error. Ingenious and charming low-budget film led to a sequel, *The Daring Dobermans.* **(CC)**

DOC SAVAGE: THE MAN OF BRONZE 1975
★★ G Action-Adventure 1:40
Dir: Michael Anderson *Cast:* Ron Ely, Darrell Zwerling, Paul Gleason, Paul Wexler, Michael Miller, Pamela Hensley
▶ Pulp superhero Doc Savage (Ely) and five associates travel to 1930s Latin America to investigate the murder of Ely's father and battle the villainous Wexler. Adaptation of the Kenneth Robeson novels is generally friendly and appealing. John Phillip Sousa score is corny, and special effects from producer George Pal surprisingly tame, but strapping Ely is perfectly cast.

DOCTOR AND THE DEVILS, THE 1985
★ R Horror 1:33
☑ Nudity, explicit language, violence
Dir: Freddie Francis *Cast:* Timothy Dalton, Jonathan Pryce, Twiggy, Julian Sands, Stephen Rea, Beryl Reid
▶ Nineteenth-century British laws limit doctor Dalton's access to a steady source of cadavers for his students; vagabonds Pryce and Rea come up with a gruesome grave-robbing scheme to supply his needs. Old-fashioned horror film adapted from a 1940s Dylan Thomas screenplay was based on a famous 1830s body-snatching case. Filmed in England. **(CC)**

DOCTOR AT SEA 1955 British
★ NR Comedy 1:34
Dir: Ralph Thomas *Cast:* Dirk Bogarde, Brigitte Bardot, Brenda de Banzie, James Robertson Justice, Maurice Denham
▶ Doctor Bogarde avoids a forced marriage by signing on as a freighter's medic. The crew takes an instant dislike to him but eventually he wins their respect and the love of pretty French lass Bardot. Simple but quite pleasant comedy with fine Bogarde in a rare comedic role and a charming young Bardot. Sequel to the 1954 *Doctor in the House.*

DOCTOR DETROIT 1983
★★ R Comedy 1:30
☑ Nudity, adult situations, explicit language, violence, adult humor
Dir: Michael Pressman *Cast:* Dan Aykroyd, Howard Hesseman, Donna Dixon, T. K. Carter, Fran Drescher, Kate Murtagh
▶ Academia collides with street life when nerdy professor Aykroyd is roped into impersonating a Chicago pimp. Prof's fright-wigged, claw-handed "Doctor Detroit" persona helps him gallantly save beleaguered hookers-with-hearts-of-gold from dreaded mobster known as "Mom" (Murtagh). Durable premise, frantic execution; given life by Dan's clowning and the attractive ladies. James Brown performs at the climactic Hooker's Ball. Aykroyd met future wife Dixon on the set.

DOCTOR DOLITTLE 1967
★★★★ NR Musical/Family 2:24
Dir: Richard Fleischer *Cast:* Rex Harrison, Samantha Eggar, Anthony Newley, Richard Attenborough, Peter Bull, Geoffrey Holder
▶ Musical adaptation of Hugh Lofting's children's classic. Eccentric doctor Harrison, who prefers beasts to people, goes on journey with fiancée Eggar and discovers strange creatures. Pacing lags in this mammoth production, but some decent moments from Rex and the Leslie Bricusse score (Oscar-winning Best Song, "Talk to the Animals"). **(CC)**

DOCTORS' WIVES 1971
★★ R Drama 1:42
☑ Strong sexual content
Dir: George Schaefer *Cast:* Dyan Cannon, Richard Crenna, Gene Hackman, Carroll O'Connor, Ralph Bellamy, Rachel Roberts
▶ Trashy Cannon decides to seduce four other doctor husbands but is shot by her own jealous mate; incident provokes the other doctors' wives to grapple with their failing marriages. Bad-taste soap opera evokes tongue-in-cheek humor; Roberts's description of a lesbian encounter is the film's low-comedy high point.

DOCTOR TAKES A WIFE, THE 1940
★★★★ NR Comedy 1:28 B&W

Dir: Alexander Hall *Cast:* Loretta Young, Ray Milland, Reginald Gardiner, Gail Patrick, Edmund Gwenn
▶ Lively little romantic comedy about two marriage-haters forced to live together for publicity purposes. Young and Milland star as the bachelorette/authoress and medical college instructor who lock horns in a sprightly battle of the sexes.

DOCTOR ZHIVAGO 1965
★★★★★ PG Drama 3:17
Dir: David Lean *Cast:* Omar Sharif, Julie Christie, Tom Courtenay, Rod Steiger, Geraldine Chaplin, Alec Guinness
▶ Sweeping epic of the Russian Revolution seen through the eyes of sensitive doctor Sharif and his beautiful lover, Christie. Enormously popular romance, based on the novel by Nobel Laureate Boris Pasternak, is filled with thrilling spectacle. Winner of five Oscars, including Screenplay (Robert Bolt) and score (Maurice Jarre). **(CC)**

DODES'KA-DEN 1970 Japanese
☆ NR Drama 2:20
☑ Explicit language
Dir: Akira Kurosawa *Cast:* Yoshitaka Zushi, Kin Sugai, Toshiyuki Tonomura, Tomoko Yamazaki
▶ The lives of various dwellers of a squalid Tokyo slum examined with sympathy and insight by the master Japanese director. Virtually plotless story line follows a man who dreams of building a palace while his son begs for food; a homeless retarded boy; a daughter who supports her father by making artificial flowers, etc. Slowly paced and extremely sentimental. ⑤

DODGE CITY 1939
★★★ NR Western 1:45
Dir: Michael Curtiz *Cast:* Errol Flynn, Olivia de Havilland, Ann Sheridan, Bruce Cabot, Frank McHugh, Alan Hale
▶ Rousing, large-scale adventure with Flynn (in his first Western) donning a sheriff's star to clean up a corrupt frontier town. The dashing star shows off his prowess by stopping a stampede, a burning runaway train, and an enormous barroom brawl (a classic of its kind). Provided the story line for Mel Brooks's Western satire *Blazing Saddles.*

DODSWORTH 1936
★★★ NR Drama 1:41 B&W
Dir: William Wyler *Cast:* Walter Huston, Ruth Chatterton, Paul Lukas, Mary Astor, David Niven, Maria Ouspenskaya
▶ Intelligent, moving drama about retired auto tycoon Huston, social-climbing wife Chatterton, and the changes they undergo during a European vacation. Niven plays a gigolo who seduces Chatterton; Astor, a divorcée who comforts Huston. Sincere adaptation of a Sinclair Lewis novel is notable for its sympathetic, adult treatment of marriage. Nominated for seven Academy Awards, including Best Picture, Actor, Director, and Screenplay.

DOG DAY AFTERNOON 1975
★★★★ R Drama 2:04
☑ Adult situations, explicit language, violence
Dir: Sidney Lumet *Cast:* Al Pacino, John Cazale, James Broderick, Charles Durning, Chris Sarandon
▶ Pacino stars in true story of New York City man who holds up bank to finance sex change operation for lover Sarandon. Plan goes awry and Pacino is forced to negotiate with cops. Pacino's no-holds-barred performance is tops. Gritty suspense, masterfully directed by Sidney Lumet. Oscar-nominated for Picture, Director, Actor (Pacino), and Supporting Actor (Sarandon). Oscar for Best Original Screenplay.

DOG OF FLANDERS, A 1959
★★★★ NR Family 1:36
Dir: James B. Clark *Cast:* David Ladd, Donald Crisp, Theodore Bikel, Max Croiset, Monique Ahrens, Siohban Taylor
▶ Turn-of-the-century Belgium provides picturesque backdrop for heartwarming story of orphaned Ladd's efforts to save sickly dog. Crippled grandfather Crisp, a milkman, sacrifices his meager food to help the canine. Third film version of Ouida's beloved children's novel retains original's bittersweet charm. Ideal for younger viewers.

DOGS OF WAR, THE 1980 British
★★★ R Action-Adventure 2:02
☑ Explicit language, violence
Dir: John Irvin *Cast:* Christopher Walken, Tom Berenger, Colin Blakely, Hugh Millais, Paul Freeman, JoBeth Williams
▶ Perceptive adaptation of Frederick Forsyth's best-seller about mercenaries concentrates on callous American Walken, captured and tortured in the tiny African republic of Zangaro. He escapes

and returns home to organize a coup against Zangaro's tyrant. Jarring battle scenes frame an unusually detailed look at Third World politics.

DOIN' TIME ON PLANET EARTH 1988
☆ **PG Comedy 1:25**
☑ Adult situations, explicit language
Dir: Charles Matthau *Cast:* Nicholas Strouse, Hugh Gillin, Gloria Henry, Hugh O'Brian, Adam West, Andrea Thompson
▶ Arizona lad Strouse learns from his computer that he's an alien, but can't return home until he unlocks code secreted in his DNA. To open his DNA package, he must seduce singer Thompson. Offbeat black comedy suffers from low budget and hit-or-miss gags. Directing debut for Matthau (son of actor Walter Matthau) features amusing cameos by Maureen Stapleton and Roddy McDowall.

$ (DOLLARS) 1971
★★★ **R Action-Adventure 2:01**
☑ Nudity, adult situations, explicit language
Dir: Richard Brooks *Cast:* Warren Beatty, Goldie Hawn, Gert Frobe, Robert Webber, Scott Brady, Arthur Brauss
▶ Breezy heist film set in Germany features a charming Beatty as a security expert who loots three safe deposit boxes with the help of Hamburg hooker Hawn. The victims—dope dealer Brauss, mob courier Webber, and crooked Army sergeant Brady—pursue Beatty and Hawn in a clever climactic chase.

DOLLS 1987
★★ **R Horror 1:18**
☑ Explicit language, violence
Dir: Stuart Gordon *Cast:* Ian Patrick Williams, Carolyn Purdy-Gordon, Carrie Lorraine, Stephen Lee, Guy Rolfe, Bunty Bailey
▶ London family caught in a storm takes refuge in a gloomy mansion filled with handmade dolls. Young Lorraine notices something odd about the toys, but cruel stepmother Purdy-Gordon and weak-willed father Williams ignore her warnings. Satisfying effort has ingenious special effects, nice comic sensibility, and relatively toned-down gore.

DOMINICK AND EUGENE 1988
★★★★ **PG-13 Drama 1:51**
☑ Adult situations, explicit language
Dir: Robert M. Young *Cast:* Tom Hulce, Ray Liotta, Jamie Lee Curtis, Todd Graff, Mimi Cecchini, Robert Levine
▶ Hulce, mildly retarded twin of medical student Liotta, works as a Pittsburgh garbageman to pay his brother's tuition. Their carefully balanced relationship is threatened when Liotta considers transferring to school in California. Emotionally charged soap opera boasts terrific acting in difficult roles. Curtis is appealing as Liotta's girlfriend.

DOMINO PRINCIPLE, THE 1977
★★★★ **R Mystery-Suspense 1:35**
☑ Violence
Dir: Stanley Kramer *Cast:* Gene Hackman, Candice Bergen, Edward Albert, Mickey Rooney, Richard Widmark
▶ Prisoner Hackman is busted out of jail by mysterious organization that wants him to commit a political assassination. He demurs and they come after him and wife Bergen. Director Kramer tries to create a mood of mid-seventies post-Watergate mistrust and paranoia; fine cast.

DONA FLOR AND HER TWO HUSBANDS 1978 Brazilian
★ **R Fantasy/Comedy 1:46**
☑ Nudity, adult situations, explicit language
Dir: Bruno Barreto *Cast:* Sonia Braga, Jose Wilker, Mauro Mendonca, Dinorah Brillanti
▶ Widow Braga marries a straitlaced and sexually dull pharmacist. Her deceased husband, an irresponsible but exciting womanizer and gambler, returns in the form of a nude ghost, leading to an unusual ménage à trois. Exotic comedy with likable Braga, colorful Bahia backgrounds and tuneful Brazilian music. Extremely racy; remade and toned down in America as Sally Field's *Kiss Me Goodbye*.
Ⓢ

DON IS DEAD, THE 1973
★ **R Drama 1:54**
☑ Brief nudity, adult situations, explicit language, violence
Dir: Richard Fleischer *Cast:* Anthony Quinn, Frederic Forrest, Robert Forster, Al Lettieri, Angel Tompkins, Vic Tayback
▶ When the old Don dies, the Cosa Nostra is in danger of falling apart. Quinn is elected as the new Don, but Forrest and Lettieri refuse to obey him. They send former Playmate Tompkins to keep Quinn occupied while they declare war on his men. Bloody, violent attempt to cash in on *The Godfather* follows a routine gangster formula.

DONOVAN'S BRAIN 1953
★★ NR Sci-Fi 1:21 B&W
Dir: Felix Feist *Cast:* Lew Ayres, Gene Evans, Nancy Davis, Steve Brodie, Lisa K. Howard
▶ Scientist Ayres keeps dead man's brain alive and pulsating, then becomes possessed by its evil spirit. Wife Davis (the future Mrs. Reagan) frets in the background. Pretty good B-movie chiller with a cult following. The type of movie Steve Martin spoofed in *The Man with Two Brains*.

DONOVAN'S REEF 1963
★★★★ NR Comedy 1:39
Dir: John Ford *Cast:* John Wayne, Lee Marvin, Elizabeth Allen, Jack Warden, Cesar Romero, Dorothy Lamour
▶ Rambunctious comedy set in the South Pacific about burly bar owner Wayne, his old Navy buddy Marvin, and veteran Warden who's taken a Polynesian wife. Plot deals with the boys hiding Warden's new family from prim Boston visitor Allen. Sentimental in stretches, but the island locations make a beautiful backdrop to Wayne's slapstick fistfights with Marvin.

DON'S PARTY 1982 Australian
★★ NR Comedy 1:30
☑ Nudity, strong sexual content, explicit language, adult humor
Dir: Bruce Beresford *Cast:* John Hargreaves, Pat Bishop, Jeannie Drynan, Graeme Blundell, Veronica Lang, Graham Kennedy
▶ In 1969 Australia, a teacher throws an election night party and his friends arrive with their mates. A mood of "quiet desperation" builds as couples pair off. This sexual vaudeville, intercut with political ironies, was an early effort from director Beresford.

DON'T CRY, IT'S ONLY THUNDER 1982
★★★★ PG Drama 1:48
☑ Adult situations, explicit language, violence
Dir: Peter Werner *Cast:* Dennis Christopher, Susan Saint James, Roger Aaron Brown, Lisa Lu, James Whitmore, Jr., Thu Thuy
▶ U.S. Army medic Christopher, working in a Saigon hospital, is recruited by nuns to steal black market supplies for their orphanage. Moved by the orphans' plight, he recruits pretty young doctor Saint James to help him. Inspirational

story, based on a true incident, is handled with compassion and humor.

DON'T DRINK THE WATER 1969
★★ G Comedy 1:40
Dir: Howard Morris *Cast:* Jackie Gleason, Estelle Parsons, Ted Bessell, Michael Constantine, Joan Delaney, Richard Libertini
▶ American tourists Gleason, Parsons, and Delaney inadvertently wind up in Communist country. They are accused of being spies and become the focus of an international incident. Flat farce adapted from the Woody Allen play has a few chuckles but end results will leave both Allen and Gleason fans feeling shortchanged.

DON'T GIVE UP THE SHIP 1959
★★★ NR Comedy 1:29 B&W
Dir: Norman Taurog *Cast:* Jerry Lewis, Dina Merrill, Diana Spencer, Mickey Shaughnessy, Robert Middleton, Gale Gordon
▶ Ensign's wedding night is ruined when Navy investigators order him to find destroyer missing since World War II. Trail leads to a watery target range. Lewis's fans consider this one of his best; Shaughnessy offers good support as his musclebound friend.

DON'T LOOK NOW 1973 British/Italian
★★ R Drama 1:50
☑ Nudity, adult situations, explicit language
Dir: Nicolas Roeg *Cast:* Julie Christie, Donald Sutherland, Hilary Mason, Clelia Matania, Massimo Serato, Renato Scarpa
▶ After the death of their daughter, art historian Sutherland and wife Christie are approached by blind seer Mason, who claims she can contact the deceased girl. Haunting, richly detailed occult thriller from a Daphne du Maurier story makes marvelous use of gloomy Venice settings. Confusing plot doesn't detract from violent climax or charged love scenes between Sutherland and Christie.

DON'T RAISE THE BRIDGE, LOWER THE RIVER 1968
★★ G Comedy 1:39
Dir: Jerry Paris *Cast:* Jerry Lewis, Terry-Thomas, Jacqueline Pearce, Bernard Cribbins, Patricia Routledge
▶ Wide-eyed American expatriate Lewis finds his marriage to Pearce in trouble as a result of his bizarre money-making plans. Con man Terry-Thomas lures him

into scheme to steal top secret oil drill. Slapstick overwhelms plot in typical Lewis vehicle. Director Paris cameos as a baseball umpire.

DOOR TO DOOR 1984
★★ PG Comedy 1:34
☑ Explicit language
Dir: Patrick Bailey *Cast:* Ron Leibman, Arliss Howard, Jane Kaczmarek, Alan Austin, Mimi Honze
▶ Leibman shines as a glib, larcenous salesman who entices Howard into a scam to sell vacuums. Since Leibman doesn't work for the vacuum company, they're soon pursued by angry, tenacious detective Austin. Thin comedy coasts on the strength of its stars.

DOUBLE INDEMNITY 1944
★★★★ NR Mystery-Suspense 1:47 B&W
Dir: Billy Wilder *Cast:* Fred MacMurray, Barbara Stanwyck, Edward G. Robinson, Porter Hall, Jean Evans, Tom Powers
▶ Nifty crime melodrama from the James M. Cain novel about treacherous housewife Stanwyck who plots the murder of her husband with the help of cynical insurance agent MacMurray. Blistering dialogue and a devious plot by Wilder and Raymond Chandler made this one of the most memorable films of the forties. Robinson is outstanding as MacMurray's colleague, an insurance investigator who pieces together the scheme. Received seven Oscar nominations.

DOUBLE LIFE, A 1947
★★★ NR Drama 1:43 B&W
Dir: George Cukor *Cast:* Ronald Colman, Signe Hasso, Edmond O'Brien, Shelley Winters, Ray Collins, Phillip Loeb
▶ Absorbing drama won Colman an Oscar for role of a brilliant stage actor who can't separate his roles from reality. Rehearsals for *Othello* lead to tragic complications as unreasonable jealousy consumes his life. Winters's turn as a waitress attracted to Colman made her a star. Miklos Rozsa's brooding score also won an Oscar; intelligent script by Ruth Gordon and Garson Kanin received a nomination. Look for John Derek as a stenographer and Paddy Chayefsky as a photographer.

DOUBLE TROUBLE 1967
★★★ NR Musical 1:30
Dir: Norman Taurog *Cast:* Elvis Presley, Annette Day, John Williams, Yvonne

Romain, The Wiere Brothers, Chips Rafferty
▶ During a European tour Elvis helps young heiress Day elude murderous uncle Williams, who's after her inheritance. Bumbling smugglers also chase the duo in this lightweight blend of comedy, action, and music. Killer version of "Long Legged Girl" lights up the film.

DOWN AND OUT IN BEVERLY HILLS 1986
★★★★ R Comedy 1:37
☑ Brief nudity, adult situations, explicit language
Dir: Paul Mazursky *Cast:* Nick Nolte, Bette Midler, Richard Dreyfuss, Little Richard, Tracy Nelson, Elizabeth Peña
▶ Homeless bum Nolte attempts suicide in swimming pool but is rescued and taken in by wealthy coat-hanger manufacturer Dreyfuss and his vulgar, frustrated wife Midler. Mazursky's jubilant remake of Jean Renoir's French classic *Boudu Saved From Drowning* expertly mixes sexual farce (Nolte seducing various members of Dreyfuss's household) and lyricism (Nick reciting Shakespeare's "What a piece of work is man" speech to Dreyfuss). Wonderful performances from all, including star turn from Mike the dog.

DOWN BY LAW 1986
★ R Drama 1:46 B&W
☑ Nudity, adult situations, explicit language
Dir: Jim Jarmusch *Cast:* Tom Waits, John Lurie, Roberto Benigni, Nicoletta Braschi, Ellen Barkin
▶ Minimalist comedy about three losers—down-and-out DJ Waits, slimy pimp Lurie, and Italian tourist Benigni—and their unlikely escape from a Louisiana jail. Slight plot is static and uninvolving until the arrival of Benigni, who steals the film with his cheerfully mangled English. Waits and Lurie collaborated on the soundtrack. **(CC)**

DOWNHILL RACER 1969
★★★ PG Drama/Sports 1:42
☑ Adult situations, explicit language
Dir: Michael Ritchie *Cast:* Robert Redford, Gene Hackman, Camilla Sparv, Karl Michael Vogler, Jim McMullan, Christian Dormer
▶ When a top racer gets hurt, U.S. ski team coach Hackman offers tryouts for a new spot on roster. Complaining loner Redford irritates many but makes squad. Tour of European race circuit, rivalry with

McMullan, the country's best skier, and affair with Sparv, assistant to wealthy ski manufacturer Vogler, precede climax at Olympics. Racing footage, with avid downhiller Redford doing much of his own stunt work, will delight skiers, but others may be put off by cynical look at heroism and unusually cold Redford.

DRACULA 1931
★★★ NR Horror 1:15 B&W
Dir: Tod Browning *Cast:* Bela Lugosi, Helen Chandler, David Manners, Dwight Frye, Edward Van Sloan, Herbert Bunston
▶ Countless sequels, remakes, and ripoffs have not diminished the stature of this classic adaptation of the Bram Stoker novel. Lugosi is unforgettable as the Transylvanian count who moves to London, puts Chandler under his vampire spell, but meets his match in professor Van Sloan. Very, very scary.

DRACULA 1979
★★★ R Horror 1:49
☑ Adult situations, violence
Dir: John Badham *Cast:* Frank Langella, Laurence Olivier, Donald Pleasence, Kate Nelligan, Trevor Eve, Tony Haygarth
▶ Moody, atmospheric version of the famous Bram Stoker story, with Langella emphasizing the erotic nature of the notorious vampire. He moves to England and falls for Nelligan, daughter of local doctor Pleasence, while fighting off Olivier, the father of another victim. Adaptation of the hit Broadway play is much sexier than the classic 1931 version.

DRACULA'S WIDOW 1987
★ R Horror 1:26
☑ Nudity, adult situations, explicit language, violence
Dir: Christopher Coppola *Cast:* Sylvia Kristel, Josef Sommer, Lenny Von Dohlen, Marc Coppola, Stefan Schnabel, Rachel Jones
▶ Von Dohlen, owner of Hollywood Wax Museum, opens a crate from Transylvania and releases Kristel, famed vampire's lovely spouse. She embarks on a killing spree that baffles Los Angeles cop Sommer. Anemic horror semispoof fails to add much to vampire myths.

DRAGNET 1954
★★ NR Crime 1:29
Dir: Jack Webb *Cast:* Jack Webb, Ben Alexander, Richard Boone, Ann Robinson, Stacy Harris, Virginia Gregg

▶ Sergeant Joe Friday (Webb) and his partner Alexander tackle murder by the Red Spot Gang, building their case from four bullet shells and a footprint. Feature spinoff from the popular TV series predictably focuses on police tactics, not characterizations. Remade as a comedy in 1987; Webb also directed a TV movie under the same title in 1969. **(CC)**

DRAGNET 1987
★★★ PG-13 Comedy 1:46
☑ Brief nudity, explicit language, adult humor
Dir: Tom Mankiewicz *Cast:* Dan Aykroyd, Tom Hanks, Christopher Plummer, Harry Morgan, Alexandra Paul, Elizabeth Ashley
▶ Affectionate takeoff of Jack Webb's TV series updated to present-day Los Angeles. As Sgt. Joe Friday's nephew, Aykroyd gives a dead-on parody of Webb's tight-lipped delivery. With his new partner Hanks (who has the best lines), Aykroyd tackles a puzzling case involving lisping pornographer Dabney Coleman, corrupt televangelist Plummer, and "the virgin Connie Swail" (Paul). Jokes trail off after a bright start.

DRAGON SEED 1944
★★ NR Drama 2:25 B&W
Dir: Jack Conway, Harold S. Bucquet
Cast: Katharine Hepburn, Walter Huston, Aline MacMahon, Akim Tamiroff, Turhan Bey, Hurd Hatfield
▶ Sincere effort to examine the impact of Japanese invaders on rural Chinese during World War II. Hepburn must convince husband Bey to resist the invasion; father-in-law Huston disagrees with her until the Japanese reach his farm. Adaptation of Pearl S. Buck's novel suffers from slow pacing and miscasting of Caucasians as Orientals.

DRAGONSLAYER 1981
★★★ PG Fantasy 1:48
☑ Brief nudity, violence
Dir: Matthew Robbins *Cast:* Peter MacNicol, Caitlin Clarke, Ralph Richardson, John Hallam, Peter Eyre, Albert Salmi
▶ Sixth-century England: sorcerer Richardson and young apprentice MacNicol are recruited to rid kingdom of terrorizing dragon. When king Eyre tests Richardson in battle with villainous Hallam, the old wizard dies. Although his education in magic is incomplete, MacNicol takes on the dragon and soon finds he's bitten off

more than he can chew. First-rate fantasy with realistic dragon and authentic Dark Ages setting.

DRAW! 1984
★★★★ NR Western/MFTV 1:38
☑ Nudity, adult situations, explicit language, violence
Dir: Steven Hilliard Stern *Cast:* Kirk Douglas, James Coburn, Alexandra Bastedo, Graham Jarvis, Derek McGrath, Len Birman
▶ Reformed outlaw Douglas, downplaying his gunslinging reputation to live last years in peace, must unwillingly kill the sheriff in Bell City and take actress Bastedo hostage to save his skin from angry mob. While romance blooms between the captor and his prisoner, the townspeople hire lawman Coburn, Douglas's longtime nemesis, to bring the gunfighter to justice. Western with a surprise ending benefits from location shoot in Canada and presence of screen veterans Douglas and Coburn.

DREAMCHILD 1985 British
★ PG Drama 1:30
☑ Adult situations
Dir: Gavin Millar *Cast:* Coral Browne, Ian Holm, Peter Gallagher, Caris Corfman, Nicola Cowper, Amelia Shankley
▶ Elderly Browne, who as a child provided Lewis Carroll (Holm) with the inspiration for *Alice in Wonderland*, recalls her relationship with the author while on a visit to 1932 New York City. Meanwhile, young assistant Cowper is wooed by brash reporter Gallagher. Complex screenplay by Dennis Potter weaves a delicate, magical spell as it movingly explores art and memory. An unusual, underappreciated treat.

DREAMER 1979
★★ PG Drama/Sports 1:33
☑ Explicit language
Dir: Noel Nosseck *Cast:* Tim Matheson, Susan Blakely, Jack Warden, Richard B. Schull, Barbara Stuart
▶ Hollywood's stab at applying familiar sports formula to bowling. Underdog bowler Matheson tries to beat the odds and win the big match, while having problems with girlfriend Blakely. Contains an unforgettable scene in which Matheson's coach Warden literally bowls himself into a fatal heart attack. And we thought boxing was dangerous!

DREAM LOVER 1986
★★ R Drama 1:44
☑ Adult situations, explicit language, violence
Dir: Alan J. Pakula *Cast:* Kristy McNichol, Ben Masters, Paul Shenar, Justin Deas, Gayle Hunnicutt, Matthew Penn
▶ Young flutist McNichol suffers recurring nightmares after being attacked by an intruder. She turns to scientist Masters from the Yale Sleep Laboratory for help. Together they uncover a disturbing secret about her past. Intriguing subject suffers from repetitive plotting and unsettling dream sequences.

DREAMSCAPE 1984
★★★ PG-13 Sci-Fi 1:39
☑ Nudity, adult situations, explicit language, violence
Dir: Joseph Ruben *Cast:* Dennis Quaid, Max Von Sydow, Christopher Plummer, Eddie Albert, Kate Capshaw
▶ Engaging sci-fi with tantalizing premise: psychic Quaid with ability to enter other people's dreams is asked to help troubled President Albert and manages to stave off telepathic assassination attempt masterminded by right-winger Plummer. Director Ruben pulls out all the stops in the inventive dream scenes.

DRESSED TO KILL 1946
★ NR Mystery-Suspense 1:12 B&W
Dir: Roy William Neill *Cast:* Basil Rathbone, Nigel Bruce, Patricia Morison, Edmond Breon, Frederick Worlock, Carl Harbord
▶ Rathbone as Sherlock Holmes tracks down three music boxes containing Bank of England engraving plates stolen by villain Morison. Twelfth and final picture starring Rathbone as the great sleuth shows the series's age. Fearful of losing his own identity to the role that made him famous, Rathbone quit movies to pursue a career on the stage.

DRESSED TO KILL 1980
★★★ R Mystery-Suspense 1:45
☑ Nudity, explicit language, graphic violence
Dir: Brian De Palma *Cast:* Michael Caine, Angie Dickinson, Nancy Allen, Keith Gordon, Dennis Franz
▶ A psychopath stalks two women—lonely suburban housewife Dickinson and feisty hooker Allen—through the streets of New York. Caine plays a psychiatrist who may hold the clue to the killer's identity. Film's frequent shocks are made all the more frightening by De Palma's stylized direction. Buffs will enjoy the

many references to Hitchcock films.
(CC)

DRIVER, THE 1978
★★★★ **PG Action-Adventure 1:31**
☑ Explicit language, violence
Dir: Walter Hill *Cast:* Ryan O'Neal,
Bruce Dern, Isabelle Adjani, Ronee
Blakley, Matt Clark
▶ Stripped-down, existential chase film
with O'Neal playing a crack getaway
driver pursued by obsessive cop Dern.
Adjani and Blakley have thankless roles
as love interests. Pretentious at times (the
characters don't even have names), but
the car stunts and fights are first rate.
(CC)

DRIVER'S SEAT, THE 1974 Italian
★ **R Drama 1:41**
☑ Adult situations, explicit language,
    violence
Dir: Giuseppe Patroni Griffi *Cast:* Eliza-
beth Taylor, Ian Bannen, Guido Man-
nari, Mona Washbourne, Maxence
Mailfort, Andy Warhol
▶ Flashy, confusing approach to Muriel
Spark's intricate novella follows neurotic
English spinster Taylor as she arranges a
date with a man she knows will kill her.
Filled with abstract touches and cine-
matic tricks, and perhaps too vague
even for Taylor's fans.

DR. JEKYLL AND MR. HYDE 1932
★★★ **NR Horror 1:30 B&W**
Dir: Rouben Mamoulian *Cast:* Fredric
March, Miriam Hopkins, Rose Hobart,
Holmes Herbert, Edgar Norton
▶ London doctor March's experiments in
chemistry turn him into monstrous Mr.
Hyde, who befriends lady of the night
Hopkins and sinks into depravity and
murder. Superior adaptation of the Rob-
ert Louis Stevenson classic features
March's Oscar-winning turn, the only Best
Actor award given to lead in horror film,
and Mamoulian's stylish direction.

DR. JEKYLL AND MR. HYDE 1941
★★★ **NR Horror 1:54 B&W**
Dir: Victor Fleming *Cast:* Spencer
Tracy, Ingrid Bergman, Lana Turner,
Donald Crisp, Ian Hunter, Barton Mac-
Lane
▶ Tracy stars as Dr. Jekyll, the scientist
whose experiments change him into the
beastly Mr. Hyde. The transformations
threaten his relationship with fiancée
Turner as he gets involved with prostitute
Bergman and becomes a murderer. Ad-
aptation of the Robert Louis Stevenson

novel is nicely directed and well acted,
especially by Bergman, but fails to erase
the memory of Fredric March's Oscar-
winning turn in the 1932 version.

DR. NO 1962 British
★★★★ **PG**
Espionage/Action-Adventure 1:51
☑ Adult situations, violence
Dir: Terence Young *Cast:* Sean Con-
nery, Ursula Andress, Joseph Wiseman,
Jack Lord, Bernard Lee
▶ First James Bond film set a winning for-
mula for the subsequent series. Agent
007 is sent to Jamaica to investigate the
murder of a fellow spy. With the help of
CIA contact Lord and beautiful Andress,
he uncovers a scheme by the nefarious
Dr. No (Wiseman) to divert missiles from
Cape Canaveral. More plot and less
humor than the other Bond pictures, but
the sets and stunts are amazing. As for
Connery, nobody does it better. (CC)

DROWNING POOL, THE 1975
★★★ **PG Mystery-Suspense 1:48**
☑ Adult situations, violence
Dir: Stuart Rosenberg *Cast:* Paul Newman, Joanne Woodward, Anthony
Franciosa, Murray Hamilton, Gail Strickland, Melanie Griffith
▶ Newman's second stab at detective
Lew Harper, here employed by former
lover Woodward to discover who's blackmailing her. Harper soon finds himself entangled with an oil tycoon, oversexed
teen Griffith, a hooker, and assorted
menacing types. Colorful New Orleans
settings, Newman's charm, and slick plotting make for intelligent and diverting escapism. From the Ross MacDonald novel.

DR. PHIBES RISES AGAIN 1972 British
★★ **PG Horror 1:34**
☑ Violence
Dir: Robert Fuest *Cast:* Vincent Price,
Robert Quarry, Hugh Griffith, Valli Kemp,
Peter Cushing, Terry-Thomas
▶ Mad doctor Price, seeking to revive his
late wife, goes to Egypt in search of resur-
rection formula. There he battles wealthy
Quarry for possession of the superpow-
ered stuff. Sequel to *The Abominable Dr.
Phibes* features Price's patented campy
humor.

**DR. STRANGELOVE OR: HOW I
LEARNED TO STOP WORRYING AND
LOVE THE BOMB** 1964 British
★★★★ **PG Comedy 1:35 B&W**
☑ Adult situations, adult humor
Dir: Stanley Kubrick *Cast:* Peter Sellers,

George C. Scott, Sterling Hayden, Keenan Wynn, Slim Pickens, James Earl Jones

▶ General Jack D. Ripper (Hayden) launches an unauthorized nuclear attack on Russia; amid escalating tensions, President Sellers and his advisors fruitlessly try to halt the bombers. Peerless Cold War black comedy won Oscar nominations for Best Picture; biting script by Kubrick, Terry Southern, and Peter George; direction; and Sellers's tour-de-force performance in a triple role (he also plays a British Group Captain and the lunatic Strangelove).

DRUM 1976
★★★ R Drama 1:40
☑ Brief nudity, strong sexual content, graphic violence
Dir: Steve Carver   *Cast:* Warren Oates, Ken Norton, Isela Vega, Yaphet Kotto, Pam Grier, Fiona Lewis
▶ Sequel to *Mandingo* reprises the original's look at life on a squalid nineteenth-century Southern plantation. Sold into slavery, former heavyweight boxer Norton rebels against owner Oates's cruelty. Rainbeaux Smith, Oates's daughter, further incites the slaves with her scanty attire.

DRUMS 1938 British
★★ NR Action-Adventure 1:36
Dir: Zoltan Korda   *Cast:* Sabu, Raymond Massey, Valerie Hobson, Roger Livesey, Desmond Tester, David Tree
▶ High-spirited adventure set in colonial India with Sabu playing a prince forced into hiding by Massey, his evil uncle. He takes refuge in a British garrison, where kindly captain Livesey adopts him as the troop's mascot. Sabu proves his courage when Massey mounts an ambush on the British.

DRUMS ALONG THE MOHAWK 1939
★★★★★ NR Drama 1:43
☑ Adult situations, mild violence
Dir: John Ford   *Cast:* Claudette Colbert, Henry Fonda, Edna May Oliver, John Carradine, Jessie Ralph, Ward Bond
▶ Sturdy frontier saga set in Revolutionary New York: cultured newlywed Colbert must adjust to the wilderness when husband Fonda goes off to fight marauding Indians. Superb slice of Americana is filled with battles, romance, humor, and tragedy. Oliver received an Oscar nomi-

nation as a feisty frontier matriarch. (CC)

DU BARRY WAS A LADY 1943
★★ NR Musical 1:41
Dir: Roy Del Ruth   *Cast:* Red Skelton, Lucille Ball, Gene Kelly, Virginia O'Brien, Zero Mostel
▶ Sanitized version of a bawdy Cole Porter play with Skelton and Kelly both pursuing Ball, a gorgeous showgirl. Skelton wins the Irish Sweepstakes, accidentally drinks a mickey, and dreams he's back in the court of Louis XIV. Includes a few great Porter tunes: "Katie Went to Haiti," "Friendship," "Did You Evah?" Tommy Dorsey and his Orchestra (in period costumes and wigs!) do "I'm Getting Sentimental Over You."

DUCHESS AND THE DIRTWATER FOX, THE 1976
★★★ PG Comedy 1:44
☑ Adult situations, violence, adult humor
Dir: Melvin Frank   *Cast:* George Segal, Goldie Hawn, Conrad Janis, Thayer David, Jennifer Lee, Roy Jenson
▶ Flat comedy set in the Wild West pairs gambler Segal and saloon singer Hawn in offbeat adventures trying to keep proceeds of a bank robbery from outlaws, Mormon settlers, and a Jewish wedding party. Song-and-dance numbers prove as irritating as Segal's mugging.

DUCK SOUP 1933
★★★ NR Comedy 1:10 B&W
Dir: Leo McCarey   *Cast:* The Marx Brothers, Louis Calhern, Margaret Dumont, Raquel Torres, Edgar Kennedy
▶ In the mythical kingdom of Fredonia, petty tyrant Rufus T. Firefly (Groucho) declares war on neighboring Sylvania; Chico and Harpo are inept spies out to steal his war plans. Purists rate this unique blend of slapstick and savage political satire the Brothers' best work. Among the many highlights are a dazzling mirror sequence and Harpo's unforgettable encounter with lemonade vendor Kennedy. Zeppo's last film.

DUCK, YOU SUCKER! 1972 Italian
★★★ PG Western 2:19
☑ Adult situations, explicit language, violence
Dir: Sergio Leone   *Cast:* Rod Steiger, James Coburn, Romolo Valli, Maria Monti, Rick Battaglia, Franco Graziosi
▶ Lavish, action-filled epic about the Mexican revolution, with Coburn out-

standing as an Irish terrorist who teams up with bandit Steiger—a disarmingly unwilling hero—to rob a bank. Stunning set pieces include an unforgettable train collision. Another strong work by Leone, but as with most of his films there are a number of versions available. Alternate title *A Fistful of Dynamite* is twenty minutes shorter.

DUDES 1988
★ **R Action-Adventure 1:30**
☑ Explicit language, violence
Dir: Penelope Spheeris *Cast:* Jon Cryer, Daniel Roebuck, Catherine Mary Stewart, Flea, Lee Ving, Calvin Bartlett
▶ Aimless punk rockers Cryer, Roebuck, and Flea set off on cross-country trek. Camping out in the desert, they are attacked by tattooed tough Ving and his gang of sadistic rednecks, who steal their money and slay Flea. When police offer no help, Cryer and Roebuck, aided by sharp-shooting Stewart, seek their own revenge. Hodgepodge of comedy, drama, and fantasy sabotages standard action premise.

DUEL 1971
★★★★ **PG Drama/MFTV 1:30**
☑ Explicit language
Dir: Steven Spielberg *Cast:* Dennis Weaver, Eddie Firestone, Gene Dynarksi, Tim Herbert, Charles Seel, Alexander Lockwood
▶ Driving through the desert, salesman Weaver is menaced by the unseen driver of a ten-ton diesel truck. Streamlined plot by Richard Matheson, relentless pacing, and impressive technical credits helped establish director Spielberg's reputation. Originally made for TV, then released theatrically with peripheral scenes about Weaver's family added. Jack A. Marta's slick photography received an Emmy nomination.

DUEL AT DIABLO 1966
★★★ **NR Western 1:43**
☑ Adult situations, violence
Dir: Ralph Nelson *Cast:* James Garner, Sidney Poitier, Bibi Andersson, Dennis Weaver, Bill Travers, William Redfield
▶ Trailsman Garner guides a shipment of ammunition through hostile Indian country while defusing racial tensions caused by black horsemaster Poitier and the half-breed son of Andersson, raped by the Apaches. Garner's rival, greenhorn Army lieutenant Travers, provokes further trouble when he breaks down during an Indian ambush. Old-fashioned Western is often excessively violent.

DUEL IN THE SUN 1946
★★★ **NR Western 2:10**
Dir: King Vidor *Cast:* Jennifer Jones, Joseph Cotten, Gregory Peck, Lionel Barrymore, Lillian Gish, Walter Huston
▶ Overwrought, controversial Western has an improbable plot, but triumphs through sheer spectacle. Thousands of extras and an extravagant production frame the tragic story of half-breed Jones torn between amoral cowpoke Peck and his refined brother Cotten. Barrymore is commanding as their invalid father; Gish (Barrymore's wife) and Jones were Oscar-nominated. Narrated by Orson Welles.

DUELLISTS, THE 1978 British
★★ **PG Drama 1:41**
☑ Violence
Dir: Ridley Scott *Cast:* Keith Carradine, Harvey Keitel, Albert Finney, Edward Fox, Cristina Raines
▶ Sober, beautifully filmed account of a feud between two French officers during the Napoleonic Wars. Keitel pursues Carradine for sixteen years before they resolve their argument. Adaptation of a Joseph Conrad story is most notable for its remarkable photography and attention to period detail. Scott's directing debut.

DUET FOR ONE 1986
★★ **R Drama 1:47**
☑ Brief nudity, adult situations, explicit language
Dir: Andrei Konchalovsky *Cast:* Julie Andrews, Alan Bates, Max Von Sydow, Rupert Everett, Margaret Courtenay
▶ Old-fashioned three-hanky weeper stars Andrews as a world-famous violinist stricken with multiple sclerosis. Forced to retire at the peak of her career and dumped by husband Bates for a secretary, she is left to contemplate suicide as her body degenerates. Andrews's perky disposition adds some light to this terminally grim fare.

DUMBO 1941
★★★★★ **G Animation 1:04**
Dir: Ben Sharpsteen *Cast:* Voices of Edward Brophy, Sterling Holloway, Verna Felton, Herman Bing, Cliff Edwards
▶ Infant circus elephant Dumbo is ridiculed for oversized ears until he discovers his deformity allows him to fly and becomes the star of the show. Flawless Disney classic will delight all ages; young-

sters will especially identify with shy, non-speaking Dumbo and the ugly duckling story line. Musical score won an Oscar; songs include "Look Out For Mr. Stork," Oscar-nominated "Baby of Mine," and unforgettable "Pink Elephants on Parade." (CC)

DUNE 1984
★★★ PG-13 Sci-Fi 2:20
☑ Explicit language, violence
Dir: David Lynch *Cast:* Kyle MacLachlan, Francesca Annis, Jose Ferrer, Brad Dourif, Linda Hunt, Freddie Jones
► Great-looking but ultimately disappointing sci-fi epic from Frank Herbert's elaborate cult classic, once thought to be unfilmable. The time is A.D. 10,991. Young messiah MacLachlan travels to the planet Dune, an arid wasteland containing a valuable narcotic spice guarded by giant sandworms. He leads its lowly inhabitants to victory over an evil emperor and his minions. Rock-star Sting plays a minor role as a smiling dispenser of pain. (CC)

DUNGEONMASTER, THE 1985
★ PG-13 Sci-Fi 1:14
☑ Violence
Dir: Rose Marie Turko, John Buechler, Charles Band, David Allen, Steve Ford, Peter Manoogian, Ted Nicolaou *Cast:* Jeffrey Byron, Leslie Wing, Richard Moll, Danny Dick
► Sword and sorcery goes yuppie when computer whiz Byron travels back in time to rescue aerobics instructor sweetheart Wing from mad magician Moll. With the help of his "pet" computer Cal, Byron zaps every bad dude in sight with just a flick of his wrist. Special effects are purely primitive. Also known as *Ragewar.*

DUSTY 1982 Australian
★★★★ NR Drama 1:28
Dir: John Richardson *Cast:* Bill Kerr, Noel Trevarthen, Carol Burns, Nick Holland, John Stanton
► An Australian rancher raises a dingo pup into a prize-winning sheep dog. When the call of the wild lures "Dusty" back to the bush, other ranchers blame the dog for an increase in slaughtered sheep. A touching, nicely produced family film both interesting and educational.

EACH DAWN I DIE 1939
★★★ NR Action-Adventure 1:32 B&W
Dir: William Keighley *Cast:* James Cagney, George Raft, Jane Bryan, George Bancroft, Maxie Rosenbloom, Victor Jory
► Framed by corrupt politicians, reporter Cagney is sent to jail, where he becomes friends with gangster Raft. Cagney is blamed when Raft escapes, so Raft returns to the pen to rescue him. Smashing prison drama is preposterous at times, but Cagney ("I'll get out if I have to kill every screw in the hole") is dynamic, and Raft matches him with a superior tough-guy performance.

EAGLE HAS LANDED, THE 1977
★★★★ PG Mystery-Suspense 2:03
☑ Mild violence
Dir: John Sturges *Cast:* Michael Caine, Donald Sutherland, Robert Duvall, Jenny Agutter, Donald Pleasence
► During World War II, German operatives led by Caine and IRA man Sutherland infiltrate a small English town in a plot to kill Winston Churchill. Well-crafted, satisfying action-adventure from the Jack Higgins best-seller presented from the point of view of sympathetic Germans. Nifty surprise ending, solid work from Caine, Sutherland, and Duvall.

EARLY FROST, AN 1985
★★★★ NR Drama/MFTV 1:37
Dir: John Erman *Cast:* Gena Rowlands, Ben Gazzara, Sylvia Sidney, Aidan Quinn, D. W. Moffett, John Glover
► Rowlands and Gazzara are shocked to discover their son Quinn is not only gay but is dying of AIDS. Made-for-television drama, one of the first to deal with the controversial subject, soars way above average because of a power-packed cast and an Emmy-winning script by Rom Cowen and Daniel Lipman, based on a Sherman Yellen story.

EARTHLING, THE 1980 Australian
★★★★ PG Drama 1:37
☑ Adult situations, violence
Dir: Peter Collinson *Cast:* William Holden, Ricky Schroder, Jack Thompson, Olivia Hamnett, Alwyn Kurts
► "City kid" Schroder is orphaned while camping in the Australian wilderness. Chased by packs of wild animals, he seems doomed until he meets grizzled traveler Holden, who teaches him the rudiments of survival. Features stunning nature footage.

EARTHQUAKE 1974
★★★★ PG Action-Adventure 2:09
☑ Explicit language, violence

Dir: Mark Robson *Cast:* Charlton Heston, Ava Gardner, Lorne Greene, George Kennedy, Victoria Principal, Walter Matthau
▶ California crumbles in this early disaster movie, startling audiences with ear-splitting "Sensurround," which created shock waves inside the theatre. Kennedy is a policeman who takes charge of the rescue operation while buildings quiver and collapse, streets buckle, and crammed elevators plummet. Packed with action and suspense.

EARTH VS. THE FLYING SAUCERS 1956
★★ NR Sci-Fi 1:23 B&W
Dir: Fred F. Sears *Cast:* Hugh Marlowe, Joan Taylor, Donald Curtis, Morris Ankrum, Tom Browne Henry
▶ Friendly flying saucers land on Earth and are greeted by gunfire, so the angry aliens respond with full-scale warfare. Marlowe stars as a scientist who discovers the space-creatures' weakness. Outstanding early special effects by Ray Harryhausen include the destruction of the Lincoln memorial and other Washington monuments.

EASTER PARADE 1948
★★★★★ NR Musical 1:43
Dir: Charles Walters *Cast:* Fred Astaire, Judy Garland, Ann Miller, Peter Lawford, Jules Munshin
▶ After partner Miller leaves him, dancer Astaire plucks Garland from the chorus to be his new sidekick. Garland and Astaire end up making beautiful professional and personal music together. A joy from start to finish; top-notch period (early-twentieth-century New York) re-creation with the stars at their peak. Many wonderful Irving Berlin songs include the title tune, Astaire and Garland clowning as "A Couple of Swells," and the beautiful and unjustly overlooked "It Only Happens When I Dance With You." Oscar for Musical Scoring.

EAST OF EDEN 1955
★★★★★ NR Drama 1:55
Dir: Elia Kazan *Cast:* James Dean, Julie Harris, Raymond Massey, Burl Ives, Richard Davalos, Jo Van Fleet
▶ In World War I Salinas Valley, Dean, rebellious son of stern father Massey, seeks truth about estranged mother Van Fleet (Supporting Actress Oscar winner) and finds love with Harris, his brother's girlfriend. Stirring, passionate direction by Kazan; lovely, winsome performance by

Harris; intense but vulnerable work by Dean; and haunting Leonard Rosenman score make this adaptation of John Steinbeck novel a memorable and emotional piece of Americana.

EASY COME, EASY GO 1967
★★ NR Musical 1:35
Dir: John Rich *Cast:* Elvis Presley, Dodie Marshall, Pat Priest, Pat Harrington, Skip Ward, Frank McHugh
▶ Romantic comedy with a nautical theme: Navy frogman Presley, go-go dancer Marshall, and old wharf rat McHugh team up to salvage treasure from a sunken Spanish galleon. Elsa Lanchester offers a kooky character bit for comic relief; Elvis sings "Yoga Is As Yoga Does" and "You Gotta Stop."

EASY LIVING 1937
★★★ NR Comedy 1:28 B&W
Dir: Mitchell Leisen *Cast:* Jean Arthur, Edward Arnold, Ray Milland, Luis Alberni, Franklin Pangborn, William Demarest
▶ Millionaire Arnold, furious over his wife's bills, throws her fur coat out his penthouse window. When stenographer Arthur retrieves the coat, Wall Street gossips identify her as Arnold's new mistress. Delightful screwball farce written by Preston Sturges never loses steam. Highlighted by a delirious slapstick riot in an automat.

EASY LIVING 1949
★★ NR Drama 1:17 B&W
Dir: Jacques Tourneur *Cast:* Victor Mature, Lucille Ball, Lizabeth Scott, Sonny Tufts, Lloyd Nolan, Jack Paar
▶ Mature, the aging halfback star of the New York Chiefs, faces endless nagging from wife Scott as retirement nears. Medical problems and loss of coaching job to rival Tufts bring him to edge of despair, but team secretary Ball offers unexpected support. Earnest sports soap opera features credible performances.

EASY MONEY 1983
★★★ R Comedy 1:39
☑ Nudity, adult situations, explicit language, adult humor
Dir: James Signorelli *Cast:* Rodney Dangerfield, Joe Pesci, Geraldine Fitzgerald, Candice Azzara, Taylor Negron, Jennifer Jason Leigh
▶ Fun-loving Dangerfield stands to inherit $10 million if he can abstain from his favorite vices—boozing, gambling, and cavorting—for a year. With Pesci as his plumber pal and Leigh as his blond

daughter married to a Puerto Rican gang member. Co-writer Dangerfield may get no respect, but fans adore his one-liners. **(CC)**

EASY RIDER 1969
★ ★ ★ **R Drama 1:35**
☑ Explicit language, violence
Dir: Dennis Hopper   *Cast:* Peter Fonda, Dennis Hopper, Jack Nicholson, Luana Anders, Robert Walker, Jr., Karen Black
▶ The sixties classic that encouraged an American generation to tune in, turn on, and drop out. Fonda and Hopper motorcycle from Southern California to New Orleans encountering drugs, hippies, hookers, and death. For his performance as an alcoholic lawyer, Nicholson won his first Academy Award nomination. Debut directorial effort by Hopper garnered international acclaim at Cannes.

EATING RAOUL 1982
★ **R Comedy 1:23**
☑ Nudity, adult situations, violence, adult humor
Dir: Paul Bartel   *Cast:* Paul Bartel, Mary Woronov, Buck Henry, Robert Beltran
▶ Cult film about Paul and Mary Bland (Bartel and Woronov), a mild-mannered modern couple who resort to murder to finance their dream of owning a gourmet restaurant. With Beltran as Raoul, a local thief who meets an unhappy fate when he tries to horn in on their plans. Offbeat black comedy for those with exotic tastes.

EAT MY DUST 1976
★ ★ **PG Action-Adventure 1:30**
☑ Explicit language, violence
Dir: Charles B. Griffith   *Cast:* Ron Howard, Christopher Norris, Warren Kemmerling, Dave Madden, Paul Bartel
▶ Sheriff Kemmerling organizes a posse after son Howard steals stock car from pro racer Big Bubba Jones (Madden). But no one can stop Howard and his girl Norris. Fast-paced but relentless Roger Corman production is essentially one long car chase.

EAT THE RICH 1988 British
☆ **R Comedy 1:32**
☑ Explicit language, violence
Dir: Peter Richardson   *Cast:* Ronald Allen, Robbie Coltrane, Sandra Dorne, Jimmy Fagg, Lemmy, Lamah Pellay
▶ Pellay, an androgynous black waiter fired from posh London restaurant, gets revenge by forming revolutionary gang, taking over the place, killing wealthy folk,

and then putting them on the menu. Irreverent, Monty Pythonesque comedy is bizarre and darkly comic. Definitely not for all tastes.

ECHOES 1981
★ **R Drama 1:31**
☑ Nudity, adult situations, explicit language
Dir: Arthur Allan Seidelman   *Cast:* Richard Alfieri, Nathalie Nell, Mercedes McCambridge, Ruth Roman, Gale Sondergaard
▶ Psychological examination of young painter Alfieri tormented by a past incarnation. Nell is his French dancer/love interest trying to understand his violent dreams. Very arty and theatrical; may be too farfetched and dreamlike for some.

ECHO PARK 1986 U.S./Austrian
★ **R Comedy/Drama 1:32**
☑ Brief nudity, adult situations, explicit language
Dir: Robert Dornhelm   *Cast:* Tom Hulce, Susan Dey, Christopher Walker, Michael Bowen, Shirley Jo Finney
▶ Aspiring poet/pizza delivery man Hulce, mother/stripper/aspiring actress Dey and Austrian weightlifter Bowen share an old duplex apartment house in Echo Park, a low-rent, hilly address in East L.A., and wait for their big breaks. Offbeat, sweet, and occasionally very funny.

EDDIE AND THE CRUISERS 1983
★ ★ ★ ★ **PG Drama 1:35 C**
☑ Adult situations, explicit language, mild violence
Dir: Martin Davidson   *Cast:* Tom Berenger, Michael Paré, Ellen Barkin, Helen Schneider, Joe Pantoliano
▶ Variation on the rock nostalgia formula in which TV reporter Barkin investigates early sixties band, Eddie (Paré) and the Cruisers. The group dissolved after Eddie's mysterious car crash but his body was never found and tapes of their last album disappeared. Music startlingly Springsteen-esque. With Berenger as the first ex-band member to be interviewed.

EDDIE MACON'S RUN 1983
★ ★ ★ ★ **PG Action-Adventure 1:31**
☑ Rape, brief nudity, adult situations, explicit language, violence
Dir: Jeff Kanew   *Cast:* Kirk Douglas, John Schneider, Lee Purcell, Leah Ayres, Lisa Dunsheath
▶ In his first film, Schneider, wrongly convicted on trumped-up charges, escapes from jail and heads for Mexico. Douglas

is the vengeful cop who pursues him in a grueling chase; Purcell, the heiress who helps him cross Texas. Based on James McLendon's novel, car chase movie is surprisingly acceptable.

EDDIE MURPHY RAW 1987
★★ R Documentary/Comedy 1:31
☑ Explicit language, adult humor
Dir: Robert Townsend *Cast:* Eddie Murphy
▶ No-frills film of Murphy's one-man show at New York's Felt Forum is a must for his fans. His targets include Mr. T, Bill Cosby, Michael Jackson, and sex—all handled in hilarious but coarse language that may offend unsuspecting viewers. (CC)

EDGE OF DARKNESS 1943
★★★ NR War 2:00 B&W
Dir: Lewis Milestone *Cast:* Errol Flynn, Ann Sheridan, Walter Huston, Helmut Dantine, Ruth Gordon, Judith Anderson
▶ During World War II, the Nazis invade a Norwegian town but find more trouble than they could have imagined: fisherman Flynn, his girlfriend Sheridan, widow Anderson, and doctor Huston are among the leaders of an underground resistance movement that battles the Germans through both nonviolent and violent means. Tense and well-crafted. (CC)

EDUCATION OF SONNY CARSON, THE 1974
★★ R Drama 1:44
☑ Explicit language, violence
Dir: Michael Campus *Cast:* Rony Clayton, Don Gordon, Joyce Walker, Paul Benjamin, Thomas Hicks
▶ Honest, hard-edged look at black ghetto life follows Carson's (Clayton) descent into crime after joining a gang. Powerful assault on racism and inescapable poverty, with a sincere, positive outlook that overcomes the film's budget limitations.

EGG AND I, THE 1947
★★★ NR Comedy 1:48 B&W
Dir: Chester Erskine *Cast:* Claudette Colbert, Fred MacMurray, Marjorie Main, Percy Kilbride, Louise Allbritton
▶ MacMurray and Colbert are delightful as the city-bred MacDonalds, who buy a chicken farm and cope with rural life. Main and Kilbride team for their roles as Ma and Pa Kettle, the hick couple next door who have so many children they don't know what to do. Based on the best-selling novel by Betty MacDonald; a box-office smash in 1947.

EGYPTIAN, THE 1954
★★★ NR Drama 2:20
Dir: Michael Curtiz *Cast:* Edmund Purdom, Jean Simmons, Victor Mature, Gene Tierney, Michael Wilding, Peter Ustinov
▶ Sprawling, soap opera treatment of ancient Egypt. Wilding plays an epileptic Pharaoh; Purdom, the Pharaoh's physician, has affairs with Simmons and Bella Darvi; Mature, a valiant soldier, must choose between the Pharaoh's religion or traditional creeds. Expensive costume epic delivers spectacle with elephantine pacing.

EIGER SANCTION, THE 1975
★★★★ R
Espionage/Action-Adventure 2:08
☑ Adult situations, explicit language, violence
Dir: Clint Eastwood *Cast:* Clint Eastwood, George Kennedy, Vonetta McGee, Jack Cassidy, Thayer David
▶ Ex-spy Eastwood is lured out of retirement to assassinate a hit man. After the mission, black stewardess McGee tricks him into killing another spy, one of three men climbing the dangerous Eiger mountain. Espionage themes are upstaged by thrilling, brutal climbing sequences in Monument Valley and the Alps. Based on a best-seller by Trevanian.

8½ 1963 Italian
☆ NR Drama 2:18 B&W
Dir: Federico Fellini *Cast:* Marcello Mastroianni, Claudia Cardinale, Anouk Aimee, Sandra Milo, Barbara Steele
▶ Classic autobiographical "film within a film" from Italian master moviemaker Fellini. A visual diary about a film director's difficulties making the very film we are seeing, it offers the viewer the chance to glimpse Fellini's memories, fantasies, and problems. Won an Academy Award for Best Foreign Film in 1963. A masterpiece for sophisticated tastes. Ⓢ

18 AGAIN 1988
★★★★ PG Comedy 1:40
☑ Brief nudity, adult situations, explicit language
Dir: Paul Flaherty *Cast:* George Burns, Charlie Schlatter, Tony Roberts, Anita Morris, Red Buttons
▶ Entry in the popular body switch genre has eighty-one-year-old tycoon Burns wishing he were eighteen again like his

grandson Schlatter. He gets his wish: after a car crash, his mind possesses Schlatter's body. Personable Schlatter has Burns's trademarks (leer, pause, cigar) down pat, and Burns is even better in this affectionate comedy. **(CC)**

EIGHT MEN OUT 1988
★★ **PG Drama/Sports 2:00**
☑ Explicit language
Dir: John Sayles *Cast:* John Cusack, Clifton James, D. B. Sweeney, Christopher Lloyd, Charlie Sheen, David Strathairn
▶ Tragic true story of the 1919 "Black Sox" scandal, the fixing of the World Series by the Chicago White Sox and a group of gamblers. Sayles's handsome period piece about our national pastime basically sides with the players who were motivated by the stinginess of team owner Charles Comiskey (James). Sober drama with many standouts in the large cast: Cusack as Buck Weaver, the player who may have been the scandal's biggest victim, Strathairn as the aging pitcher Eddie Cicotte, Sayles and author Studs Terkel as the sportwriters who blew open the scandal.

8 MILLION WAYS TO DIE 1986
★★★ **R Drama 1:55**
☑ Nudity, explicit language, violence
Dir: Hal Ashby *Cast:* Jeff Bridges, Rosanna Arquette, Alexandra Paul, Randy Brooks, Andy Garcia
▶ Hard-boiled melodrama about vendetta of alcoholic ex-cop Bridges against Garcia, head of a drug and prostitution ring. Arquette is a high-priced call girl who plays the two off each other. Adaptation of Lawrence Block's cult thriller inexplicably drops New York setting, but makes good use of tawdry Los Angeles locations. Oliver Stone worked on the screenplay. **(CC)**

84 CHARING CROSS ROAD 1987
★★★ **PG Drama 1:39**
☑ Explicit language
Dir: David Jones *Cast:* Anne Bancroft, Anthony Hopkins, Judi Dench, Maurice Denham, Jean De Baer
▶ Struggling New York writer Helene Hanff (Bancroft) orders rare books from London book dealer Frank Doel (Hopkins) and a warm relationship, spanning many years, develops by mail. True story (adapted from Hanff's memoir) of lovers who never meet is literate, civilized entertainment. All talk, little action, but the talk's good and two pros shine.

EL CID 1961
★★★★★ **NR Action-Adventure 3:04**
Dir: Anthony Mann *Cast:* Charlton Heston, Sophia Loren, Raf Vallone, Genevieve Page, Hurd Hatfield
▶ Story of the great eleventh-century Spanish warrior El Cid (Heston), who battled Moorish invaders. Mammoth costume spectacle has grand sweep and pageantry. Stiff dialogue but spectacular battle scenes, larger-than-life performances by Heston and Loren (as the great love of El Cid's life), surging musical score by Miklos Rozsa.

EL CONDOR 1970
★ **R Western 1:42**
☑ Nudity, explicit language, violence
Dir: John Guillermin *Cast:* Jim Brown, Lee Van Cleef, Patrick O'Neal, Marianna Hill, Iron Eyes Cody
▶ Outlaws Brown and Van Cleef team up to steal a treasure of gold hidden in a remote Mexican fortress. Mexican general O'Neal tries to thwart them. Undistinguished story and wooden acting but plenty of action, gunfire, and sex in this scenic made-in-Spain Western.

EL DORADO 1967
★★★★★ **NR Western 2:06**
Dir: Howard Hawks *Cast:* John Wayne, Robert Mitchum, James Caan, Arthur Hunnicutt, Edward Asner, Christopher George
▶ Rousing Howard Hawks Western with plenty of action. Gunslinger Wayne and drifter Caan help sober up drunken sheriff Mitchum and the trio find themselves in the midst of a blood feud between ranchers. The stars are in top two-fisted form and George provides nifty support as a badman with a code of honor.

ELECTRA GLIDE IN BLUE 1973
★ **PG Drama 1:53**
☑ Explicit language, violence
Dir: James William Guercio *Cast:* Robert Blake, Billy Green Bush, Mitchell Ryan, Jeannine Riley, Elisha Cook, Jr.
▶ Diminutive Arizona motorcycle cop Blake dreams of being a detective and gets his chance when he discovers an apparent suicide in a desert shack. Overly arty direction by Guercio goes too heavy on the close-ups, but Blake is solid and there's a fine motorcycle chase.

ELECTRIC DREAMS 1984
★ ★ ★ PG Romance 1:36
☑ Adult situations, explicit language,
   mild violence, adult humor
Dir: Steve Barron *Cast:* Lenny Von
Dohlen, Virginia Madsen, Maxwell
Caulfield, Bud Cort, Don Fellows
▶ Supersmart computer (voice of Bud
Cort) helps bumbling architect Von
Dohlen woo gorgeous neighbor Madsen.
Machine develops human feelings for
the girl and turns against its owner. Leads
are appealing but script doesn't develop
interesting premise. Rock video director
Barron directs this unusual love story in
high-tech fashion. Liberal use of pop
music includes Culture Club's overlooked
gem, "Love Is Love."

ELECTRIC HORSEMAN, THE 1979
★ ★ ★ ★ ★ PG Drama 2:00
☑ Adult situations, explicit language
Dir: Sydney Pollack *Cast:* Robert Redford, Jane Fonda, Valerie Perrine, Willie
Nelson, John Saxon, Wilford Brimley
▶ Pleasant modern-day Western about
alcoholic ex-rodeo champ Redford who
sobers up long enough to hijack a prize
horse exploited by an evil Las Vegas conglomerate. Skeptical TV reporter Fonda
publicizes his ride across Utah to find a
wilderness home for the horse. Disarmed
by Redford's sincerity, she gradually falls
in love. Film debut for country-western
star Willie Nelson, who plays Redford's
rodeo pal and sings his hit "Mama Don't
Let Your Babies Grow Up to Be Cowboys."

ELENI 1985
★ ★ ★ PG Biography/Drama 1:57
☑ Violence
Dir: Peter Yates *Cast:* Kate Nelligan,
John Malkovich, Linda Hunt, Oliver Cotton, Ronald Pickup
▶ True story of *New York Times* reporter
Nicholas Gage's (Malkovich) present-
day search for the Communist guerrillas
who murdered his mother Eleni (Nelligan)
during the 1948 Greek Civil War. Film cuts
between Gage's investigations and
flashbacks explaining the reasons for
Eleni's execution. Nelligan is impressive in
a demanding role. **(CC)**

ELEPHANT BOY 1937 British
★ ★ NR Drama/Family 1:21 B&W
Dir: Robert Flaherty, Zoltan Korda
Cast: Sabu, Walter Hudd, Allan Jeayes,
W. W. Holloway, Bruce Gordon, D. J.
Williams
▶ Dated but intriguing adventure about

young animal trainer Sabu whose favorite elephant is sold to a mean dealer.
Sabu steals the elephant and escapes
into the jungle, where he discovers
a herd of wild pachyderms. Film's
semidocumentary approach provides a
fascinating view of India in the 1930s;
heartwarming subject matter should
please children. Film debut for Sabu, a
former stableboy who later starred in *The
Thief of Bagdad*.

ELEPHANT CALLED SLOWLY, AN 1970
British
★ ★ ★ G Drama/Family 1:31
Dir: James Hill *Cast:* Bill Travers, Virginia McKenna, George Adamson,
Vinay Inambar
▶ McKenna and Travers, the acting couple from *Born Free*, arrive in Kenya to
house-sit and find their camp already occupied by three elephants (including
baby Slowly). Concerned the baby will
not adjust to the wild, the couple study a
nearby herd to teach Slowly survival skills.
George Adamson (the naturalist played
by Travers in *Born Free*) provides helpful
tips.

ELEPHANT MAN, THE 1980
★ ★ ★ ★ PG Drama 2:03 B&W
☑ Adult situations
Dir: David Lynch *Cast:* Anthony Hopkins, John Hurt, Anne Bancroft, John
Gielgud, Wendy Hiller, Freddie Jones
▶ Moving true story probes the real life of
John Merrick (Hurt), the horribly deformed
"Elephant Man" rescued from life as a
sideshow attraction by compassionate
doctor Hopkins in Victorian England. Unsensational account deliberately and
gracefully directed by Lynch. Exquisite
black-and-white photography, top performances by a restrained Hopkins and a
poignant Hurt (under tons of extraordinary makeup). Eight Oscar nominations
(Hurt, Lynch, and Best Picture). Not based
on the Broadway play.

11 HARROWHOUSE 1974 British
★ ★ PG Comedy/Crime 1:38
☑ Explicit language, violence
Dir: Aram Avakian *Cast:* Charles Gro-
din, Candice Bergen, James Mason,
Trevor Howard, John Gielgud
▶ Fast-paced, amusing heist film stars
Grodin as a diamond merchant who en-
lists the help of girlfriend Bergen to rob
the vault of a gem cartel headed by
Gielgud. Howard plays a seedy million-
aire who initiates the whole scheme.

Based on Gerald A. Browne's best-selling novel, which Grodin adapted. **(CC)**

ELIMINATORS, THE 1986
★★ PG Action-Adventure 1:36
☑ Explicit language, violence
Dir: Peter Manoogian *Cast:* Patrick Reynolds, Denise Crosby, Andrew Prine, Conan Lee, Roy Dotrice
► Injured flyer Reynolds, turned into "mandroid" (half-man, half robot) by mad doctor Dotrice, teams with jungle guide Prine, pretty scientist Crosby, and ninja Lee to seek his revenge. Comic book sci-fi adventure, loaded with gadgets, cute robots, and special effects, doesn't take itself too seriously. **(CC)**

ELMER GANTRY 1960
★★★★ NR Drama 2:26
Dir: Richard Brooks *Cast:* Burt Lancaster, Jean Simmons, Arthur Kennedy, Shirley Jones, Dean Jagger, Edward Andrews
► Adaptation of Sinclair Lewis novel stars Lancaster as the titular salesman-turned-evangelist. In the 1920s Midwest, he sees barnstorming preacher Simmons in action and cons her into letting him join her troupe. Gripping exposé of commercialized religion has even more impact today. Oscars went to writer/director Brooks, Lancaster, and Jones as Gantry's jilted girlfriend who turns to prostitution; also nominated for Best Picture and Scoring by André Previn. Cameo by singer Patti Page.

EL NORTE 1984
★★★ R Drama 2:19
☑ Adult situations, explicit language, violence
Dir: Gregory Nava *Cast:* Zaide Silva Gutierrez, David Villalpando, Ernesto Gomez Cruz, Alicia Del Lago, Lupe Ontiveros, Trinidad Silva
► When their father is killed and mother kidnapped by the army, a Guatemalan brother and sister decide to escape to America. After an arduous border crossing, they find life in the promised land not what was promised. Visually accomplished direction by Nava evokes the plight of the immigrant with emotion and intelligence. Oscar-nominated for Best Original Screenplay. ⓢ

ELVIRA MADIGAN 1967 Swedish
★ PG Romance 1:35
☑ Brief nudity, adult situations
Dir: Bo Widerberg *Cast:* Pia Deger-

mark, Thommy Berggren, Lennart Malmen, Nina Widerberg, Cleo Jensen
► Poetic, expressionistic love story from Sweden about an affair in 1900 between an army officer and a circus tightrope walker that ends in suicide. Visually striking art film is slowly paced and has little in the way of conventional plot development, characterization, or dialogue. Beautiful Mozart score.

ELVIRA, MISTRESS OF THE DARK 1988
★★ PG-13 Comedy 1:36
☑ Adult situations, explicit language, violence, adult humor
Dir: James Signorelli *Cast:* Cassandra Peterson, Edie McClurg, Daniel Greene, W. Morgan Sheppard, Susan Kellermann, Pat Crawford Brown
► Friendly witch inherits New England home, incurring wrath of puritanical parents with her eye-opening wardrobe and uninhibited approach to sex. Teens naturally love her, and rally to her support when she's sentenced to burn at the stake. Crude but good-natured comedy capitalizing on Peterson's TV horror movie hostess role offers an encyclopedia of breast jokes.

ELVIS 1979
★★★★ G Biography/MFTV 2:29
Dir: John Carpenter *Cast:* Kurt Russell, Shelley Winters, Season Hubley, Pat Hingle, Bing Russell
► Story of Elvis Presley's rise from truck driver to superstar and his drug-infused fall. Russell is nothing short of extraordinary in an electrifying, magnetic portrayal that sets the standard for Elvis impersonations. Excellent support from Winters as his mother. Made for television but doesn't look it—Carpenter's direction provides a big-screen feel. Russell and Hubley fell in love while doing the movie and married, but were later divorced.

ELVIS: THAT'S THE WAY IT IS 1970
★★★★ NR Documentary/Music 1:37
Dir: Denis Sanders *Cast:* Elvis Presley
► Documentary of Elvis preparing for and performing his act at Las Vegas's International Hotel. Interspersed are many brief interviews with aids, fans, hotel personnel. The Elvis of 1970 was still in pretty good shape and he puts on a rousing and thoroughly professional show. Songs include "All Shook Up," "Blue Suede Shoes," "Bridge Over Troubled Water."

EMBRYO 1976
★★★ PG Sci-Fi 1:43

☑ Nudity, violence
Dir: Ralph Nelson   *Cast:* Rock Hudson, Barbara Carrera, Diane Ladd, Roddy McDowall, Anne Schedeen, John Elerick
▶ Scientist Hudson administers growth hormone to fetus of dying pregnant woman. Result is beautiful, full-grown Carrera, gifted with brilliant mind but lacking normal life experience. Hudson promptly falls for her, but since he's tampered with nature Carrera turns out to be more than he'd anticipated. A few notches above average sci-fi fare.

EMERALD FOREST, THE 1985
★ ★ ★ ★ R Action-Adventure 1:53
☑ Nudity, violence
Dir: John Boorman   *Cast:* Powers Boothe, Meg Foster, Charley Boorman, Estee Chandler, Tetchie Agbayani
▶ American construction engineer Boothe spends ten years searching for his son Boorman, kidnapped by a remote tribe in the Amazon jungle. Decidedly different adventure from director Boorman supposedly based on fact. Exotic locations, dazzling camerawork, and convincing native cast transport the audience into another world. **(CC)**

EMIGRANTS, THE 1971 Swedish
★ ★ ★ ★ PG Drama 2:31
☑ Adult situations, explicit language, violence
Dir: Jan Troell   *Cast:* Max Von Sydow, Liv Ullmann, Eddie Axberg, Svenoloff Bern, Allan Edwall
▶ Von Sydow, his wife Ullmann, and his brother Axberg leave 1850s Sweden in search of a better life in America but must survive an arduous ocean voyage and a cross-country journey to Minnesota. Exquisitely crafted; however, slow pace requires viewer patience. Followed by 1972 sequel *The New Land.* Received Oscar nominations for Best Picture, Actress (Ullmann), Director, and Adapted Screenplay. Dubbed.

EMIL AND THE DETECTIVES 1964
★ ★ ★ NR Mystery-Suspense 0:49
Dir: Peter Tewksbury   *Cast:* Walter Slezak, Brian Russell, Roger Mobley, Heinz Schubert, Peter Erlich
▶ In West Berlin, a group of precocious kids band together to thwart the plans of a trio of comically sinister thieves. Polished entertainment in the wholesome Disney tradition. Based on a children's novel by Erich Kastner.

EMMANUELLE 1974 French
★ ★ X Sex 1:32
☑ Rape, nudity, strong sexual content, explicit language
Dir: Just Jaeckin   *Cast:* Sylvia Kristel, Alain Cuny, Marika Green, Daniel Sarky
▶ In Bangkok, Kristel, the young wife of French diplomat Sarky, gets involved with experienced older man, Cuny, who introduces her to kinky pleasures. One of the breakthrough erotic films still generates enough heat to light up your VCR.
⑤

EMPEROR JONES, THE 1933
☆ NR Drama 1:12 B&W
Dir: Dudley Murphy   *Cast:* Paul Robeson, Dudley Digges, Frank Wilson, Fredi Washington, Ruby Elzy
▶ Dated adaptation of the Eugene O'Neill play is of interest today as one of Robeson's best vehicles. He plays a brooding, egotistical railroad porter who flees to Haiti after murdering a friend. Trader Digges (the only white member of the cast) hires Jones to keep his native workers in line. Jones becomes a tyrant, and declares himself emperor of the island. Unusual studio sets enhance the story's gloomy atmosphere.

EMPEROR OF THE NORTH, THE 1973
★ ★ PG Action-Adventure 1:59
☑ Violence
Dir: Robert Aldrich   *Cast:* Lee Marvin, Ernest Borgnine, Keith Carradine, Charles Tyner, Malcolm Atterbury, Simon Oakland
▶ Unusually vicious drama about sadistic Depression-era railroad guard Borgnine, who uses any means available to rid his train of hitching hoboes. Marvin and his protégé Carradine test Borgnine's will in a epic battle of wits and brawn. Striking Oregon locations. Originally titled *Emperor of the North Pole.*

EMPIRE OF THE ANTS 1977
★ PG Sci-Fi 1:29
☑ Violence
Dir: Bert I. Gordon   *Cast:* Joan Collins, Robert Lansing, John David Carson, Albert Salmi, Jacqueline Scott
▶ "This is no picnic!" Good-natured thrills and chills about a colony of gigantic ants who've grown by eating radioactive waste. The insects attack pre-*Dynasty* Collins, head of a group of crooked real estate investors, and her colleagues. They make their way to a village only to discover the sugar refinery is controlled

by the ants. Based on an H. G. Wells story; sometimes silly, but mostly fun.

EMPIRE OF THE SUN 1987
★★★★ **PG Drama 2:25**
☑ Adult situations, explicit language, violence
Dir: Steven Spielberg *Cast:* Christian Bale, John Malkovich, Miranda Richardson, Joe Pantoliano, Rupert Frazer, Nigel Havers
▶ Spielberg's poetic, hallucinatory account of eleven-year-old Jim's harrowing adventures in Japanese-occupied China during World War II. Separated from his upper-class British parents, bruised and ignored, Jim (Bale) is "adopted" by shady Yank seaman Malkovich and his pal Pantoliano. Together, they survive the grueling conditions of a refugee camp and, from afar, Jim witnesses the nuking of Nagasaki before being reunited with his family. Screenplay by Tom Stoppard, adapted from J. G. Ballard's fictionalized account of his childhood in Shanghai. (CC)

EMPIRE STRIKES BACK, THE 1980
★★★★★ **PG Sci-Fi/Action-Adventure 2:04**
☑ Adult situations, violence
Dir: Irvin Kershner *Cast:* Mark Hamill, Harrison Ford, Carrie Fisher, Billy Dee Williams, Alec Guinness, Frank Oz
▶ Second episode of the *Star Wars* trilogy delivers the expected action and amazing special effects while rounding out the characters. Han Solo (Ford) and Princess Leia (Fisher) battle an organic asteroid; Luke Skywalker (Hamill) furthers his training with the irascible Yoda (Oz); and Darth Vader reveals a startling secret about his past. New characters include Williams as Lando Calrissian, an untrustworthy trader. Winner of an Oscar for Sound and a special award for Special Effects. Sequel: *Return of the Jedi*. (CC)

ENCHANTED COTTAGE, THE 1945
★★★ **NR Fantasy 1:31 B&W**
Dir: John Cromwell *Cast:* Dorothy McGuire, Robert Young, Herbert Marshall, Mildred Natwick, Spring Byington, Richard Gaines
▶ Suicidal veteran Young, horribly disfigured in World War I, finds romance with plain girl McGuire. They move into a honeymoon cottage in New England, where the power of love reveals the true beauty behind their physical shortcomings. Deli-

cate adaptation of an Arthur Pinero play offers endearingly understated performances and tone.

ENCORE 1951 British
★★ **NR Drama 1:29 B&W**
Dir: Harold French, Pat Jackson, Anthony Pelissier *Cast:* Nigel Patrick, Roland Culver, Kay Walsh, Noel Purcell, Glynis Johns, Terence Morgan
▶ Pleasant omnibus of three W. Somerset Maugham short stories: "The Ant and the Grasshopper" (brothers feud over money); "Winter Cruise" (Walsh makes life miserable for passengers on a luxury liner); "Gigolo and Gigolette" (Johns wants her husband to quit high diving). Smoothly diverting.

END, THE 1978
★★★ **R Comedy 1:40**
☑ Adult situations, explicit language
Dir: Burt Reynolds *Cast:* Burt Reynolds, Sally Field, Dom DeLuise, Strother Martin, David Steinberg
▶ Ambitious black comedy about real estate huckster Reynolds, who believes he has a fatal blood disease and decides to kill himself. DeLuise is hilarious as a schizophrenic who assists Reynolds in his suicide attempts. Reynolds's second stab at directing is uneven but often wildly funny, and filled with hilarious cameos: Joanne Woodward, Norman Fell, Myrna Loy, Kristy McNichol, Robby Benson, Carl Reiner, etc.

ENDANGERED SPECIES 1982
★★★ **R Drama 1:37**
☑ Brief nudity, adult situations, explicit language, graphic violence
Dir: Alan Rudolph *Cast:* Robert Urich, JoBeth Williams, Paul Dooley, Hoyt Axton, Peter Coyote
▶ Ex-cop Urich moves to Colorado for peace and quiet, then stumbles across a series of bizarre cattle mutilations that threatens his daughter's safety. Williams plays a spunky sheriff who helps him on the case. Odd blend of romantic thriller and science fiction was based on fact.

ENDLESS LOVE 1981
★★ **R Romance 1:55**
☑ Nudity, adult situations, explicit language
Dir: Franco Zeffirelli *Cast:* Brooke Shields, Martin Hewitt, Shirley Knight, Don Murray, Richard Kiley, Beatrice Straight
▶ Teenage Hewitt takes revenge on girlfriend Shields's family when her parents

break up their precocious romance. Lush, romantic adaptation of Scott Spencer's novel was a popular examination of lost love. Knight is compelling as Shields's bright but insecure mother. Oscar-nominated title song by Lionel Ritchie.

END OF THE LINE 1987
★★★ PG Drama 1:45
☑ Explicit language
Dir: Jay Russell *Cast:* Wilford Brimley, Levon Helm, Mary Steenburgen, Barbara Barrie, Bob Balaban, Holly Hunter
► Hard times hit the small town of Clifford, Arkansas, when the Southland conglomerate closes its railyard. Best friends Brimley and Helm hijack an old engine and ride to the company's headquarters in Chicago to force management to reopen the yard. Upbeat, folksy comedy was a labor of love for Steenburgen, who also produced. Kevin Bacon has a small role as Brimley's raffish ex-son-in-law. (CC)

END OF THE ROAD 1970
★ X Drama 1:50
☑ Nudity, adult situations, explicit language, violence
Dir: Aram Avakian *Cast:* Stacy Keach, Harris Yulin, Dorothy Tristan, James Earl Jones, Grayson Hall, James Coco
► Peculiar, haunting adaptation of John Barth's novel centers on teacher Keach, recently released from mental institution, and his affair with faculty wife Tristan, but story veers into meditations on abortion, drug use, the NASA moon program, and quack Jones's shock treatments for depression. Screenplay by director Avakian, Dennis McGuire, and Terry Southern. (CC)

ENEMY BELOW, THE 1957
★★★ NR War 1:38
Dir: Dick Powell *Cast:* Robert Mitchum, Curt Jurgens, Theodore Bikel, Russell Collins, Kurt Kreuger, Al (David) Hedison
► Tense account of cat-and-mouse battle between Mitchum's destroyer escort and Jurgens's Nazi U-boat in the North Atlantic during World War II is a compelling study of bravery in unforgiving circumstances. Streamlined direction, realistic performances, and accurate portrayal of military tactics contribute to nail-biting suspense. Based on a novel by D. A. Rayner; Walter Rossi's special effects received an Oscar.

ENEMY MINE 1985
★★★★ PG-13 Sci-Fi 1:48
☑ Explicit language violence
Dir: Wolfgang Petersen *Cast:* Dennis Quaid, Louis Gossett, Jr., Brion James, Richard Marcus, Carolyn McCormick
► In the twenty-first century, astronaut Quaid and reptilian Drac (Gossett) are marooned on the forbidding planet Fryine IV. Although enemies, they learn they must work together to survive. Gossett, almost unrecognizable under his scaly makeup, is surprisingly sympathetic. (CC)

ENEMY TERRITORY 1987
★★ R Action-Adventure 1:29
☑ Explicit language, graphic violence
Dir: Peter Manoogian *Cast:* Gary Frank, Ray Parker, Jr., Jan-Michael Vincent, Frances Foster, Tony Todd, Deon Richmond
► Engrossing but violent exploitation film about meek white insurance agent Frank trapped overnight in a ghetto high-rise controlled by Todd and his Vampires gang. Frank teams up with crippled Vietnam vet Vincent and a Good Samaritan telephone repairman (pop singer Parker in his acting debut) to fight his way out of the building. High body count will please action fans. (CC)

ENFORCER, THE 1976
★★★★★ R Action-Adventure 1:36
☑ Brief nudity, explicit language, graphic violence
Dir: James Fargo *Cast:* Clint Eastwood, Harry Guardino, Tyne Daly, Bradford Dillman, John Mitchum
► Third Dirty Harry film pits him against Revolutionary Strike Force terrorists who have kidnapped San Francisco's mayor. What's worse, he's been given feisty feminist Daly as his new partner. Eastwood, in fine form, trades in his .44 for a bazooka at the climax. Followed by *Sudden Impact.*

ENIGMA 1983 British/French
★★★★ PG Drama 1:41
☑ Brief nudity, adult situations, explicit language, mild violence
Dir: Jeannot Szwarc *Cast:* Martin Sheen, Sam Neill, Brigitte Fossey, Derek Jacobi, Michael Lonsdale, Frank Finlay
► East German defector Sheen is ordered back to East Berlin to stop the KGB assassination of five dissidents. Desperate for information, he forces old girlfriend Fossey to start an affair with Neill, the Russian mastermind behind the plot.

Solid cast emphasizes the personal aspects of espionage.

ENSIGN PULVER 1964
★★ NR Comedy 1:44
Dir: Joshua Logan *Cast:* Robert Walker, Jr., Burl Ives, Walter Matthau, Tommy Sands, Millie Perkins
▶ Follow-up to the classic *Mister Roberts* details the further adventures of free-spirited Ensign Pulver (Walker assumes the role Jack Lemmon played in the original). Genial service comedy but not in the same league as the earlier film. Large cast includes bit parts by young Jack Nicholson and Larry Hagman.

ENTERTAINER, THE 1960 British
★★★ NR Drama 1:36 B&W
Dir: Tony Richardson *Cast:* Laurence Olivier, Brenda de Banzie, Joan Plowright, Roger Livesey, Alan Bates, Albert Finney
▶ One of the high points of Olivier's career is his Oscar-nominated performance as Archie Rice, a music hall has-been who refuses to admit his lack of talent. John Osborne's relentlessly bleak play describes Rice's brutal treatment of his family, brought to vivid life by a wonderful supporting cast. Film debut for Plowright, who later married Olivier. Remade as a TV movie with Jack Lemmon in 1975.

ENTER THE DRAGON 1973
★★★★ R Martial Arts 1:39
☑ Violence
Dir: Robert Clouse *Cast:* Bruce Lee, John Saxon, Jim Kelly, Ahna Capri, Shih Kien, Yang Tse
▶ Lee's last role before his death is one of the best of all kung-fu pictures. On a mission to avenge his sister's death, he teams up with ex–Army buddies Saxon and Kelly to infiltrate druglord Kien's island fortress. Strong production values and a nice comic sensibility add depth to the formulaic plot. An excellent showcase for Lee's grace and skill (he also choreographed the fights).

ENTER THE NINJA 1981
★★ R Martial Arts 1:39
☑ Adult situations, explicit language, graphic violence
Dir: Menahem Golan *Cast:* Franco Nero, Susan George, Sho Kosugi, Alex Courtney, Will Hare, Christopher George
▶ Martial arts expert Nero enlists the aid of his friend Courtney to defend his Filipino plantation from Venarius (Christo-

pher George), a greedy real estate developer. Susan George, Nero's sexy wife, proves just as adept as the men in fighting off the villains. Characters and plot take a back seat to the action scenes.

ENTRE NOUS 1983 French
★ PG Drama 1:50
☑ Brief nudity, adult situations, explicit language, violence
Dir: Diane Kurys *Cast:* Miou-Miou, Isabelle Huppert, Guy Marchand, Jean-Pierre Bacri
▶ Huppert and Miou-Miou, both survivors of World War II, form a close, fifteen-year friendship that sustains them through the breakup of their respective marriages. Compassionate yet tough-minded drama from French director Kurys with fully rounded, three-dimensional characterizations. Not so much a "woman's film" as a human one which concedes the male point of view without condescension or dogma. Ⓢ

EQUUS 1977
★★ R Drama 2:18
☑ Nudity, adult situations, explicit language, violence
Dir: Sidney Lumet *Cast:* Richard Burton, Peter Firth, Colin Blakely, Joan Plowright, Eileen Atkins, Jenny Agutter
▶ Disillusioned shrink Burton probes the mind of teenager Firth, who blinded six horses. Burton begins to envy the troubled youth's passion. Thought-provoking, passionate drama about insanity vs. repression from the play by Peter Shaffer. Overly literal direction by Lumet (especially in the horse-blinding scene), dynamic Oscar-nominated work by Burton.

ERASERHEAD 1978
☆ NR Horror 1:30 B&W
☑ Adult humor
Dir: David Lynch *Cast:* John Nance, Charlotte Stewart, Allen Joseph, Jeanne Bates, Judith Anna Roberts
▶ Grotesquely fascinating cult film from director Lynch. In a squalid tenement apartment, a horribly mutated baby is born to a repressed couple. Exploration of the relationship between monster and man marked Lynch's auspicious but unsettling feature debut.

ERNEST GOES TO CAMP 1987
★★ PG Comedy 1:33
☑ Mild violence
Dir: John Cherry *Cast:* Jim Varney, Victoria Racimo, John Vernon, Iron Eyes Cody, Lyle Alzado

▶ Film debut for Varney's popular TV commercial character has Ernest baby-sitting six tough inner-city kids at Camp Kikakee. Meanwhile, an evil building contractor tries to trick Indian chief Iron Eyes Cody into giving up the camp's lease. Critics hated this film, but audiences were delighted by its goofy sense of humor and outlandish slapstick stunts. (CC)

ERNEST SAVES CHRISTMAS 1988
★ ★ PG Comedy 1:29
☑ Explicit language
Dir: John Cherry *Cast:* Jim Varney, Douglas Seale, Oliver Clark, Noelle Parker, Gailard Sartain, Billie Bird
▶ Seale plays Santa Claus, eager to retire and looking for a replacement, but his first choice, Florida kiddie show host Clark, turns down the offer. Worse yet, customs men seize Santa's reindeer and a teen hoodlum swipes his bag of gifts. To the rescue comes oddball cab driver Varney. Fans of Varney's mugging, rubber-faced Ernest P. Worrell, made famous in TV commercials and *Ernest Goes to Camp*, won't be disappointed, but others may miss the point.

ERRAND BOY, THE 1962
★ ★ NR Comedy 1:32 B&W
Dir: Jerry Lewis *Cast:* Jerry Lewis, Brian Donlevy, Howard McNear, Fritz Feld, Sig Ruman, Doodles Weaver
▶ Wacky Lewis gets Hollywood movie studio job and Tinseltown will never be the same. *Bonanza* stars Lorne Greene, Michael Landon, Dan Blocker, and Pernell Roberts, along with Stooge Joe Besser, have cameos.

ESCAPE ARTIST, THE 1982
★ ★ ★ PG Drama 1:36
☑ Explicit language
Dir: Caleb Deschanel *Cast:* Griffin O'-Neal, Raul Julia, Teri Garr, Joan Hackett, Gabriel Dell, Desi Arnaz
▶ Whimsical, family-oriented story about famous magician's gifted son O'Neal (in his film debut) who uses his skills to expose mayor Arnaz's corrupt administration. Plenty of amusing magic tricks for children; adults will appreciate the unusual set design and nostalgic cameos by Jackie Coogan and former Bowery Boys Dell and Huntz Hall. From the makers of *The Black Stallion*.

ESCAPE FROM ALCATRAZ 1979
★ ★ ★ ★ PG Mystery-Suspense 1:52
☑ Adult situations, explicit language, violence
Dir: Don Siegel *Cast:* Clint Eastwood, Patrick McGoohan, Roberts Blossom, Jack Thibeau, Fred Ward, Paul Benjamin
▶ Taut, authentic account of the only successful escape from the notorious Alcatraz Island prison. Eastwood is Frank Morris, a hardened con who masterminds the breakout with his pals Thibeau and Ward. McGoohan plays a remarkably chilling warden. Expert direction and a streamlined, unsentimental script add to the suspense.

ESCAPE FROM FORT BRAVO 1953
★ ★ ★ NR Western 1:38
Dir: John Sturges *Cast:* William Holden, Eleanor Parker, John Forsythe, William Demarest, Polly Bergen
▶ Above-average Western with Holden giving a gritty performance as the strict warden of a Union stockade in Civil War Arizona. He falls in love with Southern spy Parker, who engineers the escape of important Confederate captain Forsythe. Holden rounds up the prisoners, only to fall prey to an Indian ambush.

ESCAPE FROM NEW YORK 1981
★ ★ ★ R Sci-Fi 1:39
☑ Brief nudity, adult situations, explicit language, graphic violence
Dir: John Carpenter *Cast:* Kurt Russell, Lee Van Cleef, Ernest Borgnine, Donald Pleasence, Isaac Hayes, Adrienne Barbeau
▶ Manhattan in 1997 is a walled-in maximum security prison for murderers, terrorists, and perverts. Hayes, the Duke of New York, kidnaps President Pleasence; war hero-turned-convict Snake Plissken (Russell) has twenty-four hours to free him. Brutal, lightning-paced stunts, inventive special effects and Russell's marvelously macho hero will delight action fans. Borgnine is amusing as the Big Apple's last cabbie.

ESCAPE FROM THE PLANET OF THE APES 1971
★ ★ ★ G Sci-Fi 1:38
Dir: Don Taylor *Cast:* Roddy McDowall, Kim Hunter, Bradford Dillman, Natalie Trundy, Eric Braeden, Sal Mineo
▶ Third episode in the simian series is set in the human world of 1971. Apes Cornelius (McDowall), Zira (Hunter), and Milo (Mineo) flee their exploding world to Earth in the spaceship Charlton Heston

left behind in the first film. Fearing that pregnant Zira's child will cause the overthrow of the human race, U.S. government officials hunt the "dangerous" chimps. Two more sequels followed. (CC)

ESCAPE TO ATHENA 1979 British
★★★★ **PG Action-Adventure 1:42**
☑ Explicit language, violence
Dir: George Pan Cosmatos *Cast:* Roger Moore, Telly Savalas, David Niven, Claudia Cardinale, Richard Roundtree, Sonny Bono
▶ Odd World War II comedy-adventure about an unlikely group of Allied POWs who team up with art-loving Nazi warden Moore and Greek Resistance leader Savalas to both destroy a German missile base and loot ancient art treasures. Elliott Gould and Stefanie Powers play USO entertainers who join the plot when their plane is shot down.

ESCAPE TO WITCH MOUNTAIN 1975
★★★★★ **G Fantasy 1:37**
Dir: John Hough *Cast:* Eddie Albert, Ray Milland, Donald Pleasence, Kim Richards, Ike Eisenmann, Denver Pyle
▶ Monterey provides the setting for an amiable Disney fantasy about Richards and Eisenmann, orphans with peculiar powers who are coerced by Milland and Pleasence into predicting the stock market. Albert is a gruff old bachelor who helps the kids escape. Smooth entertainment features some unusual sci-fi twists.

E.T. THE EXTRA-TERRESTRIAL 1982
★★★★★ **PG Family/Fantasy 2:00**
☑ Explicit language, mild violence
Dir: Steven Spielberg *Cast:* Dee Wallace, Henry Thomas, Drew Barrymore, Peter Coyote, Robert MacNaughton
▶ Extraterrestrial, stranded on Earth, is befriended by young Thomas. Soon the kid's brother MacNaughton, sister Barrymore, and mom Wallace share the secret but government authorities lurk close behind. The #1 box-office champ of all time, Spielberg's fantasy weaves a magical spell, combining realistic suburban detail with flights of fancy, and the moving Thomas/E.T. relationship puts the film's many imitators to shame. Uplifting, sweet, original, and E.T. is totally convincing. A Best Picture nominee.

EUREKA 1984 British
★ **R Drama 2:09**
☑ Nudity, explicit language, violence
Dir: Nicolas Roeg *Cast:* Gene Hackman, Theresa Russell, Rutger Hauer, Jane Lapotaire, Ed Lauter, Mickey Rourke
▶ Gold prospector Hackman strikes it rich in Canada, but is too paranoid about enemies to enjoy his success. Retiring to a tropical island, he watches wife Lapotaire sink into alcoholism and daughter Russell be seduced by gigolo Hauer. Gloomy melodrama about obsession has a typically creditable performance from Hackman.

EVEL KNIEVEL 1971
★ **PG Biography 1:30**
☑ Mild violence
Dir: Marvin J. Chomsky *Cast:* George Hamilton, Sue Lyon, Rod Cameron, Bert Freed, Dub Taylor
▶ Campy biography of Evel Knievel (Hamilton), king of stuntmen, whose daredevil motorcycle jumps earned him fortune and fame. Story traces his youth in Butte, Montana, to the jump over the fountain at Caesar's Palace that almost killed him.

EVERYBODY'S ALL-AMERICAN 1988
★★★★ **R Drama 2:07**
☑ Brief nudity, adult situations, explicit language, violence
Dir: Taylor Hackford *Cast:* Dennis Quaid, Jessica Lange, Timothy Hutton, John Goodman, Raymond Baker, Carl Lumbly
▶ Football star Quaid, Louisiana's "Grey Ghost," and beauty queen Lange seem destined for a perfect marriage, but their relationship sours once Quaid's sports career is over. Ambitious soap opera covering a twenty-five-year span is smoothly entertaining rather than incisive. Goodman, a bigoted tackle addicted to gambling, and Lumbly, a black athlete defeated by discrimination, are impressive.

EVERY WHICH WAY BUT LOOSE 1978
★★★★ **PG Comedy 1:55**
☑ Brief nudity, explicit language, violence
Dir: James Fargo *Cast:* Clint Eastwood, Sondra Locke, Geoffrey Lewis, Beverly D'Angelo, Ruth Gordon
▶ Eastwood, playing a boozy truck driver and barroom brawler, chases beautiful singer Locke from California to Denver. Along the way he fights off slimy bikers and redneck cops. Extremely broad comedy was a gigantic pop hit, inspiring the sequel *Any Which Way You Can.* Filled with wacky fights, great country-

western songs (by Mel Tillis, Charlie Rich, and others), and scene-stealing comic relief from Clyde, Eastwood's ribald pet orangutan.

EVIL, THE 1978
★★★★ R Horror 1:28
☑ Explicit language, graphic violence
Dir: Gus Trikonis *Cast:* Richard Crenna, Joanna Pettet, Victor Buono, Andrew Prine, Cassie Yates
▶ Doctor Crenna rents huge gothic mansion in the country for his drug rehabilitation summer program. The building is haunted by the Evil One (Buono), who imprisons the group inside. Scary excursion into the realm of the supernatural that won favorable critical attention.

EVIL DEAD, THE 1983
★ NR Horror 1:25
☑ Adult situations, graphic violence
Dir: Sam Raimi *Cast:* Bruce Campbell, Ellen Sandweiss, Betsy Baker, Hal Delrich, Sarah York
▶ Energetic blend of fun and fear. Clean-cut kids camp out in a deserted cabin with resurrected evil spirits. Grisly, campy special effects include contorted faces, dismembered limbs, and geysers of spurting blood. Sequel appeared four years later.

EVIL DEAD II 1987
★ X Horror 1:25
☑ Explicit language, graphic violence
Dir: Sam Raimi *Cast:* Bruce Campbell, Sarah Berry, Dan Hicks, Cassie Wesley, Rick Francis
▶ Campbell and girlfriend Berry go to mountain cabin where they find recording which literally raises the dead; Campbell must fight the demons when they turn Berry into one of them. Skillful camerawork and inventive humorous touches bring horrific life to genre clichés; however, silly-looking monster and excessive violence wear out viewer patience.

EVIL THAT MEN DO, THE 1984
★★★ R Action-Adventure 1:30
☑ Nudity, adult situations, explicit language, graphic violence
Dir: J. Lee Thompson *Cast:* Charles Bronson, Theresa Saldana, Jose Ferrer, Joseph Maher, Raymond St. Jacques, John Glover
▶ Slickly made, vengeance-glorifying actioner stars Bronson as a former political assassin. He's recruited out of retirement to rub out Dr. Molloch (Maher), an evil sadist working for a fascist Central American government. Filmed entirely in Mexico. **(CC)**

EVIL UNDER THE SUN 1982 British
★★★★ PG Mystery-Suspense 1:56
☑ Explicit language, violence
Dir: Guy Hamilton *Cast:* Peter Ustinov, Maggie Smith, Diana Rigg, James Mason, Roddy McDowall, Sylvia Miles
▶ Agatha Christie's super-sleuth Hercule Poirot (Ustinov) sets out to salvage his reputation and solve the murder of famous, bitchy actress Rigg found strangled at a sunny Adriatic resort. Smith, McDowall, and Mason are among the many guests with potential motives. Soundtrack is an anthology of Cole Porter hits.

EXCALIBUR 1981 British
★★★★ PG Action-Adventure 2:20
☑ Nudity, adult situations, violence
Dir: John Boorman *Cast:* Nigel Terry, Helen Mirren, Nicholas Clay, Cherie Lunghi, Nicol Williamson, Robert Addie
▶ Beautiful but long-winded historical epic traces the rise of King Arthur (Terry), the fall of Camelot, the destruction of the evil Mordred (Addie), the quest for the Holy Grail, and the sword-in-the-stone legend. Williamson is superb as Merlin, a virile wizard/trickster. Filmed in breathtaking Irish locales. Adapted from the Malory classic *Le Morte d'Arthur*.

EXECUTIONER, THE 1970 British
★★ PG Action-Adventure 1:47
☑ Adult situations
Dir: Sam Wanamaker *Cast:* George Peppard, Joan Collins, Keith Michell, Judy Geeson, Oscar Homolka
▶ British intelligence agent Peppard tracks down fellow agent Michell suspected of double dealing with the Soviets, but is sidetracked by an old flame. Talky spy-drama that's heavier on drama than action.

EXECUTIONER'S SONG, THE 1982
★★★★ NR Biography/MFTV 3:20
☑ Nudity, adult situations, violence
Dir: Lawrence Schiller *Cast:* Tommy Lee Jones, Rosanna Arquette, Christine Lahti, Eli Wallach, Steven Keats, Jordan Clarke
▶ Norman Mailer adapted his own bestseller about Gary Gilmore (Jones), the parolee who turned to robbery and murder when he was unable to make it in the outside world and then begged the state to execute him so he could die with

dignity. Searing portrait of a man who could find no peace in this life; bravura Emmy-winning performance by Jones complemented by Arquette's sizzling turn as his girlfriend Nicole Baker.

EXECUTIVE ACTION 1973
★★ PG Drama 1:31
☑ Adult situations, violence
Dir: David Miller *Cast:* Burt Lancaster, Robert Ryan, Will Geer, Gilbert Green, Ed Lauter, Deanna Darrin
▶ Political melodrama explains the assassination of John F. Kennedy in terms of a military conspiracy instigated by high-placed officials Lancaster and Ryan. Far-fetched in the extreme, with an exploitative use of Dallas newsreel footage. Ryan's last film.

EXODUS 1960
★★★ NR Drama 3:33
Dir: Otto Preminger *Cast:* Paul Newman, Eva Marie Saint, Lee J. Cobb, Sal Mineo, Ralph Richardson
▶ Preminger's large-scale epic about the founding of the state of Israel details the efforts of Jewish underground rebel Newman leading the battles against the British and the Arabs. Overlong but exciting with a sweeping, Oscar-winning Ernest Gold score. Based on Leon Uris's best-seller.

EXORCIST, THE 1973
★★★★ R Horror 1:58
☑ Adult situations, explicit language graphic violence
Dir: William Friedkin *Cast:* Ellen Burstyn, Linda Blair, Max Von Sydow, Jason Miller, Lee J. Cobb
▶ Well-wrought horror classic of extraordinarily powerful impact adapted from William Peter Blatty's best-selling novel about a demonically possessed child. When Blair, daughter of movie star Burstyn, is transformed into a repellent monster, young priest Miller tries and fails to rid her body of the spirit. He calls in Father Merrin (Von Sydow) for an elaborate exorcism. Nominated for ten Oscars including Best Picture, Actress, and Director; won for Sound and Blatty's screenplay. One of the top-grossing films of all time.

EXORCIST II: THE HERETIC 1977
★★ R Horror 1:43
☑ Explicit language, violence
Dir: John Boorman *Cast:* Linda Blair, Richard Burton, Louise Fletcher, Kitty Winn, James Earl Jones, Max Von Sydow

▶ Chilling sequel to the 1974 megahit resumes Regan's (Blair) story four years later. Subjected to terrifying nightmares, she's treated by psychoanalyst Fletcher and, under hypnosis, discovers she's still possessed by the demon Pazuzu. Father Lamont (Burton) searches throughout Africa for Kakumo (Jones), who'd been exorcised of Pazuzu years ago by Father Merrin (Sydow). Professional cast, good production values and special effects.

EXPERIENCE PREFERRED . . . BUT NOT ESSENTIAL 1983 British
★ PG Drama 1:14
☑ Nudity, adult situations
Dir: Peter John Duffell *Cast:* Elizabeth Edmonds, Sue Wallace, Geraldine Griffith, Karen Meagher, Ron Bain
▶ Edmonds is an innocent college student working at a Welsh seaside summer resort in 1962. With the help of Scottish chef Bain, she is initiated into certain rites of passage. Charmingly told; honest and surprising, but may be too "small" and British for some tastes.

EXPLORERS 1985
★★★ PG Sci-Fi 1:50
☑ Explicit language, mild violence
Dir: Joe Dante *Cast:* Ethan Hawke, River Phoenix, Jason Presson, Amanda Peterson, Dick Miller
▶ Junior high misfits—dreamer Hawke, computer goon Phoenix, and rebel Presson—create a blue soap bubble that can rocket to outer space. Enchanting story and well-executed high-flying effects. **(CC)**

EXPOSED 1983
★★ R Mystery-Suspense 1:39
☑ Nudity, adult situations, explicit language, violence
Dir: James Toback *Cast:* Nastassja Kinski, Rudolf Nureyev, Ian McShane, Harvey Keitel, Bibi Andersson
▶ Kinski, a young Midwestern beauty, seeks her fortune in New York, where she is discovered by fashion photographer McShane. Her luck changes when eccentric violinist Nureyev enlists her to thwart vicious South American terrorist Keitel, who has a weakness for pretty women. Bizarre political thriller is often confusing and senseless.

EXTERMINATOR, THE 1980
★★★ R Action-Adventure 1:41
☑ Explicit language, graphic violence
Dir: James Glickenhaus *Cast:* Christo-

pher George, Samantha Eggar, Robert Ginty, Steve James

▶ Low-budget melodrama about former-soldier-turned-vigilante Ginty who seeks revenge on the punks who attacked and paralyzed his friend. He kills them and is pursued, in turn, by police. Excessively violent production was successful enough to spawn a sequel.

EXTERMINATOR 2 1984
★ ★ ★ **R Action-Adventure 1:28**
☑ Nudity, adult situations, explicit language, graphic violence
Dir: Mark Buntzman *Cast:* Robert Ginty, Deborah Geffner, Frankie Faison, Mario Van Peebles, Bruce Smolanoff
▶ In this sequel, urban crime avenger Ginty fights New York punks with his own special weapon, an armed city sanitation truck. Every bit as violent and action-packed as the original. With Geffner as his dancer girlfriend who gets her legs broken, inciting Ginty to get revenge.

EXTREME PREJUDICE 1987
★ ★ ★ **R Action-Adventure 1:45**
☑ Brief nudity, adult situations, explicit language, graphic violence
Dir: Walter Hill *Cast:* Nick Nolte, Powers Boothe, Rip Torn, Maria Conchita Alonso, Michael Ironside
▶ Texas Ranger Nolte and his partner Torn battle white-suited drug peddler Boothe and Ironside's high-tech bank robbers in an effort to keep their border town safe. When Boothe kidnaps Alonso, a singer in a honky tonk, Nolte infiltrates his Mexican hideout to rescue her—unaware that Ironside is planning a massacre there. Highly stylized mayhem convincingly updates Western themes in contemporary settings.

EXTREMITIES 1986
★ ★ ★ ★ **R Drama 1:30**
☑ Rape, nudity, explicit language, violence
Dir: Robert M. Young *Cast:* Farrah Fawcett, James Russo, Alfre Woodard, Diana Scarwid, Sandy Martin
▶ Unpleasant but gripping story of Fawcett who turns the tables on rapist Russo. Brutal, tense and talky. Fawcett's striking performance as victim-vanquisher catapulted her beyond "Charlie's Angels" status. Based on William Mastrosimone's off-Broadway hit, with Fawcett and Russo reprising their stage roles. **(CC)**

EYE FOR AN EYE, AN 1981
★ ★ ★ **R Martial Arts 1:44**

☑ Nudity, adult situations, explicit language, violence
Dir: Steve Carver *Cast:* Chuck Norris, Christopher Lee, Richard Roundtree, Mako, Matt Clark
▶ Actioner pits kung-fu goodness against human madness. Norris stars as an ex-cop called in to solve the murder of a TV newswoman. He discovers she was investigating a large heroin-smuggling ring and proceeds to dish out physical punishment to a small army of stuntmen. Lots of bone-shattering encounters and narrow escapes to please kick-fight fans.

EYE OF THE NEEDLE 1981
★ ★ ★ ★ **R Mystery-Suspense 1:52**
☑ Nudity, adult situations, violence
Dir: Richard Marquand *Cast:* Donald Sutherland, Kate Nelligan, Ian Bannen, Christopher Cazenove, Philip Martin Brown
▶ While attempting to complete a crucial mission during World War II, ruthless German spy Sutherland is shipwrecked on a deserted Scottish island and befriended by lonely woman Nelligan. Despite the presence of Cazenove, her crippled, embittered husband, they have an affair. Based on Ken Follett's best-selling suspense novel.

EYE OF THE TIGER 1987
★ ★ ★ ★ **R Action-Adventure 1:32**
☑ Explicit language, violence
Dir: Richard Sarafian *Cast:* Gary Busey, Yaphet Kotto, Seymour Cassel, William Smith, Denise Galik
▶ Vigilante film pits lean and mean Busey against an army of desert bikers who've killed his wife and traumatized his daughter. Using tricks he learned in Vietnam and prison (he was framed for a murder he didn't commit), Busey begins his one-man cleanup operation. When his daughter is kidnapped from the hospital, Busey really gets mad. Good-looking vengeance exploitation film combines *Walking Tall* and *Death Wish*.

EYES OF A STRANGER 1981
★ ★ ★ **R Mystery-Suspense 1:25**
☑ Nudity, adult situations, explicit language, violence
Dir: Ken Wiederhorn *Cast:* Lauren Tewes, Jennifer Jason Leigh, John DiSanti, Peter DePre, Gwen Lewis
▶ TV star Tewes makes her feature-film debut as a Miami newscaster who discovers the identity of a killer/rapist. Coin-

cidentally, he lives in her apartment building and, when he corners Tewes's deaf-dumb-blind sister, the film culminates in a vividly bloody and gruesome finale. Strictly a stalk-and-slaughter affair offering the molestation and murder of women as entertainment; with shopworn clichés, including a woman-in-the-shower scene.

EYES OF LAURA MARS, THE 1978
★★★★ R Mystery-Suspense 1:43
☑ Nudity, explicit language, graphic violence
Dir: Irvin Kershner   *Cast:* Faye Dunaway, Tommy Lee Jones, Raul Julia, René Auberjonois, Brad Dourif
▶ Classy and haunting whodunit with Dunaway as a chic fashion photographer obsessed and possessed by deadly accurate premonitions about a series of murders involving her friends and associates. Though she can see the murders she is powerless to prevent them. Magnetic Jones is the policeman assigned to the case. Screenplay by John Carpenter and David Zelag Goodman (from a story by Carpenter) provides a twisty, kinky, and genuinely scary conclusion to this stylish thriller. Title song "Prisoner" sung by Barbra Streisand. **(CC)**

EYEWITNESS 1981
★★★ R Mystery-Suspense 1:42
☑ Adult situations, explicit language, violence
Dir: Peter Yates   *Cast:* William Hurt, Sigourney Weaver, Christopher Plummer, Kenneth McMillan, Pamela Reed
▶ When a man is murdered in his building, janitor Hurt pretends to know something about the crime in order to entice the interest of beautiful TV news reporter Weaver. Quirky, interesting thriller with less emphasis on conventional suspense (though there's plenty) than on the unusual love story and complex characterizations. Terrific dialogue (especially Hurt's deadpan come-ons) from writer Steve Tesich, skillful use of New York City locations, and great performances.

FABULOUS DORSEYS, THE 1947
★★ NR Biography/Musical 1:28 B&W
Dir: Alfred E. Green   *Cast:* Tommy Dorsey, Jimmy Dorsey, Janet Blair, Paul Whiteman, William Lundigan, Sara Allgood
▶ Sanitized biography of the feuding big band leaders and their musical growth from a grim Pennsylvania steel town to the top of the charts. Songs include "Marie," "The Object of My Affection," "Green Eyes," and a wild version of "Art's Blues" by Art Tatum and Charlie Barnet.

FACE IN THE CROWD, A 1957
★★ NR Drama 2:06 B&W
Dir: Elia Kazan   *Cast:* Andy Griffith, Patricia Neal, Anthony Franciosa, Walter Matthau, Lee Remick
▶ Fascinating, still topical look at a media-created monster. Homespun hobo Lonesome Rhodes (Griffith), promoted into TV stardom by reporter Neal, rises in politics but is corrupted by power. Griffith, totally convincing in his first movie role, is ably supported by Neal, Matthau, and a breathtakingly beautiful Remick as the teenage baton twirler who is Lonesome's undoing. Incisive script and direction from the *On the Waterfront* team.

FADE TO BLACK 1980
★ R Horror 1:42
☑ Brief nudity, adult situations, explicit language, violence
Dir: Vernon Zimmerman   *Cast:* Dennis Christopher, Linda Kerridge, Tim Thomerson, Morgan Paull, Marya Small
▶ Young film buff Christopher exacts revenge on his various tormentors by staging their murders in the style of his favorite movies. Mixture of suspense and comedy doesn't always gel but contains good shocks, lots of cinematic references, and decent performances from Christopher and Australian Marilyn Monroe look-alike Kerridge.

FAHRENHEIT 451 1967 British
★ NR Sci-Fi 1:52
Dir: François Truffaut   *Cast:* Julie Christie, Oskar Werner, Cyril Cusack, Anton Diffring, Jeremy Spenser
▶ Books are outlawed and burned in a futuristic totalitarian state. Fireman Montag (Werner) turns against the government when young rebel Christie introduces him to the joys of reading. Truffaut's visually stylized adaptation of the Ray Bradbury novel is literate and intelligent.

FAIL-SAFE 1964
★★★★ NR Drama 1:52 B&W
Dir: Sidney Lumet   *Cast:* Henry Fonda, Walter Matthau, Fritz Weaver, Dan O'Herlihy, Sorrell Booke, Larry Hagman
▶ Supposedly error-proof codes are scrambled, sending bombers armed with nuclear weapons to destroy Moscow. As President, Fonda pleads with the Rus-

sians not to retaliate while his military advisors try to stop the planes. Uniformly strong performances add to the nail-biting tension in this intelligent adaptation of the Eugene Burdick/Harvey Wheeler best-seller.

FAKE OUT 1982
★★ NR Drama 1:36
☑ Rape, nudity, adult situations, explicit language, violence
Dir: Matt Cimber *Cast:* Pia Zadora, Telly Savalas, Desi Arnaz, Jr., Larry Storch
▶ Las Vegas entertainer/mobster's girl Zadora is thrown into prison after refusing to testify against her boyfriend. Even though she leads the inmates in Jane Fonda exercise classes, they gang-rape her anyway. She agrees to talk, falls in love with her police bodyguard, dodges several gun barrages, and takes twelve baths. After she and her bodyguard turn the tables on crooked detective Savalas, they win $50,000 at the roulette wheel. Cheap and trashy entertainment with plenty of unintentional laughs.

FALCON AND THE SNOWMAN, THE 1985
★★★★ R Biography/Drama 2:11
☑ Nudity, adult situations, explicit language, violence
Dir: John Schlesinger *Cast:* Timothy Hutton, Sean Penn, David Suchet, Lori Singer, Pat Hingle, Dorian Harewood
▶ True story of Christopher Boyce (Hutton) and Daulton Lee (Penn), suburban California kids who sold secrets to the Russians. Downbeat but absorbing docudrama made with craftsmanlike precision by director Schlesinger. Penn is stunning in a performance that's flamboyant without ever seeming overdone; Hutton is equally effective as the quieter Boyce. **(CC)**

FALCON'S BROTHER, THE 1942
★★ NR Mystery-Suspense 1:03 B&W
Dir: Stanley Logan *Cast:* George Sanders, Tom Conway, Jane Randolph, Don Barclay, Cliff Clark, Ed Gargan
▶ Writer Michael Arlen's dashing troubleshooter Sanders, aided by his brother Conway, investigates a ring of Nazi spies in South America. When Sanders is murdered, Conway assumes his role as the Falcon and solves the case. Fair example of the B-movie series has one unusual aspect: Sanders, tired of his role, was killed

off and replaced by his real-life brother Conway.

FALCON TAKES OVER, THE 1942
★★ NR Mystery-Suspense 1:03 B&W
Dir: Irving Reis *Cast:* George Sanders, Lynn Bari, James Gleason, Allen Jenkins, Helen Gilbert, Ward Bond
▶ Third in a series of modest B-films based on Michael Arlen's roguish detective is a loose adaptation of Raymond Chandler's *Farewell, My Lovely* (remade with Dick Powell in 1944's *Murder My Sweet* and again with Robert Mitchum in 1975 under the original title). Bond plays Moose Malloy, a hulking ex-con who hires the Falcon (Sanders) to find his old girlfriend. Bari is a reporter who helps crack the case.

FALLEN IDOL, THE 1948 British
★★★ NR Drama 1:34 B&W
Dir: Carol Reed *Cast:* Ralph Richardson, Michele Morgan, Bobby Henrey, Sonia Dresdel, Denis O'Dea, Jack Hawkins
▶ Deceptively low-key suspense story about ambassador's young son Henrey who idolizes Richardson, a butler trapped in an unhappy marriage to Dresdel. When she dies in a suspicious accident, the boy tries to protect Richardson from the police. Engrossing, superbly crafted film successfully captures a child's point of view without stinting on tension. Won Oscar nominations for director Reed and screenwriter Graham Greene, who next collaborated on *The Third Man*.

FALLING IN LOVE 1984
★★★★ PG-13 Romance 1:46
☑ Adult situations, explicit language
Dir: Ulu Grosbard *Cast:* Robert De Niro, Meryl Streep, Harvey Keitel, Jane Kaczmarek, David Clennon, Dianne Wiest
▶ Westchester commuters De Niro and Streep, each happily married, fall in love. Michael Christopher's script realistically captures the way two ordinary (and often inarticulate) people might stumble into romance. Old-fashioned love story with crisp cinematography, nice use of New York City locations, pleasant Dave Grusin score, and sweet, scaled-down performances from two acting heavyweights. **(CC)**

FALLING IN LOVE AGAIN 1980
★★ PG Drama 1:39
☑ Adult situations, explicit language

Dir: Steven Paul   *Cast:* Elliott Gould, Susannah York, Stuart Paul, Kaye Ballard, Michelle Pfeiffer
▶ Wistful and modestly entertaining story of husband Gould and wife York reminiscing about youthful times. While vacationing in New York, they rediscover their lost love. Debut directorial effort from then twenty-one-year-old Paul.

FALL OF THE ROMAN EMPIRE, THE 1964
★★ NR Drama 2:26
Dir: Anthony Mann   *Cast:* Sophia Loren, Stephen Boyd, James Mason, Alec Guinness, Christopher Plummer, Omar Sharif
▶ Power corrupts Emperor Commodus (Plummer), bringing about the decline and fall of Rome despite the efforts of noble reformer Mason and rival Boyd in this big, colorful epic that shows its massive budget. Strong cast, sumptuous sets, wall-to-wall armies and action make up for excess length and flawed story.

FAME 1980
★★★ R Drama/Musical 2:13
☑ Nudity, adult situations, explicit language
Dir: Alan Parker   *Cast:* Irene Cara, Lee Curreri, Paul McCrane, Barry Miller, Gene Anthony Ray, Maureen Teefy
▶ Feverish musical drama follows students of New York's High School for the Performing Arts from opening auditions to graduation. Some contrived, melodramatic plotting (especially in Cara's dealings with a sleazeball photographer) but plenty of music, dancing, humor (watch for one student's O. J. Simpson impression), stunning cinematography and youthful high spirits. Won Best Song and Score Oscars. Ray and fellow cast members Debbie Allen and Albert Hague re-created their roles for the TV series.

FAMILY, THE 1973 Italian
★★ R Action-Adventure 1:34
☑ Explicit language, violence
Dir: Sergio Sollima   *Cast:* Charles Bronson, Jill Ireland, Telly Savalas, Umberto Orsini, George Savalas
▶ Hired killer Bronson is romanced by Ireland, a police agent trying to solve some murders. Bronson must ambush her as the cops pick up his trail. Straightforward story provides enough action and violence to satisfy hard-core fans; sturdy performances by Bronson and Savalas

but rather tacky-looking production values.

FAMILY JEWELS, THE 1965
★★ NR Comedy 1:40
Dir: Jerry Lewis   *Cast:* Jerry Lewis, Sebastian Cabot, Donna Butterworth, Gene Baylor, Milton Frome, Herbie Faye
▶ A field day for Lewis fans: he wrote, produced, directed, and played seven roles in this sentimental comedy. Young Butterworth inherits a fortune, then must decide which of seven uncles (that's right, they're all Jerry) will be her guardian. Nonfans beware.

FAMILY PLOT 1976
★★★★ PG Mystery-Suspense 2:00
☑ Explicit language, violence
Dir: Alfred Hitchcock   *Cast:* Karen Black, Bruce Dern, Barbara Harris, William Devane, Ed Lauter, Cathleen Nesbitt
▶ Possibly bogus psychic Harris and companion Dern are hired to find long-lost heir Devane, who happens to be extortionist in midst of kidnapping scheme. Lighthearted mystery/comedy, Hitchcock's last effort, finds the director in sprightly form. Some nifty chases and filmmaking with a very appealing performance by Harris.

FAN, THE 1981
★★ R Mystery-Suspense 1:35
☑ Adult situations, explicit language, graphic violence
Dir: Edward Bianchi   *Cast:* Lauren Bacall, James Garner, Maureen Stapleton, Michael Biehn
▶ Bacall, a well-known movie star rehearsing her first Broadway musical, is stalked by psychotic fan Biehn. Rather one-note performance by Biehn but Bacall anchors the film with her solid, sympathetic performance. Straightforward thriller with dark mood, plot holes, and quite graphic violence.

FANCY PANTS 1950
★★★★ NR Comedy 1:33
Dir: George Marshall   *Cast:* Bob Hope, Lucille Ball, Bruce Cabot, Jack Kirkwood, Lea Penman, Hugh French
▶ Hope does a funny impersonation of an Englishman with a very stiff upper lip who accompanies rough-hewn oil businesswoman Ball to her home on the New Mexico frontier. Riotous cricket match and encounter with Rough Rider Teddy Roosevelt highlight this genial remake of 1935's *Ruggles of Red Gap.*

FANDANGO 1985
★★ PG Comedy 1:31
☑ Brief nudity, explicit language
Dir: Kevin Reynolds *Cast:* Kevin Costner, Sam Robards, Judd Nelson, Chuck Bush, Brian Cesak
▶ Five University of Texas college buddies have a final fling before assuming official adulthood. Nelson stars as the group scold and Costner as the ringleader. Sweet, stylish, and romantic. Originally a student film called *Proof*, the film attracted Stepven Spielberg's attention and was expanded into a feature.

FANNY 1961
★★★★ NR Drama 2:13
Dir: Joshua Logan *Cast:* Leslie Caron, Maurice Chevalier, Charles Boyer, Horst Buchholz, Baccaloni, Lionel Jeffries
▶ Ambitious Buchholz abandons pregnant girlfriend Caron for the sea; she sadly enters a marriage of convenience with the adoring but older Chevalier. American adaptation of Marcel Pagnol's Marseilles Trilogy (which also included *Marius* and *Cesar*) was originally a Broadway musical scored by Harold Rome; film inexplicably omits songs, but earthy, sentimental plot is still moving. Received five Oscar nominations, including one for Jack Cardiff's beautiful photography.

FANNY AND ALEXANDER 1983 Swedish
★★ R Drama 3:11
☑ Brief nudity, adult situations, explicit language
Dir: Ingmar Bergman *Cast:* Pernilla Allwin, Bertil Guve, Ewa Froling, Jan Malmsjo, Harriet Andersson, Erland Josephson
▶ Siblings Fanny and Alexander are raised in a warmhearted theatrical family, then must adjust when their father dies and mom remarries a stern pastor. Rich, almost Dickensian sense of character, sensitive evocation of childhood viewpoint, exquisite cinematography, and lavish period details. Very demanding but rewarding for discerning viewers. Four Oscars, including Best Foreign Film and Cinematography. Dubbed.

FANTASTIC VOYAGE 1966
★★★★ NR Sci-Fi 1:40
Dir: Richard Fleischer *Cast:* Stephen Boyd, Raquel Welch, Edmond O'Brien, Donald Pleasence, Arthur O'Connell
▶ Scientists and their craft are minaturized and injected inside defector's body

in order to save his life, but there's a spy on board who must be handled. Eye dazzling: imaginative special effects and production design, plus Raquel in tight-fitting suit.

FAR COUNTRY, THE 1955
★★★ NR Western 1:37
Dir: Anthony Mann *Cast:* James Stewart, Ruth Roman, Corinne Calvet, Walter Brennan, John McIntire, Jay C. Flippen
▶ Stewart and Brennan bring a herd of cattle from Wyoming to Alaska to exploit the gold boom but lose the steers to evil sheriff McIntire. Stewart refuses to take revenge until two close friends are murdered. First-rate Western written by Borden Chase features a stinging performance by Stewart and incisive direction by Mann.

FAREWELL, MY LOVELY 1975 British
★★★★ R Mystery-Suspense 1:31
☑ Brief nudity, adult situations, explicit language, violence
Dir: Dick Richards *Cast:* Robert Mitchum, Charlotte Rampling, John Ireland, Sylvia Miles, Jack O'Halloran, Sylvester Stallone
▶ In 1940s L.A., private eye Philip Marlowe (Mitchum) is hired by overgrown ex-con O'Halloran to track down ex-lover Rampling. Solidly plotted, true-blue adaptation of Raymond Chandler novel (filmed previously as *Murder, My Sweet* and *The Falcon Takes Over*) expertly evokes neon-drenched film noir atmosphere. Terrific cast (Miles was Oscar-nominated) led by Mitchum, who is simply perfect as the weary Marlowe.

FAREWELL TO ARMS, A 1957
★★★★ NR Romance 2:28
Dir: Charles Vidor *Cast:* Rock Hudson, Jennifer Jones, Vittorio De Sica, Oscar Homolka, Mercedes McCambridge
▶ During World War I, American ambulance driver Hudson falls in love with English nurse Jones but the romance ends tragically. Works well as a romantic tearjerker. Fine supporting turn by Oscar-nominated De Sica as Hudson's doctor friend. Adaptation of Ernest Hemingway novel (filmed previously in 1932 with Gary Cooper and Helen Hayes) was final film for producer David O. Selznick.

FAREWELL TO THE KING 1988
★★★ PG-13 Drama 1:57
☑ Adult situations, violence
Dir: John Milius *Cast:* Nick Nolte, Nigel

Havers, James Fox, Marily Tokuda, Frank McRae, Aki Aleong

▶ Nolte, a World War II deserter, becomes leader of an Iban tribe in remote Borneo. British captain Havers parachutes in to warn them of impending Japanese attack, but Nolte is determined to keep his jungle kingdom a sanctuary from civilization. Beautiful locations and rousing action sequences help compensate for superficial plot.

FARMER'S DAUGHTER, THE 1947
★★★ NR Comedy 1:37 B&W
Dir: H. C. Potter *Cast:* Loretta Young, Joseph Cotten, Ethel Barrymore, Charles Bickford, Rose Hobart, Rhys Williams

▶ Swedish farm girl Young moves to the big city and secures work as a maid for congressman Cotten and his kingmaker mom Barrymore. Young proves a model servant until her outspoken candor wins her nomination for a congressional seat from Cotten's rival party. Lively romantic comedy pokes fun at back-room politics and uptight city slickers. Young won an Oscar for her delightful performance.

FAR NORTH 1988
★★ PG-13 Comedy 1:30
☑ Adult situations, explicit language
Dir: Sam Shepard *Cast:* Jessica Lange, Charles Durning, Tess Harper, Donald Moffat, Ann Wedgeworth, Patricia Arquette

▶ Durning, patriarch of an all-female rural Minnesota family, demands the death of his horse Mel when he's thrown in a riding accident. The assignment falls to daughter Lange, who must also cope with her bitter sister Harper, flighty mother Wedgeworth, and promiscuous niece Arquette. Shepard's directing debut is intermittently amusing but also shrill and aimless.

FAR PAVILIONS, THE 1984
★★★★ NR Romance/MFTV 1:50
☑ Adult situations, mild violence
Dir: Peter John Duffell *Cast:* Ben Cross, Amy Irving, Omar Sharif, John Gielgud, Christopher Lee

▶ Cross, an India-born Englishman, has dual allegiances as an officer to the Corps of Guides and as the lover of Anjuli (Irving), a beautiful Indian princess. Epic tale of treachery and romantic intrigue set during the British raj. Originally made for cable and released in reedited version for home video. Based on the best-selling book.

FAST BREAK 1979
★★★★ PG Comedy 1:47
☑ Explicit language, adult humor
Dir: Jack Smight *Cast:* Gabe Kaplan, Harold Sylvester, Mike Warren, Bernard King, Reb Brown

▶ In Kaplan's first film he plays a New York deli cashier/basketball coach who gets a shot to coach college ball and make the Top Ten. Lighthearted, fun-filled comedy with a secret: the fifth man on his team is a girl.

FAST COMPANY 1979 Canadian
★ R Action-Adventure 1:32
☑ Adult situations, explicit language
Dir: David Cronenberg *Cast:* William Smith, Claudia Jennings, John Saxon, Nicholas Campbell, Cedric Smith

▶ Champion race-car driver Smith crashes his Top Fuel Dragster and is threatened by corrupt sponsor. Low-budget production stars Saxon, appropriately oily, as the villain.

FASTEST GUN ALIVE, THE 1956
★★★ NR Western 1:29 B&W
Dir: Russell Rouse *Cast:* Glenn Ford, Jeanne Crain, Broderick Crawford, Russ Tamblyn

▶ Mild-mannered storekeeper Ford, son of famous sheriff who has inherited skill with the gun, tries to live quiet life with wife Crain. Their peace is threatened when outlaw Crawford, eager for a challenge, comes to town. Well-played if somewhat predictable Western.

FAST FORWARD 1985
★★★ PG Drama/Dance 1:51
☑ Explicit language, mild violence
Dir: Sidney Poitier *Cast:* John Scott Clough, Don Franklin, Tamara Mark, Gretchen Palmer, Tracy Silver

▶ Eight young dancers from Ohio compete in a New York City dance contest but have to struggle to make ends meet. Hey, let's put on a show! Eight stars are born overnight. Clough plays fast-talking Matt, the leader of the bright young cast. Lively choreography by Rick Atwell enriched by New York City street breakdancers. (CC)

FAST TIMES AT RIDGEMONT HIGH 1982
★★★ R Drama 1:30
☑ Nudity, adult situations, explicit language

Dir: Amy Heckerling *Cast:* Sean Penn, Jennifer Jason Leigh, Judge Reinhold, Phoebe Cates, Robert Romanus, Brian Backer
▶ Lively, often quite raunchy, look at Southern California high school students transcends its youth comedy origins, thanks to Heckerling's amazingly subtle and compassionate direction. Leigh supplies the movie's soul as girl experiencing loss of innocence and Cates the spice as the woman of Reinhold's dreams. Penn provides the laughs as surfer boy Jeff Spicoli, dueling with history teacher Mr. Hand (Ray Walston).

FAST-WALKING 1981
★★ R Drama 1:56
☑ Nudity, explicit language, violence
Dir: James B. Harris *Cast:* James Woods, Tim McIntire, Kay Lenz, Robert Hooks
▶ "Fast-Walking" Miniver (Woods) is a smirking, laid-back prison guard/part-time pimp who helps inmates smuggle drugs and sneak into a nearby brothel. When famous black activist Hooks is convicted, Fast-Walking concocts a get-rich-quick scam to arrange the militant's escape. Bleak and cynical but well-made prison drama.

FATAL ATTRACTION 1987
★★★★★ R Drama 2:00
☑ Nudity, adult situations, explicit language, violence
Dir: Adrian Lyne *Cast:* Michael Douglas, Glenn Close, Anne Archer, Ellen Hamilton Latzen, Stuart Pankin
▶ Cautionary tale about the dangers of extramarital affairs stars Douglas as a happily married lawyer forced to deal with the repercussions of a one-night stand with sexy but neurotic book editor Close. Box-office smash garnered national attention for its antiadultery themes and thrill-packed suspense. Extremely well cast; Oscar-nominated for Best Picture, Director, Actor, Supporting Actress.

FATAL BEAUTY 1987
★★★ R Action-Adventure 1:44
☑ Nudity, adult situations, explicit language, graphic violence
Dir: Tom Holland *Cast:* Whoopi Goldberg, Sam Elliott, Ruben Blades, Harris Yulin, John P. Ryan
▶ Surefire crowd pleaser. Whoopi ("Don't call me Bitch!") Goldberg plays a tough-but-tender narcotics detective hot on the trail of a drug dealer pushing a particularly potent and deadly cocaine called "fatal beauty." As the bodies pile up, Whoopi gets involved with the drug king's chief bodyguard Elliott. Shoot-outs and chase scenes directed with technical competence; excessive killings and relentless violence deliver power-packed antidrug message. **(CC)**

FAT CITY 1972
★★ PG Drama 1:31
☑ Adult situations, explicit language
Dir: John Huston *Cast:* Stacy Keach, Jeff Bridges, Susan Tyrrell, Candy Clark, Nicholas Colasanto
▶ Keach, a boozing, battered pug, attempts boxing comeback while younger naive Bridges enters fight game. Huston's adaptation of Leonard Gardner's novel is not for the upbeat *Rocky* crowd. A gritty, painfully real look at losers on the sleazier side of the tracks. Short on plot, long on atmosphere.

FATHER GOOSE 1964
★★★ NR Comedy 1:55
Dir: Ralph Nelson *Cast:* Cary Grant, Leslie Caron, Trevor Howard, Jack Good, Pip Sparke, Nicole Felsette
▶ Good-natured World War II comedy with Grant in a change-of-pace role as an alcoholic beachcomber coerced by Howard into monitoring Japanese planes on a South Seas island. Grant's troubles multiply when prim French schoolteacher Caron and her young students are stranded on the island. Light romantic adventure won a Best Screenplay Oscar for Frank Tarloff and Peter Stone.

FATHER OF THE BRIDE 1950
★★★★ NR Comedy 1:33 B&W
Dir: Vincente Minnelli *Cast:* Spencer Tracy, Elizabeth Taylor, Joan Bennett, Don Taylor, Billie Burke
▶ A honey of a picture about American family life circa 1950. Tracy is tops as the tightly squeezed, self-important father of the bride—alternately torn by jealousy, devotion, pride, and righteous wrath. Champagne cast includes Bennett as the adoring mother, breathtakingly beautiful Liz as the bride-to-be, and Taylor as the overshadowed groom. Adapted from Edward Streeter's novel and nominated for Best Picture, Actor, and Screenplay. Spawned equally delightful sequel, *Father's Little Dividend.* **(CC)**

FATHER'S LITTLE DIVIDEND 1951
★★★★ NR Comedy 1:21 B&W
Dir: Vincente Minnelli *Cast:* Spencer Tracy, Elizabeth Taylor, Joan Bennett, Don Taylor, Billie Burke
► Charming sequel to *Father of the Bride* reassembles the same popular cast of characters. Tracy has just settled into life as a father-in-law when daughter Taylor announces her pregnancy. Disapproving at first, Tracy eventually succumbs to baby-talk, even though the kid starts bawling whenever grandpa comes close.

FATSO 1980
★★ PG Comedy 1:30
☑ Brief nudity, explicit language
Dir: Anne Bancroft *Cast:* Dom DeLuise, Anne Bancroft, Ron Carey, Candice Azzara, Michael Lombard
► Sentimental love story about overweight DeLuise who can't stop eating, even when he chains and bolts his refrigerator door. His nagging sister, Bancroft, screeches when poor Dom eats the "ONY" off the "HAPPY BIRTHDAY ANTHONY" cake. Dom seems hopeless until he meets angelic salesgirl Azzara, and finds the best diet is love. Even though Dom gives one of his best screen performances, the real stars of this movie are Hershey bars, chocolate pudding, and lasagne. Bancroft's debut as writer/director. (CC)

FBI STORY, THE 1959
★★★ NR Crime 2:29
Dir: Mervyn LeRoy *Cast:* James Stewart, Vera Miles, Murray Hamilton, Nick Adams, Larry Pennell, Diane Jergens
► History of the FBI as reflected in agent Stewart's illustrious career as he battles the KKK, killers, Nazis, gangsters, and Communists. The job puts a strain on his marriage to Miles but the couple reconcile. Episodic but generally satisfying; Stewart is top-notch.

FEAR 1988
★ R Mystery-Suspense 1:36
☑ Adult situations, explicit language, violence
Dir: Robert Ferretti *Cast:* Cliff De Young, Kay Lenz, Robert Factor, Scott Schwartz, Geri Betzler, Frank Stallone
► De Young and Lenz and their kids head to a remote mountain cabin to patch up family problems. Their domestic strife seems insignificant when they are taken hostage by four homicidal escaped convicts. Low-budget suspenser offers nothing new to genre.

FEAR CITY 1985
★★★ R Action-Adventure 1:36
☑ Nudity, explicit language, graphic violence
Dir: Abel Ferrara *Cast:* Jack Scalia, Tom Berenger, Melanie Griffith, Billy Dee Williams, Rossano Brazzi, Rae Dawn Chong
► Excellent cast elevates this familiar story of psycho-killer who wipes out topless dancers in New York's "fleshpot" district. Starring Berenger as a handsome ex-boxer hero; Griffith as a stripper who almost gets slashed. Acres of skin.

FEAR IN THE NIGHT 1972 British
★ PG Mystery-Suspense 1:22
☑ Adult situations, explicit language, violence
Dir: Jimmy Sangster *Cast:* Joan Collins, Peter Cushing, Judy Geeson, Ralph Bates, James Cossins
► Lurid account of Collins, wife of crippled boys' school headmaster Cushing, conspiring with teacher Bates to drive his wife Geeson insane. Her ultimate plan is to have Geeson murder Cushing. Monotonous drama suffers most from Collins's shrill acting.

FEARLESS VAMPIRE KILLERS, THE, OR PARDON ME, BUT YOUR TEETH ARE IN MY NECK 1967 British
★ NR Comedy 1:07
☑ Adult situations, mild violence
Dir: Roman Polanski *Cast:* Jack MacGowran, Roman Polanski, Alfie Bass, Jessie Robins, Sharon Tate, Ferdy Mayne
► Gruff professor MacGowran and bumbling assistant Polanski infiltrate a mountain castle to save innkeeper's daughter Tate from vampires celebrating their annual ball. Uneven but often devastating horror satire has a strong cult reputation. Also known as *Dance of the Vampires*. Various reedited versions are available.

FEAR STRIKES OUT 1957
★★★ NR Biography/Sports 1:40 B&W
Dir: Robert Mulligan *Cast:* Anthony Perkins, Karl Malden, Norma Moore, Adam Williams, Peter J. Votrian, Perry Wilson
► True story of baseball player Jimmy Pearsall (Perkins) whose promising career was nearly ruined by bout with mental illness. His uneasy relationship with dad Malden plays major role in his condition.

Interesting look at price of sports stardom; Perkins is quite credible and sympathetic.

FEDS 1988
★★★ **PG-13 Comedy 1:31**
☑ Adult situations, explicit language, violence
Dir: Dan Goldberg *Cast:* Rebecca De Mornay, Mary Gross, Ken Marshall, Fred Dalton Thompson, Larry Cedar, James Luisi
▶ Broad comedy about FBI recruits Gross, a bookworm unaccustomed to physical activity, and De Mornay, an ex-Marine stymied by lack of legal expertise, who become partners during slapstick training program. Amiable jokes include picking up sailors, mastering firearms, and winning simulated terrorist exercise.

FELLINI'S SATYRICON 1969 Italian
☆ **R Drama 2:09**
☑ Nudity, explicit language
Dir: Federico Fellini *Cast:* Martin Potter, Hiram Keller, Max Born, Capucine, Salvo Randone
▶ Two best friends, in love with the same boy, pursue the object of their affections through the Roman Empire. Along the way, they encounter orgies, feasts, festivals, and murders. Outrageous cinematic journey. Vivid colors and shocking visuals as director Fellini creates an entire world of illusion. Based on a first century A.D. novel by Petronius. Certainly not for all tastes.

FERRIS BUELLER'S DAY OFF 1986
★★★ **PG-13 Comedy 1:43**
☑ Explicit language
Dir: John Hughes *Cast:* Matthew Broderick, Alan Ruck, Mia Sara, Jennifer Grey, Jeffrey Jones
▶ Teenpic maestro Hughes's story about free-spirited, suburban whiz kid Broderick who fakes out his parents and takes the day off from school with his girlfriend Sara and reclusive best friend Ruck. Smart-alecky Ferris engages in a battle of wits with frustrated school principal Jones, treats his friends to an expensive lunch and a baseball game, and leads a parade through the streets of Chicago. Will Ferris get home before his mom? A treat for anyone who ever played hooky—or wanted to. (CC)

FEVER PITCH 1985
★★★ **R Drama 1:35**
☑ Brief nudity, adult situations, explicit language, mild violence

Dir: Richard Brooks *Cast:* Ryan O'Neal, Catherine Hicks, Rafael Campos, Bridgette Andersen, Chad Everett
▶ Los Angeles sportswriter O'Neal investigates the world of gambling and becomes addicted himself. Everett stars as his loan shark, and Andersen as his daughter who takes him to Gamblers Anonymous. Downbeat and intense. (CC)

FFOLKES 1980
★★★★ **PG Mystery-Suspense 1:40**
☑ Adult situations, explicit language, graphic violence
Dir: Andrew V. McLaglen *Cast:* Roger Moore, Anthony Perkins, James Mason, Michael Parks, David Hedison
▶ Mr. ffolkes (Moore), frogman–connoisseur–misogynist–cat lover, is called in by the British Admiral to ffoil the takeover of two oil rigs in the North Sea. Thoroughly plausible and pithy suspense. ("F" rendered "ff" was a common practice until the seventeenth century.)

FIDDLER ON THE ROOF 1971
★★★★★ **G Musical 2:59**
Dir: Norman Jewison *Cast:* Chaim Topol, Norma Crane, Leonard Frey, Molly Picon, Paul Mann
▶ Rich and spectacular big-budget movie version of one of Broadway's longest-running musicals, about Tevye, the Jewish milkman in Czarist Russia, his tart-tongued wife Golde, and his five nubile but dowry-less daughters. As persecution of the Jews intensifies, Tevye and his family are forced to leave their home. Bock/Harnick score includes "If I Were a Rich Man." Adapted from Shalom Aleichem stories and nominated for five Oscars (including Best Picture, Actor, Director); won for Oswald Morris's cinematography.

FIENDISH PLOT OF DR. FU MANCHU, THE 1980 British
★★ **PG Comedy 1:40**
☑ Explicit language, adult humor
Dir: Piers Haggard *Cast:* Peter Sellers, Sid Caesar, Helen Mirren, David Tomlinson, Simon Williams, Steve Franken
▶ In his last film, Sellers plays a dual role as both the devilish Dr. Fu Manchu, now 168 years old and hunting for the elixir of youth, and Fu's adversary Nayland Smith, the retired Scotland Yard inspector tracking him down. Lightweight, daffy comedy in the *Pink Panther* vein.

FIFTH FLOOR, THE 1980
★★ **R Drama 1:30**

☑ Nudity, adult situations, explicit language

Dir: Howard Avedis **Cast:** Bo Hopkins, Dianne Hull, Sharon Farrell, Mel Ferrer
► Young disco dancer Hull is wrongly committed to a mental institution where there's more violence, sadism, and rape than therapy. Hopkins is effectively creepy as the guard who takes advantage of Hull. Spartan production was allegedly based on an actual account.

FIFTH MUSKETEER, THE 1979 Austrian
★★★ PG Action-Adventure 1:43
☑ Adult situations, mild violence
Dir: Ken Annakin **Cast:** Beau Bridges, Sylvia Kristel, Ursula Andress, Cornel Wilde, Lloyd Bridges, Jose Ferrer
► Louis XIV secures his throne by imprisoning his twin brother Philippe (Beau Bridges in a dual role), but with the help of the elderly Four Musketeers (Wilde, Ferrer, Bridges, and Alan Hale, Jr.) Philippe escapes and mounts an attack on the king. Lavish but slowly paced swashbuckler, based on Alexander Dumas's *The Man in the Iron Mask*, features steady support from veteran actors Ian McShane, Helmut Dantine, Olivia de Havilland, and Rex Harrison as the king's minister Colbert.

55 DAYS AT PEKING 1963
★★★ NR Action-Adventure 2:30
Dir: Nicholas Ray **Cast:** Charlton Heston, Ava Gardner, David Niven, Flora Robson, John Ireland, Harry Andrews
► Boxer Rebellion of 1900 traps diplomatic staffs from eleven countries inside a walled compound; supplies run low during protracted siege as prisoners await rescue by their armies. Large-scale action sequences, impressive sets, and Dimitri Tiomkin score outweigh frequently confusing plot in this sprawling epic. Robson gives the best performance as the Empress Dowager.

52 PICK-UP 1986
★★★ R Mystery-Suspense 1:54
☑ Nudity, adult situations, explicit language, graphic violence
Dir: John Frankenheimer **Cast:** Roy Scheider, Ann-Margret, Vanity, John Glover, Robert Trebor, Lonny Chapman
► Successful businessman Scheider, blackmailed by creepy pornographers Glover, Trebor, and Clarence Williams III, breaks all the rules in a cunning revenge scheme. Hard-edged adaptation of Elmore Leonard's novel revels in its lurid,

sleazy atmosphere. Glover is exceptionally sinister as he sedates Scheider's wife Ann-Margret with heroin. **(CC)**

FIGHTING BACK 1982
★★★★ R Action-Adventure 1:38
☑ Brief nudity, explicit language, graphic violence
Dir: Lewis Teague **Cast:** Tom Skerritt, Patti LuPone, Michael Sarrazin, Yaphet Kotto, David Rasche, Donna Devarona
► Outraged at the crime in his South Philadelphia neighborhood, deli owner Skerritt organizes a security patrol to rid the area of crooks. But his crusade turns ugly when the patrol takes on vigilante overtones. Crude but effective thriller in the *Death Wish* mold is graced with an unusually capable cast.

FIGHTING KENTUCKIAN, THE 1949
★★★ NR Western 1:40
Dir: George Waggner **Cast:** John Wayne, Vera Ralston, Philip Dorn, Oliver Hardy, Marie Windsor, John Howard
► Heading home after the 1810 Battle of New Orleans, Wayne falls in love with Ralston, the daughter of an evil French aristocrat. Wayne calls on his fellow Kentucky rifleman to defeat the aristocrat's attempt to steal farmland. In one of his few roles without Stan Laurel, Hardy is endearing as a stout-hearted sidekick. Briskly entertaining film was also produced by Wayne.

FIGHTING PRINCE OF DONEGAL, THE 1966
★★★ NR Action-Adventure 1:52
Dir: Michael O'Herlihy **Cast:** Peter McEnery, Susan Hampshire, Tom Adams, Gordon Jackson, Andrew Keir, Maurice Roeves
► Stirring period drama about the efforts of prince McEnery to rally rival clans against British oppressors in eleventh-century Ireland. When his mother and fiancée are kidnapped by Jackson's troops, McEnery mounts an assault on his castle. Excellent Disney adaptation of Robert T. Reilly's *Red Hugh, Prince of Donegal*.

FINAL ASSIGNMENT 1982
★★★ PG Drama 1:37
☑ Adult situations, explicit language
Dir: Paul Almond **Cast:** Genevieve Bujold, Michael York, Burgess Meredith, Colleen Dewhurst, Alexandra Stewart, Richard Gabourie
► Intrepid TV reporter Bujold, on assignment in Moscow, has an affair with Rus-

sian press officer York while unearthing deadly steroid experiments on children. With the KGB hot on her trail, she agrees to smuggle out of Russia a child who needs a brain operation. Jewish fur trader Meredith helps her in the scheme.

FINAL CHAPTER: WALKING TALL 1977
★★★★ R Action-Adventure 1:52
☑ Adult situations, explicit language, violence
Dir: Jack Starrett *Cast:* Bo Svenson, Margaret Blye, Forrest Tucker, Lurene Tuttle, Morgan Woodward, Leif Garrett
▶ Third and last feature about real-life Tennessee sheriff Buford Pusser (Svenson) rehashes the formula started in *Walking Tall*: Pusser and his baseball bat make mincemeat out of villains who try to corrupt his small town. Followed by a short-lived TV series.

FINAL CONFLICT, THE 1981
★★★ R Horror 1:48
☑ Nudity, strong sexual content, explicit language, graphic violence
Dir: Graham Baker *Cast:* Sam Neill, Rossano Brazzi, Don Gordon, Lisa Harrow, Mason Adams
▶ Third episode in the *Omen* trilogy follows a middle-aged Damien Thorn (Neill) as he plots control of the world from his post as U.S. Ambassador to Britain. Monks led by Brazzi gather seven magical daggers—the only weapons that can kill the Antichrist. Gut-wrenching gore includes murder by incineration and steam iron.

FINAL COUNTDOWN, THE 1980
★★★★ PG Sci-Fi 1:43
☑ Adult situations, explicit language, mild violence
Dir: Don Taylor *Cast:* Kirk Douglas, Martin Sheen, Katharine Ross, James Farentino, Ron O'Neal, Charles Durning
▶ On December 7, 1979, the nuclear aircraft carrier *Nimitz* slips through a time warp into 1941. Captain Douglas must decide whether to interfere with Japan's attack on Pearl Harbor and thereby change the course of history. Intriguing premise undermined by talky plot. Shot with the Navy's cooperation, the film provides a fascinating look at the *Nimitz*.

FINAL MISSION 1984
★★★ NR Action-Adventure 1:41
☑ Nudity, adult situations, explicit language, graphic violence
Dir: Cerio Santiago *Cast:* Richard Young, John Dresden, Kaz Garaz, Christine Tudor

▶ Los Angeles SWAT-team cop's family is killed by a drug kingpin, his sworn enemy since their days as Green Berets in Laos. The cop tracks the dealer to Northern California, where they have a bloody confrontation. Low-budget exploitation delivers extremely violent action.

FINAL OPTION, THE 1983 British
★★★ R Drama 2:05
☑ Adult situations, explicit language, violence
Dir: Ian Sharp *Cast:* Lewis Collins, Judy Davis, Richard Widmark, Edward Woodward, Robert Webber, Tony Doyle
▶ Crackerjack secret agent Collins infiltrates an antinuclear terrorist group headed by sociopath Davis. Collins's bravery is tested when the terrorists seize the American Embassy, demanding the destruction of a nuclear submarine base. Misleading billing for Widmark, who has exactly one scene as the Secretary of State. Originally titled *Who Dares Wins*.

FINAL TERROR, THE 1983
★★ R Horror 1:24
☑ Nudity, explicit language, graphic violence
Dir: Andrew Davis *Cast:* John Friedrich, Adrian Zmed, Daryl Hannah, Rachel Ward, Mark Metcalf, Ernest Harden, Jr.
▶ Mysterious evil force in the California forest kills two motorcycle riders, then, one by one, picks off a group of teenage campers. They rush back to their bus, only to discover that the evil force still lurks among them. Well-made but routine horror film notable only for the presence of future stars Ward, Hannah, and Zmed.

FINDERS KEEPERS 1984
★★ R Comedy 1:35
☑ Adult situations, explicit language, mild violence
Dir: Richard Lester *Cast:* Michael O'Keefe, Beverly D'Angelo, Louis Gossett, Jr., David Wayne, Ed Lauter, Brian Dennehy
▶ Frantic nonstop slapstick about various crooks and con artists after $5 million hidden in a veteran's coffin. Failed roller derby manager O'Keefe dons a soldier's uniform to guard the coffin on its train journey to Nebraska; D'Angelo plays his sexy accomplice and Gossett, his foster father. Wayne stands out as the world's oldest conductor. (CC)

FINE MADNESS, A 1966
★★ NR Comedy 1:43
Dir: Irvin Kershner *Cast:* Sean Connery,

Joanne Woodward, Jean Seberg, Patrick O'Neal, Colleen Dewhurst
▶ One of Sean Connery's best and most overlooked non-Bond performances, showing off his comedic side. He plays rebellious poet Samson Shillitoe, continually running afoul of the women in his life and various forms of authority in this black satire.

FINE MESS, A 1986
★★★ PG Comedy 1:30
☑ Adult situations, explicit language
Dir: Blake Edwards *Cast:* Ted Danson, Howie Mandel, Maria Conchita Alonso, Richard Mulligan, Paul Sorvino, Jennifer Edwards
▶ Actor Danson learns that gangsters have doped a horse so he and waiter pal Mandel bet on it. The chase is on when the bad guys discover the duo's involvement. Slapstick shenanigans are overly broad and done at breakneck speed. Edwards's daughter Jennifer is likable as Howie's girlfriend. **(CC)**

FINGERS 1978
☆ R Drama 1:30
☑ Strong sexual content, explicit language, violence
Dir: James Toback *Cast:* Tisa Farrow, Harvey Keitel, Jim Brown, Tanya Roberts, Michael V. Gazzo, Marian Seldes
▶ Keitel leads double life thanks to mismatched parents: he works as collector for mobster dad Gazzo while practicing to follow in pianist mom Seldes's footsteps. He goes deeper into underworld when he falls for black gangster Brown's girlfriend Farrow. Lots of raw verve and energy but audience will have trouble identifying with unsympathetic hero.

FINIAN'S RAINBOW 1968
★★★★ G Musical/Comedy 2:21
Dir: Francis Ford Coppola *Cast:* Fred Astaire, Petula Clark, Tommy Steele, Keenan Wynn, Al Freeman, Jr.
▶ Screen legend Astaire's last major musical. Irish rascal Finian McLonergan buries a pot of leprechaun gold in Rainbow Valley. Daughter Sharon (Clark) gets three wishes and turns Wynn, racist white Southern senator, black. Nimble dancing and tuneful score includes "How Are Things in Glocca Morra?" Carefully adapted from Harburg and Saidy's Broadway play. Early directorial effort from Coppola.

FINNEGAN BEGIN AGAIN 1985
★★★★ NR Drama/MFTV 1:54
☑ Adult situations, explicit language
Dir: Joan Micklin Silver *Cast:* Robert Preston, Mary Tyler Moore, Sylvia Sidney, Sam Waterston, David Huddleston
▶ Feel-good love story of the touching and funny relationship between Moore and Preston. He plays a top-notch reporter reduced to writing a lonely hearts column; Moore's a widowed teacher having an affair with married funeral director Waterston. A platonic, mutually supportive friendship develops into a romance between the mismatched pair. Directed with style and grace by Silver.

FIRE AND ICE 1983
★★ PG Animation/Adult 1:15
☑ Mild violence
Dir: Ralph Bakshi *Cast:* Voices of Randy Norton, Cynthia Leake, Steve Sandor, Sean Hannon, Leo Gordon
▶ Sword and sorcery shenanigans from the innovative Bakshi and co-producer Frank Frazetta, an influential comic book artist. In a vaguely prehistoric jungle occupied by reptilian creatures, a fire princess is kidnapped by an evil ice king and then rescued by a brave warrior. Predictable story but innovative production techniques stretch the confines of animation.

FIRE AND ICE 1987
★ PG Drama/Sports 1:20
☑ Adult situations
Dir: Willy Bogner *Cast:* John Eaves, Suzy Chaffee, Tom Sims, Steve Link, John Denver
▶ *Flashdance* on skis! Ski bum Eaves, Canadian freestyle champ, hitchhikes to Aspen in pursuit of ski bunny Chaffee. His frequent fantasies trigger spectacular production numbers involving acrobatic skiing, ski surfing, hang gliding, wind surfing, and other feats of derring-do; sort of "Wide World of Sports" meets MTV. Not much of a plot but lots of eye-popping athletic feats, thrilling camera work, and extraordinary international locales. **(CC)**

FIRECREEK 1968
★★★ NR Western 1:44
Dir: Vincent McEveety *Cast:* James Stewart, Henry Fonda, Inger Stevens, Gary Lockwood, Dean Jagger, Ed Begley
▶ Pacifist sheriff Stewart watches his town taken over by murderous outlaws led by Fonda. After a lynching and near-rape, Stewart realizes he must resort to vio-

lence to protect himself. Elegiac but talky Western is relentlessly grim.

FIRE DOWN BELOW 1957
★ ★ NR Action-Adventure 1:56
Dir: Robert Parrish *Cast:* Rita Hayworth, Robert Mitchum, Jack Lemmon, Herbert Lom, Anthony Newley, Bernard Lee
▶ When gorgeous Hayworth, a woman with a past, becomes a passenger on boat of smugglers Mitchum and Lemmon, a shipboard triangle is the result. Friends Lemmon and Mitchum become foes, but it is Mitchum to the rescue when Lemmon's life is endangered by a collision. Clichéd story but nice performances and Caribbean scenery.

FIREFOX 1982
★ ★ ★ ★ PG Action-Adventure 2:16
☑ Explicit language, violence
Dir: Clint Eastwood *Cast:* Clint Eastwood, Freddie Jones, David Huffman, Warren Clarke, Ronald Lacey, Kenneth Colley
▶ Guilt-driven Vietnam veteran Eastwood is the only American who can fly Russia's newest secret weapon, the "mind-controlled" Firefox jet. Will his war flashbacks endanger his efforts to infiltrate the Firefox compound? Special effects climax adds some spark to the typical Eastwood heroics.

FIREMAN'S BALL, THE 1968 Czech
★ NR Comedy 1:13
☑ Adult situations, explicit language
Dir: Milos Forman *Cast:* Vaclav Stocker, Josef Svet, Ian Vistrcil, Josef Kolb
▶ Elderly fire brigade commander, dying of cancer, is feted by former associates. However, the fireman's ball turns into a series of comic mishaps. Sophisticated audiences should enjoy this Best Foreign Film nominee, an early effort of director Forman with some hilarious moments.
⑤

FIRE OVER ENGLAND 1937 British
★ ★ ★ NR Drama 1:29 B&W
Dir: William K. Howard *Cast:* Laurence Olivier, Flora Robson, Leslie Banks, Raymond Massey, Vivien Leigh, Robert Newton
▶ Fast-paced, relatively accurate historical epic about dashing British spy (Olivier), who steals plans for the Spanish Armada invasion from the court of King Philip (Massey). Robson would repeat her interpretation of Queen Elizabeth in *The*

Sea Hawk. Olivier's scenes with Leigh, who plays a lady-in-waiting, led to their real-life affair.

FIREPOWER 1979 British
★ ★ ★ ★ R Action-Adventure 1:44
☑ Explicit language, violence
Dir: Michael Winner *Cast:* Sophia Loren, James Coburn, O. J. Simpson, Eli Wallach, Anthony Franciosa, Vincent Gardenia
▶ Widowed by a suspicious chemical plant fire, Loren vows revenge on the arsonist. She's aided by government agents, bounty hunters, and mobsters. Bang-bang film treats us to multiple explosions: a Caribbean hideaway, a yacht, a helicopter, five jeeps, and a boat dock.

FIRESTARTER 1984
★ ★ ★ ★ R Horror 1:54
☑ Explicit language, violence
Dir: Mark L. Lester *Cast:* Drew Barrymore, David Keith, George C. Scott, Martin Sheen, Art Carney
▶ In this Stephen King adaptation, gifted Barrymore can telepathically ignite fires without matches. Blessing becomes a curse when she and dad Keith are pursued by sinister government assassin Scott. Incendiary horror fun will kindle genre-fans' enthusiasm with brisk pace and first-rate cast. **(CC)**

FIREWALKER 1986
★ ★ ★ PG Action-Adventure 1:50
☑ Violence
Dir: J. Lee Thompson *Cast:* Chuck Norris, Louis Gossett, Jr., Melody Anderson, Will Sampson, Sonny Landham
▶ Norris and Gossett, American soldiers of fortune, search for lost Aztec treasure in Mexico. Billed as Norris's "first comedy role" but with enough bone-cracking and carnage to inspire fans of the kung-fu star. (CC)

FIRE WITH FIRE 1986
★ ★ ★ PG-13 Drama/Romance 1:44
☑ Adult situations, explicit language, violence
Dir: Duncan Gibbins *Cast:* Virginia Madsen, Craig Sheffer, Kate Reid, Jeffrey Jay Reid, Jon Polito, Jean Smart
▶ Convent school student Madsen meets Sheffer, an inmate at nearby work camp for delinquents, and it's love at first sight. Authorities punish Sheffer when the lovers meet clandestinely, so they run off together to a remote cabin; but disapproving nuns and police are hot on

their trail. Opposite-side-of-the-tracks romance will appeal mainly to fans of the genre.

FIRST BLOOD 1982
★ ★ ★ ★ R Action-Adventure 1:33
☑ Nudity, explicit language, graphic violence
Dir: Ted Kotcheff *Cast:* Sylvester Stallone, Richard Crenna, Brian Dennehy, David Caruso, Jack Starrett
▶ Tormented ex–Green Beret John Rambo (Stallone), honed like a machine in survival and attack skills, eludes a vicious gang of backwoods cops in this first of the riveting Rambo series. Crenna appears as his old commanding officer, who calls him back to his Green Beret family. Gigantic box-office smash.

FIRSTBORN 1984
★ ★ ★ ★ PG Drama 1:43
☑ Adult situations, explicit language, violence
Dir: Michael Apted *Cast:* Teri Garr, Peter Weller, Christopher Collet, Corey Haim, Sarah Jessica Parker, Robert Downey, Jr.
▶ Single mother Garr and sons Collet and Haim are getting along just fine until she begins a romance with drug dealer Weller. He proves a villainous interloper and sets the family at odds. Eventually, elder son Collet stands up to Weller. Fine premise and convincing job by cast sabotaged by uninspired and violent ending. **(CC)**

FIRST DEADLY SIN, THE 1980
★ ★ ★ R Action-Adventure 1:52
☑ Adult situations, explicit language, violence
Dir: Brian G. Hutton *Cast:* Frank Sinatra, Faye Dunaway, David Dukes, Brenda Vaccaro, Martin Gabel
▶ Sinatra is a battle-weary detective tracking a perverted killer who stalks the streets of New York. Dunaway appears in a thankless role as the cop's dying wife, lying in bed with nasty tubes in her nose. Stuffy, somber film based on the best-selling novel by Lawrence Sanders.

FIRST FAMILY 1980
★ R Comedy 1:40
☑ Explicit language, adult humor
Dir: Buck Henry *Cast:* Bob Newhart, Gilda Radner, Madeline Kahn, Richard Benjamin, Bob Dishy
▶ Henry wrote and directed this White House spoof. Newhart plays the dim-witted President with drunk wife Kahn and

nymphomaniac daughter Radner. The Prez trades white middle-class Americans to an African nation in return for a tank of dung with magical veggie-growing properties. Lively, tacky comedy worthy of a few laughs.

FIRST LOVE 1977
★ ★ ★ R Romance 1:28
☑ Nudity, adult situations, explicit language
Dir: Joan Darling *Cast:* William Katt, Susan Dey, John Heard, Beverly D'Angelo, Robert Loggia
▶ College students Katt and Dey fall in love for the first time and deal with fidelity, responsibility, and passion. Refreshingly frank yet old-fashioned love story with a very attractive cast.

FIRST MAN INTO SPACE 1959 British
★ NR Sci-Fi 1:18 B&W
Dir: Robert Day *Cast:* Marshall Thompson, Marla Landi, Bill Edwards, Robert Ayres, Bill Nagy, Carl Jaffe
▶ Daring astronaut flies through a meteor cloud and returns to Earth with an alien hidden inside his body. Since the alien needs human blood to survive, the astronaut turns into a vampirelike killer. His brother must defeat the menace. Stark thriller's effectiveness limited by cheap production values.

FIRST MEN IN THE MOON 1964 British
★ ★ ★ NR Sci-Fi 1:43
Dir: Nathan Juran *Cast:* Edward Judd, Lionel Jeffries, Martha Hyer, Erik Chitty, Betty McDowall, Miles Malleson
▶ Tongue-in-cheek adaptation of H. G. Wells's novel follows the crew of an 1899 expedition to the moon, where they are attacked by Ray Harryhausen's devilish special effects monsters. Broad but entertaining story should please younger viewers. Peter Finch has a bit part as a process server.

FIRST MONDAY IN OCTOBER 1981
★ ★ ★ ★ R Comedy/Drama 1:39
☑ Brief nudity, explicit language
Dir: Ronald Neame *Cast:* Jill Clayburgh, Walter Matthau, Barnard Hughes, James Stephens, Jan Sterling
▶ Matthau is a crusty old Supreme Court justice shocked to learn the very female Clayburgh is filling the newly vacated Court seat. Though they disagree on nearly every critical issue, lovable sourpuss Matthau and high-spirited Clayburgh make an appealing pair.

FIRST NUDIE MUSICAL, THE 1976
★ R Comedy 1:37
☑ Nudity, explicit language
Dir: Mark Haggard *Cast:* Stephen Nathan, Cindy Williams, Bruce Kimmel, Leslie Ackerman, Diana Canova
▶ Nathan, the son of a movie mogul, tries to salvage his father's studio by producing and performing in the world's first pornographic musical. Williams plays his performing love interest, but doesn't bare any skin. Ersatz erotica with naughty talk. Screenplay and songs by actor Kimmel.

FIRST TIME, THE 1981
★ R Comedy 1:36
☑ Adult situations, explicit language, adult humor
Dir: Charlie Loventhal *Cast:* Tim Choate, Krista Errickson, Marshall Effron, Wendy Fulton, Raymond Patterson, Wallace Shawn
▶ Blossom College film student Choate schemes to lose his virginity with the advice of black roommate Patterson and school psychologist Effron. His chances drop drastically when mother Cathryn Damon unexpectedly enrolls. Clever adolescent comedy with an amusing turn by Shawn as an eccentric professor. Directing debut for twenty-two-year-old Loventhal, a Brian De Palma protégé.

FISH CALLED WANDA, A 1988
★ ★ ★ R Comedy 1:47
☑ Nudity, adult situations, explicit language, violence
Dir: Charles Crichton *Cast:* John Cleese, Jamie Lee Curtis, Kevin Kline, Michael Palin, Maria Aitken, Tom Georgeson
▶ In London, Brits Georgeson and Palin and Yanks Curtis and Kline steal diamonds and quickly start double-crossing each other. Georgeson winds up in jail, but he's hidden the loot, so Curtis comes on to his lawyer Cleese to learn the hiding spot. Meanwhile, meek Palin fails miserably in mission to kill little old lady, the crime's only witness. Side-splitting farce marries Monty Python irreverence and American caper comedy. Sleeper hit, written by Cleese and Crichton, given sure-handed treatment by the seventy-seven-year-old director. Oscar nominations for Crichton (Best Director and Screenplay) and Cleese (Screenplay); Kline won for Supporting Actor.

FISH HAWK 1980 Canadian
★ ★ ★ ★ G Family 1:34
Dir: Donald Shebib *Cast:* Will Sampson, Charlie Fields, Geoffrey Bowes, Mary Pirie, Don Francks
▶ Turn-of-the-century tale of Fish Hawk (Sampson), an elderly alcoholic Indian who befriends Ozark farm boy Fields, but dreams of returning to his people. Nicely mounted, high-quality family fare with enthralling wildlife footage.

FISH THAT SAVED PITTSBURGH, THE 1979
★ ★ PG Comedy 1:43
☑ Explicit language
Dir: Gilbert Moses *Cast:* Julius Irving, Jonathan Winters, Meadowlark Lemon, Kareem Abdul-Jabbar, Stockard Channing, Flip Wilson
▶ Channing is an astrologer who assembles a team of Pisces-only basketball players that turns the Pittsburgh franchise into a winner. Real-life NBA superstar Irving, as the team's best player, demonstrates his spectacular slam dunk. Lots of basketball, fast action, and laughs.

F.I.S.T. 1978
★ ★ ★ ★ PG Drama 2:23
☑ Explicit language, violence
Dir: Norman Jewison *Cast:* Sylvester Stallone, Rod Steiger, Peter Boyle, Melinda Dillon, David Huffman, Tony Lo Bianco
▶ Episodic tale traces Stallone's Hoffa-like rise from Hungarian immigrant to president of a trucking union in the late 1930s. Along the way, he accepts mob favors that eventually lead to a senate hearing investigation. First-rate acting delivers professional and convincing portraits, especially Steiger as the prosecuting senator, Boyle as a double-dealing union boss, and Lo Bianco as an oily Mafia connection. Excellent set decoration, use of color, and photography by the master Laslo Kovacs.

FISTFUL OF DOLLARS, A 1967 Italian
★ ★ ★ NR Western 1:36
☑ Violence
Dir: Sergio Leone *Cast:* Clint Eastwood, Marianna Koch, John Wells, Pepe Calvo, Wolfgang Lukschy, Sieghardt Rupp
▶ Eastwood, a mysterious mercenary, cleans up a corrupt Mexican village by manipulating rival families against each other. First "spaghetti Western," based loosely on Kurosawa's *Yojimbo*, has dazzling direction and a haunting Ennio Morricone score. Eastwood's shrewd perform-

ance as The Man With No Name made him an international star. Highly influential and entertaining picture was followed by *For a Few Dollars More.*   **(CC)**

FISTS OF FURY 1973 Chinese
★ ★ **R Martial Arts 1:43**
☑ Explicit language, violence
Dir: Lo Wei   *Cast:* Bruce Lee, Maria Yi, Han Ying Chieh, Tony Liu, Malalene, Paul Tien
▶ Out to avenge his teacher's murder, Lee uncovers a Japanese drug smuggling ring. Extremely violent kung-fu film suffers from poor dubbing and wooden acting, although Lee's acrobatic stunts are as amazing as ever.

FITZCARRALDO 1982 German
★ ★ **PG Action-Adventure 2:37**
☑ Brief nudity, adult situations, violence
Dir: Werner Herzog   *Cast:* Klaus Kinski, Claudia Cardinale, Jose Lewgoy, Miguel Angel Fuentes, Paul Hittscher, Huerequeque Bohorquez
▶ In turn-of-the-century South America, obsessed dreamer Kinski sets out to build an opera house in the middle of the jungle—even though he has to drag a full-sized steamboat over a forbidding mountain to reach his site. Massive epic is paradoxically a highly personal achievement for Herzog, who surmounted extraordinary production difficulties to complete the film. Impressive, although very slowly paced.   Ⓢ

FIVE CARD STUD 1968
★ ★ **PG Western 1:43**
☑ Violence
Dir: Henry Hathaway   *Cast:* Dean Martin, Robert Mitchum, Inger Stevens, Roddy McDowall, Katherine Justice, Yaphet Kotto
▶ Despite Martin's objections, five poker players lynch a cheating gambler. As the five are murdered one by one, Martin teams up with stern preacher Mitchum to unmask the killer. Routine Western loses steam when the villain is identified halfway through the picture.

FIVE CORNERS 1988
★ **R Drama 1:32**
☑ Explicit language, violence
Dir: Tony Bill   *Cast:* Jodie Foster, Tim Robbins, Todd Graff, John Turturro, Daniel Jenkins, Elizabeth Berridge
▶ Slice of 1960s Bronx life has pet store worker Foster turning to peace-loving activist Robbins for help when rapist Turturro

gets out of jail and comes calling. Quirky John Patrick Shanley screenplay has touches of originality but uneasily mixes comedy with violence; Foster and company manage to overcome the uneven tone. Marvelous sixties soundtrack.

FIVE DAYS ONE SUMMER 1982
★ ★ **PG Drama 1:48**
☑ Adult situations, mild violence
Dir: Fred Zinnemann   *Cast:* Sean Connery, Betsy Brantley, Lambert Wilson, Jennifer Hilary, Anna Massey
▶ Connery and Brantley, a doctor and his niece masquerading as husband and wife, take a holiday in 1930s Switzerland, hoping to consummate a long-postponed affair. She has eyes for their handsome young mountaineer guide Wilson, so the two men vie for her love. Tasteful production; breathtakingly beautiful Alpine setting.

FIVE EASY PIECES 1970
★ ★ ★ **R Drama 1:36**
☑ Nudity, adult situations, explicit language
Dir: Bob Rafelson   *Cast:* Jack Nicholson, Karen Black, Lois Smith, Susan Anspach, Billy Green Bush, Fannie Flagg
▶ Bobby Dupea (Nicholson) forsakes his musical talent and oppressive middle-class family for oil rig work, one-night stands, and poker games. Moody study of alienation has Oscar-nominated Nicholson as one of his quintessential anti-heroes. Several powerful scenes include Jack's one-way conversation with his crippled dad and the famous bit where he orders a "chicken salad sandwich on whole wheat toast" from an authoritarian waitress. Best Picture nominee.

FIVE MILLION YEARS TO EARTH 1968 British
★ ★ **NR Sci-Fi 1:37**
Dir: Roy Ward Baker   *Cast:* James Donald, Andrew Keir, Barbara Shelley, Julian Glover, Duncan Lamont, Bryan Marshall
▶ Workers unearth a Martian spaceship beneath the London subway. Scientists examining it discover a disturbing secret about evolution, and also unleash a terrifying monster. Competent low-budget thriller was the third in the *Quatermass* series. Also known as *Quatermass and the Pit,* and followed by *Quatermass Conclusion.*

FIVE PENNIES, THE 1959
★ ★ ★ ★ **NR Biography/Musical 1:57**

Dir: Melville Shavelson *Cast:* Danny Kaye, Barbara Bel Geddes, Louis Armstrong, Bob Crosby, Harry Guardino, Tuesday Weld

▶ Biography of famed Dixieland cornetist Red Nichols (Kaye) follows his rise to fame and early retirement when daughter Weld (in her film debut) is stricken with polio. Climax, with Nichols embarking on a comeback, features a wonderful jam session with Armstrong. Maudlin plot redeemed by twenty-five tunes, including "When the Saints Go Marching In" and "Paradise." Title song, by Kaye's wife Sylvia Fine, was Oscar-nominated.

FIVE WEEKS IN A BALLOON 1962
★★ NR Action-Adventure 1:41
Dir: Irwin Allen *Cast:* Red Buttons, Fabian, Barbara Eden, Cedric Hardwicke, Peter Lorre

▶ English explorer Hardwicke, reporter Buttons, and slave trader Lorre are among the crew of a nineteenth-century balloon expedition in uncharted Africa. Diverse cast in a lighthearted adaptation of the Jules Verne adventure from disaster-movie king Allen.

FLAME AND THE ARROW, THE 1950
★★★★ NR Action-Adventure 1:28
Dir: Jacques Tourneur *Cast:* Burt Lancaster, Virginia Mayo, Robert Douglas, Aline MacMahon, Frank Allenby, Nick Cravat

▶ High-spirited swashbuckler gave Lancaster one of his zestiest roles as Dardo, a Robin Hood type who matches wits with cruel tyrant Allenby in the Italian Alps. After a daring escape from the gallows, Lancaster disguises himself as an acrobat to rescue the beautiful Mayo from Allenby's castle. Lancaster did most of his own stunts in this well-mounted production, which won Oscar nominations for Ernest Haller's cinematography and Max Steiner's score.

FLAMINGO KID, THE 1984
★★★ PG-13 Comedy 1:40
☑ Adult situations, explicit language
Dir: Garry Marshall *Cast:* Matt Dillon, Richard Crenna, Janet Jones, Jessica Walter, Hector Elizondo, Fisher Stevens

▶ Charming, extremely likable coming-of-age movie about Jeffrey Willis (Dillon), a 1963 Brooklyn teenager who gets a summer job as a cabana boy at El Flamingo, a fancy Long Island beach club. A good kid but no genius, Dillon idolizes the club's materialistic cardsharp,

Crenna, and his gorgeous niece, Jones (in real life, Mrs. Wayne Gretsky). By Labor Day, though, Jeffrey returns to the values taught by father Elizondo, a poor but honest plumber. Soundtrack is loaded with fifties rock 'n' roll hits. **(CC)**

FLAMING STAR 1960
★★★ NR Western 1:41
Dir: Don Siegel *Cast:* Elvis Presley, Barbara Eden, Steve Forrest, Dolores Del Rio, John McIntire, Rudolph Acosta

▶ Presley gives a strong performance as a half-breed Indian torn between siding with Kiowa mother Del Rio and white father McIntire when the Kiowas declare war. Rescuing brother Forrest during a foolish attack on the Indians' village, Presley incurs the wrath of his tribe. Despite two opening songs, a solid Western decrying racial prejudice rather than a musical.

FLANAGAN 1985
☆ R Drama 1:40
☑ Brief nudity, adult situations, explicit language
Dir: Scott Goldstein *Cast:* Philip Bosco, Geraldine Page, William Hickey, Linda Thorson, Olympia Dukakis

▶ Bosco, a fifty-three-year-old New York City cab driver, dreams of becoming a Shakespearean actor but is plagued with personal and professional difficulties including estranged wife Dukakis, mistress Thorson who's helpless to comfort his angst, and rejection by producers. Talky and static drama has good urban texture and wonderful Bosco.

FLASHDANCE 1983
★★★★ R Drama/Dance 1:36
☑ Nudity, explicit language
Dir: Adrian Lyne *Cast:* Jennifer Beals, Michael Nouri, Lilia Skala, Cynthia Rhodes, Belinda Bauer, Phil Burns

▶ Megahit of 1983, a Cinderella-in-Pittsburgh fantasy about beautiful welder Beals who lives to dance. By day she handles acetylene torches, by night she gyrates to a pulsating Giorgio Moroder soundtrack. Lyne directs New Wave dancing and sweaty female workouts with vim and vigor. Sizzling Irene Cara sings Oscar-winning "What a Feeling." Also nominated for the song "Maniac," Editing, and Cinematography. **(CC)**

FLASH GORDON 1980
★★★ PG Sci-Fi 1:51
☑ Explicit language, violence
Dir: Mike Hodges *Cast:* Max Von

Sydow, Timothy Dalton, Sam J. Jones, Melody Anderson, Chaim Topol, Ornella Muti

▶ Lavish high-camp revival pits comic-strip hero/pro-quarterback Flash (Jones) and pretty, putty-brained Dale Arlen (Anderson) against the merciless Emperor Ming (Von Sydow) in a battle to save the planet. Sexy innuendos abound on the planet Mongo, where inhabitants sport gold-lamé athletic supporters.

FLASH OF GREEN, A 1984
★ NR Drama 2:11
☑ Brief nudity, adult situations, explicit language, violence
Dir: Victor Nunez   *Cast:* Ed Harris, Blair Brown, Richard Jordan, George Coe, Joan Goodfellow, Jean De Baer

▶ Moody, complex melodrama about Florida Keys newspaper reporter Harris who betrays a local conservation group despite his love for its leader Brown. Producer Jordan is magnetic as a corrupt politician. Director-writer-cameraman Nunez captures the unique feel of the Keys, but his adaptation of John D. MacDonald's novel suffers from extreme length and offbeat pacing.

FLASHPOINT 1984
★★★★ R Action-Adventure 1:34
☑ Explicit language, violence
Dir: William Tannen   *Cast:* Kris Kristofferson, Treat Williams, Rip Torn, Kevin Conway, Mark Slade, Tess Harper

▶ Texas border patrolmen Kristofferson and Williams find a skeleton and a cache of 1963 money inside an abandoned jeep. Kristofferson wants to retire with the loot in Mexico, but Williams connects the money to a deadly conspiracy. Competent adventure has an accomplished performance from Torn as a sheriff.

FLESH + BLOOD 1985
★★ R Action-Adventure 2:05
☑ Nudity, adult situations, explicit language, violence
Dir: Paul Verhoeven   *Cast:* Rutger Hauer, Jennifer Jason Leigh, Tom Burlinson, Jack Thompson, Susan Tyrrell

▶ In 1501 Europe, soldier of fortune Hauer, betrayed by a lord, kidnaps the man's daughter Leigh. They fall in love but her fiancé Burlinson arrives to rescue her. Gorgeously photographed epic recreates the Dark Ages with gusto and carnage, although characters are unsympathetic. Overripe dialogue is excessively vulgar; hot tub seduction scene is quite steamy.

FLETCH 1985
★★★★ PG Comedy 1:38
☑ Adult situations, explicit language
Dir: Michael Ritchie   *Cast:* Chevy Chase, Dana Wheeler-Nicholson, Joe Don Baker, Tim Matheson, Richard Libertini, M. Emmet Walsh

▶ Rich Matheson claims to be dying and hires investigative reporter Chase to murder him so wife Wheeler-Nicholson can collect the insurance. Chase investigates and uncovers a drug smuggling ring. Relaxed, diverting comedy/mystery with Chevy's most pleasing film work to date. His offhand delivery of screenwriter Andrew Bergman's non sequiturs ("Can I borrow your towel?" he asks a half-naked Wheeler-Nicholson, "my car just hit a water buffalo") generates laughs. (CC)

FLIGHT OF THE EAGLE, THE 1983
Swedish
★ NR Drama 2:21
☑ Violence
Dir: Jan Troell   *Cast:* Max Von Sydow, Goran Stangertz, Sverre Anker, Eva von Hanno

▶ True story of the ill-fated 1897 expedition that attempted to reach the North Pole in a hydrogen-filled balloon in order to claim the land for Sweden. The three explorers were never seen alive again but, in 1930, their remains—including a detailed diary—were discovered by the crew of a Norwegian ship. Artful but slow "documentary drama" was Sweden's entry as Best Foreign Film.

FLIGHT OF THE NAVIGATOR, THE 1986
★★★★ PG Sci-Fi 1:28
☑ Explicit language
Dir: Randal Kleiser   *Cast:* Joey Cramer, Cliff De Young, Veronica Cartwright, Matt Adler, Sarah Jessica Parker, Howard Hesseman

▶ Disney time-tripper about twelve-year-old Cramer who falls into a ravine in 1978, wakes up a moment later, and discovers it's 1986! Panic-stricken, he runs home but finds his parents have moved. NASA scientists discover the kid's been riding on a flying saucer. A lively and touching adventure, grand fun for the whole family.

FLIGHT OF THE PHOENIX 1965
★★★★ NR Action-Adventure 2:27
Dir: Robert Aldrich   *Cast:* James Stewart, Richard Attenborough, Peter Finch,

Hardy Kruger, Ernest Borgnine, Ian Bannen

▶ Grueling adventure about a small band of survivors stranded in the Arabian desert after their plane crashes. Exciting tribute to endurance is realistic and unpredictable, with Stewart delivering another thoughtful performance as the pilot. Fine support from Attenborough as an alcoholic navigator, Kruger as a German designer, Dan Duryea, and George Kennedy. **(CC)**

FLIM FLAM MAN, THE 1967
★★★ NR Comedy 1:55
Dir: Irvin Kershner *Cast:* George C. Scott, Sue Lyon, Michael Sarrazin, Harry Morgan, Jack Albertson, Slim Pickens
▶ In the South, old-time bunco artist Scott hooks up with AWOL soldier Sarrazin and teaches him the tricks of the trade. Sarrazin tries to turn Scott straight but learns there's no reforming a dishonest man. Engaging; Scott and Sarrazin make an entertaining team. **(CC)**

FLIPPER 1963
★★★★ G Family 1:30
Dir: James B. Clark *Cast:* Chuck Connors, Luke Halpin, Connie Scott, Jane Rose, Joe Higgins, Mitzi the Dolphin
▶ Florida youngster Halpin nurses a wounded dolphin back to health. Connors, his fisherman father, returns Flipper to the wild, breaking Halpin's heart. Will Flipper remember his old friend? Wholesome family film, basis for the hit TV series, will enthrall kids.

FLORIDA STRAITS 1986
★★★ PG-13 Action-Adventure/MFTV 1:37
☑ Explicit language, violence
Dir: Mike Hodges *Cast:* Raul Julia, Fred Ward, Daniel Jenkins, Jaime Sanchez, Victor Argto
▶ Old-style soldier-of-fortune adventure about Cuban refugee Julia who hires a Florida charter boat owned jointly by Ward and Jenkins to track down the gold he buried twenty years ago, before going to Castro's prison. Their exciting seafaring journey is interrupted by patrol boats and a renegade army. Excellent casting, superior technical credits, and an exciting wind-up. **(CC)**

FLOWER DRUM SONG 1961
★★★ NR Musical 2:13
Dir: Henry Koster *Cast:* Nancy Kwan, James Shigeta, Miyoshi Umeki, Juanita Hall, Jack Soo

▶ Hong Kong immigrant Umeki is brought to San Francisco to wed nightclub owner Soo in an arranged marriage, but instead falls in love with handsome stranger Shigeta. Soo's top singer Kwan is also intent on marriage in this pleasant adaptation of a Broadway hit. Rodgers and Hammerstein score includes "I Enjoy Being a Girl" and "Don't Marry Me."

FLOWERS IN THE ATTIC 1987
★★★ PG-13 Mystery-Suspense 1:31
☑ Explicit language, violence
Dir: Jeffrey Bloom *Cast:* Louise Fletcher, Victoria Tennant, Kristy Swanson, Jeb Stuart Adams, Ben Granger
▶ Nasty gothic-style melodrama, adapted from V. C. Andrews's huge best-seller. Disinherited from the family fortune for marrying her uncle, truly weird, gold-digging mom Tennant hides her four kids in the attic until her daddy dies (and she can inherit his dough). Grandma Fletcher sadistically tortures kids; mom poisons them. Stiff and dreary acting; mindless, imbecilic story will only appeal to those who loved the book.

FLY, THE 1958
★★ NR Sci-Fi/Horror 1:30
Dir: Kurt Neumann *Cast:* Al (David) Hedison, Patricia Owens, Vincent Price, Herbert Marshall
▶ Housefly gets caught in machine with scientist Hedison during his matter transference experiment. Result: one man with a fly's head and one fly with a man's head. Cult favorite with the unforgettable scene of Price and Marshall encountering the fly who pleads: "Help me!" Pretty good sci-fi, not as dramatic or nearly as grisly as David Cronenberg's 1986 remake.

FLY, THE 1986
★★★ R Sci-Fi/Horror 1:36
☑ Brief nudity, adult situations, explicit language, graphic violence
Dir: David Cronenberg *Cast:* Jeff Goldblum, Geena Davis, John Getz, Joy Boushel, Les Carlson
▶ Bookish scientist Goldblum genetically fuses himself with a fly. His journalist girlfriend Davis stands by her man—even when he starts climbing walls and has skin that resembles burnt cheese. High-tech eighties gore, plus a hearty dose of black humor, updates this remake of the fifties camp classic; decidedly not for the squeamish. Sequel: 1989's *The Fly II*. Goldblum and Davis later married. **(CC)**

FLY II, THE 1989
★★★ R Sci-Fi/Horror 1:45
☑ Adult situations, violence, explicit
language
Dir: Chris Walas *Cast:* Eric Stoltz,
Daphne Zuniga, Lee Richardson, John
Getz, Frank Turner, Ann Marie Lee
▶ Stoltz, brilliant son of the Jeff Goldblum
character in the 1986 *The Fly,* follows in his
father's footsteps by conducting matter transference experiments. Girlfriend
Zuniga remains loyal even as Stoltz's
chromosomes go haywire, transforming
him into a giant fly. Competent sequel
overcomes slow start for a rousing finale;
plenty of gore and gooey special effects.
Director Walas won an Oscar for makeup
in the first film.

FLYING DOWN TO RIO 1933
★★★ NR Musical 1:29 B&W
Dir: Thornton Freeland *Cast:* Dolores
Del Rio, Gene Raymond, Raoul Roulien,
Ginger Rogers, Fred Astaire, Blanche
Frederici
▶ Dated musical romance, focusing on
pilot/bandleader Raymond's rivalry with
singer Roulien over the beautiful Del Rio,
is an amusing Depression relic with an
incredible climax: dozens of chorus girls
perform the title song while strapped to
the wings of biplanes. Notable primarily
as the first pairing of Astaire and Rogers.
Although fourth- and fifth-billed, their version of "The Carioca" helped establish
them as America's premier dancing
team.

FLYING LEATHERNECKS 1951
★★★ NR War 1:42 B&W
Dir: Nicholas Ray *Cast:* John Wayne,
Robert Ryan, Don Taylor, William Harrigan, Janis Carter, Jay C. Flippen
▶ World War II drama examines the conflict between Wayne, a harsh, demanding major of an air squadron in Guadalcanal, and Ryan, a captain who thinks
the young pilots need more compassionate treatment. Good use of newsreel
dogfights boosts familiar plot. Flippen is a
delight as a resourceful sergeant. Produced by Howard Hughes.

FLYING TIGERS 1942
★★★ NR War 1:42
Dir: David Miller *Cast:* John Wayne,
John Carroll, Anna Lee, Paul Kelly, Gor-
don Jones, Mae Clarke
▶ Tribute to American fighter pilots sta-
tioned in China during World War II has
squadron leader Wayne (in his first war

picture) coping with his unruly fliers as
well as the Japanese. Carroll has an interesting role as a recklessly mercenary
pilot (the Tigers received $500 for each
downed enemy plane).

FM 1978
★★ PG Comedy 1:44
☑ Explicit language
Dir: John A. Alonzo *Cast:* Michael
Brandon, Eileen Brennan, Alex Karras,
Cleavon Little, Martin Mull
▶ Laid-back deejays Mull, Brennan, and
Little on Los Angeles's hippest radio sta-
tion refuse to "go commercial" by airing
the Army ads sold by the corporation
that owns the station. Excellent cast and
an exciting, tune-filled score features big
name rockers Steely Dan, B. B. King, Billy
Joel, Boz Scaggs; includes "concert ap-
pearances" by Linda Ronstadt and
Jimmy Buffett.

FOG, THE 1980
★★ R Horror 1:26
☑ Violence
Dir: John Carpenter *Cast:* Adrienne
Barbeau, Hal Holbrook, Janet Leigh,
Jamie Lee Curtis, John Houseman
▶ Dense fog hides a colony of vengeful,
shipwrecked ghosts in the California
town of Antonion Bay. In her first film role,
Barbeau stars as a deejay who broad-
casts from the isolated lighthouse. Eerie
and elegant tale of the macabre.

FOLLOW ME, BOYS 1966
★★★★ G Family 2:11
Dir: Norman Tokar *Cast:* Fred MacMurray, Vera Miles, Lillian Gish, Charles
Ruggles, Kurt Russell
▶ Small-town scoutmaster (a perfectly
cast MacMurray) and wife Miles, unable
to have kids of their own, become surrogate parents to kids in their troop. Later,
they actually adopt troubled young Russell. Sentimental if sometimes melodramatic Disney film conveys genuine
lump-in-the-throat emotion.

FOLLOW THAT DREAM 1962
★★★ NR Musical 1:50
Dir: Gordon Douglas *Cast:* Elvis Pres-
ley, Arthur O'Connell, Anne Helm, Jo-
anna Moore, Jack Kruschen, Simon
Oakland
▶ Elvis and pop O'Connell claim squat-
ters' rights to government land in Florida,
then defeat thugs to establish a home for
four orphans. Mild Presley entry features
"What a Wonderful Life," "On Top of Old
Smoky," and "Home Is Where the Heart

ls." Action scenes allow the King to show off his judo moves.

FOLLOW THE FLEET 1936
★★★★ NR Musical 1:50 B&W
Dir: Mark Sandrich *Cast:* Fred Astaire, Ginger Rogers, Randolph Scott, Harriet Hilliard, Astrid Allwyn, Harry Beresford
▶ In a turnabout to their usual glamorous roles, Astaire plays a wisecracking sailor and Rogers, a dancehall hostess. Earthy setting and plot are secondary to the splendid dances and Irving Berlin score: "I'm Putting All My Eggs in One Basket," "Let Yourself Go," "Let's Face the Music and Dance," etc. Thin but charming comedy relief provided by Scott and Hilliard (Harriet of TV's *Ozzie and Harriet*). Look quickly for Lucille Ball and Betty Grable in bit parts.

FOOD OF THE GODS 1976
★★ PG Horror 1:29
☑ Violence
Dir: Bert I. Gordon *Cast:* Marjoe Gortner, Pamela Franklin, Ida Lupino, Ralph Meeker, Jon Cypher
▶ Campy low-budgeter based on H. G. Wells's foreboding sci-fi novel about ecology gone berserk. Feeding on a mysterious food substance, giant rats, wasps, and man-eating worms proliferate and roam the earth. Special effects are on par with the dialogue ("I know a rat when I see one, mister.").

FOOL FOR LOVE 1985
★ R Drama 1:45
☑ Explicit language, violence
Dir: Robert Altman *Cast:* Sam Shepard, Kim Basinger, Harry Dean Stanton, Randy Quaid, Martha Crawford
▶ Sagebrush soap opera long on talk, short on action. Obscure screenplay by Shepard (adapted from his off-Broadway play) tells the tale of the on-again, off-again, possibly incestuous romance between has-been, love-crazed rodeo cowboy Shepard and a strung-out Basinger. Ghosts from the past also visit the seedy motel on the edge of the Mojave Desert where the story takes place. Saving graces: intense, steely-eyed performance by Shepard and a sultry, Monroe-like Basinger.

FOOLIN' AROUND 1980
★★★★ PG Comedy 1:40
☑ Adult situations, explicit language
Dir: Richard T. Heffron *Cast:* Gary Busey, Annette O'Toole, Eddie Albert,

Tony Randall, Cloris Leachman, John Calvin
▶ Sweet Oklahoma bumpkin Wes (Busey) goes to college, meets rich girl O'Toole, and falls in love. She's forced to choose between Calvin, the straitlaced do-gooder approved by mother Leachman, and farm boy Wes. Modest mix of slapstick and romance makes for a cute and entertaining film.

FOOTLIGHT PARADE 1933
★★★ NR Musical 1:44 B&W
Dir: Lloyd Bacon *Cast:* James Cagney, Joan Blondell, Ruby Keeler, Dick Powell, Guy Kibbee, Frank McHugh
▶ Vintage Depression-era fun: Cagney (in his first musical) is a hard-edged director scrambling for funds while fighting off creditors. He hits on a scheme to stage lavish musical prologues to films, leading to three of Busby Berkeley's best productions: the risqué "Hollywood Hotel," "By a Waterfall," and "Shanghai Lil" (showcasing Cagney's accomplished hoofing).

FOOTLOOSE 1984
★★★★ PG Drama 1:47
☑ Brief nudity, adult situations, explicit language, mild violence
Dir: Herbert Ross *Cast:* John Lithgow, Kevin Bacon, Lori Singer, Christopher Penn, Dianne Wiest
▶ Lithgow, a Midwestern bible belt preacher, has banned dancing in his burg but he hasn't reckoned with city hipster Bacon, the new kid in town. Bacon's cocky charisma and a terrific score (including Kenny Loggins's title tune and Deniece Williams's "Let's Hear It for the Boy") helped make this one of the year's top-grossing films. Great supporting cast includes Penn as the clumsy country boy Bacon teaches to dance. (CC)

FOR A FEW DOLLARS MORE 1965
Italian
★★★ R Western 2:10
☑ Violence
Dir: Sergio Leone *Cast:* Clint Eastwood, Lee Van Cleef, Gian Maria Volonté, Jose Effer, Rosemary Dexter, Klaus Kinski
▶ Strong sequel to *A Fistful of Dollars* improves on the original with the addition of Van Cleef, a bounty hunter whose firm morals contrast sharply with Eastwood's Man With No Name. They're unlikely partners chasing Volonté, a comically blasphemous villain. Good Ennio Morricone

score and a scene-stealing performance from Kinski as a crude hunchback. (CC)

FORBIDDEN 1985
★ ★ ★ ★ NR Drama/MFTV 1:54
☑ Adult situations, mild violence
Dir: Anthony Page *Cast:* Jacqueline Bisset, Jurgen Prochnow, Irene Worth, Amanda Cannings, Avis Bunnage
▶ Nazi Germany is the harrowing background for a passionate romance between aristocratic Nina (Bisset) and Fritz (Prochnow), a Jewish publisher. Their involvement grows despite the Nuremberg Laws prohibiting relationships between Gentiles and Jews, and Nina is ultimately forced to hide Fritz from the Nazis. Gripping real-life story fictionalized by Leonard Gross in his novel *Last Jews in Berlin*.

FORBIDDEN GAMES 1952 French
★ NR Drama 1:25 B&W
Dir: René Clement *Cast:* Brigitte Fossey, Georges Powjouly, Louis Herbert, Suzanne Courtal
▶ Little girl Fossey, orphaned by World War II, is taken in by a farm family and befriended by youngest child Poujouly. After hearing about the burial of war victims, the children start a secret graveyard and conduct services for animals. Tender and heartbreaking foreign classic makes powerful antiwar statement. Won honorary Oscar as Best Foreign Film. ⓢ

FORBIDDEN PLANET 1956
★ ★ G Sci-Fi 1:38
Dir: Fred McLeod Wilcox *Cast:* Walter Pidgeon, Anne Francis, Leslie Nielsen, Warren Stevens, Jack Kelly
▶ Three space explorers journey to a distant planet to rescue scientist Pidgeon, his attractive daughter Francis, and Robby, their robot, from a mysterious "force" that's destroyed the remainder of the planet's population. Minor classic was Oscar-nominated for special effects, but seems very simplistic by today's standards.

FORCED VENGEANCE 1982
★ ★ ★ R Martial Arts 1:30
☑ Rape, nudity, adult situations, explicit language
Dir: James Fargo *Cast:* Chuck Norris, Mary Louise Weller, Camilla Griggs, Michael Cavanaugh, David Opatoshu
▶ Kung-fu's best-known Caucasian plays a Vietnam vet who heads security for a Hong Kong casino. When a series of murders is pinned on him, Norris seeks out the real killer amid maximum mayhem. Not the best-made action film; the bored can count the number of times the boom microphone bobs into view.

FORCE OF ONE, A 1979
★ ★ ★ PG Martial Arts 1:31
☑ Adult situations, explicit language, violence
Dir: Paul Aaron *Cast:* Chuck Norris, Jennifer O'Neill, Clu Gulager, Ron O'Neal, James Whitmore, Jr.
▶ Norris, solid citizen and master martial arts fighter, is reluctant to join a police war against kung-fu killers who murder L.A. narcotics agents for kicks. After his adopted son is murdered and his girlfriend molested, he changes his mind. Clearly motivated, civic-minded story of revenge.

FORCE 10 FROM NAVARONE 1978
★ ★ ★ ★ PG War 1:58
☑ Brief nudity, explicit language, violence
Dir: Guy Hamilton *Cast:* Robert Shaw, Harrison Ford, Edward Fox, Franco Nero, Barbara Bach
▶ In this sequel to Alistair MacLean's novel *The Guns of Navarone*, Shaw and Fox, members of a British sabotage squad, join an American ranger unit led by Ford into the Balkans during World War II. Their orders: destroy an enemy bridge, vital to the Wehrmacht strategy. Solid cast and well-staged action.

FOREIGN AFFAIR, A 1948
★ ★ ★ NR Comedy 1:56 B&W
Dir: Billy Wilder *Cast:* Jean Arthur, Marlene Dietrich, John Lund, Millard Mitchell, Bill Murphy
▶ Arthur, head of a congressional investigation into Berlin's postwar black market, locks horns with Lund, a cynical American officer. She forces Lund to offer his mistress, nightclub chanteuse Dietrich, as bait to catch a missing Nazi. Caustic, dark-toned comedy restored Dietrich's popularity after a long box-office decline. She sings "Black Market" and "Ruins of Berlin."

FOREIGN BODY 1986 British
★ ★ PG-13 Comedy 1:51
☑ Nudity, adult situations, explicit language
Dir: Ronald Neame *Cast:* Victor Banerjee, Warren Mitchell, Geraldine McEwan, Denis Quilley, Amanda Donohoe, Trevor Howard
▶ Wide-eyed Banerjee borrows, bribes,

and bluffs his way from Calcutta to London, where he finds romantic and financial success while posing as a doctor. Old-fashioned comedy has amiable cast and smart pacing to compensate for inconsequential plot.

FOREIGN CORRESPONDENT 1940
★ ★ ★ ★ **NR Mystery-Suspense 2:00 B&W**
Dir: Alfred Hitchcock   *Cast:* Joel McCrea, Laraine Day, Herbert Marshall, George Sanders, Albert Basserman, Robert Benchley
► Smashing wartime thriller, one of the best espionage films ever, drops naive reporter McCrea into a maelstrom of Nazi intrigue and double-crosses as he tracks a missing diplomat through Europe. Topnotch Hitchcock film delivers many of his famous set pieces (an assassination in the rain, a shocking plane crash, etc.) with devious, breathless pacing. Oscar nominations for Picture, Screenplay, and Cinematography.

FOREVER, LULU 1987
★ **R Comedy 1:26**
☑ Nudity, explicit language, violence
Dir: Amos Kollek   *Cast:* Hanna Schygulla, Deborah Harry, Alec Baldwin, Annie Golden, Paul Gleason
► Cheap imitation of *Desperately Seeking Susan* starring accomplished Polish-born actress Schygulla in her first English-language role. She plays a down-on-her-luck East Village writer/temp for a toilet seat company, who encounters a series of "only in New York" events. Harry appears to mutter ten words and add some cachet. Schygulla embarrassingly muddles through this mess.

FOR KEEPS 1988
★ ★ ★ ★ **PG-13 Comedy 1:38**
☑ Adult situations, explicit language
Dir: John G. Avildsen   *Cast:* Molly Ringwald, Randall Batinkoff, Miriam Flynn, Kenneth Mars, Conchata Ferrell
► They're very young, very much in love, and she's very pregnant. Ringwald plays a popular adolescent forced to deal with adult problems. Newcomer Batinkoff is the confused but well-meaning father. Sweet, lighthearted comedy includes documentary footage of a live birth. Fine supporting cast.

FOR LOVE OF IVY 1968
★ ★ **G Comedy 1:41**
Dir: Daniel Mann   *Cast:* Sidney Poitier,

Abbey Lincoln, Beau Bridges, Nan Martin, Carroll O'Connor, Hugh Hurd
► Worried that maid Lincoln might quit, a white Long Island family arranges a romance with Poitier, a trucking executive and part-time gambler. Undemanding comedy based on a story by Poitier includes songs by Shirley Horn and B. B. King.

FOR ME AND MY GAL 1942
★ ★ ★ **NR Musical 1:44 B&W**
Dir: Busby Berkeley   *Cast:* Judy Garland, George Murphy, Gene Kelly, Marta Eggerth, Ben Blue, Keenan Wynn
► Garland quits her vaudeville team to work with Kelly (making his film debut), but rival singer Eggerth and the onslaught of World War I sabotage their chances for success. Ragged musical sparkles during the frequent numbers, especially a disarming version of the title song and "Oh You Beautiful Doll." (CC)

FORMULA, THE 1980
★ ★ ★ **R Drama 1:57**
☑ Adult situations, explicit language, violence
Dir: John G. Avildsen   *Cast:* George C. Scott, Marlon Brando, Marthe Keller, John Gielgud, Beatrice Straight
► High-quality suspense film about L.A. detective Scott investigating a murder case that involves giant, powerful oil cartels and a Nazi formula for synthetic fuel. Brando is haggard but still fascinating in his small part as an oil executive. Complex, novelistic story written by best-selling author Steve Shagan.

FOR PETE'S SAKE 1974
★ ★ ★ ★ **PG Comedy 1:30**
☑ Explicit language, adult humor
Dir: Peter Yates   *Cast:* Barbra Streisand, Michael Sarrazin, Estelle Parsons, William Redfield, Molly Picon
► Old-time boisterous farce with Streisand as Henrietta, a Brooklyn housewife who'll do anything for her taxi-driving husband, Sarrazin. After borrowing $3,000 to pay for hubby's college education, Babs is forced by greedy loan sharks to take up prostitution, drug dealing, and cattle rustling. Action and chase scenes are aptly handled but this faux-screwball comedy is probably best suited to Streisand aficionados.

FORT APACHE 1948
★ ★ ★ ★ **NR Western 2:08 B&W**
Dir: John Ford   *Cast:* Henry Fonda,

John Wayne, Shirley Temple, Ward Bond, John Agar, Victor McLaglen
▶ Ambitious but inexperienced colonel Fonda, overriding the objections of veteran captain Wayne, endangers the soldiers at his new post by inciting nearby Apaches to war. Somber, richly detailed Western, shot in Monument Valley, has a commanding performance by Fonda in a rare villainous role. The first of director Ford's "cavalry trilogy," followed by *She Wore a Yellow Ribbon* and *Rio Grande*.

FORT APACHE, THE BRONX 1981
★★★★ R Drama 2:03
☑ Nudity, adult situations, explicit language, violence
Dir: Daniel Petrie *Cast:* Paul Newman, Edward Asner, Ken Wahl, Rachel Ticotin, Pam Grier, Danny Aiello
▶ Tough-talking street melodrama takes disturbing look at New York's South Bronx at its down-and-dirty worst. In and around Fort Apache, the embattered precinct house, cops Newman and Wahl battle nonstop crime. After witnessing two cops commit a heinous crime, a disillusioned Newman must wrestle with his conscience. Good performances, especially from Ticotin as Newman's girlfriend, and energetically directed action add up to an exciting urban nightmare story.

FOR THE LOVE OF BENJI 1977
★★★★ G Comedy/Family 1:24
Dir: Joe Camp *Cast:* Benji, Patsy Garrett, Ed Nelson, Cynthia Smith
▶ The world's most expressive, cuddly canine is back for his second comedy-adventure. Government bad-guy Nelson chases Benji, who is accidentally carrying secret information on his paw, through the crowded streets of a lovely-to-look-at Athens. Cleverly shot through Benji's point of view. Lovable, suspenseful story for all ages.

FORTRESS 1985 Australian
★★★ NR Drama/MFTV 1:28
☑ Brief nudity, adult situations, explicit language, violence
Dir: Arch Nicholson *Cast:* Rachel Ward, Sean Garlick, Marc Gray, Rebecca Rigg, Bradley Meehan
▶ Australian schoolteacher Ward and her young students are kidnapped by two mask-wearing thugs and carted off at gunpoint to an underground cavern. Hair-raising fight-for-survival story with a thrill-packed finish. Adapted from the novel by Gabrielle Lord.

FORTUNE, THE 1975
★★ PG Comedy 1:35
☑ Adult situations, explicit language
Dir: Mike Nichols *Cast:* Jack Nicholson, Warren Beatty, Stockard Channing, Scatman Crothers, Florence Stanley
▶ Twenties rich girl Channing runs off with already wed Beatty, who marries her off to pal Nicholson for cover. Nicholson and Beatty plot to kill Channing for her dough but they're too inept to succeed. Black comedy, stylishly directed by Nichols. Outlandish antics by a curly-haired Jack, having a great time in a rare farcical role. Our favorite scene: Nicholson's "mousie bed" speech.

FORTUNE COOKIE, THE 1966
★★★ NR Comedy 2:05 B&W
Dir: Billy Wilder *Cast:* Jack Lemmon, Walter Matthau, Ron Rich, Cliff Osmond, Judi West
▶ Sports cameraman Lemmon is accidentally injured by football player Rich while filming a game. Lemmon's shyster lawyer cousin, the aptly named Whiplash Willie (Matthau, in a wonderful Oscar-winning performance), tries to exploit the situation for all it's worth but Lemmon suffers pangs of guilt. Sharp demonstration of Wilder's wit and Lemmon/Matthau's comic chemistry.

FORTY CARATS 1973
★★ PG Romance/Comedy 1:50
☑ Adult situations
Dir: Milton Katselas *Cast:* Liv Ullmann, Edward Albert, Gene Kelly, Binnie Barnes, Deborah Raffin, Nancy Walker
▶ New York realtor Ullmann falls in love with Albert, a great guy half her age, but is afraid of what her friends will think. Ullmann's good-natured ex-husband Kelly urges her to follow her heart. Sweet love story with Liv learning life begins at forty.

48 HRS. 1982
★★★★ R Action-Adventure 1:36
☑ Nudity, adult situations, explicit language, violence
Dir: Walter Hill *Cast:* Nick Nolte, Eddie Murphy, Annette O'Toole, Frank McRae, James Remar, David Patrick Kelly
▶ Boozy but tough police detective Nolte takes glib con man Murphy (in a smashing film debut) out of jail to track down two psychopath cop killers. Cunning blend of rugged action and gritty comedy was a huge hit, inspiring a rash of "buddy-cop" films. This is one of the few that deliver the goods. Murphy's bit in a redneck bar has become a classic.

FORTY-SECOND STREET 1933
★★★ NR Musical 1:38 B&W
Dir: Lloyd Bacon   *Cast:* Warner Baxter,
Bebe Daniels, George Brent, Una Mer-
kel, Ruby Keeler, Dick Powell
▶ Desperate director Baxter banks every-
thing on temperamental leading lady
Daniels, but turns to newcomer Keeler
when Daniels breaks her ankle. Seminal
musical is filled with classic lines ("You're
going out a youngster, but you've *got* to
come back a star!") and extravagant
Busby Berkeley routines. Songs include
"You're Getting to Be a Habit with Me,"
"Forty-Second Street," and "Shuffle Off to
Buffalo."

FOR YOUR EYES ONLY 1981 British
★★★★ PG
Espionage/Action-Adventure 2:08
☑ Brief nudity, adult situations, explicit
   language, violence
Dir: John Glen   *Cast:* Roger Moore,
Carole Bouquet, Chaim Topol, Lynn-
Holly Johnson, Julian Glover
▶ In his fifth Bond film, Moore is trapped in
a runaway helicopter, stalked in the
snow, flung to the sharks, hurled up a
cliff—all in the name of national security.
Bouquet joins him as a Greek beauty out
to avenge her father's death and help
save the world. Critically acclaimed for
having more substance than the traditional Bond fare.

FOUL PLAY 1978
★★★★ PG Comedy 1:51
☑ Explicit language, mild violence
Dir: Colin Higgins   *Cast:* Goldie Hawn,
Chevy Chase, Burgess Meredith, Rachel Roberts, Dudley Moore, Billy Barty
▶ Slick, amusing murder/mystery finds
Hawn accidentally involved in a plot to
murder the Pope. Chevy Chase, as a
nutty police detective, stumbles his way
into her heart. Fine supporting cast features Billy Barty as a Bible salesman and
Dudley Moore in his first big American
role, which launched his movie career
here. Charming, endearing, and very
funny.

FOUNTAINHEAD, THE 1949
★★★ NR Drama 1:54 B&W
Dir: King Vidor   *Cast:* Gary Cooper, Patricia Neal, Raymond Massey, Kent
Smith, Robert Douglas
▶ Architect Cooper asserts his right to artistic integrity by blowing up apartment
house when the builders distort his original designs. You don't have to agree with
author Ayn Rand's philosophy to enjoy
this compelling adaptation of her best-
seller. Blistering sexual chemistry between Cooper and Neal and dynamic
visuals from director Vidor.

FOUR FEATHERS, THE 1939 British
★★★★ NR Action-Adventure 1:55
Dir: Zoltan Korda   *Cast:* Ralph Richardson, John Clements, June Duprez,
C. Aubrey Smith, Jack Allen
▶ In 1898, young officer Clements resigns
commission and is given feathers as a
symbol of cowardice by his disapproving
comrades and fiancée. When his regiment fights in the Sudan, Clements disguises himself as a native and proves his
bravery, returning the feathers to their
sources one by one. Riproaring, rousing
adventure with fine cast and beautiful
color photography. Genuine classic will
leave you happy and satisfied. By far the
best of four versions of the story.

FOUR FOR TEXAS 1963
★★ NR Western 2:04
Dir: Robert Aldrich   *Cast:* Frank Sinatra,
Dean Martin, Anita Ekberg, Ursula An-
dress, Charles Bronson, Victor Buono
▶ In this self-indulgent Western comedy,
Sinatra and Martin play rival con men
who battle each other and outlaw Bron-
son over an 1870s riverboat casino. Ek-
berg and Andress are typecast as the
heroes' lovers. Guest stars include Arthur
Godfrey, Bob Steele, and the Three
Stooges.

FOUR FRIENDS 1981
★★ R Drama 1:54
☑ Nudity, adult situations, explicit language, violence
Dir: Arthur Penn   *Cast:* Craig Wasson,
Jodi Thelen, Jim Metzler, Michael Huddleston, Reed Birney, James Leo Herlihy
▶ Collaboration of Penn and screenwriter Steve Tesich traces young immigrant Wasson, his pals, and Thelen, the
free-spirited girl they all love in the 1960s.
Uneven but heartfelt film conveys sense
of turbulent lives in a turbulent decade.
Some terrific moments but also loses
some of its tension after an absolutely
shocking plot twist at the hero's wedding.

**FOUR HORSEMEN OF THE
APOCALYPSE, THE** 1962
★★★★ NR Drama 2:31
Dir: Vincente Minnelli   *Cast:* Glenn
Ford, Ingrid Thulin, Lee J. Cobb, Charles
Boyer, Paul Henreid

▶ Large-scale but unrealistic remake of the 1921 Valentino silent version about a family fighting on opposing sides in war (updated to World War II). The Four Horsemen are Conquest, War, Pestilence, and Death—a biblical allusion to the end of the earth. Entertaining, old-fashioned melodrama.

400 BLOWS, THE 1959 French
★★★ NR Drama 1:44 B&W
Dir: François Truffaut *Cast:* Jean-Pierre Leaud, Albert Remy, Patrick Auffray, Claire Maurier
▶ Troubled teenager Antoine Doinel (Leaud) turns to petty crime as parents and social institutions fail him. Technically adventurous, insightful, and really quite special. Truffaut's autobiographical directorial debut is one of the most memorable films of the French New Wave. Adventures of Doinel continued in four subsequent movies. ⑤

FOUR MUSKETEERS, THE 1975
★★★★ PG Action-Adventure 1:48
☑ Adult situations, violence
Dir: Richard Lester *Cast:* Michael York, Raquel Welch, Oliver Reed, Richard Chamberlain, Faye Dunaway, Frank Finlay
▶ York, Reed, Chamberlain, and Finlay battle the evil Milady (Dunaway) in this sequel to Richard Lester's *The Three Musketeers*. Begins with the same high spirits, comedy, and adventure of its predecessor but darkens as it goes on. Larger-than-life tale is quite engrossing and surprisingly emotion-packed, especially if you've already seen the first film (shot simultaneously, the two were released as separate movies).

FOUR SEASONS, THE 1981
★★★★ PG Comedy/Drama 1:47
☑ Brief nudity, adult situations, explicit language
Dir: Alan Alda *Cast:* Alan Alda, Carol Burnett, Sandy Dennis, Len Cariou, Rita Moreno, Jack Weston
▶ Conversational comedy/drama written, directed, and starring the affable Alda concerns three middle-class, middle-aged couples who vacation together four times over the course of a year. They cook, crack jokes, quip, and engage in heart-to-heart talks. Then Dennis and Cariou divorce, causing midlife crises all around. Harmless and endearing with a few amusing moments. Lovely locations in New England and the Virgin Islands; poignant Vivaldi score. Alda was Oscar-nominated for both directing and acting.

4TH MAN, THE 1979 Dutch
☆ NR Drama 1:44
☑ Nudity, adult situations, explicit language
Dir: Paul Verhoeven *Cast:* Jeroen Krabbe, Renee Soutendijk, Thom Hoffman, Dolf de Vries, Geert De Jong, Hans Veerman
▶ Bisexual writer Krabbe seduces bewitching beautician Soutendijk because he's interested in her fiancé, then learns that her three previous husbands died in "accidents." Will he be the fourth? An art house favorite for its strong eroticism and alluring production design, but frequent symbolic interludes are heavy going. ⑤

FOURTH PROTOCOL, THE 1987 British
★★★★ R Drama 1:59
☑ Nudity, adult situations, explicit language, violence
Dir: John Mackenzie *Cast:* Michael Caine, Pierce Brosnan, Joanna Cassidy, Ned Beatty, Julian Glover, Michael Gough
▶ Unorthodox British agent Caine uncovers a KGB plot to discredit NATO by destroying a strategic airbase with a miniature nuclear bomb. Racing against time, he tracks down Brosnan, the Russian spy assembling the bomb. Efficient version of Frederick Forsyth's best-seller sacrifices characterizations for nonstop plotting.

FOXES 1980
★★ R Drama 1:46
☑ Adult situations, explicit language, violence
Dir: Adrian Lyne *Cast:* Jodie Foster, Scott Baio, Sally Kellerman, Randy Quaid, Lois Smith, Cherie Currie
▶ Earthy coming-of-age melodrama follows troubled Los Angeles teenagers Foster, Currie, Marilyn Kagan, and Kandice Stroh as they cope with broken homes, drugs, and sex. Foster is outstanding in this realistic approach to modern problems, and Quaid contributes a strong bit as Kagan's boyfriend. (CC)

FOXY BROWN 1974
☆ R Action-Adventure 1:34
☑ Rape, nudity, adult situations, explicit language, graphic violence
Dir: Jack Hill *Cast:* Pam Grier, Antonio Fargas, Peter Brown, Terry Carty, Kathryn Loder, Harry Holcombe

▶ Tough nurse Grier takes revenge on the drug dealers responsible for the murder of her cop boyfriend. First target is her junkie brother Fargas. Extremely violent exploitation features particularly repulsive punishments for druglords Brown and Loder.

FRAMED 1975
★★ R Action-Adventure 1:46
☑ Nudity, adult situations, explicit language, violence
Dir: Phil Karlson *Cast:* Joe Don Baker, Conny Van Dyke, Gabriel Dell, John Marley, Brock Peters
▶ Professional gambler Baker, framed for murder by corrupt cops, spends four years in jail plotting his revenge. Predictable story competently handled. From the makers of *Walking Tall.*

FRANCES 1982
★★★★ R Biography 2:20
☑ Rape, nudity, adult situations, explicit language, violence
Dir: Graeme Clifford *Cast:* Jessica Lange, Kim Stanley, Sam Shepard, Bart Burns, Jeffrey DeMunn, Jordan Charney
▶ Disturbing biography of volatile beauty Frances Farmer (Lange), tracing her tragic decline from promising 1930s movie career to incarceration in mental institutions. Relentlessly downbeat story despite impressive performances from Lange, Shepard (playing a steady friend), and Stanley (returning to the screen after a lengthy absence as Farmer's domineering mother). Lange and Stanley won Oscar nominations.

FRANCIS 1950
★★★ NR Comedy 1:31 B&W
Dir: Arthur Lubin *Cast:* Donald O'Connor, Patricia Medina, ZaSu Pitts, Ray Collins, John McIntire, Eduard Franz
▶ Lowbrow antics about slow-thinking G. I. O'Connor who becomes a World War II hero with the help of Francis, a talking mule. When O'Connor tries to tell his officers about Francis's powers, he's sent repeatedly to the psycho ward. Chill Wills supplies the mule's voice in this first of a long-running series. Director Lubin went on to TV's "Mr. Ed."

FRANKENSTEIN 1931
★★★ NR Horror 1:11 B&W
Dir: James Whale *Cast:* Boris Karloff, Colin Clive, Mae Clarke, John Boles, Edward Van Sloan, Dwight Frye
▶ Mad Dr. Frankenstein (Clive) creates monster Karloff out of parts of corpses but finds he cannot control his creation. Frightened townspeople storm Karloff with torches but the indestructible creature lives on in countless sequels. Adaptation of Mary Shelley's novel is a screen classic, thanks to Karloff's tremendously sympathetic monster, Clive's intensity, and Whale's shadowy, atmospheric direction.

FRANKENSTEIN MEETS THE WOLF MAN 1943
★★★ NR Horror 1:13 B&W
Dir: Roy William Neill *Cast:* Lon Chaney, Jr., Ilona Massey, Bela Lugosi, Patric Knowles, Maria Ouspenskaya, Lionel Atwill
▶ Team-up of two favorite monsters: the Wolfman (Chaney) and Frankenstein (Lugosi). Plot involves Chaney looking for Dr. Frankenstein to cure his condition. Alas, all he finds is the monster, who prefers fighting to problem-solving.

FRANKIE AND JOHNNY 1966
★★ NR Musical 1:27
Dir: Frederick De Cordova *Cast:* Elvis Presley, Donna Douglas, Harry Morgan, Sue Ane Langdon, Nancy Kovack
▶ Mildly entertaining musical based on the famous title song. Presley is Johnny, a riverboat gambler down on his luck; Douglas plays Frankie, his jealous lover. Shapely Kovack provides the spark that sets the song's plot into motion. Other numbers include "When the Saints Go Marching In," "Petunia," and "What Every Woman Lives For."

FRANTIC 1988
★★★★ R Mystery-Suspense 2:00
☑ Brief nudity, adult situations, explicit language, violence
Dir: Roman Polanski *Cast:* Harrison Ford, Betty Buckley, Emmanuelle Seigner, John Mahoney, Jimmie Ray Weeks, Gerard Klein
▶ Ford, an American doctor, searches the streets of Paris for missing wife Buckley despite the indifference of the police and embassy officials. Sexy young Seigner holds the key to the kidnapping. Polished execution from Polanski, chic French locations, and Ford's refreshingly human heroism (he even gets jet lag) overcome mechanical plotting. **(CC)**

FRATERNITY VACATION 1985
★★ R Sex/Comedy 1:34
☑ Nudity, adult situations, explicit language, violence
Dir: James Frawley *Cast:* Stephen

Geoffreys, Sheree J. Wilson, Cameron Dye, Leigh McCloskey, Tim Robbins
► Amiable sex farce about spring break in Palm Springs. Two rival fraternities bet on who can win beautiful but aloof Wilson. Geoffreys is especially adept at playing the perpetually amorous nerd, Wendall. Bouncy tunes by Bananarama. (CC)

FREAKS 1932
☆ **NR Horror 1:05 B&W**
Dir: Tod Browning *Cast:* Wallace Ford, Olga Baclanova, Leila Hyams, Roscoe Ates, Harry Earles
► A community of circus freaks takes terrible revenge upon a beautiful trapeze performer who marries one of their troupe and then tries to poison him for his money. Strangely disturbing horror flick with a cast of physically deformed people alienated audiences of its day but retains its bizarre power.

FREAKY FRIDAY 1976
★★★★ **G Comedy 1:35**
Dir: Gary Nelson *Cast:* Barbara Harris, Jodie Foster, John Astin, Patsy Kelly, Dick Van Patten, Ruth Buzzi
► Suburban teen Foster magically gets her wish to switch places with her mom Harris. Spending time in new incarnations proves neither kids nor adults have it easy. Breezy and lightweight in the Disney way; insightful adaptation of her own book by Mary Rodgers, ingratiating performances by Foster and Harris.

FREEBIE AND THE BEAN 1974
★★★★ **R Action-Adventure/Comedy 1:53**
☑ Explicit language, violence
Dir: Richard Rush *Cast:* Alan Arkin, James Caan, Loretta Swit, Valerie Harper, Jack Kruschen, Alex Rocco
► Cops Arkin and Caan battle gangsters by chasing, shooting, and slugging their way through the streets of San Francisco. Rambunctious and energetic; Caan and Arkin make an engaging pair. Funniest scene: the cops drive through a bedroom window.

FREEWAY 1988
★★ **R Drama 1:31**
☑ Nudity, adult situations, explicit language, violence
Dir: Francis Delia *Cast:* Darlanne Fluegel, James Russo, Billy Drago, Richard Belzer, Michael Callan, Joey Palese
► Sniper loose on Los Angeles freeways kills Fluegel's husband. Policeman Callan

has no leads, although the killer strikes up relationship with radio psychologist Belzer. Russo, a neurotic ex-cop, convinces revenge-obsessed Fluegel to offer herself as decoy to the sniper. Wooden acting is a major drawback to this lurid treatment of a provocative subject.

FRENCH CONNECTION, THE 1971
★★★★★ **R Crime 1:44**
☑ Adult situations, explicit language, violence
Dir: William Friedkin *Cast:* Gene Hackman, Fernando Rey, Roy Scheider, Tony Lo Bianco
► New York City cop Popeye Doyle (Hackman) obsessively tries to bust international drug ring. Cat-and-mouse caper follows between Hackman and the elusive French mastermind Rey. A stunning thriller, unsurpassed for sheer visceral excitement. Director Friedkin combines street-smart grit with gut-wrenching suspense, especially in the incredible chase where Hackman pursues a runaway subway train. Oscars for Best Picture, Director, Screenplay, Editing, and Actor (Hackman, who is brilliant).

FRENCH CONNECTION II, THE 1975
★★★ **R Crime 1:59**
☑ Adult situations, explicit language, violence
Dir: John Frankenheimer *Cast:* Gene Hackman, Fernando Rey, Bernard Fresson, Jean-Pierre Castaldi, Charles Milot
► Tough New York cop Popeye Doyle (Hackman) trails slippery drug king Rey to Marseilles. Doyle is a fish out of water and he grates on nerves of French cop Fresson but he finally nabs his man. Pretty good sequel. Not as exciting as the original but outstanding work from Hackman (especially in a harrowing sequence where he goes cold turkey after bad guys inject him with drugs), effective locations and chases. (CC)

FRENCH LIEUTENANT'S WOMAN, THE 1981
★★ **R Drama 1:59**
☑ Brief nudity, adult situations, explicit language
Dir: Karel Reisz *Cast:* Meryl Streep, Jeremy Irons, Leo McKern, Hilton McRae, Emily Morgan
► Dark-hued romance featuring a fine performance by Streep as the 1860s Victorian governess jilted by handsome foreigner Irons. Screenwriter Harold Pinter

reworks the John Fowles novel by creating a movie-within-a-movie; the leads are also twentieth-century actors falling in love while shooting the film. Well-crafted and sumptuously photographed. Garnered Oscar nominations for Best Actress, Art Direction, Editing, Costume Design, and Screenplay.

FRENCH POSTCARDS 1979
★ **PG Comedy 1:31**
☑ Brief nudity, adult situations, explicit language
Dir: Willard Huyck *Cast:* Miles Chapin, Blanche Baker, David Marshall Grant, Debra Winger, Marie-France Pisier, Valerie Quennessen
▶ American college students Chapin, Grant, and Baker arrive in Paris for a year's study and find romance and adventure. Lightweight fluff with a minimal story, given much charm and atmosphere by the Paris locations and the attractive young cast. Chapin is fine and Mandy Patinkin has a brief but funny bit as an overzealous Iranian lover.

FRENZY 1972 British
★★ **R Mystery-Suspense 1:56**
☑ Rape, nudity, adult situations, violence
Dir: Alfred Hitchcock *Cast:* Jon Finch, Barry Foster, Barbara Leigh-Hunt, Anna Massey, Alec McCowen, Vivien Merchant
▶ The "necktie murderer" is raping and killing women in London. The cops suspect the sullen Finch but they may have the wrong man. Hitchcock's second-to-last movie is quite suspenseful and one of his best later efforts. Favorite moments: the body hidden in the lorry, the camera pulling back from one of the murder scenes, and the dryly humorous dinnertime scenes between cop McCowen and wife Merchant.

FRESH HORSES 1988
★★ **PG-13 Drama 1:45**
☑ Adult situations, explicit language
Dir: David Anspaugh *Cast:* Molly Ringwald, Andrew McCarthy, Patti D'Arbanville, Ben Stiller, Leon Russom, Molly Hagan
▶ McCarthy, an industrious college student engaged to a wealthy Cincinnati girl, becomes obsessed with Ringwald, a teenage dropout from a mysterious Kentucky farm. McCarthy falls in love despite evidence that Ringwald is a pathological liar and married prostitute. Somber,

ambitious romance based on Larry Ketron's play suffers from slow pacing.

FRIDAY THE 13TH 1980
★★ **R Horror 1:35**
☑ Nudity, adult situations, explicit language, graphic violence
Dir: Sean S. Cunningham *Cast:* Harry Crosby, Betsy Palmer, Adrienne King, Laurie Bartram, Mark Nelson
▶ Psychotic Mommy (Palmer) hacks up young counselors at Camp Crystal Lake to avenge the death of her son, who drowned twenty years ago while his counselors were making love. Box office surprise smash spawned innumerable sequels and a TV series.

FRIDAY THE 13TH, PART 2 1981
★★ **R Horror 1:27**
☑ Nudity, explicit language, graphic violence
Dir: Steve Miner *Cast:* Adrienne King, Amy Steel, John Furey, Betsy Palmer, Kirsten Baker
▶ Steel, the only survivor of the first *Friday the 13th*, tries to pull her life together but mysteriously disappears. Camp Crystal Lake is rejuvenated after five years and stories of the drowned child Jason are told around the campfires. And someone is still stalking the nubile teens.

FRIDAY THE 13TH, PART 3 1982
★★ **R Horror 1:35**
☑ Brief nudity, adult situations, explicit language, graphic violence
Dir: Steve Miner *Cast:* Dana Kimmell, Richard Brooker, Paul Kratka, Tracy Savage, Jeffrey Rogers
▶ Shot in 3-D, this third in the popular brand-name series is strictly formula: vanload of brainless teens + Camp Crystal Lake = bloody massacre. Relentless slashing and gashing grow wearisome.

FRIDAY THE 13TH—THE FINAL CHAPTER 1984
★★ **R Horror 1:30**
☑ Nudity, adult situations, explicit language, graphic violence
Dir: Joseph Zito *Cast:* Crispin Glover, Kimberly Beck, Barbara Howard, Erich Anderson, Corey Feldman, Alan Hayes
▶ Is Jason dead? The folks at the morgue think so until the killer's corpse rises up to kill the coroner. Maniac then goes to Crystal Lake to prey on new teens in town. Artful Harry Manfredini score, effective sound effects, and inventive killing methods will make you scream; ludicrous ending will not. **(CC)**

FRIDAY THE 13TH PART V: A NEW BEGINNING 1985
★★ R Horror 1:32
☑ Nudity, adult situations, explicit language, graphic violence
Dir: Danny Steinmann   *Cast:* John Shepherd, Melanie Kinnaman, Shavar Ross, Richard Young, Marco St. John
▶ Shepherd, after disposing of goalie-masked killer Jason in previous sequel, checks into camp for disturbed youngsters. History repeats itself in bloody fashion as machete murders maul staff and guests. Fifth installment hits familiar menacing notes: high corpse count, scary background music, and convincingly distressed cast. **(CC)**

FRIDAY THE 13TH PART 6: JASON LIVES 1986
★★ R Horror 1:27
☑ Adult situations, explicit language, graphic violence
Dir: Tom McLoughlin   *Cast:* Thom Mathews, Jennifer Cooke, David Kagen, Kerry Noonan, Renee Jones
▶ Jason's grave is dug up and a metal fence post is driven through his heart. Lightning strikes—and the wearer of the hockey mask is resurrected to slaughter with reckless abandon. Noninventive and routine; only so many ways to slice and dice.

FRIDAY THE 13TH PART VII—THE NEW BLOOD 1988
★★ R Horror 1:30
☑ Nudity, adult situations, explicit language, graphic violence
Dir: John Buechler   *Cast:* Lar Park Lincoln, Kevin Blair, Susan Blu, Terry Kiser, Kane Hodder, Heidi Kozak
▶ Telekinetic teen Lincoln, attempting to psychically revive her late father, instead accidentally resurrects goalie-masked killer Hodder. It's bloody business as usual as Hodder uses spikes, chain saws, and his own brute strength to slay promiscuous teenagers. Up to the series's gory standard. **(CC)**

FRIENDLY PERSUASION 1956
★★★★ NR Drama 2:18
Dir: William Wyler   *Cast:* Gary Cooper, Dorothy McGuire, Anthony Perkins, Marjorie Main, Richard Eyer
▶ Acclaimed drama of Civil War violence and its effects on the lives of a peace-loving Quaker family in Indiana, based on novel by Jessamyn West. Cooper and McGuire play the parents of Perkins, Oscar-nominated for his role as the eldest son who goes off to battle. Warm and charming film notched six Academy Award nominations, including Best Picture and Director. **(CC)**

FRIENDS OF EDDIE COYLE, THE 1973
★★ R Drama 1:42
☑ Adult situations, explicit language, violence
Dir: Peter Yates   *Cast:* Robert Mitchum, Peter Boyle, Richard Jordan, Steven Keats, Alex Rocco, Joe Santos
▶ Grim, compelling account of small-time hood Mitchum forced to turn informer on the Boston mob. Taut, convincing story paints an extremely bleak portrait of the underworld. Boyle does a sterling job as an untrustworthy bartender, but Mitchum dominates the film with his wonderful performance of a likable man worn out by a life of petty crime. Based on a George V. Higgins novel.

FRIGHT NIGHT 1985
★★★ R Horror 1:46
☑ Nudity, explicit language, violence
Dir: Tom Holland   *Cast:* Chris Sarandon, William Ragsdale, Amanda Bearse, Roddy McDowall, Stephen Geoffreys
▶ Teenager Ragsdale learns that neighbor Sarandon is a vampire. When girlfriend Bearse falls under fiend's evil spell, TV horror host McDowall agrees to help Ragsdale. Some plot holes but generally ingenious blend of horror and humor. Handsome Sarandon is a creepily effective bloodsucker; nice work from McDowall and Geoffreys as the hero's nerdy buddy. **(CC)**

FRIGHT NIGHT II 1988
★★ R Horror 1:41
☑ Nudity, explicit language, violence
Dir: Tommy Lee Wallace   *Cast:* Roddy McDowall, William Ragsdale, Traci Lin, Julie Carmen, Russell Clark, Merritt Butrick
▶ Ragsdale, after visiting shrink, is about to accept events of *Fright Night* as figments of his imagination until sexy vampire Carmen and three bloodsucking pals move into friend McDowall's building. Ragsdale and McDowall reteam to fight the newcomers. Sequel will entertain fans of the original but lacks its predecessor's verve.

FRISCO KID, THE 1979
★★★★ PG Western/Comedy 1:59

☑ Explicit language, violence, adult humor
Dir: Robert Aldrich **Cast:** Gene Wilder, Harrison Ford, Ramon Bieri, Val Bisoglio, Leo Fuchs
▶ Western spoof stars Wilder as a naive Polish rabbi who crosses America to head a San Francisco congregation during the Gold Rush. Ford is hilarious as a kindhearted bank robber who takes Wild-West Wilder under his wing.

FRITZ THE CAT 1972
★ X Animation/Adult 1:18
☑ Nudity, strong sexual content, adult situations, explicit language, violence
Dir: Ralph Bakshi
▶ Countercultural cat accidentally burns down his NYU dorm, then forsakes college life for sex, drugs, battles with the police, and a cross-country jaunt with other creatures. Freewheeling and outrageously controversial cartoon is for adults only. Based on the comic strip by R. Crumb.

FROGS 1972
★ PG Horror 1:31
☑ Mild violence
Dir: George McCowan **Cast:** Ray Milland, Sam Elliott, Joan Van Ark, Adam Roarke, Judy Pace
▶ Southern despot Milland despoils surrounding bayou, enraging the reptiles and amphibians living there. They patriotically wait until the Fourth of July to attack the wheelchair-bound Milland and his family. Funny on a camp level. (CC)

FROM BEYOND 1986
★ R Horror 1:25
☑ Nudity, adult situations, explicit language, graphic violence
Dir: Stuart Gordon **Cast:** Jeffrey Combs, Barbara Crampton, Ken Foree, Ted Sorel, Carolyn Purdy-Gordon
▶ Fantastic horror entry from the warped minds that created *Re-Animator*. Dr. Pretorious (Sorel) invents a machine that allows him to see the bizarre inhabitants of the beyond, but they can also see him. Mind-boggling special effects turn the professor's assistant Crawford (Combs) into a bald-headed brain eater. (CC)

FROM BEYOND THE GRAVE 1973 British
★★ PG Horror 1:38
Dir: Kevin Connor **Cast:** Peter Cushing, Donald Pleasence, Margaret Bannen,

Ian Bannen, David Warner, Lesley-Anne Down
▶ Cushing, the sinister owner of an antiques shop, is the macabre host for four occult tales in this well-mounted horror anthology. Uneven quality, with "The Elemental" (in which Margaret Leighton plays an unconventional psychic) the standout.

FROM HERE TO ETERNITY 1954
★★★★ NR War/Drama 1:53 B&W
Dir: Fred Zinnemann **Cast:** Burt Lancaster, Montgomery Clift, Deborah Kerr, Frank Sinatra, Donna Reed, Philip Ober
▶ Classic story about Army life in Hawaii before Pearl Harbor boasts blockbuster cast and gripping script. Clift is a rebellious bugler, Lancaster a career soldier having an affair with officer's wife Kerr, which climaxes in their famous beach love scene. Nominated for thirteen Oscars and won eight, including Best Picture, Director, Supporting Actor (Sinatra), and Supporting Actress (Reed). Based on the James Jones best-seller.

FROM MAO TO MOZART: ISAAC STERN IN CHINA 1980
★★★ G Documentary/Music 1:24
Dir: Murray Lerner **Cast:** Isaac Stern, David Golub, Tan Shuzhen
▶ World-renowned violinist Stern visits China and displays his virtuosity and passionate love for music in lectures and concerts. Noteworthy for revelations by Shuhzen of the Shanghai Conservatory of Music about his imprisonment during Chairman Mao's Cultural Revolution. Spirited account of East meeting West won Oscar for Best Documentary.

FROM NOON TILL THREE 1976
★★ PG Western 1:39
☑ Adult situations, explicit language
Dir: Frank D. Gilroy **Cast:** Charles Bronson, Jill Ireland, Douglas V. Fowley, Stan Haze, Hector Morales, Bert Williams
▶ Bronson is frightened outlaw Graham Dorsey, who avoids his gang's bank robbery by seducing beautiful widow Ireland; she exploits their brief affair by turning Graham into a mythical Wild West antihero in books and songs. Gentle satire on fame with Bronson pleasantly cast against type in a light comic role.

FROM RUSSIA, WITH LOVE 1963 British
★★★ NR Espionage/Action-Adventure
1:58
Dir: Terence Young **Cast:** Sean Con-

nery, Daniela Bianchi, Lotte Lenya, Pedro Armendariz, Robert Shaw
► Action in Istanbul and the Orient Express as Agent 007 (Connery) gets involved with beautiful Russian spy Bianchi as part of sinister Soviet plot. Very exciting James Bond thriller, one of the best in the series, is more realistic than later, more comic-book efforts and features two of 007's most memorable villains in the stoic Shaw and the creepy Lenya, of the stiletto-toed shoes.

FROM THE HIP 1987
★★★ **PG Comedy 1:52**
☑ Adult situations, explicit language
Dir: Bob Clark *Cast:* Judd Nelson, Elizabeth Perkins, John Hurt, Darren McGavin, Nancy Marchand
► Outrageous tactics help advance ambitious young defense attorney Nelson but he must wrestle with his conscience when he suspects new client Hurt is guilty of murder. Some laughs, if you can suspend your disbelief, but smug hero Judd is unappealing. Glib screenplay by David E. Kelley. **(CC)**

FROM THE TERRACE 1960
★★★★ **NR Drama 2:28**
Dir: Mark Robson *Cast:* Paul Newman, Joanne Woodward, Myrna Loy, Ina Balin, Leon Ames
► Young Newman marries pampered socialite Woodward and succeeds in the rat race as his marriage deteriorates. He then falls in love with the more down-to-earth Balin. High-class soap opera version of John O'Hara's popular novel of the idle rich, power, romance, and success. Newman and Woodward make it work as an entertaining romantic drama in the lush Hollywood tradition.

FRONT, THE 1976
★★★ **PG Drama 1:31**
☑ Adult situations, explicit language
Dir: Martin Ritt *Cast:* Woody Allen, Zero Mostel, Herschel Bernardi, Michael Murphy, Andrea Marcovicci
► During the McCarthy era, cashier Allen serves as a "front," submitting scripts under his own name so that blacklisted writers can continue to work. Allen rises to the top of the TV biz but develops a conscience when a congressional committee wants him to fink on his pals. Somewhat politically oversimplified but still effective comedy/drama. Mostel stands out as an actor driven to suicide by the witchhunt. Many involved in the film were

blacklisted (including Mostel, Ritt, Bernardi, and screenwriter Walter Bernstein).

FRONT PAGE, THE 1931
★★ **NR Comedy 1:41 B&W**
Dir: Lewis Milestone *Cast:* Adolphe Menjou, Pat O'Brien, Mary Brian, Edward Everett Horton, Walter Catlett
► First film version of the Ben Hecht/Charles MacArthur play. O'Brien is the reporter and Menjou his rascal editor covering the escape of an about-to-be-executed man in Chicago. Despite its age and three subsequent remakes (*His Girl Friday*, the Lemmon-Matthau *Front Page*, *Switching Channels*), the comedy still remains fresh.

FRONT PAGE, THE 1974
★★ **PG Comedy 1:45**
☑ Adult situations, explicit language
Dir: Billy Wilder *Cast:* Jack Lemmon, Walter Matthau, Susan Sarandon, Vincent Gardenia, David Wayne, Carol Burnett
► Chicago, 1920s: newspaperman Hildy Johnson (Lemmon) wants to give up his ink-stained existence and settle down with fiancée Sarandon. Hardnosed editor Walter Burns (Matthau) lures him back with the hottest story in town: an escaped killer hiding in the press room's rolltop desk. Third cinematic go-round for the Hecht-MacArthur comedy has Lemmon and Matthau providing frenetic fun.

FUGITIVE, THE 1947
★★★ **NR Drama 1:44 B&W**
Dir: John Ford *Cast:* Henry Fonda, Dolores Del Rio, Pedro Armendariz, Ward Bond, Leo Carrillo, J. Carrol Naish
► Fonda gives a memorable performance as a doubt-wracked priest trapped in a Mexico where Catholicism has been outlawed. Although the peasants are desperate for religious guidance, Fonda faces death each time he reveals his identity. Stark photography by Gabriel Figueroa is one of the best aspects of this loose adaptation of Graham Greene's *The Power and the Glory*.

FUGITIVE KIND, THE 1960
★★ **NR Drama 2:15 B&W**
Dir: Sidney Lumet *Cast:* Marlon Brando, Anna Magnani, Joanne Woodward, Maureen Stapleton, R. G. Armstrong, Victor Jory
► Itinerant musician Brando arrives in small Southern burg, gets involved with unhappily married woman Magnani. Town tramp Woodward also becomes in-

terested in Brando. Based on Tennessee Williams's play *Orpheus Descending*; some strong moments from the three stars but not on par with the playwright's best work.

FULLER BRUSH MAN, THE 1948
★★★ NR Comedy 1:33 B&W
Dir: S. Sylvan Simon *Cast:* Red Skelton, Janet Blair, Hillary Brooke, Don McGuire, Adele Jergens
▶ Bumbling door-to-door salesman Skelton stumbles across a murder mystery which he tries to solve with girlfriend Blair. Broad slapstick climax in a factory revives some old silent-film gags. Skelton briefly reprises his role in 1950's semisequel *The Fuller Brush Girl* starring Lucille Ball.

FULL METAL JACKET 1987
★★★★ R War 1:56
☑ Adult situations, explicit language, graphic violence
Dir: Stanley Kubrick *Cast:* Matthew Modine, Arliss Howard, Vincent D'Onofrio, Dorian Harewood, Lee Ermey, Adam Baldwin
▶ Blistering anti-Vietnam indictment from director Kubrick traces group of Marine recruits, led by ironic Private Joker (Modine), from boot camp to battlefield. The basic training sequence, a mini-movie in itself, contains amazingly foul-mouthed dialogue, great work from real-life drill sarge Ermey, and a shattering climax. The Vietnam scenes provide a gripping and visually powerful portrait of war. Not to be missed. **(CC)**

FULL MOON HIGH 1981
★★ PG Horror/Comedy 1:34
☑ Brief nudity, adult situations, explicit language, adult humor
Dir: Larry Cohen *Cast:* Adam Arkin, Roz Kelly, Elizabeth Hartman, Ed McMahon, Joanne Nail, Kenneth Mars
▶ Arkin, football star of Full Moon High, travels to Romania with his right-wing CIA agent dad McMahon and gets bitten by a werewolf. Upon his return, Arkin finds himself hungry for dog food, unable to play football, and ostracized by the community. Twenty years later, the ageless Arkin returns to his school, determined to make the football squad. Zany spoof has its moments.

FULL MOON IN BLUE WATER 1988
★★ R Drama 1:34
☑ Explicit language
Dir: Peter Masterson *Cast:* Gene Hackman, Teri Garr, Burgess Meredith, Elias Koteas
▶ Southern-fried story stars Hackman as Floyd, the owner of the Blue Water Bar and Grill, unable to shake the blues after his wife's disappearance in a boating accident several years before. He indulges in fantasies of her return while Garr, a Texas schoolbus driver, struts around in high heels and miniskirt hoping to attract his attention. Amiable and leisurely with down-home humor and fine performances from the ever-reliable Hackman and the sweetly wacky Garr. **(CC)**

FULL MOON IN PARIS 1984 French
☆ R Comedy 1:42
☑ Nudity
Dir: Eric Rohmer *Cast:* Pascale Ogier, Fabrice Luchini, Tcheky Karyo, Christian Vadim, Virginia Thevenet
▶ Young Ogier is torn between boyfriends Karyo, Luchini, and Vadim and two places (Paris and surrounding suburb) while searching for elusive happiness. When she finally decides what she wants, it is no longer available to her. A shade below top Rohmer but still insightful and witty in his fashion. Ogier died tragically shortly after release. Ⓢ

FUNERAL HOME 1982 Canadian
★ R Horror 1:33
☑ Adult situations, explicit language, violence
Dir: William Fruet *Cast:* Lesleh Donaldson, Kay Hawtrey, Barry Morse, Dean Garbett, Stephen Miller
▶ Teenager Donaldson living with her grandmother Hawtrey hears strange voices from the basement. Her curiosity turns to terror when she learns grandmom's house used to be a funeral parlor. Is her dead grandfather trying to contact her? Modest shocker strongly resembles *Psycho*.

FUNERAL IN BERLIN 1966 British
★★★ NR Espionage 1:42
Dir: Guy Hamilton *Cast:* Michael Caine, Eva Renzi, Paul Hubschmid, Oscar Homolka, Guy Doleman
▶ Sequel to *The Ipcress File* finds secret agent Harry Palmer (Caine) in Berlin trying to arrange the defection of a Soviet officer through a bogus funeral. Slick production and Caine's delicious wry humor make follow-up a worthy successor.

FUNHOUSE, THE 1981
★ R Horror 1:35

☑ Nudity, explicit language, graphic violence
Dir: Tobe Hooper   *Cast:* Elizabeth Berridge, Miles Chapin, Cooper Huckabee, Largo Woodruff, Sylvia Miles, Kevin Conway
▶ Four teens hole up in carnival funhouse for the night. Witnessing barker Conway's monster son kill fortune-teller Miles, they become the murderer's next targets. Atmospheric and not without tension; game cast tries hard but the violence and downbeat tone wear thin after a while.

FUN IN ACAPULCO 1963
★★★ NR Musical 1:37
Dir: Richard Thorpe   *Cast:* Elvis Presley, Ursula Andress, Elsa Cardenas, Paul Lukas, Larry Domasin, Alejandro Rey
▶ Presley plays a trapeze artist with vertigo who settles down to an easier job as lifeguard at a resort hotel. He must conquer his fear of heights to win lovely Andress. Scenery outrates the songs, which include "The Bullfighter Was a Lady," "There's No Room to Rhumba in a Sports Car," and "You Can't Say No in Acapulco."

FUNNY FACE 1957
★★★★ NR Musical 1:43
Dir: Stanley Donen   *Cast:* Audrey Hepburn, Fred Astaire, Kay Thompson, Michel Auclair, Robert Flemyng, Suzy Parker
▶ Elegant May-December romance, with Astaire playing a fashion photographer (based on Richard Avedon) who turns young bookstore clerk Hepburn into an internationally famous model. Slight plot buoyed by beautiful Paris locations, Oscar-nominated costumes by Edith Head and Hubert de Givenchy, and a wonderful George and Ira Gershwin score: "He Loves and She Loves," "How Long Has This Been Going On," "Clap Yo' Hands."

FUNNY FARM, THE 1983
★★ R Comedy 1:30
☑ Adult situations, explicit language, adult humor
Dir: Ron Clark   *Cast:* Miles Chapin, Eileen Brennan, Howie Mandel, Peter Aykroyd, Mike MacDonald
▶ A look at the agonies and the ecstasies of struggling young comedians. Chapin stars as a sweet comic from the Midwest trying to make it at a Santa Monica comedy club owned by Brennan. Many talented new comics, notably Mandel and MacDonald, are introduced in this likable romp. **(CC)**

FUNNY FARM 1988
★★★★ PG Comedy 1:41
☑ Explicit language
Dir: George Roy Hill   *Cast:* Chevy Chase, Madolyn Smith, Kevin O'Morrison, Joseph Maher, Jack Gilpin
▶ Sports reporter Chase moves to bucolic New England town to write a novel. But his neighbors are anything but friendly, his dream house causes slapstick complications, and his marriage to Smith falls apart when she writes a successful children's book. Mildly amusing comedy suits Chase's easygoing charm.

FUNNY GIRL 1968
★★★★★ G Biography/Musical 2:27
Dir: William Wyler   *Cast:* Barbra Streisand, Omar Sharif, Kay Medford, Anne Francis, Walter Pidgeon
▶ Charismatic musical biography of Ziegfeld Follies comedienne Fanny Brice portrays a familiar backstage story of star's rise from obscurity to fame and her doomed love for no-good Sharif. Major box-office hit with Streisand singing "People," "Don't Rain on My Parade," "My Man," and more. Schmaltzy, tuneful, and funny. Nominated for eight Oscars, including Best Picture. Streisand's Best Actress Oscar was shared with Katharine Hepburn for *The Lion in Winter*.

FUNNY LADY 1975
★★★★★ PG Biography/Musical 2:21
☑ Adult situations, explicit language
Dir: Herbert Ross   *Cast:* Barbra Streisand, James Caan, Omar Sharif, Roddy McDowall, Ben Vereen, Heidi O'Rourke
▶ Successful Ziegfeld star Fanny Brice (Streisand), divorced from Nicky Arnstein (Sharif), meets and marries showman Billy Rose (Caan). They drift apart and, by the time she realizes she loves him, he's fallen for Olympic swimming star Eleanor Holm (O'Rourke). "I'm her Nick," Caan tells Streisand. Sequel to megahit *Funny Girl* features showstopping hits "How Lucky Can You Get" (Oscar-nominated) and oldies "Me and My Shadow" and "Paper Moon." Also nominated for Cinematography, Sound, Scoring, and Costume Design.

FUNNY MONEY 1983 British
★★ NR Comedy 1:32
☑ Nudity, explicit language

Dir: James Kenelm Clarke *Cast:* Gregg Henry, Elizabeth Daily, Gareth Hunt, Annie Ross, Derren Nesbitt
▶ Two Yankee con artists, lounge pianist Henry and hooker Daily, team up at a London hotel to collect as many credit cards as possible from the guests. Corny and predictable, with a smattering of sexy jokes.

FUNNY THING HAPPENED ON THE WAY TO THE FORUM, A 1966
★ ★ ★ ★ **NR Comedy 1:39**
Dir: Richard Lester *Cast:* Zero Mostel, Phil Silvers, Jack Gilford, Buster Keaton, Michael Crawford
▶ Mostel, a scheming slave in ancient Rome, tries everything to win his freedom, dragging protesting accomplice Gilford along on outrageous schemes involving pimp Silvers and naive lover Crawford. Frantic adaptation of the Broadway hit has some wonderful slapstick, particularly by Keaton in his last feature. Stephen Sondheim score (including "Comedy Tonight" and "Lovely") won an Oscar.

FUN WITH DICK AND JANE 1977
★ ★ ★ ★ **PG Comedy 1:35**
☑ Explicit language, adult humor
Dir: Ted Kotcheff *Cast:* George Segal, Jane Fonda, Ed McMahon, Dick Gautier, Allan Miller
▶ See Dick (Segal). See Jane (Fonda). They live the American dream. Dick loses his job as an aerospace engineer. They run from bill collectors. See Dick and Jane become the Bonnie and Clyde of suburbia to maintain their standard of living. Rob, Jane, rob! Beat the system, Dick! Laugh, folks, laugh, in this wry, polished comedy.

FURY 1936
★ ★ ★ **NR Drama 1:30 B&W**
Dir: Fritz Lang *Cast:* Sylvia Sidney, Spencer Tracy, Walter Abel, Bruce Cabot, Edward Ellis
▶ Lynch mob attacks innocent Tracy. He survives the battle and plots revenge against his tormentors, although girlfriend Sidney softens his thirst for vengeance. An upbeat ending can't dim the dark power of Lang's vision. Suspense with a social conscience.

FURY, THE 1978
★ ★ ★ ★ **R Mystery-Suspense 1:58**
☑ Explicit language, violence
Dir: Brian De Palma *Cast:* Kirk Douglas, Andrew Stevens, John Cassavetes, Carrie Snodgress, Amy Irving

▶ Stevens, a young man with ESP, is kidnapped by bad-guy secret-agent Cassavetes. Father Douglas desperately attempts to get him back safely. Irving plays a girl with psychokinetic powers enlisted to help. Bloody and violent, with a literally explosive ending.

FUTURE-KILL 1985
★ **R Sci-Fi 1:25**
☑ Nudity, explicit language, graphic violence
Dir: Ronald Moore *Cast:* Edwin Neal, Marilyn Burns, Doug Davis
▶ Social consciousness and blood-and-guts are combined in this unusual low-budgeter featuring the stars of *The Texas Chain Saw Massacre.* Neal plays Splatter, a punked-out No-Nukes activist who wears armor over his radiation wounds and kills with his hooklike hand. In Barbarella garb, tough-chick Burns supplies ammo to fraternity boys to get rid of Splatter and his goons.

FUTUREWORLD 1976
★ ★ ★ ★ **PG Sci-Fi 1:47**
☑ Adult situations, explicit language, mild violence
Dir: Richard T. Heffron *Cast:* Peter Fonda, Blythe Danner, Arthur Hill, Jim Antonio, John P. Ryan, Stuart Margolin
▶ Sequel to *Westworld* concerns scientist Ryan's conspiracy to replace world leaders with robot replicas. Investigative reporters Fonda and Danner find their lives in jeopardy when they stumble across the plan while touring Ryan's amusement complex. NASA's Houston Space Center provides a realistic backdrop to this entertaining fantasy. Yul Brynner repeats his *Westworld* role in a brief cameo.

FUZZ 1972
★ ★ **PG Action-Adventure 1:32**
☑ Adult situations, mild violence
Dir: Richard A. Colla *Cast:* Burt Reynolds, Jack Weston, Tom Skerritt, Raquel Welch, Yul Brynner, Charles Martin Smith
▶ Black comedy about off-the-wall cops in a tough Boston precinct is episodic but fast-paced. Welch, an alluring undercover cop, and Smith, a baby-faced punk, stand out in the large cast. Humor is often vulgar, but Reynolds in a nun's habit is a sight to see. Adapted by Evan Hunter from a novel written under his Ed McBain pseudonym.

F/X 1986
★ ★ ★ ★ **R Action-Adventure 1:48**

☑ Adult situations, explicit language, violence

Dir: Robert Mandel *Cast:* Bryan Brown, Brian Dennehy, Diane Venora, Cliff Young, Mason Adams, Jerry Orbach
▶ Justice Department official Adams hires movie special effects wizard Brown to fake the assassination of mobster Orbach. Double-crossed, Brown becomes the target of a police manhunt. Props and tricks help him survive the taut chase that makes up most of the film. Twisty plot and accurate use of New York locations enliven this smooth entertainment. (CC)

GABRIELA 1984 Brazilian
★★ R Comedy 1:42
☑ Nudity, strong sexual content, adult situations, explicit language, mild violence

Dir: Bruno Barreto *Cast:* Marcello Mastroianni, Sonia Braga, Antonio Cantafora, Paulo Goulart, Nelson Xavier
▶ Mastroianni plays a libidinous Bahian tavernkeeper who procures lusty peasant girl Braga to be his cook, lover, and eventually his bride. Sexy Braga is the film's biggest draw. Based on Jorge Amado's novel, also made into a top Brazilian soap opera. ⑤

GABY—A TRUE STORY 1987
★★★★★ R Biography/Drama 1:54
☑ Nudity, adult situations, explicit language

Dir: Luis Mandoki *Cast:* Rachel Levin, Norma Aleandro, Liv Ullmann, Lawrence Monoson, Robert Loggia
▶ Tasteful and compassionate story of Gaby Brimmer (Levin), born with such severe cerebral palsy that all but her left foot was completely paralyzed. Her fully functioning mind, however, enabled her to become a famous writer. Gaby and boyfriend Monoson are played so realistically that critics thought both actors were disabled in real life. Aleandro won an Oscar nomination for her role as the woman who devotes her life to Gaby. An inspiring, beautiful movie that will leave no one untouched.

GALAXINA 1980
☆ R Sci-Fi/Comedy 1:36
☑ Brief nudity, explicit language, adult humor

Dir: William Sachs *Cast:* Stephen Macht, Dorothy Stratten, Avery Schreiber, James David Hinton
▶ Feeble attempt at a "Star Trek"/*Star*

Wars satire falls flat with cheap production and a vulgar, humorless script. In her last film, Dorothy Stratten, former *Playboy* Playmate (whose murder was the subject of *Star 80* and *Death of a Centerfold: The Dorothy Stratten Story*), gives a wooden performance as the beautiful robot Galaxina.

GALAXY OF TERROR 1981
★ R Sci-Fi 1:21
☑ Nudity, explicit language, graphic violence

Dir: B. D. Clark *Cast:* Edward Albert, Erin Moran, Ray Walston, Bernard Behrens, Zalman King
▶ A spaceship rescue mission lands on the planet Morganthus to investigate the strange deaths of a sister ship's crew members. The team, led by Moran, is eliminated one by one when their innermost fears materialize (e.g., one worm-hating female is molested and "slimed" by a giant squishy nightcrawler). Borrows generously from *Aliens*.

GALLANT HOURS, THE 1960
★★ NR Biography 1:51 B&W
Dir: Robert Montgomery *Cast:* James Cagney, Dennis Weaver, Ward Costello, Richard Jaeckel, Les Tremayne
▶ Realistic, sober account of Admiral William "Bull" Halsey (Cagney) focuses on his strategies during the bloody fighting at Guadalcanal. Documentary approach provides a look at the human conflicts behind large-scale World War II battles (including Halsey's personal rivalry with Japanese Admiral Yamamoto). Director Montgomery narrates a portion of the film.

GALLIPOLI 1981 Australian
★★★ PG War 1:51
☑ Brief nudity, explicit language, violence

Dir: Peter Weir *Cast:* Mel Gibson, Mark Lee, Bill Kerr, Robert Grubb, David Argue
▶ Young Australian idealists Gibson and Lee join the army to fight in World War I and are sent to Gallipoli, the site of a devastating battle. Harrowing war drama boasts excellent performances and stunning production values.

GAMBIT 1966
★★★ NR Action-Adventure 1:49
Dir: Ronald Neame *Cast:* Shirley MacLaine, Michael Caine, Herbert Lom, Roger C. Carmel, John Abbott
▶ In Hong Kong, criminal Caine enlists

Eurasian MacLaine in his scheme to out-wit wealthy Arab Lom for possession of a valuable statue. Ingeniously plotted and stylishly performed by Caine and Mac-Laine. Underrated on initial release; has become a cult favorite over the years.

GAMBLER, THE 1974
★ ★ R Drama 1:51
☑ Adult situations, explicit language
Dir: Karel Reisz *Cast:* James Caan, Paul Sorvino, Lauren Hutton, Morris Carnovsky, Burt Young, Jacqueline Brookes
▶ College professor Axel Freed (Caan) is a compulsive gambler who runs up a $44,000 debt to the Mafia. Intelligent and intense character study is nicely directed by Reisz and finely acted by Caan, Sorvino, Carnovsky, and especially Brookes as Caan's concerned mother.

GAME OF DEATH 1979
★ R Martial Arts 1:41
☑ Explicit language, violence
Dir: Robert Clouse *Cast:* Bruce Lee, Gig Young, Dean Jagger, Colleen Camp, Hugh O'Brian
▶ Kung-fu film star Lee, shot in the face by an evil crime syndicate, must undergo reconstructive plastic surgery. With a new identity, he gets even by eliminating the mob with his bare hands (and feet). Martial arts idol Lee died midway during production and a double was substituted. Best sequence is a fight between the real Lee and basketball star Kareem Abdul-Jabbar.

GANDHI 1982
★ ★ ★ ★ ★ PG Biography 3:11
☑ Violence
Dir: Richard Attenborough *Cast:* Ben Kingsley, John Gielgud, Martin Sheen, Candice Bergen, Trevor Howard
▶ Epic chronicle of Mahatma Gandhi's life, from his early days as an attorney fighting prejudice in South Africa to India's spiritual and political leader. Kingsley creates an uncannily accurate portrait of the nonviolent leader, killed by an assassin in 1948. Lavish, grand-scaled production won eight Oscars, including Best Picture, Actor, Director, Cinematography, and Costumes.

GANG THAT COULDN'T SHOOT STRAIGHT, THE 1971
★ ★ PG Comedy 1:36
☑ Adult situations
Dir: James Goldstone *Cast:* Jerry Orbach, Leigh Taylor-Young, Robert De Niro, Lionel Stander, Jo Van Fleet

▶ After sponsoring a bike race that fails, small-time Brooklyn mafioso Orbach has a falling-out with mob chief Stander and decides to eliminate him. Overly broad ethnic comedy, from the Jimmy Breslin best-seller, has one saving grace: an extremely funny performance by a young De Niro as an oversexed, kleptomaniac bike racer.

GARBO TALKS 1984
★ ★ PG-13 Comedy/Drama 1:44
☑ Adult situations, explicit language, adult humor
Dir: Sidney Lumet *Cast:* Ron Silver, Anne Bancroft, Catherine Hicks, Carrie Fisher, Harvey Fierstein
▶ Loving son Silver attempts to grant dying mother Bancroft's final wish: to meet ultrareclusive Greta Garbo. Offbeat charmer with flaky humor and a sentimental heart. **(CC)**

GARDEN OF ALLAH, THE 1936
★ ★ NR Romance 1:18
Dir: Richard Boleslawski *Cast:* Marlene Dietrich, Charles Boyer, Basil Rathbone, C. Aubrey Smith, Tilly Losch, John Carradine
▶ After the death of her father, long-suffering Dietrich flees to the Algerian desert, where she falls under the spell of moody ex-monk Boyer, hiding a dark secret about his past. Murky, stilted romance won an Oscar for its ravishing Technicolor.

GARDEN OF THE FINZI-CONTINIS, THE 1971 Italian
★ ★ R Drama 1:34
☑ Brief nudity, adult situations
Dir: Vittorio De Sica *Cast:* Dominique Sanda, Lino Capolicchio, Helmut Berger, Fabio Testi, Romolo Valli
▶ In Italy, a wealthy Jewish family pays little heed to the winds of World War II, realizing too late the danger that threatens them. Testi, the lover of daughter Sanda, is killed in battle as the government orders the imprisonment of the Jews. Engrossing, cautionary tale won Best Foreign Film Oscar. ⑤

GARDENS OF STONE 1987
★ ★ ★ ★ R Drama 1:52
☑ Adult situations, explicit language
Dir: Francis Coppola *Cast:* James Caan, Anjelica Huston, James Earl Jones, D. B. Sweeney, Dean Stockwell, Mary Stuart Masterson
▶ Sober examination of the Vietnam War years told from the perspective of soldiers

assigned to Arlington National Cemetery. Caan is a grizzled sergeant who wants a transfer to an infantry training post; Huston plays his journalist girlfriend. Blustery sergeant Jones and recruit's fiancée Masterson stand out in this accomplished but curiously detached drama. **(CC)**

GAS 1981 Canadian
★ **R Comedy 1:34**
☑ Adult situations, explicit language, adult humor
Dir: Les Rose *Cast:* Donald Sutherland, Susan Anspach, Howie Mandel, Sterling Hayden, Helen Shaver, Peter Aykroyd
▶ Midwestern city goes through gasoline shortage when tycoon Hayden hoards supply to drive up prices. Reporter Anspach investigates, and wild disc jockey Sutherland circles overhead in helicopter to keep townsfolk informed as gas lines form. Crazy, nonstop slapstick humor features many outrageous stunts.

GASLIGHT 1944
★★★ **NR Mystery-Suspense 1:54 B&W**
Dir: George Cukor *Cast:* Ingrid Bergman, Charles Boyer, Joseph Cotten, Dame May Whitty, Angela Lansbury
▶ Victorian London: wealthy young Bergman marries seemingly wonderful Boyer who proceeds to make her think she's going insane. The evil plan works all too well until detective Cotten gets involved in the case. Gripping and atmospheric. Three great performances: Bergman (Oscar-winning), Boyer (Oscar-nominated), and Lansbury (also nominated for her debut as the maid). A Best Picture nominee.

GAS-S-S-S! 1970
★ **PG Comedy 1:19**
☑ Explicit language, violence
Dir: Roger Corman *Cast:* Bud Cort, Cindy Williams, Robert Corff, Ben Vereen, Talia Shire, Marshall McLuhan
▶ Nerve gas kills everyone over thirty, leaving isolated bands of murderous teens ruling the country. Corman's version of the apocalypse is an overwrought, fragmented black comedy that doesn't quite conquer its low-budget limitations. Some worthwhile moments from the young cast, many on the verge of stardom. Music by Country Joe and the Fish.

GATE, THE 1987 Canadian
★★ **PG-13 Horror 1:32**
☑ Explicit language, violence

Dir: Tibor Takacs *Cast:* Stephen Dorff, Christa Denton, Louis Tripp, Kelly Rowan, Jennifer Irvin
▶ Young Dorff and his friend Tripp explore a suburban backyard hole, unwittingly freeing the Demon Lord and his horde of ghastly trolls into contemporary suburbia. Dreary first half-hour gives way to a fun plot, clever special effects, and strong climax.

GATE OF HELL 1954 Japanese
★★ **NR Drama 1:30**
Dir: Teinosuke Kinugasa *Cast:* Machiko Kyo, Kazuo Hasegawa, Isao Yamagata, Koreya Senda
▶ In twelfth-century Japan, an emperor grants a warrior any wish he desires. He chooses another man's wife but she sacrifices herself rather than live without the man she loves. Vividly staged war scenes are combined with passionate romantic tragedy in a foreign classic with broad appeal. Won Oscars for Best Foreign Film and Costume Design, plus New York Film Critics Award and Best Film at Cannes Film Festival. ⑤

GATHERING, THE 1977
★★★★★ **NR Drama/MFTV 1:34**
Dir: Randal Kleiser *Cast:* Edward Asner, Maureen Stapleton, Bruce Davison, Veronica Hamel, Gregory Harrison, Lawrence Pressman
▶ Asner, a lonely, dying father, reaches out to alienated wife Stapleton and children for one last Christmas celebration. Exquisite Emmy-winning tearjerker pulls out all the stops on its way to a sentimental climax. Sequel, *The Gathering, Part II*, appeared in 1979.

GATHERING OF EAGLES, A 1963
★★ **NR Drama 1:55**
Dir: Delbert Mann *Cast:* Rock Hudson, Rod Taylor, Leif Erickson, Mary Peach, Barry Sullivan, Kevin McCarthy
▶ Harsh discipline of strict colonel Hudson upsets the pilots of his Strategic Air Command base. On the home front, wife Peach faces difficulties adjusting to military life. Prosaic handling of familiar material distinguished only by its peacetime setting.

GATOR 1976
★★★★ **PG Action-Adventure 1:56**
☑ Adult situations, violence
Dir: Burt Reynolds *Cast:* Burt Reynolds, Jack Weston, Lauren Hutton, Jerry Reed, Alice Ghostley, Mike Douglas
▶ Moonshiner Reynolds (reprising his

White Lightning character) is coerced by pushy New York Fed Weston into ratting on his friend, local crime czar Reed. After a romantic liaison with TV reporter Hutton, Reynolds takes on corrupt governor Douglas instead. Directing debut for Reynolds.

GAUNTLET, THE 1977
★★★★ R Action-Adventure 1:49
☑ Nudity, explicit language, violence
Dir: Clint Eastwood *Cast:* Clint Eastwood, Sondra Locke, Pat Hingle, William Prince, Kenneth McKinney
▶ Disillusioned Phoenix cop Eastwood escorts hard-bitten hooker Locke from Las Vegas to testify in a mob trial. Gradually, they realize corrupt politicians want them both dead. Escalating violence provides plenty of thrills and humor, especially during an eye-opening fight between a motorcycle and helicopter. Eastwood brings welcome depth to his character.

GAY DIVORCEE, THE 1934
★★★ NR Musical 1:47 B&W
Dir: Mark Sandrich *Cast:* Fred Astaire, Ginger Rogers, Alice Brady, Edward Everett Horton, Erik Rhodes, Eric Blore
▶ First starring vehicle for Astaire and Rogers is a dated but enjoyable farce about divorcée Rogers who mistakes Astaire for corespondent Rhodes in her court case. Achingly romantic dances include "A Needle in a Haystack," "Night and Day," and the Oscar-winning "The Continental." Low point in the strained comic relief is Horton's duet with a young Betty Grable to "Let's K-nock K-nees."

GENE KRUPA STORY, THE 1959
★★ NR Biography/Music 1:41 B&W
Dir: Don Weis *Cast:* Sal Mineo, Susan Kohner, James Darren, Susan Oliver, Yvonne Craig
▶ Mineo stars in this antiseptic biography of the great jazz drummer, portraying his fall from grace due to drug addiction. Mineo is obviously miscast, but the songs are first-rate: "Memories of You" (sung by Anita O'Day), "Indiana" (with Red Nichols), "Cherokee," "Drum Crazy," etc.

GENERAL, THE 1927
★★★★ NR Comedy 1:18 B&W
Dir: Buster Keaton *Cast:* Buster Keaton, Marion Mack, Glen Cavender, Jim Farley, Frederick Vroom, Joe Keaton
▶ Union soldiers hijack train containing Mack, Confederate engineer Keaton's girlfriend; he singlehandedly pursues them into a Northern compound in one of film's greatest chase sequences. Keaton's silent masterpiece not only contains some of his best sight gags, but also provides a meticulous reconstruction of the Civil War era. Based on a real incident. Remade by Disney in 1956 as *The Great Locomotive Chase*.

GENEVIEVE 1953 British
★★ NR Comedy 1:26
Dir: Henry Cornelius *Cast:* John Gregson, Dinah Sheridan, Kay Kendall, Kenneth More, Geoffrey Keen
▶ Gregson and More and their vintage autos compete in a London-to-Brighton road race. Their hapless mates, Sheridan and Kendall, view the battle as juvenile madness. One of the most entertaining and lighthearted romps ever to come out of England. Kendall is delightful.

GENTLE GIANT 1967
★★★★ NR Family 1:33
Dir: James Neilson *Cast:* Dennis Weaver, Vera Miles, Clint Howard, Ralph Meeker, Huntz Hall, Charles Martin
▶ Seven-year-old Florida boy Howard befriends a lumbering but harmless bear. Despite Howard's pleas, father Weaver, a wildlife officer, returns the bear to the Everglades. But the bear proves to be a hero when he saves Weaver's life. Pleasant family-oriented story led to the TV series "Gentle Ben."

GENTLEMAN JIM 1942
★★★ NR Biography/Sports 1:44 B&W
Dir: Raoul Walsh *Cast:* Errol Flynn, Alexis Smith, Jack Carson, Alan Hale, John Loder, Ward Bond
▶ Story of nineteenth-century heavyweight boxing champion "Gentleman" Jim Corbett (Flynn), whose dandyish ways outside the ring belied his skill inside it. Few directors handled male bonding as well as Walsh, especially in demonstrating Corbett's relationship with defeated rival Bond, which goes from baiting to mutual respect in quite touching fashion. **(CC)**

GENTLEMAN'S AGREEMENT 1947
★★★★★ NR Drama 1:58 B&W
Dir: Elia Kazan *Cast:* Gregory Peck, Dorothy McGuire, John Garfield, Celeste Holm, Dean Stockwell
▶ Magazine writer Peck researches anti-Semitism by pretending to be Jewish and finds himself the target of contempt and bigotry. Probing, intelligent (if somewhat

dated) drama from Laura Z. Hobson's best-seller. Landmark treatment of a then shocking subject won Oscars for Best Picture, Director, and Supporting Actress (Holm). Peck was also nominated.

GENTLEMEN PREFER BLONDES 1953
★★★★ NR Musical 1:31
Dir: Howard Hawks *Cast:* Jane Russell, Marilyn Monroe, Charles Coburn, Elliott Reid, Tom Noonan, George Winslow
► Flashy musical about the antics of Anita Loos's famous golddigger Lorelei (Monroe), en route to Paris with best friend Russell to marry a millionaire. Russell falls for private eye Reid, who's searching for incriminating evidence against Monroe. She has an innocent flirtation with elderly jeweler Coburn. Songs include Monroe's classic "Diamonds Are a Girl's Best Friend" and "Two Little Girls From Little Rock." Followed by *Gentlemen Marry Brunettes.*

GEORGY GIRL 1966 British
★★ NR Comedy 1:39 B&W
Dir: Silvio Narizzano *Cast:* Lynn Redgrave, Alan Bates, James Mason, Charlotte Rampling, Rachel Kempson, Bill Owen
► Homely Redgrave wins the heart of parents' employer Mason. Meanwhile, Redgrave falls for her promiscuous roommate Rampling's lover Bates. When Rampling has an unwanted baby, Redgrave treats the child as her own. Funny and affecting. Bates, Mason, and Rampling are excellent; Redgrave's Oscar-nominated performance is unforgettable. Hit Tom Springfield/Jim Dale theme sung by The Seekers.

GETAWAY, THE 1972
★★★★ PG Action-Adventure 2:02
☑ Adult situations, explicit language, violence
Dir: Sam Peckinpah *Cast:* Steve McQueen, Ali MacGraw, Ben Johnson, Sally Struthers, Al Lettieri, Slim Pickens
► Double-crossed after a bank robbery, ex-con McQueen and girlfriend MacGraw must kill the accomplices and crooked cop Johnson who framed them before escaping to Mexico. Violent, fast-paced version of cult favorite Jim Thompson's novel with top-notch action sequences.

GET CRAZY 1983
★ R Comedy 1:32
☑ Nudity, adult situations, explicit language, adult humor

Dir: Allan Arkush *Cast:* Malcolm McDowell, Allen Goorwitz, Daniel Stern, Gail Edwards, Miles Chapin, Ed Begley, Jr.
► Hip, good-natured rock satire takes place during a New Year's Eve concert at the Saturn Theater as rock promoter Goorwitz puts together a superstar show to save the lease on his building. Filled with amusing cameos (Bobby Sherman, Fabian, Mary Woronov, etc.) and dead-on parodies of Mick Jagger (McDowell) and Bob Dylan (Lou Reed).

GET OUT YOUR HANDKERCHIEFS 1978 French
★★ R Comedy 1:49
☑ Nudity, strong sexual content, adult situations, explicit language
Dir: Bertrand Blier *Cast:* Gerard Depardieu, Carole Laure, Patrick Dewaere, Riton
► Depardieu stars in this unconventional story of a man who will do anything to satisfy his sexually frustrated wife Laure, including introducing her to precocious thirteen-year-old Mozart prodigy, Riton. Eyebrow-raising, controversial black comedy won an Oscar for Best Foreign Film. Strictly adult fare.

GETTING EVEN 1986
★★★ R Mystery-Suspense 1:30
☑ Nudity, explicit language, violence
Dir: Dwight H. Little *Cast:* Audrey Landers, Edward Albert, Joe Don Baker, Blue Deckert, Dan Shackelford
► Big Texas corporations battle over secret-weapon nerve gas stolen from the Russians. Ridiculous plot involves recovering the poison gas (hidden on top of a Dallas skyscraper) before the city goes up with a bang. Albert stars as the dashing young hero, Tag Taggart. Farfetched, clumsy thriller with modest suspense.

GETTING OF WISDOM, THE 1977 Australian
★★ NR Drama 1:41
☑ Explicit language
Dir: Bruce Beresford *Cast:* Susannah Fowle, Barry Humphries, John Waters, Sheila Helpmann, Hilary Ryan
► Fowle is a rough-hewn country girl, sent off to a Victorian girls' school where the other students make fun of her homemade clothes and unsophisticated manners. Even the teachers are shocked by her unpolished honesty. But the strong-willed Fowle eventually wins them over with her free spirit and musical talents.

Beautifully shot turn-of-the-century recreations, but heavy Australian accents and slow pace may require more patience than most viewers want to muster.

GET TO KNOW YOUR RABBIT 1972
★ R Comedy 1:32
☑ Adult situations, explicit language
Dir: Brian De Palma *Cast:* Tom Smothers, John Astin, Suzanne Zenor, Samantha Jones, Allen Garfield, Katharine Ross
▶ Strained satire about businessman Smothers, who rejects his conservative lifestyle to enroll in a magic school run by Orson Welles. Smothers tours as a tap-dancing magician, but discovers entertainment just as stifling as business. Early De Palma effort makes some good points despite the muddled plot.

GHOST AND MRS. MUIR, THE 1947
★★★★★ NR Fantasy/Romance 1:44 B&W
Dir: Joseph L. Mankiewicz *Cast:* Rex Harrison, Gene Tierney, George Sanders, Vanessa Brown, Edna Best, Natalie Wood
▶ Widow Tierney and her daughter Wood move into a seaside cottage haunted by Harrison, the ghost of a nineteenth-century sea captain. Harrison falls in love with Tierney and rescues her from financial woes, but the material world soon interferes with the spiritual romance. Lavishly produced fantasy with two great stars is one of filmdom's most romantic stories and should not be confused with the TV series.

GHOSTBUSTERS 1984
★★★★★ PG Comedy 1:45
☑ Explicit language, violence
Dir: Ivan Reitman *Cast:* Bill Murray, Dan Aykroyd, Sigourney Weaver, Harold Ramis, Rick Moranis, Annie Potts
▶ Columbia University parapsychologists Murray, Aykroyd, and Ramis lose their grant and go into business as free-lance exorcists. Their first major gig: dealing with Weaver's haunted refrigerator ("Usually you don't see such behavior in a major appliance," deadpans Murray). Her building turns out to be a receiving tower for ghosts and spirits, and the intrepid boys battle a giant Staypuff Marshmallow man, among others. Hilarious mixture of ectoplasmic monsters, special effects, action, and comedy. Murray is a scream. The highest-grossing comedy of all time. (CC)

GHOST FEVER 1987
★ PG Comedy 1:26
☑ Adult situations, explicit language
Dir: Alan Smithee *Cast:* Sherman Hemsley, Luis Avalos, Jennifer Rhodes, Deborah Benson, Pepper Martin
▶ Low-budget comedy with breakdancing ghosts. Hemsley and Avalos are bumbling black detectives in the Deep South. Sent to evict two old ladies from a creepy mansion, they are met by a bigoted antebellum ghost.

GHOST GOES WEST, THE 1936 British
★★★ NR Comedy 1:25 B&W
Dir: René Clair *Cast:* Robert Donat, Jean Parker, Eugene Pallette, Elsa Lanchester, Ralph Bunker
▶ Eighteenth-century Scotsman Murdoch (Donat) dies a coward and is forced to haunt his castle. When American Pallette buys the castle and moves it to Florida, the ghost and his modern-day descendant Donald (also Donat) go along: Murdoch to redeem his honor, Donald to win Pallette's daughter Parker. Whimsical comedy by Robert Sherwood has an appealingly light tone.

GHOST STORY 1981
★★★ R Horror 1:51
☑ Nudity, explicit language, mild violence
Dir: John Irvin *Cast:* Fred Astaire, Melvyn Douglas, Douglas Fairbanks, Jr., John Houseman, Craig Wasson, Patricia Neal
▶ Elderly New Englanders Astaire, Houseman, Fairbanks, and Douglas assuage their guilt over a dark secret in the past by telling each other ghost stories. The appearance of Fairbanks's son Wasson and mysterious beauty Alice Krige expose the friends to new horrors. Disappointing adaptation of Peter Straub's best-seller is notable for strong performances by Astaire and Douglas (in his last film).

GHOULIES 1985
★★ PG-13 Horror 1:21
☑ Explicit language, violence
Dir: Luca Bercovici *Cast:* Peter Liapis, Lisa Pelikan, Michael Des Barres, Jack Nance, Peter Risch
▶ Corny *Gremlins* imitator. When Jonathan (Liapis) and girlfriend Rebecca (Pelikan) move into an old house, he becomes obsessed with the occult. Suddenly, nasty little minions of the Devil (John Buechler's cutesy hand puppets)

appear to wreak bloody havoc. Rebecca's only reponse: "Why, Jonathan, why?"

GHOULIES II 1987
★ **PG-13 Horror 1:35**
☑ Explicit language, violence
Dir: Albert Band *Cast:* Damon Martin, Royal Dano, Phil Fondacaro, J. Downing, Kerry Remsen
▶ In this follow-up to the campy original, the pint-size puppet beasties terrorize a carnival sideshow. Fondacaro is a sideshow star who suggests using magic to exterminate the vicious pests. With silly-looking monsters and a minimum of violence, this "horror" film plays mainly for laughs.

GIANT 1956
★★★★ **G Drama 3:18**
Dir: George Stevens *Cast:* Elizabeth Taylor, Rock Hudson, James Dean, Dennis Hopper, Mercedes McCambridge, Carroll Baker
▶ Ten Oscar nominations (and a win for director Stevens) went to this rousing multigenerational saga from the Edna Ferber best-seller. Texan Hudson brings home Eastern bride Taylor, who must contend with jealousy of his unmarried sister McCambridge, the attentions of wild young ranch hand Dean, and a racial dispute. As the years pass, Dean grows wealthy in the oil biz but disillusioned, while Hudson and Taylor raise three kids on the Riata, the largest cattle ranch in Texas. Blockbuster combines romance, comedy, and drama. Dean's final film. (CC)

G.I. BLUES 1960
★★★ **NR Musical 1:44**
Dir: Norman Taurog *Cast:* Elvis Presley, James Douglas, Robert Ivers, Juliet Prowse, Leticia Roman, The Jordanaires
▶ Presley's first film after military service capitalized on his well-publicized assignment in Germany. Leader of a combo with two other soldiers, he bets that he can spend the night with cabaret singer Prowse. Strong assortment of songs, including "Wooden Heart," "Blue Suede Shoes," and "Shopping Around."

GIDGET 1959
★★★ **NR Comedy 1:35**
Dir: Paul Wendkos *Cast:* Sandra Dee, James Darren, Cliff Robertson, Arthur O'Connell, Mary Laroche, Tom Laughlin
▶ Frothy comedy introduced famed teenybopper Gidget (Dee), an insecure

"girl midget" convinced she'll never win a boyfriend until surfers Darren and Robertson vie for her affections. Dee is ideal as the heroine (based on Frederick Kohner's novel about his daughter). Led to a string of less successful features and two TV series. Sequel: *Gidget Goes Hawaiian.*

GIDGET GOES HAWAIIAN 1961
★★ **NR Comedy 1:42**
Dir: Paul Wendkos *Cast:* James Darren, Michael Callan, Deborah Walley, Carl Reiner, Peggy Cass, Eddie Foy, Jr.
▶ Walley replaces Sandra Dee, the original Gidget, in this painless sequel to the 1959 film. The lovable teen takes a Hawaiian vacation with her parents, trying to forget Stateside boyfriend Darren by flirting with handsome surfers. She's in for a big surprise when Darren shows up unexpectedly. Led to a feature sequel (*Gidget Goes to Rome*) as well as TV movies and series.

GIDGET GOES TO ROME 1963
★★ **NR Comedy 1:44**
Dir: Paul Wendkos *Cast:* Cindy Carol, James Darren, Jessie Royce Landis, Cesare Danova, Jeff Donnell
▶ Gidget (Carol) and her longtime steady "Moondoggie" (Darren) vacation in Rome. After several lovers' quarrels, Darren serenades himself back into Gidget's heart. Last of the series is cute, scenic, simple, and predictable.

GIFT, THE 1983 French
★ **R Comedy 1:50**
☑ Nudity, adult situations, explicit language
Dir: Michel Lang *Cast:* Clio Goldsmith, Pierre Mondy, Claudia Cardinale, Jacques Francois, Cecile Magnet
▶ Instead of a gold watch, friends of retiring bank employee Mondy give him an unusual "gift": high-priced call girl Goldsmith. Routine bedroom farce based on the popular Italian stage comedy *Even Bankers Have Souls* is cheerful and silly but markedly uneven.

GIG, THE 1985
★ **NR Comedy/Drama 1:28**
☑ Adult situations
Dir: Frank D. Gilroy *Cast:* Wayne Rogers, Cleavon Little, Andrew Duncan, Jerry Matz, Daniel Nalbach
▶ Small-scale, big-hearted comedy about a group of middle-aged men who get their dream opportunity: a two-week Catskills gig for their amateur Dixieland

band. Little plays the only professional musician in the group. Jazzy mix of mid-life crisis and Borscht Belt music.

GIGI 1958
★★★★ **G Musical 1:55**
Dir: Vincente Minnelli *Cast:* Maurice Chevalier, Leslie Caron, Louis Jourdan, Hermione Gingold, Eva Gabor
▶ Director Minnelli's Oscar-winning picture, based on the spicy Colette novel. Caron plays Gigi, a turn-of-the-century Parisian tomboy who refuses to grow up, resisting her family's efforts to train her as a charming courtesan. She has no interest in love until she meets Lachaille (Jourdan). Memorable Lerner and Loewe score includes "Thank Heaven for Little Girls," sung by Chevalier, who received an honorary Oscar for career achievement. Winner of nine Academy Awards.

GILDA 1946
★★★★ **NR Drama 1:50 B&W**
Dir: Charles Vidor *Cast:* Rita Hayworth, Glenn Ford, George Macready, Joseph Calleia, Steven Geray
▶ Casino owner Macready rescues Ford from a mugger, then hires him as bodyguard to gorgeous wife Hayworth, unaware that Ford and Hayworth were once lovers. Confusing but stylish film noir gave Hayworth one of her best roles. Her striptease to "Put the Blame on Mame" has become Hollywood legend.

GILDA LIVE 1980
★★ **R Documentary/Comedy 1:30**
☑ Explicit language
Dir: Mike Nichols *Cast:* Gilda Radner, Don Novello, Paul Schaffer
▶ Filmed version of Radner's one-woman Broadway show, with material culled mostly from NBC's "Saturday Night Live." Familiar characters include crude commentator Rosanne Rosannadanna, nerd Lisa Loopner, punk-singer Candy Slice, and others. With Novello as Vatican gossip columnist Father Guido Sarducci. Aficionados of "SNL" will love Gilda, but may also yearn for the other Not Ready for Prime Time Players.

GIMME SHELTER 1970
★★ **PG Documentary/Music 1:31**
☑ Explicit language, violence
Dir: David Maysles, Albert Maysles, Charlotte Zwerin *Cast:* The Rolling Stones, Jefferson Airplane, Ike and Tina Turner, Marvin Belli, Sonny Barger, The Flying Burrito Brothers
▶ Brilliant but extremely disturbing documentary on the 1969 Rolling Stones tour of America, focusing on the notorious Altamont concert. While the Stones perform some of their best songs ("Sympathy for the Devil," "Brown Sugar," etc.), film's most compelling moments are Mick Jagger's reactions to footage of a murder in the audience by the Hell's Angels, ironically hired as security.

GINGER AND FRED 1986 Italian
★ **PG-13 Drama 2:06**
☑ Adult situations, explicit language
Dir: Federico Fellini *Cast:* Giulietta Masina, Marcello Mastroianni, Franco Fabrizi, Frederick Von Ledenburg, Martin Blau
▶ One-time forties dance stars Mastroianni and Masina, now ravaged by time, are reunited for television special. Lovely lead performances, visual inventiveness, satiric jabs at TV, and straightforward storytelling. Fairly accessible for a Fellini film but with some dull stretches; lacks the magic of his best efforts. ⑤

GIRL CAN'T HELP IT, THE 1956
★ **NR Comedy 1:37**
Dir: Frank Tashlin *Cast:* Tom Ewell, Jayne Mansfield, Edmond O'Brien, Julie London, Henry Jones, John Emery
▶ Theatrical agent Ewell, brokenhearted over ex-girlfriend London, has six weeks to turn mobster's moll Mansfield into a star. Thin, silly plot emphasizing Mansfield's anatomy redeemed by seventeen rock gems: "Blue Monday" (Fats Domino), "Be Bop a Lula" (Gene Vincent), "Ready Teddy" (Little Richard), etc.

GIRL CRAZY 1943
★★★ **NR Musical 1:39 B&W**
Dir: Norman Taurog *Cast:* Mickey Rooney, Judy Garland, Gil Stratton, Robert E. Strickland, June Allyson, Nancy Walker
▶ First-rate Rooney-Garland comedy, their eighth teaming, finds ladies' man Rooney stuck in an all-boys' school in the desert. He falls for dean's daughter Garland, and promotes a rodeo to save the school from closing. Wonderful Gershwin score includes "Fascinating Rhythm," "Embraceable You," "But Not for Me," and Busby Berkeley's stupendous production of "I Got Rhythm."

GIRLFRIENDS 1978
★ **PG Comedy/Drama 1:28**
☑ Brief nudity, adult situations, explicit language

Dir: Claudia Weill   *Cast:* Melanie Mayron, Anita Skinner, Eli Wallach, Christopher Guest, Bob Balaban
▶ Affectionate, consciousness-raising film about dumpy but likable Jewish girl Mayron and her Midwestern roommate Skinner, fresh out of college and living in Manhattan. Though made on a shoestring budget, this attention-getting first feature by documentary maker Weill garnered praise at Cannes.

GIRL FROM PETROVKA, THE 1974
★★ PG Comedy 1:43
☑ Adult situations, explicit language
Dir: Robert Ellis Miller   *Cast:* Goldie Hawn, Hal Holbrook, Anthony Hopkins, Gregoire Aslan, Anton Dolin
▶ Young Russian Hawn falls in love with American journalist Holbrook but faces government disapproval of the relationship. Pre-glasnost tale is rather flatly directed and scripted; the leads are effective but don't generate enough chemistry to overcome the flaws.

GIRL HAPPY 1965
★★★★ NR Musical 1:36
Dir: Boris Sagal   *Cast:* Elvis Presley, Shelley Fabares, Harold J. Stone, Gary Crosby, Joby Baker, Nita Talbot
▶ Chicago mobster Stone sends singer Presley to Fort Lauderdale over spring break to keep an eye on his beautiful daughter Fabares. Inevitable romance blossoms between lesser Presley numbers: "Wolf Call," "Fort Lauderdale Chamber of Commerce," "Do the Clam," etc.

GIRL IN EVERY PORT, A 1952
★★ NR Comedy 1:26 B&W
Dir: Chester Erskine   *Cast:* Groucho Marx, Marie Wilson, William Bendix, Don DeFore, Gene Lockhart
▶ Lowbrow antics about troublemaking sailors Marx and Bendix trying to switch a slowpoke horse with its speedy twin. Wilson plays a pretty cabdriver who's onto the scheme. Generally mirthless comedy represents a low point in Groucho's career.

GIRL IN THE PICTURE, THE 1986
Scottish
★★ PG-13 Romance/Comedy 1:30
☑ Adult situations
Dir: Cary Parker   *Cast:* John Gordon-Sinclair, Irina Brook, David McKay, Gregor Fisher, Caroline Guthrie
▶ Harmless, inoffensive comedy from American-born writer/director Parker,

about the break-up and reconciliation of live-in lovers Gordon-Sinclair and Brook. Charming cast and low-key humor with lovely shots of Glasgow and a guitar-tinged musical score.

GIRLS! GIRLS! GIRLS! 1962
★★★★ NR Musical 1:46
Dir: Norman Taurog   *Cast:* Elvis Presley, Stella Stevens, Laurel Goodwin, Jeremy Slate, Benson Fong
▶ Poor tuna fisherman Presley doubles as a nightclub singer to pay the mortgage on his father's boat. He's pursued by singer Stevens (who sings "The Nearness of You") and the wealthy Goodwin. Typical Presley effort has pretty Hawaiian locations and a marvelous version of "Return to Sender."

GIRLS JUST WANT TO HAVE FUN 1985
★★★ PG Musical 1:27
☑ Explicit language
Dir: Alan Metter   *Cast:* Sarah Jessica Parker, Helen Hunt, Lee Montgomery, Sharron Shayne, Jonathan Silverman
▶ Bubble-headed high school antics of a group of Chicago kids out to win a dance contest and land a spot on their favorite TV show. Relentlessly silly, predictable characters: rich bitch, army brat, Catholic-school girl, preppie, uptight dad, and misty-eyed mom. Teenybopper version of *Staying Alive* was inspired by Cyndi Lauper's hit song, although neither Cyndi nor her voice are anywhere in evidence. **(CC)**

GIRLS NIGHT OUT 1983
☆ R Horror 1:30
☑ Nudity, adult situations, explicit language, graphic violence
Dir: Robert Deubel   *Cast:* Julie Montgomery, James Carroll, Suzanne Barnes, Rutanya Alda, Hal Holbrook
▶ Mad-killer-on-campus has special grudge against cheerleaders. Fortunately for him, the only contestants in a college scavenger hunt are young women who have no qualms about journeying out on lonely streets, alone, at midnight. Numerous grotesque attacks in a strictly low-rent horror flick. Also known as *Scared to Death*.

GIVE 'EM HELL, HARRY! 1975
★★★ PG Drama 1:42
☑ Explicit language
Dir: Steve Binder   *Cast:* James Whitmore
▶ Former President Harry Truman (Whitmore) recalls his tumultuous political ca-

reer and offers opinions on subsequent Presidents (with especially unkind words for Nixon). Whitmore won well-earned Oscar nomination for his portrayal of the irreverent, salty-tongued Truman in this film version of his one-man show.

GIVE MY REGARDS TO BROAD STREET
1984 British
★★ PG Musical 1:49
☑ Adult humor
Dir: Peter Webb *Cast:* Paul McCartney, Tracey Ullman, Bryan Brown, Ringo Starr, Linda McCartney, Ralph Richardson
▶ A silly love song from an ex-Beatle. Paul plays a superstar rocker whose master tapes have mysteriously disappeared—along with one of his employees. If Paul doesn't find the tapes by midnight, his company will be taken over by a ruthless villain who wears sunglasses indoors. McCartney fans should ignore the plot and concentrate on the songs: "Ballroom Dancing," "Yesterday," "Good Day Sunshine," and many others. **(CC)**

GIZMO! 1979
★★★ G Documentary 1:16
Dir: Howard Smith
▶ Zany chronicle of eccentric American inventions: antisnore devices, dimple-making machines, wet diaper alarms, and bathing caps for beards culled from footage dating back to the 1930s. Director Smith, who won an Academy Award for his documentary *Marjoe*, displays a fine sense of the golly-gee-whiz ridiculous.

GLASS MENAGERIE, THE 1950
★★★ NR Drama 1:47 B&W
Dir: Irving Rapper *Cast:* Jane Wyman, Gertrude Lawrence, Kirk Douglas, Arthur Kennedy
▶ Shy lame-footed Wyman and her cynical brother Kennedy struggle with their Southern belle mother Lawrence. Douglas is the Gentleman Caller who precipitates a family confrontation. First film adaptation of Tennessee Williams's drama is solid and well acted.

GLASS MENAGERIE, THE 1973
★★★ NR Drama/MFTV 1:40
Dir: Anthony Harvey *Cast:* Katharine Hepburn, Sam Waterston, Joanna Miles, Michael Moriarty
▶ Made-for-television version of the Tennessee Williams play with a great cast. Hepburn is Amanda Wingfield, the flighty Southern belle who dominates the lives of her unhappy son Waterston and fragile daughter Miles. The visit of a Gentleman Caller (Moriarty) literally shatters family illusions.

GLASS MENAGERIE, THE 1987
★★★★ PG Drama 2:10
☑ Adult situations
Dir: Paul Newman *Cast:* Joanne Woodward, Karen Allen, John Malkovich, James Naughton
▶ Reverential rendition of Tennessee Williams's American stage classic about an aging Southern belle and her children: Tom, a frustrated poet, and crippled Laura, who finds solace in her cherished glass animals. Polished performances, lavish photography, and sensitive direction from Woodward's husband Newman, but production suffers from static, stagey atmosphere.

GLEAMING THE CUBE 1988
★★ PG-13 Drama 1:45
☑ Adult situations, explicit language, violence
Dir: Graeme Clifford *Cast:* Christian Slater, Steven Bauer, Min Luong, Art Chudabala, Le Tuan
▶ When cops claim that his adopted Vietnamese stepbrother Chudabula committed suicide, skateboarding teen Slater sets out to prove he was murdered. While searching through Los Angeles's Little Saigon, he uncovers evidence of evil conspiracy. Highlighted by amazing skateboarding stunts by real-life experts Mike McGill, Gator Rogowski, and others.

GLENN MILLER STORY, THE 1954
★★★ G Biography/Musical 1:56
Dir: Anthony Mann *Cast:* James Stewart, June Allyson, Charles Drake, George Tobias, Henry Morgan, Marion Ross
▶ Story of bandleader Glenn Miller from his rise to the top to his tragic death during World War II. Sweet Stewart/Allyson romance, lively big-band music, and period settings spark this highly enjoyable biography. Songs include: "Pennsylvania 6-5000," "In the Mood," "Chattanooga Choo-Choo." Sound on video version is digitally reprogrammed for stereo.

GLEN OR GLENDA 1953
☆ PG Drama 1:10 B&W
☑ Adult situations
Dir: Edward D. Wood, Jr. *Cast:* Bela Lugosi, Lyle Talbot, Daniel Davis, Dolores Fuller, Tommy Haynes, Timothy Farrell

▶ Straightfaced account of Davis's attempt to tell fiancée Fuller about his transvestism is acknowledged to be one of the world's worst movies. Delirious combination of "scientific" commentary, baffling stock footage, and Lugosi delivering curses from a prop-filled basement make this an unintentional comic delight. Directing debut for Wood, who also stars under the pseudonym Daniel Davis. Among the many variant titles are *I Led Two Lives*, *He or She*, and *The Transvestite*.

GLITTER DOME, THE 1984
★★ NR Crime/MFTV 1:34
☑ Nudity, adult situations, explicit language, violence
Dir: Stuart Margolin *Cast:* James Garner, Margot Kidder, John Lithgow, Colleen Dewhurst, Christianne Laughlin, John Marley
▶ Funny and shocking Hollywood panorama, adapted from Joseph Wambaugh's best-selling novel. Burned-out detectives Garner and Lithgow spearhead an investigation into the murder of a Tinseltown movie mogul, leading them through a maze of performers, bookies, dope dealers and users, prostitutes, roller-skaters, porn producers, and has-beens. With Kidder as a tough-talking movie star who falls for Garner.

GLORIA 1980
★★★ PG Action-Adventure 2:01
☑ Adult situations, explicit language, violence
Dir: John Cassavetes *Cast:* Gena Rowlands, Buck Henry, John Adames, Julie Carmen, Lupe Guarnica
▶ Rowlands was Oscar-nominated for her hard-boiled portrayal of a former gangster's moll with a heart of gold who rescues Adames, the son of her slain neighbor Henry, a Mafia money-counter. When the kid refuses to relinquish his dad's accounting book, Gloria turns gunslinger to keep them both from being killed. Bristling with near-misses, New York City chase scenes, sudden encounters, and shoot-outs; written and directed by Rowlands's husband, Cassavetes.

GLOVE, THE 1980
★ R Action-Adventure 1:28
☑ Explicit language, violence
Dir: Ross Hagen *Cast:* John Saxon, Rosey Grier, Jack Carter, Aldo Ray, Keenan Wynn, Joan Blondell
▶ Competent B-movie stars Saxon as an ex-ballplayer/bounty hunter who wants out of the business of tracking bad guys. First, though, he must defeat vengeful escaped prisoner Grier and his notoriously dangerous steel glove that can maim, kill, and destroy just about anything. Action fans will devour the bruiser, he-man showdown.

G-MEN 1935
★★★ NR Action-Adventure 1:25 B&W
Dir: William Keighley *Cast:* James Cagney, Ann Dvorak, Margaret Lindsay, Robert Armstrong, Barton MacLane, Lloyd Nolan
▶ Blistering gangster drama with Cagney in a change-of-pace role as an FBI agent whose underworld connections raise the suspicions of chief Armstrong. Cagney embarks on a vendetta against hood MacLane, who not only steals his old girlfriend Dvorak but kidnaps his new flame Lindsay. Strong acting by Cagney supported by frantic pacing and brutal action. Brief prologue added in 1949. Available in a colorized version.

GNOME-MOBILE, THE 1967
★★★ G Comedy 1:30
Dir: Robert Stevenson *Cast:* Walter Brennan, Tom Lowell, Matthew Garber, Ed Wynn, Karen Dotrice
▶ Marvelous Disney fantasy based on an Upton Sinclair novel features Brennan in a dual role as a curmudgeonly timber tycoon and a 943-year-old gnome who lives on the tycoon's land. Amusing plot climaxes in a wonderful car chase that frees the tycoon from a mental institution and the gnome from a freak show. Wynn's last film.

GO-BETWEEN, THE 1971 British
★ PG Drama 1:56
☑ Brief nudity, adult situations, explicit language
Dir: Joseph Losey *Cast:* Julie Christie, Alan Bates, Dominic Guard, Michael Redgrave, Margaret Leighton, Edward Fox
▶ In turn-of-the-century England, innocent young Guard delivers love letters between wealthy Fox's fiancée Christie and her farmer lover, Bates. The affair's tragic consequences haunt Guard through the rest of his life. Beautiful period evocation and fine performances in Harold Pinter's adaptation of the L. P. Hartley novel.

GODDESS, THE 1958
★★ NR Drama 1:45 B&W
Dir: John Cromwell *Cast:* Kim Stanley,

Lloyd Bridges, Patty Duke, Steven Hill, Betty Lou Holland, Joyce Van Patten
▶ First screenplay by Paddy Chayefsky (*Network*) portrays twenty years in the life of a voluptuous movie star not unlike Marilyn Monroe. Landmark performance by Stanley covers Depression-era adolescence in the squalor of a Southern slum town, two unhappy marriages (one to ex–boxing champ Bridges), rise to international stardom, and demise due to alcoholism and drug dependency.

GODFATHER, THE 1972
★★★★★ R Drama 2:55
☑ Adult situations, explicit language, violence
Dir: Francis Ford Coppola   *Cast:* Marlon Brando, Al Pacino, James Caan, Robert Duvall, Richard Castellano, John Cazale
▶ Story of the Corleones, fictionalized leaders of the Mafia empire, from the turn of the century to the 1950s. Emotion-packed story with family theme focuses on changing relationship between Don Vito (Brando) and his sons: hot-tempered Sonny (Caan), weak Fredo (Cazale), and sensitive Michael (Pacino), who is drawn into the family biz despite his desire to live apart. A movie you can't refuse. Powerhouse cast led by the stunning Brando; wonderfully crafted filmmaking from Coppola. Oscars for Best Picture, Actor (Brando), Screenplay Adaptation.

GODFATHER, PART II, THE 1974
★★★★ R Drama 3:23
☑ Brief nudity, adult situations, explicit language, graphic violence
Dir: Francis Ford Coppola   *Cast:* Al Pacino, Robert Duvall, Robert De Niro, Diane Keaton, Talia Shire, John Cazale
▶ Follow-up to *The Godfather* projects the Mafia saga into the future and reveals its past. Michael Corleone (Pacino) extends the family empire into Nevada but pays an emotionally steep price by destroying his marriage. Young Don Vito Corleone (De Niro) flees Sicily and enters organized crime in Little Italy, the immigrant ghetto. Double story line adds richness and texture to the saga and may even surpass the magnificent original. Won six Oscars: Best Picture, Director, Supporting Actor (De Niro), Screenplay Adaptation, Art Direction, and Score.

GODFATHER SAGA, THE 1977
★★★★★ NR Drama 7:30
☑ Adult situations, explicit language, violence
Dir: Francis Ford Coppola   *Cast:* Marlon Brando, Al Pacino, Robert De Niro, Robert Duvall, James Caan, Diane Keaton
▶ Television reediting combines *The Godfather* and *The Godfather, Part II* so the story unfolds in chronological order. Includes scenes that didn't make the final cuts of the theatrical films. A genuine masterpiece, no matter how you slice it. (CC)

GOD'S LITTLE ACRE 1958
★★ PG Drama 1:50 B&W
☑ Adult situations
Dir: Anthony Mann   *Cast:* Robert Ryan, Tina Louise, Aldo Ray, Buddy Hackett, Jack Lord, Vic Morrow
▶ Rural Georgia farmer Ryan and his sons Lord and Morrow obsessively search for gold on their land; son-in-law Ray goes into the mill business while Lord's wife Louise cheats on him. Adaptation of the Erskine Caldwell novel features convincing atmosphere and strong performances.

GODS MUST BE CRAZY, THE 1984
South African
★★★ PG Comedy 1:49
☑ Brief nudity, explicit language, violence
Dir: Jamie Uys   *Cast:* Marius Weyers, Sandra Prinsloo, Louw Verwey, Sam Boga, Nic De Jager
▶ Sleeper hit is an oddball comedy adventure that begins when a pilot, flying over the Kalahari desert, tosses an empty Coke bottle into the midst of a tribe of bushmen who accept it as a gift from the gods. Slapstick fun also involves a clumsy microbiologist who studies animal manure, a beautiful journalist fleeing the city, bumbling Communist guerrillas, a vainglorious safari operator, and a fine supporting cast of giraffes, elephants, and hippos. Uys does an ace job writing, directing, and producing with charm and perfect pitch.   (CC)

GOD TOLD ME TO 1977
★★ R Horror 1:35
☑ Nudity, adult situations, explicit language
Dir: Larry Cohen   *Cast:* Tony Lo Bianco, Sandy Dennis, Sylvia Sidney, Deborah Raffin
▶ New York City detective Lo Bianco investigates a string of murders with one

common thread: the killers all claim God told them to do it. He uncovers a secret society and a cosmic war between the forces of good and evil. Combination of religion and violence may upset some, but director Cohen delivers a surprisingly gripping and creepy film.

GODZILLA, KING OF THE MONSTERS
1956 Japanese
★★ NR Sci-Fi 1:20
Dir: Inoshiro Honda, Terry Morse *Cast:* Raymond Burr, Takashi Shimura, Momoko Kochi, Akira Takarada
▶ Nuclear test has unwanted side effect: gigantic creature Godzilla revives from hibernation. He attacks Tokyo, proving immune to weapons until scientist figures out how to thwart him. Spawned many sequels but clearly the best of the series; creates a genuinely ominous mood. Dubbed.

GODZILLA VS. MOTHRA 1964
Japanese
★★ NR Sci-Fi 1:30
Dir: Inoshiro Honda *Cast:* Akira Takarada, Yuriko Hoshi, Hiroshi Koizumi, Emi Ito, Yumi Ito
▶ Giant fire-breathing monster Godzilla attacks humanity once again; little twin mutant sisters Ito and Ito convince humongous moth Mothra to battle Godzilla. Plenty of destruction and special effects fireworks. Also known as *Godzilla vs. the Thing.* Dubbed.

GODZILLA 1985 1985 Japanese
★ PG Sci-Fi 1:31
☑ Explicit language, violence
Dir: Kohju Hashimoto *Cast:* Raymond Burr, Keiju Kobayashi, Ken Tanaka, Yasuko Sawaguchi, Shin Takuma
▶ Cheapo sequel to the 1956 Japanese-made exploitation hit. Basically, the same plot: fire-snorting Godzilla awakes from ocean deep to come ashore and trample Tokyo. Burr, who played a reporter in the original, returns as an international Godzilla expert. It's sayonara sucker when the not-so-jolly green giant is lured into a volcano. Cheesy-looking and badly dubbed but definitely fun for the small screen.

GOIN' ALL THE WAY 1982
★★ R Comedy 1:26
☑ Nudity, adult situations, explicit language
Dir: Robert Freedman *Cast:* Deborah Van Rhy, Dan Waldman, Josh Cadman, Sherrie Miller

▶ High school seniors go cruising in their convertibles. They pick up girls, eat french fries, roller skate, sneak into mud wrestling, watch porno movies, and discuss sex, sex, sex. Interchangeable couples, each with one partner trying to convince the other to do as the film title implies. No worse than many of the other teen sex comedies, but certainly no better. Rated R but sex is never explicit.

GOING BANANAS 1988
★★ PG Comedy 1:33
☑ Explicit language
Dir: Boaz Davidson *Cast:* Dom DeLuise, Jimmie C. Walker, David Mendenhall, Warren Berlinger, Herbert Lom
▶ On an African safari, young Mendenhall befriends a talking chimp who's been chosen for the circus by corrupt policeman Lom. High-strung custodian DeLuise and native guide Walker pose as clowns to free the ape. Harmless nonsense filled with good-natured slapstick will amuse younger viewers. (CC)

GOING IN STYLE 1979
★★★★★ PG Comedy 1:38
☑ Explicit language
Dir: Martin Brest *Cast:* George Burns, Art Carney, Lee Strasberg, Charles Hallahan, Pamela Payton-Wright
▶ Inspired casting: Burns, Carney, and Strasberg as retired seventy-year-olds who share an apartment in Queens, a park bench, and an uneventful, atrophied life. Then Burns convinces the others to rob a Manhattan bank. Tender, contemplative study of gallantry and last stands from writer/director Brest.

GOING MY WAY 1944
★★★★ NR Drama 2:06 B&W
Dir: Leo McCarey *Cast:* Bing Crosby, Barry Fitzgerald, Rise Stevens, Frank McHugh, Gene Lockhart, William Frawley
▶ Moving account of the relationship between Fitzgerald, crusty pastor of a run-down church, and Crosby, the cocky young priest who revives the parish's fortunes. Though often skirting the maudlin, direction by Oscar-winning McCarey (who copped another Oscar for Best Original Story) is too emotional and polished to resist. Grand entertainment also won Oscars for Crosby, Fitzgerald, Best Screenwriting, Best Picture, and "Swinging on a Star." Crosby's rendition of "Too-ra-loo-ra-loo-ral" is guaranteed to melt

the hardest heart. Sequel: *The Bells of St. Mary's.*

GOING PLACES 1974 French
★★★ R Comedy 1:24
☑ Rape, nudity, strong sexual content, adult situations, explicit language
Dir: Bertrand Blier   *Cast:* Gerard Depardieu, Patrick Dewaere, Miou-Miou, Jeanne Moreau, Brigitte Fossey
▶ Outlaws Depardieu and Dewaere roam around France, stealing and pillaging. They pursue several women, including beautician Miou-Miou, convict Moreau, and mom Fossey. Controversial sex comedy from French director Blier pleased some critics but outraged many others. Ⓢ

GOIN' SOUTH 1978
★★★ PG Comedy 1:48
☑ Adult situations, adult humor
Dir: Jack Nicholson   *Cast:* Jack Nicholson, Mary Steenburgen, Christopher Lloyd, John Belushi, Veronica Cartwright, Danny DeVito
▶ Shaggy horse-thief Nicholson is saved from the gallows by beautiful widow Steenburgen, who invokes a frontier law allowing her to marry him. Nicholson attacks his role with relish in this offbeat, amusing Western comedy. Film debuts for Steenburgen and Belushi, who has a small role as a Mexican bandit.

GOLD DIGGERS OF 1933 1933
★★★ G Musical 1:36 B&W
Dir: Mervyn LeRoy   *Cast:* Warren William, Joan Blondell, Aline MacMahon, Ruby Keeler, Dick Powell, Ginger Rogers
▶ Blockbuster musical combines laughs, romance, and outrageous Busby Berkeley numbers into a very satisfying entertainment. Songwriter Powell foots the bill for a new show, scandalizing his blue-blood brother William; chorines Blondell, MacMahon, and Keeler team up to save the day. Surprisingly racy; highlighted by Rogers's pig Latin version of "We're in the Money."

GOLDEN BOY 1939
★★ NR Drama/Sports 1:41 B&W
Dir: Rouben Mamoulian   *Cast:* Barbara Stanwyck, Adolphe Menjou, William Holden, Lee J. Cobb, Joseph Calleia, Sam Levene
▶ Archetypal boxing drama made Holden a star as a violinist who turns to fighting to help his immigrant father Cobb. Stanwyck is restrained and believable as the woman who corrupts Holden's dreams. Fight scenes are expertly staged, but film version softens the ending of Clifford Odets's hit play.

GOLDEN CHILD, THE 1986
★★★ PG-13 Action-Adventure 1:34
☑ Explicit language, violence
Dir: Michael Ritchie   *Cast:* Eddie Murphy, Charlotte Lewis, Charles Dance, Victor Wong, J. L. Reate
▶ Murphy is hired to locate Reate, a Tibetan child with magical powers kidnapped by equally endowed bad guy Dance. Elaborate special effects in an often illogical plot combine *Beverly Hills Cop* "fish out of water" formula with Indiana Jones–style adventure. Wisecracking Eddie, with help from villainous Dance and voluptuous Lewis, is the main attraction. **(CC)**

GOLDENGIRL 1979
★★★★ PG Drama 1:45
☑ Adult situations, explicit language
Dir: Joseph Sargent   *Cast:* Susan Anton, James Coburn, Leslie Caron, Robert Culp, Harry Guardino, Curt Jurgens
▶ Neo-Nazi doctor Jurgens experiments on adopted daughter Anton to create a Super Sprinter programmed to win three gold medals at the Moscow Olympics. Coburn is the girl's shrewd sports agent and Caron, her live-in behavioral psychologist. Plot is somewhat predictable but fans of tall, leggy blonds may not notice.

GOLDEN NEEDLES 1974
★★ PG Action-Adventure 1:28
☑ Violence
Dir: Robert Clouse   *Cast:* Joe Don Baker, Elizabeth Ashley, Jim Kelly, Burgess Meredith, Ann Sothern
▶ Yanks Baker and Ashley, evil millionaire Meredith, and Hong Kong gangster vie for possession of gold figurine with magic healing powers. Director Clouse gets maximum mileage from camp *Maltese Falcon* clone through zippy pacing and constant barrage of brawls and chases. Baker and Ashley are no Bogart and Astor but they get by on tongue-in-cheek vigor.

GOLDEN RENDEZVOUS 1977
★★★ NR Mystery-Suspense 1:42
☑ Violence
Dir: Ashley Lazarus   *Cast:* Richard Harris, Ann Turkel, David Janssen, Burgess Meredith, John Vernon

▶ Caribbean-bound casino/cargo ship is seized by terrorists who plant a nuclear device on board. Their aim: to extort bullion from nearby U.S. Treasury ship. Their foe: gallant First Officer Harris. Lively action flick marred by awkward scripting and gorgeous Turkel's stiff performance. Adapted from Alistair MacLean's novel.

GOLDEN SEAL, THE 1983
★★★ PG Action-Adventure 1:35
☑ Explicit language, mild violence
Dir: Frank Zuniga *Cast:* Steve Railsback, Michael Beck, Penelope Milford, Torquil Campbell, Seth Sakai
▶ According to legend, a golden seal will appear someday to teach man to live in harmony with nature. Youngster Campbell happens upon the mystical animal while she's giving birth. Friendship blooms and the kid must protect his animal pal from greedy adults. The seal and the spectacular Aleutian Island settings steal the story from the adult cast members.

GOLDEN VOYAGE OF SINBAD, THE
1974 British
★★★ G Fantasy 1:45
Dir: Gordon Hessler *Cast:* John Phillip Law, Caroline Munro, Tom Baker, Douglas Wilmer, Gregoire Aslan, John Garfield, Jr.
▶ Sinbad the Sailor (Law) rescues beautiful Munro and battles monsters and villainous Baker (of *Dr. Who* fame) while seeking treasure. Entertaining adventure for children features special effects whiz Ray Harryhausen's clever creatures and beasties. (CC)

GOLDFINGER 1964 British
★★★★★ PG
Espionage/Action-Adventure 1:52
Dir: Guy Hamilton *Cast:* Sean Connery, Gert Frobe, Honor Blackman, Shirley Eaton, Harold Sakata
▶ It's secret agent James Bond (Connery) to the rescue when archvillain Goldfinger (Frobe) tries to rob Fort Knox. Along the way, 007 tumbles with Goldfinger's sexy pilot Pussy Galore (Blackman) and tackles his menacing Korean bodyguard, the derby-throwing Oddjob (Sakata). Quintessential Bond is pedal-to-the-metal entertainment; great gadgets (Bond's Aston Martin with the ejector seat), fine Connery, and flip dialogue: "Do you expect me to talk, Goldfinger?" "No, Mr. Bond, I expect you to die!" (CC)

GOLD RUSH, THE 1925
★★★★ NR Comedy 1:12 B&W
Dir: Charlie Chaplin *Cast:* Charlie Chaplin, Georgia Hale, Mack Swain, Tom Murray
▶ The Little Tramp (Chaplin) prospects during the Klondike Gold Rush. He struggles with starvation (especially in the famous Thanksgiving Day shoe dinner), tangles with the villainous Black Larsen, and has a bittersweet relationship with dancehall girl Hale. Chaplin classic is moving, full of memorable visuals, and funny; deservedly one of his best-loved works.

GONE WITH THE WIND 1939
★★★★★ G Drama 3:42
Dir: Victor Fleming *Cast:* Clark Gable, Vivien Leigh, Olivia de Havilland, Leslie Howard, Hattie McDaniel, Butterfly McQueen
▶ Hollywood moviemaking at its absolute zenith. Margaret Mitchell's Civil War saga was perfectly realized under the guidance of producer David O. Selznick and four different directors. Now part of history: the search for Scarlett, the burning of Atlanta scene, the green dress made from Miss Ellen's portieres, Rhett's tears, the wimp Ashley, Prissy "birthing" Miss Mellie's baby, and Mammy's red petticoat. Perhaps the greatest love story ever told, even though Rhett didn't give a damn. Oscars for Leigh, McDaniel (the first black ever to win), Best Picture, director Fleming, Screenplay, Cinematography, Interior Decoration, and Editing. Recently restored in time for its fiftieth anniversary. (CC)

GOODBYE, COLUMBUS 1969
★★★ PG Comedy 1:45
☑ Brief nudity, adult situations, explicit language
Dir: Larry Peerce *Cast:* Richard Benjamin, Ali MacGraw, Jack Klugman, Nan Martin, Michael Meyers
▶ Poor librarian Benjamin falls for pampered Jewish-American Princess MacGraw. Her dad Klugman prods him to be more ambitious. The lovers' relationship eventually hits a snag when she goes off to college. Satiric look at life in well-heeled suburbia from Philip Roth's acclaimed novel.

GOODBYE EMMANUELLE 1978 French
★ R Sex 1:38
☑ Nudity, strong sexual content, adult situations, explicit language

Dir: François Leterrier *Cast:* Sylvia Kristel, Umberto Orsini, Alexandra Stewart, Jean-Pierre Bouvier

▶ Beautiful Emmanuelle (Kristel) lives on the Seychelles Islands with her hubby. He openly fools around but proves less than tolerant when she has a fling with a handsome Frenchman. Lovely scenery, nice color, shapely bodies, but too much talk between the too-few sex scenes.

GOODBYE GIRL, THE 1977
★ ★ ★ ★ ★ PG Comedy 1:51
☑ Explicit language
Dir: Herbert Ross *Cast:* Richard Dreyfuss, Marsha Mason, Quinn Cummings, Barbara Rhodes, Nicol Williamson

▶ Jilted by her live-in lover, hard-luck ex-dancer Mason and precocious ten-year-old daughter Cummings must adjust to weird new roommate Dreyfuss. After hating each other on sight, the leads trade insults, wisecracks, misunderstandings, and outrage—and then fall in love. Crackling original screenplay by Neil Simon (written for then-wife, Mason) helped Dreyfuss win Oscar as Elliot Garfield, an actor forced to play Richard III in full drag. One of the top-grossing films of 1978; six Oscar nominations.

GOODBYE, MR. CHIPS 1939
★ ★ ★ ★ NR Drama 1:54 B&W
Dir: Sam Wood *Cast:* Robert Donat, Greer Garson, Paul von Henreid, Terry Kilburn, John Mills

▶ Shy, rigid schoolmaster Donat marries beautiful free spirit Garson, whom he meets on vacation. She brings out his gentler side and he becomes a much beloved teacher. Donat's tremendous performance beat out Clark Gable's Rhett Butler for the Oscar. Classic tearjerker is heartwarming and heartwrenching, particularly when Donat insists on teaching his class despite a personal tragedy. (CC)

GOODBYE, NEW YORK 1985 U.S./Israeli
★ R Comedy 1:31
☑ Adult situations, explicit language
Dir: Amos Kollek *Cast:* Julie Hagerty, Amos Kollek, David Topaz, Aviva Ger, Shmuel Shiloh

▶ Fed up with her job and her unfaithful husband, pampered New Yorker Hagerty impulsively flies to Paris but overdoses on Valium and ends up in Israel minus luggage and money. She's befriended by soldier Kollek while adjusting to life in the Holy Land. Humor comfortably alternates between sophisticated culture-clash jabs and cornball slapstick. Technically crude but charming.

GOODBYE, NORMA JEAN 1976
★ R Drama 1:35
☑ Rape, nudity, explicit language
Dir: Larry Buchanan *Cast:* Misty Rowe, Terence Locke, Patch Mackenzie, Preston Hanson

▶ Norma Jean Baker (Rowe), a.k.a. Marilyn Monroe, rises from orphan to Hollywood stardom. Along the way, she is raped twice, molested several times, attempts suicide, experiences terrifying visions, and has affairs with men and women. More fiction than fact in this spicy, low-budget sexploitation flick.

GOODBYE PEOPLE, THE 1986
★ ★ PG Drama 1:44
☑ Explicit language
Dir: Herb Gardner *Cast:* Judd Hirsch, Martin Balsam, Pamela Reed, Ron Silver, Gene Saks, Michael Tucker

▶ Forty-something Hirsch, unhappy with his life and job, goes to Coney Island to observe the sunrise and gets caught up in elderly Balsam's dream of reviving his hot dog stand. Gardner adapted his Broadway play too faithfully; the self-conscious script is extremely talky, though a good cast tries hard to please. (CC)

GOOD EARTH, THE 1937
★ ★ ★ ★ NR Drama 2:18 B&W
Dir: Sidney Franklin *Cast:* Paul Muni, Luise Rainer, Walter Connolly, Tilly Losch, Charley Grapewin, Jessie Ralph

▶ Vivid drama about Chinese peasant Muni fighting backbreaking poverty with wife Rainer. Their farm ruined by drought, Rainer is later swept up in a massive revolution. Newfound wealth corrupts Muni, who faces further tragedy from a plague of locusts. Meticulous adaptation of Pearl S. Buck's Pulitzer prize–winning novel highlighted by superb special effects and Karl Freund's Oscar-winning photography. Rainer received her second consecutive Oscar (after *The Great Ziegfeld*). Last film overseen by noted producer Irving G. Thalberg.

GOOD FATHER, THE 1987 British
★ R Drama 1:30
☑ Brief nudity, adult situations, explicit language
Dir: Mike Newell *Cast:* Anthony Hopkins, Jim Broadbent, Harriet Walter,

Fanny Viner, Simon Callow, Joanne Whalley
▶ Bitter divorcé Hopkins befriends teacher Broadbent, whose marriage is also on the rocks. When his buddy's wife Viner plans to take the couple's son and move to Australia with her lesbian lover, Hopkins makes it a personal crusade to fight her. Uncompromising and well acted, but fuzzy camerawork, poor sound recording, and generally sour tone. **(CC)**

GOOD GUYS WEAR BLACK 1979
★★★ PG Martial Arts 1:36
☑ Violence, explicit language
Dir: Ted Post *Cast:* Chuck Norris, Anne Archer, James Franciscus, Lloyd Haynes, Dana Andrews
▶ Fast and furious kung-fu stunts highlight this hard-hitting, efficient action-adventure. Corrupt politician Franciscus betrays special U.S. unit led by Norris to the Vietcong. Norris and some others survive but Franciscus takes another shot at them in the States. Plausible story is given realistic treatment.

GOOD MORNING, BABYLON 1987
Italian
★ PG-13 Drama 1:58
☑ Nudity, adult situations
Dir: Paolo Taviani, Vittorio Taviani
Cast: Vincent Spano, Joaquim de Almeida, Greta Scacchi, Desiree Becker, Omero Antonutti, Charles Dance
▶ Brothers Spano and de Almeida, down-on-their-luck Italian craftsmen, set out for America. They reach Hollywood and are hired by the great film director D. W. Griffith (Dance) to help build the sets for his epic *Intolerance*, but tragedy mars their stab at the American Dream. Picturesque production but not very convincing plotting.

GOOD MORNING, VIETNAM 1987
★★★★ R Comedy/Drama 2:00
☑ Adult situations, explicit language
Dir: Barry Levinson *Cast:* Robin Williams, Forest Whitaker, Tung Thanh Tran, Chintara Sukapatana, Bruno Kirby, Robert Wuhl
▶ Fictionalized version of real-life disc jockey Adrian Cronauer's (Williams) Vietnam years during which he delighted U.S. troops and outraged his stuffy superiors with his hysterically funny brand of iconoclastic patter; a couple of less-than-stellar dramatic subplots include Williams's ro-

mance with a Vietnamese girl and his friendship with her brother, but the film comes joyously alive whenever Williams is in the booth. Williams received an Oscar nomination. **(CC)**

GOOD MOTHER, THE 1988
★★★ R Drama 1:44
☑ Nudity, adult situations, explicit language
Dir: Leonard Nimoy *Cast:* Diane Keaton, Liam Neeson, Teresa Wright, Ralph Bellamy, Jason Robards, Jr., James Naughton
▶ Divorced mother Keaton's only passion in life is her beloved daughter; then sculptor Neeson unleashes her pent-up sexuality. Keaton seems to be having it all, until ex-husband Naughton asserts that her sex life has been a bad influence on their daughter and sues for custody. Emotionally charged drama with controversial moral. Based on Sue Miller's best-selling novel.

GOOD NEIGHBOR SAM 1964
★★★ NR Comedy 2:10
Dir: David Swift *Cast:* Jack Lemmon, Romy Schneider, Edward G. Robinson, Dorothy Provine, Mike Connors, Anne Seymour
▶ Ad exec Lemmon wins account from ultrawholesome dairy magnate Robinson, then agrees to impersonate neighbor Schneider's husband so she can collect an inheritance. The plan backfires when Robinson decides to promote the couple in his ads. Winning comedy with a good performance by Lemmon as an innocent trapped in escalating disasters.

GOOD NEWS 1947
★★★ NR Musical 1:33
Dir: Charles Walters *Cast:* June Allyson, Peter Lawford, Patricia Marshall, Joan McCracken, Ray McDonald, Mel Torme
▶ Giddy, lavish, 1920s musical: Lawford is a football star tutored by librarian Allyson so he can play in the big game; Marshall is Allyson's glamorous rival. Fun score highlighted by "Varsity Drag" and the Oscar-nominated "Pass the Peace Pipe."

GOOD, THE BAD, AND THE UGLY, THE 1967 Italian/Spanish
★★★ NR Western 2:41
☑ Adult situations, violence
Dir: Sergio Leone *Cast:* Clint Eastwood, Eli Wallach, Lee Van Cleef, Aldo Giuffre, Chelo Alonso, Mario Brega
▶ Stunning climax to Leone's "Dollars"

trilogy finds bounty hunter Eastwood, crook Wallach, and Army sergeant Van Cleef all scrambling for a fortune in gold hidden in a coffin. The Civil War, shown in sweeping detail, has an increasingly violent impact on their uneasy alliance. Sequel to *For a Few Dollars More* is among the best of all spaghetti Westerns. Highly influential score by Ennio Morricone.

GOOD WIFE, THE 1987 Australian
★ **R Drama 1:37**
☑ Brief nudity, adult situations, explicit language
Dir: Ken Cameron *Cast:* Rachel Ward, Bryan Brown, Sam Neill, Steven Vidler, Jennifer Claire
▶ In 1939 New South Wales, Ward, unhappily married to crude lumberjack Brown (Ward's real-life husband), has a brief affair with brother-in-law Vidler and then develops an unrequited passion for bartender Neill. Beautifully shot period piece engages the eyes but not the mind; the plot gets increasingly contrived in the second half.

GOONIES, THE 1985
★★★★ **PG Fantasy 1:54**
☑ Explicit language, violence
Dir: Richard Donner *Cast:* Sean Astin, Josh Brolin, Corey Feldman, Martha Plimpton, Ke Huy Quan, John Matuszak
▶ Spielberg-produced fantasy about a group of overimaginative preteens in an Oregon coastal town who find a pirate map and search for the buried treasure. They must grab the loot before mean Mama Fratelli (Anne Ramsey) and her brood close in. Brisk caper gives kid cast opportunity to exude warmth and personality while providing roller-coaster thrills. **(CC)**

GORILLAS IN THE MIST 1988
★★★★ **PG-13 Biography 2:05**
☑ Adult situations, explicit language, violence
Dir: Michael Apted *Cast:* Sigourney Weaver, Bryan Brown, John Omirah Miluwi, Julie Harris, Iain Cuthbertson
▶ Fascinating true story of anthropologist Dian Fossey (Weaver) who studied the mountain gorillas of Africa and single-handedly saved them from extinction. She has affair with photographer Brown, but her real love is the animals; she protects them from poachers to the point of obsession. Heartfelt production dominated by Weaver's mesmerizing performance; her relationship with the amazing

apes has many stirring moments. Wonderful support by Miluwi, exotic African locations. Film received five Oscar nominations, including Weaver as Best Actress.

GORKY PARK 1983
★★★★ **R Mystery-Suspense 2:08**
☑ Nudity, adult situations, explicit language, graphic violence
Dir: Michael Apted *Cast:* William Hurt, Lee Marvin, Brian Dennehy, Joanna Pacula, Ian Bannen
▶ When three mutilated bodies are found in Moscow's Gorky Park, Russian inspector Hurt investigates a diverse group of suspects: American trader Marvin, New York cop Dennehy, and beautiful dissident Pacula with whom Hurt falls in love. Convoluted but atmospheric mystery with an original premise adapted from Martin Cruz Smith's best-seller. Solid work from Hurt.

GORP 1980
★★ **R Comedy 1:30**
☑ Brief nudity, adult situations, explicit language
Dir: Joseph Ruben *Cast:* Michael Lembeck, Dennis Quaid, Phillip Casnoff, Fran Drescher, David Huddleston, Rosanna Arquette
▶ Summer-camp waiters Lembeck and Casnoff have a penchant for pranks: showing porno films on Parents' Day, spiking food with speed, sneaking into the girls' dorm dressed as werewolves, upsetting camp owner Huddleston no end. Wild, vulgar little movie plays like a cross between *Animal House* and *Meatballs*.

GOSPEL 1982
★★★★ **G Documentary/Music 1:29**
Dir: David Leivick, Frederick A. Ritzenberg *Cast:* James Cleveland, Walter Hawkins, Mighty Clouds Of Joy, Shirley Caesar
▶ A series of gospel acts performed on stage before a *very* live, often frenzied audience, some of whom had to be carried out. High-energy concert works up quite a sweat. All music, no commentary. Performers are terrific; expect plenty of shouting.

GOSPEL ACCORDING TO VIC 1986 Scottish
★★★ **PG-13 Comedy/Drama 1:27**
☑ Adult situations, explicit language
Dir: Charles Gormley *Cast:* Tom Conti, Helen Mirren, David Hayman, Brian Pettifer, Jennifer Black

► In Glasgow, Conti, a teacher of remedial students, achieves notoriety when he finds he can work miracles. Slightly off-kilter story told with sincerity and blessed with Conti's quirky and captivating antihero. The script is talky and the wry humor may be too low-key for some viewers. Also known as *Heavenly Pursuits.* (CC)

GOTCHA! 1985
★★★★ PG-13 Comedy 1:41
☑ Brief nudity, adult situations, explicit language, violence
Dir: Jeff Kanew *Cast:* Anthony Edwards, Linda Fiorentino, Nick Corri, Klaus Lowitsch, Alex Rocco
► UCLA student Edwards excels at mock assassination game called "Gotcha!"; then finds himself in real-life danger when he gets involved with sexy spy Fiorentino in Europe. Personable hero, attractive leading lady, and impressive location scenery (Paris, East Berlin). Lots of easy laughs. (CC)

GO TELL THE SPARTANS 1978
★★★★ R War 1:53
☑ Adult situations, violence, explicit language
Dir: Ted Post *Cast:* Burt Lancaster, Craig Wasson, Jonathan Goldsmith, Marc Singer, Joe Unger
► Lancaster, the commanding officer of an outpost near Dienbienphu, where the French were slaughtered in 1954, tries to impart his instincts and experiences to green troops who know little of jungle fighting. A true sleeper, this unsung Vietnam-era drama predates some of the better known efforts in the genre. Lancaster and Wasson are sympathetic and believable.

GOTHIC 1987 British
☆ R Drama 1:28
☑ Nudity, adult situations, explicit language, violence
Dir: Ken Russell *Cast:* Gabriel Byrne, Julian Sands, Natasha Richardson, Myriam Cyr, Timothy Spall
► On a stormy night in 1816, the poets Shelley (Sands) and Byron (Byrne), Mary Shelley (Richardson), Byron's girlfriend Cyr, and Dr. Polidori (Spall) tell ghost stories and confront each other. Mary Shelley is inspired to write *Frankenstein.* Florid nonsense goes over the top and stays there. Russell provides lots of flash but unappealing characters grate on the nerves.

GO WEST 1940
★★ NR Comedy 1:21 B&W
Dir: Edward Buzzell *Cast:* The Marx Brothers, John Carroll, Diana Lewis, Walter Woolf King
► Groucho, Chico, and Harpo head for the wild, wild West and battle a villain over a priceless land deed. Not top-notch Marx but some funny stuff: Groucho getting bilked by his brothers, hilarious train-chase finale.

GRACE QUIGLEY 1985
★★ PG Comedy 1:27
☑ Explicit language, violence
Dir: Anthony Harvey *Cast:* Katharine Hepburn, Nick Nolte, Elizabeth Wilson, Chip Zien, William Duell
► Elderly Hepburn witnesses hitman Nolte commit murder and blackmails him into bumping off unhappy old folks who want to end their lives but can't bring themselves to commit suicide. A warm if unlikely relationship develops between Nolte and Hepburn. Two pros add class to this uneasy, sometimes bizarre mixture of killing and comedy.

GRADUATE, THE 1967
★★★★★ PG Comedy 1:45
☑ Adult situations, explicit language
Dir: Mike Nichols *Cast:* Dustin Hoffman, Anne Bancroft, Katharine Ross, William Daniels, Murray Hamilton
► Directionless college grad Hoffman (in his first starring role) has affair with much older Mrs. Robinson (Bancroft), wife of his dad's friend, and then falls for her daughter Ross. One of the most influential films of the sixties is a witty comedy of manners and a sharp portrait of a generation. Jazzily directed by Nichols, beautifully acted by all, and clever Buck Henry script with memorable dialogue: "Plastics" and "Mrs. Robinson, you're trying to seduce me . . . aren't you?" Score by Simon and Garfunkel includes, "Mrs. Robinson," "Sounds of Silence." Oscar for Best Director, nominated for Best Picture, Actor, Actress. (CC)

GRADUATION DAY 1981
★ R Horror 1:36
☑ Adult situations, explicit language, violence
Dir: Herb Freed *Cast:* Christopher George, Patch Mackenzie, E. J. Peaker, E. Danny Murphy, Michael Pataki
► As graduation day approaches, someone is killing off members of a high school track team. The suspects: creepy princi-

pal, gung-ho track coach, female Navy ensign whose sister was the first victim, and punk rocker. Low-budget entry in the kill-a-teen genre. Some suspense for hard-core blood and gore freaks but the story is strictly routine.

GRAND HOTEL 1932
★★★ NR Drama 1:55 B&W
Dir: Edmund Goulding *Cast:* Greta Garbo, John Barrymore, Joan Crawford, Wallace Beery, Lionel Barrymore, Jean Hersholt
▶ All-star spectacular weaves together lives of several guests at a Berlin hotel. Aging dancer Garbo "wants to be alone" until thief John Barrymore breaks into her room to steal her jewels but falls in love instead; dying Lionel Barrymore gets involved with secretary Crawford and her brutal boss Beery. Oscar for Best Picture. **(CC)**

GRAND ILLUSION 1937 French
★ NR Drama 1:50 B&W
Dir: Jean Renoir *Cast:* Jean Gabin, Pierre Fresnay, Erich von Stroheim, Marcel Dalio, Dita Parlo
▶ In a World War I prison camp, titled French POW Fresnay is befriended by his German captor and fellow aristocrat von Stroheim. Fresnay helps fellow inmates Dalio and Gabin escape, forcing von Stroheim to kill his pal. Deservedly legendary antiwar classic, masterfully directed by the great Renoir. §

GRAND PRIX 1966
★★★★ NR Drama 2:49
☑ Adult situations, mild violence
Dir: John Frankenheimer *Cast:* James Garner, Eva Marie Saint, Yves Montand, Toshiro Mifune, Brian Bedford, Jessica Walter
▶ American Garner, Brit Bedford, and Corsican Montand are among the drivers whose pursuit of a racing championship is complicated by on-track accidents and off-track romances. Mildly entertaining script enhanced by good cast and visually spectacular racing footage. Three Oscars: Sound, Film Editing, Sound Effects. **(CC)**

GRAND THEFT AUTO 1977
★★★ PG Action-Adventure 1:24
☑ Explicit language, violence
Dir: Ron Howard *Cast:* Ron Howard, Nancy Morgan, Marion Ross, Pete Isackson, Barry Powers, Rance Howard
▶ Young Howard and fiancée Morgan elope to Las Vegas in a Rolls Royce after her millionaire dad Cahill refuses to approve their marriage. This good-natured action comedy turns into one gigantic car chase when they're pursued by Pop and others. Directorial debut for Howard, co-written and co-starring his dad Rance.

GRANDVIEW, U.S.A. 1984
★★ R Drama 1:37
☑ Nudity, adult situations, explicit language, mild violence, adult humor
Dir: Randal Kleiser *Cast:* Jamie Lee Curtis, Patrick Swayze, C. Thomas Howell, Troy Donahue, Jennifer Jason Leigh
▶ Teenager Howell becomes involved with older Curtis who owns the local demolition derby, leading to conflict with his dad who wants to build country club on Curtis's property. Small-town slice-of-life comedy suffers from mechanical plotting and condescending humor; somewhat redeemed by the performances, particularly the always winsome Curtis. **(CC)**

GRAPES OF WRATH, THE 1940
★★★★★ NR Drama 2:09 B&W
Dir: John Ford *Cast:* Henry Fonda, Jane Darwell, John Carradine, Dorris Bowden, Charley Grapewin, John Qualen
▶ In the 1930s, the Oklahoma Dust Bowl forces farm families like the Joads to migrate to California, where the dispossessed clan become virtual slaves at a labor camp. Tom Joad (Fonda) refuses to be beaten by adversity and demands fair treatment for the workers. Grueling, heartbreaking masterpiece tells an epic story of determination and struggle. Fonda's "I'll be there" speech is one of the most moving moments in all cinema. Director Ford and Darwell (as Ma Joad) won Oscars. From John Steinbeck's Pulitzer prize–winning novel. **(CC)**

GRASS IS GREENER, THE 1960
★★ NR Comedy 1:45
Dir: Stanley Donen *Cast:* Cary Grant, Deborah Kerr, Robert Mitchum, Jean Simmons, Moray Watson
▶ Strained, talky adaptation of a minor British play about an English couple (Grant and Kerr) whose marriage is threatened by visiting Texas oilman Mitchum. Grant, in a polished performance, summons old girlfriend Simmons to stir Kerr's jealousy. Noel Coward songs ("Mad Dogs and Englishmen," "The

Stately Homes of England") provide most of the humor.

GRAY LADY DOWN 1978
★ ★ ★ ★ PG Mystery-Suspense 1:51
☑ Explicit language, mild violence
Dir: David Greene *Cast:* Charlton Heston, Stacy Keach, David Carradine, Ned Beatty
▶ A nuclear sub commanded by Heston is sunk after being rammed by a freighter. The Navy attempts to rescue the stricken ship but an earth tremor covers the escape hatch. Finally, an experimental diving vessel comes to the rescue. Undersea thriller is a tense, nail-biting affair with a solid cast.

GREASE 1978
★ ★ ★ ★ PG Musical 1:50
☑ Explicit language
Dir: Randal Kleiser *Cast:* John Travolta, Olivia Newton-John, Stockard Channing, Jeff Conaway, Didi Conn, Eve Arden
▶ The summertime romance of wholesome Sandy (Newton-John) and greaser Danny (Travolta) is disrupted by the advent of school but love eventually triumphs. Broadway sensation about the 1950s makes for a tuneful, lively movie musical. Sprightly numbers expertly choreographed by Patricia Birch, pizazz from Travolta, charm and torch songs from Newton-John, and fine supporting work from Channing.

GREASE 2 1982
★ ★ PG Musical 1:54
☑ Explicit language
Dir: Patricia Birch *Cast:* Maxwell Caulfield, Michelle Pfeiffer, Lorna Luft, Eve Arden, Connie Stevens, Tab Hunter
▶ Britisher Caulfield arrives at raucous Rydell High and falls for Stephanie (Pfeiffer), a member of the Pink Ladies gang. She thinks he's a nerd so he disguises himself as a biker to sweep her off her feet. Young, attractive cast, ample dancing, and toe-tapping tunes in this insubstantial but fast-paced sequel.

GREASED LIGHTNING 1977
★ ★ ★ ★ PG Biography/Sports 1:36
☑ Explicit language
Dir: Michael Schultz *Cast:* Richard Pryor, Beau Bridges, Pam Grier, Cleavon Little, Vincent Gardenia, Richie Havens
▶ True story of Wendell Scott (Pryor), a black stock-car racer who overcame bigotry and poverty to become a na-

tional champion. An effective change-of-pace dramatic performance by Pryor. Slowly paced at first but well-staged racing sequences rev movie up to speed.

GREAT CARUSO, THE 1951
★ ★ ★ ★ G Biography/Music 1:49
Dir: Richard Thorpe *Cast:* Mario Lanza, Ann Blyth, Dorothy Kirsten, Jarmila Novotna
▶ Life and times of legendary opera star Enrico Caruso (Lanza) details his Italian childhood, his American success and happy marriage to beautiful socialite Blyth, and his tragic early death. Lanza was born to play this role and music lovers will feast on the many operatic classics in this gorgeous MGM production.

GREAT DICTATOR, THE 1940
★ ★ ★ G Comedy 2:05 B&W
Dir: Charles Chaplin *Cast:* Charles Chaplin, Paulette Goddard, Jack Oakie, Henry Daniell, Billy Gilbert
▶ Chaplin plays a dual role: a Hitler-like dictator and his look-alike, a poor Jewish barber. An identity switch eventually thwarts the fascist. Superb spoof of totalitarianism with many memorable moments, including Chaplin's playing with a globe/balloon and the battles between Charlie and Jack Oakie (uproariously funny as a Mussolini-like leader).

GREAT ESCAPE, THE 1963
★ ★ ★ ★ NR War 2:48
Dir: John Sturges *Cast:* Steve McQueen, James Garner, Richard Attenborough, Charles Bronson, James Coburn, David McCallum
▶ Allied prisoners plan a daring mass escape from a German POW camp by digging three underground tunnels. Thrilling adventure offers all-star macho cast, humor, clever plotting, action, and the unforgettable jaunty music theme. McQueen was never cooler than as the "Cooler King," so nicknamed because of the time he spent in solitary. Script by James Clavell from a true story. (CC)

GREATEST, THE 1977
★ ★ PG Biography/Sports 1:41
☑ Explicit language
Dir: Tom Gries *Cast:* Muhammad Ali, Ernest Borgnine, Lloyd Haynes, John Marley, Robert Duvall, James Earl Jones
▶ A relaxed and confident Ali plays himself in this biography of his rise to the heavyweight championship, battles with bigotry, conversion to Islam, marriages, being stripped of the title for his refusal to

fight in Vietnam, and triumphant resurgence against George Foreman. Actual fight footage spices this predictable but entertaining movie.

GREATEST BATTLE, THE 1979
★ ★ ★ PG War 1:45
☑ Explicit language, violence
Dir: Alan Smithee *Cast:* Henry Fonda, Stacy Keach, John Huston, Helmut Berger, Samantha Eggar, Giuliano Gemma
▶ Combining action, adventure, and romance, wartime drama interweaves personal traumas with scenes of battle during the crucial 1943 North African campaign. Fonda plays an American general returning to active duty in Tunisia; Keach is his adversary, a major in the dreaded Panzer Corps; and Eggar is Keach's half-Jewish wife.

GREATEST SHOW ON EARTH, THE 1952
★ ★ ★ ★ NR Drama 2:33
Dir: Cecil B. DeMille *Cast:* Betty Hutton, Charlton Heston, Cornel Wilde, Dorothy Lamour, Gloria Grahame, James Stewart
▶ Best Picture Oscar went to this magnificent, epic look at life under the big top. Trapeze artist Hutton falls for daring new star Wilde while still harboring a yen for the boss Heston. Showgirl Grahame also loves Wilde while clown Stewart (who remains in makeup throughout) hides a mysterious past. Despite these passions (and a train wreck disaster), the show must go on.

GREATEST STORY EVER TOLD, THE 1965
★ ★ ★ ★ ★ G Drama 3:13
Dir: George Stevens *Cast:* Max Von Sydow, Charlton Heston, Roddy McDowall, Robert Loggia, Jose Ferrer, Dorothy McGuire
▶ Von Sydow is Christ in this most grandiose of biblical epics tracing His life from birth to crucifixion and resurrection. Top-quality holiday fare has one of the most star-studded casts ever assembled; John Wayne, Sidney Poitier, Claude Rains, Angela Lansbury, and Telly Savalas are among the cameos. **(CC)**

GREAT EXPECTATIONS 1947 British
★ ★ ★ ★ NR Drama 1:58 B&W
Dir: David Lean *Cast:* John Mills, Valerie Hobson, Bernard Miles, Finlay Currie, Jean Simmons, Alec Guinness
▶ Pip, a young orphan devoted to the wealthy Estella, receives a mysterious bequest that enables him to improve his social standing. From the thrilling opening in a gloomy cemetery to the fiery climax, this remarkable masterpiece is generally regarded as the best of all Charles Dickens adaptations, unsurpassed after more than forty years. Mills, the older Pip, and Guinness, Pip's raffish London friend, are superb, but the most remarkable performance is Martita Hunt's haunting Miss Havisham. Won Oscars for set design and Guy Green's cinematography. **(CC)**

GREAT GATSBY, THE 1949
★ ★ ★ NR Drama 1:32 B&W
Dir: Elliott Nugent *Cast:* Alan Ladd, Betty Field, Macdonald Carey, Ruth Hussey, Barry Sullivan, Howard da Silva
▶ Ladd portrays F. Scott Fitzgerald's tragic hero Gatsby, a bootlegger who uses illicit wealth to buy a mansion near old flame Field, now married to boorish Sullivan. Ladd renews his relationship with Field with disastrous results. Lacks the splendor of the 1974 version although Ladd is effective.

GREAT GATSBY, THE 1974
★ ★ ★ PG Drama 2:23
☑ Adult situations, explicit language
Dir: Jack Clayton *Cast:* Robert Redford, Mia Farrow, Sam Waterston, Bruce Dern, Karen Black, Lois Chiles
▶ In the Roaring Twenties, mysterious self-made millionaire Jay Gatsby (Redford) throws mammoth parties at his Long Island estate. He hopes to get close to Daisy Buchanan (Farrow), the woman he loved and lost years back, now married to boorish blueblood Dern. Overly literal adaptation of F. Scott Fitzgerald's magnificent novel fails to do justice to book's serious themes and suffers from miscast leads. Enjoyable, though, for the lavish period re-creation and for Waterston's sharp performance as narrator Nick.

GREAT IMPOSTOR, THE 1961
★ ★ NR Biography 1:52 B&W
Dir: Robert Mulligan *Cast:* Tony Curtis, Edmond O'Brien, Karl Malden, Arthur O'Connell, Gary Merrill, Raymond Massey
▶ Doctor, Marine, prison warden, academic, and monk are some of the roles assayed in the colorful life of impostor Ferdinand Demara (Curtis). Fanciful true story is generally enjoyable, thanks to Curtis's panache and a good supporting cast.

GREAT LOVER, THE 1949
★★★ NR Comedy 1:20 B&W
Dir: Alexander Hall   *Cast:* Bob Hope,
Rhonda Fleming, Roland Young, Roland Culver, Jim Backus, George
Reeves
▶ Scoutmaster Hope takes troop on European cruise. He falls in love with penniless duchess Fleming and must save the day when a murderer appears on board. Lighthearted suspense comedy in a sophisticated milieu with an irresistible Hope compensating for some weak songs and a tentative Fleming.

GREAT McGINTY, THE 1940
★★★ NR Comedy 1:21 B&W
Dir: Preston Sturges   *Cast:* Brian Donlevy, Muriel Angelus, Akim Tamiroff, Allyn Joslyn, William Demarest
▶ In a corrupt election, bum Donlevy votes thirty-seven times for the same politician, rises to governor, is stricken by conscience, and has a falling-out with Boss Tamiroff. Marvelous satire from writer/director Sturges with unforgettable characterizations (Tamiroff as the politician so corrupt he controls both machine and reform party) and scenes (Donlevy reading children's story to his stepkids). Oscar for Best Screenplay.

GREAT MOUSE DETECTIVE, THE 1986
★★★★★ G Animation 1:12
Dir: Barry Mattinson   *Cast:* Voices of Vincent Price, Barrie Ingham, Val Bettin, Susanne Pollatschek, Candy Candido, Alan Young
▶ Sherlock Holmes and Dr. Watson return as animated characters, Basil of Baker Street and faithful companion Dr. Dawson. In foggy London town, the dynamic duo foil the evil scheme of rat Professor Rattigan (voice of Vincent Price). Pleasing story moves at fast clip with delightful visuals (best Disney animation in ages). A family entertainment winner.

GREAT MUPPET CAPER, THE 1981
★★★★ G Comedy/Family 1:38
Dir: Jim Henson   *Cast:* The Muppets, Charles Grodin, Diana Rigg, John Cleese, Peter Falk, Robert Morley
▶ Fired from their jobs as reporters for a big-city paper, Kermit and company investigate a jewel theft in London. Good-natured charm and innocence, inspired routines (Kermit dances like Fred Astaire, Miss Piggy swims in an Esther Williams number), and London locations deliver

delightful fun. Rigg and Grodin bring panache to their Muppets interactions.

GREAT NORTHFIELD, MINNESOTA RAID, THE 1972
★★★ PG Western 1:31
☑ Adult situations, explicit language, violence
Dir: Philip Kaufman   *Cast:* Cliff Robertson, Robert Duvall, Luke Askew, R. G. Armstrong, Dana Elcar, Donald Moffat
▶ Famed badman Cole Younger (Robertson) considers hanging up his gun, but his friend Jesse James (Duvall) will have none of the straight life. The pair and their gang then team up for Minnesota bank robbery. Intelligent direction by Kaufman and good performances from Robertson and Duvall.

GREAT OUTDOORS, THE 1988
★★★ PG Comedy 1:30
☑ Explicit language
Dir: Howard Deutsch   *Cast:* Dan Aykroyd, John Candy, Stephanie Faracy, Annette Bening, Chris Young, Ian Giatti
▶ Auto parts salesman Candy takes his Chicago family to bucolic lakeside retreat, but his serenity is destroyed by arrival of obnoxious brother-in-law Aykroyd and his snobby family. Broad comedy from John Hughes relies heavily on stars' charm and silly sight gags.

GREAT RACE, THE 1965
★★★ NR Comedy 2:33
Dir: Blake Edwards   *Cast:* Jack Lemmon, Tony Curtis, Natalie Wood, Peter Falk, Keenan Wynn, Larry Storch
▶ Grand-scaled comedy about a 1908 transcontinental road race. *Some Like It Hot* co-stars Curtis and Lemmon are reunited on opposite sides: Curtis is the handsome hero who wins suffragette Wood, Lemmon has a scenery-chewing field day as the mustache-twirling villain. Highlight: the most lavish pie-throwing fight ever filmed.

GREAT SANTINI, THE 1980
★★★★ PG Drama 1:55
☑ Explicit language
Dir: Lewis John Carlino   *Cast:* Robert Duvall, Blythe Danner, Michael O'Keefe, Stan Shaw, Lisa Jane Persky
▶ Duvall is utterly superb as Bull Meechum, a tough Marine pilot without any real battles to fight, who runs his household like a boot camp. O'Keefe was Oscar-nominated for his portrayal of Duvall's emotionally torn adolescent son. A luminous Danner plays a sensitive and

loving Southern belle mother. Originally released as *The Ace*; based on Pat Conroy's novel.

GREAT SCOUT AND CATHOUSE THURSDAY, THE 1976
★★★ PG Comedy 1:36
☑ Adult situations
Dir: Don Taylor *Cast:* Lee Marvin, Oliver Reed, Robert Culp, Elizabeth Ashley, Strother Martin, Kay Lenz
▶ Trapper Marvin and Harvard-educated Indian Reed team up to retrieve fortune in gold stolen by Culp, who has used the money to buy into what passes for high society in the Wild West. Lenz is attractive as a prostitute romanced by Marvin, but lumbering Western spoof lacks inspiration.

GREAT TEXAS DYNAMITE CHASE, THE 1976
★★★ R Action-Adventure 1:28
☑ Nudity, violence
Dir: Gus Trikonis *Cast:* Claudia Jennings, Jocelyn Jones, Johnny Crawford, Chris Pennock
▶ Bonnie and Clyde with a twist of women's lib: two pretty Texas girls, escaped con (*Playboy* centerfold) Jennings and obnoxious ex-bank teller Jones, join forces to rob banks, outsmart the cops, and enrapture various men. Workable and offbeat, with bits of real humor.

GREAT TRAIN ROBBERY, THE 1979
British
★★★★ PG Drama 1:51
☑ Explicit language
Dir: Michael Crichton *Cast:* Sean Connery, Donald Sutherland, Lesley-Anne Down, Alan Webb, Malcolm Terris
▶ In 1855, arch-criminal Connery enlists mistress Down and master lockpicker Sutherland in a daring scheme to hijack gold bullion from a train. Sly caper film, based on a real incident, features an excellent cast and gorgeous production values. Connery, who did his own stunts, is especially impressive. Director Crichton wrote the screenplay from his best-selling novel.

GREAT WALDO PEPPER, THE 1975
★★★ PG Drama 1:47
☑ Adult situations, explicit language
Dir: George Roy Hill *Cast:* Robert Redford, Bo Svenson, Bo Brundin, Margot Kidder, Susan Sarandon, Phil Bruns
▶ After World War I, pilot Redford barnstorms through the countryside before getting his long-delayed chance to battle German ace Brundin when both are hired as movie stuntmen. Eye-boggling aerial footage was obviously a labor of love for director Hill, a licensed pilot, but the script meanders. Redford exudes charisma in the title role.

GREAT WALL, A 1986 U.S./Chinese
★★★ PG Comedy 1:40
☑ Explicit language
Dir: Peter Wang *Cast:* Peter Wang, Sharon Iwai, Kelvin Han Yee, Li Qinqin, Hu Xiaoguang, Shen Guanglan
▶ Chinese-American computer executive Wang takes his family to Peking to visit his sister; resulting clash of values is shown with amusing insight in this lighthearted comedy. First U.S./Chinese co-production is short on plot, but scenery and characters are fascinating. Ⓢ

GREAT ZIEGFELD, THE 1936
★★★ NR Biography/Musical 2:56 B&W
Dir: Robert Z. Leonard *Cast:* William Powell, Luise Rainer, Myrna Loy, Frank Morgan, Reginald Owen, Nat Pendleton
▶ Long, detailed account of showman Flo Ziegfeld (Powell), his turbulent affair with Anna Held (Rainer), his up-and-down career, and his happy but tragically brief marriage to Billie Burke (Loy). Filled with cameos from Fanny Brice, Ray Bolger, etc., and memorable songs like "A Pretty Girl Is Like a Melody," "Rhapsody in Blue," "Look for the Silver Lining," and many more. Won three Oscars, including Best Picture and Actress (Rainer).

GREEK TYCOON, THE 1978
★★★ R Drama 1:46
☑ Adult situations, explicit language
Dir: J. Lee Thompson *Cast:* Anthony Quinn, Jacqueline Bisset, Raf Vallone, Edward Albert, Camilla Sparv, Charles Durning
▶ Greek shipping magnate Theo Tomasis (Quinn) marries Liz Cassidy (Bisset), the stylish widow of an assassinated President. Despite unimaginable wealth, they grapple with the same emotional problems as couples everywhere. Lush scenery provides a dramatic backdrop to this provocative romance loosely based on the life of billionaire Aristotle Onassis.

GREEN BERETS, THE 1968
★★★ G War 2:21
Dir: John Wayne, Ray Kellogg *Cast:* John Wayne, David Janssen, Jim Hut-

ton, Aldo Ray, Raymond St. Jacques, Bruce Cabot

▶ Wayne's tribute to the Special Forces soldiers based in Vietnam is an old-fashioned war adventure filled with large-scale action scenes. Wayne commands a regiment defending a strategic hill from swarming Vietcong, then leads his men on a mission to kidnap an enemy general. Janssen is a cynical reporter gradually won over to the Berets' methods. Received scathing reviews on release for its right-wing tone. Based on Robin Moore's novel.

GREEN FOR DANGER 1946 British
★★ NR Mystery-Suspense 1:31 B&W
Dir: Sidney Gilliat *Cast:* Alastair Sim, Trevor Howard, Leo Genn, Sally Gray, Rosamund John

▶ In a World War II English hospital, a nurse is killed after announcing that a patient who died on the operating table was actually murdered. Scotland Yard detective Sim tries to solve the case. Superior little whodunit held together by Sim's droll wit. Never a dull moment; keeps the audience guessing until the end.

GREEN ICE 1981 British
★★★ PG Action-Adventure 1:55
☑ Adult situations, explicit language, violence
Dir: Ernest Day *Cast:* Ryan O'Neal, Anne Archer, Omar Sharif, Domingo Ambriz, John Larroquette

▶ On-the-skids electronics engineer O'Neal teams up with sophisticated Archer to rob a fortune in emeralds from Colombian tycoon Sharif. Black-market thugs and left-wing guerrillas add to the tension. Highlighted by a daring raid by hot-air balloon. **(CC)**

GREGORY'S GIRL 1982 Scottish
★★ PG Comedy 1:29
☑ Adult situations, explicit language
Dir: Bill Forsyth *Cast:* Gordon John Sinclair, Dee Hepburn, Chic Murray, Clare Grogan, Jake D'Arcy

▶ Gawky high school student Sinclair falls for Hepburn, his soccer team's female goalie, but eventually finds true love with one of her friends, Grogan. Filmmaker Forsyth transforms a seemingly mundane story of an adolescent crush into something truly magical, romantic, and slyly humorous. Thick Scottish brogues may prove too wearying for the impatient.

GREMLINS 1984
★★★★ PG Fantasy/Comedy 1:46
☑ Adult situations, explicit language, violence
Dir: Joe Dante *Cast:* Zach Galligan, Phoebe Cates, Hoyt Axton, Frances Lee McCain, Polly Holliday, Keye Luke

▶ Failed inventor Axton gives son Galligan a cuddly "mogwai" for Christmas, but Galligan ignores warnings against feeding the pet after midnight and getting it wet. The result: hordes of vicious gremlins prone to deadly practical jokes invade the small town. Steven Spielberg production has fascinating special effects and a mordant sense of humor. **(CC)**

GREY FOX, THE 1983 Canadian
★★★★ PG Western 1:31
☑ Adult situations, explicit language, mild violence
Dir: Philip Borsos *Cast:* Robert Farnsworth, Jackie Burroughs, Wayne Robson, Ken Pogue, Timothy Webber, Gary Reineke

▶ After decades in jail, "Gentleman Bandit" Farnsworth must adjust to a new world of steam trains and motion pictures. Burroughs plays an early feminist who befriends the robber. Warm, elegiac Western, set in turn-of-the-century Canada, is a good showcase for ex-stuntman Farnsworth's thoughtful, expressive performance.

GREYSTOKE: THE LEGEND OF TARZAN, LORD OF THE APES 1984
★★★ PG Drama 2:10
☑ Brief nudity, violence
Dir: Hugh Hudson *Cast:* Ralph Richardson, Christopher Lambert, Ian Holm, Andie MacDowell, Nigel Davenport

▶ Sophisticated, lavish retelling of the Edgar Rice Burroughs classic stars Lambert as the Sixth Earl of Greystoke, born in the jungle to shipwrecked parents and raised by apes. "Civilized" by Belgian explorer Holm, Tarzan is brought to England to claim his inheritance. Incredible ape makeup by Rick Baker is one of the highlights. Film debut for Andie MacDowell (whose Southern voice was dubbed over by Glenn Close). Ralph Richardson's final film. **(CC)**

GRISSOM GANG, THE 1971
★★ R Action-Adventure 2:07
☑ Adult situations, explicit language, violence
Dir: Robert Aldrich *Cast:* Kim Darby,

Scott Wilson, Tony Musante, Robert Lansing, Irene Dailey, Connie Stevens
▶ In the 1930s, gangster mom Dailey and her clan nab rich girl Darby and demand ransom; Dailey's son Wilson and Darby fall in love. Slam-bang action in an off-beat story; characterizations and performances are bizarre but compelling (especially the over-the-top Wilson).

GRIZZLY 1976
★★★ PG Action-Adventure 1:32
☑ Explicit language, graphic violence
Dir: William Girdler **Cast:** Christopher George, Andrew Prine, Richard Jaeckel, Joan McCall, Joe Dorsey
▶ Enraged grizzly goes on the rampage in a Georgia forest; heroic ranger George and dedicated naturalist Jaeckel pursue the beast, hampered by meddling reporter McCall. Violent action takes precedence over characterizations in this low-budget mayhem modeled after *Jaws.*

GROOVE TUBE, THE 1974
★★ R Comedy 1:13
☑ Nudity, adult situations, explicit language, adult humor
Dir: Ken Shapiro **Cast:** Ken Shapiro, Chevy Chase, Richard Belzer, Buzzy Linhart
▶ In ten sketches masquerading as the program "The Groove Tube," writer/director/producer Shapiro takes a jaundiced look at TV commercials, Hollywood glitz, children's shows (where a clown reads from *Fanny Hill*), and more. Cult curio is wildly irreverent, with loads of scatological humor. Pre–"Saturday Night Live" Chevy Chase appears as a newscaster.

GROUNDSTAR CONSPIRACY, THE 1972
★★ PG Mystery-Suspense 1:35
☑ Violence
Dir: Lamont Johnson **Cast:** George Peppard, Michael Sarrazin, Christine Belford, Cliff Potts, James Olson, James McEachin
▶ Bomb goes off at government space project, killing several researchers. Is scientist/survivor Sarrazin involved? Inquiring agent Peppard wants to know. Overlooked and underrated suspenser features taut direction, first-rate performances, and intricate plotting.

GROUND ZERO 1988 Australian
★★★ PG-13 Mystery-Suspense 1:40
☑ Explicit language, violence
Dir: Michael Pattinson, Bruce Myles
Cast: Colin Friels, Jack Thompson, Donald Pleasence, Natalie Bate
▶ Cameraman Friels connects his father's death thirty years ago to nuclear bomb tests and battles government thugs intent on preserving a cover-up. Paranoid thriller gets off to a slow start but builds logically to create a fair amount of tension; Friels is quite sympathetic.

GROUP, THE 1966
★★★ NR Drama 2:30
Dir: Sidney Lumet **Cast:** Candice Bergen, Joan Hackett, Elizabeth Hartman, Shirley Knight, Joanna Pettet, Jessica Walter
▶ Eight women friends graduate from Vassar in the 1930s and find the real world fraught with difficulties. Walter becomes a successful but lonely author, Bergen turns to lesbianism, Knight gets involved with a married man, and Pettet suffers through a bad marriage with tragic consequences. Juicy all-star soap opera from the Mary McCarthy bestseller.

GUADALCANAL DIARY 1943
★★★★ NR War 1:33 B&W
Dir: Lewis Seiler **Cast:** Preston Foster, Lloyd Nolan, William Bendix, Richard Conte, Anthony Quinn
▶ One of Hollywood's finest World War II flag-waving actioners about Marines battling the Japanese to capture a strategic Pacific base. Features the usual disparate cast of characters brought together to fight like brothers, with Bendix stealing the show as a Brooklyn taxi driver. Based on the book by Richard Tregaskis.

GUARDIAN, THE 1984
★★★★ NR Crime/MFTV 1:41
☑ Rape, adult situations, explicit language, graphic violence
Dir: David Greene **Cast:** Louis Gossett, Jr., Martin Sheen, Arthur Hill, Tandy Cronyn
▶ No-nonsense ex–military man Gossett is hired as a security guard for a crime-plagued Manhattan apartment building. He is pitted against ultra-liberal tenant Sheen, who's concerned that Gossett is taking the law into his own hands. Engrossing crime drama.

GUESS WHO'S COMING TO DINNER 1967
★★★★★ NR Drama 1:48
Dir: Stanley Kramer **Cast:** Spencer

Tracy, Katharine Hepburn, Sidney Poitier, Katharine Houghton, Cecil Kellaway
► College senior Houghton announces to upper-middle-class parents Tracy and Hepburn her intention to marry brilliant research physician Poitier, who happens to be black. Graceful, entertaining story about the social turmoil experienced by both her family and his. Perhaps best known as the final film pairing of Hepburn and Tracy (he died a few weeks after the movie was shot). Garnered a Best Actress Oscar for Hepburn; nomination for Tracy. (CC)

GUIDE FOR THE MARRIED MAN, A
1967
★★★ NR Comedy 1:29
Dir: Gene Kelly *Cast:* Walter Matthau, Robert Morse, Inger Stevens, Lucille Ball, Jack Benny, Art Carney
► Although married to beautiful Stevens, Matthau is led down the path of infidelity by his womanizing pal Morse before seeing the error of his ways. Ball, Benny, and Carney are among the cameo guest stars in sequences illustrating Morse's advice. Broad, obvious, but very amusing; Morse and Matthau are quite funny together.

GULAG 1985
★★★★★ NR Drama/MFTV 2:10
☑ Nudity, explicit language, violence
Dir: Roger Young *Cast:* David Keith, Malcolm McDowell, David Suchet, Warren Paul
► American sportscaster Keith is railroaded by the KGB into a Russian labor camp. Struggling with the bitter cold and the cruelty of the guards, he plots a daring breakout with fellow prisoner McDowell. Top-notch escape drama.

GUMBALL RALLY, THE 1976
★★★ PG Action-Adventure 1:47
☑ Adult situations
Dir: Chuck Bail *Cast:* Michael Sarrazin, Gary Busey, Norman Burton, John Durren, Susan Flannery
► Oddball motorists stage a cross-country auto race. Violating every traffic law from New York to Los Angeles, they escape the vengeful cop out to stop them. Harmless and fast-moving, with some good gags and tons of car crashes. Perfect tonic for those summer months when you just want to put your mind in neutral.

GUMSHOE 1972 British
★ PG Comedy 1:28

☑ Adult situations, violence
Dir: Stephen Frears *Cast:* Albert Finney, Billie Whitelaw, Janice Rule, Frank Finlay, Fulton MacKay, Carolyn Seymour
► Ordinary Brit Finney decides to try his hand at the private eye business. He soon finds himself up to his neck in intrigue and danger with gunrunner Rule and members of his own family. English parody of American genre films will appeal to sophisticated tastes. Musical score by theatrical composer Andrew Lloyd Webber.

GUN CRAZY 1949
★★ NR Crime/Drama 1:26 B&W
Dir: Joseph H. Lewis *Cast:* Peggy Cummins, John Dall, Berry Kroeger, Morris Carnovsky, Anabel Shaw
► Carnival markswoman Cummins and paranoid World War II vet Dall exploit their mutual love of firearms in a widespread crime spree. Compact B movie with *Bonnie and Clyde* overtones has become a cult favorite for Lewis's stylish film noir direction. Bank robbery shot in real time is the most effective sequence.

GUNFIGHT, A 1971
★★★ PG Western 1:33
☑ Adult situations, explicit language
Dir: Lamont Johnson *Cast:* Kirk Douglas, Johnny Cash, Jane Alexander, Karen Black, Raf Vallone, Eric Douglas
► Former gunfighter Douglas now lives quietly with wife Alexander and works as celebrity bouncer at a local bar. Into town rides over-the-hill gunslinger Cash, prompting speculation about a shoot-out between the two legends. Cash and Douglas decide to make a buck on the local tongue-wagging and charge admission to their showdown. Unusual, atmospheric Western was screen debut for Cash. Financed solely by oil-rich Jicarilla Apaches of New Mexico.

GUNFIGHT AT THE O.K. CORRAL 1957
★★★★ NR Western 2:02
Dir: John Sturges *Cast:* Burt Lancaster, Kirk Douglas, Rhonda Fleming, Jo Van Fleet, John Ireland, Lyle Bettger
► Gripping, authentic account of the friendship between lawman Wyatt Earp (Lancaster) and gunslinger Doc Holliday (Douglas), and the events leading up to their famous shoot-out with the Clanton gang. Memorable acting, richly detailed script, and taut direction aided film's popular success and helped reestablish the importance of the Western genre.

Large cast includes Earl Holliman, Dennis Hopper, Lee Van Cleef, and Jack Elam. Director Sturges returned to the subject in 1967's *Hour of the Gun*.

GUNFIGHTER, THE 1950
★★★★ NR Western 1:24 B&W
Dir: Henry King *Cast:* Gregory Peck, Helen Westcott, Millard Mitchell, Jean Parker, Karl Malden, Skip Homeier
▶ Peck gives a bravura performance as Johnny Ringo, an aging gunslinger haunted by his past as he waits in a grimy frontier town for a glimpse of estranged wife Westcott and son. Somber, thoughtful Western is first-rate on all levels, particularly the assured, steady direction and Homeier's memorable turn as a novice gunman trying to goad Peck into a confrontation.

GUN FURY 1953
★★ NR Western 1:23
Dir: Raoul Walsh *Cast:* Rock Hudson, Donna Reed, Phil Carey, Roberta Haynes, Lee Marvin, Neville Brand
▶ Compact Western set in Arizona, with Hudson and Reed playing newlyweds terrorized by Carey, a genuinely disturbing villain. When Reed is kidnapped, Hudson must sink to Carey's level to rescue her. Originally released in 3-D.

GUNGA DIN 1939
★★★★ NR Action-Adventure 1:57 B&W
Dir: George Stevens *Cast:* Cary Grant, Victor McLaglen, Douglas Fairbanks, Jr., Sam Jaffe, Eduardo Ciannelli, Joan Fontaine
▶ An outstandingly heroic trio of British sergeants (Grant, McLaglen, and Fairbanks) grapple with a murderous Thugee cult in colonial India, helped by native water boy Jaffe, who dreams of becoming a soldier. Rousing blend of action, humor, and romance, loosely based on the Rudyard Kipling poem, is one of Hollywood's greatest adventures.

GUNG HO 1986
★★★★ PG-13 Comedy 2:00
☑ Adult situations, explicit language
Dir: Ron Howard *Cast:* Michael Keaton, George Wendt, Gedde Watanabe, Mimi Rogers, John Turturro, Soh Yamamura
▶ Car plant foreman Keaton convinces Japanese company to take over his hometown's abandoned auto factory, then is caught in the middle when the new bosses' strict ways clash with Ameri-

can methods. Terrific premise, cheerfully directed, niftily acted by cocky Keaton and uptight Watanabe. Script could have used some more fine tuning, but overall, quite pleasing. **(CC)**

GUNS OF NAVARONE, THE 1961
★★★★★ NR War 2:39
Dir: J. Lee Thompson *Cast:* Gregory Peck, David Niven, Anthony Quinn, Anthony Quayle, Stanley Baker
▶ On the Greek island of Kheros, a worn-out World War II garrison faces Axis annihilation, unless a group of Allied commandos led by Peck can dismantle the two radar-controlled German cannons guarding their evacuation route. High-powered Hollywood triumph-over-impossible-odds story based on Alistair MacLean's best-seller. Nominated for seven Academy Awards, deservedly winning Best Special Effects. Spawned lesser 1978 sequel *Force 10 From Navarone*.

GUS 1976
★★★ G Comedy 1:36
Dir: Gary McEveety *Cast:* Edward Asner, Don Knotts, Gary Grimes, Tim Conway, Liberty Williams
▶ More family fun from the folks at Disney. Owner Asner and coach Knotts of a struggling football team find fortunes reversed by an unlikely new player: a field-goal-kicking mule. Former pros Johnny Unitas and Dick Butkus appear, but realism is not film's strong suit.

GUY NAMED JOE, A 1944
★★★★ NR Fantasy 2:00 B&W
Dir: Victor Fleming *Cast:* Spencer Tracy, Irene Dunne, Van Johnson, Ward Bond, James Gleason, Lionel Barrymore
▶ Killed in battle, pilot Tracy finds himself assigned as a guardian angel to novice flier Johnson. To Tracy's consternation, Johnson pursues his old girlfriend Dunne, herself a flying ace. Large-scale fantasy was a popular World War II hit, although blend of whimsy, sentimentality, and ghosts seems forced today. Cast also includes Esther Williams, Barry Nelson, and future director Blake Edwards.

GUYS AND DOLLS 1955
★★★★ NR Musical 2:29
Dir: Joseph L. Mankiewicz *Cast:* Marlon Brando, Jean Simmons, Frank Sinatra, Vivian Blaine, Stubby Kaye
▶ In Damon Runyon's New York, Nathan Detroit (Sinatra) tries to finance his floating crap game by betting gambler Sky Masterson (Brando) that he can't win the

heart of Salvation Army lady Simmons. All-star cast (even the singing Brando) delivers the goods in this very professional and entertaining adaptation of Frank Loesser's Broadway smash. Hummable songs include "Luck Be a Lady," "If I Were a Bell." **(CC)**

GYMKATA 1985
★ **R Martial Arts 1:30**
☑ Graphic violence
Dir: Robert Clouse *Cast:* Kurt Thomas, Tetchie Agbayani, Richard Norton, Edward Bell, John Barrett
▶ Gymnastics gold medalist Thomas is sent to compete in a remote Himalayan country's life-and-death endurance contest that grants the winner one wish. Loud bone-crunching outshines acting and dialogue. Based on Dan Tyler Moore's novel, *The Terrible Game.*

GYPSY 1963
★★★ **NR Biography/Musical 2:23**
Dir: Mervyn LeRoy *Cast:* Rosalind Russell, Natalie Wood, Karl Malden, Paul Wallace, Betty Bruce, Ann Jillian
▶ Stage mother Russell pushes daughters Wood as Gypsy Rose Lee and Jillian as Baby June into theatrical careers, which proceed on a downward course until Wood finds a niche as a stripper. Although she overacts, Russell is effective. Brassy musical adaptation of the Jule Styne/Stephen Sondheim Broadway hit. Songs include "Everything's Coming Up Roses" and "Let Me Entertain You."

HADLEY'S REBELLION 1984
★★★ **PG Drama 1:36**
☑ Explicit language, mild violence
Dir: Fred Walton *Cast:* Griffin O'Neal, William Devane, Charles Durning, Adam Baldwin
▶ O'Neal, a kid from Georgia, attends California boarding school and tries to prove himself to the other kids with his wrestling prowess. Sensitively crafted coming-of-age drama with decent performances. **(CC)**

HAIL! HAIL! ROCK 'N' ROLL 1987
★★ **PG Documentary/Music 2:00**
☑ Explicit language
Dir: Taylor Hackford *Cast:* Chuck Berry, Keith Richards, Eric Clapton, Robert Cray, Etta James, Julian Lennon
▶ Marvelous tribute to rock pioneer Chuck Berry on his sixtieth birthday. Interviews from top musicians combine with fascinating concert footage that climaxes in an all-star bash in his St. Louis

hometown. Astute direction and editing reveal Berry as a complex, contradictory figure. Richards, Bruce Springsteen, Little Richard, and many others contribute valuable insights. Also known as *Chuck Berry Hail! Hail! Rock 'n' Roll.*

HAIL MARY 1985 French/Swiss
☆ **NR Drama 1:10**
☑ Nudity, strong sexual content, adult situations, explicit language
Dir: Jean-Luc Godard *Cast:* Myriem Roussel, Thierry Rode, Philippe Lacoste, Juliette Binoche, Manon Anderson
▶ In this modern retelling of the Nativity, Virgin Mary works at a gas station, Joseph is her moody cabdriver boyfriend, and the angel Gabriel is a seedy stranger. Story provides the peg for Godard's voice-over reveries about womanhood, spirituality, and sex. Controversial drama was condemned by the Catholic Church.

HAIL THE CONQUERING HERO 1944
★★★★★ **NR Comedy 1:41 B&W**
Dir: Preston Sturges *Cast:* Eddie Bracken, Ella Raines, Bill Edwards, Raymond Walburn, William Demarest, Freddie Steele
▶ Demarest and his fellow Marines, veterans of Guadalcanal, donate their medals to embarrassed 4-F reject Bracken so he can return home a hero. Despite Bracken's protests, his gullible neighbors nominate him for mayor. Devastating satire on wartime patriotism is a sheer delight from start to finish. Familiar Sturges actors (Demarest, Franklin Pangborn, Jimmy Conlin, Alan Bridge, etc.) handle the sparkling dialogue with aplomb. Nominated for Best Screenplay.

HAIR 1979
★★ **PG Musical 2:01**
☑ Nudity, explicit language
Dir: Milos Forman *Cast:* John Savage, Treat Williams, Beverly D'Angelo, Annie Golden, Dorsey Wright, Miles Chapin
▶ Oklahoma farm boy Williams, in New York City for his induction, gets sidetracked by a tribe of hippies obsessed with turning him on to drugs, sex, and peace so he'll forget about the Army. Forman's glowing tribute to the euphoria of flower children, adapted from the 1968 Broadway love-rock musical, features be-ins, draft dodgers, hippie rags, and lots of hair. Far-out performances, exuberant Twyla Tharp choreography, and

seminal sixties soundtrack: "Aquarius," "Easy to Be Hard," "White Boys/Black Boys," more.

HAIRSPRAY 1988
★★ **PG Comedy 1:34**
☑ Explicit language
Dir: John Waters *Cast:* Divine, Ricki Lake, Deborah Harry, Sonny Bono, Jerry Stiller, Pia Zadora
▶ With the support of parents Divine and Stiller, perky chubette Lake auditions for a popular teen dance show in 1960s Baltimore. She wows the kids with her Mashed Potato but garners the wrath of rival Amber and Amber's parents Harry and Bono. Bubble-headed series of teenage crises and crushes also touches on the civil rights movement, but plot is secondary to the campy acting and lacquered bouffants. Cult director Waters at his most goofball benign. Film was his most popular success, crossing over to mainstream audiences. **(CC)**

HALF A LIFETIME 1986
★★ **NR Drama/MFTV 0:57**
☑ Explicit language
Dir: Daniel Petrie *Cast:* Keith Carradine, Gary Busey, Nick Mancuso, Saul Rubinek
▶ A friendly poker game turns into a serious, soul-searching encounter as four buddies realize they've reached their mid-thirties without attaining their high school dreams. Over-the-hill jock Busey, mild-mannered insurance salesman Rubinek, childless teacher Mancuso, and penniless cop Carradine must each consider what to do with his remaining half a lifetime. Adapted by Stephen Metcalfe from his off-Broadway play.

HALF MOON STREET 1986
★★ **R Drama 1:30**
☑ Nudity, strong sexual content, explicit language, violence
Dir: Bob Swaim *Cast:* Michael Caine, Sigourney Weaver, Patrick Kavanagh, Faith Kent, Ram John Holder
▶ Unconventional Weaver is a scholar by day, high-class hooker by night. Caine, a diplomat and client, involves her in the world of international intrigue. Film boasts remarkable technical credits (costumes, production, etc.), a too-violent climax, and lots of Sigourney-in-the-buff shots. Based on Paul Theroux's novella. **(CC)**

HALLOWEEN 1978
★★★ **R Horror 1:31**

☑ Brief nudity, adult situations, explicit language, violence
Dir: John Carpenter *Cast:* Donald Pleasence, Jamie Lee Curtis, P. J. Soles, Nancy Loomis, Charles Cyphers
▶ A young boy is institutionalized after killing his sister. Fifteen years later, on Halloween, he escapes to menace babysitter Curtis and her high school pals. Evocative direction by Carpenter (who also wrote the chilling music score) uses inventive camerawork and deceptively peaceful settings to create a fantastic fright flick. Curtis is quite good as the terrorized heroine. Spawned three sequels.

HALLOWEEN II 1981
★★ **R Horror 1:32**
☑ Nudity, explicit language, graphic violence
Dir: Rick Rosenthal *Cast:* Jamie Lee Curtis, Donald Pleasence, Charles Cyphers, Pamela Susan Shoop, Lance Guest
▶ Just when you thought it was safe to go trick-or-treating . . . Sequel begins where the first left off: Curtis is in the hospital recovering from her ordeal when the crazed killer, not really dead as believed, tracks her down. Not nearly as subtle or confident as the first flick but delivers blood, gore, and a few solid jolts.

HALLOWEEN III: SEASON OF THE WITCH 1982
★★ **R Horror 1:38**
☑ Adult situations, explicit language, graphic violence
Dir: Tommy Lee Wallace *Cast:* Tom Atkins, Stacey Nelkin, Dan O'Herlihy, Ralph Strait
▶ After one of his patients is killed, doctor Atkins and the murdered man's daughter Nelkin investigate. They uncover a scheme by mad toy manufacturer O'Herlihy to kill children via deadly Halloween masks. Slickly mounted horror film is well executed but series fans be warned: story is unrelated to first two *Halloween* flicks.

HALLOWEEN IV: THE RETURN OF MICHAEL MYERS 1988
★★★ **R Horror 1:28**
☑ Brief nudity, explicit language, graphic violence
Dir: Dwight H. Little *Cast:* Donald Pleasence, Ellie Cornell, Danielle Harris, George P. Wilbur, Michael Pataki
▶ En route to a new mental home, homicidal slasher Michael Myers (Wilbur) escapes and heads for his hometown to

ravage his sole surviving relative, little niece Harris (who's the daughter of the Jamie Lee Curtis character from the first movie in the series). Wilbur is pursued by gimpy-legged doctor Pleasence. Special effects include an exploding gas station, a gruesome electrocution, and lots of prerequisite corpses. Film's twist ending sets the stage for a whole new series of sequels.

HAMBONE AND HILLIE 1984
★★★★ PG Family 1:30
☑ Violence
Dir: Roy Watts *Cast:* Lillian Gish, O. J. Simpson, Timothy Bottoms, Candy Clark, Jack Carter
▶ Elderly Gish, returning to L.A. after visiting grandson Bottoms in New York City, loses mutt Hambone at the airport. The resilient pet makes a cross-country journey and is eventually reunited with owner. Simple story provides vehicle for the cutest cinematic canine since Benji. Only those immune to doggie charms can resist little Hambone.

HAMBURGER HILL 1987
★★★★ R War 1:34
☑ Nudity, adult situations, explicit language, graphic violence
Dir: John Irvin *Cast:* Michael Patrick Boatman, Tegan West, Dylan McDermott, Courtney Vance, Tommy Swerdlow, Steven Weber
▶ In 1969, fresh American recruits are launched into a hellish battle against the North Vietnamese for possession of a hill. Forthright staging by Irvin and raw script by Vietnam vet James Carabatsos give an authentic grunt's-eye-view of war's carnage and confusion. Very graphic violence makes for disturbing end; difficult to view but hard to ignore.

HAMBURGER . . . THE MOTION PICTURE 1986
★ R Comedy 1:30
☑ Nudity, adult situations, explicit language
Dir: Mike Marvin *Cast:* Leigh McCloskey, Dick Butkus, Randi Brooks, Chuck McCann, Jack Blessing, Debra Blee
▶ After being expelled from four colleges, young McCloskey must clean up his act or be disinherited. He enrolls in a twelve-week course at Burgerbuster University for a degree in the fast-food biz. A few laughs and some nubile topless coeds: cinematic equivalent of a Big Mac. **(CC)**

HAMLET 1948 British
★★ NR Drama 2:33 B&W
Dir: Laurence Olivier *Cast:* Laurence Olivier, Eileen Herlie, Basil Sydney, Jean Simmons, Norman Wooland, Stanley Holloway
▶ Overwhelming performance by Olivier as the mad prince of Denmark distinguishes this noteworthy drama. Although play is abridged somewhat, cast and directing rank this among the best of Shakespeare adaptations. Simmons is suitably ethereal as Ophelia; John Gielgud supplies the voice of Hamlet's father's ghost. Best Picture winner also received Oscars for Olivier and the stark set design.

HAMLET 1969 British
★ G Drama 1:58
Dir: Tony Richardson *Cast:* Nicol Williamson, Gordon Jackson, Anthony Hopkins, Judy Parfitt, Mark Dignam, Marianne Faithfull
▶ Respectable adaptation of Shakespeare's tragedy pits Williamson's intense interpretation of Hamlet against Hopkins's larger-than-life performance as Claudius. Peculiar casting of pop star Faithfull as Ophelia is surprisingly successful. Look for Anjelica Huston as one of the court ladies.

HAMMETT 1982
★ PG Mystery-Suspense 1:37
☑ Brief nudity, adult situations, explicit language, violence
Dir: Wim Wenders *Cast:* Frederic Forrest, Peter Boyle, Marilu Henner, Roy Kinnear, Elisha Cook, Jr., Lydia Lei
▶ In 1928, Pinkerton detective Boyle asks aspiring mystery writer Dashiell Hammett (Forrest) for help on a baffling case involving missing Chinese woman Lei. Francis Ford Coppola produced this atmospheric but confusing thriller. Evocative sets, outstanding photography, and amusing in-jokes almost salvage the often tedious plot.

HAND, THE 1981
★ R Horror 1:44
☑ Nudity, adult situations, explicit language, graphic violence
Dir: Oliver Stone *Cast:* Michael Caine, Andrea Marcovicci, Annie McEnroe, Bruce McGill, Viveca Lindfors
▶ Intellectually challenging thriller about cartoonist Caine whose drawing hand is severed in a car accident. Psychologically as well as physically damaged, he

destroys his marriage and sinks into murderous fantasies. Caine gives an astute performance in this sometimes gory shocker.

HANDFUL OF DUST, A 1988 British
★ **PG Drama 1:58**
☑ Brief nudity, adult situations, explicit language
Dir: Charles Sturridge *Cast:* James Wilby, Kristin Scott Thomas, Rupert Graves, Anjelica Huston, Judi Dench, Alec Guinness
▶ England, 1930s: stuffy Wilby is devoted to country estate, while bored wife Thomas takes social-climbing lover Graves in the city. Affair plus family tragedy prove fatal to the marriage. "Masterpiece Theatre"–style filmmaking meticulously re-creates the period, but heartless characters make for unsatisfying experience. Based on the Evelyn Waugh novel.

HANDLE WITH CARE 1977
★★ **PG Comedy 1:38**
☑ Adult situations, explicit language
Dir: Jonathan Demme *Cast:* Paul LeMat, Candy Clark, Ann Wedgeworth, Bruce McGill, Hobert S. Blossom, Charles Napier
▶ Inventive comedy, released at the height of the CB craze, examines the wacky inhabitants of a Southwestern town—all fascinated with citizen-band radios—in a series of winsome vignettes. Napier, as a bigamist trucker, shines in this smoothly entertaining story. Originally titled *Citizens Band.*

HANDS OF STEEL 1986 Italian
★ **R Action-Adventure 1:34**
☑ Explicit language, violence
Dir: Martin Dolman (Sergio Martino)
Cast: Daniel Greene, Janet Agren, John Saxon, George Eastman, Amy Werba
▶ Mysterious Italian assassin Greene bungles an assignment and flees to Arizona desert, where he befriends beautiful Agren. Greene defends her from brutal arm wrestlers who later ambush him in a trap. When Agren rescues him, he reveals that he's a high-tech mandroid. Low-budget exploitation suffers from poor dubbing and special effects.

HANG 'EM HIGH 1968
★★★ **R Western 1:54**
☑ Adult situations, explicit language, violence
Dir: Ted Post *Cast:* Clint Eastwood, Inger Stevens, Ed Begley, Bruce Dern, Dennis Hopper, Ben Johnson
▶ Innocent rancher Eastwood swears revenge on the men who tried to lynch him. Derivative Hollywood version of Eastwood's highly successful spaghetti Westerns is violent, technically polished, and filled with strong supporting work, including Western veteran Bob Steele as a dungeon prisoner.

HANKY PANKY 1982
★★★ **PG Comedy 1:43**
☑ Explicit language, violence
Dir: Sidney Poitier *Cast:* Gene Wilder, Gilda Radner, Kathleen Quinlan, Richard Widmark, Robert Prosky, Josef Sommer
▶ Neurotic Chicago architect Wilder is chased by cops, spies, and villains because of a tape containing secret weapons data. Attempt to recapture the success of *Stir Crazy* is a limp mistaken-identity thriller notable for the first screen teaming of Wilder and Radner, his wife-to-be. **(CC)**

HANNAH AND HER SISTERS 1986
★★ **PG-13 Comedy 1:47**
☑ Adult situations, explicit language
Dir: Woody Allen *Cast:* Woody Allen, Mia Farrow, Michael Caine, Barbara Hershey, Dianne Wiest, Max Von Sydow
▶ In the tradition of *Annie Hall,* Allen's fourteenth film as writer/director is warmhearted, wise, and funny. Quirky contemporary drama concerns very different sisters Farrow, Wiest, and Hershey and their relationships with men, women friends, showbiz parents Maureen O'Sullivan and Lloyd Nolan, and each other. Sterling cast. Three cheers and three Oscars (Caine, Wiest, and Screenplay).

HANNA K 1983
★ **R Drama 1:50**
☑ Adult situations, explicit language, mild violence
Dir: Costa-Gavras *Cast:* Jill Clayburgh, Jean Yanne, Gabriel Byrne, Mohammed Bakri
▶ Quirky Hanna Kaufman (Clayburgh) practices law in Jerusalem. While defending Moslem Bakri for illegally crossing the border, she finds herself caught between her growing personal involvement with him, her pregnancy by Israeli Byrne, and her estranged husband Yanne. Controversial because of its ambiguous Palestinian stand.

HANNA'S WAR 1988
★★ PG-13 Biography 2:30
☑ Adult situations
Dir: Menahem Golan *Cast:* Ellen Burstyn, Maruschka Detmers, Anthony Andrews, Donald Pleasence, David Warner, Vincenzo Ricotta
▶ True story of Jewish martyr Hanna Senesh (Detmers), who fled anti-Semitism in her native Hungary for Palestine in the 1930s, but then returned as a British operative to help her people. Sincere but rather overlong and oversimplified; spirited Detmers well supported by Burstyn as her mother.

HANOI HILTON, THE 1987
★★★ R War 2:10
☑ Explicit language, violence
Dir: Lionel Chetwynd *Cast:* Michael Moriarty, Jeffrey Jones, Paul LeMat, Gloria Carlin, David Soul, Aki Aleong
▶ In a Vietnamese camp, American prisoners of war suffer torture under major Aleong's iron hand. Moriarty leads the men who resist Aleong; LeMat is among those who are not quite so principled. Grueling drama is solidly acted but rather heavy-handed, with a right-wing viewpoint unique among recent Vietnam films. Carlin plays a Jane Fonda figure who visits the camp and is resented by the Americans. **(CC)**

HANOVER STREET 1979
★★★★ PG Romance 1:49
☑ Brief nudity, adult situations, explicit language
Dir: Peter Hyams *Cast:* Harrison Ford, Lesley-Anne Down, Christopher Plummer, Alec McCowen, Richard Masur
▶ Ford, an American bomber pilot, and Down, a married Englishwoman, meet in London during the Blitzkrieg and fall in love. Coincidentally, Down's husband Plummer, a British intelligence officer, and Ford are brought together on a crucial mission behind enemy lines, not knowing they love the same woman. Old-fashioned, nostalgic romance.

HANS BRINKER AND THE SILVER SKATES 1979
★★★ NR Family 1:43
Dir: Robert Scheerer *Cast:* Eleanor Parker, Richard Basehart, Cyril Ritchard, John Gregson, Robin Askwith
▶ The beloved story of poor Dutch boy Gregson's determination to help his invalid father and win a pair of silver skates. Expert acting from Parker; Basehart and Ritchard add class. Wholesome family classic shot on location in Amsterdam.

HANS CHRISTIAN ANDERSEN 1952
★★★★★ NR Biography/Musical 1:52
Dir: Charles Vidor *Cast:* Danny Kaye, Farley Granger, (Renee) Jeanmaire, John Brown, Roland Petit
▶ Kaye shines in this musical biography of Hans Christian Andersen, a storytelling cobbler forced to leave his Danish village because children play hooky to listen to his wonderful stories. He journeys to Copenhagen, where he falls in love with beautiful ballerina Jeanmaire, who inspires one of his most famous stories, "The Little Mermaid." Well-crafted production. Music by Frank Loesser and Franz Liszt adds imagination and vibrancy.

HAPPIEST MILLIONAIRE, THE 1967
★★★★ NR Musical/Family 2:24
Dir: Norman Tokar *Cast:* Fred MacMurray, Lesley Ann Warren, Tommy Steele, Greer Garson, John Davidson
▶ MacMurray is a Philadelphia blueblood. His chaotic household includes patient wife Garson, teenage daughter Warren, two sons, Irish butler Steele, and twelve pet alligators. MacMurray is training for World War I Marines while Warren gets engaged to a New York gentleman (Davidson). Most hummable tune: "Fortuosity." Patriotic Disney production with old-fashioned Hollywood professionalism: lavish sets and beautiful costumes (even the alligators look glamorous).

HAPPY BIRTHDAY TO ME 1981
★★ R Horror 1:51
☑ Brief nudity, adult situations, explicit language, graphic violence, adult humor
Dir: J. Lee Thompson *Cast:* Glenn Ford, Melissa Sue Anderson, Tracy Bregman, Jack Blum, Matt Craven
▶ Anderson, a preppie at Crawford Academy, is welcomed into "The Top Ten," an elite social clique. A jealous maniac takes revenge, reducing them to "The Top Nine" . . . and so on. Cutlery is the murder weapon of choice in this unappetizing teen slaughter film.

HAPPY HOOKER, THE 1975
★ R Sex/Comedy 1:37
☑ Brief nudity, strong sexual content, explicit language
Dir: Nicholas Sgarro *Cast:* Lynn Redgrave, Jean-Pierre Aumont, Tom Pos-

ton, Nicholas Powell, Conrad Janis, Anita Morris

▶ Dutch girl Redgrave arrives in New York to get married, has change of heart, becomes high-class prostitute, and eventually starts her own establishment. Silly comedy plays quite tamely now. Based on real-life hooker Xaviera Hollander's best-selling memoir.

HAPPY NEW YEAR 1973 French
☆ **PG Comedy 1:54**
Ⓥ Explicit language, violence
Dir: Claude Lelouch *Cast:* Lino Ventura, Françoise Fabian, Charles Gerard, Andre Falcon

▶ It starts off as a happy new year for crook Ventura when he is released from prison. Plotting a new heist, he gets involved with store owner Fabian and is pursued by the cops. Caper benefits from director Lelouch's sure touch. American remake appeared in 1987. Also available in dubbed version. Ⓢ

HAPPY NEW YEAR 1987
★★ **PG Comedy 1:26**
Ⓥ Explicit language
Dir: John G. Avildsen *Cast:* Peter Falk, Charles Durning, Wendy Hughes, Tom Courtenay, Joan Copeland

▶ Ex-con Falk plots jewel heist with buddy Durning while romancing antique dealer Hughes in West Palm Beach. Agreeable American remake of Claude Lelouch's French film with Falk donning some neat disguises. Gently humorous and diverting though moves rather slowly and fails to deliver the big laughs.

HARDBODIES 1984
★★ **R Comedy 1:27**
Ⓥ Nudity, adult situations, explicit language
Dir: Mark Griffiths *Cast:* Grant Cramer, Gary Wood, Teal Roberts, Michael Rapport, Sorrells Pickard

▶ Middle-aged clods Wood, Rapport, and Pickard rent a house on Venice beach and hire local blond surfer-stud Cramer to teach them how to score. The lessons pay off, and soon the place is wall-to-wall bimbettes. Witless and obvious, but successfully delivers a good-looking young cast that lives up to the title. **(CC)**

HARDBODIES 2 1986
★ **R Comedy 1:28**
Ⓥ Nudity, adult situations, explicit language
Dir: Mark Griffiths *Cast:* Brad Zutaut,

Fabiana Udenio, James Karen, Sam Temeles, Alba Francesca, Roberta Collins

▶ Zutaut, Temeles, and Curtis Scott Wilmot arrive in Greece to work on a low-budget picture. The leading lady has not yet been cast; auditions are held on a cruise ship/floating university right out of an adolescent boy's fantasy, with mandatory topless attendance.

HARD CHOICES 1986
★★ **NR Drama 1:31**
Ⓥ Nudity, explicit language, violence
Dir: Rick King *Cast:* Margaret Klenck, Gary McCleery, John Seitz, John Sayles, John Snyder, Spalding Gray

▶ Tennessee teen McCleery is jailed as accomplice in robbery/cop shooting. Social worker Klenck, unable to provide help, springs him and they become lovers on the lam. Commendable low-budget ($500,000) effort with naturalistic settings and performances. Slightly slow-paced but soap opera star Klenck is outstanding. Based on a true story.

HARDCORE 1979
★★★ **R Drama 1:48**
Ⓥ Nudity, adult situations, explicit language
Dir: Paul Schrader *Cast:* George C. Scott, Peter Boyle, Season Hubley, Dick Sargent, Leonard Gaines

▶ Scott, an upright, God-fearing Midwesterner, sees his runaway daughter in a porn movie and searches for her through L.A.'s sleazy netherworld of prostitution and pornography. Hubley plays a hooker with a gold-plated heart who helps him. Strong, hard-hitting drama pulls no punches.

HARD COUNTRY 1981
★★★ **NR Drama 1:42**
Ⓥ Adult situations, explicit language
Dir: David Greene *Cast:* Jan-Michael Vincent, Kim Basinger, Michael Parks, Gailard Sartain, Daryl Hannah, Tanya Tucker

▶ Poor man's *Urban Cowboy* about unhappy factory worker Vincent and his frustrated girlfriend Basinger, living in a dreary west Texas town. They dream of California, where he can escape his brother, who's got an eye for Basinger, and she can become a stewardess. In her film debut, country-western singer Tucker plays a local-girl-made-good and Hannah appears as Basinger's kid sister. Original R rating was revoked when producers inserted additional graphic violence.

HARD DAY'S NIGHT, A 1964 British
★★★★ G Musical/Comedy 1:27 B&W
Dir: Richard Lester *Cast:* John Lennon, Paul McCartney, George Harrison, Ringo Starr, Wilfred Brambell, Victor Spinetti
▶ The Beatles head for a TV gig in London while Paul's grandfather Brambell gets into trouble. "At least he's a clean old man," the boys muse. Exuberant direction by Lester employs all sorts of playful cinematic techniques to convey the youth, humor, and enthusiasm of the Fab Four. One of the most entertaining musicals ever; enjoyable even to non-Beatles fans.

HARDER THEY COME, THE 1973 Jamaican
★★ R Drama/Musical 1:38
☑ Nudity, adult situations, explicit language, violence
Dir: Perry Henzell *Cast:* Jimmy Cliff, Carl Bradshaw, Janet Bartley, Ras Daniel Hartman
▶ Jamaican singer Cliff turns to crime when corrupt producer wrecks his dream for a recording contract. Cliff becomes legendary outlaw as his songs rise on the charts. Cult classic manages to be raw and uncompromising yet upbeat and exciting at the same time. Exhilarating reggae score by the charismatic Cliff includes title tune, "You Can Get It If You Really Want," "Many Rivers to Cross," "Sitting in Limbo." (In English but subtitles get you through the thick accents.) ⑤

HARDER THEY FALL, THE 1956
★★★★ NR Drama 1:49 B&W
Dir: Mark Robson *Cast:* Humphrey Bogart, Rod Steiger, Jan Sterling, Mike Lane, Max Baer, Jersey Joe Walcott
▶ Promoter Steiger exploits glass-jawed boxer Lane, fixing his fights all the way to a title shot. Ex-sportswriter Bogart is hired to publicize the pug but ends up exposing fight game corruption. Bogart, in his last screen role, does a fine job in this brutally effective inside look at boxing.

HARDLY WORKING 1981
★★★ PG Comedy 1:29
☑ Explicit language, adult humor
Dir: Jerry Lewis *Cast:* Jerry Lewis, Susan Oliver, Roger C. Carmel, Deanna Lund, Billy Barty
▶ Predictable Lewis vehicle about an out-of-work clown bungling a series of jobs. Lewis appears in every frame to fall down, spill drinks, or mug in front of the camera. He even tries to score with an ugly woman who turns out to be Jerry in drag. For Lewis fans only.

HARD ROCK ZOMBIES 1985
☆ R Comedy 1:34
☑ Nudity, adult situations, explicit language
Dir: Krishna Shah *Cast:* E. J. Curcio, Sam Mann, Geno Andrews, Mick McMains, Jennifer Coe, Lisa Toothman
▶ Heavy metal rockers murdered by Hitler cult are turned into zombies by singer Curcio, a specialist in Satanic lyrics. Teens flock to the living dead musicians, prompting local authorities to ban rock music. Low-budget comedy scores some good points about heavy metal, although horror elements are silly. Shot in conjunction with horror spoof *American Drive-In*, in which it appears as film-within-film.

HARD TIMES 1974
★★★★★ PG Drama 1:33
☑ Adult situations, explicit language, violence
Dir: Walter Hill *Cast:* Charles Bronson, James Coburn, Jill Ireland, Strother Martin, Maggie Blye, Michael McGuire
▶ Nineteen-thirties New Orleans provides colorful backdrop for episodic tale of burly streetfighter Bronson and his rise to wealth through a series of no-holds-barred bouts staged by manager Coburn. Vivid atmosphere and brutal fights compensate for sketchy plot. Bronson, fifty-four at the time, is in amazing shape. Promising directorial debut for Hill.

HARD TO HOLD 1984
★★ PG Romance 1:33
☑ Brief nudity, strong sexual content, explicit language
Dir: Larry Peerce *Cast:* Rick Springfield, Patti Hansen, Janet Eilber, Albert Salmi, Gregory Itzen
▶ Springfield plays a famous rock musician in love with frosty psychologist Eilber, who's far too serious for his frivolous world. Fashion model Hansen is his songwriting collaborator/sometime girlfriend. Made-for-teens movie has all the vim and spontaneity of a broken record, but Springfield fans may not notice. (CC)

HARD WAY, THE 1980 British
★ NR Mystery-Suspense 1:28
☑ Adult situations, violence

Dir: Michael Dryhurst *Cast:* Patrick McGoohan, Lee Van Cleef, Donal McCann, Edna O'Brien
▶ Burned-out hitman McGoohan wants to quit his profession, but boss Van Cleef won't let him. To make matters worse, McGoohan's sympathetic wife O'Brien is threatened by the crime syndicate. Very understated; more of a character study than an action-packed thriller. Filmed on location in Ireland.

HAREM 1985 French
★ **NR Drama 1:53**
☑ Nudity, explicit language
Dir: Arthur Joffe *Cast:* Nastassja Kinski, Ben Kingsley, Dennis Goldson, Zohra Segal, Michel Robin
▶ Love-struck Arab sheik Kingsley kidnaps New York career girl Kinski and deposits her in his desert harem, where the ladies watch porno movies on the VCR. Yet, despite appearances, the sensitive sheik has been saving himself for the woman he loves. Color, cinematography, and Kinski are visual treats but muddled, confusing story can be exasperating.

HARLOW 1965
★★★★ **NR Biography 2:05**
Dir: Gordon Douglas *Cast:* Carroll Baker, Peter Lawford, Red Buttons, Mike Connors, Angela Lansbury
▶ "Blonde bombshell" Jean Harlow (Baker) rises to Hollywood stardom in the 1930s. Marriage to studio executive Lawford ends in his suicide and leads to drink, promiscuity, and her own tragic demise. Superior of the two 1965 film bios of Harlow (the other starred Carol Lynley) plays fast and loose with fact but is nonetheless entertaining.

HAROLD AND MAUDE 1971
★★★ **PG Comedy 1:32**
☑ Adult situations, explicit language, mild violence
Dir: Hal Ashby *Cast:* Ruth Gordon, Bud Cort, Cyril Cusack, Vivian Pickles, Ellen Geer
▶ Macabre black comedy starring Cort and Gordon as a taboo odd couple. Twenty-year-old Harold is rich and suicidal; Maude is old, poor, and full of life. They meet at a funeral and fall in love. Director Ashby captures a goofy sentimentality—happily bizarre and, occasionally, madly funny. Movie has devoted cult following. Written by Colin Higgins.

HARPER 1966
★★★★ **NR Mystery-Suspense 2:01**
Dir: Jack Smight *Cast:* Paul Newman, Lauren Bacall, Julie Harris, Arthur Hill, Janet Leigh, Pamela Tiffin
▶ Newman's first detective role finds him pursuing kidnappers of Bacall's millionaire husband; his investigation uncovers a deadly smuggling ring involving drug-addicted nightclub singer Harris. Expert cast is fun to watch; screenwriter William Goldman adapted Ross MacDonald's *The Moving Target.*

HARPER VALLEY P.T.A. 1978
★★★ **PG Comedy 1:42**
☑ Adult situations, explicit language
Dir: Richard Bennett *Cast:* Barbara Eden, Nanette Fabray, Ronny Cox, Susan Swift, Louis Nye, Pat Paulsen
▶ Jeannie C. Riley's hit song is transformed into a broad attack on small-town hypocrisy, with sexy mother Eden turning tables on the snobbish leaders of her local P.T.A. Fabray is delightful as Eden's friend. Popular comedy led to a TV series.

HARRAD EXPERIMENT, THE 1973
★★ **R Drama 1:36**
☑ Nudity, adult situations
Dir: Ted Post *Cast:* James Whitmore, Tippi Hedren, Don Johnson, Laurie Walters, Robert Middleton, Victoria Thompson
▶ University faculty couple Whitmore and Hedren conduct sexuality studies, guiding their students in premarital relationship experiments. Somewhat dated attitudes and talky script are drawbacks, but cast is pleasant (featuring a pre-stardom Johnson as one of the college kids). Based on the Robert Rimmer best-seller.

HARRY AND SON 1984
★★★★ **PG Drama 1:57**
☑ Brief nudity, adult situations, explicit language, adult humor
Dir: Paul Newman *Cast:* Paul Newman, Robby Benson, Joanne Woodward, Ellen Barkin, Wilford Brimley
▶ Heartfelt family drama describes the clash between aging blue-collar widower Newman and his free-spirited son Benson, an aspiring writer. A labor of love for Newman, who worked on the script and produced as well as directed.

HARRY AND THE HENDERSONS 1987
★★★★ **PG Comedy 1:51**
☑ Adult situations, mild violence
Dir: William Dear *Cast:* John Lithgow,

Melinda Dillon, Don Ameche, Joshua Rudoy, Margaret Langrick, Kevin Peter Hall
▶ The Hendersons, a typical suburban Seattle family, run over the legendary Bigfoot on a camping trip. Dad Lithgow brings Bigfoot (played by Hall) home, where the lovable monster wreaks widespread chaos. Family-oriented comedy from Steven Spielberg features an amusing performance from Ameche as a skeptical Bigfoot expert. **(CC)**

HARRY AND TONTO 1974
★ ★ ★ ★ R Comedy/Drama 1:15
☑ Adult situations, explicit language
Dir: Paul Mazursky *Cast:* Art Carney, Ellen Burstyn, Chief Dan George, Geraldine Fitzgerald, Larry Hagman, Melanie Mayron
▶ Touching, bittersweet tale about an independent, seventy-two-year-old New York City widower/retired teacher, Harry (Carney), rejuvenated by a cross-country trip with his pet cat, Tonto. Oscar-winner Carney maintains a gentle dignity and resilience throughout various encounters with his obnoxious offspring, hitchhiker Mayron, grandson Josh Mostel, an aging radical, former sweetheart, homicidal Indian chief, and happy hooker. Not a hard R rating at all. **(CC)**

HARRY AND WALTER GO TO NEW YORK 1976
★ ★ ★ PG Comedy 2:00
☑ Adult situations, explicit language
Dir: Mark Rydell *Cast:* James Caan, Elliott Gould, Michael Caine, Diane Keaton, Charles Durning
▶ Turn-of-the-century farce about fleabag vaudevillians Gould and Caan trying to safe-crack their way into Caine's exclusive upper-crust criminal set. Zany antics, song and dance, a couple of sight gags, and a few stretches of ho-hum. A disappointment from director Rydell and all-star cast.

HARUM SCARUM 1965
★ ★ ★ NR Musical 1:25
Dir: Gene Nelson *Cast:* Elvis Presley, Mary Ann Mobley, Fran Jeffries, Michael Ansara, Jay Novello, Billy Barty
▶ Movie star Presley is kidnapped by band of assassins while on Middle East tour. He finds himself in the midst of a murder plot, rescues maidens in distress, and wins the heart of beautiful princess Mobley. Tune-filled Presley adventure as the King brings his big beat to Baghdad.

HARVEY 1950
★ ★ NR Comedy 1:44 B&W
Dir: Henry Koster *Cast:* James Stewart, Josephine Hull, Peggy Dow, Charles Drake, Cecil Kellaway, Jesse White
▶ Elwood P. Dowd (Stewart) is the nicest man you'd ever want to meet but there's a problem: his best pal is a six-foot-tall invisible rabbit. Sister Hull considers having him committed in this popular screen comedy featuring one of Stewart's drollest performances. Hull won Oscar for Best Supporting Actress.

HARVEY GIRLS, THE 1946
★ ★ ★ NR Musical 1:41
Dir: George Sidney *Cast:* Judy Garland, John Hodiak, Ray Bolger, Angela Lansbury, Preston Foster, Cyd Charisse
▶ High-spirited, beautifully photographed musical based on the real-life Fred Harvey chain of railroad restaurants and their Eastern waitresses who helped civilize frontier towns in the Old West. Garland, playing a mail-order bride, is at the peak of her talent, singing the Oscar-winning "On the Atchison, Topeka and the Santa Fe."

HATARI! 1962
★ ★ ★ ★ ★ NR Action-Adventure 2:37
Dir: Howard Hawks *Cast:* John Wayne, Elsa Martinelli, Red Buttons, Hardy Kruger, Gerard Blain
▶ American Wayne leads team that traps wild animals in East Africa for zoos around the world. Wayne clashes with photographer Martinelli, who does story on the operation, but they end up together. Simple plot is dominated by terrific footage of animals, especially two baby elephants, and African settings. Overlong but will appeal to kids. Score by Henry Mancini is a highlight.

HATFUL OF RAIN, A 1957
★ ★ NR Drama 1:49 B&W
Dir: Fred Zinnemann *Cast:* Eva Marie Saint, Don Murray, Anthony Franciosa, Lloyd Nolan, Henry Silva, Gerald S. O'Loughlin
▶ Korean War hero Murray, addicted to dope as the result of a combat injury, battles his drug problem with the help of wife Saint, brother Franciosa, and father Nolan. Harrowing drama benefits greatly from concentration on the various reactions of family members to the issue. Fine photography gives picture an intriguing documentary feel, but wide-screen

CinemaScope effect will not translate to video.

HAUNTED HONEYMOON 1986
★ ★ PG Comedy 1:23
☑ Explicit language, violence
Dir: Gene Wilder *Cast:* Gene Wilder, Gilda Radner, Dom DeLuise, Jonathan Pryce, Paul Smith
▶ Thirties radio stars Wilder and Radner intend to wed but first Wilder must overcome his fears during a weekend at his spooky ancestral home. Strange things happen: a werewolf goes on the prowl and someone is after Aunt Kate's (DeLuise) fortune. Despite all the promising elements, this one's real short on laughs. Radner's given little to work with, and DeLuise in drag is still no relief from the tedium.

HAUNTED PALACE, THE 1963
★ ★ NR Horror 1:23
Dir: Roger Corman *Cast:* Vincent Price, Debra Paget, Lon Chaney, Jr., Frank Maxwell, Leo Gordon
▶ Price, a descendant of devil worshipers, moves into New England family home with bride Paget and becomes possessed by his dead relative. Corman adaptation of an H. P. Lovecraft story is full of fog, thunder, eerie music, and other haunted-house effects. Fun to watch Price go bonkers amid the overstuffed nineteenth-century furniture.

HAUNTING, THE 1963
★ ★ ★ G Horror 1:52 B&W
Dir: Robert Wise *Cast:* Julie Harris, Claire Bloom, Richard Johnson, Russ Tamblyn, Lois Maxwell
▶ In order to do research, anthropologist Johnson takes a group of people to an allegedly haunted house, where supernatural forces plague them. Promising idea never quite coalesces but good performances and amusingly gothic direction by Wise, who opts for suggestiveness over blood and gore.

HAUNTING OF JULIA, THE 1981 British/Canadian
★ R Horror 1:36
☑ Adult situations, explicit language, violence
Dir: Richard Loncraine *Cast:* Mia Farrow, Keir Dullea, Tom Conti, Jill Bennett, Robin Gammell
▶ Distraught over the death of her daughter, Farrow moves into mansion with husband Dullea determined to forge a new life. Unfortunately, evil spirit possessing the house has malevolent designs on the couple. Some effective shocks marred by predictable plotting.

HAWAII 1966
★ ★ ★ NR Drama 2:57
Dir: George Roy Hill *Cast:* Julie Andrews, Max Von Sydow, Richard Harris, Gene Hackman, Jocelyne La Garde, Manu Tupou
▶ Von Sydow, a straitlaced missionary, attempts to convert Hawaiian natives in the 1820s; wife Andrews is torn between defending his methods and her love for sea captain Harris. Overlong, sprawling drama covers the first half of James Michener's *Hawaii.* Received six Oscar nominations, including La Garde's role as the native queen. Large cast includes Carroll O'Connor, George Rose, and Bette Midler. *The Hawaiians* covers the second half of the book.

HAWKS 1988 British
★ ★ ★ NR Drama 1:50
☑ Nudity, adult situations, explicit language
Dir: Robert Ellis Miller *Cast:* Timothy Dalton, Anthony Edwards, Janet McTeer, Jill Bennett, Sheila Hancock, Connie Booth
▶ Terminally ill patients Dalton and Edwards escape British hospital together and head for final fling at Amsterdam bordello. They pick up pregnant McTeer along the way; romance develops between Dalton and McTeer with Edwards playing matchmaker. Gallant mixture of sentiment and wry humor; pungent performances with McTeer a standout.

HAWK THE SLAYER 1980 British
★ ★ NR Action-Adventure 1:35
☑ Adult situations, violence
Dir: Terry Marcel *Cast:* Jack Palance, John Terry, Bernard Bresslaw, Ray Charleson, Peter O'Farrell
▶ Sword and sorcery tale with a plot lifted right from the comic books. Hawk (Terry) vows to avenge the death of his father and takes on the forces of darkness headed by Voltan (Palance). Plenty of swordplay and solid action keep things moving at a brisk pace. Teens may enjoy but violence is unsuitable for younger kids.

HEAD 1968
★ ★ ★ G Comedy 1:26
Dir: Bob Rafelson *Cast:* David Jones, Michael Nesmith, Mickey Dolenz, Peter Tork, Teri Garr, Frank Zappa

▶ The Monkees, TV's answer to the Beatles, hired Rafelson and Jack Nicholson (who appears in one scene) to assemble this plotless time capsule of the psychedelic era. Resulting pastiche of film clips, newsreel footage, cheerful tunes, and bizarre cameos (Annette Funicello, Sonny Liston, Victor Mature, etc.) has enough far-out laughs to appeal to cultists.

HEAD OFFICE 1986
★★ **PG-13 Comedy 1:31**
☑ Brief nudity, adult situations, explicit language, adult humor
Dir: Ken Finkelman *Cast:* Judge Reinhold, Eddie Albert, Jane Seymour, Danny DeVito, Rick Moranis, Wallace Shawn
▶ Business school grad Reinhold enters corporation and encounters diverse group: ruthless boss Albert, tax cheat DeVito, female exec Seymour sleeping her way to top, and burnouts Shawn and Moranis. Reinhold romances the boss's rebellious daughter Lori-Nan Engler and teams with her to stop company corruption. Snappy satire with amusing cast of goofballs, although fun wears thin in second half.

HEARSE, THE 1980
★★ **PG Horror 1:39**
☑ Adult situations, explicit language
Dir: George Bowers *Cast:* Trish Van Devere, Joseph Cotten, David Gautreaux, Donald Hotton, Perry Lang
▶ After the death of her aunt, an unstable Van Devere returns to her family home. She is menaced by a mysterious man driving a large black hearse. Is she going crazy or is there really something evil going on? Formula shocker with sympathetic work from Trish as the beleaguered heroine.

HEART 1987
☆ **R Drama 1:31**
☑ Explicit language, violence
Dir: James Lemmo *Cast:* Brad Davis, Frances Fisher, Steve Buscemi, Robinson Frank Adu, Jesse Doran, Bill Costello
▶ Washed-up boxer Davis is chosen to fight up-and-coming contender Costello. Girlfriend Fisher thinks Davis is a fool to accept the challenge and his greedy manager Buscemi takes a bribe to fix the fight. However, Davis proves he has the heart of a winner. If you've seen *Rocky*, you know the ending, but performances by Davis and Buscemi transcend genre clichés.

HEARTACHES 1981 Canadian
★★★ **R Drama 1:32**
☑ Adult situations, explicit language
Dir: Donald Shebib *Cast:* Margot Kidder, Annie Potts, Robert Carradine, Winston Reckert
▶ Pregnant Potts runs away from husband Carradine rather than fess up that another man fathered her child. In Toronto, she hooks up with brassy blond Kidder who has romantic problems of her own. Harmless lightweight fluff with an appealing Potts.

HEART BEAT 1980
★ **R Drama 1:48**
☑ Nudity, adult situations, explicit language
Dir: John Byrum *Cast:* Nick Nolte, Sissy Spacek, John Heard, Ray Sharkey, Ann Dusenberry
▶ An intriguing subject: Beat Generation founder Jack Kerouac's (Heard) unconventional relationship with his pal Neal Cassady (Nolte) and the woman they both love, Cassady's wife Carolyn (Spacek). First-rate production and cinematography, but script fails to penetrate the surface. Superlative Sissy outshines her two male co-stars.

HEARTBEEPS 1981
★ **PG Fantasy 1:17**
☑ Explicit language
Dir: Allan Arkush *Cast:* Andy Kaufman, Bernadette Peters, Randy Quaid, Melanie Mayron, Kenneth McMillan, Christopher Guest
▶ At a futuristic factory, robots Kaufman and Peters, trained as helpers to humans, decide they prefer each other to the company of people. They create a child out of spare parts and set out to see the world. Sweet but insubstantial flight of fancy stymies talented players in robot makeup and doesn't develop inventive premise.

HEARTBREAKERS 1984
★★ **R Drama 1:38**
☑ Nudity, adult situations, explicit language
Dir: Bobby Roth *Cast:* Peter Coyote, Nick Mancuso, Carole Laure, Kathryn Harrold, James Laurenson, Carol Wayne
▶ Artist Coyote and best pal Mancuso look for meaning in their lives as they approach middle age. Their attraction to the same woman, Laure, causes a rift between them. Generally insightful look at

male-female relationships, with sharp performances (notably Coyote, Mancuso, and Wayne) and wonderful cinematography.

HEARTBREAK HOTEL 1988
★★★★ PG-13 Comedy 1:30
☑ Adult situations, explicit language
Dir: Chris Columbus *Cast:* David Keith, Tuesday Weld, Charlie Schlatter, Angela Goethals, Jacque Lynn Colton, Chris Mulkey
▶ In 1972 Ohio, teen Schlatter's mom Weld drinks too much. Who wouldn't? Her husband has left her, her boyfriend Mulkey beats her, and she gets in a car accident. Schlatter decides to cheer up mom by kidnapping her idol Elvis Presley (Keith). Outrageous concept gets talky execution, but Schlatter is sympathetic and Keith does a fabulous Elvis impersonation. Most heartwarming scene: Elvis teaching Schlatter's sister not to be afraid of the dark.

HEARTBREAK KID, THE 1972
★★ PG Comedy 1:44
☑ Adult situations, explicit language
Dir: Elaine May *Cast:* Charles Grodin, Cybill Shepherd, Eddie Albert, Jeannie Berlin, Audra Lindley
▶ While honeymooning with his clinging bride Berlin, newlywed Grodin falls for WASP dream girl Shepherd. He wins her over the objections of her stern Midwestern pop Albert but finds victory bittersweet. Grodin's ironic demeanor is engaging, but it's the Oscar-nominated Berlin (May's daughter) who will break your heart when Grodin gives her the bad news. A comedy of intelligence and nuance as screenwriter Neil Simon (adapting Bruce Jay Friedman's story) eschews his usual one-liners. Expert direction by May.

HEARTBREAK RIDGE 1986
★★★★ R War 2:10
☑ Brief nudity, explicit language, violence
Dir: Clint Eastwood *Cast:* Clint Eastwood, Marsha Mason, Everett McGill, Moses Gunn, Eileen Heckart, Bo Svenson
▶ Unorthodox, foulmouthed gunnery sergeant Eastwood turns a squadron of misfits into gung-ho fighting machines ready to tackle the Communists in Grenada. Handled with flair by Eastwood, who shows a welcome sensitive side in scenes with his ex-wife Mason. Mario Van Pee-

bles is a standout among the recruits. (CC)

HEARTBURN 1986
★★★ R Comedy 1:48
☑ Adult situations, explicit language, adult humor
Dir: Mike Nichols *Cast:* Meryl Streep, Jack Nicholson, Maureen Stapleton, Jeff Daniels, Stockard Channing, Richard Masur
▶ New York writer Streep marries Washington columnist Nicholson but then finds he's fooling around. Witty dialogue, classy production, but ultimately unsatisfying story development and conclusion. A dark-haired Streep shows another side of her amazing range, finding humor and heartbreak as the wronged wife. Nicholson has less to do but does have film's comic highlight, serenading pregnant Streep with a medley of songs about babies. From Nora Ephron's roman à clef about her breakup with Watergate reporter Carl Bernstein. (CC)

HEART IS A LONELY HUNTER, THE 1968
★★★★ G Drama 2:04
Dir: Robert Ellis Miller *Cast:* Alan Arkin, Sondra Locke, Laurinda Barrett, Stacy Keach, Chuck McCann, Cicely Tyson
▶ Touching adaptation of a Carson McCullers novel about the efforts of small-town deaf-mute Arkin to help the people around him. Earnest, episodic, extremely downbeat story won Oscar nominations for Arkin and for Locke as a spoiled teenager. Film debuts for Locke and Keach. (CC)

HEARTLAND 1981
★★★ PG Drama 1:36
☑ Adult situations, mild violence
Dir: Richard Pearce *Cast:* Rip Torn, Conchata Ferrell, Barry Primus, Lilia Skala, Megan Folson, Amy Wright
▶ Wyoming, 1910: widow Ferrell with young daughter Folson is hired as housekeeper by dour rancher Torn. They marry and see each other through the hardships and isolation of pioneer life. Slow and thoughtful with fine performances and gorgeous photography of the Wyoming countryside.

HEART LIKE A WHEEL 1983
★★★ PG Biography/Sports 1:53
☑ Adult situations, explicit language, violence
Dir: Jonathan Kaplan *Cast:* Bonnie Bedelia, Beau Bridges, Leo Rossi, Hoyt Axton, Bill McKinney, Dean Paul Martin

▶ True story about drag racer Shirley Muldowney (Bedelia), a housewife who battled the odds to win the national championship an unprecedented three times. Honest, engrossing biography has a sensational performance from Bedelia. Bridges plays her rival/lover Connie Kalitta. **(CC)**

HEARTS AND ARMOUR 1982 Italian
☆ **NR Action-Adventure 1:41**
☑ Rape, adult situations, violence
Dir: Giacomo Battiato *Cast:* Tanya Roberts, Barbara De Rossi, Zeudi Araya, Rick Edwards, Leigh McCloskey
▶ Christian knight Orlando battles the Moors while his lover Angelica fights off would-be rapists in an action-filled sword-and-sorcery epic based on *Orlando Furioso*. Pillage and swordplay dominate this often confusing Italian production.

HEARTS AND MINDS 1974
☆ **R Documentary 1:52**
☑ Nudity, adult situations, explicit language, violence
Dir: Peter Davis
▶ Groundbreaking documentary on the Vietnam War combines newsreel footage (some of it quite horrifying) with interviews covering a wide assortment of individuals, from General Westmoreland to a paraplegic vet. Offended some rightwingers when it won an Oscar, but overall a reasoned approach to a troubling period in history.

HEARTS OF FIRE 1988
★ **R Drama 1:35**
☑ Adult situations, explicit language
Dir: Richard Marquand *Cast:* Bob Dylan, Fiona, Rupert Everett, Julian Glover, Suzanne Bertish, Richie Havens
▶ Aspiring rock star Fiona gets involved with aging superstar Dylan. The romance hits hard times when her success eclipses his and she gets involved with younger rocker Everett. Well-staged concert footage and music-world atmosphere. Problem: Dylan can sing but can't act, Everett can act but can't sing, and the slushy love triangle plot is pretty weak, but Fiona is likable. **(CC)**

HEARTS OF THE WEST 1975
★ ★ **PG Comedy 1:42**
☑ Adult situations, explicit language
Dir: Howard Zieff *Cast:* Jeff Bridges, Andy Griffith, Donald Pleasence, Blythe Danner, Alan Arkin
▶ In the 1930s, Bridges, a naive Iowan, heads west to write cowboy stories and ends up a star in B-movie Westerns. Along the way, he finds romance with script girl Danner and meets veteran stuntman Griffith and egotistical director Arkin. Amiable comedy highlighted by sweetness of Bridges and Danner.

HEAT 1987
★ ★ ★ **R Action-Adventure 1:42**
☑ Adult situations, explicit language, violence
Dir: Dick Richards *Cast:* Burt Reynolds, Peter MacNicol, Karen Young, Neill Barry, Howard Hesseman, Diana Scarwid
▶ In Las Vegas, adventurer/compulsive gambler Reynolds helps friend Young avenge a beating at the hands of gangster Barry and thus runs afoul of the mob. A nice turn by MacNicol as a wimpy rich guy Reynolds teaches how to fight. Glittery backgrounds, action, sex, violence, and Burt's trademark macho posing.

HEAT AND DUST 1983 British
★ **R Drama 2:10**
☑ Nudity, adult situations, mild violence
Dir: James Ivory *Cast:* Julie Christie, Greta Scacchi, Christopher Cazenove, Shashi Kapoor, Susan Fleetwood
▶ In India, modern Englishwoman Christie investigates the life of her great-aunt Scacchi, who caused scandal in the 1920s by running off with Indian prince Kapoor. As past intercuts with present, Christie also falls for native man. Visually extravagant, superbly acted drama; epic in scope, but may be too leisurely paced for most.

HEATED VENGEANCE 1985
★ ★ **R Action-Adventure 1:30**
☑ Nudity, explicit language, violence
Dir: Edward Murphy *Cast:* Richard Hatch, Jolina Mitchell-Collins, Michael J. Pollard, Robert Walker, Jr., Dennis Patrick
▶ In Bangkok, Vietnam vet Hatch looks up old girlfriend Mitchell-Collins. Reunion is rudely disrupted when he's kidnapped by the head of a heroin ring, an ex-comrade Hatch court-martialed during the war. Survival training enables Hatch to escape his tormentors. Okay low-budget actioner.

HEATHERS 1989
★ ★ **R Comedy 1:42**
☑ Explicit language, violence
Dir: Michael Lehman *Cast:* Winona

Ryder, Christian Slater, Shannen Doherty, Kim Walker, Lisanne Falk, Penelope Milford

▶ Ryder is the fourth wheel in a powerful high school clique composed of three other girls all named Heather (Doherty, Falk, Walker). Tired of their cruel put-downs, Ryder joins seductive newcomer Slater to rebel against the Heathers' tyranny. She has a change of heart when Slater's plans include killing the girls and their sexist jock cohorts and making the deaths appear to be suicides. Biting script and attractive young cast carry this black comedy, but teen suicide subject matter and dark humor may disturb some.

HEAT OF DESIRE 1984 French
★ R Comedy 1:29
☑ Nudity, adult situations, explicit language, mild violence
Dir: Luc Beraud *Cast:* Patrick Dewaere, Clio Goldsmith, Jeanne Moreau, Guy Marchand, Pierre Dux
▶ Against the background of political upheavals, professor Dewaere leaves his wife for sexy Goldsmith. His obsession grows even as she manipulates him. Half-baked plotting but Clio radiates heat, desire, spontaneity, and grace as she glides unclothed from moonlit balcony to bedroom. ⑤

HEATWAVE 1983 Australian
★★ R Drama 1:33
☑ Nudity, adult situations, explicit language, violence
Dir: Phillip Noyce *Cast:* Judy Davis, Richard Moir, Chris Haywood, Bill Hunter
▶ Davis, the leader of squatters protesting housing development, has affair with project's architect Moir. He turns against the corrupt developers. Intelligent and sincere, with Davis giving her usual accomplished performance, but overly preachy and excessively talky. Limited appeal to American audiences.

HEAVEN 1987
★ PG-13 Documentary 1:20
☑ Adult situations, explicit language
Dir: Diane Keaton
▶ An unseen Keaton interviews diverse group—kids, hippies, Salvation Army officers, Hawaiians, oldsters, boxing promoter Don King—on their views of God and heaven. Interspersed are clips from Hollywood movies on these subjects. Keaton's candid camera captures some bizarrely funny responses but this quirky documentary is certain to offend some.

HEAVEN CAN WAIT 1943
★★★★ NR Fantasy/Comedy 1:52
Dir: Ernst Lubitsch *Cast:* Gene Tierney, Don Ameche, Charles Coburn, Marjorie Main, Laird Cregar, Eugene Pallette
▶ Elegant, lighthearted fantasy about sophisticated rake Ameche trying to convince the Devil he deserves damnation for his busy love life. Flashbacks set in the Gay Nineties show Ameche's genuine love for the beautiful Tierney. Effortless comedy is a prime example of the suave "Lubitsch touch."

HEAVEN CAN WAIT 1978
★★★★★ PG Fantasy/Comedy 1:40
☑ Adult situations, explicit language
Dir: Warren Beatty, Buck Henry *Cast:* Warren Beatty, Julie Christie, James Mason, Jack Warden, Dyan Cannon, Charles Grodin
▶ "Does the phrase 'not being a good sport' have any meaning to you?" asks inept angel Buck Henry when pro football player Beatty protests celestial foul-up that killed him too early. Henry's superior Mason gives Beatty the new body of a millionaire threatened by murderous wife Cannon and her lover Grodin. Beatty plays in the Super Bowl and falls for environmentalist Christie. Absolutely wonderful romantic comedy/fantasy won nine Oscar nominations including Best Picture and Actor (Beatty). Remake of 1941's *Here Comes Mr. Jordan.*

HEAVEN HELP US 1985
★★★ R Comedy 1:44
☑ Brief nudity, explicit language, adult humor
Dir: Michael Dinner *Cast:* Donald Sutherland, John Heard, Andrew McCarthy, Kevin Dillon, Mary Stuart Masterson, Malcolm Danare
▶ Brooklyn, 1965: Catholic schoolboys—new kid McCarthy, tough guy Dillon, and brainy but fat Danare—form an unlikely friendship and rebel against a stern Brother's rule. Solid performances by all, and the McCarthy/Masterson romance is quite fetching. Anyone who has ever been to Catholic school will relate to this diverting mix of teen high jinks and serious drama. Overlooked but worth watching.

HEAVEN KNOWS, MR. ALLISON 1957
★★★ NR Drama 1:47

Dir: John Huston   *Cast:* Deborah Kerr, Robert Mitchum
► During World War II, burly Marine Mitchum and Roman Catholic novitiate Kerr are stranded on a South Seas island infested with Japanese soldiers. Initially antagonistic, they learn to respect each other while struggling to escape detection. Bittersweet romance with strong action elements won Oscar nominations for Kerr and the screenplay (by Huston and John Lee Mahin).

HEAVENLY BODIES 1985 Canadian
★★ R Musical 1:29
☑ Brief nudity, adult situations, explicit language, violence
Dir: Lawrence Dane   *Cast:* Cynthia Dale, Richard Rebiere, Laura Henry, Walter George Alton, Stuart Stone
► Young Dale opens her own aerobics studio, falls in love with football player Rebiere, and gets job with TV station. Life should be great, but then rival aerobicist schemes against her. Climax has the two women facing off in a dance contest. *Flashdance* clone offers enough jumping around and hot bods to last a lifetime.

HEAVENLY KID, THE 1985
★★★★ PG-13 Fantasy/Comedy 1:27
☑ Adult situations, explicit language, mild violence
Dir: Cary Medoway   *Cast:* Lewis Smith, Jason Gedrick, Jane Kaczmarek, Richard Mulligan, Mark Metcalf
► Mild-mannered comedy/fantasy with a familiar plot. In the early 1960s, James Dean-like hipster Smith dies in a drag race. Up in heaven, he's given the assignment to return to Earth and help present-day klutzy teen Gedrick, who turns out to be his illegitimate son.

HEAVENS ABOVE! 1963 British
★ NR Comedy 1:58 B&W
Dir: Roy Boulting   *Cast:* Peter Sellers, Cecil Parker, Isabel Jeans, Eric Sykes, Bernard Miles
► Sellers, a guileless small-town parson, inadvertently causes nationwide uproar when he convinces the rich to share with poor. Eventually, he is shipped off to outer space to stop him from causing further trouble. Religious satire, considered daring in 1963, lacks impact now. Heavy British dialects, at times difficult to understand, may hinder enjoyment. Strictly for Sellers fans.

HEAVEN'S GATE 1980
★★ R Western 3:40
☑ Nudity, adult situations
Dir: Michael Cimino   *Cast:* Kris Kristofferson, Christopher Walken, John Hurt, Sam Waterston, Isabelle Huppert, Jeff Bridges
► Wyoming, 1890: sheriff Kristofferson sides with immigrants as wealthy cattlemen make land grab, setting off the Johnson County War. Kris also vies with foe Walken for the affections of French madam Huppert. Cimino's megabudget Western is famous for sinking the United Artists studio. Murkily plotted and overlong, but the mammoth production has some moments of epic grandeur: a dance in Harvard, a community roller skate in Wyoming. An edited-down version failed to bring any cohesion to the story.

HEAVY TRAFFIC 1973
★ R Animation/Adult 1:16
☑ Strong sexual content, violence
Dir: Ralph Bakshi   *Cast:* Voices of Joseph Kaufman, Beverly Hope Atkinson, Frank De Kova, Terri Haven, Mary Dean Lauria, Jamie Farr
► Young aspiring cartoonist living with his parents fails in attempt to lose virginity when he accidentally bumps local tramp off the roof. Later, he falls for a black woman as his life intersects with mobsters and other neighborhood types. Gritty New York atmosphere captured by Bakshi's deft, daring animation. Bittersweet tale for adults.

HEDDA 1975 British
★★ PG Drama 1:43
Dir: Trevor Nunn   *Cast:* Glenda Jackson, Timothy West, Jennie Linden, Patrick Stewart, Peter Eyre
► Two-time Oscar winner Jackson received another Best Actress nomination for her stunning portrayal of Ibsen's Hedda Gabler, the intelligent, well-bred but quite lethal wife of the scholarly Eyre. She's well-matched by supporting cast: West as moralizing judge, Stewart as possible former lover, and Linden as the woman who idolizes Stewart and rouses Jackson's willful destructiveness.

HEIDI 1937
★★★★★ NR Family 1:27 B&W
Dir: Allan Dwan   *Cast:* Shirley Temple, Jean Hersholt, Arthur Treacher, Helen Westley, Pauline Moore, Thomas Beck
► Temple is perfectly cast as a German orphan sent to live with grandfather Hersholt in the Alps; she wins his heart but is

sold by her evil aunt to a wealthy family. Fans clamored for Temple to appear in Johanna Spyri's enduring classic, which proved one of her most popular films. (CC)

HEIDI 1968
★★★★ G Family 1:44
Dir: Delbert Mann *Cast:* Maximilian Schell, Jennifer Edwards, Jean Simmons, Michael Redgrave, Walter Slezak
▶ Living in the Swiss Alps with her kindly grandfather, the orphan Heidi is taken to the city to be a playmate for her crippled cousin. Respected group of actors, including Blake Edwards's daughter, Jennifer, as Heidi, adds class to this well-loved story. Script by Earl Hamner, Jr.

HEIRESS, THE 1949
★★★★ NR Drama 1:55 B&W
Dir: William Wyler *Cast:* Olivia de Havilland, Montgomery Clift, Ralph Richardson, Miriam Hopkins, Vanessa Brown
▶ Five-star adaptation of the 1881 Henry James novel and successful Broadway play. De Havilland won her second Oscar for an awesome performance as the plain-looking daughter of tyrannical Richardson. She falls tragically in love with fortune-hunter Clift, who abandons Olivia when her father threatens to disown her and then returns seven years after Richardson's death. A true Hollywood classic. Also won Oscars for Score, Art Direction, Costumes.

HE KNOWS YOU'RE ALONE 1980
★★ R Horror 1:30
☑ Nudity, explicit language, violence
Dir: Armand Mastroianni *Cast:* Don Scardino, Caitlin O'Heaney, Elizabeth Kemp, Tom Rolfing, Tom Hanks, Patsy Pease
▶ Killer Rolfing, jilted by his beloved, stalks brides-to-be. His next intended victim O'Heaney escapes with the help of old boyfriend Scardino. Effective thriller manages to avoid genre's gory tactics. Predictable plotting but acceptable scare ratio.

HELLBOUND: HELLRAISER II 1988
U.S./British
★ R Horror 1:38
☑ Nudity, explicit language, graphic violence
Dir: Tony Randel *Cast:* Clare Higgins, Ashley Laurence, Kenneth Cranham, Imogen Boorman
▶ Laurence is treated by shrink Cranham

after witnessing her returned-from-dead uncle murdering her father in *Hellraiser*. Laurence then teams with fellow patient Boorman to rescue dad from hell. Flashy sequel boasts impressive special effects and imaginative monsters from the mind of writer Clive Barker. However, repulsive violence and indecipherable plotting grow wearisome.

HELLCATS OF THE NAVY 1957
★★ NR War 1:21 B&W
Dir: Nathan Juran *Cast:* Ronald Reagan, Nancy Davis, Arthur Franz, Robert Arthur, William Leslie
▶ In World War II, submarine commander Reagan is criticized by first officer Franz for leaving behind diver during an operation. Reagan eventually proves his heroism and works things out with long-suffering nurse/girlfriend Davis. Okay war drama was the only film pairing of America's future first couple.

HELL COMES TO FROGTOWN 1988
★★★ R Horror 1:26
☑ Nudity, adult situations, explicit language, violence
Dir: R. J. Kizer *Cast:* Roddy Piper, Sandahl Bergman, Nicholas Worth, Cec Ferrell, Rory Calhoun
▶ In a postnuclear world where most of the men are sterile, Piper, one of the last virile men, and government woman Bergman battle mutants who have kidnapped fertile women. Loony plot played for chuckles. Appealing leads and fantastic mutant makeup add up to futuristic fun.

HELLFIGHTERS 1969
★★★ G Action-Adventure 2:01
Dir: Andrew V. McLaglen *Cast:* John Wayne, Katharine Ross, Jim Hutton, Vera Miles, Jay C. Flippen, Bruce Cabot
▶ Wayne circles the globe snuffing out dangerous oil-well fires, but has a tougher time dealing with ex-wife Miles—especially when his right-hand man Hutton proposes to their daughter Ross. Middling Wayne vehicle (based on real-life hero Red Adair) has excellent special effects.

HELLHOLE 1985
★ R Mystery-Suspense 1:35
☑ Nudity, explicit language, violence
Dir: Pierre de Moro *Cast:* Judy Landers, Ray Sharkey, Mary Woronov, Marjoe Gortner, Edy Williams, Terry Moore

▶ Amnesiac Landers, sent to "hellhole" sanatorium after witnessing mother's death, encounters mom's killer Sharkey and lesbian mad scientist Woronov. Lurid piece of exploitation delivers the sleazy goods: nudity, violence, dreadful dialogue, preposterous story, bad acting (save for delightful Woronov). **(CC)**

HELL IN THE PACIFIC 1968
★★★ G War 1:43
Dir: John Boorman *Cast:* Lee Marvin, Toshiro Mifune
▶ During World War II, American pilot Marvin finds himself stranded on Pacific island with Japanese officer Mifune. At first, the two fight each other but then team up to survive together. Two-character battle is well acted and generally exciting.

HELL NIGHT 1981
★★ R Horror 1:42
☑ Adult situations, explicit language, graphic violence
Dir: Tom DeSimone *Cast:* Linda Blair, Vincent Van Patten, Kevin Brophy, Peter Barton
▶ College frat pledges must spend a night in a haunted house for initiation. Students are bumped off one by one by the thing that lurks below the house in an underground labyrinth. Standard genre fare: a few goose bumps, okay production values, effective special effects, some charm from chubby Linda.

HELLO AGAIN 1987
★★★ PG Comedy 1:36
Dir: Frank Perry *Cast:* Shelley Long, Corbin Bernsen, Judith Ivey, Sela Ward, Gabriel Byrne
▶ Klutzy Long chokes to death on a South Korean chicken ball, then returns from the dead to find hubby Bernsen and best friend Ward in bed together. Screwball dialogue plays off variations on: "I wouldn't be caught dead in that dress." Funny feature turn by Ivey as Long's psychic sister. Director Perry and writer Susan Isaacs also collaborated on *Compromising Positions*.

HELLO, DOLLY 1969
★★★★ G Musical 2:26
Dir: Gene Kelly *Cast:* Barbra Streisand, Walter Matthau, Louis Armstrong, Michael Crawford, Tommy Tune, E. J. Peaker
▶ Turn-of-the-century New York: matchmaker Streisand gets involved in romantic intrigues with wealthy Matthau's employees (including Crawford) and family, all the while hoping to snag Matthau for herself. Bouncy Jerry Herman score, extravagant period re-creation, and Armstrong/Streisand title tune duet highlight adaptation of Broadway musical hit, in turn based on Thornton Wilder's play *The Matchmaker*. **(CC)**

HELLO MARY LOU: PROM NIGHT II
1987 Canadian
★★ R Horror 1:36
☑ Nudity, adult situations, explicit language, violence
Dir: Bruce Pittman *Cast:* Lisa Schrage, Michael Ironside, Wendy Lyon, Justin Louis, Richard Monette
▶ Thirty years after slutty Hamilton High prom queen Mary Lou was set afire by a jealous beau, a nice girl is possessed by her ghost to wreak some violent havoc. Carrie's prom was high tea at the Plaza compared to the carnage in these corridors. Stylish staging gets new-minted thrills out of recycled plot; sequel to *Prom Night*. **(CC)**

HELLRAISER 1987
★★ R Horror 1:33
☑ Explicit language, graphic violence
Dir: Clive Barker *Cast:* Andrew Robinson, Clare Higgins, Ashley Laurence, Sean Chapman, Oliver Smith, Robert Hines
▶ Magical box causes all sorts of problems for two brothers, turning one into a monster who enlists the other's wife into helping him satisfy his blood thirst. Excessive gore will surely turn off some, but those who can watch may enjoy writer/director Barker's original touches. **(CC)**

HELL'S ANGELS ON WHEELS 1967
★ NR Action-Adventure 1:35
Dir: Richard Rush *Cast:* Adam Roarke, Jack Nicholson, Sabrina Scharf, Jana Taylor, John Garwood, Sonny Barger
▶ Bored gas station attendant Nicholson joins Hell's Angels to steal away girlfriend of leader Roarke. Typical low-budget biker nonsense redeemed somewhat by Nicholson's broad performance and the presence of real-life Angels leader Barger.

HELLSTROM CHRONICLE, THE 1971
★★★★ G Documentary 1:30
Dir: Walon Green *Cast:* Lawrence Pressman
▶ Fact-based theories of fictional doctor Pressman, who opines that insects will inherit the earth. Vibrant photography

captures the beauty of nature with up-close insect footage. Fascinating and educational. Academy Award winner, Best Documentary.

HELP! 1965 British
★★★★ G Musical/Comedy 1:30
Dir: Richard Lester   *Cast:* John Lennon, Paul McCartney, George Harrison, Ringo Starr, Leo McKern, Eleanor Bron
▶ Religious zealots McKern and Bron need a sacred ring to complete a human sacrifice; Starr, who received the ring from a fan, becomes their target. Second Beatles film sacrifices irreverent wit of *A Hard Day's Night* for slapstick, James Bond parodies, and beautiful locations in Austria and the Bahamas. Still a consistent delight, especially the superb score ("You've Got to Hide Your Love Away," "Ticket to Ride," "You're Gonna Lose That Girl," etc.).

HELTER SKELTER 1976
★★★ NR Drama/MFTV 3:14
Dir: Tom Gries   *Cast:* George DiCenzo, Steve Railsback, Nancy Wolfe, Marilyn Burns, Christina Hart
▶ Made-for-television adaptation of the best-seller details the investigation of the Sharon Tate murders and the subsequent trial of Charles Manson (Railsback) and his murderous "family." Well done, with a haunting performance by Railsback and a very convincing supporting cast. Bloody scenes added for the theatrical version don't really make much difference. **(CC)**

HENNESSY 1975 British
★★★ PG Drama 1:43
Dir: Don Sharp   *Cast:* Rod Steiger, Lee Remick, Richard Johnson, Trevor Howard, Peter Egan, Ian Hogg
▶ When his wife and child are murdered in a Belfast gunfight, Steiger plots to blow up the British Parliament during an appearance by the Royal Family. Both Scotland Yard and the IRA are determined to thwart the scheme. Farfetched plot undermines standard heroics.

HENRY V 1944
★★★★ NR Drama 2:17
Dir: Laurence Olivier   *Cast:* Laurence Olivier, Robert Newton, Leslie Banks, Renee Asherson, Esmond Knight, Leo Genn
▶ Brilliant adaptation of Shakespeare's play, with swashbuckling Olivier as the young Prince of Wales who leads his men to victory against the French. A sweeping, visually stunning production justly famed for its elaborate framing device (opening as a typical seventeenth-century Globe Theatre production, then expanding into dazzling location footage). Olivier received a special Oscar for "outstanding achievement as actor, producer, and director."

HER ALIBI 1988
★★★★ PG Comedy 1:31
☒ Adult situations, explicit language, mild violence
Dir: Bruce Beresford   *Cast:* Tom Selleck, Paulina Porizkova, William Daniels, James Farentino, Tess Harper, Patrick Wayne
▶ Mystery writer Selleck provides the alibi for murder suspect Porizkova and decides to use her real-life case as the source for his next book. The two hole up in his country house, where he falls in love with her. There's only one complication: he begins to suspect she really is a killer who has targeted him as her next victim.

HERBIE RIDES AGAIN 1974
★★★★★ G Comedy 1:28
Dir: Robert Stevenson   *Cast:* Helen Hayes, Ken Berry, Stefanie Powers, John McIntire, Keenan Wynn, Huntz Hall
▶ Bright sequel to *The Love Bug* continues the adventures of the Volkswagen bug with magical powers. This time Herbie teams up with Hayes to thwart real estate developer Wynn's plot to build the world's tallest building.

HERCULES 1959 Italian
★★★ G Action-Adventure 1:43
Dir: Pietro Francisci   *Cast:* Steve Reeves, Sylva Koscina, Gianna Maria Canale, Ivo Garrani, Fabrizio Mioni
▶ Hercules (the well-developed Reeves) searches for the missing Jason and the Argonauts, wins beautiful princess Koscina, and fights ape men, amazons, animals, and monsters. Lousy dubbing, but this comic-book muscleman adventure is undeniably fun.

HERCULES 1983 Italian
★ PG Action-Adventure 1:38
☒ Explicit language, violence
Dir: Lewis Coates (Luigi Cozzi)   *Cast:* Lou Ferrigno, Mirella D'Angelo, Sybil Danning, Ingrid Anderson, William Berger, Brad Harris
▶ Ferrigno battles evil gods and deadly monsters to rescue his beloved Cassiopeia (Anderson) from fiery doom in a volcano. Plodding, witless version of the

Hercules legend relies too much on shoddy special effects. Followed by *Adventures of Hercules*. **(CC)**

HERE COMES MR. JORDAN 1941
★★★★ NR Fantasy/Comedy 1:33 B&W
Dir: Alexander Hall *Cast:* Robert Montgomery, Evelyn Keyes, Claude Rains, Rita Johnson, Edward Everett Horton, James Gleason
▶ Heavenly mixup kills boxer Montgomery before his time; angels Rains and Horton find him a replacement body—a millionaire about to be murdered by scheming wife Johnson. Charming, sophisticated fantasy is one of Hollywood's enduring classics. Received Oscar nominations for Best Picture, Direction, Actor (Montgomery), and Supporting Actor (Gleason as a skeptical fight manager); Harry Segall won for Best Story; and Sidney Buchman and Seton I. Miller won for Best Screenplay. Remade by Warren Beatty in 1978 as *Heaven Can Wait*.

HERE COMES SANTA CLAUS 1984
★★★ G Family 1:18
Dir: Christian Gion *Cast:* Emeric Chapuis, Armand Meffre, Karen Cheryl, Dominique Hulin, Jeanne Herviale
▶ Seven-year-old Chapuis asks teacher Cheryl for advice when his parents disappear; she sends him to Santa Claus (Meffre) who finds the missing parents held captive by African natives. Acceptable fare for youngsters, with good special effects and a bouncy Frances Lai score.

HERE COME THE TIGERS 1978
★★★ PG Comedy 1:30
☑ Explicit language
Dir: Sean S. Cunningham *Cast:* Richard Lincoln, James Zvanut, Samantha Grey, Manny Lieberman, William Caldwell, Fred Lincoln
▶ Rookie cop Lincoln takes on thankless task of coaching racially mixed Little League team composed of foulmouthed, inept no-accounts. Team seems destined to be the league doormat until arrival of new talent, including a Japanese power-hitting karate champ, a rehabilitated Hispanic delinquent, and a deaf pitcher. Dime store knockoff of *The Bad News Bears*.

HERO AIN'T NOTHIN' BUT A SANDWICH, A 1978
★★★ PG Drama 1:47
☑ Adult situations, explicit language
Dir: Ralph Nelson *Cast:* Cicely Tyson,

Paul Winfield, Larry B. Scott, Helen Martin, Glynn Turman, David Groh
▶ Troubled Los Angeles ghetto boy Scott turns to drugs as mother Tyson and foster father Winfield struggle to set him on a constructive course. Sincere, realistic drama suffers somewhat from preachy tone and distracting subplot between high school teachers Turman and Groh. Well-meaning drama based on a book by Alice Childress.

HERO AND THE TERROR 1988
★★★ R Action-Adventure 1:36
☑ Adult situations, explicit language, violence
Dir: William Tannen *Cast:* Chuck Norris, Brynn Thayer, Steve James, Jack O'Halloran, Jeffrey Kramer, Ron O'Neal
▶ Broadening his macho image, Norris plays an L.A. cop who feels guilty about undeserved credit in nabbing serial killer O'Halloran. He's understandably dismayed when the "Terror" killer escapes from jail and resumes his butchery. Accomplished thriller shortchanges kung-fu scenes, but has a strong climax in the Wiltern Theater.

HERO AT LARGE 1980
★★★★ PG Comedy 1:38
☑ Explicit language
Dir: Martin Davidson *Cast:* John Ritter, Anne Archer, Bert Convy, Kevin McCarthy, Harry Bellaver, Anita Dangler
▶ Aspiring actor Ritter makes public appearances as the heroic Captain Avenger; when he foils a holdup, the city thinks a real hero now protects them. The mayor's agents Convy and McCarthy exploit the actor for an upcoming election. Ritter excels in a "Three's Company"–type nice-guy role.

HEROES 1977
★★★ PG Comedy 1:53
☑ Explicit language
Dir: Jeremy Paul Kagan *Cast:* Henry Winkler, Sally Field, Harrison Ford, Val Avery, Olivia Cole, Hector Elias
▶ Vietnam vet Winkler escapes from a mental institution and travels cross-country to start a worm farm. Field plays a fiancée on the run who aids him. Uneven blend of whimsy and melodrama gave Winkler his first starring role in films.

HE'S MY GIRL 1987
★★ PG-13 Comedy 1:44
☑ Brief nudity, adult situations, explicit language
Dir: Gabrielle Beaumont *Cast:* T. K.

Carter, David Hallyday, Misha McK, Jennifer Tilly, Warwick Sims, David Clennon
► Missouri rocker Hallyday wins a trip to Los Angeles; his manager Carter resorts to dressing in drag to accompany him. Clennon, a sleazy L.A. hustler, sets his sights on Hallyday's beautiful "date." Cute sex farce gets a tremendous lift from Carter's lively performance.

HESTER STREET 1975
★ **PG Drama 1:32 B&W**
☑ Adult situations
Dir: Joan Micklin Silver *Cast:* Steven Keats, Carol Kane, Mel Howard, Dorrie Kavanaugh, Doris Roberts, Stephen Strimpell
► New York, 1896: Jewish immigrant Keats adjusts to American ways; his Old World wife Kane alienates him by sticking to tradition. Keats forsakes Kane for another woman but eventually gets his comeuppance. Wonderfully expressive performance by Kane was Oscar-nominated; slow pace and muted dramatic impact may limit appeal.

HEY GOOD LOOKIN' 1982
★ **R Animation/Adult 1:16**
☑ Nudity, adult situations, explicit language, adult humor
Dir: Ralph Bakshi *Cast:* Voices of Richard Romanus, David Proval, Jesse Welles, Tina Bowman, Danny Wells
► Ambitious animated drama uses the adventures of gang leader Romanus and his friend Proval as a metaphor for life in Brownsville during the early 1950s. Occasionally interesting visuals and a realistic atmosphere can't compensate for routine gang war plot.

HIDDEN, THE 1987
★★★ **R Sci-Fi 1:37**
☑ Explicit language, violence
Dir: Jack Sholder *Cast:* Michael Nouri, Kyle MacLachlan, Ed O'Ross, Clu Gulager, Claudia Christian, Clarence Christian
► Ingenious thriller with sci-fi overtones: oddball FBI agent MacLachlan joins Los Angeles homicide cop Nouri on a manhunt for a psycho killer who's apparently already dead. But then why does a meek accountant go on a wild crime spree? And why does MacLachlan chew his Alka-Seltzer tablets? Enjoyable low-budget sleeper starts with a dynamite car chase and rarely lets up.

HIDDEN FORTRESS, THE 1958
Japanese
★ **NR Action-Adventure 2:06 B&W**
Dir: Akira Kurosawa *Cast:* Toshiro Mifune, Misa Uehara, Minoru Chiaki, Kamatari Fujiwara, Susumu Fujita, Takashi Shimura
► Two bumbling mercenaries join forces with fugitive general Mifune in guiding a fortune in gold and haughty deposed princess Uehara across enemy territory. Influential "samurai Western" will delight Kurosawa fans; others may find its stately pacing and uneven acting hard to take. Characters and rousing action sequences were the original inspiration for *Star Wars*. Japanese version contains additional footage. [S]

HIDE IN PLAIN SIGHT 1980
★★★★ **PG Drama 1:32**
☑ Explicit language, mild violence
Dir: James Caan *Cast:* James Caan, Jill Eikenberry, Robert Viharo, Joe Grifasi, Barbara Rae
► Caan plays a Buffalo, New York, factory worker who becomes the innocent victim of the federal witness protection program. His ex-wife marries a two-bit crook who testifies against the mob and, overnight, disappears with Caan's family. The government refuses to reveal the whereabouts of Caan's children, now living under an assumed identity with their mother and stepfather. Based on a true story; Caan's directorial debut.

HIDING OUT 1987
★★★★ **PG-13 Comedy 1:39**
☑ Explicit language, violence
Dir: Bob Giraldi *Cast:* Jon Cryer, Keith Coogan, Annabeth Gish, Gretchen Cryer, Oliver Cotton
► Cryer, a twenty-seven-year-old Boston commodities trader, testifies against mobsters and then poses as a high school student in Delaware to avoid getting killed. Within a week, he becomes the most popular kid in school, runs for student council president, and dates class beauty Gish; then the Feds and the bad guys catch up with him. Affable teen comedy from Giraldi, king of the music video, also features Cryer's real-life mom, Gretchen, as Aunt Lucy.

HIGH ANXIETY 1977
★★★ **PG Comedy 1:30**
☑ Explicit language
Dir: Mel Brooks *Cast:* Mel Brooks,

Madeline Kahn, Cloris Leachman, Harvey Korman, Ron Carey
▶ Psychiatrist Thorndyke (Brooks), head of the Psycho-Neurotic Institute for the Very, Very Nervous, hides the fact he suffers from high anxiety—sort of like vertigo but worse. He must deal with his neurosis, a sadistic Nurse Diesel (Leachman), several flipped-out patients, and a hint of murderous skullduggery in the padded cells. Witty homage to Hitchcock features Brooks's usual brand of lunacy and lowbrow humor.

HIGH COUNTRY, THE 1981 Canadian
★★★★ **PG Drama 1:38**
☑ Nudity, explicit language
Dir: Harvey Hart *Cast:* Timothy Bottoms, Linda Purl, George Sims, Jim Lawrence, Bill Berry
▶ Escaped con Bottoms hooks up with learning-disabled runaway Purl. They hide out in the mountains and fall in love. Thin story, shallow characterizations, but beautiful scenery and genuine romantic chemistry between the appealing leads.

HIGHEST HONOR, THE 1984 Australian/Japanese
★★★ **R War 1:39**
☑ Explicit language, violence
Dir: Peter Maxwell, Seiji Maruyama
Cast: John Howard, Atsuo Nakamura, Stuart Wilson, Michael Aitkens
▶ Disguised as Malaysians, members of Australia's Z Force infiltrate Singapore on a daring mission to destroy enemy ships during World War II. Captured by the Japanese, Captain Page (Howard) develops an unusual relationship with interpreter Nakamura. Well-meaning; based on a true story. ⑤

HIGHLANDER 1986
★★★★ **R Action-Adventure 1:51**
☑ Nudity, adult situations, explicit language, graphic violence
Dir: Russell Mulcahy *Cast:* Christopher Lambert, Sean Connery, Roxanne Hart, Clancy Brown, Beatie Edney
▶ Two parallel stories, set in medieval Scotland and modern-day New York, where immortal heroes Connery and Lambert battle for several centuries to win the ultimate prize of Total Knowledge. Sort of a Tarzan-meets-007, with enough head-chopping for even the most jaded fan. Flashy directing, costumes, settings; score combines rock group Queen with traditional Scottish folk music. **(CC)**

HIGH NOON 1952
★★★★ **NR Western 1:25 B&W**
Dir: Fred Zinnemann *Cast:* Gary Cooper, Grace Kelly, Lloyd Bridges, Thomas Mitchell, Katy Jurado, Lon Chaney, Jr.
▶ On his wedding day, about-to-retire sheriff Cooper learns that outlaw gang is gunning for him at high noon. He must stand alone as no one in town will help him; even his Quaker wife Kelly doesn't want him to get involved. Unforgettable Western generates maximum suspense by unfolding in real time. Oscars to the great Coop and Dimitri Tiomkin's score and theme song.

HIGH PLAINS DRIFTER 1973
★★★★ **R Western 1:45**
☑ Rape, adult situations, explicit language, graphic violence
Dir: Clint Eastwood *Cast:* Clint Eastwood, Verna Bloom, Marianna Hill, Mitchell Ryan, Jack Ging, Billy Curtis
▶ Inhabitants of a corrupt mining town hire mysterious gunman Eastwood to protect them from three vengeful ex-cons. Eastwood proceeds to destroy the town and everyone in it. Provocative, harshly violent Western has extraordinary locations and a subtle sense of humor.

HIGHPOINT 1984 Canadian
★★ **PG Action-Adventure 1:28**
☑ Explicit language, violence
Dir: Peter Carter *Cast:* Richard Harris, Christopher Plummer, Beverly D'Angelo, Kate Reid, Peter Donat, Robin Gammell
▶ Industrialist Plummer double-crosses the Mafia and CIA, in the process framing unemployed accountant Harris for a $10 million theft. Jumbled thriller with comic overtones boils down to a series of routine chases.

HIGH RISK 1981
★★★ **R Action-Adventure 1:32**
☑ Explicit language, violence
Dir: Stewart Raffill *Cast:* James Brolin, Lindsay Wagner, Anthony Quinn, Cleavon Little, Bruce Davison, James Coburn
▶ Filmmaker Brolin and three friends rob Colombian druglord Coburn but fall prey to Quinn's banditos before they can flee the country. Offbeat caper film with plenty of humor and an unusual cast. Ernest Borgnine has an amusing cameo as an arms dealer.

HIGH ROAD TO CHINA 1983
★★★★ **PG Action-Adventure 1:45**
☑ Explicit language, violence
Dir: Brian G. Hutton   *Cast:* Tom Selleck, Bess Armstrong, Jack Weston, Robert Morley, Wilford Brimley
▶ Asia, 1920s: heiress Armstrong hires hard-drinking pilot Selleck to locate her missing dad Brimley before his business partner Morley can have him declared legally dead and take over their empire. Nice aerial photography, plenty of action, and a pleasing Selleck in this entertaining high flyer.

HIGH SCHOOL CONFIDENTIAL 1958
★ **NR Drama 1:25 B&W**
Dir: Jack Arnold   *Cast:* Russ Tamblyn, Jan Sterling, John (Drew) Barrymore, Mamie Van Doren, Diane Jergens, Charles Chaplin, Jr.
▶ Narcotics agent Tamblyn goes undercover in a California high school to break up a heroin ring. Unintentionally hilarious exposé with bizarre casting is a revealing time capsule of the late 1950s. Former child star Jackie Coogan plays the drug kingpin. Look for Michael Landon as one of the students. Jerry Lee Lewis opens with a killer version of the title song.

HIGH SEASON 1988 British
★★ **R Comedy 1:44**
☑ Nudity, adult situations, explicit language
Dir: Clare Peploe   *Cast:* Jacqueline Bisset, James Fox, Irene Papas, Paris Tselios, Sebastian Shaw, Kenneth Branagh
▶ Estranged couple (photographer Bisset and sculptor Fox) live in separate houses on the beautiful Greek island of Rhodes with their teenage daughter. Even though they all become involved with several expatriates, tourists, artists, and spies, plot never gels. Nice scenery, though. Directorial debut for Peploe, real-life wife of Bernardo Bertolucci.

HIGH SIERRA 1941
★★★ **NR Drama 1:40 B&W**
Dir: Raoul Walsh   *Cast:* Humphrey Bogart, Ida Lupino, Arthur Kennedy, Joan Leslie, Henry Travers
▶ Aging gangster Mad Dog Earle (Bogart) befriends a crippled Leslie and reluctantly participates in one last caper. The plan goes awry, setting the stage for a tragic mountainside conclusion. Poignant performance by Bogart, brisk direction by Walsh in this Warner Brothers classic.

HIGH SOCIETY 1956
★★★ **NR Musical 1:47**
Dir: Charles Walters   *Cast:* Grace Kelly, Bing Crosby, Frank Sinatra, Celeste Holm, John Lund, Louis Armstrong
▶ Top-drawer musical remake of *The Philadelphia Story* stars Kelly as a frosty Newport society beauty dithering over three men: her priggish fiancé Lund; her ex-husband Crosby, a wealthy jazz devotee; and brash reporter Sinatra, on hand to cover her wedding for a gossip magazine. Cole Porter hits include "Did You Evah?" "You're Sensational," and the Oscar-nominated "True Love." Bing and Satchmo sing "Now You Have Jazz."

HIGH SPIRITS 1988 U.S./British
★★ **PG-13 Fantasy/Comedy 1:36**
☑ Adult situations, explicit language
Dir: Neil Jordan   *Cast:* Daryl Hannah, Peter O'Toole, Steve Guttenberg, Beverly D'Angelo, Jennifer Tilly, Liam Neeson
▶ Faced with losing ancestral castle, Irish hotel owner O'Toole hires locals to impersonate ghosts to lure tourist trade. Not all of the spirits turn out to be fake: guest Guttenberg forsakes shrewish wife D'Angelo for spectacular spectre Hannah. Perky concept benefits from vivacious cast and beguiling local color. Special effects, however, are merely passable. (CC)

HIGH TIDE 1987 Australian
★★★ **PG-13 Drama 1:41**
☑ Adult situations, explicit language
Dir: Gillian Armstrong   *Cast:* Judy Davis, Jan Adele, Claudia Karvan, Colin Friels, John Clayton
▶ Davis shines as a backup singer and dancer left to fend for herself in a remote trailer park. She forms a friendship with teenaged Adele, gradually revealing that she is the mother who abandoned Adele years before. Moving drama reunited Davis with Armstrong, her director in *My Brilliant Career.*

HIGH WIND IN JAMAICA, A 1965
★★ **NR Drama 1:44**
Dir: Alexander Mackendrick   *Cast:* Anthony Quinn, James Coburn, Lila Kedrova, Gert Frobe, Deborah Baxter, Martin Amis
▶ Pirates led by Quinn inadvertently kidnap young schoolchildren while looting a ship; his second mate Coburn wants to

kill the youngsters, but Quinn slowly develops a fondness for them. Intriguing Victorian-age adventure, based on the novel by Richard Hughes, offers an unsettling view of adolescence.

HILLS HAVE EYES, THE 1977
★ R Horror 1:29
☑ Nudity, explicit language, graphic violence
Dir: Wes Craven *Cast:* Susan Lanier, Robert Houston, Virginia Vincent, Russ Grieve, Dee Wallace
▶ A typical American family goes camping and is harassed by man-eating mutants. Gory cult film loaded with plot twists. Popular film spawned a sequel also directed by horror master Craven.

HILLS HAVE EYES PART II, THE 1985
★ R Horror 1:27
☑ Nudity, explicit language, graphic violence
Dir: Wes Craven *Cast:* Michael Berryman, John Laughlin, Tamara Stafford, Kevin Blair, John Bloom, Janus Blyth
▶ A group of motocross enthusiasts, late for the big race, take a shortcut across the desert and are chased by a family of cannibal mutants. Chock-full of footage from the first film, including the first doggie flashback in movie history.

HINDENBURG, THE 1975
★★★★ PG Mystery-Suspense 2:05
☑ Violence
Dir: Robert Wise *Cast:* George C. Scott, Anne Bancroft, Roy Thinnes, Gig Young, Burgess Meredith, Charles Durning
▶ Star-studded spectacle combines actual newsreel footage with loony dialogue to dramatize the 1937 explosion of the German zeppelin in Lakehurst, New Jersey. Special effects provide ample thrills. Disaster movie fans may not mind such lackluster scripting as Scott, the good German, saying: "I have an uneasy sense of disaster."

HIROSHIMA, MON AMOUR 1959
French
★ NR Drama 1:28 B&W
☑ Nudity, adult situations
Dir: Alain Resnais *Cast:* Emmanuelle Riva, Eiji Okada, Bernard Fresson, Stella Dassas, Pierre Barnaud
▶ Japanese architect Okada and French actress Riva, both scarred by World War II tragedies, have a sensual affair in Hiroshima circa 1960. Resnais's meditation on memory is one of the most important films of the French New Wave. Rich in content, lovely to look at, but slow, talky, and extremely esoteric. ⑤

HIS GIRL FRIDAY 1940
★★★ NR Comedy 1:32 B&W
Dir: Howard Hawks *Cast:* Cary Grant, Rosalind Russell, Ralph Bellamy, Gene Lockhart, Helen Mack, Porter Hall
▶ Scheming editor Grant tries everything to keep star reporter and ex-wife Russell from marrying insurance agent Bellamy. Outstanding remake of *The Front Page* rates among Hollywood's best comedies. Razor-sharp dialogue, breathless pacing, savagely cynical plot, and a brilliant cast (including superb supporting work from Ernest Truex, Roscoe Karns, John Qualen, Billy Gilbert, and Alma Kruger) add up to first-rate entertainment. Recently remade into the lackluster *Switching Channels.*

HISTORY IS MADE AT NIGHT 1937
★★★ NR Drama 1:37 B&W
Dir: Frank Borzage *Cast:* Charles Boyer, Jean Arthur, Colin Clive, Leo Carrillo, George Meeker, Lucien Prival
▶ Fascinating melodrama about insanely jealous husband's efforts to ruin wife Arthur's life by framing her lover (Boyer) for murder. Wildly improbable, but compelling direction and intensely romantic tone give story rare depth and resonance. Highlighted by a stunning climax aboard a luxury liner threatened by icebergs.

HISTORY OF THE WORLD—PART I 1981
★★★ R Comedy 1:32
☑ Nudity, explicit language
Dir: Mel Brooks *Cast:* Mel Brooks, Dom DeLuise, Madeline Kahn, Harvey Korman, Cloris Leachman, Hugh Hefner
▶ String of burlesque blackouts and slapstick vignettes takes potshots at mankind. Brooks looks at cave dwellers, unholy Christian hosts, the Romans, highstepping torturers of the Spanish Inquisition, and the French Revolution. No-holds-barred comedy epic for the legion of Mel's fans, featuring cameo appearances by Sid Caesar, Gregory Hines, Orson Welles, Bea Arthur, Jackie Mason, Henny Youngman, many more.

HIT, THE 1985 British
★ R Mystery-Suspense 1:39
☑ Adult situations, explicit language, violence
Dir: Stephen Frears *Cast:* John Hurt,

Terence Stamp, Tim Roth, Laura Del Sol, Fernando Rey

▶ Gang boss hires hitmen Hurt and Roth to kidnap squealer Stamp. Stamp doesn't put up a struggle; he actually seems to enjoy the bumpy journey as the others transport him to his doom. Beautiful Spanish countryside and strong performances by Stamp and Roth. However, this offbeat film works overtime not to be taken seriously; unfortunately it succeeds.

HITCHER, THE 1986
★ ★ ★ ★ R Mystery-Suspense 1:37
☑ Explicit language, graphic violence
Dir: Robert Harmon   *Cast:* Rutger Hauer, C. Thomas Howell, Jennifer Jason Leigh, Jeffrey DeMunn, Henry Darrow

▶ In Texas, a young Howell picks up hitchhiker Hauer who turns out to be murderous lunatic. Hauer stalks Howell and Leigh, the waitress he befriends. Harrowing thriller creates edge-of-your-seat suspense. Classy cinematography by John Seale. **(CC)**

HITLER: THE LAST TEN DAYS 1973
British/Italian
★ PG Drama 1:45
☑ Adult situations, explicit language
Dir: Ennio De Concini   *Cast:* Alec Guinness, Doris Kunstmann, Simon Ward, Adolfo Celi, Diane Cilento, Eric Porter

▶ Claustrophobic account of the last ten days of Hitler's (Guinness) life set exclusively in the bunker where he hid with Eva Braun (Kunstmann) and a handful of staff members. Brilliant Riefenstahl footage from *Triumph of the Will* leaves the rest of the film looking cheap and unimaginative. Talky and painfully uneventful.

HOBSON'S CHOICE 1954 British
★ ★ ★ NR Comedy 1:47 B&W
Dir: David Lean   *Cast:* Charles Laughton, John Mills, Brenda de Banzie, Prunella Scales, Daphne Anderson, Richard Wattis

▶ Hard-drinking bootmaker Laughton makes life miserable for his three single daughters. De Banzie, the eldest, rebels by marrying Mills, dad's assistant, and turning him into Laughton's business rival. A comedy with heart, laughs, and fine performances from Laughton, Mills, and de Banzie.

HOLCROFT COVENANT, THE 1985
British
★ ★ ★ R Mystery-Suspense 1:52

☑ Nudity, adult situations, explicit language, violence
Dir: John Frankenheimer   *Cast:* Michael Caine, Anthony Andrews, Victoria Tennant, Lilli Palmer, Michael Lonsdale

▶ Caine stars as the son of a Nazi financial wizard. He's supposed to use his inheritance to make amends for Hitler's crimes. A series of creepy events leads his mother Palmer to believe the money is being used to build a new Nazi empire. Unconvincing, muddled thriller with modest suspense. Based on the Robert Ludlum novel.

HOLD THAT GHOST 1941
★ ★ NR Comedy 1:26 B&W
Dir: Arthur Lubin   *Cast:* Bud Abbott, Lou Costello, Richard Carlson, Evelyn Ankers, Joan Davis, The Andrews Sisters

▶ Delightful Abbott and Costello foolishness with an unusually strong supporting cast. Haunted high jinks are the order of the day when the boys come into possession of a dead gangster's house. Davis shines in a wacky duet with Bud; the Andrews Sisters and vaudeville great Ted Lewis offer four songs.

HOLIDAY 1938
★ ★ ★ ★ NR Comedy 1:31 B&W
Dir: George Cukor   *Cast:* Cary Grant, Katharine Hepburn, Edward Everett Horton, Doris Nolan, Lew Ayres

▶ Successful young Grant would like to retire at thirty and enjoy the world; wealthy fiancée Nolan disapproves, as do her stuffy parents. Grant finds a more sympathetic ear—and true love—in Nolan's free-thinking sister Hepburn. Glorious adaptation of Philip Barry's play boasts amazing ensemble acting.

HOLIDAY INN 1942
★ ★ ★ ★ ★ NR Musical 1:41 B&W
Dir: Mark Sandrich   *Cast:* Bing Crosby, Fred Astaire, Marjorie Reynolds, Virginia Dale, Walter Abel, Louise Beavers

▶ Crosby retires from show biz to New England but finds farm chores harder than singing. Solution: turn the farm into an inn open only on holidays. Extremely slight plot about romantic triangle with Astaire and Reynolds barely gets in the way of first-rate Irving Berlin songs, including Oscar-winning perennial "White Christmas," "Happy Holidays," and "Easter Parade." Fred's routine with firecrackers is one of his best specialty numbers.

HOLLYWOOD BOULEVARD 1976
★ R Comedy 1:22

☑ Nudity, adult situations, explicit language

Dir: Joe Dante, Allan Arkush *Cast:* Candice Rialson, Mary Woronov, Rita George, Jeffrey Kramer, Dick Miller, Paul Bartel

▶ Innocent blond Rialson arrives in Hollywood and gets gig at Miracle Pictures, a studio churning out one B movie a week. She becomes a target when reigning star Woronov tries to eliminate the competition. Some uproarious satire and inside moviemaking jokes from producer/mogul Roger Corman. Low budget shows, but generally fun stuff in this early Dante effort.

HOLLYWOOD GHOST STORIES 1986
★★ NR Documentary 1:15
☑ Violence

Dir: James Forsher *Cast:* John Carradine, Elke Sommer, Susan Strasberg, William Peter Blatty

▶ Documentary is the cinematic equivalent of a Halloween grab bag. A little of everything: from *Exorcist* scribe Blatty introducing highlights from Hollywood's haunted house films to actresses Sommer and Strasberg discussing their experiences with the spirit world. Also includes a look at cinematic spook comedies and investigations into the deaths and afterlives of Rudolph Valentino and George Reeves.

HOLLYWOOD HIGH 1977
★ R Comedy 1:21
☑ Nudity, adult situations, explicit language

Dir: Patrick Wright *Cast:* Marcy Albrecht, Sherry Hardin, Rae Sperling, Susanne, Marla Winters

▶ Four beach bunnies attend Hollywood High but are more preoccupied with surfing, giggling, and making out. Winters, an aging movie sexpot, lets the girls hang out at her place, as long as she can ogle their young male friends.

HOLLYWOOD HIGH II 1981
★ R Comedy 1:20
☑ Brief nudity, adult situations, explicit language

Dir: Caruth C. Byrd *Cast:* April May, Donna Lynn, Camille Warner, Brad Cowgill, Drew Davis

▶ Teen clan at Hollywood High are now seniors but their penchant for bad marks, sex, drugs, and rotten manners may put graduation out of reach. Once again, they prefer romping on the beach to hitting the books. Along the way, they pull pranks on a cop. Inane dialogue, rude teenagers, bad acting. Your move.

HOLLYWOOD HOT TUBS 1984
★ R Comedy 1:43
☑ Nudity, adult situations, explicit language, mild violence

Dir: Chuck Vincent *Cast:* Paul Gunning, Donna McDaniel, Michael Andrew, Katt Shea, Jewel Shepard

▶ Arrested for desecrating the famed HOLLYWOOD sign, spoiled California teen Gunning avoids the slammer by working as a hot-tub repairman. Big event: a wild hot-tub party whose guests include a wacked-out horror movie star, overaged Hell's Angels, a woman with whips, a chimpanzee, and a marimba band. Mindless, hedonistic fluff.

HOLLYWOOD OR BUST 1956
★★★ NR Comedy 1:35
Dir: Frank Tashlin *Cast:* Dean Martin, Jerry Lewis, Anita Ekberg, Pat Crowley, Maxie Rosenbloom, Willard Waterman

▶ Lewis is dying to meet Ekberg, his favorite star; Martin forges the winning lottery ticket for a car to drive his pal cross-country for a blind date with her. Strained comedy was the duo's last film together. Songs include "The Wild and Woolly West."

HOLLYWOOD SHUFFLE 1987
★★ R Comedy 1:21
☑ Adult situations, explicit language, violence

Dir: Robert Townsend *Cast:* Robert Townsend, Anne-Marie Johnson, Helen Martin, Keenan Ivory Wayans, Paul Mooney

▶ Fresh and unexpected satire from actor/writer/director/producer Townsend. He plays a black middle-class actor who struggles to become a star, but only encounters roles for pimps, muggers, and slaves. NAACP members appear to say, "You'll never play the Rambos till you stop playing the Sambos!" Funny, sweet, and amazingly well made for its low budget.

HOMBRE 1967
★★★★ NR Western 1:51
☑ Adult situations, explicit language, mild violence

Dir: Martin Ritt *Cast:* Paul Newman, Fredric March, Richard Boone, Diane Cilento, Cameron Mitchell

▶ Newman, an Apache-raised white man, boards a stagecoach full of prejudiced passengers. When the travelers are attacked by bandits, Newman leads them to safety in the hills and defends them from the marauders. Film successfully crossbreeds 1960s social consciousness with classic genre elements. Newman makes a terrific antihero. From an Elmore Leonard novel.

HOMECOMING, THE 1971
★ NR Drama/MFTV 1:20
Dir: Fielder Cook *Cast:* Richard Thomas, Patricia Neal, Edgar Bergen, Ellen Corby, Cleavon Little, Andrew Duggan
▶ Heartwarming pilot movie for long-running TV series "The Waltons" recounts the events of Christmas Day, 1933, in the lives of a rural American family. Neal, Cook, and writer Earl Hamner, Jr., were all nominated for Emmys; Hamner's autobiographical source novel was previously filmed as the 1963 Henry Fonda/Maureen O'Hara vehicle *Spencer's Mountain.* Seasonally rebroadcast as *The Homecoming—A Christmas Story.* (CC)

HOME OF THE BRAVE 1949
★★★ NR War 1:25 B&W
Dir: Mark Robson *Cast:* James Edwards, Douglas Dick, Steve Brodie, Jeff Corey, Lloyd Bridges, Frank Lovejoy
▶ Black soldier Edwards is paralyzed while on a South Seas mission during World War II. Under psychiatrist Corey's guidance, he confronts the racism that caused his injury. Provocative message drama was one of the first Hollywood films to deal with discrimination. Intelligent screenplay by Carl Foreman based on a Broadway play by Arthur Laurents.

HOMEWORK 1982
☆ R Comedy 1:30
☑ Nudity, adult situations, explicit language
Dir: James Beshears *Cast:* Joan Collins, Michael Morgan, Shell Kepler, Lanny Horn, Carrie Snodgress
▶ Adolescent tease about good-looking but virginal punk-rock singer Morgan, with Collins as the older woman who makes a man of him. Crude and sloppy; more embarrassing than libido-stirring.

HONEYMOON KILLERS, THE 1970
★ R Mystery-Suspense 1:50 B&W
☑ Adult situations, mild violence
Dir: Leonard Kastle *Cast:* Shirley Stoler, Tony Lo Bianco, Doris Roberts, Mary Jane Higby
▶ Stark, hypnotic, true story of obese nurse Stoler and her charming boyfriend Lo Bianco, electrocuted in 1951 for murdering "lonely hearts club" women after robbing them of their savings. Bizarre drama has a cult following.

HONEYSUCKLE ROSE 1980
★★★ PG Drama 1:59
☑ Adult situations, explicit language
Dir: Jerry Schatzberg *Cast:* Willie Nelson, Dyan Cannon, Amy Irving, Slim Pickens, Charles Levin, Bobbie Nelson
▶ Nelson's first starring film is a semi-autobiographical account about the conflict between a country-western musician's heavy touring schedule and his home life. Nelson's wife Cannon is understandably upset when he starts an affair with young musician Irving. First-rate music (including Nelson's Oscar-nominated "On the Road Again") outweighs sometimes improbable plot. C&W fans can spot many stars: Johnny Gimble, Hank Cochran, Emmylou Harris, etc.

HONKY TONK FREEWAY 1981
★★ PG Comedy 1:46
☑ Adult situations, explicit language, adult humor
Dir: John Schlesinger *Cast:* Beau Bridges, Hume Cronyn, Beverly D'Angelo, William Devane, George Dzundza, Teri Garr
▶ Devane, Mayor of Ticlaw, a small Florida town heavily dependent on tourists, resorts to bribery and kidnapping when the state fails to build the town an exit ramp on the new interstate. Broad slapstick and episodic vignettes result in a chaotic structure that's only intermittently amusing. Large cast (including Geraldine Page, Howard Hesseman, and Jessica Tandy) strikes some sparks, but can't salvage the film (a notorious failure on release).

HONKYTONK MAN 1982
★★★ PG Drama 2:03
☑ Adult situations, explicit language, mild violence
Dir: Clint Eastwood *Cast:* Clint Eastwood, Kyle Eastwood, John McIntire, Alexa Kenin, Verna Bloom, Matt Clark
▶ Consumptive country singer Eastwood and nephew Kyle (Eastwood's son) travel the backroads of Depression-era South in hopes of arranging Grand Ole Opry audition. Atypical Eastwood effort is both subtle and charming: excellent production values capture the 1930s; strong cast adds unpredictable touches. Linda Hop-

kins and Marty Robbins (who died before the film's release) are among the musicians contributing to the soundtrack.

HOOPER 1978
★★★★ **PG Action-Adventure 1:39**
☑ Explicit language
Dir: Hal Needham *Cast:* Burt Reynolds, Jan-Michael Vincent, Sally Field, Brian Keith, John Marley, Robert Klein
▶ Affectionate tribute to stuntmen concentrates on the rivalry between aging pro Reynolds and newcomer Vincent, who challenges him to an especially dangerous stunt. Large-scale set pieces are predictably impressive (both Reynolds and director Needham started out in stunts); strong ensemble acting adds to the fun. Klein is marvelous as an egomaniacal director.

HOOSIERS 1986
★★★★ **PG Drama 1:55**
☑ Adult situations
Dir: David Anspaugh *Cast:* Gene Hackman, Barbara Hershey, Dennis Hopper, Sheb Wooley, Fern Persons
▶ Heartwarming slice of Americana stars Hackman as a scandal-haunted, unconventional basketball coach leading a losing high school team to victory, and redeeming himself. Set in small-town Indiana, where basketball is worshipped. With Hopper as the town drunk/ex-basketball star Hackman hires as his assistant coach. Both screenwriter Angelo Pizzo and director Anspaugh are real-life Hoosiers. Oscar nominations went to Hopper for Best Supporting Actor and the film's musical score. **(CC)**

HOPE AND GLORY 1987 British
★★★ **PG-13 Drama 1:53**
☑ Adult situations, explicit language
Dir: John Boorman *Cast:* Sebastian Rice Edwards, Sarah Miles, David Hayman, Derrick O'Connor, Sammi Davis, Ian Bannen
▶ World War II England: the London Blitz as seen through the eyes of a ten-year-old boy (Edwards) whose mother Miles tries to hold together the family, including rebellious daughter Davis. Boorman's memoir takes an unusual child's point of view: the war seems like one great happy adventure (when the bombing cancels school, one lad thanks Hitler!). A magical movie, alternately funny and dramatic, with a wonderful feel for the past. A Best Picture nominee. **(CC)**

HOPSCOTCH 1980
★★★★ **R Comedy 1:45**
☑ Adult situations, explicit language
Dir: Ronald Neame *Cast:* Walter Matthau, Glenda Jackson, Ned Beatty, Sam Waterston, Herbert Lom
▶ Polished performances from pros Matthau and Jackson. He's a CIA agent put out to pasture; she's his girlfriend/co-conspirator helping him to expose the bureau's misdeeds and dirty tricks. Light-as-a-feather espionage caper capitalizes on leads' chemistry proven in their first film, *House Calls*.

HORROR OF DRACULA 1958 British
★★★ **NR Horror 1:22**
Dir: Terence Fisher *Cast:* Christopher Lee, Peter Cushing, Michael Gough, Melissa Stribling, Carol Marsh, John Van Eyssen
▶ Adaptation of the Bram Stoker classic introduced Lee's uniquely sinister yet charismatic portrayal of Count Dracula, who moves to London, puts pretty young Marsh under his spell, but finds opposition from Cushing. Measures up well to the 1931 Bela Lugosi version and certainly surpasses its own six sequels.

HORROR OF FRANKENSTEIN, THE 1970 British
★★ **R Horror 1:35**
☑ Graphic violence
Dir: Jimmy Sangster *Cast:* Ralph Bates, Kate O'Mara, Graham James, Veronica Carlson, Dennis Price, David Prowse
▶ Bates plays Victor Frankenstein, son of the monster-making count, who kills his dad and then takes the family business to new lows of depravity by murdering locals to provide body parts for his own creation, the hulking Prowse.

HORSE FEATHERS 1932
★★★ **NR Comedy 1:09 B&W**
Dir: Norman Z. McLeod *Cast:* The Marx Brothers, Thelma Todd, David Landau, Robert Greig, Nat Pendleton
▶ The brothers go to college: Groucho is the president who advocates tearing down the dorms ("Where will the students sleep?" "Where they always sleep, in the classroom."); Zeppo is the son fooling around with the college widow; Chico and Harpo a speakeasy worker and dogcatcher Groucho mistakes for football stars. Sidesplitting fun from Groucho's opening credo (expressed in the clever

song, "I'm Against It") to the gridiron finale.

HORSE IN THE GRAY FLANNEL SUIT, THE 1968
★★★★ G Comedy/Family 1:54
Dir: Norman Tokar *Cast:* Dean Jones, Diane Baker, Lloyd Bochner, Fred Clark, Ellen Janov
▶ Advertising man Jones purchases a horse to use in campaign to boost sagging aspirin sales. His plan fails but all isn't lost: the horse turns out to be a steeplechase champ and wins the big race. Family comedy from Disney.

HORSEMEN, THE 1971
☆ PG Action-Adventure 1:50
☑ Brief nudity, violence
Dir: John Frankenheimer *Cast:* Omar Sharif, Leigh Taylor-Young, Jack Palance, David De, Peter Jeffrey, Mohammed Shamsi
▶ Unusual look at the Afghani sport of buzkashi, a type of superviolent polo played with a headless calf for a ball. Sharif is the player who overcomes an amputated leg and an uneasy relationship with father Palance to win the championship. Looks better than it sounds; scenery and action compensate for unfocused story.

HORSE SOLDIERS, THE 1959
★★★ NR Western 1:59
Dir: John Ford *Cast:* John Wayne, William Holden, Constance Towers, Hoot Gibson, Althea Gibson
▶ Stirring Ford adventure. Wayne is a Union officer leading a march through the Confederacy. Along the way, he has conflicts with liberal doctor Holden and pretty Southern sympathizer Towers. All the elements of a Ford cavalry picture, including great action and pageantry, yet falls short of his classic trilogy. (CC)

HORSE WITHOUT A HEAD, THE 1963
★★★ NR Action-Adventure/Family 1:29
Dir: Don Chaffey *Cast:* Jean-Pierre Aumont, Herbert Lom, Leo McKern, Pamela Franklin, Vincent Winter
▶ A kindly junk dealer gives a group of poor children a headless toy horse. Soon both the law and criminals are in pursuit of the kids, for the horse contains stolen loot. Fine Disney family fare, shot in Britain, was originally aired in two parts on TV.

HOSPITAL, THE 1972
★★★ PG Comedy 1:44
☑ Adult situations, explicit language
Dir: Arthur Hiller *Cast:* George C. Scott, Diana Rigg, Barnard Hughes, Nancy Marchand, Lenny Baker, Stockard Channing
▶ Best Screenplay Oscar went to Paddy Chayefsky for this acerbic black comedy, which does for hospitals what his *Network* did for TV. Impotent doctor Scott has his sexual confidence restored by free spirit Rigg but must deal with a series of crises, including psychopathic murderer on the loose in the corridors. Greatly enhanced by Scott's sardonic performance. (CC)

HOSTAGE 1987
★★ R Action-Adventure 1:34
☑ Explicit language, violence
Dir: Hanro Moehr *Cast:* Wings Hauser, Karen Black, Kevin McCarthy, Nancy Locke, Robert Whitehead, Billy Second
▶ Arab terrorists hijack South African plane; vets Hauser and McCarthy assemble mission to rescue Locke (Hauser's real-life wife) and her ailing son. Hang-glider assault provides some chills to offset perfunctory script; Black offers good comic support as fading sexpot passenger.

HOT CHILD IN THE CITY 1987
★★ NR Mystery-Suspense 1:25
☑ Brief nudity, adult situations, explicit language, violence
Dir: John Florea *Cast:* Leah Ayres Hendrix, Shari Shattuck, Geof Prysirr, Antony Alda, Will Bledsoe
▶ Hendrix is up to her teased hair in danger when she plays detective to solve big sister Shattuck's murder. Plot contrived to fit Nick Gilder and James McCullouch's familiar pop song.

HOT DOG . . . THE MOVIE 1984
★★ R Comedy 1:36
☑ Nudity, adult situations, explicit language, mild violence, adult humor
Dir: Peter Markle *Cast:* David Naughton, Tracy N. Smith, Patrick Houser, John Patrick Reger, Shannon Tweed
▶ Set in Lake Tahoe, *Hot Dog* (ski lingo for showing off) is mostly spectacular ski stunts and naked women. Plot concerns ski-slope rivalry between the American team led by wholesome farm boy Houser and the Australian team led by ruthless Reger. With Naughton as the American team's oldest member; Playmate Tweed

as ski bunny on the make. Includes a major wet T-shirt contest. **(CC)**

HOTEL 1967
★ ★ ★ ★ **PG Drama 2:05**
☑ Adult situations, explicit language
Dir: Richard Quine *Cast:* Rod Taylor, Karl Malden, Catherine Spaak, Melvyn Douglas, Richard Conte
▶ Adaptation of Arthur Hailey's novel about the glamorous guests and management of New Orleans's venerable St. Gregory Hotel, forced either to modernize or to sell. Large and colorful cast includes a superb Douglas as the gentleman owner who loves his hotel but is resistant to change and Malden as an amusingly elusive thief. Eventually adapted into a successful TV series.

HOTEL COLONIAL 1987 U.S./Italian
★ ★ **R Action-Adventure 1:43**
☑ Brief nudity, explicit language, violence
Dir: Cinzia Torrini *Cast:* John Savage, Rachel Ward, Robert Duvall, Massimo Troisi
▶ Savage searches the Amazon for brother Duvall's murderer. He encounters friendly embassy aide Ward, bad-guy locals, a filthy jail, a colorful cockfight, a comfy hotel—and his brother, very much alive. Meandering, slow-paced, and unusually cast. Excellent location shooting in Mexico.

HOTEL NEW HAMPSHIRE, THE 1984
★ **R Comedy 1:48**
☑ Rape, adult situations, explicit language, violence, adult humor
Dir: Tony Richardson *Cast:* Jodie Foster, Beau Bridges, Rob Lowe, Nastassja Kinski, Wilford Brimley, Jennifer Dundas
▶ Lives and loves of New England hotel man Bridges and his children, including homosexual Paul McCrane, writer Dundas who won't grow, and Lowe and Foster, both in love with one another. Wild plot includes shy Kinski who hides in bear suit, revolutionaries, and family's revenge against Foster's rapist Matthew Modine. Visually inventive adaptation of John Irving's best-seller captures the author's bittersweet, whimsical tone. Enjoyable for those tuned in to Irving's wavelength; others may find characters relentlessly eccentric.

HOT LEAD AND COLD FEET 1978
★ ★ ★ ★ **G Western/Comedy 1:59**
Dir: Robert Butler *Cast:* Jim Dale, Darren McGavin, Karen Valentine, Jack Elam, Don Knotts
▶ Cowtown is turned upside down when a rich, cantankerous codger named Jasper Bloodshy dies, leaving his estate to one of two identical twin sons; a sweet-tempered Salvation Army officer and crazed bandit "Wild Billy" fight it out for their inheritance. Dale plays all three parts. With Knotts as the sheriff preparing for a shoot-out. Boisterous, fast-paced Disney fun.

HOT MOVES 1984
★ **R Comedy 1:26**
☑ Nudity, adult situations, explicit language, mild violence, adult humor
Dir: Jim Sotos *Cast:* Michael Zorek, Adam Silbar, Jeff Fishman, Johnny Timko, Jill Schaelen
▶ Four Southern California teens vow to lose their virginity before summer ends. Fishman tries to score with hookers on Hollywood Boulevard, Zorek hits on a bowling alley waitress, and Silbar plays up to his reluctant girlfriend. Conversely, Timko is pursued by a female impersonator disguised as a housewife.

HOT PURSUIT 1987
★ ★ ★ **PG-13 Comedy 1:33**
☑ Adult situations, explicit language, mild violence
Dir: Steven Lisberger *Cast:* John Cusack, Wendy Gazelle, Robert Loggia, Monte Markham, Shelley Fabares, Jerry Stiller
▶ Due to a failed chemistry exam, likable preppie Cusack misses a Caribbean cruise with girlfriend Gazelle and her folks Markham and Fabares. When he's granted a reprieve, Cusack embarks on a hellish three-day odyssey to catch up to Gazelle. Appealing comedy, thanks to Cusack's charisma and the picturesque locales.

HOT RESORT 1985
★ **R Comedy 1:31**
☑ Nudity, explicit language, adult humor
Dir: John Robins *Cast:* Tom Parsekian, Michael Berz, Bronson Pinchot, Daniel Schneider, Linda Kenton, Frank Gorshin
▶ Cut off from the beautiful girls at a St. Kitts resort, three summer employees go on strike until management agrees to let them compete in a boat-race audition for a TV commercial. Leering teen comedy with an emphasis on bikinis and gross-out humor marks an early effort for

Pinchot. Kenton was 1985 *Penthouse* Pet of the Year.

HOT ROCK, THE 1972
★ ★ ★ PG Comedy/Crime 1:45
☑ Explicit language, mild violence
Dir: Peter Yates *Cast:* Robert Redford, George Segal, Paul Sand, Ron Leibman, Zero Mostel, Moses Gunn
▶ Gunn, ambassador of an African nation, recruits pro thieves/brothers-in-law Redford and Segal to steal priceless diamond from a museum, claiming the gem rightfully belongs in his home country. Two enlist aid of Sand and Leibman and successfully pull off the heist, but Sand swallows the jewel when police apprehend him. Further misadventures ensue in this thoroughly entertaining comic caper, although Redford sometimes seems out of place. Sequel: *The Bank Shot.*

HOT STUFF 1979
★ ★ ★ ★ PG Comedy 1:31
☑ Adult situations, explicit language
Dir: Dom DeLuise *Cast:* Dom DeLuise, Suzanne Pleshette, Jerry Reed, Luis Avalos, Ossie Davis
▶ Nutty action comedy stars DeLuise as a Miami cop. With partners Reed, Avalos, and sexy sergeant Pleshette, he sets up a fencing front to bust clients selling stolen goods. Amiable, entertaining fluff.

HOT TO TROT 1988
★ ★ PG Comedy 1:23
☑ Adult situations, explicit language
Dir: Michael Dinner *Cast:* Bob Goldthwait, Dabney Coleman, Virginia Madsen, Cindy Pickett, Jim Metzler
▶ Goldthwait inherits talking horse (voice of John Candy) and half-share in brokerage. Horse's tips propel Goldthwait to fortune, but scheming stepbrother Coleman plots to discover the success formula. Outrageously strident performances and flimsy screenplay; tolerable for kids and Goldthwait fans. Danny Elfman score includes nifty Muzak version of "We're in the Money."

HOT TOUCH 1981
★ ★ NR Drama 1:33
☑ Nudity, adult situations, explicit language, violence
Dir: Roger Vadim *Cast:* Wayne Rogers, Samantha Eggar, Marie-France Pisier, Patrick Macnee, Melvyn Douglas
▶ Caper film about cop Rogers, who goes undercover as an artist and is blackmailed into forging a pair of missing masterpieces. With gorgeous girlfriend Pisier, he uncovers a crooked art dealer. Unbalanced mixture of romance, comedy, drama, and suspense; lackluster and punchless.

HOT T-SHIRTS 1979
★ R Comedy 1:26
☑ Nudity, adult situations, explicit language, adult humor
Dir: Chuck Vincent *Cast:* Ray Holland, Glenn Marc, Stephanie Landor, Pauline Rose, Corinne Alphen
▶ Small-town bar owner revives his flagging business by instituting a wet T-shirt competition, leading to a heated rivalry between the local girls and snooty college co-eds. Despite suggestive subject matter, leering comedy fails to deliver the goods.

HOUND OF THE BASKERVILLES, THE 1939
★ ★ ★ NR Mystery-Suspense 1:20 B&W
Dir: Sidney Lanfield *Cast:* Basil Rathbone, Nigel Bruce, Wendy Barrie, Lionel Atwill, Richard Greene, John Carradine
▶ It's Sherlock Holmes (Rathbone) and Dr. Watson (Bruce) to the rescue when young nobleman Greene is menaced by a legendary beast. Cerebral Rathbone and bumbling Bruce left an indelible impression in these roles. Intelligently mounted adaptation retained Sir Arthur Conan Doyle's Victorian period (later efforts were updated to World War II era) and an explicit reference to Holmes's drug habit in the closing line, "Watson, the needle!"

HOUND OF THE BASKERVILLES, THE 1959 British
★ ★ NR Mystery-Suspense 1:26
Dir: Terence Fisher *Cast:* Peter Cushing, Andre Morell, Christopher Lee, Marla Landi
▶ Not bad Hammer Studios remake of the Holmes classic with horror star Cushing as the great detective and Morell as his Watson. They take on the case of Sir Baskerville (Lee) whose estate is haunted by the curse of a murderous dog. (CC)

HOUR OF THE GUN 1967
★ ★ ★ NR Western 1:40
Dir: John Sturges *Cast:* James Garner, Jason Robards, Jr., Robert Ryan, Albert Salmi, Charles Aidman, Steve Ihnat
▶ Strong, compact Western about Wyatt Earp picks up where director Sturges's *Gunfight at O.K. Corral* left off. Garner

delivers an impassioned performance as the famous sheriff, driven by unhealthy revenge as he tracks his brothers' killers. Robards adds a jaunty note as Earp's best friend Doc Holliday. Look for Jon Voight in a small but telling role as gunslinger Curly Bill Brocius.

HOUSE 1986
★★★ R Horror 1:32
☑ Explicit language, graphic violence
Dir: Steve Miner *Cast:* William Katt, Kay Lenz, George Wendt, Richard Moll, Mary Stavin
▶ After his aunt commits suicide, writer Katt moves into her big old house. She claimed the house was haunted and, when monsters start coming out of closets, he suspects she was right. Familiar story enlivened by inventive touches, emphasizing chuckles over tingles. Not really scary (monsters look fake) but well-produced fun should play nicely on the small screen. **(CC)**

HOUSE II: THE SECOND STORY 1987
★★ PG-13 Horror 1:28
☑ Explicit language, violence
Dir: Ethan Wiley *Cast:* Arye Gross, Jonathan Stark, Royal Dano, Bill Maher, Lar Park Lincoln, John Ratzenberger
▶ Sequel in name only. Gross, his girlfriend Lincoln, and hustling best pal Stark move into creepy digs where Gross's parents were done in twenty-five years earlier. The horror begins when Gross resurrects long-dead great-great-grandfather Dano. Arbitrary plotting, a few jolts. **(CC)**

HOUSEBOAT 1958
★★★★ NR Comedy 1:50
Dir: Melville Shavelson *Cast:* Cary Grant, Sophia Loren, Martha Hyer, Harry Guardino, Paul Petersen, Murray Hamilton
▶ Widowed Washington lawyer Grant hires music conductor's daughter Loren to look after his three children on Potomac houseboat. Grant and Loren, although pursued by others, fall in love. Lighthearted and lots of fun; Grant and Loren interact beautifully with each other and the children. Sam Cooke sings the Oscar-nominated "Almost in Your Arms"; screenplay was also nominated.

HOUSE CALLS 1978
★★★★★ PG Comedy 1:38
☑ Adult situations, explicit language
Dir: Howard Zieff *Cast:* Walter Matthau, Glenda Jackson, Art Carney,

Richard Benjamin, Candice Azzara, Dick O'Neill
▶ Slapstick hospital antics combine with sophisticated sexual innuendos when recently widowed surgeon/would-be lady-killer Matthau falls for divorcée Jackson while rewiring her broken jaw. He's forced to choose between the hectic single life and Glenda's home and hearth. Middle-age comedy/romance serves as apt vehicle for powerhouse leads, with strong support from Carney as an out-to-lunch doctor going senile.

HOUSEKEEPER, THE 1987 Canadian
★ R Mystery-Suspense 1:37
☑ Brief nudity, adult situations, explicit language, violence
Dir: Ousama Rawi *Cast:* Rita Tushingham, Ross Petty, Tom Kneebone, Shelley Peterson, Jonathan Crombie, Jessica Steen
▶ Dyslexic Tushingham kills her dad after he makes fun of her impediment. She then takes a job with a doctor's family without telling of her handicap, leading to friction and a violent (and rather repellent) climax. Tushingham is memorable, but this feature fails to build sufficient suspense.

HOUSEKEEPING 1987
★★★ PG Drama 1:56
☑ Adult situations
Dir: Bill Forsyth *Cast:* Christine Lahti, Andrea Burchill, Sara Walker, Anne Pitoniak, Barbara Reese
▶ Beautifully observed, quirky drama about sisters Walker and Burchill, orphaned by their mother's suicide and cared for by their long-lost eccentric Aunt Sylvie (Lahti). Haunting performances (especially from Lahti and Walker) examine the nature of impossible attachments and vagrant lives. Based on Marilynne Robinson's well-regarded novel. **(CC)**

HOUSE OF FEAR, THE 1945
★★ NR Mystery-Suspense 1:08 B&W
Dir: Roy William Neill *Cast:* Basil Rathbone, Nigel Bruce, Aubrey Mather, Dennis Hoey, Paul Cavanagh, Holmes Herbert
▶ After attempting to move Sherlock Holmes and Dr. Watson into World War II era, long-running series returned the duo to Victorian times. In a dreary Scottish mansion, someone is killing off the seven middle-aged members of the "Good Comrades Club." A curse on the manor

decrees that no inhabitant shall go to the grave in one piece. Indeed, those slain die in ways that make identification impossible, posing a formidable test for Holmes's renowned powers of deduction.

HOUSE OF GAMES 1987
★★ R Mystery-Suspense 1:41
☑ Adult situations, explicit language, violence
Dir: David Mamet   *Cast:* Lindsay Crouse, Joe Mantegna, Mike Nussbaum, Lilia Skala, J. T. Walsh
▶ Repressed shrink Crouse attempts to study con man Mantegna and his gang and becomes involved in a series of scams. Twisty, satisfying plot has a few predictable spots but generally keeps the audience off balance. Playwright Mamet's feature debut is a visually sleek thriller. Frosty Crouse (Mrs. Mamet) and frisky Mantegna work beautifully together.

HOUSE OF THE LONG SHADOWS 1983 British
★★★ PG Horror 1:42
☑ Explicit language, violence
Dir: Peter Walker   *Cast:* Peter Cushing, Vincent Price, Christopher Lee, John Carradine, Desi Arnaz, Jr., Richard Todd
▶ Spooky spoof about young author Arnaz who tries to write his new novel in a deserted gothic mansion, only to be interrupted by murder. Price, Lee, Cushing, and Carradine are the film's most menacing bogeymen.

HOUSE OF THE RISING SUN 1986
★ NR Mystery-Suspense 1:26
☑ Brief nudity, adult situations, explicit language, violence
Dir: Greg Gold   *Cast:* Frank Annese, Jamie Barrett, Tawny Moyer
▶ Newspaper reporter Barrett goes undercover as high-class escort to get the goods on murderer, stylishly dressed pimp Annese. She finds herself attracted to him and becomes his lover, but he gives chase when he learns her true identity. Suspenser plays like a full-length music video.

HOUSE OF WAX 1953
★★★ PG Horror 1:28
Dir: Andre de Toth   *Cast:* Vincent Price, Frank Lovejoy, Carolyn Jones, Phyllis Kirk, Paul Picerni, Charles Buchinski
▶ Sculptor Price disappears after fire started by evil partner and then returns with a new wax museum. People begin to wonder: how does he get those figures

so realistic? It wouldn't have anything to do with some murders, would it? Originally filmed in 3-D but ingenious thriller works just fine without the gimmick. Macabre wax museum atmosphere, deliciously mad Vincent.

HOUSE ON CARROLL STREET, THE 1988
★★★ PG Mystery-Suspense 1:41
☑ Explicit language, mild violence
Dir: Peter Yates   *Cast:* Kelly McGillis, Jeff Daniels, Mandy Patinkin, Jessica Tandy, Jonathan Hogan
▶ An old-fashioned thriller set in 1950s New York City. Blacklisted McGillis uncovers mysterious goings-on at the house next door involving Joe McCarthyish senator Patinkin. G-man Daniels helps her through treacherous maze of murder and espionage. New York never looked spiffier in this splendid period re-creation, although the plot relies too heavily on coincidence. **(CC)**

HOUSE ON HAUNTED HILL 1958
★★ NR Horror 1:15 B&W
Dir: William Castle   *Cast:* Vincent Price, Carol Ohmart, Richard Long, Alan Marshal
▶ Mysterious millionaire Price invites group of people to spend the night at his haunted mansion, offering ten grand each if they stay until dawn. Murder is on the menu for the guests, including Price's unfaithful wife and her lover. William Castle gimmick movie, originally filmed in "Percepto" (skeleton flying over the audience), is enjoyable but not to be taken seriously. **(CC)**

HOUSE ON SORORITY ROW, THE 1983
★★ R Horror 1:31
☑ Brief nudity, explicit language, violence
Dir: Mark Rosman   *Cast:* Kathryn McNeil, Eileen Davidson, Janis Zido, Robin Meloy
▶ Sorority girls accidentally kill their bitchy housemother and dump the corpse into the pool. Then someone starts killing the girls. Could the housemother have risen from the dead? Bad acting plus a plot with few surprises in an already oversaturated genre. Many false scares, too few real ones.

HOUSE THAT DRIPPED BLOOD, THE 1971 British
★ PG Horror 1:41
☑ Violence
Dir: Peter John Duffell   *Cast:* Denholm

Elliott, Peter Cushing, Christopher Lee, Ingrid Pitt, John Bennett, Jon Pertwee
▶ Anthology features four stories set in an English country mansion: writer Elliott is stalked by killer, the house becomes a wax museum and setting for more murders, Lee falls victim to voodoo doll, and actor Pertwee takes vampire role too seriously. Sturdy cast and literate screenplay by Robert Bloch combine scares and laughs.

HOUSE WHERE EVIL DWELLS, THE 1982
★ R Horror 1:28
☑ Nudity, adult situations, explicit language, graphic violence
Dir: Kevin Connor *Cast:* Susan George, Edward Albert, Doug McClure, Amy Barrett, Mayo Hattori
▶ Americans Albert and George rent a house outside Kyoto, unaware the place is haunted by ghosts of a samurai, his unfaithful wife, and her lover. All hell breaks loose as the spirits menace the tenants. Offensive characters (you may be rooting for the ghosts), silly special effects (like giant crabs), plenty of sex and violence.

HOWARDS OF VIRGINIA, THE 1940
★★ NR Drama 1:58 B&W
Dir: Frank Lloyd *Cast:* Cary Grant, Martha Scott, Cedric Hardwicke, Alan Marshal, Richard Carlson, Paul Kelly
▶ Revolutionary War epic traces surveyor Grant's growing involvement with the rebel cause against a backdrop of familiar events (the Boston Tea Party, Valley Forge, etc.). Although shot in Williamsburg, dull historical pageant feels contrived and inauthentic.

HOWARD THE DUCK 1986
★★ PG Fantasy 1:50
☑ Adult situations, explicit language
Dir: Willard Huyck *Cast:* Lea Thompson, Jeffrey Jones, Tim Robbins, Ed Gale, Chip Zien
▶ George Lucas's mega-mess features the cigar-chomping comic-book alien accidentally transported to Cleveland via a wayward laser. Befriended by aspiring rock star Thompson, the feathered hero defends her against a gang of punks. Mild satire then turns into overproduced orgy of frenetic chase scenes, car crashes, and light shows as Howard saves the world from an evil Duck Warlord (Jones). Critics and audiences alike found this wise-quacking water fowl a turkey. (CC)

HOW GREEN WAS MY VALLEY 1941
★★★★ NR Drama 1:58 B&W
Dir: John Ford *Cast:* Walter Pidgeon, Maureen O'Hara, Donald Crisp, Anna Lee, Roddy McDowall, Sara Allgood
▶ Emotionally powerful adaptation of Richard Llewellyn's novel shows changes in a nineteenth-century Welsh coal-mining village, seen through the eyes of a young boy whose parents sacrifice to give him a better life. Inspiring, often heartbreaking film received ten Oscar nominations, winning for Best Picture, Ford's magnificent direction, Crisp's stern but loving father, Arthur Miller's lyrical photography, and impressive set design.

HOW I WON THE WAR 1967 British
★ NR Comedy 1:51
☑ Violence
Dir: Richard Lester *Cast:* Michael Crawford, John Lennon, Roy Kinnear, Lee Montague, Jack MacGowran
▶ In World War II North Africa, eccentric officer Crawford drives his troops crazy with his ridiculous demands. Impressively shot black comedy makes sharp contrast between its lunatic characters and the realistic horrors of war, but the very British accents and humor may not be readily accessible to Americans. Crawford is remarkable and Lennon (who appears briefly) is fascinating.

HOWLING, THE 1981
★★ R Horror 1:30
☑ Nudity, explicit language, graphic violence
Dir: Joe Dante *Cast:* Dee Wallace, Patrick Macnee, Dennis Dugan, John Carradine, Christopher Stone, Slim Pickens
▶ TV reporter Wallace survives attack from a lunatic and then recuperates with husband Stone at a secluded retreat. Bad idea: the place turns out to be a coven of werewolves who intend to make Wallace their next furry member. Very convincing special effects provide lots of gore, but director Dante and co-writer Sayles (who appears in a cameo) deliver a beautifully conceived and executed movie that transcends its B-movie origins.

HOWLING II: YOUR SISTER IS A WEREWOLF 1985
★ R Horror 1:24
☑ Nudity, adult situations, explicit language, graphic violence
Dir: Philippe Mora *Cast:* Christopher

Lee, Annie McEnroe, Reb Brown, Sybil Danning, Marsha Hunt

► In L.A., Brown investigates the death of his sister, rumored to be a werewolf. Then, accompanied by reporter McEnroe and psychic investigator Lee, it's off to Transylvania to confront werewolf leader Danning. Feeble sequel, inferior to the original. Production values are good; script and performances aren't, although Danning outcleavages Hunt.

HOWLING III: THE MARSUPIALS 1987
Australian
★ **PG-13 Horror 1:34**
☑ Nudity, explicit language, violence
Dir: Philippe Mora *Cast:* Barry Otto, Imogen Annesley, Leigh Biolos, Max Fairchild, Dasha Blahova

► Marsupial werewolf Annesley gets a job in a horror flick and falls for a crew member. Meanwhile, her cohorts track her down. More professional than *Howling II* but not as good as the superior original. Hammy acting, ridiculous script, intrusive rock score, more laughs than scares although some fine camerawork and a few audacious ideas.

HOW THE WEST WAS WON 1963
★★★★★ **G Western 2:25**
Dir: John Ford, Henry Hathaway, George Marshall *Cast:* John Wayne, James Stewart, Debbie Reynolds, Gregory Peck, Carroll Baker, George Peppard

► Tale traces family of New England farmers as they head West in the 1830s through two subsequent generations of trials and tribulations. This one has it all: comedy, romance, drama, adventure. Wide-screen Western classic loses scope on the TV screen but all-star cast and sweep of the story make it almost like a mammoth (and very engrossing) mini-series. Divided into chapters, each with its own director. A Best Picture nominee.

HOW TO BEAT THE HIGH COST OF LIVING 1980
★★★★ **PG Comedy 1:44**
☑ Nudity, adult situations, explicit language
Dir: Robert Scheerer *Cast:* Susan Saint James, Jane Curtin, Jessica Lange, Dabney Coleman, Richard Benjamin, Fred Willard

► Caper comedy about Oregon ladies St. James, Curtin, and Lange, who are mad as hell about skyrocketing prices and decide not to take it anymore. They pull off a shopping mall heist. Predictable but happy high jinks—sort of like "Charlie's Housewives"—will be familiar to TV watchers everywhere.

HOW TO MARRY A MILLIONAIRE 1953
★★★★ **NR Comedy 1:35**
Dir: Jean Negulesco *Cast:* Marilyn Monroe, Betty Grable, Lauren Bacall, William Powell, David Wayne, Rory Calhoun

► Trying to land millionaire husbands, models Monroe, Gable, and Bacall pool their funds to rent a posh Manhattan penthouse into which they plan to lure their victims. The golddiggers' plans go awry when two fall for men who appear to be poor. Frothy fun with sprightly dialogue from writer/producer Nunnally Johnson. First comedy to use wide-screen CinemaScope process.

HOW TO STEAL A MILLION 1966
★★★ **NR Comedy 2:07**
Dir: William Wyler *Cast:* Audrey Hepburn, Peter O'Toole, Eli Wallach, Hugh Griffith, Charles Boyer, Marcel Dalio

► Delicious comedy caper set in Paris. Hepburn, daughter of art forger Griffith, must steal one of her father's fakes from heavily guarded museum before authenticators examine it. She turns to security expert O'Toole, who concocts an elaborate break-in. Smoothly entertaining film features a winning performance by Boyer.

HOW TO STUFF A WILD BIKINI 1965
★★ **NR Comedy 1:30**
Dir: William Asher *Cast:* Annette Funicello, Dwayne Hickman, Brian Donlevy, Harvey Lembeck, Beverly Adams, Buster Keaton

► Witch doctor Keaton's flying bikini makes Adams the hit of the beach; she steals Hickman away from Funicello, who's also pining over Naval Reserve recruit Frankie Avalon. Sixth *Beach Party* entry shows its age. Guests include the Kingsmen, Mickey Rooney, and Brian Wilson as one of the surf bums. Sequel *Ghost in the Invisible Bikini* sinks even further.

HUCKLEBERRY FINN 1974
★★★★ **G Musical/Family 1:54**
Dir: J. Lee Thompson *Cast:* Jeff East, Paul Winfield, Harvey Korman, David Wayne

► Charming musical adaptation of Mark Twain's classic. Among the adventures facing young Huck (East) and freedom-bound slave Jim (Winfield) is hooking up with the rascally "King" (Korman). Score by Robert and Richard Sherman (*Mary Poppins, Chitty Chitty Bang Bang*). **(CC)**

HUCKLEBERRY FINN 1975
★★★★ NR Family/MFTV 1:16
Dir: Robert Totten *Cast:* Ron Howard, Antonio Fargas, Jack Elam, Merle Haggard, Donny Most, Sarah Selby
▶ Made-for-television adaptation of Mark Twain's classic about young Huck Finn (Howard) and runaway slave Jim (Fargas) journeying down the Mississippi via raft. Simply presented, well produced, but rather uninspired. Howard is convincing, if not endearing, as Huck; Fargas is miscast as Jim. Easy-to-take lesson in tolerance for younger kids.

HUD 1963
★★★ NR Drama 1:52 B&W
☑ Rape, adult situations, violence
Dir: Martin Ritt *Cast:* Paul Newman, Patricia Neal, Melvyn Douglas, Brandon de Wilde, John Ashley, Whit Bissell
▶ Ne'er-do-well Newman returns to father Douglas, feuds with the honorable old man about how to save struggling ranch, tries to rape maid Neal, and loses the respect of nephew de Wilde. Great drama still remarkably fresh thanks to Newman's Oscar-nominated performance. Equally fine are Oscar-winning Neal and Douglas. Based on a Larry McMurtry novel.

HUMAN COMEDY, THE 1943
★★★ NR Drama 1:58 B&W
Dir: Clarence Brown *Cast:* Mickey Rooney, Frank Morgan, James Craig, Marsha Hunt, Fay Bainter, Ray Collins
▶ Warmly sentimental look at how the people of a small California town are affected by World War II. Rooney excels as a telegraph messenger, a job that means delivering tragic news to friends. Large cast is filled with familiar faces: Donna Reed, Van Johnson, a young Robert Mitchum, etc., but child star "Butch" Jenkins steals the picture as Rooney's brother. William Saroyan won an Oscar for his story; film received four other nominations.

HUMAN FACTOR, THE 1979
★ R Drama 1:55
☑ Nudity, adult situations, explicit language
Dir: Otto Preminger *Cast:* Nicol Williamson, Richard Attenborough, John Gielgud, Robert Morley, Iman, Derek Jacobi
▶ Family man Williamson is unlikely suspect when a double agent is discovered in British Secret Service. Williamson turns out to be the culprit: years before he made deal with USSR to get black wife Iman out of South Africa. He must leave his family behind when the net tightens around him. Subtle, understated acting from Williamson but lovely model Iman is rather lifeless as his wife. Intimate spy drama, sturdily adapted from Tom Stoppard from Graham Greene novel, suffers from below-average production values.

HUMANOIDS FROM THE DEEP 1980
★ R Horror 1:20
☑ Rape, nudity, explicit language, graphic violence
Dir: Barbara Peeters *Cast:* Doug McClure, Ann Turkel, Vic Morrow, Cindy Weintraub, Anthony Penya, Denise Galik
▶ Gruesome monsters attack a fishing community, prompting an investigation by scientist Turkel and fisherman McClure. Lurid but enjoyable low-budget shocker, with a heavy emphasis on gore and nudity, scores some points with its pro-environment stance.

HUMONGOUS 1982 Canadian
★★ R Horror 1:34
☑ Rape, adult situations, explicit language, graphic violence
Dir: Paul Lynch *Cast:* Janet Julian, David Wallace, Janit Baldwin, John Wildman
▶ In 1946, a woman survives a rape attempt on an island. In the present, a group of teens lost in a fog are shipwrecked on the island where the rape victim still lives in isolation. Someone (or something) starts bumping off the teens. Adequate suspense, distasteful violence.

HUNCHBACK OF NOTRE DAME, THE 1939
★★★★ NR Drama 1:57 B&W
Dir: William Dieterle *Cast:* Charles Laughton, Maureen O'Hara, Thomas Mitchell, Cedric Hardwicke, Edmond O'Brien, Walter Hampden
▶ Fifteenth-century Paris: at Notre Dame Cathedral, hideous hunchback Quasimodo (Laughton) rescues gypsy O'Hara from angry crowd but ultimately becomes tragic victim of church officials. Laughton's poignant performance is a magnificent blending of makeup and

acting. Based on the often-filmed Victor Hugo novel; Lon Chaney starred in the 1923 silent version, Anthony Quinn in the 1957, and Anthony Hopkins in the tele-movie.

HUNDRA 1984 Italian
☆ NR Action-Adventure 1:49
☑ Rape, nudity, adult situations, explicit language, graphic violence
Dir: Matt Cimber *Cast:* Laurene Landon, John Ghaffari, Marissa Casel, Romiro Oliveros
▶ Landon, sole survivor of a woman warrior tribe massacred by male marauders, ventures into the city to get impregnated and continue her race. She finds love with a handsome healer but must overcome an evil king. Intentionally silly adventure/parody. Landon plays this like a valley girl with a thorn in her side, but her comic flair and athletic sexiness keep this spoof moving.

HUNGER, THE 1983
★★ R Horror 1:36
☑ Nudity, adult situations, explicit language, violence
Dir: Tony Scott *Cast:* Catherine Deneuve, David Bowie, Susan Sarandon, Cliff De Young, Beth Ehlers
▶ In present-day New York City, two-hundred-year-old vampire Bowie is rapidly aging. His immortal mate Deneuve tries to reverse the process by recruiting brilliant scientist Sarandon. Deneuve seduces Sarandon and then tries to lay claim to her soul. Arresting visuals and vivid sex scenes but muddled storytelling and lurid bloodletting.

HUNK 1987
★ PG Comedy 1:42
☑ Explicit language, adult humor
Dir: Lawrence Bassoff *Cast:* John Allen Nelson, Steve Levitt, Deborah Shelton, Rebeccah Bush, James Coco, Robert Morse
▶ Brainy computer wimp Levitt, jilted by girlfriend for aerobics instructor, is lured by sexy witch Shelton into making deal with the Devil (Coco). Result: Levitt's turned into handsome hunk Nelson. Slapdash direction, but flimsy froth provides handsome bods and mindless fun for teens.

HUNTER, THE 1980
★★★★ PG Action-Adventure 1:37
☑ Adult situations, explicit language, violence
Dir: Buzz Kulik *Cast:* Steve McQueen,

Eli Wallach, Kathryn Harrold, LeVar Burton, Ben Johnson
▶ Old-fashioned bounty hunter McQueen tries to catch up with a new breed of leaner, meaner criminal. After nabbing bail jumpers, he must get pregnant girlfriend Harrold to the hospital. Several excellent chase scenes (in a Nebraska cornfield and a Chicago elevated train), convincingly seedy environment, energetic Burton, and vitality from McQueen (dying when this was made) in his last film.

HUNTER'S BLOOD 1987
★★★ R Action-Adventure 1:41
☑ Explicit language, graphic violence
Dir: Robert C. Hughes *Cast:* Sam Bottoms, Kim Delaney, Clu Gulager, Mayf Nutter, Ken Swofford, Joey Travolta
▶ City boy Bottoms and four friends take hunting trip in backwoods Oklahoma. They run afoul of redneck poachers, who stalk the vacationers and kidnap Bottoms's girlfriend Delaney. Well directed, but characters are stereotypes and plot seems recycled from better movies. (CC)

HURRICANE, THE 1937
★★★ NR Action-Adventure 1:43 B&W
Dir: John Ford *Cast:* Jon Hall, Dorothy Lamour, Mary Astor, Raymond Massey, C. Aubrey Smith
▶ Rousing, first-class adventure and South Seas spectacular from master director Ford. Massey plays an uncompromising governor obsessed with capturing runaway native Hall, who eventually saves Massey's wife Astor during the relentless hurricane finale. Spellbinding disaster climax directed by special effects wizard James Basevi. Alfred Newman's score includes the pop hit "Moon of Manakoora."

HURRICANE 1979
★★★ PG Action-Adventure 2:00
☑ Brief nudity, explicit language
Dir: Jan Troell *Cast:* Timothy Bottoms, Jason Robards, Mia Farrow, Max Von Sydow, Trevor Howard, Dayton Ka'Ne
▶ Dino De Laurentiis's $22 million remake of John Ford's 1937 classic of love and torrential rain. There's trouble in Pago Pago when Farrow defies stern father Robards and falls for native Ka'ne, whose dialogue includes such gems as: "I see you are getting very wet." Most of the cast drowns in the waterlogged climax—and not a moment too soon.

HUSH . . . HUSH, SWEET CHARLOTTE
1965
★★★★ NR Horror 2:13
Dir: Robert Aldrich *Cast:* Bette Davis, Olivia de Havilland, Joseph Cotten, Agnes Moorehead, Cecil Kellaway
▶ Not a sequel, more a blood relation to *Whatever Happened to Baby Jane?* featuring the same producer/director Aldrich, star Davis, and gothic gore and bitchery. Old-pro bravura performances include Oscar-nominated Moorehead as Velma, housekeeper to the deteriorating Southern mansion where de Havilland and Cotten plot to turn poor Bette into a blabbering maniac. Also received six other nominations. (CC)

HUSTLE 1975
★★★★ R Mystery-Suspense 2:00
☑ Nudity, strong sexual content, violence
Dir: Robert Aldrich *Cast:* Burt Reynolds, Catherine Deneuve, Ben Johnson, Paul Winfield, Eileen Brennan, Eddie Albert
▶ Los Angeles detective Reynolds, involved with high-class hooker Deneuve, investigates death of young woman found on beach. The trail leads to Albert, a lawyer with mob connections. Johnson, the dead girl's father, is also involved in the investigation. Cynical stuff with a powerful kick; Reynolds is quite sympathetic.

HUSTLER, THE 1961
★★★★ NR Drama 2:15 B&W
Dir: Robert Rossen *Cast:* Paul Newman, Jackie Gleason, Piper Laurie, George C. Scott, Myron McCormick, Murray Hamilton
▶ Pool hustler "Fast" Eddie Felson (Newman) takes on Minnesota Fats (Gleason), has a doomed affair with crippled woman Laurie, and almost loses his soul to gambler Scott. Tense, highly compelling drama with Newman in one of his most complex and full-bodied performances as the self-destructive Eddie. Scott, Laurie, and Gleason offer superb support. Razor-sharp cinematography and editing, magnificently directed by Rossen. Followed up, twenty-five years later, by Scorsese's *The Color of Money.* (CC)

I AM A CAMERA 1955 British
★★ NR Drama 1:38 B&W
Dir: Henry Cornelius *Cast:* Julie Harris, Laurence Harvey, Shelley Winters, Ron Randell, Lea Seidl, Anton Diffring
▶ In pre–World War II Berlin, Harris is a fun-loving chanteuse while Winters is a Jewish girl who encounters the first wave of Hitler's anti-Semitism. Harvey portrays poor, struggling writer Christopher Isherwood, whose *Berlin Stories* inspired John van Druten's play from which this intelligent film was adapted. Source material later evolved into the Broadway musical and hit film *Cabaret.*

I AM A FUGITIVE FROM A CHAIN GANG 1932
★★★★★ NR Drama 1:33 B&W
Dir: Mervyn LeRoy *Cast:* Paul Muni, Glenda Farrell, Helen Vinson, Preston Foster, Edward J. McNamara
▶ World War I vet Muni, unwilling accomplice in a petty crime, is caught and sentenced to brutal Southern chain gang. He escapes and establishes a law-abiding life, but the past catches up with him. Gripping Depression-era drama, relentlessly directed by LeRoy and stunningly acted by Muni. Absolutely shattering climax: "How do you live?" asks Muni's friend. "I steal," he says from the shadows. Fact-based drama remade by HBO as *The Man Who Broke a Thousand Chains.* Based on Robert E. Burns's autobiographical story.

I AM THE CHEESE 1983
★★ PG Drama 1:35
☑ Explicit language
Dir: Robert Jiras *Cast:* Robert MacNaughton, Robert Wagner, Hope Lange, Don Murray, Cynthia Nixon
▶ Troubled teen MacNaughton recalls childhood traumas that led to his institutionalization. Past and present are intercut as therapist Wagner tries to help the kid. Quiet but high-quality, low-budget drama from Robert Cormier's popular novel for young adults. Nonlinear story requires concentration to follow.

ICE CASTLES 1979
★★★★ PG Drama 1:49
☑ Explicit language
Dir: Donald Wrye *Cast:* Robby Benson, Lynn-Holly Johnson, Colleen Dewhurst, Tom Skerritt, Jennifer Warren
▶ Teen ice-skater Johnson forsakes beau Benson and widowed dad Skerritt to rise to the top. When an accident nearly blinds her, she reaffirms her ties to them and beats the odds to skate again. Well-done sentiment evokes laughs and tears. Ice Capades star Johnson makes a winsome debut. Moving Marvin Hamlisch

score features Melissa Manchester singing Oscar-nominated "Through the Eyes of Love."

ICEMAN 1984
★ ★ ★ **PG Action-Adventure 1:40**
☑ Explicit language, violence
Dir: Fred Schepisi *Cast:* Timothy Hutton, Lindsay Crouse, John Lone, Josef Sommer, David Strathairn, Danny Glover
▶ Caveman Lone is found preserved in ice. Revived by scientists, he makes a painful adjustment to his new surroundings, although anthropologist Hutton develops a strong rapport with him (even teaching him to sing Neil Young's "Heart of Gold"). Intriguing adventure with a magnetic performance by Lone and solid work from Hutton, but an overly mystical ending.

ICE PALACE 1960
★ ★ ★ **NR Drama 2:23**
Dir: Vincent Sherman *Cast:* Richard Burton, Robert Ryan, Martha Hyer, Jim Backus, Carolyn Jones, Ray Danton
▶ The drive for Alaskan statehood is the backdrop for the rivalry between Burton and Ryan. Burton ruthlessly pursues money, battles Ryan for Jones's affections, goes against public opinion on the statehood question, and is reconciled with his former enemy through marriage. Based on the Edna Ferber novel.

ICE PIRATES, THE 1984
★ ★ **PG Sci-Fi 1:34**
☑ Adult situations, violence, adult humor
Dir: Stewart Raffill *Cast:* Robert Urich, Mary Crosby, Michael D. Roberts, Anjelica Huston, John Matuszak, Ron Perlman
▶ Pirate leader Urich and his buccaneer band aid princess Crosby in a battle against an evil empire for the most valuable commodity in the universe: water. Tongue-in-cheek attempt to crossbreed swashbuckler genre with sci-fi trappings. Aimless script, bland effects, some fun for the younger set.

ICE STATION ZEBRA 1968
★ ★ ★ ★ **G Action-Adventure 2:30**
Dir: John Sturges *Cast:* Rock Hudson, Ernest Borgnine, Patrick McGoohan, Jim Brown, Tony Bill, Lloyd Nolan
▶ Nuclear submarine races to the North Pole to retrieve a strategic Russian satellite. Hudson, the commander, must also identify a saboteur among suspects including Communist defector Borgnine, British secret agent McGoohan, and Brown, a captain bitter over discrimination. Despite impressive Arctic settings, large-scale adventure based on Alistair MacLean's best-seller is typical Cold War espionage.

I CONFESS 1953
★ ★ ★ ★ **NR Mystery-Suspense 1:35 B&W**
Dir: Alfred Hitchcock *Cast:* Montgomery Clift, Anne Baxter, Karl Malden, Brian Aherne, Roger Dann
▶ Priest Clift hears murderer's confession. Religious code keeps him silent about what he knows, so he becomes cop Malden's number-one suspect. Somber but involving thriller from the master. Intense performance by Clift, evocative use of Quebec locations.

I COVER THE WATERFRONT 1933
★ ★ ★ **NR Drama 1:10 B&W**
Dir: James Cruze *Cast:* Ben Lyon, Claudette Colbert, Ernest Torrence, Hobart Cavanaugh, Maurice Black, Harry Beresford
▶ Muckraking reporter Lyon starts an affair with Colbert to dig up evidence against her father Torrence, an unscrupulous fisherman smuggling illegal aliens into San Diego. Antique curio of interest only to die-hard film buffs. Torrence died before film's release.

IDIOT'S DELIGHT 1939
★ ★ **NR Comedy 1:45 B&W**
Dir: Clarence Brown *Cast:* Norma Shearer, Clark Gable, Edward Arnold, Charles Coburn, Joseph Schildkraut, Burgess Meredith
▶ Glamorous adaptation of Robert Sherwood's Pulitzer prize–winning play concerns a mixed bag of travelers stranded in an Alpine retreat at the outbreak of World War II. Gable, leader of a cut-rate song-and-dance troupe, rekindles a romance with Shearer, now mistress to munitions industrialist Arnold. Antiwar stance seems naive today, but Gable does a delightful version of "Puttin' on the Ritz."

IDOLMAKER, THE 1980
★ ★ ★ **PG Drama 1:59**
☑ Adult situations, explicit language
Dir: Taylor Hackford *Cast:* Ray Sharkey, Peter Gallagher, Tovah Feldshuh, Paul Land, Maureen McCormick
▶ In the late 1950s, failed-songwriter-turned-producer Sharkey stops at nothing to make stars out of unknown Phila-

delphia kids Land and Gallagher. Flashy inside look at the music biz, inspired by the careers of Fabian and Frankie Avalon, with nice period detail, exciting concert footage, and an energetic performance by Sharkey.

IF . . . 1969 British
☆ **R Drama 1:51 C/B&W**
☑ Nudity, explicit language
Dir: Lindsay Anderson *Cast:* Malcolm McDowell, David Wood, Christine Noonan, Richard Warwick
▶ At a British boarding school, student McDowell leads violent rebellion against the establishment. Exemplary performances with McDowell making an unforgettable debut in this strikingly original film. Sharply satiric but avant-garde narrative techniques (film alternates between black-and-white and color) may alienate the casual viewer.

IF EVER I SEE YOU AGAIN 1978
★★★ **PG Romance 1:45**
☑ Adult situations, explicit language
Dir: Joe Brooks *Cast:* Joe Brooks, Shelley Hack, Jimmy Breslin, Jerry Keller, George Plimpton
▶ Composer/widower Brooks looks up old school flame Hack and they renew their affair. He loses her again but then wins her back. Actor/co-writer/director Brooks also wrote the swooning music (a chore he repeated in *You Light Up My Life*).

IF YOU COULD SEE WHAT I HEAR 1982
★★★★★ **PG Biography 1:43**
☑ Adult situations, explicit language
Dir: Eric Till *Cast:* Marc Singer, R. H. Thomson, Sarah Torgov, Shari Belafonte Harper
▶ True story traces the college years of the blind singer/TV personality Tom Sullivan (Singer) as he deals with the realities of his condition and has several affairs before settling down with Torgov. Focus is on the humorous aspects of Sullivan's situation rather than the usual teary-eyed manipulation. Sunny and uplifting.

IGOR AND THE LUNATICS 1985
☆ **R Horror 1:24**
☑ Nudity, explicit language
Dir: Billy Parolini *Cast:* Joseph Eero, Joe Niola, T. J. Michaels, Mary Ann Schacht
▶ In the 1960s, commune leaders enjoy sawing women in half. They are finally arrested and jailed. In the present, one of

the killers is released and he reassembles his old pals for more terror. Amateurish acting and production values.

ILLEGALLY YOURS 1988
★★ **PG Comedy 1:34**
☑ Adult situations, mild violence
Dir: Peter Bogdanovich *Cast:* Rob Lowe, Colleen Camp, Kenneth Mars, Kim Myers, L. B. Stratten
▶ When Camp, the object of Lowe's childhood crush nineteen years ago, goes on trial for attempted murder, Lowe lies about the relationship to get on the jury. Love develops as Lowe helps Camp prove her innocence. Breezy style recalls thirties screwball comedy; paper-thin plot overloads the shtick but the leads are pleasant. Stratten, Bogdanovich's current wife and sister of the late Dorothy Stratten, has a small role. **(CC)**

ILLUSTRATED MAN, THE 1969
★ **PG Sci-Fi 1:43**
☑ Adult situations, violence
Dir: Jack Smight *Cast:* Rod Steiger, Claire Bloom, Robert Drivas, Jason Evers, Don Dubbins, Tim Weldon
▶ In 1933 California, hobo Drivas encounters Steiger, who is covered with magical tattoos that come to life to illustrate three different stories: Steiger and Bloom—then real-life spouses—as parents of superpowered children, Steiger as astronaut caught in endless downpour, and Steiger and Bloom caught in nuclear conflict. Based on the book by Ray Bradbury.

I LOVE MY WIFE 1970
★★ **R Comedy 1:35**
☑ Nudity, adult situations, explicit language
Dir: Mel Stuart *Cast:* Elliott Gould, Brenda Vaccaro, Angel Tompkins, Dabney Coleman, Joan Tompkins, Leonard Stone
▶ When wife Vaccaro becomes pregnant, med student Gould seduces nurses and has affair with model Tompkins. Vaccaro learns of his infidelity and rebuffs him; he eventually sees the error of his ways, but will she take him back? Risqué Robert Kaufman screenplay provides little entertainment.

I LOVE YOU, ALICE B. TOKLAS 1968
★★ **R Comedy 1:33**
☑ Nudity, adult situations
Dir: Hy Averback *Cast:* Peter Sellers, Jo Van Fleet, Leigh Taylor-Young, David Arkin, Joyce Van Patten

▶ Successful L.A. lawyer Sellers jilts fiancée Van Patten in favor of young hippie Taylor-Young after munching marijuana brownies. He grows his hair long and moves into his car, but finds the hippie world just as constraining as the straight life. Freaked-out Sellers has never been more charming. Although obviously dated, script by Paul Mazursky and Larry Tucker remains surprisingly funny.

IMAGEMAKER, THE 1986
★ **R Drama 1:29**
☑ Nudity, adult situations, violence
Dir: Hal Weiner *Cast:* Michael Nouri, Jessica Harper, Anne Twomey, Jerry Orbach, Farley Granger
▶ Former Presidential media consultant Nouri attempts to expose corruption while the government tries to stop him. Nouri must also deal with his wife's suicide in this well-acted but only intermittently successful political thriller. Script is rather vague at critical points, so the movie is not always easy to follow.

IMAGINE: JOHN LENNON 1988
★★★ **R Documentary/Biography 1:43**
☑ Brief nudity, adult situations, explicit language
Dir: Andrew Solt *Cast:* John Lennon, Yoko Ono, Paul McCartney, Ringo Starr, George Harrison, Julian Lennon
▶ Interviews, rare live concert footage, and astounding home movies trace Lennon's rise to Beatle stardom, his eventful relationship with wife Ono, the break-up of the group, involvement in drugs and other controversies, solo career, and death. Like its subject, film is quirky, abrasive, moving, funny, and sometimes brilliant. Superbly remixed music soundtrack.

I'M ALL RIGHT, JACK 1959 British
★★★ **NR Comedy 1:48**
Dir: John Boulting, Roy Boulting *Cast:* Ian Carmichael, Peter Sellers, Terry-Thomas, Richard Attenborough, Dennis Price, Margaret Rutherford
▶ Naive youth Carmichael enters industry and upsets union leaders by improving plant efficiency. The union calls a strike that spreads and cripples Britain. Astute, biting satire features a remarkable cast of comics in peak form. Sellers's pompous shop steward is one of his best performances.

I MARRIED A MONSTER FROM OUTER SPACE 1958
★ **NR Sci-Fi 1:18 B&W**

Dir: Gene Fowler *Cast:* Tom Tryon, Gloria Talbott, Ken Lynch, John Eldredge, Jean Carson, Maxie Rosenbloom
▶ Newlywed Talbott begins to realize husband Tryon (the future best-selling author) is acting bizarre. You would too, if you were possessed by a horrifying alien! Terse and moody B-movie, far from the exploitation flick the title suggests.

I MARRIED A WITCH 1942
★★★★ **NR Fantasy/Comedy 1:16 B&W**
Dir: René Clair *Cast:* Fredric March, Veronica Lake, Robert Benchley, Susan Hayward, Cecil Kellaway, Robert Warwick
▶ Delightful fantasy about father/daughter witches Kellaway and Lake who wait four hundred years for revenge against their persecutors, the Wooley family. Modern-day Wooley (March) is a stuffy gubernatorial candidate; through devilish tricks, Lake breaks up his engagement to Hayward. First-rate comedy boasts sharp dialogue, funny special effects, and a twisty plot from Thorne Smith.

I'M DANCING AS FAST AS I CAN 1982
★★★ **R Drama 1:46**
☑ Adult situations, explicit language, violence
Dir: Jack Hofsiss *Cast:* Jill Clayburgh, Nicol Williamson, Dianne Wiest, Geraldine Page, Joe Pesci, Ellen Greene
▶ True story of TV producer Barbara Gordon (Clayburgh), who finds refuge from her stressful existence in Valium and then battles to overcome her addiction. Well-acted but very grim (until the uplifting ending) psychological drama pulls no punches in indicting medical profession and drug companies. Clayburgh, strongly supported by Page and Wiest, is in top form. Based on Gordon's best-selling book.

I'M GONNA GIT YOU SUCKA 1988
★★★ **R Comedy 1:27**
☑ Nudity, explicit language, violence
Dir: Keenan Ivory Wayans *Cast:* Keenan Ivory Wayans, Bernie Casey, Antonio Fargas, John Vernon, Isaac Hayes, Jim Brown
▶ After a ten-year Army stint, Wayans returns home to discover his brother has died of an overdose of gold neck chains and left behind a debt to Vernon, the "Mr. Big" of local crime syndicate. When

Vernon gets rough with Wayans's family and the police are no help, Wayans enlists the aid of Casey, Hayes, Brown, and Fargas, all over-the-hill former black heroes/role models. Wild and woolly spoof does to blaxploitation movies what *Airplane* did to the disaster genre.

IMITATION OF LIFE 1959
★★★★ NR Drama 2:04
Dir: Douglas Sirk *Cast:* Lana Turner, John Gavin, Sandra Dee, Dan O'Herlihy, Susan Kohner, Juanita Moore
▶ Actress Turner and black maid Moore are close to each other but not to their daughters; Turner ignores Dee to rise to the top while Kohner rejects Moore to pass for white. Tearjerker benefits from Sirk's sure hand and Turner's strong performance. Remake of 1934 Claudette Colbert vehicle is based on the Fannie Hurst novel.

IMPORTANCE OF BEING EARNEST, THE 1952 British
★★ NR Comedy 1:35
Dir: Anthony Asquith *Cast:* Michael Redgrave, Michael Denison, Edith Evans, Joan Greenwood, Dorothy Tutin, Margaret Rutherford
▶ Debonair London bachelor Redgrave uses the nom de plume "Ernest" to cover up his escapades while he's courting country beauty Gwendolen (Greenwood). His plans go awry when his friend Denison pretends to be Ernest to woo Redgrave's ward Cecily (Tutin). Spirited adaptation of Oscar Wilde's classic comedy of errors is played to the hilt by an extraordinary cast. Greenwood is especially alluring as the secretly daring Gwendolen.

IMPOSSIBLE SPY, THE 1987
★★★★ NR Espionage/MFTV 1:29
☑ Explicit language, violence
Dir: Jim Goddard *Cast:* John Shea, Eli Wallach, Michal Bat-Adam, Sasson Gabai, Rami Danon, Haim Girafi
▶ True story of the Israeli spy Elie Cohen (Shea) who infiltrates Syrian government, befriends Arab bigwig Gabai, and rises in the corridors of power. Shea risks his life to provide Israel with information that later leads to victory in the Six Day War. Gripping tale portrays the costs of espionage in very human terms.

IMPROPER CHANNELS 1981 Canadian
★★★★ PG Comedy 1:32
☑ Adult situations, explicit language, violence

Dir: Eric Till *Cast:* Alan Arkin, Mariette Hartley, Monica Parker, Harry Ditson, Sarah Stevens
▶ Parents Arkin and Hartley fight the bureaucracy to get their daughter back when overzealous social worker mistakenly institutionalizes her. Winning performances, appealing "little guys vs. the system" theme. Unevenly paced but generally satisfying.

IMPULSE 1984
★★ R Sci-Fi 1:31
☑ Nudity, adult situations, explicit language, graphic violence, adult humor
Dir: Graham Baker *Cast:* Tim Matheson, Meg Tilly, Hume Cronyn, John Karlen, Bill Paxton
▶ City girl Tilly and med student beau Matheson return to small town when her mom attempts suicide. They discover people are suddenly and violently acting out their impulses without any moral restraints. A toxic waste leak turns out to be the cause. Interesting concept, disappointing development.

IN COLD BLOOD 1968
★★★★ R Crime 2:14 B&W
☑ Adult situations, explicit language, violence
Dir: Richard Brooks *Cast:* Robert Blake, Scott Wilson, John Forsythe, Paul Stewart, Gerald S. O'Loughlin
▶ A true story of life at its harshest and most heartbreaking. Adaptation of Truman Capote's best-seller traces killers Blake and Wilson (both giving the performances of their lives) from the motiveless murder of a Midwest family to their capture and eventual execution. Chilling masterpiece exudes a constant sense of foreboding with a minimum of blood and gore and a maximum of intelligence and skill. Outstanding editing and black-and-white photography. Four Oscar nominations including Best Director.

INCREDIBLE JOURNEY, THE 1963
★★★ G Family 1:20
Dir: Fletcher Markle *Cast:* Emile Genest, John Drainie, Tommy Tweed, Sandra Scott, Syme Jago, Marion Finlayson
▶ When their owners leave for the summer, three pets—bull terrier Bodger, Siamese cat Lao, and Labrador retriever Luath—are sent to stay with a friend 250 miles away. The pets embark on an action-filled adventure across the Canadian wilderness to rejoin the family, en-

countering bears, lynx, and porcupines as well as some eccentric humans. Highly enjoyable Disney picture with beautiful scenery and amazing animal stunts.

INCREDIBLE SHRINKING MAN, THE
1957
★ ★ ★ ★ NR Sci-Fi 1:21 B&W
Dir: Jack Arnold *Cast:* Grant Williams, Randy Stuart, April Kent, Paul Langton, William Schallert
▶ After passing through radioactive cloud, Williams begins to shrink. Science is unable to reverse the process and Williams faces personal humiliation and life-and-death battles with house pets and spiders. Director Arnold skillfully creates a disturbing mood in this strikingly original sci-fi classic. From Richard Matheson's novel; also inspired Lily Tomlin's 1981 comedy *The Incredible Shrinking Woman.*

INCREDIBLE SHRINKING WOMAN, THE
1981
★ ★ ★ PG Comedy 1:28
☑ Explicit language, adult humor
Dir: Joel Schumacher *Cast:* Lily Tomlin, Charles Grodin, Ned Beatty, Henry Gibson, Elizabeth Wilson, Mark Blankfield
▶ Amusing reworking of *The Incredible Shrinking Man*: Tomlin, a typical suburban housewife, is bombarded with so many pollutants that she starts to shrink. Uneven as satire, but plenty of laughs. Special effects master Rick Baker does an impressive turn as a gorilla; Tomlin briefly reprises her Ernestine character.

IN CROWD, THE 1988
★ ★ ★ PG Drama 1:35
☑ Adult situations
Dir: Mark Rosenthal *Cast:* Donovan Leitch, Joe Pantoliano, Jennifer Runyon, Wendy Gazelle
▶ Wealthy teen Leitch (son of 1960s pop star Donovan) sacrifices girlfriend Gazelle and college goals to appear on a TV dance show, where he disrupts a troubled romance between hoodlum Pantoliano and Runyon, the show's dancing star. Modest teen romance set in 1960s Philadelphia has an outstanding oldies soundtrack and plenty of dance numbers. **(CC)**

INCUBUS, THE 1982 Canadian
★ ★ R Horror 1:32
☑ Rape, nudity, adult situations, explicit language, graphic violence
Dir: John Hough *Cast:* John Cassavetes, Kerrie Keane, Helen Hughes, Erin Flannery, Duncan McIntosh, John Ireland
▶ Rapist terrorizes small Wisconsin town, leading surgeon Cassavetes to suspect daughter's boyfriend McIntosh. With the help of beautiful reporter Keane, he sets a trap for the villain. Weak low-budget horror effort relies too much on violence and silly special effects.

INDEPENDENCE DAY 1983
★ ★ ★ ★ R Drama 1:50
☑ Brief nudity, adult situations, explicit language, violence
Dir: Robert Mandel *Cast:* Kathleen Quinlan, David Keith, Dianne Wiest, Frances Sternhagen, Cliff De Young
▶ Spunky small-town waitress Quinlan dreams of big-city photography career. Can she leave behind her lover, mechanic Keith? Both have problems: her mother Sternhagen is dying and his sister Wiest is being abused by husband De Young. Naturalistic atmosphere and forceful performances (notably Wiest's) in this pleasing soap opera drama.

INDIANA JONES AND THE TEMPLE OF DOOM 1984
★ ★ ★ ★ PG Action-Adventure 1:58
☑ Explicit language, violence
Dir: Steven Spielberg *Cast:* Harrison Ford, Kate Capshaw, Ke Huy Quan, Amrish Puri, Roshan Seth
▶ Adventurer Indiana Jones (Ford), sidekick Quan, and nightclub singer Capshaw (who opens the movie with a nifty Chinese version of "Anything Goes") flee Shanghai gang and land in India. There Indy helps villagers recover sacred stone from an evil cult. Breakneck-paced sequel to *Raiders of the Lost Ark* crams in enough amazing derring-do and outrageous stunts for ten movies. Lags a bit in the Temple of Doom sequence (and small kids may be upset when a cultist rips out a human heart from a victim's chest), but otherwise, Spielberg never gives you a chance to catch your breath. **(CC)**

INDISCREET 1958
★ ★ ★ NR Romance 1:40
Dir: Stanley Donen *Cast:* Cary Grant, Ingrid Bergman, Cecil Parker, Phyllis Calvert, Megs Jenkins, David Kossoff
▶ Single financier Grant, pretending to be married to keep from getting involved in a serious relationship, woos film star Bergman. She eventually discovers the truth. Generally stylish romance with Cary

and Ingrid generating class and charm, as always.

I NEVER PROMISED YOU A ROSE GARDEN 1977
★★★ R Drama 1:29
☑ Nudity, explicit language
Dir: Anthony Page *Cast:* Bibi Andersson, Kathleen Quinlan, Reni Santoni, Susan Tyrrell, Signe Hasso, Diane Varsi
► Teenager Quinlan is institutionalized by her parents. With the help of understanding therapist Andersson, she comes to grips with her private demons. Harrowing, realistic drama; strong performances by Quinlan and Andersson. Based on the Joanne Greenberg best-seller.

I NEVER SANG FOR MY FATHER 1970
★★★ PG Drama 1:30
☑ Adult situations
Dir: Gilbert Cates *Cast:* Melvyn Douglas, Gene Hackman, Dorothy Stickney, Estelle Parsons, Elizabeth Hubbard, Conrad Bain
► New Yorker Hackman plans to move to California with divorcée Hubbard but mom Stickney's death and cantankerous dad Douglas's opposition complicate the plan. Douglas-Hackman sparring is worth the price of admission; both were Oscar-nominated. Based on the Robert Anderson play.

INFORMER, THE 1935
★★★ NR Drama 1:31 B&W
Dir: John Ford *Cast:* Victor McLaglen, Heather Angel, Preston Foster, Margot Grahame, Wallace Ford, Una O'Connor
► Searing adaptation of Liam O'Flaherty's novel gave McLaglen the role of his life as Gypo Nolan, a hulking Dubliner who betrays his IRA friend to the British for twenty pounds. Stark, uncompromising classic builds to an unbearable climax. Won Oscars for McLaglen, director Ford, screenplay by Dudley Nichols, and Max Steiner's score. Remade in 1968 as *Up Tight,* with the setting changed from 1922 Ireland to black American ghetto.

INHERIT THE WIND 1960
★★★ NR Drama 2:07 B&W
Dir: Stanley Kramer *Cast:* Spencer Tracy, Fredric March, Gene Kelly, Florence Eldridge, Dick York
► Tennessee, 1925: teacher York is put on trial for advocating evolution. Clarence Darrow-like attorney Tracy defends him against William Jennings Bryan–like fundamentalist March while cynical H. L. Menckenish reporter Kelly looks on.

Movie version of the Lawrence and Lee Broadway play (inspired by the Scopes "Monkey" Trial) provides glib but entertaining courtroom theatrics and larger-than-life performances by Tracy and March.

INITIATION, THE 1984
★ R Horror 1:37
☑ Nudity, adult situations, explicit language, graphic violence
Dir: Larry Stewart *Cast:* Clu Gulager, Vera Miles, James Read, Daphne Zuniga, Marilyn Kagan
► Sorority initiation turns into a real-life Hell Night when a knife-wielding asylum escapee terrorizes nubile coeds. Formula slasher film with a surprise ending. Filmed on location in the Dallas–Fort Worth area.

IN-LAWS, THE 1979
★★★★ PG Comedy 1:43
☑ Explicit language, adult humor
Dir: Arthur Hiller *Cast:* Peter Falk, Alan Arkin, Richard Libertini, Nancy Dussault, Penny Peyser, Michael Lembeck
► Conservative dentist Arkin does a favor for his future in-law, CIA agent Falk, and winds up facing a firing squad in a South American dictatorship. Madcap farce is often side-splittingly funny, with Libertini a standout for his performance as a crazed tyrant. Charming leads were reteamed to lesser effect in 1985's *Big Trouble.*

IN NAME ONLY 1939
★★★ NR Drama 1:42 B&W
Dir: John Cromwell *Cast:* Carole Lombard, Cary Grant, Kay Francis, Charles Coburn, Helen Vinson, Peggy Ann Garner
► Francis marries Grant for his family's money. Grant sees through her act but his parents don't; they side with her when Cary finds real love with Carole. Emotion-packed tearjerker with a superb cast.

INNERSPACE 1987
★★★★ PG Fantasy/Comedy 2:00
☑ Explicit language
Dir: Joe Dante *Cast:* Dennis Quaid, Martin Short, Meg Ryan, Kevin McCarthy, Fiona Lewis, Vernon Wells
► Quaid, a guinea pig for a top-secret government miniaturization experiment, is accidentally injected into the body of nerdish grocery clerk Short. As spies pursue Short, Quaid's girlfriend Ryan helps him evade the bad guys. Steven Spielberg production has typically good special effects, inventive premise, and cheerful tone. Short is outstanding; his

SCTV pals Joe Flaherty and Andrea Martin have brief cameos. Won a Visual Effects Oscar. **(CC)**

INNOCENT, THE 1979 Italian
★ R Drama 1:41
☑ Nudity, adult situations
Dir: Luchino Visconti *Cast:* Giancarlo Giannini, Laura Antonelli, Jennifer O'Neill, Rina Morelli, Massimo Girotti
▶ In nineteenth-century Italy, wealthy nobleman Giannini ignores beautiful wife Antonelli to pursue mistress O'Neill, but regrets his actions when he learns Antonelli is having her own affair. Lush, beautifully photographed romance became an art house favorite for its highly charged eroticism. Visconti's last film. Ⓢ

INNOCENTS, THE 1962 British
★★★ NR Drama 1:39 B&W
Dir: Jack Clayton *Cast:* Deborah Kerr, Michael Redgrave, Peter Wyngarde, Pamela Franklin, Martin Stephens, Megs Jenkins
▶ In nineteenth-century England, repressed governess Kerr is hired to look after children Franklin and Stephens at a country estate. Kerr becomes convinced that the children are possessed by ghosts—or is she just imagining? Magnificent adaptation of Henry James's *The Turn of the Screw* weaves a supremely chilling spell. Superbly directed by Clayton.

INN OF THE SIXTH HAPPINESS, THE 1958
★★★★ NR Biography 2:41
Dir: Mark Robson *Cast:* Ingrid Bergman, Curt Jurgens, Robert Donat, Ronald Squire
▶ Biography of Gladys Alward (Bergman), an Englishwoman who opened a mission in China and won the love and respect of the locals. She falls for Eurasian colonel Jurgens and helps war orphans during World War II. Mandarin Donat converts to Christianity out of esteem for her. Bergman shines in this satisfying combination of religion, romance, and adventure. Donat is also superb in his last screen appearance.

IN OLD CHICAGO 1938
★★★ NR Drama 1:35 B&W
Dir: Henry King *Cast:* Tyrone Power, Alice Faye, Don Ameche, Alice Brady, Andy Devine, Brian Donlevy
▶ Lively Hollywood version of events leading up to famous 1871 fire that destroyed Chicago concentrates on washerwoman Brady (who won the Supporting Oscar) and her sons Power and Ameche. Power romances singer Faye while dominating city's corrupt underworld from his saloon; Ameche must battle him after winning election as reform mayor. Climactic fire features astounding special effects.

IN PRAISE OF OLDER WOMEN 1979 Canadian
★★ R Drama 1:48
☑ Nudity, strong sexual content, explicit language
Dir: George Kaczender *Cast:* Tom Berenger, Karen Black, Susan Strasberg, Alexandra Stewart, Helen Shaver
▶ Succession of various older women (Black, Strasberg, Stewart, and Shaver) initiate young Berenger into the pleasures of sex, love, and literature. Plenty of heavy breathing but the doltish dialogue and stilted (though explicit) love scenes are ultimately more embarrassing than erotic.

INQUIRY, THE 1987 Italian
★★ NR Drama 1:50
☑ Violence
Dir: Damiano Damiani *Cast:* Keith Carradine, Harvey Keitel, Phyllis Logan, Angelo Infanti, Lina Sastri, John Forgeham
▶ Roman authorities send officer Carradine to Palestine to investigate rumors that the body of Christ, crucified three years earlier, is missing. Carradine, unsatisfied with explanations by Pontius Pilate (Keitel), questions witnesses who knew Christ personally. Biblical epic's offbeat premise proves unexpectedly absorbing.

IN SEARCH OF A GOLDEN SKY 1984
★★★★ PG Family 1:35
☑ Mild violence
Dir: Jefferson Richard *Cast:* Charles Napier, George "Buck" Flower, Cliff Osmond, Anne Szesny, Shane Wallace
▶ Crusty old coot Flower, a hermit in the Pacific Northwest, is dismayed when two nephews and a niece arrive for an unexpected visit, but grows to appreciate their youthful spirits. Wholesome wilderness story features beautiful photography and scene-stealing fun from a raccoon and bear cub. **(CC)**

IN SEARCH OF THE CASTAWAYS 1962
★★★ G Fantasy/Family 1:40
Dir: Robert Stevenson *Cast:* Maurice Chevalier, Hayley Mills, George Sand-

ers, Wilfrid Hyde-White, Michael Anderson, Jr., Inia Te Wiata

▶ Young Mills enlists singing professor Chevalier to find her missing sea captain father. The search leads from South America to Australia, with Chevalier's expedition battling giant condors, earthquakes, volcanoes, and cannibals. Enjoyable Disney fantasy based on a Jules Verne story.

INSERTS 1976 British
☆ X Drama 1:39
☑ Nudity, strong sexual content, adult situations, explicit language, violence
Dir: John Byrum *Cast:* Richard Dreyfuss, Jessica Harper, Veronica Cartwright, Bob Hoskins, Stephen Davies
▶ In 1930s Hollywood, big-time director Dreyfuss has hit the professional and personal skids and now makes porno films. Dreyfuss becomes sexually involved with actress Harper while porn star Cartwright suffers drug overdose. Good cast tries vainly to breathe life into overwrought script.

INSIDE MOVES 1980
★★★★ PG Drama 1:53
☑ Adult situations, explicit language
Dir: Richard Donner *Cast:* John Savage, David Morse, Diana Scarwid, Harold Russell, Bert Remsen, Tony Burton
▶ Crippled after a suicide attempt, Savage finds solace with similarly handicapped patrons of a San Francisco bar. He falls in love with waitress Scarwid and befriends injured basketball star Morse. Donner, director of such heralded films as *Superman* and *The Omen*, did some of his best work with this sleeper; a movie full of warmth, humor, fine ensemble acting, and sharply observed, totally sympathetic characters.

INSIDE OUT 1987
☆ R Drama 1:27
☑ Adult situations, explicit language
Dir: Robert Taicher *Cast:* Elliott Gould, Howard Hesseman, Jennifer Tilly, Beah Richards, Nicole Norman, John Bleifer
▶ Gould gives a strong performance as a New York gambler trapped in his apartment by agoraphobia. Despite help from best friend Hesseman and call girl Tilly, his fear of open spaces leads to tragedy. Intriguing idea undermined by static presentation.

INSIGNIFICANCE 1985 British
★ R Drama 1:48

☑ Adult situations, explicit language, violence
Dir: Nicolas Roeg *Cast:* Michael Emil, Theresa Russell, Tony Curtis, Gary Busey, Will Sampson
▶ New York, 1953: political, emotional, intellectual, and sexual machinations between Albert Einsteinish scientist Emil, Marilyn Monroe-like film star Russell, her ballplayer husband Busey, and McCarthyish senator Curtis. Ambitious concept works as an intellectual exercise but script is somewhat obscure for general tastes. Affecting performances by Russell and Emil.

INSPECTOR GENERAL, THE 1949
★★★★ NR Comedy 1:42
Dir: Henry Koster *Cast:* Danny Kaye, Walter Slezak, Barbara Bates, Elsa Lanchester, Gene Lockhart, Alan Hale
▶ Clumsy Kaye benefits from case of mistaken identity in czarist Russia: locals think he is a bigwig and give him red carpet treatment. Adaptation of the Nikolai Gogol play provides effective vehicle for Kaye, whose wife, Sylvia Fine, wrote the lyrics for the musical numbers.

INSTANT JUSTICE 1986 British
★★ R Action-Adventure 1:41
☑ Brief nudity, explicit language, violence
Dir: Denis Amar *Cast:* Michael Paré, Tawny Kitaen, Peter Crook, Charles Napier, Linda Bridges
▶ Tough, two-fisted Marine Paré leaves the Corps to avenge death of his sister Bridges in Madrid. Kitaen plays a prostitute who reluctantly agrees to help Paré. Solid action helps camouflage flimsy plot.

INTERIORS 1978
★★ PG Drama 1:32
Dir: Woody Allen *Cast:* Diane Keaton, Geraldine Page, Maureen Stapleton, Mary Beth Hurt, E. G. Marshall, Sam Waterston
▶ Allen's first serious work as a writer-director (he does not appear) is populated by members of a desperately unhappy family. Keaton, a successful poet in analysis, and her sisters Hurt and Kristin Griffith deal with the divorce of their parents Page and Marshall and his subsequent remarriage to Stapleton. Memorable and heartbreaking, in the style of Ingmar Bergman. Warning: Woody Allen fans looking for laughs, look elsewhere.

INTERMEZZO 1939
★★★ NR Drama/Romance 1:10 B&W

Dir: Gregory Ratoff *Cast:* Leslie Howard, Ingrid Bergman, Edna Best, John Halliday, Cecil Kellaway, Enid Bennett
▶ American remake of Swedish film of same name has Bergman reprising her role as a bright-eyed piano teacher. Married, world-weary violinist Howard falls for Bergman; he abandons wife Best and kids for new love, but is haunted by familial responsibilities. In her first English-speaking role, Bergman electrified American audiences in this touching, tender romance. Memorable theme music by Heinz Provost became an enormously popular hit.

INTERNATIONAL HOUSE 1933
★★ NR Comedy 1:10 B&W
Dir: Edward Sutherland *Cast:* W. C. Fields, Peggy Hopkins Joyce, George Burns, Gracie Allen, Bela Lugosi, Cab Calloway
▶ Inventor displays his television device at a Chinese hotel, bringing all sorts of crazy types, like Soviet military man Lugosi, to bid for it. Cockeyed plot is terrific excuse for Fields to interact with great cast of vaudevillians and clowns.

INTERNATIONAL VELVET 1978 British
★★★★ PG Drama/Family 2:07
☑ Adult situations
Dir: Bryan Forbes *Cast:* Tatum O'Neal, Christopher Plummer, Anthony Hopkins, Nanette Newman
▶ Long-delayed sequel to the 1944 classic *National Velvet.* English Steeplechase winner Velvet Brown (Newman) is now forty and her American niece O'Neal is destined to follow in auntie's equestrienne footsteps. Plummer plays Newman's writer boyfriend; Hopkins is first-class as O'Neal's stern, no-nonsense trainer. Polished family entertainment.

INTERNS, THE 1962
★★ NR Drama 2:02 B&W
Dir: David Swift *Cast:* Michael Callan, Cliff Robertson, James MacArthur, Nick Adams, Suzy Parker, Haya Harareet
▶ Glossy soap opera about a year in the lives of four interns at a big-city hospital. Adams falls for a dying patient; Robertson struggles with his ethics when model Parker requests an abortion; Callan juggles affairs with a nurse and a socialite; MacArthur pursues a nurse who hates doctors. Predictable material notable for many future TV stars (Telly Savalas, Stefanie Powers, Buddy Ebsen). Led to a 1964 sequel, *The New Interns,* as well as a brief TV series.

IN THE GOOD OLD SUMMERTIME 1949
★★★★★ NR Musical 1:43
Dir: Robert Z. Leonard *Cast:* Judy Garland, Van Johnson, S. Z. Sakall, Spring Byington, Clinton Sundberg, Buster Keaton
▶ Charming musical remake of *The Shop Around the Corner* switches the setting of the 1940 film to turn-of-the-century Chicago. Garland and Johnson, impersonal co-workers in Sakall's music shop, are unaware they're secretly romantic pen pals. Tuneful score includes the title song and "I Don't Care."

IN THE HEAT OF THE NIGHT 1967
★★★★ NR Mystery-Suspense 1:49
Dir: Norman Jewison *Cast:* Sidney Poitier, Rod Steiger, Warren Oates, Lee Grant, William Schallert, Scott Wilson
▶ "They call me Mister Tibbs!" says Philadelphia detective Poitier, trying to command respect from redneck sheriff Steiger in a Mississippi town. Teaming to solve a murder, the two warily grow to respect one another. Magnificent mystery with a message features powerhouse performances from Steiger and Poitier. Oscars for Best Picture, Actor (Steiger), Editing, Sound, and Screenplay. Poitier reprised Tibbs in *They Call Me Mister Tibbs* and *The Organization.*

IN THE MOOD 1987
★★★★ PG-13 Biography 1:38
☑ Brief nudity, adult situations, explicit language
Dir: Phil Alden Robinson *Cast:* Patrick Dempsey, Beverly D'Angelo, Talia Balsam, Michael Constantine, Betty Jinett
▶ True story of Sonny Wisecarver (Dempsey), a.k.a. "The Woo Woo Kid," a teenager who caused a sensation in 1944 by running off with a married mother of two, played by Balsam. After that relationship is annulled, he finds romance and more legal trouble with D'Angelo, another older woman. Consistently buoyant romantic comedy with classy period details and likable performances. A neglected treat. **(CC)**

IN THE REALM OF THE SENSES 1976
Japanese/French
☆ NR Drama 1:55
☑ Nudity, strong sexual content, adult situations, explicit language, violence

Dir: Nagisa Oshima *Cast:* Tatsuya Fuji, Eiko Matsuda, Aio Nakajima, Meika Seri
▶ In 1930s Japan, geisha Matsuda develops an irrational obsession with married man Fuji that leads to murder. Based on a real incident, this stylish but gloomy drama consists almost entirely of sexual couplings filmed in graphic detail. Gained some notoriety when it was seized by United States Customs officials. ⑤

INTIMATE CONTACT 1987 British
★★★★ NR Drama/MFTV 2:39
☑ Adult situations, explicit language
Dir: Waris Hussein *Cast:* Claire Bloom, Daniel Massey, Sylvia Sims, Abigail Cruttenden, Mark Kingston, Lizzy McInnerny
▶ Affluent Englishman Massey contracts AIDS from a prostitute. Wife Bloom supports him through the fatal ordeal, befriends other victims of the disease, faces ostracism from neighbors, and becomes crusader against ignorance and prejudice. Sensitive and realistic portrayal of controversial medical issue; Bloom is outstanding.

INTO THE HOMELAND 1987
★★★ NR Drama/MFTV 1:55
☑ Violence
Dir: Lesli Linka Glatter *Cast:* Powers Boothe, C. Thomas Howell, Paul LeMat, Cindy Pickett, David Caruso, Arye Gross
▶ Ex-cop Boothe infiltrates white supremacist group to find his runaway teenage daughter. Boothe abducts her boyfriend Howell, the son of group leader LeMat, and attempts to deprogram him. Riveting drama with unsettling contemporary political overtones. Script by Anna Hamilton Phelan, who also wrote *Mask.*

INTO THE NIGHT 1985
★★★★ R Mystery-Suspense 1:55
☑ Nudity, adult situations, explicit language, graphic violence
Dir: John Landis *Cast:* Jeff Goldblum, Michelle Pfeiffer, David Bowie, Richard Farnsworth, Vera Miles, Dan Aykroyd
▶ Insomniac Goldblum finds something to do with his restless nights when he accidentally gets involved with the beautiful Pfeiffer, who is battling Arabs for possession of some stolen emeralds. Uneven but stylish mixture of comedy, romance, and intrigue. Occasionally marred by excessive violence, but flick is often fun and exciting. Cameo appearances from many Hollywood directors including Lawrence Kasdan, David Cronenburg, and Jonathan Demme. **(CC)**

INVADERS FROM MARS 1953
★★ NR Sci-Fi 1:20
Dir: William Cameron Menzies *Cast:* Jimmy Hunt, Helena Carter, Arthur Franz, Morris Ankrum, Leif Erickson
▶ Young Hunt is the only witness when aliens invade a small town. He tries in vain to convince the authorities of what he's seen. B-movie sci-fi enlivened by striking visuals from director Menzies, best remembered as the *Gone With the Wind* production designer. Remade in 1986. **(CC)**

INVADERS FROM MARS 1986
★★ PG Sci-Fi 1:33
☑ Explicit language, violence
Dir: Tobe Hooper *Cast:* Karen Black, Hunter Carson, Timothy Bottoms, Laraine Newman, James Karen, Louise Fletcher
▶ Carson witnesses spaceship land outside his bedroom window but no one in town believes the boy's tale of aliens, perhaps because they're being possessed by the invaders. Hooper creates some crackerjack tension in the movie's first half, sort of a child's-eye paranoid thriller. Second half, with silly-looking monsters and military response to the threat, bogs down. Remake of the 1953 B-movie. **(CC)**

INVASION OF THE BEE GIRLS 1974
★ R Sci-Fi 1:25
☑ Nudity, explicit language, violence
Dir: Denis Sanders *Cast:* Victoria Vetri, William Smith, Anitra Ford, Cliff Osmond, Wright King
▶ Nude mutant women come on to guys, buzzing sounds begin, and then each man instantly dies. Motif is repeated over and over. Awful music, cheapo production values; for fans of gratuitous nudity only.

INVASION OF THE BODY SNATCHERS 1956
★★★★ NR Sci-Fi 1:20 B&W
Dir: Don Siegel *Cast:* Kevin McCarthy, Dana Wynter, Carolyn Jones, King Donovan, Larry Gates, Sam Peckinpah
▶ Small-town doctor McCarthy and girlfriend Wynter try to hold on to their humanity and their lives when friends and neighbors are turned into emotionless "pod people" by alien force. Siegel's low-key, evocative direction creates classic moments of terror: the greenhouse

confrontation, McCarthy yelling "You're next!" as passing drivers ignore him. Based on the Jack Finney novel.

INVASION OF THE BODY SNATCHERS
1978
★★★ PG Sci-Fi 1:56
☑ Brief nudity, explicit language, violence
Dir: Philip Kaufman *Cast:* Donald Sutherland, Brooke Adams, Leonard Nimoy, Jeff Goldblum, Veronica Cartwright, Art Hindle
▶ Jazzy remake of the 1956 classic effectively takes terror out of 1950s small town and into modern-day San Francisco, where city health official Sutherland and colleague Adams find epidemic of soulless alien automatons in their midst. Celebrity shrink Nimoy also gets involved. Literate screenplay and glittery cinematography create credibly creepy atmosphere.

INVASION OF THE FLESH HUNTERS
1982 Italian/Spanish
☆ NR Horror 1:31
☑ Nudity, adult situations, explicit language, graphic violence
Dir: Anthony M. Dawson (Antonio Margheriti) *Cast:* John Saxon, Elizabeth Turner, John Morghen, Cindy Hamilton, Tony King
▶ More gross than engrossing tale of ex-Vietnam G.I.s infected with a strange virus that turns them into cannibals who devour innocent Atlantans. Veteran actor Saxon plays the commanding officer trying to resist the disease, despite being infected. Blood and gore galore.

INVASION U.S.A. 1985
★★★ R Action-Adventure 1:48
☑ Brief nudity, adult situations, explicit language, graphic violence
Dir: Joseph Zito *Cast:* Chuck Norris, Richard Lynch, Melissa Prophet, Alexander Zale, Alex Colon
▶ Villainous Soviet agent Lynch and cohorts shamelessly seek to destroy the American way of life by blowing up shopping malls at Christmastime and shooting innocent suburbanites at home. One-man National Guard Norris is called in to kill the Russian terrorists and save democracy. Overwrought and extremely violent melodrama.

INVISIBLE KID, THE 1988
★★★ PG Fantasy/Comedy 1:36
☑ Nudity, explicit language
Dir: Avery Crouse *Cast:* Karen Black,

Jay Underwood, Wally Ward, Chynna Phillips, Brother Theodore
▶ High school nerd Underwood invents a green slime that renders swallower invisible for half an hour, just enough time to peek in the cheerleaders' locker room with wimpy pal Ward or help win the big basketball game. Black, sporting countless curlers and a huge bathrobe, plays Grover's ditsy mom. Lightweight screwball comedy for kids.

INVISIBLE MAN, THE 1933
★★★ NR Horror 1:11 B&W
Dir: James Whale *Cast:* Claude Rains, Gloria Stuart, William Harrigan, Henry Travers, Una O'Connor, E. E. Clive
▶ Scientist Rains invents process to render himself invisible. Unfortunately, his mind is affected and he becomes a raving megalomaniac. Amazing special effects (even by today's standards), wonderfully atmospheric direction by Whale, incredible vocal performance by the unseen Rains ("Power to rule, power to make the world grovel at my feet," he says in that magnificent voice). A classic, from the H. G. Wells novel.

INVITATION TO A WEDDING 1982
British
★★ PG Comedy 1:38
☑ Adult situations, explicit language
Dir: Joseph Brooks *Cast:* Ralph Richardson, John Gielgud, Susan Brooks, Paul Nicholson
▶ Implausible, nonsensical tale of young Nicholson who fills in for a busy groom at his wedding rehearsal and is accidentally betrothed to bride-to-be Brooks. Richardson is the befuddled English minister who marries them. In an extremely unlikely role, Gielgud is a born-again Texan evangelist.

INVITATION TO THE DANCE 1956
★ NR Dance 1:32
Dir: Gene Kelly *Cast:* Gene Kelly, Igor Youskevitch, Claire Sombert, David Kasday, David Paltenghi, Daphne Dale
▶ Three-part film told entirely in dance and mime. In "Circus," Kelly plays a lovestruck clown trying to win Sombert from trapeze artist Youskevitch; "Ring Around the Rosy" reworks the circular love affairs of *La Ronde*; "Sinbad the Sailor" is a fun version of the genie-in-a-lamp classic set in a magical animated world. Ambitious attempt to popularize dance features music by Jacques Ibert, André Previn, and Roger Edens.

IN WHICH WE SERVE 1942 British
★★★ NR War 1:55 B&W
Dir: Noel Coward, David Lean *Cast:*
Noel Coward, John Mills, Bernard Miles,
Celia Johnson, Kay Walsh, Michael
Wilding
▶ Tribute to the crew of the British destroyer *Torrin* and their battles in Dunkirk
and Crete during World War II is a landmark war film for its subtle direction, incisive script, and understated heroics.
Debuts for Johnson, Richard Attenborough, and co-director Lean. Coward,
who produced, co-directed, wrote
(based on Lord Mountbatten's wartime
exploits), and starred, received a special
Oscar for "outstanding production
achievement."

I OUGHT TO BE IN PICTURES 1982
★★★★ PG Comedy 1:47
☑ Brief nudity, adult situations, explicit
language
Dir: Herbert Ross *Cast:* Walter Matthau, Ann-Margret, Dinah Manoff,
Lance Guest, Lewis Smith
▶ New Yorker Manoff arrives in Hollywood
to look up long-lost father Matthau, a bitter screenwriter who spends more time at
the racetrack than at the typewriter. Father and daughter, with dad's sympathetic girlfriend Ann-Margret mediating,
eventually resolve their problems. Solid
acting in a funny Neil Simon script.

IPCRESS FILE, THE 1965 British
★★★★ NR Espionage 1:47
Dir: Sidney J. Furie *Cast:* Michael
Caine, Nigel Green, Sue Lloyd, Guy
Doleman, Gordon Jackson
▶ British agent Harry Palmer (Caine) in-
vestigates kidnappings of top scientists;
the trail leads to a traitor in his own orga-
nization. Twisty and intelligent; Caine
gives a marvelously low-key and subtle
performance. First and best of the Harry
Palmer series adapted from the Len
Deighton novel. Spawned sequels *Fu-
neral in Berlin* and *Billion Dollar Brain*.

I REMEMBER MAMA 1948
★★★★★ NR Drama 2:14 B&W
Dir: George Stevens *Cast:* Irene
Dunne, Barbara Bel Geddes, Oscar Ho-
molka, Philip Dorn, Edgar Bergen, Ellen
Corby
▶ Norwegian family emigrates to San
Francisco, where they cheerfully struggle
to make ends meet as loving mama
Dunne pulls them through ups and
downs. Shy aunt Corby and blustering

uncle Homolka are among those who inspire eldest daughter Bel Geddes to
write about her family. Old-fashioned
heartwarmer with humor and genuine
emotion. Oscar nominations to Dunne,
Corby, Bel Geddes, Homolka. Based on
the play by John Van Druten and the
book *Mama's Bank Account* by Kathryn
Forbes.

IRMA LA DOUCE 1963
★★ NR Comedy 2:26
Dir: Billy Wilder *Cast:* Shirley MacLaine,
Jack Lemmon, Lou Jacobi, Herschel
Bernardi, Joan Shawlee, Hope Holiday
▶ Adaptation of Broadway play concerns overzealous, bumbling Parisian
cop Lemmon who raids Jacobi's bistro to
rid it of prostitutes and winds up arresting
his boss Bernardi. Sacked from the force,
Lemmon works as streetwalker Mac-
Laine's procurer but, smitten by love,
grows jealous of her work. To keep her
away from other men, he poses as elderly
English customer, but ruse backfires. Amiable comedy won Oscar for André Previn
score.

IRON EAGLE 1986
★★★★ PG-13 Action-Adventure 1:57
☑ Explicit language, violence
Dir: Sidney J. Furie *Cast:* Louis Gossett,
Jr., Jason Gedrick, David Suchet, Tim
Thomerson
▶ Macho movie about young Gedrick's
attempt to rescue his pilot father Thomer-
son, shot down in a small Arab country.
Aided by combat veteran Gossett, he
breaks into the top secret Air Force com-
puter, steals two jets, drops a few bombs,
and fights it out with rival MIGs. Turns into
battle between teen Rambo and entire
Middle East country. Striking aerial photography. **(CC)**

IRON EAGLE II 1988
★★★★ PG Action-Adventure 1:40
☑ Explicit language, violence
Dir: Sidney J. Furie *Cast:* Louis Gossett,
Jr., Mark Humphrey, Stuart Margolin,
Alan Scarfe, Sharon H. Brandon, Maury
Chaykin
▶ Sequel to popular aviation adventure
finds Gossett, now a general, recruiting
multinational team of pilots to destroy
Third World nuclear weapons plant. Hot-
dog flier Humphrey, bitterly anti-Soviet,
finds himself falling for beautiful Russian
aviatrix Brandon during grueling training
sessions. Inventive dogfights provide
plenty of excitement.

IRON TRIANGLE, THE 1989
★★ R War 1:31
☑ Adult situations, explicit language, violence
Dir: Eric Weston *Cast:* Beau Bridges, Haing S. Ngor, Johnny Hallyday, Liem Whatley, James Ishida
▶ During the Vietnam War, American Army captain Bridges is captured by Vietcong guerrilla Whatley and Communist disciple Ishida, who hates Whatley and Bridges with equal vehemence. On the trip north, Whatley flees with Bridges to spare him from Ishida; the pragmatic American and idealistic North Vietnamese learn to respect each other. Portrayal of war from the Vietcong perspective is more intriguing for its premise than for the result.

IRON WARRIOR 1987 Italian
☆ PG-13 Action-Adventure 1:22
☑ Nudity, violence
Dir: Al Bradley *Cast:* Miles O'Keeffe, Savina Gersak, Iris Peynado, Elisabeth Kaza, Tim Lane
▶ Evil goddess steals one of two twins raised by good goddess and, eighteen years later, the two do battle. Sample dialogue: "And what if they kill you?" "Then I'll be dead." Senseless plot, lackluster swordplay, and mix-and-match mythology with K Mart special effects. **(CC)**

IRONWEED 1987
★★ R Drama 2:23
☑ Nudity, explicit language, violence
Dir: Hector Babenco *Cast:* Jack Nicholson, Meryl Streep, Carroll Baker, Tom Waits, Fred Gwynne, Michael O'Keefe
▶ Prestigious but grim tale of late 1930s bag people. Homeless bum Nicholson, haunted by the death of his infant son, hangs out with fellow boozer Streep, visits ex-wife Baker, and returns to hobo camp which is burned out by Albany townspeople. Relentlessly downbeat despite impressive performances by Oscar-nominated leads. Based on the Pulitzer prize–winning novel by William Kennedy (who also wrote the screenplay).

IRRECONCILABLE DIFFERENCES 1984
★★★★ PG Comedy 1:53
☑ Adult situations
Dir: Charles Shyer *Cast:* Drew Barrymore, Ryan O'Neal, Shelley Long, Sharon Stone, Sam Wanamaker
▶ West-coast version of *Kramer vs. Kramer* with a hip twist. Coy nine-year-old Barrymore hires lawyer Wanamaker and sues to divorce bickering parents Long and O'Neal. Flashbacks recall the couple's relationship. Set in the world of Hollywood writers and directors with many in-jokes. **(CC)**

ISADORA 1969 British
★★ PG Biography/Dance 2:11
☑ Adult situations, explicit language
Dir: Karel Reisz *Cast:* Vanessa Redgrave, James Fox, Jason Robards, Ivan Tchenko, John Fraser, Bessie Love
▶ True story of the controversial and free-spirited dancer Isadora Duncan (Redgrave) traces her involvements with artist Fox, tycoon Robards, and poet Tchenko, her innovations in modern dance, the deaths of her children, and her own tragic demise. Ambitious but overly precious direction by Reisz frames interesting performance by Redgrave. Also known as *The Loves of Isadora.*

I SAILED TO TAHITI WITH AN ALL-GIRL CREW 1968
☆ NR Comedy 1:35
Dir: Richard Bare *Cast:* Gardner McKay, Fred Clark, Pat Buttram, Diane McBaine, Richard Denning, Edy Williams
▶ Unscrupulous Clark and his scheming crew beat McKay and his gorgeous sailors to Tahiti by cheating; McKay turns the tables by challenging Clark to race his "baboons" (actually Polynesian sailors) home. Hard to live up to that title, and the film doesn't.

I SEE A DARK STRANGER 1947 British
★★ NR Mystery-Suspense 1:52 B&W
Dir: Frank Launder *Cast:* Deborah Kerr, Trevor Howard, Raymond Huntley, Michael Howard, Norman Shelley
▶ Kerr, a young Irish girl, hates the English and unwittingly becomes a pawn of a Nazi agent until English officer Howard helps her. Perky, spirited performance by beautiful Kerr highlights fine suspense drama with touches of witty comedy. Also known as *The Adventuress.*

I SENT A LETTER TO MY LOVE 1981 French
★ PG Drama 1:42
☑ Adult situations
Dir: Moshe Mizrahi *Cast:* Simone Signoret, Jean Rochefort, Delphine Seyrig
▶ Middle-aged Signoret cares for invalid brother Rochefort. When he places a personal ad, she inadvertently answers and, unable to reveal the coincidence, con-

tinues the correspondence. Good premise, but tepid drama is slowly paced. Some touching moments; Seyrig is delightful as the neighbor who eventually wins Rochefort's heart. ⑤

ISHTAR 1987
★ PG-13 Comedy 1:47
☑ Brief nudity, explicit language
Dir: Elaine May *Cast:* Warren Beatty, Dustin Hoffman, Isabelle Adjani, Charles Grodin, Tess Harper, Jack Weston
▶ Forty-million-dollar rocky road caper about dunderheaded songwriters Beatty and Hoffman booked by agent Weston into a club in strife-torn North Africa. Once there, they become patsies for gorgeous terrorist Adjani and manipulative CIA agent Grodin. After several misadventures with a blind camel and a flock of hungry vultures, they survive to record a live album. Awful songs are constantly repeated, killing all the humor. The cast tries hard, but the reverse casting backfires. Overall, a far from entertaining box-office bust and artistic embarrassment for writer/director Elaine May. **(CC)**

ISLAND, THE 1980
★★ R Mystery-Suspense 1:54
☑ Nudity, adult situations, explicit language, graphic violence
Dir: Michael Ritchie *Cast:* Michael Caine, David Warner, Angela Punch-McGregor, Don Henderson, Jeffrey Frank
▶ New York journalist Caine travels to Bermuda Triangle island to investigate reports of bizarre disappearances. He unwisely brings along his twelve-year-old son Frank. They are soon abducted by a incest-ridden gang of toothless pirates led by Warner. Excessive blood and gore, sloppy photography, stilted action scenes, and waterlogged plot from Peter Benchley.

ISLAND OF DR. MOREAU, THE 1977
★★ PG Horror 1:38
☑ Brief nudity
Dir: Don Taylor *Cast:* Burt Lancaster, Michael York, Barbara Carrera, Nigel Davenport, Richard Basehart
▶ Classic 1896 H. G. Wells story about mad scientist Lancaster working on his wild-beast-into-man serum. Shipwrecked sailor York falls for the doc's beautiful adopted daughter Carrera and discovers his evil experiments. Not as good as the 1933 original *Island of Lost Souls* but does boast fine performances from an admirable cast and appropriately lush jungle background.

ISLAND OF THE BLUE DOLPHINS 1964
★ NR Family 1:33
Dir: James B. Clark *Cast:* Celia Kaye, Larry Domasin, Ann Daniel, George Kennedy, Carlos Romero, Hal Jon Norman
▶ In the early 1800s, Kaye, a young Aleutian girl, is marooned on a remote Alaskan island. For twenty years she survives on perseverance and luck, until she is finally rescued by hunters. Offbeat adventure, adapted from Scott O'Dell's popular children's novel, was based on a true incident.

ISLANDS IN THE STREAM 1977
★★★★ PG Drama 1:44
☑ Explicit language
Dir: Franklin J. Schaffner *Cast:* George C. Scott, David Hemmings, Claire Bloom, Susan Tyrrell, Gilbert Roland
▶ On the eve of World War II, famous sculptor Scott enjoys a solitary existence in the West Indies. Visits by his three sons and one of his ex-wives cause him to reexamine his life. Adaptation of Ernest Hemingway's unfinished last novel is heartfelt and emotion-packed. Classy cinematography (Oscar-nominated) and a great Scott.

ISLE OF THE DEAD 1945
★★ NR Horror 1:12 B&W
Dir: Mark Robson *Cast:* Boris Karloff, Ellen Drew, Marc Cramer, Katherine Emery, Helen Thimig, Jason Robards, Sr.
▶ In 1912, Greek general Karloff uncovers evidence of grave-robbing on a remote Balkan island. He pursues the culprits despite rumors of vampires and an outbreak of the plague. Highly unusual horror film has a gripping, unsettling tone and an eerie performance by Drew, one of the suspected vampires.

IT CAME FROM BENEATH THE SEA 1955
★★ NR Sci-Fi 1:20 B&W
Dir: Robert Gordon *Cast:* Faith Domergue, Kenneth Tobey, Ian Keith, Donald Curtis, Dean Maddox, Jr.
▶ San Francisco is the target of an enraged giant octopus. Navy sub commander Tobey tries to thwart the beast, who creates Bay City havoc before being nuked. Sci-fi thriller most notable for Ray Harryhausen's special effects.

IT CAME FROM HOLLYWOOD 1982
★ **PG Comedy 1:20 C/B&W**
☑ Explicit language, adult humor
Dir: Malcolm Leo, Andrew Solt *Cast:* Dan Aykroyd, John Candy, Cheech Marin, Thomas Chong, Gilda Radner
▶ Casserole of clips from Hollywood's most laughably bad movies, including the forgettable *I Married a Monster From Outer Space*, *Glen or Glenda*, and *Attack of the 50-Foot Woman*. Hosted by popular comedians Aykroyd, Radner, and others. Awful, campy fun is perfect for midnight movie fans.

IT CAME FROM OUTER SPACE 1953
★★ **NR Sci-Fi 1:20 B&W**
Dir: Jack Arnold *Cast:* Richard Carlson, Barbara Rush, Russell Johnson, Kathleen Hughes, Charles Drake
▶ In an Arizona desert town, astronomer Carlson witnesses spaceship landing and then finds townspeople's personalities suddenly changed. Ultimately benign view of aliens rare for the paranoid fifties. Eerie and intelligent chiller, nicely directed by Arnold. Originally filmed in 3-D and based on a Ray Bradbury story.

IT HAPPENED AT THE WORLD'S FAIR 1963
★★★ **NR Musical 1:45**
Dir: Norman Taurog *Cast:* Elvis Presley, Joan O'Brien, Gary Lockwood, Vicky Tiu, H. M. Wynant
▶ Presley plays a daredevil pilot who romances nurse O'Brien at the 1962 Seattle World's Fair. Charming subplot involves young Tiu's efforts to stay out of an orphanage. Ten Elvis tunes, including "One Broken Heart for Sale," "Cotton Candy Land," and "I'm Falling in Love Tonight." Look for young Kurt Russell in this, his first film. He was later to play the King in the telemovie *Elvis*.

IT HAPPENED ONE NIGHT 1934
★★★★ **NR Comedy 1:45 B&W**
Dir: Frank Capra *Cast:* Clark Gable, Claudette Colbert, Walter Connolly, Roscoe Karns, Alan Hale
▶ Pampered heiress Colbert runs away from dad Connolly and travels incognito. Hard-edged reporter Gable pretends he doesn't recognize her to get the big scoop. They hit the road together and antagonism gives way to love. Terrific romantic comedy with many classic scenes: Colbert and Gable arguing over hitchhiking methods, Gable putting up "Walls of Jericho" when they share a hotel room, sing-along on a bus. Oscar sweep: Picture, Director, Actor, Actress, Screenplay (only film besides *One Flew Over the Cuckoo's Nest* to accomplish this feat). **(CC)**

IT HAPPENED TOMORROW 1944
★★★ **NR Fantasy 1:24 B&W**
Dir: René Clair *Cast:* Dick Powell, Linda Darnell, Jack Oakie, Edgar Kennedy, Edward Brophy
▶ Reporter Powell finds himself in possession of tomorrow's newspaper. Its stories come true, and Powell exploits the situation for his own gain; however, he then sees article about his own impending demise. Imaginative premise and lighthearted charm are hard to resist; endearing performances by Powell, Darnell, and Oakie.

I, THE JURY 1982
★★★ **R Action-Adventure 1:51**
☑ Nudity, strong sexual content, adult situations, explicit language, violence
Dir: Richard T. Heffron *Cast:* Armand Assante, Barbara Carrera, Alan King, Laurene Landon, Geoffrey Lewis, Paul Sorvino
▶ Tough private eye Mike Hammer (Assante) investigates the murder of his Vietnam buddy and gets involved with sex therapist Carrera, whose clinic may be connected to the case. The pace is fast, the violence frequent, the atmosphere seedy, and the women numerous and often unclad in this flavorful adaptation of Mickey Spillane's pulp classic.

IT LIVES AGAIN 1978
★ **R Horror 1:31**
☑ Adult situations, explicit language, graphic violence
Dir: Larry Cohen *Cast:* Frederic Forrest, Kathleen Lloyd, John P. Ryan, John Marley, Eddie Constantine
▶ Lurid sequel to *It's Alive* with Ryan reprising his earlier role as the distressed father of a homicidal infant. He warns parents Forrest and Lloyd that their child may also be a monster, while police conduct a manhunt for two other killer babies. Good special effects by Rick Baker and lush Bernard Herrmann score helped make this a cult favorite among horror fans.

IT'S A GIFT 1934
★★★ **NR Comedy 1:13 B&W**
Dir: Norman Z. McLeod *Cast:* W. C. Fields, Jean Rouverol, Julian Madison,

Kathleen Howard, Tom Bupp, Baby LeRoy
▶ Henpecked grocer Harold Bissonette (Fields) drags his protesting family cross-country to a ramshackle orange grove. Unforgettable comedy may be the best, and bitterest, of Fields's work. Contains one classic scene after another: Baby LeRoy's encounter with molasses, Fields's herculean efforts to get to sleep, insufferable salesman T. Roy Barnes looking for Carl LaFong, etc. Highly recommended to Fields's fans.

IT'S ALIVE 1974
★ PG Horror 1:30
☑ Adult situations, graphic violence
Dir: Larry Cohen *Cast:* John P. Ryan, Sharon Farrell, Andrew Duggan, Guy Stockwell, James Dixon
▶ Infant mutant bounds out of the womb to bite and claw people to shreds. Escaping the hospital, it crawls around L.A., killing innocents and assaulting milk trucks. Ryan and Farrell play the horrified parents. Led to two sequels.

IT'S ALIVE III: ISLAND OF THE ALIVE 1987
★ R Horror 1:30
☑ Adult situations, explicit language, graphic violence
Dir: Larry Cohen *Cast:* Michael Moriarty, Karen Black, Laurene Landon, Gerrit Graham, James Dixon
▶ Third go-round (after *It Lives Again*) for the killer babies, now quarantined on a desert island. Moriarty, father of one of the mutants, accompanies an expedition to the island to save them from extermination. After considerable carnage (much of it tongue-in-cheek), the tots escape and kidnap Black, their mom. Clever exploitation scores some effective satirical points.

IT'S ALWAYS FAIR WEATHER 1955
★★★ NR Musical 1:42
Dir: Stanley Donen, Gene Kelly *Cast:* Gene Kelly, Cyd Charisse, Dan Dailey, Dolores Gray, Michael Kidd
▶ World War II buddies Kelly, Dailey, and Kidd vow to meet in ten years. Their reunion proves to be bittersweet as youthful hopes and dreams have fallen by the wayside. Wide-screen production may lose something on video but first-rate musical scenes such as the trash-can dance and a roller skating number highlight third Donen/Kelly collaboration (after *On the Town* and *Singing in the Rain*).

IT'S A MAD, MAD, MAD, MAD WORLD 1963
★★★ G Comedy 3:12
Dir: Stanley Kramer *Cast:* Spencer Tracy, Edie Adams, Milton Berle, Sid Caesar, Ethel Merman, Jonathan Winters
▶ Three hours of wackiness with huge all-star cast. Story has comedians racing wildly to find a hidden cache of stolen money, under the watchful eye of sober sheriff Tracy. Big and splashy, lots of fun. Cameos by Buddy Hackett, Mickey Rooney, Dick Shawn, Phil Silvers, Peter Falk, The Three Stooges, Buster Keaton, Jimmy Durante, Jim Backus, Don Knotts, and many more.

IT'S A WONDERFUL LIFE 1946
★★★★★ NR Drama 2:09 B&W
Dir: Frank Capra *Cast:* James Stewart, Donna Reed, Lionel Barrymore, Thomas Mitchell, Henry Travers, Gloria Grahame
▶ Small-towner George Bailey (Stewart) finds his dreams thwarted by rich and greedy Barrymore. He's driven to the point of suicide until angel Travers shows him what life would be like if he'd never been born. Christmas classic grows more popular every year, and deservedly so; combines whimsical humor, romance, and fantasy with realistic despair. Towering performance by Stewart; Reed is touching as his sweet wife; Travers a delight as the bumbling angel. Wonderful movie with life-affirming ending. Available in a colorized version.

IT SHOULD HAPPEN TO YOU 1954
★★★ NR Comedy 1:27 B&W
Dir: George Cukor *Cast:* Judy Holliday, Jack Lemmon, Peter Lawford, Michael O'Shea
▶ Kooky New Yorker Holliday wants to feel special and important, so she purchases billboard space to advertise her name in huge letters. Soap company executive Lawford makes a deal with her to get the prime space; in return he buys her several other billboards. Boyfriend Lemmon is nonplussed by her sudden notoriety. Vibrant performance by Holliday in this breezy comedy. Lemmon's film debut.

IT'S MY TURN 1980
★★★ R Romance/Comedy 1:31
☑ Adult situations, explicit language
Dir: Claudia Weill *Cast:* Jill Clayburgh, Michael Douglas, Charles Grodin, Teresa Baxter

▶ Smart but spacey mathematician Clayburgh lives in Chicago with aloof architect Grodin, but falls for her stepmother's brash, bearded ex–baseball player son Douglas in New York. A warm, witty look at romance. Title song by Diana Ross.

IT TAKES TWO 1988
★★★ PG-13 Comedy 1:21
☑ Adult situations, explicit language
Dir: David Beaird *Cast:* George Newbern, Leslie Hope, Kimberly Foster, Barry Corbin, Anthony Geary, Bill Bolender
▶ Jittery Texas groom-to-be Newbern buys sports car in Dallas for a last fling before his wedding, but the adventure turns into a comic nightmare that changes his life forever. Amiable plot has engaging offbeat style and appealing performances by Newbern and fiancée Hope.

IVANHOE 1952
★★★ NR Action-Adventure 1:46
Dir: Richard Thorpe *Cast:* Robert Taylor, Elizabeth Taylor, Joan Fontaine, George Sanders, Emlyn Williams, Robert Douglas
▶ In twelfth-century England, the noble Saxon knight Ivanhoe (Taylor) defeats a Norman plot against the king while rescuing both his betrothed Fontaine and beautiful Jewess Taylor from the dastardly De Bois-Builbert (Sanders). Faithful, lavish adaptation of Sir Walter Scott's medieval epic offers dazzling sweep and spectacle.

I WALKED WITH A ZOMBIE 1943
★★ NR Horror 1:09 B&W
Dir: Jacques Tourneur *Cast:* Frances Dee, Tom Conway, James Ellison, Edith Barrett, Christine Gordon, Teresa Harris
▶ American planter Conway hires nurse Dee to look after his mysteriously catatonic wife Barrett on Haiti. While denying her love for Conway, Dee tries voodoo to "cure" Barrett. Imaginative film uses evocative atmosphere to suggest rather than show horror, emphasizing tension over shocks. A treat for sophisticated viewers (who will also appreciate plot's close resemblance to *Jane Eyre*).

I WANNA HOLD YOUR HAND 1978
★ PG Comedy 1:44
☑ Explicit language
Dir: Robert Zemeckis *Cast:* Nancy Allen, Bobby DiCicco, Marc McClure, Susan Newman, Theresa Saldana, Eddie Deezen

▶ February 1964: the Beatles are set to appear on the Ed Sullivan show. Several New Jersey teenagers travel to New York City to see their idols. Nostalgic look at Beatlemania captures fan hysteria with energetic crowd shots, inventive comic plot, a fresh young cast, and numerous Fab Four hits on the soundtrack. Overlooked early effort from the director of *Back to the Future* and *Who Framed Roger Rabbit*.

I WANT TO LIVE! 1958
★★★ NR Biography 2:00 B&W
Dir: Robert Wise *Cast:* Susan Hayward, Simon Oakland, Virginia Vincent, Theodore Bikel, Wesley Lau, Philip Coolidge
▶ Relentlessly downbeat story of Barbara Graham (Hayward), a hardened convict and drug addict sentenced to death in 1955 for the murder of a widow. Hayward is mesmerizing in an Oscar-winning performance, but film raised considerable controversy by insisting (without evidence) Graham was innocent. Bleak but compelling story received five other Oscar nominations.

I WAS A TEENAGE ZOMBIE 1987
★ NR Horror 1:32
☑ Nudity, adult situations, explicit language, graphic violence
Dir: John Elias Michalakias *Cast:* Michael Rubin, George Seminara, Steve McCoy, Peter Bush, Cassie Madden, Cindy Keiter
▶ Five teens victimized by unscrupulous pusher McCoy kill him and dump his body in polluted river. Toxic wastes revive McCoy as a zombie who murders Rubin. Remaining teens use the river to transform Rubin into a "good guy" zombie who engages McCoy in battle. Campy exploitation film shot on shoestring budget has become cult favorite at midnight shows. Extraordinary soundtrack includes tunes by the Fleshtones, Smithereens, Del Fuegos, Violent Femmes, Alex Chilton, and Los Lobos.

I WILL, I WILL . . . FOR NOW 1976
★★★★ R Comedy 1:47
☑ Explicit language
Dir: Norman Panama *Cast:* Elliott Gould, Diane Keaton, Paul Sorvino, Victoria Principal, Robert Alda, Candy Clark
▶ Divorced couple Gould and Keaton are still attracted to one another. They negotiate a contract to guide their renewed relationship and then go to a sex

clinic for further help. Meanwhile, lawyer Sorvino pursues Keaton. Good cast in a bawdy and sometimes bittersweet sex comedy.

I WONDER WHO'S KILLING HER NOW
1976
☆ **PG Comedy 1:24**
☑ Explicit language, adult humor
Dir: Steven Hilliard Stern *Cast:* Bob Dishy, Joanna Barnes, Bill Dana, Steve Franken
▶ Hapless Dishy, whose life is falling apart, puts out a contract on his wife in order to collect insurance money. When Dishy discovers she's not insured, he must track down the killer to prevent the murder. Inconsistent black comedy: some of the jokes are outrageous and original but much of it backfires.

JABBERWOCKY 1977 British
★ **PG Comedy 1:40**
☑ Brief nudity, graphic violence
Dir: Terry Gilliam *Cast:* Michael Palin, Max Wall, John Le Mesurier, Annette Badland, Terry Jones
▶ Monty Python meets Lewis Carroll in Gilliam's daft adaptation of the famous poem. Befuddled Palin seeks his fortune in the realm of King Bruno the Questionable so that he can marry Griselda Fishfinger (Badland). Sophomoric farce, predictably insane, with plenty of blood splatterings. Warning: when the King says, "Off with his head!" Gilliam obeys.

JACKNIFE 1989
★★★★ **R Drama 1:42**
☑ Adult situations, explicit language, violence
Dir: David Jones *Cast:* Robert De Niro, Ed Harris, Kathy Baker, Tom Isbell, Charles Dutton, Loudon Wainwright III
▶ After a long separation, Vietnam vet De Niro tries to pull his old buddy Harris out of an alcohol-induced depression over the war. Harris resents De Niro's help and courtship of his sister Baker, but De Niro's tactics ultimately force Harris to confront his memories of the war. Powerhouse casting sparks Stephen Metcalfe's adaptation of his off-Broadway play.

JACK'S BACK 1988
★★ **R Mystery-Suspense 1:35**
☑ Nudity, adult situations, explicit language, violence
Dir: Rowdy Herrington *Cast:* James Spader, Cynthia Gibb, Rod Loomis, Rex Ryon, Robert Picardo
▶ Pulse-pounding thriller, set in Los An-

geles, one hundred years to the day after each of Jack the Ripper's famous London murders. Young medic Spader, cute doctor Gibb, uptight chief doctor Ryon, and intern Loomis track the serial killer who's murdered four hookers in the same manner as his English counterpart. Twisty plot with intriguing psychological details keeps audience guessing right up to the action-packed climax. **(CC)**

JACKSON COUNTY JAIL 1976
★★ **R Action-Adventure 1:23**
☑ Rape, strong sexual content, explicit language, violence
Dir: Michael Miller *Cast:* Yvette Mimieux, Tommy Lee Jones, Robert Carradine, Howard Hesseman, Betty Thomas
▶ While driving cross country, producer Mimieux is unjustly imprisoned and then raped by her jailer. She kills her attacker and escapes with convicted murderer Jones. Roger Corman–produced film really gets the audience on the side of antiheroes. Zippy pacing, lots of action, exceptional performances by Jones and Mimieux. Warning: rape scene is extremely graphic.

JAGGED EDGE 1985
★★★★★ **R Mystery-Suspense 1:49**
☑ Brief nudity, adult situations, explicit language, violence
Dir: Richard Marquand *Cast:* Jeff Bridges, Glenn Close, Peter Coyote, Robert Loggia, Leigh Taylor-Young
▶ Solid courtroom drama with lawyer Close defending newspaper publisher Bridges on charges of ruthlessly murdering his wife. Vulnerable but strong, she finds herself falling for him. Close's unmannered acting is perfectly balanced by Bridges's finely shaded performance, adding crackling tension to the riveting conclusion. Loggia shines in an Oscar-nominated performance as a seedy private investigator with a memorable exit line. **(CC)**

JAILHOUSE ROCK 1957
★★★ **NR Musical 1:36 B&W**
Dir: Richard Thorpe *Cast:* Elvis Presley, Judy Tyler, Mickey Shaughnessy, Jennifer Holden, Dean Jones, The Jordanaires
▶ Presley kills a man while defending a woman's honor, then learns to sing in prison. With Tyler's help he becomes a rock 'n' roll sensation, but turns on his old friends when fame goes to his head.

Stark plot and outstanding songs ("Treat Me Nice," "Baby I Don't Care," "Don't Leave Me Now," etc.) set this well above other Presley vehicles. Elvis sizzles throughout, particularly during the title tune.

JAKE SPEED 1986
★★ **PG Action-Adventure 1:45**
☑ Explicit language, violence
Dir: Andrew Lane *Cast:* Wayne Crawford, Dennis Christopher, Karen Kopins, John Hurt, Leon Ames, Donna Pescow
▶ Fictional paperback hero Jake Speed (Crawford) and sidekick Christopher come to life to help Kopins rescue her kidnapped sister in Africa. Tongue-incheek derring-do, reminiscent of *Romancing the Stone*, suffers from erratic pacing and storytelling, and co-writer Crawford's blandness in the lead. **(CC)**

JANE AND THE LOST CITY 1987 British
☆ **PG Action-Adventure 1:32**
☑ Adult situations, explicit language, violence
Dir: Terry Marcel *Cast:* Sam J. Jones, Maud Adams, Kirsten Hughes, Jasper Carrott, Elsa O'Toole
▶ Lackluster British entry into Indiana Jones territory is based on the long-running World War II comic strip, "Jane," about a nubile heroine who's constantly losing her dress in battle. In this adventure, Churchill orders Jane into the African jungle to search for diamonds to support the war effort. And, yes, Jane disrobes several times while escaping the Nazis.

JANE EYRE 1944
★★★★ **NR Drama 1:37 B&W**
Dir: Robert Stevenson *Cast:* Joan Fontaine, Orson Welles, Margaret O'Brien, Peggy Ann Garner, John Sutton
▶ In nineteenth-century England, shy governess Fontaine takes a job with mysterious, wealthy Welles. They fall in love but he has a dark secret that could threaten their happiness. Sterling adaptation of the classic Charlotte Brontë novel. Moody camerawork captures atmosphere of the moors and strong performances by the leads. **(CC)**

JANIS 1975
★★★ **R Documentary/Biography 1:36**
☑ Explicit language
Dir: Howard Alk, Seaton Findley *Cast:* Janis Joplin, Big Brother and the Holding Company
▶ Documentary on rock star Janis Joplin concentrates on concert footage, showing her in performance between 1967 and 1970. Includes her classic songs ("Piece of My Heart," "Ball and Chain," "Me and Bobby McGee"), but glosses over her drug addiction and death. Visit to her tenth high school reunion provides a revealing glimpse into her character.

JANUARY MAN, THE 1989
★★ **R Mystery-Suspense 1:37**
☑ Brief nudity, adult situations, explicit language, mild violence
Dir: Pat O'Connor *Cast:* Kevin Kline, Susan Sarandon, Mary Elizabeth Mastrantonio, Harvey Keitel, Rod Steiger
▶ When serial killer claims eleventh victim, unorthodox detective Kline is assigned to the case. Romance blooms between Kline and Mastrantonio, the mayor's daughter, as they bumble their way to a solution. Quirky John Patrick Shanley screenplay combines genres but disappoints greatly after his wonderful *Moonstruck;* O'Connor's misdirection makes matters worse. A talented cast is left stranded in this critical and box-office bomb.

JASON AND THE ARGONAUTS 1963
★★★ **G Fantasy 1:44**
Dir: Don Chaffey *Cast:* Todd Armstrong, Nancy Kovack, Gary Raymond, Laurence Naismith, Niall MacGinnis, Honor Blackman
▶ Cheated out of his birthright, Jason (Armstrong) assembles a band of heroes to retrieve the golden fleece and claim his throne. Captivating adventure based on Greek mythology with outstanding Ray Harryhausen special effects. The giant statue Talos, monstrous harpies, and deadly skeleton warriors are only a few of the highlights in this immensely entertaining fantasy.

JAWS 1975
★★★★★ **PG Action-Adventure 2:04**
☑ Graphic violence, explicit language
Dir: Steven Spielberg *Cast:* Roy Scheider, Robert Shaw, Richard Dreyfuss, Lorraine Gary, Murray Hamilton
▶ Triple-Oscar-winning fish-tale about an Atlantic resort town terrorized by a twenty-five-foot man-eating great white shark. Chief of police Scheider, salty old shark-hunter Shaw, and cocky young oceanographer Dreyfuss battle the killer

creature to the death. Spielberg's first major triumph spawned three sequels and numerous imitators. Based on best-selling novel by Peter Benchley and filmed on Martha's Vineyard. Considered by many to be among the best of its genre. The evocative score by John Williams has become synonymous with terror.

JAWS 2 1978
★ ★ ★ PG Action-Adventure 1:56
☑ Explicit language, violence
Dir: Jeannot Szwarc *Cast:* Roy Scheider, Lorraine Gary, Murray Hamilton, Joseph Mascolo, Jeffrey Kramer
▶ Scheider reprises his role as resort-town sheriff, convinced another killer shark is stalking vacationing swimmers. No one believes him until the fish rears its mechanical head to gobble teens tartare. Sequel lacks the quality cast and meticulously calculated suspense that made the original a box-office splash.

JAWS 3 1983
★ ★ PG Action-Adventure 1:38
☑ Explicit language, graphic violence
Dir: Joe Alves *Cast:* Dennis Quaid, Bess Armstrong, Simon MacCorkindale, Louis Gossett, Jr., John Putch, Lea Thompson
▶ Third entry in the Jaws series shifts the setting to Florida's Sea World theme park, where Quaid (supposedly the son of sheriff Roy Scheider of the earlier films) and marine biologist Armstrong capture a great white shark. Mother shark arrives for bloody revenge. Shot in 3-D, film's best effects will be lost on TV.

JAWS THE REVENGE 1987
★ ★ PG-13 Action-Adventure 1:30
☑ Explicit language, graphic violence
Dir: Joseph Sargent *Cast:* Michael Caine, Lorraine Gary, Lance Guest, Karen Young, Mitchell Anderson
▶ Holding a personal grudge against the Brody clan, the killer shark swims all the way to the Bahamas to stalk widow Gary and her only remaining son Guest. Caine plays a rakish pilot romantically pursuing Gary. By now, the fourth remake in the Jaws series has lost most of its bite. (CC)

JAZZ SINGER, THE 1927
★ ★ NR Musical 1:28 B&W
Dir: Alan Crosland *Cast:* Al Jolson, May McAvoy, Werner Oland, Eugene Besserer, Bobby Gordon, William Demarest

▶ Pioneering sound movie changed movie industry forever, although large portions of the film are actually silent. Jolson plays an aspiring Broadway star whose mainstream ambitions conflict with those of cantor father Oland, who wants son to follow in his professional and religious footsteps. Jolson is unforgettable, singing "Mammy," "Toot, Toot, Tootsie Goodbye," and others.

JAZZ SINGER, THE 1980
★ ★ ★ ★ ★ PG Drama/Musical 1:56
☑ Adult situations, explicit language
Dir: Richard Fleischer *Cast:* Neil Diamond, Laurence Olivier, Lucie Arnaz, Catlin Adams, Franklyn Ajaye, Paul Nicholas
▶ Singer Diamond reaches for the pop music pinnacle, but Jewish cantor dad Olivier wants him to follow in family footsteps. Diamond has affair with promoter Arnaz but eventually sees the emptiness of success. Old-fashioned sentiment laid on with conviction is a guaranteed audience pleaser. Most heartrending moment: Olivier declaring "I have no son." Diamond's score includes "Love on the Rocks," "Hello Again," and "America." Earlier versions starred Al Jolson (1927) and Danny Thomas (1953).

JEAN DE FLORETTE 1987 French
★ ★ PG Drama 2:02
☑ Explicit language
Dir: Claude Berri *Cast:* Yves Montand, Gerard Depardieu, Daniel Auteuil, Elisabeth Depardieu, Ernestine Mazurowna
▶ Hunchback Depardieu moves to the French countryside from the city and tries to make it as a farmer. Greedy neighbors Montand and Auteuil plot against him. Placidly paced but lovingly rendered French drama with excellent performances, beautiful production, and old-fashioned literary feel. Story reaches its conclusion in *Manon of the Spring.*
⑤

JEKYLL AND HYDE . . . TOGETHER AGAIN 1982
★ ★ ★ R Comedy 1:27
☑ Nudity, adult situations, explicit language
Dir: Jerry Belson *Cast:* Mark Blankfield, Bess Armstrong, Tim Thomerson, Krista Errickson
▶ Raunchy parody of Robert Louis Stevenson's *The Strange Case of Dr. Jekyll and Mr. Hyde.* Straitlaced surgeon Blank-

field inhales white powder that turns him into a bushy-haired, gold-chain-wearing swinger. Irreverent, tasteless humor, heavy on the sex and drug references.

JEREMIAH JOHNSON 1972
★ ★ ★ ★ ★ **PG Western 1:51**
☑ Violence
Dir: Sydney Pollack *Cast:* Robert Redford, Will Geer, Stefan Gierasch, Allyn Ann McLerie, Josh Tyner
▶ Nineteenth-century mountain man Redford survives winter, wilderness, and rival trappers. After Indians kill his family, Redford seeks revenge. Rambles at times but excellent photography and locations, thoughtful direction by Pollack, respectful view of Indians, and convincing performance by Redford combine for an extraordinary adventure.

JERK, THE 1979
★ ★ ★ **R Comedy 1:34**
☑ Adult situations, explicit language, adult humor
Dir: Carl Reiner *Cast:* Steve Martin, Bernadette Peters, Bill Macy, Catlin Adams, Mabel King, Richard Ward
▶ Eager-beaver, happy idiot Martin discovers he's not the natural son of black sharecroppers King and Ward and sets out to find his place in the world. An off-the-wall inventor, he makes and loses a fortune, then marries Peters, the cornet-playing cosmetologist of his dreams. Goofy, innocent, nonstop lunacy reminiscent of Jerry Lewis.

JESSE JAMES 1939
★ ★ ★ **NR Western 1:46**
Dir: Henry King *Cast:* Tyrone Power, Henry Fonda, Nancy Kelly, Randolph Scott, Brian Donlevy, Jane Darwell
▶ When their mother Darwell is murdered by villainous railroad agent Donlevy, Jesse James (Power) and his brother Frank (Fonda) are forced into a life of crime. Large-scale adventure is pure hokum as biography, but for action and entertainment it's hard to beat. Outstanding production values and cast, with John Carradine memorably evil as Bob Ford. Fonda starred in the sequel, *The Return of Frank James.*

JESSE JAMES MEETS FRANKENSTEIN'S DAUGHTER 1966
☆ **NR Western/Horror 1:28**
Dir: William Beaudine *Cast:* John Lupton, Cal Bolder, Narda Onyx, Steven Geray, Felipe Turich, Rosa Turich
▶ Unwilling outlaw Jesse James (Lupton)

and his pal Bolder hide from a posse with Baron Frankenstein's granddaughter (Onyx). She proceeds to transplant the famous monster's brain into Bolder, turning him into the deadly Igor. Can Jesse escape? Low-budget cross-genre nonsense offers plenty of unintentional laughs.

JESUS 1979
★ ★ ★ ★ **G Drama 1:56**
Dir: Peter Sykes, John Kirsh *Cast:* Brian Deacon, Rivka Noiman, Joseph Shiloah, Niko Nitai, Gadi Rol
▶ Unusually faithful approach to the life of Jesus Christ in an almost literal adaptation of the Gospel of Luke. Filmed in the Holy Land with an all-Israeli cast (with the exception of Shakespearean actor Deacon, in the lead). Sober and quite satisfying. Narration by Alexander Scourby.

JESUS CHRIST SUPERSTAR 1973
★ ★ ★ **G Musical 1:46**
Dir: Norman Jewison *Cast:* Ted Neeley, Carl Anderson, Yvonne Elliman, Barry Dennen, Bob Bingham, Josh Mostel
▶ Controversial rock opera version of the final weeks of Jesus's life, including the Last Supper and the Crucifixion. Interesting visuals as director Jewison injects relevance by including modern jets and tanks during Judas's production number. Energetic Andrew Lloyd Webber/Tim Rice score includes "I Don't Know How to Love Him."

JEWEL OF THE NILE, THE 1985
★ ★ ★ ★ **PG Action-Adventure 1:46**
☑ Brief nudity, explicit language, violence
Dir: Lewis Teague *Cast:* Michael Douglas, Kathleen Turner, Danny DeVito, Avner Eisenberg, Spiros Focas
▶ *Romancing the Stone* alumni Douglas, Turner, and DeVito return six months later to track down yet another valuable "jewel"—this one lost somewhere in the blistering Sahara desert. Lots of cliff-hanging action, expensive-looking explosions, and good technical credits, but the Douglas/Turner matchup feels a little like a retread. **(CC)**

JEZEBEL 1938
★ ★ ★ **NR Drama 1:44 B&W**
Dir: William Wyler *Cast:* Bette Davis, Henry Fonda, George Brent, Fay Bainter, Margaret Lindsay, Richard Cromwell
▶ Pre–Civil War New Orleans: belle Davis

causes scandal by wearing red dress to the big ball instead of traditional white. Move leads to breakup with beau Fonda; later, Fonda reenters her life and she gets chance for redemption. Oscar-winning performance by Davis is magnificent. Large-scale production received five other nominations, with Bainter garnering Best Supporting Actress.

JIGSAW MAN, THE 1984 British
★★ **PG Espionage 1:31**
☑ Explicit language, violence
Dir: Terence Young *Cast:* Laurence Olivier, Michael Caine, Susan George, Robert Powell, Eric Sevareid
▶ Double-crosses run rampant when defector Caine returns to England to recover a microfilmed list of Soviet agents he hid long before. Not to worry: British Secret Service agent Olivier is on Caine's case. The fourth pairing of two British superstars (*Sleuth, A Bridge Too Far, The Battle of Britain*) makes for an appealing caper. From the best-seller by Dorothea Bennett (Mrs. Terence Young.)

JIMMY THE KID 1982
★★★★ **PG Family 1:26**
☑ Explicit language, mild violence
Dir: Gary Nelson *Cast:* Gary Coleman, Paul LeMat, Ruth Gordon, Dee Wallace, Don Adams, Cleavon Little
▶ Tried-and-true caper in which a precocious kid outwits scatterbrained adults. Unhappy, rich, twelve-year-old Coleman learns to have fun and make friends after being kidnapped by bumbling bad guys LeMat, Wallace, and Gordon. Nonthreatening, above-average family film. Based on the novel by Donald E. Westlake.

JIM THORPE—ALL-AMERICAN 1951
★★★★ **NR Biography/Sports 1:47 B&W**
Dir: Michael Curtiz *Cast:* Burt Lancaster, Phyllis Thaxter, Charles Bickford, Steve Cochran
▶ Rags-to-riches-to-rags true life story of the famous Indian athlete from Oklahoma. Thorpe (Lancaster) leaves the reservation, excels in football, marries co-ed Thaxter, and wins the pentathlon and decathlon at the 1912 Olympics in Sweden. Tragedy strikes when his son dies and his career and marriage crumble. Lancaster is believable and inspirational.

JINXED! 1982
★★ **R Comedy 1:42**
☑ Brief nudity, adult situations, explicit language

Dir: Don Siegel *Cast:* Bette Midler, Ken Wahl, Rip Torn, Val Avery
▶ Way-off-the-mark romantic triangle begins like hard-boiled drama, sways toward romance, and turns into slapstick. Blackjack dealer Wahl, jinxed by Torn, steals his girl Midler. Then Wahl and Midler plot to murder Torn for his insurance. Bette chickens out; Torn commits suicide; Wahl suspects the double-cross. Confusing plot and mismatched cast never gel.

JOAN OF ARC 1948
★ **NR Drama 1:40**
Dir: Victor Fleming *Cast:* Ingrid Bergman, Jose Ferrer, J. Carroll Naish, Ward Bond, Francis L. Sullivan
▶ Farm girl Joan of Arc (Bergman) leads French armies against England and is later tried as a heretic and burned at the stake. Opulent spectacle, with stalwart Ingrid breathing life into slack pacing and musty screenplay.

JOCKS 1987
★ **R Comedy 1:31**
☑ Nudity, adult situations, explicit language, adult humor
Dir: Steve Carver *Cast:* Scott Strader, Perry Lang, Mariska Hargitay, Richard Roundtree, R. G. Armstrong, Christopher Lee
▶ Juvenile pranksters must get their act together and win big tennis tournament or their program will be cancelled. By-the-numbers teen fare won't disappoint genre fans: frantic pacing, idiotic situations, clichéd characters, muscular guys, busty gals, and raunchy shenanigans including strip blackjack game.

JOE 1970
★★ **R Drama 1:47**
☑ Nudity, explicit language, violence
Dir: John G. Avildsen *Cast:* Peter Boyle, Dennis Patrick, Susan Sarandon, Audrey Caine, K. Callan, Patrick McDermott
▶ Business exec Patrick accidentally murders his daughter Sarandon's junkie boyfriend and then meets bigoted hard-hat Joe (Boyle), who convinces him, "Plenty of people would consider you a hero." Controversial flower people–vs.–Archie Bunker drama made big impression when first released. Noted for fine performance by Boyle; early effort from Avildsen, who later directed *Rocky.* Sarandon's film debut.

JOE KIDD 1972
★★★★ **PG Western 1:27**

☑ Explicit language, violence
Dir: John Sturges *Cast:* Clint Eastwood, Robert Duvall, John Saxon, Don Stroud, Stella Garcia, James Wainwright
▶ When his ranch in New Mexico is raided, Eastwood joins a posse to catch the Mexican-American guerrillas responsible. But posse leader Duvall proves as dangerous as the fugitives. Despite marvelous locomotive climax, muddled Western is a disappointment. Written by Elmore Leonard.

JOEY 1985
★★★ PG Drama 1:37
☑ Adult situations, explicit language, mild violence
Dir: Joseph Ellison *Cast:* Neill Barry, Linda Thorson, Elisa Heinsohn, James Quinn, John Snyder
▶ Ode to doo-wop music follows the lives of rebellious teen rocker Barry and his once famous 1950s crooner dad Quinn, now an alcoholic who works in a gas station. Music from the Ramones, Stray Cats, the Silhouettes, Jay Hawkins, the Elegants; with songs, "Why Do Fools Fall in Love?," "Boy From New York City," "Get a Job," and more.

JOHN AND JULIE 1955 British
★★ NR Family 1:22
Dir: William Fairchild *Cast:* Constance Cummings, Colin Gibson, Lesley Dydley, Noel Middleton, Wilfrid Hyde-White, Peter Sellers
▶ Two English schoolchildren, determined to see the coronation of Queen Elizabeth II, run away to London (150 miles away) and have a series of adventures en route. Very appealing child actors backed by a swell adult supporting cast make this superior family programming.

JOHN AND MARY 1969
★★ PG Romance 1:23
☑ Brief nudity, adult situations, explicit language
Dir: Peter Yates *Cast:* Dustin Hoffman, Mia Farrow, Michael Tolan, Sunny Griffin, Tyne Daly, Stanley Beck
▶ In this dated slice of New York singles life, John (Hoffman) meets Mary (Farrow) at a bar. Without knowing each other's names, they become lovers and their one-night stand grows into a possibly deeper commitment. Not the finest moment for either star. Olympia Dukakis has the small role of Hoffman's mom.

JOHNNY ANGEL 1945
★★ NR Mystery-Suspense 1:19 B&W
Dir: Edwin L. Marin *Cast:* George Raft, Claire Trevor, Signe Hasso, Lowell Gilmore, Hoagy Carmichael, Marvin Miller
▶ Well-shot but talky film noir, with Raft playing a hard-bitten sea captain who noses around the New Orleans underworld for the men who killed his father. With the help of glib cabbie Carmichael, Raft uncovers a plot involving $5 million in gold bullion. Strong support from Miller as a mentally unstable villain and Trevor as his untrustworthy wife.

JOHNNY BE GOOD 1988
★★★ R Comedy 1:26
☑ Nudity, adult situations, explicit language
Dir: Bud Smith *Cast:* Anthony Michael Hall, Paul Gleason, Robert Downey, Jr., Uma Thurman, Seymour Cassel
▶ Star high school quarterback Hall is tempted by aggressive college recruiters promising cash, fast cars, and willing cheerleaders. With Downey as his best friend, Thurman as his girl. Cameos by Jim McMahon and Howard Cosell. **(CC)**

JOHNNY BELINDA 1948
★★★★ NR Drama 1:42 B&W
Dir: Jean Negulesco *Cast:* Jane Wyman, Lew Ayres, Charles Bickford, Stephen McNally, Agnes Moorehead
▶ In rural New England, deaf-mute Wyman is befriended by doctor Ayres. She is put on trial when she kills McNally, who raped and impregnated her. Moving drama with an outstanding performance by Wyman that copped Best Actress Oscar.

JOHNNY DANGEROUSLY 1984
★★★ PG-13 Comedy 1:30
☑ Explicit language, adult humor
Dir: Amy Heckerling *Cast:* Michael Keaton, Dom DeLuise, Maureen Stapleton, Joe Piscopo, Danny DeVito, Griffin Dunne
▶ Spoof of gangster movies and the Prohibition era. Keaton plays Johnny Dangerously, a mamma's boy/hoodlum; Dunne, his straight-arrow D.A. brother; Piscopo, a sleazy mobster named Vermin; and Stapleton, Johnny's ailing mother who talks dirty. Dopey slapstick humor, fun for those who appreciate opening song by Weird Al Yankovic. (CC)

JOHNNY GOT HIS GUN 1971
★ PG War 1:51

☑ Brief nudity, adult situations, explicit language
Dir: Dalton Trumbo   *Cast:* Timothy Bottoms, Jason Robards, Donald Sutherland, Diane Varsi, Kathy Fields
▶ Frightening and depressing story of young World War I soldier Bottoms who loses most of his body, face, and limbs in a bomb blast; only his mind survives intact. His flashbacks include past experiences with father Robards and girlfriend Fields, and strange visions of Jesus Christ (Sutherland). Jarring antiwar film was based on Trumbo's novel.

JOHNNY GUITAR 1954
★★★ NR Western 1:50
Dir: Nicholas Ray   *Cast:* Joan Crawford, Sterling Hayden, Mercedes McCambridge, Scott Brady, Ward Bond, Ben Cooper
▶ Bizarre Western pits Crawford, saloon owner with a shady past, against McCambridge, a two-fisted moral crusader determined to drive her out of Arizona. Hayden is a worn-out gunfighter who observes the duel from the sidelines. Interpreted variously as a Freudian psychodrama, an anti-McCarthy parable, and an auteur classic, film wavers precariously between high camp and enjoyable nonsense.

JOHNNY TREMAIN 1957
★★★ NR Drama 1:20
Dir: Robert Stevenson   *Cast:* Hal Stalmaster, Luana Patten, Jeff York, Sebastian Cabot, Richard Beymer, Walter Sande
▶ In 1773 Boston, silversmith's apprentice Stalmaster, victimized by British nobleman Cabot, is persuaded by Paul Revere to join the revolutionary movement. Involving Disney adaptation of Esther Forbes's novel explains the war for independence in human terms; accurate, exciting production is perfect for the entire family.

JO JO DANCER, YOUR LIFE IS CALLING 1986
★★★ R Comedy/Drama 1:37
☑ Nudity, adult situations, explicit language
Dir: Richard Pryor   *Cast:* Richard Pryor, Debbie Allen, Carmen McRae, Diahnne Abbott, Barbara Williams
▶ This is your life, Richard Pryor. Extremely personal account of funny man's near-fatal accident freebasing cocaine. Half dead, the spirit of Jo Jo Dancer rises from the hospital bed to relive his life and discover the reason for his drug dependency. Odd mixture of maudlin drama, self-absorbed fantasy, and hard reality enlivened by a few uproarious monologues.

JOKER IS WILD, THE 1957
★★★ NR Biography 2:06 B&W
Dir: Charles Vidor   *Cast:* Frank Sinatra, Mitzi Gaynor, Jeanne Crain, Eddie Albert, Beverly Garland, Jackie Coogan
▶ Sinatra gives a compelling performance in this true story of Joe E. Lewis, a Roaring Twenties nightclub singer whose throat is slashed by gangsters. He battles depression and alcoholism to become a famous comic. Grim but ultimately uplifting story features the Oscar-winning "All the Way."

JOLSON SINGS AGAIN 1949
★★★ NR Biography/Musical 1:36
Dir: Henry Levin   *Cast:* Larry Parks, Barbara Hale, William Demarest, Bill Goodwin, Ludwig Donath, Tamara Shayne
▶ Sequel to popular musical biography picks up the singer's life after his divorce. Singing for the troops overseas during World War II, Jolson (Parks) falls in love with nurse Hale. After their wedding, work begins on the original picture, setting up unusual scene in which Parks as Jolson meets Parks as Parks. Once again, story is merely an excuse for a tune-a-thon, with "Give My Regards to Broadway," "You Made Me Love You," and "I'm Looking Over a Four-Leaf Clover" among the many numbers.

JOLSON STORY, THE 1946
★★★ NR Biography/Musical 2:08
Dir: Alfred E. Green   *Cast:* Larry Parks, Evelyn Keyes, William Demarest, Bill Goodwin, Ludwig Donath, Tamara Shayne
▶ Parks plays singing great Al Jolson, as picture charts his rise through vaudeville to top of pop charts and star role in *The Jazz Singer*, the first talkie. Jolson assisted with the production and dubbed the songs in this sanitized biopic. Resulting sing-along concentrates on the many tunes such as "Swanee," "My Mammy," "April Showers," "You Made Me Love You," and "By the Light of the Silvery Moon."

JONATHAN LIVINGSTON SEAGULL 1973
★★ G Drama 1:55
Dir: Hall Bartlett

▶ Based on Richard Bach's early-seventies best-selling book. Allegorical tale of a seagull who forsakes his flock to fly to new heights and learn the meaning of perfection. Shot from a spectacular bird's-eye view. With effective music by Neil Diamond.

JOSEPH ANDREWS 1977 British
★ R Comedy 1:39
☑ Nudity, adult situations, explicit language, adult humor
Dir: Tony Richardson *Cast:* Ann-Margret, Peter Firth, Michael Hordern, Beryl Reid, Jim Dale, Natalie Ogle
▶ Eighteenth-century footman Firth becomes the object of Lady Booby's (Ann-Margret) amorous attentions in a farcical plot of escalating mistaken identities. Gorgeously mounted adaptation of Henry Fielding's novel lacks the bawdy humor and rapid pacing of director Richardson's earlier *Tom Jones*, but Reid is outstanding as Mrs. Slipslop. Cameos by John Gielgud, Hugh Griffith, and Peggy Ashcroft.

JOSHUA THEN AND NOW 1985 Canadian
★★★ R Comedy 1:58
☑ Nudity, adult situations, explicit language
Dir: Ted Kotcheff *Cast:* James Woods, Alan Arkin, Gabrielle Lazure, Michael Sarrazin, Linda Sorensen
▶ Joshua Shapiro (Woods), a Jewish-Canadian writer, recalls his life and times through flashbacks. Joshua then: ex-gangster dad Arkin tells him about sex and uninhibited mom does a striptease at his bar mitzvah. Joshua now: caught in a trumped-up homosexual scandal and abandoned by aristocratic gentile wife Lazure. Based on Mordechai Richler's semiautobiographical novel. **(CC)**

JOURNEY INTO FEAR 1942
★★ NR Mystery-Suspense 1:11 B&W
Dir: Norman Foster *Cast:* Orson Welles, Joseph Cotten, Dolores Del Rio, Ruth Warrick, Agnes Moorehead, Everett Sloane
▶ American munitions expert Cotten becomes the target of Nazi assassins in Istanbul; Turkish spy Welles assures him he'll be safe aboard a rusty freighter, but as the ship leaves port, Cotten sees that the killers are also on board. Taut, realistic thriller (scripted by Welles and Cotten from Eric Ambler's best-seller) is filled with brilliant touches. Welles was replaced by director Foster after filming started.

JOURNEY OF NATTY GANN, THE 1985
★★★★ PG Action-Adventure/Family 1:45
☑ Explicit language, mild violence
Dir: Jeremy Paul Kagan *Cast:* Meredith Salenger, John Cusack, Lainie Kazan, Verna Bloom, Scatman Crothers
▶ Feisty fourteen-year-old tomboy Natty Gann (Salenger) embarks on a cross-country journey to find her father, sent to Seattle on a logging job. She rides the rails with teen drifter Cusack, escapes a train wreck, and thwarts a charging bull, accompanied by a friendly wolf. Authentic Depression-era setting helps this spirited Disney adventure appeal to sophisticated youths without sacrificing family values.

JOURNEY TO THE CENTER OF THE EARTH 1959
★★★ NR Sci-Fi 2:09
Dir: Henry Levin *Cast:* James Mason, Pat Boone, Arlene Dahl, Diane Baker, Peter Ronson
▶ Scientist Mason, his star pupil Boone, widow Dahl, and Nordic assistant Ronson and his pet duck Gertrude attempt an underground expedition to the center of the earth. They encounter landslides, volcanic tremors, giant reptiles, a subterranean shipwreck, the lost city of Atlantis, and an evil Count during their arduous trek. Perfect casting, top cinematography and special effects, first-rate Bernard Herrmann score enhance a Jules Verne adaptation that delivers fun, fantasy, and adventure. **(CC)**

JOURNEY TO THE FAR SIDE OF THE SUN 1969 British
★★ G Sci-Fi 1:39
Dir: Robert Parrish *Cast:* Roy Thinnes, Ian Hendry, Patrick Wymark, Lynn Loring, Loni von Friedl, Herbert Lom
▶ Scientists discover a new planet hidden behind the sun; astronauts Thinnes and Hendry are sent to explore it. A crash landing leaves them trapped in a strange new world. Good special effects and a devious trick ending highlight this tidy low-budget effort.

JOURNEY TO THE 7TH PLANET 1961
☆ NR Sci-Fi 1:20
Dir: Sidney Pink *Cast:* John Agar, Greta Thyssen, Ann Smyrner, Mimi Heinrich, Carl Ottosen, Ove Sprogoe
▶ At the dawn of the twenty-first century,

Agar leads a five-man United Nations expedition to Uranus. Planet's bitterly cold landscape hides a terrifying monster who preys on the astronauts' fears with startling illusions. Dated special effects and dubbing of Danish cast members lessen the story's impact.

JOY OF SEX 1984
★ **R Comedy 1:33**
☑ Nudity, explicit language, adult humor
Dir: Martha Coolidge *Cast:* Michelle Meyrink, Cameron Dye, Christopher Lloyd, Charles Van Eman
▶ The kids at Southern California's Richard M. Nixon High School hold farting contests and try to lose their virginity. Tasteless teen comedy no worse than others in the genre, but that's not saying much. Bears no resemblance to the best-selling book of the same title.

JOYRIDE 1977
★★★ **R Drama 1:32**
☑ Nudity, adult situations, explicit language
Dir: Joseph Ruben *Cast:* Desi Arnaz, Jr., Robert Carradine, Melanie Griffith, Anne Lockhart, Tom Ligon
▶ Disenchanted young Californians Arnaz, Carradine, and Griffith dump their boring jobs and head to Alaska for adventure. When their money runs out, they rob a bank, take Lockhart hostage, and flee from the police. Well-acted, good-looking, low-budget production.

JOYSTICKS 1983
★ **R Comedy 1:28**
☑ Nudity, explicit language, adult humor
Dir: Greydon Clark *Cast:* Joe Don Baker, Leif Green, Jim Greenleaf, Scott McGinnis
▶ Offensive low-grade farce features Baker as a parent who disapproves of decadent teenage fun at the local video arcade. With Green as the nerd and Greenleaf as an overweight slob who redeems himself through video game expertise. Originally titled *Video Madness*.

JUAREZ 1939
★★ **NR Biography 2:12 B&W**
Dir: William Dieterle *Cast:* Paul Muni, Bette Davis, Brian Aherne, Claude Rains, John Garfield, Donald Crisp
▶ True story of Mexican leader Benito Pablo Juarez (Muni), who led revolution against Emperor Aherne, Empress Davis, and Napoleon III (Rains), the power be-

hind the throne. Epic-scaled and entertaining; Muni and Rains are terrific.

JUBAL 1956
★★★ **NR Western 1:41**
Dir: Delmer Daves *Cast:* Glenn Ford, Ernest Borgnine, Rod Steiger, Valerie French, Felicia Farr, Noah Beery, Jr.
▶ Ford, a Wyoming drifter, signs on with Steiger's ranch, attracting Steiger's wife Farr. Jealous Borgnine claims that Ford and Farr are lovers, leading to a series of tense shoot-outs. Gloomy, adult Western will make more sense to viewers familiar with *Othello*.

JUDGE PRIEST 1934
★★★ **NR Comedy 1:19 B&W**
Dir: John Ford *Cast:* Will Rogers, Henry B. Walthall, Tom Brown, Anita Louise, Rochelle Hudson, Hattie McDaniel
▶ Southern man faces assault charges in a trial rather than reveal he's the father of "orphan" Louise. Slim plot is an undemanding framework for enjoyable Rogers vehicle. As a no-nonsense judge, the famous humorist offers wry observations on small-town foibles. Sentimental comedy's beautifully realized atmosphere is marred only by some racist caricatures. Director Ford remade story in 1953 as *The Sun Shines Bright*.

JUDGMENT AT NUREMBERG 1961
★★★★ **NR Drama 3:09 B&W**
Dir: Stanley Kramer *Cast:* Spencer Tracy, Maximilian Schell, Richard Widmark, Judy Garland, Montgomery Clift, Burt Lancaster
▶ Nuremberg, Germany, 1948: American judge Tracy presides over Nazi war crimes trials, resisting pressure from power sources for a "not guilty" verdict as testimony from Holocaust survivors Garland and Clift (both Oscar-nominated) proves damning. Absorbing and intelligent, if overlong, examination of the issues. Phenomenal cast includes Schell's mesmerizing, Oscar-winning turn as the German defense attorney. A Best Picture nominee.

JUDGMENT IN BERLIN 1988
★★ **PG Drama 1:32**
☑ Adult situations, mild violence
Dir: Leo Penn *Cast:* Martin Sheen, Sean Penn, Sam Wanamaker, Max Gail, Jurgen Heinrich, Heinz Hoenig
▶ True story of East German couple who hijacked Polish plane to U.S. base in West Berlin. Seeking to avoid an international incident, American authorities summon

judge Sheen to decide the hijackers' fate. Penn (whose father directed) shines in the small but key part of a witness.

JUGGERNAUT 1974 British
★★★ PG Action-Adventure 1:49
☑ Explicit language, violence
Dir: Richard Lester *Cast:* Richard Harris, Omar Sharif, David Hemmings, Anthony Hopkins, Shirley Knight, Ian Holm
▶ Blackmailer plants several bombs aboard a luxury liner; Harris and a band of demolitions experts race against time to defuse them. Tense, realistic thriller is a nerve-wracking battle of wits. Strong cast performs capably. **(CC)**

JULES AND JIM 1962 French
★★ NR Drama 1:50 B&W
Dir: François Truffaut *Cast:* Oskar Werner, Jeanne Moreau, Henri Serre, Marie Dubois, Vanna Urbino
▶ Best friends Werner and Serre share a love for Moreau in pre–World War I France. An unusual three-way triangle unfolds with ultimately tragic consequences. Magnificently directed by Truffaut, mixing humor, romance, and melancholy. The charismatic and sexy Moreau is completely convincing as the restless focus of passion in bohemian Paris. ⑤

JULIA 1977
★★★★ PG Drama 1:57
☑ Adult situations, mild violence
Dir: Fred Zinnemann *Cast:* Jane Fonda, Vanessa Redgrave, Maximilian Schell, Jason Robards, Meryl Streep
▶ Vibrant and mesmerizing story adapted from a chapter in Lillian Hellman's popular memoir *Pentimento.* Oscar-winner Redgrave plays Julia, Hellman's wealthy childhood friend, who becomes a political activist in 1930s Europe and involves Lillian (Fonda) in the intrigue. Robards also snagged an Oscar for his role as tough but tender mystery writer Dashiell Hammett. In her film debut, Streep appears briefly as Hellman's friend.

JULIA AND JULIA 1988 Italian
★ R Mystery-Suspense 1:37
☑ Nudity, adult situations, explicit language
Dir: Peter Del Monte *Cast:* Kathleen Turner, Sting, Gabriel Byrne, Gabriele Ferzetti, Angela Goodwin
▶ Psychological thriller stars Turner as the beautiful, long-widowed Julia, still trying to forget husband Byrne's tragic death.

When she comes home one day to find him alive and tending to their supposed son, the intrigue has only just begun. Promising premise gets muddled in its own illogical plot turns. Sting shows up as Turner's ominous lover. **(CC)**

JUMPIN' JACK FLASH 1986
★★★★ R Mystery-Suspense/Comedy 1:45
☑ Adult situations, explicit language, mild violence
Dir: Penny Marshall *Cast:* Whoopi Goldberg, Stephen Collins, John Wood, Carol Kane, Annie Potts, Jon Lovitz
▶ New York City bank computer programmer Goldberg receives messages on her screen from spy caught behind the Iron Curtain. When she tries to aid him, she's caught up in chases and intrigue. Upbeat comedy/thriller with bright moments and blue language from Whoopi. The computer terminal relationship between Whoopi and the unseen spy is novel and affecting. Oddball cast of co-workers adds some spice. Feature directorial debut of Marshall. **(CC)**

JUNGLE BOOK, THE 1942
★★★ NR Drama/Family 1:55
Dir: Zoltan Korda *Cast:* Sabu, Joseph Calleia, John Qualen, Rosemary DeCamp, Ralph Byrd, Frank Puglia
▶ Rudyard Kipling's classic tale of Mowgli (Sabu), the boy raised by wolves and then introduced to society in India. Mowgli grows disenchanted with violent but civilized society and decides to return to the jungle. Family fare, remade in the late 1960s as an animated Disney film.

JUNGLE RAIDERS 1986 Italian
★ PG-13 Action-Adventure 1:42
☑ Adult situations, explicit language, violence
Dir: Anthony M. Dawson (Antonio Margheriti) *Cast:* Christopher Connelly, Marina Costa, Lee Van Cleef, Alan Collins, Dario Pontonutti
▶ In 1938 Malaya, museum curator Costa hires dashing mercenary Connelly to retrieve the Ruby of Gloom, a jewel hidden in booby-trapped caves. Routine treatment of predictable action fare hampered by sloppy dubbing and poor special effects.

JUNGLE WARRIORS 1984 German/Mexican
☆ R Action-Adventure 1:33
☑ Nudity, explicit language, violence
Dir: Ernst R. von Theumer *Cast:* Nina

Van Pallandt, Paul Smith, Marjoe Gortner, John Vernon, Woody Strode, Sybil Danning

▶ A fashion crew's plane is forced to land in the jungle by some evil drug traders. Danning, the drug king's sister, tortures the models, who are also molested by horny locals and then caught in the middle of a battle between the druggies, the mob, and the Feds. Lame dialogue with performances to match; cheap thrills for the exploitation crowd.

JUNIOR BONNER 1972
★★★ PG Drama 1:40
☑ Adult situations, explicit language
Dir: Sam Peckinpah *Cast:* Steve McQueen, Robert Preston, Ida Lupino, Ben Johnson, Joe Don Baker, Barbara Leigh

▶ Aging rodeo rider McQueen returns to his small hometown after many years to discover that his parents Preston and Lupino are estranged and his brother Baker, now a phony real estate wheeler-dealer, has subdivided the family homestead. During a local rodeo, brief fling with Leigh, and barroom brawl, McQueen stands out as the cowboy who learns you can't go home on the range again. Unusual and whimsical effort from director Peckinpah, known for his essays in violence.

JUST ANOTHER MISSING KID 1987
Canadian
★★★★ NR Documentary/MFTV 1:27
☑ Adult situations, explicit language
Dir: John Zaritsky *Cast:* Narrated by Ian Parker

▶ A disturbing true story: Canadian teenager Eric Wilson disappears in the U.S. and his family hires a private eye because authorities are indifferent to "just another missing kid." Wilson was murdered and the killers eventually caught but given lenient sentences. Fascinating indictment of flawed U.S. justice system won Best Documentary Oscar.

JUST BETWEEN FRIENDS 1986
★★★★ PG-13 Drama 1:51
☑ Brief nudity, adult situations, explicit language
Dir: Allan Burns *Cast:* Mary Tyler Moore, Christine Lahti, Ted Danson, Sam Waterston, Jane Geer

▶ Moore is unaware that her new pal Lahti is having an affair with her husband Danson. When tragedy strikes, the friendship is tested by the revelation that Lahti

is pregnant with Danson's child. Old-fashioned, agreeable mixture of laughter and tears. Lahti is the standout among four good performances.

JUSTINE 1969
★ R Drama 1:55
☑ Nudity, adult situations
Dir: George Cukor *Cast:* Anouk Aimee, Dirk Bogarde, Robert Forster, Anna Karina, John Vernon, Michael York

▶ Aimee, a Jewish woman living in Egypt, attempts to send weapons to Palestine Jews. Also involved in the plan: her husband Vernon, her lover York, York's girlfriend Karina, and her British friend Bogarde. Atmospheric, beautifully shot adaptation of Lawrence Durrell's *The Alexandria Quartet.* (CC)

JUST ONE OF THE GUYS 1985
★★★★ PG-13 Comedy 1:40
☑ Brief nudity, explicit language, mild violence, adult humor
Dir: Lisa Gottlieb *Cast:* Joyce Hyser, Clayton Rohner, Billy Jacoby, Toni Hudson, William Zabka, Leigh McCloskey

▶ Cute high school journalism student Hyser finds she isn't taken seriously so she decides to disguise herself as a boy. In her male incarnation, she befriends nerd Rohner, bolsters his confidence, and then falls for him. Teen *Tootsie* has some funny moments ("Of course you're confused," Hyser's little brother tells her, "you're wearing my underwear") but suffers from obvious plotting. (CC)

JUST TELL ME WHAT YOU WANT 1980
★★ R Comedy 1:53
☑ Brief nudity, adult situations, explicit language
Dir: Sidney Lumet *Cast:* Ali MacGraw, Alan King, Peter Weller, Myrna Loy, Dina Merrill, Tony Roberts

▶ TV producer MacGraw tries to break free of her powerful mogul beau King by marrying young writer Weller. But King outmaneuvers her at every turn and wins her back. Slick and sophisticated, joyfully cynical romantic comedy with an amusingly bombastic performance by King and able support from Loy, Merrill, Roberts, and Keenan Wynn. Screenplay by Jay Presson Allan was based on her novel.

JUST THE WAY YOU ARE 1984
★★★★ PG Drama 1:35
☑ Nudity, adult situations
Dir: Edouard Molinaro *Cast:* Kristy

McNichol, Michael Ontkean, Robert Carradine, Lance Guest, Timothy Daly, Kaki Hunter

▶ Unhappy disabled musician McNichol takes skiing vacation and has doctor put a cast on her leg to disguise her condition. Life turns into a glorious adventure and she meets Mr. Right (Ontkean)—but how will he react when he learns the truth? Spunky Kristy takes the potential sappiness out of the story and makes a very sympathetic heroine. **(CC)**

KAGEMUSHA 1980 Japanese
★★ **PG Action-Adventure 2:39**
☑ Violence
Dir: Akira Kurosawa **Cast:** Tatsuya Nakadai, Tsutomu Yamazaki, Kenichi Hagiwara, Kota Yui, Hideji Otaki
▶ Sixteenth-century Japan: small-time crook Nakadai, look-alike for a great warlord, is used by the clan to impersonate the leader after his death. Nakadai slowly grows into his new role. Grand epic from Japan's master director combines magnificent battle scenes and beautiful color photography with moments of psychological insight. Loses some grandeur on TV. ⑤

KANDYLAND 1987
★ **R Drama 1:29**
☑ Nudity, adult situations, explicit language, violence
Dir: Robert Schnitzer **Cast:** Kim Evenson, Charles Laulette, Sandahl Bergman, Cole Stevens, Bruce Baum
▶ Perky Evenson, bored with her dry-cleaning job, gets the stage bug when she enters a bikini contest. She becomes a stripper under Bergman's tutelege but almost loses the love of Laulette, her hot-tempered boyfriend. Glossy T-and-A vehicle for former *Playboy* Playmate Evenson.

KANGAROO 1987 Australian
☆ **R Drama 1:45**
☑ Brief nudity, adult situations, explicit language, violence
Dir: Tim Burstall **Cast:** Colin Friels, Judy Davis, John Walton, Julie Nihill, Hugh Keays-Byrne
▶ Controversial English writer Friels and his German-born wife Davis move to Australia in the 1920s. Friels falls under the spell of right-wing radical leader Keays-Byrne but later turns against him. Good performances by real-life husband and wife Friels and Davis, but adaptation of a

semiautobiographical D. H. Lawrence novel is torturously talky.

KANSAS 1988
★★★ **R Drama 1:48**
☑ Adult situations, explicit language, mild violence
Dir: David Stevens **Cast:** Matt Dillon, Andrew McCarthy, Leslie Hope, Alan Toy, Brent Jennings, Andy Romano
▶ Ordinary guy McCarthy meets vagrant Dillon and finds himself passive participant in latter's bank robbery. They separate and McCarthy becomes involved with farmer's daughter Hope; fugitive Dillon's return threatens McCarthy's future. Authentic Corn Belt ambiance provides background for young leads to stretch their talents. **(CC)**

KARATE KID, THE 1984
★★★★★ **PG Drama 2:07**
☑ Explicit language, violence
Dir: John G. Avildsen **Cast:** Ralph Macchio, Noriyuki "Pat" Morita, Elisabeth Shue, Martin Kove, William Zabka
▶ New Jersey teen Macchio moves to Southern California and runs afoul of martial arts bully. Kindly Oriental handyman (Oscar-nominated Morita) comes to the rescue with karate lessons, training Macchio for a karate tournament showdown with his tormentor. The Macchio-Morita relationship is warm and appealing. A winner; you'll cheer for the underdog. **(CC)**

KARATE KID, PART II, THE 1986
★★★★★ **PG Drama 1:53**
☑ Explicit language, violence
Dir: John G. Avildsen **Cast:** Ralph Macchio, Noriyuki "Pat" Morita, Nobu McCarthy, Danny Kamekona, Tamlyn Tomita, Yuji Okumoto
▶ With Macchio in tow, Morita returns to his native Okinawa to visit his dying father, resolve a thirty-year-old feud, and resume a romance with his childhood sweetheart (McCarthy). Macchio finds love of his own with the charming Tomita and also battles a bully. Sequel repeats likable characters and inspiring, warm-hearted plotting. **(CC)**

KEEP, THE 1983
★★ **R Horror 1:38**
☑ Rape, nudity, adult situations
Dir: Michael Mann **Cast:** Scott Glenn, Alberta Watson, Jurgen Prochnow, Robert Prosky, Gabriel Byrne, Ian McKellen

▶ Nazi soldiers under the command of sensitive officer Prochnow hole up in imposing Rumanian edifice known as "the keep." Monster hidden within its walls murders soldiers and threatens all humanity. Artful visual style from "Miami Vice" creator Mann fails to compensate for ponderous pacing, stilted script, and lack of real shocks. Pulsating score by Tangerine Dream.

KEEPING TRACK 1987 Canadian
★ R Mystery-Suspense 1:42
☑ Brief nudity, explicit language, violence
Dir: Robin Spry *Cast:* Margot Kidder, Michael Sarrazin, Ken Pogue, Alan Scarfe
▶ Bank executive Kidder and TV news anchorman Sarrazin witness a shooting and find themselves battling killers, cops, and a government cover-up. Standard suspenser features acceptable performances and scenic Montreal locations, but suffers from creaky, farfetched plotting. **(CC)**

KELLY'S HEROES 1970
★★★★ PG War 2:24
☑ Adult situations, explicit language, violence
Dir: Brian G. Hutton *Cast:* Clint Eastwood, Telly Savalas, Don Rickles, Donald Sutherland, Carroll O'Connor, Gavin McLeod
▶ During World War II, Eastwood learns where a fortune in gold is hidden behind enemy lines. As the Allies advance, he assembles a ragtag band of misfits to steal the gold. Sprawling, consistently entertaining adventure has an expert cast and pleasant tongue-in-cheek tone.

KENTUCKIAN, THE 1955
★★★ NR Western 1:44
Dir: Burt Lancaster *Cast:* Burt Lancaster, Dianne Foster, Diana Lynn, John McIntire, Una Merkel, Walter Matthau
▶ Rugged frontier adventure finds Lancaster and his son involved in a vicious family feud when they leave Kentucky for Texas. Lancaster's only directing effort gave Matthau his film debut as a whip-wielding villain.

KENTUCKY 1938
★★★★ NR Drama/Romance 1:35
Dir: David Butler *Cast:* Loretta Young, Richard Greene, Walter Brennan, Douglas Dumbrille, Karen Morley, Moroni Olsen
▶ A long-standing family feud disrupts the romance between horse fanciers Young and Greene, but the Kentucky Derby helps resolve the crisis. Blue Grass State romance has gorgeous photography and an Oscar-winning performance by Brennan as one of the feud's instigators.

KENTUCKY FRIED MOVIE, THE 1977
★★ R Comedy 1:24
☑ Nudity, explicit language
Dir: John Landis *Cast:* Evan C. Kim, Bill Bixby, Henry Gibson, George Lazenby, Master Bong Soo Han, Donald Sutherland
▶ From the director of *Animal House* and the creators of *Airplane*: a generally amusing and frequently off-color collection of skits satirizing 1950s TV shows, disaster movies, kung-fu flicks, sexploitation movies, and commercials. Some terrible jokes but many very funny ones too.

KEY EXCHANGE 1985
★ R Romance/Comedy 1:36
☑ Nudity, adult situations, explicit language
Dir: Barnett Kellman *Cast:* Brooke Adams, Ben Masters, Daniel Stern, Danny Aiello, Tony Roberts
▶ Writer Masters enjoys sexual freedom and resists girlfriend Adams's request for commitment while his best pal Stern separates from his wife. Adaptation of Kevin Wade's off-Broadway play has attractive cast, but insights into singles scene are pretty dated. Comic highlight: Masters pretending to be a "Sterile Single" on TV talk show. **(CC)**

KEY LARGO 1948
★★★ NR Drama 1:41 B&W
Dir: John Huston *Cast:* Humphrey Bogart, Lauren Bacall, Edward G. Robinson, Lionel Barrymore, Claire Trevor
▶ During a hurricane, gangster Robinson takes hostages in a Florida hotel. Disillusioned World War II vet Bogart is reluctant to get involved until Bacall gives him the inspiration to fight back. Strongly acted if overly talky drama. Trevor won Best Supporting Actress Oscar as a lush.

KEYS OF THE KINGDOM, THE 1945
★★★★ NR Drama 2:17 B&W
Dir: John M. Stahl *Cast:* Gregory Peck, Thomas Mitchell, Vincent Price, Roddy McDowall, Edmund Gwenn, Cedric Hardwicke
▶ In China, humble missionary Peck overcomes personal hardships and the horrors of war to affect the lives of many peo-

ple with his devout faith. An inspiring story that touches the heart. Lavishly produced; Peck won his first Oscar nomination for his performance. Based on the A. J. Cronin novel.

KHARTOUM 1966 British
★★ NR Action-Adventure 2:14
Dir: Basil Dearden **Cast:** Charlton Heston, Laurence Olivier, Richard Johnson, Ralph Richardson, Johnny Sekka, Michael Hordern
▶ True story of the 1885 siege of Khartoum, in which Sudanese natives, led by holy man "The Mahdi" (Olivier), eventually defeated British troops led by Sir Charles "Chinese" Gordon (Heston) after a long and arduous siege. Intelligent screenplay and superb performances by Heston and Olivier make this epic a cut above the genre norm.

KID, THE 1921
★ NR Comedy 1:00 B&W
Dir: Charlie Chaplin **Cast:** Charlie Chaplin, Jackie Coogan, Carl Miller, Edna Purviance
▶ The Little Tramp adopts abandoned boy Coogan and serves as father and mother to him. Their relationship is threatened when the child's actual mother seeks to reclaim him. Silent classic is heartwarming and always amusingly sentimental; Chaplin and young Coogan made an unbeatable team.

KIDCO 1984
★★★★ PG Comedy/Family 1:44
☑ Adult situations, explicit language
Dir: Ronald F. Maxwell **Cast:** Scott Schwartz, Cinnamon Idles, Tristine Skyler, Elizabeth Gorcey, Maggie Blye
▶ Sixth-grader Schwartz and his pals go into business, cornering the local manure market. Adult competition and the IRS are no match for these pint-sized entrepreneurs. Predictable, but as cheerfully produced as a corn flakes commercial; inspired by a true story. **(CC)**

KID FROM BROOKLYN, THE 1946
★★★★ NR Musical/Comedy 1:54
Dir: Norman Z. McLeod **Cast:** Danny Kaye, Virginia Mayo, Vera-Ellen, Steve Cochran, Eve Arden, Lionel Stander
▶ Mild-mannered milkman Kaye gets into nightclub tussle with middleweight boxing champ Cochran. The press wrongly reports that Kaye knocked out Cochran, thus setting the stage for milkman's pugilistic career. Broadly appealing Kaye vehicle highlighted by "Pav-

lova," a nifty modern dance parody number. Wisecracking Arden steals her scenes. Remake of the 1936 Harold Lloyd comedy The Milky Way.

KID GALAHAD 1962
★★ NR Musical 1:35
Dir: Phil Karlson **Cast:** Elvis Presley, Gig Young, Lola Albright, Joan Blackman, Charles Bronson, Ned Glass
▶ Boxing promoter Young discovers young fighter Presley at his Catskills camp and turns him into title contender Kid Galahad. Weak remake of a 1937 Edward G. Robinson film includes "King of the Whole Wide World" and "Love Is for Lovers." Bronson is effectively understated as Presley's incorruptible trainer.

KID MILLIONS 1934
★ NR Musical 1:30 C/B&W
Dir: Roy Del Ruth **Cast:** Eddie Cantor, Ann Sothern, Ethel Merman, George Murphy, Edgar Kennedy, Nicholas Brothers
▶ Lower East Side singer Cantor inherits $77 million and goes on a wild spending spree with his girlfriend Sothern. Dated but tuneful comedy works best during the frequent specialty numbers. Songs include "When My Ship Comes In," "Mandy," and "Ice Cream Fantasy" (look quickly for Goldwyn Girl Lucille Ball in this number).

KIDNAPPED 1960
★★★★ G Action-Adventure 1:34
Dir: Robert Stevenson **Cast:** Peter Finch, James MacArthur, Bernard Lee, Niall MacGinnis, Finlay Currie, Peter O'Toole
▶ In eighteenth-century Scotland, young MacArthur is tricked out of a fortune and impressed as a cabin boy on a ship to the New World. He befriends Scottish rebel Finch, who leads him on a series of daring adventures against the English. Third film version of Robert Louis Stevenson's adventure receives typically polished Disney treatment.

KIDNAPPED 1986
★★ R Action-Adventure 1:38
☑ Nudity, strong sexual content, explicit language, violence
Dir: Howard Avedis **Cast:** David Naughton, Barbara Crampton, Lance LeGault, Chick Vennera, Kim Evenson, Jimmie C. Walker
▶ Young Evenson is abducted and forced into pornographic films. Her older sister Crampton joins forces with Santa

Barbara police detective Naughton to rescue her. Low-budget exploitation film with a full quota of nudity and sadistic violence.

KIDNAPPING OF THE PRESIDENT, THE
1980 Canadian
★★★ R Drama 1:33
☑ Adult situations, explicit language, violence
Dir: George Mendeluk *Cast:* William Shatner, Hal Holbrook, Van Johnson, Ava Gardner, Miguel Fernandes, Cindy Girling
▶ During a Toronto visit, the President (Holbrook) is taken hostage by South American terrorists; Secret Service agent Shatner must rescue him. The Vice President (Johnson) and wife Gardner want Shatner to fail. Workmanlike thriller with a good performance from Fernandes as the terrorist leader.

KIDS ARE ALRIGHT, THE 1979 British
★★ PG Documentary/Music 1:47
☑ Explicit language
Dir: Jeff Stein *Cast:* Pete Townshend, Roger Daltrey, John Entwistle, Keith Moon, Kenny Jones
▶ Fascinating look at rock supergroup the Who is a chaotic collection of concert footage, rock videos, and interviews with the group and their friends Ringo Starr, Tom Smothers, etc. Includes fourteen first-rate songs: "Happy Jack," "Baba O'Riley," "Won't Get Fooled Again," etc. Final sequence, filmed in Dolby Stereo, features deceased drummer Moon's replacement Jones.

KILL AND KILL AGAIN 1981
★★ PG Martial Arts 1:40
☑ Violence
Dir: Ivan Hall *Cast:* James Ryan, Anneline Kriel, Ken Gampu, Norman Robinson, Stan Schmidt, Bill Flynn
▶ Sequel to *Kill or Be Killed* with Ryan repeating his role as a heroic martial arts master. This time he battles a mad billionaire who plans to poison the world's water supply. Ryan is alerted to the case by former Miss World Kriel, whose scientist father has been kidnapped. Fast, lighthearted action should please kung-fu fans.

KILLER ELITE, THE 1975
★★★★ PG Action-Adventure 2:00
☑ Explicit language, graphic violence
Dir: Sam Peckinpah *Cast:* James Caan, Robert Duvall, Arthur Hill, Gig Young, Mako, Bo Hopkins

▶ While protecting Asian politician Mako, bodyguard Caan learns that his nemesis Duvall is assembling an assassination team. Extended chases and double-crosses are the best aspects of this political thriller. Caan makes a strong impression as the badly wounded hero.

KILLER FISH 1979 Italian/Brazilian
☆ PG Action-Adventure 1:41
☑ Explicit language, violence
Dir: Anthony M. Dawson (Antonio Margheriti) *Cast:* Lee Majors, Karen Black, James Franciscus, Margaux Hemingway, Marisa Berenson, Gary Collins
▶ Laconic tough guy Majors and his neurotic partner Black steal a fortune in gems from a Brazilian industrial complex. They hide the loot in the bottom of a lake, unaware that villain Franciscus has stocked it with hungry piranha. Mindless, fast-paced thriller is perfectly cast. Also known as *Treasure of the Piranha.* (CC)

KILLER FORCE 1975
★★ R Action-Adventure 1:40
☑ Adult situations, explicit language, violence
Dir: Val Guest *Cast:* Telly Savalas, Peter Fonda, Hugh O'Brian, O. J. Simpson, Maud Adams, Christopher Lee
▶ Savalas, chief of security at a South African diamond mine, asks local deputy Fonda to investigate a series of thefts, unaware that Fonda is masterminding an assault on the mine's vaults. Competent adventure highlighted by an extended break-in sequence.

KILLER INSIDE ME, THE 1976
★★ R Drama 1:39
☑ Brief nudity, adult situations, explicit language, violence
Dir: Burt Kennedy *Cast:* Stacy Keach, Susan Tyrrell, Tisha Sterling, Keenan Wynn, Charles McGraw, John Dehner
▶ Battling redneck hoodlums, Montana sheriff Keach succumbs to a violent psychosis brought on by childhood traumas. Disappointing, flashback-ridden adaptation of Jim Thompson's cult novel is worth a look for Keach's thoughtful performance and a superb turn by Tyrrell as a hard-bitten hooker.

KILLER PARTY 1986
★ R Horror 1:32
☑ Nudity, adult situations, explicit language, violence
Dir: William Fruet *Cast:* Martin Hewitt,

Ralph Seymour, Elaine Wilkes, Paul Bartel, Sherry Willis-Burch, Alicia Fleer
▶ Sorority pledges plan a series of practical jokes for an April Fool's party at a haunted house, but something goes terribly wrong as the guests meet gruesome deaths. Minor horror piece sticks to a familiar formula.

KILLERS, THE 1964
★★ NR Drama 1:35
Dir: Don Siegel *Cast:* Lee Marvin, Angie Dickinson, John Cassavetes, Ronald Reagan, Clu Gulager, Claude Akins
▶ Marvin and Gulager assassinate Cassavetes and then pursue Reagan, a gangster who sold out Cassavetes in robbery scheme. Fast-paced film is notable for Reagan's atypical bad guy role in his last film. Based on the Ernest Hemingway story and originally made for TV. Previously filmed in 1946 with Burt Lancaster.

KILLING AFFAIR, A 1988
★★ R Drama 1:40
☑ Nudity, adult situations, explicit language, violence
Dir: David Saperstein *Cast:* Peter Weller, Kathy Baker, John Glover, Bill Smitrovich, Rhetta Hughes
▶ In 1943 West Virginia, a vicious labor boss is found murdered. Widow Baker strikes up an unsettling relationship with Weller, a drifter who might be the killer. Bleak Southern gothic melodrama is often confusing. Directing debut for Saperstein, author of *Cocoon*.

KILLING FIELDS, THE 1984
★★★★ R Drama 2:22
☑ Adult situations, explicit language, graphic violence
Dir: Roland Joffe *Cast:* Sam Waterston, Haing S. Ngor, John Malkovich, Craig T. Nelson, Julian Sands, Athol Fugard
▶ Morally overwhelming masterwork about friendship, survival, and war based on a true story. *New York Times* journalist Sydney Schanberg (Waterston) escapes the fall of Cambodia aided by his native assistant Dith Pran (Ngor) but can't help Pran, who's left behind to face the horrors of the Khmer Rouge holocaust. Real-life Cambodian survivor Ngor is astonishing. Three Oscars, including Best Supporting Actor (Ngor), Editing, and Cinematography. Also nominated for Picture, Director, and Actor (Waterston). **(CC)**

KILLING OF SISTER GEORGE, THE 1968
British
☆ R Drama 2:19
☑ Nudity, strong sexual content, adult situations, explicit language
Dir: Robert Aldrich *Cast:* Beryl Reid, Susannah York, Coral Browne, Ronald Fraser, Patricia Medina, Hugh Paddick
▶ Lesbian actress Reid faces personal and professional problems: she's written out of her BBC soap opera and her lover York gets involved with another woman. Subject matter may offend some; Reid's powerhouse performance dominates. Lengthy seduction scene near film's conclusion originally earned X rating.

KILLING TIME, THE 1987
★★★ R Mystery-Suspense 1:35
☑ Nudity, adult situations, explicit language, violence
Dir: Rick King *Cast:* Beau Bridges, Kiefer Sutherland, Wayne Rogers, Joe Don Baker, Camelia Kath, Janet Carroll
▶ Small-town California sheriff Bridges and his ex-lover Kath plot the death of her arrogant developer husband Rogers, but their plan is threatened by the arrival of new deputy Sutherland. Scheme is further complicated when Bridges discovers Sutherland is actually a serial killer. Twisty modern-day film noir has an unpredictable story line and agreeably unsavory characters.

KILL OR BE KILLED 1980
★★ PG Martial Arts 1:30
☑ Violence
Dir: Ivan Hall *Cast:* James Ryan, Norman Combes, Charlotte Michelle, Danie DuPlessis
▶ Ex-Nazi karate coach forces his star students to compete against a Japanese team led by his nemesis from World War II. Martial arts master Ryan rebels, leading to an action-filled climax involving his kidnapped girlfriend. Fast-paced exploitation picture, filmed in South Africa, led to sequel *Kill and Kill Again*.

KILLPOINT 1984
★ R Action-Adventure 1:32
☑ Rape, nudity, adult situations, explicit language, graphic violence
Dir: Frank Harris *Cast:* Leo Fong, Richard Roundtree, Cameron Mitchell, Stack Pierce, Hope Holiday, Diana Leigh
▶ Vicious thugs led by Mitchell and Pierce overwhelm a small-town arsenal, then use the weapons to terrorize local

citizens. Kung-fu expert Fong and Federal agent Roundtree battle the gang. Standard low-budget thriller is often uncomfortably racist.

KIM 1951
★★★★ G Action-Adventure 1:53
Dir: Victor Saville   *Cast:* Errol Flynn, Dean Stockwell, Paul Lukas, Robert Douglas, Thomas Gomez, Cecil Kellaway
► Young Stockwell, orphaned in colonial India, befriends horse-thief Flynn and ascetic Lukas; disguised as a native, he takes part in a secret plot to repel a Russian invasion of the Khyber Pass. Adaptation of Rudyard Kipling's classic adventure captures the novel's exotic atmosphere and sweeping action. Remade as a TV movie in 1984.

KIND HEARTS AND CORONETS 1949 British
★★★ NR Comedy 1:45 B&W
Dir: Robert Hamer   *Cast:* Dennis Price, Alec Guinness, Joan Greenwood, Valerie Hobson, Miles Malleson, Audrey Fildes
► Conniving cad Price, the unacknowledged offspring of a duke, conspires to kill those who stand between him and the inheritance he believes is rightfully his. In an unparalleled acting feat, Guinness plays the eight family members, including the duke himself, whom Price must slay in order to acquire the title. Memorable and notorious black comedy made Guinness an international star; witty dialogue and wicked send-up of English manners still amuse today.

KIND OF LOVING, A 1962 British
★★ NR Drama 1:52 B&W
Dir: John Schlesinger   *Cast:* Alan Bates, June Ritchie, Thora Hird, Bert Palmer, Gwen Nelson, Malcolm Patton
► Factory workers Bates and Ritchie, forced to marry when she becomes pregnant, move in with her domineering mother Hird. Marriage goes awry when she miscarries and forsakes sex and he hits the bottle; two eventually realize they must escape Hird's clutches to save the marriage and achieve a "kind of loving." Simple story sustained by grimy realism, fine performances from unknown cast (save for Bates), and sure-handed direction by Schlesinger.

KINDRED, THE 1987
★★ R Horror 1:29
☑ Explicit language, violence

Dir: Jeffrey Obrow   *Cast:* David Allen Brooks, Rod Steiger, Amanda Pays, Talia Balsam, Kim Hunter
► Geneticist Brooks discovers late scientist's mom Hunter created nasty things in the lab (such as turning Brooks's brother into a tentacled creature). Mad doctor Steiger complicates Brooks's efforts to annihilate mom's experiments. Above-par "don't go in the basement" flick. Fair number of chills as well as unintentional chuckles.

KING AND I, THE 1956
★★★★ NR Musical 2:13
Dir: Walter Lang   *Cast:* Deborah Kerr, Yul Brynner, Rita Moreno, Martin Benson, Terry Saunders
► Stern Siamese monarch Brynner is softened by the influence of English governess Kerr as their clashing cultures and personalities eventually give way to an unspoken love. Magnificent performance by Brynner (who won one of film's three Oscars) in this sumptuously produced and moving adaptation of the Broadway musical. Brynner/Kerr "Shall We Dance?" duet highlights a wonderful Rodgers and Hammerstein score. A Best Picture nominee. Story was originally brought to the screen in 1946's *Anna and the King of Siam.*

KING CREOLE 1958
★★★★ NR Musical 1:56 B&W
Dir: Michael Curtiz   *Cast:* Elvis Presley, Carolyn Jones, Dolores Hart, Dean Jagger, Liliane Montevecchi, Walter Matthau
► Presley plays a New Orleans singer drawn into the underworld by his love for Jones, mistress to nightclub owner Matthau. Vic Morrow made a good impression as a young gang leader. Unusually dramatic plot for a musical was adapted from Harold Robbins's early best-seller *A Stone for Danny Fisher.* Elvis's last film before entering the Army includes "Hard-Headed Woman" and "Trouble."

KING DAVID 1985
★★★ PG-13 Drama 1:54
☑ Rape, brief nudity, violence
Dir: Bruce Beresford   *Cast:* Richard Gere, Edward Woodward, Alice Krige, Denis Quilley, Hurd Hatfield
► Biblical epic of the story of David (Gere), from his battle with Goliath through his ascension to the throne. He falls for Bathsheba (Krige) and has her husband killed. Although film is respectful

and well produced, Gere is miscast and the pacing lags. Visual appeal doesn't always grab you emotionally. **(CC)**

KING KONG 1933
★★★★ NR Sci-Fi 1:40 B&W
Dir: Merian C. Cooper, Ernest B. Schoedsack *Cast:* Fay Wray, Bruce Cabot, Robert Armstrong, Frank Reicher, Sam Hardy
▶ Enduring classic stands head and shoulders above any of the remakes and imitators. On a trip to Skull Island, Wray is captured by a fifty-foot gorilla known as Kong. After her rescue, Kong is brought to New York, where he is billed as the Eighth Wonder of the World. He wreaks havoc on the city when he escapes and seeks out true love Wray. Climax atop the Empire State Building is one of filmdom's great moments.

KING KONG 1976
★★★★ PG Sci-Fi 2:14
Dir: John Guillermin *Cast:* Jessica Lange, Jeff Bridges, Charles Grodin, John Randolph, René Auberjonois
▶ Showman De Laurentiis's $24 million remake of the 1933 classic boasts touches of feminism, Freud, and ecology in the script; a wealth of special effects including an updated climax where Kong climbs on one of the World Trade Center towers; and Lange in her film debut. Fun family entertainment, enlivened by bravura performances from Grodin and the marvelous mechanical beast. Not as charming as the original but will kids care?

KING KONG LIVES 1986
★★ PG-13 Sci-Fi 1:45
☑ Adult situations, explicit language, violence
Dir: John Guillermin *Cast:* Brian Kerwin, Linda Hamilton, John Ashton, Peter Michael Goetz, Peter Elliot, George Yiasomi
▶ Sequel to 1976 film reveals giant ape kept on life-support systems after fall from World Trade Center. Borneo hunter Kerwin brings enormous female Kong to help doctor Hamilton perform needed surgery on the King. Two apes fall in love, escape, but fall prey to bloodthirsty hunters. Despite improved special effects, pointless adventure strains credibility. **(CC)**

KING LEAR 1988 U.S./Swiss
☆ PG Drama 1:31
☑ Explicit language
Dir: Jean-Luc Godard *Cast:* Burgess

Meredith, Molly Ringwald, Jean-Luc Godard, Peter Sellars, Norman Mailer
▶ Ancestor of William Shakespeare (American theater director Sellars) follows retired mobster Meredith and daughter Ringwald as they reenact scenes from *King Lear.* French director Godard (working in English) uses Shakespeare's text as a vehicle for obscure critique of pop culture that may appeal to his following but will leave most in the cold.

KING OF COMEDY, THE 1983
★ PG Comedy/Drama 1:49
☑ Adult situations, explicit language, mild violence
Dir: Martin Scorsese *Cast:* Robert De Niro, Jerry Lewis, Sandra Bernhard, Diahnne Abbott, Shelley Hack
▶ Show-biz junkie and general nebbish Rupert Pupkin (De Niro) worships urbane TV talk-show host Lewis. Desperate to become a celebrity and win an appearance on late night TV, De Niro and sidekick Bernhard kidnap Lewis and hold him hostage. Top-notch acting from entire cast (especially the restrained Lewis) but some critics found De Niro's character too unlikable; others were put off by Scorsese's moralizing tone.

KING OF HEARTS 1967 French/British
★★ NR Comedy 1:42
Dir: Philippe de Broca *Cast:* Alan Bates, Genevieve Bujold, Adolfo Celi, Pierre Brasseur, Jean-Claude Brialy
▶ Funny and touching parable was an enormous underground hit with college kids of the late sixties/early seventies. Amiable Scotsman Bates is sent to a small village during World War I to defuse a bomb. He doesn't realize that the townsfolk have fled, replaced by charming lunatics from a local asylum. Now a little dated and simpleminded, but definitely worth a look.

KING OF KINGS 1961
★★★★★ NR Drama 2:44
Dir: Nicholas Ray *Cast:* Jeffrey Hunter, Robert Ryan, Harry Guardino, Rip Torn, Siobhan McKenna, Hurd Hatfield
▶ Story of Christ (Hunter), told against the backdrop of Jewish resistance to Roman rule, traces his life through birth in the manger, wandering in the desert, the Sermon on the Mount, and the Last Supper. Cast-of-thousands spectacular is satisfying holiday fare.

KING OF MARVIN GARDENS, THE
1972
☆ R Drama 1:44
☑ Brief nudity, adult situations, explicit language
Dir: Bob Rafelson *Cast:* Jack Nicholson, Bruce Dern, Ellen Burstyn, Julia Anne Robinson, Scatman Crothers
► Eccentric, disorienting story of two brothers—all-night FM deejay Nicholson and minor hood Dern—who meet in Atlantic City to discuss Dern's farfetched plan to buy land in Hawaii for hotel development. Dern's girlfriend, a former beauty queen (Burstyn), and her stepdaughter Robinson compete for the men's attention. Strong cult following for this original and deeply affecting drama, although slow pacing and quirky plotting may put off many viewers.

KING OF THE GYPSIES 1978
★★★★ R Drama 1:52
☑ Nudity, adult situations, explicit language
Dir: Frank Pierson *Cast:* Sterling Hayden, Shelley Winters, Susan Sarandon, Judd Hirsch, Eric Roberts, Brooke Shields
► Inside look at three generations of gypsies and the succession of power from "king" Hayden to his reluctant grandson Roberts. Colorful *Godfather* clone re-creates a very foreign, nomadic way of life replete with fortune tellers and all-night celebrations. Written and directed by Pierson; based on the nonfiction best-seller by Peter Maas.

KING OF THE MOUNTAIN 1981
★★ PG Drama 1:30
☑ Adult situations, explicit language
Dir: Noel Nosseck *Cast:* Harry Hamlin, Joseph Bottoms, Richard Cox, Dennis Hopper, Dan Haggerty, Seymour Cassel
► Three young Angelenos—garage mechanic Hamlin, aspiring songwriter Bottoms, and junior record producer Cox—pursue careers by day and drag race on Mulholland Drive by night. They pal around with over-the-hill hippie Hopper and risk their macho lives, staking claim to title: "king of the mountain."

KING RAT 1965
★★★★ NR War 2:13 B&W
Dir: Bryan Forbes *Cast:* George Segal, Tom Courtenay, James Fox, Patrick O'Neal, Denholm Elliott, John Mills
► In Singapore in 1945, POW Segal ensures his survival but incurs the hatred of his fellow prisoners by exploiting the black market in a Japanese prison camp. Officers Elliott and Mills aid him in return for money and food, while Provost Marshal Courtenay opposes him. Powerful, unvarnished drama is based on the novel by James Clavell.

KING SOLOMON'S MINES 1985
★★ PG-13 Action-Adventure 1:40
☑ Explicit language, violence
Dir: J. Lee Thompson *Cast:* Richard Chamberlain, Sharon Stone, Herbert Lom, John Rhys-Davies, Ken Gampu, Shai K. Ophir
► In Africa, adventurer Chamberlain helps Stone search for her missing father, who has been captured by Germans seeking coveted diamond-mine treasure map. Romance develops as the intrepid duo face cannibals, wild animals, and other dangers. Moves along quickly if mindlessly. Exotic scenery helps; cardboard characterizations do not. Spawned sequel *Allan Quartermain and the Lost City of Gold*.

KINJITE—FORBIDDEN SUBJECTS 1989
★★★ R Action-Adventure 1:37
☑ Nudity, explicit language, violence
Dir: J. Lee Thompson *Cast:* Charles Bronson, Perry Lopez, Juan Fernandez, Peggy Lipton, James Pax
► When pimp Fernandez kidnaps daughter of Japanese businessman Pax, Los Angeles cop Bronson investigates although he's no fan of Pax (who once made a play for Bronson's daughter). Bronson vehicle has a bit more variety than his recent outings; attempts to create three-dimensional character, but contrived story is often distasteful.

KISMET 1955
★★★ NR Musical 1:53
Dir: Vincente Minnelli *Cast:* Howard Keel, Ann Blyth, Dolores Gray, Vic Damone, Monty Woolley, Sebastian Cabot
► In ancient Baghdad, rascal con man Keel is forced by wicked Wazir (Cabot) to persuade Caliph (Damone) to wed a princess. Keel outwits the Wazir and helps daughter Blyth win Caliph's heart. Screen version of the popular Broadway musical is an Arabian Nights tale of comedy and romance. Songs include "Stranger in Paradise," "This Is My Beloved," "Baubles, Bangles and Beads." **(CC)**

KISS, THE 1988
★★ R Horror 1:40

☑ Nudity, adult situations, explicit language, graphic violence
Dir: Pen Desham *Cast:* Joanna Pacula, Meredith Salenger, Mimi Kuzyk, Pamela Collyer, Nicholas Kilbertus, Jan Rubes
▶ Beautiful model Pacula visits family of her niece Salenger. Dad Kilbertus is bewitched by gorgeous Pacula, but Salenger senses the truth: Pacula is really murderous witch who'd like to possess her. Stylishly directed and above-par acting for the genre, but gross violence and increasingly contrived plotting hurt.

KISSIN' COUSINS 1964
★★ NR Musical 1:36
Dir: Gene Nelson *Cast:* Elvis Presley, Arthur O'Connell, Glenda Farrell, Jack Albertson, Pam Austin, Yvonne Craig
▶ Dual role for Presley: he's an Air Force officer ordered to buy O'Connell's land for a missile base and a distant cousin in love with a WAC. O'Connell's moonshine operations provide most of the comedy; Elvis sings "It's a Long Lonely Highway," "Barefoot Ballad," "Smokey Mountain Boy," etc.

KISS ME DEADLY 1955
★★ NR Mystery-Suspense 1:45 B&W
Dir: Robert Aldrich *Cast:* Ralph Meeker, Albert Dekker, Paul Stewart, Maxine Cooper, Wesley Addy, Juano Hernandez
▶ Detective Mike Hammer (Meeker) wreaks vicious revenge when he is framed for a murder. In the process he uncovers a mysterious plot involving gangster Stewart and treacherous femme fatale Gaby Rodgers. Swift, hard-edged film noir is an influential cult item for its unsavory characters and relentless brutality. Highlighted by an unforgettable cameo by Cloris Leachman and a genuinely incredible climax. Based on the Mickey Spillane novel.

KISS ME GOODBYE 1982
★★★★ PG Fantasy/Comedy 1:41
☑ Adult situations, explicit language, adult humor
Dir: Robert Mulligan *Cast:* Sally Field, James Caan, Jeff Bridges, Claire Trevor, Paul Dooley
▶ Widow Field is set to wed straitlaced lawyer Bridges but her happiness is complicated by the ghostly appearance of late husband Caan. Cozy Americanized remake of the much spicier Brazilian *Dona Flor and Her Two Husbands.* The comedy has its obvious side (scenes of Field talking to Caan with everybody else, who can't see him, wondering what's going on) but perky Fields and dryly humorous Bridges are quite likable.

KISS ME, KATE 1953
★★★ NR Musical 1:50
Dir: George Sidney *Cast:* Kathryn Grayson, Howard Keel, Ann Miller, Bobby Van, Keenan Wynn, Bob Fosse
▶ Sometimes stiff adaptation of Cole Porter's Broadway hit (itself based on Shakespeare's *The Taming of the Shrew*) is a sophisticated comedy of errors about lovers, prima donnas, and gangsters staging a musical. Outstanding Oscar-nominated score includes "Wunderbar," "So in Love," "Why Can't You Behave?" and Miller's scorching tapping to "Too Darn Hot."

KISS OF DEATH 1947
★★★ NR Crime 1:39 B&W
Dir: Henry Hathaway *Cast:* Victor Mature, Brian Donlevy, Richard Widmark, Coleen Gray, Karl Malden, Mildred Dunnock
▶ Thief Mature tries to go straight by cooperating with prosecutor Donlevy but is stalked by Widmark, the psychopathic killer he implicated. Compelling and suspenseful with solid work from Mature and authentic New York City locations. The amazingly menacing turn by Widmark—in his film debut—was Oscar-nominated. The famous scene in which he pushes a wheelchair-bound old lady down a flight of steps is just one of many powerful moments.

KISS OF THE SPIDER WOMAN 1985
U.S./Brazilian
★★★ R Drama 1:59
☑ Adult situations, explicit language, violence
Dir: Hector Babenco *Cast:* William Hurt, Raul Julia, Sonia Braga, Jose Lewgoy
▶ Hurt, an apolitical gay, and Julia, a political prisoner, are cellmates in a South American jail. Hurt entertains the initially reluctant Julia by retelling scenes from old movies, and a close relationship develops between the men. Superb direction by Babenco weaves a magical spell. Magnificent Oscar-winning performance by Hurt is tender, subtle, and completely convincing. Julia holds his own in this enthralling drama. A Best Picture nominee. **(CC)**

KITCHEN TOTO, THE 1988 British
★★ PG-13 Drama 1:36
☑ Violence
Dir: Harry Hook *Cast:* Edwin Mahinda, Bob Peck, Phyllis Logan, Kirsten Hughes, Robert Urquhart, Nicholas Chase
▶ In politically troubled 1950 Kenya, young black Mahinda becomes houseboy for British family after his father is killed. Mahinda finds his allegiance divided between his white employers and the black rebels. Beautifully filmed and socially conscious, but melancholy tone and slow pace limit appeal. Mahinda gives a beguilingly natural performance.

KITTY FOYLE 1940
★★★ NR Drama 1:45 B&W
Dir: Sam Wood *Cast:* Ginger Rogers, Dennis Morgan, James Craig, Eduardo Ciannelli, Gladys Cooper
▶ Ambitious Kitty Foyle (Rogers) dumps fiancée Craig to marry wealthy Morgan. Unhappy, she leaves Morgan, only to discover she is pregnant. Tragedy and then eventual happiness follow in this soap opera, which nabbed Rogers a Best Actress Oscar. A Best Picture nominee.

KLONDIKE FEVER 1980
★★★ PG Action-Adventure 1:58
☑ Adult situations, explicit language, violence
Dir: Peter Carter *Cast:* Rod Steiger, Angie Dickinson, Jeff East, Lorne Greene, Barry Morse
▶ During his Alaskan Gold Rush youth, writer Jack London (East) stands up to the brutality and corruption of the gold miners, helps a madam, Dickinson, set up her own saloon, saves a husky dog from being mistreated and battles town tyrant Steiger. Fast-paced adventure. Also known as *Jack London's Klondike Fever.*

KLUTE 1971
★★★★ R Mystery-Suspense 1:54
☑ Adult situations, explicit language, mild violence
Dir: Alan J. Pakula *Cast:* Jane Fonda, Donald Sutherland, Charles Cioffi, Roy Scheider, Dorothy Tristan, Rita Gam
▶ Pennsylvania detective Sutherland investigates friend's disappearance in New York City and gets involved with hooker Fonda, who's being stalked by psychopath. Consistently provocative adult thriller with a nail-biting finale. Fascinating Oscar-winning performance by Fonda dominates the film, with Sutherland providing understated support.

KNIGHTRIDERS 1981
★ R Action-Adventure 2:26
☑ Brief nudity, adult situations, explicit language, violence
Dir: George A. Romero *Cast:* Ed Harris, Gary Lahti, Tom Savini, Amy Ingersoll
▶ A traveling troupe of entertainers combines medieval costumes with motorcycles and live according to the laws of Camelot. The group's king is challenged by a pretender to the throne. Unusual film is a wry change-of-pace for horror director Romero.

KNIGHTS OF THE CITY 1986
★ R Drama/Music 1:29 C/B&W
☑ Adult situations, explicit language, violence
Dir: Dominic Orlando *Cast:* Leon Isaac Kennedy, John Mengatti, Nicholas Campbell, Janine Turner
▶ When not making music, street gang led by Kennedy battles rivals over turf. Kennedy romances record company executive's daughter Turner and the gang wins a talent contest. However, they must revert to knives to settle their final confrontation. Noisy, crudely shot entry in the breakdance/rap craze represents last gasp of the dying genre.

KNIGHTS OF THE ROUND TABLE 1953
★★★ NR Action-Adventure 1:55
Dir: Richard Thorpe *Cast:* Robert Taylor, Ava Gardner, Mel Ferrer, Anne Crawford, Stanley Baker, Felix Aylmer
▶ Medieval England: Sir Lancelot (Taylor) faithfully serves King Arthur (Ferrer) but his heart roams in the direction of Arthur's wife Queen Guinevere (Gardner). Well-mounted version of a now-familiar triangle.

KNOCK ON ANY DOOR 1949
★★ NR Drama 1:40 B&W
Dir: Nicholas Ray *Cast:* Humphrey Bogart, John Derek, George Macready, Allene Roberts, Susan Perry
▶ Socially conscious drama stars Bogart as an attorney defending cop-killer Derek on the grounds of his deprived childhood. This liberal philosophy may seem quaint to some, but Bogart's climactic courtroom "knock on any door" speech is a rouser.

KNOCK ON WOOD 1954
★★ NR Musical/Comedy 1:43
Dir: Melvin Frank, Norman Panama *Cast:* Danny Kaye, Mai Zetterling, Torin Thatcher, David Burns, Leon Askin
▶ Perfect showcase for the multitalented

Kaye. He stars as a professional ventrilo-quist on the verge of a nervous break-down who sleepwalks in a women's hotel, gets involved with an international spy ring, and falls in love with his shrink, Zetterling. Lots of singing and dancing. All the songs ("All About You," "Monahan O'Han," etc.) were written by Sylvia Fine (Mrs. Danny Kaye).

KNUTE ROCKNE—ALL AMERICAN 1940
★ ★ ★ ★ **NR Biography/Sports 1:36 B&W**
Dir: Lloyd Bacon *Cast:* Pat O'Brien, Ronald Reagan, Gale Page, Donald Crisp, Albert Basserman
▶ Biography of football coach Knute Rockne (O'Brien), who guided Notre Dame to many gridiron victories, is con-ventional but still entertaining. Reagan is George Gipp, the dying player who asks O'Brien to "tell the boys to win one for the Gipper." O'Brien does just that in an inspi-rational speech that is now part of cin-ema, sports, and political history. Availa-ble in a colorized version.

KOTCH 1971
★ ★ ★ ★ **PG Comedy 1:53**
☑ Adult situations, explicit language
Dir: Jack Lemmon *Cast:* Walter Mat-thau, Deborah Winters, Felicia Farr, Ellen Geer, Charles Aidman, Lucy Saroyan
▶ Senior citizen Matthau lives with son Aidman and daughter-in-law Farr. Farr and Matthau fight. She tries to send him to an old age home; he responds by run-ning away and befriending unmarried mother-to-be Winters. Affecting comedy won Oscar nominations for the wonderful Matthau, editing, sound, and the Johnny Mercer/Marvin Hamlisch song, "Life Is What You Make It." Lemmon's only direc-torial effort to date.

KOYAANISQATSI 1983
☆ **NR Documentary 1:27**
Dir: Godfrey Reggio
▶ Reggio collaborated with composer Philip Glass and cinematographer Ron Fricks to illuminate Hopi Indian concept of "life out of balance." Powerful score and stunning photographic techniques show natural wonders and man's tech-nological invasion of them. Assault daz-zles the senses, though mainstream audi-ences may be overwhelmed by the experience.

KRAMER VS. KRAMER 1979
★ ★ ★ ★ ★ **PG Drama 1:45**

☑ Brief nudity, adult situations, explicit language
Dir: Robert Benton *Cast:* Dustin Hoff-man, Meryl Streep, Justin Henry, JoBeth Williams, Jane Alexander, Howard Duff
▶ Enormously moving, intimate, and classy film about parental love examines the relationship between father Hoffman and son Henry after they're abandoned by wife/mother Streep. A fierce child-cus-tody battle ensues when Streep returns to claim her son. The growing attach-ment between Hoffman and Henry, ex-quisitely played, is guaranteed to bring tears to your eyes. Oscars for Best Picture and Benton's screenplay, adapted from the Avery Corman novel. Hoffman's and Streep's superior acting also received Os-cars. **(CC)**

KRULL 1983
★ ★ ★ **PG Fantasy 1:56**
☑ Adult situations, violence
Dir: Peter Yates *Cast:* Ken Marshall, Lysette Anthony, Freddie Jones, Fran-cesca Annis, David Battley, Liam Nee-son
▶ Once upon a time on a far-off planet, prince Marshall was aided by a bandit, a sorcerer, and a cyclops in a quest to res-cue his beloved Anthony, kidnapped by an evil monster. Elaborate fantasy ad-venture will entertain kids but adults may find it laughable. Fanciful special effects and set design, but awkwardly directed by the usually dependable Yates. **(CC)**

KRUSH GROOVE 1985
★ ★ ★ **R Musical 1:34**
☑ Brief nudity, adult situations, explicit language
Dir: Michael Schultz *Cast:* Blair Under-wood, Sheila E. (Escovedo), Run-D.M.C., Kurtis Blow, Fat Boys, L.L. Cool J
▶ Slight plot about young entrepreneur Underwood and his fledgling record company provides the framework for top-notch songs performed by rap's greatest musicians. Sheila E. makes the strongest impression, but film catches Run-D.M.C., the Fat Boys, and the Beastie Boys (in a brief cameo) on the verge of stardom. Soundtrack album was a huge success. **(CC)**

LA BAMBA 1987
★ ★ ★ ★ **PG-13 Biography/Music 1:49**
☑ Brief nudity, adult situations, explicit language
Dir: Luis Valdez *Cast:* Lou Diamond

Phillips, Esai Morales, Rosana de Soto, Elizabeth Peña, Danielle von Zerneck, Joe Pantoliano

▶ Uplifting musical about migrant laborer Ritchie Valens (Phillips), who bucks the odds against Hispanics by becoming a rock star. Film concentrates on Valens's problems with his criminal brother Morales and romance with Donna (von Zerneck) before his tragic death in a plane crash. Rock stars Marshall Crenshaw and Brian Setzer join Los Lobos on the soundtrack, which includes "Come On Let's Go" and the title tune. **(CC)**

LABYRINTH 1986
★★★★ **PG Fantasy/Family 1:42**
☑ Explicit language
Dir: Jim Henson *Cast:* David Bowie, Jennifer Connelly, Toby Froud, Shelley Thompson, Christopher Malcolm, Natalie Finland

▶ When goblins kidnap her baby brother, teenager Connelly enters a magical labyrinth to find him. She's aided by a helpful dwarf and other odd creatures. Henson's puppets should delight the kiddies but, aside from David Bowie as the king of the goblins, there's not much here for adults. **(CC)**

LA CAGE AUX FOLLES 1979
French/Italian
★★ **R Comedy 1:37**
☑ Adult situations, explicit language
Dir: Edouard Molinaro *Cast:* Ugo Tognazzi, Michel Serrault, Michel Galabru, Claire Maurier

▶ Gay nightclub owner Tognazzi and his star performer/lover Serrault attempt to impersonate a straight couple to please their son's priggish prospective in-laws. Hilarious boulevard farce with Serrault especially amusing. Most sidesplitting scene: Tognazzi teaching Serrault how to act like a "man." Three Oscar nominations; inspired the Tony-winning Broadway musical. Spawned several sequels. ⑤

LA CAGE AUX FOLLES II 1981
French/Italian
★ **R Comedy 1:39**
☑ Adult situations, explicit language, violence, adult humor
Dir: Edouard Molinaro *Cast:* Ugo Tognazzi, Michel Serrault, Mark Bodin, Benny Luke, Gianrico Tondinelli, Michel Galabru

▶ Gay nightclub owner Tognazzi and his transvestite companion Serrault become involved with cops and spies when Serrault unwittingly gets his hands on stolen microfilm. The lovers flee to Italy but find little peace there. Re-creating their original roles, Tognazzi and Serrault still evoke laughs. ⑤

LA CAGE AUX FOLLES 3: THE WEDDING 1985 French
★ **PG-13 Comedy 1:31**
☑ Adult situations, explicit language
Dir: Georges Lautner *Cast:* Ugo Tognazzi, Michel Serrault, Michel Galabru, Benny Luke

▶ The St. Tropez nightclub of lovers Serrault and Tognazzi has fallen on hard times. One glimmer of hope: Serrault will inherit a fortune if he can marry and produce an heir within eighteen months. Third in the popular comedy series from France. Some fun but the original is still the best. ⑤

LA DOLCE VITA 1960 Italian
★★ **NR Drama 2:55 B&W**
Dir: Federico Fellini *Cast:* Marcello Mastroianni, Yvonne Furneaux, Anita Ekberg, Anouk Aimee, Magali Noel, Alain Cuny

▶ Roman gossip columnist Mastroianni has serious literary aspirations but craves money too much to pursue them. Instead, his life is an aimless round of womanizing and trivial glamour events beloved of tabloid readers. Part slice-of-life look at Italy, part satire of money as route to happiness, and part elaborate joke by director Fellini. Trendsetting film will delight buffs, but length, rambling structure, and often banal dialogue will bore those with conventional tastes. ⑤

LADY AND THE TRAMP 1955
★★★★★ **G Animation 1:16**
Dir: Hamilton Luske, Clyde Geronomi, Wilfred Jackson *Cast:* Voices of Peggy Lee, Barbara Luddy, Larry Roberts, Stan Freberg, Verna Felton

▶ Lady, a pampered pedigreed spaniel, runs away when forced to play second fiddle to her owners' new baby. She falls in puppy love with a mutt named Tramp from the other side of the tracks after their famous romantic spaghetti dinner scene. Peggy Lee provides the voice for a blowsy Pekinese and Si and Am, two slinky cats who sing "We Are Siamese If You Please." Charming and witty Disney effort has become a popular favorite. **(CC)**

LADY BEWARE 1987
★★ R Mystery-Suspense 1:48
☑ Nudity, strong sexual content, explicit language, violence
Dir: Karen Arthur *Cast:* Diane Lane, Michael Woods, Cotter Smith, Peter Nevargic, Tyra Ferrell
▶ Lane, a sultry Pittsburgh window dresser, turns the tables on a psychopathic Peeping Tom who's been torturing her with foul mind games. With Smith as the journalist boyfriend she jilts. Lane has one provocative bath-time nude scene. Mildly exploitive thriller.

LADY CHATTERLEY'S LOVER 1982
French/British
★★ R Drama 1:43
☑ Nudity, strong sexual content, adult situations, explicit language, mild violence
Dir: Just Jaeckin *Cast:* Sylvia Kristel, Shane Briant, Nicholas Clay, Ann Mitchell
▶ After husband Briant is wounded in World War I, Lady Chatterley (Kristel) takes handsome caretaker Clay for a lover. Classy production values enhance tasteful sex scenes, but this sappy rendering of D. H. Lawrence's novel suffers from overwrought music, marginal characterizations, and languid pacing.

LADY EVE, THE 1941
★★★★ NR Comedy 1:34 B&W
Dir: Preston Sturges *Cast:* Barbara Stanwyck, Henry Fonda, Charles Coburn, Eugene Pallette, William Demarest, Eric Blore
▶ Shipboard romance flounders when wealthy paleontologist Fonda discovers cardsharp Stanwyck originally intended to bilk him. She plots delicious revenge by posing as British royalty. Fonda is charmingly innocent (he thinks it can't be same girl because "they look too much alike"), Stanwyck devastatingly sexy (especially in the hair-ruffling scene), and the Sturges stock company swell, especially Demarest as the aide who insists: "It's the same dame."

LADY FROM SHANGHAI, THE 1948
★ NR Mystery-Suspense 1:27 B&W
Dir: Orson Welles *Cast:* Rita Hayworth, Orson Welles, Everett Sloane, Glenn Anders, Ted de Corsia
▶ Sailor Welles gets involved with femme fatale Hayworth (then Mrs. Welles) and is implicated in a murder plot by her crippled husband Sloane. Twisty film noir

highlighted by Welles's exciting cinematic technique (as exemplified by the celebrated hall of mirrors finale).

LADYHAWKE 1985
★★★★ PG-13 Fantasy 2:01
☑ Explicit language, violence
Dir: Richard Donner *Cast:* Rutger Hauer, Matthew Broderick, Michelle Pfeiffer, Leo McKern, John Wood
▶ Offbeat and original story of thirteenth-century cursed lovers. Young pickpocket Broderick meets mysterious knight Hauer who's always accompanied by a hawk. Every night, the hawk turns into Pfeiffer and the knight becomes a wolf; they are actually lovers trapped in an awful spell cast by jealous bishop Wood. This romantic medieval fantasy features handsome stars, strong period flavor, and rousing adventure. **(CC)**

LADY IN A CAGE 1964
★ NR Mystery-Suspense 1:33 B&W
Dir: Walter Grauman *Cast:* Olivia de Havilland, Jeff Corey, Ann Sothern, James Caan, Scatman Crothers
▶ De Havilland plays a wealthy woman trapped in an elevator and menaced by a trio of thugs including a young Caan. Taut thriller builds up a great deal of claustrophobic tension.

LADY IN RED, THE 1979
★★★ R Biography/Crime 1:29
☑ Nudity, adult situations, explicit language, graphic violence
Dir: Lewis Teague *Cast:* Pamela Sue Martin, Robert Conrad, Louise Fletcher, Robert Hogan, Laurie Heineman
▶ Gangster saga from gun moll's point of view. Abused by her dad, Polly Franklin (Martin) moves to Chicago, works in a sweatshop, goes to prison, and becomes a prostitute. She falls for John Dillinger (Conrad) and, after he's gunned down, turns to a life of crime. Lurid, frenzied plotting with lots of stabbings, sadistic murders, and scintillating sex. Roger Corman production has a screenplay by John Sayles.

LADY IN THE LAKE 1947
★★ NR Mystery-Suspense 1:43 B&W
Dir: Robert Montgomery *Cast:* Robert Montgomery, Audrey Totter, Lloyd Nolan, Tom Tully, Leon Ames
▶ Detective Philip Marlowe (Montgomery) investigates a wife's disappearance. Generally interesting experiment in subjective camera (the tale is told entirely from Marlowe's point of view as we only

see him in reflections) becomes a little much when sexy femme fatale Totter kisses the lens. Adapted from the Raymond Chandler novel.

LADY IN WHITE 1988
★★★ **PG-13 Mystery-Suspense 1:52**
☑ Explicit language, violence
Dir: Frank LaLoggia *Cast:* Lukas Haas, Katherine Helmond, Len Cariou, Alex Rocco, Lucy Lee Flippin
▶ Enthralling chiller about sweet, imaginative nine-year-old Haas who gets locked in a spooky school closet on Halloween night. He sees the ghost of a murdered girl and is almost strangled by a mysterious killer. Absorbing blend of comedy, horror, the supernatural, and fantasy; may be too frightening for children. (CC)

LADY JANE 1986 British
★★★ **PG-13 Biography 2:22**
☑ Brief nudity, adult situations
Dir: Trevor Nunn *Cast:* Helena Bonham Carter, Cary Elwes, John Wood, Jane Lapotaire, Joan Bennett
▶ Classy, old-fashioned historical epic based on the life of Lady Jane Grey (Carter), who was crowned Queen of England at the age of sixteen in 1553 and reigned for only nine days. With Elwes as Guilford Dudley, Jane's handsome teenaged husband, and Lapotaire as her rival, the vehemently pro-Catholic Princess Mary (who became legendary queen "Bloody" Mary). (CC)

LADYKILLERS, THE 1955 British
★★★★ **NR Comedy 1:30**
Dir: Alexander Mackendrick *Cast:* Alec Guinness, Katie Johnson, Cecil Parker, Herbert Lom, Peter Sellers
▶ Gang of crooks led by a false-toothed Guinness moves in with old lady Johnson, who's unaware of their true professions. They plot to kill her but accidents do them in. Black comedy evokes more smiles than belly laughs but is still quite amusing.

LADY ON THE BUS 1978 Brazilian
★ **R Comedy 1:26**
☑ Nudity, strong sexual content, adult situations
Dir: Neville d'Almeida *Cast:* Sonia Braga, Nuno Leal Maia, Jorge Doria, Paulo Cesar Pereio, Yara Amaral
▶ Bewitching Brazilian temptress Braga is a frigid newlywed, unresponsive to her handsome husband Maia. Her solution is to try other lovers, from her husband's best friend (Cesar Pereio), to his father, to casual strangers riding the bus. Shot on location in Rio de Janeiro. Ⓢ

LADY SINGS THE BLUES 1972
★★★★ **R Biography/Musical 2:22**
☑ Brief nudity, adult situations, explicit language, violence
Dir: Sidney J. Furie *Cast:* Diana Ross, Billy Dee Williams, Richard Pryor, James Callahan, Paul Hampton
▶ In her film debut, Diana Ross plays Billie Holiday, the legendary black jazz singer whose life and brilliant career was destroyed by drug addiction. With Richard Pryor as "Piano Man" and Williams as her lover. Songs include: "Strange Fruit" and "God Bless the Child." Based on Holiday's book co-written with William Duffy. Nominated for five Oscars (Actress, Screenplay, Art Direction, Score, and Costumes).

LADY VANISHES, THE 1938 British
★★★★ **NR Mystery-Suspense 1:37 B&W**
Dir: Alfred Hitchcock *Cast:* Margaret Lockwood, Michael Redgrave, Paul Lukas, Dame May Whitty, Naunton Wayne, Basil Radford
▶ Returning home from a Balkan vacation, young Lockwood strikes up a friendship with elderly Whitty. When Whitty disappears during a train journey, Lockwood turns to arrogant folklorist Redgrave for help. They uncover a sinister spy conspiracy in this deft mixture of suspense and comedy, one of Hitchcock's most enjoyable movies. Cricket fanciers Wayne and Radford proved so popular as comic relief that they teamed up in many subsequent films.

LAGUNA HEAT 1987
★★★★ **NR Mystery-Suspense/MFTV 1:50**
☑ Brief nudity, adult situations, explicit language, violence
Dir: Simon Langton *Cast:* Harry Hamlin, Jason Robards, Jr., Rip Torn, Catherine Hicks, Anne Francis
▶ Wry, witty suspense drama about the sleepy picture-postcard town of Laguna Beach, jolted awake by two brutal murders. In a plot full of razor-sharp twists and turns, former police detective Hamlin investigates the crimes and discovers a long-buried secret that hits painfully close to home. Based on T. Jefferson Parker's best-selling thriller.

LAIR OF THE WHITE WORM, THE 1988
British
★ R Horror 1:34
☑ Nudity, adult situations, explicit language, violence
Dir: Ken Russell *Cast:* Amanda Donohoe, Hugh Grant, Catherine Oxenberg, Sammi Davis, Peter Capaldi, Stratford Johns
▶ Archaeologist Capaldi unearths ancient skull that proves a crucial element in neighbor Donohoe's search for virgins to feed local giant white worm. Delirious horror extravaganza, loosely based on a Bram Stoker novel, is nifty fun on a camp level. Donohoe is amazingly alluring as an aristocratic vampire priestess.

LAND BEFORE TIME, THE 1988
★★★★ G Animation 1:13
Dir: Don Bluth *Cast:* Voices of Pat Hingle, Helen Shaver, Gabriel Damon, Candice Houston, Burke Barnes
▶ In a time when dinosaurs rule the earth, changes in climate make the land inhospitable for plant eaters. Baby brontosaurus Littlefoot and his family leave their home in search of the bountiful Great Valley. Separated from his elders and pursued by a flesh-eating tyrannosaurus, Littlefoot must team with child dinosaurs from differing species to find the promised land. Superb animation from purist Bluth stands out among today's static, cost-cutting cartoons.

LA RONDE 1950 French
★★ NR Drama 1:37 B&W
Dir: Max Ophuls *Cast:* Simone Signoret, Anton Walbrook, Serge Reggiani, Simone Simon, Daniel Gelin, Danielle Darrieux
▶ Walbrook serves as the cynical master of ceremonies for an elegant, sophisticated, but bleak comedy of manners about the intertwined affairs of various lovers, starting and ending with young prostitute Signoret. Jean-Louis Barrault and Gerard Philipe add distinguished performances. Witty, polished adaptation of Arthur Schnitzler's play was nominated for Best Screenplay. Ⓢ

LASSITER 1984
★★★★ R Action-Adventure 1:40
☑ Nudity, adult situations, explicit language, violence
Dir: Roger Young *Cast:* Tom Selleck, Jane Seymour, Lauren Hutton, Bob Hoskins, Joe Regalbuto, Ed Lauter
▶ Pre–World War II intrigue set in London follows the exploits of suave cat burglar Selleck, forced by the police to steal uncut diamonds from the German embassy. Selleck's mission includes seducing beautiful Nazi courier Hutton. Glamorous adventure sparked by Hoskins's hard-boiled cop.

LAST AMERICAN HERO, THE 1973
★★★ PG Biography/Sports 1:33
☑ Nudity, adult situations, explicit language, mild violence
Dir: Lamont Johnson *Cast:* Jeff Bridges, Valerie Perrine, Geraldine Fitzgerald, Art Lund, Gary Busey, Ned Beatty
▶ When his dad is busted for moonshining, hot-rodder Bridges joins the racing circuit to pay for a lawyer. He rises to pro stardom, remaining his own man despite the demands of promoters and sponsors. Underrated movie with good work from Bridges and exciting demo derby and stock car footage. Based on the life of flamboyant auto racer Junior Jackson. Retitled *Hard Driver.*

LAST AMERICAN VIRGIN, THE 1982
★★ R Comedy 1:33
☑ Nudity, adult situations, explicit language
Dir: Boaz Davidson *Cast:* Lawrence Monoson, Diane Franklin, Steve Antin, Joe Rubbo, Louisa Moritz, Brian Peck
▶ Three horny teenagers—ladies' man Antin, chubby Rubbo, and shy Monoson—set their sights on beautiful Franklin. Predictable teen comedy scores some points for its fairly realistic look at high school rituals and knockout soundtrack featuring the Cars, the Police, Devo, Blondie, Commodores, and others.

LAST DAYS OF POMPEII, THE 1935
★★ NR Action-Adventure 1:36 B&W
Dir: Ernest B. Schoedsack *Cast:* Preston Foster, Alan Hale, Basil Rathbone, John Wood, Louis Calhern, Dorothy Wilson
▶ When his family is killed by a nobleman, blacksmith Foster becomes an amoral gladiator. Sent to Judea, he allies himself with the weak-willed Pontius Pilate (Rathbone). He repents in time to save Christians from the eruption of Mount Vesuvius. Long-winded historical epic is of interest only for Rathbone's superb acting and the famous special effects climax.

LAST DETAIL, THE 1974
★★ R Drama 1:44

☑ Adult situations, explicit language
Dir: Hal Ashby *Cast:* Jack Nicholson, Otis Young, Randy Quaid, Carol Kane, Michael Moriarty
► Career sailors Nicholson and Young are assigned to escort petty thief Quaid from Virginia to a New Hampshire naval prison. On the road, the two lifers teach the hapless Quaid about life, but the brief taste of freedom proves bittersweet. Powerhouse movie, alternately bawdy and moving, with a blistering performance by Jack as "Badass" Buddusky and some of the saltiest dialogue in film history. Oscar nominations went to Nicholson, Quaid, Robert Towne's screenplay.

LAST DRAGON, THE 1985
★★★ PG-13 Action-Adventure 1:48
☑ Explicit language, violence
Dir: Michael Schultz *Cast:* Taimak, Vanity, Julius J. Carry III, Faith Prince, Leo O'Brien, Jim Moody
► The world's first kung-fu musical has a cluttered plot that makes almost no sense, but its high-tech, action-packed style has a goofy charm. Taimak plays a young black who idolizes Bruce Lee; he's drawn into various battles with gangsters and the Shogun of Harlem when he falls for nightclub VJ Vanity. Romance between the attractive leads is credible, and humor sparks the inevitable martial arts showdowns. Also known as *Berry Gordy's The Last Dragon.*

LAST EMBRACE 1979
★★★ R Mystery-Suspense 1:43
☑ Nudity, violence
Dir: Jonathan Demme *Cast:* Roy Scheider, Janet Margolin, Sam Levene, John Glover, Christopher Walken, Jacqueline Brookes
► Government agent Scheider, having suffered a nervous breakdown after his wife's death, receives a death threat in Hebrew and becomes involved in a series of murders. Some farfetched plotting but inventive direction by Demme keeps the thrills coming quickly. Evocative Miklos Rozsa score, exciting Niagara Falls finale.

LAST EMPEROR, THE 1987
Italian/British/Chinese
★★★★ PG-13 Biography 2:46
☑ Brief nudity, adult situations, explicit language, violence
Dir: Bernardo Bertolucci *Cast:* John Lone, Joan Chen, Peter O'Toole, Ying Ruocheng, Dennis Dun, Ryuichi Sakamoto
► Epic biography of Pu Yi (Lone), who was crowned Chinese emperor at age three in 1908 but whose rule was essentially powerless and anachronistic. Eventually arrested by the Communists and reeducated, he lived out his days as a common gardener. Stunning imagery, filmed on location in China's Forbidden City, highlights this rare epic that is essentially an intimate character study. Gorgeous sets, costumes, art direction, although some may find it remote emotionally. Nine Oscars, including Best Picture. **(CC)**

LAST FIGHT, THE 1983
★★★ R Drama/Sports 1:29
☑ Nudity, adult situations, explicit language, violence
Dir: Fred Williamson *Cast:* Willie Colon, Ruben Blades, Fred Williamson, Joe Spinell, Darlanne Fluegel, Don King
► Singer-turned-boxer Blades signs with shady promoter Colon but then turns against him when Colon's thugs kill his girlfriend. Despite a blood clot in his head, Blades gets revenge and a shot at the title. Low-budget boxing film leaves no cliché unturned. Captures environment with conviction, but characters are not sympathetic.

LAST HOLIDAY 1950 British
★★ NR Drama 1:29 B&W
Dir: Henry Cass *Cast:* Alec Guinness, Beatrice Campbell, Kay Walsh, Wilfrid Hyde-White, Bernard Lee
► Told by his doctor that he has three months to live, Guinness withdraws his savings and goes to a posh resort. His warmth and generosity help other guests live happier lives in this superbly balanced mixture of drama, comedy, and romance. Excellent performances.

LAST HOUSE ON THE LEFT, THE 1972
☆ R Horror 1:31
☑ Rape, nudity, graphic violence
Dir: Wes Craven *Cast:* David Hess, Lucy Grantham, Sandra Cassell, Marc Sheffler, Jeramie Rain
► After a rock concert, two young girls are abducted by a demented Manson-like foursome who torture, rape, and murder them. The gang, in turn, meets an even more gruesome death from one of the girls' vengeful parents. Absolutely sickening violence, blood, and gore turn off any sympathy toward the parents and

emphasize the antivigilante theme common in director Craven's films.

LAST HURRAH, THE 1958
★★★★ NR Drama 2:01 B&W
Dir: John Ford *Cast:* Spencer Tracy, Jeffrey Hunter, Dianne Foster, Pat O'Brien, Basil Rathbone, Donald Crisp
▶ Long-time Boston mayor Frank Skeffington (Tracy) enters his last campaign against a weak candidate backed by conservative patrician forces. Compelling Tracy vehicle based on Edwin O'Connor's best-seller features outstanding character actors: James Gleason, Edward Brophy, John Carradine, Frank McHugh, Jane Darwell, Edmund Lowe, etc.

LAST INNOCENT MAN, THE 1987
★★★★★ NR Mystery-Suspense/MFTV
1:53
☑ Adult situations, explicit language, violence
Dir: Roger Spottiswoode *Cast:* Ed Harris, Roxanne Hart, Clarence Williams III, Darrell Larson, Bruce McGill, David Suchet
▶ Hot-shot Portland lawyer Harris, disillusioned with defending guilty clients, falls for Hart, estranged wife of murder suspect Larson. Harris accepts Larson's case and is quickly trapped in a baffling web of deceit and treachery. Superior courtroom drama adapted from attorney Phillip Margolin's novel raises engrossing ethical questions. Excellent acting and steamy love scenes add to the already high quality.

LAST MARRIED COUPLE IN AMERICA, THE 1980
★★★ R Comedy 1:42
☑ Nudity, adult situations, explicit language
Dir: Gilbert Cates *Cast:* George Segal, Natalie Wood, Richard Benjamin, Arlene Golonka, Valerie Harper
▶ When all their friends start getting divorced, happily married Segal and Wood wonder if they should, too. With Dom DeLuise as their jolly porno film star/plumber friend who eggs them on. Popular, ribald comedy concludes traditional ways are still the best.

LAST METRO, THE 1981 French
★★ PG Drama 2:13
☑ Adult situations, mild violence
Dir: François Truffaut *Cast:* Catherine Deneuve, Gerard Depardieu, Jean Poiret, Heinz Bennent, Andrea Ferreol

▶ Elegant yet empty melodrama set in Nazi-occupied Paris features Deneuve as the wife of a theater director. She tries to produce a play while hiding Jewish husband Bennent underneath the stage. Deneuve is the film's best asset. Nominated for Best Foreign Film. Ⓢ

LAST OF SHEILA, THE 1973
★★ PG Mystery-Suspense 1:59
☑ Adult situations, explicit language
Dir: Herbert Ross *Cast:* James Mason, James Coburn, Dyan Cannon, Raquel Welch, Ian McShane
▶ Movie producer Coburn invites six urbane Hollywood friends on a Mediterranean cruise aboard his yacht *Sheila.* Playing whodunit parlor games, Coburn searches for the person who caused his wife's death. A slew of red herrings keeps audience guessing. Script by Stephen Sondheim and Anthony Perkins.

LAST OF THE RED HOT LOVERS 1972
★ PG Comedy 1:38
☑ Adult situations, explicit language
Dir: Gene Saks *Cast:* Alan Arkin, Sally Kellerman, Paula Prentiss, Renée Taylor, Bella Bruck, Sandy Balson
▶ Married restaurateur Arkin, in throes of mid-life crisis, dreams of restoring passion to his life. Using his mother's unoccupied apartment, he tries to start affairs with Kellerman, Prentiss, and Taylor. Commercially unsuccessful adaptation of Neil Simon's play.

LAST PLANE OUT 1983
★★★ PG Action-Adventure 1:37
☑ Explicit language, mild violence
Dir: David Nelson *Cast:* Jan-Michael Vincent, Mary Crosby, Julie Carmen, William Windom, David Huffman
▶ American journalist Vincent has an affair with Nicaraguan Carmen during the last days of the Samosa regime. When Samosa is toppled, Vincent is pursued by rebels who suspect him of working for the CIA. Blandly directed, though it picks up steam as it goes along. Based on the true story of film's co-producer, Jack Cox. (CC)

LA STRADA 1956 Italian
★★ NR Drama 1:45 B&W
Dir: Federico Fellini *Cast:* Anthony Quinn, Giulietta Masina, Richard Basehart, Aldo Silviani, Marcella Rovere, Livia Venturini
▶ Circus strongman Quinn, realizing his one-man show needs an extra attraction, acquires dim-witted peasant

Masina to play trumpet and drums while he performs. He treats his sidekick/mistress poorly during their itinerant life; at a carnival, sympathetic clown/acrobat Basehart seeks to free Masina from servitude. Spare direction from Fellini, simple story, and Chaplinesque Masina yielded Oscar for Best Foreign Film. Released in Europe in 1954. Ⓢ

LAST REMAKE OF BEAU GESTE, THE
1977
★★ PG Comedy 1:23
☑ Explicit language, adult humor
Dir: Marty Feldman   *Cast:* Marty Feldman, Ann-Margret, Michael York, Peter Ustinov, James Earl Jones, Trevor Howard
▶ Spoof of the three film versions of P. C. Wren's novel stars bug-eyed Feldman and blond Adonis York as an unlikely pair of identical twins who join the French Foreign Legion. With Ann-Margret as the femme fatale who weds Howard, the Geste twins' father, and nearly kills him in bed. Uneven, bawdy comedy.

LAST RESORT 1986
★ R Comedy 1:19
☑ Nudity, explicit language, adult humor
Dir: Zane Busby   *Cast:* Charles Grodin, Robin Pearson Rose, John Ashton, Ellen Blake, Megan Mullally, Jon Lovitz
▶ Businessman Grodin takes wife and kids for a Caribbean vacation at Club Sand that turns into a series of comic disasters. Talented Chuck deserves much better. Frantic pacing, smutty and predictable humor, and crude slapstick.

LAST STARFIGHTER, THE 1984
★★★★ PG Sci-Fi 1:40
☑ Explicit language, violence
Dir: Nick Castle   *Cast:* Robert Preston, Lance Guest, Barbara Bosson, Dan O'Herlihy, Catherine Mary Stewart
▶ Videogame whiz Guest, living in a trailer, gets whisked away to another galaxy by alien headhunter Preston. He helps save the universe from evil invaders. O'Herlihy, underneath layers of lizard makeup, plays an intergalactic good guy. Sweet-natured sci-fi tale for kids.

LAST SUMMER 1969
★★★ R Drama 1:37
☑ Rape, nudity, adult situations, explicit language
Dir: Frank Perry   *Cast:* Barbara Hershey, Richard Thomas, Bruce Davidson,

Cathy Burns, Ernesto Gonzalez, Peter Turgeon
▶ Adaptation of an Evan Hunter novel concerns unchaperoned teens on the loose in New York's Fire Island resort. They get drunk, play revealing game of "truth or dare," smoke marijuana, and experiment with sex. Rivalry between sluttish Hershey and shy Burns leads to brutality. Fine, insightful look at teen gamesmanship and cruelty.

LAST TANGO IN PARIS 1973
French/Italian
☆ X Drama 2:09
☑ Nudity, strong sexual content, explicit language
Dir: Bernardo Bertolucci   *Cast:* Marlon Brando, Maria Schneider, Jean-Pierre Leaud, Massimo Girotti, Darling Legitimus, Catherine Allegret
▶ Highly controversial film about an obsessive affair between Brando and Schneider, a young stranger he meets in a deserted apartment. Notorious for its frank treatment of sexuality, story is rewarding as a psychological case study. Expert direction and Brando's startling performance were awarded Oscar nominations. Memorable Gato Barbieri score. Ⓢ

LAST TEMPTATION OF CHRIST, THE
1988
★★ R Drama 2:40
☑ Nudity, adult situations, violence
Dir: Martin Scorsese   *Cast:* Willem Dafoe, Harvey Keitel, Barbara Hershey, David Bowie, Andre Gregory, Harry Dean Stanton
▶ Despite miracles and a growing following, Jesus Christ (Dafoe) struggles with his sense of mission. Condemned to the cross by the Romans, Dafoe has a vivid fantasy of what his life might be as a normal man. Scorsese directs with a blazing intensity that matches the protagonist's restless searching. Unconventional story created much controversy but actually arrives at a quite pious (and moving) conclusion. Scorsese was nominated for an Oscar. From the novel by Nikos Kazantzakis.

LAST TIME I SAW PARIS, THE 1954
★★★★ NR Romance 1:56
Dir: Richard Brooks   *Cast:* Elizabeth Taylor, Van Johnson, Donna Reed, Walter Pidgeon, Eva Gabor
▶ Tragic love story of Johnson and Taylor, a young couple in post–World War II Paris

who strike it rich with Texas oil stocks. Their once-happy marriage turns sour when they start living frivolously and drinking heavily. With Pidgeon as Taylor's expatriate father. Glossy, slightly altered adaptation of F. Scott Fitzgerald's "Babylon Revisited."

LAST TRAIN FROM GUN HILL 1959
★★★ NR Western 1:34
Dir: John Sturges   *Cast:* Kirk Douglas, Anthony Quinn, Carolyn Jones, Earl Holliman, Ziva Rodann, Brad Dexter
▶ Sheriff Douglas tracks down Holliman, his wife's killer and the son of his best friend Quinn. Quinn's henchmen are determined to rescue Holliman before Douglas takes him out of town. Sturdy Western is an intriguing study of loyalty.

LAST TYCOON, THE 1976
★★★ PG Drama 2:02
☑ Adult situations
Dir: Elia Kazan   *Cast:* Robert De Niro, Robert Mitchum, Jeanne Moreau, Tony Curtis, Jack Nicholson, Ingrid Boulting
▶ In 1930s Hollywood, brilliant young movie mogul De Niro pursues an elusive Boulting, who reminds him of his late wife, but he is unable to control her as he does his film productions. Intelligent, meticulously crafted adaptation of F. Scott Fitzgerald's last, unfinished novel features one of De Niro's subtlest and most effective performances.

LAST WALTZ, THE 1978
★★ PG Documentary/Music 1:56
☑ Explicit language
Dir: Martin Scorsese   *Cast:* The Band, Bob Dylan, Neil Young, Van Morrison, Eric Clapton, Emmylou Harris
▶ The 1976 farewell performance of The Band (supplemented by guest stars Ringo Starr, Neil Diamond, Dr. John, Joni Mitchell, and others) is arguably the best rock concert film ever. First-rate direction by Scorsese, intercutting onstage numbers with penetrating backstage interviews. Highlights: guitar duet between Clapton and Robbie Robertson of The Band so intense that Eric breaks a string, and a climactic sing-along of "I Shall Be Released." Songs include "The Night They Drove Old Dixie Down," "The Weight," "Up on Cripple Creek," many more.

LAST WAVE, THE 1977 Australian
★ PG Mystery-Suspense 1:46
☑ Explicit language, violence
Dir: Peter Weir   *Cast:* Richard Chamberlain, Olivia Hamnett, David Gulpilil, Frederick Parslow
▶ Dazzling and unusual Australian thriller about lawyer Chamberlain defending five aborigines accused of murdering their friend. After witnessing a rain of frogs and apocalyptic winds, he suspects ancient tribal rituals and black magic were responsible for the killing. Spine-tingling and spooky.

LAST WORD, THE 1980
★★★ PG Drama 1:42
☑ Explicit language
Dir: Roy Boulting   *Cast:* Richard Harris, Karen Black, Martin Landau, Dennis Christopher, Biff McGuire, Penelope Milford
▶ Inventor Harris refuses to leave his apartment when the government decides to tear down his neighborhood. He takes a cop hostage, becomes a hero when the story is nationally televised, and uses some of his inventions to ward off an invading SWAT team. Socially conscious and well-meaning.

LATE SHOW, THE 1977
★★★ PG Mystery-Suspense 1:34
☑ Explicit language, violence
Dir: Robert Benton   *Cast:* Art Carney, Lily Tomlin, Bill Macy, Howard Duff, Joanna Cassidy
▶ Elderly private eye Carney is hired by wacky Tomlin to find her missing cat. The trail leads them into a complex web of murder and blackmail. Sophisticated contemporary mystery has comic chemistry; complex characterizations from Carney and Tomlin make this a treat.

LA TRAVIATA 1982 Italian
★★★★ G Music 1:50
Dir: Franco Zeffirelli   *Cast:* Teresa Stratas, Placido Domingo, Cornell MacNeil, Alan Monk
▶ Courtesan Stratas falls in love with wealthy MacNeil's son Domingo. MacNeil convinces Stratas she'll ruin Domingo's life, and she breaks off the relationship before a deathbed reconciliation. Lavish all-star production of Verdi's timeless opera. Based on the same story that inspired *Camille*. ⑤

LAUGHING POLICEMAN, THE 1974
★★ R Drama 1:51
☑ Adult situations
Dir: Stuart Rosenberg   *Cast:* Walter Matthau, Bruce Dern, Louis Gossett, Jr., Albert Paulsen, Anthony Zerbe, Val Avery

▶ Working on tips from a dangerously untrustworthy informer, cop partners Matthau and Dern track a violent killer through the seamy underside of San Francisco's homosexual community. Brutal thriller is somewhat dated, but plot is realistic and bloody. Based on a novel by Per Wahloo and Maj Sjowall. **(CC)**

LAURA 1944
★★★★ NR Mystery-Suspense 1:27 B&W
Dir: Otto Preminger *Cast:* Gene Tierney, Dana Andrews, Clifton Webb, Vincent Price, Judith Anderson, Dorothy Adams
▶ Investigating a murder, detective Andrews falls under the spell of the beautiful victim (Tierney). Witty, stylish mystery a landmark film noir of the 1940s. Highlighted by Webb's delicious role as acerbic columnist Waldo Lydecker, film received five Oscar nominations (winning for Joseph LaShelle's photography). Romantic theme by David Raksin became a classic ballad.

LAVENDER HILL MOB, THE 1951 British
★★★ NR Comedy/Crime 1:22 B&W
Dir: Charles Crichton *Cast:* Alec Guinness, Stanley Holloway, Sidney James, Alfie Bass, Marjorie Fielding, John Gregson
▶ Mild-mannered bank worker Guinness enlists aid of sculptor pal Holloway and pro crooks James and Bass to hijack armored car containing gold bullion. Thieves melt the loot into small, souvenir Eiffel Towers for smuggling to Paris; plan goes awry when English schoolgirls purchase some of the miniatures. Hilarious, tongue-in-cheek comedy features delightful Guinness and madcap antics. Oscar winner for screenplay. Look for young Audrey Hepburn in opening sequence.

LAWRENCE OF ARABIA 1962 British
★★★★★ G
Biography/Action-Adventure 3:25
Dir: David Lean *Cast:* Peter O'Toole, Alec Guinness, Omar Sharif, Anthony Quinn, Jack Hawkins, Jose Ferrer
▶ Seven Oscars, including Best Picture and Director, went to this magnificent screen biography of T. E. Lawrence (O'Toole), the enigmatic Britisher who attempted to unite Arab factions to revolt against the Turks during World War I. In the process, he befriends tribal leader Sharif (Oscar-nominated), faces self-

doubt over his own love of killing, and survives torture. Oscar-nominated O'Toole is brilliant and Lean's direction conveys epic sweep and grandeur, as does Maurice Jarre's score. Recently restored and re-released theatrically.

LEADER OF THE BAND 1987
★★★ PG Comedy 1:31
☑ Adult situations, explicit language
Dir: Nessa Hyams *Cast:* Steve Landesberg, Gailard Sartain, Mercedes Ruehl, James Martinez, Calvert Deforest
▶ Itinerant musician Landesberg takes job conducting unruly high school marching band and whips his charges into championship form. Bland story is nevertheless peppy and heartwarming, thanks in large measure to engaging comic timing from Landesberg.

LEAGUE OF GENTLEMEN, THE 1960 British
★★ NR Comedy 1:53 B&W
Dir: Basil Dearden *Cast:* Jack Hawkins, Nigel Patrick, Roger Livesey, Richard Attenborough, Bryan Forbes
▶ A shady group of ex-servicemen are recruited for a complicated bank heist by Hawkins, their former sergeant. They almost pull it off until fate trips them up. Engrossing and witty caper flick performed and directed with great style.

LEARNING TREE, THE 1969
★★★★ PG Drama 1:47
☑ Adult situations
Dir: Gordon Parks *Cast:* Kyle Johnson, Estelle Evans, Dana Elcar, Mita Waters, Alex Clarke
▶ In a small 1920s Kansas town, young black Johnson gets a taste of racial prejudice when a murder he witnesses is wrongly pinned on a black. *Life* magazine photographer Parks adapted his own autobiographical novel with satisfying results.

LEFT-HANDED GUN, THE 1958
★★ NR Western 1:42 B&W
Dir: Arthur Penn *Cast:* Paul Newman, Lita Milan, John Denner, Hurd Hatfield, James Congdon, James Best
▶ Debunking the myth of Billy the Kid, Newman portrays the legendary gunfighter as a stupid, backstabbing killer. Outraged by the murder of his only friend, Newman and saddlemates Best and Congdon go on a killing spree. After a fling with blacksmith's wife Milan, Newman is pursued by his old pal Sheriff Pat Garrett (Denner). Popping in and out of

the story is pulp writer Hatfield, who creates the Billy the Kid of folklore and berates Newman for not living up to his fabrication. Newman stands out in psychological Western.

LEFT HAND OF GOD, THE 1955
★★ NR Action-Adventure 1:27
Dir: Edward Dmytryk *Cast:* Humphrey Bogart, Gene Tierney, Lee J. Cobb, Agnes Moorehead, E. G. Marshall, Jean Porter
▶ China, 1947: American soldier-of-fortune Bogart disguises himself as a monk to flee employ of local warlord Cobb. In a small village, Bogart must continue pretense to appease missionaries Moorehead and Marshall; he even brings comfort to the locals with his phony ceremonies and sermons. Plot thickens when Bogart falls for mission nurse Tierney and Cobb arrives to insist Bogart rejoin him. Bogart excels in one of his last roles, while luscious Tierney made comeback after sanatorium stay.

LEGACY, THE 1979
★★★ R Horror 1:40
☑ Adult situations, explicit language, violence
Dir: Richard Marquand *Cast:* Katharine Ross, Sam Elliott, John Standing, Ian Hogg, Margaret Tyzack
▶ In England to do interior design work, American couple Elliott and Ross find themselves unwilling guests in a haunted manor. Competent suspenser. Workmanlike direction by Marquand generates tension even though the story is predictable.

LEGAL EAGLES 1986
★★★★ PG Mystery-Suspense 1:56
☑ Adult situations, explicit language, violence
Dir: Ivan Reitman *Cast:* Robert Redford, Debra Winger, Daryl Hannah, Brian Dennehy, Terence Stamp
▶ Prosecutor Redford and defense lawyer Winger team up when flaky but beautiful performance artist Hannah gets involved in art fraud and murder. Sophisticated comedy/mystery scores with plenty of action, old-fashioned romance, and clever verbal sparring. Husky-voiced Debra and charming Robert make an immensely appealing team. **(CC)**

LEGEND 1986 British
★★★ PG Fantasy 1:30
☑ Violence
Dir: Ridley Scott *Cast:* Tom Cruise, Mia

Sara, David Bennent, Tim Curry, Alice Playten, Billy Barty
▶ It's Cruise to the rescue when the Lord of Darkness (Curry) kidnaps the unicorn that prevents evil from taking over the world. Lovely production design, vibrant cinematography, and intricate costumes bring fairy tale world to life, but sappy story has the sophistication of a greeting card. **(CC)**

LEGEND OF BILLIE JEAN, THE 1985
★★★ PG-13 Drama 1:36
☑ Adult situations, explicit language, violence
Dir: Matthew Robbins *Cast:* Helen Slater, Keith Gordon, Christian Slater, Richard Bradford, Peter Coyote, Martha Gehmen
▶ Texas teenager Billie Jean (Slater) demands reimbursement when bullies trash her brother's motorcycle. The brother (Christian Slater, no relation to Helen) accidentally shoots bully's dad Bradford. The siblings go on the lam and Billie Jean becomes a folk hero. Agreeable cast but simplistic story lacks dramatic weight. **(CC)**

LEGEND OF BOGGY CREEK, THE 1972
★ G Horror 1:30
Dir: Charles B. Pierce *Cast:* Willie E. Smith, John P. Hixon, John W. Oates, Jeff Crabtree, Buddy Crabtree
▶ Docudrama concerns alleged Bigfootlike monster running wild near small town of Foulke, Arkansas. Creature attacks several people, roots around garbage cans, and occasionally sticks its arm through a living room window. Tame stuff for horror fans, but G rating offered scares to small kids and made crude picture a hit. Followed by *Return to Boggy Creek* and *The Barbaric Beast of Boggy Creek Part II*.

LEGEND OF HELL HOUSE, THE 1973 British
★★★ PG Horror 1:34
☑ Adult situations, explicit language, violence
Dir: John Hough *Cast:* Pamela Franklin, Roddy McDowall, Clive Revill, Gayle Hunnicutt, Roland Culver, Peter Bowles
▶ Millionaire Culver hires four people to spend a week in an allegedly haunted house to determine truth of the rumors. McDowall is a veteran of the house's eerie effects, Franklin is a spiritualist in touch with the spooks, Revill is a skeptical scientist, and Hunnicutt is Revill's wife.

Occasionally harrowing look at occult phenomena.

LEGEND OF THE LONE RANGER, THE
1981
★ ★ ★ PG Western 1:38
☑ Explicit language, violence
Dir: William A. Fraker *Cast:* Klinton Spilsbury, Michael Horse, Christopher Lloyd, Jason Robards, Richard Farnsworth
▶ The Lone Ranger (Spilsbury) dons mask to track his brother's murderer. Teaming up with his childhood Indian friend Tonto (Horse), he gets his man and rescues President Grant (Robards) in the process. Old-fashioned Western, classily produced and photographed. Action aplenty and rousing score (including the familiar "William Tell Overture") but lackluster leads. Robards and Silver the horse are delightful, however.

LEMON DROP KID, THE 1951
★ ★ ★ NR Comedy 1:31 B&W
Dir: Sidney Lanfield *Cast:* Bob Hope, Marilyn Maxwell, Lloyd Nolan, Jane Darwell, Andrea King, Fred Clark
▶ Fast-paced comedy with Hope in top form as a bookie who gives a bad tip to gangster Nolan. He has a month to pay back Nolan's money, but his schemes backfire hilariously. Sweet version of "Silver Bells" caps off this adaptation of a Damon Runyon story.

LENNY 1974
★ ★ R Biography 1:51 B&W
☑ Nudity, adult situations, explicit language
Dir: Bob Fosse *Cast:* Dustin Hoffman, Valerie Perrine, Jan Miner, Stanley Beck, Gary Morton
▶ Rise and fall of controversial comedian and social gadfly Lenny Bruce (Hoffman), as seen by the people who knew him best: self-destructive stripper/wife Perrine, overbearing mother Miner, and ruthless manager Beck. Fosse brilliantly blends elements of documentary, drama, and stand-up comedy. Critically acclaimed biography was nominated for several Oscars including Best Actor, Director, Picture, and Screenplay. (CC)

LEONARD PART VI 1987
★ PG Comedy 1:25
☑ Adult situations, explicit language
Dir: Paul Weiland *Cast:* Bill Cosby, Tom Courtenay, Joe Don Baker, Moses Gunn, Pat Colbert
▶ Such a super dud that Cosby offered to buy back the film from Columbia Pictures—and with good cause. He plays 007-type agent fighting to save the world from homicidal house cats, brook trout, and lobsters. No zip, no laughs, no go. (CC)

LEOPARD MAN, THE 1943
★ ★ NR Mystery-Suspense 1:06 B&W
Dir: Jacques Tourneur *Cast:* Dennis O'Keefe, Margo, Jean Brooks, Isabel Jewell, James Bell, Margaret Landry
▶ New Mexican nightclub promoter O'Keefe rents a leopard to increase business, but the cat escapes just before a series of brutal murders terrifies the town. Snug little thriller from producer Val Lewton (*Cat People*) has terrific atmosphere and tension. Highly recommended to film buffs.

LEPKE 1974
★ ★ ★ R Biography/Crime 1:38
☑ Adult situations, explicit language, violence
Dir: Menahem Golan *Cast:* Tony Curtis, Anjanette Comer, Michael Callan, Warren Berlinger, Milton Berle
▶ Jewish gangster Curtis rises from New York delinquent to narcotics king and leader of "Murder Inc." but is eventually arrested by the Feds. Reminiscent of (although not as good as) the gangster classics of the 1930s. May appeal to genre fans.

LES COMPERES 1984 French
★ ★ PG Comedy 1:32
☑ Adult situations, explicit language, violence
Dir: Francis Veber *Cast:* Gerard Depardieu, Pierre Richard, Anny Duperey, Bruno Allain, Patrick Blondell, Stephane Bierry
▶ When teen Bierry vanishes en route to the Riviera with his girlfriend, his mom Duperey persuades two of her former lovers that the boy is his son. Macho reporter Depardieu and meek poet Richard then search for the boy and, when they meet and learn of their common goal, each seeks to prove more worthy of Bierry's affection than the other. Fine, fast-paced French farce. ⑤

LES GIRLS 1957
★ ★ ★ ★ NR Musical 1:54
Dir: George Cukor *Cast:* Gene Kelly, Mitzi Gaynor, Kay Kendall, Taina Elg, Jacques Bergerac
▶ An MGM winner. Former dancer Kendall writes sensational book and is sued

for libel by another member of her troupe. Conflicting stories come out in courtroom flashbacks. Sumptuous musical with energetic dancing, lavish production numbers, excellent Cole Porter tunes, terrific cast (especially Kendall) and Oscar-winning costumes.

LES MISERABLES 1935
★★★★ NR Drama 1:49 B&W
Dir: Richard Boleslawski *Cast:* Fredric March, Charles Laughton, John Beal, Cedric Hardwicke, Rochelle Hudson
▶ Nineteenth-century France: starving peasant Jean Valjean (March) is imprisoned for stealing a loaf of bread. He emerges from prison and becomes respectable citizen but is relentlessly pursued by inspector Laughton. Most highly regarded of the four Hollywood filmings of Victor Hugo classic which also inspired the recent Broadway musical. Shows its age in spots but still succeeds.

LESS THAN ZERO 1987
★★ R Drama 1:38
☑ Nudity, adult situations, violence
Dir: Marek Kanievska *Cast:* Andrew McCarthy, Jami Gertz, Robert Downey, Jr., James Spader, Tony Bill
▶ College student McCarthy returns to Beverly Hills for Christmas vacation, rekindles romance with coke-snorting model Gertz, and tries to save his self-destructive pal Downey from pusher Spader. Candid peek at the rich and debauched, junior division, based on the best-selling novel by Bret Easton Ellis. Gorgeous graphics, superbly sardonic performance by Downey, but self-absorbed adolescents generate little sympathy. (CC)

LETHAL WEAPON 1987
★★★★★ R Action-Adventure 1:49
☑ Brief nudity, explicit language, violence
Dir: Richard Donner *Cast:* Mel Gibson, Danny Glover, Gary Busey, Mitchell Ryan, Tom Atkins, Darlene Love
▶ Veteran cop Glover, a staid family man, is paired with Gibson, an undercover narc on the verge of a nervous breakdown. Together they discover that a routine suicide is a cover-up for a drug ring. High-voltage thriller with a driven performance from Gibson, breathless pacing, and stunning action pieces. Huge popular success. (CC)

LET IT BE 1970 British
★★ G Documentary/Music 1:21
Dir: Michael Lindsay-Hogg *Cast:* John Lennon, Paul McCartney, George Harrison, Ringo Starr, Billy Preston, Yoko Ono
▶ Documentary on the Beatles' recording session for their last album drags at times, but provides revealing glimpses of their methods and personalities. The music is, of course, wonderful: "Get Back," "I Dig a Pony," "Two of Us," etc. Climaxes with their last live performance, a rooftop concert. Won an Oscar for Best Score. A must for their fans, as it includes songs not found on the album ("Shake, Rattle, and Roll," "Besame Mucho," "Kansas City," etc.).

LET'S DO IT AGAIN 1975
★★★★ PG Comedy 1:53
☑ Explicit language, adult humor
Dir: Sidney Poitier *Cast:* Sidney Poitier, Bill Cosby, Calvin Lockhart, John Amos, Jimmie C. Walker, Ossie Davis
▶ Fun sequel to *Uptown Saturday Night*, with Poitier and Cosby reprising their roles as larcenous brothers of "The Sons and Daughters of Shaka Lodge." This time they use Poitier's hexing powers to hypnotize bony Walker into thinking he's a prizefighter. Followed by *A Piece of the Action*.

LET'S GET HARRY 1986
★★★★ R Action-Adventure 1:47
☑ Explicit language, violence
Dir: Stuart Rosenberg *Cast:* Michael Schoeffling, Tom Wilson, Glen Frey, Gary Busey, Robert Duvall, Mark Harmon
▶ When his brother Harmon is kidnapped by Colombian terrorists, Schoeffling and three Illinois friends set out to rescue him. Shallow but well-made thriller with a full quota of exciting violence. Duvall gives a wonderful performance as the mercenary who aids the heroes.

LET'S MAKE LOVE 1960
★★★ NR Musical/Comedy 1:58
Dir: George Cukor *Cast:* Marilyn Monroe, Yves Montand, Tony Randall, Frankie Vaughan, Wilfrid Hyde-White, David Burns
▶ Wealthy industrialist Montand investigates rehearsals of Off-Broadway play satirizing him and, mistaken for an actor by the director, is asked to play himself in the spoof. Stunned by the beauty of leading lady Monroe, Montand accepts the part and hires guest stars Bing Crosby, Milton Berle, and Gene Kelly to give him a cram course in the tricks of the trade. Not as funny as it could be, but

worthy for luminous Monroe and sly Randall as Montand's PR man. Songs include superb version of "My Heart Belongs to Daddy" by Monroe.

LET'S SPEND THE NIGHT TOGETHER 1983
★ ★ PG Documentary/Music 1:30
☑ Explicit language
Dir: Hal Ashby   *Cast:* Mick Jagger, Keith Richards, Charlie Watts, Bill Wyman, Ron Wood, Ian Stewart
▶ Well-staged documentary of the Rolling Stones' 1981 American tour features twenty-five of their songs performed in concert. Apart from a few oldies ("Time Is on My Side," "Satisfaction"), songs are from later stages in their career: "Start Me Up," "Miss You," "Waiting on a Friend," etc. Best for their fans.

LETTER, THE 1940
★ ★ ★ ★ NR Drama 1:35 B&W
Dir: William Wyler   *Cast:* Bette Davis, Herbert Marshall, James Stephenson, Gale Sondergaard, Bruce Lester, Elizabeth Earl
▶ While rubber plantation owner Marshall is away from Malaysian home, wife Davis kills her secret lover and pleads self-defense. Then dead man's widow (Sondergaard) produces letter from Davis luring victim to his death. Potentially melodramatic adaptation of a W. Somerset Maugham story elevated by dynamic Davis in unsympathetic role. Her most memorable line: "I still love the man I killed."

LETTER TO BREZHNEV 1986 British
★ R Romance 1:34
☑ Nudity, adult situations, explicit language
Dir: Chris Bernard   *Cast:* Alexandra Pigg, Alfred Molina, Peter Firth, Margi Clarke, Tracy Lea, Ted Wood
▶ In Liverpool, young Englishwoman Pigg has quick fling with Russian sailor Firth while her friend Clarke gets involved with Firth's pal Molina. After the Russians leave, a lovesick Pigg writes a letter to Soviet premier Brezhnev about the situation and gets a surprising answer. Good performances and buoyant feel, but accents are so thick subtitles would have come in handy.   (CC)

LETTER TO THREE WIVES, A 1949
★ ★ ★ ★ NR Drama 1:43 B&W
Dir: Joseph L. Mankiewicz   *Cast:* Jeanne Crain, Linda Darnell, Ann Soth-

ern, Kirk Douglas, Paul Douglas, Jeffrey Lynn
▶ During a day trip, three wives learn that one of their husbands is running off with notorious flirt Addie Ross (Celeste Holm). Crain worries that she doesn't fit into spouse Lynn's social set; Sothern wonders if Kirk Douglas resents her writing income; Darnell is convinced that burly Paul Douglas has lost interest in her. Ingenious and witty, with Mankiewicz winning Oscars for his directing and screenplay.

LIANNA 1983
★ R Drama 1:55
☑ Nudity, strong sexual content, adult situations, explicit language
Dir: John Sayles   *Cast:* Linda Griffiths, Jane Halloren, Jon DeVries, Jo Henderson
▶ Lianna (Griffiths), married to insensitive film professor DeVries, finds she prefers Halloran to him and leaves husband and children to be with her lover. Humanistic lesbian love story with naturalistic dialogue from the screenwriter/director.

LIAR'S MOON 1982
★ ★ ★ ★ PG Drama 1:45
☑ Nudity, adult situations
Dir: David Fisher   *Cast:* Matt Dillon, Cindy Fisher, Christopher Connelly, Hoyt Axton, Yvonne De Carlo, Broderick Crawford
▶ Texas, 1949: youngsters Dillon and pregnant Fisher run off to get married, only to discover they may be brother and sister. Fisher goes for an abortion before the truth is learned. Intimate melodrama with an appealing Dillon; nicely produced and quite affecting.

LIBELED LADY 1936
★ ★ ★ NR Comedy 1:38 B&W
Dir: Jack Conway   *Cast:* Jean Harlow, William Powell, Myrna Loy, Spencer Tracy, Walter Connolly
▶ Newspaper editor Tracy, facing libel suit from heiress Loy, hires Powell to romance her into an embarrassing position. Plan backfires when Powell really falls in love. Furiously fast and funny romantic comedy with brisk dialogue, ingenious plotting, and terrific performances.

LIBERATION OF L.B. JONES, THE 1970
★ ★ R Drama 1:44
☑ Adult situations, explicit language, violence
Dir: William Wyler   *Cast:* Lee J. Cobb, Anthony Zerbe, Roscoe Lee Browne,

Lola Falana, Lee Majors, Barbara Hershey
▶ Southern attorney Cobb and nephew Majors represent black funeral director Browne; he wants to sue wife Falana for divorce over her affair with white policeman Zerbe. Zerbe wants Falana not to contest the divorce, but she needs alimony to raise his child. Zerbe then turns violent. Too many subplots overcomplicate final work of director Wyler's distinguished career.

LICENSE TO DRIVE 1988
★★★ PG-13 Comedy 1:28
☑ Adult situations, explicit language
Dir: Greg Beeman *Cast:* Corey Haim, Corey Feldman, Heather Graham, Carol Kane, Richard Masur, Grant Goodeve
▶ Teenager Haim is obsessed with getting his driver's license. He fails road test but "borrows" stepfather's Cadillac anyway for date with dream girl Graham. A series of comic disasters ensues in this furiously paced lightweight comedy with lots of wild stunts, car crashes, and colorful supporting characters. **(CC)**

LIES MY FATHER TOLD ME 1975
Canadian
★★★ PG Drama 1:42
☑ Explicit language
Dir: Jan Kadar *Cast:* Yossi Yadin, Len Birman, Marilyn Lightstone, Jeffrey Lynas
▶ Engrossing, sentimental tale of young Lynas, who worships his story-spinning, rag-peddler grandfather Yadin. Czech Director Kadar (*Little Shop on Main Street*) strongly evokes life in the Jewish/Canadian ghetto of Montreal in the 1920s. Tender and moving; screenplay was nominated for Oscar.

LIFE AND DEATH OF COLONEL BLIMP, THE 1943 British
★★ NR Drama 2:43
Dir: Michael Powell *Cast:* Roger Livesey, Deborah Kerr, Anton Walbrook, Roland Culver, James McKechnie, Albert Lieven
▶ Extraordinary portrait of a stereotypical British soldier examines his career from dashing officer in the Boer War to outmoded reactionary during World War II. Livesey is remarkable in a difficult part; Kerr excels in multiple roles as the women in his life. Heavily cut after harsh criticism from Winston Churchill and recently restored to full length on videocassettes.

LIFE AND TIMES OF JUDGE ROY BEAN, THE 1972
★★★★ PG Western 2:00
☑ Adult humor
Dir: John Huston *Cast:* Paul Newman, Ava Gardner, Jacqueline Bisset, Anthony Perkins, Victoria Principal, John Huston
▶ Revisionist Western spoof about outlaw Bean (Newman), who takes over a Texas frontier town and proceeds to rob and hang assorted travelers. Violent, disjointed, occasionally funny tall tale is filled with cameos: Stacy Keach, Tab Hunter, Roddy McDowall, Ned Beatty, etc. Gardner plays Lily Langtry, Bean's idol.

LIFEBOAT 1944
★★★★★ NR Drama 1:37 B&W
Dir: Alfred Hitchcock *Cast:* Tallulah Bankhead, William Bendix, Walter Slezak, Mary Anderson, John Hodiak, Henry Hull
▶ During World War II, survivors of a German sub attack are stranded on a lifeboat in the middle of the Atlantic. Despite mixed backgrounds, they team together to defeat a Nazi threat. Although limited to one set, technological tour de force is a riveting thriller. Bankhead gives her best screen performance; Hume Cronyn and Canada Lee also register strongly. Hitchcock and writer John Steinbeck received Oscar nominations. **(CC)**

LIFEFORCE 1985
★★ R Sci-Fi 1:41
☑ Nudity, adult situations, explicit language, violence
Dir: Tobe Hooper *Cast:* Steve Railsback, Peter Firth, Frank Finlay, Mathilda May
▶ Space mission led by Railsback discovers bodies of alien vampires and brings them to London. The creatures come to life and suck the lifeforce out of people. Railsback must finally confront sexy head vampire May. A good start but story gets pretty silly. Special effects and the naked-throughout Ms. May are eye-filling.

LIFEGUARD 1976
★★★ PG Drama 1:33
☑ Adult situations, explicit language
Dir: Daniel Petrie *Cast:* Sam Elliott, Anne Archer, Kathleen Quinlan, Stephen Young, Parker Stevenson
▶ California lifeguard Elliott, past thirty

and feeling insecure, considers getting a more stable job and settling down with his high school sweetheart Archer. A simple story nicely played by Elliott and Archer.

LIFE OF EMILE ZOLA, THE 1937
★★★ NR Biography 1:56 B&W
Dir: William Dieterle *Cast:* Paul Muni, Gale Sondergaard, Joseph Schildkraut, Gloria Holden, Donald Crisp
▶ Life and times of Zola (Muni), France's most famous crusading journalist and author. Story focuses on Zola helping unjustly accused Jewish soldier Schildkraut in the notorious Dreyfus Affair. Effective biography with a strong Oscar-nominated performance by Muni. Oscar wins for Best Picture and Schildkraut as Best Supporting Actor.

LIFE WITH FATHER 1947
★★★★ NR Comedy 1:58
Dir: Michael Curtiz *Cast:* William Powell, Irene Dunne, Elizabeth Taylor, Edmund Gwenn, ZaSu Pitts, Jimmy Lydon
▶ First-rate adaptation of the Broadway hit is a warm, nostalgic look at the foibles of irascible Victorian father Powell and his often unruly family. Essentially a series of reminiscences, beautifully shot film is consistently funny and touching. Based on the book by Clarence Day, Jr.

LIGHTHORSEMEN, THE 1988 Australian
★★★ PG War 1:56
☑ Brief nudity, explicit language, violence
Dir: Simon Wincer *Cast:* Jon Blake, Peter Phelps, Tony Bonner, Bill Kerr, John Walton, Anthony Andrews
▶ Old-fashioned adventure about the Australian cavalrymen who played a decisive role in the battle of Beersheba during World War I. Episodic plot follows four friends preparing for the battle, in particular Phelps, a young recruit with pacifist leanings. Sincere but plodding, apart from the rousing climax.

LIGHT IN THE FOREST, THE 1958
★★★ NR Western/Family 1:33
Dir: Herschel Daugherty *Cast:* James MacArthur, Fess Parker, Wendell Corey, Carol Lynley, Joanne Dru, Jessica Tandy
▶ Intriguing Disney adaptation of the Conrad Richter novel tells of MacArthur, a young white man raised by Indians who must readjust to life in white society. Army scout Parker helps him make the transition, but MacArthur despises his

racist uncle Corey. MacArthur falls in love with Corey's indentured servant Lynley, but romance is threatened when his old tribe wants to use him as ploy in war against whites.

LIGHTNING SWORDS OF DEATH 1974
Japanese
★★ R Martial Arts 1:29
☑ Rape, nudity, graphic violence
Dir: Kenji Musumi *Cast:* Tomisaburo Wakayama, Goh Kato, Masahiro Tomikawa, Katsu Wakayama
▶ Renegade samurai, formerly the Shogun's executioner, is hired to kill an insane leader who has surrounded himself with a private army. Extremely violent period adventure is part of the *Sword of Vengeance* series, esteemed by cultists for its highly stylized mayhem. Original title *Kozure Ohkami* (*Baby Cart in Hell*) refers to the hero's unusual sidekick, his infant son in a weapon-filled carriage. Sequel (of sorts): *Shogun Assassin*, recut by producers for American audiences.

LIGHT OF DAY 1987
★★ PG-13 Drama 1:47
☑ Explicit language
Dir: Paul Schrader *Cast:* Michael J. Fox, Gena Rowlands, Joan Jett, Michael McKean, Thomas G. Waites, Cherry Jones
▶ Honest but grim account about the efforts of Fox and Jett, a Cleveland brother and sister, to break out of their blue-collar background through rock 'n' roll. Jett's painful relationship with cancer-ridden mother Rowlands exacerbates her problems. Story tends to wander, but rock star Jett is impressive in her film debut. Originally named *Born in the USA* until Bruce Springsteen borrowed the title for his rock anthem; the Boss returned the favor by writing film's theme song.

LIGHTSHIP, THE 1986
★★ PG-13 Drama 1:30
☑ Explicit language, violence
Dir: Jerzy Skolimowski *Cast:* Robert Duvall, Klaus Maria Brandauer, Michael Lyndon, Tom Bower, Robert Costanzo, Badja Djola
▶ Ship captain Brandauer and his estranged son Lyndon resolve their differences after they are taken hostage by Duvall's gang of fugitives. Some claustrophobic tension in the psychological duel, but film is hindered by overly mannered performance by Duvall (his accent is so thick you may not understand what he's

saying), meandering story, and excessive talk. **(CC)**

LIKE FATHER LIKE SON 1987
★★★★ **PG-13 Comedy 1:39**
☑ Adult situations, explicit language
Dir: Rod Daniel *Cast:* Dudley Moore, Kirk Cameron, Margaret Colin, Catherine Hicks, Patrick O'Neal, Sean Astin
▶ Thanks to an Indian brain transference serum, prominent heart surgeon Moore and his sixteen-year-old son Cameron accidentally exchange bodies and have to live each other's lives. Adult/teen switcheroo is hardly a new premise, but the leads are charming and Moore generates some genuine laughs as a befuddled teen.

LILI 1953
★★★★ **G Musical 1:21**
Dir: Charles Walters *Cast:* Leslie Caron, Mel Ferrer, Jean-Pierre Aumont, Zsa Zsa Gabor, Kurt Kasznar, Amanda Blake
▶ Sixteen-year-old French orphan Caron joins carnival and falls in love with magician Aumont. Heartbroken to learn that Aumont's assistant Gabor is also his wife, Caron is consoled by puppeteer Ferrer, a crippled former dancer whose bitterness she has mistaken for cruelty. Delightful Caron was nominated for an Oscar; music won Academy Award. Turned into the 1961 Broadway hit *Carnival*. Best bit: Caron and Ferrer's puppets sing famous "Hi-Lili, Hi-Lo."

LILIES OF THE FIELD 1963
★★★ **NR Drama 1:34 B&W**
Dir: Ralph Nelson *Cast:* Sidney Poitier, Lilia Skala, Lisa Mann, Isa Crino
▶ Black handyman Poitier builds church under the watchful supervision of German nuns led by Skala. Moving, humanistic drama with an Oscar-winning performance by Poitier (the first black actor ever to win in this category). Also received nominations for Best Picture and Supporting Actress Skala. **(CC)**

LILITH 1964
★★ **NR Drama 1:54 B&W**
Dir: Robert Rossen *Cast:* Warren Beatty, Jean Seberg, Peter Fonda, Kim Hunter, Jessica Walter, Gene Hackman
▶ Beatty, occupational therapist at an exclusive mental institution, is drawn against his will into an affair with alluring patient Seberg. Respectful adaptation of J. R. Salamanca's novel has thoughtful

performances to offset its slow pacing and downbeat tone.

LILY IN LOVE 1985 U.S./Hungarian
★ **PG-13 Comedy 1:46**
☑ Adult situations
Dir: Karoly Makk *Cast:* Christopher Plummer, Maggie Smith, Elke Sommer, Adolph Green, Szabo Sandor
▶ Writer Smith doesn't feel her ham actor hubby Plummer is quite right for her script. He disguises himself as an Italian matinee idol to seduce her and win the role. Genteel continental fluff with lovely Hungarian locations. Smith and Plummer transcend the flat dialogue with smooth timing and poise.

LIMELIGHT 1952
★★★ **NR Comedy/Drama 2:25 B&W**
Dir: Charles Chaplin *Cast:* Charles Chaplin, Claire Bloom, Nigel Bruce, Buster Keaton, Sydney Chaplin
▶ Elderly vaudevillian Chaplin rescues suicidal ballet dancer Bloom and they support each other through career ups and downs. The innocence and goodness of the central relationship is hard to resist in this sweetly sentimental Chaplin talkie. Stiff performance by Chaplin's son Sydney but Buster shines in his too-brief routine with Charlie. Chaplin co-wrote the Oscar-winning score.

LINK 1986
★★★ **R Horror 1:43**
☑ Brief nudity, violence
Dir: Richard Franklin *Cast:* Elisabeth Shue, Terence Stamp, Steven Pinner, Richard Garnett, David O'Hara
▶ American student Shue takes housekeeping gig with Stamp, an English doctor studying apes. She becomes the object of a rampaging orangutan's affections. Pace lags until orangutan goes ape in the last part of the movie. Weak screenplay leaves the human actors stranded although the monkey shines in this brutal thriller.

LIONHEART 1987
★★ **PG Action-Adventure 1:44**
☑ Explicit language, violence
Dir: Franklin J. Schaffner *Cast:* Eric Stoltz, Gabriel Byrne, Nicola Cowper, Dexter Fletcher, Deborah Barrymore, Nicholas Clay
▶ Young knight Stoltz leads group of sideshow escapees and orphans to join the Crusades but must battle Black Knight Byrne who seeks to enslave them. Promising story gets lost in clumsy telling.

Stoltz lacks the charisma to carry this large-scale production, although villainous Byrne does well.

LION IN WINTER, THE 1968
★★★★ PG Drama 2:14
☑ Adult language
Dir: Anthony Harvey *Cast:* Katharine Hepburn, Peter O'Toole, Anthony Hopkins, Timothy Dalton, Jane Merrow
► Hepburn won her third Oscar as Eleanor of Aquitaine, the imprisoned wife of King Henry II (O'Toole). Amid jousting contests and period pageants, the King and Queen squabble over which of their three sons should inherit the throne in twelfth-century England. Elaborate plotting and witty dialogue. Also won Oscars for Screenplay and Musical Score.

LION OF AFRICA, THE 1987
★★★★ NR Action-Adventure/MFTV 1:49
Dir: Kevin Connor *Cast:* Brian Dennehy, Brooke Adams, Joseph Shiloa, Don Warrington
► In West Africa, no-nonsense doctor Adams hires feisty trader Dennehy and his battered truck to fetch desperately needed medical shipment. Friction blossoms into romance during their adventurous trek. Old-fashioned entertainment with exotic Kenyan locales.

LION OF THE DESERT 1981
Libyan/British
★★★★ PG Drama 2:40
☑ Graphic violence
Dir: Moustapha Akkad *Cast:* Anthony Quinn, Oliver Reed, Raf Vallone, Rod Steiger, John Gielgud
► Libya, 1929–31: Bedouin Omar Mukhtar (Quinn) leads his people against Italian invaders led by vicious general Reed. True story is impressive in scope with well-staged battle scenes, spectacular desert vistas, and grand Maurice Jarre score. Very long; requires some patience to sit through.

LION, THE WITCH & THE WARDROBE, THE 1979
★★★★ NR Animation 1:40
Dir: Bill Melendez *Cast:* Voices of Dick Vosborough, Rachel Warren, Victor Spinetti, Don Parker, Liz Proud, Beth Porter
► Four children pass through an antique wardrobe in a old country house and enter a magical land called Narnia where many adventures await them. Superior adaptation of the classic fairy tale from the first of the seven books in *The*

Chronicles of Narnia by C. S. Lewis. (CC)

LIPSTICK 1976
★★★ R Drama 1:29
☑ Rape, nudity, violence, explicit language
Dir: Lamont Johnson *Cast:* Margaux Hemingway, Chris Sarandon, Anne Bancroft, Mariel Hemingway, Perry King
► Model Margaux Hemingway is raped by Sarandon. Despite the efforts of prosecutor Bancroft, he gets off. When Sarandon attacks her little sister Mariel, Margaux takes the law into her own hands. Volatile antirape drama; you'll be rooting for Margaux, but the graphic rape scenes are difficult to watch.

LIQUID SKY 1983
☆ R Sci-Fi 1:52
☑ Rape, nudity, adult situations, explicit language, violence
Dir: Slava Tsukerman *Cast:* Anne Carlisle, Paula Sheppard, Susan Doukas, Otto Von Wernherr, Bob Brady, Elaine Grove
► Lesbian model Carlisle, reeling from a brutal rape, is attacked by miniature UFO seeking brain secretions formed during intercourse. Eccentric low-budget combination of sci-fi, black comedy, New Wave fashion, and punk sensibilities has mild cult following, but underground humor has already dated badly. Carlisle's androgynous beauty is an asset in her dual role (she's also a male heroin addict).

LIST OF ADRIAN MESSENGER, THE 1963
★★ NR Mystery-Suspense 1:38 B&W
Dir: John Huston *Cast:* George C. Scott, Dana Wynter, Clive Brook, Gladys Cooper, Herbert Marshall, John Merivale
► Scott, a retired British colonel, is given a list of eleven names by Merivale, the title character. When Merivale dies, Scott learns that the eleven have met similar fates; all were World War II POWs whose escape plans were betrayed to the Japanese by a cohort. Scott pursues the murderer, a master of disguise, before he kills again. Numerous red herrings feature uncredited appearances by Tony Curtis, Kirk Douglas, Burt Lancaster, Robert Mitchum, Frank Sinatra, and director Huston, all in heavy disguise. Fine mystery even without the gimmick; shot in Ireland.

LISZTOMANIA 1975 British
☆ **R Biography/Music 1:44**
☑ Nudity, strong sexual content, adult situations, explicit language
Dir: Ken Russell *Cast:* Roger Daltrey, Sara Kestelman, Paul Nicholas, Fiona Lewis, Veronica Quilligan, Ringo Starr
▶ Daltrey is composer Franz Liszt and Nicholas is his buddy Richard Wagner in this surreal, outrageous, and sexually obsessed biographical fantasy. Director Russell re-creates Liszt as the first rock idol, with the composer's music updated by English rocker Rick Wakeman. Russell is always flamboyant, but here he aims to shock even the most adventurous.

LITTLE BIG MAN 1970
★★★★★ **PG Western 2:13**
☑ Adult situations, violence
Dir: Arthur Penn *Cast:* Dustin Hoffman, Faye Dunaway, Martin Balsam, Richard Mulligan, Chief Dan George, Jeff Corey
▶ Adaptation of Thomas Berger's novel about Jack Crabb (Hoffman), a 121-year-old-man who reminisces about his days as a young pioneer, adopted Indian, drinking pal of Wild Bill Hickok, medicine show hustler, and survivor of Custer's Last Stand. Monumental, enthralling epic with superior performances and compassionate view of Indians. **(CC)**

LITTLE CAESAR 1930
★★★ **NR Crime 1:17 B&W**
Dir: Mervyn LeRoy *Cast:* Edward G. Robinson, Douglas Fairbanks, Jr., Glenda Farrell, Stanley Fields, Sidney Blackmer, Ralph Ince
▶ The rise and fall of crime kingpin Robinson. Hard-hitting gangster film with a magnetic performance by the great Eddie G. Includes one of the great curtain lines in cinema history: "Mother of mercy, is this the end of Rico?"

LITTLE COLONEL, THE 1935
★★ **NR Family 1:20 C/B&W**
Dir: David Butler *Cast:* Shirley Temple, Lionel Barrymore, Evelyn Venable, John Lodge, Hattie McDaniel, Bill "Bojangles" Robinson
▶ Superior Temple vehicle, set in the post–Civil War South, has Shirley smoothing over a feud between her grandfather Barrymore, a Confederate colonel, and mother Venable, who made the mistake of marrying Yankee Lodge. Temple does one of her most famous routines, a stair-step tap dance with Robinson. **(CC)**

LITTLE DARLINGS 1980
★★★ **R Comedy 1:34**
☑ Adult situations, explicit language, adult humor
Dir: Ronald F. Maxwell *Cast:* Kristy McNichol, Tatum O'Neal, Matt Dillon, Armand Assante, Maggie Blye
▶ Teen campers McNichol and O'Neal bet on who'll be first to lose her virginity. O'Neal tries to score with camp counselor Assante while McNichol falls for fellow camper Dillon. Tasteful handling of a tricky theme elicits sympathetic performances from the leads. Amusing and occasionally touching.

LITTLE DRUMMER GIRL, THE 1984
★★★ **R Espionage 2:10**
☑ Brief nudity, adult situations, explicit language, violence
Dir: George Roy Hill *Cast:* Diane Keaton, Klaus Kinski, Yorgo Voyagis, Sami Frey, Michael Cristofer
▶ Crack Israeli intelligence team headed by Kinski recruits flaky American actress Keaton to help catch a Palestinian terrorist. She falls for Israeli agent Voyagis, assigned to teach her the espionage business. Faithful adaptation of John le Carré's best-selling novel is often contrived, but leads give uniformly powerful performances and European and Middle Eastern locations are spectacular. **(CC)**

LITTLE FOXES, THE 1941
★★★★ **NR Drama 1:56 B&W**
Dir: William Wyler *Cast:* Bette Davis, Herbert Marshall, Teresa Wright, Richard Carlson, Patricia Collinge, Dan Duryea
▶ In the turn-of-the-century South, a family of greedy carpetbaggers scheme among and against one another to build a factory on a former lovely plantation. Seven Oscar nominations (Picture, Director, Davis, Collinge, Wright) went to this juicy film version of Lillian Hellman's play. Davis gives one of her best performances as a woman willing to risk everything, even her husband's life, to get what she wants.

LITTLE GIRL WHO LIVES DOWN THE LANE, THE 1976
★★ **PG Mystery-Suspense 1:33**
☑ Violence
Dir: Nicholas Gessner *Cast:* Jodie Foster, Martin Sheen, Scott Jacoby, Mort Shuman, Alexis Smith
▶ Reclusive thirteen-year-old Foster, who lives in isolated house, is befriended by

handicapped teen Jacoby. Foster is endangered when child molester Sheen discovers her. Subtle thriller with an effective performance by Foster.

LITTLE LORD FAUNTLEROY 1936
★★★ NR Drama 1:44 B&W
Dir: John Cromwell *Cast:* Freddie Bartholomew, C. Aubrey Smith, Dolores Costello, Mickey Rooney, Guy Kibbee
▶ Warmhearted adaptation of the classic Frances Hodgson Burnett story about poor Brooklyn boy Bartholomew, who is the heir to a fortune and a title if he can win the heart of grumpy English grandfather Smith. Rooney stands out in a small part as a shoeshine boy. **(CC)**

LITTLE MISS MARKER 1980
★★★★ PG Comedy 1:42
☑ Explicit language
Dir: Walter Bernstein *Cast:* Walter Matthau, Julie Andrews, Bob Newhart, Lee Grant, Sara Stimson
▶ Crabby bookie Sorrowful Jones (Matthau) gets stuck with six-year-old Stimson, left as collateral after her father commits suicide because of his racetrack losses. Sorrowful and the kid are befriended by beautiful widow Andrews. Matthau magic and Andrews charm make this sentimental Damon Runyon story good for family viewing. Remake of the 1934 Shirley Temple vehicle.

LITTLE NIGHT MUSIC, A 1977
★ PG Musical 2:05
☑ Adult situations
Dir: Harold Prince *Cast:* Elizabeth Taylor, Diana Rigg, Len Cariou, Lesley-Anne Down, Hermione Gingold, Lawrence Guittard
▶ Vienna, 1905: lawyer Cariou, his virginal wife Down, his old flame Taylor, his teenage son, and Taylor's lover Guittard gather for a summer weekend at Gingold's estate. Couples break up and reunite in new pairs. Stiff staging by theater director Prince but nice work from Rigg and Cariou and wonderfully witty, sophisticated Stephen Sondheim score (including "Send in the Clowns"). Adaptation of the Broadway hit based on Bergman's *Smiles of a Summer Night.* Oscar for Best Song Score.

LITTLE NIKITA 1988
★★★★ PG Mystery-Suspense 1:38
☑ Explicit language, violence
Dir: Richard Benjamin *Cast:* Sidney Poitier, River Phoenix, Richard Jenkins, Caroline Kava, Richard Bradford
▶ While tracking KGB man, FBI agent Poitier interviews teenaged Phoenix whose parents turn out to be Russian agents themselves. A stunned Phoenix is then kidnapped by Poitier's quarry. Farfetched tale has some plot holes but maintains interest throughout. **(CC)**

LITTLE PRINCE, THE 1974 British
★★★ G Musical 1:28
Dir: Stanley Donen *Cast:* Richard Kiley, Steven Warner, Bob Fosse, Gene Wilder, Joss Ackland, Clive Revill
▶ Pilot Kiley crash-lands in the desert and meets young interplanetary traveler Warner. Warner has encounters with a snake (Fosse) and a fox (Wilder) and learns about life. Tender adaptation of the Antoine de Saint-Exupéry children's classic. Lerner and Loewe score highlighted by Wilder singing "Closer and Closer."

LITTLE PRINCESS, THE 1939
★★ NR Family 1:33
Dir: Walter Lang *Cast:* Shirley Temple, Richard Greene, Anita Louise, Cesar Romero, Ian Hunter
▶ Legendary charmer with Temple as a poor little rich girl sent to boarding school after her father is killed in the Boer War. Shirley escapes and discovers her father's still alive in a military hospital but stricken with amnesia. Predictably, the sight of his darling daughter quickly cures him. Top-notch entertainment.

LITTLE ROMANCE, A 1979
★★★ PG Romance/Comedy 1:50
☑ Explicit language
Dir: George Roy Hill *Cast:* Laurence Olivier, Sally Kellerman, Diane Lane, Arthur Hill, Thelonious Bernard
▶ Precocious teens Lane and Bernard, hassled by their parents, run away from Paris to Italy. Dapper, elderly ex-con Olivier helps them in their quest to reach Venice and kiss under the Bridge of Sighs. A sweet movie that will leave you with a nice feeling. Pretty locations, the kids are winning and natural, and Lord Larry is a sly scene-stealer.

LITTLE SEX, A 1982
★★ R Romance/Comedy 1:35
☑ Adult situations, explicit language, adult humor
Dir: Bruce Paltrow *Cast:* Tim Matheson, Kate Capshaw, Edward Herrmann, John Glover, Wallace Shawn
▶ After Matheson marries Capshaw, older brother Herrmann bets him that he

can't stay faithful. Tempted by beautiful women at every turn, the poor newlywed is in danger of losing Capshaw to ex-beau Glover when he strays. Harmless sit-com romantic comedy.

LITTLE SHOP OF HORRORS, THE 1960
★ NR Horror/Comedy 1:10 B&W
Dir: Roger Corman *Cast:* Jonathan Haze, Jackie Joseph, Dick Miller, Mel Welles, Jack Nicholson
▶ On Skid Row, lowly florist's assistant Haze becomes popular when he creates a new plant. However, Audrey, Jr. (named after the girl of his dreams), snacks on human blood and is soon de-manding, "Feed Me!" B-movie cult clas-sic, shot in two days, is raw and quite funny. Young Nicholson is hysterically funny as a masochistic dental patient. Inspired the off-Broadway musical and 1986 film.

LITTLE SHOP OF HORRORS 1986
★★ PG-13 Musical 1:34
☑ Explicit language, violence
Dir: Frank Oz *Cast:* Rick Moranis, Ellen Greene, Vincent Gardenia, Steve Mar-tin, John Candy, Bill Murray
▶ Funny, fractured production, set in a Skid Row flower shop. Life of nebbish Sey-mour (Moranis) changes after he buys a mysterious plant during a solar eclipse. But to keep the plant alive, Seymour must feed it fresh blood. Singing and dancing with Seymour are his love interest Audrey (Greene), ruthless boss Gardenia, and demented dentist Martin. Original, outra-geous, tuneful, and fun; based on Roger Corman's 1960 horror-movie spoof. Levi Stubbs, the voice of the plant, shines; screamingly funny Martin defames an entire profession. **(CC)**

LITTLEST HORSE THIEVES, THE 1977
★★★ G Comedy/Family 1:44
Dir: Charles Jarrott *Cast:* Alastair Sim, Peter Barkworth, Maurice Colbourne, Andrew Harrison, Benje Bolgar, Chloe Franks
▶ Franks, daughter of coal mine man-ager in turn-of-the-century England, mounts a campaign to protect ponies from abuse in the mines. With her friends Harrison and Bolger, she hides the ponies in a church while the miners vote on their fate. Sim's last film has interesting moral points. Strong Disney effort.

LITTLEST REBEL, THE 1935
★★ NR Musical/Family 1:10 B&W
Dir: David Butler *Cast:* Shirley Temple,
John Boles, Bill "Bojangles" Robinson, Jack Holt, Karen Morley
▶ Memorable Temple feature set in the South during the Civil War. Temple saves soldier daddy Boles, convicted as a spy, from the death sentence by persuading Abe Lincoln to let him go free. Songs in-clude "Those Endearing Young Charms" and "Polly Wolly Doodle" in a famous tap-dancing duet with "Bojangles" Rob-inson. **(CC)**

LITTLE TREASURE 1985
★★ R Action-Adventure 1:38
☑ Brief nudity, explicit language, mild violence
Dir: Alan Sharp *Cast:* Margot Kidder, Ted Danson, Burt Lancaster, Joseph Hacker, Malena Doria
▶ Stripper Kidder, told by dying dad Lan-caster of buried stolen loot in New Mex-ico ghost town, teams with lapsed semi-nary student Danson to find the treasure. It's a bumpy road to love and money for this mismatched pair in Sharp's easy-to-take adventure. **(CC)**

LITTLE WOMEN 1933
★★★★ NR Drama 1:55 B&W
Dir: George Cukor *Cast:* Katharine Hepburn, Joan Bennett, Paul Lukas, Edna May Oliver, Jean Parker, Frances Dee
▶ Faithful adaptation of Louisa May Al-cott's classic about the coming-of-age of four New England sisters during the Civil War is an irresistible tearjerker. Luminous performance by Hepburn as Jo, an aspir-ing writer who fears the family may fall apart when sister Meg (Dee) marries Brooke (John Lodge). Nominated for three Oscars, winning for superb screen-play by Sarah Y. Mason and Victor Heer-man.

LIVE AND LET DIE 1973 British
★★★★★ PG
Espionage/Action-Adventure 2:01
☑ Adult situations, explicit language, violence
Dir: Guy Hamilton *Cast:* Roger Moore, Yaphet Kotto, Jane Seymour, Clifton James, Geoffrey Holder
▶ The trail leads from Harlem to New Or-leans as secret agent James Bond (Moore) goes after Kotto, a villain who mixes voodoo with drug dealings. Action includes a wild chase through the Louisi-ana swamps with good-ol'-boy sheriff James providing comic relief so effec-tively they brought him back for *The Man*

With the Golden Gun. Moore makes a debonair debut as agent 007, Seymour provides the love interest as Solitaire, and Paul McCartney does the theme song in this typically effective Bond concoction.

LIVES OF A BENGAL LANCER, THE
1935
★★★ NR Action-Adventure 1:49 B&W
Dir: Henry Hathaway *Cast:* Gary Cooper, Franchot Tone, Richard Cromwell, Guy Standing, C. Aubrey Smith, Monte Blue
▶ Rousing adventure set in colonial India: daredevil Tone and nervous Cromwell, neglected son of troop commander Standing, join Cooper in foiling a native uprising. A delight from start to finish, with a snake-charming sequence and a grueling torture session among the highlights. Unusually accurate classic received six Oscar nominations.

LIVING DAYLIGHTS, THE 1987 British
★★★★ PG
Espionage/Action-Adventure 2:11
☑ Violence
Dir: John Glen *Cast:* Timothy Dalton, Maryam d'Abo, Jeroen Krabbe, Joe Don Baker, John Rhys-Davies, Art Malik
▶ The sixteenth installment of the world's most popular secret agent features Dalton as the newest James Bond. Helping with the defection of KGB agent Krabbe, 007 and svelte blond d'Abo toboggan their way over the Iron Curtain. Then the unflappable Bond gets mixed up with ruthless American arms dealer Baker and Afghan freedom-fighter Malik. Exotic scenery, breathless chase scenes, and socko production values add up to Bond business as usual. (CC)

LIVING DESERT, THE 1953
★★★★ G Documentary 1:39
Dir: James Algar
▶ Trendsetting documentary uses striking footage to portray the seasonal life cycle of an American desert and its inhabitants. Oscar winner for Best Documentary despite controversy surrounding some staged animal rituals. First in Disney's True-Life Adventure series. Narrated by Winston Hibler.

LIVING FREE 1972 British
★★★★ G Drama/Family 1:31
Dir: Jack Couffer *Cast:* Susan Hampshire, Nigel Davenport, Geoffrey Keen, Edward Judd, Peter Lukoye
▶ Sequel to *Born Free* continues the efforts of real-life conservationist Joy

Adamson to protect Elsa's three lion cubs. Less inspired than the original, although the Kenya locations are beautiful.

LLOYDS OF LONDON 1936
★★★★ NR Drama 1:58 B&W
Dir: Henry King *Cast:* Freddie Bartholomew, Madeleine Carroll, Guy Standing, Tyrone Power, George Sanders, C. Aubrey Smith
▶ Fictionalized drama about the rise of the famous English insurance house in the eighteenth century, seen from the eyes of young apprentice Bartholomew who, as an adult (played by Power), saves the company from bankruptcy. Against a backdrop of the Napoleonic Wars, he pursues an affair with Carroll, wife of dastardly lord Sanders. Power's first major role skyrocketed him to stardom.

LOCAL HERO 1983 Scottish
★★ PG Comedy 1:51
☑ Adult situations, explicit language
Dir: Bill Forsyth *Cast:* Peter Riegert, Burt Lancaster, Fulton MacKay, Dennis Lawson, Peter Capaldi, Jenny Seagrove
▶ Houston oil company executive Riegert is sent by boss to buy seaside Scottish town where petrol has been discovered. He falls under the spell of the place—and who wouldn't? Everything is slightly and magically off kilter: there's biologist Seagrove who may be a mermaid, innkeeper Lawson who doubles as a lawyer/town spokesman, and the sky's nightly show of northern lights. Forsyth's lyrical comedy is intelligent and subtle, full of unexpected and joyfully unexplained juxtapositions. A marvelous Lancaster stars as Riegert's visionary boss. Mainstream audiences, however, may not have patience for Scottish brogues and film's brand of whimsy.

LOGAN'S RUN 1976
★★★ PG Sci-Fi 2:00
☑ Brief nudity, adult situations
Dir: Michael Anderson *Cast:* Michael York, Jenny Agutter, Richard Jordan, Peter Ustinov, Farrah Fawcett-Majors, Roscoe Lee Browne
▶ In the year 2274, an enclosed society encourages a pleasure-seeking lifestyle but then kills its citizens at age thirty. Cop York rebels against the system and flees with fellow resister Agutter. York's colleague Jordan pursues. Fast-paced sci-fi

mixes action, ingenious effects, and provocative ideas.

LOLA MONTES 1955 French
★ NR Drama 1:50
Dir: Max Ophuls *Cast:* Martine Carol, Peter Ustinov, Anton Walbrook, Ivan Desny, Oskar Werner
▶ A New Orleans circus ringmaster (Ustinov) tells the story of his main attraction, the famous courtesan Lola Montes (Carol). Through flashbacks we see her affairs with various European lovers, including the King of Bavaria (Walbrook). Technically breathtaking but emotionally distant period drama is considered a critical masterpiece; Ophuls's last film.
Ⓢ

LOLITA 1962 British
★ NR Comedy 2:32 B&W
Dir: Stanley Kubrick *Cast:* James Mason, Sue Lyon, Shelley Winters, Peter Sellers, Marianne Stone, Diana Decker
▶ Mason, a middle-aged professor, marries sex-starved widow Winters in order to start an affair with her daughter Lyon, a precocious teen. Peculiar black comedy tones down the controversial novel; still an unnerving look at sexual obsession and hypocrisy. Outstanding acting, particularly Sellers in multiple disguises as a rake who pursues Lolita. Vladimir Nabokov received an Oscar nomination for adapting his novel.

LONELINESS OF THE LONG DISTANCE RUNNER, THE 1962 British
★★★★ NR Drama 1:43 B&W
Dir: Tony Richardson *Cast:* Tom Courtenay, Michael Redgrave, Avis Bunnage, Peter Madden, Alec McCowen, James Fox
▶ Eighteen-year-old Courtenay robs bakery, is sent to reformatory, and encounters strict governor Redgrave. Redgrave believes in rehabilitation through sports. Courtenay's running ability gains him some freedom and recognition, but competition fails to curb his rebellious instincts. Critically acclaimed but bleak look at alienated youth.

LONELY ARE THE BRAVE 1962
★★★ NR Western 1:47 B&W
Dir: David Miller *Cast:* Kirk Douglas, Walter Matthau, Gena Rowlands, Michael Kane, Carroll O'Connor
▶ Nonconformist cowboy Douglas, indifferent to the social order of the modern Southwest, escapes from jail after intentionally getting arrested to help a friend.

Sheriff Matthau pursues but grows to respect his quarry. Crisply told and thoughtful; from a Dalton Trumbo screenplay.

LONELY GUY, THE 1984
★★ R Comedy 1:30
☑ Adult situations, explicit language
Dir: Arthur Hiller *Cast:* Steve Martin, Charles Grodin, Judith Ivey, Robyn Douglass, Steve Lawrence, Dr. Joyce Brothers
▶ Greeting card writer Martin is exposed to the perils of singlehood when girlfriend Douglass kicks him out. Fellow "lonely guy" Grodin provides solace. Martin eventually finds new love with divorcée Ivey. Mild-mannered but sometimes poignant comedy is at its best when it sticks to the realities of urban life (as when Martin tries to eat alone inconspicuously). Nicely mournful chemistry between Grodin and Martin. Uneven script co-written by Neil Simon from Bruce Jay Friedman's *The Lonely Guy's Book of Life*.

LONELYHEARTS 1958
★★ NR Drama 1:42 B&W
Dir: Vincent J. Donehue *Cast:* Montgomery Clift, Robert Ryan, Myrna Loy, Dolores Hart, Maureen Stapleton, Jackie Coogan
▶ Cynical editor Ryan assigns sensitive reporter Clift to write an advice column for the lovelorn. Against his will, Clift is drawn into the personal problems of his readers. Turgid melodrama, based very loosely on Nathanael West's *Miss Lonelyhearts*, is worth a look for its strong cast. Stapleton received an Oscar nomination in her film debut.

LONELY LADY, THE 1983
★ R Drama 1:31
☑ Rape, nudity, explicit language
Dir: Peter Sasdy *Cast:* Pia Zadora, Lloyd Bochner, Bibi Besch, Joseph Cali, Anthony Holland, Ray Liotta
▶ Aspiring writer Zadora endures rape, abortion, lesbianism, a nervous breakdown, and professional jealousy during her climb to fame in Hollywood. Sloppy adaptation of a Harold Robbins bestseller takes a glamorous view of the seedy side of show biz. Best for Zadora's fans, who will treasure her Oscar acceptance speech.

LONELY PASSION OF JUDITH HEARNE, THE 1987 British
★★ R Drama 1:50

☑ Nudity, adult situations, explicit language

Dir: Jack Clayton **Cast:** Maggie Smith, Bob Hoskins, Wendy Hiller, Alan Devlin, Prunella Scales
▶ In 1950s Dublin, repressed alcoholic piano teacher Smith is wooed by con man Hoskins, her landlady's brother. Well-acted but downbeat British drama. Sad characters are beautifully rendered by a perfect cast.

LONE RUNNER 1988 Italian
☆ PG Action-Adventure 1:25
☑ Explicit language, violence
Dir: Ruggero Deodato **Cast:** Miles O'Keeffe, Savina Gersak, Michael J. Aronin, John Steiner, Hal Yamanouchi
▶ In the Arab desert, a modern-day Robin Hood known as Lone Runner (O'Keeffe) rescues wealthy young Gersak from kidnappers. God-awful juvenile action-adventure with one-note acting from tight-lipped O'Keeffe, bad dialogue badly dubbed, and tedious action. (CC)

LONE WOLF McQUADE 1983
★★★★ PG Action-Adventure 1:47
☑ Nudity, adult situations, explicit language, graphic violence
Dir: Steve Carver **Cast:** Chuck Norris, David Carradine, Barbara Carrera, Leon Isaac Kennedy, Robert Beltran
▶ Trashy, obvious, heavy-handed and a great deal of fun. Norris plays the title character, an independent Texas Ranger assigned Mexican partner Beltran to combat his "Lone Wolf" image. They uncover Carradine's gun-smuggling operation with the help of federal agent Kennedy. Tight-knit action flick climaxes with a to-the-death karate fight between martial arts masters Norris and Carradine.

LONG DARK NIGHT, THE 1977
★★★ R Mystery-Suspense 1:39
☑ Explicit language, violence
Dir: Robert Clouse **Cast:** Joe Don Baker, Hope Alexander-Willis, Richard B. Shull, R. G. Armstrong, Ned Wertimer, Bibi Besch
▶ Well-made thriller from the director of *Enter the Dragon*. A pack of dogs, abandoned by vacationing tourists, starts attacking people on a resort island. Marine biologist Baker, his girlfriend Alexander-Willis, fisherman Armstrong, and country store owner Shull are among the menaced humans who make a last stand. Originally titled *The Pack*.

LONG DAY'S JOURNEY INTO NIGHT 1962
★★ NR Drama 2:54 B&W
Dir: Sidney Lumet **Cast:** Katharine Hepburn, Ralph Richardson, Jason Robards, Jr., Dean Stockwell, Jeanne Barr
▶ Recriminations and arguments afflict the Tyrone family—drug-addicted mother Hepburn, stingy actor father Richardson, alcoholic son Robards, and his sickly writer brother Stockwell—in their Connecticut home as Hepburn makes a long day's journey into madness. Masterful adaptation of Eugene O'Neill play features superb performances. Hepburn was Oscar-nominated.

LONGEST DAY, THE 1962
★★★ G War 3:00 B&W
Dir: Ken Annakin, Andrew Marton, Bernhard Wicki **Cast:** John Wayne, Robert Mitchum, Henry Fonda, Robert Ryan, Rod Steiger, Robert Wagner
▶ Extravagant epic with an all-star cast repeats in exhaustive detail the events of D-Day, June 6, 1944, when the Allies launched the crucial invasion of Normandy. Told in three parts: preparations by the high command, activities by Resistance heroes and paratroopers, and the bloody assault on Omaha Beach. Among the many actors are Richard Burton, Mel Ferrer, Jeffrey Hunter, Richard Todd, Jean-Louis Barrault, Red Buttons, Stuart Whitman, and Gert Frobe.

LONGEST YARD, THE 1974
★★★★ R Comedy/Sports 1:59
☑ Explicit language, violence
Dir: Robert Aldrich **Cast:** Burt Reynolds, Eddie Albert, Ed Lauter, Michael Conrad, James Hampton, Bernadette Peters
▶ Ex-pro-football-star-turned-convict Reynolds organizes other prisoners into a team to take on the brutal guards. Corrupt warden Albert schemes to insure the guards' victory. Brawny football comedy with uproarious, literally bone-crunching humor. Rousing football game finale; one of Burt's best performances.

LONG GONE 1987
★★★★ NR Comedy/MFTV 1:52
☑ Brief nudity, adult situations, explicit language
Dir: Martin Davidson **Cast:** William L. Petersen, Virginia Madsen, Dermot Mulroney, Larry Riley, Henry Gibson, Teller Lasarow
▶ Winning baseball comedy set in the

1950s follows the misadventures of the Tampico Stogies, a third-rate minor league team managed by hard-bitten pitcher Petersen. He recruits talent that turns the club into a contender, but at the risk of losing his job and his girlfriend Madsen. Solid cast and nostalgic settings add to the fun.

LONG GOOD FRIDAY, THE 1982 British
★★★ **R Crime/Drama 1:54**
☑ Brief nudity, adult situations, explicit language, violence
Dir: John Mackenzie *Cast:* Bob Hoskins, Helen Mirren, Eddie Constantine, Dave King
▶ Swift and sharp-edged British gangster film. While cajoling American mobsters to invest in a major real estate deal, crime kingpin Hoskins and his mistress Mirren are threatened by terrorist bomb attacks from unknown sources. Complicated plot and heavy Cockney accents require concentration, but Hoskins's riveting transformation from smooth talker to raging ogre desperate for revenge is well worth the effort.

LONG, HOT SUMMER, THE 1958
★★★ **NR Drama 1:57**
Dir: Martin Ritt *Cast:* Paul Newman, Joanne Woodward, Anthony Franciosa, Orson Welles, Lee Remick, Angela Lansbury
▶ Drifter Newman enters into a sharecropping contract with Welles, richest man in a backwater Mississippi county, while pursuing his spinster daughter Woodward. Seamless adaptation of several William Faulkner stories captures the author's atmospheric view of corruption and redemption in the small-town South. First teaming of Newman and Woodward led to their marriage. Remade as a TV movie in 1985.

LONG RIDERS, THE 1980
★★★ **R Western 1:39**
☑ Adult situations, explicit language, graphic violence
Dir: Walter Hill *Cast:* David Carradine, Keith Carradine, James Keach, Stacy Keach, Dennis Quaid, Randy Quaid
▶ First-rate Western about the James-Younger gang has an unusual gimmick: the notorious outlaws are played by real-life brothers. The Carradines (along with younger brother Robert) are the Youngers; the Keaches play Frank and Jesse James; the Quaids are the Miller brothers; and Christopher and Nicholas Guest portray the villainous Ford brothers. Historically accurate, brutally violent, and consistently engrossing. Pamela Reed is a memorably sexy Belle Starr. Ry Cooder soundtrack adds to film's authencity.

LONGSHOT, THE 1986
★★ **PG-13 Comedy 1:29**
☑ Explicit language, adult humor
Dir: Paul Bartel *Cast:* Tim Conway, Jack Weston, Harvey Korman, Ted Wass, Anne Meara, Stella Stevens
▶ Working on a tip from a Mexican stableboy, four friends borrow money from gangsters to bet on a sure shot. But they pick the wrong horse, leading to long chases and slapstick complications. Not to be confused with Conway's family-oriented efforts: humor here is often scatological and racist. A bizarre project for executive producer Mike Nichols.

LONG VOYAGE HOME, THE 1940
★★★ **NR Drama 1:44 B&W**
Dir: John Ford *Cast:* John Wayne, Thomas Mitchell, Ian Hunter, Barry Fitzgerald, John Qualen, Ward Bond
▶ Moving drama about merchant marines in 1939, drawn from four Eugene O'Neill one-act plays. Wayne gives one of his best performances as a naive Swede protected by more experienced seamen on a dangerous ammunition convoy. Mildred Natwick has a memorable role as a waterfront prostitute. Nominated for six Oscars, including Best Picture and Screenplay (Dudley Nichols).

LOOK BACK IN ANGER 1959 British
★★ **NR Drama 1:39 B&W**
Dir: Tony Richardson *Cast:* Richard Burton, Claire Bloom, Mary Ure, Edith Evans, Donald Pleasence, Gary Raymond
▶ In England, impoverished Burton takes out his frustrations on wife Ure and has an affair with her friend Bloom. A passionate performance from young Burton and a fragile and sensuous one from Ure are featured in this high-quality drama based on John Osborne's play.

LOOKER 1981
★★ **PG Mystery-Suspense 1:30**
☑ Nudity, explicit language, violence
Dir: Michael Crichton *Cast:* Albert Finney, Susan Dey, James Coburn, Leigh Taylor-Young, Dorian Harewood
▶ Successful Los Angeles plastic surgeon Finney is set up as the fall guy for a string of murders involving beautiful models who were also his patients. He teams with

Dey, tracks down the real killers, and uncovers an ambitious politician's plot to hypnotize people via TV commercials. Glossy but farfetched thriller.

LOOKING FOR MR. GOODBAR 1977
★★★ R Drama 2:16
☑ Strong sexual content, explicit language, graphic violence
Dir: Richard Brooks *Cast:* Diane Keaton, Tuesday Weld, William Atherton, Richard Kiley, Richard Gere, Tom Berenger
▶ Catholic schoolteacher Keaton leads a self-destructive double life. She helps deaf children by day and cruises seedy singles bars to pick up men by night. Keaton gives a tour-de-force performance as an emotionally and physically crippled woman; but the film's brutal murder scene, violent sex, and harsh language don't do justice to Judith Rossner's sensitive novel. Gere and Berenger play some of the men in Keaton's life.

LOOKING GLASS WAR, THE 1970 British
★★ PG Espionage 1:46
☑ Adult situations, explicit language
Dir: Frank Pierson *Cast:* Christopher Jones, Pia Degermark, Ralph Richardson, Anthony Hopkins, Paul Rogers, Susan George
▶ Polish refugee Jones is forced by British Intelligence into a suicidal mission behind the Iron Curtain. Despite help from free-spirited hippie Degermark, he is unable to shake his KGB pursuers. Dreary Cold War thriller based on a John le Carré novel has a good performance by Richardson as an untrustworthy British agent.

LOOKIN' TO GET OUT 1982
★ R Drama 1:45
☑ Brief nudity, adult situations, explicit language, violence
Dir: Hal Ashby *Cast:* Jon Voight, Ann-Margret, Burt Young, Bert Remsen, Richard Bradford
▶ Voight and Young are New York gamblers in debt to loan sharks. They flee to Las Vegas and, helped by over-the-hill cardsharp Remsen, sneak into a high-stakes blackjack game. With Ann-Margret as Voight's former flame. Haphazard story co-written and co-produced by Voight was a flop at the box office.

LOONEY LOONEY LOONEY BUGS BUNNY MOVIE 1981
★★★★★ G Animation 1:15

Dir: Friz Freleng *Cast:* Voices of Mel Blanc, June Foray, Frank Nelson
▶ Oscar-winning animator Freleng displays his talents in this festival of Bugs Bunny's greatest hits. Featuring Yosemite Sam, Tweetie and Sylvester, plus a fire-breathing dragon, a black knight, and a little red Devil. In a spoof of the Academy Awards, the gang attends "The Oswald Awards," a gala that highlights clips of their stellar careers. Solid family fun.

LOOSE SCREWS 1985 Canadian
★★ R Comedy 1:17
☑ Nudity, explicit language, adult humor
Dir: Rafal Zielinski *Cast:* Brian Genesse, Karen Wood, Alan Deveau, Jason Warren, Lance Van Der Kolk
▶ Rude and crude *Screwballs* sequel about teens Hugh G. Rection (Deveau) and Steve Hardman (Van Der Kolk), kicked out of Beaver High and sent to Coxwell Academy for summer school. Their French teacher's name is Mona Lott. Lewd and predictable.

LOOSE SHOES 1980
★ R Comedy 1:16
☑ Nudity, explicit language, adult humor
Dir: Ira Miller *Cast:* Bill Murray, Howard Hesseman, Avery Schreiber, Buddy Hackett, Susan Tyrrell
▶ Wacky series of fake movie trailers which are actually parodies of Woody Allen movies, biker pictures, sci-fi films, and other genre movies. Skits vary wildly, including "Welcome to Bacon County," Jewish "Star Wars," and a Chaplin take-off, "The Yid and the Kid." Some of the material was criticized for being offensive and racist. Originally titled *Coming Attractions*.

LORD JIM 1965 British
★★★★ NR Drama 2:34
Dir: Richard Brooks *Cast:* Peter O'Toole, James Mason, Curt Jurgens, Eli Wallach, Jack Hawkins, Paul Lukas
▶ Ambitious but uneven version of Joseph Conrad's novel, with O'Toole giving a fascinating performance as a British officer who spends a lifetime making up for one moment of cowardice. South Seas period adventure filmed in Cambodia and Hong Kong has plenty of spectacle and an outstanding supporting cast, particularly Mason's unscrupulous mercenary.

LORD OF THE RINGS, THE 1978
★★★★ PG Animation/Adult 2:13
☑ Mild violence
Dir: Ralph Bakshi *Cast:* Voices of Christopher Guard, John Hurt, William Squire, Michael Sholes
► Fantasy based on a portion of Tolkien's trilogy about a hobbit named Frodo and other creatures in Middle Earth competing for a magic ring. Ambitious adventure, but you need to be familiar with the books to understand what's happening; strictly for Tolkien fans.

LORDS OF DISCIPLINE, THE 1983
★★★ R Drama 1:42
☑ Brief nudity, explicit language, graphic violence
Dir: Franc Roddam *Cast:* David Keith, Judge Reinhold, Robert Prosky, G. D. Spradlin, Barbara Babcock, Rick Rossovich
► Well-crafted, hard-hitting drama about 1960s cadet life in a strict Southern military academy. To preserve decorum, senior cadet Keith is asked by his cigar-chomping colonel Prosky to watch out for the school's first black student, Mark Breland. Keith soon uncovers a sadistic secret society, the Ten, that uses Klan-like tactics to terrorize and humiliate certain undesirable cadets. Absorbing but brutal film about military macho was based on Pat Conroy's dynamic novel.

LORDS OF FLATBUSH, THE 1974
★ PG Drama 1:25
☑ Adult situations, explicit language, mild violence
Dir: Stephen F. Verona, Martin Davidson *Cast:* Perry King, Sylvester Stallone, Henry Winkler, Susan Blakely, Paul Mace
► In 1950s Brooklyn, leather jacketed high school students Stallone, Winkler, King, and Mace hang out together and cause havoc. King falls for new student Blakely; Stallone is reluctantly dragged into marriage by his pregnant girlfriend. Limited budget shows, but those nostalgic for the era (or curious for glimpses at pre-stardom King, Winkler, and a quite pudgy Sly) might take a look.

LOSIN' IT 1983
★★ R Comedy 1:40
☑ Nudity, explicit language, violence
Dir: Curtis Hanson *Cast:* Tom Cruise, Jackie Earle Haley, Shelley Long, John Stockwell, John P. Navin, Jr.
► Teens Cruise, Haley, Stockwell, and Navin go to Tijuana to lose their virginity. Cruise hooks up with married Long, in town to seek a divorce, while the others get involved in some wild misadventures of their own. Modest, agreeable youth comedy; above average for the genre.

LOST AND FOUND 1979
★★★ PG Comedy 1:45
☑ Adult situations, explicit language
Dir: Melvin Frank *Cast:* George Segal, Glenda Jackson, Maureen Stapleton, Hollis McLaren, John Cunningham, Paul Sorvino
► Affable widowed professor Segal and persnickety British divorcée Jackson meet by accident—in a car crash—and fall in love. Sophisticated adult comedy tries to capture the spirit of *A Touch of Class* but falls far short. Cameo appearances by Martin Short and John Candy.

LOST BOYS, THE 1987
★★★★ R Horror 1:37
☑ Explicit language, violence
Dir: Joel Schumacher *Cast:* Jason Patric, Corey Haim, Dianne Wiest, Barnard Hughes, Kiefer Sutherland, Jami Gertz
► Divorced Wiest moves with her kids Patric and Haim to a California town that contains a pack of bike-riding teen vampires (led by scary Sutherland). Haim tries to save Patric after the bloodsuckers add him to their group. Slick and flashy fun, outrageously mixing comedy and horror in music video style. Should make the younger crowd shriek for joy. **(CC)**

LOST EMPIRE, THE 1983
★ R Sci-Fi/Comedy 1:26
☑ Nudity, strong sexual content, adult situations, explicit language, graphic violence
Dir: Jim Wynorski *Cast:* Melanie Vincz, Angela Aames, Raven de la Croix, Paul Coufos, Angus Scrimm
► On the Pacific isle of Golgotha, a bevy of beautiful, busty, and half-clothed women warriors investigate a death cult run by the sinister Dr. Sin Do (Scrimm). Bob Tessier, a familiar baddie, wears ridiculous paste-on eyebrows that vary from scene to scene. Raunchy, low-budget adventure spoof borders on soft porn.

LOST HORIZON 1937
★★★★ NR Action-Adventure 2:13 B&W
Dir: Frank Capra *Cast:* Ronald Colman, H. B. Warner, Sam Jaffe, Jane Wyatt, Thomas Mitchell
► A planeload of passengers is forced

down in Tibet, where they discover Shangri-La, a paradise where the weather is always perfect and people live forever and are gentle to each other. Capra's version of James Hilton's utopian novel creaks a little but, overall, still stands as an unusual, lavish, and entertaining film classic. Colman won Best Actor Oscar; nominations for Picture, Supporting Actor (Warner) and Score. Remade unsuccessfully in 1973 as a musical. Recently restored with footage cut from the original version.

LOST IN AMERICA 1985
★★ R Comedy 1:31
☑ Adult situations, explicit language
Dir: Albert Brooks *Cast:* Albert Brooks, Julie Hagerty, Maggie Roswell, Michael Greene, Tom Tarpey
▶ Advertising exec Brooks and his wife Hagerty decide to drop out, sell everything, and hit the road to find America, mimicking their *Easy Rider* idol, Peter Fonda. Roughing it in a $40,000 Winnebago, complete with microwave oven, they arrive in Vegas where their life and luck changes after Hagerty goes crazy at the roulette wheel. Brooks's right-on-the-money look at a yuppie mid-life crisis may not appeal to all, but those who appreciate his humor will howl. (CC)

LOST PATROL, THE 1934
★★ NR War 1:14 B&W
Dir: John Ford *Cast:* Victor McLaglen, Boris Karloff, Wallace Ford, Reginald Denny, Billy Bevan, Alan Hale
▶ British cavalry troops stranded at an oasis in the Mesopotamian desert are picked off one by one by Arab snipers. Grim, fast-paced World War I adventure features steady direction, engrossing performances (particularly Karloff's religious fanatic), and surprisingly enjoyable sense of gloom.

LOST WEEKEND, THE 1945
★★★ NR Drama 1:41 B&W
Dir: Billy Wilder *Cast:* Ray Milland, Jane Wyman, Phillip Terry, Howard da Silva, Frank Faylen
▶ Writer Milland hits the bottle instead of the typewriter. His brother Terry and girlfriend Wyman can do little to stop him and he goes through hell before pulling himself together. Landmark film about alcoholism, vividly directed by Wilder and superbly acted by the Oscar-winning Mil-

land. Also Oscars for Best Picture, Director, Screenplay.

LOST WORLD, THE 1960
★★ NR Sci-Fi 1:37
Dir: Irwin Allen *Cast:* Michael Rennie, Jill St. John, Claude Rains, David Hedison, Fernando Lamas, Richard Haydn
▶ Professor Rains leads expedition into a region of South America where dinosaurs still roam the earth. The giant creatures and Indians are among the perils faced by the intrepid crew. Rousing fun if not taken seriously. Acting honors go to Rains as the blustery Professor Challenger in this adaptation of the Arthur Conan Doyle novel.

LOUISIANA 1984
★★★ NR Drama/MFTV 2:06
☑ Adult situations, explicit language, violence
Dir: Philippe de Broca *Cast:* Margot Kidder, Ian Charleson, Victor Lanoux, Lloyd Bochner, Len Cariou
▶ In the nineteenth-century South, Kidder survives the loss of her children and two husbands. Despite the destruction of her pre–Civil War life, she manages to hang on to her beloved planatation and Charleson, the man she truly loves. Romantic saga in the tradition of *Gone With the Wind*.

LOVE AND BULLETS 1979 British
★★★★ PG Action-Adventure 1:43
☑ Adult situations, explicit language, violence
Dir: Stuart Rosenberg *Cast:* Charles Bronson, Rod Steiger, Jill Ireland, Bradford Dillman, Strother Martin
▶ Bronson is a tough Arizona cop sent to Switzerland to bring back mobster's moll Ireland. When he falls in love with her, the mobsters fear she'll leak information and have her killed. Bronson takes private revenge. Inoffensive adventure yarn with pleasing Swiss location shots. (CC)

LOVE AND DEATH 1975
★★★ PG Comedy 1:25
☑ Adult humor
Dir: Woody Allen *Cast:* Woody Allen, Diane Keaton, Frank Adu, Olga Georges-Picot, Harold Gould
▶ Woody's super-goofy spoof of *War and Peace*. Boris (Allen), a nineteenth-century Slav, is imprisoned for attempting to assassinate Napoleon and has two hours to review his life. He muses about Keaton, his unrequited love, Russian philosophy, art, war, and religion ("I will dwell in the

House of the Lord for six months with an option to buy"). Vintage, not-to-be-missed Allen.

LOVE AT FIRST BITE 1979
★★★ PG Comedy 1:36
☑ Explicit language
Dir: Stan Dragoti *Cast:* George Hamilton, Susan Saint James, Richard Benjamin, Dick Shawn, Arte Johnson
▶ Evicted from his Transylvania castle, modern-day Count Dracula (Hamilton) jets to New York, gets drunk on a skid-row wino's blood, and meets the girl of his dreams, Saint James, in a disco. Her psychiatrist boyfriend Benjamin frantically tries to warn Saint James but she falls for the sexy Prince of Darkness anyway. Hammy, lightweight, and amusing.

LOVE AT STAKE 1988
☆ R Comedy 1:26
☑ Explicit language
Dir: John Moffitt *Cast:* Patrick Cassidy, Kelly Preston, Bud Cort, David Graf, Stuart Pankin, Dave Thomas
▶ In 1692 Salem, Cassidy and Preston fall in love as judge Pankin and mayor Thomas plot to exploit the witch trials for their own financial gain. Preston is then accused of witchcraft. Dreadful premise for a comedy; simpleminded humor includes enema and chastity belt jokes. Formerly known as *Burnin' Love*.

LOVE BUG, THE 1968
★★★★★ G Family 1:50
Dir: Robert Stevenson *Cast:* Dean Jones, Michele Lee, Buddy Hackett, David Tomlinson, Joe Flynn
▶ Herbie, a perky green Volkswagen Bug with human feelings, adopts high-spirited but losing race-car driver Jones and carries him to victory. With Tomlinson as the villain who gets Herbie drunk before the road race. Charming Disney family fantasy spawned three sequels: *Herbie Rides Again*, *Herbie Goes to Monte Carlo*, and *Herbie Goes Bananas*. **(CC)**

LOVE CHILD 1982
★★★★ R Drama 1:37
☑ Nudity, adult situations, explicit language
Dir: Larry Peerce *Cast:* Amy Madigan, Beau Bridges, Mackenzie Phillips, Albert Salmi, Joanna Merlin
▶ Young convict Madigan has a secret affair with Bridges, a guard at Florida's Broward Correctional Institute. She then fights for the right to give birth behind bars. Sporting a greased-back ducktail,

Phillips plays a tough lesbian inmate who befriends Madigan. Rough around the edges, but the intriguing drama was based on a true story.

LOVE IN THE AFTERNOON 1957
★★★ NR Comedy 2:10 B&W
Dir: Billy Wilder *Cast:* Gary Cooper, Audrey Hepburn, Maurice Chevalier, Van Doude, John McGiver
▶ Texas millionaire Cooper, intrigued by a chance encounter with beautiful Parisian Hepburn, hires detective Chevalier to trace her but doesn't realize Chevalier is her father. Chevalier's charm and the fabulous locations more than compensate for Cooper's stiff performance in this breezy May-December romance. **(CC)**

LOVE IS A DOG FROM HELL 1988
Belgian
☆ NR Drama 1:30
☑ Nudity, adult situations, explicit language
Dir: Dominique Deruddere *Cast:* Josse De Pauw, Geert Hunaerts, Michael Pas, Gene Bervoets, Amid Chakir, Florence Beliard
▶ Adaptation of stories by American writer Charles Bukowski traces luckless young man's misadventures with women over twenty-year period; acne and drinking prove obstacles to success until he finally finds perfect woman (who happens to be a corpse). Odd, terribly sad tale is done with honesty and candor but never works up much sympathy for the hapless hero. ⑤

LOVE IS A MANY SPLENDORED THING 1955
★★★ NR Romance 1:42
Dir: Henry King *Cast:* Jennifer Jones, William Holden, Torin Thatcher, Isobel Elsom, Murray Matheson, Richard Loo
▶ Jones garnered a well-earned Oscar nomination as real-life Han Suyin, a Eurasian doctor who falls in love with married American reporter Holden. Racial prejudice, Holden's wife, and the Korean War keep the lovers apart in this extremely romantic and moving love story. Best Picture nominee; won for Score, Song, and Costume Design.

LOVELESS, THE 1983
★ R Drama 1:24
☑ Nudity, adult situations, explicit language, violence
Dir: Kathryn Bigelow, Monty Montgomery *Cast:* Willem Dafoe, Robert Gor-

don, Marin Kanter, J. Don Ferguson, Tina L'Hotsky, Lawrence Matarese
▶ In the late 1950s, motorcycle gang led by Dafoe invades small Georgia town, taking over a diner and saloon and menacing local girls. Dafoe's encounter with Kanter forces a deadly confrontation with her father Ferguson. Ambitious homage to *The Wild One* has stunning visuals but pretentious attitude. Good soundtrack includes songs by Gordon, Marshall Crenshaw, and Little Richard.

LOVE LETTERS 1984
★★ R Romance **1:28**
☑ Nudity, strong sexual content
Dir: Amy Jones *Cast:* Jamie Lee Curtis, James Keach, Amy Madigan, Bud Cort, Matt Clark
▶ Romantic drama about young L.A. disc jockey Curtis, who discovers old love letters that reveal her deceased mother once had an adulterous affair. Curtis then begins a passionate romance of her own with Keach, a married man. With Cort as a spaced-out DJ.

LOVELINES 1984
★★ R Comedy **1:34**
☑ Nudity, explicit language, adult humor
Dir: Rod Amateau *Cast:* Greg Bradford, Mary Beth Evans, Michael Winslow, Don Michael Paul, Tammy Taylor
▶ Low-budget teen sex comedy stars former coverboy Bradford and Evans as students from rival high schools and lead singers of competitive bands. Despite protests from their peers, the two fall in love and play a duet. No-think entertainment with strictly mainstream music. **(CC)**

LOVE MACHINE, THE 1971
★ R Drama **1:48**
☑ Adult situations, explicit language
Dir: Jack Haley, Jr. *Cast:* John Phillip Law, Dyan Cannon, Robert Ryan, Jackie Cooper, David Hemmings
▶ Dated adaptation of Jacqueline Susann's steamy 1960s best-seller about handsome Robin Stone (Law), a ruthless and libidinous TV newscaster who uses people to reach the top of the network pile. The frequent love scenes are fairly tame by 1980s standards. Borders on campy when seen today.

LOVE ME OR LEAVE ME 1955
★★★★ NR Biography/Musical **2:02**
Dir: Charles Vidor *Cast:* Doris Day,

James Cagney, Cameron Mitchell, Robert Keith, Tom Tully, Harry Bellaver
▶ Gangster Martin "the Gimp" Snyder (Cagney) turns dance-hall singer Ruth Etting (Day) into one of the most popular stars of the Roaring Twenties. But Snyder's insane jealousy leads to tragedy when Etting starts an affair with her pianist, Mitchell. Absorbing biography has strong performances from the leads and a standard-filled soundtrack ("Mean to Me," "Ten Cents a Dance," "I'll Never Stop Loving You," etc.). Received six Oscar nominations, winning for the story by Daniel Fuchs. **(CC)**

LOVE ME TENDER 1956
★★★★ NR Western **1:29** B&W
Dir: Robert D. Webb *Cast:* Elvis Presley, Richard Egan, Debra Paget, Mildred Dunnock, William Campbell, James Drury
▶ The Civil War sets brother against brother. Elvis marries Paget because sibling Egan is presumed dead in battle. Trouble begins when Egan returns in possession of a stolen payroll. Motion picture debut of a young and vibrant Elvis. He sings "Poor Boy," "Old Shep," and the title song, among others.

LOVE OR MONEY 1988
★★ NR Romance/Comedy **1:31**
☑ Adult situations, explicit language
Dir: Todd Hallowell *Cast:* Timothy Daly, Haviland Morris, Kevin McCarthy, Shelley Fabares
▶ In the Hamptons, young business hotshot Daly falls for marine biologist Morris, daughter of a major client, but they clash over his development of Long Island coast. Yuppie love story offers slick production and attractive leads but smug characterizations and unwieldy screenplay.

LOVER COME BACK 1962
★★★ NR Romance/Comedy **1:47**
Dir: Delbert Mann *Cast:* Rock Hudson, Doris Day, Tony Randall, Edie Adams, Jack Oakie, Ann B. Davis
▶ Sprightly Madison Avenue comedy: Day is an ad executive furious over rival Hudson's sneaky tactics, especially when she learns that the product in his latest campaign doesn't even exist. Leads are charming, and they receive fine support from Randall and Adams.

LOVERS AND LIARS 1981 Italian
★★ R Comedy/Drama **1:36**
☑ Nudity, explicit language

Dir: Mario Monicelli *Cast:* Goldie Hawn, Giancarlo Giannini, Auroré Clément, Claudine Auger

▶ Giannini, a Cassanova type, tries to whisk fun-loving American tourist Hawn to Pisa for a tryst, but is foiled by a series of mishaps. Potentially good setup falls flat; Giannini and Hawn, as she declares in the movie, "simply don't get along." Also known as *Travels With Anita.*

LOVERS AND OTHER STRANGERS 1970
★ ★ PG Comedy 1:44
☑ Adult situations, adult humor
Dir: Cy Howard *Cast:* Gig Young, Beatrice Arthur, Bonnie Bedelia, Anne Jackson, Harry Guardino, Michael Brandon

▶ Honest, frequently hilarious comedy about the surfacing tensions between two families as they prepare for Bedelia's marriage to Brandon. Incisive vignettes and accomplished cast (including Anne Meara, Bob Balaban, Cloris Leachman, and Diane Keaton in her film debut) add up to delightful entertainment. Received nominations for Richard Castellano (introducing the phrase "So what's the story?") and screenplay (based on a play by Renée Taylor and Joseph Bologna); "For All We Know" won Best Song Oscar.

LOVESICK 1983
★ ★ PG Romance/Comedy 1:36
☑ Adult situations, explicit language, adult humor
Dir: Marshall Brickman *Cast:* Dudley Moore, Elizabeth McGovern, Alec Guinness, John Huston, Wallace Shawn

▶ Moore, a psychiatrist with a posh Manhattan office and pretty wife, develops an obsessive crush on his latest patient, McGovern. Disregarding professional ethics and supposedly good sense, they begin a passionate romance. Alec Guinness, as a comic Sigmund Freud, occasionally appears to ask Moore: "Didn't you read my chapter on termination?"

LOVES OF CARMEN, THE 1948
★ ★ ★ NR Drama 1:37 B&W
Dir: Charles Vidor *Cast:* Rita Hayworth, Glenn Ford, Victor Jory, Arnold Moss

▶ Amoral temptress Hayworth, married to gypsy Jory, has affair with handsome soldier Ford that brings misfortune to them both. Follow-up to the Hayworth/Ford *Gilda* has the same sizzling sexual chemistry of its predecessor.

LOVE STORY 1970
★ ★ ★ PG Drama 1:39

Dir: Arthur Miller *Cast:* Ali MacGraw, Ryan O'Neal, Ray Milland, John Marley, Katherine Balfour

▶ Rich Ivy Leaguer O'Neal falls for poor but sassy co-ed MacGraw and, despite objections of his dad Milland, they marry. Their happiness is shattered when she becomes terminally ill. Most often-quoted line: "Love means never having to say you're sorry." Megahit tearjerker was based on Erich Segal's best-seller and won an Oscar for Francis Lai's score. Sequel: *Oliver's Story.*

LOVE STREAMS 1984
★ PG-13 Drama 2:02
☑ Adult situations, explicit language, violence
Dir: John Cassavetes *Cast:* Gena Rowlands, John Cassavetes, Diahnne Abbott, Seymour Cassel

▶ Intensely emotional drama about alienated writer Cassavetes and his sister Rowlands helping each other work through their various (and many) neuroses and discovering that life is really worth living. A brilliant roller coaster of human emotion for Cassavetes fans; long, rambling psychodrama for everyone else.

LOVING COUPLES 1980
★ ★ ★ PG Comedy 1:37
☑ Adult situations, explicit language
Dir: Jack Smight *Cast:* Shirley MacLaine, James Coburn, Susan Sarandon, Stephen Collins, Sally Kellerman

▶ Saucy sex comedy about MacLaine and Coburn taking up with younger lovers Collins and Sarandon before realizing there's no bed like home. Smooth cast of professionals give polish to routine screenplay.

LOVING YOU 1957
★ ★ ★ ★ NR Musical 1:41
Dir: Hal Kanter *Cast:* Elvis Presley, Lizabeth Scott, Wendell Corey, Dolores Hart, James Gleason, The Jordanaires

▶ Promoter Scott and country-western star Corey turn hillbilly truckdriver Presley into a rock 'n' roll star, but Presley has second thoughts about his new career when he loses girlfriend Hart. Elvis, at the height of his powers, does a fine acting job in a story loosely based on his own life. Great soundtrack: "Teddy Bear," "Hot Dog," "Mean Woman Blues," title song, etc.

LUCAS 1986
★ ★ ★ ★ PG-13 Comedy/Drama 1:40

☑ Explicit language
Dir: David Seltzer   *Cast:* Corey Haim, Kerri Green, Charlie Sheen, Courtney Thorne-Smith, Winona Horowitz (Ryder)
► Brainy but shrimpy high schooler Lucas (Haim) falls for friend Green, although she prefers sensitive jock Sheen. To prove himself, Haim tries out for the football team. Seltzer has created three-dimensional teenage characters in a sweetly affecting little movie. Intelligent dialogue and winning performances; modest in scope but quite evocative. **(CC)**

LUCKY JIM 1957 British
★★ NR Comedy 1:35
Dir: John Boulting   *Cast:* Ian Carmichael, Terry-Thomas, Hugh Griffith, Sharon Acker, Jean Anderson, Maureen Connell
► At a small English college, professor Carmichael's efforts to impress his superiors run aground on a series of comic disasters. Amusing performances by Carmichael and Terry-Thomas highlight this entertaining adaptation of the Kingsley Amis novel.

LUCKY LUCIANO 1974
U.S./French/Italian
★★ R Drama 1:50
☑ Adult situations, explicit language, violence
Dir: Francesco Rosi   *Cast:* Gian Maria Volonté, Rod Steiger, Charles Siragusa, Edmond O'Brien, Vincent Gardenia, Silverio Blasi
► Intriguing account of famed gangster's career after deportation to Italy in the 1950s. Real-life narcotics investigator Siragusa adds touch of authenticity in showing the ten-year campaign to end Luciano's criminal empire; Steiger is convincing as an informer.

LUNCH WAGON GIRLS 1981
★ R Comedy 1:30
☑ Nudity, strong sexual content, explicit language, adult humor
Dir: Ernest Pintoff   *Cast:* Pamela Bryant, Rosanne Katon, Candy Moore, Jimmy Van Patten, Chuck McCann, Rose Marie
► Three lovely young ladies quit their gas station gig and take over a traveling lunch wagon. Hot pants and tight sweaters lure more customers than the cuisine. Mindless sex comedy is technically amateurish, full of juvenile humor, and provides plenty of nudity and profanity.

LUST FOR LIFE 1956
★★★★ NR Biography 2:02
Dir: Vincente Minnelli   *Cast:* Kirk Douglas, Anthony Quinn, James Donald, Pamela Brown, Everett Sloane
► Painter Vincent Van Gogh (Douglas) struggles with poverty, heartbreak, mental illness, and a world that ignores his artistic genius. Compelling drama may be the best movie ever made about an artist; Douglas's magnificently intense performance captures Van Gogh's inner workings. Stunning color photography, Oscar-winning supporting performance by Quinn as Van Gogh's friend, the artist Gauguin.

LUST IN THE DUST 1985
★ R Western/Comedy 1:24
☑ Nudity, explicit language, violence, adult humor
Dir: Paul Bartel   *Cast:* Tab Hunter, Divine, Lainie Kazan, Geoffrey Lewis, Cesar Romero
► Offbeat camp Western, decidedly tasteless but often fun. Big mama Rosie (drag queen Divine) and singer Margarita (Kazan) vie for gunslinger Hunter's attention. The rivalry ends, however, when by matching derriere tattoos they realize they are long-lost sisters! Saucy and irreverent. **(CC)**

LUV 1967
☆ NR Comedy 1:35
Dir: Clive Donner   *Cast:* Jack Lemmon, Peter Falk, Elaine May, Nina Wayne, Eddie Mayehoff
► Lemmon plays an inept loser who's rescued from a suicide attempt by old school friend Falk; in return, Falk asks Lemmon to help him divorce May. Lemmon marries May, Falk ends up with buxom gym teacher Wayne—but both couples are still unhappy. Plodding adaptation of a Murray Schisgal play fails to reproduce the original's comic tone.

M 1931 German
★★★ NR Drama 1:39 B&W
Dir: Fritz Lang   *Cast:* Peter Lorre, Otto Wernicke, Gustav Grundgens, Theo Lingen, Theodore Loos, Georg John
► Child murderer Lorre terrifies and outrages Berlin. When the police prove incompetent, the city's criminals conduct their own manhunt. Provocative, critically praised film suffers from dated passages, but its cumulative impact is astonishing and nerve-wracking. Lorre's chilling film

debut made him an international star.
S

MAC AND ME 1988
★ ★ ★ PG Fantasy/Family 1:33
☑ Explicit language
Dir: Stewart Raffill *Cast:* Jade Calegory, Christine Ebersole, Jonathan Ward, Katrina Caspary, Lauren Stanley, Vinnie Torrente
▶ Baby alien Mac (Mysterious Alien Creature) is left behind when government scientists attempt to nab his family. Mac hides out in California home and is befriended by handicapped boy Calegory. Resemblance to *E.T.* very apparent but sweet story evokes its own charm.

MACARONI 1985 Italian
★ ★ PG Comedy/Drama 1:44
☑ Explicit language
Dir: Ettore Scola *Cast:* Jack Lemmon, Marcello Mastroianni, Daria Nicolodi, Isa Danieli, Maria Luisa Saniella, Patrizzia Sacchi
▶ Uptight American businessman Lemmon arrives in Naples and is reunited with Mastroianni, brother of his World War II flame Danieli. Mastroianni has kept the romance alive by writing his sister love letters and signing Lemmon's name. Lemmon loosens up under Mastroianni's guidance. Pleasing performances by the two stars. In English and (sporadically) subtitled Italian.

MACARTHUR 1977
★ ★ ★ ★ PG Biography 2:10
☑ Violence
Dir: Joseph Sargent *Cast:* Gregory Peck, Dan O'Herlihy, Ed Flanders, Marj Dusay
▶ The life and times of General Douglas MacArthur (Peck) from World War II to his dismissal during the Korean War. Sacrifices cinematic excitement in favor of historical accuracy, but the excellent portrayal by Peck and the fine supporting players (Flanders as Truman, O'Herlihy as FDR) make it worthwhile.

MACBETH 1971 British
★ ★ R Drama 2:20
☑ Nudity, graphic violence
Dir: Roman Polanski *Cast:* Jon Finch, Francesca Annis, Martin Shaw, Nicholas Shelby, John Stride, Stephan Chase
▶ Macbeth (Finch), egged on by scheming wife Annis and witches' prophecy, attempts to usurp the crown of Scotland. Bloody version of Shakespeare's tragedy seems like a catharsis for director Po-

lanksi (he made it after wife's murder by the Charles Manson family). Unusual interpretation of the classic has some terrific swordplay and stunning visuals.

MACK, THE 1973
★ R Drama 1:50
☑ Explicit language
Dir: Michael Campus *Cast:* Max Julien, Richard Pryor, Roger Mosley, Don Gordon
▶ Black pimp Julien rises to the top of his profession and comes into conflict with corrupt white cops and the Mafia. Dated black exploitation; even Pryor's small part as Julien's sidekick doesn't help enliven stereotyped plot.

MACKENNA'S GOLD 1969
★ ★ ★ PG Western 2:08
☑ Explicit language, violence
Dir: J. Lee Thompson *Cast:* Gregory Peck, Omar Sharif, Telly Savalas, Camilla Sparv, Keenan Wynn, Julie Newmar
▶ Sheriff Peck memorizes and burns Indian map to a mythical golden canyon; he becomes the target of innumerable greedy prospectors and killers in this long, disappointing Western. Large cast (including Lee J. Cobb, Raymond Massey, Burgess Meredith, Anthony Quayle, Edward G. Robinson, and Eli Wallach) fails to spark episodic story.

MACKINTOSH MAN, THE 1973
★ ★ ★ PG Espionage 1:38
☑ Violence
Dir: John Huston *Cast:* Paul Newman, James Mason, Dominique Sanda, Harry Andrews, Ian Bannen
▶ British intelligence sends out Interpol agent Newman to trap Mason, a parliament member who is actually working for the Communists. Good characters, charismatic cast, atmospheric Maurice Jarre score, and colorful locations in England, Ireland, and Malta; but contrived plotting makes for a less than satisfying whole.

MACON COUNTY LINE 1975
★ ★ ★ R Action-Adventure 1:29
☑ Adult situations, explicit language, violence
Dir: Richard Compton *Cast:* Alan Vint, Cheryl Waters, Max Baer, Jr., Geoffrey Lewis, Joan Blackman, Jesse Vint
▶ Baer, who also wrote and produced, stars as a redneck sheriff whose wife Blackman is brutally murdered. The prime suspects are outsiders Waters, Alan Vint,

and Jesse Vint; a deputy finds out too late that Baer is pursuing the wrong people. Taut Southern thriller set in the early 1950s led to a sequel, *Return to Macon County*.

MADAME BOVARY 1949
★★★★ NR Drama 1:55 B&W
Dir: Vincente Minnelli *Cast:* Jennifer Jones, James Mason, Van Heflin, Louis Jourdan, Gene Lockhart, Gladys Cooper
▶ Lavish production of Gustave Flaubert's classic, with Mason portraying the writer as he defends himself from censors. Through flashbacks, he reveals the story of Emma Bovary (Jones), a nineteenth-century libertine whose extramarital affairs lead to tragedy. Novel's plot is softened considerably, but passion and spectacle remain intact. "Emma Bovary Waltz" stands among Minnelli's best dances.

MADAME ROSA 1977 French
★★ PG Drama 1:45
☑ Adult situations, explicit language
Dir: Moshe Mizrahi *Cast:* Simone Signoret, Claude Dauphin, Sammy Ben Youb, Gabriel Jabbour
▶ Profoundly moving, Oscar-winning Best Foreign Film about an aging ex-prostitute/Auschwitz survivor and an orphaned fourteen-year-old Arab boy, Ben Youb. Her dying mission in life is to save him from becoming a "fancy man" of the French quarter. Huffing and puffing her way up tenement stairs, painfully aware her mind is slipping into senility, Signoret is unforgettable and heartbreaking. A very different kind of love story, often quite funny in spite of its downbeat subject, about two brave, immensely appealing characters.

MADAME SOUSATZKA 1988 British
★★ PG-13 Drama 2:02
☑ Adult situations, explicit language
Dir: John Schlesinger *Cast:* Shirley MacLaine, Peggy Ashcroft, Twiggy, Navin Chowdhry, Leigh Lawson, Shabana Azmi
▶ In London, eccentric piano teacher MacLaine takes Indian teenager Chowdhry under her wing, teaching him not only how to play but how to live. Prodigy blossoms under her tutelage, but rift eventually occurs between pupil and mentor. Flamboyant MacLaine performance is hard to resist, as is the very appealing Chowdhry.

MADAME X 1966
★★★ NR Drama 1:40
Dir: David Lowell Rich *Cast:* Lana Turner, John Forsythe, Ricardo Montalban, Burgess Meredith, Constance Bennett, Keir Dullea
▶ Version of an oft-filmed Alexandre Bisson play is a smoothly produced soap opera about bored diplomat's wife Turner whose affair with playboy Montalban leads to prostitution, blackmail, and murder. In a tragic twist, she is defended in court by Dullea, the son who never knew her. Turner's dedicated performance overcomes the often maudlin plot.

MAD DOG MORGAN 1976 Australian
★★ R Western 1:42
☑ Adult situations, explicit language, violence
Dir: Philippe Mora *Cast:* Dennis Hopper, Jack Thompson, David Gulpilil, Frank Thring, Michael Pate, Walls Eaton
▶ After failing as a prospector during the mid-1800s, Hopper turns to robbery and winds up in prison. Once released, he teams with aborigine Gulpilil for an infamous crime spree. Well-made, extremely violent Western is based on the legendary outlaw of Australia's gold rush era.

MADE FOR EACH OTHER 1939
★★★★ NR Drama 1:31 B&W
Dir: John Cromwell *Cast:* Carole Lombard, James Stewart, Lucile Watson, Charles Coburn, Ward Bond
▶ First-rate melodrama, set in the late 1930s, about young love on an uphill climb. Stewart and Lombard, in fine comedic form, struggle with marriage, parenting, and interfering in-laws. The engaging script by Jo Swerling climaxes in the near death of the couple's first child. Also available in a colorized version. **(CC)**

MADE IN HEAVEN 1987
★★ PG Fantasy/Romance 1:41
☑ Brief nudity, adult situations
Dir: Alan Rudolph *Cast:* Timothy Hutton, Kelly McGillis, Maureen Stapleton, Ann Wedgeworth, Mare Winningham, Debra Winger
▶ Fairy-tale romance begins in the 1940s when Hutton dies while saving a drowning child. Up in heaven, he falls for fellow angel, McGillis. When she's returned to earth to fulfill her destiny, he follows. Featherweight concoction sags as the couple try to find each other on earth. Includes surprising cameo appearances

by Winger as a man, Neil Young, Ellen Barkin, and Tom Petty.

MADE IN THE U.S.A. 1987
★ R Drama 1:26
☑ Nudity, adult situations, explicit language
Dir: Ken Friedman *Cast:* Christopher Penn, Lori Singer, Adrian Pasdar, Jackie Murphy, Judy Baldwin, Dean Paul Martin
▶ Punks Penn and Pasdar pick up Singer and go on a crime spree across America. Downbeat road movie with unpleasant characters and heavy-handed preaching against the evils of toxic waste. Well made but not much fun to sit through.

MADHOUSE 1974 British
★ PG Horror 1:29
☑ Violence
Dir: Jim Clark *Cast:* Vincent Price, Peter Cushing, Robert Quarry, Adrienne Corri, Natasha Pyne
▶ Horror actor Price, famous for his role as Doctor Death, spends twelve years in an asylum after finding his fiancée beheaded. He is released but his comeback is sabotaged by a series of murders. Above-average genre plot features noteworthy Price but is pretty tame in the fright department.

MADIGAN 1968
★★★ NR Action-Adventure 1:41
Dir: Don Siegel *Cast:* Richard Widmark, Henry Fonda, Inger Stevens, Harry Guardino, Susan Clark, James Whitmore
▶ Cops Madigan (Widmark) and Guardino, in hot water with police commissioner Fonda for letting killer get away, attempt to recapture him. Gritty, intelligent thriller with good performances (Widmark re-created his role in the subsequent TV series), authentic New York City locations, and a shattering finale.

MAD MAX 1980 Australian
★ R Action-Adventure 1:33
☑ Explicit language, graphic violence
Dir: George Miller *Cast:* Mel Gibson, Joanne Samuel, Hugh Keays-Byrne, Steve Bisley, Tim Burns
▶ Australia, the near future: policeman Gibson goes on a rampage of revenge when vicious biker gang attacks his wife and child. Visceral excitement, fast-paced action, and well-executed stunts in this tough and unusual futuristic fantasy. Dubbed voices substitute for the

Australian accents. Spawned two sequels.

MAD MAX BEYOND THUNDERDOME 1985 Australian
★★ PG-13 Action-Adventure 1:47
☑ Violence
Dir: George Miller, George Ogilvie *Cast:* Mel Gibson, Tina Turner, Helen Buday, Bruce Spence, Angelo Rossitto, Frank Thring
▶ "Two men enter, one man leaves," announces feudal society queen Turner as Max (Gibson) prepares for gladiatorial combat in the futuristic arena known as Thunderdome. Gibson also befriends a tribe of wild children in this third entry in the Mad Max series. Less action-oriented than its predecessors, with a higher budget, more elaborate costumes and sets, and Mel adding some humanity to his charismatic hero. Still, plenty of thrills (especially in the rousing Thunderdome sequence) and Tina is a high-style villain. (CC)

MAGIC 1978
★★★ R Mystery-Suspense 1:38
☑ Brief nudity, explicit language, violence
Dir: Richard Attenborough *Cast:* Anthony Hopkins, Ann-Margret, Burgess Meredith, Ed Lauter, E. J. Andre, Jerry Houser
▶ Ventriloquist-magician Hopkins, insecure about the success of his latest dummy Fats, flees a lucrative TV contract for his Catskills hometown. There he rekindles a romance with high school sweetheart Ann-Margret (delivering another fine performance), who's trapped in an unhappy marriage with redneck Lauter. Similar to an episode in thriller *Dead of Night*, it gives away most of its surprises in the first half hour. Screenplay by William Goldman from his novel.

MAGIC CHRISTIAN, THE 1970 British
★ PG Comedy 1:33
☑ Adult situations, explicit language, adult humor
Dir: Joseph McGrath *Cast:* Peter Sellers, Ringo Starr, Richard Attenborough, Laurence Harvey, Christopher Lee, Spike Milligan
▶ Millionaire Sellers sets out to prove to adopted son Starr that people will do anything for money. Irreverent, often tasteless satire is structurally a mess, but many of the vignettes are priceless. Filled with cameos: Graham Chapman, John

Cleese, Spike Milligan, Raquel Welch, etc. Typical scene: Yul Brunner in drag singing "Mad About the Boy" to Roman Polanski. Other songs include Badfinger's "Come and Get It."

MAGIC FLUTE, THE 1974 Swedish
★ G Music 2:14
Dir: Ingmar Bergman   *Cast:* Ulric Cold, Josef Kostlinger, Erik Saeden, Birgit Nordin, Trina Urrila
▶ Superior adaptation of Mozart's opera about a prince who must rescue the kidnapped daughter of the Queen of the Night. Assured direction captures intimate details as well as the sweep of Mozart's score. Only drawbacks: cast sings in Swedish, not German; length may be excessive for non-opera fans. On all other levels a delightful, rewarding experience.
S

MAGIC OF LASSIE, THE 1978
★★★★★ G Family 1:40
Dir: Don Chaffey   *Cast:* James Stewart, Mickey Rooney, Pernell Roberts, Stephanie Zimbalist, Michael Sharrett, Alice Faye
▶ Evil millionaire Roberts, unable to buy neighbor Stewart's vineyard, steals Stewart's dog instead. Can Lassie find her way home across the vast Rockies? Children will love the canine star's comeback (her first film since 1952); adults will enjoy the singing by Faye, Stewart, and Pat and Debby Boone.

MAGNIFICENT AMBERSONS, THE 1942
★★★ NR Drama 1:28 B&W
Dir: Orson Welles   *Cast:* Joseph Cotten, Dolores Costello, Anne Baxter, Tim Holt, Agnes Moorehead, Ray Collins
▶ Fascinating study of the Amberson family, wealthy Midwesterners who fail to adapt to changing times. Technically innovative film is also rich in characterizations: Cotten as a compassionate inventor, Holt an insufferable heir, Oscar-nominated Moorehead his spinster aunt. Director Welles wrote the screenplay from Booth Tarkington's novel. Laserdisk version contains additional information about the uneven ending (which was reshot by the studio).

MAGNIFICENT OBSESSION 1954
★★★★ NR Drama 1:48
Dir: Douglas Sirk   *Cast:* Jane Wyman, Rock Hudson, Barbara Rush, Otto Kruger, Agnes Moorehead
▶ Playboy Hudson is responsible for blinding Wyman in an accident. He changes his lifestyle, becomes a doctor, and gets a chance to help the woman he injured. They fall in love although she is unaware of her benefactor's true identity. Soap opera love story acted with conviction and emotion by the leads.

MAGNIFICENT SEVEN, THE 1960
★★★★ NR Western 2:06
Dir: John Sturges   *Cast:* Yul Brynner, Eli Wallach, Steve McQueen, Charles Bronson, Robert Vaughn, James Coburn
▶ Americanized version of Japanese classic *The Seven Samurai* depicts Mexican village terrorized by outlaw Wallach and his band of cutthroats. Townsfolk hire tough hombre Brynner and six other mercenaries, including McQueen, Bronson, Vaughn, and Coburn, to fight for them. Rousing and perpetually popular Western carried by fine performances from cast of relative unknowns (save for Brynner) who later became stars. Elmer Bernstein score so enthralled audiences it became the signature tune of Marlboro cigarettes. Three sequels followed.

MAGNUM FORCE 1973
★★★★★ R Action-Adventure 2:02
☑ Nudity, explicit language, violence
Dir: Ted Post   *Cast:* Clint Eastwood, Hal Holbrook, Felton Perry, Mitchell Ryan, David Soul, Tim Matheson
▶ Brutal sequel to *Dirty Harry*: rogue cops form an execution squad to rid San Francisco of its crime leaders. Detective Harry Callahan (Eastwood) is the one man who can stop them, because "shooting is all right, as long as the right people get shot." Fast, violent, and more popular than the original, with a thrilling car chase and an unnerving bomb sequence. Followed by *The Enforcer*.

MAHLER 1974 British
★ PG Biography/Music 1:55
☑ Adult situations, adult humor
Dir: Ken Russell   *Cast:* Robert Powell, Georgina Hale, Richard Morant, Lee Montague, Rosalie Crutchley
▶ Biography of composer Gustav Mahler (Powell) traces his troubled relationship with wife Hale, religious problems, and tortured inner life. Nice photography and classical music, but overwrought imagery and odd mixture of fact and fantasy à la Ken Russell are for very specialized tastes only.

MAHOGANY 1975
★★★★ PG Drama 1:48 B&W

☑ Adult situations
Dir: Berry Gordy *Cast:* Diana Ross, Billy Dee Williams, Anthony Perkins, Jean-Pierre Aumont, Nina Foch
▶ Gay photographer Perkins turns Ross, a poor Chicago girl, into the internationally famous model Mahogany. Rich Frenchman Aumont helps develop her wildly successful clothing designs, but Mahogany realizes she can only be happy with struggling politician Williams. Glossy soap opera with an emphasis on fashion. Oscar-nominated theme, "Do You Know Where You're Going To," became a pop hit for Ross.

MAID TO ORDER 1987
★★★ PG Comedy 1:36
☑ Brief nudity, explicit language
Dir: Amy Jones *Cast:* Ally Sheedy, Beverly D'Angelo, Michael Ontkean, Valerie Perrine, Tom Skerritt, Dick Shawn
▶ Fairy tale reversal for pouty brat packer Sheedy who's transformed from bored Beverly Hills heiress to maid by flaky fairy godmother D'Angelo. Household chores and a romance with the chauffeur humanize Sheedy, educating her about what's really important in life. Riches-to-rags tale spun with simplicity and enthusiasm. Comic turns by Perrine and Shawn as Sheedy's wealthy, snobby employers who hoard tin foil.

MAIN EVENT, THE 1979
★★★★ PG Comedy 1:49
☑ Adult situations, explicit language
Dir: Howard Zieff *Cast:* Barbra Streisand, Ryan O'Neal, Paul Sand, Patti D'Arbanville, Whitman Mayo
▶ After her business manager flees with all her money, bankrupt perfume company owner Streisand has only one asset left: O'Neal, a boxer she once acquired as a tax write-off. She nags him back into the ring; they fall in love. Attempts to recapture the chemistry the leads displayed in *What's Up Doc?*

MAJOR BARBARA 1941 British
★★ NR Comedy 2:00 B&W
Dir: Gabriel Pascal *Cast:* Wendy Hiller, Rex Harrison, Robert Morley, Robert Newton, Emlyn Williams, Deborah Kerr
▶ Salvation Army Major Barbara (Hiller) clashes with her surprisingly benevolent munitions mogul father Morley. Her admirer Harrison is caught in between the two. Cynically amusing film version of the George Bernard Shaw play features Kerr in her film debut.

MAJOR DUNDEE 1965
★ NR Western 2:04
Dir: Sam Peckinpah *Cast:* Charlton Heston, Richard Harris, Jim Hutton, James Coburn, Senta Berger, Warren Oates
▶ Apaches attack a Southwestern jail; Union Army warden Heston assembles his prisoners—including Confederate captain Harris, who's been sentenced to death—to chase the Indians into Mexico. Good cast and violent action.

MAKING CONTACT 1986
★★★ PG Fantasy 1:19
☑ Explicit language
Dir: Roland Emmerich *Cast:* Joshua Morrell, Eva Kryll, Jan Zierold, Tammy Shields
▶ Nine-year-old Morrell, mourning the death of his father, finds a mysterious dummy with magical but deadly powers. Some impressive special effects but the ending is pretty weird. Too intense for younger kids, okay for the older ones.

MAKING LOVE 1982
★★ R Drama 1:51
☑ Adult situations, strong sexual content, explicit language
Dir: Arthur Hiller *Cast:* Kate Jackson, Michael Ontkean, Harry Hamlin, Wendy Hiller, Arthur Hill
▶ Doctor Ontkean, seemingly happily married to TV executive Jackson, discovers that he has a preference for men, particularly Hamlin. His marriage falls apart when Jackson learns the truth. Attractive cast in a compassionate (if somewhat sanitized) look at once-taboo subject matter.

MAKING MR. RIGHT 1987
★★ PG-13 Comedy 1:38
☑ Adult situations, explicit language
Dir: Susan Seidelman *Cast:* John Malkovich, Ann Magnuson, Ben Masters, Glenne Headly, Laurie Metcalf, Polly Bergen
▶ Miami PR exec Magnuson despairs of finding Mr. Right until she is hired to publicize naive android Malkovich, made in his own image by grouchy scientist (Malkovich again). Magnuson teaches the robot social graces and falls for him. Kooky comedy with inventive visuals and production design, delightful Magnuson, and Malkovich having fun with his dual role. However, pacing and too many of the bits fall flat.

MAKING THE GRADE 1984
★★ R Comedy 1:45
☑ Nudity, adult situations, explicit language
Dir: Dorian Walker *Cast:* Judd Nelson, Jonna Lee, Gordon Jump, Walter Olkewicz, Ronald Lacey, Dana Olsen
▶ Youth comedy version of *The Prince and the Pauper*: obnoxious young millionaire Olsen hires street-smart punk Nelson to impersonate him at prep school while he bops across Europe. Nelson turns the snooty academy upside down in this predictable if above-average genre effort.

MALCOLM 1986 Australian
★★ PG-13 Comedy 1:30
☑ Adult situations, explicit language, mild violence
Dir: Nadia Tass *Cast:* Colin Friels, John Hargreaves, Lindy Davies, Chris Haywood, Charles Tingwell
▶ Mechanical genius Friels loses his job and to improve his finances takes in excon Hargreaves and his girlfriend Davies as roommates. The trio form a close relationship and plot a heist together. Some charm and wit but gets off to a slow start.

MALIBU BIKINI SHOP, THE 1987
★★ R Comedy 1:38
☑ Nudity, adult situations
Dir: David Wechter *Cast:* Michael David Wright, Bruce Greenwood, Barbara Horan, Debra Blee, Jay Robinson
▶ Stuffy yuppie Wright and his ne'er-do-well brother Greenwood inherit bikini store from their aunt. Wright loosens up under the influence of would-be designer Horan and then battles a guru for possession of the place. Inconsequential comedy features miles of tan lines. **(CC)**

MALIBU EXPRESS 1985
★ R Sex 1:41
☑ Nudity, strong sexual content, violence
Dir: Andy Sidaris *Cast:* Darby Hinton, Sybil Danning, Barbara Edwards, Brett Clark, Kimberly McArthur, Lorraine Michaels
▶ Mysterious Contessa Danning hires slow-talking Texas private eye Hinton to investigate sale of computer secrets to the Russians. Hayseed dialogue, wooden acting, and nonstop nudity featuring four *Playboy* Playmates (including Playmate of the Year Edwards) as well as some beefcake for the ladies.

MALONE 1987
★★★ R Action-Adventure 1:32
☑ Explicit language, violence
Dir: Harley Cokliss *Cast:* Burt Reynolds, Cliff Robertson, Lauren Hutton, Kenneth McMillan, Scott Wilson, Cynthia Gibb
▶ In a remote mountain town, burnt-out CIA assassin Reynolds befriends gas station owner Wilson and his daughter Gibb. He protects them against Robertson, a fascist trying to take over the burg. Standard Burt vehicle has pleasant scenery and pert Gibb but overly solemn Reynolds and slow pacing.

MALTESE FALCON, THE 1941
★★★★★ NR Mystery-Suspense 1:40 B&W
Dir: John Huston *Cast:* Humphrey Bogart, Mary Astor, Peter Lorre, Sydney Greenstreet, Lee Patrick, Elisha Cook, Jr.
▶ Detective Sam Spade is hired by an enigmatic Astor to find a valuable antique, but she doesn't tell him that a gang of swindlers is also after the bird. Irresistible mystery based on Dashiell Hammett's novel set a high standard for private eye films. Bogart excels in his first major role as the hard-boiled Spade; outstanding support from Lorre as an effeminate con man, Greenstreet (in his film debut) as the notorious fat man, and Cook, a jittery gunman. Directing debut for Huston (whose father Walter appears in a cameo). Available in a colorized version. **(CC)**

MAME 1974
★★ PG Musical 2:13
Dir: Gene Saks *Cast:* Lucille Ball, Robert Preston, Beatrice Arthur, Jane Connell, Bruce Davison, Joyce Van Patten
▶ Ball, at sixty-two and no great singer, was miscast as the eccentric Auntie Mame in this musical version of the durable Patrick Dennis novel. Arthur is her best friend, Van Patten plays Gooch, and Preston is Mame's southern love interest. Funniest scene: Ball, pretending to ride in the fox hunt, passes the master of the hounds, then the hounds, then the fox. Excellent score includes "We Need a Little Christmas" and "If He Walked Into My Life."

MAN AND A WOMAN, A 1966 French
★★★ NR Romance 1:43
Dir: Claude Lelouch *Cast:* Anouk Aimee, Jean-Louis Trintignant, Pierre Barouh, Valerie Lagrange

▶ Two widowed people, script girl Aimee and race-car driver Trintignant, embark on a love affair haunted by memories of the tragic past. Lyrical contemporary classic won two Oscars (Best Foreign Film, Screenplay) and is one of the most popular French films ever in America. Outstanding musical score by Frances Lai. Spawned a sequel twenty years later. (CC) ⑤

MAN AND A WOMAN, A: 20 YEARS LATER 1986 French
★ **PG Romance 1:52**
☑ Adult situations, mild violence
Dir: Claude Lelouch *Cast:* Anouk Aimee, Jean-Louis Trintignant, Evelyne Bouix, Marie-Sophie Pochat
▶ Film producer Aimee, making a movie about her old love Trintignant, realizes she still loves him. She switches to another topic for her movie and uncovers a murderer. Self-indulgent and convoluted, although film buffs may admire Lelouch's intricate editing. Swoony romantic moments mix with a mystery subplot. Great music from the original is used again. ⑤

MAN AND BOY 1971
★★ **G Western 1:38**
Dir: E. W. Swackhamer *Cast:* Bill Cosby, Gloria Foster, George Spell, Leif Erickson, Douglas Turner Ward, Yaphet Kotto
▶ Homesteader Cosby returns from the Civil War to discover his horses have been stolen. Accompanied by son Spell and burly sidekick Kotto, he sets out on an odyssey across the Southwest to recover them. Earnest family-oriented adventure with Cosby in an unusual noncomic performance.

MAN, A WOMAN AND A BANK, A 1979 Canadian
★★★ **PG Comedy 1:42**
☑ Adult situations, explicit language
Dir: Noel Black *Cast:* Donald Sutherland, Brooke Adams, Paul Mazursky, Allen Magicovsky, Nick Rice
▶ Standard caper movie with an offbeat love story. Electronic masterminds Mazursky and Sutherland break the code of a bank's computer, but while stealing the building's blueprints, they get photographed by Adams. Trying to recover the pictures, Sutherland falls in love with her. Originally titled *A Very Big Withdrawal.*

MAN CALLED HORSE, A 1970
★★★★★ **PG Western 1:49**

☑ Graphic violence
Dir: Elliot Silverstein *Cast:* Richard Harris, Judith Anderson, Jean Gascon, Manu Tupou, Corinna Tsopei
▶ While hunting in the Dakota Territory in the early 1800s, English aristocrat Harris is captured by Sioux Indians. He endures torturous rituals (shown in horrifying detail) and proves his manhood. Eventually, he becomes the tribe's great white chief and marries Indian princess Tsopei (Miss Universe 1964). Features authentic Sioux rituals and language. Sequels: *Return of a Man Called Horse* and *Triumphs of a Man Called Horse.* (CC)

MANCHURIAN CANDIDATE, THE 1962
★★★★ **NR Mystery-Suspense 2:06 B&W**
Dir: John Frankenheimer *Cast:* Frank Sinatra, Laurence Harvey, Janet Leigh, Angela Lansbury, James Gregory, Henry Silva
▶ Korean War vet Harvey returns to the U.S. as a hero. No one suspects at first, save his nightmare-plagued pal Sinatra, that Harvey is actually a killing machine brainwashed by his Communist captors. Audacious thriller works on many levels: crackerjack suspense, political satire, social comment, and even prophecy (film predates the Kennedy assassination it so chillingly resembles). Magnificently intricate direction by Frankenheimer and wonderful acting all around; Harvey is quite poignant and Lansbury does an Oscar-nominated turn as his monstrous mom. Not to be missed. Video version includes interviews with Sinatra and Frankenheimer. (CC)

MANDELA 1987
★★★★ **NR Biography/MFTV 2:15**
Dir: Philip Saville *Cast:* Danny Glover, Alfre Woodard, John Indi, John Matshikiza, Nathan Dambusa Mdledle
▶ True story of Nelson Mandela (Glover), black South African lawyer whose stand against apartheid awakened the world's conscience. Film traces his involvement with the African National Congress, treason trial, decision to support armed resistance, imprisonment since the 1960s, and the dedication of his wife Winnie (Woodard). Inspiring drama with outstanding performances by Glover and Woodard.

MANDINGO 1975
★★★ **R Drama 2:07**
☑ Nudity, adult situations, explicit language, violence

Dir: Richard Fleischer   *Cast:* James Mason, Susan George, Perry King, Richard Ward, Ken Norton, Brenda Sykes
▶ Lurid adaptation of Kyle Onstott's bestseller about a Southern plantation ruled with an iron hand by Mason. Heir King ignores wife George for an affair with slave Sykes, at the same time exploiting her husband (heavyweight boxer Norton, in his film debut) in brutal match fights. Norton reprised his role in the sequel *Drum.*

MAN FOR ALL SEASONS, A 1966
★ ★ ★ ★ ★ G Drama 2:00
Dir: Fred Zinnemann   *Cast:* Paul Scofield, Robert Shaw, Wendy Hiller, Susannah York, Leo McKern, Orson Welles
▶ Refusing to endorse the divorce of King Henry VIII (Shaw), Chancellor of England Thomas More (Scofield) pays the price in martyrdom. Asked to conform for the sake of "fellowship," More replies, "When you go to heaven for following your conscience and I go to hell for not following mine, will you join me, then, for fellowship?" Towering, superbly mounted film version of the Robert Bolt play, which he adapted. Justifiably acclaimed with Scofield's immensely moving portrait leading a great cast. Oscars for Best Picture, Director, Actor (Scofield), Screenplay, Costumes, and Cinematography. **(CC)**

MAN FRIDAY 1975 British
★ ★ ★ PG Drama 1:55
☑ Explicit language, brief nudity
Dir: Jack Gold   *Cast:* Peter O'Toole, Richard Roundtree, Peter Cellier, Christopher Cabot, Sam Seabrook, Stanley Clay
▶ Variation on Daniel Defoe's *Robinson Crusoe* emphasizes the racial conflicts between marooned sailor O'Toole and black native Roundtree, a fugitive who washes up on the island. In this version, O'Toole establishes a master-slave relationship which the wily Roundtree manages to reverse. Offbeat and extremely talky.

MAN FROM LARAMIE, THE 1955
★ ★ ★ ★ NR Western 1:44
Dir: Anthony Mann   *Cast:* James Stewart, Arthur Kennedy, Donald Crisp, Cathy O'Donnell, Alex Nicol
▶ Mysterious stranger Stewart seeks the identity of the man who sold rifles to the Apaches and was thus responsible for his brother's death. The trail leads to powerful rancher Crisp, his evil son Nicol,

and his foreman Kennedy. Taut and suspenseful psychological Western with scenes of quite shocking violence (such as the bad guys shooting Stewart in the hand while they hold him down).

MAN FROM SNOWY RIVER, THE 1982 Australian
★ ★ ★ ★ PG Action-Adventure 1:44
☑ Explicit language, mild violence
Dir: George Miller   *Cast:* Kirk Douglas, Jack Thompson, Tom Burlinson, Sigrid Thornton, Lorraine Bayly, Chris Haywood
▶ After his father's death, young Burlinson gets a job with wealthy rancher Douglas who objects when his daughter Thornton falls for him. Burlinson proves himself by rescuing a missing prized colt. Sweeping adventure with gorgeous cinematography, incredible landscapes, exciting horse stampedes, and stirring music. Douglas has fun in a dual role as the rancher and his brother.

MANHATTAN 1979
★ ★ R Comedy 1:36 B&W
☑ Adult situations, explicit language, adult humor
Dir: Woody Allen   *Cast:* Woody Allen, Diane Keaton, Michael Murphy, Mariel Hemingway, Meryl Streep, Anne Byrne
▶ TV writer Allen has his share of romantic problems: wife Streep left him for another woman, his affair with teenager Hemingway makes him uncomfortable, and his pursuit of flighty Keaton is complicated by her love for her married best pal Murphy. Sophisticated ode to New York City with superb black-and-white photography and Gershwin score. Funniest scene: Woody, having been told by Keaton about her gorgeously attractive ex-boyfriend, runs into the guy and discovers he's shrimpy Wallace Shawn.

MANHATTAN PROJECT, THE 1986
★ ★ ★ ★ PG-13 Drama 1:58
☑ Explicit language
Dir: Marshall Brickman   *Cast:* John Lithgow, Christopher Collet, Jill Eikenberry, Cynthia Nixon, John Mahoney
▶ In Ithaca, amateur high school physicist Collet suspects that new government scientist Lithgow is making nuclear warheads. Collet steals a bottle of plutonium and constructs an atom bomb to show how dangerous Lithgow's facility is. Topical thriller has a professional performance from Lithgow and pleasant comic touches. **(CC)**

MANHUNT, THE 1986 Italian
★ NR Western 1:30
☑ Explicit language, violence
Dir: Larry Ludman *Cast:* Ernest Borgnine, John Ethan Wayne, Bo Svenson, Henry Silva, Henry Harmstorf
▶ Modern-day Western features son of film legend John Wayne as a would-be horse trainer wrongfully accused of stealing and imprisoned in a sadistic Arizona jail. Borgnine is sufficiently sinister as the wealthy rancher intent on keeping Wayne in the slammer.

MANHUNTER 1986
★★★★ R Action-Adventure 1:58
☑ Violence
Dir: Michael Mann *Cast:* William L. Petersen, Kim Greist, Dennis Farina, Brian Cox, Joan Allen, Tom Noonan
▶ Gripping, nerve-wracking thriller about psychopathic killer Noonan who murders entire families. He's pursued by ex–FBI forensic specialist Peterson. Cox is splendidly creepy as a mad psychiatrist in contact with the killer. Based on Thomas Harris's novel *Red Dragon.* **(CC)**

MANIAC 1977
☆ PG Mystery-Suspense 1:27
☑ Explicit language, violence
Dir: Richard Compton *Cast:* Oliver Reed, Deborah Raffin, Stuart Whitman, Jim Mitchum, Paul Koslo
▶ Maniac Koslo, dressed as a war-painted Indian, terrorizes the wealthy Arizona town of Paradise. After murdering several people with a bow and arrow, he demands a $5 million ransom. Stone-faced Reed does his best to track down the killer. Sturdy suspense with stunning desert photography.

MANIAC COP 1988
★★★ R Horror 1:32
☑ Nudity, adult situations, explicit language, graphic violence
Dir: William Lustig *Cast:* Tom Atkins, Bruce Campbell, Laurene Landon, Richard Roundtree, Sheree North
▶ Well-made crime/horror feature about a monstrously strong killer cop—who may or may not be human—stalking the streets of New York. Atkins plays the no-nonsense lieutenant investigating the case; North has an unusual part as the maniac's crippled girlfriend. Gory chiller with a touch of black comedy.

MAN IN LOVE, A 1987 French/Italian
★ R Romance 1:48
☑ Nudity, adult situations, explicit language
Dir: Diane Kurys *Cast:* Peter Coyote, Greta Scacchi, Peter Riegert, Jamie Lee Curtis, Claudia Cardinale, John Berry
▶ In Rome to make a movie, American leading man Coyote falls in love with leading lady Scacchi. Jeopardizing the affair: her dying mother Cardinale and his wife Curtis. Lush production with steamy love scenes marred by a banal soap opera plot.

MAN IN THE WHITE SUIT, THE 1952 British
★★ NR Comedy 1:25 B&W
Dir: Alexander Mackendrick *Cast:* Alec Guinness, Joan Greenwood, Cecil Parker, Michael Gough, Ernest Thesiger
▶ Shy chemist Guinness develops a wondrous white fabric that never gets dirty or wears out. Its acceptance by consumers poses a serious threat to both labor and management and they plot to thwart him. Marvelous satire boasts one of Sir Alec's best performances.

MANITOU, THE 1978
★★★ PG Horror 1:43
☑ Brief nudity, graphic violence
Dir: William Girdler *Cast:* Tony Curtis, Susan Strasberg, Stella Stevens, Michael Ansara, Ann Sothern, Burgess Meredith
▶ Con man Curtis is shocked when a lump on his girlfriend Strasberg's back turns into the fetus of a 400-year-old evil medicine man. Indian variation on *The Exorcist* has an improbable script that the cast plays tongue in cheek. Good special effects brighten last effort from director Girdler, who was killed in a helicopter crash before film's release.

MANNEQUIN 1987
★★★★ PG Comedy 1:30
☑ Explicit language
Dir: Michael Gottlieb *Cast:* Andrew McCarthy, Kim Cattrall, Estelle Getty, James Spader, Meshach Taylor, Carole Davis
▶ McCarthy, a struggling Philadelphia window dresser, skyrockets to fame with the help of mannequin Cattrall, actually an Egyptian princess brought to life by a magic spell. Airy fantasy makes good use of Wanamaker's department store setting; Taylor adds some fun as McCarthy's effeminate colleague. Starship's "Noth-

ing's Gonna Stop Us Now" was an Oscar-nominated song. **(CC)**

MAN OF LA MANCHA 1972
★★★ PG Musical 2:09
☑ Adult situations, explicit language
Dir: Arthur Hiller *Cast:* Peter O'Toole, Sophia Loren, James Coco, Harry Andrews, John Castle, Brian Blessed
▶ In seventeenth-century Spain, rich nobleman Don Quixote (O'Toole) imagines himself to be a knight and charges at windmills, seeing them as dragons. Everyone thinks he's crazy, but servant Sancho Panza (Coco) sticks by him and even Loren, the hardened prostitute he loves, is moved by his valor. Gallant performance by O'Toole, Loren's beauty, and the unforgettable musical score (including "The Impossible Dream") overcome Hiller's lumbering direction.

MANON OF THE SPRING 1987 French
★★ PG Drama 1:53
☑ Brief nudity
Dir: Claude Berri *Cast:* Yves Montand, Daniel Auteuil, Emmanuelle Beart, Hippolyte Girardot, Elisabeth Depardieu
▶ Beautiful shepherd Beart gets revenge on Auteuil and Montand, villains who dammed up her father's spring, leading to his accidental death. Classy continuation of *Jean de Florette*. Perfect acting, tasteful atmosphere and production values, but slow pacing. **S**

MAN OUTSIDE 1986
★ PG-13 Drama 1:49
☑ Explicit language, violence
Dir: Mark Stouffer *Cast:* Kathleen Quinlan, Robert Logan, Bradford Dillman, Levon Helm
▶ Attorney Logan, a recluse since his wife's death, teams with teacher Quinlan to prove his innocence when he is wrongly accused of killing children. Low-budget independent film has slick production values and sincere acting but suffers from awkward scripting and direction.

MAN'S FAVORITE SPORT? 1964
★★★ NR Comedy 2:00
Dir: Howard Hawks *Cast:* Rock Hudson, Paula Prentiss, Maria Perschy, Charlene Holt, John McGiver, Roscoe Karns
▶ Public relations expert Prentiss pushes sporting goods salesman Hudson into entering a fishing contest, even though he's never fished before. Attempt to capture the lunacy of screwball comedies is

marked by broad slapstick and an energetic cast.

MAN WHO BROKE 1,000 CHAINS, THE 1987
★★★★ NR Biography/MFTV 1:53
☑ Explicit language, violence
Dir: Daniel Mann *Cast:* Val Kilmer, Charles Durning, Elisha Cook, Jr., Kyra Sedgewick, Sonia Braga
▶ True story of Robert Ellis Burns (Kilmer), World War I vet sentenced to hard labor in a brutal Georgia work camp after being forced to participate in an armed robbery. Burns escapes and establishes a new life as a respected Chicago magazine publisher. When his real identity emerges, his captors want him to serve out his term. Strong drama inspired previous Hollywood classic *I Am a Fugitive From a Chain Gang*.

MAN WHO FELL TO EARTH, THE 1976 British
★ R Sci-Fi 2:20
☑ Nudity, strong sexual content, explicit language
Dir: Nicolas Roeg *Cast:* David Bowie, Rip Torn, Candy Clark, Buck Henry, Bernie Casey
▶ Alien Bowie comes to Earth to get water for his drought-stricken planet. He sets up a company and makes a fortune, only to be plotted against by mysterious business interests. Great-looking, thought-provoking sci-fi with intricate direction by Roeg and strong performance by Bowie (his film debut). Occasionally murky plotting loses steam towards the end. Based on the novel by Walter Tevis.

MAN WHO KNEW TOO MUCH, THE 1934 British
★★ NR Mystery-Suspense 1:15 B&W
Dir: Alfred Hitchcock *Cast:* Leslie Banks, Edna Best, Peter Lorre, Hugh Wakefield, Nova Pilbeam, Pierre Fresnay
▶ While vacationing in Switzerland with their daughter Pilbeam, Best and Banks learn from dying Fresnay of Lorre's plot to assassinate a foreign dignitary in London. When Lorre and his associates kidnap Pilbeam to prevent the couple from going to the authorities, Banks and Best must try to rescue their girl and stop the killing on their own. Gripping suspenser boasts Lorre's first English-speaking role. Remade by Hitchcock in 1956.

MAN WHO KNEW TOO MUCH, THE
1956
★★★★ NR Mystery-Suspense 2:00
Dir: Alfred Hitchcock *Cast:* James Stewart, Doris Day, Brenda de Banzie, Bernard Miles, Ralph Truman, Christopher Olsen
▶ Vacationing in Morocco, American doctor Stewart and his wife Day, a retired singing star, stumble across a clue to an assassination. But they can't tell the police because their son Olsen has been kidnapped by the killers. Expansive reworking of Hitchcock's 1935 classic is preferred by some critics for Stewart's engaging performance and the famous Albert Hall climax. Day's version of "Que Sera, Sera" won an Oscar for Best Song.

MAN WHO LOVED CAT DANCING, THE
1973
★★ PG Western 1:51
Dir: Richard Sarafian *Cast:* Burt Reynolds, Sarah Miles, Lee J. Cobb, Jack Warden, George Hamilton, Bo Hopkins
▶ Fugitive outlaw Reynolds and his gang kidnap Hamilton's wife Miles. Hamilton and bounty hunter Cobb pursue as captive and captor fall in love. Unusual and at times somewhat turgid; however, Reynolds and Miles demonstrate a good deal of chemistry.

MAN WHO LOVED WOMEN, THE 1977
French
★★ NR Comedy 1:59
Dir: François Truffaut *Cast:* Charles Denner, Brigitte Fossey, Leslie Caron, Nelly Borgeaud
▶ A large number of women attend Denner's funeral. Through flashbacks, his womanizing adventures are recounted. Low-key Truffaut comedy with gentle comic ironies (like the hero being rejected by an older woman who prefers younger men) and a memorable performance by the underrated Denner. Remade in America by Blake Edwards. [S]

MAN WHO LOVED WOMEN, THE 1983
★★ R Comedy 1:50
☑ Nudity, explicit language
Dir: Blake Edwards *Cast:* Burt Reynolds, Julie Andrews, Kim Basinger, Marilu Henner, Cynthia Sikes, Jennifer Edwards
▶ Compulsive womanizer Reynolds just can't say no to beautiful women, including psychiatrist Andrews who tries to probe his psyche. American remake of Truffaut's French film is sober and repetitive but sometimes affecting. Funniest scenes involve Reynolds getting accidentally glued to a dog and delightful Basinger as a Texan who enjoys making love in public places. (CC)

MAN WHO SAW TOMORROW, THE
1981
★★★★ PG Documentary 1:28
☑ Violence
Dir: Robert Guenette *Cast:* Narrated by Orson Welles
▶ Welles narrates this provocative exploration of the prophecies of the sixteenth-century writer Nostradamus. Among the seer's predictions: the rise of Hitler, the assassinations of Lincoln and JFK, a devastating California earthquake in 1988, and World War III in 1994.

MAN WHO SHOT LIBERTY VALANCE, THE 1962
★★★★ NR Western 2:02 B&W
Dir: John Ford *Cast:* James Stewart, John Wayne, Vera Miles, Lee Marvin, Edmond O'Brien, Andy Devine
▶ Greenhorn lawyer Stewart, trying to bring civilization to the frontier town of Shinbone, runs up against Valance (Marvin), a bullying killer. Stewart turns to rancher Wayne for help. Sprawling, elegiac drama eloquently sums up director Ford's favorite Western themes. Notable supporting work from Woody Strode, Lee Van Cleef, and Strother Martin; Gene Pitney's version of the theme song became a pop hit.

MAN WHO WOULD BE KING, THE
1975
★★★★ PG Action-Adventure 2:09
☑ Violence
Dir: John Huston *Cast:* Sean Connery, Michael Caine, Christopher Plummer, Saeed Jaffrey, Shakira Caine
▶ Rogue British soldiers Connery and Caine leave colonial India and enter the remote kingdom of Kafiristan. Caine wants to plunder the royal treasure and move on but Connery, mistaken for a god and installed as king by the natives, develops deadly delusions of grandeur. Glorious adventure with director Huston weaving a magical narrative spell against an epic background. Exuberant Connery and crafty Caine play off each other beautifully. Plummer gives able support as the writer Rudyard Kipling (on whose story the film is based). Four Oscar

nominations (Screenplay, Costumes, Art Direction, Editing). **(CC)**

MAN WITH BOGART'S FACE, THE 1980
★★★ PG Comedy 1:51
☑ Brief nudity, adult situations
Dir: Robert Day *Cast:* Robert Sacchi, Franco Nero, Olivia Hussey, Michelle Phillips, Victor Buono, Misty Rowe
▶ Business picks up for detective Sacchi when plastic surgery turns him into a Bogart look-alike. He gets hired by two beautiful women to crack two different cases. Remarkable impersonation of Bogie by Sacchi in a likable parody plot that should please film buffs. The one joke does wear a little thin by the end.

MAN WITH ONE RED SHOE, THE 1985
★★★ PG Comedy 1:32
☑ Adult situations, mild violence
Dir: Stan Dragoti *Cast:* Tom Hanks, Dabney Coleman, Lori Singer, James Belushi, Charles Durning, Edward Herrmann
▶ Eccentric musician Hanks is the patsy caught between CIA rivals Durning and Coleman. Beautiful spy Singer helps Hanks to escape. More frantic than truly funny but Hanks makes the frenzy easy to take. Lots of physical humor in this American remake of the French *The Tall Blond Man with One Black Shoe*. **(CC)**

MAN WITHOUT A STAR 1955
★★★ NR Western 1:29
Dir: King Vidor *Cast:* Kirk Douglas, Jeanne Crain, Claire Trevor, William Campbell, Richard Boone, Jay C. Flippen
▶ Drifting cowboy Douglas befriends young farmboy Campbell; both are hired by Crain, a rancher who is plotting a range war. Although unwilling to fight, Douglas must confront sadistic killer Boone. Intelligent Western also features a song from Douglas ("And the Moon Grew Brighter and Brighter").

MAN WITH THE GOLDEN ARM, THE 1955
★★ NR Drama 1:59 B&W
Dir: Otto Preminger *Cast:* Frank Sinatra, Kim Novak, Eleanor Parker, Darren McGavin, Arnold Stang
▶ Heroin addict Sinatra tries to go straight. Nagging wife Parker provides little understanding and pusher McGavin pressures him. Only local vamp Novak can help him. Unrelenting drama tackles difficult subject honestly. One of Sinatra's

best performances and a classic jazz score by Elmer Bernstein.

MAN WITH THE GOLDEN GUN, THE 1974 British
★★★★ PG
Espionage/Action-Adventure 2:05
☑ Violence, explicit language
Dir: Guy Hamilton *Cast:* Roger Moore, Christopher Lee, Britt Ekland, Maud Adams, Herve Villechaize, Clifton James
▶ James Bond (Moore) takes on Scaramanga (Lee), a three-nippled golden-gun-wielding assassin plotting to corner the market on solar energy, and his midget sidekick Villechaize. Moore's second 007 outing has gadgets, gimmicks, beautiful women, exotic Southeast Asia locations, and Lee, one of the best villians of the series. James reprises his Southern sheriff from *Live and Let Die*.

MAN WITH TWO BRAINS, THE 1983
★★ R Comedy 1:30
☑ Nudity, explicit language, adult humor
Dir: Carl Reiner *Cast:* Steve Martin, Kathleen Turner, David Warner, Paul Benedict, Richard Brestoff, James Cromwell
▶ Brilliant brain surgeon Dr. Michael Hfuhruhurr (Martin) marries sexy but unfaithful Turner. Frustrated in his marriage, Martin finds true love with a disembodied female brain that is able to communicate (voice provided by Sissy Spacek). Nutty mad-scientist parody is uneven but frequently sidesplitting and occasionally endearing. Funniest moments: a lakeside love scene with his beloved brain, the drunk test, and Merv Griffin's cameo.

MAN, WOMAN AND CHILD 1983
★★★★ PG Drama 1:41
☑ Adult situations, explicit language
Dir: Dick Richards *Cast:* Martin Sheen, Blythe Danner, Craig T. Nelson, Sebastian Dungan, David Hemmings, Nathalie Nell
▶ Sheen, a happily married family man, and his wife Danner are shocked when he learns he has illegitmate child Dungan from a fling ten years ago in France. High-grade, sentimental soap opera pulls out all the stops and gets the tear ducts going. Based on an Erich Segal novel.

MARATHON MAN 1976
★★★★★ R Mystery-Suspense 2:05

☑ Adult situations, explicit language, violence
Dir: John Schlesinger *Cast:* Dustin Hoffman, Laurence Olivier, Roy Scheider, William Devane, Marthe Keller, Fritz Weaver
▶ "Is it safe?" demands escaped Nazi war criminal Olivier as he tortures Columbia grad student Hoffman with a dentist drill in a now-classic scene. This is just one of Hoffman's predicaments when Scheider, his intelligence-agent brother, becomes embroiled in Olivier's diamond-smuggling scheme. Tense thriller with bravura direction by Schlesinger providing nonstop excitement. Olivier was nominated for an Oscar.

MARIA'S LOVERS 1985
★ R Drama 1:49
☑ Nudity, adult situations, explicit language
Dir: Andrei Konchalovsky *Cast:* Nastassja Kinski, John Savage, Robert Mitchum, Keith Carradine, Vincent Spano, Anita Morris
▶ World War II hero Savage comes home and marries old girlfriend Kinski. He turns out to be impotent and skips town. She becomes pregnant by itinerant musician Carradine. Will Savage take her back? Turgid, off-beat romance rarely works up any emotional urgency.

MARIE 1985
★★★★ PG-13 Biography 1:51
☑ Explicit language, violence
Dir: Roger Donaldson *Cast:* Sissy Spacek, Jeff Daniels, Keith Szarabajka, Lisa Banes, Morgan Freeman, Fred Thompson
▶ True story of how Marie Ragghianti (Spacek), an abused mother of three, left her husband, went to college, and rose to become the first female chief of Tennessee's parole board. Uncovering widespread political corruption, she singlehandedly took the administration to court. Gutsy little-person-versus-the-establishment theme is given class and substance by believable cast, compelling Spacek, and virtuoso directing from Donaldson. Adapted from book by Peter Maas. (CC)

MARKED WOMAN 1937
★★★ NR Drama 1:36 B&W
Dir: Lloyd Bacon *Cast:* Bette Davis, Humphrey Bogart, Jane Bryan, Eduardo Ciannelli, Isabel Jewell, Allen Jenkins
▶ Rapid, hard-hitting crime exposé

about vicious gangster Ciannelli who mistreats the "hostesses" at his posh gambling den. Crusading DA Bogart begs Davis to testify against Ciannelli, but his thugs threaten her with death. Based on the real-life trial of Lucky Luciano, with Davis giving a fiery performance. (CC)

MARK OF ZORRO, THE 1940
★★★★★ NR Action-Adventure 1:33 B&W
Dir: Rouben Mamoulian *Cast:* Tyrone Power, Linda Darnell, Basil Rathbone, Gale Sondergaard, Eugene Pallette, J. Edward Bromberg
▶ Preening fop by day and masked avenger by night, Power battles greedy governor Bromberg and his ruthless aide Rathbone to free the people of nineteenth-century California from tyranny of taxation and terror. Whether romancing governor's daughter Darnell or dueling with Rathbone, Power is a marvel in this smashing swashbuckler.

MARLENE 1986 German
★★ NR Documentary 1:36
Dir: Maximilian Schell *Cast:* Marlene Dietrich
▶ Documentary features film clips from Dietrich's best movies (*Blue Angel, Destry Rides Again, Touch of Evil*), stage appearances, and photos, intercut with an audio interview of Marlene today (she refused to be photographed). The star is still feisty and opinionated, as this unusual documentary proves. Subtitles are used when she lapses into German.

MARLOWE 1969
★★★ PG Mystery-Suspense 1:36
☑ Adult situations, explicit language, mild violence
Dir: Paul Bogart *Cast:* James Garner, Gayle Hunnicutt, Carroll O'Connor, Rita Moreno, Sharon Farrell, William Daniels
▶ Updating of Raymond Chandler's *The Little Sister* to the 1960s, with Garner effective as the famous private eye Philip Marlowe. He's hired by Farrell to find her missing brother, a case that also involves TV star Hunnicutt, stripper Moreno, and a string of ice-pick murders. Confusing mystery notable for kung-fu master Bruce Lee's film debut in a brief but unforgettable encounter with Marlowe.

MARNIE 1964
★★ PG Drama 2:10
☑ Adult situations, violence
Dir: Alfred Hitchcock *Cast:* Sean Con-

nery, Tippi Hedren, Diane Baker, Martin Gabel, Louise Latham, Bruce Dern
▶ Wealthy Philadelphia scion Connery becomes obsessed with kleptomaniac secretary Hedren. She resists him but he blackmails her into marriage and tries to discover the roots of her neurosis. The director's startling use of color highlights this intense drama which emphasizes psychological exploration over conventional suspense.

MAROONED 1969
★★★ G Mystery-Suspense 2:14
Dir: John Sturges *Cast:* Gregory Peck, Richard Crenna, James Franciscus, David Janssen, Gene Hackman, Lee Grant
▶ American astronauts Crenna, Hackman, and Franciscus are stranded in outer space. Concerned NASA official Peck struggles to rescue them before their oxygen runs out. Tense and quite plausible thriller won Oscar for Best Special Effects.

MARRIAGE OF MARIA BRAUN, THE 1978 German
★★ R Drama 2:00
☑ Nudity, adult situations, explicit language
Dir: Rainer Werner Fassbinder *Cast:* Hanna Schygulla, Klaus Lowitsch, Ivan Desny, Gottfried John, Gisela Uhlen, Gunter Lamprecht
▶ In the ruins of postwar Berlin, a liberated but vulnerable Schygulla (in a splendid performance) forges financial independence despite a tragic affair with a black American soldier (George Byrd) that sends husband Lowitsch to jail. Challenging look at German society will delight sophisticated viewers with its subtle humor. ⑤

MARRIED TO THE MOB 1988
★★★★ R Comedy 1:43
☑ Adult situations, explicit language, violence
Dir: Jonathan Demme *Cast:* Michelle Pfeiffer, Matthew Modine, Dean Stockwell, Mercedes Ruehl, Alec Baldwin, Joan Cusack
▶ When her hit man husband is rubbed out, Pfeiffer tries to flee the Long Island Mafia by moving into a New York tenement. She's pursued by Mafia don Stockwell and FBI agent Modine in a comedy of errors. Screwball approach to gangsters is colorful, although plot runs out of steam despite fine performances by

Pfeiffer and Stockwell. Amusing cast also includes David Johansen and Sister Carol East; score by David Byrne features songs by New Order, Deborah Harry, and Brian Eno. Stockwell received an Oscar nomination as Best Supporting Actor.

MARTIN'S DAY 1985 Canadian
★★★★ PG Drama 1:39
☑ Explicit language
Dir: Alan Gibson *Cast:* Richard Harris, Justin Henry, James Coburn, Lindsay Wagner, Karen Black, John Ireland
▶ Escaped convict Harris kidnaps young Henry. As cop Coburn and lady shrink Wagner close in, the kid and the con grow to be friends. Well-handled formula story given substance by an impressive cast. (CC)

MARTY 1955
★★★ NR Drama 1:39 B&W
Dir: Delbert Mann *Cast:* Ernest Borgnine, Betsy Blair, Esther Minciotti, Karen Steele, Jerry Paris, Frank Sutton
▶ Bronx butcher Borgnine spends lonely nights hanging out with his male pals. They object when he finally finds romance with plain Blair. Wonderful and heartwarming with a superb Ernie. Paddy Chayefsky's sensitive script has lines that have achieved classic status ("Whaddaya wanna do tonight, Marty?"). Oscars for Best Picture, Actor (Borgnine), Screenplay (Chayefsky), Director.

MARVIN AND TIGE 1983
★★★★ PG Drama 1:44
☑ Adult situations, explicit language
Dir: Eric Weston *Cast:* John Cassavetes, Billy Dee Williams, Gibran Brown, Denise Nicholas-Hill
▶ In Atlanta, orphaned black kid Brown is talked out of committing suicide by white alcoholic Cassavetes. A father-son relationship develops between the two. Extremely predictable slice-of-life realism. Fine performances can't compensate for uninspired plotting, glacial pacing, and an excess of pathos.

MARY OF SCOTLAND 1936
★★ NR Biography/Drama 2:03 B&W
Dir: John Ford *Cast:* Katharine Hepburn, Fredric March, Florence Eldridge, Douglas Walton, John Carradine, Moroni Olsen
▶ Fictionalized account of the conflict between Mary (Hepburn), the Catholic Queen of Scotland, and Elizabeth (Eldridge), the Anglican Queen of Britain. March, Mary's third husband, gives the

strongest performance in this somber, gloomy historical epic. Adapted from a Maxwell Anderson play.

MARY POPPINS 1964
★★★★★ G Musical/Family 2:26
Dir: Robert Stevenson *Cast:* Julie Andrews, Dick Van Dyke, David Tomlinson, Glynis Johns, Ed Wynn
▶ Julie Andrews won an Oscar for her effervescent performance as the world's greatest nanny, Mary Poppins. She and whimsical chimney sweep Uncle Bert (Van Dyke) take the Banks children for tea parties on the ceiling and other fantasy adventures. When her work is finished, Mary opens her umbrella and flies away. Charming Disney adaptation of the P. L. Travers books won five Oscars, including Visual Effects, Editing, Score, and Song "Chim Chim Cher-ee." Other songs include "A Spoon Full of Sugar" and "Supercalifragilisticexpialidocious."

M*A*S*H 1970
★★★★★ PG War/Comedy 1:56
☑ Nudity, adult situations, explicit language, violence, adult humor
Dir: Robert Altman *Cast:* Donald Sutherland, Elliott Gould, Sally Kellerman, Robert Duvall, Tom Skerritt, Gary Burghoff
▶ Korean War, a Mobile Army Surgical Hospital: irreverent, fun-loving doctors Sutherland, Gould, and Skerritt contend with straitlaced surgeon Duvall and his lover, head nurse Kellerman. Antics include exposing Kellerman in the shower to prove she's a blond, curing a suicidal dentist's impotence, and climactic, unorthodox football game with rival unit. Ring Lardner's hilarious screenplay won an Oscar; nominated for Best Picture, Director, and Supporting Actress (Kellerman). Spawned one of most successful series in TV history, with Burghoff reprising his role as Radar O'Reilly.

M*A*S*H: GOODBYE, FAREWELL & AMEN 1983
★★★★★ NR Comedy/MFTV 2:00
Dir: Alan Alda *Cast:* Alan Alda, Mike Farrell, Harry Morgan, David Ogden Stiers, Loretta Swit, Jamie Farr
▶ Concluding two-hour episode of the popular network series "M*A*S*H" explores the final days of the Korean War, as Hawkeye (Alda), BJ (Farrell), Colonel Potter (Morgan), Charles (Stiers), Margaret (Swit), Klinger (Farr), and the rest of the 4077th learn of the declaration of peace,

watch the camp (including the infamous Swamp) be dismantled, and bid fond farewells to each other. Broadcast debut scored one of the highest Nielsen ratings in TV history.

MASK 1985
★★★★★ PG-13 Drama 2:00
☑ Adult situations, explicit language
Dir: Peter Bogdanovich *Cast:* Cher, Sam Elliott, Eric Stoltz, Estelle Getty, Richard Dysart, Laura Dern
▶ Stoltz, a grotesquely disfigured teen with a sense of humor ("You never seen anyone from the planet Vulcan before?") lives with hard-living motorcycle mom Cher. He wins the heart of blind rich girl Dern before succumbing to his disease. Fictional tearjerker, based on a true story, features uniformly outstanding performances and a touching spirit of hope and courage. (CC)

MASQUE OF THE RED DEATH, THE 1964
★★ NR Horror 1:26
Dir: Roger Corman *Cast:* Vincent Price, Hazel Court, Jane Asher, David Weston, Patrick Magee, Skip Martin
▶ Medieval prince Price uses murder and sadism to control his peasants while a deadly plague sweeps the countryside. Stylish, evocative horror based on two Edgar Allan Poe short stories is among the best of Corman's features. Superb production design and bleak touches of humor add to the fun.

MASQUERADE 1988
★★★★ R Mystery-Suspense 1:47
☑ Nudity, adult situations, explicit language, violence
Dir: Bob Swaim *Cast:* Rob Lowe, Meg Tilly, Kim Cattrall, Doug Savant, John Glover
▶ Hamptons heiress Tilly falls for penniless boat skipper Lowe, but are his motives pure or monetary? Among those interested in the answer: Tilly's malevolent stepfather Glover and Savant, the cop who loves her. Stylishly shot and cleverly plotted thriller spins a web of murder and blackmail. Beautiful Hamptons scenery provides an inside look at the lifestyles of the rich and famous.

MASSACRE AT CENTRAL HIGH 1976
★ R Drama 1:28
☑ Nudity, explicit language, violence
Dir: Renee Daalder *Cast:* Derrel Maury, Andrew Stevens, Robert Carra-

dine, Kimberly Beck, Roy Underwood, Rainbeaux Smith

▶ Transfer student Maury, tormented by bullies, wreaks clever revenge only to discover new problems in his high school's rearranged social structure. Peculiar exploitation picture has a cult reputation for offering satire as well as violence and nudity.

MASS APPEAL 1984
★★★★ PG Comedy/Drama 1:39
☑ Adult situations, explicit language
Dir: Glenn Jordan *Cast:* Jack Lemmon, Zeljko Ivanek, Charles Durning, Louise Latham

▶ Extroverted priest Lemmon clashes with young firebrand seminarian Ivanek. However, gradual respect builds between them, putting Lemmon in a dilemma when superior Durning wants to kick Ivanek out of the clergy. Lemmon and Ivanek play off each other with humanity and humor. Based on Bill C. Davis's Broadway hit. **(CC)**

MASSIVE RETALIATION 1984
★ NR Drama 1:29
☑ Explicit language, violence
Dir: Thomas A. Cohen *Cast:* Tom Bower, Karlene Crockett, Peter Donat, Marilyn Hassett, Susan O'Connell

▶ Three Northern California families are so worried about the threat of nuclear war that they establish a heavily fortified survivalists' retreat. Their worst fears come true when an atom bomb explodes during war games. Intriguing Cold War paranoia premise sabotaged by low-budget execution and lackluster plotting.

MASTER OF THE WORLD 1961
★★ NR Fantasy 1:44
Dir: William Witney *Cast:* Vincent Price, Charles Bronson, Henry Hull, Mary Webster

▶ In the nineteenth century, visionary scientist Price is determined to impose peace on the world with his invention, an advanced flying machine. American agent Bronson attempts to thwart Price when his plans get out of hand. Not bad period thriller from a Jules Verne novel.

MASTERS OF THE UNIVERSE 1987
★★★ PG Fantasy 1:46
☑ Explicit language, violence
Dir: Gary Goddard *Cast:* Dolph Lundgren, Frank Langella, Meg Foster, Billy Barty, Courteney Cox, Chelsea Field

▶ On the magical planet Eternia, super-

hero He-Man (Lundgren) battles evil Skeletor (Langella) to rescue the imprisoned Sorceress of Greyskull Castle. He-Man comes to Earth, where two teens help in his struggle. Juvenile sword-and-sorcery epic based on a line of popular Mattel toys (also the inspiration for an animated TV series). **(CC)**

MATA HARI 1985
★ R Drama 1:44
☑ Nudity, adult situations
Dir: Curtis Harrington *Cast:* Sylvia Kristel, Christopher Cazenove, Oliver Tobias, Gaye Browne, Gottfried John, William Fox

▶ Melodrama about the famous World War I spy concentrates heavily on eroticism, less on her espionage exploits. The frequently unclothed Kristel (*Emmanuelle*) is an alluring Mata Hari, but story flounders when dealing with farfetched French and German intrigues.

MATEWAN 1987
★★★ PG-13 Drama 2:12
☑ Explicit language, violence
Dir: John Sayles *Cast:* Chris Cooper, Will Oldham, Mary McDonnell, James Earl Jones, Jace Alexander, Ken Jenkins

▶ In 1920, rural West Virginia coal miners organize a union against their company's abusive tactics, but their effort is thrown into disarray with the arrival of Italian and black scabs. Somber, straightforward treatment of a real-life incident has strong ensemble acting from the large cast and impressive period details. Director Sayles has a cameo as fire-and-brimstone preacher. **(CC)**

MATTER OF TIME, A 1976 U.S./Italian
★★ PG Drama 1:37
Dir: Vincente Minnelli *Cast:* Liza Minnelli, Ingrid Bergman, Charles Boyer, Tina Aumont, Gabriele Ferzetti, Fernando Rey

▶ Director Minnelli's last film is an embarrassing mishmash about maid Liza Minnelli's rise to fame as a movie star through the inspiration of a dying contessa (Bergman). Set primarily in 1949, although flashback structure is often confusing. Film debut for Bergman's daughter Isabella Rossellini, who plays a nun at her mother's deathbed.

MAURICE 1987 British
★ R Drama 2:15
☑ Brief nudity, adult situations
Dir: James Ivory *Cast:* James Wilby,

Rupert Graves, Hugh Grant, Billie Whitelaw, Denholm Elliott, Ben Kingsley
▶ Long, arty, and genteel drama about passionate Maurice (Wilby) and scholarly Clive (Grant), who meet while studying at Cambridge. Excellent commentary on socially and sexually repressed Edwardian England. With Kingsley as quack hypnotist who advises Maurice to "take exercise and stroll around with a gun" to cure his homosexuality. Based on E. M. Forster's 1914 novel. **(CC)**

MAX DUGAN RETURNS 1983
★★★★ **PG Comedy 1:38**
☑ Adult situations, explicit language
Dir: Herbert Ross *Cast:* Marsha Mason, Jason Robards, Donald Sutherland, Matthew Broderick, Dody Goodman, Sal Viscuso
▶ Whimsical Neil Simon comedy about single mother Mason's struggle to raise son Broderick. Her long-estranged father Robards shows up unexpectedly to shower her with gifts, arousing the suspicion of amorous cop Sutherland. Polished entertainment features brief appearances by Sutherland's son Kiefer and baseball expert Charley Lau.

MAXIE 1985
★★★ **PG Fantasy/Comedy 1:38**
☑ Adult situations, explicit language
Dir: Paul Aaron *Cast:* Glenn Close, Mandy Patinkin, Ruth Gordon, Barnard Hughes, Googy Gress, Valerie Curtin
▶ Sexy 1920s flapper returns to inhabit body of clerical secretary Close, confusing both her husband Patinkin and boss Hughes. In a dual role, Close performs admirably but the screenplay, adapted from Jack Finney's novel *Marian's Wall*, is often predictable and schmaltzy. Final film for the great Ruth Gordon, who plays the landlady.

MAXIMUM OVERDRIVE 1986
★★ **R Horror 1:37**
☑ Explicit language, violence
Dir: Stephen King *Cast:* Emilio Estevez, Pat Hingle, Laura Harrington, Yeardley Smith, John Short, Ellen McElduff
▶ When Earth passes through the tail of a comet, formerly inanimate machines come to life. Malevolent trucks besiege a small group of survivors—including ex-con Estevez and hitchhiker Harrington—at a North Carolina Dixie Boy restaurant, leading to relentless crashes and carnage. Directing debut by horror master King runs out of gas after an intriguing

start. Ear-splitting score by hard-rock group AC/DC.

MAYERLING 1936 French
★ **NR Romance 1:36 B&W**
Dir: Anatole Litvak *Cast:* Charles Boyer, Danielle Darrieux, Suzy Prim, Jean Dax, Gabrielle Dorziat
▶ Sensitive, moving account of the doomed love affair in the late nineteenth century between Rudolph (Boyer), crown prince of Austria, and Marie Vetsera (Darrieux), his young mistress. Classic romance notable for its discreet, subtle handling of a real-life scandal. Superb performances from the leads made them international stars. ⑤

McCABE & MRS. MILLER 1971
★★ **R Western 2:01**
☑ Nudity, adult situations, explicit language, violence
Dir: Robert Altman *Cast:* Warren Beatty, Julie Christie, René Auberjonois, Keith Carradine, William Devane, Shelley Duvall
▶ In the turn-of-the-century Pacific Northwest, a combination saloon-bordello run by small-time gambler Beatty and ambitious prostitute Christie attracts the attention of sinister big-money interests. Innovative, richly detailed film was critically praised, but its revisionist approach to Western myths may disturb some viewers. Christie's work received an Oscar nomination. Score by Leonard Cohen.

McQ 1974
★★★★ **PG Action-Adventure 1:46**
☑ Explicit language, violence
Dir: John Sturges *Cast:* John Wayne, Eddie Albert, Diana Muldaur, Colleen Dewhurst, Clu Gulager, Al Lettieri
▶ When a colleague is murdered, McQ (Wayne) quits the Seattle police force to find his killer. The trail leads to lonely barmaid Dewhurst and evil drug dealer Lettieri, but Wayne also uncovers evidence implicating his former employers. Rare contemporary role for the Duke is a fast-paced thriller in the *Dirty Harry* mold.

McVICAR 1980 British
★ **R Biography/Crime 1:30**
☑ Brief nudity, explicit language, violence
Dir: Tom Clegg *Cast:* Roger Daltrey, Adam Faith, Cheryl Campbell, Steven Berkoff, Brian Hall
▶ Rock singer Daltrey gives an honest, gritty performance as real-life bank robber Tom McVicar, Britain's Public Enemy

No. 1 for his sensational escape from a maximum-security prison. After a reunion with common-law wife Campbell, he plots one more robbery. McVicar wrote the screenplay based on his book; soundtrack includes songs by Daltrey's group the Who.

MEAN DOG BLUES 1978
★ ★ ★ ★ R Action-Adventure 1:48
☑ Brief nudity, adult situations, explicit language, violence
Dir: Mel Stuart *Cast:* George Kennedy, Gregg Henry, Kay Lenz, Scatman Crothers, Tina Louise, William Windom
▶ Unjustly convicted of manslaughter, country-western singer Henry is sent to a brutal prison farm run by sadistic warden Kennedy, who owns a vicious Doberman. When guards attempt to rape his pregnant wife Lenz, Henry decides to escape. Modest, hard-hitting prison drama with a sympathetic underdog hero.

MEAN SEASON, THE 1985
★ ★ ★ R Drama 1:44
☑ Nudity, explicit language, graphic violence
Dir: Philip Borsos *Cast:* Kurt Russell, Mariel Hemingway, Richard Jordan, Richard Masur, Joe Pantoliano, Andy Garcia
▶ Miami reporter Russell boosts his career with exclusive stories on the "Numbers Killer," serial murderer Jordan, despite girlfriend Hemingway's fear that he's becoming a collaborator in the deaths. Taut, hard-edged thriller takes some frightening twists.

MEAN STREETS 1973
★ R Drama 1:52
☑ Brief nudity, explicit language, graphic violence
Dir: Martin Scorsese *Cast:* Harvey Keitel, Robert De Niro, Amy Robinson, David Proval, Richard Romanus, Cesare Danova
▶ New York hood Keitel sabotages his career in the Mafia by helping debt-ridden, irresponsible friend De Niro. Director Scorsese's first critical success has strong performances and impressive Little Italy atmosphere, but a gloomy, gritty, and episodic story line. David and Robert Carradine have brief cameos. **(CC)**

MEATBALLS 1979 Canadian
★ ★ ★ ★ PG Comedy 1:33
☑ Brief nudity, adult situations, explicit language, adult humor
Dir: Ivan Reitman *Cast:* Bill Murray,

Chris Makepeace, Kate Lynch, Russ Banham, Kristine DeBell, Sarah Torgov
▶ Camp counselor Murray leads his sad-sack troopers against a rival camp in a summer olympics, finding time for romance with Lynch and helping quiet kid Makepeace along the way. Some hilarious high jinks are interspersed with touching moments in this lightweight and quite winning summertime fun. Irreverent Bill is truly irresistible.

MEATBALLS PART II 1984
★ ★ PG Comedy 1:35
☑ Adult situations, explicit language
Dir: Ken Wiederhorn *Cast:* Archie Hahn, John Mengatti, Tammy Taylor, Kim Richards, Ralph Seymour, Richard Mulligan
▶ Street punk Mengatti becomes summer camp counselor, takes care of handicapped kid and extraterrestrial, and must fight in a boxing match for ownership of the camp. Follow-up contains no characters from the first film and has nowhere near its freshness and comic style. Mulligan and John Larroquette are wasted. **(CC)**

MEATBALLS III 1987
★ R Comedy 1:34
☑ Nudity, explicit language, adult humor
Dir: George Mendeluk *Cast:* Sally Kellerman, Al Waxman, Patrick Dempsey, Shannon Tweed
▶ At camp North Star, nerdy teen Dempsey makes the transition to stud under the guidance of his favorite porn queen Kellerman, who has died but been given the opportunity to return to Earth to do a good deed. Lewd and crude with none of the charm of the original.

MECHANIC, THE 1972
★ ★ ★ PG Action-Adventure 1:40
☑ Adult situations, violence
Dir: Michael Winner *Cast:* Charles Bronson, Jan-Michael Vincent, Keenan Wynn, Jill Ireland, Linda Ridgeway
▶ Bronson gives a steady performance as a "mechanic," an ace assassin under contract to the Mafia. He takes young apprentice Vincent under his wing during a series of hits in Los Angeles and Naples. Good script features an especially tricky ending. Bronson's real-life wife Ireland has a brief role as a prostitute.

MEDIUM COOL 1969
★ R Drama 1:51
☑ Nudity, explicit language, violence

Dir: Haskell Wexler *Cast:* Robert Forster, Verna Bloom, Peter Bonerz, Marianna Hill, Peter Boyle

▶ Cinematographer-turned-director Wexler blends documentary footage and fiction in this tale of TV news cameraman Forster covering the violent events of the 1968 Democratic Convention in Chicago. Sophisticated cult classic explores the question of reality versus television.

MEDUSA TOUCH, THE 1978 British
★★★★ PG Mystery-Suspense 1:50
☑ Explicit language, violence
Dir: Jack Gold *Cast:* Richard Burton, Derek Jacobi, Lee Remick, Lino Ventura, Marie-Christine Barrault

▶ Burton, a man with superhuman powers, tells psychiatrist Remick he can cause a 747 to crash, ruin a moon landing, even cause Westminster Abbey to crumble, simply by willing it. When he's mysteriously bludgeoned to death while watching TV, police inspector Ventura is recruited to solve the crime.

MEET JOHN DOE 1941
★★★ NR Drama 2:03 B&W
Dir: Frank Capra *Cast:* Gary Cooper, Barbara Stanwyck, Edward Arnold, Walter Brennan, James Gleason, Spring Byington

▶ Newspaper columnist Stanwyck creates a fictional Good Samaritan who catches the public's fancy; political candidate Arnold orders her to find the real "John Doe" to help his campaign. Washed-up pitcher Cooper agrees to take the role, but rebels when he discovers Arnold's corrupt intentions. Top-notch drama with an intriguing theme, sparkling comic touches, and outstanding performances. Director Capra filmed three different endings before settling for the final version. Available in a colorized version.

MEET ME IN ST. LOUIS 1944
★★★★★ NR Musical 1:53
Dir: Vincente Minnelli *Cast:* Judy Garland, Margaret O'Brien, Lucille Bremer, Tom Drake, Mary Astor, Leon Ames

▶ Turn-of-the-century St. Louis: papa Ames wants to move the family to New York but his children prefer the comforts of home, including boy next door Drake, Halloween trick or treating, and the fair. Heartfelt and moving, with immaculate direction by Minnelli, beautiful camerawork and period settings, and wonderful performances. Score includes "The Trolley Song," "Under the Bamboo Tree," the title tune, and "Have Yourself a Merry Little Christmas" (sung by Judy to Margaret in a scene guaranteed to bring tears to your eyes).

MEGAFORCE 1982
★★ PG Action-Adventure 1:39
☑ Explicit language, violence
Dir: Hal Needham *Cast:* Barry Bostwick, Persis Khambatta, Michael Beck, Edward Mulhare, George Furth, Henry Silva

▶ Ace Hunter (Bostwick) and his Megaforce (a multinational army of good guys using advanced weaponry) are recruited by major Khambatta to rescue her beleaguered desert nation from rebel leader Silva. Harmless fantasy packed to the gills with stunts, but Bostwick is miscast, the humor falls flat, and the comic-book plot is lifeless.

MELVIN AND HOWARD 1980
★★ R Comedy/Drama 1:35
☑ Nudity, adult situations, explicit language
Dir: Jonathan Demme *Cast:* Paul LeMat, Jason Robards, Jr., Mary Steenburgen, Michael J. Pollard, Jack Kehoe, Dabney Coleman

▶ Critically acclaimed, real-life story about Utah gas station attendant Melvin Dummar (LeMat), who once gave eccentric billionaire Howard Hughes (Robards) a ride in his truck. When Hughes died, Melvin produced a handscrawled will listing himself as beneficiary for $156 million. Robards was nominated for a Best Supporting Oscar and Steenburgen won Best Supporting Actress for her role as Melvin's quirky wife.

MEMBER OF THE WEDDING, THE 1953
★★★★ NR Drama 1:29 B&W
Dir: Fred Zinnemann *Cast:* Ethel Waters, Julie Harris, Brandon de Wilde, Arthur Franz, Nancy Gates, William Hansen

▶ Southern twelve-year-old Harris, desperate to become an adult, imposes herself on her brother's wedding plans. Black cook Waters is the only person who understands her turmoil. Splendid coming-of-age drama adapted from Carson McCullers's novel and Broadway hit is a heartbreaking examination of adolescence. Harris, in her film debut, received an Oscar nomination for her remarkable performance (she was twenty-five at the time).

MEMORIES OF ME 1988
★ ★ ★ ★ PG-13 Comedy/Drama 1:44
☑ Adult situations, explicit language
Dir: Henry Winkler *Cast:* Billy Crystal, Alan King, JoBeth Williams, Sean Connery, Janet Carroll, David Ackroyd
▶ After a heart attack, New York doctor Crystal reexamines his life and heads to Hollywood for reconciliation with estranged dad King, a career movie extra. Dad and son find making up is hard to do; Crystal's girlfriend Williams is caught in the middle. Mixture of laughter and tears aims straight at the heart. Connery contributes cameo playing himself. Funniest scene: King's rendition of "Too Pooped to Pop."

MEN, THE 1950
★ ★ ★ ★ NR Drama 1:25 B&W
Dir: Fred Zinnemann *Cast:* Marlon Brando, Teresa Wright, Everett Sloane, Jack Webb, Richard Erdman
▶ During World War II, lieutenant Brando receives a spinal injury that leaves him a paraplegic. Falling into depression, he spurns support from fiancée Wright and doctor Sloane and avoids rehabilitation therapy. An honest, sensitive account of war victims. Brando's film debut. Carl Foreman's screenplay received an Oscar nomination.

MEN 1986 German
★ NR Comedy 1:39
☑ Nudity, adult situations, explicit language, violence
Dir: Doris Dorrie *Cast:* Heiner Lauterbach, Uwe Ochsenknecht, Ulrike Kreiner, Janna Marangosoff
▶ Workaholic executive Lauterbach discovers wife Kreiner is having an affair with scruffy artist Ochsenknecht. Using a false name, Lauterbach moves in with Ochsenknecht and gets revenge by turning him into a yuppie clone of himself. A bauble with bite; savvy screenplay puts some clever twists on male bonding.

MEN'S CLUB, THE 1986
★ R Drama 1:35
☑ Nudity, adult situations, explicit language
Dir: Peter Medak *Cast:* Roy Scheider, David Dukes, Richard Jordan, Harvey Keitel, Craig Wasson, Treat Williams
▶ What do men talk about in group therapy? According to ex-baseball star Scheider, homebody Dukes, salesman

Keitel, doctor Williams, nice guy Wasson, and loony psychiatrist Jordan, they mostly discuss women and act out their hostilities. Then they relocate their session to a bordello. Talky and pretentious with a bunch of truly obnoxious characters. Based on Leonard Michaels's controversial novel about male bonding.

MEPHISTO 1981 Hungarian
★ NR Drama 2:15
☑ Nudity, adult situations, explicit language, violence
Dir: Istvan Szabo *Cast:* Klaus Maria Brandauer, Krystyna Janda, Karin Boyd, Rolf Hoppe
▶ Stylish, handsome, and well-acted film set in prewar Nazi Germany. Gifted actor Brandauer wins the admiration of a Nazi benefactor and the opportunity to rise in the theater if he will renounce his past politics and friendships. Somewhat heavy going but can be a dynamic and hypnotic experience for sophisticated audiences willing to accept rather complicated subplot. Based on the book by Klaus Mann (son of Thomas Mann) that was banned in Germany for almost forty years. Won an Oscar for Best Foreign Film.
Ⓢ

MEPHISTO WALTZ, THE 1971
★ ★ R Horror 1:48
☑ Adult situations, explicit language, violence
Dir: Paul Wendkos *Cast:* Alan Alda, Jacqueline Bisset, Barbara Parkins, Curt Jurgens, Bradford Dillman, William Windom
▶ Journalist Alda interviews dying pianist Jurgens. Jurgens turns out to be a satanist who possesses Alda; Alda's wife Bisset senses something amiss and also gets involved with the devil. Overlooked chiller is genuinely atmospheric and spooky; the ending is truly haunting.

MERCENARY FIGHTERS 1988
★ R Action-Adventure 1:31
☑ Nudity, explicit language, violence
Dir: Riki Shelach *Cast:* Peter Fonda, Reb Brown, Ron O'Neal, Jim Mitchum, Robert DoQui, Joanna Weinberg
▶ American mercenaries led by Fonda are hired to wipe out African rebels threatening massive dam project that will uproot natives from their homeland. Influenced by beautiful nurse Weinberg, Brown shifts allegiance to the rebels, provoking dissension among the Americans. Low-budget exploitation concentrates

on fights and explosions rather than plotting.

MERRY CHRISTMAS, MR. LAWRENCE
1983 British/Japanese
★★ R Drama 2:03
☑ Brief nudity, adult situations, explicit language, graphic violence
Dir: Nagisa Oshima *Cast:* David Bowie, Tom Conti, Ryuichi Sakamoto, Takeshi, Jack Thompson
▶ Heroic British soldier Bowie is held captive in a Japanese prisoner-of-war camp during World War II. Two alien cultures clash as captain Sakamoto tries to impose his own ideas of discipline, honor, order, and obedience on Bowie. Includes graphic depictions of brutal beheadings, disembowelments, and other unpleasantries. Based on a novel by Sir Laurens van der Post. Mostly in English with subtitles for occasional Japanese dialogue. Memorable score composed by Sakamoto, a music superstar in Japan. ⑤

MESSENGER OF DEATH 1989
★★★ R Action-Adventure 1:30
☑ Explicit language, violence
Dir: J. Lee Thompson *Cast:* Charles Bronson, Trish Van Devere, Laurence Luckinbill, John Ireland, Marilyn Hassett
▶ Denver reporter Bronson investigates murders of women and children. Small-town newspaper owner Van Devere helps Bronson link the killings to religious sect, powerful society types, and water rights battle. Pretty Colorado scenery is background for patented Bronson heroics, with explosions, chases, shootouts, and killings galore.

METALSTORM: THE DESTRUCTION OF JARED-SYN 1983
★ PG Sci-Fi 1:23
☑ Explicit language, violence
Dir: Charles Band *Cast:* Jeffrey Byron, Mike Preston, Tim Thomerson, Kelly Preston, R. David Smith
▶ Can peacekeeping Ranger (Byron) stop evil warlord Jared-Syn (Preston) from taking over the universe? Poor man's *Mad Max* with a muddled plot was filmed in the California desert—and looks it. Clunky and low-budget fare, for hard-core fantasy devotees only.

METEOR 1979
★★★ PG Action-Adventure 1:46
☑ Adult situations, explicit language, violence
Dir: Ronald Neame *Cast:* Sean Connery, Natalie Wood, Karl Malden, Martin Landau, Brian Keith, Trevor Howard
▶ Gigantic meteor hurtles toward Earth, causing mudslides, earthquakes, and other disasters as American scientist Connery teams with Soviet counterpart Keith to find a solution. Familiar genre formula has all-star cast, clichéd characters. Acceptable special effects generate some suspense.

METROPOLIS 1926 German
★★ NR Sci-Fi 2:00 B&W
Dir: Fritz Lang *Cast:* Brigitte Helm, Alfred Abel, Gustav Froehlich, Rudolf Klein-Rogge, Fritz Rasp
▶ Influential silent film classic about a futuristic society divided into haves and have-nots. Beautiful robot Helm controlled by mad-scientist Klein-Rogge leads exploited workers in a tragic uprising. Plot is alternately silly and dull, but extraordinary special effects set precedent for future sci-fi films. Rock producer Giorgio Moroder added a pop soundtrack to a shortened, partially colorized version in 1984.

MICKI & MAUDE 1984
★★★★ PG-13 Comedy 1:58
☑ Adult situations, explicit language
Dir: Blake Edwards *Cast:* Dudley Moore, Amy Irving, Ann Reinking, Richard Mulligan, George Gaynes, Wallace Shawn
▶ TV newsman Moore wants a child and manages to impregnate both his wife Reinking and mistress Irving. Moore compounds the difficulty by marrying Irving, trying to separate his two wives and lives. Outrageous farce has some flat moments but lots of funny stuff, too (as in the climactic double delivery scene). **(CC)**

MIDNIGHT COWBOY 1969
★★ R Drama 1:53
☑ Nudity, strong sexual content, adult situations, explicit language, violence
Dir: John Schlesinger *Cast:* Dustin Hoffman, Jon Voight, Sylvia Miles, John McGiver, Brenda Vaccaro, Barnard Hughes
▶ Seamy, downbeat look at New York street life brings young Texan Voight, an aspiring gigolo, to the big city. When his dreams don't match reality, Voight agrees to let tubercular street hustler Hoffman manage him. As winter sets in, the two dream of moving to Florida before Hoffman's health gets much

worse. First X-rated (later revised to R) movie to win Best Picture; director Schlesinger and screenwriter Waldo Salt also won Academy Awards. Hoffman, Voight, and Miles were Oscar-nominated. "Everybody's Talking," sung by Harry Nilsson, was huge hit.

MIDNIGHT CROSSING 1988
★★ R Mystery-Suspense 1:44
☑ Nudity
Dir: Roger Holzberg   *Cast:* Faye Dunaway, Daniel J. Travanti, John Laughlin, Kim Cattrall, Ned Beatty
▶ Travanti takes blind wife Dunaway on Laughlin's boat for a Caribbean cruise, supposedly to celebrate their anniversary but actually to recover a fortune in illicit loot. Love affairs, murder, double crosses follow. Thriller has enough plot twists to keep you guessing, but the acting ranges from good (Dunaway, Laughlin) to overdone (Travanti, Beatty).

MIDNIGHT EXPRESS 1978
★★★★★ R Drama 1:59
☑ Nudity, explicit language, graphic violence
Dir: Alan Parker   *Cast:* Brad Davis, Randy Quaid, Irene Miracle, Bo Hopkins, John Hurt, Paul Smith
▶ True story of Billy Hayes (Davis), a young American convicted of drug smuggling in Turkey and sentenced to an inhumane prison. Hard-hitting, well-acted (especially by Oscar-nominated Hurt as Davis's junkie prison pal), but the brutality and violence are unrelenting. Some charged the portrayal of the Turks bordered on racism. Screenwriter Oliver Stone won an Oscar, as did Giorgio Moroder's musical score.

MIDNIGHT LACE 1960
★★★ NR Mystery-Suspense 1:48
Dir: David Miller   *Cast:* Doris Day, Rex Harrison, John Gavin, Myrna Loy, Roddy McDowall, Herbert Marshall
▶ Transparent thriller about Day, recently married to wealthy tycoon Harrison, tormented by death threats regarded as lies by Scotland Yard. Day's only supporter, construction foreman Gavin, may be hiding a dangerous secret. Stars struggle gamely with implausible plot.

MIDNIGHT MADNESS 1980
★★ PG Comedy 1:52
☑ Explicit language, adult humor
Dir: David Wechter, Michael Nankin
Cast: David Naughton, Debra Clinger,

Eddie Deezen, Stephen Furst, Maggie Roswell, Michael J. Fox
▶ Games-obsessed L.A. grad student organizes nighttime scavenger hunt that pits jocks, sorority girls, nerds, and good guys against one another. Harmless teen farce from Disney Studios lacks the tasteless humor of other genre efforts.

MIDNIGHT RUN 1988
★★★★ R Action-Adventure 2:02
☑ Explicit language, violence
Dir: Martin Brest   *Cast:* Robert De Niro, Charles Grodin, Yaphet Kotto, John Ashton, Dennis Farina, Joe Pantoliano
▶ Bounty hunter De Niro accepts what looks like an easy assignment: transport mild-mannered CPA Grodin from New York to Los Angeles. Unfortunately, FBI agents and the mob are also after Grodin, leading to a frantic cross-country chase involving biplanes, buses, helicopters, freight trains, and large-scale shootouts. Brisk action sequences are balanced by stars' remarkable chemistry in this high-spirited comic adventure.

MIDSUMMER NIGHT'S DREAM, A 1935
★★ NR Comedy 2:12 B&W
Dir: Max Reinhardt, William Dieterle
Cast: James Cagney, Dick Powell, Olivia de Havilland, Mickey Rooney, Joe E. Brown, Hugh Herbert
▶ Lavish production of Shakespeare's comedy about mischievous sprites who magically disrupt the affairs of eight lovers is a surprisingly respectful version of the Bard. Cagney makes a delightful Bottom, Rooney an energetic Puck; the other roles are uneven, but Victor Jory and Billy Barty register strongly. Only film by famous impresario Reinhardt won Oscars for photography and editing. De Havilland's film debut.

MIDSUMMER NIGHT'S SEX COMEDY, A 1982
★★ PG Comedy 1:28
☑ Adult situations, adult humor
Dir: Woody Allen   *Cast:* Woody Allen, Mia Farrow, Jose Ferrer, Julie Hagerty, Mary Steenburgen, Tony Roberts
▶ Romantic complications ensue when three couples (inventor Allen and his frustrated wife Steenburgen, pompous professor Ferrer and his fiancée Farrow, doctor Roberts and his nurse/mistress Hagerty) spend a weekend at a country house. Sweet-tempered, lyrical farce with radiant cinematography and lovely

turn-of-the-century settings. Humor is gentler than in previous Woody efforts.

MIDWAY 1976
★★★★★ PG War 2:11
☑ Explicit language, violence
Dir: Jack Smight *Cast:* Charlton Heston, Henry Fonda, James Coburn, Hal Holbrook, Toshiro Mifune, Robert Mitchum
▶ Newsreel and studio-made footage are edited together in a fact-based account of the World War II Battle of Midway, in which American air and sea power combined to deliver a key blow against Japanese forces. When not fighting the battle, captain Heston helps his son deal with a Japanese-American girlfriend. Originally released in Sensurround.

MIGHTY JOE YOUNG 1949
★★ NR Sci-Fi 1:34 B&W
Dir: Ernest B. Schoedsack *Cast:* Terry Moore, Robert Armstrong, Ben Johnson, Frank McHugh
▶ Showman Armstrong brings back from Africa a great ape and the beautiful Moore whose piano rendition of "Beautiful Dreamer" soothes the savage beast. From the creators of *King Kong* and bearing more than a passing resemblance to it; neither ape nor movie is on the scale of Kong but both are appealing and rather fun. Oscar for Special Effects.

MIKE'S MURDER 1984
★★ R Drama 1:49
☑ Brief nudity, adult situations, explicit language, violence
Dir: James Bridges *Cast:* Debra Winger, Mark Keyloun, Paul Winfield, Darrell Larson, Brookers Alderson
▶ Winger walks on L.A.'s wild side, investigating the death of Mike (Keyloun), her tennis-bum lover with a sordid double life. Winfield plays a record producer who loved Mike, too. Offbeat and intriguing crime drama set against gritty atmosphere of drugs and murder.

MIKEY AND NICKY 1976
☆ R Drama 1:45
☑ Adult situations, explicit language, violence
Dir: Elaine May *Cast:* Peter Falk, John Cassavetes, Ned Beatty, Joyce Van Patten, Sanford Meisner
▶ Small-time hood Falk sells out pal Cassavetes to the mob. The duo spend a long night together as the hit man closes in. Gritty, realistic look at the underworld features high-energy performances by Falk and Cassavetes, but rather unlikable characters. Marred by slow pacing, patchwork editing and camerawork.

MILAGRO BEANFIELD WAR, THE 1988
★★★★ R Drama 1:58
☑ Explicit language, violence
Dir: Robert Redford *Cast:* Ruben Blades, Sonia Braga, Daniel Stern, John Heard, Chick Vennera, Christopher Walken
▶ Chicano handyman Vennera "borrows" water to irrigate his dried-up beanfield and sets off a confrontation with powerful interests. Local radical Braga and lawyer Heard side with Vennera, sheriff Blades is caught in the middle, while bad guy Walken is brought in to eliminate Vennera. Little-guy-versus-the-system fable plods a bit but is generally whimsical and charming. Good cast with a delightful pig stealing the show. Film won the Oscar for Best Original Score.

MILDRED PIERCE 1945
★★★★ NR Drama 1:53 B&W
Dir: Michael Curtiz *Cast:* Joan Crawford, Jack Carson, Zachary Scott, Eve Arden, Ann Blyth, Bruce Bennett
▶ Outstanding melodrama about impoverished divorcée Crawford (in one of her greatest roles) who struggles to succeed with a restaurant chain only to face disaster at the hands of her heartless lover Scott and spoiled daughter Blyth. Brilliant script (based on James M. Cain's novel) and astute direction helped Crawford win an Oscar for her portrayal of a gutsy heroine; film received five other nominations.

MILES FROM HOME 1988
★★★ R Drama 1:52
☑ Adult situations, explicit language, violence
Dir: Gary Sinise *Cast:* Richard Gere, Kevin Anderson, Penelope Ann Miller, John Malkovich, Judith Ivey, Brian Dennehy
▶ Brothers Gere and Anderson burn down the family farm rather than let the bank take possession after foreclosure. They go on the lam through the Midwest, becoming folk heroes. Provocative story contains one of Gere's most emotionally charged performances, but the film is hindered by Sinise's overblown direction. Malkovich contributes a sharply cynical cameo as a reporter.

MILLION DOLLAR MYSTERY 1987
★★ PG Comedy 1:30

☑ Explicit language, mild violence
Dir: Richard Fleischer *Cast:* Tom Bosley, Rich Hall, Kevin Pollak, Pam Matteson, Eddie Deezen, Wendy Sherman
▶ Relentlessly zany chase comedy in the style of *It's a Mad, Mad, Mad, Mad World*. Government official Bosley keels over in desert cafe, revealing to assorted onlookers that he has hidden four caches of $1 million. The hunt is on as a busty waitress, her alcoholic brother, nerdy newlyweds, a rock group, a ninja, and a cop search for the dough. Also looking: movie audiences who were offered $1 million by the producers if they could guess the hiding place.

MIND KILLER 1987
★ R Horror 1:26
☑ Nudity, adult situations, explicit language, violence
Dir: Michael Krueger *Cast:* Joe McDonald, Christopher Wade, Shirley Ross, Kevin Hart
▶ Nerdy librarian McDonald is a flop at picking up chicks until he reads a mind-control manual and brainwashes women into falling in love with him. Working overtime to satisfy his every desire, McDonald's seething brain reaches uncontrollable proportions, explodes out of his skull, and hunts his friends. Attack of the killer id is low-budget and scary, with ultra-gross special effects.

MIRACLE MILE 1988
★★ R Sci-Fi 1:35
☑ Nudity, adult situations, explicit language, violence
Dir: Steve DeJarnatt *Cast:* Anthony Edwards, Mare Winningham, Mykel T. Williamson, Denise Crosby
▶ Musician Edwards intercepts a chance phone call and learns that World War III is about to start. Can he get his waitress girlfriend Winningham out of L.A. before panic overcomes the streets and the bombs hit? Impudent thriller with house-afire pacing and visually ingenious direction, although quirky plotting and crazy dialogue relegate this to cult status.

MIRACLE OF MORGAN'S CREEK, THE 1944
★★★★ NR Comedy 1:38 B&W
Dir: Preston Sturges *Cast:* Eddie Bracken, Betty Hutton, William Demarest, Diana Lynn, Porter Hall, Alan Bridge
▶ Outrageous World War II comedy about small-town flirt Trudy Kockenlocker (Hutton) who thinks she married someone named "Ratzkiwatzki" after an all-night party with soldiers from a nearby base. Learning she's pregnant, she tricks 4F reject Bracken into marriage. All-out assault on American morals is one of the raciest and funniest farces ever filmed, with superb supporting work from a large cast of comic pros. Director Sturges received an Oscar nomination for his hilarious screenplay.

MIRACLE ON 34TH STREET 1947
★★★★★ NR Fantasy/Comedy 1:36 B&W
Dir: George Seaton *Cast:* Maureen O'Hara, John Payne, Natalie Wood, Edmund Gwenn, Thelma Ritter
▶ Enduring holiday classic features Gwenn going to work as Macy's Santa Claus for executive O'Hara. While trying to persuade O'Hara's daughter, a very young and cynical Wood, that Santa is real, Gwenn is institutionalized. O'Hara's fiancé, lawyer Payne, must convince the court of Gwenn's sanity and the very existence of Santa Claus. Heartwarming, much-beloved Christmas classic works like a charm. Gwenn, story writer Valentine Davis, and screenwriter Seaton all garnered Oscars. Available in colorized version.

MIRACLES 1986
★★★ PG Comedy/Drama 1:27
☑ Explicit language, violence
Dir: Jim Kouf *Cast:* Teri Garr, Tom Conti, Paul Rodriguez, Christopher Lloyd
▶ Newly divorced Garr and Conti are kidnapped by thieves Rodriguez and Lloyd and taken south of the border. There they get into further misadventures and rediscover their feelings for one another. Likable stars deserved a better script.

MIRACLE WORKER, THE 1962
★★★★ NR Biography 1:47 B&W
Dir: Arthur Penn *Cast:* Anne Bancroft, Patty Duke, Victor Jory, Inga Swenson, Andrew Prine
▶ Determined Annie Sullivan (Bancroft) attempts to teach deaf, dumb, and blind child Helen Keller (Duke) some semblance of language. An inspiring true story from the William Gibson Broadway play with galvanizing Oscar-winning performances by Bancroft and Duke.

MIRACLE WORKER, THE 1979
★★★★★ NR Biography/MFTV 1:38
Dir: Paul Aaron *Cast:* Patty Duke Astin,

Melissa Gilbert, Diana Muldaur, Charles Siebert

▶ TV remake of the William Gibson classic has Astin, who won an Oscar for playing Helen Keller in the original, portraying the teacher Annie Sullivan. Co-producer Gilbert plays Keller. The now-familiar story of blind deaf-mute Keller learning to communicate through Sullivan's guidance remains powerful, thanks to these two gifted actresses.

MIRROR CRACK'D, THE 1980 British
★★★ PG Mystery-Suspense 1:46
☑ Adult situations
Dir: Guy Hamilton *Cast:* Angela Lansbury, Elizabeth Taylor, Rock Hudson, Kim Novak, Tony Curtis, Geraldine Chaplin
▶ Amateur detective extraordinaire Miss Marple (Lansbury) gets on the case when a murder occurs during a reception for a film production company. Among the possible suspects: co-star Taylor, her husband/director Hudson, rival Novak, secretary Chaplin, and Novak's producer husband Curtis. Lighthearted whodunnit is a bit slowly paced but fun, especially when Taylor and Novak try to out-bitch one another.

MISCHIEF 1985
★★★ R Comedy 1:37
☑ Nudity, adult situations, explicit language
Dir: Mel Damski *Cast:* Doug McKeon, Chris Nash, Kelly Preston, Catherine Mary Stewart, Jami Gertz
▶ Fifties fable in which rebel Nash initiates shy teen McKeon into the mysteries of dating and sex. McKeon has brief fling with high school sex kitten Preston while Nash eventually splits town with new flame Stewart. Hardly virgin territory but competently rendered nostalgia piece. (CC)

MISFITS, THE 1961
★★ NR Drama 2:04 B&W
Dir: John Huston *Cast:* Clark Gable, Marilyn Monroe, Montgomery Clift, Thelma Ritter, Eli Wallach, Estelle Winwood
▶ Moody study of the stormy relationship between aging cowhand Gable and divorcée Monroe in Reno. She opposes his job: roping wild horses for dog food. More absorbing for its participants than its plot. Gable, who did his own stunts, died before film's release; Monroe never completed another picture. Script by Arthur Miller, Monroe's husband at the time.

MISHIMA 1985
☆ R Drama 2:00 C/B&W
☑ Nudity, adult situations, explicit language, violence
Dir: Paul Schrader *Cast:* Ken Ogata, Masayuki Shionoya, Hiroshi Mikami, Junya Fukuda, Shigeto Tachihara, Junkichi Orimoto
▶ Intricate, visually fascinating biography of noted Japanese author Yukio Mishima (Ogata) combines black-and-white footage of his troubled life with opulent color excerpts from three novels: *Temple of the Golden Pavilion*, *Kyoko's House*, and *Runaway Horses*. Intellectually demanding and only intermittently successful experiment features a score by Philip Glass. (CC) Ⓢ

MISSING 1982
★★★★ PG Drama 2:02
☑ Brief nudity, explicit language, violence
Dir: Costa-Gavras *Cast:* Jack Lemmon, Sissy Spacek, John Shea, Melanie Mayron, David Clennon, Janice Rule
▶ American Shea disappears during a coup in Latin America. Searching for him, his anguished wife Spacek and father Lemmon uncover possible U.S. government involvement. Intriguing political thriller, inspired by a true story. Beautifully crafted direction by Costa-Gavras. Lemmon is outstanding as the conservative businessman who gradually sees the error of his ways; Spacek is also fine. Oscar for Best Screenplay Adaptation; nominated for Picture, Actor (Lemmon), and Actress (Spacek).

MISSING IN ACTION 1984
★★★★ R Action-Adventure 1:41
☑ Nudity, explicit language, violence
Dir: Joseph Zito *Cast:* Chuck Norris, M. Emmet Walsh, Lenore Kasdorf, James Hong, David Tress
▶ Determined soldier Norris returns to Vietnam to rescue American POWs. Although he's helped by army buddy Walsh who deals in the black market, Norris wins his battles almost single-handedly. Plenty of firebombs, car chases, hand-to-hand combat, evil Vietnamese officers, and gung-ho action. Equally popular sequel: *Missing in Action 2—The Beginning.*

MISSING IN ACTION 2—THE BEGINNING 1985
★★★★ R Action-Adventure 1:35

☑ Explicit language, violence
Dir: Lance Hool *Cast:* Chuck Norris, Steven Williams, Bennett Ohta, Soon-Teck Oh, Cosie Costa
▶ Sturdy prequel to *Missing in Action*. American colonel Norris is captured when his helicopter crashes in Vietnam. He's imprisoned and tortured by the sadistic Vietcong. Among other atrocities, the V.C. put Norris's head in a bag with a rat, which really makes Chuck mad. Of course, he outfoxes his torturers and gets a large measure of revenge.

MISSING LINK, THE 1988
French/Belgian
★ ★ ★ PG Animation/Adult 1:35
☑ Nudity, adult situations, explicit language
Dir: Picha *Cast:* Voices of Ron Venable, John Graham, Bob Kaliban, Christopher Guest, Clark Warren, Mark Smith
▶ The missing link in human evolution is found and reared by dinosaurs after being abandoned by his prehistoric tribe. When he is old enough to realize the difference between himself and his adoptive parents, he searches for his people. Inventive animation from cartoonist Picha; music by Leo Sayer. In English.

MISSION, THE 1986 British
★ ★ ★ ★ PG Action-Adventure 2:05
☑ Adult situations, explicit language, violence
Dir: Roland Joffe *Cast:* Robert De Niro, Jeremy Irons, Ray McAnally, Aidan Quinn, Cherie Lunghi, Ronald Pickup
▶ The jungles of eighteenth-century Brazil provide a dramatic backdrop to an intriguing power struggle between a Jesuit religious society promoting the interests of the Indian natives and government officials determined to consolidate their power over the colony. De Niro delivers another commanding performance as a soldier whose faith is tested by politics, but film's themes are sometimes obscured by the elaborate production values. Oscar-winning cinematography by Chris Menges. (CC)

MISSIONARY, THE 1982 British
★ R Comedy 1:27
☑ Brief nudity, adult situations, explicit language, adult humor
Dir: Richard Loncraine *Cast:* Michael Palin, Maggie Smith, Trevor Howard, Denholm Elliott, Michael Hordern, Phoebe Nicholls

▶ In 1906, idealistic British missionary Palin returns from Africa and is assigned to a home for fallen women. Palin tends to his charges beyond the call of duty, falling into bed with them and being seduced by the mission's wealthy patron (Smith). Daffy comedy with thin story is longer on small chuckles than big laughs. Sumptuous period settings, delightful Smith and Nicholls.

MISSION KILL 1985
★ ★ R Action-Adventure 1:37
☑ Adult situations, explicit language, graphic violence
Dir: David Winters *Cast:* Robert Ginty, Cameron Mitchell, Merete Van Kamp, Olivia d'Abo, Henry Darrow, Eduardo Lopez Rojas
▶ Demolitions expert Ginty is trapped in the middle of a Central American revolution when his Marine pal Mitchell is killed by rebels. After witnessing atrocities ordered by dictator Rojas and his underling Darrow, Ginty conducts series of terrorist attacks that turn him into folk hero. Workmanlike low-budget action offers good stunts and competent acting.

MISSISSIPPI BURNING 1988
★ ★ ★ ★ R Drama 2:00
☑ Adult situations, explicit language, violence
Dir: Alan Parker *Cast:* Gene Hackman, Willem Dafoe, Frances McDormand, Brad Dourif, Lee Ermey, Gailard Sartain
▶ In 1964, young, by-the-book FBI honcho Dafoe and good ol' boy assistant Hackman investigate the suspicious disappearance of three civil rights workers in backwoods Jessup County. When it seems likely that local citizens killed the three using KKK nighttime terror tactics, Dafoe ups the ante by calling in hundreds of Bureau men. Disastrous results force Dafoe to yield to Hackman's more unorthodox approach. Based on real events, gripping, often disturbing drama takes more than a few liberties with the facts but always entertains. Nominated for seven Oscars, including Best Picture, Actor (Hackman), Supporting Actress (McDormand), and Director; won for Cinematography.

MISSOURI BREAKS, THE 1976
★ ★ ★ ★ PG Western 2:06
☑ Violence
Dir: Arthur Penn *Cast:* Marlon Brando, Jack Nicholson, Randy Quaid, Frederic

Forrest, Harry Dean Stanton, Kathleen Lloyd
▶ Nicholson plays a bumbling horse thief pursued by the mercenary lawman Brando. Despite an unusual showdown in a bubble bath, the picture rambles, neither a straight Western nor a spoof. A dream cast, talented director, and stylish screenwriter (novelist Tom McGuane) produced a resounding box office dud. Critics were especially hard on Brando for a performance deemed overblown and completely at odds with the rest of the film.

MISTER ROBERTS 1955
★ ★ ★ ★ NR Comedy 1:56
Dir: John Ford, Mervyn LeRoy *Cast:* Henry Fonda, James Cagney, Jack Lemmon, William Powell, Betsy Palmer
▶ During World War II, cargo ship officer Mister Roberts (Fonda) battles authoritarian captain Cagney on behalf of his men (including Lemmon's jaunty Ensign Pulver and Powell's kindly doctor) while yearning for the excitement of real wartime action. Terrific adaptation of the Pulitzer prize–winning novel and play is alternately funny and moving. Perfectly cast Fonda is solid and Oscar-winning Lemmon steals the show. A Best Picture nominee.

MISTY 1961
★ ★ ★ ★ NR Family 1:31
Dir: James B. Clark *Cast:* David Ladd, Arthur O'Connell, Pam Smith, Anne Seymour, Duke Farley
▶ Charming children's adventure about orphaned siblings Ladd and Smith, who help round up the wild horses on Chincoteaque, an island off the coast of Virginia. The children fall in love with Misty, a colt, and set out to earn enough money to buy the pony. Adaptation of Marguerite Henry's book aided by beautiful locations and realistic acting.

MISUNDERSTOOD 1984
★ ★ ★ ★ PG Drama 1:35
☑ Adult situations
Dir: Jerry Schatzberg *Cast:* Gene Hackman, Rip Torn, Henry Thomas, Huckleberry Fox, Susan Anspach
▶ Melodrama about Hackman, a workaholic shipping magnate based in Tunisia who neglects his sons Thomas and Fox. The three come to terms with each other after Mom dies (cameo by Anspach). As usual Hackman rises above sudsy material.

MOBY DICK 1956
★ ★ NR Action-Adventure 1:56
Dir: John Huston *Cast:* Gregory Peck, Richard Basehart, Leo Genn, Orson Welles, Harry Andrews, Bernard Miles
▶ New Bedford, 1840: despite warnings from ominous preacher Welles, seaman Basehart sets sail aboard a whaling ship. The obsessed Captain Ahab (Peck), scarred and peg-legged, then announces to the crew they are on a vengeance mission to kill Moby Dick, the great white whale that disfigured him. Fine adaptation of the Herman Melville classic, with screenplay by director Huston and sci-fi author Ray Bradbury.

MODEL BEHAVIOR 1985
☆ NR Comedy 1:26
☑ Nudity, adult situations
Dir: Bud Gardner *Cast:* Richard Bekins, Bruce Lyons, Anne Howard, Lisa McMillan, Antonio Fargas
▶ Two guys, a hustler and an ad agency drone, scheme to meet beautiful women by pretending to be a photographer and a Hollywood talent agent. Not bad sex comedy premise but execution lacks wit and imagination. Some nice looking bodies but actual nudity and sex is downplayed.

MODERN PROBLEMS 1981
★ ★ PG Comedy 1:31
☑ Explicit language, adult humor
Dir: Ken Shapiro *Cast:* Chevy Chase, Patti D'Arbanville, Mary Kay Place, Dabney Coleman, Nell Carter
▶ Hapless air traffic controller Chase acquires telekinetic powers, transforming his jealous tirades over girlfriend D'Arbanville and ex-wife Place into special effects showcases. Chase and the underutilized cast often seem on automatic pilot as the script drags, but some comic bits are memorable.

MODERN ROMANCE 1981
★ R Comedy 1:34
☑ Nudity, adult situations, explicit language
Dir: Albert Brooks *Cast:* Kathryn Harrold, Albert Brooks, Bruno Kirby, Jane Hallaren, James L. Brooks
▶ Breaking up is hard to do for Brooks and on-again/off-again girlfriend Harrold. Mostly one-man show features Brooks's jealous neuroses, but Harrold is a stunner in her limited screen time. Famed director James L. Brooks (no relation) makes cameo appearance spoofing the

filmmaking biz. Cult followers of Brooks and his quirky, angst-driven humor won't be disappointed, but nonbelievers will wonder what all the fuss is about.

MODERNS, THE 1988
★★ R Drama 2:06
☑ Nudity, adult situations, explicit language, violence
Dir: Alan Rudolph *Cast:* Keith Carradine, Linda Fiorentino, Genevieve Bujold, Geraldine Chaplin, Wallace Shawn, John Lone
▶ Paris, 1926: struggling painter Carradine romances ex-wife Fiorentino under the nose of her current husband Lone, a wealthy collector, and gets involved in an art forging scheme. Colorful but not very compelling drama of American expatriates. Pretty music and cinematography but overlong, with absurd portrayals of famous figures (Hemingway, Gertrude Stein, Alice B. Toklas).

MODERN TIMES 1936
★★★★ G Comedy 1:27 B&W
Dir: Charlie Chaplin *Cast:* Charlie Chaplin, Paulette Goddard, Henry Bergman, Chester Conklin
▶ Factory worker Chaplin suffers through machine-induced nervous breakdown, a strike, a jail sentence, and other modern problems while finding companionship with an orphan (his fetching then-wife Goddard). Chaplin's last silent film does have music (including "Smile"), sound effects, brief dialogue, and Charlie singing a delightful nonsensical song. A gem, masterfully combining hilarious slapstick, machine-age satire, tenderness, and heartbreak.

MOGAMBO 1953
★★★ NR Action-Adventure 1:56
Dir: John Ford *Cast:* Clark Gable, Ava Gardner, Grace Kelly, Donald Sinden, Laurence Naismith
▶ Sparks fly in a triangle between safari guide Gable, married Englishwoman Kelly, and jet-setter Gardner during an upriver trip in Central Africa. Old-fashioned entertainment, Hollywood style. Amusing dialogue, exotic locations, romance, and bubbling star chemistry. Our favorite scene: Ava giving her bubble gum to a chimp. Remake of the 1932 *Red Dust*, which also starred Gable.

MOLLY MAGUIRES, THE 1970
★★★ PG Drama 2:05
☑ Adult situations, explicit language, violence

Dir: Martin Ritt *Cast:* Sean Connery, Richard Harris, Samantha Eggar, Frank Finlay, Anthony Zerbe, Art Lund
▶ Pennsylvania, 1876: company spy Harris infiltrates the Mollies, an Irish mineworkers union violently battling inhuman conditions. He befriends leader Connery and romances miner's daughter Eggar but eventually must betray them. Ambitious, fact-based drama has handsome period production, strong performances, and haunting Henry Mancini score.

MOMMIE DEAREST 1981
★★★ PG Drama 2:09
☑ Explicit language, violence
Dir: Frank Perry *Cast:* Faye Dunaway, Diana Scarwid, Steve Forrest, Howard da Silva, Mara Hobel
▶ In a tour-de-force performance, Dunaway transforms herself passionately and completely into Joan Crawford. Based on Christina Crawford's autobiography about growing up the adopted and abused daughter of the movie queen, the film generally lacks insight and depth. Nonetheless, it has become a kind of cult classic for its glossy good looks, memorable performances (da Silva is brilliant as L. B. Mayer), and quotable dialogue ("No wire hangers!").

MONA LISA 1986 British
★★ R Drama 1:40
☑ Nudity, adult situations, explicit language, violence
Dir: Neil Jordan *Cast:* Bob Hoskins, Cathy Tyson, Michael Caine, Clarke Peters, Kate Hardie, Robbie Coltrane
▶ Cockney ex-con Hoskins is hired by crime czar Caine as a driver for high-class call girl Tyson. Hoskins falls for Tyson and risks his life to search for her missing friend. Magnetic performance by Hoskins dominates the movie and makes his unusual relationship with the haunting Tyson quite touching. Stylish direction by Jordan conveys a convincingly sleazy atmosphere yet the movie is basically quite sentimental. Hoskins was nominated for an Oscar for his performance.

MONDO CANE 1963 Italian
★ R Documentary 1:47
☑ Nudity, adult situations, graphic violence
Dir: Gualtiero Jacopetti
▶ Documentary look at gruesome customs and sights throughout the world: puppy cooking in Formosa, hog slaughter in New Guinea, Bikini turtles dying of radi-

ation, etc. Shocking and a box office success in its time but now merely the stuff of nightmares; Oscar nomination for Best Song ("More"). Dubbed.

MONDO NEW YORK 1988
☆ NR Documentary 1:22
☑ Nudity, adult situations, explicit language, graphic violence
Dir: Harvey Keith *Cast:* Rick Aviles, Charlie Barnett, Ann Magnuson, Karen Finlay, Dean Johnson, Phoebe Legere
► Look at New York City's East Village performance art scene includes no-holds-barred turns by controversial Finlay, who breaks eggs over her naked body while reciting antiyuppie diatribe, and Johnson, a six-foot-plus bald drag queen who performs an outrageous song whose title cannot be printed here. Alternately provocative and offensive; grotesque violence includes people biting the heads off mice and chickens.

MONEY PIT, THE 1986
★★★★ PG Comedy 1:31
☑ Adult situations, explicit language
Dir: Richard Benjamin *Cast:* Tom Hanks, Shelley Long, Maureen Stapleton, Alexander Godunov, Joe Mantegna, Philip Bosco
► Flaky musician Long and her live-in lawyer/lover Hanks attempt to renovate a rundown mansion. Outlandish special effects include collapsing stairways, exploding plumbing, falling doors, and defective wiring. Godunov is Long's arrogant ex-husband. (CC)

MONKEY BUSINESS 1931
★★★★ NR Comedy 1:27 B&W
Dir: Norman Z. McLeod *Cast:* Groucho Marx, Harpo Marx, Chico Marx, Zeppo Marx, Thelma Todd, Tom Kennedy
► In the first of their films to be written directly for the screen, the loopy brothers stow away on a luxury liner. Chaos reigns, aided by a pair of gangsters and Groucho's wooing of Todd. Plenty of laughs; fine work from the brothers and Todd assure fans and newcomers a good time.

MONKEY BUSINESS 1952
★★★ NR Comedy 1:37 B&W
Dir: Howard Hawks *Cast:* Cary Grant, Ginger Rogers, Charles Coburn, Marilyn Monroe, Hugh Marlowe, George "Foghorn" Winslow
► While scientist Grant experiments to find a youth potion, one of his lab chimps laces water fountain with a successful version of the formula. Grant reverts to college shenanigans with lab secretary Monroe; he and wife Rogers later slide all the way back to preadolescence. Amusing screwball romp delivered by an expert cast.

MONKEY SHINES: AN EXPERIMENT IN FEAR 1988
★★★ R Horror 1:55
☑ Nudity, adult situations, explicit language, violence
Dir: George A. Romero *Cast:* Jason Beghe, John Pankow, Kate McNeil, Joyce Van Patten, Christine Forrest, Boo the Monkey
► When law student Beghe is rendered quadraplegic, scientist Pankow provides experimental monkey Boo to assist him with daily chores. Boo takes task too close to heart, going on murderous rampage against Beghe's enemies. After low-gear start, Romero masterfully builds to hair-raising shudders; amazing performance by Boo the monkey. (CC)

MON ONCLE 1958 French
☆ NR Comedy 1:50
Dir: Jacques Tati *Cast:* Jacques Tati, Jean-Pierre Zola, Adrienne Servantie, Alain Becourt, Lucien Fregis, Betty Schneider
► Director Tati plays a disheveled, unaffected man, in contrast to his brother-in-law Zola, who resides in a sanitized suburban home cluttered with the latest gadgets. Tati's nephew Becourt prefers his uncle's simple life, but neither can completely escape modernization. In this sight-gag satire of technology addicts, Tati reprises the character he created in *Mr. Hulot's Holiday.* Oscar winner for Best Foreign Film. Dubbed version available. Ⓢ

MON ONCLE D'AMERIQUE 1980 French
★ PG Drama 2:05
☑ Adult situations
Dir: Alain Resnais *Cast:* Gerard Depardieu, Nicole Garcia, Roger Pierre, Marie Dubois, Nelly Bourgeaud, Henri Laborit
► Real-life behavioral scientist Laborit provides commentary on executive Depardieu's adjustment to corporate upheaval and married man Pierre's affair with actress Garcia. Rather talky and dry but still provocative; the fictional situations interweave with Laborit's theories in complex and surprisingly humorous fashion. Recommended only for discerning moviegoers. Ⓢ

MONSIEUR VERDOUX 1947
★ ★ ★ ★ **NR Comedy 2:04 B&W**
Dir: Charles Chaplin   *Cast:* Charles
Chaplin, Martha Raye, Maddy Correll,
Isobel Elsom, William Frawley
▶ Former bank teller Chaplin supports his
crippled wife and child by wedding rich
ladies and murdering them for their
money. Cynical black comedy, a depar-
ture for writer/director/star/composer
Chaplin. Overlong and belabors its point
but original and unusual. Best scenes pair
Chaplin with his gabby would-be victim
Raye.

MONSIGNOR 1982
★ ★ ★ **R Drama 2:02**
☑ Nudity, adult situations, explicit language, violence
Dir: Frank Perry   *Cast:* Christopher
Reeve, Genevieve Bujold, Fernando
Rey, Jason Miller, Joe Cortese, Leo-
nardo Cimino
▶ Corrupt priest Reeve rises to Vatican
treasurer, making deals with the mob
and seducing novice Bujold. Earnest,
classily photographed story mixes religion, crime, and passion. Soap opera
level is sometimes unintentionally laugh-
provoking, as when Bujold stops short in
church on discovering her lover is a priest,
causing a silly traffic jam of nuns bunch-
ing up behind her.

MONSTER IN THE CLOSET 1986
☆ **PG Horror/Comedy 1:27**
☑ Brief nudity, explicit language, violence
Dir: Bob Dahlin   *Cast:* Donald Grant,
Denise DuBarry, Claude Akins, Howard
Duff, Henry Gibson, Paul Dooley
▶ Comedy of terrors attempts to spoof
1950s horror classics. Grant, a Clark Kent–
type reporter, investigates a baffling series of brutal closet murders. Along with
biology teacher DuBarry, madly in love
with him, and Nobel Prize–winning scientist Gibson, he discovers the culprit is a
ravenous, hunchback monster. High
point: DuBarry on national TV, pleading,
"Destroy all closets!"   **(CC)**

MONSTER SQUAD, THE 1987
★ ★ ★ **PG-13 Horror/Comedy 1:22**
☑ Explicit language, violence
Dir: Fred Dekker   *Cast:* Andre Gower,
Robby Kiger, Stephen Macht, Duncan
Regehr, Tom Noonan, Brent Chalam
▶ It's up to a group of monster-movie-
loving schoolchildren to save the day
when Frankenstein, Dracula, the Mummy,

the Wolfman, and the Creature from the
Black Lagoon descend on a small town.
Simple story geared for the younger set,
who should love it. Not really that scary
but appealing kid actors and tongue-in-
cheek humor.

MONTENEGRO 1981 Swedish/British
★ **R Comedy 1:34**
☑ Nudity, adult situations, explicit language
Dir: Dusan Makavejev   *Cast:* Susan Anspach, Erland Josephson, Jamie Marsh,
Per Oscarsson, Bora Todorovic, Svetzo-
var Cvetkovic
▶ Upscale American housewife Anspach, living in Sweden with husband Josephson and children, forsakes her boring marriage for a quick and passionate
affair with Yugoslavian hunk Cvetkovic.
Off-beat, quite steamy comedy from
avant-garde director Makavejev.

MONTEREY POP 1968
★ ★ ★ **NR Documentary/Music 1:28**
Dir: James Desmond, Barry Feinstein,
D. A. Pennebaker, Albert Maysles, Roger
Murphy, Richard Leacock, Nick Proferes
Cast: Jefferson Airplane, Janis Joplin,
Jimi Hendrix, The Mamas and Papas,
Otis Redding, The Who
▶ Landmark documentary about the
1967 rock 'n' roll festival at Monterey captures some of the sixties' brightest stars at
their peaks. Highlights include Joplin's
mesmerizing "Ball and Chain," a white-
hot performance by Redding, Hendrix's
dazzling guitar workout, and a blockbuster rendition of "My Generation" by
the Who.

MONTE WALSH 1970
★ ★ ★ ★ **PG Western 1:40**
☑ Adult situations
Dir: William A. Fraker   *Cast:* Lee Marvin,
Jeanne Moreau, Jack Palance, Mitch
Ryan, Jim Davis, John "Bear" Hudkins
▶ Cowpoke chums Marvin and Palance
face dwindling options when their ranch
is closed by Eastern money interests; Marvin must also confront his lover Moreau's
fatal consumption in this somber Western. Noted photographer Fraker's directorial debut eloquently describes passing of an era.   **(CC)**

MONTH IN THE COUNTRY, A 1988
British
★ ★ **PG Drama 1:36**
☑ Adult situations
Dir: Pat O'Connor   *Cast:* Colin Firth,

Kenneth Branagh, Natasha Richardson, Patrick Malahide
▶ Art restorer Firth, still haunted by memories of service in World War I, falls in love with parson's wife Richardson while solving the mystery of an unmarked grave. Exceedingly tasteful British drama; well-acted but terribly genteel and slowly paced.

MONTY PYTHON AND THE HOLY GRAIL
1974 British
★ ★ ★ PG Comedy 1:29
☑ Adult situations, explicit language, violence, adult humor
Dir: Terry Gilliam, Terry Jones *Cast:* Graham Chapman, John Cleese, Eric Idle, Michael Palin, Terry Jones, Terry Gilliam
▶ Merry takeoff on medieval era features the Python gang as King Arthur and the knights of the Round Table on a quest for the Holy Grail. Obstacles in their path include renegade knights obsessed with shrubbery and a bridge guard who demands answers to three questions (like "What's your favorite color?"). Many priceless moments: Cleese apologizing after slaughtering party of innocents, cowardly Idle objecting to minstrel's singing of how he "runneth away," and knight continuing duel despite severed limbs.

MONTY PYTHON LIVE AT THE HOLLYWOOD BOWL 1982 British
★ ★ ★ R Documentary/Comedy 1:21
☑ Explicit language, adult humor
Dir: Terry Hughes *Cast:* Graham Chapman, John Cleese, Terry Gilliam, Eric Idle, Terry Jones, Michael Palin
▶ Inimitable Pythons perform new skits and re-create old favorites in front of a crowd of adoring Angelenos. Troupe's acid wit and bawdy antics are at their finest here. Those who have acquired the taste will be amused; those who tire of dead parrot jokes should stay away.

MONTY PYTHON'S LIFE OF BRIAN
1979 British
★ ★ R Comedy 1:34
☑ Explicit language, violence, adult humor
Dir: Terry Jones *Cast:* Graham Chapman, John Cleese, Eric Idle, Michael Palin, Terry Jones, Terry Gilliam
▶ The life and times of one Brian of Nazareth (Chapman), a somewhat reluctant messiah born the same day as Jesus. Religious satire has moments of in-spired lunacy, such as crucified people singing the cheery "Always Look on the Bright Side of Life." Python fans will love it although others may be offended by ir-reverant humor.

MONTY PYTHON'S THE MEANING OF LIFE 1983 British
★ ★ R Comedy 1:47
☑ Nudity, adult situations, explicit language, violence, adult humor
Dir: Terry Jones *Cast:* Terry Gilliam, John Cleese, Eric Idle, Terry Jones, Graham Chapman, Michael Palin
▶ Plotless grab bag of skits from the ever-irreverent Brits. Here the Pythons cast their satirical eye at big issues: death, the afterlife, contraception, and twenty-five-course meals, with typically rude and raucous results. Fans will no doubt be delighted, although many find the sketches of uneven quality. Warning: do not view this movie on a full stomach.

MOON IN THE GUTTER, THE 1983 French
☆ R Drama 2:06
☑ Nudity, explicit language, violence
Dir: Jean-Jacques Beineix *Cast:* Nastassia Kinski, Gerard Depardieu, Victoria Abril, Vittorio Mezzogiorno
▶ Hulking dockworker Depardieu seeks the rapist who drove his sister to suicide. Enter sultry rich brat Kinski to distract him from the squalor of his life; exit all semblance of a coherent plot. Lots of pretty images. ⑤

MOON IS BLUE, THE 1953
★ ★ ★ PG Comedy 1:39 B&W
☑ Adult situations
Dir: Otto Preminger *Cast:* William Holden, David Niven, Maggie McNamara, Tom Tully, Dawn Addams, Gregory Ratoff
▶ New York architect Holden falls for young actress McNamara, who disrupts his home by flirting with Niven, his prospective father-in-law. Mild adaptation of a dated Broadway farce stirred some controversy for its adult themes. Title song and McNamara (in her film debut) received Oscar nominations.

MOONLIGHTING 1982 British
★ ★ PG Drama 1:37
☑ Explicit language
Dir: Jerzy Skolimowski *Cast:* Jeremy Irons, Eugene Lipinski, Jiri Stanislav, Eugeniusz Hacziewicz
▶ Four Polish workers are sent to London to remodel a townhouse. Foreman Irons is

the only one who speaks English. When he learns of Solidarity upheavals back home, he keeps the news from the others so they will finish the job. Quiet and reflective political meditation; well acted by Irons but placid pace may try patience. For sophisticated tastes. **(CC)** ⑤

MOON OVER PARADOR 1988
★ ★ ★ PG-13 Comedy 1:45
☑ Adult situations, explicit language, violence
Dir: Paul Mazursky   *Cast:* Richard Dreyfuss, Raul Julia, Sonia Braga, Jonathan Winters, Fernando Rey, Sammy Davis, Jr.
▶ When a Latin American dictator dies, power-behind-the-throne Julia convinces New York actor Dreyfuss to impersonate the dead man. Dreyfuss gets involved with the dictator's mistress Braga, CIA man Winters, and land reform plan. Fizzy farce has infectious spirit; Dreyfuss struts his stuff amusingly, Davis contributes a hilarious cameo, and scattershot humor frequently hits home.

MOON PILOT 1962
★ ★ ★ NR Sci-Fi 1:38
Dir: James Neilson   *Cast:* Tom Tryon, Brian Keith, Edmond O'Brien, Dany Saval, Tommy Kirk
▶ Playful chimp "volunteers" astronaut Tryon to be the first man in orbit; beautiful alien Saval suddenly arrives with a rocket-fuel formula to ensure the mission's success. Pleasant Disney comedy pokes harmless fun at NASA; romance between Saval and Tryon (later a best-selling author) provides plenty of laughs.

MOONRAKER 1979 British
★ ★ ★ ★ PG
Espionage/Action-Adventure 2:06
☑ Adult situations, explicit language
Dir: Lewis Gilbert   *Cast:* Roger Moore, Lois Chiles, Michael Lonsdale, Richard Kiel, Corinne Clery
▶ This time around (the eleventh in the series) aeronautics tycoon Lonsdale threatens the world with nerve gas dispensed from his personal fleet of space shuttles. Bond saves the planet by overcoming a vendetta by Venetian gondoliers and a tram car tango in Rio with Jaws (Kiel). Glossy, action-packed fun with standard exotic locales, nifty spy hardware, ribald wit, and an explosive finale in space.

MOONSHINE COUNTY EXPRESS 1977
★ ★ PG Action-Adventure 1:36

☑ Adult situations, explicit language, violence
Dir: Gus Trikonis   *Cast:* John Saxon, Susan Howard, William Conrad, Morgan Woodward, Claudia Jennings, Maureen McCormick
▶ Sexy sisters Howard, Jennings, and McCormick go after evil bootlegger Conrad, who they think killed their moonshining father. Bankrolled by a stash of Prohibition liquor, and with help from Conrad's underling Saxon, the girls take over their county. Lightweight low-budget drama with plenty of action.

MOON-SPINNERS, THE 1964
★ ★ ★ ★ NR Mystery-Suspense 1:58
Dir: James Neilson   *Cast:* Hayley Mills, Eli Wallach, Pola Negri, Peter McEnery, Joan Greenwood, Irene Papas
▶ While vacationing in Crete, young Mills befriends wounded Englishman McEnery, a suspect trying to clear his name of robbery charges. Modest Disney thriller, based on a Mary Stewart novel, has beautiful settings and good work from Wallach and Negri as the villains.

MOONSTRUCK 1987
★ ★ ★ ★ PG Romance/Comedy 1:43
☑ Adult situations, explicit language
Dir: Norman Jewison   *Cast:* Cher, Nicolas Cage, Vincent Gardenia, Olympia Dukakis, Danny Aiello, John Mahoney
▶ Magical look at love, Italian-American style. Brooklyn widow Cher, about to settle into a passionless marriage with Aiello, is pursued by his wild one-handed brother Cage. Meanwhile, Cher's dad Gardenia showers trinkets on a red-headed cutie while her long-suffering mom· Dukakis meets wolfish NYU professor Mahoney. Perfect combination of romantic atmosphere, warmth, and deadpan dialogue, especially in the conversations between Cher and caustic-tongued Dukakis. Oscars for Cher, Dukakis, and John Patrick Shanley's brilliant script. A Best Picture nominee. **(CC)**

MORE AMERICAN GRAFFITI 1979
★ ★ PG Drama 1:51
☑ Adult situations, explicit language, violence
Dir: B.W.L. Norton   *Cast:* Candy Clark, Mackenzie Phillips, Ron Howard, Paul LeMat, Cindy Williams, Charles Martin Smith
▶ George Lucas produced but did not direct this satisfying sequel to his 1973 hit,

American Graffiti. Follow-up takes original characters into turbulent sixties: nerdy Smith fights in Vietnam, while on the homefront Williams and Howard marry and get caught in antiwar demonstrations. Clark becomes part of San Francisco counterculture, and LeMat finds romance with an Icelandic beauty. Some may find ambitious techniques and structure distracting. Great period score.

MORE THE MERRIER, THE 1943
★★★★ NR Comedy 1:44 B&W
Dir: George Stevens   *Cast:* Jean Arthur, Joel McCrea, Charles Coburn, Richard Gaines, Bruce Bennett
▶ Popular comedy based on Washington's World War II housing shortage, with Arthur a single woman who rents out a room to genial Coburn. Concerned about her love life, Coburn rents half his space to handsome Air Force mechanic McCrea. Buoyant romantic comedy received six Oscar nominations, with Coburn winning for his crusty Cupid. Remade with Cary Grant as *Walk, Don't Run.*

MORGAN: A SUITABLE CASE FOR TREATMENT 1966 British
★ NR Comedy 1:37 B&W
Dir: Karel Reisz   *Cast:* David Warner, Vanessa Redgrave, Robert Stephens, Irene Handl
▶ Talented but unstable painter Warner is divorced by wife Redgrave. Refusing to accept her remarriage to wealthy art dealer Stephens, he kidnaps her. Bittersweet comedy is sometimes eccentric, funny, and endearing but suffers from Reisz's dated visual tricks. Warner is super but it's hard to sympathize with his self-destructive character.

MORGAN STEWART'S COMING HOME 1987
★★★ PG-13 Comedy 1:28
☑ Explicit language
Dir: Alan Smithee   *Cast:* Jon Cryer, Lynn Redgrave, Nicholas Pryor, Paul Gleason, Viveka Davis
▶ Confused seventeen-year-old Cryer is brought home after years of boarding school to bolster dad Pryor's Senate campaign, which is based on family values. Redgrave, his uptight, no-nonsense mom, displays little patience or understanding. Convoluted plot involves corrupt aide Gleason, blackmail, a safe-deposit box, and a wild chase on girlfriend Davis's moped.

MORNING AFTER, THE 1986
★★★★ R Mystery-Suspense 1:43
☑ Brief nudity, adult situations, explicit language, violence
Dir: Sidney Lumet   *Cast:* Jane Fonda, Jeff Bridges, Raul Julia, Diane Salinger, Richard Foronjy, Geoffrey Scott
▶ Alcoholic actress Fonda wakes up with the ultimate hangover: a dead body in her bed and no memory of the night before. Bridges is the mysterious redneck who may be her saviour or her undoing. A quite satisfying thriller with Oscar-nominated Fonda and Bridges giving their all to unusually complex characterizations for the genre. Effectively moody direction by Lumet. **(CC)**

MORNING GLORY 1933
★★ NR Drama 1:14 B&W
Dir: Lowell Sherman   *Cast:* Katharine Hepburn, Douglas Fairbanks, Jr., Adolphe Menjou, Mary Duncan, C. Aubrey Smith
▶ Hepburn, a stagestruck New England girl, receives an indifferent welcome in New York until she meets promising playwright Fairbanks. Touching, small-scale, and somewhat dated drama was based on Zoe Akins's Broadway hit. Hepburn won her first Oscar for her glowing performance.

MOROCCO 1930
★★ NR Drama 1:32 B&W
Dir: Josef von Sternberg   *Cast:* Gary Cooper, Marlene Dietrich, Adolphe Menjou, Ulrich Haupt, Juliette Compton, Francis McDonald
▶ Moody drama about exotic nightclub singer Dietrich's infatuation with Foreign Legionnaire Cooper moves slowly, but Lee Garmes's stunning Oscar-nominated photography provides dazzling backdrop for romantic drama. Dietrich, who also received an Oscar nomination in her Hollywood debut, performs one of her most notorious songs, "What Am I Bid for These Apples."

MORONS FROM OUTER SPACE 1985 British
☆ PG-13 Comedy 1:26
☑ Explicit language, adult humor
Dir: Mike Hodges   *Cast:* Jimmy Nail, Mel Smith, Paul Brown, Joanne Pearce, Griff Rhys Jones, James B. Sikking
▶ Less-than-brilliant alien tourists from the planet Blob land in England, where they are transformed into international singing stars. Broad spoof has an engag-

ing opening and pockets of laughter, but overall it's predictable and lowbrow.

MORTUARY 1983
★ R Horror 1:31
☑ Nudity, adult situations, explicit language, violence
Dir: Howard Avedis *Cast:* Mary McDonough, David Wallace, Bill Paxton, Lynda Day George, Christopher George
▶ Young McDonough suspects her father's death was no accident and traces the killing to a crazed mortician's son who works in his father's embalming room. Gross low-budget horror.

MOSCOW DOES NOT BELIEVE IN TEARS 1980 Russian
★ ★ NR Drama 2:30
Dir: Vladimir Menschow *Cast:* Vera Alentova, Irina Muravyova, Raisa Ryazanova, Alexei Batalov, Alexander Fatiushin
▶ Three country women move to Moscow to seek fortunes and husbands. One marries an alcoholic hockey player, a second is impregnated and deserted by the father but becomes a successful factory boss, and the third has a happy marriage to a simple man. Old-fashioned, rambling soap opera offers insight into Russian lifestyle. Oscar for Best Foreign Film. Ⓢ

MOSCOW ON THE HUDSON 1984
★ ★ ★ R Comedy 1:57
☑ Nudity, adult situations, explicit language, mild violence
Dir: Paul Mazursky *Cast:* Robin Williams, Maria Conchita Alonso, Cleavant Derricks, Alejandro Rey, Savely Kramarov, Elya Baskin
▶ Russian musician Williams defects in Bloomingdale's and faces difficult (if often comic) adjustment to life in America. Making the transition easier are new girlfriend Alonso and black pal Derricks. A gentle and compassionate melting pot of laughter and tears. Brave and winning performance from Williams; his accent is perfect. **(CC)**

MOSQUITO COAST, THE 1986
★ ★ PG Action-Adventure 1:59
☑ Explicit language, violence
Dir: Peter Weir *Cast:* Harrison Ford, Helen Mirren, River Phoenix, Martha Plimpton, Andre Gregory
▶ Eccentric inventor Ford, disillusioned with life in America, moves his family to a Central American jungle. His attempt to build an ideal community is noble but misguided and ultimately tragic. Original and interesting adventure, beautifully mounted and artfully directed. Problem: although Ford brilliantly extends his acting range, it's almost impossible to empathize with his near-lunatic character. Based on Paul Theroux's best-selling novel. **(CC)**

MOST DANGEROUS GAME, THE 1932
★ ★ NR Mystery-Suspense 1:03 B&W
Dir: Ernest B. Schoedsack, Irving Pichel *Cast:* Joel McCrea, Fay Wray, Leslie Banks, Robert Armstrong, Steve Clemento, Noble Johnson
▶ McCrea, Wray, and Armstrong are shipwrecked on an island ruled by Russian count Banks. Although treated hospitably at first, the three quickly learn that Banks intends to use them as prey in a sadistic hunt. Gripping, genuinely frightening adaptation of Richard Connell's famous story has been the unofficial inspiration for countless chase films.

MOTEL HELL 1980
★ R Horror 1:43
☑ Nudity, explicit language, graphic violence
Dir: Kevin Connor *Cast:* Rory Calhoun, Paul Linke, Nancy Parsons, Nina Axelrod, Wolfman Jack, Elaine Joyce
▶ Uneasy blend of horror and black comedy centered around the remote hotel where Farmer Vincent (Calhoun) prepares his famous sausages. Beautiful biker Axelrod discovers Vincent's horrifying secret ingredient, leading to bloody confrontations. Dueling chainsaws sequence provides the most laughs.

MOTHER LODE 1983
★ ★ PG Action-Adventure 1:43
☑ Explicit language, violence
Dir: Charlton Heston *Cast:* Charlton Heston, Nick Mancuso, Kim Basinger, John Marley
▶ City dwellers Mancuso and Basinger crash-land on a mountain lake while searching for a missing friend. They encounter Scottish prospector Heston whose crazy brother (also Heston) is killing anyone who comes near his claim. Gorgeous Canadian wilderness scenery, colorful if overbearing Heston (whose son Fraser wrote the script), and a rather turgid narrative.

MOTHRA 1962 Japanese
★ ★ NR Sci-Fi 1:41
Dir: Inoshiro Honda, Lee Kresel *Cast:*

Franky Sakai, Hiroshi Koizumi, Kyoko Kagawa, Emi Ito, Yumi Ito, Jerry Ito

► Six-inch-tall twin princesses are kidnapped from their island home by unscrupulous Kagawa for display in his nightclub. The girls pray to god Mothra for help and soon an enormous caterpillar hatches on their island. Creature makes its way to Tokyo in search of the girls, laying waste to Japan. Dubbed into English by Toho Studios, creators of the Godzilla and Gammera monsters.

MOUNTAIN FAMILY ROBINSON 1979
★★★★ G Family 1:39

Dir: John Cotter *Cast:* Robert Logan, Susan Damante Shaw, William Bryant, Heather Rattray, Ham Larsen, George "Buck" Flower

► Pa Robinson (Logan) and his family build a log cabin on the site of his uncle's mining claim in the Colorado Rockies. A mining agent wants to run them off the land, but friendly prospector Flower helps save the day. Good-natured family adventure from the makers of the *Wilderness Family* series.

MOUNTAIN MEN, THE 1980
★★★★ R Western 1:40

☑ Rape, adult situations, explicit language, graphic violence

Dir: Richard Lang *Cast:* Charlton Heston, Brian Keith, Victoria Racimo, Stephen Macht, John Glover, David Ackroyd

► Aided by sidekick Keith, Wyoming fur trapper Heston protects Racimo, the runaway wife of sadistic Indian chief Macht. Throwback to old-fashioned Westerns, written by Heston's son Fraser Clarke Heston. An extremely violent adventure.

MOUSE THAT ROARED, THE 1959 British
★★★ NR Comedy 1:23

Dir: Jack Arnold *Cast:* Peter Sellers, Jean Seberg, David Kossoff, William Hartnell, Monty Landis

► Grand Fenwick, the smallest nation on Earth, declares war on the U.S. in the hopes of being defeated and reaping the benefits of foreign aid. The country accidentally captures a bomb inventor and becomes a feared power. Nifty political satire with Sellers hilarious in three roles: the wily prime minister, a bumbling field marshal, and the Grand Duchess.

MOVE OVER, DARLING 1963
★★★ NR Comedy 1:43

Dir: Michael Gordon *Cast:* Doris Day,

James Garner, Polly Bergen, Chuck Connors, Thelma Ritter, Don Knotts

► Garner is set to marry Bergen when his wife Day, believed dead after a plane crash five years before, shows up very much alive and attempts to win him back. Day is perky and Garner solid in this consistently amusing remake of 1940's *My Favorite Wife.*

MOVERS & SHAKERS 1985
★ PG Comedy 1:19

☑ Adult situations

Dir: William Asher *Cast:* Walter Matthau, Charles Grodin, Vincent Gardenia, Tyne Daly, Bill Macy, Gilda Radner

► Hollywood studio head Matthau paid $1 million for the film rights to "Sex in Love," a self-help manual; now he has to convince screenwriter Grodin to turn it into a romance. Wry show biz satire written and produced by Grodin has a great cast, including cameos from Steve Martin and Penny Marshall, but takes too broad an approach to easy targets.

MOVIE MOVIE 1978
★★ PG Comedy 1:46 C/B&W

☑ Explicit language

Dir: Stanley Donen *Cast:* George C. Scott, Trish Van Devere, Red Buttons, Barry Bostwick, Harry Hamlin, Art Carney

► Delightful comedy/homage to 1930s flicks is divided into two parts: the black-and-white "Dynamite Hands" about delivery boy Hamlin who turns boxer to pay for his sister's eye operation, and the color musical "Baxter's Beauties of 1933" about dying producer Scott putting together one last Broadway hit. Never less than genial and often quite diverting. A great cast with droll Scott and disarming Bostwick (singing and dancing "Just Shows to Go Ya") the standouts.

MOVING 1988
★★ R Comedy 1:29

☑ Explicit language, adult humor

Dir: Alan Metter *Cast:* Richard Pryor, Beverly Todd, Dave Thomas, Dana Carvey, Randy Quaid, Stacey Dash

► New Jersey transit engineer Pryor uproots his family for a new job in Idaho. Slapstick complications include Ramboesque neighbor Quaid, psychopathic driver Carvey, and the world's worst moving team. Small cameos by Rodney Dangerfield and Morris Day add to the fun. (CC)

MOVING VIOLATIONS 1985
★★★ PG-13 Comedy 1:31
☑ Adult situations, explicit language, adult humor
Dir: Neil Israel   *Cast:* John Murray, Jennifer Tilly, James Keach, Brian Backer, Ned Eisenberg, Clara Peller
▶ Rambunctious comedy about students in a compulsory driver education class consists of a series of broad skits in the style of *Police Academy*. Leading man Murray delivers a studied imitation of his brother Bill; Sally Kellerman and Fred Willard offer amusing cameos. (CC)

MR. & MRS. SMITH 1941
★★★ NR Comedy 1:35 B&W
Dir: Alfred Hitchcock   *Cast:* Carole Lombard, Robert Montgomery, Gene Raymond, Jack Carson, Philip Merivale, Lucile Watson
▶ Sprightly screwball farce about quarrelsome but devoted husband and wife, Montgomery and Lombard, who discover that their marriage isn't legal. Comic misunderstandings force Montgomery to move to his men's club while his law partner Raymond pursues Lombard. Unusual project for Hitchcock, who directed as a favor for his close friend Lombard.

MR. BILLION 1977
★★ PG Action-Adventure 1:33
☑ Explicit language
Dir: Jonathan Kaplan   *Cast:* Terence Hill, Valerie Perrine, Jackie Gleason, Slim Pickens, Chill Wills, Dick Miller
▶ Italian mechanic Hill inherits a billion dollars, but he must reach San Francisco within twenty days to inherit the money. Gleason, a lawyer who covets the fortune, throws every possible obstacle in Hill's way. Cross-country chase with comic overtones offers a full range of cliff-hanging situations. (CC)

MR. BLANDINGS BUILDS HIS DREAM HOUSE 1948
★★★★ NR Comedy 1:34 B&W
Dir: H. C. Potter   *Cast:* Cary Grant, Myrna Loy, Melvyn Douglas, Reginald Denny, Sharyn Moffett, Connie Marshall
▶ Tired of their cramped apartment, Manhattanites Grant and Loy purchase a dream house in Connecticut. Their troubles start when architect Denny informs them he'll have to raze the house and build a new one from scratch. Homeowners will sympathize with this amusing adaptation of Eric Hodgins's best-selling novel. An interesting contrast to the similar plot of 1986's *The Money Pit*.

MR. DEEDS GOES TO TOWN 1936
★★★ NR Comedy 1:58 B&W
Dir: Frank Capra   *Cast:* Gary Cooper, Jean Arthur, Lionel Stander, George Bancroft, Douglas Dumbrille
▶ Small-town tuba player Longfellow Deeds (Cooper) inherits $20 million dollars. Big-city reporter Arthur exploits him to sell papers but then falls for the big galoot. When Coop wants to give his fortune to the needy, unscrupulous business types attempt to have him declared insane. Funny, sweet, and endearing Capra classic is a joy. Marvelous chemistry between Cooper and Arthur. Film introduced phrase "pixilated" to the American public. Oscar for Best Director, nominations for Picture, Actor (Cooper), Screenplay, Sound.

MR. HOBBS TAKES A VACATION 1962
★★★★ NR Comedy 1:57
Dir: Henry Koster   *Cast:* James Stewart, Maureen O'Hara, Fabian, Lauri Peters, Lili Gentle, John Saxon
▶ Witty satire on family togetherness. St. Louis banker Stewart and wife O'Hara rent a ramshackle West Coast beach house, but their vacation is almost ruined by a series of humorous calamities. O'Hara fends off advances from amorous yacht club member Reginald Denny, daughter Peters is so upset by her new braces that she won't go on dates, etc. As expected, Stewart handles each disaster with aplomb. (CC)

MR. HULOT'S HOLIDAY 1954 French
★ NR Comedy 1:26 B&W
Dir: Jacques Tati   *Cast:* Jacques Tati, Nathalie Pascaud, Michelle Rolla, Valentine Camax, Louis Perrault, Andre DuBois
▶ Shy and clumsy bachelor Tati takes a vacation on the Britanny coast, oblivious to the chaos created by his every move. Gags include misadventures in a kayak, disruption of several card games, and finale in a fireworks factory. Employing slapstick humor and his superb skills as a mime, writer/director/star Tati uses very little dialogue and nonstop visual comedy in a style reminiscent of the early silent films. ⓢ

MR. LOVE 1986 British
★★ PG-13 Comedy 1:31

☑ Adult situations, explicit language, mild violence
Dir: Roy Battersby *Cast:* Barry Jackson, Maurice Denham, Margaret Tyzack, Julia Deakin
▶ Meek gardener Jackson, trapped in a bad marriage and despised by his own daughter, finds romance with several different lonely women, including usher Deakin. Odd film is slowly paced and may try your patience. Jackson is sympathetic and Deakin does an absolutely magnificent Ingrid Bergman impression. (CC)

MR. LUCKY 1943
★★★ NR Comedy 1:38 B&W
Dir: H. C. Potter *Cast:* Cary Grant, Laraine Day, Charles Bickford, Gladys Cooper, Alan Carney, Paul Stewart
▶ Breezy romantic comedy set in World War II. Crooked gangster Grant prepares a gambling night for a wealthy charity, planning to steal the money for his shipboard casino. He has second thoughts about the scheme when he meets beautiful charity official Day. Debonair Grant shows off his Cockney rhyming slang in this popular hit that led to a TV series.

MR. MAJESTYK 1974
★★ PG Action-Adventure 1:43
☑ Adult situations, explicit language, violence
Dir: Richard Fleischer *Cast:* Charles Bronson, Al Lettieri, Linda Cristal, Lee Purcell, Paul Koslo
▶ Watermelon grower Bronson, unjustly jailed for exploiting migrant workers, helps crimelord Lettieri escape from prison in return for his own freedom. Lettieri's men subsequently terrorize Bronson until he sets out for revenge. Unexpected plotting by Elmore Leonard raises this above other Bronson vehicles.

MR. MOM 1983
★★★★★ PG Comedy 1:31
☑ Adult situations, explicit language
Dir: Stan Dragoti *Cast:* Michael Keaton, Teri Garr, Martin Mull, Ann Jillian, Christopher Lloyd
▶ Detroit auto engineer Keaton loses his job and turns househusband, taking care of the kids while wife Garr gets a job in advertising. Garr is pursued by boss Mull and Keaton by neighbor Jillian but they stick together and overcome the problems of role reversal. Hugely popular comedy is uplifting and quite endearing. Keaton is more restrained than usual but

very appealing and the children are adorable. (CC)

MR. NICE GUY 1987
★ PG-13 Comedy 1:32
☑ Nudity, adult situations, explicit language
Dir: Henry Wolford *Cast:* Mike MacDonald, Jan Smithers, Joe Silver, Harvey Atkin, Howard Jerome
▶ Security guard MacDonald is hired by company specializing in killings and assassinations. MacDonald proves good at the gig, wins the heart of lady shrink Smithers, and takes on her mafioso father. Broad burlesque jokes but few real laughs.

MR. NORTH 1988
★★ PG Comedy 1:32
☑ Adult situations
Dir: Danny Huston *Cast:* Anthony Edwards, Robert Mitchum, Lauren Bacall, Harry Dean Stanton, Anjelica Huston, Mary Stuart Masterson
▶ In 1926 Newport, Edwards, a young tutor with mysterious powers, helps ailing millionaire Mitchum and foils scheming heirs. Sunny fable offers beguiling hero and comforting message although whimsical style is not for all tastes. Adaptation of a Thornton Wilder novel was final film for executive producer/co-writer John Huston; directing mantle was passed to son Danny.

MR. PEABODY AND THE MERMAID 1948
★★ NR Fantasy/Comedy 1:29 B&W
Dir: Irving Pichel *Cast:* William Powell, Ann Blyth, Irene Hervey, Andrea King, Clinton Sundberg
▶ Pre-*Splash* oddity features Powell as a fifty-year-old married man on the brink of a mid-life crisis. Vacationing in the Caribbean, he goes fishing and, instead of supper, snags mermaid Blyth. The problem: no one else can see her. Funniest scene: Powell tries to convince Blyth to wear a bra. Doesn't really work but, as always, the charming Powell can do no wrong. Script by Nunnally Johnson.

MR. SKEFFINGTON 1944
★★★ NR Drama 2:07 B&W
Dir: Vincent Sherman *Cast:* Bette Davis, Claude Rains, Walter Abel, Richard Waring, Marjorie Riordan, Charles Drake
▶ When her brother Waring steals money from Rains's bank, socialite Davis agrees to marry the banker if he'll drop charges.

After Waring dies in World War I, she divorces Rains for a life of hedonism in Europe. Diphtheria, a dishonest daughter, and World War II help bring about a reconciliation in this tumultuous soap opera. Tour-de-force Davis performance compensates for frequently soggy passages.

MR. SMITH GOES TO WASHINGTON 1939
★★★★ NR Drama 2:10 B&W
Dir: Frank Capra *Cast:* James Stewart, Jean Arthur, Claude Rains, Thomas Mitchell, Edward Arnold
▶ Innocent scout leader Stewart is appointed Senator and soon uncovers Washington corruption. Feeling that "lost causes are the only ones worth fighting for" and helped by secretary Arthur, Smith battles his one-time mentor Rains and ruthless boss Arnold over a fraudulent land scam. Stirring and memorable Capra classic; Stewart and Rains (both Oscar nominees) are superb. Climactic filibuster, with Stewart fighting fatigue and loss of voice to keep going, is enough to restore your faith in democracy. Best Picture nominee.

MRS. SOFFEL 1984
★★★ PG-13 Drama 1:51
☑ Adult situations, violence
Dir: Gillian Armstrong *Cast:* Diane Keaton, Mel Gibson, Matthew Modine, Edward Herrmann, Trini Alvarado
▶ A true story set in 1901 Pittsburgh: repressed warden's wife Keaton falls in love with prisoner Gibson and helps him escape. They become lovers on the lam, pursued by the law. Keaton and Gibson provide passion but sluggish script and dim lighting dampen their fire. Resourceful but heavy-handed direction from Australian Armstrong. **(CC)**

MUGSY'S GIRLS 1985
☆ R Comedy 1:30
☑ Adult situations, explicit language
Dir: Kevin Brodie *Cast:* Ruth Gordon, Laura Brannigan, Eddie Deezen, James Marcel, Joanna Dierek, Rebecca Forstadt
▶ Sorority girls need money to pay off their house mortgage so they enter a Las Vegas mud wrestling tournament. Singer Brannigan (making her film debut) and old pro Gordon (as the house mother) deserve better than this crude college comedy.

MUMMY, THE 1932
★★★ NR Horror 1:12 B&W
Dir: Karl Freund *Cast:* Boris Karloff, Zita Johann, David Manners, Edward Van Sloan, Arthur Byron, Bramwell Fletcher
▶ Archaeologists ignore warnings on an Egyptian sarcophagus, unleashing a malicious mummy condemned to eternal life for a taboo love affair. Spunky heroine Johann, who resembles his ancient sweetheart, summons Egyptian goddesses to escape his dusty embrace. Eerie horror film accomplishes more through suggestive atmosphere than explicit violence. Inspired four sequels and a British remake in 1959.

MUMMY, THE 1959 British
★★ NR Horror 1:28
Dir: Terence Fisher *Cast:* Peter Cushing, Christopher Lee, Yvonne Fumeaux, Eddie Byrne, Felix Aylmer, Raymond Huntley
▶ Lively remake of the 1932 classic shows the dire consequences when arrogant archaeologist Cushing robs an ancient Egyptian grave. Mummy Lee pursues Cushing's expedition back to London, where he kidnaps beautiful reincarnation of his dead lover. Fast-paced and frightening production helped rejuvenate moribund horror genre.

MUNCHIES 1987
★ PG Comedy 1:22
☑ Adult situations, explicit language, violence
Dir: Bettina Hirsch *Cast:* Harvey Korman, Charles Stratton, Nadine Van Der Velde, Alix Elias, Charlie Phillips, Paul Bartel
▶ Anthropologist Korman discovers a lovable furry creature, which his son Stratton hopes to market. The scientist's brother steals the animal, which unexpectedly multiplies and transforms into a bevy of vicious killers. Low-budget thriller modeled after *Gremlins* takes some funny digs at consumerism.

MUPPET MOVIE, THE 1979
★★★★★ G Comedy/Family 1:34
Dir: James Frawley *Cast:* The Muppets, Charles Durning, Richard Pryor, Steve Martin, Bob Hope, Mel Brooks
▶ Kermit heads for Hollywood to break into show biz and is pursued by Doc Hopper (Durning), who wants him as spokesfrog for a chain of fried-frogs'-legs franchises. "A whole nation of frogs on little tiny crutches," fears Kermit. Great family

entertainment: kids will love the antics of Miss Piggy and company, adults will enjoy movie references and big star cameos (the funniest is Martin's surly waiter). Hummable Paul Williams songs include the Oscar-nominated "Rainbow Connection."

MUPPETS TAKE MANHATTAN, THE
1984
★ ★ ★ ★ ★ G Comedy/Family 1:34
Dir: Frank Oz *Cast:* The Muppets, Dabney Coleman, Art Carney, Joan Rivers, Liza Minnelli, Lonny Price
▶ Kermit and friends, a big hit with a college variety show, try to make it on the Great White Way. Shyster lawyer Coleman and a case of frog amnesia are two of the obstacles on the road to Broadway success and a possible Kermit/Miss Piggy wedding. Well-honed fun from Jim Henson's troupe. Our favorite scene: the rats cook breakfast. **(CC)**

MURDER BY DEATH 1976
★ ★ ★ ★ PG Comedy 1:34
☑ Adult situations, explicit language
Dir: Robert Moore *Cast:* Peter Falk, Peter Sellers, Alec Guinness, Maggie Smith, Eileen Brennan, James Coco
▶ Eccentric millionaire Lionel Twain (Truman Capote) invites the world's super sleuths to dinner and a murder in Neil Simon's hysterically funny parody of great fictional film detectives. Guests include Sam Diamond (Falk), Sidney Wang (Sellers), Nick and Nora Charleston (Smith and David Niven), Jessica Marbles (Elsa Lancaster), and Milo Perrier (Coco). Guinness is the blind butler, Nancy Walker the deaf cook. Tour-de-force performances from sterling cast; twisty plot done with mirrors.

MURDER BY DECREE 1979
Canadian/British
★ ★ ★ ★ PG Mystery-Suspense 2:04
☑ Graphic violence
Dir: Bob Clark *Cast:* Christopher Plummer, James Mason, Donald Sutherland, Genevieve Bujold, David Hemmings, John Gielgud
▶ Sherlock Holmes (Plummer) investigates Jack the Ripper's murders of prostitutes in Victorian London and comes across a cover-up involving highly placed people. Satisfying mystery provides sturdy, old-fashioned plotting with a dash of post-Watergate cynicism. Director Clark creates a nice sense of danger lurking in the foggy streets. Amusing

chemistry between Plummer's surprisingly outgoing Holmes and Mason's deliciously droll Watson.

MURDERERS' ROW 1966
★ NR Espionage/Action-Adventure 1:48
Dir: Henry Levin *Cast:* Dean Martin, Ann-Margret, Karl Malden, Camilla Sparv, Beverly Adams, Jacqueline Fontaine
▶ Madman Malden threatens Washington with a deadly Helio Beam; dashing secret agent Matt Helm (Martin) defeats him while rescuing the beam's inventor and his mod daughter, Ann-Margret. Poor sequel to *The Silencers* is a strained spy spoof with music ("I'm Not the Marrying Kind," "If You're Thinking What I'm Thinking," etc.).

MURDER, MY SWEET 1944
★ ★ ★ NR Mystery-Suspense 1:35 B&W
Dir: Edward Dmytryk *Cast:* Dick Powell, Claire Trevor, Anne Shirley, Otto Kruger, Mike Mazurki, Miles Mander
▶ Hulking ex-con Mazurki hires private eye Philip Marlowe (Powell) to find his girlfriend, but the seemingly easy case turns into a nightmare of drugs, theft, and murder. First-rate adaptation of Raymond Chandler's *Farewell, My Lovely* ranks among the best of 1940s mysteries. Crooner Powell revived a flagging career with his first tough-guy role, and received excellent support from Trevor and Shirley as the treacherous women in the mystery.

MURDER ONE 1988 Canadian
★ R Crime 1:35
☑ Rape, nudity, adult situations, explicit language, graphic violence
Dir: Graeme Campbell *Cast:* Henry Thomas, James Wilder, Stephen Shellen, Errol Slue
▶ A grim true story: Georgia convicts Wilder and Shellen break out of prison, pick up little brother Thomas, and go on a brutal spree of rape and murder. Straightforward, generally well acted (although Thomas has little to do but look shocked), but repellent; the violent last half hour is especially hard to watch.

MURPHY'S LAW 1986
★ ★ ★ ★ R Action-Adventure 1:37
☑ Nudity, explicit language, graphic violence
Dir: J. Lee Thompson *Cast:* Charles Bronson, Kathleen Wilhoite, Carrie

Snodgrass, Robert F. Lyons, Richard Romanus, Angel Tompkins

▶ Tough cop Bronson is framed for murdering his ex-wife by Snodgrass, a killer he once sent to jail. Bronson escapes while handcuffed to foulmouthed teen Wilhoite. They grow to be friends while he attempts to nab Snodgrass. Violent and distasteful although Bronson fans will like the action. Suitably nasty performance by Snodgrass. **(CC)**

MURPHY'S ROMANCE 1985
★ ★ ★ ★ ★ **PG-13 Romance/Comedy 1:48**
☑ Brief nudity, adult situations, explicit language
Dir: Martin Ritt   **Cast:** Sally Field, James Garner, Brian Kerwin, Corey Haim, Dennis Burkley

▶ Newly divorced Field and twelve-year-old son Haim move to a small town in Arizona to run a horse ranch. Crusty town druggist Garner helps her establish the ranch. Their budding, May-September romance is threatened by the unexpected appearance of her ne'er-do-well ex-husband Kerwin. Effortlessly good, comic leads glorify old-fashioned values. *Saturday Evening Post* feeling to homespun details: all-American drug store, barbeque, and square dance. Fresh and flavorful. **(CC)**

MUSCLE BEACH PARTY 1964
★ ★ **NR Comedy 1:34**
Dir: William Asher   **Cast:** Frankie Avalon, Annette Funicello, Luciana Paluzzi, John Ashley, Don Rickles, Rock Stevens

▶ "Surf's up!" Frankie and Annette take on weight-lifting bullies hogging the beach. Great example of 1960s camp has surprising bonuses: songs by Beach Boys' Brian Wilson, "Little" Stevie Wonder's screen debut, Peter Lorre's last performance (in an unbilled cameo), and early role by Rock Stevens (later Peter Lupus of TV's "Mission: Impossible"). Followed by *Bikini Beach*.

MUSIC MAN, THE 1962
★ ★ ★ ★ ★ **G Musical 2:31**
Dir: Morton Da Costa   **Cast:** Robert Preston, Shirley Jones, Buddy Hackett, Hermione Gingold, Paul Ford, Ron Howard

▶ Professor Harold Hill (Preston) convinces the gullible townsfolk of River City, Iowa, that he can teach their children music through his so-called Think Method. His conscience is pricked when

he falls for local librarian Jones. Brassy, supremely entertaining Meredith Wilson musical is as American as apple pie. Preston is marvelous as the charismatic con man in a role he created on Broadway. Won Oscar for Best Song Score (including such well-loved tunes as "Till There Was You" and "Seventy-Six Trombones"). **(CC)**

MUSSOLINI: THE DECLINE AND FALL OF IL DUCE 1985
★ ★ ★ **NR Biography/MFTV 1:52**
☑ Violence
Dir: Alberto Negrin   **Cast:** Susan Sarandon, Anthony Hopkins, Bob Hoskins, Annie Girardot, Barbara De Rossi

▶ Sweeping portrait focuses on the years 1943–45 in the life of the Italian dictator Mussolini (Hoskins) and the bitter political and family struggle as his son-in-law Hopkins opposes the Germans, who order Il Duce to execute him. Well-crafted epic filmed on location in Italy.

MUTANT 1984
★ **R Horror 1:39**
☑ Adult situations, explicit language, violence
Dir: John Cardos   **Cast:** Wings Hauser, Lee Montgomery, Jody Medford, Mark Clement, Cary Guffey, Jennifer Warren

▶ When his brother is killed by zombies, products of nearby toxic waste, Hauser seeks revenge. Some good chills and zombie transformations but plagued by poor production: the film quality is so murky that it's difficult to figure out what's going on.

MUTILATOR, THE 1985
☆ **R Horror 1:26**
☑ Nudity, adult situations, explicit language, violence
Dir: Buddy Cooper   **Cast:** Matt Mitler, Ruth Martinez, Bill Hitchcock, Frances Raines, Morley Lampley

▶ Father is driven crazy when his little son accidentally kills mom. Ten years later at a beach house, the son and his teen pals are savagely mutilated one by one. Is it dad on the loose? Few surprises in this amateurish entry in the slasher genre.

MUTINY ON THE BOUNTY 1935
★ ★ ★ ★ **NR Action-Adventure 2:12 B&W**
Dir: Frank Lloyd   **Cast:** Clark Gable, Charles Laughton, Franchot Tone, Herbert Mundin, Eddie Quillan, Donald Crisp

▶ Virile, commanding adventure outshines its subsequent remakes. The familiar story of the 1787 mutiny has Gable as mutiny leader Fletcher Christian, Laughton as evil Captain Bligh, and Tone as the midshipman caught between the two. Oscar for Best Picture and Best Actor nominations to the three leads.

MY AMERICAN COUSIN 1985
Canadian
★ PG Drama 1:25
☑ Adult situations, explicit language
Dir: Sandy Wilson *Cast:* Margaret Langrick, John Wildman, Richard Donat, Jane Mortifee
▶ Rural Canada, summer 1959: bored twelve-year-old Langrick, battling with mom Mortifee about boys and rock music, develops a wild crush on her California cousin Wildman, a James Dean-like stud. Wry observations, believable performances, gorgeous scenery, but a little too predictable and low-key.

MY BEAUTIFUL LAUNDRETTE 1986 British
★★ R Comedy/Drama 1:38
☑ Nudity, adult situations, explicit language
Dir: Stephen Frears *Cast:* Daniel Day-Lewis, Gordon Warnecke, Saeed Jaffrey, Roshan Seth, Shirley Anne Field, Rita Wolf
▶ In a shabby, racially torn London neighborhood, young Pakistani Warnecke and his Cockney lover Day-Lewis take over a failing laundry and turn it into a sleek neon moneymaker. Warnecke also deals with bigotry and sexual intrigue within his own upwardly mobile family. Alternately jolly and sad art film makes sharp social comment; overloaded plot and thick accents may render it inaccessible to some. **(CC)**

MY BEST FRIEND IS A VAMPIRE 1988
★★★ PG Comedy 1:29
☑ Explicit language
Dir: Jimmy Huston *Cast:* Robert Sean Leonard, Evan Mirand, Cheryl Pollak, René Auberjonois, Fannie Flagg, David Warner
▶ Texas grocery boy Leonard, seduced by a mysterious woman, is puzzled by his growing teeth and sudden aversion to garlic until Auberjonois explains that he's become a vampire. Can he still win a date with pretty musician Pollak while avoiding demented vampire killer Warner? Predictable but pleasant comedy with a nice soundtrack (Blondie, Timbuk 3, etc.). **(CC)**

MY BLOODY VALENTINE 1981
Canadian
★★ R Horror 1:31
☑ Adult situations, explicit language, graphic violence
Dir: George Mihalka *Cast:* Paul Kelman, Lori Hallier, Neil Affleck, Keith Knight, Alf Humphreys
▶ After a twenty-year hiatus, the people of Valentine Bluffs hold a fair in honor of their patron saint. Youngsters explore a nearby cave, ignoring warnings about the murderer buried there during the last fair. Subsequent pickax killings include good jolts for gore fans.

MY BODYGUARD 1980
★★★★ PG Comedy 1:35
☑ Explicit language, violence
Dir: Tony Bill *Cast:* Chris Makepeace, Adam Baldwin, Matt Dillon, Joan Cusack, Ruth Gordon, Martin Mull
▶ Makepeace, a transfer student at a Chicago high school, becomes the victim of punks led by Dillon until he hires menacing older classmate Baldwin as his bodyguard. Modest, appealing comedy benefits from an honest script, realistic characters, and fine supporting cast.

MY BRILLIANT CAREER 1979 Australian
★★★ G Drama 1:40
Dir: Gillian Armstrong *Cast:* Judy Davis, Sam Neill, Wendy Hughes, Robert Grubb, Max Cullen, Pat Kennedy
▶ In the nineteenth-century Australian outback, a headstrong girl of limited means rejects the safety of marriage to become a writer. Davis is remarkable in her film debut as the unconventional heroine; Neill, her suitor, is properly romantic. Stunning locations enhance this uplifting drama, based on a semiautobiographical novel by Miles Franklin.

MY CHAUFFEUR 1986
★★ R Comedy 1:37
☑ Nudity, adult situations, explicit language
Dir: David Beaird *Cast:* Deborah Foreman, Sam J. Jones, Sean McClory, Howard Hesseman, E. G. Marshall, Penn and Teller
▶ Exclusive limo service is forced to hire woman driver Foreman; manager Hesseman gives her horrible assignments to break her spirit. But Foreman's bubbly personality wins over the other drivers, and she also manages to snag boss's son Jones. Disarming throwback to 1930s screwball comedies is effectively light

and smooth. Film debut for magician team Penn and Teller.

MY DARLING CLEMENTINE 1946
★ ★ ★ ★ NR Western 1:37 B&W
Dir: John Ford *Cast:* Henry Fonda, Linda Darnell, Victor Mature, Walter Brennan, Tim Holt, Cathy Downs
▶ When his brother is murdered on a cattle drive, Wyatt Earp (Fonda) becomes sheriff of Tombstone to find his killers. Earp forms an uneasy alliance with the tubercular Doc Holliday (Mature) while gathering evidence against the evil Clanton gang. Vivid characters, particularly Brennan as Old Man Clanton, exceptional photography, and a plot crammed with memorable sequences—climaxing in an exciting rendering of the famous gunfight at OK Corral—make this outstanding Western one of the true classics of the genre. **(CC)**

MY DEMON LOVER 1987
★ PG-13 Comedy 1:26
☑ Adult situations, explicit language, violence
Dir: Charlie Loventhal *Cast:* Scott Valentine, Michelle Little, Arnold Johnson, Robert Trebor, Alan Fudge, Gina Gallego
▶ Uneven blend of horror and comedy: young Little is a loser in love until she meets Valentine, who has the unfortunate habit of turning into various monsters whenever he's aroused. Little sets out to prove that her new boyfriend isn't a serial killer dubbed the Mangler. Stars outdo iffy special effects.

MY DINNER WITH ANDRE 1981
☆ PG Drama 1:50
☑ Explicit language
Dir: Louis Malle *Cast:* Wallace Shawn, Andre Gregory, Jean Lenauer, Roy Butler
▶ Playwright Shawn meets his friend Gregory, an experimental theater director, for dinner. Over their meal Gregory regales Shawn with stories about his search for the meaning of life. One-of-a-kind film was a surprise art-house hit despite divided critical reception. Nonstop talk is occasionally engrossing, sometimes obscure and pretentious.

MY FAIR LADY 1964
★ ★ ★ ★ ★ G Musical 2:50
Dir: George Cukor *Cast:* Rex Harrison, Audrey Hepburn, Stanley Holloway, Wilfrid Hyde-White, Gladys Cooper, Jeremy Brett
▶ Upper-crust English professor Henry Higgins (Harrison) attempts to transform Cockney flower girl Eliza Doolittle (Hepburn) into a respectable lady. Simply grand: Harrison is wonderfully imperious, Hepburn is winningly winsome, and the showstopping Lerner and Loewe score includes "The Rain in Spain," "On the Street Where You Live," and "Get Me to the Church on Time" (sung by Oscar-nominated Holloway). Eight Oscars, for Best Picture, Director, Actor (Harrison), Cinematography, Costume Design (Cecil Beaton), Music, Art Direction, and Sound. Based on the Broadway musical inspired by George Bernard Shaw's *Pygmalion*. **(CC)**

MY FAVORITE BRUNETTE 1947
★ ★ ★ NR Comedy 1:29 B&W
Dir: Elliott Nugent *Cast:* Bob Hope, Dorothy Lamour, Peter Lorre, Lon Chaney, Jr., Reginald Denny
▶ Glamorous Lamour mistakes baby photographer Hope for a hard-boiled private eye, and involves him in a search for a missing baron. Prime Hope vehicle crammed with quips, sight gags, and funny performances (particularly Lorre's self-parody of a menacing villain). Also available in a colorized version.

MY FAVORITE WIFE 1940
★ ★ ★ ★ NR Comedy 1:28 B&W
Dir: Garson Kanin *Cast:* Cary Grant, Irene Dunne, Randolph Scott, Gail Patrick, Ann Shoemaker, Scotty Beckett
▶ Dunne, lost at sea for seven years, returns home to find hubby Grant married to Patrick. Grant calls off his honeymoon, only to learn that Dunne was marooned with handsome bodybuilder Scott. Stars are in peak form in this delightfully effervescent comedy of errors. Received three Oscar nominations, including Best Story.

MY FAVORITE YEAR 1982
★ ★ ★ PG Comedy 1:29
☑ Adult situations, explicit language, adult humor
Dir: Richard Benjamin *Cast:* Peter O'Toole, Mark Linn-Baker, Jessica Harper, Joseph Bologna, Lainie Kazan, Bill Macy
▶ "If I were truly plastered, could I do this?" asks flamboyant film star O'Toole as he drunkenly somersaults into rehearsals for a live comedy TV show in 1950s New York. Concerned host Bologna assigns young writer Linn-Baker to keep O'Toole

out of trouble. Linn-Baker fails miserably but memorably as the two men form a close relationship. Wonderfully sweet and winning; dominated by O'Toole's glorious Oscar-nominated turn as the aging swashbuckler. Highlights: O'Toole's gallant dance with an elderly admirer and the Central Park ride on horseback.

MY FRIEND FLICKA 1943
★★★★★ NR Family 1:29
Dir: Harold Schuster *Cast:* Roddy McDowall, Preston Foster, Rita Johnson, James Bell, Jeff Corey
▶ Rancher's son McDowall yearns for a horse, but chooses a colt his father (Foster) thinks too wild to tame. McDowall persists, and through hard work trains Flicka to be a loyal companion. Sensitive, moving adaptation of Mary O'Hara's novel is an excellent example of a children's film that parents can also enjoy. Led to a long-running TV series.

MY LIFE AS A DOG 1987 Swedish
★★ PG-13 Comedy/Drama 1:41
☑ Nudity, adult situations
Dir: Lasse Hallstrom *Cast:* Anton Glanzelius, Tomas von Bromssen, Anki Liden, Melinda Kinnaman, Kicki Rundgren
▶ When his mother falls fatally ill, young Glanzelius is packed off to live with relatives in a rural village populated by a cast of endearing eccentrics. Beneath the adolescent high jinks lurks the boy's ongoing struggles with guilt, loss, and his first love. More than just another coming-of-age tale, this Oscar nominee is graced with compelling warmth, wit, and wisdom and a sweetly artless performance by Glanzelius. Hallstrom was nominated for Best Director. Also available in a dubbed version. ⑤

MY LITTLE CHICKADEE 1940
★★★ NR Comedy 1:23 B&W
Dir: Edward Cline *Cast:* W. C. Fields, Mae West, Joseph Calleia, Dick Foran, Margaret Hamilton, Donald Meek
▶ West loves mysterious masked bandit Calleia, but enters a marriage of convenience with Fields, a card sharp who takes their marriage vows a bit too seriously. Low-key Western spoof never catches fire, but the card games and a memorable wedding night with a goat are prime Fields scenes. The two stars wrote the screenplay.

MY LITTLE PONY, THE MOVIE 1986
★★★★★ G Animation 1:30
Dir: Michael Joens *Cast:* Voices of Danny DeVito, Madeline Kahn, Cloris Leachman, Rhea Perlman, Tony Randall
▶ Wicked witch threatens carefree Ponyland with a living slime called "the Smooze." Will the pastel Ponies see their world turned to shades of gray? Tiny tots will be kept in suspense by this feature-length pitch for Little Pony products. (CC)

MY MAN ADAM 1985
★★ R Comedy 1:24
☑ Nudity, adult situations, explicit language, violence
Dir: Roger L. Simon *Cast:* Raphael Sbarge, Page Hannah, Veronica Cartwright, Dave Thomas
▶ Restless teen Sbarge daydreams of being a famous journalist. His fantasies and much more come true when Hannah involves him in exposing a car-theft ring. He gets the scoop and the girl. Walter Mitty–like premise is sabotaged by meandering plot. (CC)

MY MAN GODFREY 1936
★★★★ NR Comedy 1:35 B&W
Dir: Gregory La Cava *Cast:* William Powell, Carole Lombard, Alice Brady, Eugene Pallette, Gail Patrick, Mischa Auer
▶ Daffy heiress Lombard wins a society treasure hunt with the help of Powell, a down-and-out but curiously civilized hobo. When she hires him as a butler, Powell straightens out her wacky household. Exceptional screwball comedy whose social points make sense today; received six Oscar nominations, including Auer's hilarious supporting role as a gorilla-impersonating gigolo.

MYRA BRECKENRIDGE 1970
☆ R Comedy 1:34
☑ Rape, nudity, strong sexual content, adult situations, explicit language
Dir: Michael Sarne *Cast:* Mae West, John Huston, Raquel Welch, Rex Reed, Farrah Fawcett, Jim Backus
▶ West, starring in her first film in thirty-seven years at the age of seventy-eight, plays a film critic who undergoes a sex-change operation before launching an attack on America's love affair with virile male movie stars. Embarrassingly bad adaptation of Gore Vidal's controversial novel concentrates exclusively on leering innuendos and double entendres.

MY SCIENCE PROJECT 1985
★★★ PG Sci-Fi/Comedy 1:35

☑ Explicit language, violence
Dir: Jonathan Betuel *Cast:* John Stockwell, Fisher Stevens, Danielle von Zerneck, Raphael Sbarge, Dennis Hopper, Richard Masur
▶ High school senior Stockwell needs a science project to graduate and comes up with a whopper when he stumbles upon a relic from outer space. Soon he's warping through time and wreaking havoc on his hometown until he decides some things are better left alone. Hopper steals the show as a hippie science teacher.

MY STEPMOTHER IS AN ALIEN 1988
★★★ PG-13 Sci-Fi/Comedy 1:50
☑ Adult situations, explicit language, adult humor
Dir: Richard Benjamin *Cast:* Dan Aykroyd, Kim Basinger, Jon Lovitz, Alyson Hannigan
▶ Alien Basinger arrives on Earth to learn how scientist Aykroyd sent her planet off course. Basinger finds both earthly phenomena (like cheeseburgers and Jimmy Durante songs) and Aykroyd fascinating, leading to intergalactic marriage. Cheerful fun as Aykroyd effectively plays straight man to the effervescent Basinger. Lovitz adds some mirth as Aykroyd's horny brother.

MYSTERIOUS ISLAND 1961
★★★ NR Fantasy/Action-Adventure 1:41
Dir: Cy Endfield *Cast:* Michael Craig, Joan Greenwood, Michael Callan, Gary Merrill, Herbert Lom
▶ Union soldiers escape Confederate prison via balloon, crash-land at sea, and are washed up on the shores of a strange island containing giant creatures, pirates, Captain Nemo (Lom), and a live volcano. Exciting escapist fantasy from the pages of Jules Verne. Ray Harryhausen special effects wizardry and Bernard Herrmann score add to the fun. (CC)

MYSTERY MANSION 1984
★★ PG Family 1:35
☑ Violence
Dir: David E. Jackson *Cast:* Dallas McKennon, Greg Wynne, Randi Brown, Jane Ferguson
▶ Young Brown explores the secrets of a spooky mansion with crusty old caretaker McKennon. A pair of escaped convicts in pursuit of buried treasure terrorize the girl and kidnap her aunt, but McKennon

scares them away with fake ghosts. Standard family fare with enough diversion for young and old alike.

MYSTIC PIZZA 1988
★★★ R Romance 1:42
☑ Adult situations, explicit language
Dir: Donald Petrie *Cast:* Julia Roberts, Annabeth Gish, Lili Taylor, Vincent D'Onofrio, William R. Moses, Adam Storke
▶ Roberts, Gish, and Taylor, waitresses at Mystic Pizza restaurant in Connecticut, have summer of romantic ups and downs: Taylor faints before fiancée D'Onofrio at the altar, Gish falls for married Moses, and poor girl Roberts gets involved with rich law student Storke. Winning cast transcends familiar material.

MY TUTOR 1983
★★★ R Comedy 1:37
☑ Nudity, strong sexual content, adult situations, explicit language, adult humor
Dir: George Bowers *Cast:* Caren Kaye, Matt Lattanzi, Kevin McCarthy, Bruce Bauer, Arlene Golonka, Crispin Glover
▶ Sexy tutor Kaye is retained by wealthy Southern California family to assure that son Lattanzi gets into Yale. Guess what she winds up teaching him? Credible romance and some better-than-average comic bits. Look for Glover in a small turn as a horny high school chum.

NADINE 1987
★★★ PG Comedy 1:23
☑ Explicit language, violence
Dir: Robert Benton *Cast:* Jeff Bridges, Kim Basinger, Rip Torn, Gwen Verdon, Glenne Headly, Jerry Stiller
▶ In 1954 Austin, manicurist Basinger is trying to recover revealing photos from photographer Stiller when someone murders him over a valuable map. Basinger and her soon-to-be-ex-husband Bridges fall in love all over again as they battle bad guy Torn for possession of the map. Good-natured, if unoriginal, diversion. Handsome Bridges and saucy Basinger make an attractive couple. (CC)

NAKED AND THE DEAD, THE 1958
★★★ NR War 2:13
Dir: Raoul Walsh *Cast:* Aldo Ray, Cliff Robertson, Raymond Massey, William Campbell, Richard Jaeckel, James Best
▶ Hard-hitting World War II adventure about a doomed platoon's efforts to occupy a Pacific island. Officers Robertson and Massey argue over the welfare of

their unit; Ray and his men—including Joey Bishop and L. Q. Jones—encounter fierce resistance from the Japanese. Adapted from Norman Mailer's novel.

NAKED CAGE, THE 1986
★ R Action-Adventure 1:37
☑ Nudity, adult situations, explicit language, violence
Dir: Paul Nicholas *Cast:* Shari Shattuck, Angel Tompkins, Lucinda Crosby, Christina Whitaker, Faith Minton, Stacey Shaffer
▶ Innocent bank clerk Shattuck takes the rap for a robbery masterminded by Whitaker. They are sentenced to a women's prison run by Tompkins, an evil lesbian warden. Crosby, a guard trying to expose Tompkins's corruption, befriends Shattuck and rescues her during a tear gas attack. Low-budget exploitation relies on predictable material.

NAKED CITY, THE 1948
★★★ NR Crime 1:36 B&W
Dir: Jules Dassin *Cast:* Barry Fitzgerald, Howard Duff, Dorothy Hart, Don Taylor, Ted de Corsia, House Jameson
▶ Veteran New York cop Fitzgerald and young partner Taylor investigate the brutal slaying of a blond and bring the killer to justice by persistent legwork. Quite gripping. Landmark semidocumentary style effectively uses New York locations. Oscars for Cinematography and Editing. Spawned TV series.

NAKED FACE, THE 1985
★★★ R Drama 1:45
☑ Brief nudity, adult situations, explicit language, violence
Dir: Bryan Forbes *Cast:* Roger Moore, Rod Steiger, Elliott Gould, Art Carney, Anne Archer, David Hedison
▶ Cops Steiger and Gould try to pin a series of murders on Chicago psychiatrist Moore (in a change of pace from his James Bond roles) whose court testimony endangered a colleague. Moore hires eccentric private eye Carney to clear his name. Slick adaptation of Sidney Sheldon's first novel with an above-average cast.

NAKED GUN, THE: FROM THE FILES OF POLICE SQUAD 1988
★★★★ PG-13 Comedy 1:30
☑ Adult situations, explicit language, adult humor
Dir: David Zucker *Cast:* Leslie Nielsen, Priscilla Presley, Ricardo Montalban, George Kennedy, O. J. Simpson, Reggie Jackson
▶ When partner Simpson is nearly killed, L.A. cop Nielsen investigates and uncovers crooked mogul Montalban's plot to assassinate visiting Queen Elizabeth. Hilarious from beginning (Simpson turns getting shot into comic art), through middle (Nielsen and Presley frolicking in MTV-style romantic montage), to end (Nielsen disguised as umpire in the funniest baseball game in recent memory). Straight-faced Nielsen demonstrates genuine comic flair; amusing cameo from Jackson as outfielder turned brainwashed assassin.

NAKED JUNGLE, THE 1954
★★★ NR Action-Adventure 1:35
Dir: Byron Haskin *Cast:* Eleanor Parker, Charlton Heston, William Conrad, Abraham Sofaer
▶ In South America, mail-order bride Parker finds her plantation-owner husband Heston a cold fish. When an army of soldier ants descends on the place, they band together to fight them and fall in love. Interesting, unusual premise generates maximum suspense. Great special effects, strong chemistry between Parker and Heston. Underrated and worth a look.

NAKED PREY, THE 1966
★★★★ NR Action-Adventure 1:34
Dir: Cornel Wilde *Cast:* Cornel Wilde, Gert van de Berg, Ken Gampu, Patrick Mynhardt, Jose Sithole, Richard Mashiya
▶ In the 1860s, an ivory expedition is ambushed by natives led by Gampu. Wilde, the only survivor, is given a short head start before murderous warriors chase him through the jungle. Harrowing adventure shot in a documentary style on fascinating African locations received a Best Screenplay nomination.

NAKED SPUR, THE 1953
★★★★ NR Western 1:31
Dir: Anthony Mann *Cast:* James Stewart, Janet Leigh, Robert Ryan, Ralph Meeker, Millard Mitchell
▶ Obsessed bounty hunter Stewart and two untrustworthy partners—grizzled prospector Mitchell and dishonorably discharged soldier Meeker—capture bandit Ryan in the Colorado Rockies. As they return to Abilene, Ryan preys on the weaknesses of his captors, using greed and fear to arrange an escape. Unusu-

ally sophisticated Western features taut direction, masterful acting, and an incisive, Oscar-nominated screenplay. Highly recommended to fans of the genre.

NAME OF THE ROSE, THE 1986
Italian/German/French
★★★ R Mystery-Suspense 2:09
☑ Nudity, adult situations, violence
Dir: Jean-Jacques Annaud   *Cast:* Sean Connery, F. Murray Abraham, Christian Slater, William Hickey, Ron Perlman, Michael Lonsdale
▶ From the Umberto Eco best-seller set in Northern Italy, 1327. Liberal monk Connery and young protégé Slater solve a series of monastery murders. The shadow of the Inquisition (led by evil Abraham) looms over the investigation. A thinker's mystery plot, eerily atmospheric, marred by dismal pacing. Wise and witty performance by Connery holds it together. Best scenes: Connery's advice to Slater about women and his confession of his own dark secret.   (CC)

NAPOLEON 1927 French
★ G Biography 3:55 C/B&W
Dir: Abel Gance   *Cast:* Albert Dieudonne, Gina Manes, Vladimir Roudenko, Antonin Artaud, Pierre Batcheff, Abel Gance
▶ Monumental silent epic on the life of Napoleon (Dieudonne), from his childhood through his courtship of Josephine (Manes) and triumphant military campaign in Italy. Lost for years, this version was reconstructed in 1981 by historian Kevin Brownlow and released with a new score by Carmine Coppola. Film's best effects (particularly the stunning, hand-colored, three-screen climax) may not transfer well to TV.

NAPOLEON AND SAMANTHA 1972
★★★★ G Action-Adventure/Family 1:31
Dir: Bernard McEveety   *Cast:* Johnnie Whitaker, Jodie Foster, Michael Douglas, Will Geer, Henry Jones, Rex Holman
▶ Oregon kids Whitaker and Foster adopt a circus lion. When Whitaker's grandfather Geer dies, the kids, preferring the company of mountain man Douglas to being put in a state institution, run away with their feline friend. First-rate Disney fare.

NASHVILLE 1975
★ R Comedy/Drama 2:39

☑ Nudity, adult situations, explicit language, violence
Dir: Robert Altman   *Cast:* Lily Tomlin, Keith Carradine, Ronee Blakley, Henry Gibson, Karen Black, Gwen Welles
▶ Altman's look at country music characters and the dreams that bring them to Nashville. The most memorable: mother of two deaf children (Tomlin) having an affair with womanizing singer Carradine, country music star Blakley suffering nervous breakdown, and no-talent Welles humiliated into becoming a stripper. Some may find the seeming lack of focus disconcerting; however, the film is as richly populated as a Dickens novel. Five Oscar nominations included Best Picture and Supporting Actresses Blakley and Tomlin; won for Best Song (Keith Carradine's "I'm Easy").

NASHVILLE GIRL 1976
★★ R Drama 1:30
☑ Nudity, adult situations, explicit language
Dir: Gus Trikonis   *Cast:* Monica Gayle, Glenn Corbett, Roger Davis, Johnny Rodriguez, Jesse White
▶ Raped by a neighbor, young Gayle leaves her farm for Nashville, determined to become a country-western star. But success doesn't come easy: she is forced to work in a massage parlor and sleep with phony agents and producers before recording her songs. Sincere but predictable drama with a strong country-western soundtrack. Film debut for pop star Rodriguez, who plays himself. Also known as *New Girl in Town* and *Country Music Daughter.*

NASTY HABITS 1977
★ PG Comedy 1:32
☑ Adult situations, explicit language
Dir: Michael Lindsay-Hogg   *Cast:* Glenda Jackson, Melina Mercouri, Geraldine Page, Sandy Dennis, Anne Jackson, Anne Meara
▶ The Watergate scandal in nun's clothing: scheming sister Jackson plots to win election to succeed the dying abbess through burglary and bugging. Great cast, ingenious idea—but the one joke wears thin very quickly and the Nixonian satire is now dated.

NATE AND HAYES 1983 U.S./New Zealand
★★★ PG Action-Adventure 1:40
☑ Explicit language, graphic violence
Dir: Ferdinand Fairfax   *Cast:* Tommy

Lee Jones, Michael O'Keefe, Max Phipps, Jenny Seagrove

▶ In a characterization based on an actual historical figure, good-hearted pirate Bully Hayes (Jones) teams up with missionary O'Keefe to rescue Seagrove, O'Keefe's kidnapped fiancée. Convincing period re-creation of 1880s South Seas, lovely New Zealand scenery, plenty of action, but unconvincing performances, feeble humor and screenplay.

NATIONAL LAMPOON'S CLASS REUNION 1982
★ R Horror/Comedy 1:25
☑ Nudity, adult situations, explicit language, violence
Dir: Michael Miller *Cast:* Gerrit Graham, Michael Lerner, Stephen Furst, Zane Buzby, Anne Ramsey, Shelley Smith

▶ Tenth-year reunion for the class of 1972 at Lizzie Borden High. Gathered for the festivities are a stuffy yacht salesman, the class prig, a fat guy, and other odd types. The antics get out of hand when someone starts bumping off the alumni. Overstated satire, ludicriously scripted and unevenly acted, has a few clever bits. Chuck Berry guest stars but doesn't even sing one whole song.

NATIONAL LAMPOON'S EUROPEAN VACATION 1985
★★★ PG-13 Comedy 1:30
☑ Nudity, explicit language, adult humor
Dir: Amy Heckerling *Cast:* Chevy Chase, Beverly D'Angelo, Dana Hill, Jason Lively, Victor Lanoux, Eric Idle

▶ All-American dad Clark W. Griswold (Chase) from *National Lampoon's Vacation* is back with his family on a European jaunt won on a game show. Perils of London driving, French women, and Italian kidnappings are some of the comic mishaps that befall the merry bunch. Chase is funny and there is some amusing slapstick although not quite up to the original. **(CC)**

NATIONAL LAMPOON'S VACATION 1983
★★★★ R Comedy 1:38
☑ Nudity, adult situations, explicit language, adult humor
Dir: Harold Ramis *Cast:* Chevy Chase, Beverly D'Angelo, Imogene Coca, Randy Quaid, Anthony Michael Hall, John Candy

▶ Middle-class dad Clark Griswold (Chase) takes wife D'Angelo and kids on a cross-country trip to "Wally World," a Disneyland-like theme park. Some unlucky but very funny situations follow: visits with redneck relative Quaid, obnoxious aunt Coca, a St. Louis ghetto detour, and an encounter with stunning blond model Christie Brinkley who flirts with Chase. Lively, outrageous, frequently rib-tickling; Chase anchors the craziness with surprising humanity.

NATIONAL VELVET 1945
★★★★★ G Drama/Family 2:05
Dir: Clarence Brown *Cast:* Mickey Rooney, Elizabeth Taylor, Donald Crisp, Anne Revere, Angela Lansbury, Juanita Quigley

▶ Heartwarming family film follows the adventures of young Taylor and ex-jockey Rooney as they train a long shot for England's Grand National steeplechase. Sterling performances by all involved, with Crisp in grand form as Taylor's crusty father. Revere received a Supporting Oscar as her sensitive mother; climactic race helped win an Oscar for editor Robert Kern. Followed in 1977 by *International Velvet.* **(CC)**

NATIVE SON 1986
★ PG Drama 1:52
☑ Explicit language, violence
Dir: Jerrold Freedman *Cast:* Victor Love, Matt Dillon, Elizabeth McGovern, Geraldine Page, Oprah Winfrey, Akosua Busia

▶ Chicago, 1930s: young black Love is hired as chauffeur to wealthy white family. He accidentally kills their daughter, is caught, and put on trial. Well-intentioned but rather slow-moving adaptation of Richard Wright's classic novel. Good cast but subdued filmmaking never catches fire. **(CC)**

NATURAL, THE 1984
★★★★★ PG Drama/Sports 2:18
☑ Adult situations, explicit language, violence
Dir: Barry Levinson *Cast:* Robert Redford, Robert Duvall, Glenn Close, Kim Basinger, Barbara Hershey

▶ Redford plays Roy Hobbs, the baseball natural whose promising career is cut short by madwoman Hershey's bullet. Sixteen years later, Hobbs makes a comeback, overcoming his injury, self-doubts, and the allure of femme fatale Basinger to win the World Series and first love Close. Purists disliked this slick and sanitized adaptation of Bernard Malamud's darkly Arthurian fable, but Redford and the all-star cast shimmer in Caleb Deschanel's lustrous cinematography. (CC)

NAVIGATOR, THE 1924
★★★ NR Comedy 1:00 B&W
Dir: Donald Crisp, Buster Keaton *Cast:* Buster Keaton, Kathryn McGuire, Frederick Vroom, Noble Johnson, Clarence Burton, Donald Crisp
▶ Keaton, a millionaire completely inept in the real world, is stranded on a luxury liner adrift in the ocean and deserted except for McGuire, a dizzy heiress who has repeatedly rejected his marriage proposals. Classic silent comedy is filled with unusually inventive and daring sight gags.

NEAR DARK 1987
★ R Horror 1:35
☑ Explicit language, graphic violence
Dir: Kathryn Bigelow *Cast:* Adrian Pasdar, Jenny Wright, Lance Henriksen, Bill Paxton, Jenette Goldstein, Joshua Miller
▶ Young cowboy Pasdar is lured into a traveling pack of vampires by strange but pretty Wright. He reluctantly takes part in their deadly games but eventually turns against them. Wonderfully fresh and original variation on vampire theme is technically and visually superb. Some may find the strong violence unpleasant.

NECROPOLIS 1987
☆ R Horror 1:17
☑ Nudity, adult situations, explicit language, violence
Dir: Bruce Hickey *Cast:* Leeanne Baker, Jacquie Fitz, Michael Conte, William K. Reed, Jett Julian
▶ Baker, a three-hundred-year-old witch disguised as a black-leather punker, preys on Manhattan's homeless. Local reverend Reed joins puzzled cop Conte in battling her. Dismal low-budget effort with poor acting and shoddy special effects.

NEIGHBORS 1981
★ R Comedy 1:35
☑ Adult situations, explicit language
Dir: John G. Avildsen *Cast:* John Belushi, Dan Aykroyd, Cathy Moriarty, Kathryn Walker, Igors Gavon, Tim Kazurinsky
▶ There goes the neighborhood as shameless couple Aykroyd and Moriarty move next door to stoical suburbanite

Belushi and wife Walker. New arrivals proceed to disrupt Belushi's staid existence. Adaptation of the Thomas Berger novel gets off to a strong start with Belushi doing surprisingly well in his quiet role; humor lags in the second half.

NEON MANIACS 1986
★★ R Horror 1:31
☑ Brief nudity, adult situations, explicit language, violence
Dir: Joseph Mangine *Cast:* Alan Hayes, Leilani Sarelle, Donna Locke, Victor Elliott Brandt
▶ Monsters ambush teenagers partying under San Francisco's Golden Gate Bridge. Police won't believe Sarelle, the only survivor, so she teams up with boyfriend Hayes and amateur filmmaker Locke to destroy the menace. Average horror entry with an agreeable sense of humor and a full quota of gore.

NETWORK 1976
★★★★ R Comedy 2:01
☑ Brief nudity, adult situations, explicit language
Dir: Sidney Lumet *Cast:* Faye Dunaway, William Holden, Peter Finch, Robert Duvall, Ned Beatty, Beatrice Straight
▶ "I'm mad as hell and I'm not gonna take it anymore!" With these words, TV news anchorman Finch revives his faltering career and becomes the popular "mad prophet of the airwaves." Although veteran newsman Holden worries that friend Finch is really mad as a hatter, ruthless executive Dunaway exploits the situation for big ratings. Blistering and brilliant satire of television with Oscarwinning performances by Finch (his last role), Dunaway, and Straight (for one great scene as Holden's wronged wife); also won for Original Screenplay (Paddy Chayefsky).

NEVADA SMITH 1966
★★★ NR Western 2:15
Dir: Henry Hathaway *Cast:* Steve McQueen, Karl Malden, Brian Keith, Arthur Kennedy, Suzanne Pleshette, Pat Hingle
▶ When his parents are murdered by outlaws, half-breed McQueen enlists the aid of sharpshooter Keith in tracking them down. Sturdy Western features hardedged action and a strong cast (including Martin Landau's sneaky villain). McQueen's character is based on a role played by Alan Ladd in 1964's *The Car-*

petbaggers. Remade for TV in 1975 with Cliff Potts.

NEVER CRY WOLF 1983
★ ★ ★ ★ PG Action-Adventure 1:45
☑ Nudity, adult situations, explicit language, violence
Dir: Carroll Ballard *Cast:* Charles Martin Smith, Brian Dennehy, Zachary Ittimangnaq, Samson Jorah, Hugh Webster, Martha Ittimangnaq
▶ Biologist Smith is sent into the Canadian arctic to study wolves. The relationship that develops between him and the animals is moving yet subtle. Breathtaking cinematography and locations, intelligent ecological message, and humor (as when Smith snacks on mice to better understand his charges). Absorbing arctic adventure based on Farley Mowat's best-seller.

NEVERENDING STORY, THE 1984
German/British
★ ★ ★ ★ PG Fantasy/Family 1:34
☑ Violence
Dir: Wolfgang Petersen *Cast:* Noah Hathaway, Barret Oliver, Tami Stronach, Moses Gunn, Patricia Hayes, Gerald McRaney
▶ Little boy Oliver reads "special" book that tells of young warrior Hathaway's quest to stop a stormlike entity from destroying a fantasy world. Oliver enters the story to help save the day. Good-natured family adventure, filled with charming monsters, magic, and special effects. Imaginative direction by Petersen. (CC)

NEVER GIVE A SUCKER AN EVEN BREAK 1941
★ ★ NR Comedy 1:11 B&W
Dir: Edward Cline *Cast:* W. C. Fields, Gloria Jean, Margaret Dumont, Leon Errol, Franklin Pangborn, Susan Miller
▶ Crazy, wildly surreal bit of nonsense starts with Fields pitching movie idea to producer Pangborn. Story within the story has Fields falling out of an airplane in pursuit of his beloved bottle and visiting the mountaintop home of wealthy but monstrous Dumont. Free-falling fun was the great comic's last starring role.

NEVER ON SUNDAY 1960 Greek
★ ★ ★ NR Comedy 1:31 B&W
Dir: Jules Dassin *Cast:* Melina Mercouri, Jules Dassin, Titos Vandis, Mitsos Liguisos, Despo Diamantidou, George Foundas
▶ Greek prostitute Mercouri plies her trade six days a week but "never on Sunday." Visiting American intellectual Dassin takes Mercouri (his wife in real life) under his wing and tries to teach her a more legit lifestyle; in the end, it is Dassin who ends up learning from Mercouri. Mercouri's marvelous Oscar-nominated turn dominates this frisky tale. Title tune won Best Song Oscar; also nominated for screenplay and direction.

NEVER SAY NEVER AGAIN 1983
★ ★ ★ ★ PG
Espionage/Action-Adventure 2:14
☑ Brief nudity, adult situations, explicit language, violence
Dir: Irvin Kershner *Cast:* Sean Connery, Klaus Maria Brandauer, Max Von Sydow, Barbara Carrera, Kim Basinger, Bernie Casey
▶ Arch-villain Brandauer hijacks two cruise missiles to hold the world hostage, but doesn't count on the resolute superagent 007. High-spirited James Bond adventure based on *Thunderball,* with Connery making a welcome return after a thirteen-year absence to the role he originated. Carrera is especially alluring as the evil Fatima Blush.

NEVER TOO YOUNG TO DIE 1986
★ ★ R Action-Adventure 1:37
☑ Nudity, adult situations, explicit language, violence
Dir: Gil Bettman *Cast:* John Stamos, Vanity, Gene Simmons, George Lazenby, Peter Kwong
▶ Hermaphrodite Simmons kills agent Lazenby and plots to pollute Los Angeles water supply. Lazenby's son Stamos and lover Vanity team up to thwart Simmons and get revenge. Teenage James Bond–style thriller is poorly written but may appeal to fans of soap star Stamos and rock star Vanity. (CC)

NEW ADVENTURES OF PIPPI LONGSTOCKING, THE 1988
★ ★ ★ G Family 1:40
Dir: Ken Annakin *Cast:* Tami Erin, Eileen Brennan, Dennis Dugan, Dianne Hull, George DiCenzo, Dick Van Patten
▶ Separated from her sea captain father by a tidal wave, young Pippi washes ashore in small Florida town, where her pranks and practical jokes incur the wrath of mean orphanage mistress Brennan. Kids should enjoy elaborate food fights and special effects. Erin, in her film debut, is the perfect physical type for the

pigtailed heroine of Astrid Lindgren's classic children's novels.

NEW CENTURIONS, THE 1972
★ ★ ★ R Crime 1:43
☑ Adult situations, explicit language, graphic violence
Dir: Richard Fleischer *Cast:* George C. Scott, Stacy Keach, Jane Alexander, Scott Wilson, Rosalind Cash, Erik Estrada
▶ Rookie Los Angeles cop Keach is shown the ropes by grizzled old pro Scott. Keach's marriage to Alexander deteriorates under the pressures of police lifestyle; Scott falls apart when he is sent into retirement. Strong performances by Scott and Keach, but fans of the Joseph Wambaugh best-seller may be disappointed by the less-than-faithful screenplay.

NEW KIDS, THE 1985
★ ★ ★ R Mystery-Suspense 1:29
☑ Rape, explicit language, graphic violence
Dir: Sean S. Cunningham *Cast:* Shannon Presby, Lori Loughlin, James Spader, Eddie Jones, John Philbin, Eric Stoltz
▶ Orphaned by a car crash, teen siblings Presby and Loughlin move in with Florida relatives and run afoul of vicious local bullies. After the gang tries to rape Loughlin, the brother and sister fight back. Competently filmed but banal junior version of *Death Wish.* **(CC)**

NEW LAND, THE 1973 Swedish
★ ★ ★ ★ PG Drama 2:41
☑ Adult situations, explicit language, violence
Dir: Jan Troell *Cast:* Max Von Sydow, Liv Ullmann, Eddie Axberg, Monica Zetterlund, Hans Alfredson, Halvar Bjork
▶ Continuation of *The Emigrants,* set in the 1850s. Immigrant Swedish couple Von Sydow and Ullmann battle Indians, the rigors of the Minnesota climate, and personal hardships. Von Sydow's brother Axberg is lured to the California gold rush with tragic results. Lovely epic is grandly shot and acted, but leisurely pace requires patience. Nominated for Best Foreign Film Oscar.

NEW LEAF, A 1971
★ ★ G Comedy 1:42
☑ Adult situations
Dir: Elaine May *Cast:* Walter Matthau, Elaine May, Jack Weston, George Rose, William Redfield, James Coco
▶ His trust fund exhausted, aging liber-

tine Matthau woos wealthy but woefully klutzy botanist May, planning to murder her after their wedding. Uneven black comedy is not for all tastes, but director/writer/star May's script contains some priceless moments. Excellent support by Rose as an imperturbable valet and Weston as a scheming lawyer.

NEW LIFE, A 1988
★ ★ ★ PG-13 Comedy/Drama 1:45
☑ Adult situations, explicit language
Dir: Alan Alda *Cast:* Alan Alda, Ann-Margret, Hal Linden, Veronica Hamel, John Shea, Mary Kay Place
▶ Workaholic Wall Streeter Alda is divorced by wife Ann-Margret and gingerly enters the Manhattan singles scene. Both find new relationships with younger lovers: he with heart specialist Hamel and she with sculptor Shea. Alda's willingness to laugh at himself is endearing. Sometimes reaches for easy laughs but credible characters and situations pleasantly evoke real-life pains and joys. **(CC)**

NEWSFRONT 1978 Australian
★ PG Drama 1:51 C/B&W
☑ Brief nudity, adult situations, explicit language
Dir: Phillip Noyce *Cast:* Bill Hunter, Gerard Kennedy, Wendy Hughes, Angela Punch, Chris Haywood
▶ Original, absorbing drama about the rivalry between Hunter and Kennedy, brothers who work for competing newsreel companies in post–World War II Australia. Fresh approach to the subject uses actual documentary footage to round out the characters' lives. Technically impressive film provides a rewarding, nostalgic look at the period.

NEW YORK, NEW YORK 1977
★ ★ ★ PG Musical 2:43
☑ Explicit language
Dir: Martin Scorsese *Cast:* Liza Minnelli, Robert De Niro, Lionel Stander, Mary Kay Place, Diahnne Abbott, Dick Miller
▶ Lavish but downbeat musical about the troubled affair between saxophonist De Niro and singer Minnelli during the post–World War II Big Band era boasts a strong score by John Kander and Fred Ebb (title song, "There Goes the Ball Game," etc.) and good performances from the leads, but unfocused plot has tedious stretches. Abbott does a great "Honeysuckle Rose." Reissue and cassette versions also include "Happy End-

ings," a song cut from the original release.

NEW YORK NIGHTS 1984
★ R Sex 1:43
☑ Nudity, strong sexual content, adult situations, explicit language
Dir: Simon Nuchtern *Cast:* Corinne Alphen, George Ayer, Bobbi Burns, Cynthia Lee, Marcia McBroom, Willem Dafoe
▶ Anthology of nine erotic stories, set in modern-day New York and loosely based on *La Ronde.* In "The Porno Star and the Financier," Lee seduces William Dysart for a part in a mainstream film; "The Authoress and the Photographer" features a female boxing match; etc. Alphen, 1982 *Penthouse* Pet of the Year, performs an explicit striptease.

NEW YORK STORIES 1989
★ ★ PG Comedy/Drama 2:10
☑ Adult situations, explicit language
Dir: Woody Allen, Francis Coppola, Martin Scorsese *Cast:* Nick Nolte, Rosanna Arquette, Heather McComb, Talia Shire, Woody Allen, Mae Questel
▶ Anthology of three stories about Manhattan: in Scorsese's "Life Lessons," artist Nolte suffers through obsessive passion for Arquette; Coppola's "Life Without Zoe" concerns lively young McComb's adventures in and around the Sherry-Netherland hotel; Allen's "Oedipus Wrecks" takes a nagging mother joke to absurd and hilarious lengths. Among the many performers are Mia Farrow, Giancarlo Giannini, Don Novello, and Carole Bouquet.

NEXT STOP, GREENWICH VILLAGE 1976
★ ★ R Comedy 1:51
☑ Nudity, adult situations, explicit language
Dir: Paul Mazursky *Cast:* Lenny Baker, Shelley Winters, Ellen Greene, Christopher Walken, Antonio Fargas, Lois Smith
▶ In 1953, young Brooklynite Baker moves to Greenwich Village to live the life of a struggling actor. He endures romantic crisis with girlfriend Greene, hangs out with Village types like black homosexual Fargas, and deals with his overbearing Jewish mother Winters. Gently nostalgic coming-of-age story, quite warm and funny, was based on director Mazursky's own experience as an actor.

NIAGARA 1953
★ ★ ★ NR Mystery-Suspense 1:29
Dir: Henry Hathaway *Cast:* Marilyn Monroe, Joseph Cotten, Jean Peters, Casey Adams, Denis O'Dea, Richard Allan
▶ Disturbing film noir about newlywed femme fatale Monroe plotting the murder of her weak-willed husband Cotten, a veteran just released from a mental institution. Peters, a bride honeymooning at the same Niagara Falls motel, finds her loyalty and courage tested when the scheme takes an unexpectedly grim twist. Gritty drama catches Monroe on the verge of superstardom.

NICE GIRLS DON'T EXPLODE 1987
★ PG Comedy 1:32
☑ Brief nudity
Dir: Chuck Martinez *Cast:* Barbara Harris, Wallace Shawn, Michelle Meyrink, William O'Leary, Belinda Wells, James Nardini
▶ Slight, whimsical comedy about young Meyrink, who sets objects on fire when she thinks about romance—a major drawback when she falls in love. Mother Harris, who shares the curse, concocts goofy methods for dealing with men while Meyrink tries to explain her problem to boyfriend O'Leary.

NICHOLAS AND ALEXANDRA 1971
British
★ ★ ★ PG Drama 3:03
☑ Adult situations
Dir: Franklin J. Schaffner *Cast:* Michael Jayston, Janet Suzman, Roderic Noble, Tom Baker, Harry Andrews, Irene Worth
▶ Historically accurate epic about Nicholas (Jayston), the last Russian czar, and the events surrounding the 1917 Bolshevik revolution. Suzman is superb as Alexandra, the czarina mesmerized by mad monk Rasputin (Baker). Filled with interesting cameos (Laurence Olivier, Michael Redgrave, John Wood, etc.). Received six Oscar nominations, winning for Art Design and Costumes.

NICHOLAS NICKLEBY 1947
★ ★ NR Drama 1:48 B&W
Dir: Alberto Cavalcanti *Cast:* Derek Bond, Cedric Hardwicke, Alfred Drayton, Sally Ann Howes, Stanley Holloway
▶ When his father dies, young Nicholas Nickleby (Bond) takes teaching position at an orphanage run by a cruel family, then flees with a crippled pupil. Nicholas also protects his sister and his beloved

against rich, manipulative uncle Hardwicke. Old-fashioned sentiment and morality, painstakingly detailed costumes and sets, fascinating performances (especially Hardwicke) in this adaptation of the Charles Dickens classic.

NICKEL MOUNTAIN 1985
★★★★ NR Drama 1:28
☑ Brief nudity, adult situations, explicit language, violence
Dir: Drew Denbaum *Cast:* Michael Cole, Heather Langenkamp, Patrick Cassidy, Brian Kerwin, Grace Zabriskie, Don Beddoe
▶ Rural waitress Langenkamp refuses to have an abortion when boyfriend Cassidy deserts her for college. She forms a relationship with older diner owner Cole that deepens into true love. Polished, low-key tearjerker with a winning performance from Langenkamp. Based on a John Gardner novel.

NIGHT AND DAY 1946
★★ NR Biography/Musical 2:08
Dir: Michael Curtiz *Cast:* Cary Grant, Alexis Smith, Monty Woolley, Ginny Simms, Jane Wyman, Eve Arden
▶ Star-studded biography of Cole Porter (Grant), wealthy Ivy Leaguer who became a legendary composer only to suffer a crippling accident. Smith plays his loyal wife. Well-mounted production ignores controversy surrounding his private life for excellent renditions of his remarkable songs. Grant attempts "You're the Top"; Mary Martin re-creates her Broadway hit "My Heart Belongs to Daddy." Other tunes include "Begin the Beguine," "I've Got You Under My Skin," "Just One of Those Things," "What Is This Thing Called Love."

NIGHT AT THE OPERA, A 1935
★★★★ NR Comedy 1:32 B&W
Dir: Sam Wood *Cast:* The Marx Brothers, Allan Jones, Kitty Carlisle, Margaret Dumont, Sig Rumann
▶ Riotously funny classic has the brothers helping opera singer Jones outwit a nasty rival while Groucho battles Rumann for wealthy patron Dumont's affections. Highlights: the stateroom scene, Chico and Groucho negotiating the "sanity clause," the boys trying to disguise themselves as aviators for a City Hall ceremony.

NIGHT BEFORE, THE 1988
★★ PG-13 Comedy 1:25

☑ Adult situations, explicit language, mild violence
Dir: Thom Eberhardt *Cast:* Keanu Reeves, Lori Loughlin, Theresa Saldana, Trinidad Silva, Suzanne Snyder
▶ School beauty Loughlin attends prom with wimpy Reeves because she lost a bet. Date escalates into disaster as couple ends up on wrong side of the tracks and pimp Silva nabs Loughlin. Reeves rescues her and wins her heart. Engaging youth comedy gets better as it goes along; Reeves and Loughlin are tart and attractive. (CC)

NIGHTCOMERS, THE 1972 British
★★ R Drama 1:36
☑ Nudity, violence
Dir: Michael Winner *Cast:* Marlon Brando, Stephanie Beacham, Thora Hird, Harry Andrews, Verna Harvey, Christopher Ellis
▶ On a turn-of-the-century English estate, children Ellis and Harvey become obsessed with mysterious gardener Brando, who has an affair with their governess Beacham. Powerfully brooding performance by Brando. Inspired by Henry James's novel *The Turn of the Screw.*

NIGHT CROSSING 1982
★★★★ PG Action-Adventure/Family 1:46
☑ Mild violence
Dir: Delbert Mann *Cast:* John Hurt, Jane Alexander, Glynnis O'Connor, Beau Bridges, Doug McKeon, Ian Bannen
▶ Two dissident East German families attempt to escape their country via hot-air balloon. Their first effort fails so they try again while the authorities investigate. Terrific true story from Walt Disney Productions.

NIGHT FLYERS 1987
☆ R Sci-Fi 1:29
☑ Explicit language, violence
Dir: T. C. Blake (Robert Collector)
Cast: Catherine Mary Stewart, Michael Praed, John Standing, Lisa Blount, Michael Des Barres
▶ Something is menacing the crew aboard a twenty-first-century spaceship mission to an unexplored planet. Suspects include captain Praed and the craft's computer. Pleasing production values but *Alien* clone lacks the jolts that made its role model special.

NIGHTFORCE 1986
★★ R Action-Adventure 1:22
☑ Nudity, adult situations, explicit language, violence
Dir: Lawrence D. Foldes *Cast:* Linda Blair, James Van Patten, Chad McQueen, Cameron Mitchell, Richard Lynch, Dean R. Miller
▶ Central American revolutionary group kidnaps daughter of U.S. Senator Mitchell so he will reverse his position on their country. Blair leads the kidnapped girl's young pals in a rescue raid. Unbelievable and overly familiar, with dreadful script and direction. Almost succeeds at being unintentionally funny.

NIGHT GAMES 1980
★ R Drama 1:43
☑ Nudity, explicit language
Dir: Roger Vadim *Cast:* Cindy Pickett, Joanna Cassidy, Barry Primus, Paul Jenkins
▶ Memories of being raped leaves Californian Pickett frigid, much to husband Primus's chagrin. She retreats into a sexual fantasy world that becomes all too real when a scorned suitor tries to kill her. Titillating pulp has perky Cindy and lots of skin. Sunk by feeble flashbacks and laughable psychology.

NIGHTHAWKS 1981
★★★★ R Action-Adventure 1:39
☑ Adult situations, explicit language, graphic violence
Dir: Bruce Malmuth *Cast:* Sylvester Stallone, Billy Dee Williams, Lindsay Wagner, Rutger Hauer, Persis Khambatta, Nigel Davenport
▶ New York City cops Stallone and Williams pursue vicious international terrorist Hauer. Fast-paced and exciting action, especially when Hauer hijacks the Roosevelt Island tramway, overcomes story contrivances. Sly gives one of his best non-*Rocky* performances and Hauer is supremely menacing. Wagner is wasted in an undeveloped role as Stallone's ex-wife.

NIGHT IN CASABLANCA, A 1946
★★★ NR Comedy 1:25 B&W
Dir: Archie Mayo *Cast:* Groucho Marx, Harpo Marx, Chico Marx, Charles Drake, Lois Collier, Lisette Verea
▶ Groucho takes job at Hotel Casablanca not knowing that his three predecessors have been murdered. Treasure-seeking Nazis are the key to the killings; Groucho teams with Chico and Harpo to thwart them. Perhaps the best of the brothers' later efforts. Funniest bit: Harpo's classic reaction when criticized for leaning against building.

NIGHT IN HEAVEN, A 1983
★★ R Drama 1:23
☑ Nudity, adult situations, explicit language, mild violence
Dir: John G. Avildsen *Cast:* Christopher Atkins, Lesley Ann Warren, Robert Logan, Deborah Rush, Carrie Snodgress
▶ Teacher Warren, unhappily married to aerospace worker Logan, finds solace in the arms male stripper Atkins, who is also one of her students. Dull drama has uncertain tone and half-baked story. Includes brief scene of frontal male nudity. (CC)

NIGHT IN THE LIFE OF JIMMY REARDON, A 1988
★★ R Comedy 1:32
☑ Brief nudity, adult situations, explicit language
Dir: William Richert *Cast:* River Phoenix, Ann Magnuson, Meredith Salenger, Ione Skye, Louanne, Matthew Perry
▶ Phoenix plays a glib teen Lothario in a "what-a-night-I'm-having" comedy. Amid seductions and chaos, he tries to scam up airfare to escape to Hawaii with his girl, Salenger. Featuring director Richert's usual lunacy and literacy, film will disappoint those expecting ordinary coming-of-age fare; recommended for anyone with a taste for the ironic and offbeat. (CC)

NIGHTMARE ON ELM STREET, A 1984
★★★ R Horror 1:31
☑ Adult situations, explicit language, graphic violence
Dir: Wes Craven *Cast:* John Saxon, Ronee Blakley, Robert Englund, Heather Langenkamp, Amanda Wyss, Nick Corri
▶ The first appearance of now-infamous Freddy Krueger (Englund), the disfigured, finger-knived bogeyman who preys on promiscuous teens. Years ago vigilantes torched child murderer Freddy; he returns to lethally haunt the dreams of his killers' kids. Some slice-and-dice clichés, but for the most part director Craven manages to find real horror amid ordinary life. Mainly for fans of the genre. (CC)

NIGHTMARE ON ELM STREET, PART 2, A: FREDDY'S REVENGE 1985
★★★ R Horror 1:25

☑ Brief nudity, adult situations, explicit language, graphic violence
Dir: Jack Sholder *Cast:* Mark Patton, Robert Englund, Kim Myers, Robert Rusler, Clu Gulager, Hope Lange
▶ More rude awakenings from Freddy (Englund). New kid in town Patton learns too late to leave on his night light. Freddy takes over Patton's body; teen makes few new friends during spree of mayhem and murder. Patton's girlfriend Myers saves the day with exorcism, but only the naive believe Freddy won't crawl under the covers again soon. Squeamish stay away. **(CC)**

NIGHTMARE ON ELM STREET 3, A: DREAM WARRIORS 1987
★ ★ ★ R Horror 1:36
☑ Brief nudity, adult situations, explicit language, graphic violence
Dir: Chuck Russell *Cast:* Robert Englund, Heather Langenkamp, John Saxon, Patricia Arquette, Craig Wasson
▶ Seven nightmare-plagued Elm Street kids are sent to a psychiatric hospital, where intern Langenkamp (reprising her role from the series original) realizes Freddy is at work once again. Freddy's undying appeal and clever visual effects compensate for illogical script and some truly bad acting. Cameos by Dick Cavett and Zsa Zsa Gabor. **(CC)**

NIGHTMARE ON ELM STREET 4, A: THE DREAM MASTER 1988
★ ★ ★ R Horror 1:33
☑ Brief nudity, adult situations, explicit language, graphic violence
Dir: Renny Harlin *Cast:* Robert Englund, Lisa Wilcox, Rodney Eastman, Danny Hassel, Andras Jones, Tuesday Knight
▶ When Freddy returns to Elm Street (yes, a few people still live there) and quickly offs his dream dates from prior flicks, it's up to Wilcox, the new kid on the block, to do the screaming. She ultimately employs the services of the Dream Master, the guardian of good dreams. More body counts, quips from the affably demonic Freddy, and expensive special effects.

NIGHTMARES 1983
★ ★ R Horror 1:40
☑ Explicit language, graphic violence
Dir: Joseph Sargent *Cast:* Emilio Estevez, Richard Masur, Cristina Raines, Veronica Cartwright, Lance Henriksen, Moon Zappa

▶ Anthology pic featuring four horror tales of varying quality. Originally shot on a low budget for network TV but released theatrically, so effects are not up to par with rest of genre. Critics admired direction but felt writing was uneven. For dedicated thrillseekers only.

'NIGHT, MOTHER 1986
★ ★ ★ PG-13 Drama 1:36
☑ Adult situations, explicit language
Dir: Tom Moore *Cast:* Anne Bancroft, Sissy Spacek
▶ Overwhelmed by despair, Spacek calmly and methodically prepares to kill herself. Over the course of an hour and a half, her mother Bancroft tries to convince her life is worth living, no matter how bleak. Not for all tastes (some might be put off by the soul-baring), but two topflight actresses shine in a faithful adaptation of the Pulitzer prize-winning play by Marsha Norman. **(CC)**

NIGHT MOVES 1975
★ ★ R Mystery-Suspense 1:39
☑ Nudity, adult situations, violence
Dir: Arthur Penn *Cast:* Gene Hackman, Jennifer Warren, Susan Clark, Edward Binns, Melanie Griffith, James Woods
▶ L.A. detective Hackman, hired to find runaway teen Griffith, tracks her down to the Florida Keys and brings her home. The mystery deepens when someone is murdered in the seemingly cut-and-dried case. Moody, intelligent film noir, as much an allegory about social malaise as it is a mystery. Muddled plotting but solid performance by Hackman, sizzling one from the underrated Warren. One of the most overlooked films of the 1970s.

NIGHT OF THE COMET 1984
★ ★ PG-13 Sci-Fi 1:35
☑ Explicit language, violence
Dir: Thom Eberhardt *Cast:* Catherine Mary Stewart, Kelli Maroney, Robert Beltran, Mary Woronov, Geoffrey Lewis, Sharon Farrell
▶ Campy day-after saga of Southern Cal sisters Stewart and Maroney who are among the few to weather a comet's impact and lethal fallout. Battling zombies and survivalists, the valley girls search for the remnants of civilization and a couple of cute dudes. At least as silly as it sounds but nonetheless diverting. **(CC)**

NIGHT OF THE CREEPS 1986
★ ★ R Horror/Comedy 1:28 C/B&W
☑ Nudity, explicit language, graphic violence

Dir: Fred Dekker *Cast:* Jason Lively, Steve Marshall, Jill Whitlow, Tom Atkins
▶ In 1959, a young man is killed by an alien slug. In 1986, college students Lively and Marshall steal his corpse from lab for frat initiation, thus unleashing little creatures that turn people into murderous zombies. Dekker's tongue-in-cheek wit enlivens standard scare plot. Best line comes as zombies approach sorority house: "The good news is that your dates are here . . . the bad news is they're dead!"

NIGHT OF THE GENERALS 1967 British
★ ★ NR War/Mystery-Suspense 2:28
Dir: Anatole Litvak *Cast:* Peter O'Toole, Omar Sharif, Tom Courtenay, Donald Pleasence, Joanna Pettet, Christopher Plummer
▶ When a prostitute is brutally slain in 1942 Warsaw, German intelligence agent Sharif narrows the suspects to three top-ranking Nazi generals, including the ruthless O'Toole. Sharif tries to bring the killer to justice; the mystery widens to include a plot against Hitler and extends twenty years beyond the war. Tension-filled.

NIGHT OF THE HUNTER, THE 1955
★ ★ ★ ★ NR Drama 1:33 B&W
Dir: Charles Laughton *Cast:* Robert Mitchum, Shelley Winters, Lillian Gish, Evelyn Varden, Billy Chapin, Sally Jane Bruce
▶ Mitchum delivers an unforgettable performance as a psychopath posing as a minister who marries convict's widow Winters to search her house for hidden loot. Her children Chapin and Bruce escape with the money, but are pursued downriver by the preacher. Unnerving, dreamlike study of innocence and corruption was Laughton's only film as a director. Screenplay by James Agee.

NIGHT OF THE IGUANA, THE 1964
★ ★ ★ NR Drama 2:05 B&W
Dir: John Huston *Cast:* Richard Burton, Ava Gardner, Deborah Kerr, Sue Lyon, James Ward, Grayson Hall
▶ In Puerto Vallarta, hard-drinking former priest Burton works as tour guide and gets entangled with three women—pretty, young Lyon, spinsterish artist Kerr, and slatternly hotel owner Gardner—one of whom may be able to halt his physical and mental deterioration. Generally engrossing Tennessee Williams adaptation.

Burton, Gardner, and Kerr are outstanding; Oscar for Best Costume Design.

NIGHT OF THE JUGGLER 1980
★ ★ ★ R Action-Adventure 1:41
☑ Explicit language, graphic violence
Dir: Robert Butler *Cast:* James Brolin, Cliff Gorman, Richard Castellano, Abby Bluestone, Dan Hedaya, Julie Carmen
▶ Deranged kidnapper Gorman mistakenly abducts ex-cop Brolin's daughter. Brolin defies the police in an effort to rescue her. Well-executed chases dominate this relentless revenge film exploiting realistically seedy New York locations.

NIGHT OF THE LIVING DEAD 1968
★ ★ ★ ★ NR Horror 1:36 B&W
☑ Graphic violence
Dir: George A. Romero *Cast:* Duane Jones, Judith O'Dea, Russell Steiner, Karl Hardman, Keith Wayne, Judith Ridley
▶ Pursued by man-eating zombies, seven people in a farmhouse struggle to survive a night of terror. Grainy, low-budget pic was panned by critics for its ghoulish and graphic effects, but today the gore seems tame. Became one of the most successful cult films ever, acknowledged as genre classic and now frequently aped in commercials and videos. Romero went on to complete trilogy with *Dawn of the Dead* and *Day of the Dead*. Also available in a colorized version.

NIGHT PATROL 1984
★ ★ R Comedy 1:22
☑ Nudity, adult situations, explicit language, adult humor
Dir: Jackie Kong *Cast:* Linda Blair, Pat Paulsen, Jaye P. Morgan, Jack Riley, Billy Barty, Murray Langston
▶ Rookie cop Langston is transferred to the rough night shift—a schedule that interferes with his career as the Unknown Comic. He runs into further trouble when a thief steals his stand-up costume. Extremely broad slapstick with hit-or-miss gags and a lifeless performance by Blair. (CC)

NIGHT PORTER, THE 1974 Italian
★ R Drama 1:58
☑ Rape, nudity, strong sexual content
Dir: Liliana Cavani *Cast:* Dirk Bogarde, Charlotte Rampling, Philippe Leroy, Gabriele Ferzetti, Giuseppe Addobbati
▶ Unsettling examination of the sadomasochistic relationship between concentration camp guard Bogarde

and Rampling, one of his victims. Meeting again in 1958, they resume their affair. Controversial film takes a serious, nonexploitative approach to the subject, but graphic sexuality may offend some viewers.

NIGHT SCHOOL 1981
★ R Horror 1:28
☑ Nudity, adult situations, explicit language, graphic violence
Dir: Ken Hughes *Cast:* Leonard Mann, Rachel Ward, Drew Snyder, Joseph R. Sicari, Nicholas Cairis
▶ Boston cop Mann investigates a series of decapitations which lead to Snyder, a promiscuous anthropology professor at a women's college. Evidence of demonic cults hamper Mann's work. Routine slasher film enlivened by Ward, a sexy student, in her first major film role.

NIGHT SHIFT 1982
★★★★ R Comedy 1:46
☑ Nudity, adult situations, explicit language, violence
Dir: Ron Howard *Cast:* Michael Keaton, Shelley Long, Henry Winkler, Gina Hecht, Pat Corley, Bobby DiCicco
▶ Much-abused nebbish Winkler seeks peace through night job at a morgue, only to encounter manic colleague Keaton. Soon the odd couple are running an escort service out of the morgue and expanding into legit businesses. Winkler falls in love with Long, the sweetest of the hookers. Sanitized sitcom about prostitution, but many laughs, fine performances, and engaging romance. Keaton's feature debut made him a star.

NIGHTS IN WHITE SATIN 1986
★★ NR Musical 1:36
☑ Adult situations, explicit language
Dir: Michael Barnard *Cast:* Kenneth David Gilman, Priscilla Harris, Kim Waltrip, Michael Laskin, Pierre Manasse
▶ Successful fashion photographer Gilman discovers beautiful waif Harris and elevates her from skid row as she teaches him about life on the street. She becomes a hot model while he completes a photo book about the homeless. Fine soundtrack, pretty faces, and no soul or substance—for those who want their MTV in long doses.

NIGHTS OF CABIRIA 1957 Italian
★★ NR Drama 1:50
Dir: Federico Fellini *Cast:* Giulietta Masina, François Périer, Amadeo Nazzari, Aldo Silvani, Dorian Gray

▶ Kindhearted prostitute Masina has brief affair with movie star Nazzari and then falls for Périer. Her hopes for the straight life with him are cruelly dashed, but her essential optimism remains. Bittersweet drama has knockout performance by Masina (Fellini's wife). Oscar for Best Foreign Film; inspired the Broadway musical *Sweet Charity*. ⑤

NIGHT STALKER, THE 1987
★★★ R Mystery-Suspense 1:31
☑ Nudity, adult situations, explicit language, graphic violence
Dir: Max Kleven *Cast:* Charles Napier, Michelle Reese, Katherine Kelly Lang, Robert Viharo, Joey Gian, Robert Zdar
▶ Hard-drinking, often-suspended cop Napier pursues ritualistic murderer of prostitutes who appears to get stronger each time he kills. Standard rehashing of B-movie premise boasts brisk action, some barbed dialogue, and skid row hero.

NIGHTSTICK 1987
★★ R Action-Adventure 1:32
☑ Violence, explicit language
Dir: Joseph Scanlan *Cast:* Bruce Fairbairn, Kerrie Keane, Robert Vaughn, John Vernon, Leslie Nielsen
▶ Lone-wolf cop Fairbairn tracks three terrorists threatening to blow up Manhattan unless they're paid a $5 million ransom. Cop's bosses Vaughn and Nielsen argue, girlfriend Keane gets kidnapped, and he confronts the bad guys for a climatic shoot-out in a deserted warehouse.

NIGHT THE LIGHTS WENT OUT IN GEORGIA, THE 1981
★★★ PG Drama 1:52
☑ Brief nudity, adult situations, explicit language
Dir: Ronald F. Maxwell *Cast:* Kristy McNichol, Dennis Quaid, Mark Hamill, Don Stroud, Arlen Dean Snyder
▶ Country singer Quaid and his sister McNichol travel to Nashville. After getting into trouble with the law, Quaid is sentenced to a work farm; McNichol falls in love with cop Hamill, who tries to help him. Agreeable drama bears little resemblance to the hit title song. Quaid and McNichol perform on the soundtrack (which also includes country-western stars Glen Campbell and George Jones).

NIGHT THEY RAIDED MINSKY'S, THE 1969
★★★ PG Comedy 1:40

☑ Adult situations
Dir: William Friedkin   *Cast:* Jason Robards, Britt Ekland, Norman Wisdom, Forrest Tucker, Denholm Elliott, Elliott Gould
▶ Vaudeville comic Robards persuades naive Amish girl Ekland to perform a religious dance in order to thwart attempts by censors to close his theater. Flavorful account of the history of striptease humorously re-creates famous burlesque skits. Film debut for Gould; charming cameo by Bert Lahr in his last role. Narrated by Rudy Vallee. **(CC)**

NIGHT TO REMEMBER, A 1958 British
★★★★ NR Drama 2:03 B&W
Dir: Roy Ward Baker   *Cast:* Kenneth More, Ronald Allen, Robert Ayres, Honor Blackman, Anthony Bushell, David McCallum
▶ Authentic, documentary-style reconstruction of the famous 1912 wreck of the "unsinkable" *Titanic*, told from the perspective of second officer More as he oversees rescue operations. Large cast is uniformly impressive; vignettes of passengers are alternately touching and uplifting. Adapted by Eric Ambler from Walter Lord's best-selling book.

NIGHT TRAIN TO MUNICH 1940 British
★★★ NR Mystery-Suspense 1:35 B&W
Dir: Carol Reed   *Cast:* Margaret Lockwood, Rex Harrison, Paul Henreid, Basil Radford, Naunton Wayne
▶ On the eve of World War II, Nazi agent Henreid tries to use Lockwood to lead him to her father, an inventor, while British spy Harrison attempts to get her out of Germany. Nonstop thrills and tension in this absorbing wartime classic.

NIGHT WATCH 1973 British
★★ PG Drama 1:35
☑ Explicit language, violence
Dir: Brian G. Hutton   *Cast:* Elizabeth Taylor, Laurence Harvey, Billie Whitelaw, Robert Lang, Tony Britton
▶ When her husband dies in a car accident, Taylor suffers a nervous breakdown. After recovering, she witnesses what may be a murder across the street, but her suave second husband Harvey insists she's hallucinating. Uneven thriller from a Lucille Fletcher play relies too heavily on red herrings.

NIGHTWING 1979
★★ PG Horror 1:45
☑ Explicit language, violence
Dir: Arthur Hiller   *Cast:* Nick Mancuso,

David Warner, Kathryn Harrold, Stephen Macht, Strother Martin, Ben Piazza
▶ Mancuso, a sheriff on an Arizona Indian reservation, and his girlfriend Harrold, a nurse, join exterminator Warner in battling a plague of vampire bats. Infrequent tense moments are obscured by subplots involving spiritualism, Indian rights, and Macht's scheme to steal mineral deposits. Based on Martin Cruz Smith's novel.

9½ WEEKS 1986
★★ R Romance/Drama 1:53
☑ Nudity, strong sexual content, adult situations, explicit language
Dir: Adrian Lyne   *Cast:* Mickey Rourke, Kim Basinger, Margaret Whitton, David Margulies, Christine Baranski
▶ Screen adaptation of Elizabeth McNeill's novel about an obsessive, all-consuming love affair between Wall Street wheeler-dealer Rourke and art gallery employee Basinger that lasts as long as the title indicates. Recently divorced, Basinger is shy about sex until Rourke seduces her into some of his kinky fantasies. Plenty of erotic spark between the leads. Video version is more explicit than theatrical release.

9 DEATHS OF THE NINJA 1985
★★★ R Martial Arts 1:34
☑ Adult situations, explicit language, graphic violence
Dir: Emmett Alston   *Cast:* Sho Kosugi, Brent Huff, Emmila Leshah, Blackie Dammett, Regina Richardson
▶ Manila tourist bus is hijacked by a lesbian ringleader and her amazon army; passengers are dragged through the desert. Antiterrorist team, headed by Japanese martial arts master Kosugi, is dispatched to rescue the hostages. Lots of kicking and maiming.

1918 1985
★ NR Drama 1:32
Dir: Ken Harrison   *Cast:* Matthew Broderick, Hallie Foote, William Converse-Roberts, Michael Higgins, Rochelle Oliver
▶ Atmospheric period piece, adapted by Horton Foote from his stage play and set in a small Texas town during the last weeks of World War I. Broderick wants to enlist in the army while his father Higgins wants to send him off to work. The family is struck down by the Spanish influenza epidemic. Deliberately restrained, very

talky and slow-moving; requires an inordinate amount of patience. **(CC)**

1984 1985 British
★ **R Drama 1:51**
☑ Nudity, adult situations, violence
Dir: Michael Radford *Cast:* John Hurt, Suzanna Hamilton, Richard Burton, Cyril Cusack, Gregor Fisher
▶ Chilling film adaptation of George Orwell's futuristic classic. In a totalitarian society, under Big Brother's constant surveillance, civil servant Hurt works at the Ministry of Truth, shows signs of dissatisfaction, and is arrested for having sex with clandestine rebel Hamilton. He's tortured and "cured" by interrogator Burton. Brilliant production design and superior work from distinguished cast, but the tone is uniformly dark and depressing.

1941 1979
★★★ **PG Comedy 1:58**
☑ Explicit language, adult humor
Dir: Steven Spielberg *Cast:* Dan Aykroyd, John Belushi, Lorraine Gary, Robert Stack, John Candy, Eddie Deezen
▶ After the bombing of Pearl Harbor, a Japanese sub sighted off the coast of California panics the people of Los Angeles. Mammoth comedy about war hysteria suffers from overkill, but the special effects are extraordinary. Enormous cast features Toshiro Mifune, Christopher Lee, Warren Oates, Murray Hamilton, Tim Matheson, Slim Pickens, Joe Flaherty, etc.

1900 1977 Italian
★ **R Drama 4:05**
☑ Nudity, adult situations, explicit language
Dir: Bernardo Bertolucci *Cast:* Burt Lancaster, Robert De Niro, Gerard Depardieu, Dominique Sanda, Donald Sutherland, Sterling Hayden
▶ Monumental epic chronicles the history, politics and social changes of a small Italian province from 1900 to the defeat of Mussolini in 1945. Considered the *Gone With the Wind* of Italy, story concerns two boys, best friends, both born on January 1, 1900. One is fatherless peasant Depardieu and the other, De Niro, is heir to a vast estate. Their relationship is shaped by volatile social forces. Visually stunning but the excessive length requires unlimited patience.

1969 1988
★★ **R Drama 1:35**

☑ Nudity, adult situations, explicit language
Dir: Ernest Thompson *Cast:* Bruce Dern, Kiefer Sutherland, Robert Downey, Jr., Mariette Hartley, Winona Ryder, Joanna Cassidy
▶ Flower power finds its way to small-town Maryland as college students Sutherland and Downey contend with the Vietnam War and domestic woes. Downey turns on, flunks out, and gets arrested for breaking into his draft board office; Sutherland's pacifism alienates his dad Dern but attracts Downey's sister Ryder. Sutherland and Ryder excel, but psychedelic melodrama from writer/director Thompson can be overly earnest.

NINE TO FIVE 1980
★★★★★ **PG Comedy 1:49**
☑ Explicit language, adult humor
Dir: Colin Higgins *Cast:* Jane Fonda, Lily Tomlin, Dolly Parton, Dabney Coleman, Sterling Hayden
▶ Slapstick sermon on job equality. Office workers Fonda, Tomlin, and Parton, pushed to the wall by their chauvinist boss Coleman, kidnap him while they wait for proof he's an embezzler. Terrific team acting but Tomlin steals the show. ("I'm no fool. I killed the boss . . . they're going to fire me for that.") Spawned a TV series. Parton, in her screen debut, sings hit title song she also wrote.

90 DAYS 1986 Canadian
★ **NR Comedy 1:40**
☑ Adult situations, explicit language
Dir: Giles Walker *Cast:* Stefan Wodoslowsky, Christine Pak, Sam Grana, Fernanda Tavares, Daisy De Bellefeville
▶ Charming, low-budget comedy about two men in crisis. Womanizer Wodoslowsky has been dumped by both his wife and mistress; lovelorn Grana has ninety days to decide whether to marry Korean mail-order bride Pak before her visa expires. Deft comic performances. **(CC)**

99 AND 44/100% DEAD 1974
☆ **PG Comedy 1:38**
☑ Adult situations, explicit language, violence
Dir: John Frankenheimer *Cast:* Richard Harris, Ann Turkel, Bradford Dillman, Edmond O'Brien, Chuck Connors, Katherine Baumann
▶ Hired gun Harris accepts task of knocking off crook Dillman on behalf of gangster O'Brien; Harris then finds himself in-

volved with beautiful Turkel (his real-life wife at the time), shoot-outs, chases, and metal claw–handed thug Connors. Frankenheimer's stylishness brings some life to broad, comic book–style material.

92 IN THE SHADE 1975
★ **R Drama 1:33**
☑ Nudity, adult situations, explicit language, violence
Dir: Thomas McGuane *Cast:* Peter Fonda, Warren Oates, Margot Kidder, Burgess Meredith, Harry Dean Stanton, Sylvia Miles
▶ Drifter Fonda returns home to Key West to open a fishing charter business, provoking a dangerous feud with rival captain Oates. Subtle, picturesque cult favorite was adapted by director McGuane from his novel. Interesting cast also includes Elizabeth Ashley, William Hickey, and Louise Latham.

NINJA III—THE DOMINATION 1984
★★ **R Martial Arts 1:35**
☑ Nudity, adult situations, explicit language, violence
Dir: Sam Firstenberg *Cast:* Lucinda Dickey, Sho Kosugi, Jordan Bennett, David Chung, T. J. Castronova
▶ Telephone worker Dickey, possessed by the spirit of an evil ninja, perplexes cop boyfriend Bennett when she goes on a killing spree. Kosugi is the only ninja who can exorcise the demon. Lively sequel to *Revenge of the Ninja* blends martial arts action (expertly choreographed by Kosugi) with touches of the supernatural.

NINJA TURF 1986
★★ **R Martial Arts 1:26**
☑ Explicit language, violence
Dir: Richard Park *Cast:* Jun Chong, Phillip Rhee, James Lew, Rosanna King, Bill Wallace, Dorin Mukama
▶ Teenager Chong, a kung-fu whiz with a boozing mom, gets involved in gang warfare and drug dealing while battling arch-rival Rhee. The action is sometimes impressive; the acting and production values are not. Chong and Rhee acted, respectively, as executive producer and producer of the film.

NINOTCHKA 1939
★★★★ **NR Comedy 1:50 B&W**
Dir: Ernst Lubitsch *Cast:* Greta Garbo, Melvyn Douglas, Ina Claire, Sig Rumann, Felix Bressart, Bela Lugosi
▶ Garbo, in her first comedy, is stunning as a stern Communist sent to Paris to rep-

rimand comrades indulging in the luxuries of capitalism. Debonair gigolo Douglas does his best to seduce the icy Ninotchka. Elegant comedy takes some gentle stabs at social satire, but succeeds best as a delightful romance. Both Garbo and the screenplay by Charles Brackett, Walter Reisch, and Billy Wilder received Oscar nominations.

NINTH CONFIGURATION, THE 1980
★ **R Drama 1:55**
☑ Nudity, explicit language, graphic violence
Dir: William Peter Blatty *Cast:* Stacy Keach, Scott Wilson, Jason Miller, Ed Flanders, Neville Brand, Robert Loggia
▶ Keach plays a new psychiatrist at a military mental institution who may be more insane than his patients. Obscure, jumbled concoction of pompous speeches and sadistic violence was cut into several confusing versions by the studio. Director Blatty also produced and wrote the screenplay from his novel *Twinkle, Twinkle, Killer Kane.*

NOBODY'S FOOL 1986
★★ **PG-13 Comedy 1:47**
☑ Adult situations, explicit language
Dir: Evelyn Purcell *Cast:* Rosanna Arquette, Eric Roberts, Mare Winningham, Jim Youngs, Louise Fletcher, Gwen Welles
▶ Kooky small-town waitress Arquette, broken-hearted over losing a local boy to a rich girl, falls for Roberts, the lighting director of a visiting theatrical troupe. Oddball romance by Beth Henley is filled with disarming peripheral characters and her trademark touches of black comedy. **(CC)**

NOBODY'S PERFEKT 1981
★★ **PG Comedy 1:36**
Dir: Peter Bonerz *Cast:* Gabe Kaplan, Alex Karras, Robert Klein, Susan Clark, Paul Stewart
▶ When Kaplan's car is totalled in a Miami pothole, friends Karras and Klein convince him to sue the city. But their scheme intersects with a gangland heist that leads to comic chases. Likable stars can't salvage this extremely obvious comedy.

NO DEPOSIT, NO RETURN 1976
★★★★★ **G Comedy/Family 1:58**
Dir: Norman Tokar *Cast:* David Niven, Darren McGavin, Don Knotts, Herschel Bernardi, Barbara Feldon, Kim Richards
▶ Lonely children Richards and Brad Sav-

age persuade bumbling crooks McGavin and Knotts to stage a phony kidnapping so they can visit their mother in Hong Kong. Grandfather Niven, a multimillion-aire, turns detective to track down the kids. Disney blend of comedy and action has an unusually good cast of comic veterans.

NOMADS 1986
★ R Action-Adventure 1:35
☑ Nudity, adult situations, explicit language, violence
Dir: John McTiernan   *Cast:* Pierce Brosnan, Lesley-Anne Down, Adam Ant, Hector Mercado, Anna-Maria Montecelli, Mary Woronov
▶ French anthropologist Brosnan transmits his soul to Los Angeles doctor Down; she discovers he was battling evil spirits in the form of punk rockers led by a mute Ant. Intriguing body-switching premise undermined by confusing crosscutting; still, some successful shocks.

NO MAN'S LAND 1987
★★★ R Drama 1:46
☑ Adult situations, explicit language, violence
Dir: Peter Werner   *Cast:* Charlie Sheen, D. B. Sweeney, Lara Harris, Randy Quaid, Bill Duke, M. Emmet Walsh
▶ Rookie cop Sweeney takes undercover job in a "chop shop" specializing in stolen Porsches. Under the influence of seductive car thief Sheen, Sweeney turns to crime. Stylish, fast-paced thriller with above-average car chases raises interesting moral issues. **(CC)**

NO MERCY 1986
★★★★ R Action-Adventure 1:48
☑ Adult situations, explicit language, graphic violence
Dir: Richard Pearce   *Cast:* Richard Gere, Kim Basinger, Jeroen Krabbe, George Dzundza, Gary Basaraba, William Atherton
▶ Undercover Chicago cop Gere, vowing revenge for his partner's murder, tracks the killers to the Louisiana bayous. There he uncovers a conspiracy involving pony-tailed druglord Krabbe and his illiterate moll Basinger. Sexy leads and tense action enliven familiar plot.

NONE BUT THE LONELY HEART 1944
★★★ NR Drama 1:53 B&W
Dir: Clifford Odets   *Cast:* Cary Grant, Ethel Barrymore, Barry Fitzgerald, June Duprez, Jane Wyatt, George Coulouris
▶ Ambitious but grim story of the London slums: Cockney con man Grant drifts into a crime ring run by Coulouris. He repents when he learns his impoverished mother Barrymore is dying of cancer. Grant received an Oscar nomination for his change-of-pace role; Barrymore won Best Supporting Actress.

NO RETREAT, NO SURRENDER 1986
★★★ PG Martial Arts 1:24
☑ Explicit language, violence
Dir: Corey Yuen   *Cast:* Kurt McKinney, Jean-Claude Van Damme, J. W. Fails, Kathie Sileno, Kim Tai Chong
▶ Seattle karate student McKinney, tormented by local thugs, turns to the ghost of Bruce Lee (Chong) for help. McKinney vindicates himself by battling psychopathic Russian athlete Van Damme. Amateurish martial arts drama picks up some steam during the frequent fights.

NORMA RAE 1979
★★★★★ PG Drama 1:54
☑ Adult situations, explicit language, mild violence
Dir: Martin Ritt   *Cast:* Sally Field, Ron Leibman, Beau Bridges, Pat Hingle, Barbara Baxley, Gail Strickland
▶ Small-town Southern worker Norma Rae (Field) helps fast-talking Jewish organizer Leibman to unionize the cotton mill where her family has worked for generations. The friendship between Field and Leibman is played against her marriage to Bridges, a good-hearted but confused electrician. Enormously affecting, intelligent film with plenty of heart showcases a spectacular Oscar-winning performance by Field.

NORTH BY NORTHWEST 1959
★★★★★ NR Mystery-Suspense 2:16
Dir: Alfred Hitchcock   *Cast:* Cary Grant, Eva Marie Saint, James Mason, Jessie Royce Landis, Martin Landau, Leo G. Carroll
▶ Madison Avenue exec Grant finds his world turned upside down when he is mistaken for a CIA agent. Pursued by both cops and enemy spies (led by Mason), he gets involved with mysterious Saint on a cross-country chase. One of Hitchcock's best films is fast-paced, witty, and tremendously exciting. Many classic scenes: the murder at the UN, the crop-duster sequence, and the cliff-hanging Mount Rushmore climax.

NORTH DALLAS FORTY 1979
★★★ R Comedy/Sports 1:58

☑ Nudity, adult situations, explicit language
Dir: Ted Kotcheff ***Cast:*** Nick Nolte, Mac Davis, Charles Durning, Dayle Haddon, Bo Svenson, Steve Forrest
▶ Over-the-hill wide receiver Nolte, needing drugs to overcome his aches and pains, gradually realizes the corruption of the owners and coaches. A winner, both on and off the field: convincing bone-crunching football action, terrific buddy-buddy relationship between Nolte and quarterback pal Davis, and some great raucous humor (especially in Davis's bawdy "Wait til I get to the weird part" story). Based on the Peter Gent novel.

NORTHERN PURSUIT 1943
★★ NR War 1:34 B&W
Dir: Raoul Walsh ***Cast:*** Errol Flynn, Julie Bishop, Helmut Dantine, John Ridgely, Gene Lockhart
▶ During World War II, Flynn, a Canadian mountie of German descent, befriends Nazi spy Dantine in order to infiltrate an enemy cabal. Top-level wartime thriller with some fine action (the avalanche, a ski chase).

NORTH SHORE 1987
★★★ PG Drama 1:36
☑ Explicit language
Dir: William Phelps ***Cast:*** Matt Adler, Nia Peeples, John Philbin, Gregory Harrison, Gerry Lopez
▶ Arizona surfer Adler rejects the security of college to challenge the waves at Hawaii's famous North Shore. While training for a dangerous pipeline contest, Adler meets beautiful native Peeples and receives inspiration from older "soul surfer" Harrison. Undemanding fare with above-average wave footage.

NORTH TO ALASKA 1960
★★★★ NR Western 2:00
Dir: Henry Hathaway ***Cast:*** John Wayne, Stewart Granger, Ernie Kovacs, Fabian, Capucine, Mickey Shaughnessy
▶ Light-hearted Western romp with gold-mining partners Wayne and Granger battling over saucy Capucine, a replacement for Granger's Seattle mail-order bride. Kovacs, an unctuous con man and Capucine's former lover, attempts to steal the mine with a rival claim. Good vehicle for Wayne, who revels in his comic role. Title tune became a pop hit for Johnny Horton. **(CC)**

NOSFERATU, THE VAMPYRE 1979
German
★ PG Horror 1:47
☑ Violence
Dir: Werner Herzog ***Cast:*** Klaus Kinski, Isabelle Adjani, Bruno Ganz, Jacques Dufilho, Roland Topor
▶ Eerie but slow-paced remake of a 1922 silent film presents an intellectual version of the Dracula legend. Ganz plays a lawyer who stumbles across the horrid secret behind mysterious count Kinski; Ganz's wife Adjani sacrifices herself to destroy the vampire. Visually stunning picture benefits from oddly comic touches and Kinski's magnetic performance. Shorter English-language version also available. ⑤

NO SMALL AFFAIR 1984
★★ R Comedy 1:42
☑ Brief nudity, adult situations, explicit language
Dir: Jerry Schatzberg ***Cast:*** Jon Cryer, Demi Moore, George Wendt, Peter Frechette, Elizabeth Daily, Ann Wedgeworth
▶ Precocious teen photographer Cryer sets his sights on an indifferent "older" woman, aspiring rock singer Moore. Predictable adolescent comedy salvaged by Cryer's ingratiating performance and glossy San Francisco locations. **(CC)**

NOT FOR PUBLICATION 1984
★ R Comedy 1:27
☑ Adult situations, explicit language
Dir: Paul Bartel ***Cast:*** Nancy Allen, David Naughton, Laurence Luckinbill, Alice Ghostley, Richard Paul, Barry Dennen
▶ Old-fashioned farce set in the 1950s about the double life of plucky heroine Allen, who's both a muckraking reporter for an exposé rag and assistant to reform mayoral candidate Luckinbill. Romance blossoms between Allen and Naughton, a photographer she's hired to check into Luckinbill's background. Fitfully amusing but rarely inspired.

NOTHING IN COMMON 1986
★★★★ PG Comedy/Drama 1:59
☑ Brief nudity, adult situations, explicit language
Dir: Garry Marshall ***Cast:*** Tom Hanks, Jackie Gleason, Eva Marie Saint, Bess Armstrong, Hector Elizondo, Barry Corbin
▶ High-flying advertising whiz kid Hanks is grounded by the divorce of parents

Gleason and Saint and their sudden dependence on him. Hanks's transformation from hilarious-but-unlikable yuppie to responsible, loving son is, by turns, funny, touching, and overly sentimental. Fine supporting help from Elizondo as Hanks's boss and Armstrong as his girlfriend. Gleason's final film.

NOTHING SACRED 1937
★★★★ NR Comedy 1:15
Dir: William Wellman *Cast:* Carole Lombard, Fredric March, Charles Winninger, Walter Connolly, Sig Rumann, Frank Fay
▶ Ambitious New York reporter March plans a sob story on dying Vermonter Lombard. When her incompetent doctor Winninger reverses his initial diagnosis, March won't back off and persuades Lombard to feign illness and journey to the city in style. She's honored by a grief-stricken populace until her ruddy good health raises eyebrows. Classic screwball comedy provides nonstop laughs at a breakneck pace, with script by Ben Hecht and additional dialogue by Ring Lardner, Jr., and Budd Schulberg.

NO TIME FOR SERGEANTS 1958
★★★★ NR Comedy 1:51 B&W
Dir: Mervyn LeRoy *Cast:* Andy Griffith, Nick Adams, Myron McCormick, Murray Hamilton, Howard Smith, Don Knotts
▶ Hillbilly Will Stockdale (Griffith) joins the Air Force, where his down-home ways bring him into conflict with no nonsense sarge McCormick. Fresh, alive, and very funny with marvelous performances by Griffith and McCormick. Griffith's second film was adapted from Ira Levin's Broadway play and Mac Hyman's novel.

NOTORIOUS 1945
★★★★ NR Mystery-Suspense 1:41 B&W
Dir: Alfred Hitchcock *Cast:* Cary Grant, Ingrid Bergman, Claude Rains, Louis Calhern, Leopoldine Konstantin, Reinhold Schunzel
▶ In post–World War II South America, Federal agent Grant blackmails German playgirl Bergman into marrying Nazi Rains. When she uncovers a conspiracy involving uranium, Rains slowly poisons her. Fascinating drama executed with breathless pacing and superlative plotting; on top of the suspense, Grant and Bergman conduct a memorably passionate romance. Rains and screenwriter Ben

Hecht both received Oscar nominations. (CC)

NOT QUITE PARADISE 1986 British
★ R Drama 1:46
☑ Brief nudity, adult situations, explicit language, violence
Dir: Lewis Gilbert *Cast:* Joanna Pacula, Sam Robards, Kevin McNally, Todd Graff, Selina Cadell
▶ Foreign workers on an Israeli kibbutz encounter a variety of adventures, ranging from a run-in with Arabs to a budding romance between American medical student Robards and Pacula, a no-nonsense native in charge of the kibbutz. Uneven mixture of drama, comedy, and romance offers a good performance by Cadell as a neurotic Englishwoman.
Ⓢ

NOW AND FOREVER 1983 Australian
★★★★ R Romance 1:32
☑ Nudity, adult situations, explicit language, violence
Dir: Adrian Carr *Cast:* Cheryl Ladd, Robert Coleby, Carmen Duncan, Christine Amor, Alex Scott
▶ Boutique owner Ladd turns to alcohol and pills when her writer husband Coleby is wrongly convicted of rape. Beautiful Australian countryside, lush visuals. Unfortunately, the soap opera plot has many holes and Cheryl's characterization generates little sympathy. Based on the Danielle Steel novel.

NO WAY OUT 1987
★★★★★ R Mystery-Suspense 1:54
☑ Nudity, adult situations, explicit language, violence
Dir: Roger Donaldson *Cast:* Kevin Costner, Gene Hackman, Sean Young, Will Patton, Howard Duff, George Dzundza
▶ Gripping thriller about Navy career man Costner assigned as a CIA liaison to Secretary of Defense Hackman. While searching for a Russian mole, Costner realizes he is being framed for the murder of Hackman's mistress Young. Taut, convincing plot was loosely based on Kenneth Fearing's novel *The Big Clock* and filmed under that title in 1948.

NO WAY TO TREAT A LADY 1968
★★★ NR Mystery-Suspense 1:48
Dir: Jack Smight *Cast:* Rod Steiger, Lee Remick, George Segal, Eileen Heckart, Murray Hamilton, Michael Dunn
▶ Deranged serial killer Steiger, a master

of disguise, slays New York women while in costume. Police detective Segal romances key witness Remick as he pursues Steiger in a battle of wits. Well-crafted romantic suspenser is both humorous and grisly.

NOWHERE TO HIDE 1987 Canadian
★★★ R Mystery-Suspense **1:30**
☑ Explicit language, violence
Dir: Mario Azzopardi *Cast:* Amy Madigan, Daniel Hugh Kelly, Robin MacEachern, Michael Ironside, John Colicos, Charles Shamata
▶ When her husband is murdered while investigating suspicious helicopter crashes, ex-Marine and mother Madigan must recover his work before assassins find her. Competent thriller features an above-average performance by Madigan as the indomitable heroine. **(CC)**

NOW, VOYAGER 1942
★★★★ NR Romance **1:57** B&W
Dir: Irving Rapper *Cast:* Bette Davis, Claude Rains, Paul Henreid, Gladys Cooper, Bonita Granville, Ilka Chase
▶ Davis, the ugly duckling in a New England family, is transformed into swan under guidance of kindly shrink Rains. She finds shipboard romance with married Henreid and helps his troubled daughter. Davis is superb in one of the most romantic movies ever made. Many unforgettable moments: Henreid lighting two cigarettes at once; Davis's famous line, "Don't let's ask for the moon! We have the stars!" Oscar-winning score by Max Steiner.

NUMBER ONE WITH A BULLET 1987
★★★ R Action-Adventure **1:41**
☑ Adult situations, explicit language, violence
Dir: Jack Smight *Cast:* Robert Carradine, Billy Dee Williams, Valerie Bertinelli, Peter Graves, Bobby DiCicco, Doris Roberts
▶ Los Angeles narcotics cops Carradine and Williams attempt to nab drug dealing bigwig and uncover corruption in the police department. Fast-moving genre film does not ignore the human side: Carradine deals with ex-wife Bertinelli and mom Roberts while teaming with Williams for a pleasing buddy relationship.

NUN'S STORY, THE 1959
★★★ NR Drama **2:29**
Dir: Fred Zinnemann *Cast:* Audrey Hepburn, Peter Finch, Edith Evans, Peggy Ashcroft, Dean Jagger, Mildred Dunnock
▶ Young Hepburn becomes a nun. Serving as a nurse in a Belgian mental institution and a Congolese hospital, she begins to question stern church doctrine. World War II proves to be a turning point in wrestling with her conscience. Outstanding and quite engrossing drama features one of Oscar-nominated Hepburn's most complex performances. A Best Picture nominee.

NUTCRACKER: THE MOTION PICTURE 1986
★★★ G Dance/Family **1:25**
Dir: Carroll Ballard *Cast:* Hugh Bigney, Vanessa Sharp, Patricia Barker, Wade Walthall, Russell Burnett
▶ Sophisticated, ambitious approach to classical ballet with Tchaikovsky score. In twelve-year-old Clara's dream, her Christmas gift, the Nutcracker, and a legion of toy soldiers wage battle with mice while the tree decorations come to life. Charmingly sinister sets and creatures were designed by children's book illustrator, Maurice Sendak. Ballet lovers will rejoice. Performed by the Pacific Northwest Ballet and narrated by Julie Harris.

NUTS 1987
★★★★ R Drama **1:58**
☑ Adult situations, explicit language, violence
Dir: Martin Ritt *Cast:* Barbra Streisand, Richard Dreyfuss, Maureen Stapleton, Eli Wallach, Robert Webber, Karl Malden
▶ High-priced prostitute Streisand is indicted for manslaughter after killing a customer. Against the advice of court-appointed attorney Dreyfuss, she refuses to plead insanity, demanding her day in court. Psychological fireworks erupt when her stepfather Malden takes the stand. High-powered, well-cast courtroom drama was adapted from Tom Topor's Broadway play. **(CC)**

NUTTY PROFESSOR, THE 1963
★★ NR Comedy **1:47**
Dir: Jerry Lewis *Cast:* Jerry Lewis, Stella Stevens, Kathleen Freeman, Ned Flory, Norman Alden, Howard Morris
▶ Hoping to win the love of beautiful student Stevens, nerdy professor Julius Kelp (Lewis) creates a potion that transforms him into the obnoxious but dashing Buddy Love (also Lewis). The double life

gets complicated when the formula wears off at inconvenient times. Lewis's best and deservedly most popular film; his usual broad clowning is tempered with heart.

OBJECTIVE, BURMA! 1945
★★★ NR War 2:22 B&W
Dir: Raoul Walsh *Cast:* Errol Flynn, William Prince, James Brown, Warner Anderson, George Tobias, Henry Hull
► Major Flynn leads unit of Allied soldiers on parachute drop into Japanese-occupied Burma. After achieving initial objective, the men must elude brutal enemy pursuit to get out alive. Blistering wartime excitement directed for maximum tension by reliable Walsh.

OBLONG BOX, THE 1969 British
★ PG Horror 1:31
☑ Violence
Dir: Gordon Hessler *Cast:* Vincent Price, Christopher Lee, Alistair Williamson, Hilary Dwyer, Peter Arne, Harry Baird
► British aristocrat Price injects his brother Williamson, mutilated on African safari, with witch doctor's drug that gives the appearance of death before entombing him. But grave robbers take the body to scientist Lee, who revives the "corpse." Price must confront Williamson to stop subsequent murders. Slowly paced adaptation of an Edgar Allan Poe story sacrifices genuine chills for too much talk.

OBSESSION 1976
★★★★ PG Mystery-Suspense 1:38
☑ Adult situations, explicit language, mild violence
Dir: Brian De Palma *Cast:* Cliff Robertson, Genevieve Bujold, John Lithgow, Sylvia Kuumba Williams, Wanda Blackman
► In 1959, New Orleans businessman Robertson cooperates with police when his wife Bujold and daughter are kidnapped; as a result, they are killed. Sixteen years later in Rome, the guilt-ridden Robertson meets his late wife's look-alike (also Bujold) and marries her. History repeats itself when she is kidnapped. Lush, emotional Hitchcockian thriller. Sweeping Bernard Herrmann score, sincere performances, and bravura camerawork create a rich mood of danger and romance.

O.C. AND STIGGS 1987
☆ R Comedy 1:50
☑ Brief nudity, adult situations, explicit language
Dir: Robert Altman *Cast:* Neill Barry, Daniel Jenkins, Martin Mull, Jane Curtin, Dennis Hopper, Paul Dooley
► Boisterous Phoenix teens Barry and Jenkins spend idle summer persecuting insurance mogul Dooley and his kin. Overly ambitious, anarchic satire of Sun Belt life is alternately hilarious and dumb. Director Altman's foray into teen comedy sports individual gags and splendid supporting cast, but don't expect it all to add up to much. (CC)

OCEAN'S ELEVEN 1960
★★★ NR Comedy 2:08
Dir: Lewis Milestone *Cast:* Frank Sinatra, Dean Martin, Sammy Davis, Jr., Peter Lawford, Angie Dickinson, Richard Conte
► All-star caper film built around a clever premise: Sinatra and ten buddies, all Airborne veterans, come up with a scheme to rob five Las Vegas casinos on New Year's Eve. Complications set in when local gangster Cesar Romero hears of the plot. Besides the Rat Pack, cast includes Akim Tamiroff, Henry Silva, Red Skelton, Shirley MacLaine, and George Raft.

OCTAGON, THE 1980
★★★ R Martial Arts 1:44
☑ Brief nudity, adult situations, explicit language, graphic violence
Dir: Eric Karson *Cast:* Chuck Norris, Lee Van Cleef, Karen Carlson, Art Hindle, Kim Lankford, Tadashi Yamashita
► Retired martial arts champ Norris makes comeback when gang of Ninja killers slay his date Lankford. Soon Norris is on the trail of kung-fu terrorists. Climactic battle at gang's HQ, the Octagon, leads to duel-to-death between Norris and villains' leader Yamashita. Better-than-average chop socky with usual Oriental mysticism, sultry girls, and violence a-plenty.

OCTOPUSSY 1983 British
★★★★ PG
Espionage/Action-Adventure 2:10
☑ Adult situations, explicit language, violence
Dir: John Glen *Cast:* Roger Moore, Maud Adams, Louis Jourdan, Kristina Wayborn, Kabir Bedi, Steven Berkoff
► Hawkish Soviet general Berkoff attempts to start a superpower war, assisted by beautiful smuggler Adams and

villainous art dealer Jourdan. Many exotic locales including Indian island populated only by scantily-clad women. Breath-taking stunts, droll and urbane Jourdan, and Moore's best turn as 007. Thirteenth installment in the always popular series.

ODD COUPLE, THE 1968
★★★★ G Comedy 1:45
Dir: Gene Saks *Cast:* Jack Lemmon, Walter Matthau, John Fiedler, Herb Edelman, Carole Shelley, Monica Evans
▶ When his wife leaves him, finicky Felix Unger (Lemmon) moves in with his sloppy sportswriter pal, Oscar Madison (Matthau). Felix's obsessively neat behavior quickly conflicts with Oscar's messy poker games. Time and the popular Tony Randall/Jack Klugman TV series have not diminished the appealing Lemmon/Matthau teamwork in this hilarious and endearing adaptation of Neil Simon's smash Broadway hit.

ODD JOBS 1986
★ PG-13 Comedy 1:29
☑ Adult situations, explicit language, mild violence
Dir: Mark Story *Cast:* Paul Reiser, Robert Townsend, Scott McGinnis, Paul Provenza, Rick Overton, Julianne Phillips
▶ When their schemes to get rich quick with summer jobs fail, Reiser and four college friends form a moving company that draws the wrath of rival Cabrezzi Brothers goons. Capable cast does wonders with the story's breezy high jinks, but inventive writing is undercut by scattershot direction. Notable for appearances by Phillips (then Mrs. Bruce Springsteen), radio personality Don Imus, and "Body by Jake" Steinfeld.

ODD MAN OUT 1947 British
★★★ NR Mystery-Suspense 1:55 B&W
Dir: Carol Reed *Cast:* James Mason, Kathleen Ryan, Robert Newton, F. J. McCormick, Cyril Cusack, Dan O'Herlihy
▶ Irish rebel Mason, critically wounded during a robbery, seeks refuge in the slums of Belfast while a British manhunt closes in on him. An unforgettable masterpiece of suspense written, directed, and performed with almost unbearable tension. Mason is especially remarkable in what may be his best role.

ODESSA FILE, THE 1974 British
★★★ PG Action-Adventure 2:08
☑ Adult situations, explicit language, violence

Dir: Ronald Neame *Cast:* Jon Voight, Maximilian Schell, Maria Schell, Mary Tamm, Derek Jacobi, Peter Jeffrey
▶ After reading a concentration camp survivor's diary, German journalist Voight is determined to find Schell, a missing SS agent responsible for mass murders. Israelis train him to infiltrate Odessa, a secret neo-Nazi organization harboring Schell. Brooding adaptation of a Frederick Forsyth best-seller showcases a strong performance by Voight, but plot is often confusing. **(CC)**

ODE TO BILLY JOE 1976
★★★ PG Drama 1:46
☑ Adult situations
Dir: Max Baer *Cast:* Robby Benson, Glynnis O'Connor, Joan Hotchkis, Sandy McPeak, James Best
▶ Feature-length interpretation of Bobbie Gentry's 1976 hit song concerns young lovers Benson and O'Connor facing problems in rural 1953 South. Benson, hiding a tragic secret, commits suicide; O'Connor comes to maturity when she discovers his past. Accurate period details help this sincere but overwrought melodrama.

OFF BEAT 1986
★★ PG Comedy 1:33
☑ Adult situations, explicit language
Dir: Michael Dinner *Cast:* Judge Reinhold, Meg Tilly, Cleavant Derricks, Joe Mantegna, Jacques d'Amboise, Amy Wright
▶ Pal of librarian Reinhold doesn't want to perform in a police dance benefit; Reinhold takes his place and falls in love with police hostage negotiator Tilly. Ensuing impersonation leads to amusing but predictable complications; supporting actors (Anthony Zerbe, Fred Gwynne, Harvey Keitel, etc.) provide most of the laughs in this middling comedy.

OFFICER AND A GENTLEMAN, AN 1982
★★★★★ R Drama/Romance 2:04
☑ Nudity, adult situations, explicit language, violence
Dir: Taylor Hackford *Cast:* Richard Gere, Debra Winger, Louis Gossett, Jr., David Keith, Robert Loggia, Lisa Blount
▶ Loner pilot-in-training Gere meets his match in hardnosed drill instructor Gossett while romancing local Puget Sound girl, Winger. Gere's best buddy Keith drops out and then blows it with his townie belle; but Gere has the right stuff

and learns to become both a warrior and a lover. Hugely popular if somewhat obvious film combines old-style steamy romance and boot camp rite-of-passage. Gossett won an Oscar for his fine supporting portrayal of a tough but humane mentor.

OFFICIAL STORY, THE 1985 Argentinian
★★ NR Drama 1:53
☑ Adult situations
Dir: Luis Puenzo *Cast:* Norma Aleandro, Hector Alterio, Chela Ruiz, Chunchuna Villafane, Hugo Arana
▶ Argentinian Aleandro finds her comfortable, upper-class life disrupted when she suspects her adopted daughter is the offspring of political prisoner killed by the military dictatorship. Her right-wing husband Alterio seeks to allay her concerns, but her investigation reveals he is a partner in the corrupt government. Winner of an Oscar for Best Foreign Film, picture shrewdly reveals its politics through a moving human story. ⑤

OFF LIMITS 1953
★★ NR Comedy 1:29 B&W
Dir: George Marshall *Cast:* Bob Hope, Mickey Rooney, Marilyn Maxwell, Eddie Mayehoff, Stanley Clements, Marvin Miller
▶ Boxing promoter Hope calls it quits when he's drafted, despite pleas from young recruit Rooney to help him train. Hope changes his mind when he learns Rooney's aunt (Maxwell) is a gorgeous nightclub singer. Fast-paced comedy filled with Army gags features an amusing cameo by Jack Dempsey.

OFF LIMITS 1988
★★★ R Mystery-Suspense 1:42
☑ Nudity, explicit language, violence
Dir: Christopher Crowe *Cast:* Willem Dafoe, Gregory Hines, Fred Ward, Amanda Pays, Kay Tong Lim, Scott Glenn
▶ Saigon 1968 provides an unusual setting for a nasty murder mystery; undercover Army detectives Dafoe and Hines search the grimy underworld for a high-ranking superior who's murdering prostitutes. Pays is a nun whose missionary work helps the cops. Conventional thriller graced by unusually good leads and taut atmosphere. (CC)

OF HUMAN BONDAGE 1934
★★★ NR Drama 1:23 B&W
Dir: John Cromwell *Cast:* Leslie Howard, Bette Davis, Frances Dee, Reginald Owen, Reginald Denny, Kay Johnson
▶ Howard, a sensitive, clubfooted medical student, falls under the spell of cockney waitress Davis, a heartless tramp who destroys his life. Powerful adaptation of W. Somerset Maugham's novel still packs an emotional punch. Davis approaches her breakthrough role with relish. Remade in 1946 and 1964.

OF HUMAN BONDAGE 1964
★★★★ NR Drama 1:39 B&W
Dir: Ken Hughes *Cast:* Kim Novak, Laurence Harvey, Robert Morley, Siobhan McKenna, Roger Livesey
▶ Third film version of W. Somerset Maugham's classic novel about clubfooted medical student Harvey's obsession with unfaithful Cockney waitress Novak lacks the honesty and resonance of the 1934 Bette Davis vehicle. Novak's accomplished performance and grim view of Edwardian London bring some life to the sentimental plot.

OF UNKNOWN ORIGIN 1983
Canadian
★★ R Horror 1:29
☑ Nudity, explicit language, violence
Dir: George Pan Cosmatos *Cast:* Peter Weller, Jennifer Dale, Lawrence Dane, Kenneth Welsh, Shannon Tweed
▶ New York bank executive Weller sends his family to Vermont while he completes a company project, but his privacy is disrupted by a large, extremely aggressive rodent. Shrewd psychological twists perk up an otherwise predictable story line.

O'HARA'S WIFE 1982
★★★★ PG Drama 1:27
☑ Adult situations, explicit language
Dir: William S. Bartman *Cast:* Edward Asner, Mariette Hartley, Jodie Foster, Perry Lang, Tom Bosley, Ray Walston
▶ Hard-working attorney Asner suffers when wife Hartley suddenly dies; then she reappears as a ghost. She offers counsel on his career and travails with daughter Foster and son Lang, but since her ghost is visible only to Asner he's presumed to have gone bonkers. Fine performances from quality cast.

OH, GOD! 1977
★★★★ PG Comedy 1:38
☑ Adult humor
Dir: Carl Reiner *Cast:* George Burns, John Denver, Teri Garr, Donald Pleasence, Ralph Bellamy, Dinah Shore
▶ God (Burns) chooses California super-

market manager Denver to spread his good word. This suburban Moses meets some skepticism from the secular world, but soon the media can't get enough of him. Divine inspiration was casting Burns as Supreme Being who admits that ostriches and avocados were mistakes and claims the 1969 Mets as His last big miracle. First entry in popular series.

OH, GOD! BOOK II 1980
★★★★ PG Comedy 1:34
☑ Adult humor
Dir: Gilbert Cates *Cast:* George Burns, Suzanne Pleshette, David Birney, Louanne, John Louie, Conrad Janis
▶ Less-than-inspired sequel with Burns reprising his role as the Big Guy. This time preteen Louanne gets tapped to persuade a disbelieving world that God is not dead. Havoc ensues at school and at home until Burns intervenes to convince the girl's estranged parents, Pleshette and Birney, and a team of doctors that Louanne isn't loony. Mildly diverting family fare, but the original's edge is gone, especially when Burns is off-screen.

OH, GOD! YOU DEVIL 1984
★★★★ PG Comedy 1:36
☑ Explicit language, adult humor
Dir: Paul Bogart *Cast:* George Burns, Ted Wass, Ron Silver, Roxanne Hart, Eugene Roche, Robert Desiderio
▶ New gimmick here: Burns plays both God and the Devil. Struggling musician Wass sells his soul to become a rock superstar, only to find wealth and fame don't compensate for loss of love from his previous life. Ultimately God plays poker with the Devil to save Wass from suicide. Burns, always a rascal, is even better as Satan and supremely carries the picture. **(CC)**

OH HEAVENLY DOG! 1980
★★★★ PG Comedy/Family 1:43
☑ Explicit language, mild violence
Dir: Joe Camp *Cast:* Chevy Chase, Jane Seymour, Omar Sharif, Robert Morley, Alan Sues, Benji
▶ Private eye Chase, murdered during a case, is reincarnated as dog Benji to capture his killers. While pursuing the villains, Chase discovers he's still attracted to girlfriend Seymour, despite his canine appearance. Third Benji film is racier than expected, with an amazing performance by the adorable pooch. **(CC)**

OKLAHOMA! 1955
★★★★★ G Musical 2:23

Dir: Fred Zinnemann *Cast:* Gordon MacRae, Shirley Jones, Charlotte Greenwood, Gloria Grahame, Eddie Albert, Rod Steiger
▶ Rodgers and Hammerstein's landmark musical receives a first-rate, full-bodied film adaptation capturing all the joy and energy of the stage hit. Plot concerns the love affair between Sooner cowboy MacRae and young Laurey (Jones, in her film debut), but supporting cast (particularly Grahame, Greenwood, and Steiger) is most impressive. Oscar-winning score includes "People Will Say We're in Love" and "The Surrey With the Fringe on Top." Choreography by Agnes DeMille. **(CC)**

OKLAHOMA CRUDE 1973
★★★ PG Drama 1:48
☑ Adult situations, violence
Dir: Stanley Kramer *Cast:* George C. Scott, Faye Dunaway, John Mills, Jack Palance, William Lucking
▶ In 1913, stubborn protofeminist Dunaway rejects the help of her estranged father Mills while defending her wildcat rig from sneaky Pan-Oklahoma oil agent Palance. Mills hires Scott, an irascible drifter who tames Dunaway while fighting off Palance's men. Scott's comic hobo is the highlight of this diverting adventure.

OKLAHOMA KID, THE 1939
★★ NR Western 1:25 B&W
Dir: Lloyd Bacon *Cast:* James Cagney, Humphrey Bogart, Rosemary Lane, Donald Crisp, Harvey Stephens, Hugh Sothern
▶ Contrived but enjoyable Western ostensibly about the founding of Tulsa. Bogart, a land-grabbing villain, arranges the lynching of a sheriff; Cagney, a noble outlaw nicknamed the Oklahoma Kid who is the sheriff's long-lost son, rides into town for revenge. Stars overcome miscasting by adopting a tongue-in-cheek approach—Cagney even gets to sing "I Don't Want to Play in Your Yard."

OLD BOYFRIENDS 1979
★★ R Drama 1:42
☑ Brief nudity, adult situations, explicit language
Dir: Joan Tewkesbury *Cast:* Talia Shire, Richard Jordan, Keith Carradine, John Belushi, John Houseman, Buck Henry
▶ Los Angeles psychologist Shire conquers depression over her husband's death by contacting past lovers: Jordan, a divorced filmmaker; Belushi, leader of a tacky lounge band; and Carradine,

younger brother of a Vietnam fatality. Intriguing premise undone by choppy script (by Paul and Leonard Schrader) and vague point of view. Belushi and Henry offer good comic bits.

OLD CURIOSITY SHOP, THE 1975 British
★★★ G Musical 1:58
Dir: Michael Tuchner *Cast:* Anthony Newley, David Hemmings, David Warner, Mona Washbourne, Michael Hordern, Sarah Jane Varley
▶ Nineteenth-century England: Little Nell (Varley) and grandfather Hordern flee from hunchbacked miser Newley, to whom the old man owes money. Adaptation of the Charles Dickens classic is reminiscent of *Oliver.* Plush costumes and sets; Newley also wrote the songs. Entertaining family fare also known as *Mr. Quilp.* **(CC)**

OLD ENOUGH 1984
★ PG Comedy 1:28
☑ Adult situations, explicit language
Dir: Marisa Silver *Cast:* Sarah Boyd, Rainbow Harvest, Neill Barry, Danny Aiello, Susan Kingsley
▶ Wealthy young New Yorker Boyd strikes up an unlikely friendship with streetwise teenager Harvest, who teaches her about makeup and shoplifting. Modest, low-key coming-of-age comedy features a strong performance by Boyd. First-time director Silver, daughter of Joan Micklin Silver, developed her script at Robert Redford's Sundance Institute.

OLD MAID, THE 1939
★★★★ NR Drama 1:35 B&W
Dir: Edmund Goulding *Cast:* Bette Davis, Miriam Hopkins, George Brent, Donald Crisp, Jane Bryan
▶ Davis secretly has an affair with Brent, who is supposed to marry her sister Hopkins. After Brent is killed in the Civil War, Davis gives birth to a girl and then joins Hopkins's household as the spinster aunt. No one knows the secret of daughter Bryan's birth, and Davis fights a losing battle for her love. One of Bette's best performances.

OLD MAN AND THE SEA, THE 1958
★★★★ NR Drama 1:27
Dir: John Sturges *Cast:* Spencer Tracy, Felipe Pazos, Harry Bellaver, Donald Diamond
▶ Adaptation of Ernest Hemingway's novel about an old Cuban fisherman (Tracy), his affecting relationship with young Pazos, and his battle to land a

giant marlin. Tour-de-force for the great Tracy, who was Oscar-nominated, and great cinematography by James Wong Howe. Oscar for Best Music Scoring. One-of-a-kind classic.

OLD YELLER 1957
★★★★★ G Family 1:23
Dir: Robert Stevenson *Cast:* Dorothy McGuire, Fess Parker, Tommy Kirk, Jeff York, Chuck Connors, Kevin Corcoran
▶ Left in charge of the family while father Parker joins a cattle drive, young Texas frontier boy Kirk befriends Old Yeller, a mischievous mongrel with a fearless heart. Their adventures include encounters with bears, wild boars, and a plague of rabies. Heartwarming adaptation of Fred Gipson's novel is an enduring Disney favorite. Followed by *Savage Sam.*

OLIVER! 1968 British
★★★★ G Musical 2:29
Dir: Carol Reed *Cast:* Ron Moody, Oliver Reed, Mark Lester, Shani Wallis, Jack Wild
▶ Romanticized musical version of Dickens's novel *Oliver Twist.* Young orphan Lester is tossed into the London streets where he falls in with gang of London pickpockets and then is rescued by a wealthy gent who turns out to be his uncle. Fine performances by Moody as head thief, Reed as street thug, and Wild as spunky waif. Film classic won six Oscars including Best Picture and Director. Lionel Bart's score (from his play) includes rambunctious "Food, Glorious Food" and plaintive "Where Is Love?" Striking sets vividly re-create London of the 1830s. **(CC)**

OLIVER & COMPANY 1988
★★★★★ G Animation 1:12
Dir: George Scribner *Cast:* Voices of: Bette Midler, Billy Joel, Cheech Marin, Richard Mulligan, Dom DeLuise, Robert Loggia
▶ Disney variation on Dickens's *Oliver Twist* tells of orphaned New York kitten befriended by canine Dodger (Joel), human Fagin (DeLuise), and their gang of thieves. Oliver is adopted by rich girl but must team with pals to save her from mobster Loggia. Snappy music and fun characterizations (notably Midler's pampered poodle and Marin's street-smart Chihuahua) make satisfying family fare.

OLIVER'S STORY 1978
★★★ PG Romance 1:30
☑ Adult situations, explicit language

Dir: John Korty *Cast:* Ryan O'Neal, Candice Bergen, Nicola Pagett, Edward Binns, Ray Milland
▶ Sequel to the huge hit *Love Story*. Young attorney O'Neal, still in mourning over wife's death, is all work and no play until he meets fashion heiress Bergen. Both are prisoners of their self-centered, upper-class backgrounds and their romance eventually flounders. Adapted from Erich Segal's novel, well-acted film looks slick but lacks its predecessor's gripping melodrama.

OLIVER TWIST 1948 British
★★★ NR Drama 1:45 B&W
Dir: David Lean *Cast:* Alec Guinness, John Howard Davies, Robert Newton, Kay Walsh, Anthony Newley, Henry Stephenson
▶ In nineteenth-century England, orphan Oliver Twist (Davies), after daring to ask keepers for more gruel, finds himself out on the street and in the company of thief Fagin (Guinness), the Artful Dodger (Newley), and their gang of teen pickpockets. Magnificently acted and directed adaptation of the Charles Dickens classic; Guinness's performance, although viewed as anti-Semitic upon film's first release, remains especially unforgettable. (CC)

OLLY, OLLY, OXEN FREE 1978
★★★ G Family 1:28
Dir: Richard A. Colla *Cast:* Katharine Hepburn, Kevin McKenzie, Dennis Dimster, Peter Kilman
▶ Spinster junk dealer Hepburn befriends McKenzie and Dimster and helps them rebuild an antique hot-air balloon. Screen immortal Hepburn always worth a watch, but plot seems little more than excuse for some lovely aerial photography.

O LUCKY MAN! 1973 British
★ R Drama 3:01
☑ Strong sexual content, adult situations, explicit language
Dir: Lindsay Anderson *Cast:* Malcolm McDowell, Ralph Richardson, Rachel Roberts, Arthur Lowe, Helen Mirren
▶ Hustling young salesman McDowell pushes his way to the top in bleak, post-industrial England. Superbly acted by topnotch cast, complex and thought-provoking film was a favorite of most critics. However, length, surrealism, allegorical intent, and cynicism ("If you've found the reason to live on and not to die—you

are a lucky man!") make it rough going for most viewers. Beware of severely edited versions.

OLYMPIA 1936 German
★ NR Documentary/Sports 3:40 B&W
Dir: Leni Riefenstahl
▶ Massive documentary on the 1936 Berlin Olympics is one of the most comprehensive and beautiful records of the games. Shot with an eye towards extolling Nazi virtues, film downplays non-Aryans like Jesse Owens, but otherwise presents a fascinating, intimate look at athletes. Several sequences—in particular the majestic diving competition—are edited with breathtaking virtuosity. Various shorter versions are also available. ⓢ

OMEGA MAN, THE 1971
★★★ PG Sci-Fi 1:38
☑ Brief nudity, adult situations, explicit language, violence
Dir: Boris Sagal *Cast:* Charlton Heston, Anthony Zerbe, Rosalind Cash, Paul Koslo, Lincoln Kilpatrick, Eric Laneuville
▶ Most of human life has been killed by germ warfare. Los Angeles scientist Heston immunizes himself and must battle plague-stricken albino mutants known as the Family. Heston discovers a group of disease-free youngsters who may be the key to saving mankind. Visually striking and generally gripping.

OMEGA SYNDROME 1987
★★ R Action-Adventure 1:29
☑ Adult situations, explicit language, violence
Dir: Joseph Manduke *Cast:* Ken Wahl, Doug McClure, George DiCenzo, Nicole Eggert
▶ Hard-drinking, down-on-his-luck journalist Wahl shakes out of his doldrums when daughter Eggert is kidnapped by neo-Nazi terrorists known as Omega. Teamed with Vietnam buddy DiCenzo, Wahl infiltrates Omega, rescues his daughter, and wastes the fascists in a climactic shoot-out. Formula actioner for diehards only.

OMEN, THE 1976
★★★★ R Horror 1:51
☑ Explicit language, graphic violence
Dir: Richard Donner *Cast:* Gregory Peck, Lee Remick, David Warner, Billie Whitelaw, Harvey Stephens, Leo McKern
▶ Peck, American ambassador to England, and wife Remick learn that an-

gelic-looking surrogate son Stephens is actually the Antichrist, offspring of Satan. Many gory deaths later, Peck must attempt to kill the boy to avert Armageddon. Lurid and extremely popular film spawned sequels *Damien—Omen II* and *The Final Conflict*.

ON A CLEAR DAY YOU CAN SEE FOREVER 1970
★ ★ ★ **G Musical 2:09**
Dir: Vincente Minnelli *Cast:* Barbra Streisand, Yves Montand, Bob Newhart, Larry Blyden, Simon Oakland, Jack Nicholson
▶ Shrink Montand becomes fascinated with patient Streisand who can recall past lives under hypnosis. Unaware of the true nature of his experiments (she just wants to beat the smoking habit), she falls in love with him. Tuneful, underrated Streisand vehicle; spectacular cinematography (especially in the flashbacks), melodic Lerner and Lane score (including title tune and "Come Back to Me"), fine support from Newhart and Nicholson as Barbra's stepbrother.

ONCE BITTEN 1985
★ ★ **PG-13 Comedy 1:33**
☑ Brief nudity, adult situations, explicit language, adult humor
Dir: Howard Storm *Cast:* Lauren Hutton, Cleavon Little, Jim Carrey, Karen Kopins, Skip Lackey
▶ Frustrated Los Angeles teenager Carrey has a one-night stand with alluring countess Hutton—unaware that she preys on the blood of virgins. Can Carrey's girlfriend Kopins rescue him from the undead? Despite sultry Hutton, stylish but uninspired comedy quickly grows tedious. **(CC)**

ONCE IN PARIS 1978
★ ★ **PG Romance 1:39**
☑ Adult situations, explicit language
Dir: Frank D. Gilroy *Cast:* Wayne Rogers, Gayle Hunnicutt, Jack Lenoir, Phillippe March, Clement Harari, Tanya Lopert
▶ American screenwriter Rogers, on assignment in Paris, is shown the town by know-it-all chauffeur Lenoir. Rogers romances beautiful Englishwoman Hunnicutt until Lenoir also beds her. The guys remain buddies after she returns to Britain. Slight, sedate, and highly personal romance (Lenoir was originally Paris chauffeur to writer/director Gilroy).

ONCE IS NOT ENOUGH 1975
★ **R Drama 2:01**
☑ Nudity, adult situations, explicit language
Dir: Guy Green *Cast:* Kirk Douglas, Alexis Smith, David Janssen, George Hamilton, Melina Mercouri, Deborah Raffin
▶ Glossy, superficial adaptation of Jacqueline Susann's best-selling soap opera describes the affairs of various jet-setters, in particular Douglas, an over-the-hill movie producer who marries wealthy lesbian Smith to please his spoiled daughter, Raffin. Raffin then seduces playboy Hamilton and writer Janssen. Also known as *Jacqueline Susann's Once Is Not Enough.*

ONCE UPON A HONEYMOON 1942
★ **NR Comedy 1:57 B&W**
Dir: Leo McCarey *Cast:* Ginger Rogers, Cary Grant, Walter Slezak, Albert Dekker, Albert Basserman
▶ Romantic triangle set before World War II, with Grant a reporter who lures an American stripper-turned-society-woman Rogers from her "businessman" husband Slezak. Slezak, actually a Nazi agent, then chases the couple across Europe. Stars outshine lackluster script.

ONCE UPON A TIME IN THE WEST 1969 U.S./Italian
★ ★ ★ **PG Western 2:45**
☑ Rape, explicit language, graphic violence
Dir: Sergio Leone *Cast:* Charles Bronson, Henry Fonda, Claudia Cardinale, Jason Robards, Gabriele Ferzetti, Keenan Wynn
▶ Culmination of director Leone's spaghetti Westerns is an extraordinary look at the settling of the frontier. Cardinale, newly widowed, is drawn into a land war with a railroad magnate. Bronson and Robards are outlaws who defend her against hired killers led by Fonda (outstanding in a rare villainous role). From its brilliant opening credits (featuring Woody Strode and Jack Elam) to its final shootout, a film of breathtaking scope and detail. Avoid the re-edited shorter version.

ONCE UPON A TIME IN AMERICA 1984
★ ★ ★ ★ **R Crime/Drama 3:48**
☑ Rape, nudity, explicit language, graphic violence
Dir: Sergio Leone *Cast:* Robert De

Niro, James Woods, Elizabeth McGovern, Tuesday Weld, William Forsythe, James Hayden

▶ Lengthy, convoluted gangster epic traces the uneasy friendship between Brooklyn thugs De Niro and Woods over a fifty-year span of rape, extortion, and murder. Film's visual sweep achieves an almost operatic intensity, but plot is often incomprehensible. First released here in two drastically shortened and re-edited versions; cassette copies still lack some footage shown in Europe. **(CC)**

ONCE WE WERE DREAMERS 1987 Israeli
★ **NR Drama 1:40**
☑ Violence
Dir: Uri Barbash *Cast:* Kelly McGillis, John Shea, Christine Boisson, Arnon Zadok

▶ Sincere, high-minded drama about the early days of Israel, focusing on a Galilee commune dedicated to equality. A forbidden love affair between McGillis, a beautiful Viennese woman, and violinist Shea threatens to disrupt the delicate balance of the community. Good intentions can't salvage film's plodding style.

ONE AND ONLY, THE 1978
★★ **PG Comedy 1:38**
☑ Explicit language
Dir: Carl Reiner *Cast:* Henry Winkler, Kim Darby, Gene Saks, William Daniels, Harold Gould, Herve Villechaize

▶ Brash Midwesterner Winkler moves to New York confident he will become an acting star, but finds success elusive until manager Saks introduces him to the world of professional wrestling. Easygoing comedy presents a warmly nostalgic view of the 1950s.

ONE CRAZY SUMMER 1986
★★★ **PG Comedy 1:33**
☑ Adult situations, explicit language, adult humor
Dir: Savage Steve Holland *Cast:* John Cusack, Demi Moore, Joel Murray, Bob Goldthwait, Curtis Armstrong, Joe Flaherty

▶ Vacationing on Nantucket, aspiring cartoonist Cusack falls for singer Moore, who's leading a protest against land developer William Hickey. Loose collection of sight gags and brief animated sequences add up to a pleasant but standard teen comedy. **(CC)**

ONE DARK NIGHT 1983
★★ **PG Horror 1:29**

☑ Adult situations, explicit language, violence
Dir: Tom McLoughlin *Cast:* Meg Tilly, Robin Evans, Leslie Speights, Elizabeth Daily, Adam West, Melissa Newman

▶ Teen Tilly must spend a night in a local mausoleum as part of a sorority initiation. A Russian psychic is buried there and his powers survive the grave to cause trouble for Tilly and her sorority sisters. Some original touches but farfetched plot and mediocre special effects.

ONE DEADLY SUMMER 1983 French
★ **R Mystery-Suspense 2:10**
☑ Rape, nudity, strong sexual content, adult situations, explicit language, violence
Dir: Jean Becker *Cast:* Isabelle Adjani, Alain Souchon, Suzanne Flon, Francois Cluzet, Jenny Cleve, Manuel Gelin

▶ Emotionally unstable young Adjani seeks to kill the men who once raped her mother. Only after she has seduced the three en route to her planned revenge does she learn they are not guilty. She is institutionalized while her husband mistakenly slays the innocent men. Adjani sizzles in otherwise pretentious and confused story. **(CC)** Ⓢ

ONE-EYED JACKS 1961
★★★★ **NR Western 2:21**
Dir: Marlon Brando *Cast:* Marlon Brando, Karl Malden, Pina Pillicer, Katy Jurado, Ben Johnson, Slim Pickens

▶ Bank robber Brando, betrayed by partner Malden, spends five years in a Mexican prison. On release, he confronts Malden, now a sheriff, in Monterey. Brando's only turn at directing is a rambling but often intriguing psychological Western with stunning, Oscar-nominated photography.

ONE FLEW OVER THE CUCKOO'S NEST 1975
★★★★★ **R Comedy/Drama 2:13**
☑ Adult situations, explicit language
Dir: Milos Forman *Cast:* Jack Nicholson, Louise Fletcher, Will Sampson, Brad Dourif, Scatman Crothers, Danny DeVito

▶ Entertaining and moving adaptation of Ken Kesey's antiestablishment novel. Troublemaking convict Nicholson is transferred to a mental hospital. There he tries to rally patients Dourif, DeVito, and Sampson against the iron rule of head nurse Fletcher. Picture swept top five

Academy Awards, first to do so in forty years. Nicholson soars.

ONE FROM THE HEART 1982
★ R Romance/Comedy 1:40
☑ Brief nudity, adult situations, explicit language
Dir: Francis Coppola *Cast:* Frederic Forrest, Teri Garr, Raul Julia, Nastassia Kinski, Harry Dean Stanton, Lainie Kazan
▶ Longtime Las Vegas lovers Forrest and Garr quarrel on their anniversary. Each cavorts with respective one-night stands Kinski and Julia while wishing they were reunited. Director Coppola hoped to create a homage to old-style Hollywood tinsel, but insubstantial script sabotaged his intent. Picture is lushly gorgeous, with breath-taking sets from Dean Tavoularis and striking cinematography by Vittorio Storaro, but dull result lacks heart.

101 DALMATIONS 1961
★ ★ ★ ★ ★ G Animation 1:19
Dir: Wolfgang Reitherman, Hamilton Luske, Clyde Geronimi *Cast:* Voices of: Rod Taylor, Betty Lou Gerson, J. Pat O'-Malley, Martha Wentworth
▶ Male dalmation Pongo arranges for bachelor master to meet pretty woman with female dalmation Perdita. The humans marry, and puppies are soon born. When villainous Cruella De Ville kidnaps the pups to make a fur coat, it's Pongo and Perdita to the rescue. Enthralling family fare has thrills, chills, suspense, romance, comedy, and Disney's most memorable villainess.

100 RIFLES 1969
★ ★ ★ PG Western 1:50
☑ Adult situations, explicit language, violence
Dir: Tom Gries *Cast:* Jim Brown, Raquel Welch, Burt Reynolds, Fernando Lamas, Dan O'Herlihy
▶ Sheriff Brown pursues renegade half-breed Reynolds, who has just stolen a shipment of guns for an uprising against sadistic Mexican officer Lamas and railroad tycoon O'Herlihy. Brown's priorities are tested when he falls for Welch, Reynolds's squaw and a Yaqui Indian guerrilla leader. Reynolds's ingratiating performance steals this violent but routine Western.

ONE MAGIC CHRISTMAS 1985
★ ★ ★ ★ G Drama/Family 1:40
Dir: Philip Borsos *Cast:* Mary Steenburgen, Gary Basaraba, Harry Dean Stan-

ton, Arthur Hill, Elisabeth Harnois, Robbie Magwood
▶ Impoverished mother Steenburgen sinks into despair as the holidays near, but guardian angel Stanton renews her faith with a series of unexpected miracles. Sincere but surprisingly dark Disney fantasy is an extremely effective Yuletide tearjerker. Climax features Jan Rubes as a touchingly realistic Santa Claus.

ONE MILLION YEARS B.C. 1966
U.S./British
★ NR Action-Adventure 1:40
Dir: Don Chaffey *Cast:* Raquel Welch, John Richardson, Percy Herbert, Robert Brown, Martine Beswick, Jean Waldon
▶ Prehistoric Romeo and Juliet with dinosaurs. Richardson, an outcast from the Rock People, romances Welch, one of the Shell People. Performance in animal-skin bikini made Welch a household name. Real stars of pic are the dinosaurs created by special-effects legend Ray Harryhausen.

ONE MORE SATURDAY NIGHT 1986
★ R Comedy 1:31
☑ Brief nudity, adult situations, explicit language
Dir: Dennis Klein *Cast:* Tom Davis, Al Franken, Moira Harris, Frank Howard, Bess Meyer
▶ Uneventful comedy about mishaps and mixups in the small town of St. Cloud, Minnesota. "Saturday Night Live" veterans Franken and Davis play visiting rock musicians on the prowl for dates; other subplots involve a widower dating for the first time in years and teens wrecking a house during an unplanned party. Bland film was produced by Dan Aykroyd.

ONE OF OUR DINOSAURS IS MISSING 1975
★ ★ ★ G Comedy 1:41
Dir: Robert Stevenson *Cast:* Peter Ustinov, Helen Hayes, Clive Revill, Derek Nimmo, Joan Sims
▶ Chinese spies steal a dinosaur fossil containing top-secret microfilm from a British museum. Scotland Yard is baffled until nanny Hayes and her friends tackle the case. Lower-grade Disney offering filled with weak slapstick chases.

ONE ON ONE 1977
★ ★ ★ ★ PG Drama 1:38
☑ Explicit language
Dir: Lamont Johnson *Cast:* Robby Benson, Annette O'Toole, G. D. Spradlin, Gail Strickland, Melanie Griffith

▶ Benson, a small-town high schooler, wins a basketball scholarship to a large university, but is quickly overwhelmed by coach Spradlin's demanding training regimen. Beautiful tutor O'Toole helps him cope with classes and sports. Inspiring underdog drama was written by Benson and his father, Jerry Segal.

ONE SUMMER LOVE 1976
★★ **PG Drama 1:35**
☑ Adult situations, violence
Dir: Gilbert Cates *Cast:* Beau Bridges, Susan Sarandon, Mildred Dunnock, Michael B. Miller, Linda Miller, Ann Wedgeworth
▶ Connecticut mental patient Bridges has trouble adjusting to the real world upon release and seeks comfort from a variety of surrogate mothers. Sarandon, a movie theater concession clerk, falls for his naive view of life and helps him trace his parents. Earnest drama suffers from predictable plotting.

1001 ARABIAN NIGHTS 1959
★★★★ **NR Animation 1:16**
Dir: Jack Kinney *Cast:* Voices of Jim Backus, Kathryn Grant, Dwayne Hickman, Hans Conried, Herschel Bernardi
▶ Baghdad merchant Abdul Azziz Magoo discovers a genie in one of his lamps, leading to magical adventures involving his nephew Aladdin. Charming animated version of the famous Arabian Nights tales was nearsighted Mr. Magoo's feature-film debut. Pleasant musical score by George Duning.

ONE TRICK PONY 1980
★ **R Drama 1:40**
☑ Nudity, adult situations, explicit language
Dir: Robert M. Young *Cast:* Paul Simon, Blair Brown, Rip Torn, Joan Hackett, Allen Goorwitz, Mare Winningham
▶ Earnest but predictable drama about Simon, a once-popular musician confronting various crises: pressure from record company execs for a new hit, an impending divorce, an affair with a married woman, etc. Simon, who also wrote the script and score (including "Late in the Evening"), gives a creditable performance. Appearances by the B-52's, Sam and Dave, the Lovin' Spoonful, and Lou Reed as an egotistical producer.

ONE, TWO, THREE 1961
★★★ **NR Comedy 1:48 B&W**
Dir: Billy Wilder *Cast:* James Cagney,

Horst Buchholz, Pamela Tiffin, Arlene Francis
▶ In West Berlin, Coca-Cola executive Cagney, told to look after the boss's daughter (Tiffin), tries to turn her Communist husband Buchholz into a proper capitalist. Fast-paced and very funny Cold War satire, dominated by Cagney's wonderfully blustering characterization.

ONE WOMAN OR TWO 1985 French
☆ **PG-13 Romance/Comedy 1:37**
☑ Nudity, explicit language
Dir: Daniel Vigne *Cast:* Gerard Depardieu, Sigourney Weaver, Michel Aumont, Dr. Ruth Westheimer, Zabou, Jean-Pierre Bisson
▶ Archaeologist Depardieu discovers remnants of prehistoric woman. Mistaking ad exec Weaver for Westheimer, a philanthropist with cash for future research, Depardieu whisks Weaver off to his dig and falls in love. Harmless romp with fine cast aspires to lunacy of classic screwball comedies but often falls short of the mark.

ON GOLDEN POND 1981
★★★★★ **PG Drama 1:49**
☑ Explicit language
Dir: Mark Rydell *Cast:* Katharine Hepburn, Henry Fonda, Jane Fonda, Dabney Coleman, Doug McKeon, William Lanteau
▶ Crotchety Yankee retiree Henry Fonda and spunky wife Hepburn find idyllic summer on New England lake disrupted when daughter Jane Fonda and fiancé Coleman leave his unruly son McKeon in their care. Kid learns to be civil while old man learns to loosen up and love, so that he and daughter can overcome lifelong hostility. Screenplay by Ernest Thompson from his touching Broadway hit. Splendid performances from all, but Fonda steals the show in his last film. Oscars went to Fonda (his first in a long and accomplished career), Hepburn, and Thompson.

ON HER MAJESTY'S SECRET SERVICE 1969 British
★★★ **PG Espionage/Action-Adventure 2:20**
☑ Violence
Dir: Peter Hunt *Cast:* George Lazenby, Diana Rigg, Telly Savalas, Ilse Steppat, Gabriele Ferzetti, Bernard Lee
▶ James Bond (Lazenby), while battling archvillain Blofeld's (Savalas) plan to poison international food supply, falls in love

with gangster's daughter Rigg and gets married. First non-Connery Bond movie lacks Sean's charisma (although George tries gallantly) but is otherwise first-class, with terrific chase scenes, more depth and fewer gimmicks than usual, fetching Diana. The ill-fated romance provides some of the most poignant moments in the whole series.

ONION FIELD, THE 1979
★★★★ R Drama 2:01
☑ Brief nudity, explicit language, violence
Dir: Harold Becker   *Cast:* John Savage, James Woods, Franklyn Seales, Ronny Cox, Ted Danson, David Huffman
▶ In 1963, small-time criminals Woods and Seales kidnap two cops, kill one, and are later apprehended. As surviving policeman Savage struggles with his guilt, the killers manage to frustrate the justice system and avoid the death penalty. Gutsy, realistic, and strongly crafted indictment of the legal system based on the book (a true story) by Joseph Wambaugh. Exceptional performances by Woods and Savage.

ONLY ANGELS HAVE WINGS 1939
★★★ NR Drama 2:01 B&W
Dir: Howard Hawks   *Cast:* Cary Grant, Jean Arthur, Richard Barthelmess, Rita Hayworth, Thomas Mitchell, Sig Rumann
▶ Stylized, highly charged adventure about foolhardy aviators under pressure to deliver mail over the Andes Mountains despite constant bad weather. Arrival of showgirl Arthur, who's immediately drawn to top pilot Grant, increases tension among the fliers. Perfect example of golden-era Hollywood storytelling is filled with memorable scenes, particularly a grim dinner after a crash.

ONLY GAME IN TOWN, THE 1970
★★ PG Drama 1:53
☑ Adult situations, explicit language
Dir: George Stevens   *Cast:* Elizabeth Taylor, Warren Beatty, Charles Braswell, Hank Henry, Olga Valery
▶ Las Vegas mistress Taylor, despairing of marrying lover Braswell, starts a casual affair with hard-gambling musician Beatty. Pleasant but slight adaptation of a Frank D. Gilroy play was filmed in Paris so Taylor could remain close to then-husband Richard Burton. Gilroy used his experiences on this film to write *Once in Paris.*

ONLY WHEN I LAUGH 1981
★★★★ R Comedy/Drama 1:55
☑ Brief nudity, adult situations, explicit language adult humor
Dir: Glenn Jordan   *Cast:* Marsha Mason, Kristy McNichol, James Coco, Joan Hackett, David Dukes
▶ After a stay in a rehab clinic, actress Mason tries to rebuild her relationship with daughter McNichol. Mason, fighting the temptation to drink again when personal and professional problems surface, is wonderful and sympathetic; Coco and Hackett provide able support (all were Oscar-nominated) and McNichol holds her own in this august company. Quite satisfying Neil Simon screenplay combines one-liners with realistic look at life's disappointments and triumphs.

ON THE BEACH 1959
★★★ NR Drama 2:13 B&W
Dir: Stanley Kramer   *Cast:* Gregory Peck, Ava Gardner, Fred Astaire, Anthony Perkins, Donna Anderson
▶ After a nuclear explosion devastates the world, the sole survivors (the crew of a sub captained by Peck and the people of Australia) deal with their impending radioactive doom. Haunting and powerful, superbly performed; one of the strongest antiwar statements ever made. So disturbing some may find it depressing. From the novel by Nevil Shute.

ON THE EDGE 1985
★★ PG-13 Drama 1:35
☑ Brief nudity, explicit language
Dir: Rob Nilsson   *Cast:* Bruce Dern, John Marley, Bill Bailey, Jim Haynie, Pam Grier
▶ Middle-aged runner Dern, banned from the sport for twenty years, pins his hopes for personal redemption on California's grueling Dipsea Race (renamed Cielo-Sea here), a beautiful but challenging mountain course. Sincere, uplifting film features an inspiring climax.

ON THE RIGHT TRACK 1981
★★★★ PG Comedy 1:38
☑ Adult situations, explicit language, mild violence
Dir: Lee Philips   *Cast:* Gary Coleman, Maureen Stapleton, Michael Lembeck, Norman Fell, Lisa Eilbacher, Bill Russell
▶ Ten-year-old shoeshine boy Coleman lives in Chicago's Union Station, where his friends include affable bag lady Stapleton. When Coleman uses his psychic powers to pick horses at the racetrack,

everyone wants to be his friend. Social worker Lembeck and arcade employee Eilbacher fall in love and rescue Coleman from exploitation.

ON THE TOWN 1950
★ ★ ★ NR Musical 1:37
Dir: Gene Kelly, Stanley Donen *Cast:* Gene Kelly, Frank Sinatra, Ann Miller, Vera-Ellen, Jules Munshin, Betty Garrett
▶ "Gotta pick up a date, maybe seven or eight, in a day" is the mission for sailors Kelly, Sinatra, and Munshin on a one-day leave in "New York, New York, it's a helluva town." Kelly pursues subway poster girl Vera-Ellen, Sinatra finds romance with cabbie Garrett, and cavemanish Munshin pairs off with Miller, doing a study on prehistoric days. Exuberant musical classic gives you a tour of famous New York City locations to the bounce of a tuneful Betty Comden/Adolph Green-Leonard Bernstein/Roger Edens score.

ON THE WATERFRONT 1954
★ ★ ★ ★ NR Drama 1:47 B&W
Dir: Elia Kazan *Cast:* Marlon Brando, Eva Marie Saint, Karl Malden, Lee J. Cobb, Rod Steiger, Leif Erickson
▶ "I coulda been a contender," pleads ex-boxer-turned-longshoreman Brando to his brother Steiger. Both are involved with corrupt union boss Cobb, responsible for the death of a dock worker, but Brando turns against Cobb under the influence of crusading priest Malden and the dead man's sister, Saint. Hard-hitting and incredibly powerful; deservedly one of the most acclaimed films of all time. Winner of eight Oscars including Picture, Director, Actor (Brando), Supporting Actress (Saint). **(CC)**

ON THE YARD 1979
★ ★ ★ R Drama 1:41
☑ Explicit language, violence
Dir: Raphael D. Silver *Cast:* Thomas Waites, John Heard, Mike Kellin, Richard Bright, Joe Grifasi
▶ Conflict escalates between Waites, an inmate who runs the prison black market, and Heard, a convict who cannot pay him back for fifteen packs of cigarettes. Convincing ensemble acting, excellent jazz score, and realistic prison environment. However, plot lacks focus and tone is generally downbeat.

ON VALENTINE'S DAY 1986
★ PG Drama 1:46
☑ Adult situations, explicit language
Dir: Ken Harrison *Cast:* William Con-verse-Roberts, Hallie Foote, Michael Higgins, Steven Hill, Rochelle Oliver, Matthew Broderick
▶ Second in Horton Foote's semiautobiographical cycle of nine plays about a small Texas town is a literate but slow-moving account of various members of the Robedaux family, in particular pregnant Foote, wife of Converse-Roberts. Having eloped on Valentine's Day 1917, she hopes for a reconciliation with her parents over Christmas. A prequel to *1918*, paired together as *Story of a Marriage* for TV.

OPERATION PETTICOAT 1959
★ ★ ★ NR Comedy 2:04
Dir: Blake Edwards *Cast:* Cary Grant, Tony Curtis, Joan O'Brien, Dina Merrill, Arthur O'Connell
▶ Extremely popular service comedy about a crippled sub captained by Grant but controlled by smooth-talking con man Curtis. As a result of one of Curtis's schemes, Grant finds five beautiful nurses squeezed into the sub's tight confines. Stars make a great comic pair, and they're supported by consistently strong gags. Financially Grant's most successful effort, film inspired a TV movie and short series.

OPERATION THUNDERBOLT 1978 Israeli
★ ★ ★ ★ PG Action-Adventure 2:00
☑ Violence
Dir: Menahem Golan *Cast:* Yehoram Gaon, Klaus Kinski, Assaf Dayan, Sybil Danning, Ori Levy, Arik Lavi
▶ True story of the raid on Entebbe Airport: terrorists hijack Tel Aviv–Paris flight and bring it to Uganda. Israeli soldiers stage a daring mission to rescue them. Straightforward and exciting; enough action to overcome crude direction and unconvincing performances. Some subtitles but most of the dialogue is in English. Nominated for Oscar as Best Foreign Film. Other films about the same event: *Raid on Entebbe* and *Victory at Entebbe*. **S**

OPPOSING FORCE 1986
★ ★ ★ R Action-Adventure 1:37
☑ Rape, nudity, adult situations, explicit language, violence
Dir: Eric Karson *Cast:* Tom Skerritt, Lisa Eichhorn, Anthony Zerbe, Richard Roundtree, Robert Wightman, John Considine
▶ Air Force recruits, including one female, Eichhorn, are dropped on a de-

serted Philippine island for war games which get murderously out of hand when psychotic commander Zerbe plays for keeps. Well-staged action, good cast, and generally entertaining although short on logic.

ORCA 1977
★★★★ PG Mystery-Suspense 1:32
☑ Explicit language, violence
Dir: Michael Anderson *Cast:* Richard Harris, Charlotte Rampling, Will Sampson, Keenan Wynn, Bo Derek
▶ When fisherman Harris kills pregnant killer whale, he finds himself stalked by her revenge-minded mate. Generates plenty of farfetched tension and spectacular scares, as when the whale knocks over a house to snack on Bo's leg. Effective Ennio Morricone score; pompous dialogue from Rampling, unbelievably cast as a whale expert.

ORDEAL BY INNOCENCE 1985
★★ PG-13 Mystery-Suspense 1:30
☑ Brief nudity, adult situations, violence
Dir: Desmond Davis *Cast:* Donald Sutherland, Sarah Miles, Faye Dunaway, Ian McShane, Christopher Plummer
▶ Dr. Arthur Calgary (Sutherland) returns from a polar expedition to discover that he was the alibi for a man hanged two years earlier for murder. When the police won't reopen the case, Calgary decides to investigate the murder himself. A moderately entertaining mystery marred by a less than riveting plot and rather wooden performances. Still, genre fans will enjoy the usual Agatha Christie mix of suspects and clues.

ORDINARY PEOPLE 1980
★★★★ R Drama 2:04
☑ Adult situations, explicit language
Dir: Robert Redford *Cast:* Donald Sutherland, Mary Tyler Moore, Judd Hirsch, Timothy Hutton, Elizabeth McGovern, Dinah Manoff
▶ After a boating accident that kills his older brother and a suicide attempt, Hutton visits shrink Hirsch to deal with his guilt and his emotionally repressed mother Moore. Dad Sutherland and mom gradually grow apart. Oscars for Best Picture, Director, and Supporting Actor (Hutton) went to this immaculately crafted, emotionally wrenching examination of upper-middle-class angst. Superbly performed

(especially by Hutton), with wonderful use of suburban Chicago locations.

ORGANIZATION, THE 1971
★★ PG Drama 1:47
☑ Adult situations, explicit language, violence
Dir: Don Medford *Cast:* Sidney Poitier, Barbara McNair, Gerald S. O'Loughlin, Sheree North, Fred Beir, Allen Garfield
▶ Poitier reprises his *In the Heat of the Night* role as Virgil Tibbs, a hard-boiled cop trying to break up a drug ring. Anti-drug vigilantes are framed for a murder; when Poitier tries to clear them, he's suspended from the force. Above-average cop film with driving action and a strong climax. Look for Ron O'Neal and Raul Julia in small roles. **(CC)**

ORPHANS 1987
★★ R Drama 2:00
☑ Adult situations, explicit language, violence
Dir: Alan J. Pakula *Cast:* Albert Finney, Matthew Modine, Kevin Anderson, John Kellogg, Anthony Heald
▶ Orphaned brothers, manipulative Modine and naive Anderson, kidnap alcoholic gangster Finney. A strange family relationship develops as captive becomes a father figure to his captors. Grandstanding performances by the talented trio get the most out of the juicy dialogue. However, weird characterizations and claustrophobic conflict will limit appeal. From Lyle Kessler's Off-Broadway play. **(CC)**

OSCAR, THE 1966
★ NR Drama 1:59
Dir: Russell Rouse *Cast:* Stephen Boyd, Elke Sommer, Eleanor Parker, Joseph Cotten, Milton Berle, Jill St. John
▶ Romanticized hokum about actor Boyd nervously waiting through the awards ceremony to see if he's won an Oscar. Best friend Tony Bennett recounts his sordid career from strip joint emcee to over-the-hill matinee idol. Fun on a camp level, and filled with stars: Ernest Borgnine, Walter Brennan, Hedda Hopper, Bob Hope, Merle Oberon, Frank Sinatra, Edie Adams, Peter Lawford, etc.

OSTERMAN WEEKEND, THE 1983
★★★ R Mystery-Suspense 1:42
☑ Nudity, explicit language, violence
Dir: Sam Peckinpah *Cast:* Rutger Hauer, John Hurt, Burt Lancaster, Craig T. Nelson, Dennis Hopper, Chris Sarandon

▶ Television journalist Hauer, told by CIA agent Hurt that his best friends Nelson, Hopper, and Sarandon are Soviet spies, hosts a CIA-monitored gathering. Double crosses and kidnapping are on the weekend agenda. Virile direction by Peckinpah and decent acting, but confused plotting generates little emotional empathy. From the Robert Ludlum novel.

OTELLO 1986 Italian
★ ★ ★ ★ **PG Music 2:02**
☑ Adult situations
Dir: Franco Zeffirelli *Cast:* Placido Domingo, Katia Ricciarelli, Justino Diaz, Petra Malakova
▶ Pathologically jealous Moorish general Domingo is driven into a murderous frenzy toward his wife Ricciarelli by the machinations of scheming ensign Diaz. Overblown production of Verdi opus may please opera fans. Domingo sings beautifully but looks (thanks to ridiculous dark makeup) awful.

OTHER, THE 1972
★ ★ ★ **PG Horror 1:40**
☑ Adult situations, explicit language, violence
Dir: Robert Mulligan *Cast:* Uta Hagen, Diana Muldaur, Chris Udvarnoky, Martin Udvarnoky, Portia Nelson, John Ritter
▶ In 1930s New England, bizarre murders plague small town. Are the Udvarnoky twins, one good and one evil, involved? Mom Muldaur and grandma Hagen are among those who'd like some answers. Spine-tingling adaptation of the Thomas Tryon best-seller.

OTHER SIDE OF MIDNIGHT, THE 1977
★ ★ ★ ★ ★ **R Drama 2:49**
☑ Nudity, adult situations, explicit language
Dir: Charles Jarrott *Cast:* Marie-France Pisier, John Beck, Susan Sarandon, Raf Vallone, Clu Gulager
▶ During World War II, American pilot Beck seduces, impregnates, and dumps French Pisier. After having an abortion, Pisier uses her wiles to become rich and famous and then plots revenge against Beck and his wife Sarandon. Lavish, swanky, juicy pulp captures author Sidney Sheldon's standard formula for elegant melodrama. Lush Michel Legrand score.

OTHER SIDE OF THE MOUNTAIN, THE 1975
★ ★ ★ ★ **PG Biography 1:41**
☑ Adult situations, explicit language

Dir: Larry Peerce *Cast:* Marilyn Hassett, Beau Bridges, Belinda Montgomery, Dabney Coleman, Nan Martin, William Bryant
▶ True story of skier Jill Kinmont (Hassett) whose career ends when a skiing accident leaves her a paraplegic. New beau Bridges gives her hope and romance. She becomes a teacher; but then tragedy strikes Bridges. Inspirational tale will evoke tears; Hassett is excellent. Spawned sequel.

OTHER SIDE OF THE MOUNTAIN PART II, THE 1978
★ ★ ★ ★ ★ **PG Biography 1:39**
☑ Adult situations, explicit language
Dir: Larry Peerce *Cast:* Marilyn Hassett, Timothy Bottoms, Nan Martin, Belinda Montgomery, Gretchen Corbett
▶ Continuation of the true story of Olympic skier Jill Kinmont (Hassett), who suffered paralysis in a skiing accident and the death of her fiancé in a plane crash. Kinmont teaches in L.A. and then vacations in her hometown, where she meets divorced trucker Bottoms who breaks through her resistance to love. Hassett repeats her credible and sympathetic characterization. Bottoms is natural and likable, and the intimate love story delivers a good cry.

OUR MAN FLINT 1966
★ ★ ★ **NR Espionage/Comedy 1:47**
Dir: Daniel Mann *Cast:* James Coburn, Lee J. Cobb, Gila Golan, Edward Mulhare, Benson Fong, Shelby Grant
▶ When an evil organization plots to take over the world by establishing control over global weather, it is up to superspy Derek Flint (Coburn) to stop them. Perhaps the best of the countless James Bond spoofs of the 1960s, thanks to Coburn's confident tongue-in-cheek flair. Superior to its 1967 sequel *In Like Flint*.

OUR TOWN 1940
★ ★ ★ ★ ★ **NR Drama 1:30 B&W**
Dir: Sam Wood *Cast:* William Holden, Martha Scott, Frank Craven, Beulah Bondi, Thomas Mitchell, Guy Kibbee
▶ Narrator Craven is our guide to life in pre–World War I Grover's Corners, a small New England town. Holden is a doctor's son who pursues strong-willed Scott over many years; in film's eeriest scene, she encounters reminders of the frailty of human existence during a cemetery hallucination. Adaptation of Thornton Wilder's classic Pulitzer prize–winning

play is moving, funny, innocent, and wise.

OUT COLD 1988
★ ★ R Comedy 1:35
☑ Brief nudity, adult situations, explicit language, violence
Dir: Malcolm Mowbray *Cast:* John Lithgow, Teri Garr, Randy Quaid, Bruce McGill, Lisa Blount
▶ When crude butcher McGill accidentally freezes to death in his meat closet, his unfaithful wife Garr and hapless partner Lithgow, both involved in the incident, conspire to hide the body. Story owes a nod to *The Postman Always Rings Twice.* Some real belly laughs (most effective running sick joke is McGill's popsicled corpse) but despite a talented cast, humor doesn't go far enough, winding up as watered-down black comedy.

OUTLAND 1981
★ ★ R Sci-Fi 1:50
☑ Brief nudity, explicit language, graphic violence
Dir: Peter Hyams *Cast:* Sean Connery, Peter Boyle, Frances Sternhagen, James B. Sikking, Kika Markham, Steven Berkoff
▶ New marshall Connery arrives on moon of Jupiter, just in time to investigate weird mining-camp deaths. When he gets too close to the truth, he's stalked by hired killers. Sturdy story unites Western-style plot with elaborate sci-fi trappings. Violence is more explicit than necessary but sympathetic Connery transcends the flaws. Best scenes: the interplay between Connery and crusty lady doctor Sternhagen.

OUTLAW, THE 1943
★ ★ G Western 1:43 B&W
Dir: Howard Hughes *Cast:* Jane Russell, Jack Beutel, Thomas Mitchell, Walter Huston, Joe Sawyer
▶ Wounded by lawman Pat Garrett (Mitchell), famous outlaw Billy the Kid (Beutel) hides out on a desert ranch with his friend Doc Holliday (Huston). There he falls for the tempestuous Russell (in her film debut). Once-controversial Western seems dull today, although Huston is always interesting. Censored on release for Hughes's preoccupation with Russell's cleavage.

OUTLAW BLUES 1977
★ ★ ★ PG Action-Adventure 1:41
☑ Adult situations, explicit language
Dir: Richard T. Heffron *Cast:* Peter Fonda, Susan Saint James, John Crawford, James Callahan, Michael Lerner
▶ Texas ex-con Fonda has his song stolen by country singer Callahan. Fonda accidentally shoots Callahan trying to retrieve his money, then becomes the center of a statewide manhunt. Singer Saint James helps him escape police while promoting his song into a hit. Lightweight chase film has an appealing country-western score (with Fonda doing his own singing).

OUTLAW JOSEY WALES, THE 1976
★ ★ ★ ★ ★ PG Western 2:16
☑ Rape, brief nudity, explicit language, violence
Dir: Clint Eastwood *Cast:* Clint Eastwood, Chief Dan George, Sondra Locke, Bill McKinney, John Vernon, Sam Bottoms
▶ When his family is murdered by Union "Redlegs," farmer Eastwood joins Confederate guerrillas. Eastwood escapes from an ambush with a price on his head and flees across the West from his nemesis McKinney. Despite his desire for peace, he encounters violence with marauders and Indians. Strong post–Civil War Western features a large canvas of richly detailed characters and settings.

OUT OF AFRICA 1985
★ ★ ★ ★ PG Drama 2:44
☑ Adult situations, mild violence
Dir: Sydney Pollack *Cast:* Meryl Streep, Robert Redford, Klaus Maria Brandauer, Michael Kitchen, Malick Bowens
▶ True story of Danish writer Karen Blixen (Streep), known as Isak Dinesen, who arrives in 1913 Africa to run a coffee plantation. Ignored by husband Brandauer, she develops a special relationship with the land, its people, and dashing adventurer Redford. Magnificent cinematography and locations, stunning performances, unusually complex characters, and beautiful John Barry score make this a class act. Even with the epic trappings, at its heart this is an intimate and quite beautiful love story. Seven Oscars include Best Picture, Director, Screenplay. **(CC)**

OUT OF BOUNDS 1986
★ ★ ★ R Mystery-Suspense 1:29
☑ Explicit language, violence
Dir: Richard Tuggle *Cast:* Anthony Michael Hall, Jenny Wright, Jeff Kober, Glynn Turman, Raymond J. Barry, Pepe Serna
▶ Iowa teen Hall visits his brother in L.A.,

picks up the wrong bag at the airport, and finds himself the target of vicious drug dealers. Farfetched but boasts some tension, action, and surprises. Wright is appealing although Hall suffers from a poorly written part. **(CC)**

OUT OF CONTROL 1985
★ R Action-Adventure 1:18
☑ Rape, nudity, adult situations, explicit language, violence
Dir: Allan Holzman *Cast:* Martin Hewitt, Betsy Russell, Claudia Udy, Andrew J. Lederer, Cindi Dietrich, Jim Youngs
▶ After their senior prom, a group of teens take a plane ride and crash land on a deserted island. Their high jinks (including a rousing game of strip "Spin the Bottle") are rudely disrupted by drug smugglers. Well-shot but rather pointless exercise. Shallow characters, meager plotting.

OUT OF THE BLUE 1980
★★ R Drama 1:29
☑ Nudity, strong sexual content, explicit language, violence
Dir: Dennis Hopper *Cast:* Linda Manz, Dennis Hopper, Sharon Farrell, Don Gordon, Raymond Burr, Eric Allen
▶ Rebellious teen Manz, living with drug-addicted mom Farrell, is reunited with her dad Hopper, who has spent six years in prison for ramming his truck into a school bus. Hopper's drinking and the family's tortured past make the reunion eventful. Outstanding acting but devastating look at family life is tough to take; not a pretty picture.

OUT OF THE PAST 1947
★★★ NR Mystery-Suspense 1:37 B&W
Dir: Jacques Tourneur *Cast:* Robert Mitchum, Jane Greer, Kirk Douglas, Rhonda Fleming, Richard Webb
▶ Former private eye Mitchum tries to lead a quiet small-town life but ex-lover Greer and her gangster boyfriend Douglas return to both haunt and involve him in murder. Film noir cult classic has it all: an intricate and twisty plot, Tourneur's striking visuals, sizzling Greer, Mitchum at his sardonic best, and fine support from Douglas. Remade in 1984 as *Against All Odds* with Greer playing the mother of her original character.

OUT OF TOWNERS, THE 1970
★★★ G Comedy 1:37
Dir: Arthur Hiller *Cast:* Jack Lemmon, Sandy Dennis, Anne Meara, Sandy Baron, Ann Prentiss

▶ Ohio couple, Lemmon and Dennis, plan a romantic visit to New York before an important job interview, but run into a series of nightmarish disasters: lost luggage, cancelled hotel reservations, muggers, hijackers, etc. Although dismaying to Big Apple's tourist industry, Neil Simon script provides nonstop laughs at a breakneck pace.

OUTRAGEOUS! 1977 Canadian
★ R Comedy/Drama 1:36
☑ Adult situations, explicit language
Dir: Richard Benner *Cast:* Craig Russell, Hollis McLaren, Richard Easley, Allan Moyle, Helen Shaver, Gerry Salzberg
▶ Released Toronto mental patient McLaren befriends gay hairdresser/female impersonator Russell. McLaren becomes pregnant by another man but miscarries. She then joins Russell when he moves to New York to seek fame and fortune. Cult following found offbeat, low-budget feature hilarious, but not for mainstream tastes. Followed by *Too Outrageous!*, filmed ten years later.

OUTRAGEOUS FORTUNE 1987
★★★★ R Comedy 1:32
☑ Adult situations, explicit language
Dir: Arthur Hiller *Cast:* Shelley Long, Bette Midler, Peter Coyote, George Carlin, Robert Prosky, John Schuck
▶ Two would-be actresses, prim and proper Long and rude and earthy Midler, are shocked to discover they share the same lover, Coyote. Although he's apparently killed, the two are convinced he's alive and, pursued by both the KGB and the CIA, they trail Coyote to New Mexico. Assisted by 1960s burn-out Carlin, they save California from oblivion. Antagonistic chemistry between Long and Midler is uproarious while Carlin is a hoot in this briskly entertaining romp.

OUTSIDERS, THE 1983
★★★★ PG Drama 1:27
☑ Explicit language, violence
Dir: Francis Coppola *Cast:* Matt Dillon, Ralph Macchio, C. Thomas Howell, Patrick Swayze, Rob Lowe, Emilio Estevez
▶ In 1966 Oklahoma, troubled teens Dillon, Macchio, and others square off against the preppies. When Macchio accidentally kills a preppie, he and Howell must lay low. Then Macchio dies saving schoolchildren from a fire, causing grief-stricken Dillon to attempt ill-fated robbery. Fine performances from Brat Pack

actors and authentic period look. Adapted from the best-selling novel by young adult author S. E. Hinton.

OVERBOARD 1987
★★★★ PG Romance/Comedy 1:52
☑ Explicit language
Dir: Garry Marshall *Cast:* Goldie Hawn, Kurt Russell, Edward Herrmann, Katherine Helmond, Michael Hagerty, Roddy McDowall
► Amiable escapist fare about bored heiress Hawn who stiffs redneck carpenter Russell for a six-hundred dollar fee. When she falls off her yacht and washes ashore with amnesia, widower Russell persuades Hawn she's mother to his bratty children. After initial turmoil in rural pigsty home, Hawn becomes ideal mom to reformed kids. But it isn't long before devious hubby Herrmann shows up to claim her. Hawn, America's favorite airhead, is at her best with real-life beau Russell. **(CC)**

OVER THE BROOKLYN BRIDGE 1984
★★ R Romance/Comedy 1:46
☑ Nudity, adult situations, explicit language
Dir: Menahem Golan *Cast:* Elliott Gould, Margaux Hemingway, Sid Caesar, Shelley Winters, Carol Kane, Burt Young
► Brooklyn restaurateur Gould seeks to open a more upscale establishment in Manhattan but needs loan from rich uncle Caesar. Caesar and rest of Jewish clan don't approve of Gould's Catholic girlfriend Hemingway and pressure him to wed nice Jewish girl Kane. Melting-pot romantic comedy mixes lifeless direction and stereotypical characters into bland fare.

OVER THE EDGE 1979
★★ PG Action-Adventure 1:35
☑ Explicit language, violence
Dir: Jonathan Kaplan *Cast:* Matt Dillon, Vincent Spano, Michael Kramer, Patricia Ludwig, Tom Fergud, Harry Northrup
► In model suburb, young tough-guy teens Dillon, Spano, and Kramer kill time with drugs and vandalism. When hard-nosed cop Northrup slays Dillon after car theft, kids run amok in fatal binge of violence. Fine young cast in probing look at alienated youth, although story is often familiar. Fine soundtrack; Dillon's screen debut.

OVER THE SUMMER 1984
★ NR Drama 1:40
☑ Rape, nudity, explicit language
Dir: Teresa Sparks *Cast:* Laura Hunt, Willard Millan, Johnson West, Catherine Williams
► Atlanta teenager visits her relatives in rural North Carolina. In an eventful stay, she falls in love for the first time, renews her friendship with another seventeen-year-old girl, and fights a rapist. Naturalistic and fresh flavor but thin plot, slow pace, and amateurish acting.

OVER THE TOP 1987
★★★★ PG Drama/Sports 1:33
☑ Explicit language, violence
Dir: Menahem Golan *Cast:* Sylvester Stallone, Robert Loggia, Susan Blakely, Rick Zumwalt, David Mendenhall
► Gentle giant truck driver Stallone battles rich dad-in-law Loggia for custody of son Mendenhall when mom Blakely dies. To earn cash for child support Stallone enters world arm-wrestling championship. Variation on *The Champ* will delight the legions of Stallone fans. **(CC)**

OWL AND THE PUSSYCAT, THE 1970
★★★★ PG Comedy 1:37
☑ Adult situations, explicit language
Dir: Herbert Ross *Cast:* Barbra Streisand, George Segal, Robert Klein, Allen Garfield, Roz Kelly
► Would-be writer Segal informs his landlord of kooky prostitute neighbor Streisand's late-night activities. After she is evicted, she cons her way into becoming his roommate. They fight, argue, and fall in love. Charming if somewhat inconsistent comedy featured Streisand's first nonsinging role. Adapted by Buck Henry from Bill Manhoff's 1964 Broadway hit.

OX-BOW INCIDENT, THE 1943
★★★★ NR Western 1:15 B&W
Dir: William Wellman *Cast:* Henry Fonda, Dana Andrews, Harry Morgan, Anthony Quinn, Mary Beth Hughes, William Eythe
► Searing indictment of mob rule and vigilante justice is one of the all-time great westerns and director Wellman's masterpiece. Cowboys Fonda and Morgan ride into small Nevada town where local rancher is shot by rustlers. Despite pleas for reason by Fonda and others, posse forms and apprehends passing farmers Andrews and Quinn. Gritty, compelling drama uses Western setting for

morality tale with universal appeal. (CC)

OXFORD BLUES 1984
★ ★ ★ PG-13 Comedy 1:37
☑ Adult situations, explicit language
Dir: Robert Boris *Cast:* Rob Lowe, Ally Sheedy, Amanda Pays, Julian Sands, Julian Firth, Alan Howard
▶ American drop-out Lowe cons his way into Oxford to woo English beauty Pays. He's immediately disliked by the stiff British until he proves his mettle as a rower. Creaky fable of British reserve clashing with American brashness works primarily as vehicle for heartthrob Lowe. (CC)

PAINT YOUR WAGON 1969
★ ★ PG Musical 2:46
☑ Adult situations, explicit language
Dir: Joshua Logan *Cast:* Lee Marvin, Clint Eastwood, Jean Seberg, Harve Presnell, Ray Walston, The Nitty Gritty Dirt Band
▶ California prospector Marvin purchases wife Seberg from a Mormon; when she falls for his partner Eastwood, they set up a ménage à trois that shocks their straitlaced neighbors. Lavish production of a Lerner-Loewe stage hit, adapted by Paddy Chayefksy, suffers somewhat from the stars' inability to sing. Songs include "I Talk to the Trees," "They Call the Wind Maria," "Whoop-Ti-Ay."

PAJAMA GAME, THE 1957
★ ★ ★ NR Musical 1:41
Dir: George Abbott, Stanley Donen *Cast:* Doris Day, John Raitt, Carol Haney, Eddie Foy, Jr., Barbara Nichols
▶ Highly enjoyable musical about a labor disturbance in a pajama factory: workers seeking a raise appoint Day to negotiate with foreman Raitt, but she lets them down by falling in love with him. Inventive choreography by Bob Fosse complements a bright score, including "Hernando's Hideaway" and Haney's knockout "Steam Heat."

PALEFACE, THE 1948
★ ★ ★ NR Western/Comedy 1:31
Dir: Norman Z. McLeod *Cast:* Bob Hope, Jane Russell, Robert Armstrong, Iris Adrian, Robert Watson, Iron Eyes Cody
▶ Sprightly Western farce about dentist Hope with a mail-order degree who marries Calamity Jane (Russell) to keep her out of jail. Hope inadvertently corrals a gang of outlaws, but not before engaging in frequently hysterical parodies of

Western clichés. Hope and Russell duet to the Oscar-winning "Buttons and Bows." Followed by *Son of Paleface.*

PALE RIDER 1985
★ ★ ★ ★ R Western 1:56
☑ Explicit language, violence
Dir: Clint Eastwood *Cast:* Clint Eastwood, Carrie Snodgress, Michael Moriarty, Christopher Penn, Richard Dysart, Richard Kiel
▶ Miners in Idaho are harassed by robber baron Dysart and pray for salvation. Into town rides Eastwood, a stranger called the Preacher. When reason doesn't work with Dysart, Eastwood takes off his collar and straps on his six-guns, proving action speaks louder than words. Eastwood has no peer as the silent avenger and his direction brings both reverence and freshness to the Western genre that made him a star. (CC)

PAL JOEY 1957
★ ★ ★ NR Musical 1:51
Dir: George Sidney *Cast:* Frank Sinatra, Rita Hayworth, Kim Novak, Barbara Nichols, Bobby Sherwood
▶ Cynical singer Sinatra dreams of opening his own club; wealthy Hayworth will provide financing if he'll abandon his true love Novak. Sparkling Rodgers and Hart score (including "Bewitched, Bothered, and Bewildered," "My Funny Valentine," "The Lady Is a Tramp"), wonderful San Francisco locations, terrific singing and performances (particularly a fetching canine) in this entertaining adaptation of the John O'Hara story.

PALM BEACH STORY, THE 1942
★ ★ ★ NR Comedy 1:28 B&W
Dir: Preston Sturges *Cast:* Claudette Colbert, Joel McCrea, Mary Astor, Rudy Vallee, William Demarest, Sig Arno
▶ Colbert, the flighty wife of impoverished inventor McCrea, runs off to Palm Beach and attracts mild-mannered millionaire Vallee. When McCrea follows, Vallee's sister Astor sets her sights on him. Witty, cleverly plotted, breathlessly paced love quadrangle from Preston Sturges. Full of unforgettable comic scenes (McCrea luring Colbert to bed while Vallee croons outside) and characters (Astor's foreign boyfriend, the wealthy "Wienie King").

PANDEMONIUM 1982
★ PG Comedy 1:21
☑ Explicit language, violence, adult humor

Dir: Alfred Sole *Cast:* Tom Smothers, Carol Kane, Candice Azzara, Miles Chapin, Judge Reinhold
► Midwestern cheerleading academy is tormented by a series of brutal murders; Kane, a cheerleader with telekinetic powers, joins stalwart Mountie Smothers in solving the case. Silly takeoff of horror movies features cameos by Tab Hunter, Eve Arden, Pee-wee Herman, etc.

PANIC IN NEEDLE PARK 1971
★ **PG Drama 1:50**
☑ Adult situations, explicit language
Dir: Jerry Schatzberg *Cast:* Al Pacino, Kitty Winn, Alan Vint, Richard Bright, Raul Julia, Kiel Martin
► New York City drug addict/dealer Pacino and new girl in town Winn become lovers. She falls into his bad habits; the pair runs afoul of the law and one another when she becomes an informer. Grim tale rings harrowingly true; Pacino is first-rate.

PANIC IN THE STREETS 1950
★★★★ **NR Mystery-Suspense 1:33 B&W**
Dir: Elia Kazan *Cast:* Richard Widmark, Paul Douglas, Barbara Bel Geddes, Walter (Jack) Palance, Zero Mostel, Tommy Rettig
► When bubonic plague is discovered in a dead man, doctor Widmark and cop Douglas team up to find the killers and stop the disease from spreading. Taut and suspenseful with outstanding performances, excellent direction, and superb New Orleans locations. Oscar for Motion Picture Writing (Story).

PAPA'S DELICATE CONDITION 1963
★★★★ **NR Comedy 1:38**
Dir: George Marshall *Cast:* Jackie Gleason, Glynis Johns, Charles Ruggles, Laurel Goodwin, Linda Bruhl, Ned Glass
► Turn-of-the-century Texas: although fun-loving railroad supervisor Gleason drinks too much, daughter Bruhl adores him. However, wife Johns gets fed up, takes the kids, and walks out. A reconciliation eventually occurs. Gleason is quite appealing in this nostalgic charmer. Oscar for Best Song, "Call Me Irresponsible."

PAPER CHASE, THE 1973
★★★★ **PG Drama 1:51**
☑ Adult situations, explicit language
Dir: James Bridges *Cast:* Timothy Bottoms, Lindsay Wagner, John Houseman,
Graham Beckel, Edward Herrmann, James Naughton
► First-year Harvard law student Bottoms struggles under the stern tutelage of crusty professor Houseman; he also falls in love with Houseman's daughter Wagner. Incisive look at law school features stupendous, Oscar-winning performance by Houseman. Spawned television series.

PAPERHOUSE 1988
★★ **PG-13 Horror 1:34**
☑ Adult situations, explicit language, violence
Dir: Bernard Rose *Cast:* Charlotte Burke, Elliott Spiers, Glenne Headly, Ben Cross, Gemma Jones
► Young Burke, confined to home because of an illness, invents an imaginary world through her drawings. Her initially pleasant adventures there with Spiers are menaced by mysterious nemesis. Rose, a noted rock video director, brings an inventive visual style to underdeveloped plot.

PAPER LION 1968
★★ **G Drama/Sports 1:45**
Dir: Alex March *Cast:* Alan Alda, Lauren Hutton, Alex Karras, David Doyle, Ann Turkel, Sugar Ray Robinson
► To get an inside look at the NFL, writer George Plimpton (Alda) tries out for quarterback in the Detroit Lions training camp, despite the doubts of the other players. Generally entertaining with enough humor to keep even non-football fans interested. Several Lions play themselves; based on Plimpton's book.

PAPER MOON 1973
★★★★ **PG Comedy 1:42 B&W**
☑ Adult situations, explicit language, mild violence
Dir: Peter Bogdanovich *Cast:* Ryan O'Neal, Tatum O'Neal, Madeline Kahn, John Hillerman, P. J. Johnson, Randy Quaid
► In 1936, Bible-selling con artist Ryan O'Neal is forced into driving a foul-mouthed young orphan, played by his real-life daughter Tatum in her film debut, to relatives in Missouri. Along the way they develop a grudging respect for each other, despite the intrusion of flamboyant "showgirl" Trixie Delight (Kahn). Charming, flavorful period piece received a Supporting Actress Oscar for O'Neal (beating out Kahn's nomination). Aided by beautiful B&W photography and a soundtrack of vintage Depression tunes.

PAPILLON 1973
★★★★★ PG
Biography/Action-Adventure 2:34
☑ Adult situations, explicit language, violence
Dir: Franklin J. Schaffner *Cast:* Steve McQueen, Dustin Hoffman, Victor Jory, Anthony Zerbe, Don Gordon, Robert Deman
▶ True story of unjustly convicted French gangster McQueen and counterfeiter buddy Hoffman who repeatedly attempt to escape from penal colonies in Guiana. After many ordeals in solitary confinement, and a brief, bucolic respite in an Indian village, McQueen's thirst for freedom and desire to break out of the escape-proof Devil's Island grow stronger as he makes a final, desperate bid for liberation. Lengthy film boasts two star turns, exotic locales, and plot extolling human spirit. Screenplay by Dalton Trumbo and Lorenzo Semple, Jr., based on best-seller by the real Papillon, Henri Charrière.

PARADINE CASE, THE 1948
★★ NR Drama 1:56 B&W
Dir: Alfred Hitchcock *Cast:* Gregory Peck, Charles Laughton, Ann Todd, Valli, Louis Jourdan, Ethel Barrymore
▶ Courtroom drama in which married attorney Peck falls in love with client Valli, accused of murdering her wealthy husband. Peck compels Valli's stableman/lover Jourdan to testify and presents evidence that drives the innocent man to suicide. Even the great Hitchcock and a fine cast couldn't overcome a chatty and static script co-written by producer David O. Selznick. **(CC)**

PARADISE 1982
★★ R Drama 1:35
☑ Nudity, violence
Dir: Stuart Gillard *Cast:* Phoebe Cates, Willie Aames, Richard Curnock, Tuvia Tavi, Neil Vipond, Aviva Marks
▶ *Blue Lagoon* without water. In nineteenth-century Turkey, Arabs massacre a Christian caravan; only good-looking teens Cates and Aames survive. Pursued from oasis to oasis by lecherous sheik Tavi, the two unchaperoned youngsters cannot resist each other. Plenty of uncovered skin.

PARADISE ALLEY 1978
★★★ PG Drama 1:49
☑ Adult situations, explicit language
Dir: Sylvester Stallone *Cast:* Sylvester Stallone, Armand Assante, Anne Archer, Kevin Conway, Joe Spinell, Lee Canalito
▶ Brothers Stallone, Assante, and Canalito seek to escape the slums of 1940s New York by exploiting Canalito's strength in the wrestling ring. Small-time hood Conway thwarts their plan until hustling con man Stallone shifts into high gear. Sly is everywhere in this picture: star, writer, director (his debut as such), and even crooner of the title song.

PARADISE, HAWAIIAN STYLE 1966
★★ NR Musical 1:31
Dir: Michael Moore *Cast:* Elvis Presley, Suzanna Leigh, James Shigeta, Donna Butterworth, Marianna Hill
▶ When he loses his job as an airline pilot, Presley moves to Hawaii to form a charter helicopter service. Although his license is suspended, Presley risks his career to fly a wounded friend to the hospital. Weak plotting fails to capture the lighthearted spirit of the King's earlier *Blue Hawaii*; nondescript songs include "Datin'," "Queenie Wahine's Papaya," and "Bill Bailey, Won't You Please Come Home."

PARADISE MOTEL 1985
★ R Comedy 1:30
☑ Nudity, adult situations, explicit language
Dir: Cary Medoway *Cast:* Gary Hershberger, Jonna Leigh Stack, Robert Krantz, Bob Basso, Rick Gibbs, Jeffrey Jay Hea
▶ Naive teen Hershberger's father buys resort motel; local Romeo Krantz fakes friendship with him in order to use motel rooms for romantic liaisons with local beauties. Problems ensue when Hershberger falls for Krantz's true girlfriend Stack. Performers bring some spark to routine story.

PARALLAX VIEW, THE 1974
★★★ R Mystery-Suspense 1:41
☑ Adult situations, explicit language, violence
Dir: Alan J. Pakula *Cast:* Warren Beatty, Paula Prentiss, William Daniels, Walter McGinn, Hume Cronyn, Kelly Thordsen
▶ Investigative reporter Beatty probes the strange deaths of witnesses to the assassination of a presidential candidate. With help of colleague Prentiss and despite reluctance of editor Cronyn, Beatty soon finds himself neck-deep in an elaborate conspiracy. Taut, intelligent

thriller builds suspense with each new piece of evidence uncovered, bringing Beatty closer to his own death.

PARAMEDICS 1988
★★ **PG-13 Comedy 1:31**
☑ Brief nudity, adult situations, explicit language
Dir: Stuart Margolin *Cast:* George Newbern, Christopher McDonald, Javier Grajeda, Lawrence Hilton-Jacobs, John P. Ryan, Ray Walston
▶ Fun-loving paramedics Newbern and McDonald enjoy girl-chasing while lifesaving, so their boss assigns them to tough neighborhood as punishment. The guys must deal with terrorists as well as organ snatchers. Rowdy antics include laughs at the expense of ethnic stereotypes and cardiac arrest. Actors seem to be enjoying themselves, although plot is overly familiar.

PARASITE 1982
☆ **R Horror 1:25**
☑ Nudity, explicit language, graphic violence
Dir: Charles Band *Cast:* Robert Glaudini, Demi Moore, Luca Bercovici, James Davidson, Vivian Blaine
▶ In a postapocalyptic wasteland, scientist Glaudini is infected with a hideous bacteria that multiplies into bloodthirsty parasites. With the help of local lemon grower Moore, he searches for a cure as the parasites eat through his stomach. Repellant horror exploitation filmed in 3-D will lose most of its impact on TV.

PARENTS 1988
★ **R Horror 1:23**
☑ Adult situations, explicit language, violence
Dir: Bob Balaban *Cast:* Randy Quaid, Mary Beth Hurt, Sandy Dennis, Bryan Madorsky, Juno Mills-Cockell, Kathryn Grody
▶ Young Madorsky, whose father Quaid is engaged in unusual scientific research, is troubled by bloody nightmares and starts to wonder about the strange cuts of meat prepared by his doting mother Hurt. Eccentric blend of 1950s camp and eerie horror doesn't succeed entirely, but offbeat visual style and amusing soundtrack are often delightful.

PARENT TRAP, THE 1961
★★★★ **NR Comedy/Family 2:04**
Dir: David Swift *Cast:* Hayley Mills, Maureen O'Hara, Brian Keith, Charles Ruggles, Una Merkel, Leo G. Carroll

▶ Hayley Mills plays identical twins, the daughters of divorced parents O'Hara and Keith. The girls live apart but finally meet when they attend the same camp and scheme to bring their folks back together. Mills doubles delightfully in delectable Disney antics. Spawned TV movie sequel in 1986.

PARIS BLUES 1961
★★ **NR Drama 1:38 B&W**
Dir: Martin Ritt *Cast:* Paul Newman, Joanne Woodward, Sidney Poitier, Diahann Carroll, Louis Armstrong
▶ Intriguing story about two American musicians, expatriates in post–World War II Paris for the wrong reasons: Poitier fears racism at home, Newman won't give up his stalled classical career. Their lives are changed when they fall in love with tourists Carroll and Woodward. One of the better attempts to capture jazz on film. Duke Ellington received an Oscar nomination for his first-rate score, including "Mood Indigo" and "Sophisticated Lady." **(CC)**

PARIS, TEXAS 1984 West German/French
★ **R Drama 2:25**
☑ Brief nudity, adult situations, explicit language
Dir: Wim Wenders *Cast:* Harry Dean Stanton, Nastassja Kinski, Dean Stockwell, Hunter Carson, Aurore Clément
▶ Critically praised drama about drifter Stanton's efforts at reconciling with his son Carson and estranged wife Kinski. Overly long, demanding, but surprisingly positive depiction of loneliness and alienation. Carson (son of Karen Black and writer L. M. Kit Carson) is marvelous in his first film. Screenplay by Sam Shepard, outstanding photography by Robby Mueller, and moody Ry Cooder soundtrack. Some may find it slow and pretentious; not for everyone. **(CC)**

PARIS WHEN IT SIZZLES 1964
★★ **NR Comedy 1:50**
Dir: Richard Quine *Cast:* William Holden, Audrey Hepburn, Gregoire Aslan, Raymond Bussieres, Noel Coward, Tony Curtis
▶ Facing a tight deadline, screenwriter Holden hires secretary Hepburn to help him finish his latest script. Instead of working, they fall in love while acting out fantasy versions of film plots. Despite beautiful locations and numerous cameos (Marlene Dietrich, Mel Ferrer, etc.), a

disappointing comedy that fails to establish a consistent tone, but fans of Hepburn and Holden might not care.

PARK IS MINE, THE 1985
★★★★ NR Drama/MFTV 1:39
☑ Brief nudity, adult situations, explicit language, violence
Dir: Steven Hilliard Stern *Cast:* Tommy Lee Jones, Helen Shaver, Yaphet Kotto, Eric Peterson, Lawrence Dane, Peter Devorsky
▶ Emotionally shattered Vietnam vet Jones, using techniques of jungle warfare, captures New York's Central Park to protest government indifference to the plight of his fellow vets. Freelance TV reporter Shaver risks life to get the scoop while cop Kotto tries to undermine Jones's plan. Thriller with a message. (CC)

PARTING GLANCES 1986
★ NR Drama 1:30
☑ Adult situations, explicit language
Dir: Bill Sherwood *Cast:* Richard Ganoung, John Bolger, Steve Buscemi, Adam Nathan, Kathy Kinney, Patrick Tull
▶ Gay lovers Ganoung and Bolger must separate when Bolger is transferred to Africa. Their last hours together are disrupted by quarrel over care for friend Buscemi, dying of AIDS. Honest, straightforward depiction of contemporary homosexual life mixes laughs and tears while confronting AIDS crisis. (CC)

PARTNERS 1982
★★★ R Comedy 1:32
☑ Nudity, adult situations, explicit language, mild violence
Dir: James Burrows *Cast:* Ryan O'Neal, John Hurt, Kenneth McMillan, Robyn Douglass, Jay Robinson, Denise Galik
▶ Macho cop O'Neal must pose as homosexual with genuine gay policeman Hurt to find murderer of male models. Hurt, smitten with his new partner, sulks when O'Neal beds gorgeous photographer Douglass who's linked to killings. Despite his jealousy Hurt comes to the rescue when O'Neal's life is on the line. Shallow parody of homosexual lifestyles may please some fans of very broad humor.

PARTY CAMP 1986
★ R Comedy 1:37
☑ Nudity, adult situations, explicit language
Dir: Gary Graver *Cast:* Andrew Ross,

Kerry Brennan, Billy Jacoby, Jewel Shepard, Peter Jason, Kirk Cribb
▶ Party-animal counselor Ross butts heads with disciplinarian camp director Jason. Ross overcomes interference to teach fun-loving to campers and woo sexy lifeguard Brennan. Silly clone of *Meatballs* without laughs or Bill Murray.

PASCALI'S ISLAND 1988 British
★ PG-13 Drama 1:41
☑ Nudity, adult situations, explicit language, violence
Dir: James Dearden *Cast:* Ben Kingsley, Charles Dance, Helen Mirren, George Murcell, Sheila Allen, Stefan Gryff
▶ Political and emotional intrigue on Greek island in 1908. Kingsley, a two-bit spy for the Turks, helps archaeologist Dance dig up ancient artifacts. When Dance romances Austrian expatriate painter Mirren, Kingsley becomes jealous, setting into motion a tragic climax. Low-key drama features fine cast and much local flavor, but may be too cerebral for some.

PASSAGE TO INDIA, A 1984 British
★★★★ PG Drama 2:46
☑ Adult situations, explicit language
Dir: David Lean *Cast:* Alec Guinness, Judy Davis, Peggy Ashcroft, James Fox, Victor Banerjee, Nigel Havers
▶ In the 1920s, Havers's mother Ashcroft escorts his bethrothed, young Englishwoman Davis, to India to see him. Alarmed by prevailing British racial prejudice, Davis and Ashcroft seek out locals with help of like-minded scholar Fox and soon befriend affable Indian doctor Banerjee. On an ill-fated picnic to rural caves, Davis accuses Banerjee of attempted rape. Intimate story of sexual repression set against sweeping backdrop garnered eleven Oscar nominations with Ashcroft taking Best Supporting Actress. Based on the novel by E. M. Forster. (CC)

PASSAGE TO MARSEILLES 1944
★★ NR Action-Adventure 1:50 B&W
Dir: Michael Curtiz *Cast:* Humphrey Bogart, Claude Rains, Michele Morgan, Philip Dorn, Sydney Greenstreet, Peter Lorre
▶ Anti-Nazi French reporter Bogart leads escapes of like-minded Frenchmen from a prison and a ship captained by German sympathizer Greenstreet. Action-packed but far from top-notch Bogie,

due to excessive flashbacks in the cluttered plot.

PASSENGER, THE 1975 Italian
★ PG Drama 1:59
☑ Violence
Dir: Michelangelo Antonioni *Cast:* Jack Nicholson, Maria Schneider, Jenny Runacre, Ian Hendry, Steven Berkoff
▶ In Africa, disaffected journalist Nicholson switches identities with a dead gun runner, gets involved with beautiful young Schneider, and finds himself in danger. Subtle and intelligent performance by Nicholson. Virtuoso camerawork from Antonioni includes one of the most complex final shots in film history. Unusual, provocative, and quite absorbing but strictly for sophisticated tastes.

PASSION OF JOAN OF ARC, THE 1928 French
★★ NR Drama 1:54 B&W
Dir: Carl Theodor Dreyer *Cast:* Maria Falconetti, Eugene Silvain, Maurice Schutz, Michel Simon, Antonin Artaud
▶ Meticulous approach to the inquisition and martyrdom of Joan of Arc in the fifteenth century relies on actual trial transcripts to provide a realistic, often harrowing view of the events. Falconetti, in her only screen role, is unforgettable as the young saint. Silent masterpiece is historically significant for director Dreyer's unprecedented use of close-ups.

PASSPORT TO PIMLICO 1948 British
★★ NR Comedy 1:25 B&W
Dir: Henry Cornelius *Cast:* Stanley Holloway, Hermione Baddeley, Margaret Rutherford, Basil Radford, Naunton Wayne
▶ Post–World War II excavation reveals an ancient French deed granting political autonomy to a London neighborhood. The citizens react by establishing their own country whose new, relaxed laws give government officials a fit. Delightful ensemble comedy with an Oscar-nominated screenplay is highly recommended to fans of British humor.

PASS THE AMMO 1988
★★★ R Comedy 1:37
☑ Adult situations, explicit language
Dir: David Beaird *Cast:* Bill Paxton, Linda Kozlowski, Tim Curry, Annie Potts, Dennis Burkley, Glenn Withrow
▶ Swindled out of $50,000 by phony TV evangelists Curry and Potts, lovers Paxton and Kozlowski try to steal back the cash from the preachers' broadcast studio.

Caught in the act, the thieves take Curry and Potts hostage and go public with their plight, leading to raucous climax. Broad and uneven satire of born-again biz has its moments.

PAT AND MIKE 1952
★★★★ NR Comedy 1:35 B&W
Dir: George Cukor *Cast:* Spencer Tracy, Katharine Hepburn, Aldo Ray, William Ching, Sammy White, Charles Buchinski (Bronson)
▶ Sportswoman Hepburn is convinced to turn pro by manager/promoter Tracy. Business relationship turns personal, causing problems with her fiancé Ching. Tracy's woes include shady deal with underworld partner Buchinski. Deft comedy with Oscar-nominated script by reknowned duo Garson Kanin and Ruth Gordon was seventh teaming for Tracy and Hepburn. Look for Chuck Connors, on leave from pro baseball career, in film debut, golfer Babe Didrikson, and scene-stealing Ray as oafish boxer.

PATCH OF BLUE, A 1966
★★★★ NR Drama 1:45 B&W
Dir: Guy Green *Cast:* Sidney Poitier, Shelley Winters, Elizabeth Hartman, Wallace Ford, Ivan Dixon, John Qualen
▶ Shut-in, blind Hartman, used as housekeeper by prostitute mom Winters, meets young black businessman Poitier on rare trip to park. Shocked by uneducated Hartman's forlorn life, Poitier befriends her despite racist Winters's ire; soon she's in love with him. Poitier arranges for her to attend school for blind; marriage may be in the cards but only once she's learned of life. Sensitive, thoughtful drama avoids sentimentality. Five Oscar nominations with Winters taking Best Supporting Actress.

PATERNITY 1981
★★★★ PG Comedy 1:33
☑ Adult situations, explicit language, adult humor
Dir: David Steinberg *Cast:* Burt Reynolds, Beverly D'Angelo, Paul Dooley, Norman Fell, Elizabeth Ashley, Lauren Hutton
▶ Confirmed bachelor Reynolds wants heir but not wife. With help of doctor Fell and attorney Dooley, he contracts with musician/waitress D'Angelo for her to bear his child. Deal sours when she falls in love with him. Lightweight comedy will please Reynolds's fans.

PAT GARRETT AND BILLY THE KID
1973
★ R Western 1:46
☑ Nudity, adult situations, explicit language, graphic violence
Dir: Sam Peckinpah **Cast:** James Coburn, Kris Kristofferson, Bob Dylan, Richard Jaeckel, Jason Robards, Jr., Slim Pickens
▶ Outlaw-turned-sheriff Coburn pursues buddy Kristofferson, a notorious gunslinger, in 1881 New Mexico. Lawman apprehends his old friend, who then escapes for final violent confrontation. Blue-chip director, quality cast, legendary Western story, and soundtrack by Dylan (also his debut as screen actor), but end result is an uneven and unexciting muddle.

PATHS OF GLORY 1957
★★ NR War/Drama 1:26 B&W
Dir: Stanley Kubrick **Cast:** Kirk Douglas, Ralph Meeker, Adolphe Menjou, George Macready, Wayne Morris, Richard Anderson
▶ During World War I, pompous French generals Menjou and Macready order regiment to assault impregnable German position despite protests of commander Douglas. When the attack fails utterly, three soldiers are court-martialed and executed for cowardice in an attempt to cover the high command's ineptitude. Considered by many one of the finest antiwar pics ever, harrowing drama boasts ultrarealistic trench scenes, seamless direction, and stellar performances with Douglas arguably at his best.

PATRIOT, THE 1986
★ R Action-Adventure 1:25
☑ Nudity, adult situations, explicit language, violence
Dir: Frank Harris **Cast:** Gregg Henry, Simone Griffeth, Leslie Nielsen, Michael J. Pollard, Stack Pierce, Jeff Conaway
▶ When lunatics steal a nuclear warhead to sell to the Soviets, scuba expert (Henry) is called out of retirement. With help of admiral Neilsen and his beautiful daughter Griffeth, Henry saves the day. Clumsy script and technical ineptitude mar underwater action pic.

PATTI ROCKS 1988
★★ R Comedy 1:26
☑ Nudity, adult situations, explicit language
Dir: David Burton Morris **Cast:** Chris Mulkey, John Jenkins, Karen Landry, David L. Turk
▶ Married Mulkey cons buddy Jenkins into helping break news of wife and kids to pregnant girlfriend Landry. Jenkins beds Landry and decides to help her raise Mulkey's child. Chatty comedy skewers male chauvinism and sexual myths.

PATTON 1970
★★★★★ PG Biography 2:51
☑ Explicit language, violence
Dir: Franklin J. Schaffner **Cast:** George C. Scott, Karl Malden, Stephen Young, Michael Strong, Frank Latimore, James Edwards
▶ Compelling bio of World War II General George Patton (Scott). A genius of tank warfare, Patton's fits of temper and public outspokeness put him at odds with his superiors and eventually cause General Omar Bradley (Malden) to relieve him of his command in Sicily. Scott is simply brilliant as a born warrior doomed to live in an age that no longer glorifies war. Film took eight Academy Awards, including Best Picture, Director, and Actor, which Scott refused on the premise actors shouldn't compete with each other.

PATTY HEARST 1988
★★ R Biography 1:48
☑ Nudity, adult situations, explicit language
Dir: Paul Schrader **Cast:** Natasha Richardson, William Forsythe, Ving Rhames, Frances Fisher, Jodi Long, Olivia Barash
▶ True story of heiress Patty Hearst (Richardson), kidnapped, imprisoned, and brainwashed by the radical Symbionese Liberation Army. She participates in SLA bank robbery before arrest by FBI. Grim rehash of recent history features innovative direction and superb Richardson.

PAULINE AT THE BEACH 1983 French
☆ R Comedy 1:35
☑ Nudity, explicit language
Dir: Eric Rohmer **Cast:** Amanda Langlet, Arielle Dombasle, Pascal Greggory, Feodor Atkine, Simon de la Brosse, Rosette
▶ Fifteen-year-old Langlet spends summer at Normandy beach with relatives and learns about sex, love, and the French passion for talking about both topics. Relatively plotless and very chatty, airy comedy is for fans of director Rohmer only. Striking cinematography

by the reknowned Nestor Almendros. S

PAWNBROKER, THE 1965
★★★ NR Drama 1:56 B&W
Dir: Sidney Lumet *Cast:* Rod Steiger, Geraldine Fitzgerald, Brock Peters, Jaime Sanchez, Thelma Oliver, Marketa Kimbrell
▶ In Harlem, Jewish pawnbroker Steiger, bitter survivor of the Holocaust, has lost all faith and doesn't care that shop's black owner Peters is a pimp and gangster. Social worker Fitzgerald and employee Sanchez try to shake Steiger out of his apathy but fail until Sanchez makes the ultimate sacrifice. Grim social realism, breakthrough depiction of minorities, and captivating, Oscar-nominated performance by Steiger distinguish this important and controversial film.

PAYDAY 1973
★ R Drama 1:43
☑ Nudity, adult situations, explicit language
Dir: Daryl Duke *Cast:* Rip Torn, Ahna Capri, Elayne Heilveil, Michael C. Gwynne, Jeff Morris, Cliff Emmich
▶ Chronicle of last thirty-six hours in life of on-the-skids country singer Torn. Hard-hitting look at groupies, bribes, drugs, and hardship of the road skewers the myth of glamorous performing life. Well-honed script and solid acting, especially bravura Torn, mark this often overlooked but well-regarded film. Discriminating viewers should take a look.

PEANUT BUTTER SOLUTION, THE 1986 Canadian
★★ PG Family 1:31
☑ Explicit language
Dir: Michael Rubbo *Cast:* Mathew Mackay, Siluck Saysanasy, Alison Podbrey, Michael Hogan, Michel Maillot, Helen Hughes
▶ Visiting a haunted house, eleven-year-old Mackay is so scared that his hair literally falls out. Ghosts later supply baldness cure, whose recipe includes peanut butter, but resulting hair growth is so phenomenal that further misadventures occur. Offbeat family fare features imaginative story line, likable characters, and fine production values.

PEARL OF DEATH, THE 1944
★★ NR Mystery-Suspense 1:09 B&W
Dir: Roy William Neill *Cast:* Basil Rathbone, Nigel Bruce, Evelyn Ankers, Dennis Hoey, Miles Mander, Rondo Hatton

▶ Rathbone and Bruce as London's ace detective Sherlock Holmes and his bumbling sidekick Dr. Watson pursue pearl thief Mander. Mander employs an evil henchman, the "Oxford Creeper," who kills his victims by snapping their third vertebrae. One of the better offerings in the Rathbone series climaxes with battle between Holmes and the Creeper.

PEEPING TOM 1960 British
★★★ NR Mystery-Suspense 1:49
☑ Brief nudity, adult situations, explicit language
Dir: Michael Powell *Cast:* Carl Boehm, Moira Shearer, Anna Massey, Maxine Audley, Esmond Knight, Bartlett Mullins
▶ Disturbed movie cameraman Boehm tours London murdering women and photographing their death throes. Unique examination of voyeurism is both provocative and distasteful. Savaged by critics on release, cult favorite is now touted by many as a classic psychological study.

PEE-WEE'S BIG ADVENTURE 1985
★★ PG Comedy 1:27
☑ Mild violence
Dir: Tim Burton *Cast:* Pee-wee Herman, Elizabeth Daily, Mark Holton, Diane Salinger, James Brolin, Morgan Fairchild
▶ When his beloved bicycle is stolen, Pee-wee travels cross-country to the Alamo to recover it. Along the way, he hooks up with an escaped convict, a waitress who dreams of France, and bikers whom he entertains with a "Tequila" clog dance. Insanely surreal bit of nonsense, full of lunatic gags and bizarrely clever production design. Will appeal to Pee-wee fans of all ages. Fun moment: Pee-wee's encounter with "Large Marge." (CC)

PEGGY SUE GOT MARRIED 1986
★★★★ PG-13 Fantasy 1:43
☑ Adult situations, explicit language
Dir: Francis Coppola *Cast:* Kathleen Turner, Nicolas Cage, Barry Miller, Catherine Hicks, Maureen O'Sullivan, Leon Ames
▶ Peggy Sue (Turner), the mother of two, is separated from her husband, TV appliance pitchman Cage. She attends her twenty-fifth high school reunion where she's crowned queen, blacks out, and time travels back to 1960. As a teenager with the brain of a grown woman, Peggy Sue has the chance to change her des-

tiny. Will she repeat the same mistakes? Delightful adult fairy tale with a 1980s sensibility is provocative, well-acted, and stylishly directed. **(CC)**

PELLE THE CONQUEROR 1988 Danish
★ **PG-13 Drama 2:30**
☑ Adult situations, violence, nudity
Dir: Billie August *Cast:* Max Von Sydow, Pelle Hvenegaard, Erik Paaske, Kristina Tornqvists, Morten Jorgensen
▶ Impoverished Swede Von Sydow and son Hvenegaard go to Denmark to work on farm. Hvenegaard comes of age as they face many hardships, including a tyrannical overseer. Long, stately epic with affecting moments and insightful political points. Actors (especially the Oscar-nominated Von Sydow) are cast to perfection, but slow pace limits appeal to the discriminating. Won Academy Award as Best Foreign Film. **S**

PENDULUM 1969
★★ **PG Drama 1:46**
☑ Adult situations, explicit language, violence
Dir: George Schaefer *Cast:* George Peppard, Jean Seberg, Richard Kiley, Charles McGraw, Madeleine Sherwood, Robert F. Lyons
▶ After convicted rapist-murderer Lyons wins release on technicality argued by liberal attorney Kiley, irate police captain Peppard takes leave. He's promptly arrested for murder of wife Seberg and her lover and retains Kiley for defense, but breaks out of jail when conviction appears likely. Fascinating premise is given too soft a treatment to be completely satisfying.

PENITENT, THE 1988
★ **PG-13 Drama 1:34**
☑ Brief nudity, adult situations
Dir: Cliff Osmond *Cast:* Raul Julia, Armand Assante, Rona Freed, Julie Carmen, Lucy Reina
▶ Struggling farmer Julia learns that his frigid wife Freed is having an affair with his best friend Assante. Julia retaliates by forcing Assante to play Christ in the local village's yearly reenactment of the Crucifixion. Ponderous melodrama loses focus despite attractive cast.

PENITENTIARY 1979
★★ **R Action-Adventure 1:39**
☑ Nudity, adult situations, explicit language, graphic violence
Dir: Jamaa Fanaka *Cast:* Leon Isaac Kennedy, Thommy Pollard, Hazel

Spears, Badja Djola, Chuck Mitchell, Floyd Chatman
▶ Framed for murder, Kennedy relies on his fists to avoid homosexual advances in prison. His fighting skill leads to a chance for early parole in a boxing championship, but he must first thwart a murder plot by a jealous inmate. Tough, honest prison drama benefits from Kennedy's gritty performance as "Too Sweet." Led to two inferior sequels.

PENITENTIARY II 1982
★ **R Action-Adventure 1:49**
☑ Rape, nudity, adult situations, explicit language, graphic violence
Dir: Jamaa Fanaka *Cast:* Leon Isaac Kennedy, Ernie Hudson, Glynn Turman, Peggy Blow, Ebony Wright, Mr. T
▶ Sequel to *Penitentiary* finds Too Sweet (Kennedy) ordered to throw his nationally televised boxing match with a prison champ by the villainous Half Dead (Hudson), who's holding Sweet's family hostage. Ugly, violent melodrama will disappoint fans of the original.

PENITENTIARY III 1987
★ **R Action-Adventure 1:31**
☑ Adult situations, explicit language, graphic violence
Dir: Jamaa Fanaka *Cast:* Leon Isaac Kennedy, Anthony Geary, Steve Antin, Ric Mancini, Kessler Raymond, Magic Schwarz
▶ Boxer Too Sweet (Kennedy), drugged during a match, kills his opponent and winds up in the pen again. Refusing a chance to fight for jailed mobster Geary, he is set upon by Raymond, a vicious midget (and real-life wrestler Haiti Kid). Too Sweet subdues Raymond before facing Geary's monstrous fighter Schwarz. Sequel to *Penitentiary II* continues formula's emphasis on sadism and wooden acting. **(CC)**

PENNIES FROM HEAVEN 1981
☆ **R Musical 1:48**
☑ Nudity, adult situations, explicit language
Dir: Herbert Ross *Cast:* Steve Martin, Bernadette Peters, Christopher Walken, Jessica Harper, Vernel Bagneris
▶ Stylized, off-beat entertainment, set in 1930s Depression era. Unhappily married sheet-music salesman Martin fantasizes about a more glamorous life with mistress Peters; the two frequently break into song just like Fred and Ginger. Before they can run away together, he's arrested for mur-

der and she becomes a streetwalker. Extraordinary cameo by Walken who strips to "Let's Misbehave." Startlingly bold and risky, but not for all tastes. Adapted from the well-received BBC TV series written by Dennis Potter.

PENNY SERENADE 1941
★★★★ NR Drama 2:00 B&W
Dir: George Stevens *Cast:* Irene Dunne, Cary Grant, Beulah Bondi, Edgar Buchanan, Ann Doran
▶ Journalist Grant weds Dunne and brings her to Japan, where she becomes pregnant but miscarries. Back in the States, the couple adopt a baby but tragedy strikes again. Get out your handkerchiefs for this well-made weeper. Sentimental classic boasts strong performances by Grant (Oscar-nominated), Dunne, and Buchanan. Available in a colorized version.

PEOPLE NEXT DOOR, THE 1970
★ R Drama 1:33
☑ Adult situations, explicit language
Dir: David Greene *Cast:* Deborah Winters, Eli Wallach, Julie Harris, Stephen McHattie, Hal Holbrook, Cloris Leachman
▶ Suburban parents Wallach and Harris discover that their daughter Winters is strung out on LSD. After much handwringing, they take action to break her habit and expose the neighborhood drug pusher. Based on a network teleplay, dated cautionary tale has been surpassed by many subsequent and more gut-wrenching efforts.

PEOPLE WILL TALK 1951
★★★★ NR Comedy 1:50 B&W
Dir: Joseph L. Mankiewicz *Cast:* Cary Grant, Jeanne Crain, Finlay Currie, Hume Cronyn, Walter Slezak, Sidney Blackmer
▶ Unorthodox doctor Grant treats unhappy, unwed mother-to-be Crain. They fall in love and get married, but Grant must then defend himself against charges of professional misconduct brought by professor Cronyn. Adult approach is way ahead of its time; Grant and Crain are perfect.

PERFECT 1985
★★ R Drama 2:00
☑ Brief nudity, adult situations, explicit language
Dir: James Bridges *Cast:* John Travolta, Jamie Lee Curtis, Marilu Henner,

Laraine Newman, Anne De Salvo, Jann Wenner
▶ *Rolling Stone* magazine reporter Travolta falls for aerobics instructor Curtis while researching a story about the health club/singles scene. They quarrel about his ethics but when the government harasses him to reveal his sources on a computer scandal he uncovers, she stands by her man. Slick, glossy, and superficial but those sweaty bodies, especially Curtis's, are easy to watch. Appearances by Carly Simon and real-life *Rolling Stone* publisher Wenner. (CC)

PERFORMANCE 1970 British
☆ R Drama 1:46
☑ Adult situations, explicit language, violence
Dir: Donald Cammell, Nicolas Roeg
Cast: James Fox, Mick Jagger, Anita Pallenberg, Michele Breton, Ann Sidney, John Bindon
▶ After killing the wrong man, London gangster Fox hides out in townhouse of decadent rock star Jagger (in his first starring role). Accompanied by groupies Pallenberg and Breton, they embark on an odyssey of drugs, sex, and psychological games. Perverse, sadistic, deliberately bizarre film has some arresting moments (notably Jagger's striptease to his "Memo From Turner") despite an incomprehensible plot.

PERILS OF GWENDOLINE, THE 1984 French
☆ R Action-Adventure 1:28
☑ Nudity, strong sexual content, adult situations, explicit language, graphic violence, adult humor
Dir: Just Jaeckin *Cast:* Tawny Kitaen, Brent Huff, Zabou, Bernadette Lafont, Jean Rougerie
▶ Excessively silly parody of action movies (in particular *Raiders of the Lost Ark*) teams virginal but buxom heroine Kitaen with macho adventurer Huff in a search for her missing father. Their journey includes encounters with cannibals, Asian thugs, and an underground Amazon empire. Based on a 1930s erotic comic strip by John Wilie. Full title: *The Perils of Gwendoline in the Land of the Yik Yak.*

PERMANENT RECORD 1988
★★★ PG-13 Drama 1:31
☑ Adult situations, explicit language
Dir: Marissa Silver *Cast:* Alan Boyce, Keanu Reeves, Michelle Meyrink, Jennifer Rubin, Pamela Gidley

▶ Subtle, sensitive account of how the lives of various high schoolers are irrevocably changed when their talented classmate Boyce commits suicide. Best friend Reeves suffers the most, but learns to cope with Boyce's decision. Perceptive, low-key drama features music by Joe Strummer, formerly of the Clash. Lou Reed has a brief cameo as himself. (CC)

PERSONA 1967 Swedish
☆ NR Drama **1:21** B&W
Dir: Ingmar Bergman *Cast:* Liv Ullmann, Bibi Andersson, Gunnar Bjornstrand, Margaretha Krook
▶ Nurse Andersson takes care of actress Ullmann who has suffered a nervous breakdown and been rendered mute. As the relationship grows closer, a personality transference occurs. Landmark, brilliantly made drama with tremendous performances. Director Bergman's technique is dazzling but demanding; may be too abstract for the casual viewer (especially in the climactic repeated confession sequence). Ⓢ

PERSONAL BEST 1982
★★ R Drama/Sports **2:01**
☑ Nudity, adult situations, explicit language
Dir: Robert Towne *Cast:* Mariel Hemingway, Scott Glenn, Patrice Donnelly, Kenny Moore, Jim Moody
▶ Female track-and-field athletes Hemingway and Donnelly become lovers but their relationship hits the rocks under the pressures of competition. Hemingway eventually finds a new love in male athlete Moore. Compassionate, tasteful handling of the lesbian theme, winning performances (especially Glenn as the coach), intelligent direction, and exciting track footage; plotting is somewhat thin, however.

PERSONALS, THE 1982
★ PG Comedy **1:28**
☑ Adult situations, explicit language
Dir: Peter Markle *Cast:* Bill Schoppert, Karen Landry, Paul Eiding, Michael Laskin, Vicki Dakil
▶ "Straight, White, Male, recently divorced, thirty-two, interested in Picasso, Prokofiev, roller skating and Chicken Kiev." With this personals ad, nerdy-but-nice Schoppert meets pretty, literate psychologist Landry. Everything is wonderful until he discovers she's married. Amiable, winsome comedy, set in Minneapolis,

features steady performances but no surprises.

PERSONAL SERVICES 1987 British
★ R Comedy/Drama **1:43**
☑ Nudity, strong sexual content, adult situations, explicit language, mild violence
Dir: Terry Jones *Cast:* Julie Walters, Alec McCowen, Shirley Stelfox, Danny Schiller, Victoria Hardcastle, Tim Woodward
▶ Waitress Walters supplements her income by managing apartments rented by prostitutes. When she owes money to her own landlord, she repays him with sexual favors and falls into a new career as call girl and madam. Kinky and witty but overly talky and strictly for adults. Based on the life of English madam Cynthia Payne.

PETE KELLY'S BLUES 1955
★★★ NR Drama **1:35**
Dir: Jack Webb *Cast:* Jack Webb, Janet Leigh, Edmond O'Brien, Peggy Lee, Andy Devine, Lee Marvin
▶ Interesting, unsentimental gangster drama set in Kansas City during the Roaring Twenties. Webb leads a jazz combo who take on crimelord O'Brien and his extorting henchmen. Lee won an Oscar nomination for her role as O'Brien's alcoholic mistress. Best for the good score and rare appearances by top jazz musicians Ella Fitzgerald, George Van Eps, Joe Venuti, etc.

PETE 'N' TILLIE 1972
★★★ PG Drama **1:40**
☑ Adult situations, explicit language
Dir: Martin Ritt *Cast:* Walter Matthau, Carol Burnett, Geraldine Page, Barry Nelson, René Auberjonois, Lee H. Montgomery
▶ Ambitious, often charming drama blends comedy and pathos while examining unlikely marriage between compulsive jokester Matthau and Burnett, an aging woman afraid of spinsterhood. Verges on the mawkish, but redeemed by thoughtful performances. Julius Epstein's adaptation of *Witch's Milk* by Peter DeVries received an Oscar nomination.

PETE'S DRAGON 1977
★★★★★ G Musical/Family **2:17**
Dir: Don Caffey *Cast:* Helen Reddy, Mickey Rooney, Sean Marshall, Red Buttons, Shelley Winters, Jim Dale
▶ Popular Disney fantasy mixes animation with real characters in this playful

romp through Passamaquoddy, Maine, with orphan Pete and his friend Elliot, a bright green dragon with pink wings and the power to make himself invisible. Escaping from awful backwoods Winters, Pete and Elliot share many adventures with friendly lighthouse keeper Rooney and his fair daughter Reddy. Kids will cheer as Elliot's clowning gets Pete into all kinds of trouble. Lots of singing and dancing. **(CC)**

PETRIFIED FOREST, THE 1936
★★★ NR Drama 1:23 B&W
Dir: Archie Mayo *Cast:* Bette Davis, Leslie Howard, Humphrey Bogart, Genevieve Tobin, Dick Foran
▶ Waitress Davis and disillusioned writer Howard are among the captives when criminal Duke Mantee (Bogart) takes hostages at a southwestern diner. Adaptation of Robert Sherwood play, which both Howard and Bogart starred in on Broadway, is dated and stagy but still engrossing, thanks to Bogart's breakthrough performance and the wistfully romantic Davis.

PETULIA 1968
★★ R Drama 1:45
☑ Adult situations, explicit language
Dir: Richard Lester *Cast:* Julie Christie, George C. Scott, Richard Chamberlain, Arthur Hill, Shirley Knight, Joseph Cotten
▶ Unsettling, beautifully photographed drama about the bittersweet romance between divorced doctor Scott and wealthy Christie, who may be the victim of abuse from her husband Chamberlain. Penetrating look at San Francisco's hippie movement provides a satirical backdrop to superb cast and absorbing script.

PHANTASM 1979
★★ R Horror 1:29
☑ Nudity, explicit language, graphic violence
Dir: Don Coscarelli *Cast:* Michael Baldwin, Bill Thornbury, Reggie Bannister, Angus Scrimm, Ken Jones, Kathy Lester
▶ Oregon orphan Baldwin investigates when friend of older brother Thornbury is murdered. Murderous mortician Scrimm is the number-one suspect. Visually imaginative and often quite terrifying, especially when Scrimm and a lethal flying ball are on screen; audiences may find the farfetched plot too silly. Spawned a sequel.

PHANTASM II 1988
★★ R Horror 1:30
☑ Nudity, explicit language, violence
Dir: Don Coscarelli *Cast:* James Le Gros, Reggie Bannister, Angus Scrimm, Paula Irvine, Samantha Phillips, Kenneth Tiger
▶ Le Gros, put in psychiatric clinic after events of *Phantasm*, gets out and finds he wasn't imagining things: murderous mortician Scrimm is back with his flying silver ball to create deadly havoc. Flashy production an improvement over its low-budget predecessor, but farfetched script lacks the first entry's originality. Effective use of special effects and music.

PHANTOM OF THE OPERA 1943
★★★ NR Horror 1:32
Dir: Arthur Lubin *Cast:* Nelson Eddy, Susanna Foster, Claude Rains, Edgar Barrier, Leo Carillo, Jane Farrar
▶ Acid-scarred violinist Rains haunts Paris opera house and promotes the career of protégé Foster. Her beau Eddy finds himself involved when Rains goes on a murderous rampage. Lavish, music-filled production with less emphasis on terror than other versions; nice work by Rains as a sympathetic Phantom.

PHANTOM OF THE PARADISE 1974
★★ PG Musical 1:32
☑ Explicit language, violence
Dir: Brian De Palma *Cast:* Paul Williams, William Finley, Jessica Harper, George Memmoli, Gerrit Graham
▶ Surprisingly sturdy parody of *The Phantom of the Opera* and *Faust:* evil rock promoter Williams steals songs from naive composer Finley who's then horribly scarred in an accident. Finley haunts Williams's rock palace, where he becomes obsessed with young singer Harper. Despite unfocused plot, scores some satirical points, particularly Graham's overdone macho singer. Williams's score received an Oscar nomination.

PHANTOM TOLLBOOTH, THE 1970
★★★ G Animation 1:30
Dir: Chuck Jones, David Monahan, Abe Levitow *Cast:* Butch Patrick; voices of Mel Blanc, Daws Butler, Candy Candido, Hans Conried, June Foray
▶ Bored youngster Patrick drives his toy car through a "phantom tollbooth" which appears in his bedroom. He's then transported (and animated) into a wonderful world disrupted by conflict between Letters and Numbers, as each

group believes it's more important to society. Charming children's picture offers likable characters, diverting songs, and educational impact.

PHAR LAP 1984 Australian
★★★★ **PG Drama/Sports 1:47**
☑ Explicit language
Dir: Simon Wincer *Cast:* Tom Burlinson, Ron Leibman, Martin Vaughan, Judy Morris, Celia Deburgh
▶ True story of champion come-from-behind racehorse, Phar Lap, a huge money winner and symbol of hope for Australians in the early 1930s. Owned by American Jewish businessman Leibman, who had to fight anti-Semitism to race the horse, Phar Lap was trained by brutish fanatic Vaughan, but the love of stable boy Burlinson made him the winner of thirty-seven races in three years. Thoroughbred family entertainment. **(CC)**

PHASE IV 1974
★★ **PG Sci-Fi 1:26**
☑ Violence
Dir: Saul Bass *Cast:* Nigel Davenport, Michael Murphy, Lynne Frederick, Alan Gifford, Robert Henderson, Helen Horton
▶ When humanity is threatened by superpowered race of ants, scientists Davenport, Murphy, and Frederick attempt to find a solution at an Arizona desert lab. Bass, who designed the credits for classic Hitchcock films like *Vertigo* and *North by Northwest*, makes a stylish directorial debut.

PHILADELPHIA EXPERIMENT, THE 1984
★★★★ **PG Sci-Fi 1:41**
☑ Explicit language, violence
Dir: Stewart Raffill *Cast:* Michael Paré, Nancy Allen, Bobby DiCicco, Kene Holiday, Eric Christmas
▶ Sailors Paré and DiCicco time travel from 1940s to 1984 when a clandestine government experiment goes awry. Chased by military men, Paré finds himself confused by a world in which an actor is President. Allen helps him elude capture. Quite lively and inventive; zippy direction by Raffill overcomes plot illogic and uneven performances. An entertaining surprise.

PHILADELPHIA STORY, THE 1940
★★★★ **NR Comedy 1:52 B&W**
Dir: George Cukor *Cast:* Cary Grant, Katharine Hepburn, James Stewart, Ruth Hussey, John Howard, Roland Young
▶ Priceless romantic comedy about the chaos before heiress Hepburn's second wedding when her ex-husband Grant and meddling reporter Stewart unexpectedly arrive. Extraordinary acting throughout, with special kudos to James Stewart's Oscar-winning turn and Virginia Weidler's sharp-tongued youngster. Glossy adaptation of Philip Barry's Broadway hit betrays its stage origins, but Donald Ogden Stewart's Oscar-winning screenplay retains enough sparkling dialogue to make this consistently delightful. Also available in a colorized version.

PHONE CALL FROM A STRANGER 1952
★★ **NR Drama 1:36 B&W**
Dir: Jean Negulesco *Cast:* Shelley Winters, Gary Merrill, Michael Rennie, Keenan Wynn, Bette Davis, Beatrice Straight
▶ On a plane flight to Los Angeles, lawyer Merrill befriends three strangers: failed actress Winters, blustering salesman Wynn, and Rennie, a doctor whose drunken driving has caused three deaths. Plane crash kills the three; Merrill decides to break the news to their survivors, including Wynn's wife Davis. Intriguing anthology drama features good performances by talented cast. **(CC)**

PHYSICAL EVIDENCE 1989
★★★ **R Mystery-Suspense 1:39**
☑ Explicit language, violence
Dir: Michael Crichton *Cast:* Burt Reynolds, Theresa Russell, Ned Beatty, Kay Lenz, Ted McGinley
▶ Reynolds, a suspended Boston cop who is the chief suspect in mobster's murder, is forced to accept ambitious but inexperienced attorney Russell as his lawyer. Spurning prosecutor Beatty's plea-bargaining deal, she sets out to prove Reynolds was framed. Formulaic courtroom drama finds Russell out of her element, but Reynolds turns in one of his best performances in years.

PICK-UP ARTIST, THE 1987
★★ **PG-13 Comedy/Drama 1:21**
☑ Adult situations, explicit language
Dir: James Toback *Cast:* Molly Ringwald, Robert Downey, Jr., Dennis Hopper, Danny Aiello, Harvey Keitel
▶ Downey makes a career out of conquering women, until he meets his match in Ringwald who condescends to a one-night stand but won't supply her phone number. Convoluted subplot involves

Ringwald's alcoholic gambling father Hopper and gangster Keitel to whom he owes a fortune. Ringwald projects sweetness and sensuality. Lively rock soundtrack with title song by Stevie Wonder. (CC)

PICNIC 1956
★★★★ NR Drama 1:53
Dir: Joshua Logan *Cast:* William Holden, Rosalind Russell, Kim Novak, Betty Field, Arthur O'Connell, Cliff Robertson
▶ Wanderer Holden hooks up with old pal Robertson in Kansas town. Robertson's girlfriend Novak falls for Holden, as does teacher Russell. Holden runs afoul of law after dispute with Robertson. Probing and atmospheric adaptation of the Pulitzer prize–winning William Inge play. Electric Holden/Novak chemistry; tremendous performance from Russell.

PICNIC AT HANGING ROCK 1979 Australian
★★ PG Drama 1:50
☑ Adult situations, explicit language
Dir: Peter Weir *Cast:* Rachel Roberts, Dominic Guard, Helen Morse, Anne Lambert, Margaret Nelson
▶ On Valentine's Day, 1900, teachers and students from an exclusive Australian girls' boarding school prepare for an excursion to the mysterious Hanging Rock near Mt. Macedon. Three girls and a teacher disappear without explanation. Challenging, inventive adaptation of a John Lindsay novel has an evocative but puzzling atmosphere.

PICTURE OF DORIAN GRAY, THE 1945
★★★ NR Drama 1:50 C/B&W
Dir: Albert Lewin *Cast:* George Sanders, Hurd Hatfield, Donna Reed, Angela Lansbury, Lowell Gilmore, Peter Lawford
▶ Exemplary adaptation of Oscar Wilde's classic novel about nineteenth-century rake Hatfield, who makes a satanic pact to retain his youthful looks while his portrait ages hideously. Strong support from Sanders, as the man who initially corrupts Hatfield, and Oscar-nominated Lansbury as a jilted singer. Harry Stradling's scintillating photography won an Oscar. Original release showed the portrait in Technicolor.

PIECE OF THE ACTION, A 1977
★★★★ PG Comedy 2:15
☑ Explicit language
Dir: Sidney Poitier *Cast:* Sidney Poitier,
Bill Cosby, James Earl Jones, Denise Nicholas, Hope Clarke
▶ Follow-up to *Let's Do It Again* is a high-spirited romp about genial con men Poitier and Cosby, forced into supervising tough juvenile delinquents at a community service center. Uplifting social message blends nicely with action and slapstick. Impressive work by Jones as an imposing cop and a good score by Curtis Mayfield add to the fun.

PIECES 1983 Italian/Spanish
☆ NR Horror 1:25
☑ Nudity, adult situations, explicit language, graphic violence
Dir: Juan Piquer Simon *Cast:* Christopher George, Lynda Day George, Edmund Purdom, Paul Smith
▶ Puzzled detective George pursues a psychotic killer who is dismembering Boston coeds to assemble a life-sized jigsaw puzzle of a naked woman. George's real-life wife Lynda Day plays a screaming tennis tutor. Wretched, extremely graphic nonsense fails on all levels.

PILLOW TALK 1959
★★★★ NR Romance/Comedy 1:45
Dir: Michael Gordon *Cast:* Rock Hudson, Doris Day, Tony Randall, Thelma Ritter, Nick Adams, Julia Meade
▶ First Hudson-Day teaming is a light-hearted romantic farce about a Manhattan playboy and a no-nonsense interior designer who grow to hate each other when they're forced to share a party line. Hate turns to love when Hudson finally meets Day at auditions for a Broadway musical. Received five Oscar nominations (including Day and Ritter, her unflappable maid), winning for screenplay by Russell Rouse, Clarence Greene, Stanley Shapiro, and Maurice Richlin.

PINK FLAMINGOS 1974
☆ NR Comedy 1:35
☑ Rape, nudity, strong sexual content, explicit language, violence, adult humor
Dir: John Waters *Cast:* Divine, David Lochary, Mink Stole, Mary Vivian Pearce, Edith Massey, Danny Mills
▶ Seminal midnight cult movie, an all-out assault on taste, gleefully breaks every imaginable taboo in telling story of obese transvestite Divine's competition against Lochary and Stole to become the filthiest person in the world. Written, shot, edited, directed, and produced by

Waters, film's humorous scenes of cannibalism, white slavery, heroin addiction, and coprophagy are considered high camp by fans. Also starring Paul Swift as the Eggman.

PINK FLOYD: THE WALL 1982 British
★ **R Music 1:39**
☑ Nudity, adult situations, explicit language, violence
Dir: Alan Parker *Cast:* Bob Geldof, Christine Hargreaves, James Laurenson, Eleanor David, Bob Hoskins
▶ Music from Pink Floyd's best-selling album *The Wall* inspired this relentlessly bleak examination of Pink (Geldof), a tormented rock star who sinks into insanity in his isolated hotel room. Written by former Floyd bassist Roger Waters (although the group itself doesn't appear), and featuring harsh animation by political caricaturist Gerald Scarfe. Good antiwar themes countered by offensively misogynist touches.

PINK PANTHER, THE 1964
★★★★ **NR Comedy 1:53**
Dir: Blake Edwards *Cast:* David Niven, Peter Sellers, Capucine, Robert Wagner, Claudia Cardinale
▶ Hilariously incompetent Inspector Clouseau (Sellers) has problems: not only is international jewel thief Niven one step ahead of him but he's also sleeping with Sellers's wife! The film that started all the comic madness (spawning six sequels) introduces the familiar trademarks: Sellers's malapropisms and pratfalls, Edwards's slick slapstick, the animated credits, and Henry Mancini theme music. Still fresh and funny.

PINK PANTHER STRIKES AGAIN, THE 1976 British
★★★★ **PG Comedy 1:43**
☑ Adult situations
Dir: Blake Edwards *Cast:* Peter Sellers, Herbert Lom, Lesley-Anne Down, Colin Blakely, Leonard Rossiter
▶ Ex–chief inspector Lom is about to be released from the insane asylum—until an appearance by the bumbling Clouseau (Sellers) causes a relapse. Lom escapes, hires a gang of assassins, and builds a doomsday machine that will destroy an entire city if Sellers is not eliminated. Fourth in the successful free-form comedy series features on-the-mark slapstick antics and the winning Sellers/Lom team.

PINKY 1949
★★ **NR Drama 1:42 B&W**
Dir: Elia Kazan *Cast:* Jeanne Crain, Ethel Barrymore, Ethel Waters, William Lundigan, Nina Mae McKinney, Basil Ruysdael
▶ Fair-skinned black Crain, educated in the North where she passed for white, returns to small hometown in deep South and reencounters racial prejudice. She cares for elderly rich white woman Barrymore and inherits her estate, only to be accused of foul play by Barrymore's racist relatives. Thoughtful but hard-hitting attack on racial bigotry withstands the test of time. Oscar nominations to Crain, Barrymore, and Waters.

PINOCCHIO 1940
★★★★★ **G Animation 1:28**
Dir: Ben Sharpsteen, Hamilton Luske *Cast:* Voices of Dickie Jones, Christian Rub, Cliff Edwards, Evelyn Venable, Walter Catlett
▶ Magical fantasy about young marionette's efforts to become a flesh-and-blood boy is among the most accomplished of all Disney features. Rich characterizations (wisecracking Jiminy Cricket, the insidious fox J. Worthington Foulfellow, etc.), astonishing animation, an Oscar-winning score (including Cliff Edwards's version of "When You Wish Upon a Star"), and a plot that alternates between whimsical humor and genuinely frightening sequences has made this a family favorite for five decades. Highly recommended. **(CC)**

PIRANHA 1978
★★ **R Horror 1:34**
☑ Brief nudity, explicit language, graphic violence
Dir: Joe Dante *Cast:* Bradford Dillman, Heather Menzies, Kevin McCarthy, Keenan Wynn, Richard Deacon
▶ Killer fish, developed at scientist McCarthy's lab, invade local river, menacing summer camp kids and vacationers. Mountain man Dillman and skip tracer Menzies try to warn the populace. Pretty scary stuff, stylishly directed by Dante and appealingly acted by Dillman and Menzies, although the story can't be taken seriously.

PIRANHA II: THE SPAWNING 1983 U.S./Italian
★ **R Horror 1:30**
☑ Nudity, adult situations, explicit language, violence

Dir: James Cameron *Cast:* Tricia O'Neil, Lance Henriksen, Steve Marachuk, Ricky G. Paull, Ted Richert
▶ Diving teacher O'Neil and biochemist Marachuk investigate when guests start dropping like flies at a tropical resort. The culprits: deadly piranha. Predictable story but well-done fright scenes, like opening bit of critters attacking couple making love underwater. Enticing-looking scenery and lead actors.

PIRATE, THE 1948
★★★ NR Musical 1:42
Dir: Vincente Minnelli *Cast:* Judy Garland, Gene Kelly, Walter Slezak, Gladys Cooper, Reginald Owen, The Nicholas Brothers
▶ Nineteenth-century Caribbean: performer Kelly pretends to be a pirate to win Garland away from her older fiancé Slezak. Overly broad MGM musical with a production design almost too loudly colorful. Can be enjoyed for Kelly's acrobatics and the Cole Porter score, which includes "Be a Clown".

PIRATE MOVIE, THE 1982 Australian
★★ PG Musical 1:39
☑ Explicit language
Dir: Ken Annakin *Cast:* Kristy McNichol, Christopher Atkins, Ted Hamilton, Bill Kerr, Maggie Kirkpatrick, Garry McDonald
▶ Plain young McNichol, stranded on a beach, dreams of being wooed by handsome pirate's apprentice Atkins. He helps McNichol retrieve her family's stolen treasure from the pirate gang. Modernized version of Gilbert and Sullivan's *The Pirates of Penzance* with clumsily staged dances, bubblegum music, and Atkins's stiff performance. McNichol charmingly emerges unscathed.

PIRATES 1986 French/Tunisian
★ PG-13 Action-Adventure/Comedy 2:04
☑ Explicit language, mild violence, adult humor
Dir: Roman Polanski *Cast:* Walter Matthau, Cris Campion, Charlotte Lewis, Damien Thomas, Richard Pearson
▶ Peglegged English pirate Matthau and his young mate Campion are imprisoned by Spanish captain Thomas. The pirates attempt mutiny as Matthau seeks treasure and Campion falls for Lewis, Thomas's intended. Burlesque of pirate genre is a gorgeous eyeful of sets and costumes, not to mention attractive Lewis and Campion. The downside: unsympathetic characters, repetitive swashbuckling action, a mush-mouthed Matthau, and a disgusting rat-eating sequence.

PIRATES OF PENZANCE, THE 1983
★ G Musical 1:52
Dir: Wilford Leach *Cast:* Kevin Kline, Angela Lansbury, Linda Ronstadt, George Rose, Rex Smith, Tony Azito
▶ Young pirate Smith goes ashore and falls for Ronstadt, daughter of Major General Rose, but is torn between love and duty when Pirate King Kline bounds him to further swashbuckling servitude on a technicality. Leach sweetly re-creates his Broadway staging of the Gilbert and Sullivan operetta; his deliberately artificial-looking production is amusing (especially when Rose romps through multicolored cows) but somewhat off-putting. Kline does a wonderfully funny and charismatic Errol Flynn parody; Ronstadt sings beautifully, acts less well.

PIT AND THE PENDULUM, THE 1961
★★ NR Horror 1:20
Dir: Roger Corman *Cast:* Vincent Price, John Kerr, Barbara Steele, Luana Anders, Anthony Carbone
▶ Price, the son of a Spanish Inquisition torturer, goes off his rocker after the death of wife Steele. When Steele's brother Kerr investigates, Price hooks him up to the title device. Solid, chilling adaptation of the Edgar Allan Poe short story. One of Corman's and Price's better efforts.

PIXOTE 1981 Brazilian
★ NR Drama 2:07
☑ Nudity, strong sexual content, explicit language, violence
Dir: Hector Babenco *Cast:* Fernando Ramos da Silva, Marilia Pera, Jardel Filho, Rubens de Falco, Elke Maravilha, Tony Tornado
▶ Young da Silva is mistreated in harsh São Paulo reform school and escapes after authorities kill two of his pals. He becomes a drug dealer and then hooks up with prostitute Pera. Very realistic brutal atmosphere and the nonprofessional cast is quite good; so unrelentingly grim and violent that it may be too hard to sit through for most. Actor da Silva was recently shot dead during an armed robbery. ⑤

PLACE IN THE SUN, A 1951
★★★★ NR Drama 1:42 B&W

Dir: George Stevens *Cast:* Montgomery Clift, Elizabeth Taylor, Shelley Winters, Raymond Burr, Anne Revere, Herbert Hayes
▶ Weak-willed Clift gets romantically involved with factory co-worker Winters until he falls in love with heiress Taylor. Clift plans to wed Taylor until Winters announces she's pregnant. Confrontation between Clift and Winters, who insists on marriage, ends in tragedy. Sensational cast; intense close-ups of beautiful, similar-looking lovers Clift and Taylor are one of the film's distinctions, as well as lush score by Franz Waxman. Remake of *An American Tragedy* (from Theodore Dreiser's novel) won six Academy Awards, including Best Director and Screenplay.

PLACES IN THE HEART 1984
★★★★★ PG Drama 1:51
☑ Adult situations, explicit language, violence
Dir: Robert Benton *Cast:* Sally Field, Danny Glover, Lindsay Crouse, John Malkovich, Ed Harris, Amy Madigan
▶ Heartfelt story of family endurance features Oscar-winning performance by Field as a feisty widow and mother of two who fights tornadoes, falling cotton prices, and the KKK to save her Texas farm from foreclosure in 1935. She hires itinerant Glover and takes in blind tenant Malkovich to help make ends meet. Benton's screenplay, a celebration of traditional American values, also won an Oscar. Nominations included Picture, Director, Supporting Actress (Crouse) and Actor (Malkovich), and Costumes. (CC)

PLAGUE DOGS, THE 1982
★★★ NR Animation 1:26
☑ Explicit language, violence
Dir: Martin Rosen *Cast:* Voices of John Hurt, Christopher Benjamin, James Bolam, Nigel Hawthorne, Warren Mitchell
▶ Two dogs escape from the laboratory where scientists have been tormenting them and roam the English countryside. When the scientists reveal they've exposed the dogs to the bubonic plague, the canine hunt intensifies. Striking animation distinguishes this adaptation of Richard Adams's novel, but grim, often unsettling story is unusual family fare. (CC)

PLAIN CLOTHES 1988
★★★ PG Mystery-Suspense 1:38
☑ Explicit language, mild violence
Dir: Martha Coolidge *Cast:* Arliss Howard, Suzy Amis, George Wendt, Diane Ladd, Seymour Cassel, Robert Stack
▶ When a teacher is murdered, young cop Howard, whose brother is the number-one suspect, poses as a high school student in order to investigate. Howard finds romance with English teacher Amis while cracking the case. Mildly amusing humor, promising performances by newcomers Howard and Amis, and sleek production values. (CC)

PLAINSMAN, THE 1936
★★★ NR Western 1:53 B&W
Dir: Cecil B. DeMille *Cast:* Gary Cooper, Jean Arthur, James Ellison, Charles Bickford, Porter Hall, Anthony Quinn
▶ Extravagant, fast-paced version of a fictional romance between Wild Bill Hickok (Cooper) and Calamity Jane (Arthur) interrupted by villain Bickford's scheme to sell guns to the Indians. Facts may be inaccurate, but the stars' bickering affair is disarming, and the action (with a proverbial cast of thousands) is furious.

PLANES, TRAINS & AUTOMOBILES 1987
★★★ R Comedy 1:33
☑ Explicit language, adult humor
Dir: John Hughes *Cast:* Steve Martin, John Candy, Laila Robbins, Michael McKean, William Windom, Kevin Bacon
▶ Uptight Chicago executive Martin, desperate to get home for Thanksgiving despite an indefinitely delayed plane, hooks up with overbearing shower-curtain-ring salesman Candy to make the trip by car and train. Although their trek is a series of comic disasters, Candy slowly melts Martin's reserve. Candy and Martin make a winning team in a contrived (but frequently funny) tale of travel's travails. Highlights: Candy warbling the Flintstones theme and the "Those aren't pillows" bedroom encounter. (CC)

PLANET OF BLOOD 1966
☆ NR Sci-Fi 1:21
Dir: Curtis Harrington *Cast:* John Saxon, Basil Rathbone, Dennis Hopper, Judi Meredith, Florence Marly
▶ Earth astronauts, responding to strange signals from Mars, rescue alien woman from a wrecked spacecraft. Bad

move: she turns out to be a vampire and starts killing off the crew members. Surprisingly effective chiller whose plot may remind you of *Alien*. Also known as *Queen of Blood*.

PLANET OF THE APES 1968
★★★★ G Sci-Fi 1:52
Dir: Franklin J. Schaffner *Cast:* Charlton Heston, Roddy McDowall, Kim Hunter, Maurice Evans, James Whitmore, James Daly
▶ Astronaut Heston crash-lands on planet where evolution has taken an upside-down turn: talking apes rule and humans are mute and enslaved. When Heston is captured by the simian rulers, sympathetic scientist ape couple Hunter and McDowall rally to his side. Terrific sci-fi adventure; witty, thought-provoking, visually exciting, and original. Heston has never been more heroic; marvelous Oscar-winning monkey makeup, and the twist ending still packs a punch. Spawned four sequels and a TV series. (CC)

PLANET OF THE VAMPIRES 1965 Italian
☆ NR Sci-Fi 1:26
Dir: Mario Bava *Cast:* Barry Sullivan, Norma Bengell, Angel Aranda, Evi Mirandi
▶ Spaceship captain Sullivan investigates eerie transmission from the planet Aura. Mysterious killings plague his crew. The culprit: advanced minds seeking bodies to escape Aura. Also known as *The Demon Planet*.

PLAN 9 FROM OUTER SPACE 1959
★ NR Sci-Fi 1:19 B&W
Dir: Edward D. Wood, Jr. *Cast:* Gregory Walcott, Mona McKinnon, Duke Moore, Tom Keene, Bela Lugosi, Vampira
▶ Aliens invade Earth, reviving the dead to take over the planet. First target is Vampira, Lugosi's recently deceased wife. Pilot Walcott and his friends are the only people who can save humanity. Revered by cultists as the worst movie ever made, staggeringly inept horror adventure is actually funnier than many intentional comedies.

PLATOON 1986
★★★★ R War 1:59
☑ Explicit language, graphic violence
Dir: Oliver Stone *Cast:* Charlie Sheen, Willem Dafoe, Tom Berenger, Forest Whitaker, Francesco Quinn, John C. McGinley
▶ Harrowing account of life on the front line in Vietnam. Seen through the eyes of young idealist-turned-cynic Sheen, portrait of war as hell pits decent sergeant Dafoe against vicious counterpart Berenger. Blockbuster hit noteworthy for excellent ensemble acting, realistic depiction of jungle warfare, and sympathetic look at individual struggle to cope with the insanity of an unpopular war. Film won four Oscars, including Best Picture and Director. (CC)

PLATOON LEADER 1988
★★ R War 1:40
☑ Adult situations, explicit language, graphic violence
Dir: Aaron Norris *Cast:* Michael Dudikoff, Robert F. Lyons, Rick Fitts, Michael De Lorenzo, Jesse Dabson, William Smith
▶ Rookie first lieutenant Dudikoff must win the respect of battle-scarred veterans in his new platoon while battling hordes of Vietcong on debilitating daily raids. Well-mounted, bloody Vietnam War drama undermined by routine plotting and thin characterizations.

PLAYERS 1979
★★ PG Drama 2:00
☑ Adult situations, explicit language
Dir: Anthony Harvey *Cast:* Ali MacGraw, Dean Paul Martin, Maximilian Schell, Steve Guttenberg, Melissa Prophet, Pancho Gonzalez
▶ In Mexico, young tennis hustler Martin falls in love with older, kept woman MacGraw, but her wealthy sugar daddy Schell drops in at the most inopportune times. Will MacGraw choose true romance? Will the final score be Money: 40, Love: Love? Great-looking actors, exotic locales, and cameo appearances by tennis stars of the era, including a youthful John McEnroe.

PLAYING FOR KEEPS 1986
★★ PG-13 Comedy 1:43
☑ Brief nudity, adult situations, explicit language
Dir: Bob Weinstein, Harvey Weinstein *Cast:* Danny Jordano, Matthew Penn, Leon Grant, Mary B. Ward, Marisa Tomei
▶ Teenager Jordano and his family inherit run-down hotel which he and buddies Penn and Grant decide to rehab into rock 'n' roll resort. Obstacles include back taxes, suspicious townfolk, and politician's plan for chemical waste dump on

the site. Lightweight teen comedy sports foot-tapping soundtrack and energetic style.

PLAYING FOR TIME 1980
★★★★ NR Drama/MFTV 2:31
Dir: Daniel Mann *Cast:* Vanessa Redgrave, Jane Alexander, Maud Adams, Shirley Knight, Melanie Mayron
▶ True story of Fania Fenelon (Redgrave), a French cabaret singer who survived Auschwitz concentration camp by performing in the women's orchestra. Conducted by Alma Rose (Alexander), they were forced to play while inmates were led to the crematoriums. First-rate, uncompromising, and shattering made-for-TV film won four Emmys including Drama Special, Actress (Redgrave), Supporting Actress (Alexander), and Writing (Arthur Miller).

PLAY IT AGAIN, SAM 1972
★★★ PG Comedy 1:25
☑ Explicit language
Dir: Herbert Ross *Cast:* Woody Allen, Diane Keaton, Tony Roberts, Jerry Lacy, Susan Anspach, Jennifer Salt
▶ Timid San Francisco film critic Allen, abandoned by bored wife Anspach, is such a mess he can't bring himself to heat up TV dinners—he sucks them frozen. Enter the ghost of Humphrey Bogart (Lacy) to teach Allen about being a man, especially with women ("I never met one who didn't understand a slap in the mouth"). After a series of nightmarish dates, Allen has one-night fling with Keaton, the wife of his best friend Roberts, and gets to live out his *Casablanca* fantasy. From Allen's Broadway play.

PLAY MISTY FOR ME 1971
★★★★ R Mystery-Suspense 1:42
☑ Adult situations, violence
Dir: Clint Eastwood *Cast:* Clint Eastwood, Jessica Walter, Donna Mills, John Larch, Jack Ging, Irene Hervey
▶ Spooky thriller about obsessive love predates *Fatal Attraction*. Late-night DJ Eastwood has one-night stand with fan Walter who calls every evening requesting tune "Misty." She refuses to let go of him, making life miserable for him and his girlfriend Mills with invasions of privacy, a suicide attempt, and eventually homicidal mayhem. Sure-handed directorial debut for Eastwood was box office smash. Song "The First Time Ever I Saw Your Face", sung by Roberta Flack, was a Top-Ten hit.

PLAZA SUITE 1971
★★★ PG Comedy 1:55
☑ Adult situations
Dir: Arthur Hiller *Cast:* Walter Matthau, Maureen Stapleton, Barbara Harris; Lee Grant, Louise Sorel, Jenny Sullivan
▶ Matthau assays three different roles in three different episodes taking place in one New York Plaza Hotel suite: Stapleton's unfaithful husband, producer attempting to seduce old flame Harris, and father of nervous bride Sullivan, who locks herself in room before wedding. Neil Simon adaptation of his Broadway hit provides good vehicle for Matthau's clowning.

PLENTY 1985
★★★ R Drama 2:04
☑ Adult situations, explicit language
Dir: Fred Schepisi *Cast:* Meryl Streep, Charles Dance, Sting, Tracey Ullman, John Gielgud, Ian McKellen
▶ Faithful film version of David Hare's play traces the life of Susan Traherne (Streep). Her happiest moments are as World War II resistance fighter; then her life deteriorates even though she prospers through several careers. Unhappily married to Foreign Service member Dance, she's given to teary pronouncements ("I want to change everything and I don't know how") and, eventually, suffers a nervous breakdown. High-powered supporting cast includes Ullman as Streep's wisecracking friend and Gielgud as a diplomat.

PLOUGHMAN'S LUNCH, THE 1984
British
☆ R Drama 1:47
☑ Adult situations, explicit language
Dir: Richard Eyre *Cast:* Jonathan Pryce, Tim Curry, Charlie Dore, Rosemary Harris, Frank Finlay, Simon Stokes
▶ Burnt-out journalist Pryce is enamored of young intellectual Dore. He interviews her historian mother Harris and is invited to stay for the weekend. Instead of making his play for Dore, Pryce makes love to Harris. He later regrets his decision when his friend Curry is intimate with Dore. Well-crafted but static study of class differences and cynically detached youth in Thatcher England will appeal only to those with taste for things veddy British.

POCKETFUL OF MIRACLES 1961
★★★★ NR Comedy 2:16
Dir: Frank Capra *Cast:* Glenn Ford,

Bette Davis, Hope Lange, Peter Falk, Arthur O'Connell, Ann-Margret

▶ Soft-hearted gangster Ford sets up alcoholic street vendor Davis in posh Manhattan digs so she can impress European-educated daughter Ann-Margret and her fiancé's wealthy father O'Connell. Chaotic and comic encounters between mobsters, socialites, and street people follow. Capra's last feature is a remake of his earlier and briefer *Lady for a Day*, adapted from a Damon Runyon short story. **(CC)**

POCKET MONEY 1972
★★ PG Western/Comedy 1:42
☑ Adult situations, explicit language
Dir: Stuart Rosenberg *Cast:* Paul Newman, Lee Marvin, Strother Martin, Christine Belford, Wayne Rogers, Hector Elizondo

▶ Dumb cowpoke Newman and boozer buddy Marvin deal in rodeo cattle with crooked businessman Martin. One disaster follows another as the good ol' boys botch every opportunity for success. Curious comedy from screenplay by Terence Malick drew mixed responses, but Newman and Marvin have a great time hamming it up. The real star of the film, however, is the enormous white Caddy with longhorns on the hood that Marvin drives.

POINT BLANK 1967
★★ NR Action-Adventure 1:32
☑ Violence
Dir: John Boorman *Cast:* Lee Marvin, Angie Dickinson, Keenan Wynn, Carroll O'Connor, Lloyd Bochner, John Vernon

▶ Marvin, a San Francisco gangster double-crossed by his wife and partner after a gang heist, infiltrates their L.A. mob for revenge. Working with crooked accountant Wynn, he wipes out a series of mobsters while searching for his missing loot. Tense, hard-edged thriller was based on a Donald Westlake novel. **(CC)**

POLICE ACADEMY 1984
★★★★ R Comedy 1:36
☑ Nudity, adult situations, explicit language
Dir: Hugh Wilson *Cast:* Steve Guttenberg, Kim Cattrall, George Gaynes, G. W. Bailey, Michael Winslow, Bubba Smith

▶ Assorted misfits, including failed parking lot attendant Guttenberg, bored socialite Cattrall, and hulking florist Smith, enroll in police academy when admissions standards are eliminated. Mil-

quetoast commander Gaynes meekly accepts inept new trainees, but hard-nosed chief instructor Bailey is determined to make their lives miserable. Inevitable clashes between Bailey and rookies result until the trainees prove their worth. Raucous and extremely popular comedy pushes limits of taste, usually with outrageous results. **(CC)**

POLICE ACADEMY 2: THEIR FIRST ASSIGNMENT 1985
★★★★ PG-13 Comedy 1:27
☑ Brief nudity, explicit language, adult humor
Dir: Jerry Paris *Cast:* Steve Guttenberg, Bubba Smith, Michael Winslow, Howard Hesseman, George Gaynes, Art Metrano

▶ Sequel to comedy hit. Fresh from their academy training, endearing rookies Guttenberg, Smith, and Winslow are assigned to a crime-ridden precinct run by besieged captain Hesseman. Ambitious lieutenant Metrano, with eye on Hesseman's job, tries to thwart the new cops, but the bumbling misfits fight crime with laughs and soon the neighborhood is safe again. **(CC)**

POLICE ACADEMY 3: BACK IN TRAINING 1986
★★★ PG Comedy 1:24
☑ Adult situations, adult humor
Dir: Jerry Paris *Cast:* Steve Guttenberg, Bubba Smith, David Graf, Michael Winslow, George Gaynes, Art Metrano

▶ City decides to close one of two police academies, one run by underhanded tough guy Metrano and the other by lovable numbskull Gaynes. All-thumbs alums Guttenberg, Smith, etc., return for decisive drill competition but make poor impression on evaluators. However, when the governor is kidnapped at a regatta, the misfits prove their true mettle. More boffo laughs in third of series. **(CC)**

POLICE ACADEMY 4: CITIZENS ON PATROL 1987
★★★ PG Comedy 1:27
☑ Explicit language
Dir: Jim Drake *Cast:* Steve Guttenberg, Bubba Smith, Michael Winslow, David Graf, George Gaynes, G. W. Bailey

▶ More law and little order from the bumbling boys in blue. Academy commander Gaynes initiates civilian crime-fighting program so the Keystone Klones

(Guttenberg and rest of the gang) are enlisted to train volunteers. Original nemesis Bailey tries to sabotage their efforts. Prisoners escape and must be apprehended in bang-up finale. Formula losing gas. Gags even more juvenile, but still popular. **(CC)**

POLICE ACADEMY 5: ASSIGNMENT MIAMI BEACH 1988
★★★ **PG Comedy 1:30**
☑ Explicit language
Dir: Alan Myerson *Cast:* Bubba Smith, David Graf, Michael Winslow, George Gaynes, G. W. Bailey, Janet Jones
▶ Academy commander Gaynes is to be honored at Miami cop convention, so he, obnoxious rival Bailey, and customary crew of klutzes (Smith, Graf, etc.) fly south. Gaynes accidentally picks up bag of stolen gems at airport and is kidnapped by jewel thieves. In typically inept style, the comic coppers save the day. More silly high jinks from the same boneheaded lawmen, although Steve Guttenberg bowed out of this round. **(CC)**

POLICE SQUAD! HELP WANTED 1982
★★★ **NR Comedy/MFTV 1:15**
Dir: Jim Abrahams, Jerry Zucker, David Zucker, Joe Dante, Reza Badiyi *Cast:* Leslie Nielsen, Alan North, Rex Hamilton, Peter Lupus, Lorne Greene, Florence Henderson
▶ Three episodes of the TV series "Police Squad" featuring Nielsen as the square-jawed cop Frank Drebin. He solves a murder at a check cashing outfit, battles an extortion ring, and takes on a corrupt boxing promoter. Freewheeling humor, often very funny. Best bits: the visit to Little Italy and "no sax before the fight." Spawned the hugely popular 1988 feature *The Naked Gun*.

POLLYANNA 1960
★★★★★ **NR Family 2:14**
Dir: David Swift *Cast:* Hayley Mills, Jane Wyman, Richard Egan, Karl Malden, Nancy Olson, Adolphe Menjou
▶ Orphan Mills, taken in by her New England aunt Wyman, brings sunshine and happiness to previously glum neighbors, including hermit Menjou and hellfire preacher Malden. Wonderful Disney adaptation of Eleanor Porter's novel is sentimental without being sticky. Excellent cast also includes Donald Crisp and Agnes Moorehead. In her American debut, Mills received Oscar statuette for

her "outstanding juvenile performance." Menjou's last film. **(CC)**

POLTERGEIST 1982
★★★★ **PG Horror 1:54**
☑ Adult situations, explicit language, graphic violence
Dir: Tobe Hooper *Cast:* JoBeth Williams, Craig T. Nelson, Dominique Dunne, Heather O'Rourke, Oliver Robins, Zelda Rubinstein
▶ Suburban couple Williams and Nelson and kids Dunne, O'Rourke, and Robins, who've moved into a new home, are harassed by poltergeists (German for "noisy ghosts"). At first the unseen critters merely rearrange the furniture, but then they turn nasty and abduct little O'Rourke. As chaos breaks out, diminutive exorcist Rubinstein, who's pretty spooky herself, must calm the angry spirits and return O'Rourke. Sensational special effects in spine-tingling and gruesome ghost story co-written and co-produced by Steven Spielberg. Not for younger kids.

POLTERGEIST II: THE OTHER SIDE 1986
★★★ **PG-13 Horror 1:31**
☑ Explicit language, graphic violence
Dir: Brian Gibson *Cast:* JoBeth Williams, Craig T. Nelson, Heather O'Rourke, Oliver Robins, Will Sampson, Geraldine Fitzgerald
▶ "They're back!" in sequel to megahit ghost thriller. On the skids after their first bout with poltergeists, downtrodden family Williams, Nelson, etc., move in with Williams's psychic mother Fitzgerald. When Fitzgerald dies, vicious spirits invade the house, wreaking stunning visual havoc. Indian mystic Sampson assists family in warding off evil spirits. Family crosses over into netherworld to battle their nemeses with help from ghost of Fitzgerald. Generally satisfying encore, with spellbinding special effects. **(CC)**

POLTERGEIST III 1988
★★ **PG-13 Horror 1:37**
☑ Explicit language, violence
Dir: Gary A. Sherman *Cast:* Heather O'Rourke, Zelda Rubinstein, Tom Skerritt, Nancy Allen, Lara Flynn Boyle, Kip Wentz
▶ Reprising her role from prior two films, O'Rourke now lives in care of aunt Allen and uncle Skerritt in their chic Chicago high-rise. But nasty evil spirits just won't leave her alone and soon abduct her and her cousin Boyle to the netherworld.

Once again sweet little exorcist Rubinstein comes to the rescue. Story getting awfully familiar; as usual, real stars are special effects. Dedicated to O'Rourke, who passed away during emergency surgery following film's completion.

POLYESTER 1981
★ R Comedy 1:30
☑ Explicit language, violence, adult humor
Dir: John Waters *Cast:* Divine, Tab Hunter, Stiv Bators, Edith Massey, Mink Stole
▶ Intentionally tacky domestic comedy will probably be appreciated only by cult followers of writer/producer/director John Waters. Transvestite Divine plays the much-beleaguered Baltimore housewife Francine Fishpaw, who fantasizes about dream lover Hunter. Theatrical release gimmick was Odorama card with scratch-and-sniff smells (when Francine smelled something, a number appeared on the screen and audience could sniff the same scent). Definitely not for all tastes or scents.

POM POM GIRLS, THE 1976
☆ PG Comedy 1:30
☑ Nudity, adult situations, explicit language, violence
Dir: Joseph Ruben *Cast:* Robert Carradine, Jennifer Ashley, Lisa Reeves, Michael Mullins, Bill Adler, James Gammon
▶ Rivalry between two Southern Cal high schools spawns antagonism between big men on each campus, Carradine and Adler, climaxing in chicken run over oceanside cliff. Meanwhile, football player Mullins quits the team to romance pom-pom girl Ashley; Carradine gets into the action with another cheerleader, Reeves. Episodic anecdotes provide humor in good-natured exploitation film.

POOR LITTLE RICH GIRL 1936
★★ NR Musical/Family 1:12 B&W
Dir: Irving Cummings *Cast:* Shirley Temple, Alice Faye, Jack Haley, Gloria Stuart, Michael Whalen, Sara Haden
▶ Little rich girl Temple dodges boarding school and, claiming to be an orphan, hooks up with vaudeville duo Faye and Haley. They dance their way to success, ultimately reuniting Temple with her widowed father Whalen and his new love Stuart. One of finer vehicles for puckish moptop, with first-rate production values. Song-and-dance numbers include oft-excerpted "Military Man" (Temple in uniform with rifle) and "You've Got To Eat Your Spinach, Baby." **(CC)**

POPE OF GREENWICH VILLAGE, THE
1984
★★★ R Drama 2:00
☑ Adult situations, explicit language, violence
Dir: Stuart Rosenberg *Cast:* Eric Roberts, Mickey Rourke, Daryl Hannah, Geraldine Page, Burt Young, Kenneth McMillan
▶ Off-beat slice-of-life tale about punk cousins Roberts and Rourke who rob a Mafia safe and accidently kill a cop, landing them in deep trouble with both organized crime in Little Italy and the police. Rourke's live-in girl Hannah makes off with the money as the leads struggle desperately to stay alive. Authentic New York City locations. Best performance: Geraldine Page as the slain cop's frumpy mother. Adapted from Vincent Patrick's best-seller.

POPEYE 1980
★★★ PG Musical 1:54
☑ Explicit language, violence
Dir: Robert Altman *Cast:* Robin Williams, Shelley Duvall, Ray Walston, Paul Dooley, Paul Smith, Richard Libertini
▶ Sailor Popeye (Williams) rows into Sweethaven port searching for his long-lost Pappy (Walston). He falls in love with Olive Oyl (Duvall) though she's engaged to Bluto (Smith); together Popeye and Olive care for foundling Swee'Pea. Eccentric live-action comedy was box-office dud despite inspired casting. Worthy family fare.

PORK CHOP HILL 1959
★★ NR War 1:37 B&W
Dir: Lewis Milestone *Cast:* Gregory Peck, Harry Guardino, Rip Torn, George Peppard, James Edwards, Bob Steele
▶ Peck gives a quietly heroic performance as a Korean War lieutenant ordered to take a strategically worthless hill just as cease-fire talks commence. Despite horrendous fatalities and minimal backup support, Peck and his men battle their way to the top, then learn they must hold the hill against overwhelming enemy onslaughts. Realistic, hard-hitting film features excellent support from Woody Strode, Robert Blake, and Martin Landau. **(CC)**

PORKY'S 1982 Canadian
★★★★ R Comedy 1:38

☑ Nudity, adult situations, explicit language, adult humor
Dir: Bob Clark **Cast:** Kim Cattrall, Scott Colomby, Kaki Hunter, Nancy Parsons, Alex Karras, Susan Clark
► Good-natured but extremely raunchy comedy set in 1950s Florida is basically a fast-paced collection of locker room jokes as high school friends—primarily Don Monahan, Mark Herrier, Wyatt Knight, and Roger Wilson—try to lose their virginity at a local tavern notorious for its loose women. Megahit comedy inspired a number of sequels; four male stars appeared in the follow-up, *Porky's II: The Next Day.*

PORKY'S II: THE NEXT DAY 1983
Canadian
★ ★ ★ R Comedy 1:38
☑ Nudity, adult situations, explicit language, mild violence, adult humor
Dir: Bob Clark **Cast:** Dan Monahan, Wyatt Knight, Mark Herrier, Tony Ganios, Kaki Hunter, Scott Colomby
► The *Porky's* gang production of *Romeo and Juliet* is disrupted by a fundamentalist minister and the Ku Klux Klan who object to the racy language and casting of a Seminole in the lead. Not to worry, the kids manage to outwit their tormentors. Outrageous pranks and sophomoric gags of the original are mixed with a dash of social consciousness.

PORKY'S REVENGE 1985
★ ★ R Comedy 1:33
☑ Nudity, adult situations, explicit language, graphic violence
Dir: James Komack **Cast:** Dan Monahan, Wyatt Knight, Tony Ganios, Mark Herrier, Kaki Hunter, Chuck Mitchell
► Pee Wee (Monahan), Meat (Ganios), and cohorts foil their old nemesis Porky's (Mitchell) plan to fix the high school basketball championship and force Meat to marry his ugly daughter. Tried-and-true horny high jinks superior to the second movie, not as good as the first. Soundtrack, featuring Dave Edmunds, Willie Nelson, and Clarence Clemons, really rocks. **(CC)**

PORTNOY'S COMPLAINT 1972
★ R Drama 1:42
☑ Nudity, adult situations, explicit language
Dir: Ernest Lehman **Cast:** Richard Benjamin, Karen Black, Lee Grant, Jack Somack, Jeannie Berlin, Jill Clayburgh
► Attempt to film Philip Roth's profane

novel, a virtual monologue about the miseries of growing up, was universally panned by critics upon its release. Portnoy (Benjamin) recites his sexual hangups to his shrink while describing his nagging mother Grant, constipated father Somack, and gentile girlfriend Black. For curiosity seekers only.

POSEIDON ADVENTURE, THE 1972
★ ★ ★ ★ ★ PG Action-Adventure 1:57
☑ Explicit language, mild violence
Dir: Ronald Neame **Cast:** Gene Hackman, Ernest Borgnine, Shelley Winters, Red Buttons, Roddy McDowall, Stella Stevens
► The first and best of the seventies disaster films. Trapped when their luxury liner is capsized by a tidal wave, an all-star cast of survivors must undertake a perilous journey to the bottom—now the top—of the ship. Thrills, chills, and action all the way, with juicy performances from everyone. Our favorite scene: Jewish mama Winters taking her big dive underwater. Oscars for theme song, "The Morning After," and Special Effects; Winters was nominated. Sequel: *Beyond the Poseidon Adventure.*

POSITIVE I.D. 1986
★ R Mystery-Suspense 1:31
☑ Adult situations, explicit language, violence
Dir: Andy Anderson **Cast:** Stephanie Rascoe, John Davies, Steve Fromholz, Laura Lane, Gail Cronauer
► Fort Worth housewife Julie (Rascoe), recovering slowly from a brutal rape-torture and subsequent media-sensation trial, manufactures a new identity as "Bobbie," a blond bombshell who hangs out at a seedy downtown bar. The reason for her double life is revealed when her rapist is released from prison. Compelling low-budget film displays a surprisingly good mix of dark humor and convincing tension.

POSTMAN ALWAYS RINGS TWICE, THE 1946
★ ★ ★ ★ NR Drama 1:53 B&W
Dir: Tay Garnett **Cast:** Lana Turner, John Garfield, Cecil Kellaway, Hume Cronyn, Leon Ames, Audrey Totter
► Drifter Garfield accepts handyman job at roadside diner in order to seduce owner Kellaway's wife Turner; she responds with a plot to kill her husband. Classic film noir notable for torrid teaming of Garfield and Turner (who's irresistible in

almost all-white wardrobe) and daring plot. Shrewd adaptation of James M. Cain's novel suggests a great deal despite censorship restrictions. Remade in 1981.

POSTMAN ALWAYS RINGS TWICE, THE 1981
★★★ R Drama 1:56
☑ Strong sexual content, adult situations, explicit language, violence
Dir: Bob Rafelson *Cast:* Jack Nicholson, Jessica Lange, John Colicos, Michael Lerner, Anjelica Huston
▶ Steamy remake of the 1946 Lana Turner/John Garfield vehicle, based on James M. Cain's novel. In the Depression thirties, drifter Nicholson begins a torrid affair with Lange, wife of roadhouse owner Colicos. The lovers succeed in murdering Colicos and even manage to escape justice but get their just desserts in the end. Most notorious scene: Nicholson and Lange on the floury kitchen table.

POT O' GOLD 1941
★★ NR Comedy 1:25 B&W
Dir: George Marshall *Cast:* James Stewart, Paulette Goddard, Charles Winninger, Mary Gordon, Frank Melton, Horace Heidt
▶ Inconsequential comedy about the efforts of wealthy harmonica whiz Stewart to promote Heidt's band while pursuing Goddard, the beautiful daughter of a tenement landlady. Stewart succeeds in placing the band on a new radio show financed by his uncle Winninger. Frail story line isn't helped by Stewart's singing or songs like "Hi Cy, What's Cookin'?" Based on a once-popular radio series.

POWAQQATSI 1988
☆ G Documentary 1:37
Dir: Godfrey Reggio
▶ Reggio's follow-up to *Koyaanisqatsi* contrasts modern urban life with images of nature and Third World cultures. Reggio eschews conventional storytelling and dialogue in favor of an extravagant visual style and bravura editing that make this a treat for the eye and ear if not the mind and heart. Score by Philip Glass.

POWER, THE 1984
★★ R Horror 1:26
☑ Explicit language, graphic violence
Dir: Jeffrey Obrow, Stephen Carpenter
Cast: Susan Stokey, Warren Lincoln, Lisa Erickson, J. Dinan Myrtetus, Chad Christian

▶ Aztec relic that possesses people falls into the hands of teens who give it to reporter Stokey. Reporter's rejected beau Lincoln falls under statue's influence and goes on a murderous spree. Good special effects and makeup but atrocious acting, clichéd story, and excessive violence.

POWER 1986
★★ R Drama 1:51
☑ Brief nudity, adult situations, explicit language
Dir: Sidney Lumet *Cast:* Richard Gere, Julie Christie, Gene Hackman, Kate Capshaw, Denzel Washington, E. G. Marshall
▶ Media consultant Gere is handsome, ruthless, and for a big enough fee, will transform anyone into a front-running political contender. His ex-mentor Hackman, ex-wife Christie, and Senator Marshall, who's involved in a real-estate swindle, ultimately convince Gere to redeem himself by backing an ethical candidate. Well-meaning but rather witless film with lots of pretty clothes and hip set decorations. (CC)

POWER PLAY 1978 Canadian
★ NR Action-Adventure 1:42
☑ Brief nudity, graphic violence
Dir: Martyn Burke *Cast:* Peter O'Toole, David Hemmings, Donald Pleasence, Barry Morse, Jon Granik, Dick Cavett
▶ In a European country, army officers conspire to overthrow the corrupt government. The coup is a success but O'Toole, one of the conspirators, turns on his erstwhile allies and assumes power himself. Believable performances, acceptable action, but somewhat leisurely pacing and overly dry dialogue.

P.O.W. THE ESCAPE 1986
★★ R War 1:30
☑ Nudity, explicit language, violence
Dir: Gideon Amir *Cast:* David Carradine, Charles R. Floyd, Mako, Steve James, Phil Brock
▶ North Vietnam, 1973: captured American colonel Carradine is slated for execution but offered freedom if he'll help captor Mako escape to the U.S. with his cache of gold. Carradine enters Norris/Stallone territory, delivering the expected macho heroics and nonstop action.

PRAYER FOR THE DYING, A 1987 British
★★ R Drama 1:48
☑ Brief nudity, adult situations, explicit language, violence

Dir: Mike Hodges *Cast:* Mickey Rourke, Bob Hoskins, Alan Bates, Sammi Davis, Christopher Fulford, Liam Neeson
▶ Rourke, a disillusioned IRA man, does a hit for mobster Bates. When priest Hoskins witnesses the deed, Rourke uses the confessional to ensure Hoskins's silence but finds himself pursued by the police and his employers. Well-mounted and strongly cast but hindered by incomplete characterizations, heavy accents, and overwrought symbolism. Based on the Jack Higgins best-seller. **(CC)**

PRAY FOR DEATH 1985
★ ★ R Martial Arts 1:34
☑ Explicit language, graphic violence
Dir: Gordon Hessler *Cast:* Sho Kosugi, Donna Kei Benz, James Booth, Norman Burton, Michael Constantine
▶ Japanese businessman Kosugi moves to New York and opens a restaurant. When thugs kidnap his son and kill his wife, Kosugi comes out of ninja retirement for revenge. Rousing fight scenes, acrobatic action, formula plot, and wooden performances.

PREDATOR 1987
★ ★ ★ ★ R Sci-Fi/Action-Adventure 1:46
☑ Explicit language, graphic violence
Dir: John McTiernan *Cast:* Arnold Schwarzenegger, Carl Weathers, Elpidia Carrillo, Bill Duke, Jesse Ventura, Sonny Landham
▶ Schwarzenegger leads a team of mercenaries into the jungles of Latin America, but they're double-crossed by CIA agent Weathers and forced to battle their way back to a distant rendezvous point. Tension increases as half-seen enemy (Kevin Peter Hall) with amazing powers picks them off one by one. Solid adventure with good special effects is sure to please Schwarzenegger's fans. **(CC)**

PREMATURE BURIAL, THE 1962
★ ★ NR Horror 1:21
Dir: Roger Corman *Cast:* Ray Milland, Hazel Court, Richard Ney, Heather Angel, Alan Napier, Dick Miller
▶ Nineteenth-century medical student Milland's one great fear—of being buried alive—becomes reality when doctor mistakenly declares him dead. Milland escapes to get revenge. Middling entry in Corman's series of Edgar Allan Poe adaptations.

PREPPIES 1984
★ R Sex/Comedy 1:23
☑ Nudity, adult situations, explicit language
Dir: Chuck Vincent *Cast:* Dennis Drake, Peter Reardon, Steven Holt, Nitchie Barrett, Cindy Manion, Lynda Wiesmeier
▶ Preppie Drake will blow his inheritance if he doesn't pass upcoming exams, so his scheming cousin, who covets the family fortune himself, hires sexy sluts to distract Drake and his pals from their books. Second-rate sex gags, heavy on lame verbal foreplay. Plenty of skin with former *Playboy* Playmate Wiesmeier in an especially steamy role.

PRESENTING LILY MARS 1943
★ ★ ★ NR Musical 1:44 B&W
Dir: Norman Taurog *Cast:* Judy Garland, Van Heflin, Fay Bainter, Richard Carlson, Spring Byington, Marta Eggerth
▶ Garland enhances this predictable tale of a stagestruck Indiana girl who convinces Broadway producer Heflin to make her a chorus girl in his next show. Despite objections of star Eggerth, Garland becomes a success. Routine songs ("Three O'Clock in the Morning," "Broadway Rhythm") overwhelm slight plot (based on a novel by Booth Tarkington). With Tommy Dorsey, Bob Crosby, and their orchestras.

PRESIDENT'S ANALYST, THE 1967
★ ★ NR Comedy 1:43
☑ Adult situations, explicit language, violence
Dir: Theodore J. Flicker *Cast:* James Coburn, Godfrey Cambridge, Severn Darden, Joan Delaney, Pat Harrington, William Daniels
▶ Shrink Coburn learns too much in his sessions with the President and tries to escape the pressures of his job, only to become the target of both the U.S. and foreign spies. Wacky satire takes on the CIA, FBI, and international political intrigue. Uneven but Coburn's cool and some delicious bits (especially the revelation of the identity of "TPC," one of the groups hounding Coburn) make it work.

PRESIDENT'S LADY, THE 1953
★ ★ ★ NR Biography 1:36 B&W
Dir: Henry Levin *Cast:* Charlton Heston, Susan Hayward, John McIntire, Fay Bainter, Whitfield Connor, Carl Betz
▶ While trying to end her marriage to an unfaithful businessman, Rachel Donelson

(Hayward) falls in love with attorney Andrew Jackson (Heston). After they marry, Jackson must cope with malicious gossip during his 1828 campaign for the presidency. Surprisingly accurate and engrossing adaptation of Irving Stone's best-selling novel features spirited performances by Heston and Hayward.

PRESIDIO, THE 1988
★ ★ ★ ★ **R Mystery-Suspense 1:39**
☑ Adult situations, explicit language, violence
Dir: Peter Hyams *Cast:* Sean Connery, Mark Harmon, Meg Ryan, Jack Warden, Dana Gladstone, Mark Blum
► When a young female soldier is slain while patrolling the Presidio, the San Francisco Army base, hot-headed police detective Harmon and tough, by-the-book base chief Connery must settle jurisdictional dispute and team to solve the case. Connery's hostility is increased by daughter Ryan's romance with Harmon. Flinty team of Connery and Harmon create sparks in fast-paced, action-packed crime drama.

PRETTY BABY 1978
★ ★ **R Drama 1:50**
☑ Nudity, adult situations, explicit language
Dir: Louis Malle *Cast:* Keith Carradine, Susan Sarandon, Brooke Shields, Frances Faye, Antonio Fargas, Gerrit Graham
► New Orleans, 1917: young Shields follows in the professional footsteps of prostitute mom Sarandon. Photographer Carradine takes pictures of the women and eventually marries Shields. Beautiful period re-creation, snazzy ragtime score, several shocking scenes (mostly involving Shields) but slow pace and stiff acting hinder story.

PRETTY IN PINK 1986
★ ★ ★ ★ **PG-13 Romance/Comedy 1:36**
☑ Adult situations, explicit language
Dir: Howard Deutsch *Cast:* Molly Ringwald, Harry Dean Stanton, Jon Cryer, Andrew McCarthy, Annie Potts, James Spader
► Snooty high schoolers look down on poor teen Ringwald with unemployed dad Stanton although her nerdy best pal Cryer loves her. Rich kid McCarthy falls for Ringwald but will peer pressure ruin their prom date? Slight but very sweet: witty dialogue from producer/writer John

Hughes, adorable Ringwald, amusing support from Cryer, good rock standards score, and an upbeat finale. **(CC)**

PRETTYKILL 1987
★ **R Mystery-Suspense 1:35**
☑ Nudity, adult situations, explicit language, violence
Dir: George Kaczender *Cast:* David Birney, Season Hubley, Suzanne Snyder, Yaphet Kotto, Susannah York
► High-class hooker Hubley takes Snyder under her professional wing. Can Hubley's cop boyfriend Birney save her when Snyder turns out to be a schizoid killer? Unconvincing thriller with cardboard characters, silly screenplay, average production values.

PRETTY POISON 1968
★ ★ ★ **R Mystery-Suspense 1:29**
☑ Nudity, adult situations, violence
Dir: Noel Black *Cast:* Anthony Perkins, Tuesday Weld, Beverly Garland, John Randolph, Dick O'Neill, Clarice Blackburn
► Paroled arsonist Perkins, released under Randolph's supervision, works in local lumber mill. Bored with small-town life, he tells precocious high schooler Weld he's a CIA agent investigating the lumber outfit and asks for her help. Eager to escape stern rule of her mother Garland, Weld teams with Perkins and pushes his plans for adventure further than he'd anticipated. Taut drama with sensational Weld as the pretty poison.

PRETTY SMART 1987
★ **R Comedy 1:24**
☑ Nudity, strong sexual content, adult situations, explicit language
Dir: Dimitri Logothetis *Cast:* Tricia Leigh Fisher, Lisa Lorient, Dennis Cole, Patricia Arquette, Paris Vaughan
► Sisters Fisher and Lorient at posh girls' academy in Greece are divided by their choice of clique. Fisher joins the rebel Subs while Lorient opts for the snooty 'Premes. They are, however, united in their effort to thwart drug-smuggling scheme of principal Cole. Lots of nudity in a silly story.

PREY, THE 1983
★ **R Horror 1:21**
☑ Brief nudity, adult situations, violence
Dir: Edwin Scott Brown *Cast:* Debbie Thureson, Steve Bond, Lori Lethin, Robert Wald, Gayle Gannes
► Teens take their van into the moun-

tains to go camping but something tall, gross, and ugly begins to stalk and kill them. A ranger aids the survivors but is soon in danger himself. Routine formula story, blandly cast and dully directed. Fails to deliver requisite thrills.

PRICK UP YOUR EARS 1987 British
☆ R Drama 1:51
☑ Strong sexual content, adult situations, explicit language
Dir: Stephen Frears *Cast:* Gary Oldman, Alfred Molina, Vanessa Redgrave, Wallace Shawn, Lindsay Duncan
▶ True story of the late British playwright Joe Orton (Oldman) who gained reknown for his black comedies in the 1960s. His male lover Molina's jealousy of Orton's success led to a tragic conclusion. Literate, candid, superbly performed by Oldman and Molina but very depressing. Definitely not for all tastes.

PRIDE AND PREJUDICE 1940
★★★★ NR Comedy 1:58 B&W
Dir: Robert Z. Leonard *Cast:* Greer Garson, Laurence Olivier, Mary Boland, Edna May Oliver, Maureen O'Sullivan, Edmund Gwenn
▶ First-rate adaptation of Jane Austen's classic comedy of manners about the efforts of early nineteenth-century English couple Boland and Gwenn to marry off their five eligible daughters. Garson and Olivier, extremely appealing as antagonistic lovers, make the most of the witty, polished dialogue (by Aldous Huxley and Jane Murfin). Gorgeous set designs by Cedric Gibbons and Paul Groesse received an Oscar.

PRIDE AND THE PASSION, THE 1957
★★ NR Action-Adventure 2:12
Dir: Stanley Kramer *Cast:* Cary Grant, Frank Sinatra, Sophia Loren, Theodore Bikel, John Wengraf, Jay Novello
▶ Overblown historical epic about a strategic cannon left behind by retreating Spaniards during 1810 war. Guerrilla leader Sinatra convinces British artillery expert Grant to bring the weapon to Avila, where it will be used against the French. During the perilous journey Grant falls in love with beautiful camp follower Loren. Large-scale spectacle lacks emotion.

PRIDE OF THE YANKEES, THE 1942
★★★★★ NR Biography/Sports 2:08 B&W
Dir: Sam Wood *Cast:* Gary Cooper,

Teresa Wright, Babe Ruth, Walter Brennan, Dan Duryea, Elsa Janssen
▶ Top-notch story of Lou Gehrig (Cooper), Hall-of-Fame Yankee first baseman, charts his undergrad years at Columbia, choice of pro baseball over postgrad work to pay for operation for mother Janssen, romance with wife-to-be Wright, and spectacular career as part of legendary "Murderer's Row" of twenties and thirties Yanks. After setting still-unbroken record for 2,130 consecutive games played, "Iron Horse" Gehrig succumbed to the degenerative muscle disease that bears his name, bowing out of baseball in an emotional farewell. First-class production earned ten Oscar nominations; won for Best Editing. **(CC)**

PRIEST OF LOVE 1981 British
★★ R Biography 2:05
☑ Nudity, adult situations, explicit language
Dir: Christopher Miles *Cast:* Ian McKellen, Janet Suzman, Ava Gardner, John Gielgud, Sarah Miles, Penelope Keith
▶ The life and loves of the writer D. H. Lawrence (McKellen), including relationships with wife (Suzman) and patroness of the arts Mabel Dodge Luhan (Gardner). Interesting casting (Gardner looks especially fit) and colorful locations, but rather shapeless narrative fails to give sufficient insight into what made Lawrence tick.

PRIME CUT 1972
★★★ R Action-Adventure 1:26
☑ Brief nudity, explicit language, violence
Dir: Michael Ritchie *Cast:* Lee Marvin, Gene Hackman, Angel Tompkins, Gregory Walcott, Sissy Spacek
▶ Stylish but brutal thriller about gang warfare between a Chicago mob represented by Marvin and Kansas City upstarts led by Hackman features a memorable opening sequence in which a thug is reduced to sausages. Spacek makes her film debut as a drugged prostitute auctioned off in a cattle warehouse by Hackman's wife Tompkins. **(CC)**

PRIME RISK 1985
★★ PG-13 Drama 1:38
☑ Brief nudity, explicit language, violence
Dir: Michael Farkas *Cast:* Lee Montgomery, Toni Hudson, Sam Bottoms, Clu Gulager, Keenan Wynn
▶ When computer expert Hudson is

turned down for a job by a sexist bank officer, she teams up with aspiring pilot Montgomery, whose bank account has been frozen, in a plot to rob automated teller machines. Unfortunately, they stumble into a deadly conspiracy by foreign spies to undermine the Federal Reserve Bank. Taut, enjoyable thriller with an impressive script by first-time director Farkas.

PRINCE AND THE PAUPER, THE 1937
★★★ NR Action-Adventure 2:00 B&W
Dir: William Keighley *Cast:* Errol Flynn, Claude Rains, Henry Stephenson, Barton MacLane, Billy Mauch, Bobby Mauch
▶ Young prince Bobby Mauch, soon to be crowned King Edward VI, trades places with a look-alike beggar Billy Mauch for a first-hand look at sixteenth-century London slums. Enemies at court learn of the switch, and proceed with plans to crown the wrong boy. The only one who listens to the prince's pleas is dissolute rake Flynn. Large-scale adaptation of Mark Twain's classic played with high spirits and wit. Also available in a colorized version. **(CC)**

PRINCE AND THE SHOWGIRL, THE 1957
★★ NR Comedy 1:57
Dir: Laurence Olivier *Cast:* Marilyn Monroe, Laurence Olivier, Sybil Thorndike, Richard Wattis, Jeremy Spenser
▶ Charming but low-key comedy set in 1911 London. Carpathian prince Olivier, in town for King George's coronation, invites dizzy showgirl Monroe to dinner in hopes of a quick seduction. Instead, she falls in love and settles a feud between the prince and his son Spenser. Based on a hit play by Terence Rattigan.

PRINCE OF DARKNESS 1987
★★ R Horror 1:41
☑ Explicit language, graphic violence
Dir: John Carpenter *Cast:* Donald Pleasence, Jameson Parker, Lisa Blount, Victor Wong, Dennis Dun, Susan Blanchard
▶ Priest Pleasence, scientist Wong, and graduate students, including Parker and Blount, team to fight Satan (imprisoned for centuries in a church basement in the form of a liquid green mass) when the demon threatens to return to life. Carpenter provides genuine jolts, moody atmosphere, intense special effects, and interesting ideas; there may be times,

however, when you wish his talky characters would just shut up.

PRINCE OF THE CITY 1981
★★★ R Drama 2:50
☑ Adult situations, explicit language, violence
Dir: Sidney Lumet *Cast:* Treat Williams, Jerry Orbach, Richard Foronjy, Don Billett, Kenny Marino, Lindsay Crouse
▶ New York narc Williams is torn between moral obligation and loyalty to his partners when he agrees to cooperate in a corruption investigation. Gripping drama manages a complex balancing act, portraying all sides of the characters and issues while evoking utmost sympathy for the tortured Williams. Moving work from Williams, strongly supported by Orbach. Powerfully directed and co-written by Lumet; Oscar-nominated screenplay inspired by a true story.

PRINCESS ACADEMY, THE 1987
★ R Comedy 1:30
☑ Adult situations, explicit language, adult humor
Dir: Bruce Block *Cast:* Eva Gabor, Lu Leonard, Lar Park Lincoln, Richard Paul, Carole Davis
▶ Reform-school teen Lincoln nabs scholarship to posh Swiss academy where pâté eating and shopping are part of the curriculum. Lincoln foils corrupt headmistress Leonard and wins the heart of a titled twit. Crass comedy features lots of jokes about losing virginity and close-ups of manure.

PRINCESS AND THE PIRATE, THE 1944
★★ NR Comedy 1:34
Dir: David Butler *Cast:* Bob Hope, Virginia Mayo, Walter Brennan, Walter Slezak, Victor McLaglen
▶ Princess Mayo, fleeing arranged marriage, is kidnapped by pirates of the Spanish Main. Actor Hope, longer on shtick than talent, helps her escape. Mindless, glossy period story shows off Hope, Mayo, and Brennan (who provides many of the laughs) to good advantage.

PRINCESS BRIDE, THE 1987
★★★★ PG Fantasy/Comedy 1:38
☑ Explicit language, mild violence
Dir: Rob Reiner *Cast:* Cary Elwes, Robin Wright, Mandy Patinkin, Chris Sarandon, Wallace Shawn, Andre the Giant
▶ Grandfather Peter Falk's bedtime story features fencing, fighting, torture, giants, monsters, Miracle Max (Billy Crystal), and

yes, some kissing. Princess Buttercup (Wright) becomes engaged to Prince Humperdink (Sarandon) after learning her true love Elwes has been killed by pirates. When she's abducted by Shawn, Patinkin, and Andre, a masked stranger appears to rescue her. Enchanting, high-spirited fun is actually an adult fantasy disguised as a children's story. Adapted by William Goldman from his cult novel. A true delight for all ages. **(CC)**

PRINCIPAL, THE 1987
★ ★ ★ ★ **R Drama 1:50**
☑ Explicit language, violence
Dir: Christopher Cain   *Cast:* James Belushi, Louis Gossett, Jr., Rae Dawn Chong, Michael Wright, J. J. Cohen, Esai Morales
▶ Unruly teacher Belushi is punished with "promotion" to principal of war-zone high school dominated by drug-dealing ganglord Wright. Teaming with security chief Gossett, baseball bat-wielding Belushi attempts to instill discipline in rowdy students and pride in apathetic teachers. Efforts lead to climactic showdown with Wright. Picture blends comedy and drama, often with unsettling results, but Belushi shines in this ultimately compelling tale.

PRISON 1988
★ ★ **R Horror 1:42**
Dir: Renny Harlin   *Cast:* Lane Smith, Viggo Mortensen, Chelsea Field, Andre de Shields, Lincoln Kilpatrick, Ivan Kane
▶ Prison guard Smith stands by as innocent man is electrocuted. Twenty years later, Smith, now warden of the very same prison, is haunted by the vengeful electric ghost of the wrongfully executed man. Low-budget horror pic offers few surprises. **(CC)**

PRISONER OF SECOND AVENUE, THE 1975
★ ★ ★ ★ **PG Comedy 1:38**
☑ Explicit language, adult humor
Dir: Melvin Frank   *Cast:* Jack Lemmon, Anne Bancroft, Gene Saks, Elizabeth Wilson, Florence Stanley, Maxine Stuart
▶ His nerves already frayed by New York hassles, ad executive Lemmon suffers nervous breakdown when fired by failing firm. His rock-solid wife Bancroft gets a job and supports Lemmon through hardships with apathetic shrink, obnoxious neighbors, and meddling relatives, but then is also dismissed. Fine comic outing with melancholy edge in another play-into-

film by prolific Neil Simon. Look for pre-*Rocky* Stallone in bit part.

PRISONER OF SHARK ISLAND, THE 1936
★ ★ **NR Biography 1:34 B&W**
Dir: John Ford   *Cast:* Warner Baxter, Gloria Stuart, Joyce Kay, Fred Kohler, Jr., Harry Carey, John Carradine
▶ In 1865, Maryland doctor Samuel Mudd (Baxter) sets a stranger's broken ankle, unaware he's John Wilkes Booth. In the hysteria surrounding Lincoln's assassination, Mudd is convicted of conspiracy and sentenced to life imprisonment on Shark Island. Despite harsh mistreatment, he redeems himself during a yellow fever epidemic. Masterful treatment of an absorbing true story remains consistently interesting despite gloomy tone.

PRISONER OF ZENDA, THE 1952
★ ★ ★ **NR Action-Adventure 1:40**
Dir: Richard Thorpe   *Cast:* Stewart Granger, Deborah Kerr, James Mason, Louis Calhern, Jane Greer, Robert Douglas
▶ Third version of Anthony Hope's novel about political intrigue in the mythical kingdom of Ruritania. When crown prince Granger is kidnapped, a look-alike Englishman (also Granger) steps in to replace him and falls in love with beautiful princess Kerr. Thrilling climax features swashbuckling swordplay with oily villain Mason.

PRISONER OF ZENDA, THE 1979
★ ★ ★ **PG Comedy 1:48**
☑ Adult situations
Dir: Richard Quine   *Cast:* Peter Sellers, Lynne Frederick, Lionel Jeffries, Elke Sommer, Gregory Sierra, Jeremy Kemp
▶ Send-up of many previous incarnations of film by same name. In late nineteenth-century London, cabbie is enlisted to impersonate the crown prince of Ruritania (Sellers in both roles) since the prince's evil half-brother Kemp has plans for an assassination. Complications ensue when cabbie Sellers falls in love with the prince's fiancée Frederick. Tepid costume comedy worthy for the always entertaining Sellers.

PRIVATE BENJAMIN 1980
★ ★ ★ ★ ★ **R Comedy 1:50**
☑ Brief nudity, explicit language
Dir: Howard Zieff   *Cast:* Goldie Hawn, Eileen Brennan, Armand Assante, Albert Brooks, Sam Wanamaker, Barbara Barrie

▶ Spoiled, rich Hawn, distraught after death of hubby Brooks six hours after wedding, enlists in Army expecting country club life. Imagine Hawn's dismay when she encounters the spartan military, personified by no-nonsense captain Brennan determined to make a woman out of her. Bouncy and popular comedy is splendid vehicle for Hawn, but Brennan and Brooks are also terrific. Hawn, Brennan, and screenplay were Oscar nominees.

PRIVATE EYES, THE 1980
★★★ PG Comedy/Family 1:31
☑ Mild violence
Dir: Lang Elliot   *Cast:* Tim Conway, Don Knotts, Trisha Noble, Bernard Fox, Grace Zabriskie, Jogn Fujioka
▶ Klutzy American detectives Conway and Knotts assigned to Scotland Yard must solve the murder of two British aristocrats. Bluebloods' daughter Noble is in danger, since family servants inherit fortune if she also expires. Lightweight but amiable comedy (co-written by Conway) aims for kids, with plenty of secret passageways, pratfalls, and silly sight gags.

PRIVATE FILES OF J. EDGAR HOOVER, THE 1977
★★ PG Biography 1:22
☑ Explicit language, violence
Dir: Larry Cohen   *Cast:* Broderick Crawford, Jose Ferrer, Rip Torn, Dan Dailey, Michael Parks, Ronee Blakley
▶ Sensationalist biopic of the late FBI chief Hoover (Crawford), whose ironfisted rule over the bureau lasted from 1924 until his death in 1972, is not for admirers of the man. Film paints unflattering portrait of Hoover's professional tactics and private life, acknowledging his contribution in building the agency into respected crime-fighting outfit but questioning his disregard for individual rights and pointedly touching on his hypocritical personal standards. Fine portrayal of feud with RFK (Parks).

PRIVATE FUNCTION, A 1985 British
★ R Comedy 1:33
☑ Adult situations, explicit language
Dir: Malcolm Mowbray   *Cast:* Michael Palin, Maggie Smith, Denholm Elliott, Liz Smith, Richard Griffiths, Tony Haygarth
▶ Food rationing causes havoc in World War II English town as snobby big-shot Elliott and pals illegally raise a pig for a banquet. Wimpy podiatrist Palin, badgered by his social-climber wife Smith, pignaps the main course but can't butcher it. Smith, Palin, Elliott, and the pig all deliver oustanding performances, but droll comedy will appeal only to fans of British humor.

PRIVATE INVESTIGATIONS 1987
★★ R Drama 1:31
☑ Adult situations, explicit language, violence
Dir: Nigel Dick   *Cast:* Clayton Rohner, Ray Sharkey, Paul LeMat, Talia Balsam, Anthony Zerbe, Martin Balsam
▶ Newspaper editor Zerbe investigates drug-dealing cop Sharkey who frames his son Rohner for murder. Rohner seeks sanctuary with new girlfriend Balsam. The young couple, pursued by Sharkey and his murderous cohorts (including LeMat), seek to establish Rohner's innocence and help Zerbe expose police corruption. Serviceable thriller employs brisk action to disguise somewhat familiar tale.

PRIVATE LESSONS 1981
★★ R Comedy 1:27
☑ Nudity, adult situations, explicit language
Dir: Alan Myerson   *Cast:* Sylvia Kristel, Howard Hesseman, Eric Brown, Patrick Piccininni, Ed Begley, Jr., Pamela Bryant
▶ Unscrupulous chauffeur Hesseman takes advantage of teen Brown's preoccupation with sex by having beautiful housekeeper Kristel seduce him. Hesseman then fakes Kristel's death in a blackmail scheme, but true love saves the day. A popular hit on release for its ample nudity, but leering tone grows tedious.

PRIVATE LIFE OF HENRY VIII, THE 1933 British
★★ NR Biography 1:37 B&W
Dir: Alexander Korda   *Cast:* Charles Laughton, Robert Donat, Binnie Barnes, Elsa Lanchester, Merle Oberon, Wendy Barrie
▶ Laughton won an Oscar for his vibrant, full-bodied impersonation of the notorious sixteenth-century English king in this sumptuous historical epic. Story covers Henry's last five marriages, with Laughton's wife Lanchester a standout as the card-cheating Anne of Cleves. Although technically dated, film's blend of spectacle and bawdy humor remains delightful.

PRIVATE LIFE OF SHERLOCK HOLMES, THE 1970
★★ PG Mystery-Suspense 2:05

☑ Adult situations, explicit language
Dir: Billy Wilder   *Cast:* Robert Stephens, Colin Blakely, Genevieve Page, Christopher Lee, Irene Handl, Stanley Holloway
▶ Sherlock Holmes (Stephens) and Doctor Watson (Blakely) investigate a baffling case that involves midgets, the Loch Ness monster, and mystery woman Page. Unusual and absorbing; Wilder takes an adult, revisionist approach to Holmes that brings new complexity to the character.

PRIVATE LIVES OF ELIZABETH AND ESSEX, THE 1939
★★★ NR Drama 1:46
Dir: Michael Curtiz   *Cast:* Bette Davis, Errol Flynn, Olivia de Havilland, Donald Crisp, Alan Hale, Vincent Price
▶ Elaborate but historically inaccurate costume epic about the tempestuous relationship between the aging Queen of England and the dashing Earl of Essex is a fine showcase for Davis's marvelous acting. Adapted from Maxwell Anderson's play *Elizabeth the Queen*, with a stirring score by Wolfang Korngold. Davis would repeat her role in 1955's *The Virgin Queen*.

PRIVATE RESORT 1985
★★ R Comedy 1:22
☑ Nudity, adult situations, explicit language
Dir: George Bowers   *Cast:* Rob Morrow, Johnny Depp, Emily Longstreth, Karyn O'Bryan, Hector Elizondo, Dody Goodman
▶ Still another adolescent farce about young boys looking for girls, this time at a Jamaican resort. Jack (teen heartthrob Depp) falls for older woman Longstreth; his friend Morrow chases a waitress. Slapstick plot complications are provided by jewel thief Elizondo.

PRIVATE ROAD 1987
★ R Drama 1:37
☑ Nudity, explicit language, mild violence
Dir: Raphael Nussbaum   *Cast:* Greg Evigan, George Kennedy, Mitzi Kapture, Brian Patrick Clarke
▶ Hotheaded mechanic Evigan is the victim of a hit-and-run accident by unstable heiress Kapture. Afraid of the police, her father Kennedy hides him at home until he recovers. Evigan insinuates himself into the family but faces a set-

back in a blackmail plot. Twisty plot compensates for a low budget.

PRIVATE SCHOOL 1983
★★ R Comedy 1:25
☑ Nudity, explicit language, adult humor
Dir: Noel Black   *Cast:* Phoebe Cates, Betsy Russell, Matthew Modine, Michael Zorek, Ray Walston, Sylvia Kristel
▶ Leering teen comedy about the efforts of prep school boys to spy on the luscious girls at Cherryvale Academy. Modine's tricks backfire when he's pursued by naughty flirt Russell as well as shy virgin Cates. Plenty of skin on display, but smirking screenplay by humorist Dan Greenburg is a disappointment.

PRIVATES ON PARADE 1984 British
☆ R Comedy 1:38
☑ Nudity, adult situations, explicit language, violence
Dir: Michael Blakemore   *Cast:* John Cleese, Denis Quilley, Patrick Pearson, Michael Elphick, Nicola Pagett, Bruce Payne
▶ Adaptation of Peter Nichols's stage play concerns song-and-dance troupe entertaining British soldiers in 1948 Singapore. Farce pits gung-ho, not-too-bright officer Cleese against aging homosexual chorus director Quilley. Uneven mixture of camp musical comedy and antiwar intrigue doesn't work, although Cleese and especially Quilley are fine.

PRIVILEGE 1967 British
★ NR Drama 1:43
Dir: Peter Watkins   *Cast:* Paul Jones, Jean Shrimpton, Mark London, Max Bacon, Jeremy Child, William Job
▶ In the 1970s, English rock idol Jones is used by government and church to control nation's youth. Inspired by artist Shrimpton, Jones rebels against the authorities and their attempts to manipulate the masses. Attempt to satirize future of British welfare state suffers from uneven direction. Jones is former singer for rock group Manfred Mann.

PRIZE FIGHTER, THE 1979
★★★ PG Comedy 1:39
☑ Explicit language
Dir: Michael Pierce   *Cast:* Tim Conway, Don Knotts, David Wayne, Robin Clarke, Cisse Cameron, Mary Ellen O'Neill
▶ In the 1930s, inept boxer Conway and trainer Knotts get involved with fight-fixing gangsters without realizing Conway's

sudden winning streak is due to the mob's scams rather than his skills. Third feature teaming of Conway and Knotts is silly, harmless fun with family appeal.

PRIZZI'S HONOR 1985
★★★★ R Comedy/Drama 2:09
☑ Brief nudity, adult situations, explicit language, violence
Dir: John Huston *Cast:* Jack Nicholson, Kathleen Turner, William Hickey, Anjelica Huston, Robert Loggia, John Randolph
► Charlie Partana (Nicholson), super hit man for the Prizzi family, especially the Don (Hickey), falls for classy Irene (Turner). When he discovers she also kills for a living and, even worse, may have stolen from the Prizzis, Nicholson is confused. "Do I ice her? Do I marry her?" he asks ex-girlfriend Maerose (Oscar winner Anjelica Huston), who replies: "Just because she's a thief and a hitter don't mean she ain't a good woman in all other departments." The double cross turns somersaults in the John Huston/Janet Roach sceenplay, adapted from Richard Condon's witty novel and enhanced by riveting performances from all. Copped eight Oscar nominations.

PRODUCERS, THE 1967
★★★★ NR Musical/Comedy 1:28
Dir: Mel Brooks *Cast:* Zero Mostel, Gene Wilder, Dick Shawn, Kenneth Mars, Estelle Winwood, Renée Taylor
► Has-been theatrical producer Mostel and neurotic accountant Wilder conspire to raise money from rich old ladies to produce sure-fire flop, *Springtime for Hitler.* If the show closes on opening night, the swindlers will get rich. To insure failure, they hire terrible writer Mars, transvestite director Christopher Hewett, and drugged-out hippie actor Shawn. Topnotch Brooks screenplay won an Oscar. A rare comedy that gets funnier with every viewing.

PROFESSIONALS, THE 1966
★★★★ PG Western 1:57
☑ Brief nudity, adult situations
Dir: Richard Brooks *Cast:* Burt Lancaster, Lee Marvin, Robert Ryan, Jack Palance, Claudia Cardinale, Woody Strode
► Cattle baron Ralph Bellamy hires four mercenaries to retrieve kidnapped wife Cardinale from Mexican bandit Palance. The team consists of specialized experts: explosives wizard Lancaster, sharp-shooter Marvin, horse trainer Ryan, and archer Strode. After a daring raid on the bandit's hideout, the heroes learn they've been double-crossed. Thoroughly enjoyable Western with a superb cast features Oscar-nominated photography by Conrad Hall.

PROJECT X 1987
★★★★ PG Drama 1:47
☑ Explicit language, mild violence
Dir: Jonathan Kaplan *Cast:* Matthew Broderick, Helen Hunt, Bill Sadler, Johnny Ray McGhee, Jonathan Stark, Robin Gammell
► Unruly Air Force pilot Broderick is punished with a new assignment: experimenting on chimps at a top-secret weapons research center. With the help of animal psychologist Hunt, he learns the chimps are being prepared for an unnecessarily fatal test. Sincere plea for animal rights enhanced by a marvelous performance by Willie as a chimp with the ability to read sign language. (CC)

PROMISED LAND 1988
★★ R Drama 1:35
☑ Adult situations, explicit language, violence
Dir: Michael Hoffman *Cast:* Jason Gedrick, Kiefer Sutherland, Meg Ryan, Tracy Pollan, Googy Gress
► Two years after high school, jock-turned-cop Gedrick is visited by old girl-friend Pollan; his shy friend Sutherland also returns home. Tragedy is set in motion when Sutherland falls on the wrong side of the law. Ambitious coming-of-age story covers familiar ground but does it well. Nicely nuanced performances by the lead foursome, beautiful cinematography; sometimes too self-consciously arty.

PROMISES IN THE DARK 1979
★★★★★ PG Drama 1:58
☑ Adult situations, explicit language
Dir: Jerome Hellman *Cast:* Marsha Mason, Ned Beatty, Kathleen Beller, Susan Clark, Michael Brandon
► Beller, a gallant teenager dying of cancer, is treated by compassionate but personally troubled doctor Mason who must decide whether or not to keep the beautiful child on life support. Modern melodrama featuring first-rate acting and ultrarealistic production design is an assured tearjerker.

PROM NIGHT 1980 Canadian
★ R Horror 1:31
☑ Brief nudity, adult situations, explicit language, graphic violence
Dir: Paul Lynch *Cast:* Leslie Nielsen, Jamie Lee Curtis, Casey Stevens, Eddie Benton, Antoinette Bower
▶ Four preteens tease a friend until she commits suicide. Six years later they're stalked by a masked madman on the night of a big dance. Derivative horror film with a predictably gory plot benefits from a professional turn by Curtis as the daughter of high school principal Nielsen.

PROPHECY 1979
★★ PG Horror 1:42
☑ Explicit language, graphic violence
Dir: John Frankenheimer *Cast:* Talia Shire, Robert Foxworth, Armand Assante, Richard Dysart, Victoria Racimo
▶ In Maine, government agent Foxworth and wife Shire investigate when a pollution-caused monster goes on bloody killing spree. Some effective scares and nice natural backgrounds. Unfortunately, the plot is tired, the monster looks phony, and some may find the violence distasteful.

PROTECTOR, THE 1985
★★ R Action-Adventure 1:34
☑ Nudity, explicit language, graphic violence
Dir: James Glickenhaus *Cast:* Jackie Chan, Danny Aiello, Roy Chao, Bill Wallace, Victor Arnold, Kim Bass
▶ New York cops Chan and Aiello bust the rules and plenty of heads pursuing a Hong Kong drug kingpin who kidnaps an heiress. Nonstop action includes no-holds-barred barroom brawl, speedboat chase, and a big fight between Chan and karate champ Wallace. Gratuitous nudity and violence; Chan has muscles but little screen presence. **(CC)**

PROTOCOL 1984
★★★★ PG Comedy 1:35
☑ Explicit language, violence
Dir: Herbert Ross *Cast:* Goldie Hawn, Chris Sarandon, Andre Gregory, Cliff De Young, Richard Romanus, Ed Begley, Jr.
▶ Washington cocktail waitress Hawn becomes a national heroine when she accidentally foils an assassination attempt on Arab sheik Romanus. Hired by the State Protocol Department, she becomes involved in several misadventures, including a brawl at a gay-Arab-

biker sushi bar. Breezy and lighthearted romp was tailor-made for Hawn's talents. **(CC)**

PROUD REBEL, THE 1958
★★★★ G Western/Family 1:43
Dir: Michael Curtiz *Cast:* Alan Ladd, Olivia de Havilland, Dean Jagger, David Ladd
▶ When son David Ladd becomes mute after seeing mom killed in the Civil War, father Alan Ladd takes him north for medical help. Along the way, the Ladds are helped by spinster de Havilland as they battle local villains for possession of the boy's beloved dog. Wholesome, heartwarming, quite satisfying; fine father-and-son teamwork from the Ladds.

PROVIDENCE 1977 French
★ R Drama 1:50
☑ Adult situations, explicit language
Dir: Alain Resnais *Cast:* Dirk Bogarde, Ellen Burstyn, John Gielgud, David Warner, Elaine Stritch
▶ On his deathbed, British novelist Gielgud spins imaginary stories about son Bogarde, daughter-in-law Burstyn, and their respective lovers Stritch and Warner. Baffling adult puzzle dealing with themes of creativity and death requires an effort to watch; easier to admire than enjoy.

PROWLER, THE 1982
★ R Horror 1:28
☑ Nudity, adult situations, explicit language, violence
Dir: Joseph Zito *Cast:* Vicki Dawson, Christopher Goutman, Cindy Weintraub, Farley Granger, John Seitz, Lawrence Tierney
▶ Returning World War II vet catches his girlfriend cheating on him and kills the lovers with a pitchfork. Thirty-five years later, a killer goes on a murder spree, wearing an Army helmet and wielding a pitchfork and other exotic weapons. B-grade attempt to cash in on success of *Halloween* is for hard-core fans only.

PSYCHIC KILLER 1976
★★★ PG Mystery-Suspense 1:30
☑ Nudity, graphic violence
Dir: Raymond Danton *Cast:* Jim Hutton, Paul Burke, Della Reese, Rod Cameron, Aldo Ray, Julie Adams
▶ Hutton, wrongly accused of murder, is committed to an asylum where he learns the secret of astral projection. Upon his release, he uses this power to get revenge against his enemies. Unusual premise given overly gruesome treat-

ment; above-average B-movie may please genre fans.

PSYCHO 1960
★ ★ ★ ★ R Mystery-Suspense 1:49 B&W
☑ Adult situations, violence
Dir: Alfred Hitchcock *Cast:* Anthony Perkins, Janet Leigh, Vera Miles, John Gavin, Martin Balsam, John McIntire
▶ Bank employee Leigh steals money and takes a room at the spooky Bates Motel. Proprietor Perkins seems like such a nice young man, but his mom is a tad strange; Leigh then meets a tragic fate in cinema's most famous shower scene. Hitchcock's fiendishly clever tale of madness and murder masterfully creates tension through camera and editing techniques. Much more frightening than today's gory movies. Brilliant Bernard Herrmann score. Spawned two sequels more than twenty years later.

PSYCHO II 1983
★ ★ ★ R Horror 1:53
☑ Nudity, adult situations, explicit language, graphic violence
Dir: Richard Franklin *Cast:* Anthony Perkins, Vera Miles, Meg Tilly, Robert Loggia, Dennis Franz, Hugh Gillin
▶ Released after twenty-two years in a mental institution, murderer Norman Bates (Perkins, re-creating his most famous role) moves back into the old digs, and tries to go straight with the help of waitress friend Tilly. However, the cycle of killings begins once more. Surprisingly effective sequel/homage to the Hitchcock classic. Twisty, ironic plot and ominous camera angles keep you guessing.

PSYCHO III 1986
★ ★ R Horror 1:33
☑ Nudity, explicit language, violence
Dir: Anthony Perkins *Cast:* Anthony Perkins, Diana Scarwid, Jeff Fahey, Roberta Maxwell, Hugh Gillin
▶ Norman Bates (Perkins) saves ex-nun Scarwid who tries to kill herself at his motel. Other guests are not so lucky: someone is murdering them. Norman, is that you? Assured direction by Perkins, who still can twitch effectively, and the underrated Scarwid offers sturdy support. However, plot is pretty thin and predictable. Few scares; not in the league of the original or *Psycho II*. (CC)

PSYCHO GIRLS 1987
☆ R Horror 1:32

☑ Adult situations, explicit language, graphic violence
Dir: Gerard Ciccoritti *Cast:* John Haslett Cuff, Darlene Mignacco, Agi Gallus, Rose Graham, Silvio Oliviero, Pier Giorgio Dicicco
▶ When her parents are poisoned on their anniversary, Mignacco is sentenced to an insane asylum. Fifteen years later she escapes in search of her sister Gallus, the real culprit. Private eye Cuff is trapped in the middle of their deadly confrontation in this low-budget exploitation.

PSYCH-OUT 1968
★ ★ NR Drama 1:22
☑ Brief nudity, adult situations, explicit language, violence
Dir: Richard Rush *Cast:* Susan Strasberg, Jack Nicholson, Bruce Dern, Dean Stockwell, Adam Roarke, Max Julien
▶ Deaf teenager Strasberg searches Haight-Ashbury for missing brother Dern. Hippies Nicholson, Roarke, and Julien help her. Meager storyline provides vehicle for quaintly dated period atmosphere and dialogue ("Hey, man, I'm hip") and a young Nicholson. A curiosity item.

PT 109 1963
★ ★ NR Biography 2:20
Dir: Leslie H. Martinson *Cast:* Cliff Robertson, Ty Hardin, James Gregory, Robert Culp, Grant Williams
▶ World War II experiences of John F. Kennedy in the South Pacific are the basis for this serviceable naval drama. Robertson turns in a creditable performance as the future President who assumes command of his first vessel and engages in dangerous missions on islands held by the Japanese. Climaxes in a daring escape after the PT boat is rammed by an enemy destroyer.

PUBERTY BLUES 1983 Australian
★ R Comedy 1:27
☑ Nudity, adult situations, explicit language
Dir: Bruce Beresford *Cast:* Neil Schofield, Jad Capelja, Geoff Rhoe, Tony Hughes, Sandy Paul, Leander Brett
▶ Title says it all: the adolescent woes of surfer girls Schofield and Capelja in Sydney. Neither is especially attractive so they must drink, smoke, and swear to get the attention of boys interested only in a little groping. Standard rite-of-passage

tale distinguished by candor and Aussie setting.

PUBLIC ENEMY 1931
★★★ NR Crime 1:23 B&W
Dir: William Wellman *Cast:* James Cagney, Jean Harlow, Eddie Woods, Beryl Mercer, Joan Blondell, Donald Cook
▶ Gritty cautionary tale about short and violent life of gangster Cagney is still compelling. Cagney and Irish tough buddy Woods embrace lives of crime in south side of Chicago, stealing booze for resale during Prohibition. Soon they're in the thick of gang warfare and its inevitable tragedy, as director Wellman pulls no punches depicting the characters' vicious immorality. Picture made Cagney and his rough-hewn mannerisms an overnight star. Most familiar scene: Cagney smashing grapefruit into face of Mae Clark, who's worn out her welcome.

PULSEBEAT 1986 Spanish
☆ NR Drama 1:32
Dir: Marice Tobias *Cast:* Daniel Greene, Lee Taylor Allen, Bob Small, Alice Moore, Helga Line, Peter Lupus
▶ Limp drama about rivalry between two aerobics spas, one owned by American Greene, the other by his Spanish mother Line. After various schemes to snare talented instructors, they put aside their differences for climactic aerobics competition. Filmed in Spain, and marred by obvious dubbing.

PUMPING IRON 1977
★★ PG Documentary 1:25
☑ Explicit language
Dir: George Butler *Cast:* Arnold Schwarzenegger, Lou Ferrigno, Matty Ferrigno, Victorio Ferrigno, Franco Columbu, Mike Katz
▶ Intriguing look at the Mr. Olympia contest in which Schwarzenegger seeks to defend his title against challenger Ferrigno and others. Ferrigno has the better physique but, even with help of his doting parents and homespun Brooklyn philosophy, he's no match for Schwarzenegger's psych-out ruses. Observant and often witty documentary noteworthy for introducing Schwarzenegger to the American public.

PUMPING IRON II: THE WOMEN 1985
★★ NR Documentary 1:47
☑ Brief nudity, explicit language
Dir: George Butler *Cast:* Rachel McLish, Bev Francis, Carla Dunlap, Lori

Bowen, Kris Alexander, George Plimpton
▶ World's best female body builders gather in Vegas for competition. Judges debate two views of feminine ideal, represented by kittenish McLish and densely muscle-bound Francis. Emceed by "the one and only" Plimpton. **(CC)**

PUMPKINHEAD 1989
★★ R Horror 1:26
☑ Adult situations, explicit language, graphic violence
Dir: Stan Winston *Cast:* Lance Henriksen, John Diaquino, Joel Hoffman, Kimberly Ross, Florence Shauffler, Kerry Remsen
▶ When his son is killed in a motorcycle accident, grieving father Henriksen seeks out local witch for revenge against the visitors responsible. She summons Pumpkinhead, a hideous demon whose indiscriminate murders force Henriksen to reconsider his plan. Good intentions and frightening special effects elevate routine plot and characters.

PURPLE HEARTS 1984
★★★★ R Drama 1:55
☑ Nudity, explicit language, violence
Dir: Sidney J. Furie *Cast:* Ken Wahl, Cheryl Ladd, Paul McCrane, Stephen Lee, Annie McEnroe, Cyril O'Reilly
▶ Surgeon Wahl, tending wounded troops in Vietnam, woos nurse Ladd at another Army base. Individual trips to the front and special assignments make their courtship arduous. Then Wahl is shot down behind enemy lines and must fight his way home.

PURPLE RAIN 1984
★★★ R Musical 1:51
☑ Nudity, adult situations, explicit language, violence
Dir: Albert Magnoli *Cast:* Prince, Morris Day, Apollonia Kotero, Clarence Williams III, Jerome Benton, Olga Karlatos
▶ Triple-platinum music sensation Prince, in his smashing screen debut as a performer with on- and off-stage problems. He doesn't get along with his troubled parents Karlatos and Williams, quarrels with his band Revolution, and has romance problems with his new girl, stunning Kotero. Jazzy melodrama has color, energy, and lots of rock 'n' roll hits: "Let's Go Crazy," "When Doves Cry," "I Would Die 4 U," "Darling Nikki" and title song. Score won Oscar. **(CC)**

PURPLE ROSE OF CAIRO, THE 1985
★★ PG Comedy 1:22
☑ Adult situations
Dir: Woody Allen *Cast:* Mia Farrow,
Jeff Daniels, Danny Aiello, Van Johnson,
Alexander Cohen, Milo O'Shea
▶ Frumpy Depression Era waitress Farrow,
unhappily married to unemployed lout
Aiello, finds solace at the movies. On fifth
viewing of her favorite flick, *The Purple
Rose of Cairo*, handsome actor Daniels
steps off the silver screen and into her
heart. ("He's fictional, but you can't have
everything," muses Farrow.) Meanwhile,
pandemonium breaks out on the screen
as the stranded actors debate how to
end the movie without their leading man.
Fresh and inventive, although criticized
by some as a one-joke movie.   **(CC)**

PURPLE TAXI, THE 1977
French/Italian/Irish
★★ R Drama 1:44
☑ Nudity, adult situations, explicit language
Dir: Yves Boiset *Cast:* Charlotte Rampling, Philippe Noiret, Agostina Belli,
Peter Ustinov, Fred Astaire, Edward Albert
▶ Rich American playboy Albert and seductress sister Rampling visit Ireland. They
befriend dying Frenchman Noiret, his
puckish Irish doctor Astaire, mysterious
local landowner Ustinov, and mute Belli
who is either Ustinov's mistress and/or
daughter. Thereafter all sorts of dark secrets surface in this talkative, overly literary film adapted from novel by Frenchman Michel Deon. Taxing fare.

PURSUIT OF D. B. COOPER, THE 1981
★★★ PG Action-Adventure 1:40
☑ Brief nudity, adult situations, explicit
language
Dir: Roger Spottiswoode *Cast:* Robert
Duvall, Treat Williams, Kathryn Harrold,
Paul Gleason, Ed Flanders, R. G. Armstrong
▶ Comedy caper about D. B. Cooper
(Williams), real-life antihero who hijacked
plane with phony bomb and para-
chuted into legend with $200,000 of ex-
tortion money. Speculative film follows attempts of insurance investigator Duvall to
track Williams and wife Harrold cross-
country to Mexican border. Plenty of
chases and amiable characters.

PURSUIT OF HAPPINESS, THE 1971
★ PG Drama 1:38
☑ Adult situations, explicit language

Dir: Robert Mulligan *Cast:* Michael
Sarrazin, Barbara Hershey, Robert Klein,
Sada Thompson, Ralph Waite, Arthur
Hill
▶ Dated message drama about Sarrazin, an alienated youth who refuses to
defend himself against the "establishment" during a trial for a hit-and-run accident. Sentenced to prison, he escapes
after a knifing incident and flees to Canada with girlfriend Hershey. Suffers from
improbable plotting, although Klein is
amusing as Sarrazin's hippie friend.

PURSUIT TO ALGIERS 1945
★★ NR Mystery-Suspense 1:05 B&W
Dir: Roy William Neill *Cast:* Basil Rathbone, Nigel Bruce, Marjorie Riordan,
Rosalind Ivan, Martin Kosleck, Leslie
Vincent
▶ World's greatest detective Sherlock
Holmes (Rathbone) and sidekick Dr. Watson (Bruce) encounter foul play when
they escort a Mediterranean prince on
sea voyage from England to his home
country. Modern take on Arthur Conan
Doyle's *The Return of Sherlock Holmes*
plays up melodrama while neglecting
logic and deduction.

PUTNEY SWOPE 1969
☆ R Comedy 1:25 C/B&W
☑ Adult situations, explicit language
Dir: Robert Downey *Cast:* Arnold Johnson, Antonio Fargas, Laura Greene,
Pepi Hermine, Ruth Hermine, Allen Garfield
▶ Token black ad agency exec Johnson
catapulted to helm of firm promptly re-
vamps it into the Truth and Soul agency,
firing most whites and refusing to promote booze, cigarettes, or war toys.
Madcap, subversive agency is an immediate success but soon falls victim to new
internal strife. Influential underground
classic, with its anarchic and irreverent
sixties style, now seems more artifact
than art, although TV commercial spoofs
are still hilarious.

PYGMALION 1938 British
★★★★ NR Comedy 1:35 B&W
Dir: Anthony Asquith, Leslie Howard
Cast: Leslie Howard, Wendy Hiller, Wil-
frid Lawson, Marie Lohr, David Tree,
Scott Sunderland
▶ Top-notch adaptation of the G. B.
Shaw play concerns stuffy phonetics pro-
fessor Howard who bets friend Lawson he
can transform uneducated Cockney
flower girl Hiller into an English lady. How-

ard's rigorous course of diction and etiquette is quite successful: Hiller not only passes for a duchess at London society ball but also wins the love of her tutor. Superior romantic comedy preserved much of the play's barbed dialogue; in fact, Shaw won Oscar for screenplay. Later remade as musical *My Fair Lady.*

Q 1982
★★ **R Horror 1:32**
☑ Nudity, explicit language, graphic violence
Dir: Larry Cohen *Cast:* Michael Moriarty, David Carradine, Richard Roundtree, Candy Clark, Malachi McCourt, Ron Cey
▶ Giant winged creature hides out in the top of the Chrysler Building, swooping down on unsuspecting New Yorkers. Detective Carradine investigates while small-time crook Moriarty gets involved. Campy monster flick; more silly than scary. Preposterous plot but Moriarty hams it up, yelling, "Eat him, eat him!" as the beast munches on one of his enemies.

QUACKSER FORTUNE HAS A COUSIN IN THE BRONX 1970 Irish
★★ **PG Comedy 1:30**
☑ Brief nudity, adult situations
Dir: Waris Hussein *Cast:* Gene Wilder, Margot Kidder, Eileen Colgan, Seamus Ford, May Ollis, Liz Davis
▶ Dubliner Wilder makes living recycling horse manure from streets as fertilizer, enjoying independence, the outdoors, and an affair with customer Colgan. His life takes turn for worse when he falls in love with wealthy American Kidder and Dublin authorities order horses off the streets in favor of cars. Amiable, offbeat comedy features charming Dublin locale and fine, controlled performance by Wilder.

QUADROPHENIA 1979 British
☆ **R Drama/Music 1:55**
☑ Adult situations, explicit language, violence
Dir: Franc Roddam *Cast:* Phil Daniels, Mark Wingett, Philip Davis, Leslie Ash, Garry Cooper, Sting
▶ Gritty visualization of rock opera written by the Who's Pete Townshend. In 1964 England, young Mod Daniels in dead-end mailroom job joins mates to seek kicks in pills, casual sex, and rumbles with rival Rockers. Solid, involving story of angry young man for fans of the Who's

music. Convincing screen debut by rock star Sting as an over-the-hill Mod.

QUARTET 1949 British
★★★★ **NR Comedy/Drama 2:00 B&W**
Dir: Ken Annakin, Arthur Crabtree, Harold French, Ralph Smart *Cast:* Hermione Baddeley, Dirk Bogarde, Mervyn Johns, Cecil Parker, Honor Blackman, Mai Zetterling
▶ Four W. Somerset Maugham tales, introduced by the author: a young man ignores his conservative dad's advice and outwits an adventuress, an aspiring pianist faces a harsh evaluation of his talent, a clerk's obsession with kites upsets his wife and mother, an aging womanizer is angry when his wife writes poems about a younger man (not realizing her subject is the younger him). Excellent; crisply produced, swiftly paced, well acted.

QUATERMASS CONCLUSION, THE 1980 British
★ **NR Sci-Fi 1:47**
Dir: Piers Haggard *Cast:* John Mills, Simon MacCorkindale, Barbara Kellerman, Margaret Tyzack, Brewster Mason
▶ Evil alien employs death ray to suck energy from Earth's children. Scientist Mills and his cohorts feed atom bomb to extraterrestrial to induce terminal indigestion. Intriguing script overcomes mediocre effects and direction. Based on the lead character from popular British TV show and film series.

QUEEN CHRISTINA 1933
★★ **NR Drama 1:37 B&W**
Dir: Rouben Mamoulian *Cast:* Greta Garbo, John Gilbert, Ian Keith, Lewis Stone, C. Aubrey Smith, Elizabeth Young
▶ Seventeenth-century Swedish queen Garbo flees arranged marriage to pursue Spanish ambassador Gilbert. To learn his real nature she dons men's clothes and pals with him before revealing her true sex. When her romance with commoner Gilbert angers the public, she considers abdicating her throne. Chemistry between off-screen lovers Garbo and Gilbert is electrifying and enhances the heartbreaking ending. A classic; arguably Garbo's best performance.

QUEEN OF SPADES, THE 1949 British
★★ **NR Fantasy 1:39 B&W**
Dir: Thorold Dickinson *Cast:* Anton Walbrook, Edith Evans, Yvonne Mitchell,

Ronald Howard, Mary Jerrold, Anthony Dawson

▶ Walbrook, an impoverished officer in the nineteenth-century Russian army, learns that elderly countess Evans has a secret for winning at faro. He tries various schemes to pry the information from her but accidentally frightens her to death. Eerie adaptation of classic Alexander Pushkin tale builds smoothly to a sinister climax.

QUEEN OF THE ROAD 1985 Australian
★★ NR Drama 1:45
☑ Adult situations, explicit language, mild violence
Dir: Bruce Best *Cast:* Joanne Samuel, Amanda Muggleton, Shane Withington, Jonathan Sweet, Chris Hession
▶ After the death of her father, a schoolteacher attempts to follow in his footsteps as a professional trucker. Among the obstacles in her way: her own inexperience and thugs searching for a box containing $1 million. Overblown, rambling, and slimly plotted. Australian accents and terminology don't help; talented Amanda does.

QUERELLE 1983 German
☆ R Drama 1:46
☑ Strong sexual content, explicit language, violence
Dir: Rainer Werner Fassbinder *Cast:* Brad Davis, Jeanne Moreau, Franco Nero, Laurent Malet, Hanno Poschl, Gunter Kaufmann
▶ Sailor Davis in seedy port deals in opium and murder and has both hetero- and homosexual relations. Confused saga of decadence and decay doesn't work at all despite occasionally intriguing visual experimentation. Difficult-to-watch film was also director Fassbinder's last. ⑤

QUEST FOR FIRE 1982
French/Canadian
★★ R Action-Adventure 1:40
☑ Nudity, strong sexual content, adult situations, graphic violence, adult humor
Dir: Jean-Jacques Annaud *Cast:* Everett McGill, Rae Dawn Chong, Ron Perlman, Nameer El-Kadi, Gary Schwartz
▶ Prehistoric tribe loses its source of fire and sends McGill, Perlman, and El-Kadi in search of flame. Their adventures include encounters with cannibals, marshnymph Chong and her more advanced tribe, wooly mammoths, and a saber-

toothed tiger. Chong and McGill become mates; she teaches him both tenderness and the art of firemaking. Ambitious saga is generally diverting and often sweetly comic. Remarkably effective languages by novelist Anthony Burgess and body movements by zoologist Desmond Morris. Oscar for costumes.

QUESTION OF SILENCE, A 1984 Dutch
☆ R Drama 1:32
☑ Brief nudity, adult situations, explicit language, violence
Dir: Marleen Gorris *Cast:* Cox Habbema, Nelly Fridja, Edda Barends, Henriette Tol, Eddy Brugman, Dolf de Vries
▶ Fridja, Barends, and Tol are arrested for murder of male shopkeeper, whom they beat to a pulp in show of solidarity when he caught one shoplifting. The women, strangers prior to the event, are analyzed by psychiatrist Habbema, who comes to share their hostility to world run by men. Feminist parable is based on fact. Director Gorris displays originality and attention to character in film with unusual premise. Not for all tastes. ⑤

QUICK AND THE DEAD, THE 1987
★★★ NR Western/MFTV 1:30
☑ Adult situations, violence
Dir: Robert Day *Cast:* Sam Elliott, Tom Conti, Kate Capshaw, Kenny Morrison, Matt Clark
▶ Devoutly religious frontier family struggles across the harsh Wyoming wilderness to their new homestead. Although attacked by bandits, father Conti refuses to fight and spurns the help of vengeful drifter Elliott. But as the journey progresses, Conti grows so dependent on Elliott that his marriage to Capshaw is threatened. Strong, vigorous adaptation of a Louis L'Amour novel captures the scope and themes of a Western classic. Aided considerably by Dick Bush's stark, beautiful photography.

QUICKSILVER 1986
★★★ PG Drama 1:46
☑ Explicit language, violence
Dir: Tom Donnelly *Cast:* Kevin Bacon, Jami Gertz, Paul Rodriguez, Rudy Ramos, Andrew Smith, Gerald S. O'Loughlin
▶ Busted stockbroker Bacon takes job as bicycle messenger. He locks horns with Ramos, drug dealer on wheels, and saves gullible Gertz from Ramos's clutches. Bacon returns to stock market to earn money for messenger buddy Ro-

driguez, who hopes to open own hot-dog stand. Implausible premise and too many subplots detract from fine performances and slick, MTV filming. Real stars of picture are stuntmen on bicycles and pounding soundtrack. **(CC)**

QUIET COOL 1986
★★ R Action-Adventure 1:20
☑ Explicit language, graphic violence
Dir: Clay Borris *Cast:* James Remar, Adam Howard, Daphne Ashbrook, Jared Martin, Nick Cassavetes, Fran Ryan
▶ Remar, a New York cop with a low boiling point, travels to Northern California to aid old girlfriend Ashbrook, whose brother and sister-in-law have been slain by violent marijuana growers. Ashbrook's vengeful nephew Howard and Remar team up to waste the druggies and their leader Cassavetes. Leads convincing in action pic with often brutal violence.

QUIET EARTH, THE 1985 New Zealand
★ R Drama 1:31
☑ Nudity, adult situations, explicit language
Dir: Geoff Murphy *Cast:* Bruno Lawrence, Alison Routledge, Peter Smith
▶ Scientist Lawrence working on malfunctioning top-secret project discovers his efforts have eliminated all human life save for himself, pretty redhead Routledge, and menacing Maori Smith. Lawrence enjoys free material amenities and the company of Routledge until confronted by mystical Smith. Often implausible and inconclusive, antinuke film has fans for Lawrence's performance and technical achievements. **(CC)**

QUIET MAN, THE 1952
★★★★ NR Drama/Romance 2:09
Dir: John Ford *Cast:* John Wayne, Maureen O'Hara, Barry Fitzgerald, Victor McLaglen, Ward Bond, Mildred Natwick
▶ American boxer Wayne seeks peace in native Ireland after killing man in the ring. Obstacles include tempestuous local beauty O'Hara, who weds Wayne but resents his refusal to demand traditional dowry from her bullying brother McLaglen. When O'Hara tries to run away, Wayne shelves his pacifism for rollicking fight with McLaglen. Spirited and vibrant drama won Best Director Oscar for Ford and Best Cinematography for gorgeous portrayal of Ireland. A classic.

QUILLER MEMORANDUM, THE 1966
British
★★★ NR Espionage 1:45
Dir: Michael Anderson *Cast:* George Segal, Alec Guinness, Max Von Sydow, Senta Berger, George Sanders, Robert Helpman
▶ American secret agent Segal is recruited by Brit spy chief Guinness to replace operatives killed during investigation of modern neo-Nazi conspiracy in Berlin. Nazi leader Von Sydow nabs Segal and tortures him to reveal whereabouts of Guinness. Thoughtful spy intrigue, with screenplay by Harold Pinter, forsakes guns and stunts. **(CC)**

QUINTET 1979
★ R Drama 1:58
☑ Adult situations, graphic violence
Dir: Robert Altman *Cast:* Paul Newman, Bibi Andersson, Fernando Rey, Vittorio Gassman, Nina Van Pallandt, Brigitte Fossey
▶ During the future Ice Age, people play a life-or-death game known as Quintet. Into this frozen apocalypse enters life-affirming newcomer Newman, determined to beat the odds of the game. Arty, high-falutin' allegory falls flat on its face. A major disappointment from usually intriguing director Altman.

QUO VADIS 1951
★★★★ NR Action-Adventure 2:52
Dir: Mervyn LeRoy *Cast:* Robert Taylor, Deborah Kerr, Peter Ustinov, Leo Genn, Patricia Laffan, Finlay Currie
▶ Roman commander Taylor falls in love with Christian slave Kerr. When Nero (Ustinov) burns Rome and blames the Christians, Taylor and Kerr are seized for mass executions in the arena. Taylor then leads mob of Christians and disgruntled Romans against the hated Nero. Sweeping costume epic produced with lavish care to detail was box office smash and earned eight Oscar nominations. Somewhere among the thousands of extras are Sophia Loren and Elizabeth Taylor, but attention is better paid to the scene-stealing Ustinov. **(CC)**

RABBIT TEST 1978
★ PG Comedy 1:24
☑ Explicit language, adult humor
Dir: Joan Rivers *Cast:* Billy Crystal, Joan Prather, Alex Rocco, Doris Roberts, Margaret Adachi
▶ Rivers's directing debut is a strained, often tasteless comedy about the world's

first pregnant man, Crystal. His condition draws immense media attention, allowing a large cast of comics to deliver some undeniably funny Rivers one-liners. Guests include Imogene Coca, Valerie Curtin, Alice Ghostley, George Gobel, Michael Keaton, Paul Lynde, Sheree North, Tom Poston, and Jimmie Walker.

RABID 1977 Canadian
★ **R Horror 1:31**
☑ Nudity, explicit language, graphic violence
Dir: David Cronenberg *Cast:* Marilyn Chambers, Frank Moore, Joe Silver, Howard Ryshpan, Patricia Gage, Susan Roman
▶ An accident and subsequent surgery turns young Chambers into a rabies-infected vampire who terrorizes Montreal and turns her victims into killers like herself. Gruesome and unappealing, although former porn star/Ivory Snow girl Chambers does well enough in her first dramatic role.

RACE FOR YOUR LIFE, CHARLIE BROWN 1977
★★★★★ **G Animation 1:15**
Dir: Bill Melendez *Cast:* Voices of Duncan Watson, Greg Felton, Stuart Brotman, Gail Davis, Liam Martin, Kirk Jue
▶ Charlie Brown and company go to summer camp, where they run afoul of bullies who challenge them to a dangerous river-raft race. Heroic efforts by Charlie and Snoopy (riding a motorcycle *Easy Rider* style) pull the gang through. Solid family fare; bright animation and jazzy musical score.

RACE WITH THE DEVIL 1975
☆ **PG Drama 1:28**
☑ Adult situations, explicit language, violence
Dir: Jack Starrett *Cast:* Peter Fonda, Warren Oates, Loretta Swit, Lara Parker, R. G. Armstrong, Clay Tanner
▶ Couples Fonda and Parker and Oates and Swit share camper while vacationing in Texas. First night out they see a Satanic cult sacrifice humans and flee in horror. Devil worshippers give chase, pursuing camper across Texas with intent to kill witnesses to their worship. Uneasy blend of horror and chases at least moves quickly.

RACHEL AND THE STRANGER 1948
★★★★ **NR Romance 1:19 B&W**
Dir: Norman Foster *Cast:* Loretta

Young, William Holden, Robert Mitchum, Tom Tully, Sara Haden
▶ In 1820, widowed backwoodsman Holden buys bondswoman Young out of servitude and marries her so that his son will have a mother. Holden's guitar-playing friend Mitchum falls for Young and a love triangle results. Agreeable, appealing performances with Mitchum warbling five songs.

RACHEL, RACHEL 1968
★★★ **R Drama 1:41**
☑ Adult situations, explicit language
Dir: Paul Newman *Cast:* Joanne Woodward, James Olson, Kate Harrington, Estelle Parsons, Donald Moffat, Geraldine Fitzgerald
▶ Spinsterish schoolteacher Woodward, upset at the lack of emotional involvement in her life, rejects the lesbian advances of friend Parsons and has her first affair with old classmate, Olson. Deeply moving; highlighted by sensitive Oscar-nominated performances by Woodward and Parsons. Also nominated for Best Picture and Director. Newman's first outing behind the camera.

RACING WITH THE MOON 1984
★★★ **PG Drama 1:49**
☑ Nudity, adult situations, explicit language
Dir: Richard Benjamin *Cast:* Sean Penn, Elizabeth McGovern, Nicolas Cage, John Karlen, Rutanya Alda, Carol Kane
▶ Northern California, World War II: on the eve of their enlistment in the marines, best pals Penn and Cage hang out together while Penn woos McGovern, who he thinks is a wealthy "Gatsby Girl" but who is actually a maid's daughter. Lightweight but likable story has immaculate period details, sweet chemistry between Penn and McGovern, and a warm, nostalgic tone. **(CC)**

RACKET, THE 1951
★★ **NR Crime 1:28 B&W**
Dir: John Cromwell *Cast:* Robert Mitchum, Lizabeth Scott, Robert Ryan, William Talman, Ray Collins, William Conrad
▶ Honest police chief Mitchum battles for control of Midwestern city with violent mobster Ryan and corrupt government officials Collins and Conrad. Mitchum finds Ryan's weak point and brings him to heel, setting trap for crooked politicos. Briskly paced film noir with splendid Ryan

as throwback hoodlum pressured by Mafia chiefs to assume modern, business-like demeanor.

RAD 1986
★ ★ ★ PG Drama 1:30
☑ Explicit language
Dir: Hal Needham *Cast:* Bill Allen, Lori Loughlin, Talia Shire, Ray Walston, Bart Conner, Jack Weston
▶ Allen, a local boy, rises from paper route obscurity to take on arrogant champ Conner (the former Olympic gold-medal gymnast) in BMX bike competition sponsored by greedy promoter Weston. Allen also wins the heart of racer Loughlin. Kids may enjoy the action and freestyle bike acrobatics. **(CC)**

RADIOACTIVE DREAMS 1986
★ R Sci-Fi 1:35
☑ Nudity, explicit language, violence
Dir: Albert Pyun *Cast:* John Stockwell, Michael Dudikoff, Lisa Blount, George Kennedy, Don Murray, Michelle Little
▶ Raised in a fallout shelter after a nuclear war, Stockwell and Dudikoff receive their entire education from pulp mystery novels. They travel through a wasteland filled with mutants, bikers, punks, and beautiful but untrustworthy molls Blount and Little—all searching for the keys to the world's last atomic bomb. Clever but overdone premise wears thin quickly due to confusing plot.

RADIO DAYS 1987
★ ★ ★ PG Comedy 1:28
☑ Brief nudity, adult situations, explicit language
Dir: Woody Allen *Cast:* Mia Farrow, Seth Green, Julie Kavner, Michael Tucker, Dianne Wiest, Danny Aiello
▶ Depression era lives of young Green and his close-knit if far-from-rich Rockaways family—mom Kavner, dad Tucker, unmarried aunt Wiest—are intercut with more glamorous stories of the radio stars they adore, like rags-to-riches rise of cigarette girl Farrow. Nostalgic, affectionate look back is a series of vignettes, alternately gentle, sweet, and amusing. Best scenes: Green's punishment by a rabbi, Wiest's disastrous date during "War of the Worlds," Farrow's encounter with gangster Aiello.

RAFFERTY AND THE GOLD DUST TWINS 1975
★ ★ ★ R Comedy 1:32
☑ Explicit language
Dir: Dick Richards *Cast:* Alan Arkin,

Sally Kellerman, Mackenzie Phillips, Alex Rocco, Harry Dean Stanton, Charles Martin Smith
▶ In Los Angeles, motor vehicles bureau inspector Arkin is kidnapped by aspiring singer Kellerman and teenage runaway Phillips, who demand he take them to New Orleans. Along the way, the threesome draw closer as Kellerman and Arkin become lovers. Good performances with a fresh improvised air although rambling story, not quite comedy or drama, is eccentric and unsatisfying.

RAGE 1972
★ ★ ★ PG Action-Adventure 1:39
☑ Explicit language, violence
Dir: George C. Scott *Cast:* George C. Scott, Richard Basehart, Martin Sheen, Barnard Hughes
▶ Rancher Scott realizes Army's chemical warfare tests are responsible for his son's death. When major Sheen plots a cover-up, Scott is provoked into an explosive vendetta. Scott's directorial debut successfully works up a mood of righteous anger; after a slow start, story will have you rooting for revenge.

RAGE OF HONOR 1987
★ ★ R Martial Arts 1:31
☑ Adult situations, explicit language, violence
Dir: Gordon Hessler *Cast:* Sho Kosugi, Lewis Van Bergen, Robin Evans, Gerry Gibson
▶ Phoenix-based narc Kosugi is determined to get revenge after his partner is tortured and murdered. When his boss (who is in cahoots with the killer) won't cooperate, Kosugi quits his job and tracks the murderer to Buenos Aires. Kosugi delivers the expected action for genre fans but struggles with the English dialogue in the predictable story.

RAGGEDY ANN AND ANDY 1977
★ ★ ★ G Animation 1:26
Dir: Richard Williams *Cast:* Claire Williams; voices of Didi Conn, Mark Baker, Fred Stuthman, George S. Irving, Arnold Stang
▶ A little girl's dolls come to life while she sleeps. When a pirate kidnaps their owner's new doll, Raggedy Ann and Andy team up for a rescue. Among the creatures aiding them is a homeless camel. Quite satisfying children's fare from the director of the Pink Panther animated titles features lively animation

and songs from "Sesame Street" composer Joe Raposo. **(CC)**

RAGGEDY MAN 1981
★ ★ ★ ★ **PG Drama 1:34**
☑ Brief nudity, adult situations, violence
Dir: Jack Fisk *Cast:* Sissy Spacek, Eric Roberts, Sam Shepard, William Sanderson, Tracey Walter, Henry Thomas
▶ During World War II, Texas divorcée Spacek struggles to support her two kids while having an affair with sailor Roberts. Mysterious "raggedy man" Shepard intervenes when angry locals try to rape her. Intimate, sensitive, and low-key with convincing tenderness between Spacek and Roberts. Naturalistic dialogue and fine period atmosphere transcend understated plotting. Favorite scene: Spacek's "Rum & Coca-Cola" dance. Director Fisk is Spacek's husband.

RAGING BULL 1980
★ ★ ★ **R Biography/Sports 2:09 C/B&W**
☑ Adult situations, explicit language, violence
Dir: Martin Scorsese *Cast:* Robert De Niro, Cathy Moriarty, Joe Pesci, Frank Vincent, Nicholas Colasanto, Theresa Saldana
▶ De Niro won an Oscar for his astonishing portrayal of Jake LaMotta, a furious, inarticulate boxer who briefly held the middleweight championship. Told in flashbacks as he prepares for a nightclub performance, unusually intelligent script covers his career, his brush with the mob, and his painful decline. Fights are shown with frightening intensity and brutality, but take second place to uniformly strong acting. Received eight Oscar nominations overall, also winning for Thelma Schoonmaker's dynamic editing.

RAGTIME 1981
★ ★ ★ ★ **PG Drama 2:38**
☑ Nudity, adult situations, explicit language, violence
Dir: Milos Forman *Cast:* James Cagney, Howard E. Rollins, Jr., Elizabeth McGovern, Mandy Patinkin, Mary Steenburgen, James Olson
▶ Turn-of-the-century New York: white family Olson, Steenburgen, and Brad Dourif find themselves involved when black Rollins seeks justice from racist fireman Kenneth McMillan who humiliated him. Police chief Cagney takes charge as the dispute escalates. Other figures in the period panarama: actress McGovern at apex of violent love triangle and immigrant moviemaker Patinkin. Engrossing, superbly produced adaptation of the E. L. Doctorow best-seller. Cagney, who came out of retirement, and Oscar-nominated Rollins stand out in the great cast. Eight Oscar nominations include Randy Newman's score.

RAIDERS OF THE LOST ARK 1981
★ ★ ★ ★ ★ **PG Action-Adventure 1:55**
☑ Explicit language, violence
Dir: Steven Spielberg *Cast:* Harrison Ford, Karen Allen, Wolf Kahler, Paul Freeman, John Rhys-Davies, Denholm Elliott
▶ In 1936, archaeologist/adventurer Indiana Jones (Ford) and his spunky girlfriend Allen battle Nazi-backed rival Freeman in a search for the Lost Ark of the Covenant, a biblical relic that contains powerful supernatural force. Riproaring, old-fashioned adventure anchored by a wonderfully gritty Ford is perhaps more pure fun than any other recent movie. Rousing John Williams score. Among many exciting scenes: Ford's brief duel with a swordsman, the runaway boulder. Eight Oscar nominations (including Best Picture); won Sound, Visual Effects, Editing, Art Direction. **(CC)**

RAID ON ENTEBBE 1977
★ ★ ★ **NR Drama/MFTV 2:32**
Dir: Irvin Kershner *Cast:* Charles Bronson, Peter Finch, Jack Warden, Horst Buchholz, Martin Balsam, Sylvia Sidney
▶ Israeli general Finch leads Bronson, Buchholz, and a team of commandos on a daring rescue of 103 Israeli hostages from a hijacked plane in Uganda. Thoughtful and thrilling made-for-TV drama based on a true 1976 incident. Finch's last screen appearance earned Emmy nomination. Same incident was depicted in *Victory at Entebbe* and *Operation Thunderbolt*.

RAID ON ROMMEL 1971
★ **PG War 1:39**
☑ Adult situations, explicit language, violence
Dir: Henry Hathaway *Cast:* Richard Burton, John Colicos, Clinton Greyn, Wolfgang Preiss, Danielle De Metz, Karl Otto Alberty
▶ British World War II commando Burton and cohorts penetrate Nazi lines by deliberately allowing capture. Once in POW camp, they escape for sabotage mis-

sion. Second-rate actioner recycles desert footage from earlier film *Tobruk.*

RAILWAY CHILDREN, THE 1971 British
★★★ G Family 1:35
Dir: Lionel Jeffries *Cast:* Dinah Sheridan, Bernard Cribbins, William Mervyn, Iain Cuthbertson, Jenny Agutter, Sally Thomsett
▶ With her husband wrongly imprisoned for treason, Sheridan must move her children to a lower-class home near a railroad on the Yorkshire moors. Wealthy aristocrat Mervyn takes a liking to the youngsters, and helps them clear their father's name. Above-average family-oriented story makes good use of its turn-of-the-century settings.

RAIN 1932
★★ NR Drama 1:32
Dir: Lewis Milestone *Cast:* Joan Crawford, Walter Huston, William Gargan, Guy Kibbee, Walter Catlett, Beulah Bondi
▶ Dated adaptation of W. Somerset Maugham's story finds Crawford, a notorious South Seas prostitute, stranded on Pago Pago with dedicated missionary Huston and amorous but naive sergeant Gargan. Huston attempts to reform her but falls prey to her temptations instead. Strong atmosphere and Huston's superb performance are still interesting. Remade as *Miss Sadie Thompson* in 1953.

RAINBOW BRITE AND THE STAR STEALER 1985
★★★★ G Animation 1:25
Dir: Bernard Deyries, Kimio Yabuki
Cast: Voices of Bettina, Patrick Fraley, Peter Cullen, Robbie Lee, Andre Stojka
▶ An evil princess steals the planet Spectra, the source of all light in the universe. Armed with a magical belt and aided by her horse Starlite, Rainbow Brite sets out to restore light and color to Rainbow Land. Engaging fantasy featuring popular Hallmark characters is a perfect pacifier for preschoolers. **(CC)**

RAINMAKER, THE 1956
★★★★ NR Comedy/Drama 2:01
Dir: Joseph Anthony *Cast:* Burt Lancaster, Katharine Hepburn, Wendell Corey, Lloyd Bridges, Earl Holliman, Cameron Prud'homme
▶ Drought-striken Southwestern town mirrors the arid emotional life of lonely spinster Hepburn (receiving her seventh Oscar nomination) courted half-heartedly by sheriff Corey. Arrival of brash con

man Lancaster, who promises rain for one hundred dollars, exposes Hepburn to true romance for the first time. Lancaster's sly performance dominates this pleasant comedy. **(CC)**

RAIN MAN 1988
★★★★ R Drama 2:13
☑ Adult situations, explicit language
Dir: Barry Levinson *Cast:* Dustin Hoffman, Tom Cruise, Valeria Golino, Jerry Molen, Jack Murdock, Michael D. Roberts
▶ High-pressure Los Angeles salesman Cruise is depending on his estranged father's estate to save his auto franchise but discovers he has an autistic brother Raymond (Hoffman), who has inherited everything except a '49 Buick. Cruise kidnaps Hoffman for a cross-country trip and learns to appreciate his brother's unusual talents. Inspired directing, deeply affecting script, and stellar acting in demanding roles bring unexpected humor and warmth to this unusual road movie. Won four Oscars, including Best Picture, Actor (Hoffman), Director, and Original Screenplay.

RAIN PEOPLE, THE 1969
★★ R Drama 1:41
☑ Adult situations, explicit language
Dir: Francis Ford Coppola *Cast:* James Caan, Shirley Knight, Robert Duvall, Marya Zimmet, Tom Aldredge
▶ When she learns she's pregnant, housewife Knight flees Long Island on a cross-country odyssey to find herself. She befriends mildly retarded football player Caan and later has a disturbing encounter with Nebraska cop Duvall. Impressive acting and sympathetic treatment of feminist themes are pluses in this early Coppola film.

RAINTREE COUNTY 1957
★★★★ NR Drama 2:49
Dir: Edward Dmytryk *Cast:* Elizabeth Taylor, Montgomery Clift, Eva Marie Saint, Lee Marvin, Rod Taylor, Agnes Moorehead
▶ Idealist Clift drifts away from high school sweetheart and marries New Orleans belle Taylor. He discovers Taylor's mom died of insanity and it becomes apparent she has inherited family curse. Lavishly mounted Civil War epic; quite entertaining with Oscar-nominated Taylor expressing surprising range. Movie has grim history of being shot at time when Clift had his disfiguring car accident, re-

vealing the effects in the scenes filmed after his recovery.

RAINY DAY FRIENDS 1985
★★ R Drama 1:45
☑ Explicit language, mild violence
Dir: Gary Kent *Cast:* Esai Morales, Chuck Bail, Janice Rule, Carrie Snodgress, Tomi Barrett, John Phillip Law
▶ L.A. street punk Morales learns he has cancer; with the help of fellow patient Bail, he battles his own drug habit and authorities who object to his illegal immigrant background. Gutsy little movie packs a surprising punch on a small budget; Morales is sensational and you'll be rooting for him. A sleeper.

RAISE THE TITANIC 1980
★★★ PG Action-Adventure 1:54
☑ Explicit language
Dir: Jerry Jameson *Cast:* Jason Robards, Jr., Richard Jordan, Alec Guinness, Anne Archer, David Selby
▶ When valuable metal is located in the wreck of the *Titanic*, an American team led by Robards and Jordan seek to salvage it before the Russians. Underwater mishaps threaten their effort. Good special effects, especially in the spectacular raising-of-the-*Titanic* sequence, help the unevenly paced story.

RAISING ARIZONA 1987
★★ PG-13 Comedy 1:32
☑ Explicit language, mild violence
Dir: Joel Coen *Cast:* Nicolas Cage, Holly Hunter, Trey Wilson, John Goodman, William Forsythe, Randall (Tex) Cobb
▶ Highly stylized comedy starts brilliantly with a ten-minute prologue describing the marriage between career petty con Cage and police mug shot photographer Hunter. Childless, they kidnap one of five quints, then confront a series of disasters involving two escaped convicts, deadly biker Cobb, and assorted cops. Intellectual approach to Three Stooges material is alternately grating and hilarious, with good performances undermined by too much silliness. **(CC)**

RAISIN IN THE SUN, A 1961
★★★★ NR Drama 2:08 B&W
Dir: Daniel Petrie *Cast:* Sidney Poitier, Ruby Dee, Claudia McNeil, Diana Sands, Ivan Dixon, Louis Gossett, Jr.
▶ Black family, living in Chicago ghetto, must decide what to do with $10,000 insurance payment. Poitier's dream of starting his own business leads to conflict with mom McNeil, wife Dee, and sister Sands. Towering drama from Lorraine Hansberry's Pulitzer prize–winning play; perfect performances in complex, unstereotyped characterizations evoke laughter and tears.

RAMBO: FIRST BLOOD, PART II 1985
★★★★ R Action-Adventure 1:36
☑ Explicit language, violence
Dir: George Pan Cosmatos *Cast:* Sylvester Stallone, Richard Crenna, Charles Napier, Steven Berkoff, Julia Nickson, Martin Kove
▶ Rambo (Stallone) is freed from prison by the U.S. Army to locate POWs still being held in Vietnam. He is captured by the Vietnamese and deserted by his own government but that doesn't stop his one-man rescue effort. Literally explosive sequel. Breathless pacing, killings and stunts aplenty, impressive special effects; Stallone perfectly embodies a lean, mean fighting machine and Nickson, as the Vietnamese woman who helps him, adds a touch of humanity. **(CC)**

RAMBO III 1988
★★★★ R Action-Adventure 1:41
☑ Explicit language, violence
Dir: Peter MacDonald *Cast:* Sylvester Stallone, Richard Crenna, Marc de Jonge, Sasson Gabai, Doudi Shoua, Spiros Focus
▶ When his mentor Crenna is captured by the Russians in Afghanistan, Rambo (Stallone) teams up with the Afghan rebels to rescue him and wipe out the Soviets. Third in the series sticks to tried-and-true formula: convincing explosions, narrow escapes, little dialogue, lots of action. Large budget shows on screen: the film looks great. Stallone fans will cheer.

RAMPAGE 1987
★★ R Drama 1:37
☑ Adult situations, explicit language, graphic violence
Dir: William Friedkin *Cast:* Michael Biehn, Alex McArthur, Nicholas Campbell, Deborah Van Valkenburgh, John Harkins, Billy Green Bush
▶ Prosecutor Biehn, although personally against capital punishment, is assigned to seek death penalty for serial killer McArthur. McArthur's lawyer Campbell tries to get client off via insanity plea. Becomes a conservative courtroom drama after a lurid opening detailing McArthur's crimes. Interesting presenta-

tion of all sides of the issue, convincing performances, compulsively watchable.

RAN 1985 Japanese
★★★ R Drama 2:40
☑ Violence
Dir: Akira Kurosawa *Cast:* Tatsuya Nakadai, Akira Terao, Jinpachi Nezu, Daisuke Ryu, Mieko Harada, Yoshiko Miyazaki
▶ In sixteenth-century Japan an aging lord gives kingdom to eldest son, not realizing his ambitious daughter-in-law is plotting against him. Youngest son opposes the arrangement and is banished by the foolish old man, who later realizes the truth. Lavish adaptation of Shakespeare's *King Lear* is exciting but long and arduous, with stunning use of color and expert choreography of grueling battle scenes. Will lose some impact on the small screen. ⑤

RANCHO DELUXE 1975
★ R Western/Comedy 1:33
☑ Nudity, adult situations, explicit language
Dir: Frank Perry *Cast:* Jeff Bridges, Elizabeth Ashley, Sam Waterston, Clifton James, Slim Pickens, Harry Dean Stanton
▶ Two-bit rustlers Bridges and Waterston make living stealing odd cattle from big rancher James. When personal problems prove too annoying, the two gamble on huge heist of cows. Offbeat and episodic, this contemporary Western has a cult following for its whimsical humor and laid-back philosophy. Screenplay by novelist Thomas McGuane and music by Jimmy Buffett.

RANCHO NOTORIOUS 1952
★★★ NR Western 1:29
Dir: Fritz Lang *Cast:* Marlene Dietrich, Arthur Kennedy, Mel Ferrer, Lloyd Gough, Gloria Henry, William Frawley
▶ When his girlfriend is murdered by bandits, innocent cowboy Kennedy embarks on a vendetta that transforms him into a hardened killer. His only clue—"Chuck-a-Luck"—turns out to be an outlaw hideout ruled by glamorous Dietrich. Tensions simmer as Kennedy continues his search by courting Dietrich. Unusually somber Western is an intriguing exploration of hatred and revenge. Gough's name was removed from the credits when he was blacklisted as a Communist.

RANDOM HARVEST 1942
★★★ NR Drama 2:04 B&W

Dir: Mervyn LeRoy *Cast:* Ronald Colman, Greer Garson, Susan Peters, Philip Dorn, Reginald Owen, Edmund Gwenn
▶ Shell-shocked World War II soldier Colman suffers amnesia and cannot recall his wealthy past. He is nursed to health by dancer Garson and falls in love with her. When new trauma causes him to forget her and return to family and business, she gets job as secretary to woo him anew. Despite creaky amnesia gimmick, entertaining melodrama moves without being too maudlin, thanks to splendid work by Colman and Garson.

RAPPIN' 1985
★★ PG Drama/Musical 1:32
☑ Adult situations, explicit language, mild violence
Dir: Joel Silberg *Cast:* Mario Van Peebles, Tasia Valenza, Charles Flohe, Melvin Plowden, Leo O'Brien, Eriq La Salle
▶ Van Peebles, a reformed street tough with the gift of gab, returns from prison to Pittsburgh ghetto. There he woos ex-girlfriend Valenza, beats up gang leader Flohe, defeats attempt by greedy landlord to evict tenants prior to gentrification, and cuts a rap record to earn the dough to save kid brother O'Brien from jail, all in time to rap with homeboys Plowden and La Salle in the musical finale. Sweet and good-natured hokum mainly for urban teens.

RARE BREED, THE 1966
★★★ NR Western 1:37
Dir: Andrew V. McLaglen *Cast:* James Stewart, Maureen O'Hara, Brian Keith, Juliet Mills, Don Galloway, David Brian
▶ British widow O'Hara travels to the States for an experiment with Texas rancher Keith: can English Hereford cows be crossbred with longhorns? Cynical cowboy Stewart must transport O'Hara, daughter Mills, and bull from St. Louis to Keith's ranch and grows to admire O'Hara and her vision. Romantic rivalry between Stewart and Keith begins at ranch. Wholesome oater sometimes bogged down by sentimentality.

RARE BREED, A 1981
★★ PG Drama 1:34
☑ Explicit language, mild violence
Dir: David Nelson *Cast:* George Kennedy, Forrest Tucker, Tracy Vaccaro, Tom Hallick, Don DeFore, William Hicks
▶ Rich rancher Kennedy buys filly Carnauba for Vaccaro, daughter of best friend Tucker. She raises the horse and stows

away when Carnauba is shipped to Italy for further training. Carnauba wins races until filly, Vaccaro, and trainer Hallick are kidnapped for ransom. Wholesome but unsurprising family fare. Based on a true story.

RASHOMON 1950 Japanese
★★ **NR Drama 1:27 B&W**
Dir: Akira Kurosawa *Cast:* Toshiro Mifune, Machiko Kyo, Masayuki Mori, Takashi Shimura
▶ Twelfth-century Japan: bandit kills a husband and rapes his wife—or does he? Participants and witnesses give four differing accounts of the tragic incident. Truly timeless work about the nature of truth and justice, magnificently filmed and acted, although American audiences may find stylized performances somewhat remote. Received an honorary Oscar.

RATBOY 1986
★ **PG-13 Drama 1:44**
☑ Adult situations, explicit language
Dir: Sondra Locke *Cast:* Sondra Locke, Robert Townsend, Christopher Hewett, Larry Hankin, Gerrit Graham, S. L. Baird
▶ Directing debut for Clint Eastwood paramour Locke is a decidedly offbeat parable about half-boy, half-rat outcast Baird, exploited by opportunistic journalist Locke. When the ratboy escapes from his guardian Townsend, Locke must choose between imprisoning him again or granting him freedom. Despite good satirical moments, superficial story fails to generate sympathy.

RAVEN, THE 1935
★★ **NR Horror 1:01 B&W**
Dir: Louis Friedlander (Lew Landers) *Cast:* Boris Karloff, Bela Lugosi, Irene Ware, Lester Matthews, Samuel S. Hinds, Inez Courtney
▶ Teaming of horror greats features Lugosi as a mad doctor who performs plastic surgery on gangster Karloff and makes him look worse. Lugosi then plots vengeance against the family of the woman who jilted him, but Karloff tries to thwart him.

RAVEN, THE 1963
★★ **G Horror 1:26**
Dir: Roger Corman *Cast:* Vincent Price, Peter Lorre, Boris Karloff, Hazel Court, Jack Nicholson, Olive Sturgess
▶ Evil magician Karloff steals good magician Price's wife Court. Price teams up with fellow conjurer Lorre and Lorre's son

Nicholson to battle Karloff. Loosely inspired by Edgar Allan Poe's classic poem; Price and Corman mock their more serious Poe films with high spirits and good humor.

RAW DEAL 1986
★★★ **R Action-Adventure 1:37**
☑ Explicit language, graphic violence
Dir: John Irvin *Cast:* Arnold Schwarzenegger, Kathryn Harrold, Sam Wanamaker, Paul Shenar, Robert Davi, Ed Lauter
▶ Disgraced former FBI agent Scwharzenegger busts up the Chicago mobs to redeem himself. Middling action fare doesn't compare well to better Schwarzeneggger outings. For those who favor automatic weapons and automatic plot lines. **(CC)**

RAWHEAD REX 1987
★ **R Horror 1:29**
☑ Adult situations, explicit language, graphic violence
Dir: George Pablou *Cast:* David Dukes, Kelly Piper, Ronan Wilmot, Niall Tobin, Heinrich von Schellendorf, Niall O'Brien
▶ Ugly, red-eyed monster von Schellendorf, a.k.a. Rawhead Rex, Lord of the Dark Times, is unearthed from his tomb in Ireland and goes on a murder spree, assisted by vicar's aide Wilmot. American historian Dukes and wife Piper arrive in town and are soon in the thick of the mayhem. Gory, poorly acted, low-budget horror with formula plot. Nice Irish setting and colorful brogues, though.

RAZORBACK 1984 Australian
★★ **R Horror 1:35**
☑ Rape, explicit language, graphic violence
Dir: Russell Mulcahy *Cast:* Gregory Harrison, Arkie Whitely, Bill Kerr, Chris Haywood, David Argue, Judy Morris
▶ Giant razorback hog in Australian outback devours American newscaster Morris. Hubby Harrison investigates and is illtreated by suspicious locals. Harrison teams with pretty zoologist Whitely to lead posse that slays marauding pig. Director Mulcahy, weaned on music videos, shoots the Aussie wilderness as a surreal nightmare, but style alone can't overcome plot that's neither scary nor campy.

RAZOR'S EDGE, THE 1946
★★★★ **NR Drama 2:26 B&W**
Dir: Edmund Goulding *Cast:* Tyrone

Power, Gene Tierney, John Payne, Anne Baxter, Clifton Webb, Herbert Marshall
▶ Adaptation of W. Somerset Maugham novel, with Marshall in the role of the observant author. Idealistic young Power, his life philosophy askew after horror of World War I, struggles with materialistic America and searches abroad for truth. Elegantly shot and well acted, episodic and novelistic picture is engrossing. Baxter got Academy Award for Best Supporting Actress.

RAZOR'S EDGE, THE 1984
★★★ PG-13 Drama 2:09
☑ Adult situations, explicit language, violence
Dir: John Byrum *Cast:* Bill Murray, Theresa Russell, Catherine Hicks, Denholm Elliott, James Keach, Peter Vaughn
▶ After eye-opening stint as ambulance driver in World War I, young Murray postpones his marriage to Midwestern sweetheart Hicks. He seeks enlightenment in India while she weds his buddy Keach. The three are reunited in Paris, where Russell and Keach live with her dour rich uncle Elliott, but friendships sour when Hicks ruins Murray's plans to marry local prostitute Russell. Confusing plot and Murray's discomfort with dramatic material detract; 1946 version holds up better. (CC)

REAL GENIUS 1985
★★★★ PG Comedy 1:46
☑ Adult situations, explicit language
Dir: Martha Coolidge *Cast:* Val Kilmer, William Atherton, Gabe Jarret, Patti D'Arbanville, Michelle Meyrink, Jonathan Gries
▶ Fifteen-year-old science whiz Jarret enrolls in college and rooms with unorthodox genius senior Kilmer. Each learns from the other amid campus high jinks until they go to work on laser project for unethical prof Atherton. The boys then discover their research will aid development of deadly weapon for the Pentagon. Amiable hybrid comedy combines standard sex jokes and sight gags with more clever lines and sharp satire. (CC)

REAL LIFE 1979
★ PG Comedy 1:38
☑ Explicit language
Dir: Albert Brooks *Cast:* Albert Brooks, Charles Grodin, Frances Lee McCain,

Matthew Tobin, J. A. Preston, Lisa Urette
▶ Documentary filmmaker Brooks, backed by think tank and Hollywood studio, moves in with "typical" American family Grodin, McCain, and two kids to chronicle their day-to-day life. Family quickly disintegrates under continual scrutiny of cameras while Brooks grows ever more rabid in pursuit of his vision. Spoof of Hollywood filmmaking and the PBS "American Family" docu-series doesn't hold together, but many individual pieces are terrific.

REAL MEN 1987
★★★ PG-13 Comedy 1:36
☑ Explicit language, violence
Dir: Dennis Feldman *Cast:* James Belushi, John Ritter, Barbara Barrie, Bill Morey, Iva Anderson, Gail Berle
▶ When Russians kill a CIA agent in touch with aliens about an ecology conspiracy that threatens the world, rogue agent Belushi must convince Milquetoast lookalike Ritter to replace the dead spy. Amid shoot-'em-ups with the Russkies on a wild cross-country trek, Ritter learns to be aggressive and Belushi picks up some manners. Far-fetched and frantic spy spoof occasionally hits its target. (CC)

RE-ANIMATOR 1985
★★ NR Horror 1:26
☑ Nudity, explicit language, graphic violence
Dir: Stuart Gordon *Cast:* Jeffrey Combs, Bruce Abbott, Barbara Crampton, David Gale, Robert Sampson, Gerry Block
▶ Based on stories by H. P. Lovecraft, film concerns medical student Combs, who develops serum to bring the dead back to life. Unfortunately, the re-animated return in very bad moods. Combining 1930s-style horror story with 1980s special effects gore, grisly but comically macabre picture has substantial cult following. Original R rating was revoked when producers inserted additional graphic violence on videocassette version.

REAP THE WILD WIND 1942
★★★ NR Action-Adventure 2:04
Dir: Cecil B. DeMille *Cast:* Ray Milland, John Wayne, Paulette Goddard, Raymond Massey, Robert Preston, Susan Hayward
▶ Ship captain Wayne falls prey to pirates off the coast of Florida; lawyer Milland investigates the case and falls for

Wayne's girl Goddard, the feisty owner of a salvage operation. Two-fisted DeMille epic set in the 1840s is immensely entertaining, climaxed by duel with a giant red squid, a stunt that won an Oscar for Special Effects.

REAR WINDOW 1954
★ ★ ★ ★ ★ **PG Mystery-Suspense 1:52**
☑ Adult situations
Dir: Alfred Hitchcock *Cast:* James Stewart, Grace Kelly, Raymond Burr, Thelma Ritter, Wendell Corey, Judith Evelyn
► Magazine photographer Stewart, laid up in his Greenwich Village apartment with a broken leg, has nothing to do but spy on his neighbors. He begins to suspect that Burr, the man across the courtyard, has killed his suddenly missing wife. Hitchcock gem has a deceptively simple surface, amazingly sharp psychological insight, and a serious look at voyeurism encased in a gripping thriller plot. Dazzling technique, letter-perfect performances by Stewart and Kelly as his girlfriend. Not to be missed.

REBECCA 1940
★ ★ ★ ★ **NR Drama 2:10 B&W**
Dir: Alfred Hitchcock *Cast:* Laurence Olivier, Joan Fontaine, George Sanders, Judith Anderson, Nigel Bruce, C. Aubrey Smith
► After a whirlwind romance, shy Fontaine marries dashing aristocrat Olivier. Moving to his Manderley estate, Fontaine finds herself puzzled and then haunted by his deceased wife Rebecca. Dazzling adaptation of Daphne du Maurier's novel is a beautifully tense and compelling romance, with an outstanding performance by Anderson as a grim housekeeper. Received an Oscar for George Barnes's cinematography, as well as seven other nominations. Hitchcock's first American work is also his only film to win the Best Picture Oscar. (CC)

REBECCA OF SUNNYBROOK FARM 1938
★ ★ **NR Musical/Family 1:20 B&W**
Dir: Allan Dwan *Cast:* Shirley Temple, Randolph Scott, Jack Haley, Gloria Stuart, William Demarest, Bill "Bojangles" Robinson
► Aspiring radio star Temple stays at aunt's farm; Scott is the talent scout next door who discovers the little girl's potential. Very loosely based on the classic novel; plot is an excuse for Temple to perform "On the Good Ship Lollipop," "Animal Crackers," and others.

REBEL 1986 Australian
★ **R Drama 1:34**
☑ Nudity, adult situations, explicit language, violence
Dir: Michael Jenkins *Cast:* Matt Dillon, Bryan Brown, Debbie Byrne, Bill Hunter, Ray Barrett, Julie Nihill
► In Sydney during World War II, American Marine Dillon goes AWOL and falls in love with married nightclub singer Byrne, whose hubby is off fighting the Axis. Amid shenanigans with waterfront con man Brown, Dillon romances the reluctant Byrne while dodging the local police and American MPs. Low-grade romantic drama with thin plot and confused mix of 1980s tunes sung in wartime setting. For Dillon fans only. (CC)

REBEL LOVE 1985
★ ★ **R Drama 1:30**
☑ Nudity, adult situations, explicit language
Dir: Milton Bagby, Jr. *Cast:* Jamie Rose, Terence Knox, Fran Ryan, Carl Spurlock, Rick Waln
► The solitary Indiana farm life of Yankee widow Rose is changed by an affair with Confederate spy Knox. It's so nice to have a man around the homestead again, even if he is the enemy. Cut-rate Civil War drama.

REBEL ROUSERS 1970
★ ★ **R Action-Adventure 1:18**
☑ Adult situations, explicit language, violence
Dir: Martin B. Cohen *Cast:* Cameron Mitchell, Jack Nicholson, Bruce Dern, Diane Ladd, Harry Dean Stanton, Lou Procopio
► In a remote Arizona town, Dern and his motorcycle buddies abduct pregnant girlfriend of architect Mitchell; he turns to local Mexicans armed with pitchforks for help. Violent but predictable low-budget exploitation highlighted by Nicholson's amusing turn as "Bunny."

REBEL WITHOUT A CAUSE 1955
★ ★ ★ ★ **NR Drama 1:51**
☑ Adult situations, violence
Dir: Nicholas Ray *Cast:* James Dean, Natalie Wood, Sal Mineo, Jim Backus, Ann Doran, William Hopper
► Chronic delinquent teenager Dean tries for fresh start at L.A. school, only to find himself baited into contest of cour-

age by Wood, girlfriend of local tough. Thus begins night of tragedy, as Dean, Wood, and oddball peer Mineo find brief solace with one another from pressures to conform, parents who don't understand, and the longing for adult identity. Bona fide classic still hits all the right notes of teen angst. Splendid performances from Mineo, Wood, and the smoldering Dean; energetic filmmaking from director Ray.

RECKLESS 1984
★★ R Drama 1:30
☑ Nudity, adult situations, explicit language, violence
Dir: James Foley *Cast:* Daryl Hannah, Aidan Quinn, Kenneth McMillan, Adam Baldwin, Cliff De Young, Lois Smith
▶ In small West Virginia town, moody, rebellious teenager Quinn quits football but still manages to romance straitlaced cheerleader Hannah. He battles alcoholic steelworker father McMillan while she copes with dullsville boyfriend Baldwin and mother Smith, whose idea of a tribal rite-of-passage is getting her first credit card. Familiar opposite-side-of-the-tracks teen romance burdened by cumbersome screenplay but boasts great-looking leads, torrid sex scenes, distinctive direction from Foley, and dynamic score.

RECRUITS 1986
☆ R Comedy 1:22
Dir: Rafal Zeilinski *Cast:* Steve Osmond, Doug Annear, Annie McAuley, Alan Deveau, John Terrell, Lolita David
▶ In beach town Clam Cove, sheriff cleans up the streets by deputizing all the thieves, hookers, winos, and bums. Ragtag recruits aren't as inept as expected—they thwart corrupt police chief and run bikers out of town. Cheap carbon copy of Police Academy series offers few laughs and technical incompetence.

RED BADGE OF COURAGE, THE 1951
★★★★ NR War/Drama 1:09 B&W
☑ Adult situations, mild violence
Dir: John Huston *Cast:* Audie Murphy, Bill Mauldin, Douglas Dick, Royal Dano, John Dierkes, Andy Devine
▶ Adaptation of well-known Stephen Crane novel depicts struggle of Union soldier Murphy with cowardice during first battle with Confederates. Despite his confidence behind the lines, Murphy freezes at the sight of the enemy, then seeks to hide his panic from his fellow soldiers. Classic film boasts compelling battle sequences and down-home dialogue from writer/director Huston. Murphy was most-decorated soldier of World War II.

RED DAWN 1984
★★★★ PG-13 Action-Adventure 1:54
☑ Adult situations, explicit language, violence
Dir: John Milius *Cast:* Patrick Swayze, Charlie Sheen, C. Thomas Howell, Lea Thompson, Powers Boothe, Harry Dean Stanton
▶ Soviet and Cuban troops invade the U.S. after limited nuke attack and occupy Calumet, Colorado, killing many and dispatching remaining adults to "reeducation camps." Cause of freedom is left in hands of teen refugees Swayze, Sheen, Howell, and Thompson, known as the Wolverines. Adopting guerrilla tactics and assisted by downed flyer Boothe, the once-disorganized crew becomes effective nemesis to the Commies. Intriguing premise and fine cast.

RED-HEADED STRANGER 1987
★★ R Western 1:45
☑ Explicit language, violence
Dir: William Wittliff *Cast:* Willie Nelson, Katharine Ross, Morgan Fairchild, Royal Dano, Sonny Carl Davis
▶ Eastern parson Nelson travels with unfaithful wife Fairchild to run church in Montana and finds town dominated by bully Dano and his clan. Nelson battles with Dano for the freedom of the townfolk and gets rid of philandering Fairchild for sweet-natured widow Ross. Somber western, with origin in 1975 album by Nelson, will disappoint fans of the genre, although Nelson is always likable and production values are better than average. (CC)

RED HEAT 1988
★★★★ R Action-Adventure 1:46
☑ Adult situations, explicit language, graphic violence
Dir: Walter Hill *Cast:* Arnold Schwarzenegger, James Belushi, Peter Boyle, Ed O'Ross, Gina Gershon, Larry Fishburne
▶ Tough, hard-nosed Moscow cop Schwarzenegger is dispatched to Chicago to extradite Soviet narcotics gangster O'Ross. When O'Ross escapes, Schwarzenegger pairs with slovenly, cynical U.S. counterpart Belushi. The two mix

like oil and water at first, but soon develop rapport needed to nab the ruthless Russian and his cohorts. Plenty of shootouts, chases, and a good measure of humor in this clever take on the buddy-action formula.

RED PONY, THE 1949
★★★★ NR Family 1:19
Dir: Lewis Milestone *Cast:* Myrna Loy, Robert Mitchum, Louis Calhern, Shepperd Strudwick, Peter Miles, Margaret Hamilton
► Young Miles idolizes Mitchum, a hired hand on father Strudwick's ranch. Strudwick's marital problems with Loy upset the youngster; he's comforted when Mitchum helps him train a frail horse. Moving family drama boasts superb photography, beautiful Aaron Copland score, and effectively understated sentiment. Adapted by John Steinbeck from three of his short stories and remade for TV in 1972.

RED RIVER 1948
★★★★ NR Western 2:05 B&W
Dir: Howard Hawks *Cast:* John Wayne, Montgomery Clift, Joanne Dru, Walter Brennan, Coleen Gray, John Ireland
► Seminal Western about mammoth cattle drive along the Chisholm Trail to Abilene is one of the true classics of the genre. Wayne is remarkable as cattle baron Tom Dunson; Clift became a star as a foster son who rebels against Dunson's unreasonable discipline. Magnificent photography, rousing score, and hard-as-nails script by Borden Chase contribute to film's epic sweep.

REDS 1981
★★★ PG Biography 3:19
☑ Adult situations, explicit language, violence
Dir: Warren Beatty *Cast:* Warren Beatty, Diane Keaton, Jack Nicholson, Maureen Stapleton, Gene Hackman, Edward Herrmann
► Radical journalist John Reed (Beatty) gets involved with writer Louise Bryant (Keaton), who leaves behind her middle-class life to marry him. Reed makes his mark when he reports on the tumultuous Russian Revolution. Ambitious, impressive epic successfully mixes passion and politics; interviews with real-life survivors of the period like Henry Miller and Adela Rogers St. John are one of the brilliant strokes. Nominated for Best Picture, Actor (Beatty), Actress (Keaton), Supporting

Actor (Nicholson, magnificently cynical as Bryant's lover, the playwright Eugene O'Neill). Oscars for Best Director, Supporting Actress (Stapleton), Cinematography.

RED SHOES, THE 1948 British
★★★★ NR Drama/Dance 2:13
Dir: Michael Powell, Emeric Pressburger
Cast: Moira Shearer, Anton Walbrook, Marius Goring, Robert Helpmann, Albert Basserman, Leonide Massine
► Ambitious ballerina Shearer loves composer Goring but ruthless company director Walbrook disapproves of the relationship. Shearer's conflict between love and career is paralleled by the tragic ballet that made her famous, "The Red Shoes." Grandly romantic and beautifully produced; perhaps responsible for several generations of young girls taking ballet lessons. Best Picture nominee; won for Art/Set Decoration and Score.

RED SONJA 1985
★ PG-13 Action-Adventure 1:29
☑ Adult situations, violence
Dir: Richard Fleischer *Cast:* Arnold Schwarzenegger, Brigitte Nielsen, Sandahl Bergman, Paul Smith, Ernie Reyes, Jr., Ronald Lacey
► Female warrior Nielsen acquires special skill at swordplay but must pledge never to make love to a man unless he beats her in a fair fight. Some years later, well-developed Nielsen, aided by even-better-developed mercenary Schwarzenegger, embarks on mission to retrieve magic talisman from evil queen Bergman and thus save the world from destruction. Adapted from stories by Robert E. Howard, also creator of *Conan the Barbarian.* Humorless sword-and-sorcery exercise for fans only. (CC)

RED TENT, THE 1971 Italian/Russian
★★★ G Action-Adventure 2:01
Dir: Mikhail K. Kalatozov *Cast:* Sean Connery, Claudia Cardinale, Hardy Kruger, Peter Finch, Massimo Girotti, Luigi Vannucchi
► Finch commands Italian dirigible expedition to North Pole in 1928. When his airship crashes in the North Atlantic, Kruger races team led by Norwegian explorer Roald Amundsen (Connery) to the rescue. Impressive location photography adds scope to this exciting drama based on a real-life disaster.

REEFER MADNESS 1936
☆ PG Drama 1:12 B&W

☑ Adult situations
Dir: Louis Gasnier *Cast:* Dorothy Short, Kenneth Craig, Lillian Miles, Dave O'Brien, Thelma White, Carleton Young
▶ Cautionary tale about youngsters who experiment with marijuana and soon become addicted to the evil weed. Depths of debauchery include necking, close dancing, and fast boogie-woogie piano playing; drug use ultimately leads to prison and death. Unintentionally comic, camp classic is favorite of midnight movie audiences.

REFLECTION OF FEAR, A 1973
★ ★ ★ PG Mystery-Suspense 1:29
☑ Violence
Dir: William A. Fraker *Cast:* Robert Shaw, Mary Ure, Sally Kellerman, Sondra Locke, Signe Hasso
▶ Young Locke, given strange upbringing by mother Ure and grandmother Hasso, makes hazy distinctions between fantasy and reality and believes her doll Aaron is alive. When her dad Shaw shows up to demand divorce so he can marry his girlfriend Kellerman, Locke goes on killing spree. Standard shocker.

REFLECTIONS IN A GOLDEN EYE 1967
★ NR Drama 1:49
☑ Adult situations, explicit language
Dir: John Huston *Cast:* Elizabeth Taylor, Marlon Brando, Brian Keith, Julie Harris, Zorro David, Robert Forster
▶ Army major Brando hides his homosexuality behind stern discipline and neglects sexpot wife Taylor, leading her to begin affair with colonel Keith, whose psychotic wife Harris enjoys company of gay houseboy David. Add to the equation Peeping Tom underwear fetishist Forster, who stirs Brando's repressed longings, and things really get kinky. Heavyhanded melodrama of interest for stars only. Based on the Carson McCullers novel.

REFORM SCHOOL GIRLS 1986
★ R Action-Adventure 1:34
☑ Nudity, adult situations, explicit language, violence
Dir: Tom DeSimone *Cast:* Sybil Danning, Wendy O. Williams, Pat Ast, Linda Carol, Charlotte McGinnis, Sherri Stoner
▶ Innocent young Carol is convicted and sentenced to nightmarish reform school where she encounters Bible-spouting warden Danning, nasty cell-block matron Ast, and tough lesbian inmate Williams. Campy send-up of women-be-hind-bars pics has a few yuks but is generally flimsy excuse for hair-pulling brawls and many shower scenes. Williams was former singer for punk group The Plasmatics; Ast appeared in numerous Andy Warhol films.

REINCARNATION OF PETER PROUD, THE 1975
★ ★ R Mystery-Suspense 1:45
☑ Nudity, adult situations, explicit language, violence
Dir: J. Lee Thompson *Cast:* Michael Sarrazin, Jennifer O'Neill, Margot Kidder, Cornelia Sharpe, Paul Hecht, Tony Stephano
▶ Young professor Sarrazin discovers he's inhabited by spirit of cheating husband killed by angry wife Kidder years ago. Kidder realizes Sarrazin is her husband reincarnated and feels some of her original passion return. Matters grow more complex when Kidder's daughter O'Neill falls for Sarrazin. Adaptation of Max Ehrlich's best-selling novel devotes considerable effort to character development, unusual for occult yarns.

REIVERS, THE 1969
★ ★ ★ ★ PG Comedy 1:47
☑ Adult situations, explicit language
Dir: Mark Rydell *Cast:* Steve McQueen, Sharon Farrell, Will Geer, Michael Constantine, Rupert Crosse, Mitch Vogel
▶ Young rich boy Vogel, chauffeur McQueen, and McQueen's black buddy Crosse drive an expensive auto from Mississippi to Memphis. There Vogel samples the fare at a bordello as McQueen romances vet hooker Farrell. When Crosse trades car for racehorse, the trio must finagle its return to save Vogel from paying the consequences. Colorful yarn peopled by eccentrics based on William Faulkner's last novel.

REMBRANDT 1936 British
★ ★ ★ ★ NR Biography 1:26 B&W
Dir: Alexander Korda *Cast:* Charles Laughton, Gertrude Lawrence, Elsa Lanchester, Edward Chapman, Walter Hudd, Roger Livesey
▶ Laughton's restrained performance dominates this romanticized version of the final three decades in the master Dutch painter's life. Newly widowed, Rembrandt turns to his housekeeper and sometime-model Lawrence for companionship. Crippling debts and a third marriage to his maid Lanchester leave him

on the brink of senility. While not factually accurate, film is an honest, incisive study of the creative process. Magnificent photography illustrates the sources of Rembrandt's inspirations.

REMOTE CONTROL 1988
☆ **R Sci-Fi 1:28**
☑ Explicit language, violence
Dir: Jeff Lieberman *Cast:* Kevin Dillon, Deborah Goodrich, Christopher Wynne, Frank Beddor, Jennifer Tilly, Bert Remsen
▶ Aliens fabricate sci-fi home video that sends viewers on homicidal rampage. Vid store employee Dillon is fingered by police for subsequent murders and must go on lam with boss Wynne and dream girl Goodrich while attempting to thwart alien plan to take over world by videocassette. Less-than-serious sci-fi mixes suspense and inside jokes. Kids and teens will enjoy it the most.

REMO WILLIAMS: THE ADVENTURE BEGINS 1985
★★★★ **PG-13 Action-Adventure 2:01**
☑ Explicit language, violence
Dir: Guy Hamilton *Cast:* Fred Ward, Joel Grey, Wilford Brimley, Kate Mulgrew, J. A. Preston, George Coe
▶ Tough New York City cop Ward is unwillingly enlisted by government higher-up Brimley to assassinate bad guys beyond the reach of justice. After training in martial arts and Zen from oriental mystic Grey, Ward is thrust into conspiracy so elaborate he barely has time for romantic interest Mulgrew. Live-action comic-book movie, based on best-selling pulp novels, boasts impressive stunts and a shrewd turn from Grey, who tells Ward "You move like a pregnant yak."

RENT-A-COP 1988
★★★ **R Action-Adventure 1:36**
☑ Explicit language, violence
Dir: Jerry London *Cast:* Burt Reynolds, Liza Minnelli, James Remar, Richard Masur, Dionne Warwick, Robby Benson
▶ Reduced to working as security guard when a drug bust ends in everyone except him being killed, ex-cop Reynolds is hired as a bodyguard by high-priced hooker Minnelli who also witnessed the event. Suspects include drug dealer Remar, cop-gone-bad Masur, and high-tech madam Warwick, among others. No surprises and few sparks from this poorly plotted shoot-'em-up. **(CC)**

RENTED LIPS 1988
★★ **R Comedy 1:22**
☑ Nudity, adult situations, explicit language
Dir: Robert Downey *Cast:* Martin Mull, Dick Shawn, Jennifer Tilly, Robert Downey, Jr., Edy Williams, Kenneth Mars
▶ Mull and Shawn, documentary filmmakers of such epics as *Hello, Mr. Spermwhale,* are lured by promise of funds for pic on Indian farming techniques into taking over helm of porno film stalled in midshoot by director's death. Amid on-set mayhem, including romance between Mull and ditzy singer Tilly and obstruction by fundamentalist preacher Mars, filmmakers attempt to shoot both porno and docu as musicals.

REPO MAN 1984
★ **R Action-Adventure/Comedy 1:32**
☑ Adult situations, explicit language, violence
Dir: Alex Cox *Cast:* Harry Dean Stanton, Emilio Estevez, Olivia Barash, Tracey Walter, Sy Richardson, Susan Barnes
▶ Middle-class punk Estevez learns how to repossess cars from mentor Stanton, an old-timer who knows all the tricks of the trade. They get involved with pretty Barash and a Chevy Malibu worth $20,000 to someone. Imagine their surprise when they find radioactive aliens in the trunk of the Chevy. Zany and offbeat low-budget film features good performances from the leads, but may be too weird for mainstream audiences.

REPORT TO THE COMMISSIONER 1975
★★ **PG Action-Adventure 1:52**
☑ Adult situations, explicit language, violence
Dir: Milton Katselas *Cast:* Michael Moriarty, Susan Blakely, Yaphet Kotto, Hector Elizondo, Tony King, Michael McGuire
▶ During bust of drug czar King, rookie detective Moriarty kills undercover agent Blakely, not realizing she's also a cop. Other cops, including Moriarty's partner Kotto, derail investigation into Blakely's death. Moriarty and Kotto try to do their jobs but get caught in bureaucratic infighting. Uneven mix of character study and social commentary is not for action fans. Look for Richard Gere in screen debut as sleazy pimp.

REPULSION 1965 British
★ **NR Mystery-Suspense 1:45 B&W**

☑ Rape, adult situations, violence
Dir: Roman Polanski **Cast:** Catherine Deneuve, Ian Hendry, Patrick Wymark, John Fraser, Yvonne Furneaux
▶ Extremely repressed Belgian manicurist Deneuve lives in London with her sister Furnaux. She is driven into a mad, murderous rampage when Furneaux brings a lover home and then goes away for two weeks. Scary and controversial; quite shocking after a slow opening.

REQUIEM FOR A HEAVYWEIGHT 1962
★★ NR Drama/Sports 1:40 B&W
Dir: Ralph Nelson **Cast:** Anthony Quinn, Jackie Gleason, Mickey Rooney, Julie Harris, Stanley Adams, Cassius Clay
▶ Over-the-hill boxer Quinn is advised to retire by doctor after beating from younger, faster fighter Clay (before he changed his name to Muhammad Ali). Gleason, Quinn's manager, has lost large bet to mob and fears loss of his meal ticket. Gleason sabotages attempt by social worker Harris to land decent job for Quinn and persuades him to try pro wrestling. Feature version of Rod Serling's Emmy-winning teledrama is still fine, but extra scenes are redundant. Superb Quinn and Gleason, plus cameo by boxing legend Jack Dempsey.

RESCUE, THE 1988
★★★ PG Action-Adventure 1:38
☑ Explicit language, mild violence
Dir: Ferdinand Fairfax **Cast:** Kevin Dillon, Christina Harnos, Marc Price, Ned Vaughn, Charles Haid, Edward Albert
▶ Four American servicemen are captured by the North Koreans. When the State Department abandons a rescue plan, the captured men's Navy brat offspring (led by punky teen Dillon) stage their own daring mission to liberate their fathers. Heart-tugging flag-waver provides foolproof entertainment. Several exciting chase scenes.

RESURRECTION 1980
★★★★ PG Drama 1:43
☑ Adult situations, explicit language
Dir: Daniel Petrie **Cast:** Ellen Burstyn, Sam Shepard, Eva Le Gallienne, Richard Farnsworth, Roberts Blossom
▶ Burstyn, after car accident and near-death experience (represented in an visually eerie sequence), discovers she has a miraculous power to heal others. Her lover Shepard is uneasy about her newfound ability. Simply told yet power-

ful and fascinating. Graceful, stirring performance by Burstyn (Oscar-nominated, as was Le Gallienne as the grandmother).

RETALIATOR, THE 1987
☆ R Action-Adventure 1:31
☑ Nudity, adult situations, explicit language, violence
Dir: Allan Holzman **Cast:** Robert Ginty, Sandahl Bergman, James Booth, Alex Courtney, Paul W. Walker, Louise Caire Clark
▶ Mercenary Ginty captures Mideast terrorist Bergman; CIA scientists turn her into cyborg programmed to kill her PLO colleagues. But Bergman short-circuits and embarks on rampage against American agents. Can Ginty stop the robot? Standard action exploitation suffers from mechanical acting.

RETURN, THE 1980
★★ NR Sci-Fi 1:31
☑ Explicit language, violence
Dir: Greydon Clark **Cast:** Jan-Michael Vincent, Cybill Shepherd, Martin Landau, Raymond Burr, Neville Brand
▶ Deputy Vincent and scientist Shepherd, having witnessed UFO while still children, are reunited in a New Mexico town where they confront an alien visitor. Although story is somewhat implausible, pleasing special effects and likable leads succeed in evoking a sense of wonder. Will appeal to older kids.

RETURN FROM THE RIVER KWAI 1988
★★★ NR War 2:00
☑ Explicit language, violence
Dir: Andrew V. McLaglen **Cast:** Edward Fox, Denholm Elliott, Christopher Penn, Timothy Bottoms, George Takei
▶ Thailand, 1945: allied POWs are being shipped to Japan for factory work; Aussie Bottoms plots escape although British officer Fox is doubtful. American pilot Penn eventually comes to their aid. Gets off to a flat start but improves as it goes along; good performances and a rousing ending. Doesn't live up to its 1957 predecessor but doesn't disgrace it either.

RETURN FROM WITCH MOUNTAIN 1978
★★★★ G Action-Adventure/Family 1:33
Dir: John Hough **Cast:** Bette Davis, Christopher Lee, Kim Richards, Ike Eisenmann, Jack Soo, Anthony James
▶ Psychic-powered alien siblings Richards and Eisenmann vacation in Los An-

geles. When Eisenmann is kidnapped by mad-scientist Lee and cohort Davis, Richards teams with a street gang to rescue him. First-rate sequel to Disney's 1975 *Escape to Witch Mountain* has appealing performances by Davis, Lee, and the children.

RETURN OF A MAN CALLED HORSE 1976
★★★★ PG Western 2:05
☑ Graphic violence
Dir: Irvin Kershner   *Cast:* Richard Harris, Gale Sondergaard, Geoffrey Lewis, William Lucking, Jorge Luke, Enrique Lucero
▶ In 1830, English lord Harris, bored with life among whites, returns to the Yellow Hands, his adopted Indian tribe in America. Tribe is suffering under the attacks of a trader (Lewis), but Harris reverses the trend after undergoing the breast-piercing Sun Vow ritual once more. As exciting and memorable as the original. Excellent photography but excruciating torture sequences.

RETURN OF FRANK JAMES, THE 1940
★★★★ NR Western 1:33
Dir: Fritz Lang   *Cast:* Henry Fonda, Gene Tierney, Jackie Cooper, Henry Hull, John Carradine, Donald Meek
▶ Continuation of 1939's *Jesse James* opens with Jesse's murder at the hands of the Ford brothers (Carradine, Charles Tannen). When they're pardoned, brother Frank (Fonda) vows revenge. Framed for an accidental death during a robbery, he is brought to trial while Carradine gloats in the audience. With the help of intrepid reporter Tierney (in her film debut), justice prevails. Trim, fast-paced Western with a winning performance by Fonda and good photography.

RETURN OF MARTIN GUERRE, THE 1983 French
★ NR Drama 1:51
☑ Adult situations, violence
Dir: Daniel Vigne   *Cast:* Gerard Depardieu, Nathalie Baye, Roger Planchon, Bernard Pierre Donnadieu, Maurice Barrier
▶ Sixteenth-century France: peasant Martin Guerre leaves wife Baye and child. Nine years later, stranger Depardieu arrives in town and claims to be Guerre; Baye vouches for him but others are not so sure. Absorbing story with fine acting, beautiful photography, and ex-

pert period details; slow pacing requires patience.   Ⓢ

RETURN OF THE DRAGON 1974 Hong Kong
★★ R Martial Arts 1:31
☑ Explicit language, violence
Dir: Bruce Lee   *Cast:* Bruce Lee, Chuck Norris, Nora Miao, Huang Chung Hsun
▶ In Rome, Lee helps family trying to stop evil gang from taking over their restaurant. Among the bad guys: fellow martial arts master Norris. Bad dubbing, ho-hum crime plot, stiff characters and dialogue, but Lee and Norris provide plenty of acrobatic action. Lee, who also wrote screenplay, died before film's completion.

RETURN OF THE FLY 1959
★ NR Horror 1:20 B&W
Dir: Edward Bernds   *Cast:* Vincent Price, Brett Halsey, David Frankham, John Sutton, Dan Seymour
▶ Halsey, son of the ill-fated scientist in 1958's *The Fly*, decides to repeat his dad's work. He too becomes a half-man/half-fly when spy Frankham disrupts the experiment. Halsey's uncle Price helps him. Okay genre effort not in the league of its predecessor.

RETURN OF THE JEDI 1983
★★★★★ PG Sci-Fi/Action-Adventure 2:12
☑ Adult situations, violence
Dir: Richard Marquand   *Cast:* Mark Hamill, Harrison Ford, Carrie Fisher, Billy Dee Williams, Anthony Daniels, Alec Guinness
▶ Much-awaited finale to the Star Wars trilogy. Luke (Hamill), Han (Ford), Lando (Williams), Princess Leia (Fisher), and their robot pals are befriended by furry Ewoks in their final battle with Darth Vader and the evil Empire. Along the way, Luke learns the series's most shocking secret: Vader's true identity. Smashing sequel to the elaborate space opera introduces colorful new creatures and features stunning three-way battle climax, adding thrills to the tried-and-true formula. Most exciting scene: the flying chase through the forest. Special effects won an Oscar. (CC)

RETURN OF THE LIVING DEAD, THE 1985
★★ R Horror/Comedy 1:31
☑ Nudity, explicit language, graphic violence
Dir: Dan O'Bannon   *Cast:* Clu Gulager,

James Karen, Don Calfa, Thom Mathews, Beverly Randolph, Jewel Shepard
▶ Medical supply house workers Karen and Mathews accidentally bring zombies back to life by releasing gas from a sealed government drum. Some genuine laughs, clever situations, and pleasing tongue-in-cheek acting, but quite gory; brain-eating zombies will not be to everyone's taste.

RETURN OF THE LIVING DEAD II, THE 1988
★★ R Horror/Comedy 1:29
☑ Explicit language, violence
Dir: Ken Wiederhorn   *Cast:* James Karen, Thom Mathews, Michael Kenworthy, Marsha Dietlein, Suzanne Snyder, Dana Ashbrook
▶ Can of zombie gas falls off an Army truck and kids break it open. Big mistake: the gas floats into the local graveyard and brings the dead to life to menace the locals. Some laughs and gory effects but few surprises; the original film had a lot more humor. **(CC)**

RETURN OF THE PINK PANTHER, THE 1975 British
★★★★ G Comedy 1:53
Dir: Blake Edwards   *Cast:* Peter Sellers, Christopher Plummer, Catherine Schell, Herbert Lom, Peter Arne, Burt Kwouk
▶ Pink Panther diamond is stolen and ex-thief Plummer is blamed. While Plummer seeks real thief to clear his name, chief inspector Lom reluctantly puts blundering detective Sellers on the trail of the crooks. Usual assortment of pratfalls, sight gags, and quotable Clouseau-isms result. Fourth Pink Panther picture featured return of inimitable Sellers as Inspector Clouseau after Alan Arkin tried role in third of series.

RETURN OF THE SECAUCUS 7 1981
★ R Comedy/Drama 1:48
☑ Nudity, adult situations, explicit language
Dir: John Sayles   *Cast:* Mark Arnott, Gordon Clapp, Maggie Renzi, Karen Trott, John Sayles
▶ Earnest and intelligent, very-low budget first directorial effort by Sayles predates similar but more polished *The Big Chill.* Seven political activists from the 1960s, now in their thirties, reunite to spend a weekend in New Hampshire. The group includes a hippie couple, two Washington activists, and several grown-up children who refuse to face the responsibilities of adulthood. Wall-to-wall talk, but much of it is interesting. Mainstream audiences may not have the patience, though.

RETURN OF THE SOLDIER, THE 1985 British
★ NR Drama 1:42
☑ Adult situations, explicit language
Dir: Alan Bridges   *Cast:* Alan Bates, Julie Christie, Glenda Jackson, Ann-Margret, Ian Holm
▶ Soldier Bates, shellshocked and amnesiac after World War I, returns home. Snobby wife Christie, old flame Jackson, and Ann-Margret, the cousin who secretly loves him, must deal with his condition. Heavy, ponderous, and depressing despite fine performances and classy production values.

RETURN TO BOGGY CREEK 1977
★★ G Mystery-Suspense 1:27
Dir: Tom Moore   *Cast:* Dawn Wells, Dana Plato, David Sobiesk
▶ Giant monster terrorizes inhabitants of Arkansas swamp communities. Decent-looking, low-budget production may hold the attention of kids but unsubtle acting, cardboard characters, dull direction, and simplistic script make it more laughable than scary for adults. Sequel to *The Legend of Boggy Creek.*

RETURN TO HORROR HIGH 1987
★ R Horror 1:35
☑ Nudity, adult situations, explicit language, violence
Dir: Bill Froehlich   *Cast:* Lori Lethin, Brendan Hughes, Alex Rocco, Scott Jacoby, Vince Edwards, Maureen McCormick
▶ Movie company shoots at a high school where murders took place a few years back. Someone starts knocking off crew members. A few clever moments elevate this above standard slasher fare, but not many scares and the jokey finale will leave viewers feeling cheated.

RETURN TO MACON COUNTY 1975
★★ PG Action-Adventure 1:30
☑ Explicit language, violence
Dir: Richard Compton   *Cast:* Nick Nolte, Don Johnson, Robin Mattson, Robert Viharo, Eugene Daniels, Matt Greene
▶ Hot-rodding pals Nolte and Johnson pick up crazy Mattson for drag duel with toughs Daniels and Greene and run-in with cop Viharo. Cheapo exploitation flick used allure of sex and violence to

cash in on success of *Macon County Line*. Young Nolte and Johnson are wasted on inane script.

RETURN TO OZ 1985
★ ★ **PG Fantasy/Family 1:50**
☑ Violence
Dir: Walter Murch *Cast:* Fairuza Balk, Nicol Williamson, Jean Marsh, Piper Laurie, Matt Clark
▶ Dorothy (Balk) returns to the Emerald City, now turned into a wasteland by the evil Nome King (Williamson) and Princess Mombi (Marsh). Dorothy sets off to restore order with the help of her talking chicken, a moosehead, a tin man, and a pump-kinhead. Balk is appealing and there are some nice special effects but downbeat tone may alienate those looking for a lighthearted sequel to *The Wizard of Oz*. Dorothy's mechanical companions lack the charm and humanity of the original's predecessors.

RETURN TO SALEM'S LOT 1987
★ **R Horror 1:40**
☑ Nudity, adult situations, explicit lan-guage, violence
Dir: Larry Cohen *Cast:* Michael Mori-arty, Samuel Fuller, Evelyn Keyes, An-drew Duggan, June Havoc
▶ Sequel to TV movie based on the Ste-phen King novel. Anthropologist Moriarty arrives in Maine for research and soon learns the place is infested with vam-pires. When Moriarty's son Duggan ap-pears to be on his way to eternal life of bloodsucking, dad teams with Nazi/vampire killer Fuller to rescue son and es-cape from Salem's Lot. Average vampire effort plays for laughs with scene-stealing turn by legendary director Fuller. History will note this the first film to discuss AIDS risk to vampires.

RETURN TO SNOWY RIVER 1988
Australian
★ ★ ★ ★ **PG Western 1:40**
☑ Explicit language, mild violence
Dir: Geoff Burrowes *Cast:* Tom Burlin-son, Sigrid Thornton, Brian Dennehy, Nicholas Eadie, Mark Hembrow, Bryan Marshall
▶ Adventurer Burlinson returns to reclaim beloved Thornton but faces opposition from dad Dennehy and banker's son Eadie, who covets her for himself. Burlin-son pursues when Eadie steals his horses. Sequel to *The Man from Snowy River* sus-tains hardy formula with grand, wide-

open scenery, handsome horseflesh and humans, and swift pace.

REUBEN, REUBEN 1983
★ ★ **R Comedy/Drama 1:40**
☑ Brief nudity, adult situations, explicit language
Dir: Robert Ellis Miller *Cast:* Tom Conti, Kelly McGillis, Roberts Blossom, Cynthia Harris, Lois Smith, Kara Wilson
▶ Conti plays a freeloading poet who's lazy, irresponsible, and fascinating to women. A puckish Scotsman, he's trans-planted to Connecticut and has roving eyes for farm-bred college girl McGillis. Sophisticated fare, adapted from the Peter DeVries novel, was nominated for two Oscars (Best Actor and Screenplay) but will move slowly for many viewers. (CC)

REVENGE OF THE NERDS 1984
★ ★ ★ ★ **R Comedy 1:30**
☑ Nudity, adult situations, explicit lan-guage
Dir: Jeff Kanew *Cast:* Robert Carra-dine, Anthony Edwards, Curtis Arm-strong, Andrew Cassese, Julie Mont-gomery, Melanie Meyrink
▶ College freshmen Carradine and Ed-wards, humiliated by loutish jocks and re-jected by cheerleaders, enlist fellow campus outcasts and join previously all-black fraternity. Nerds then gain a mea-sure of vengeance in resulting rivalry with the elitists. Raucous romp was quite pop-ular. Carradine and Edwards excel as the geek leads. (CC)

REVENGE OF THE NERDS II: NERDS IN PARADISE 1987
★ ★ **PG-13 Comedy 1:29**
☑ Brief nudity, explicit language
Dir: Joe Roth *Cast:* Robert Carradine, Curtis Armstrong, Timothy Busfield, An-drew Cassese, Larry B. Scott, Courtney Thorne-Smith
▶ The house of geeks, played by Carra-dine and crew, heads south to Fort Lau-derdale for an interfraternity conference. Arch-rival jocks nearly sabotage fun in the sun, but you can't keep a good nerd down, especially when he steals a tank to assure entry into exclusive meetings. Popular sequel features more wacky high jinks, including romance for Carradine with comely hotel clerk Thorne-Smith and nerd pride rap number. (CC)

REVENGE OF THE NINJA 1983
★ ★ ★ **R Martial Arts 1:28**

☐ Nudity, explicit language, graphic violence

Dir: Sam Firstenberg *Cast:* Sho Kosugi, Keith Vitali, Virgil Frye, Arthur Roberts, Mario Gallo, Grace Oshita

▶ Kosugi, a Japanese immigrant in U.S., conceals ninja heritage until unscrupulous Roberts kidnaps his son. Then it's no-blows-barred action, capped by rooftop free-for-all. Sequel to *Enter the Ninja*, also starring Kosugi (who choreographed fight scenes). For diehard kung-fu fans.

REVENGE OF THE PINK PANTHER 1978
★★★★ PG Comedy 1:39
☑ Explicit language
Dir: Blake Edwards *Cast:* Peter Sellers, Herbert Lom, Dyan Cannon, Robert Webber, Burt Kwouk, Robert Loggia

▶ Chief Inspector Clouseau (Sellers) is on the loose again in fifth outing (and last for Sellers) of the perennially popular series. In Paris, American heroin dealer Webber plans to kill Clouseau to prove his clout to Mafia. Webber's secretary Cannon spills the beans to Clouseau and the duo team up to thwart heroin ring in Hong Kong climax. Standard Sellers vehicle includes many disguises (look for takeoffs on Toulouse-Lautrec and Don Corleone) and customary brushes with addled former boss Lom and karate-crazy valet Kwouk. Plenty of mileage left.

REVOLUTION 1985
★★ PG Drama 2:01
☑ Explicit language, graphic violence
Dir: Hugh Hudson *Cast:* Al Pacino, Donald Sutherland, Nastassja Kinski, Joan Plowright, Dexter Fletcher, Annie Lennox

▶ Large-scale spectacle of the American Revolution seen from the eyes of Pacino, a New York trapper who becomes an unwilling rebel when his son Fletcher is drafted into the British Army by villainous sergeant Sutherland. He joins a movement that includes wealthy aristocrat Kinski and a loud "Liberty Woman" (rock star Lennox). Stirring battle scenes can't salvage miscasting, incongruous accents, and English locations doubling as American landmarks. **(CC)**

RHINESTONE 1984
★★ PG Musical/Comedy 1:51
☑ Explicit language
Dir: Bob Clark *Cast:* Sylvester Stallone, Dolly Parton, Richard Farnsworth, Ron Leibman, Tim Thomerson, Steven Apostle Pec

▶ Country-western singer Parton bets club owner Leibman she can turn anyone into passable country crooner in two weeks. Leibman selects shiftless cabbie Stallone as guinea pig. Parton whisks Stallone off to ol' Tennessee home where she and pappy Farnsworth turn him into Roy Rogers with muscles in time for acid test at Leibman's club. Formulaic but good-natured clash of cultures, with superior supporting cast and romance in form-fitting clothes between the two stars. **(CC)**

RICH AND FAMOUS 1981
★★★ R Drama 1:57
☑ Nudity, adult situations, explicit language
Dir: George Cukor *Cast:* Jacqueline Bisset, Candice Bergen, David Selby, Hart Bochner, Steven Hill, Meg Ryan

▶ Glossy remake of 1943's *Old Acquaintance* examines a twenty-year friendly rivalry between two Smith College grads: Bisset, a serious novelist who must settle for critical rather than financial success, and Bergen, the author of best-selling soap operas. Despite explicit language and preoccupation with sex, doesn't improve on the original. Cukor's last film.

RICHARD PRYOR HERE AND NOW 1983
★★★ R Documentary/Comedy 1:34
☑ Adult situations, explicit language, adult humor
Dir: Richard Pryor *Cast:* Richard Pryor

▶ Filmed in a Bourbon Street theater in New Orleans, fourth Pryor concert film offers the comedian's caustic and obscene comments on such subjects as his acting career, Ronald Reagan, drunks, and racism. Quirkier, funkier, and sometimes more rambling than his earlier performance films. Not for delicate sensibilities. **(CC)**

RICHARD PRYOR—LIVE IN CONCERT 1979
★★★★ NR Documentary/Comedy 1:18
☑ Explicit language, adult humor
Dir: Jeff Margolis *Cast:* Richard Pryor

▶ First of Pryor's concert films (and arguably the best) records the comedian's rib-tickling reactions to being arrested for shooting his car, suffering a heart attack, and being confronted by his grandmother about cocaine use. Also included are diatribes against macho men and rapists. Uncensored and uncut Pryor talks a blue streak—strictly for adults.

RICHARD PRYOR LIVE ON THE SUNSET STRIP 1982
★★★ R Documentary/Comedy 1:21
☑ Explicit language, adult humor
Dir: Joe Layton *Cast:* Richard Pryor
▶ Third Pryor concert film, shot in Los Angeles's Palladium, is another blistering, hilarious monologue on a variety of controversial subjects, particularly sex. Explicit, provocative, and at times oddly moving, especially when Pryor discusses his freebasing accident. Followed by *Richard Pryor Here and Now.*

RICHARD III 1956 British
★★★ NR Drama 2:18
Dir: Laurence Olivier *Cast:* Laurence Olivier, John Gielgud, Ralph Richardson, Claire Bloom, Alec Clunes, Cedric Hardwicke
▶ Olivier is riveting as Shakespeare's hunchback king, a volatile combination of cunning and malice who proved to be England's most dangerous ruler. Excellent support from an outstanding cast, beautiful photography, and meticulous production values showcase Olivier's superb Oscar-nominated interpretation.

RICH KIDS 1979
★★★ PG Drama 1:36
☑ Adult situations, explicit language
Dir: Robert M. Young *Cast:* Trini Alvarado, Jeremy Levy, Kathryn Walker, John Lithgow, Paul Dooley, Irene Worth
▶ Twelve-year-old Alvarado knows upper-class New Yorker parents Walker and Lithgow are headed for divorce and seeks advice from classmate Levy, who's already been through the mill. Puppy love and parental manipulation ensue. Lightweight drama examines divorce and its innocent victims with intelligence and conviction, but dry, upscale setting and copious talk may be turnoffs.

RIDDLE OF THE SANDS, THE 1984 British
★★ NR Action-Adventure 1:42
☑ Brief nudity, mild violence
Dir: Tony Maylam *Cast:* Michael York, Jenny Agutter, Simon MacCorkindale, Alan Badel, Jurgen Andersen, Olga Lowe
▶ College chums York and MacCorkindale go on sailing venture off northern Germany and make acquaintance of rich German yachtsman Badel and his daughter Agutter. As MacCorkindale romances Agutter, he and York suspect that Badel is helping to plan a German invasion of England, and attempt to thwart the attack on their homeland. Picturesque spy drama too slow for savvy audiences, but fine for older kids.

RIDE IN THE WHIRLWIND 1965
★★ G Western 1:22
Dir: Monte Hellman *Cast:* Cameron Mitchell, Jack Nicholson, Tom Filer, Millie Perkins, Katherine Squire, Harry Dean Stanton
▶ Returning from cattle roundup, cowpokes Mitchell, Nicholson, and Filer share an innocent meal with Stanton, who turns out to be the leader of a gang of killers. Pursued across Utah by murderous vigilantes, Nicholson decides to take homesteader's daughter Perkins hostage. Standard Western of interest for an early Nicholson performance (he also wrote the script). Filmed simultaneously with the superior *The Shooting.*

RIDER ON THE RAIN 1970
French/Italian
★★ PG Mystery-Suspense 1:54
☑ Rape, violence
Dir: René Clement *Cast:* Charles Bronson, Marlene Jobert, Annie Cordy, Jill Ireland, Gabriele Tinti, Jean Gaven
▶ Jobert plays a French housewife who's raped by a mysterious stranger. She murders him in self-defense and hides his body from the authorities, then is menaced by American agent Bronson, who claims the rapist stole $60,000. Unnerving thriller with a thoughtful, unpredictable script and a polished performance by Bronson. His real-life wife Ireland has a small role as the owner of a boutique.

RIDERS ON THE STORM 1988
★★ R Comedy 1:32
☑ Adult situations, explicit language, violence
Dir: Maurice Phillips *Cast:* Dennis Hopper, Michael J. Pollard, Eugene Lipinski, James Aubrey, Al Matthews, Nigel Pegram
▶ Madcap Vietnam veterans, led by Hopper, monitor American TV from a B-29 crammed with state-of-the-art technology, jamming political broadcasts with their own propaganda. Their latest target is right-wing Presidential candidate Willa Westinghouse (Pegram). Inventive but extremely broad satire is sexist, racist, bizarre, and only infrequently on target.

RIDE THE HIGH COUNTRY 1962
★ ★ ★ ★ NR Western 1:34
☑ Adult situations, adult humor
Dir: Sam Peckinpah *Cast:* Randolph Scott, Joel McCrea, Mariette Hartley, Ronald Starr, R. G. Armstrong, Edgar Buchanan
▶ Two aging former lawmen—McCrea still idealistic and dedicated, Scott out for his own interests—escort a shipment of gold from a mountain mining camp. They also rescue young bride Hartley from her hideous in-laws, leading to a gripping chase to safety. Handsome, bittersweet tribute to old Western values is a memorable success due to the stars' subdued performances. Scott's last film.

RIGHT HAND MAN, THE 1987
Australian
★ ★ ★ R Drama 1:41
☑ Nudity, adult situations, explicit language, violence
Dir: Di Drew *Cast:* Rupert Everett, Hugo Weaving, Catherine McClements, Arthur Dignam, Jennifer Claire
▶ Diabetic aristocrat Everett loses his arm in a riding accident. He hires dashing stagecoach driver Weaving to exercise his horses, a move with dire repercussions for Everett's lovely fiancée McClements. Lushly photographed romance set in 1860 Australia undermined by talky, unconvincing plot.

RIGHT OF WAY 1983
★ ★ ★ ★ NR Drama/MFTV 1:42
☑ Adult situations, explicit language
Dir: George Schaefer *Cast:* Bette Davis, James Stewart, Melinda Dillon, Priscilla Morrill, John Harkins, Jacque Lynn Colton
▶ Elderly Santa Monica couple have a secret: wife Davis has terminal disease and husband Stewart can't bear to live alone, so they've made a suicide pact. When they reveal plan to daughter Dillon she contacts a social worker. Soon Davis and Stewart face obstruction from city officials, lawyers, and the press. Drama with healthy dose of humor is first pairing of screen legends Davis and Stewart.

RIGHT STUFF, THE 1983
★ ★ ★ ★ PG Action-Adventure 3:16
☑ Adult situations, explicit language
Dir: Philip Kaufman *Cast:* Sam Shepard, Scott Glenn, Ed Harris, Dennis Quaid, Fred Ward, Barbara Hershey
▶ Rousing, often witty adaptation of Tom Wolfe's best-seller, chronicling heroics of test pilot Chuck Yeager (Shepard) and the Mercury program astronauts, particularly John Glenn (Harris), Alan Shepard (Glenn), and Gordon Cooper (Quaid). Spectacular flight scenes, genuine depiction of human side of astronauts and their wives, and moving portrayal of Yeager as unsung hero more than compensate for some uneven scenes. Stellar ensemble cast. Film won four technical Oscars. **(CC)**

RIKKY AND PETE 1988 Australian
★ R Comedy 1:47
☑ Nudity, adult situations, explicit language
Dir: Nadia Tass *Cast:* Stephen Kearney, Nina Landis, Bruno Lawrence, Tetchie Agbayani, Bill Hunter, Bruce Spence
▶ Loopy inventor Kearney and his overachiever sister Landis leave Melbourne for mining town in middle of nowhere. There Kearney woos dizzy Filipino Agbayani and Landis romances terse miner Lawrence. Siblings begin own mining operation employing Kearney's Rube Goldberg-style drilling gizmo. Rustic bliss is briefly interrupted by arrival of parents and vengeful Melbourne policeman Hunter, but bang-up finale solves all problems. Whimsical, off-beat comedy with likable cast, stunning scenery, and Kearney's remarkable inventions; may not appeal to audiences with broader tastes.

RING OF BRIGHT WATER 1969 British
★ ★ ★ G Family 1:47
Dir: Jack Couffer *Cast:* Bill Travers, Virginia McKenna, Peter Jeffrey, Jameson Clark
▶ London writer Travers adopts Mij the otter, then leaves the city for Scotland, where man and beast cavort against scenic backgrounds. One heartrending scene toward the end may upset smaller children, but overall this is warm and wonderful family fare.

RIO BRAVO 1959
★ ★ ★ ★ NR Western 2:20
Dir: Howard Hawks *Cast:* John Wayne, Dean Martin, Ricky Nelson, Angie Dickinson, Walter Brennan, Claude Akins
▶ Wayne is John T. (for "Trouble") Chance, a border town sheriff who jails murderer Akins even though his wealthy brother controls the county. Under siege by hired killers, Wayne turns to a motley crew for help: drunken deputy Martin,

who's lost his self-respect; crippled old-ster Brennan; greenhorn gunslinger Nel-son; and the aggressive, leggy showgirl Feathers (Dickinson). Polished, extremely entertaining Western was reworked by director Hawks in the similar *El Dorado* and *Rio Lobo*.

RIO CONCHOS 1964
★★★★ NR Western 1:47
Dir: Gordon Douglas *Cast:* Richard Boone, Stuart Whitman, Tony Franciosa, Wende Wagner, Jim Brown, Edmond O'Brien
▶ Union captain Whitman orders bigot Boone to discover source of stolen rifles. Joined by Mexican bandit Franciosa and black sergeant Brown, they track the weapons to unrepentant Confederate O'Brien, who is trading them to Apaches to start another Civil War. Hard-edged, action-packed Western features excep-tional performance by Boone. Brown's film debut.

RIO GRANDE 1950
★★★★ NR Western 1:45 B&W
Dir: John Ford *Cast:* John Wayne, Maureen O'Hara, Ben Johnson, Claude Jarman, Jr., Harry Carey, Jr., Victor McLaglen
▶ Wayne, the commander of a remote Army outpost, repulses Apache attacks while coping with personal problems. His son Jarman, a West Point dropout, has been assigned to the post after enlisting; his estranged wife O'Hara wants Jarman sent home to safety. Leisurely, richly de-tailed Western, an excellent climax to di-rector Ford's "cavalry trilogy" (*Fort Ap-ache*, *She Wore a Yellow Ribbon*), features stirring Sons of the Pioneers tunes and a fine performance by Johnson as a fugitive horseman.

RIO LOBO 1970
★★★★ G Western 1:54
Dir: Howard Hawks *Cast:* John Wayne, Jennifer O'Neill, Jorge Rivero, Sherry Lansing, Jack Elam, Chris Mitchum
▶ Howard Hawks's last film features the Duke as a Union soldier who teams with ex-Confederate Rivero to search for a gold-shipment thief and help belea-guered townsfolk against corrupt sheriff. Lively, fun, and action-packed; interest-ing cast features future producer/studio head Lansing as the woman who gets revenge against the man who scarred her and pairs off with Wayne in the finale. (CC)

RISKY BUSINESS 1983
★★★★ R Comedy 1:39
☑ Nudity, strong sexual content, adult situations, explicit language, adult humor
Dir: Paul Brickman *Cast:* Tom Cruise, Rebecca De Mornay, Curtis Armstrong, Bronson Pinchot, Raphael Sbarge, Joe Pantoliano
▶ Wealthy, sex-starved Chicago teen Cruise uses chance encounter with pros-titute De Mornay to establish a one-night bordello in his parents' house while they're out of town. But pimps clean out Cruise's house just as his parents are due back. Although morally vague, disarming comedy is inventive and good-natured. Cruise has a great air-guitar solo to Bob Seeger's "Old Time Rock and Roll."

RITA, SUE AND BOB TOO 1987 British
★★ R Comedy 1:35
☑ Brief nudity, strong sexual content, explicit language
Dir: Alan Clarke *Cast:* Michelle Holmes, Siobhan Finneran, George Costigan, Lesley Sharp, Willie Ross, Ghir Kulvindar
▶ Yorkshire teens Holmes and Finneran babysit for married couple Costigan and Sharp. Soon both girls lose their virginity to Costigan. They share him happily until Sharp wises up and packs off with the kids. Further complicating their once-happy triangle is Finneran's pregnancy and Holmes's new Pakistani boyfriend Kulvindar. Deliberately outrageous com-edy blends wistful sadness and cheery raunchiness. Not for the narrow-minded, but others will be tickled.

RITZ, THE 1976
★★ R Comedy 1:31
☑ Nudity, strong sexual content, adult situations, explicit language
Dir: Richard Lester *Cast:* Rita Moreno, Jack Weston, Jerry Stiller, Kaye Ballard, F. Murray Abraham, Treat Williams
▶ Small-time businessman Weston, flee-ing murderous mobster brother-in-law Stiller, seeks refuge for night in gay bath-house. Flirtations and much confusion of sexual preference ensue as Weston meets off-key singer Moreno, trench-coated detective Williams, and sharp-tongued gay Abraham. The ante is upped when Stiller and sister Ballard ar-rive at the bathhouse. Terrence McNally's hit Broadway farce is given a stagy screen adaptation, but much of the wit is still here.

RIVER, THE 1984
★ ★ ★ ★ PG-13 Drama 2:02
☑ Adult situations, explicit language, violence
Dir: Mark Rydell *Cast:* Mel Gibson, Sissy Spacek, Scott Glenn, Shane Bailey, Becky Jo Lynch, Don Hood
▶ Hard-headed, debt-ridden farmer Gibson and wife Spacek struggle to keep their riverside farm in business. Gibson must auction belongings and take factory job to make ends meet while Spacek fends off advances of Glenn, an ex-lover who would like to buy the farm. Then rains cause severe flooding and the river becomes foremost threat to survival. Grimly realistic portrait of plight of today's small farmer. Picture nominated for four Oscars, including Spacek as Best Actress. (CC)

RIVER OF NO RETURN 1954
★ ★ ★ NR Western 1:31
Dir: Otto Preminger *Cast:* Robert Mitchum, Marilyn Monroe, Rory Calhoun, Tommy Rettig, Murvyn Vye, Douglas Spencer
▶ During the Canadian gold rush, ex-con Mitchum makes arduous raft journey with son Rettig and singer Monroe in pursuit of bad guy Calhoun. Mitchum wins Monroe's love and the respect of his son. River trip provides plenty of physical excitement and star chemistry.

RIVER RAT, THE 1984
★ ★ ★ PG Drama 1:29
☑ Explicit language, violence
Dir: Tom Rickman *Cast:* Tommy Lee Jones, Martha Plimpton, Brian Dennehy, Shawn Smith, Nancy Lea Owen
▶ Touching family drama about ex-con Jones trying to win the affection of Plimpton, the thirteen-year-old daughter he's met for the first time. Together they renovate an old boat that used to cruise the Mississippi, but Jones's crooked past reappears in the form of corrupt parole officer Dennehy searching for robbery loot. Moving story was developed at Robert Redford's Sundance Institute. (CC)

RIVER'S EDGE 1987
★ ★ R Drama 1:39
☑ Adult situations, explicit language, violence
Dir: Tim Hunter *Cast:* Dennis Hopper, Crispin Glover, Keanu Reeves, Daniel Roebuck, Ione Skye Leitch, Joshua Miller

▶ Young teenager Roebuck murders his girl and friends numbly agree not to inform on him. But one boy, Reeves, feels compelled to speak with the police, setting up conflict with stoned clique leader Glover. Roebuck flees to home of hermit drug-dealer Hopper. Based on fact, critically acclaimed portrait of alienated, small-town youth hits hard. Some may find bleak depiction of violence, drug use, and utter apathy too unsettling. (CC)

ROAD GAMES 1981 Australian
★ ★ PG Mystery-Suspense 1:41
☑ Adult situations, explicit language, graphic violence
Dir: Richard Franklin *Cast:* Stacy Keach, Jamie Lee Curtis, Marion Edward, Grant Page, Bill Stacey, Thaddeus Smith
▶ Truck driver Keach, on long haul from Melbourne to Perth, finds his load getting heavier—someone has been stashing corpses in the rig. Police suspect Keach is the highway killer, so with help of sympathetic hitchhiker Curtis he tries to apprehend the true murderer and prove his innocence. Offbeat suspenser with plenty of action and Aussie color.

ROADHOUSE 66 1984
★ ★ R Action-Adventure 1:34
☑ Nudity, adult situations, explicit language, violence
Dir: John Mark Robinson *Cast:* Willem Dafoe, Judge Reinhold, Kaaren Lee, Kate Vernon, Stephen Elliot, Alan Autry
▶ Ivy Leaguer Reinhold and hitchhiker Dafoe are stranded overnight in a small Arizona town. After taunts from bullies and a touch of romance with sisters Lee and Vernon, they enter their 1955 T-bird in a drag race. Interesting cast and great soundtrack (including the Pretenders, Dave Edmunds, Los Lobos, etc.) set this a notch above typical action films.

ROAD TO RIO 1947
★ ★ ★ NR Comedy 1:40 B&W
Dir: Norman Z. McLeod *Cast:* Bing Crosby, Bob Hope, Dorothy Lamour, Gale Sondergaard, Frank Faylen, Joseph Vitale
▶ Musician stowaways Crosby and Hope are nonplussed by beautiful passenger Lamour's erratic behavior until they learn she's been hypnotized by Sondergaard into marrying a Brazilian villain. Fifth "Road" entry is one of the best in the series, with the usual array of gags and

tunes supported by the zany Wiere Brothers and singing guests the Andrews Sisters.

ROAD TO UTOPIA 1945
★★★ NR Comedy 1:30 B&W
Dir: Hal Walker *Cast:* Bing Crosby, Bob Hope, Dorothy Lamour, Hillary Brooke, Douglas Dumbrille, Jack LaRue
▶ Fourth Crosby-Hope teaming could be their best: washed up as vaudevillians, they head for gold-rush Alaska with a stolen mine deed. There they encounter saloon singer Lamour (who croons the pop hit "Personality"), the actual owner of the mine, as well as slimy villain Dumbrille. Full complement of sight gags and one-liners topped off with an amusing voice-over commentary by Robert Benchley.

ROAD WARRIOR, THE 1982 Australian
★★★ R Action-Adventure 1:35
☑ Rape, nudity, explicit language, violence
Dir: George Miller *Cast:* Mel Gibson, Bruce Spence, Vernon Wells, Emil Minty, Mike Preston, Virginia Hey
▶ Sequel to *Mad Max* continues the story of loner cop Gibson, who battles injustice in a harsh future where fuel is the most precious commodity. Minimalist plot concerns a desert commune besieged by punk villains for their primitive refinery. Influential international hit contains striking sets, startling violence, and some of the most incredible high-velocity chases every filmed. Followed by *Mad Max Beyond Thunderdome*.

ROARING TWENTIES, THE 1939
★★★ NR Crime 1:44 B&W
Dir: Raoul Walsh *Cast:* James Cagney, Humphrey Bogart, Priscilla Lane, Gladys George, Jeffrey Lynn
▶ Cagney and Bogart are World War I buddies who make bootlegging fortune. After the stock market crash, Cagney goes straight and turns against Bogart when he menaces Lane, the woman Cagney loves. Riproaring, hugely entertaining gangster classic. Great last line: "He used to be a big shot." Available in a colorized version.

ROBE, THE 1953
★★★★ NR Drama 2:15
Dir: Henry Koster *Cast:* Richard Burton, Jean Simmons, Victor Mature, Michael Rennie, Jay Robinson, Dean Jagger
▶ Episodic but richly inspirational drama about the impact of Christianity on the Roman tribune (Burton) ordered to crucify Christ. His slave (Mature) obtains Christ's miraculous robe, an object later coveted by mad emperor Caligula. Burton and his lover Simmons must choose between Christian martyrdom and obeying Caligula. Noteworthy as the first feature shot in CinemaScope; won Oscars for Best Costume Design and Art Direction. Mature would repeat his role in the sequel, *Demetrius and the Gladiators*.

ROBERTA 1935
★★★ NR Musical 1:45 B&W
Dir: William A. Seiter *Cast:* Irene Dunne, Fred Astaire, Ginger Rogers, Randolph Scott, Helen Westley, Luis Alberni
▶ Wispy plot about romance between football player Scott and Russian emigré clothes designer Dunne in Paris detracts somewhat from the beautiful Jerome Kern–Dorothy Fields–Jimmy McHugh score (including "Smoke Gets in Your Eyes," "Yesterdays," and the Oscar-nominated "Lovely to Look At"). Fred and Ginger play subsidiary roles in this fashion-oriented musical, but they steal the film with their witty duets to "I'll Be Hard to Handle" and "I Won't Dance."

ROBIN AND MARIAN 1976
★★★ PG Romance/Action-Adventure 1:47
☑ Adult situations, explicit language, violence
Dir: Richard Lester *Cast:* Sean Connery, Audrey Hepburn, Robert Shaw, Nicol Williamson, Richard Harris, Ronnie Barker
▶ Aging Robin Hood (Connery) returns to Sherwood Forest after twenty years' fighting in the Crusades and discovers Maid Marian (Hepburn) has become a nun in his absence. Robin renews their love affair and his battle with the evil Sheriff of Nottingham (Shaw). A supremely moving love story with touches of revisionist satire. Sweet chemistry between Connery and Hepburn (who returned to the screen after a decade in retirement), superb support from Williamson as the loyal Little John, literate screenplay and direction.

ROBIN AND THE SEVEN HOODS 1964
★★★ NR Musical 2:00
Dir: Gordon Douglas *Cast:* Frank Sinatra, Dean Martin, Sammy Davis, Jr., Bing Crosby, Peter Falk, Barbara Rush
▶ Pleasant musical comedy set in Prohibition-era Chicago. Gangster Sinatra inadvertently donates money to Crosby's

orphanage and enjoys the public's acclaim so much he steps up his contributions. Rival mobster Falk doesn't like the competition and sets out to ruin Sinatra's gang. Last Rat Pack film features Oscar-nominated "My Kind of Town" and Falk's amusing rendition of "All for One."

ROBINSON CRUSOE ON MARS 1964
★★★ NR Sci-Fi 1:49
Dir: Byron Haskin *Cast:* Paul Mantee, Adam West, Vic Lundin, Mona the Monkey
▶ Producer George Pal's sci-fi adaptation of the Daniel Defoe classic: Mantee is an astronaut who must survive on Mars after his spaceship crashes. Faithful monkey Mona is his only company until Friday shows up in the form of Lundin, an alien slave whom Mantee rescues from his captors. Literate and imaginative; Death Valley provides the eerie Martian backgrounds.

ROBOCOP 1987
★★★★ R Sci-Fi 1:43
☑ Explicit language, graphic violence
Dir: Paul Verhoeven *Cast:* Peter Weller, Nancy Allen, Daniel O'Herlihy, Ronny Cox, Kurtwood Smith, Miguel Ferrer
▶ In a grim Detroit future, Weller, a patrolman killed on duty, is reassembled into Robocop, a deadly anticrime machine. Weller's human memories interfere with Robocop's computer programs, leading him on a search for his killers that brings him dangerously close to the leaders of an android company. Eye-opening special effects and nonstop action made this a megahit. (CC)

ROBOT MONSTER 1953
☆ NR Sci-Fi 1:03 B&W
Dir: Phil Tucker *Cast:* George Nader, Claudia Barrett, Selena Royle, Gregory Moffett, John Mylong, George Barrows
▶ Alien creature, played by Barrows in a gorilla costume and diving helmet, is ordered to destroy life on Earth; Nader and Barrett are two of the humans who try to escape his wrath. Low-budget sci-fi is so ludicrous it has achieved the status of a camp classic. Originally released in 3-D.

ROCK AND ROLL HIGH SCHOOL 1979
★ PG Musical 1:32
☑ Explicit language
Dir: Allan Arkush *Cast:* P. J. Soles, Vincent Van Patten, Clint Howard, Dey Young, Mary Woronov, The Ramones
▶ At Vince Lombardi High, evil principal

Woronov tries to suppress her high-spirited student body, led by the bouncy Soles. Soles succeeds in bringing her favorite group, the Ramones, to the school, setting off a rockin' revolt against authority. Lightweight youth antics set to an energetic beat has inventive humor but little to offer adults.

ROCK & RULE 1985 Canadian
★★★ PG Animation/Adult 1:18
☑ Explicit language, adult humor
Dir: Clive A. Smith *Cast:* Voices of Don Francks, Paul LeMat, Susan Roman, Catherine O'Hara
▶ Feature-length rock cartoon set in the futuristic city of Ohmtown, where an aging rock star kidnaps a young singer as a human sacrifice to evil demons. Inventive visuals can't overcome predictable plot. Soundtrack includes Deborah Harry, Lou Reed, Iggy Pop, Cheap Trick, and Earth, Wind & Fire in a knockout version of "Dance, Dance, Dance."

ROCK AROUND THE CLOCK 1956
★★ NR Musical 1:18 B&W
Dir: Fred F. Sears *Cast:* Bill Haley and the Comets, The Platters, Tony Martinez and His Band, Frankie Bell and His Bellboys, Alan Freed, Johnny Johnston
▶ Freed, playing himself, discovers Bill Haley and the Comets and brings them to New York, where the band becomes a sensation by performing "See You Later, Alligator," "Razzle Dazzle," and the famous title tune. Almost nonexistent plot showcases "The Great Pretender" by the Platters, but also includes ephemera like "Codfish and Potatoes" by Tony Martinez.

ROCKET GIBRALTAR 1988
★★★ PG Drama 1:40
☑ Adult situations, explicit language
Dir: Daniel Petrie *Cast:* Burt Lancaster, Suzy Amis, Patricia Clarkson, Frances Conroy, Sinead Cusack, John Glover
▶ Grown children and grandchildren gather for dying patriarch Lancaster's birthday party. The little kids decide to grant the old man's wish for a Viking funeral while the adults are too busy to notice. Sweet and gentle; Lancaster interacts beautifully with the children, and the ending will leave you in tears.

ROCKIN' ROAD TRIP 1986
☆ PG-13 Comedy 1:41
☑ Adult situations, explicit language
Dir: William Olsen *Cast:* Garth McLean, Margaret Currie, Katherine Harrison, Steve Boles

► Rock band Cherry Suicide takes road trip from Boston to North Carolina. Pursued by robbers and a jealous boyfriend, they land a gig at a Christian revival meeting. Some chuckles and rousing tunes in cheesy drive-in fare.

ROCK, ROCK, ROCK 1956
★★ NR Musical 1:23 B&W
Dir: Will Price   *Cast:* Tuesday Weld, Jacqueline Kerr, Ivy Schulman, Jack Collins, Carol Moss, Alan Freed
► Mean father of teenybopper Weld (in her film debut) closes her charge account before she can buy a strapless gown for her prom. Ridiculous plot is fun on a camp level, but film's real appeal is an amazing collection of rock 'n' roll artists: Chuck Berry ("You Can't Catch Me"), Frankie Lymon and the Teenagers ("I'm Not a Juvenile Delinquent"), the Moonglows, the Flamingos, LaVern Baker, etc.

ROCKY 1976
★★★★★ PG Drama/Sports 1:59
☑ Explicit language, violence
Dir: John G. Avildsen   *Cast:* Sylvester Stallone, Talia Shire, Burt Young, Carl Weathers, Burgess Meredith, Thayer David
► Stallone, a club boxer/Mafia thumb-breaker from South Philly, gets unlikely title shot against publicity-hungry heavyweight champ Weathers. Mercilessly conditioned by gruff old trainer Meredith and inspired by shy girlfriend Shire, the Italian Stallion is determined to prove he's no palooka by going the distance with Weathers. Superior Hollywood hokum left crowds cheering and spawned three more films about America's favorite screen pugilist. Oscars for Best Picture, Director, and Editing. Inspirational soundtrack also a hit.

ROCKY II 1979
★★★★★ PG Drama/Sports 1:58
☑ Explicit language, violence
Dir: Sylvester Stallone   *Cast:* Sylvester Stallone, Talia Shire, Burt Young, Carl Weathers, Burgess Meredith, Tony Burton
► In the wake of his stunning draw against world champ Weathers, artless club fighter Stallone copes with sudden fame and inability to find work. After marriage to mousy girlfriend Shire, he cannot resist Weathers's taunting challenge for a rematch and resumes training under watchful eye of mentor Meredith, despite objections of Shire. When Shire

lapses into coma after childbirth, Stallone may lose will to fight. Generally successful sequel with another spirited finale bout.

ROCKY III 1982
★★★★★ PG Drama/Sports 1:39
☑ Explicit language, violence
Dir: Sylvester Stallone   *Cast:* Sylvester Stallone, Talia Shire, Carl Weathers, Burt Young, Burgess Meredith, Mr. T
► Now a superstar going soft, series hero Stallone loses title to tough and hungry challenger Mr. T in wake of death of longtime trainer Meredith. Determined to regain the heavyweight championship, Stallone learns quickness and moves from previous nemesis Weathers for showdown with Mr. T. Popular myth survives one more installment without losing too much vitality. Look for pre-Hulkamania Hogan in charity exhibition at movie's start.

ROCKY IV 1985
★★★★ PG Drama/Sports 1:31
☑ Explicit language, violence
Dir: Sylvester Stallone   *Cast:* Sylvester Stallone, Talia Shire, Burt Young, Carl Weathers, Dolph Lundgren, Brigitte Nielsen
► To avenge the death of friend and ex-champ Weathers and to defend the honor of his homeland, beloved boxer Stallone journeys to Russia for grudge match against seemingly superhuman Soviet Lundgren. Lundgren uses science and steroids to prepare for bout, but Rocky preps the old-fashioned way in frigid Siberia while wife Shire reluctantly decides to back him for another headbanger. Critics kvetched about tired boxing formula, but fans stayed in Rocky's corner all the way. (CC)

ROCKY HORROR PICTURE SHOW, THE
1975 British
★ R Musical/Sci-Fi 1:35
☑ Brief nudity, adult situations, explicit language
Dir: Jim Sharman   *Cast:* Tim Curry, Susan Sarandon, Barry Bostwick, Meat Loaf, Nell Campbell, Richard O'Brien
► Riotous, campy, and sexy horror spoof takes innocent couple Sarandon and Bostwick to Gothic home of Transylvanians led by transvestite mad-scientist Curry. Curry and his weirdo minions teach the straitlaced duo a thing or two about loosening up. Picture was originally box-office dud, but word-of-mouth devel-

oped unprecedented cult following based on audience interaction with the movie. Actor O'Brien also wrote songs, including "The Time Warp," "Science Fiction Double Feature," and "Sweet Transvestite." For midnight movie types only. Followed by *Shock Treatment*.

RODAN 1958 Japanese
★★ NR Sci-Fi 1:10 B&W
Dir: Inoshiro Honda *Cast:* Kenji Sawara, Yumi Shirakawa, Akihiko Hirata, Akio Kobori, Yasuko Nakata
▶ Just when you thought it was safe to go to Tokyo, flying reptile Rodan comes out of hibernation inside a mountain and proceeds to destroy all in its wake. Pretty silly, although those who enjoy *Godzilla* and *Mothra* will be entertained. Dubbed.

ROLLERBALL 1975
★★★ R Action-Adventure 2:03
☑ Adult situations, explicit language, violence
Dir: Norman Jewison *Cast:* James Caan, John Houseman, John Beck, Maud Adams, Moses Gunn, Pamela Hensley
▶ The future: man's need for violence (now outlawed) is fulfilled by spectator sport rollerball, an amalgam of football, roller derby, hockey, judo, and motorcycle racing. Caan, the best athlete in the game, is told to retire because he's grown too popular, but he refuses. Corporate/government elite make the game even deadlier to kill Caan. Director Jewison intended to condemn glorification of violence, but gripping rollerball action scenes often have opposite effect.

ROLLER BOOGIE 1979
★★ PG Comedy 1:44
☑ Adult situations, explicit language
Dir: Mark L. Lester *Cast:* Linda Blair, Jim Bray, Beverly Garland, Roger Perry, Jimmy Van Patten, Kimberly Beck
▶ Carefree rich girl Blair runs away from Beverly Hills home for roller-skating life in Venice Beach with boyfriend Bray. When mobsters threaten to take over the kids' favorite roller rink, Blair returns home to enlist aid of lawyer father Perry and eventually competes in climactic disco skating contest. Quickie effort to cash in on now defunct roller disco craze looks dated.

ROLLERCOASTER 1977
★★★★ PG Action-Adventure 1:58
☑ Explicit language, violence
Dir: James Goldstone *Cast:* George Segal, Richard Widmark, Timothy Bottoms, Henry Fonda, Susan Strasberg, Harry Guardino
▶ Extortionist Bottoms hides bombs in amusement parks and threatens to set them off unless he is paid $1 million. Safety inspector Segal tries to thwart Bottoms. Intelligent and quite involving; solid performances (especially Bottoms), canny use of everyday settings to increase the tension, sensational rollercoaster sequences. Originally released in Sensurround.

ROLLING THUNDER 1977
★★★★ R Action-Adventure 1:39
☑ Explicit language, graphic violence
Dir: John Flynn *Cast:* William Devane, Tommy Lee Jones, Linda Haynes, James Best, Dabney Coleman, Lisa Richards
▶ After eight years in a Vietcong POW camp, Devane returns to his Texas hometown a hero. But thieves murder his wife and son, and mutilate his hand in a garbage disposal. Aided by fellow ex-POW Jones, Devane sets out to execute the villains. Unusually good action film has an unpredictable script (by Paul Schrader and Heywood Gould) and strong interpretations of intense, complicated characters by Devane and Jones.

ROLLING VENGEANCE 1987
★★ R Action-Adventure 1:31
☑ Rape, adult situations, explicit language, violence
Dir: Steven Hilliard Stern *Cast:* Don Michael Paul, Lawrence Dane, Ned Beatty, Lisa Howard, Todd Duckworth, Michael J. Reynolds
▶ When he learns that his family has been murdered and his girlfriend raped by redneck thugs who hang out at Beatty's sleazy tavern, young trucker Paul constructs a Monster Truck with seventy-three-inch tires and a 600-horsepower engine to wreak revenge. Fast-paced exploitation features spectacular stunts that demolish over sixty vehicles.

ROLLOVER 1981
★★★ R Drama 1:55
☑ Adult situations, explicit language, violence
Dir: Alan J. Pakula *Cast:* Jane Fonda, Kris Kristofferson, Hume Cronyn, Josef Sommer, Bob Gunton
▶ Widow Fonda has affair with wheeler-dealer Kristofferson, who helps her take

over late husband's business. High-powered conspiracy involving Arab investment threatens the firm. Complex, disturbing, and topical. Fine Fonda, slick direction, and polished production marred somewhat by excessive talk and miscast Kristofferson.

ROMANCING THE STONE 1984
★★★★ PG Action-Adventure 1:46
☑ Adult situations, explicit language, violence
Dir: Robert Zemeckis *Cast:* Michael Douglas, Kathleen Turner, Danny DeVito, Zack Norman, Alfonso Arau, Manuel Ojeda
▶ Turner, the author of pulp romances, travels with mysterious package to South America to seek kidnapped sister. Norman, DeVito, Ojeda, and other assorted criminals pursue her for the treasure map she unwittingly possesses and soon she's lost in the wilds in her high heels. To her rescue comes adventurer Douglas. They team up to flee the bad guys and seek the treasure. Boisterous, wildly successful adventure with laughs, romance, and real sparks between the leads. Sequel: *The Jewel of the Nile.* **(CC)**

ROMAN HOLIDAY 1953
★★★★★ NR Romance 1:58 B&W
Dir: William Wyler *Cast:* Gregory Peck, Audrey Hepburn, Eddie Albert, Hartley Power, Tullio Carminati
▶ Sheltered princess Hepburn sneaks away from her official duties to enjoy the sights of Rome. Cynical reporter Peck befriends her, pretending not to know her true identity in hopes of getting the big scoop; but then they fall in love. Rome and Hepburn were never lovelier than in this gloriously romantic tale. The leads and Albert (as Peck's photographer pal) are splendid and the ending movingly bittersweet. Nine Oscar nominations—including Best Picture, Director, and Supporting Actor (Albert)—with Hepburn, scriptwriter Ian McLellan Hunter, and costumer Edith Head winning.

ROMAN SCANDALS 1933
★ NR Musical 1:31 B&W
Dir: Frank Tuttle *Cast:* Eddie Cantor, Ruth Etting, Gloria Stuart, David Manners, Edward Arnold, Alan Mowbray
▶ Amusing romp sends Cantor, an Oklahoma delivery boy, to ancient Rome in an extended dream. Food taster for evil emperor Arnold, he's thrown into a wild chariot race parodying *Ben Hur.* Dated

but enjoyable comedy highlighted by daring Busby Berkeley numbers, one featuring women (including young Lucille Ball) dressed only in long blond wigs.

ROMAN SPRING OF MRS. STONE, THE 1961
★★ NR Drama 1:44
Dir: Jose Quintero *Cast:* Vivien Leigh, Warren Beatty, Lotte Lenya, Jill St. John, Coral Browne, Jeremy Spenser
▶ Aging actress Leigh finds Rome romance with young Italian gigolo Beatty. Leigh's obsession grows but Beatty eventually jilts her for younger St. John. Poignant but dark love story features solid work from Leigh, Beatty, and Lenya (Oscar-nominated). Based on the Tennessee Williams novel.

ROMANTIC COMEDY 1983
★★★ PG Romance/Comedy 1:42
☑ Adult situations, explicit language, adult humor
Dir: Arthur Hiller *Cast:* Dudley Moore, Mary Steenburgen, Frances Sternhagen, Janet Eilber, Ron Leibman, Robyn Douglass
▶ As playwrights, the sophisticated Moore and the shy Steenburgen find collaborating on Broadway hits much easier than love; both go through other lovers and spouses before realizing their true feelings for one another. Likable leads but the writing and directing are lackluster. Lush Marvin Hamlisch score, some amusing moments. Based on Bernard Slade's play. **(CC)**

ROMANTIC ENGLISHWOMAN, THE 1975 British
★ R Drama 1:56
☑ Strong sexual content
Dir: Joseph Losey *Cast:* Glenda Jackson, Michael Caine, Helmut Berger, Kate Nelligan, Beatrice Romand, Michael Lonsdale
▶ Writer Caine works on tale of infidelity and finds life imitating art when wife Jackson has affair with smuggler Berger. Ambitious, sharply acted (by Caine and Jackson) and written (by Tom Stoppard) but overly complex and unsatisfying; for sophisticated tastes only.

ROMEO AND JULIET 1968 British/Italian
★★★★ PG Romance 2:17
☑ Brief nudity, adult situations, mild violence
Dir: Franco Zeffirelli *Cast:* Olivia Hussey, Leonard Whiting, Milo O'Shea, Michael York, John McEnery, Robert Stephens

▶ In Verona, teenagers Romeo (Whiting) and Juliet (Hussey) fall in love; however, their warring families insure the romance will be starcrossed. Definitive movie version of Shakespeare's play is gloriously romantic (Hussey and Whiting's balcony scene will take your breath away) and gorgeously mounted. Nominated for Best Picture and Director; won for Cinematography and Costume Design. Haunting music by Nino Rota.

ROOM AT THE TOP 1959 British
★★ NR Drama 1:57 B&W
Dir: Jack Clayton *Cast:* Laurence Harvey, Simone Signoret, Heather Sears, Donald Wolfit, Hermione Baddeley, Ambrosine Philpotts
▶ Incisive story about the rise of ambitious but amoral clerk Harvey in a grimy industrial town. Received six Oscar nominations, winning for Neil Paterson's screenplay and Signoret's haunting performance as an older woman whose life is ruined by Harvey when he leaves her for Sears, the daughter of a prominent businessman. Early example of the new wave of British realistic films was based on a novel by John Braine. Led to a 1965 sequel, *Man at the Top.*

ROOM SERVICE 1938
★★ NR Comedy 1:18 B&W
Dir: William A. Seiter *Cast:* The Marx Brothers, Lucille Ball, Ann Miller, Frank Albertson, Donald MacBride
▶ The John Murray–Allen Boretz Broadway comedy, adapted rather uneasily into a Marx Brothers vehicle. Groucho is the struggling producer of a play, trying to get his show off the ground while staying one step ahead of his creditors. Chico is the cheerfully obtuse director and Harpo his sidekick.

ROOM WITH A VIEW, A 1986 British
★★★ NR Drama 1:55
☑ Nudity, adult situations
Dir: James Ivory *Cast:* Maggie Smith, Denholm Elliott, Helena Bonham Carter, Julian Sands, Daniel Day-Lewis, Simon Callow
▶ Florence, 1907: well-to-do Englishwoman Carter begins to fall in love with socially unsuitable young Sands, son of rough-edged self-made businessman Elliott. Her alarmed chaperone Smith whisks Carter back to England where she's soon engaged to dull, blue-blooded fop Day-Lewis. By coincidence, Elliott and Sands move to the same vil-

lage so Carter is caught between passion and propriety. Beautiful production, quality performances, and witty-and-wise screenplay adapted from E. M. Forster novel. Won three Oscars. **(CC)**

ROOSTER COGBURN 1975
★★★★★ PG Western 1:47
☑ Violence
Dir: Stuart Millar *Cast:* John Wayne, Katharine Hepburn, Anthony Zerbe, Richard Jordan, Strother Martin, John McIntyre
▶ Hard-drinking one-eyed lawman Wayne, reprising his Oscar-winning role from *True Grit*, pursues outlaws Jordan and Zerbe, who have heisted Army wagon laden with nitroglycerin. On their trail he meets Bible-thumping schoolmarm Hepburn, whose preacher father has been slain by the bad guys. Male chauvinist Wayne has his doubts until feisty Hepburn proves a crack shot and ace horsewoman, so the two old coots team up to avenge her father's murder. Sometimes creaky and overly sentimental attempt at Western version of *The African Queen* is saved by presence of two movie legends.

ROOTS 1977
★★★★★ NR Drama/MFTV 9:00
Dir: David Greene *Cast:* LeVar Burton, John Amos, Ben Vereen, Edward Asner, Louis Gossett, Jr., Sandy Duncan
▶ In 1750, black African Kunte Kinte (played by Burton as a young man, Amos as an older one) is captured by slave traders and taken to America. Kinte attempts to escape several times, but freedom is something only his descendents will know. Massive miniseries, part of television history, is unmatched for sheer dramatic impact; from Alex Haley's best-selling account of his own African roots. Available in six ninety-minute tapes.

ROPE 1948
★★★ NR Mystery-Suspense 1:20
Dir: Alfred Hitchcock *Cast:* James Stewart, Farley Granger, John Dall, Cedric Hardwicke, Joan Chandler, Dick Hogan
▶ Bright but amoral college pals Granger and Dall murder friend Hogan for the intellectual thrill, strangling him with a rope in their apartment. To further their macabre game they hide the corpse on the premises and invite over Hogan's father Hardwicke, fiancée Chandler, and professor Stewart, whose

lectures inspired the slaying. As the evening wears on and Hogan's absence becomes alarming, Stewart grows suspicious of his pupils. An experiment for Hitchcock, film was shot in ten-minute takes spliced together to create the illusion of one seamless shot.

ROPE OF SAND 1949
★ ★ NR Action-Adventure 1:44 B&W
Dir: William Dieterle *Cast:* Burt Lancaster, Paul Henreid, Claude Rains, Peter Lorre, Corinne Calvet, Sam Jaffe
▶ In South Africa, thief/adventurer Lancaster attempts to recover hidden stolen diamonds while mining company chief Rains and his strongman Henreid use torture and the allure of prostitute Calvet to beat him to the treasure. Plenty of intrigue and action for adventure fans, with Rains, Henreid, and Lorre reunited in an effort to recapture *Casablanca* magic.

ROSARY MURDERS, THE 1987
★ ★ ★ R Mystery-Suspense 1:41
☑ Adult situations, explicit language, violence
Dir: Fred Walton *Cast:* Donald Sutherland, Charles Durning, Josef Sommer, Belinda Bauer, James Murtaugh, John Danelle
▶ Serial killer terrorizes Detroit, leaving rosary beads as clues. Unorthodox priest Sutherland tackles the case with beautiful reporter Bauer. Plodding mystery from a script by director Walton and Elmore Leonard. (CC)

ROSE, THE 1979
★ ★ ★ R Musical 2:14
☑ Adult situations, explicit language
Dir: Mark Rydell *Cast:* Bette Midler, Alan Bates, Frederic Forrest, Harry Dean Stanton, David Keith
▶ Oscar-nominated Midler is the heart and soul of this grandly tragic tale of hard rock, the road, and redemption. Bette's first feature performance, a composite portrait of several 1960s singers, especially Janis Joplin, is a powerhouse in every way. Enhanced by solid supporting roles from Bates as her overbearing manager and Forrest (nominated for Supporting Actor) as her lover. Electrifying concert footage features great music: "Stay With Me" and her swan song, "The Rose." Also nominated for Sound and Editing. (CC)

ROSEBUD BEACH HOTEL, THE 1984
★ R Comedy 1:22
☑ Nudity, adult situations, explicit language
Dir: Harry Hurwitz *Cast:* Colleen Camp, Peter Scolari, Christopher Lee, Fran Drescher, Eddie Deezen, Monique Gabrielle
▶ Scolari signs on as manager of a second-rate Florida hotel at the suggestion of girlfriend Camp. They deal with the odd staff which includes bellhop/call girl Drescher, while Camp's tycoon father Lee plots to blow up the place for the insurance money. Frantic and silly; the supporting cast (especially Drescher) steals it.

ROSELAND 1977
★ PG Drama 1:44
☑ Adult situations
Dir: James Ivory *Cast:* Joan Copeland, Geraldine Chaplin, Lilia Skala, Lou Jacobi, Christopher Walken, Teresa Wright
▶ Three stories set in New York City's Roseland Ballroom: widow Wright is obsessed with her dead husband until she meets the uncouth but sensitive Jacobi; gigolo Walken gets involved with three different women; and an old German woman, Skala, dreams of winning a dance contest. Affecting performances, great dancing, but talky and slow; the stories are rather depressing.

ROSE MARIE 1936
★ ★ ★ NR Musical 1:53 B&W
Dir: W. S. Van Dyke II *Cast:* Jeanette MacDonald, Nelson Eddy, Reginald Owen, Allan Jones, James Stewart, Alan Mowbray
▶ Lavish musical set in Canada: opera star MacDonald enlists Mountie Eddy's help in finding her brother Stewart. Discards most of the Otto Harbach–Oscar Hammerstein II play, but the soaring duets to "Indian Love Call" and others should please fans of light opera. Also known as *Indian Love Call*.

ROSEMARY'S BABY 1968
★ ★ ★ R Horror 2:17
☑ Rape, nudity, adult situations, explicit language
Dir: Roman Polanski *Cast:* Mia Farrow, John Cassavetes, Ruth Gordon, Maurice Evans, Ralph Bellamy, Charles Grodin
▶ Stylish classic based on Ira Levin's bestselling novel. When Farrow and Cassavetes move into a beautiful old New York City apartment building, it's to start

a new family. Little does Farrow realize that a coven of witches living next door is also eager for her to get pregnant—for a very diabolical reason! Gordon won Best Supporting Actress; Grodin's first film.

ROSE TATTOO, THE 1955
★★ **NR Drama 1:57 B&W**
Dir: Daniel Mann *Cast:* Anna Magnani, Burt Lancaster, Marisa Pavan, Ben Cooper, Jo Van Fleet, Virginia Grey
▶ In Louisiana, Sicilian widow Magnani remains obsessed with her late husband until truck driver Lancaster enters her life. Discovery of the dead man's infidelity helps pave way for new romance. Terrific adaptation of the Tennessee Williams play is dominated by Magnani's magnetic Oscar-winning performance (although Oscar-nominated Pavan holds her own as Magnani's daughter). Best Picture nominee also won for Cinematography and Art Direction/Set Decoration.

ROUGH CUT 1980
★★★★ **PG Mystery-Suspense 1:51**
☑ Adult situations, explicit language
Dir: Don Siegel *Cast:* Burt Reynolds, Lesley-Anne Down, David Niven, Timothy West, Patrick Magee, Susan Littler
▶ In England, American jewel thief Reynolds plans diamond caper and meets gorgeous socialite Down, who is working for Scotland Yard inspector Niven. Down falls for Reynolds and becomes his partner in crime. Escapist fare of a high order; slick production, attractive and charming performances, pleasant European locations.

'ROUND MIDNIGHT 1986 U.S./French
★★★ **R Drama/Music 2:11**
☑ Adult situations, explicit language
Dir: Bertrand Tavernier *Cast:* Dexter Gordon, François Cluzet, Gabrielle Haker, Sandra Reaves-Philips, Lonette McKee, Herbie Hancock
▶ Heartfelt tribute to 1950s jazz features a magnetic performance by real-life musician Gordon as Dale Turner, a talented but self-destructive saxophonist whose career is rescued by French fan Cluzet. Loosely based on the friendship between jazz great Bud Powell and Francis Paudras, film is more a series of vignettes than a coherent story. Herbie Hancock's score (which includes the title song and "How Long Has This Been Going On?") won an Oscar. Martin Scorsese has

a chilling cameo during a brief sequence in New York. (CC) ⑤

ROUSTABOUT 1964
★★ **NR Musical 1:41**
Dir: John Rich *Cast:* Elvis Presley, Barbara Stanwyck, Joan Freeman, Leif Erickson, Sue Ane Langdon, Pat Buttram
▶ Presley takes a job with Stanwyck's financially troubled carnival, and saves her from bankruptcy with his singing while falling in love with fellow worker Freeman. Enjoyable vehicle for the King, who sings "Little Egypt," "One Track Heart," "Wheels on My Heels," and "Big Love, Big Heartache." Unusual cast includes Jack Albertson, Billy Barty, Richard Kiel, and Raquel Welch in her film debut.

ROXANNE 1987
★★★ **PG Romance/Comedy 1:47**
☑ Adult situations, explicit language
Dir: Fred Schepisi *Cast:* Steve Martin, Daryl Hannah, Shelley Duvall, Rick Rossovich, Fred Willard, Michael J. Pollard
▶ Fire chief Martin has a big nose and a bigger problem: he loves astronomer Hannah, who is hung up on his hunky coworker Rossovich. Too shy to woo Hannah, Rossovich asks Martin to provide him with love letters and dialogue. Update of *Cyrano de Bergerac* is one of the best comedies of recent years; funny, charming, and lyrical. Imaginatively directed by Schepisi, delightfully acted by an acrobatic and poignant Martin. Funniest moment in Martin's screenplay: the barroom list of twenty nasal put-downs. (CC)

ROYAL FLASH 1975 British
★★ **PG Action-Adventure/Comedy 1:38**
☑ Adult situations, violence, explicit language
Dir: Richard Lester *Cast:* Malcolm McDowell, Alan Bates, Oliver Reed, Florinda Bolkan, Britt Ekland, Alastair Sim
▶ Nineteenth-century British swordsman Harry Flashman (McDowell) is a liar, coward, and braggart. He's also the hero as he battles Bates and Otto Von Bismarck (Reed), who attempt to use him as a pawn in a power-grabbing scheme. Unjustly overlooked and underrated adventure has the same combination of cynical humor, narrative drive, and romantic derring-do that made Lester's "Musketeer" films so delightful.

ROYAL WEDDING 1951
★★★ **NR Musical 1:33**

Dir: Stanley Donen   *Cast:* Fred Astaire, Jane Powell, Peter Lawford, Sarah Churchill, Keenan Wynn

▶ Queen Elizabeth II's wedding to Prince Philip provides the background to a slight romantic comedy about brother-sister team, Astaire and Powell, who find love with dancer Churchill (Sir Winston's daughter) and aristocrat Lawford in London. Despite a smooth score by Alan Jay Lerner and Burton Lane (Oscar-nominated "Too Late Now," "You're All the World to Me," etc.), memorable chiefly for two amazing Astaire routines: one a dance with a hat rack, the other his celebrated dancing-on-the-ceiling sequence.

R.P.M. 1970
★ R Drama 1:30
☑ Adult situations, explicit language, violence

Dir: Stanley Kramer   *Cast:* Anthony Quinn, Ann-Margret, Gary Lockwood, Paul Winfield, Graham Jarvis

▶ Student radicals take over university, naming popular liberal professor Quinn the new president. Unable to meet their demands, he must call in cops to quell a sit-in. Unintentionally funny when released, "hip" drama written by Erich Segal now seems as dated as the corny "Revolutions Per Minute" title.

R.S.V.P. 1984
★ R Sex 1:26
☑ Nudity, strong sexual content, explicit language

Dir: John Amero, Lem Amero   *Cast:* Ray Colbert, Veronica Hart, Lynda Wiesmeier, Harry Reems, Adam Mills, Lola Mason

▶ Colbert and Hart throw a Hollywood party for the publication of *Picnic Lunch*, a sex exposé. Guests include starlets, agents, and politicians who indulge in a wild orgy of sex and drugs culminating in an earthquake that proves fatal to a governor. Unexpectedly sophisticated sex comedy features a cast of famous porno stars.

RUBY GENTRY 1952
★★★ NR Drama 1:22 B&W
Dir: King Vidor   *Cast:* Jennifer Jones, Charlton Heston, Karl Malden, Tom Tully, Bernard Phillips

▶ Jones, sexy girl from the wrong side of the Carolina swamps, loves Heston but is embittered when he marries someone else. She marries his wealthy rival Malden

and plots revenge. Lurid, overheated, and quite entertaining melodrama with an intense love/hate relationship between Heston and Jones.

RUCKUS 1980
★★★★ PG Action-Adventure 1:31
☑ Adult situations, explicit language, violence

Dir: Max Kleven   *Cast:* Dirk Benedict, Linda Blair, Ben Johnson, Richard Farnsworth, Matt Clark

▶ Burnt-out Vietnam vet Benedict arrives in small town, runs afoul of local big-shot Johnson and townspeople. Only Johnson's widowed daughter-in-law Blair sides with Benedict as he uses his fighting skills against his tormentors. Well-staged action, good performances, credible middle-American atmosphere; story will have you rooting for Benedict.

RUDE BOY 1980 British
★★ R Musical 2:13
☑ Explicit language

Dir: Jack Hazan   *Cast:* The Clash, Ray Gange, Johnny Green, Barry Baker, Terry McQuade, Caroline Coon

▶ With little direction in life, cashier Gange gets gig as roadie for his favorite band, the Clash, but manages to mess up and get fired. Good rock music numbers, convincing portrait of alienated punk generation, but unintelligible accents and uneven production values. Strictly for the band's fans.

RUGGLES OF RED GAP 1935
★★★ NR Comedy 1:30 B&W
Dir: Leo McCarey   *Cast:* Charles Laughton, Mary Boland, Charles Ruggles, ZaSu Pitts, Roland Young

▶ Very proper English butler Laughton is won by vulgar American millionaire Ruggles in poker game and makes a surprisingly deft transition to the wild, wild West. Charming, sweet, and quite amusing; Laughton eschews his usual theatrics to deliver a quietly droll and touching performance.

RULES OF THE GAME 1939 French
☆ NR Comedy/Drama 1:46 B&W
Dir: Jean Renoir   *Cast:* Marcel Dalio, Nora Gregor, Mila Parely, Jean Renoir, Roland Toutain, Paulette Dubost

▶ On eve of World War II, French aristocrats, including famous aviator Toutain and his confidant (played by director Renoir), gather at home of dapper toy collector Dalio and his wife Gregor. During weekend of hunting and partying, various flirtations among both rich and servants merge in chaos ("Stop this farce!" demands Dalio; "Which one?" asks his butler) until one too many cases of mistaken identity brings a tragic end to the high jinks. Satire of morals and manners features striking compositions, deep-focus photography, and splendid performances, especially Dalio and Renoir. Ⓢ

RULING CLASS, THE 1972 British
★★ PG Comedy/Drama 2:24
☑ Brief nudity, adult situations, explicit language, mild violence, adult humor
Dir: Peter Medak *Cast:* Peter O'Toole, Alastair Sim, Harry Andrews, Arthur Lowe, Coral Browne
▶ "When I pray to Him, I find I'm talking to myself," explains O'Toole when asked why he fancies himself to be Jesus Christ. O'Toole's family initially indulges his fantasy so they can live off his money, but plots against him as his madness gets out of hand. Brilliant black comedy based on play by Peter Barnes loses some of its impact in screen translation. Only for devoted fans of the genre.

RUMBLE FISH 1983
★★ R Drama 1:34 B&W
☑ Nudity, explicit language, violence
Dir: Francis Coppola *Cast:* Matt Dillon, Mickey Rourke, Diane Lane, Dennis Hopper, Diana Scarwid, Vincent Spano
▶ Troubled Tulsa teenager Dillon, living with alcoholic dad Hopper, gets visit from biker older brother Rourke whom he worships. Rourke's desire to liberate rare fish from pet store leads to conflict with cop. Audacious yet emotionally remote; technically brilliant cinematography and sound but arch dialogue and cold characters are never grounded in recognizable reality. From the S. E. Hinton novel.

RUMPELSTILTSKIN 1987
★★★ G Musical/Family 1:24
Dir: David Irving *Cast:* Amy Irving, Clive Revill, Billy Barty, Priscilla Pointer, John Moulder-Brown
▶ Miller's daughter Irving must turn straw into gold or be executed by king Revill. Dwarf Barty helps her out but then demands her first born—unless she can guess his name. Straightforward fairy tale lacks the magic of Shelley Duvall's *Faerie Tale Theatre,* but is wholesome and suitable for the very young. Songs are sappy but Barty is a delight. Irving's brother directed, and her mother Priscilla Pointer makes a guest appearance. **(CC)**

RUNAWAY 1984
★★★★ PG-13 Sci-Fi 1:40
☑ Brief nudity, explicit language, violence
Dir: Michael Crichton *Cast:* Tom Selleck, Cynthia Rhodes, Kirstie Alley, Gene Simmons, Stan Shaw
▶ Pretty blond cop Rhodes is assigned to robotics expert Selleck, who suffers from vertigo. They're called in when someone's modifications transform domestic robots into murder machines. Bad guy Luther (Simmons, from rock group Kiss) kidnaps Selleck's son and holds him high atop a building under construction. Farfetched formula helped by clever special effects, terrific craftsmanship, and the always easy-to-watch Selleck. **(CC)**

RUNAWAY TRAIN 1985
★★★ R Action-Adventure 1:47
☑ Explicit language, graphic violence
Dir: Andrei Konchalovsky *Cast:* Jon Voight, Eric Roberts, Rebecca De Mornay, Kyle T. Heffner, John P. Ryan, Kenneth McMillan
▶ In Alaska, hardened convict Voight breaks out of jail with younger colleague Roberts. They hop a freight but find themselves on a runaway train when the engineer suffers a fatal heart attack. Exciting action and stunts but unsavory characterizations and pretentious dialogue. Intense performances by Voight and Roberts nabbed Oscar nominations. Based on a screenplay by Akira Kurosawa. **(CC)**

RUNNER STUMBLES, THE 1979
★★★★ PG Drama 1:50
☑ Adult situations, explicit language
Dir: Stanley Kramer *Cast:* Dick Van Dyke, Kathleen Quinlan, Beau Bridges, Ray Bolger, Tammy Grimes, Maureen Stapleton
▶ In a 1920s mining town, priest Van Dyke falls in love with rebellious young nun Quinlan. When she is murdered, he is defrocked and tried for the crime. Intriguing tale holds interest throughout; strong performances (especially Quinlan), top-notch cinematography, solid period atmosphere. From Milan Stitt's play. **(CC)**

RUNNING 1979
★★★★ PG Drama 1:42
☑ Explicit language
Dir: Steven Hilliard Stern *Cast:* Michael

Douglas, Susan Anspach, Lawrence Dane, Eugene Levy, Charles Shamata, Jim McKay
► Marathon runner Douglas, a personal and professional flop, makes one last stab at making the U.S. Olympic team. Doubted by his coach Dane but encouraged by ex-wife Anspach, he overcomes the odds against him. Douglas is quite believable and the running sequences are well shot. Rousing big race finale provides an uplifting closing kick.

RUNNING BRAVE 1983
★ ★ ★ ★ **PG Biography/Sports 1:46**
☑ Brief nudity, adult situations, mild violence
Dir: D. S. Everett *Cast:* Robby Benson, Pat Hingle, Claudia Cron, Jeff McCracken, August Schellenberg, Graham Greene
► True story of Billy Mills (Benson), the American Indian runner who overcame prejudice and personal crises to win a gold medal at the 1964 Olympics. Along the way, he gets support from his WASP wife Cron and tough coach Hingle. Irresistible story with sympathetic hero and thrilling (if predictable) finale; Benson's best screen work to date.

RUNNING MAN, THE 1987
★ ★ ★ **R Sci-Fi/Action-Adventure 1:41**
☑ Explicit language, violence
Dir: Andrew Davis *Cast:* Arnold Schwarzenegger, Maria Conchita Alonso, Yaphet Kotto, Richard Dawson, Jim Brown, Jesse Ventura
► In 2017, pilot Schwarzenegger disobeys fascist regime's orders and is forced to become contestant on deadly TV game show. He must run for his life while being hunted down by killers. "I'll be back," Schwarzenegger promises the unctuous host (perfectly cast Dawson) and you know he ain't kidding. Fast-moving futuristic fun is noisy but energetic. Based on the novel by Richard Bachman (Stephen King).

RUNNING ON EMPTY 1988
★ ★ ★ ★ **PG-13 Drama 1:55**
☑ Adult situations, explicit language
Dir: Sidney Lumet *Cast:* Christine Lahti, Judd Hirsch, River Phoenix, Martha Plimpton, L. M. Kit Carson, Steven Hill
► Sixties radicals Lahti and Hirsch have been on the lam for fifteen years after blowing up napalm lab, moving from town to town and changing their names to avoid capture by the Feds. When their

teenage son Phoenix decides to apply for a Juilliard music scholarship, it precipitates a family crisis. The adults are fine but it is the sensitive Phoenix and the marvelously natural Plimpton as his girlfriend who dominate this provocative and moving story. Quite engrossing with a haunting emotional payoff.

RUNNING SCARED 1986
★ ★ ★ ★ **R Action-Adventure 1:47**
☑ Nudity, adult situations, explicit language, violence
Dir: Peter Hyams *Cast:* Gregory Hines, Billy Crystal, Dan Hedaya, Steven Bauer, Jimmy Smits, Darlanne Fluegel
► Hectic male-bonding melodrama features top-notch team of Crystal and Hines as two cool Chicago cops looking to retire to Florida after a bloody confrontation with aspiring Spanish godfather Smits. They're forced back onto the streets when Smits kidnaps Crystal's ex-wife Fluegel. Nonstop banter is rowdy, intimate, and often very funny. Fresh action ending staged at Chicago's cavernous Illinois State Building. **(CC)**

RUNNING WILD 1973
★ ★ ★ ★ **G Drama 1:43**
Dir: Robert McCahon *Cast:* Lloyd Bridges, Dina Merrill, Pat Hingle, Morgan Woodward, Gilbert Roland
► Merrill, a journalist visiting the high country of Colorado, organizes animal rights campaign when she learns that a herd of wild horses is threatened by a local dog food canning factory. Upbeat, family-oriented drama features a strong cast and beautiful scenery.

RUN SILENT, RUN DEEP 1958
★ ★ ★ **NR War 1:33 B&W**
Dir: Robert Wise *Cast:* Clark Gable, Burt Lancaster, Jack Warden, Brad Dexter, Don Rickles, Nick Cravat
► World War II sub commander Gable is the only survivor of a Japanese attack. Distrusted by the crew of his new sub (in particular executive officer Lancaster), he embarks on a foolhardy mission to sink an enemy destroyer. Tense, claustrophobic drama adapted from Commander Edward L. Beach's best-seller features a valiant performance by Gable.

RUSSIAN ROULETTE 1975
★ ★ ★ **PG Mystery-Suspense 1:33**
☑ Explicit language, mild violence
Dir: Lou Lombardo *Cast:* George Segal, Cristina Raines, Denholm Elliott,

Louise Fletcher, Bo Brundin, Peter Donat
▶ Mountie Segal is assigned to guard Soviet premier Kosygin during Canadian visit. Segal infiltrates local agitators only to discover KGB reactionaries plan to slay the Russian leader and frame the CIA for the hit. Above-average espionage caper gets off to confusing start but soon moves into high gear with Segal effective as rogue detective.

RUSSIANS ARE COMING, THE RUSSIANS ARE COMING, THE 1966
★★★★ NR Comedy 2:06
Dir: Norman Jewison **Cast:** Carl Reiner, Eva Marie Saint, Alan Arkin, Brian Keith, Jonathan Winters, Theodore Bikel
▶ Surprise hit about a Soviet submarine that runs aground off the New England coast. A landing crew led by Arkin takes Reiner hostage and searches for a motorboat to tow the sub off the sandbar. Meanwhile, sheriff Keith and sidekick Winters have their hands full as panic spreads and the town mobilizes to defend itself from an imagined attack. Light-hearted parody of Cold War tension is still effective; Arkin was Oscar-nominated in his screen debut.

RUSSKIES 1987
★★★★ PG Drama 1:38
☑ Explicit language
Dir: Rick Rosenthal **Cast:** Whip Hubley, Peter Billingsley, Leaf Phoenix, Stefan DeSalle, Susan Walters, Carole King
▶ On the Fourth of July, Russian radio operator Hubley is shipwrecked on a Key West beach while on a mission. Local kids Billingsley, Phoenix, and DeSalle discover him. Their initial mistrust soon turns to East-West friendship. Amiable civics lesson, especially for the young, with adorable kids and comforting conclusion.

RUSTLERS' RHAPSODY 1985
★★ PG Western/Comedy 1:28
☑ Explicit language, violence, adult humor
Dir: Hugh Wilson **Cast:** Tom Berenger, G. W. Bailey, Marilu Henner, Andy Griffith, Fernando Rey, Sela Ward
▶ White-suited singing cowboy Berenger aids sheepherders in battle against evil cattlemen and wins the hearts of town "hostess" Henner and colonel's daughter Ward. Cute spoof with amusing supporting cast, especially Henner and Patrick Wayne as a good guy hired by the bad

guys to confuse Berenger; a bit skimpy on big laughs, however. **(CC)**

RUTHLESS PEOPLE 1986
★★★★ R Comedy 1:38
☑ Nudity, explicit language, adult humor
Dir: Jerry Zucker **Cast:** Bette Midler, Danny DeVito, Judge Reinhold, Helen Slater, Anita Morris
▶ Spandex miniskirt king DeVito is planning to kill heiress wife Midler when he discovers she's been kidnapped. Abductors Reinhold and Slater demand $500,000 "or else" if Sam calls the cops. He opens champagne, calls his mistress Morris, and promptly alerts the police and media. Cheerfully boisterous comedy about bad manners proves nastiness is its own reward.

RYAN'S DAUGHTER 1970 British
★★★★ PG Drama 3:18
☑ Brief nudity, adult situations, explicit language
Dir: David Lean **Cast:** Robert Mitchum, Sarah Miles, John Mills, Christopher Jones, Trevor Howard, Leo McKern
▶ Ireland, 1916: willful young Miles, married to middle-aged schoolteacher Mitchum, has affair with British major Jones that scandalizes the locals and leads to tragic consequences. Sweeping love story, directed by Lean on an epic scale. Oscars for Supporting Actor Mills as the village idiot and the lovely cinematography; Miles was nominated for Best Actress.

SABOTAGE 1936 British
★★ NR Mystery-Suspense 1:16 B&W
Dir: Alfred Hitchcock **Cast:** Sylvia Sidney, Oscar Homolka, John Loder, Desmond Tester, Joyce Barbour, Matthew Boulton
▶ Foreign terrorist Homolka establishes a cover in London as a movie theater manager. His unhappy wife Sidney gradually suspects him, and turns to Scotland Yard undercover agent Loder for help. Chilling thriller based on Joseph Conrad's *The Secret Agent* has a flawed plot despite impressive work by Sidney. Notable for two of Hitchcock's most famous scenes: a controversial depiction of an explosion and a fascinating murder performed after a screening of Walt Disney's cartoon *Who Killed Cock Robin?*

SABOTEUR 1942
★★★ PG Mystery-Suspense 1:48 B&W

☑ Violence
Dir: Alfred Hitchcock *Cast:* Robert Cummings, Priscilla Lane, Otto Kruger, Alan Baxter, Alma Kruger
► Cummings, falsely implicated for torching a war factory, embarks on cross-country chase to nab the real culprit, Nazi agent Kruger. Fast-paced thrills from the opening bit with the gas-filled fire extinguisher to the famous cliffhanging climax at the Statue of Liberty, although callow Cummings is miscast.

SABRINA 1954
★ ★ ★ ★ ★ **NR Romance/Comedy 1:53 B&W**
Dir: Billy Wilder *Cast:* Humphrey Bogart, Audrey Hepburn, William Holden, Walter Hampden, John Williams, Martha Hyer
► After Paris education, chauffeur's daughter Hepburn returns to Long Island estate where dad works and attracts the attention of two scions: swinging swain Holden and his stuffy older brother Bogart. Sparkling romantic triangle, nicely played by the three leads. Oscar for Costume Design.

SAD SACK, THE 1957
★ ★ **NR Comedy 1:38 B&W**
Dir: George Marshall *Cast:* Jerry Lewis, David Wayne, Phyllis Kirk, Peter Lorre, Gene Evans, Liliane Montevecchi
► George Baker's popular comic strip about the perennial Army loser gave Lewis his second starring role without Dean Martin. Loosely structured plot sends Lewis to Morocco, where he falls for slinky singer Montevecchi. Spurned, he joins the Foreign Legion, where his photographic memory is exploited by Arab bandit Lorre. Predictable high jinks buoyed by Lorre's amusing performance.

SAFARI 3000 1982
★ ★ **PG Action-Adventure 1:31**
☑ Brief nudity, adult situations, explicit language
Dir: Harry Hurwitz *Cast:* David Carradine, Stockard Channing, Christopher Lee, Hamilton Camp, Ian Yule
► American stunt-driver Carradine teams with live-wire journalist Channing for the African International Rally. Various entanglements over the 2,500-mile course include crumbling bridges, irritable locals, hostile competitors. Amid such adversity, antagonism betweens the leads turns to love. Only mild humor but very attractive visuals of African landscape and fauna.

SAFETY LAST 1923
★ ★ **NR Comedy 1:18 B&W**
Dir: Sam Taylor, Fred Newmeyer *Cast:* Harold Lloyd, Mildred Davis, Noah Young, Bill Strother, Mickey Daniels
► Country boy Lloyd moves to the city, attempts to succeed while winning the girl of his dreams. Upward mobility takes a comic turn when circumstances force him to climb a skyscraper, an amazing sequence (done without camera trickery) that features the immortal image of Lloyd hanging from the face of a clock. Silent classic is filled with nifty sight gags. Lloyd's upbeat persona is quite winning.

SAHARA 1943
★ ★ ★ ★ **NR War 1:37 B&W**
Dir: Zoltan Korda *Cast:* Humphrey Bogart, Bruce Bennett, Lloyd Bridges, Rex Ingram, J. Carrol Naish, Dan Duryea
► Top-notch World War II adventure about an American tank led by Bogart fleeing the Germans after the fall of Tobruk. Bogart rescues a band of stragglers and finds refuge from the withering heat in the ruins of an Arabian desert village. His men make a heroic stand against a Nazi battalion desperate for water. Canny use of survival themes, racial conflicts, and thrilling battles combine into a superior film with integrity and excitement. Received three Oscar nominations, including Naish's convincing Italian POW.

SAHARA 1984
★ **PG Action-Adventure 1:51**
☑ Adult situations, mild violence
Dir: Andrew V. McLaglen *Cast:* Brooke Shields, Lambert Wilson, John Mills, Horst Buchholz, John Rhys-Davies, Steve Forrest
► In 1927, Shields poses as a man to enter Sahara road race. After winning warm-up heat, her identity is revealed and she is kidnapped by tribal leaders; handsome sheik Wilson comes to her rescue. Conventional, nicely mounted, but no surprises. Shields is pleasant to watch although she lacks the depth to be really convincing.

SAILOR WHO FELL FROM GRACE WITH THE SEA, THE 1976 British
★ ★ ★ ★ **R Drama 1:45**
☑ Nudity, adult situations, explicit language, violence
Dir: Lewis John Carlino *Cast:* Sarah

Miles, Kris Kristofferson, Jonathan Kahn, Margo Cunningham, Earl Rhodes, Paul Tropea

▶ Young Kahn is initially pleased when Kristofferson passionately courts his widowed mother Miles, but friends convince him that the sailor cannot maintain integrity on land. Solemn adaptation of a Yukio Mishima novel gained some notoriety for its graphic eroticism, but story ultimately turns glum and violent.

SAINT JACK 1979
★★ R Drama 1:50
☑ Nudity, adult situations, explicit language
Dir: Peter Bogdanovich *Cast:* Ben Gazzara, Denholm Elliott, James Villiers, Peter Bogdanovich, Lisa Lu

▶ Jack Flowers (Gazzara), a pimp with a heart of gold, runs a bordello in Singapore for U.S. soldiers recovering from the Vietnam war. When local competitors bring down the operation, Flowers works for American mobster Bogdanovich, but draws the line at blackmailing a U.S. senator. Vivid portrayal of the seamier side of Singapore, fine supporting performance from Elliott as a dreary English accountant who befriends Flowers, and a perfect role for the always interesting Gazzara.

SAINT JOAN 1957
☆ NR Drama 1:51 B&W
Dir: Otto Preminger *Cast:* Jean Seberg, Richard Widmark, Anton Walbrook, John Gielgud, Harry Andrews

▶ Lackluster historical drama set in 15th-century France about Seberg, a simple country girl who hears voices telling her to lead her people into battle, enabling the Dauphin (Widmark) to be crowned. Undermined by the Earl of Warwick (Gielgud), she is eventually burned at the stake as a witch. Tepid screen version of G. B. Shaw play; strong cast with exception of Seberg who's way beyond her depth in her film debut, after being discovered by Preminger during a huge talent search. Available in a colorized version.

SAKHAROV 1984
★★★★★ NR Biography/MFTV 1:58
☑ Adult situations
Dir: Jack Gold *Cast:* Jason Robards, Glenda Jackson, Nicol Williamson, Frank Finlay, Marion Bailey, Michael Bryant

▶ Russian physicist Andrei Sakharov (Robards) speaks out against human rights abuses. He and wife Jackson suffer hardships, persecution, and exile but his actions provoke the conscience of the world; he is eventually awarded the Nobel Peace Prize. Gripping and powerful true story with stirring performances by Robards and Jackson.

SALAAM BOMBAY! 1988 Indian
★★ NR Drama 1:53
☑ Adult situations, explicit language
Dir: Mira Nair *Cast:* Shafiq Syed, Raghubir Yadav, Aneeta Kanwar, Nana Patekar, Chanda Sharma

▶ Indian youngster takes menial jobs after being forced out of home. He befriends drug addict who steals from him and teenage prostitute who seeks to escape pimp. Harrowing and often moving look at the street children of Bombay, wonderfully acted by a nonprofessional cast. Nominated for Best Foreign Film Oscar. Ⓢ

SALAMANDER 1981 U.S./British/Italian
★ NR Drama 1:41
☑ Brief nudity, adult situations, explicit language, mild violence
Dir: Peter Zinner *Cast:* Franco Nero, Anthony Quinn, Sybil Danning, Martin Balsam, Claudia Cardinale, Christopher Lee

▶ When an Italian general dies under suspicious circumstances, cop Nero investigates and uncovers a right-wing plot to take over the government. Along the way, Nero has an affair with Polish spy Danning. Serviceable premise, decent acting, breathtaking locations, but tangled plotting and stiff dialogue.

SALEM'S LOT: THE MOVIE 1979
★★★ PG Horror 1:51
☑ Mild violence
Dir: Tobe Hooper *Cast:* David Soul, James Mason, Bonnie Bedelia, Lance Kerwin, Lew Ayres, Elisha Cook, Jr.

▶ Novelist Soul returns to the Maine town of Salem's Lot and discovers his boyhood house has been sold to sinister antique dealer Mason. Supernatural hell breaks loose: vampires materialize and young children disappear. Goose-bumping gimmicks include opening graves, barking doors, creaking fences, and gusting wind. Certain to please fans of Stephen King, who wrote the original novel. Originally shown on television in two parts, videocassette version contains more explicit violence.

SALOME 1953
★★★ NR Drama 1:43
Dir: William Dieterle *Cast:* Rita Hayworth, Stewart Granger, Charles Laughton, Judith Anderson, Cedric Hardwicke, Alan Badel
▶ Costly Biblical epic completely distorts story of infamous seductress, presenting her as a secret Christian sympathizer in love with soldier/convert Granger. Still entertaining, with Hayworth especially ravishing during her dance of the seven veils and Laughton chewing the scenery as Herod.

SALOME'S LAST DANCE 1988 British
☆ R Drama 1:29
☑ Nudity, adult situations, explicit language
Dir: Ken Russell *Cast:* Glenda Jackson, Stratford Johns, Nickolas Grace, Douglas Hodge, Imogen Millais-Scott, Denis Ull
▶ In 1892, Oscar Wilde attends secret premiere of his banned play *Salome* in the homosexual brothel that would later figure in his arrest. Amateur cast for the play includes brothel proprietor Johns and his servant Millais-Scott (in her film debut). Overwrought version of already florid play may strike viewers as camp.

SALSA 1988
★★ PG Drama/Dance 1:36
☑ Adult situations, explicit language
Dir: Boaz Davidson *Cast:* Robby Rosa, Rodney Harvey, Magali Alvarado, Miranda Garrison, Moon Orona, Angela Alvarado
▶ Auto mechanic Rosa rehearses feverishly to win top prize in a Los Angeles salsa contest, trading in girlfriend Angela Alvarado for older dancing partner Orona. He also watches over young sister Magali Alvarado, who's just starting to date. Thin plot doesn't detract from sensational salsa numbers choreographed by Kenny Ortega (*Dirty Dancing*). Music by Tito Puente, Celia Cruz, Mongo Santamaria, etc. Also available in a Spanish language version.

SALTY 1974
★★★★ G Comedy/Family 1:33
Dir: Ricou Browning *Cast:* Clint Howard, Mark Slade, Nina Foch, Julius W. Harris, Linda Scruggs
▶ Orphan Howard and his brother Slade befriend an intelligent, fun-loving sea lion fond of practical jokes. Predictable fam-

ily-oriented high jinks aided by pretty Florida locations.

SALVADOR 1986
★★★★ R Action-Adventure 2:03
☑ Rape, adult situations, explicit language, graphic violence
Dir: Oliver Stone *Cast:* James Woods, James Belushi, John Savage, Michael Murphy, Cynthia Gibb, Elpidia Carrillo
▶ Journalist Woods and DJ buddy Belushi go to El Salvador. Woods uncovers the corruption and oppression of the U.S.-backed military while trying to aid girlfriend Carrillo. Vivid, unsettling, hard-hitting, and real; Stone's direction rivals his *Platoon* for its sheer intensity. Woods nabbed an Oscar nomination for his magnificently edgy performance as the real-life Richard Boyle (who was nominated for co-authoring the script with Stone). **(CC)**

SALVATION! 1987
☆ R Comedy 1:20
☑ Rape, nudity, adult situations, explicit language, violence
Dir: Beth B *Cast:* Stephen McHattie, Dominique Davalos, Exene Cervenka, Viggo Mortensen, Rockets Redglare, Billy Bastiani
▶ Sexy Davalos seduces televangelist McHattie, who's then blackmailed into starring on new TV show with her sister Cervenka. Broad lampoon of corrupt religious ministries surfaced during downfall of Jim and Tammy Faye Bakker. Scores some effective points but suffers from weak screenplay. Rock star Cervenka performs "Destroy All Evil"; other songs include director Beth B's cult rock video "The Dominatrix Sleeps Tonight." Full title: *Salvation! Have You Said Your Prayers Today?*

SALZBURG CONNECTION, THE 1972
★★ PG Drama 1:33
☑ Explicit language, violence
Dir: Lee H. Katzin *Cast:* Barry Newman, Anna Karina, Klaus Maria Brandauer, Maren Jensen, Joe Maross
▶ Trunk filled with names of Nazi collaborators is found in an Austrian lake. While authorities debate whether to reveal its contents, vacationing American lawyer Newman is drawn into a puzzling conspiracy involving the CIA and foreign agents. Austrian locations bring some life to this tepid adaptation of a Helen MacInnes novel.

SAME TIME, NEXT YEAR 1978
★★★★★ PG Romance/Comedy
1:59
☑ Adult situations, explicit language,
adult humor
Dir: Robert Mulligan *Cast:* Ellen Bur-
styn, Alan Alda, Ivan Bonar, Bernie
Kuby
► Burstyn and Alda, married but not to
each other, have an annual affair at a
California inn. Over a 26-year period, the
one-weekend-a-year lovers see each
other through several crises. Captivating,
warm, witty, and very romantic, with ex-
cellent Burstyn and Alda, well-crafted di-
rection from Mulligan, and sweet Marvin
Hamlisch score. Oscar nominations: Best
Actress (Burstyn), Screenplay Adaptation
(Bernard Slade from his Broadway hit),
Song ("The Last Time I Felt Like This"),
Cinematography.

SAMMY AND ROSIE GET LAID 1987
British
★★ R Comedy/Drama 1:40
☑ Nudity, adult situations, explicit language, violence
Dir: Stephen Frears *Cast:* Shashi Kapoor, Frances Barber, Ayub Khan Din,
Claire Bloom, Roland Gift, Wendy Gazelle
► Pakistani fascist Kapoor visits accountant son Din and his antiestablishment
English wife Barber in a racially torn London ghetto. Kapoor renews acquaintance with old flame Bloom but his son's
open marriage and countercultural lifestyle shock him. Ambitious, seething, and
rowdy comedy has complex characters
(especially Kapoor) and darkly funny sexual shenanigans (three couplings in a
montage set to "My Girl"), although political slant makes it not for all tastes.

SAMSON AND DELILAH 1950
★★★ NR Drama 2:07
Dir: Cecil B. DeMille *Cast:* Victor Mature, Hedy Lamarr, George Sanders,
Angela Lansbury, Henry Wilcoxon
► Extravagant biblical epic about the ill-
fated romance between the legendary
muscleman Samson (Mature) and the
treacherous Philistine Delilah (Lamarr).
Samson first wins the hand of beautiful
princess Lansbury by killing a lion bare-
handed; betrayed, he lays waste the
Saran's (Sanders) soldiers until he is
tricked by the wily Delilah. Enormous cast
and intricate special effects helped
make this a popular success. Won Oscars
for costumes and art direction.

SAN ANTONIO 1945
★★★ NR Western 1:51
Dir: David Butler *Cast:* Errol Flynn,
Alexis Smith, S. Z. Sakall, Victor Francen,
Florence Bates, Paul Kelly
► Rancher Flynn uncovers saloon owner
Kelly's cattle rustling operation; Smith, a
performer at Kelly's joint, becomes in-
volved with Flynn. Flynn fights, Smith sings,
and the story moves along briskly if not
memorably.

SAND PEBBLES, THE 1966
★★★ NR Action-Adventure 3:15
Dir: Robert Wise *Cast:* Steve
McQueen, Richard Attenborough, Rich-
ard Crenna, Candice Bergen, Mako,
Marayat Andriane
► In China, lone wolf McQueen is as-
signed to the engine room of a U.S. Navy
gunboat patrolling the Yangtze River.
Civil war breaks out, and ship's captain
Crenna must balance diplomacy
against self-preservation. Meanwhile,
McQueen falls in love with missionary Ber-
gen. Epic adventure about American in-
tervention abroad was nominated for
Best Picture, Actor (McQueen), Supporting Actor (Mako as McQueen's machinist
sidekick), and five technical Oscars.

SANDPIPER, THE 1965
★★★★ NR Romance 1:57
☑ Adult situations, explicit language
Dir: Vincente Minnelli *Cast:* Elizabeth
Taylor, Richard Burton, Eva Marie Saint,
Charles Bronson, Tom Drake
► Classy soap opera set against California's scenic Big Sur: artist Taylor enrolls her
son in private school run by married cler-
gyman Burton. After initial conflict, a love
affair develops between Taylor and Burton that threatens his career and marriage to Saint. Slightly dated but the stars
transcend the material. Oscar for Best
Song ("The Shadow of Your Smile").

SANDS OF IWO JIMA, THE 1949
★★★★ NR War 1:50
Dir: Allan Dwan *Cast:* John Wayne,
John Agar, Adele Mara, Forrest Tucker,
James Brown, Richard Webb
► Wayne, winning his first Oscar nomination, plays a World War II sergeant whose
expertly trained men were a major factor
in the battle of Iwo Jima. Realistic plot
follows the men through jungle exercises,
harsh fighting on Tarawa, R&R leaves,
and climactic effort to take Mt. Suribachi.
Film is enhanced by use of documentary
war footage and appearances by three

of the soldiers in the famous flag-raising photograph (Ira Hayes, Rene Gagnon, John Bradley).

SAN FRANCISCO 1936
★★★★ **NR Drama 1:55 B&W**
Dir: W. S. Van Dyke II *Cast:* Clark Gable, Jeanette MacDonald, Spencer Tracy, Jack Holt, Ted Healy, Margaret Irving
▶ Barbary Coast gambler Gable and singer MacDonald fall in love. His rough ways hinder both the romance and his friendship with priest Tracy, both of which are further disrupted by the 1906 earthquake. Lusty, brawling saga is a great deal of fun, thanks to the star power of the leads and the magnificent earthquake sequence. Many musical numbers include MacDonald's famous warbling of the title tune.

SANTA CLAUS 1985
★★★★ **PG Family 1:52**
☑ Explicit language
Dir: Jeannot Szwarc *Cast:* Dudley Moore, John Lithgow, David Huddleston, Burgess Meredith, Judy Cornwell
▶ Large-scale fantasy about the origin of Santa Claus (Huddleston), a kindly woodcutter magically transported to a toy-filled workshop at the North Pole. Conflict between bumbling elf Moore and evil toy baron Lithgow provides plot complications. Intricate special effects will enthrall young viewers. Also known as *Santa Claus: The Movie*. (CC)

SANTA CLAUS CONQUERS THE MARTIANS 1964
☆ **NR Sci-Fi 1:20**
Dir: Nicholas Webster *Cast:* John Call, Victor Stiles, Donna Conforti, Vincent Beck, Bill McCutheon, Pia Zadora
▶ Santa Claus and two Earthling children are kidnapped by Martians but all ends happily as old St. Nick introduces the joys of Christmas to the angry red planet. Silly screenplay, chintzy sets, and memorably wacky theme song ("Hurray for Santa Claus!") add up to a camp classic.

SANTA FE TRAIL 1940
★★★★ **NR Western 1:50 B&W**
Dir: Michael Curtiz *Cast:* Errol Flynn, Olivia de Havilland, Raymond Massey, Ronald Reagan, Alan Hale, Van Heflin
▶ Unusual Western set in 1854 Kansas: West Point pals Jeb Stuart (Flynn) and George Custer (Reagan) battle each other over beautiful tomboy de Havilland while infiltrating John Brown's (Massey)

dangerous abolitionist movement. Culminates in the famous Harpers Ferry siege. Muddled as history and often uncomfortably pro-slavery, but furious pacing and large-scale action scenes are exciting. Available in a colorized version.

SAPPHIRE 1959 British
★★ **NR Mystery-Suspense 1:32**
Dir: Basil Dearden *Cast:* Nigel Patrick, Yvonne Mitchell, Michael Craig, Paul Massie, Bernard Miles
▶ In London, a black woman who was passing for white is murdered. Among the many suspects: members of her boyfriend's bigoted family. Absorbing whodunit with a social conscience; fine ensemble acting, tight script, intriguing John Dankworth jazz score. Frank depiction of racial slurs could offend some.

SATISFACTION 1988
★★★ **PG-13 Drama 1:32**
☑ Adult situations, explicit language
Dir: Joan Freeman *Cast:* Justine Bateman, Liam Neeson, Trini Alvarado, Scott Coffey, Britta Phillips, Julia Roberts
▶ Four-girl, one-guy inner-city rock band Mystery wins an audition for a summer-long gig at a posh seaside resort. Lead singer Bateman has a fling with alcoholic, Grammy-winning songwriter Neeson; Phillips overdoses on pills; Roberts finds love in the back of a van. Predictable teen flick isn't helped by nondescript songs. Debbie Harry has a brief cameo. (CC)

SATURDAY NIGHT FEVER 1977
★★★ **PG Drama/Dance 1:52**
☑ Brief nudity, adult situations
Dir: John Badham *Cast:* John Travolta, Karen Lynn Gorney, Barry Miller, Donna Pescow, Julie Bovasso, Joseph Cali
▶ Blockbuster megahit made Travolta a household name. Tony Manero (Travolta), a nineteen-year-old paint store salesman in Brooklyn, lives for Saturday nights at the local disco where he's the star dancer. He enters a dance contest with new partner Gorney, ultimately decides his life is a "cliché" and moves to Manhattan. Not much on plot but great dancing scenes and phenomenally successful, pulse-pounding Bee Gees score includes hits "Night Fever," "How Deep Is Your Love," "More Than a Woman," many more. Sequel: *Staying Alive*.

SATURDAY THE 14TH 1981
★★ **PG Horror/Comedy 1:16**
☑ Explicit language, violence

Dir: Howard R. Cohen   *Cast:* Richard Benjamin, Paula Prentiss, Severn Darden, Jeffrey Tambor, Kari Michaelson, Kevin Brando
▶ Benjamin and Prentiss inherit haunted house and try to make the best of it when assorted monsters and spooks make themselves part of the household. Family tires of finding Creature from the Black Lagoon in bath tub, so they throw an exorcism party to rid themselves of the guests that won't leave. Sophomoric horror spoof.

SATURN 3 1980
★ ★ R Sci-Fi 1:27
☑ Nudity, adult situations, violence
Dir: Stanley Donen   *Cast:* Farrah Fawcett, Kirk Douglas, Harvey Keitel, Douglas Lambert, Ed Bishop
▶ Somewhere in deep, dark space, scientists Fawcett and Douglas jog around an enclosed space station. Enter creepy bad guy Keitel, who installs Hector, a lust-crazed humanoid robot who terrorizes the inhabitants of this outer-orbit Garden of Eden. Best scene: Hector's resurrection after he has been dismantled for being randy.

SAVAGE DAWN 1985
★ ★ NR Action-Adventure 1:42
☑ Adult situations, explicit language, violence
Dir: Simon Nuchtern   *Cast:* George Kennedy, Richard Lynch, Karen Black, Lance Henriksen, Claudia Udy, William Forsythe
▶ Vietnam hero Henriksen visits his vet friend Kennedy, now confined to a wheelchair. They are attacked by a gang of vicious bikers led by Forsythe. Neighbors, including paranoid preacher Lynch and surly bar owner Black, are powerless to stop the villains until Henriksen takes charge. Low-budget exploitation redeemed somewhat by inventive motorcycle stunts.

SAVAGE STREETS 1984
★ ★ R Action-Adventure 1:33
☑ Rape, nudity, explicit language, graphic violence
Dir: Danny Steinmann   *Cast:* Linda Blair, John Vernon, Robert Dryer, Johnny Venocur, Sal Landi
▶ Punks led by Dryer gang rape a deaf-mute and murder a bride on her wedding day. Blair, the deaf-mute's older sister, assembles her girlfriends for revenge. Explicit, often gratuitously violent drama

features campy dialogue and a satisfying vigilante theme.

SAVANNAH SMILES 1982
★ ★ ★ ★ ★ PG Family 1:44
☑ Mild violence
Dir: Pierre DeMoro   *Cast:* Mark Miller, Donovan Scott, Bridgette Andersen, Peter Graves, Michael Parks, Pat Morita
▶ Perfect family entertainment, a comedy/drama that delivers in every way. Poor little six-year-old rich girl Savannah (Andersen) runs away from snooty parents and hooks up with Miller and Scott, a pair of on-the-run criminals with hearts of teddy bears. Holding her for ransom, they set up what turns into a very loving household. Genuine laughs, moments of true warmth and tenderness, and an ending that defies you not to shed a tear. One of the highest-rated, best-loved movies ever shown on HBO.

SAVE THE TIGER 1973
★ ★ ★ R Drama 1:42
Dir: John G. Avildsen   *Cast:* Jack Lemmon, Jack Gilford, Laurie Heineman, Norman Burton, Thayer David
▶ Oscar-winner Lemmon in a sobering, sensitive portrait of a middle-aged clothing manufacturer whose life and business are failing. In desperation, he decides to burn his factory for the insurance money, despite the objections of partner Gilford. Serious-minded examination of the failure of the American dream feels sluggish at times but packs a powerful punch.

SAVING GRACE 1986
★ ★ ★ ★ PG Drama 1:52
☑ Explicit language, violence
Dir: Robert M. Young   *Cast:* Tom Conti, Giancarlo Giannini, Fernando Rey, Erland Josephson, Edward James Olmos
▶ Sentimental but heartfelt tale about man-of-the-people Pope (Conti) who wanders away from the Vatican one day and ends up in a remote small town without a priest, where everyone pretends to be quarantined in order to receive relief money. Vatican officials Rey and Josephson keep the Pope's absence a secret. Conti succeeds in redeeming the town, including mysterious goatherd Giannini. Pleasant, likable entertainment.   **(CC)**

SAY AMEN, SOMEBODY 1983
★ ★ ★ ★ G Documentary/Music 1:40
Dir: George T. Nierenberg   *Cast:* Willie Mae Ford Smith, Thomas A. Dorsey, Sallie Martin, The Barrett Sisters, The O'Neal Brothers, Jackson Price

▶ Jubilant documentary about gospel music, the "sanctified blues." Mixing music scenes with exploration of colorful characters, picture pays special attention to two legends of gospel's roots: "Mother" Smith and Dorsey, the acknowledged "Father of Gospel Music." Uplifting, first-class production is fine for all ages.

SAYONARA 1957
★★★★ NR Drama 2:31
☑ Adult situations, explicit language
Dir: Joshua Logan *Cast:* Marlon Brando, James Garner, Red Buttons, Miyoshi Umeki, Miiko Taka, Ricardo Montalban
▶ Adapted from the James Michener novel about the love affair between U.S. pilot Brando and Japanese singer Taka during Korean War. Features wonderful performances from quality cast, exotic locale, and convincing story. Winner of four Oscars, incuding Best Supporting Actor and Actress to Buttons and Umeki.

SAY YES 1986
★★ PG-13 Comedy 1:30
☑ Nudity, adult situations, explicit language
Dir: Larry Yust *Cast:* Lissa Layng, Art Hindle, Logan Ramsey, Jonathan Winters, Maryedith Burrell
▶ Good-natured comedy with a familiar premise: playboy Hindle must marry before his thirty-fifth birthday or lose his immense inheritance. Winters displays his delightful off-the-wall humor as the curmudgeonly grandfather, but story suffers from flat jokes.

SCALPEL 1976
★★★ PG Horror 1:36
☑ Brief nudity, explicit language, mild violence
Dir: John Grissmer *Cast:* Robert Lansing, Judith Chapman, Arlen Dean Snyder, David Scarroll, Sandy Martin
▶ Brilliant plastic surgeon Lansing murders his wife and the boyfriend of daughter Chapman. Chapman disappears just as Lansing learns she's heir to five million dollars. He remodels a bargirl's face in an effort to steal the inheritance. Tricky plot enlivens this low-budget effort shot on location in Georgia. Also known as *False Face.*

SCANDALOUS 1984
★★ PG Comedy 1:34
☑ Brief nudity, adult situations, explicit language

Dir: Rob Cohen *Cast:* John Gielgud, Robert Hays, Pamela Stephenson, Jim Dale, M. Emmet Walsh, Jim Magill
▶ Beautiful con artist Stephenson falls in love with mark Hays and tries to reshape the scam, but her veteran con man uncle Gielgud balks. Matters grow more complicated when Hays's wealthy wife is killed and detective Dale tries to pin murder rap on him. Lame-brained thriller farce gets off to fine start but runs out of gas.

SCANNERS 1981 Canadian
★★ R Horror 1:42
☑ Adult situations, graphic violence
Dir: David Cronenberg *Cast:* Jennifer O'Neill, Stephen Lack, Patrick McGoohan, Lawrence Dane, Michael Ironside, Charles Shamata
▶ Maternity drug with bizarre side effects creates "scanners," humans with telekinetic powers who can cause others' heads to explode. One such man, Lack, is recruited by weaponry corporation to infiltrate in-house conspiracy to take over the world by other scanners Dane and Ironside. Aided by beautiful scanner comrade O'Neill, Lack battles his evil counterparts. Literally mind-blowing special effects in the service of average premise and script.

SCARAMOUCHE 1952
★★★ NR Action-Adventure 1:58
Dir: George Sidney *Cast:* Stewart Granger, Eleanor Parker, Janet Leigh, Henry Wilcoxon, Mel Ferrer, Nina Foch
▶ Nobleman Granger has two good reasons to seek vengeance against marquis Ferrer: he killed Granger's best pal and is engaged to marry his beloved Leigh. Granger trains as an actor, learns to wield a mean sword, and battles his nemesis. Sterling swashbuckler based on the Rafael Sabatini novel.

SCARECROW 1973
★ R Drama 1:52
☑ Adult situations, explicit language, violence
Dir: Jerry Schatzberg *Cast:* Gene Hackman, Al Pacino, Dorothy Tristan, Ann Wedgeworth, Richard Lynch, Eileen Brennan
▶ Ex-con Hackman, hoping to open a car wash in Pittsburgh, teams up with merchant seaman Pacino, who plans reconciliation with his estranged wife in Detroit, for a journey across an extremely bleak America. Episodic road movie fea-

tures superior performances, particularly Hackman's unpredictably violent drifter, but plot often feels aimless.

SCARED STIFF 1987
★ R Horror 1:23
☐ Explicit language, graphic violence
Dir: Richard Friedman *Cast:* Andrew Stevens, Mary Page Keller, Josh Segal, David Ramsey, William Hindman
▶ Rock singer Keller, her son Segal, and her psychiatrist boyfriend Stevens move into Gothic Southern mansion. When Keller suffers terrifying hallucinations, Stevens at first believes she's having a relapse of a nervous breakdown. Soon enough the three learn that their new home is cursed—its original owner slaughtered innocents in voodoo rituals. Southern-fried chiller will appeal mainly to genre fans.

SCARFACE 1932
★★ PG Crime/Drama 1:30
☐ Violence
Dir: Howard Hawks *Cast:* Paul Muni, Ann Dvorak, George Raft, Boris Karloff, Karen Morley, Osgood Perkins
▶ Extraordinary story of Chicago hoodlum Tony Camonte (Muni), his amoral sister Dvorak, and violent henchman Raft is among the most violent and shocking gangster movies ever made. Based on the career of Al Capone, plot is uncompromising in its depiction of a ruthless, lethal underworld. Plagued by censors for its suggestions of incest and twenty-eight on-screen murders, film was recut by producer Howard Hughes, then withdrawn from circulation for forty years. Muni and Raft became overnight stars for their brutal performances. Loosely remade in 1983 with Al Pacino.

SCARFACE 1983
★★★ R Crime/Drama 2:53
☐ Nudity, adult situations, explicit language, graphic violence
Dir: Brian De Palma *Cast:* Al Pacino, Michelle Pfeiffer, Steven Bauer, Robert Loggia, Mary Elizabeth Mastrantonio, F. Murray Abraham
▶ Flashy, big-budget remake of the Howard Hawks 1932 classic tells the story of Cuban refugee Tony Montana (Pacino), who rises from cocaine courier to top kingpin of the drug world. He takes blond mistress Pfeiffer from crime boss Loggia, kills Bauer, the lover of his kid sister Mastrantonio, and spirals into a cocaine frenzy that leads to a final shootout in his Miami mansion. Written by Oliver Stone. Be warned: R rated for very strong violence: dismemberments, hangings, knifings, etc.

SCARLET CLAW, THE 1944
★★★ NR Mystery-Suspense 1:14 B&W
Dir: Roy William Neill *Cast:* Basil Rathbone, Nigel Bruce, Gerald Hamer, Paul Cavanagh, Arthur Hohl, Kay Harding
▶ Canada, 1944: Rathbone as Sherlock Holmes and Bruce as Dr. Watson attend a conference on the supernatural. The local villagers hold a legendary monster responsible for a rash of murders, but Holmes proves contemporary vengeance is behind the killings. Better-than-average outing for Rathbone and Bruce in modernized version of Arthur Conan Doyle's classics.

SCARLET PIMPERNEL, THE 1934 British
★★ NR Action-Adventure 1:35 B&W
Dir: Harold Young *Cast:* Leslie Howard, Merle Oberon, Raymond Massey, Nigel Bruce, Bramwell Fletcher, Joan Gardner
▶ As her aristocratic friends are guillotined during the eighteenth-century Reign of Terror, Oberon, a lady in the court of the Prince of Wales, loses faith in her foppish husband Howard—unaware he's secretly the daredevil freeing many of the prisoners. Howard approaches his role with relish in this rousing adaptation of Baroness Orczy's swashbuckling adventure.

SCARLET STREET 1945
★★ NR Mystery-Suspense 1:43 B&W
Dir: Fritz Lang *Cast:* Edward G. Robinson, Joan Bennett, Dan Duryea, Margaret Lindsay, Rosalind Ivan, Jess Barker
▶ Gloomy tale of mild-mannered clerk Robinson's infatuation with Bennett, a mysterious woman he rescues from a mugging. Her secret lover Duryea takes advantage of Robinson's artwork, leading to a murder with an ironic double twist. Remake of 1931's *La Chienne* re-teamed three stars from *The Woman in the Window* for a similarly bleak study of revenge.

SCARRED 1984
★ R Drama 1:25
☐ Nudity, strong sexual content, adult situations, explicit language
Dir: Rose Marie Turko *Cast:* Jennifer Mayo, Jackie Berryman, David Dean, Rico L. Richardson, Debbie Dion, Lili
▶ Single mother Mayo is forced into pros-

titution to pay the rent, reluctantly allowing Dean to pimp for her. Honest look at unsavory subject suffers from budget restrictions, but realistic view of seedy Los Angeles settings is powerful. Young Mayo is impressive as the resilient heroine.

SCARS OF DRACULA 1971 British
★★ R Horror 1:33
☑ Adult situations, explicit language, violence
Dir: Roy Ward Baker *Cast:* Christopher Lee, Dennis Waterman, Jenny Hanley, Christopher Matthews, Patrick Troughton, Michael Gwynn
▶ Lured to Count Dracula's castle by a seductive vampiress, Matthews gets fanged. Young couple Waterman and Hanley battle cobwebs, bats, and worse in search of Matthews. Climactic showdown with Lee, heir to Bela Lugosi as the Dracula of choice.

SCAVENGER HUNT 1979
★★★★ PG Comedy 1:56
☑ Explicit language
Dir: Michael Schultz *Cast:* Richard Benjamin, James Coco, Scatman Crothers, Ruth Gordon, Cloris Leachman, Cleavon Little
▶ Broad, frantic comedy with five greedy teams in a mad scramble to fulfill the weird obligations of game manufacturer's will by competing in a treasure hunt. Among their targets to find: obese people, ostriches, toilets, and beehives. All-star cast includes bizarre cameos by Arnold Schwarzenegger, Meat Loaf, Tony Randall, Avery Schreiber, Dirk Benedict, others.

SCAVENGERS 1988
★★ PG-13 Action-Adventure 1:34
☑ Explicit language, violence
Dir: Duncan McLachlan *Cast:* Kenneth David Gilman, Brenda Bakke, Crispin De Nys, Cocky Tlhothalemaj
▶ Adventure parody set primarily in Africa, with KGB and CIA agents chasing virile hero Gilman and his girlfriend Bakke for secret information hidden in a Bible. Extended chase featuring vintage planes, tanks, and jeeps is high-spirited, but generic plot and low production values are big drawbacks.

SCENE OF THE CRIME 1986 French
☆ NR Drama 1:31
☑ Nudity, adult situations, explicit language, violence
Dir: Andre Techine *Cast:* Catherine Deneuve, Danielle Darrieux, Wadeck

Stanczak, Nicolas Giraudi, Victor Lanoux, Jean Bousquet
▶ Young Giraudi, threatened by deadly drifter Stanczak, draws his repressed mother Deneuve into a mysterious plot involving murder, escaped convicts, and blackmail. Intriguing premise and a polished performance by Deneuve can't overcome murky story line. Best moments involve Deneuve's strained relationship with ex-husband Lanoux. ⑤

SCENES FROM A MARRIAGE 1974 Swedish
☆ PG Drama 2:48
☑ Adult situations, explicit language
Dir: Ingmar Bergman *Cast:* Liv Ullmann, Erland Josephson, Bibi Andersson, Jan Malmsjo, Anita Wall, Gunnel Lindblom
▶ Challenging, intimately detailed depiction of a troubled marriage focuses on Ullmann's grief at learning her husband Josephson is seeing a younger woman. Edited down from a six-part Swedish TV miniseries, film's incessant close-ups and emotionally traumatic themes are often uncomfortably vivid. ⑤

SCENES FROM THE GOLDMINE 1987
★★ R Drama/Musical 1:45
☑ Explicit language
Dir: Marc Rocco *Cast:* Catherine Mary Stewart, Steve Railsback, Cameron Dye, Joe Pantoliano, John Ford Coley, Timothy B. Schmit
▶ Keyboard player Stewart joins rock band and becomes involved with lead singer Dye. But when record magnate Pantoliano dangles dollars at Dye, he changes for the worse, stealing Stewart's songs, asking his brother Railsback to quit as band's manager, and developing cocaine addiction. Lots of tunes in credible look at cut-throat music biz.

SCHIZOID 1980
★★ R Mystery-Suspense 1:31
☑ Nudity, adult situations, explicit language, graphic violence
Dir: David Paulsen *Cast:* Klaus Kinski, Marianna Hill, Craig Wasson, Donna Wilkes, Richard Herd, Christopher Lloyd
▶ Newspaper columnist Hill, member of a therapy group run by psychiatrist Kinski, receives evidence about a series of gruesome murders that implicates both Kinski and her estranged husband Wasson. Strong acting adds to the agreeably creepy atmosphere in this crude but effective chiller.

SCHLOCK 1971
☆ **PG Comedy 1:20**
☑ Explicit language, mild violence
Dir: John Landis *Cast:* John Landis,
Saul Kahan, Joseph Piantadosi, Eliza
Garrett, Laslo Benedek
▶ Sophomoric spoof of science fiction
films stars director Landis as missing-link
ape man brought back to life in modern
California. Leaving telltale banana peels
as clues, he goes on killing spree that
baffles authorities. Landis's sometimes in-
spired directing debut is filled with film
school jokes and cameos. Also known as
The Banana Killer.

SCHOOL DAZE 1988
★ **R Musical/Comedy 1:54**
☑ Adult situations, explicit language
Dir: Spike Lee *Cast:* Larry Fishburne,
Giancarlo Esposito, Tisha Campbell,
Kyme, Ossie Davis, Spike Lee
▶ Feisty, often funny, but unstructured
and episodic chronicle of life on all-black
campus. School is split between conservative Wannabee fraternity and socially
conscious, independent Jigaboos. Over
homecoming weekend Wannabee
head Esposito and Jigaboo leader Fishburne clash over everything except the
ineptitude of young frat pledge Lee.
Many zippy dance-and-music numbers
and spirited lampooning of fraternities in
somewhat scattershot satire. **(CC)**

SCORPION 1986
★★★ **R Action-Adventure 1:39**
☑ Violence
Dir: William Riead *Cast:* Tonny Tulleners, Don Murray, Robert Logan, Allen
Williams, Kathryn Daley, Ross Elliott
▶ Secret agent Tulleners, code name
Scorpion, disposes of four hijackers
before untrustworthy government lawyer
Murray assigns him to safeguard a terrorist informant. A double cross leads Scorpion on a mission of revenge. Former karate champ Tulleners displays his martial
arts prowess in four hand-to-hand battles.

SCREAM AND SCREAM AGAIN 1970
British
★★ **PG Horror 1:35**
☑ Adult situations, explicit language,
violence
Dir: Gordon Hessler *Cast:* Vincent
Price, Christopher Lee, Peter Cushing,
Judy Huxtable, Alfred Marks
▶ Gruesome thriller about mad scientist
Price conducting amputation experi-

ments for a conspiracy led by vicious sadist Cushing. Lee's murder investigations
and subplot about military secrets add
unnecessary confusion, but three horror
stars are in top form.

SCREAM FOR HELP 1984
★★ **R Mystery-Suspense 1:30**
☑ Nudity, adult situations, explicit language, violence
Dir: Michael Winner *Cast:* Rachael
Kelly, Marie Masters, David Brooks,
Lolita Lorre, Rocco Sisto
▶ Young Kelly is convinced that her stepfather Brooks is trying to kill her mother
Masters. Police refuse to believe her,
even after murderous traps lead to the
deaths of a power company worker and
her best friend. Effective shocker from the
maker of *Death Wish* features some jar-
ringly violent scenes.

SCREEN TEST 1985
★★ **R Sex/Comedy 1:24**
☑ Nudity, strong sexual content, explicit language, adult humor
Dir: Sam Auster *Cast:* Michael Allen
Bloom, Monique Gabrielle, Robert
Bundy, David Simpatico, Paul Leuken,
William Dick
▶ Four sex-starved teens hold auditions
for phony porno video in order to meet
willing women. The aspiring stars who
show up include an aging stripper, kinky
plastic surgeon, Mafia princess, and dog
in a face mask. When daddy of Mafia
princess threatens death unless kids
come up with nonexistent video, the
boys must scramble to shoot a real picture.

SCREWBALL ACADEMY 1987 Canadian
★ **R Comedy 1:27**
☑ Nudity, adult situations, explicit language
Dir: John Blanchard *Cast:* Colleen
Camp, Kenneth Welsh, Christine Cat-
tell, Charles Dennis, Angus MacInnes,
Damian Lee
▶ Thin farce about ad executive Camp
making a low-budget feminist film on a
resort island where corrupt televangelist
Lee is dodging a Federal investigation
into his finances. Low-budget attempt at
teen-oriented slapstick was filmed in
1983 and never released theatrically.

SCREWBALLS 1983
★ **R Comedy 1:20**
☑ Nudity, explicit language, adult
humor
Dir: Rafal Zielinski *Cast:* Peter Keleg-

han, Linda Shayne, Alan Daveau, Kent Deuters, Jason Warren, Lynda Speciale
▶ Male students at Taft & Adams High School try a variety of tricks to deflower Purity Bush (Speciale), the school's sole remaining virgin. Stunts include a fraudulent medical exam, a strip bowling contest, and visits to the girls' locker room. Raunchy low-brow humor in the *Porky's* mold.

SCROOGE 1970 British
★★ G Musical 1:58
Dir: Ronald Neame *Cast:* Albert Finney, Alec Guinness, Edith Evans, Kenneth More, Michael Medwin, Laurence Naismith
▶ Glossy, big-budget musical version of classic Christmas tale by Charles Dickens. Old skinflint Finney is transformed overnight by ghosts Guinness, More, and Evans into jolly do-gooder. Distinguished cast, quality production, and music by Leslie Bricusse, author of tunes for *Dr. Doolittle*, make this decent family fare, although many critics panned it on release. **(CC)**

SCROOGED 1988
★★★★ PG-13 Comedy 1:41
☑ Explicit language
Dir: Richard Donner *Cast:* Bill Murray, Karen Allen, John Forsythe, Carol Kane, Bob Goldthwait, David Johansen
▶ Modern-day version of Dickens's *A Christmas Carol* stars Murray as a Scrooge-like network TV mogul who finally learns to put a little love in his heart when visited by ghosts Forsythe, Johansen, and Kane. Hilarious and heartwarming comedy with Murray's trademark brash humor topped off by a surprisingly emotional ending. Among many funny scenes: Murray dictating Christmas gift list ("Towel, towel, VCR . . . "), figuring out how to put antlers on mice, and watching commercial for "Robert Goulet's Cajun Christmas."

SCRUBBERS 1984 British
★ R Drama 1:33
☑ Adult situations, explicit language, violence
Dir: Mai Zetterling *Cast:* Amanda York, Chrissie Cotterill, Elizabeth Edmonds, Kate Ingram, Debby Bishop, Dana Gillespie
▶ Vivid but extremely grim look at girls' reform school, focusing on York's attempts to cope with violence and lesbianism and Cotterill's efforts to find a

guardian for her child. Unflinching portrait is uncomfortably realistic.

SEA GYPSIES, THE 1978
★★★★ G Family 1:41
Dir: Stewart Raffill *Cast:* Robert Logan, Mikki Jamison-Olson, Heather Rattray, Cjon Damitri Patterson, Shannon Saylor
▶ Seattle widower Logan sets sail around world with daughters Saylor and Rattray and two last-minute additions, cute female reporter Jamison-Olson and young black stowaway Patterson. Storm maroons motley crew on Alaskan coast. Agreeable family adventure combines spectacular wildlife and scenery with an engaging Seattle Family Robinson yarn.

SEA HAWK, THE 1940
★★★★ NR Action-Adventure 2:07 B&W
Dir: Michael Curtiz *Cast:* Errol Flynn, Brenda Marshall, Claude Rains, Donald Crisp, Flora Robson, Henry Daniell
▶ In the sixteenth century, Queen Elizabeth (Robson) suspects the Spaniards are building an armada to attack England but lacks evidence. Gallant sea captain Flynn combats plot by Spanish ambassador Rains while trying to prove worthy of the love of Rains's beautiful daughter Marshall. Rousing old-fashioned adventure, with action on seas off Spain, England, and Panama, boasts swashbuckling Flynn at his finest.

SEANCE ON A WET AFTERNOON 1964 British
★★ NR Mystery-Suspense 1:55 B&W
Dir: Bryan Forbes *Cast:* Kim Stanley, Richard Attenborough, Mark Eden, Nanette Newman, Judith Donner, Patrick Magee
▶ Inventive, gripping drama about half-crazed psychic Stanley, who forces her weak-willed husband Attenborough to stage the kidnapping of a young girl for publicity purposes. Unpredictable plot twists and cunning direction maintain story's relentless pacing. Stanley received an Oscar nomination for her bravura performance.

SEARCH AND DESTROY 1981
★★★ PG Action-Adventure 1:33
☑ Adult situations, explicit language, violence
Dir: William Fruet *Cast:* Perry King, Don Stroud, Tisa Farrow, Park Jong Soo, George Kennedy, Tony Sheer
▶ Special Forces experts King and Stroud abandon Vietnamese officer Soo to care

for a wounded buddy. Ten years later, the vindictive Soo stalks the veterans through Niagara Falls, determined to kill them. Kennedy plays a policeman seeking an end to the feud. Good locations add to film's extended chase sequences.

SEARCHERS, THE 1956
★★★★★ NR Western 1:59
Dir: John Ford   *Cast:* John Wayne, Natalie Wood, Vera Miles, Jeffrey Hunter, Ward Bond, John Qualen
▶ When his brother and sister-in-law are savagely killed by Comanches, Civil War veteran Wayne begins seven-year search for their kidnapped daughter Wood. Wayne delivers arguably the finest performance of his career as a man caught between civilization and savagery in this landmark Western. Director Ford's masterpiece, an important influence on later generations of filmmakers, uses stunning visuals and multiple perspectives to portray a haunting, morally complex story. Wayne's oft-repeated riposte, "That'll be the day," inspired the Buddy Holly tune.

SEA WOLF, THE 1941
★★★ NR Drama 1:40 B&W
Dir: Michael Curtiz   *Cast:* Edward G. Robinson, John Garfield, Ida Lupino, Alexander Knox, Gene Lockhart, Barry Fitzgerald
▶ Gripping adaptation of the Jack London novel centers around sea wolf Robinson, the egomaniacal captain of a scavenger ship who physically and mentally dominates his crew. Shipwreck survivors Knox and Lupino are rescued by the ship; scholar Knox engages in a chess game of wits with Robinson, while Lupino softens the demeanor of sullen seaman Garfield. When disease renders Robinson blind, the crew seeks to exploit his weakness.

SEA WOLVES, THE 1981 British
★★★★ PG Action-Adventure 2:00
☑ Brief nudity, adult situations, explicit language, violence
Dir: Andrew V. McLaglen   *Cast:* Gregory Peck, Roger Moore, David Niven, Trevor Howard, Barbara Kellerman, Patrick Macnee
▶ During World War II, aging members of the Calcutta Light Horse, an honorary drinking club in India, undertake a commando raid on Nazi ships anchored in neutral Goa. Led by British intelligence officer Peck, the commandos train for the mission while second spy Moore romances double agent Kellerman. Stars bring life to this large-scale adventure based on a true incident.

SECOND CHANCE 1953
★★ NR Drama 1:22
Dir: Rudolph Maté   *Cast:* Robert Mitchum, Linda Darnell, Jack Palance, Sandro Giglio, Rodolfo Hoyos, Jr., Reginald Sheffield
▶ Mitchum gives a brooding performance as a boxer who flees to Mexico after killing an opponent. He falls for gangster's moll Darnell, a fugitive from a Washington Senate investigation. Arrival of hit man Palance leads the couple to a thrilling climax aboard a damaged mountain cable car. Filmed on location in 3-D.

SECOND THOUGHTS 1983
★★★ PG Comedy 1:38
☑ Adult situations, explicit language
Dir: Lawrence Turman   *Cast:* Lucie Arnaz, Craig Wasson, Ken Howard, Anne Schedeen, Arthur Rosenberg
▶ San Diego lawyer Arnaz leaves stuffy banking husband Howard for affair with idealistic musician Wasson. Learning she's pregnant, she considers an abortion because Wasson is too immature. Wasson reacts by kidnapping her until she must give birth. Engaging performances compensate for script's labored humor.

SECRET ADMIRER 1985
★★★ R Comedy 1:38
☑ Nudity, adult situations, explicit language
Dir: David Greenwalt   *Cast:* C. Thomas Howell, Lori Loughlin, Kelly Preston, Dee Wallace Stone, Cliff De Young, Leigh Taylor-Young
▶ Bright teen farce about high school student Howell who receives an anonymous love letter. Is the writer his long-suffering pal Loughlin or sexy classmate Preston? Comic complications extend to parents as well when further letters fall into the hands of his mother Stone and Preston's father Fred Ward.

SECRET AGENT 1936 British
★★ NR Mystery-Suspense 1:26 B&W
Dir: Alfred Hitchcock   *Cast:* John Gielgud, Madeleine Carroll, Robert Young, Peter Lorre, Lilli Palmer
▶ British agent Gielgud goes to Switzerland to nab enemy agent and nearly jeopardizes the mission when he and co-

hort Lorre assassinate the wrong man. First-rate Hitchcock sets up an interesting, morally ambiguous situation and concludes with a terrific train wreck finale.

SECRET CEREMONY 1968 British
★ R Drama 1:49
☑ Nudity, adult situations, explicit language, violence
Dir: Joseph Losey   *Cast:* Elizabeth Taylor, Mia Farrow, Robert Mitchum, Peggy Ashcroft, Pamela Brown
▶ Aging prostitute Taylor, grieving over the death of her daughter, becomes obsessed with young look-alike Farrow. Entering into a symbolic familial relationship, Taylor follows her home, where stepfather Mitchum reveals Farrow is insane. Glum, murky melodrama is both tedious and confusing. Producers recut scenes and added characters for a TV version that remains equally baffling.

SECRET DIARY OF SIGMUND FREUD, THE 1984
☆ PG Comedy 1:41
☑ Adult situations, explicit language
Dir: Danford B. Greene   *Cast:* Bud Cort, Carol Kane, Klaus Kinski, Marisa Berenson, Carroll Baker, Dick Shawn
▶ Off-beat comedy about the early life of Dr. Sigmund Freud (Cort), who learns about sex by asking his mother Baker. He experiments with cocaine and hypnotizes his lisping assistant Kane who falls in love with him and becomes jealous of his first client Berenson. Mostly silly, often dreary, plays likes an old vaudeville routine but provides a few laughs.   **(CC)**

SECRET HONOR 1984
★ NR Drama 1:30
☑ Explicit language
Dir: Robert Altman   *Cast:* Philip Baker Hall
▶ One-man show depicts a frenzied President Nixon pacing around his study while holding forth on the memorable controversies and personalities of his roller-coaster career. Scathing portrait of a paranoid and vindictive politician goes beyond satire to become mean-spirited and malicious; for the curious and Nixon-haters only.

SECRET LIFE OF AN AMERICAN WIFE, THE 1968
★ R Comedy 1:33
☑ Brief nudity, adult situations, explicit language
Dir: George Axelrod   *Cast:* Walter Matthau, Anne Jackson, Patrick O'Neal, Edy Williams, Richard Bull
▶ When her press agent husband O'Neal neglects her, suburban housewife Jackson poses as a prostitute for macho film star Matthau to regain her self-esteem. Labored and leering farce fails to exploit its immoral premise.

SECRET LIFE OF WALTER MITTY, THE 1947
★★★ NR Comedy 1:50
Dir: Norman Z. McLeod   *Cast:* Danny Kaye, Virginia Mayo, Boris Karloff, Fay Bainter, Ann Rutherford, Thurston Hall
▶ Loose adaptation of James Thurber's short story gave Kaye one of his best roles as a henpecked proofreader tormented by fiancée Rutherford, mother Bainter, boss Hall, and everyday life. His solution is to star in daydreams as a gunslinger, gambler, surgeon, etc., pursuing voluptuous Mayo. Fantasy intrudes into reality when Mayo asks his help against jewel thieves. Highlighted by Kaye's performance of "Anatole of Paris."

SECRET OF MY SUCCESS, THE 1987
★★★★ PG-13 Comedy 1:50
☑ Brief nudity, adult situations, explicit language
Dir: Herbert Ross   *Cast:* Michael J. Fox, Helen Slater, Richard Jordan, Margaret Whitton, John Pankow, Fred Gwynne
▶ Breezy satire of the business world follows young Kansas college graduate Fox on his improbable climb up the corporate ladder. Combination of luck, wits, and an affair with boss's wife Whitton places him in the position to thwart corporate raider Jordan's sneaky tricks and pursue true love Slater. Stars' charm and cleverly calculating plot made this a popular hit.

SECRET OF NIMH, THE 1982
★★★★★ G Animation 1:22
Dir: Don Bluth   *Cast:* Voices of Derek Jacobi, Elizabeth Hartman, Dom DeLuise, Hermione Baddeley, John Carradine, Peter Strauss
▶ Animated adventure of mother field mouse trying to find new home for brood before spring plowing destroys old one. Task is complicated by illness of one child, so buffoon crow, wise owl, and trio of high-IQ rats come to her aid against perils of nature and man. Spectacular animation matches standards of old Disney pics while story will interest kids and adults alike. Superior family fare.

SECRET PLACES 1985 British
★★★ PG Drama 1:38
☑ Brief nudity, explicit language
Dir: Zelda Barron *Cast:* Marie-Theres Relin, Tara MacGowran, Claudine Auger, Jenny Agutter, Cassie Stuart, Klaus Barner
▶ During World War II, German refugee Relin attends English girls school and is ostracized by all students except one, MacGowran. MacGowran's home life is dull and empty so she's intrigued by Relin's colorful alternative: her mother Auger is a morphine addict while her physicist father Barner, denounced in Germany by Nazi son, is interned as enemy alien in nearby camp. Average coming-of-age melodrama. (CC)

SECRET POLICEMAN'S OTHER BALL, THE 1982 British
★★★ R Documentary/Music 1:33
☑ Adult situations, explicit language, adult humor
Dir: Julien Temple *Cast:* John Cleese, Graham Chapman, Michael Palin, Terry Jones, Peter Cook, Pamela Stephenson
▶ Compilation of two benefit concerts for Amnesty International blends classic Monty Python routines, bizarre skits by *Beyond the Fringe* founding member Cook, and above-average rock songs (including Sting, Pete Townshend, and the reunion of Eric Clapton and Jeff Beck) into an often haphazard but consistently delightful entertainment revue. Opening includes portions from 1979's *The Secret Policeman's Ball.*

SECRET WAR OF HARRY FRIGG, THE 1969
★ NR War/Comedy 1:49
Dir: Jack Smight *Cast:* Paul Newman, Sylva Koscina, Andrew Duggan, Tom Bosley, John Williams, Charles Gray
▶ Disappointing World War II comedy about five Allied generals crucial to the war effort but held prisoner in Italy. Brash private Newman, known for his ability to escape jail, is promoted to major general and dropped behind enemy lines to rescue them. Scheme comes to a halt when Newman falls for beautiful warden Koscina. Stars mug broadly in this slow-moving farce.

SEDUCTION, THE 1982
★★★ R Mystery-Suspense 1:44
☑ Nudity, explicit language, violence
Dir: David Schmoeller *Cast:* Morgan Fairchild, Michael Sarrazin, Vince Edwards, Andrew Stevens, Colleen Camp
▶ Gorgeous Los Angeles reporter Fairchild is terrorized by psychotic photographer Stevens, who pries into every aspect of her personal life. With her boyfriend Sarrazin and policeman Edwards powerless to help, Fairchild must confront Stevens alone. Uncomfortably voyeuristic plot follows a predictable story line.

SEDUCTION OF JOE TYNAN, THE 1979
★★★★ R Drama 1:47
☑ Adult situations, explicit language
Dir: Jerry Schatzberg *Cast:* Alan Alda, Meryl Streep, Barbara Harris, Rip Torn, Melvyn Douglas
▶ Alda, a U.S. senator from New York, has lovely wife Harris and two kids, but begins an affair with southern lawyer Streep who's helping him do research for senate hearing. Ignoring his conscience, he seizes the opportunity for national publicity by selling out elderly colleague Douglas. Not altogether believable script by Alda is enhanced by fine ensemble acting, especially from Streep, Harris, and Torn as an influential, skirt-chasing Southern senator.

SEDUCTION OF MIMI, THE 1974 Italian
★ R Comedy 1:29
☑ Adult situations, explicit language
Dir: Lina Wertmuller *Cast:* Giancarlo Giannini, Mariangela Melato, Agostina Belli, Elena Fiore
▶ Giannini is a slow-witted, vain, and stubborn Communist who gradually compromises his ideals in this satire of sexual and political morals. Various episodes are amusing, but end result is not on a par with director Wertmuller's *Seven Beauties* or *Swept Away.* Hollywood lifted the bare-bones story for the Richard Pryor vehicle *Which Way Is Up?*

SEEMS LIKE OLD TIMES 1980
★★★★ PG Comedy 1:42
☑ Explicit language
Dir: Jay Sandrich *Cast:* Goldie Hawn, Chevy Chase, Charles Grodin, Robert Guillaume, Harold Gould, George Grizzard
▶ Adorable, soft-hearted lawyer Hawn is torn between helping her hopeless ex-husband Chase through his bottomless legal problems and keeping up appearances for her current husband Grodin as he runs for California attorney general. Genial Neil Simon script and can't-miss

cast are hallmarks of this sweetly zany comedy.

SEE NO EVIL 1971 British
★ ★ ★ **PG Mystery-Suspense 1:29**
☑ Violence
Dir: Richard Fleischer   *Cast:* Mia Farrow, Dorothy Alison, Robin Bailey, Diane Grayson, Brian Rawlinson, Norman Eshley
▶ Blinded in an accident, Farrow recuperates in home of her uncle Bailey. A homicidal maniac murders Bailey and his family while she is horseback riding with her fiancé Eshley. Farrow returns to the house alone, discovers the deaths, and must overcome her handicap to defeat the killer. Manipulative but effective thriller offers a fair share of shocks.

SEIZE THE DAY 1986
★ **NR Drama/MFTV 1:33**
☑ Explicit language
Dir: Fielder Cook   *Cast:* Robin Williams, Jerry Stiller, Tony Roberts, Glenne Headly, William Hickey, Joseph Wiseman
▶ Harassed by his girlfriend and bled dry by his ex-wife, unemployed salesman Williams loses his job and returns home to New York. Old buddies offer smiles but no help while cold-hearted father Wiseman dismisses pleas for aid. Desperate for big score, Williams gambles his last savings with commodities broker Stiller. Williams shines in serious role, but bleak portrait of disintegrating life is not for those seeking laughs. Adapted from the Saul Bellow novella.

SEMI-TOUGH 1977
★ ★ ★ ★ **R Comedy/Sports 1:47**
☑ Brief nudity, adult situations, explicit language, adult humor
Dir: Michael Ritchie   *Cast:* Burt Reynolds, Kris Kristofferson, Jill Clayburgh, Robert Preston, Lotte Lenya, Bert Convy
▶ Star running back Reynolds and roommate wide receiver Kristofferson pal around with Clayburgh, daughter of team owner Preston. Then Kristofferson joins self-realization cult and convinces Clayburgh to both convert and marry him. Suddenly the odd man out, Reynolds joins the cult to expose its fraudulence and woo Clayburgh for himself. Amiable and often uproarious comedy satirizes both Me Decade fads and pro football. Based on best-seller by Dan Jenkins.

SENATOR WAS INDISCREET, THE 1948
★ ★ ★ **NR Comedy 1:21 B&W**
Dir: George S. Kaufman   *Cast:* William Powell, Ella Raines, Peter Lind Hayes, Arleen Whelan, Ray Collins, Allen Jenkins
▶ Inept senator Powell runs for President, using a diary recording crooked business by party bigwigs to assure nomination. Powell's press agent Hayes gets the blackmail book and must choose between keeping his job or allowing journalist girlfriend Raines to expose the politicians. Only directorial outing for renowned playwright/screenwriter Kaufman has many fine moments.

SENDER, THE 1982 British
★ **R Mystery-Suspense 1:32**
☑ Explicit language, violence
Dir: Roger Christian   *Cast:* Kathryn Harrold, Zeljko Ivanek, Shirley Knight, Paul Freeman, Sean Hewitt, Harry Ditson
▶ Beautiful psychiatrist Harrold, working with an attempted suicide Ivanek, learns he has the power to telepathically transmit dreams and nightmares. When his mother Knight, who has been raising him as the new Messiah, is murdered, Harrold realizes Ivanek is being framed. Understated psychological thriller was the debut film for director Christian, art designer for *Star Wars* and *Alien*.

SEND ME NO FLOWERS 1964
★ ★ ★ **NR Comedy 1:40**
Dir: Norman Jewison   *Cast:* Rock Hudson, Doris Day, Tony Randall, Paul Lynde, Hal March, Edward Andrews
▶ Last Hudson-Day teaming takes a slapstick approach to death. Hudson overhears the wrong prognosis at the hospital and assumes he's dying. With his best friend Randall, he searches for a second husband for his soon-to-be-widowed wife Day. She's convinced his strange behavior is a cover-up for an affair. Excellent supporting cast provides plenty of bounce. Day sings the title tune by Hal David and Burt Bacharach.

SENIORS 1978
★ **R Comedy 1:28**
☑ Nudity, explicit language
Dir: Rod Amateau   *Cast:* Jeffrey Byron, Gary Imhoff, Dennis Quaid, Priscilla Barnes, Lou Richards
▶ Four college buddies con a professor into giving them a $50,000 grant to study "Sex and the College Girl." The boys use the money to rent a lavish house for their

"interviews" with buxom coeds. Low-budget sex comedy with a heavy emphasis on nudity and juvenile jokes.

SENSUOUS NURSE, THE 1976 Italian
★★ R Sex 1:17
☑ Nudity, strong sexual content, explicit language
Dir: Nello Rossati *Cast:* Ursula Andress, Duilio Del Prete, Luciana Paluzzi, Lino Toffolo, Jack Palance
▶ When a wealthy patriarch suffers a stroke, his greedy offspring hire voluptuous nurse Andress to cause his death through sexual stimulation. Andress services various members of the family, but withholds her favors from the patriarch until he proposes marriage. Routine Italian sex farce notable primarily for Andress's astonishingly sexy body. Palance's role is negligible. **(CC)**

SENTINEL, THE 1977
★★★★ R Horror 1:32
Dir: Michael Winner *Cast:* Cristina Raines, Chris Sarandon, Martin Balsam, John Carradine, Ava Gardner, Jose Ferrer
▶ Upset over her father's death, elegant fashion model Raines moves to a Brooklyn Heights apartment, where she is plagued by nightmares, harassed by an evil real-estate agent, and bothered by a blind tenant. When she tells her boyfriend Sarandon she's found the doorway to hell, he wonders if she's losing her mind. All-star cast (including Arthur Kennedy, Burgess Meredith, Sylvia Miles, Deborah Raffin, and Eli Wallach) add gloss to a genuinely creepy plot.

SEPARATE PEACE, A 1972
★★ PG Drama 1:44
☑ Adult situations, explicit language
Dir: Larry Peerce *Cast:* Parker Stevenson, John Heyl, Peter Brush, Victor Bevine, William Roerick
▶ Sensitive adaptation of the John Knowles modern classic novel: roommates Stevenson and Heyl have a complex relationship in the insulated world of an affluent New England prep school while World War II rages. Stevenson admires and resents the popular Heyl, an emotional mix that has tragic consequences.

SEPARATE TABLES 1958
★★★ NR Drama 1:38 B&W
Dir: Delbert Mann *Cast:* Deborah Kerr, Rita Hayworth, David Niven, Wendy Hiller, Burt Lancaster, Gladys Cooper
▶ Moving drama about guests at a modest resort hotel and the tentative relationships they develop in the dining room. Niven brags about his wartime experiences, attracting Kerr, the shy daughter of domineering mother Cooper. Hotel owner Hiller worries about her lover Lancaster, an alcoholic writer whose ex-wife Hayworth arrives unexpectedly. Based on two Terence Rattigan one-act plays, this superbly acted film received seven Oscar nominations, with Niven and Hiller winning for their touching performances.

SEPARATE VACATIONS 1986
★ R Comedy 1:31
☑ Nudity, adult situations, explicit language, mild violence
Dir: Michael Anderson *Cast:* David Naughton, Jennifer Dale, Mark Keyloun, Laurie Holden, Blanca Guerra
▶ After twelve years of marriage, bored architect Naughton and his wife Dale try a vacation apart: Naughton in Mexico, where he futilely pursues various beauties; Dale at a ski resort, where she catches the eye of a handsome young instructor Keyloun. Uninspired comedy financed by Playboy Enterprises features lackluster premise, weak cast, and predictable jokes.

SEPARATE WAYS 1981
★★★ R Drama 1:32
☑ Nudity, adult situations, explicit language
Dir: Howard Avedis *Cast:* Karen Black, Tony Lo Bianco, Arlene Golonka, David Naughton, Jack Carter, Sharon Farrell
▶ Unhappy with husband Lo Bianco, a former race-car driver now bored with his auto dealership, Black tries an affair with young art student Naughton. She moves out and takes a waitressing job at Carter's strip joint when she learns that Lo Bianco is having an affair of his own. Cast tries hard to inject life into a routine melodrama.

SEPTEMBER 1987
★ PG Drama 1:22
☑ Explicit language
Dir: Woody Allen *Cast:* Mia Farrow, Denholm Elliott, Dianne Wiest, Elaine Stritch, Sam Waterston, Jack Warden
▶ In a Vermont country house, would-be suicide Farrow is visited by mom Stritch, stepdad Warden, best friend Wiest, widowed neighbor Elliott, and tenant Waterston. Elliott loves Farrow, Farrow loves Wa-

terston, Waterston loves Wiest, Wiest may or may not love her husband and kids in Philadelphia. The most burning question: who shot Stritch's lover thirty years ago, mother or daughter? Housebound, talky drama moves as slow as molasses although some of the performances are noteworthy. **(CC)**

SERGEANT RUTLEDGE 1960
★★ **NR Western 1:51**
Dir: John Ford *Cast:* Jeffrey Hunter, Woody Strode, Constance Towers, Billie Burke, Juano Hernandez, Willis Bouchey
▶ Intriguing but talky Western examines the rape and murder trial of black Ninth Cavalry sergeant Strode at a hostile outpost led by intolerant whites. Flashbacks show his heroism during an Indian ambush. Engrossing study of racism is enhanced by Strode's dignified performance.

SERGEANTS 3 1962
★★ **NR Western 1:52**
Dir: John Sturges *Cast:* Frank Sinatra, Dean Martin, Sammy Davis, Jr., Peter Lawford, Joey Bishop, Henry Silva
▶ Uninspired remake of *Gunga Din* set in the Wild West, with frontier sergeants Sinatra, Martin, and Lawford battling an Indian uprising led by Silva. "Rat Pack" high jinks grow tiresome, and Davis's version of the Gunga Din character is no match for Sam Jaffe's original.

SERGEANT YORK 1941
★★★★★ **NR Biography 2:14 B&W**
Dir: Howard Hawks *Cast:* Gary Cooper, Walter Brennan, Joan Leslie, George Tobias, Stanley Ridges, Margaret Wycherly
▶ Outstanding biography of Alvin York, the pacifist soldier who single-handedly captured 132 Germans during World War I. Although the battle scenes are shown with superb realism, film's best moments are scenes of York's backwoods upbringing in the hills of Tennessee. Cooper earned an Oscar for capturing the sincerity and nobility behind the hero's shy character. Received eleven nominations overall, also winning for editing. Available in a colorized version.

SERIAL 1980
★★ **R Comedy 1:32**
☑ Nudity, adult situations, explicit language
Dir: Bill Persky *Cast:* Martin Mull, Tom Smothers, Sally Kellerman, Tuesday Weld, Bill Macy, Christopher Less

▶ Satirical look at every seventies fad from hot tubs to religious cults, based on the best-selling novel by Cyra McFadden. In Marin County, California, relationships flounder, the drug culture flourishes, kids are in therapy "to get in touch with their childhood," teenagers run off to join Moonie-type groups, and women gather to raise their consciousness. Entertaining and right on the money, although much of it will seem dated now.

SERPENT AND THE RAINBOW, THE 1988
★★ **R Mystery-Suspense 1:38**
☑ Nudity, adult situations, explicit language, graphic violence
Dir: Wes Craven *Cast:* Bill Pullman, Cathy Tyson, Zakes Mokae, Paul Winfield, Brent Jennings, Conrad Roberts
▶ Prerevolution Haiti: Harvard researcher Pullman gets involved in black magic and battles local police while trying to get his hands on a powerful zombie-making powder. Intriguing story, good special effects, picturesque locations, outstanding Mokae; a bit overlong and overcomplicated but holds your interest throughout.

SERPENT'S EGG, THE 1978 U.S./German
☆ **R Drama 2:00**
☑ Adult situations, explicit language, violence
Dir: Ingmar Bergman *Cast:* Liv Ullmann, David Carradine, Gert Frobe, Heinz Bennent, James Whitmore, Glynn Turman
▶ Against the background of incipient Nazism in 1920s Berlin, Jewish circus performer Carradine hooks up with his brother's widow Ullmann. They encounter old friend Bennent, who may be involved in a sinister scheme. Bergman's first English-language effort is moody and atmospheric but rather slow-moving, talky, and unevenly acted.

SERPICO 1974
★★★★★ **R Biography/Crime 2:10**
☑ Adult situations, explicit language, violence
Dir: Sidney Lumet *Cast:* Al Pacino, Tony Roberts, John Randolph, Jack Kehoe, Biff McGuire, Barbara Eda-Young
▶ Galvanizing, disquieting adaptation of Peter Maas's best-selling book dramatizing the career of real-life undercover cop Frank Serpico (Pacino) whose testimony about police corruption and bribery led

to the formation of the Knapp Commission. Riveting, high-energy performance from Pacino as the obsessive "hippie" cop who takes ballet lessons, studies Spanish, and refuses to compromise.

SERVANT, THE 1963 British
☆ NR Drama 1:55 B&W
Dir: Joseph Losey *Cast:* Dirk Bogarde, Sarah Miles, Wendy Craig, James Fox, Catherine Lacey, Richard Vernon
▶ Jaded playboy Fox hires lower-class valet Bogarde to run his London mansion. Bogarde cunningly assumes control of Fox's life in a psychological battle of wits. Challenging examination of power and decadence will reward patient viewers. Screenplay by Harold Pinter, who has a brief cameo as a party-goer.

SESAME STREET PRESENTS: FOLLOW THAT BIRD 1985
★★★★★ G Family 1:28
Dir: Ken Kwapis *Cast:* The Sesame Street Gang, Sandra Bernhard, John Candy, Chevy Chase, Joe Flaherty, Dave Thomas
▶ Big Bird goes to Illinois to live with a family of dodos but misses his pals back on Sesame Street. He decides to hit the road back to New York while the Sleaze Brothers (Thomas, Flaherty) try to catch Big Bird for their amusement park. Delightful entertainment for children; all-star Muppet cast includes Cookie Monster, Oscar the Grouch (who does a neat *Patton* parody to open the film). Funny bits from Bernhard and Candy. **(CC)**

SET-UP, THE 1949
★★★ NR Drama/Sports 1:12 B&W
Dir: Robert Wise *Cast:* Robert Ryan, Audrey Totter, George Tobias, Alan Baxter, Wallace Ford, Percy Helton
▶ Aging fighter Ryan prepares for a meaningless bout, unaware his trainer Helton and local gangster Baxter have fixed the match. Unique boxing drama, played out in real time, is uncompromising in its depiction of the sport as seedy and corrupt. Fight scenes are among the most brutal ever filmed.

SEVEN BEAUTIES 1976 Italian
★★ R Comedy/Drama 1:55
☑ Nudity, explicit language, violence
Dir: Lina Wertmuller *Cast:* Giancarlo Giannini, Fernando Rey, Shirley Stoler, Elena Fiore, Enzo Vitale, Mario Conti
▶ During World War II, good-looking Giannini kills man who pimps for his sister Fiore and chooses insanity plea over

death sentence. The insane asylum becomes intolerable, so Giannini wins release by joining the army. But when he's shipped off to the Russian front he deserts, only to wind up in a Nazi concentration camp, a place so hellish he tries to seduce obese, sadistic warden Stoler to survive. Some will find director Wertmuller's masterful portrayal of survivor-without-scruples too disturbing. Ⓢ

SEVEN BRIDES FOR SEVEN BROTHERS 1954
★★★★ G Musical 1:42
Dir: Stanley Donen *Cast:* Howard Keel, Jane Powell, Jeff Richards, Russ Tamblyn, Julie Newmar, Jacques d'Amboise
▶ Bachelor brothers live a lonely existence on their Oregon farm until eldest Keel brings home pert wife Powell. She tries to domesticate the rowdy bunch; they proceed to kidnap six pretty girls for wives of their own. One of America's most beloved musicals remains fresh, thanks to strong direction, witty script, tuneful Johnny Mercer–Gene de Paul score, and outstanding choreography by Michael Kidd. A Best Picture nominee.

SEVEN DAYS IN MAY 1964
★★★ NR Mystery-Suspense 2:00 B&W
Dir: John Frankenheimer *Cast:* Kirk Douglas, Burt Lancaster, Fredric March, Ava Gardner, Edmond O'Brien, Martin Balsam
▶ Army colonel Douglas suspects right-wing general Lancaster is plotting to dispose of President March and take over the U.S. government. Douglas alerts March and attempts to thwart the coup. Blistering, topical, and tense nail-biter with terrific performances. Frankenheimer's superb direction creates the same "it can happen here" feel as his *The Manchurian Candidate*.

7 FACES OF DR. LAO 1964
★★★ NR Fantasy 1:40
Dir: George Pal *Cast:* Tony Randall, Arthur O'Connell, Barbara Eden, John Ericson, Lee Patrick, Noah Beery, Jr.
▶ In the Western frontier town of Abalone, crusading newspaper editor O'Connell battles land-grabbing villain Ericson and woos pretty widow Eden. Into town rides oriental magician Randall and circus troupe of oddities (also played by Randall) to assist O'Connell in his worthy endeavors. Diverting Old West fantasy is distinguished by excellent per-

formance from Randall in multiple roles. Received a special Oscar for makeup (not a regular Academy Award until 1981).

SEVEN HOURS TO JUDGMENT 1988
★★★ R Mystery-Suspense 1:36
☑ Explicit language, violence
Dir: Beau Bridges *Cast:* Beau Bridges, Ron Leibman, Julianne Phillips, Tiny Ron Taylor, Reggie Johnson
▶ Although he knows they are guilty of murder, judge Bridges is forced to free vicious punks on a technicality. Leibman, the victim's husband, kidnaps Bridges's wife Phillips and gives him seven hours to find the evidence necessary for conviction. Familiar vigilante story given a lift by swift pacing and realistic performances.

SEVEN LITTLE FOYS, THE 1955
★★★★ NR Biography/Musical 1:33
Dir: Melville Shavelson *Cast:* Bob Hope, Milly Vitale, George Tobias, Angela Clarke, Herbert Heyes, Richard Shannon
▶ Charming biography of vaudeville star Eddie Foy (Hope), whose marriage to ballerina Vitale results in seven children. When Vitale dies, Hope molds his brood into a top vaudeville act. Nostalgic songs ("Row, Row, Row," "I'm the Greatest Father of Them All"), surefire gags, a restrained performance by Hope, and a knockout cameo by James Cagney (reprising his George M. Cohan role from *Yankee Doodle Dandy*) add up to winning entertainment. Narrated by Eddie Foy, Jr.

SEVEN MAGNIFICENT GLADIATORS, THE 1984
★ PG Fantasy 1:26
☑ Violence
Dir: Bruno Mattei *Cast:* Lou Ferrigno, Sybil Danning, Brad Harris, Dan Vadis, Carla Ferrigno, Mandy Rice-Davies
▶ Village forced to pay tribute to evil demigod Vadis asks the barbarian Han (Ferrigno) to free them from slavery. Ferrigno hires gladiator Harris, fierce but beautiful fighter Danning, and four other unemployed warriors to do battle against the tyrant. Uncredited remake of *The Magnificent Seven* set in mythical times offers plenty of action, but poor dubbing and special effects are obvious.

SEVEN MINUTES IN HEAVEN 1986
★★★ PG-13 Comedy 1:28
☑ Explicit language
Dir: Linda Feferman *Cast:* Jennifer

Connelly, Maddie Corman, Byron Thames, Alan Boyce, Polly Draper, Marshall Bell
▶ Appealing coming-of-age comedy set in Ohio. Connelly plays a studious teen competing in an essay contest; she lets mixed-up male friend Thames stay at her house despite rumors about their relationship at school. She also competes with best friend Corman over a handsome classmate. Endearing cast and honest, sympathetic script set this above routine adolescent comedies.

SEVEN-PER-CENT SOLUTION, THE 1976
★★★ PG Action-Adventure 1:53
☑ Adult situations
Dir: Herbert Ross *Cast:* Nicol Williamson, Alan Arkin, Robert Duvall, Vanessa Redgrave, Laurence Olivier, Joel Grey
▶ Sherlock Holmes (Williamson) is lured to Vienna by Dr. Watson (Duvall) so that Sigmund Freud (Arkin) can treat the detective for cocaine addiction. The two great minds then team up to solve a mystery. Stylish, original, and an enormous amount of fun; Williamson is brilliant as a high-strung Holmes and he gets outstanding support from Arkin, Duvall, and Olivier (in a delicious cameo as a surprisingly mousy Moriarty). Handsomely mounted, beautifully paced. Literate screenplay by Nicholas Meyer from his best-selling novel.

SEVEN SAMURAI, THE 1954 Japanese
★ NR Action-Adventure 2:21 B&W
Dir: Akira Kurosawa *Cast:* Takashi Shimura, Toshiro Mifune, Yoshio Inaba, Seiji Miyaguchi, Minoru Chiaki, Daisuke Kato
▶ Seventeenth-century master samurai Shimura agrees to defend villagers from marauders. He assembles a team of six other warriors, trains the villagers in fighting, and leads them against the bandits in an astonishing battle. Sweeping epic is a highly influential classic famed for its thrilling action and sharply realized characters. Remade in the U.S. under its alternate title, *The Magnificent Seven*. Restored, 3-hour, 28-minute version is also available. ⑤

1776 1972
★★★★ G Musical 2:28
Dir: Peter H. Hunt *Cast:* William Daniels, Howard da Silva, Ken Howard, Blythe Danner, Ronald Holgate, John Cullum
▶ "I'm obnoxious and disliked," sings

acerbic John Adams (Daniels), explaining to Benjamin Franklin (da Silva) why he's a bad choice to write the Declaration of Independence at the first Continental Congress. Young Tom Jefferson (Howard) eventually accepts the job but will a divided congress approve the document? Occasionally corny but high-spirited tribute to our founding fathers. Stiff staging betrays Broadway origins but the cast is a lot of fun, especially Daniels, da Silva, and Holgate, whose boisterous "Lees of Virginia" number is a comic highlight.

SEVENTH SEAL, THE 1956 Swedish
★★ **NR Drama 1:45 B&W**
Dir: Ingmar Bergman *Cast:* Max Von Sydow, Gunnar Bjornstrand, Nils Poppe, Bengt Ekerot, Bibi Andersson, Maud Hansson
▶ Fourteenth-century Swedish knight Von Sydow returns from the Crusades to his plague-ravaged homeland. He takes on Death in a game of chess and rescues a family from its clutches. Magnificent, haunting foreign classic; Bergman's stunning direction creates a superb medieval tapestry and the performances (especially the moving Von Sydow and the fresh-faced Andersson) are unforgettable. [S]

SEVENTH SIGN, THE 1988
★★★ **R Horror 1:37**
☑ Brief nudity, adult situations, explicit language, violence
Dir: Carl Schultz *Cast:* Demi Moore, Michael Biehn, Jurgen Prochnow, Peter Friedman, Manny Jacobs
▶ Pregnant Moore, suffering from horrible nightmares while disasters occur around the world, takes in mysterious boarder Prochnow. Through him, she learns her unborn child's role in saving the world from destruction. Contemporary shocker in the vein of *The Omen*; fast-paced thrills anchored sympathetically by raspy-voiced Moore. **(CC)**

SEVENTH VEIL, THE 1945 British
★★★ **NR Drama 1:35 B&W**
Dir: Compton Bennett *Cast:* James Mason, Ann Todd, Herbert Lom, Hugh McDermott, Albert Lieven, Yvonne Owen
▶ With the aid of psychiatrist Lom, suicidal pianist Todd, an orphan, comes to terms with her feelings toward neurotic Mason, the bachelor cousin who raised her and cultivated her musical talents.

Intelligent psycholgical drama won Oscar for Best Screenplay.

7TH VOYAGE OF SINBAD, THE 1958
★★★ **G Fantasy 1:28**
Dir: Nathan Juran *Cast:* Kerwin Mathews, Kathryn Grant, Richard Eyer, Torin Thatcher, Alec Mango, Danny Green
▶ Evil magician Thatcher shrinks princess Grant to miniature size; to rescue her, hero Sinbad (Mathews) must battle a fierce Cyclops, an angry mother roc, a fire-breathing dragon, and a living skeleton. Prime example of Arabian Nights entertainment will delight parents as well as children. Lively plot, strong action, but stars and story are upstaged by Ray Harryhausen's marvelous special effects and a sweeping score by Bernard Herrmann.

SEVEN-UPS, THE 1973
★★ **PG Action-Adventure 1:43**
☑ Explicit language, violence
Dir: Philip D'Antoni *Cast:* Roy Scheider, Tony Lo Bianco, Larry Haines, Victor Arnold, Jerry Leon, Ken Kercheval
▶ Hard-nosed New York cop Scheider runs unorthodox unit employing informants to pursue crooks whose crimes merit prison sentences of seven years or longer. Chief stoolie Lo Bianco uses police info for his own profit until the scam gets one of Scheider's men killed. Director D'Antoni, producer of *Bullit* and *The French Connection*, favors action over character. Best bit: chase sequence in which head car is cut off by a tractor trailer. **(CC)**

SEVEN YEAR ITCH, THE 1955
★★★ **NR Comedy 1:45**
Dir: Billy Wilder *Cast:* Marilyn Monroe, Tom Ewell, Evelyn Keyes, Sonny Tufts, Robert Strauss, Oscar Homolka
▶ With wife Keyes and son on vacation, high-strung Manhattan publisher Ewell fantasizes an affair with new upstairs neighbor Monroe. Adaptation of a George Axelrod Broadway hit, laden with double entendres, has a disarmingly wistful performance by Monroe. Her scene over a subway grating features one of her most famous poses.

SEXTETTE 1979
☆ **PG Comedy 1:31**
☑ Adult humor
Dir: Ken Hughes *Cast:* Mae West, Timothy Dalton, Dom DeLuise, Tony Curtis, Ringo Starr, George Hamilton
▶ Much-married famous actress West

weds titled Englishman Dalton, but honeymoon consummation is interrupted by the intrusion of fans, journalists, and ex-husbands. West's last film after an eight-year layoff embarrassed everyone in it and the few viewers who bothered to see it. A sad failure even for camp aficionados.

SEX THROUGH A WINDOW 1973
★ R Sex/Drama 1:21
☑ Nudity, strong sexual content
Dir: Jeannot Szwarc *Cast:* James McMullan, James A. Watson, Kate Woodville, Bara Byrnes
▶ Los Angeles TV reporter rents high-tech surveillance equipment for a story. He soon becomes a voyeur, spying on women undressing and having sex. Potentially interesting theme is undercut by wooden performances and second-rate production values. Screenplay by Michael Crichton. Also known as *Extreme Close-Up*.

SGT. PEPPER'S LONELY HEARTS CLUB BAND 1978
★ PG Musical 1:51
Dir: Michael Schultz *Cast:* Peter Frampton, Barry Gibb, Robin Gibb, Maurice Gibb, Frankie Howerd, Paul Nicholas
▶ Misguided effort to provide a story line to the classic Beatles album interprets their songs in weak skits and some funny bits of camp. Long list of guest performers and cameo appearances (George Burns, Steve Martin, Alice Cooper, Aerosmith, Billy Preston, Peter Allen, Helen Reddy, Connie Stevens, Carol Channing, Leif Garrett, Heart, Seals and Croft, Tina Turner, and Earth, Wind & Fire, among others) can't salvage silly plot.

SHADEY 1987 British
★ PG-13 Comedy 1:46
☑ Brief nudity, adult situations, explicit language, violence
Dir: Philip Saville *Cast:* Antony Sher, Billie Whitelaw, Patrick Macnee, Leslie Ash, Bernard Hepton, Larry Lamb
▶ Auto mechanic Sher, who has the ability to project anyone's thoughts and images onto film, is courted by secret agent Whitelaw in an effort to uncover strategic Russian submarine plans. But pacifist Sher is only interested in earning enough money for a sex-change operation. Offbeat black comedy is short on satisfying laughs. **(CC)**

SHADOW OF A DOUBT 1943
★★★★ NR Mystery-Suspense 1:48 B&W
Dir: Alfred Hitchcock *Cast:* Teresa Wright, Joseph Cotten, Macdonald Carey, Henry Travers, Patricia Collinge, Hume Cronyn
▶ Young Wright's placid Santa Rosa life is disrupted by the arrival of her beloved uncle Cotten, a suave, charming intellectual who offers her a glimpse of sophistication. To her dismay, she finds evidence that he could be a notorious mass murderer, and is torn between revealing her fears to detective Carey and protecting her family. Subtle but penetrating thriller is among Hitchcock's most accomplished and unnerving stories. Screenplay by Thornton Wilder, Sally Benson, and Alma Reville.

SHADOW OF THE THIN MAN 1941
★★ NR Mystery-Suspense 1:37 B&W
Dir: W. S. Van Dyke II *Cast:* William Powell, Myrna Loy, Barry Nelson, Donna Reed, Sam Levene, Stella Adler
▶ Married sleuthes Nick (Powell) and Nora (Loy) Charles investigate the deaths of a jockey and a reporter at the racetrack. Fourth entry in the Thin Man series provides trademark blend of whodunit plotting and wit.

SHADOW PLAY 1986
★★ R Drama 1:37
☑ Brief nudity, adult situations, explicit language
Dir: Susan Shadburne *Cast:* Dee Wallace Stone, Cloris Leachman, Ron Kuhlman, Barry Laws, Al Strobel, Delia Salvi
▶ New York playwright Stone, obsessed with her lover's suicide, goes to his hometown and has visions of the dead man. Is this her imagination or is there a more sinister explanation? Stone goes crazy beautifully and Leachman underplays sweetly as the grieving mom. Tense climax, but talkiness drags down earlier sections.

SHADOWS RUN BLACK 1984
★ NR Horror 1:29
☑ Nudity, adult situations, explicit language, graphic violence
Dir: Howard Heard *Cast:* William J. Kulzer, Elizabeth Trosper, Shea Porter, George J. Engelson, Dianne Hinkler, Kevin Costner
▶ Campus killer slices and dices coeds. Cop Kulzer, whose kidnapped daughter may be one of the victims, investigates.

Among the suspects: a prestardom Kevin Costner (who appears briefly). Shabbily directed, little story momentum, rudimentary acting, gratuitous nudity.

SHAFT 1971
★★★ R Action-Adventure 1:40
☑ Brief nudity, adult situations, explicit language, violence
Dir: Gordon Parks *Cast:* Richard Roundtree, Moses Gunn, Charles Cioffi, Gwenn Mitchell, Christopher St. John, Lawrence Pressman
▶ When the Mafia kidnaps daughter of Harlem crime boss Gunn, he hires tough private eye Roundtree to retrieve her. While cop pal Cioffi frets about racially oriented mob war, Roundtree takes care of business with aid of black militant St. John. Gumshoe-with-soul was forerunner of 1970s black exploitation pics, but holds up today as urban actioner regardless of racial focus. Dynamic score by Isaac Hayes won Oscar for Best Song. Director Parks started as well-known *Life* magazine photographer.

SHAG 1988
★★★ NR Comedy 1:40
☑ Adult situations, explicit language
Dir: Zelda Barron *Cast:* Phoebe Cates, Scott Coffey, Bridget Fonda, Annabeth Gish, Page Hannah, Page Rusler
▶ Cates, Fonda, Gish, and Hannah are four friends who head to Myrtle Beach, South Carolina, for some fun in the sun in the summer of 1963. Cates, although engaged to someone else, finds true love with handsome Rusler while pudgy Gish falls for Coffey. The girls also find time for plenty of shag dancing. Pleasant beach movie is a throwback to another era.

SHAGGY D.A., THE 1976
★★★ G Comedy/Family 1:31
Dir: Robert Stevenson *Cast:* Dean Jones, Suzanne Pleshette, Tim Conway, Keenan Wynn, Jo Anne Worley, Dick Van Patten
▶ Belated sequel to *The Shaggy Dog* repeats the original's winning blend of slapstick and fantasy. Jones's campaign against comically corrupt district attorney Wynn runs into a snag when an ancient ring turns him into a sheepdog at inopportune moments. Prime Disney fun.

SHAGGY DOG, THE 1959
★★★★ G Comedy/Family 1:44 B&W
Dir: Charles Barton *Cast:* Fred MacMurray, Jean Hagen, Tommy Kirk, An-

nette Funicello, Tim Considine, Kevin Corcoran
▶ Young Kirk finds a magic ring that turns him into a sheepdog, causing no end of problems for father MacMurray, who's allergic to canines. Kirk later plays a secret part in unmasking a spy ring. Charming Disney fantasy, the studio's first attempt at live-action slapstick, led to *The Shaggy D.A.* almost twenty years later. Available in a colorized version.

SHAKEDOWN 1988
★★★ R Action-Adventure 1:40
☑ Adult situations, explicit language, violence
Dir: James Glickenhaus *Cast:* Peter Weller, Sam Elliott, Patricia Charbonneau, Blanche Baker, Antonio Fargas
▶ Legal Aid lawyer Weller, defending crack dealer accused of killing undercover cop, teams with cop Elliott to investigate police theft of money from drug pushers. Packed with action and impressive stunts; moves along nicely even though farfetched story doesn't always make sense.

SHAKER RUN 1985 New Zealand
★★★ NR Action-Adventure 1:30
☑ Adult situations, explicit language, violence
Dir: Bruce Morrison *Cast:* Cliff Robertson, Leif Garrett, Lisa Harrow, Shane Briant
▶ In New Zealand, American race-car drivers Robertson and Garrett are hired by scientist Harrow to take an experiment out of the country and quickly get involved with the army and CIA. Well-crafted with nicely orchestrated chases; characterizations and dialogue are rather simplistic, however.

SHALAKO 1968 British
★ PG Western 1:53
☑ Violence
Dir: Edward Dmytryk *Cast:* Sean Connery, Brigitte Bardot, Stephen Boyd, Jack Hawkins, Peter Van Eyck, Honor Blackman
▶ Turgid Western about stoical guide Connery who rescues British aristocrats from an Indian ambush engineered by untrustworthy range boss Boyd. When the travelers prove ungrateful, Connery shifts his attention to their guest, beautiful countess Bardot, who turns out to be a crack shot. Based on a Louis L'Amour novel.

SHALL WE DANCE 1937
★★★ NR Musical 1:56 B&W
Dir: Mark Sandrich *Cast:* Fred Astaire,
Ginger Rogers, Edward Everett Horton,
Eric Blore, Jerome Cowan, Ketti Gallian
► Seventh Astaire-Rogers teaming
skimps on the dances for thin but elegant
comedy about a publicity-inspired romance between aloof Russian ballet star
and a strong-willed American singer.
Since the Russian is really an American in
disguise, true love is inevitable. Remarkable George and Ira Gershwin score includes the Oscar-nominated "They Can't
Take That Away from Me," "Let's Call the
Whole Thing Off" (performed on roller
skates), and "Slap That Bass," but the
highlight is an irresistible duet to "They All
Laughed."

SHAME 1988 Australian
★★★ R Drama 1:30
☑ Adult situations, explicit language,
    violence
Dir: Steve Jodrell *Cast:* Deborra-Lee
Furness, Tony Barry, Simone Buchanan,
Gillian Jones, Peter Aanensen, Margaret Ford
► Rapists terrorize women in grimy Australian town; female motorcyclist Furness,
waiting for repairs to her bike, becomes
target of violence when she presses for
thugs' arrest. Good acting and unusual
approach to vigilante and feminist
themes add up to provocative drama.

SHAMPOO 1975
★★★ R Comedy 1:52
☑ Nudity, adult situations, explicit lan-
    guage
Dir: Hal Ashby *Cast:* Warren Beatty,
Julie Christie, Goldie Hawn, Lee Grant,
Jack Warden, Carrie Fisher
► Against the background of the 1968
Presidential election, Beverly Hills hair-
dresser Beatty has affairs with the three
women in wealthy Warden's life: wife
Grant, mistress Christie, and daughter
Fisher, while still seeing his own girlfriend
Hawn. However, real happiness eludes
him. Saucy, sharply satirical, and often
quite shocking (Christie's famous under-
the-table seduction of Beatty) sexual
roundelay. Ashby's direction and Paul
Simon score expertly capture mood of
the times. Oscar for Best Supporting Actress (Grant). (CC)

SHAMUS 1973
★★ PG Action-Adventure 1:31

☑ Adult situations, explicit language,
    violence
Dir: Buzz Kulik *Cast:* Burt Reynolds,
Dyan Cannon, John P. Ryan, Joe Santos, Georgio Tozzi, Ron Weyand
► Brooklyn private eye and part-time
pool hustler Reynolds stumbles across a
warehouse filled with illegal arms while
searching for stolen diamonds. Unlikely
help comes in the form of beautiful society heiress Cannon. Swift action and
sharp dialogue lift this above standard
Reynolds vehicles.

SHANE 1953
★★★★ NR Western 1:58
Dir: George Stevens *Cast:* Alan Ladd,
Jean Arthur, Van Heflin, Brandon de
Wilde, Jack Palance, Emile Meyer
► Reformed gunfighter Ladd works as
hired hand for Wyoming homesteaders
Heflin and Arthur, winning admiration of
their son de Wilde and love of Arthur. Cattle baron Meyer seeks to drive farmers
away and imports hired gun Palance as
intimidator. When Heflin decides to show
the other farmers how to face up to Palance and Meyer, Ladd must choose between apathy and return to the gunslinger's wayward life. Classic Western
was nominated for five Oscars and won
for Cinematography.

SHANGHAI SURPRISE 1986
★ PG-13 Action-Adventure 1:37
☑ Brief nudity, adult situations, explicit
    language, mild violence
Dir: Jim Goddard *Cast:* Sean Penn,
Madonna, Paul Freeman, Richard Griffiths, Philip Sayer, Clyde Kusatsu
► In 1937, missionary Madonna hires
rogue Penn to help her track down valuable opium cargo; they run afoul of various villains who also want the stash. After
a good start (credits by Maurice Binder of
James Bond fame), escapist fare falls
apart due to moldy screenplay, abysmal
dialogue, and miscast leads. Freeman
outshines the stars; ex-Beatle George
Harrison produced and provided the
music.

SHARKS' TREASURE 1975
☆ PG Action-Adventure 1:35
☑ Violence
Dir: Cornel Wilde *Cast:* Cornel Wilde,
Yaphet Kotto, John Neilson, Cliff Os-
mond, David Canary
► Aging deep-sea fisher Wilde risks his
prized boat in a search for sunken trea-
sure. Caribbean locations, good under-

water photography, and frequent shark attacks enliven middling plot and acting. Wilde also wrote and produced.

SHARKY'S MACHINE 1981
★ ★ ★ ★ **R Action-Adventure 1:58**
☑ Brief nudity, adult situations, explicit language, graphic violence
Dir: Burt Reynolds *Cast:* Burt Reynolds, Rachel Ward, Vittorio Gassman, Bernie Casey, Brian Keith, Charles Durning
▶ Atlanta cop Reynolds, demoted to vice squad after shootout, falls for Ward, the high-class call girl he has under surveillance, and uncovers corruption involving drug king Gassman. Fast and furious, with adept performance and direction from Reynolds, sexual chemistry from sultry Ward, realistic and gritty atmosphere. Very satisfying although very violent.

SHE 1983 Italian
★ **NR Fantasy 1:46**
☑ Nudity, adult situations, explicit language, graphic violence
Dir: Avi Nesher *Cast:* Sandahl Bergman, David Goss, Harrison Muller, Quinn Kessler
▶ In a post–nuclear war world, immortal amazon Bergman falls in love with traveler Goss, who is searching for his kidnapped sister. Goss and Bergman battle mutants, vampires, and a mad doctor. Repetitive story, cheap production skimpy on everything but dismembered limbs.

SHE DONE HIM WRONG 1933
★ ★ ★ **NR Comedy 1:06 B&W**
Dir: Lowell Sherman *Cast:* Mae West, Cary Grant, Gilbert Roland, Owen Moore, Noah Beery, Sr.
▶ West, a Gay Nineties Bowery bar manager involved with crime boss Beery and convict Moore, loses her heart to handsome Salvation Army captain Grant. One of West's best: she sings, delivers her patented one-liners, and makes eyes at Grant in high style against a lusty period background. Based on West's play "Diamond Lil."

SHEENA 1984
★ ★ **PG Action-Adventure 1:56**
☑ Nudity, explicit language, violence
Dir: John Guillermin *Cast:* Tanya Roberts, Ted Wass, Donovan Scott, Elizabeth of Toro, France Zobda
▶ After her parents are killed on an expedition, blond orphan Roberts grows up to be Queen of the Jungle. Her ability to communicate with animals helps her fight bad guys who have framed her mentor for an assassination. Agreeable updating of a popular comic strip has a welcome sense of humor, scenic African backgrounds, cute animals. Roberts is attractive but lacks charisma. **(CC)**

SHEILA LEVINE IS DEAD AND LIVING IN NEW YORK 1975
☆ **PG Comedy 1:53**
☑ Adult situations, explicit language
Dir: Sidney J. Furie *Cast:* Jeannie Berlin, Roy Scheider, Rebecca Dianna Smith, Janet Brandt, Sid Melton
▶ Despite her parents' objections, young Berlin forsakes suburbia for Manhattan's East Side. She falls hopelessly in love with doctor Scheider after a one-night stand, even after he rejects her for her roommate Smith. Flat adaptation of Gail Parent's comic novel lacks insight and compassion.

SHENANDOAH 1965
★ ★ ★ ★ **NR Western 1:45**
Dir: Andrew V. McLaglen *Cast:* James Stewart, Doug McClure, Glenn Corbett, Patrick Wayne, Rosemary Forsyth, Katharine Ross
▶ Stewart gives a wonderful performance as a Virginia farmer whose opposition to the Civil War doesn't prevent tragedy from striking his family. When his son is arrested by Union soldiers, Stewart gathers his clan to rescue him. Large-scale adventure uses haunting vignettes to show the personal impact of the war, with warm humor balancing heartbreaking moments. Inspired a Broadway musical.

SHERLOCK HOLMES AND THE SECRET WEAPON 1943
★ ★ ★ ★ **NR Mystery-Suspense 1:08 B&W**
Dir: Roy William Neill *Cast:* Basil Rathbone, Nigel Bruce, Lionel Atwill, Kaaren Verne
▶ During World War II, Sherlock Holmes (Rathbone) dons disguises to ferret a Swiss inventor away from the Nazis. Holmes's archnemesis Professor Moriarty (Atwill), working for the Germans, attempts to foil the great detective. Wartime thrills; Rathbone and Bruce are fine (as always) as Holmes and Watson. Available in a colorized version. **(CC)**

SHERLOCK HOLMES AND THE SPIDER WOMAN 1944
★ ★ ★ **NR Mystery-Suspense 1:02 B&W**

Dir: Roy William Neill   *Cast:* Basil Rathbone, Nigel Bruce, Gale Sondergaard, Dennis Hoey

▶ Sherlock Holmes (Rathbone) almost meets his match in the fiendishly clever "Spider Woman" (Sondergaard), who murders men so she can collect on the insurance. She tries to kill Holmes with a poisonous spider. One of the better Rathbone-Bruce efforts; Sondergaard makes a quite stylish villain.

SHERLOCK HOLMES AND THE VOICE OF TERROR 1942
★★ NR Mystery-Suspense 1:05 B&W
Dir: John Rawlings   *Cast:* Basil Rathbone, Nigel Bruce, Evelyn Ankers, Reginald Denny, Henry Daniell, Lon Chaney, Jr.

▶ Holmes (Rathbone) and Watson (Bruce) employ some lowlife types to help them infiltrate a sinister Nazi ring that announces sabotage threats on the radio and then carries them out. One of the series's better casts; the "Voice of Terror" broadcasts are quite chilling. Third Rathbone-Bruce effort was their first to place Holmes in a modern setting. (CC)

SHERLOCK HOLMES FACES DEATH 1943
★★ NR Mystery-Suspense 1:08 B&W
Dir: Roy William Neill   *Cast:* Basil Rathbone, Nigel Bruce, Dennis Hoey, Arthur Margetson, Hillary Brooke, Halliwell Hobbes

▶ Arthur Conan Doyle's nineteenth-century story is updated to the World War II era: shell-shocked officers are treated by Bruce at mansion belonging to impoverished aristocrat Brooke. When Bruce's assistant Margetson is stabbed by an unknown assailant, and the manor's clock strikes thirteen times—a legendary portent of the death of one of the residing family—Bruce calls upon his famous detective friend Rathbone to solve the mystery. (CC)

SHERLOCK HOLMES IN WASHINGTON 1943
★★ NR Mystery-Suspense 1:11 B&W
Dir: Roy William Neill   *Cast:* Basil Rathbone, Nigel Bruce, Marjorie Lord, Henry Daniell, George Zucco

▶ Matchbook containing important secret information falls into the hands of a German agent in America's capital. Holmes and Watson travel to Washington to recover it. Standard Rathbone-Bruce vehicle. (CC)

SHE'S GOTTA HAVE IT 1986
★ R Comedy 1:29 B&W
☑ Nudity, strong sexual content, explicit language
Dir: Spike Lee   *Cast:* Tracy Camilla Johns, Tommy R. Hicks, John Canada Terrell, Spike Lee, Raye Dowell, Joie Lee

▶ Black Brooklynite Johns juggles three lovers: vain actor Terrell, sensitive romantic Hicks, and jokester Lee. Rough-edged and sexually frank but fresh, vibrant, and very funny; Lee's inventiveness as a writer-director is matched only by his skill as the fast-talking Mars Blackmon. Funniest scenes: the Thanksgiving dinner where Lee boasts of his meeting with Jesse Jackson and the montage of male come-ons. (CC)

SHE'S HAVING A BABY 1988
★★★ PG-13 Comedy 1:46
☑ Adult situations, explicit language
Dir: John Hughes   *Cast:* Kevin Bacon, Elizabeth McGovern, Alec Baldwin, Isabel Lorca, William Windom, Cathryn Damon

▶ Bacon marries his high school sweetheart McGovern, takes job in advertising, and settles into suburbia. Couple has trouble conceiving and Bacon feels alienated from his new lifestyle. Nice cast and slick production. Upbeat finale will leave viewers in a good mood if mean-spirited earlier sections are overlooked. (CC)

SHE WORE A YELLOW RIBBON 1949
★★★★ NR Western 1:44
Dir: John Ford   *Cast:* John Wayne, Joanne Dru, John Agar, Ben Johnson, Harry Carey, Jr., Victor McLaglen

▶ Second of director Ford's "cavalry trilogy," and the only one in color, stars Wayne as an officer facing retirement whose region is threatened by rampaging Arapahos. Frustrated in his attempts to make peace, and unable to evacuate civilians safely, he decides to confront the Indian chief before he loses his command. Wayne gives a memorable performance in this beautifully detailed Western, with Oscar-winning photography by Winton Hoch. *Fort Apache* and *Rio Grande* are the other entries in the trilogy.

SHINING, THE 1980
★★★ R Horror 2:24

☑ Nudity, explicit language, graphic violence
Dir: Stanley Kubrick *Cast:* Jack Nicholson, Shelley Duvall, Scatman Crothers, Danny Lloyd, Barry Nelson, Philip Stone
▶ Aspiring writer Nicholson, wife Duvall, and their clairvoyant son Lloyd spend winter caretaking huge Colorado hotel where, years before, caretaker killed family and self. Lloyd suffers vivid visualizations of the violence; isolation eventually drives Nicholson insane. Longish adaptation of Stephen King novel can be confusing but has plenty of shocks and gore for horror fans. Most frequently mimicked scene: ax-wielding Nicholson hacks door open and grins, "Heeeere's Johnny!"

SHIP OF FOOLS 1965
★★ NR Drama 2:30 B&W
Dir: Stanley Kramer *Cast:* Vivien Leigh, Simone Signoret, Jose Ferrer, Lee Marvin, Oskar Werner, George Segal
▶ In 1933, events aboard a German-bound ship symbolize the rise of Nazism. Among the passengers: drug addict Signoret and her doctor lover Werner, divorcée Leigh, anti-Semite Ferrer, and dwarf Michael Dunn. Engrossing adaptation of the Katherine Anne Porter best-seller. Outstanding Oscar-nominated performances from Werner, Signoret, and Dunn. A Best Picture nominee; won for Cinematography and Art/Set Direction. **(CC)**

SHOCK TREATMENT 1981
★ PG Musical 1:34
☑ Adult situations, explicit language, adult humor
Dir: Jim Sharman *Cast:* Jessica Harper, Cliff De Young, Richard O'Brien, Patricia Quinn, Charles Gray, Ruby Wax
▶ Followup to campy cult hit *The Rocky Horror Picture Show* substitutes Harper and De Young for the naive young couple originally played by Susan Sarandon and Barry Bostwick. Duo are guests on "Marriage Maze" TV game show, leading to night of musical debauchery. Despite return of writer/actor/songwriter O'Brien, silly spin-off lacks crude fun of the original. **(CC)**

SHOES OF THE FISHERMAN, THE 1968
★★★★★ G Drama 2:28
Dir: Michael Anderson *Cast:* Anthony Quinn, Oskar Werner, John Gielgud, David Janssen, Laurence Olivier, Vittorio De Sica
▶ Archbishop Quinn emerges from twenty-year sentence in Soviet prison camp to become the first non-Italian pope in four hundred years. Quinn must deal with a world facing starvation and nuclear confrontation. Global-sized adaptation of the Morris West best-seller has a superb cast and an epic sweep.

SHOGUN 1981
★★★ NR Action-Adventure/MFTV 2:05
☑ Nudity, adult situations, violence
Dir: Jerry London *Cast:* Richard Chamberlain, Toshiro Mifune, Yoko Shimada, Frankie Sakai, Alan Badel, Michael Hordern
▶ Chamberlain, a seventeenth-century Englishman shipwrecked in Japan, becomes a pawn in feudal power struggle as local lord Mifune vies for title of shogun. Star-crossed romance between Chamberlain and concubine Shimada falls victim to politics when couple is captured by one of Mifune's rivals. Highly compressed version of ten-hour TV miniseries.

SHOGUN ASSASSIN 1980
U.S./Japanese
★★ R Martial Arts 1:26
☑ Nudity, adult situations, graphic violence
Dir: Robert Houston *Cast:* Tomisaburo Wakayama, Masahiro Tomikawa, Kayo Matsuo, Minoru Ohki, Shoji Kobayashi
▶ Curiosity item edited from two episodes in a popular Japanese martial arts series. Adding a new soundtrack and redubbing the characters, American producers fashioned an extremely violent and almost plotless story from *Sword of Vengeance* and *Baby-Cart at the River Styx*, sequels to the stylish *Lightning Swords of Death*. Nonstop action involving an outcast samurai and his young son is dazzlingly bloody, but narration adds unnecessary comic overtones. Providing new voices are Lamont Johnson and Sandra Bernhard.

SHOOTING, THE 1967
★★★ G Western 1:22
☑ Explicit language, violence
Dir: Monte Hellman *Cast:* Millie Perkins, Jack Nicholson, Warren Oates, Will Hutchins
▶ Ex–bounty hunter and sidekick hook up with mysterious woman in the desert. A gunslinger follows them, leading to a violent dispute. Offbeat and arty Western filmed simultaneously with *Ride in the*

Whirlwind is not for the John Wayne crowd. However, Nicholson is fascinating and cult favorite Hellman provides interesting direction.

SHOOTING PARTY, THE 1985 British
★★ **NR Drama 1:48**
☑ Brief nudity, explicit language, mild violence
Dir: Alan Bridges *Cast:* James Mason, Dorothy Tutin, Edward Fox, Cheryl Campbell, John Gielgud, Gordon Jackson
▶ Pre–World War I England: nobleman Mason plays host to fellow aristocrats for a weekend of hunting at his country estate. Shooting isn't the only thing on the agenda as adultery, romance, and political discussions also occur. Faultlessly acted (the one Mason-Gielgud scene is priceless) and the bucolic English countryside provides nice contrast to the violence of the hunt. However, talky drama of manners and tradition moves slowly.

SHOOTIST, THE 1976
★★★★★ **PG Western 1:39**
☑ Adult situations, explicit language, violence
Dir: Don Siegel *Cast:* John Wayne, Lauren Bacall, Ron Howard, James Stewart, Richard Boone, Hugh O'Brian
▶ Turn-of-the-century Carson City: famous gunslinger Wayne, dying of cancer, takes room in Bacall's boarding house. Her son Howard worships Wayne but bad guys Boone and O'Brien are determined to shoot him down. Tremendously moving and effective. Director Siegel emphasizes characterization and suspense over the usual genre shootouts; Wayne's quietly dignified performance ranks with his finest.

SHOOT THE MOON 1982
★★★ **R Drama 2:04**
☑ Adult situations, explicit language, violence
Dir: Alan Parker *Cast:* Albert Finney, Diane Keaton, Karen Allen, Peter Weller, Dana Hill
▶ Respected author Finney, the father of four girls, leaves Keaton for younger woman Allen. Keaton battles rejection and despair while considering a divorce and an affair with Weller. Strong acting and incisive writing by Bo Goldman are the highlights of this downbeat melodrama.

SHOOT THE PIANO PLAYER 1960
French
☆ **NR Drama 1:25 B&W**
Dir: François Truffaut *Cast:* Charles Aznavour, Marie Dubois, Nicole Berger, Michele Mercier
▶ Pianist Aznavour, haunted by his wife's suicide, plays in a cheap cafe. Aznavour's quiet existence is disrupted when he gets in a violent dispute with the bartender over the affections of waitress Dubois and his brother gets mixed up with criminals. Masterful mix of different moods from black comedy (the famous shock cut when a gangster swears on his mother's life) to tragedy (the shootout in the snow) will delight fans of the French New Wave. Soulfully magnetic performance by Aznavour, catchy score by Georges Delerue. Adapted from a David Goodis novel. ⑤

SHOOT THE SUN DOWN 1980
★ **PG Western 1:33**
☑ Violence
Dir: David Leeds *Cast:* Margot Kidder, Christopher Walken, Bo Brundin, Geoffrey Lewis
▶ Kidder flees from indentured servitude by posing as a lady. Walken saves her from desert heat prostration, but her employer attempts to steal Kidder back. One of Kidder's best performances, but one of Walken's weakest. Confusing story with little action ends on a downbeat note.

SHOOT TO KILL 1988
★★★★ **R Action-Adventure 1:46**
☑ Adult situations, explicit language, violence
Dir: Roger Spottiswoode *Cast:* Sidney Poitier, Tom Berenger, Kirstie Alley, Clancy Brown, Richard Masur, Andrew Robinson
▶ Savage killer joins a group camping trip led by Alley through Pacific Northwest mountains; San Francisco FBI agent Poitier must depend on Alley's outdoorsman boyfriend Berenger to track the killer down. Familiar manhunt benefits from extraordinary location footage, well-mounted action sequences, and first-rate performance by Poitier, starring in his first film in a decade.

SHOP AROUND THE CORNER, THE 1940
★★★ **NR Romance/Comedy 1:37 B&W**
Dir: Ernst Lubitsch *Cast:* James Stew-

art, Margaret Sullavan, Frank Morgan, Joseph Schildkraut, Sara Haden, Felix Bressart

▶ For feuding Budapest sales clerks Stewart and Sullavan, it is fight at first sight. Both fall for pen pals they've never met, not realizing that the other is actually the object of their written affections. One of the most charming and romantic confections ever to come out of Hollywood features delicately nuanced direction by Lubitsch, marvelous ensemble playing. Remade as the musical *In the Good Old Summertime* and adapted into the Broadway musical *She Loves Me*. **(CC)**

SHOP ON MAIN STREET, THE 1965
Czech
★★ NR Drama 2:08 B&W
Dir: Jan Kadar, Elmar Klos   *Cast:* Josef Kroner, Ida Kaminska, Hana Slivkova, Frantisek Zvarik, Helena Zvarikov, Martin Holly

▶ In Nazi-occupied Eastern Europe, amiable carpenter Kroner agrees to be "Aryan comptroller" for a Jewish-owned button shop on Main Street to appease nagging wife Slivkova and fascist brother-in-law Zvarik. Kroner learns the store's owner, bankrupt, deaf, and elderly Kaminska, is not even aware of the war, and he must decide whether or not to abide by an order to deport the town's Jews. Oscar winner for Best Foreign Film. [S]

SHORT CIRCUIT 1986
★★★★★ PG Sci-Fi/Comedy 1:39
☑ Explicit language, mild violence
Dir: John Badham   *Cast:* Steve Guttenberg, Ally Sheedy, Fisher Stevens, Austin Pendleton, G. W. Bailey, Brian McNamara

▶ Lightning strikes robot made for military applications, giving it human qualities. Robot escapes from lab and finds sanctuary with animal-lover Sheedy, who thinks it's an adorable alien. Robot's inventor Guttenberg and Indian colleague Stevens search for their creation while military honcho Bailey orders the errant robot destroyed. Genial box-office smash will delight children of all ages. Followed by sequel. **(CC)**

SHORT CIRCUIT II 1988
★★★★ PG Sci-Fi/Comedy 1:52
☑ Explicit language
Dir: Kenneth Johnson   *Cast:* Fisher Stevens, Michael McKean, Cynthia Gibb, Jack Weston, David Hemblen

▶ Sequel to the popular comedy continues the adventures of Johnny Five, the jerry-rigged robot with superhuman intelligence. This time he helps Stevens, one of his former guardians, foil a jewel robbery while struggling with an idea for a new toy. Lighthearted follow-up should please younger viewers.

SHORT EYES 1977
☆ R Drama 1:44
☑ Adult situations, explicit language, graphic violence
Dir: Robert M. Young   *Cast:* Bruce Davison, Jose Perez, Nathan George, Don Blakely, Shawn Elliot, Tito Goya

▶ Davison, a mild-mannered, middle-class WASP, encounters complex code of rules and dangerous existence when imprisoned in New York City's Tombs jail. The other inmates learn Davison is an accused child molester (a "short eyes" in cellblock slang) and vent their racial and sexual frustrations on him in awful ways. Powerful and hard-hitting look at underclass of American society is disturbing and unforgettable. Not for those seeking escapist fare.

SHOT IN THE DARK, A 1964
★★★★ PG Comedy 1:43
☑ Adult situations, explicit language
Dir: Blake Edwards   *Cast:* Peter Sellers, Elke Sommer, George Sanders, Herbert Lom, Burt Kwouk, Tracy Reed

▶ When Paris maid Sommer is accused of murder, bumbling Inspector Clouseau (Sellers) investigates. Despite all evidence to the contrary and an increasing body count, Clouseau insists on Sommer's innocence and solves the case in his own inimitable fashion. Hilarious follow-up to *The Pink Panther* with classic Sellers-Edwards pratfalls.

SHOUT AT THE DEVIL 1977 British
★★★★ PG Action-Adventure 2:08
☑ Explicit language, violence
Dir: Peter Hunt   *Cast:* Lee Marvin, Roger Moore, Barbara Parkins, Ian Holm, Rene Kolldehoff, Horst Janson

▶ East Africa, 1913: Irish ivory poacher Marvin and English partner Moore run afoul of German commissioner Kolldehoff. Moore and Marvin's daughter Parkins fall in love but when Kolldehoff kills their baby, they seek vengeance by blowing up a German battleship. Rousingly old-fashioned adventure is well mounted and quite pleasing.

SHOW BOAT 1936
★★ **NR Musical 1:50 B&W**
Dir: James Whale *Cast:* Irene Dunne, Allan Jones, Charles Winninger, Paul Robeson, Helen Morgan, Helen Westley
▶ Aboard a Mississippi River showboat in the 1900s, captain's daughter Dunne falls for gambler Jones while black singer Morgan tries to pass for white. Atmospheric direction from Whale; superb singing and acting by Dunne and Robeson. Magnificent Jerome Kern–Oscar Hammerstein score includes "Ol' Man River," "Can't Help Lovin' Dat Man," and "Bill." Adapted from the Broadway musical based on the Edna Ferber novel.

SHOW BOAT 1951
★★★★ **NR Musical 1:48**
Dir: George Sidney *Cast:* Howard Keel, Kathryn Grayson, Ava Gardner, Joe E. Brown, William Warfield, Agnes Moorehead
▶ MGM remake of the Kern-Hammerstein musical classic is perfectly cast: Grayson as captain Brown's daughter, Keel as her gambler beau, and Gardner as the mulatto star singer forced to flee from the sheriff because the law forbids her marriage to a white. Lovingly produced, beautifully sung, emotional and heartbreaking.

SHY PEOPLE 1987
★★ **R Drama 1:58**
☑ Rape, adult situations, explicit language, violence
Dir: Andrei Konchalovsky *Cast:* Jill Clayburgh, Barbara Hershey, Martha Plimpton, Merritt Butrick, John Philbin, Mare Winningham
▶ Manhattan magazine writer Clayburgh, unruly daughter Plimpton in tow, goes to Louisiana bayou to do article on her backwoods relative Hershey, a widowed mother of four. A sometimes violent culture clash ensues. Strong performances by Hershey (Best Actress at the Cannes Film Festival) and Clayburgh transcend overbaked script. **(CC)**

SICILIAN, THE 1987
★ **R Action-Adventure 1:55**
☑ Nudity, explicit language, violence
Dir: Michael Cimino *Cast:* Christopher Lambert, Terence Stamp, Barbara Sukowa, Joss Ackland, John Turturro, Richard Bauer
▶ Sicilian peasant Lambert kills cop, organizes outlaw band in the mountains, and becomes local folk hero as he battles powerful Mafia chieftain Ackland. Achieves some sweep and color but miscast Lambert fails to emerge as a tragic figure. Adapted from the Mario Puzo novel which reprised Michael Corleone characterization (cut from the film version) and was inspired by a true story.

SID AND NANCY 1986 British
☆ **R Biography/Music 1:53**
☑ Nudity, adult situations, explicit language, violence
Dir: Alex Cox *Cast:* Gary Oldman, Chloe Webb, David Hayman, Drew Schofield, Debby Bishop, Tony London
▶ Sordid relationship between Sex Pistols bassist Sid Vicious and junkie groupie Nancy Spungen receives a graphic but sympathetic treatment in this highly stylized punk biography. Oldman and Webb are sensational as the ill-fated pair, but film's unflinching depiction of the drug and punk underworlds is uncomfortably authentic. The music (including a re-creation of Sid's infamous "My Way" rock video) is first-rate. **(CC)**

SIDEWALKS OF LONDON 1938 British
★★ **NR Comedy 1:24 B&W**
Dir: Tim Whelan *Cast:* Charles Laughton, Vivien Leigh, Rex Harrison, Larry Adler, Tyrone Guthrie, Gus McNaughton
▶ Laughton, a London street entertainer, takes gamin Leigh under his wing when he catches her stealing from a musician. With the help of admirer Harrison, she becomes a famous music hall star, but doesn't forget the man who first helped her. Charming, bittersweet comedy features excellent performances by Laughton and Leigh.

SIESTA 1987
★★ **R Drama 1:37**
☑ Rape, nudity, adult situations, explicit language
Dir: Mary Lambert *Cast:* Ellen Barkin, Gabriel Byrne, Julian Sands, Isabella Rossellini, Martin Sheen, Jodie Foster
▶ Fragmented, experimental drama about daredevil stuntwoman Barkin whose pursuit of ex-lover Byrne brings her to the brink of madness. Told in flashbacks, story includes Barkin's encounters with jaded aristocrats in Spain and abandoned husband Sheen in Death Valley. Barkin is superb, but debut director Lambert's style is often irritating and pretentious. **(CC)**

SIGN O' THE TIMES 1987
★★★ **PG-13 Documentary/Music**
1:30
☑ Adult situations, explicit language
Dir: Prince *Cast:* Prince, Sheila E.,
Sheena Easton, Dr. Fink, Miko Weaver,
Cat
▶ Concert footage from Prince's European tour shot in Rotterdam and Ant-
werp. On stage set resembling seedy
downtown bar district, Prince and his reti-
nue rip through numbers including "Sign
o' the Times," "Little Red Corvette," "The
Cross," and "U Got the Look." Prince also
writhes his way through several dance
numbers and sports numerous outrageous costumes. Fans will be in revery
while doubters may become converts.

SILENCE OF THE NORTH 1981
Canadian
★★★★ **PG Drama 1:33**
☑ Adult situations, explicit language,
    violence
Dir: Allan King *Cast:* Ellen Burstyn, Tom
Skerritt, Gordon Pinsent, Jennifer McKinney, Colin Fox
▶ True story of Olive Frederickson (Burstyn) who accompanied her trapper husband Skerritt into the northern Canadian
wilderness in 1919. Burstyn sees her family
through harsh conditions and personal
tragedies. Little-known film deserves a
bigger reputation; strong story, solid production values, and magnificently sympathetic Burstyn.

SILENCERS, THE 1966
★★ **NR Espionage/Action-Adventure**
1:52
Dir: Phil Karlson *Cast:* Dean Martin,
Stella Stevens, Daliah Lavi, Victor
Buono, Arthur O'Connell, Robert Web-
ber
▶ Secret agent Matt Helm (Martin) bat-
tles the Big O, a spy group threatening
America's atomic missiles. Among the
obstacles to capturing Big O's leader
Buono are the Slaymates, eleven beauti-
ful but deadly models. Gaudy, leering es-
pionage spoof is the best in the series of
four Helm adventures. Theme sung by
Cyd Charisse, who also has a small role.
Sequel: *Murderers' Row.*

SILENT MADNESS 1984
★ **R Horror 1:35**
☑ Nudity, adult situations, explicit lan-
    guage, graphic violence
Dir: Simon Nuchtern *Cast:* Belinda

Montgomery, Viveca Lindfors, Solly
Marx, David Greenan, Sydney Lassick
▶ Brilliant psychiatrist Montgomery learns
that homicidal psychopath Marx has
been released by mistake from an asylum. She returns to the small-town college where he committed his original
murders, and poses as a sorority sister in
an effort to capture him. Predictably
bloody drama's interesting 3-D effects
will lose some impact on TV.

SILENT MOVIE 1976
★★★ **PG Comedy 1:27**
☑ Adult situations
Dir: Mel Brooks *Cast:* Mel Brooks,
Marty Feldman, Dom DeLuise, Ber-
nadette Peters, Burt Reynolds, Paul
Newman
▶ Has-been director Brooks and his pals
Feldman and DeLuise try to revive their
careers by convincing studio chief Sid
Caesar to back their silent movie. To win
Caesar's support, the guys attempt to
sign up big stars like Reynolds, Newman,
James Caan, and Liza Minnelli. Wild and
wacky fun with inventive visual gags. Not
strictly a silent: there are music, sound effects, and one line of dialogue spoken by
mime Marcel Marceau. Funniest scene:
the boys take a shower with Reynolds.

SILENT NIGHT, DEADLY NIGHT 1984
★ **R Horror 1:19**
☑ Nudity, explicit language, graphic
    violence
Dir: Charles E. Sellier *Cast:* Lilyan
Chauvan, Gilmer McCormick, Toni
Nero, Robert Brian Wilson, Britt Leach
▶ Little Billy witnesses parents' murder by
man in a Santa Claus suit. The kid grows
up in a Catholic orphanage, where the
Mother Superior punishes him for his anti-
Christmas feelings. When his toy-store
boss makes him don Santa gear, he goes
berserk. Lackluster slasher pic whose
premise provoked public outcry on origi-
nal release.

SILENT NIGHT, DEADLY NIGHT PART 2
1987
☆ **R Horror 1:28**
☑ Rape, nudity, adult situations, expli-
    cit language, violence
Dir: Lee Harry *Cast:* Eric Freeman,
James P. Newman, Elizabeth Cayton,
Jean Miller
▶ While institutionalized, Freeman,
younger brother of the killer from *Silent
Night, Deadly Night*, recalls emotionally
distraught childhood. Upon release, Free-

man puts on Saint Nick gear and goes on murderous rampage. Vicious sequel, poorly produced and badly acted.

SILENT PARTNER, THE 1979 Canadian
★ ★ ★ ★ R Mystery-Suspense 1:45
☑ Brief nudity, explicit language, violence
Dir: Daryl Duke   *Cast:* Elliott Gould, Susannah York, Christopher Plummer, Celine Lomez, Ken Pogue, John Candy
► When crazed robber Plummer attempts hold-up, mild-mannered teller Gould takes advantage of the heist to grab the loot for himself. Plummer menaces Gould for the dough; the two attempt to outwit one another with Lomez, involved with both men, caught in the middle. Exceptional and underrated with clever plotting, fine performances, well-rounded characterizations, and maximum tension.

SILENT RAGE 1982
★ ★ ★ R Action-Adventure 1:40
☑ Nudity, adult situations, explicit language, graphic violence
Dir: Michael Miller   *Cast:* Chuck Norris, Ron Silver, Steven Keats, Toni Kalem, Brian Libby, William Finley
► Sheriff Norris figures his job is done when his deputies kill ax murderer Libby. However, a research doctor revives the dead man with a drug, turning him into an indestructible killing machine. It's up to Norris to stop him. Fast-paced, if not quite Norris's best.

SILENT RUNNING 1972
★ ★ ★ G Sci-Fi 1:29
Dir: Douglas Trumbull   *Cast:* Bruce Dern, Cliff Potts, Ron Rifkin, Jesse Vint, Steven Brown
► Nuclear war has destroyed vegetation on Earth; the only plants left are in a space station orbiting Saturn. When the crew's botanist Dern receives orders to destroy them, he rebels and takes over the station. Intriguing but slowly paced drama was the directing debut for Trumbull, who worked on the special effects for *2001: A Space Odyssey*. Music by Peter Schickele, better known as P.D.Q. Bach.

SILENT SCREAM 1980
★ ★ R Horror 1:26
☑ Nudity, adult situations, explicit language, violence
Dir: Denny Harris   *Cast:* Rebecca Balding, Cameron Mitchell, Avery Schreiber,

Barbara Steele, Steve Doubet, Yvonne De Carlo
► College student Balding rents room in spooky boarding house, unaware that landlady De Carlo is hiding her psychotic daughter Steele upstairs. Subsequent brutal murders puzzle detectives Mitchell and Schreiber. Inventive but gory thriller builds up credible chills from a routine formula.

SILK STOCKINGS 1957
★ ★ ★ ★ NR Musical 1:57
Dir: Rouben Mamoulian   *Cast:* Fred Astaire, Cyd Charisse, Janis Paige, Peter Lorre, George Tobias, Barrie Chase
► Near-classic remake of *Ninotchka* features some good Cole Porter songs and memorable Astaire dancing. In Paris, Hollywood producer Astaire gets involved with Russian agents, in particular pretty comrade Charisse. She's all official business at first, but Astaire manages to overcome the Cold War and warm her up. While Garbo was a more convincing Russian, Charisse sure can dance. Score includes "All of You" and "Stereophonic Sound."

SILKWOOD 1983
★ ★ ★ ★ R Biography/Drama 2:11
☑ Brief nudity, adult situations, explicit language, violence
Dir: Mike Nichols   *Cast:* Meryl Streep, Kurt Russell, Cher, Craig T. Nelson, Diana Scarwid, Fred Ward
► Streep, a scrappy worker at a nuclear plant where employees include her live-in lover Russell and gay roommate Cher, grows disenchanted with lax safety procedures and becomes a union activist. When she discovers boss Nelson is deliberately concealing defects in products that could cause nuclear disasters, she gathers evidence for the press, annoying both management and her colleagues. Based on the true story of Karen Silkwood, topical drama depicts both Middle American blue-collar life and corporate greed and recklessness. Nominated for five Oscars.

SILVERADO 1985
★ ★ ★ ★ PG-13 Western 2:13
☑ Explicit language, violence
Dir: Lawrence Kasdan   *Cast:* Kevin Kline, Scott Glenn, Kevin Costner, Danny Glover, John Cleese, Rosanna Arquette
► Drifters Kline and Glenn team up with Glenn's hot-blooded younger brother

Costner and black cowboy Glover to rid town of corrupt sheriff Brian Dennehy and crooked cattle ranchers. Ripsnorter has it all: epic feel, fascinating characters, Oscar-nominated Bruce Broughton score. Relentless action and unflagging pace combine with touchingly quieter moments, like the gentle friendship between Kline and the barmaid Linda Hunt. (CC)

SILVER BEARS 1978
★★ **PG Drama 1:53**
☑ Adult situations, explicit language
Dir: Ivan Passer *Cast:* Michael Caine, Cybill Shepherd, Louis Jourdan, Tom Smothers, Martin Balsam, David Warner
▶ Wheeler-dealers Balsam and Caine hire penniless Italian count Jourdan as front for new Swiss bank. With wealthy Persian Warner, they conspire to smuggle silver from Iran. Convoluted plot includes various other bankers, brokers, and silver magnates. Shepherd plays the screwball, unfaithful wife of Smothers; Jay Leno appears as Balsam's car-thief son. Adapted from Paul Erdman's novel.

SILVER BULLET 1985
★★★ **R Horror 1:35**
☑ Explicit language, graphic violence
Dir: Dan Attias *Cast:* Gary Busey, Corey Haim, Megan Follows, Robin Groves
▶ Run-of-the-mill werewolf story, written by Stephen King and based on his novella, "Cycle of the Werewolf." Confined to a wheelchair, Haim must convince sister Follows and hard-drinking uncle Busey that a werewolf is responsible for the horrible murders in Tarker's Mills. Eventually, they confront the monster on Halloween with the assistance of a silver bullet. (CC)

SILVER CHALICE, THE 1955
★★★ **NR Drama 2:15**
Dir: Victor Saville *Cast:* Paul Newman, Virginia Mayo, Pier Angeli, Jack Palance, Natalie Wood, Lorne Greene
▶ Greek sculptor Newman is sold into slavery but wins recognition in Rome. He is commissioned by Christian leaders in Jerusalem to make a religious relic, leading to battles with evil magician Palance and the Roman emperor. Miscast Newman is awkward and self-conscious in his film debut; actor took out an ad asking people not to watch the movie, but it really isn't that bad. Based on the Thomas B. Costain novel.

SILVER DREAM RACER 1983 British
★★ **PG Drama/Sports 1:39**
☑ Adult situations, explicit language
Dir: David Wickes *Cast:* Beau Bridges, David Essex, Cristina Raines, Clarke Peters, Harry H. Corbett
▶ Essex is an aspiring world-class biker who has it in for American champ Bridges, responsible for the death of another driver. Forced out of the competition, Essex gets help financing his new motorcycle prototype, the Silver Dream Racer, from Raines, the widow of the dead driver, and enters the big British race. First-rate photography and spectacular track scenes enhance the only slightly above-average plotline.

SILVER STREAK 1976
★★★★★ **PG Comedy 1:53**
☑ Adult situations, explicit language, mild violence
Dir: Arthur Hiller *Cast:* Gene Wilder, Jill Clayburgh, Richard Pryor, Ned Beatty, Patrick McGoohan, Ray Walston
▶ All-star cast of clowns becomes embroiled in a cross-country caper when bookish Wilder, on an L.A. to Chicago train trip, seduces Clayburgh. Everything is blissful until he sees a corpse thrown from the train. With looney, petty thief Pryor, they learn of a murder plot involving missing Rembrandt letters and psychopathic art historian McGoohan. Briskly paced plot culminates in a literally smashing ending.

SIMON 1980
★ **PG Comedy 1:37**
☑ Explicit language, adult humor
Dir: Marshall Brickman *Cast:* Alan Arkin, Austin Pendleton, Judy Graubart, William Finley, Wallace Shawn, Madeline Kahn
▶ Think-tank scientists brainwash professor Arkin into believing he is an alien; experiment gets out of control when Arkin becomes a TV messiah, preaching to the masses. Some funny scenes, like Arkin's pantomine history of evolution, but the humor tends to be uneven. Graubart is quite winning as the girlfriend who tells Arkin he is not from "out of space." "That's 'outer space'!" protests Arkin.

SINBAD AND THE EYE OF THE TIGER 1977 British
★★★ **G Fantasy/Family 1:53**
Dir: Sam Wanamaker *Cast:* Patrick Wayne, Taryn Power, Margaret Whiting, Jane Seymour

▶ Sinbad (Wayne) comes to the aid of his princess-fiancée Seymour when her brother is transformed into a baboon by his evil stepmother Whiting. Along the way, the brave sailor fights numerous monsters (courtesy of special effects whiz Ray Harryhausen). Good fun for youngsters although bland acting may not hold adult viewers.

SINBAD THE SAILOR 1947
★★★★ NR Action-Adventure 1:57
Dir: Richard Wallace *Cast:* Douglas Fairbanks, Jr., Maureen O'Hara, Anthony Quinn, Walter Slezak, Jane Greer, Mike Mazurki
▶ On a mysterious island, Sinbad (Fairbanks) races against evil emir Quinn in pursuit of the legendary treasure of Alexander the Great and wins the love of the beautiful O'Hara. Saturday matinee-style escapism: alabaster palaces and slender minarets sparkle in Technicolor with Fairbanks adding a dash of panache to the many escapes.

SINCERELY YOURS 1955
★★ NR Drama 1:55
Dir: Gordon Douglas *Cast:* Liberace, Joanne Dru, Dorothy Malone, Alex Nicol, William Demarest, Lori Nelson
▶ Pianist Liberace goes deaf and becomes a recluse. He watches others through a telescope and acquires lip-reading ability. His enthusiasm for life renewed, he helps those less fortunate. Liberace fans might enjoy his patented outrageous outfits and musical numbers (including "Chopsticks"), but the script is unintentionally funny.

SINCE YOU WENT AWAY 1944
★★★★ NR Drama 2:52 B&W
Dir: John Cromwell *Cast:* Claudette Colbert, Jennifer Jones, Shirley Temple, Joseph Cotten, Monty Woolley, Robert Walker
▶ Sentimental masterpiece examines the impact of World War II on the home front, in particular housewife Colbert and daughters Jones and Temple as they wait for news from their enlisted husband and father. Cotten offers solid support as a long-term friend of the family. Filled with heartbreaking moments and warmly nostalgic views of small-town life, film received nine Oscar nominations, winning for Max Steiner's lush score. Large cast includes many familiar faces, including Lionel Barrymore, Agnes

Moorehead, Hattie McDaniel, and Keenan Wynn.

SINGIN' IN THE RAIN 1952
★★★★★ NR Musical 1:43
Dir: Gene Kelly, Stanley Donen *Cast:* Gene Kelly, Debbie Reynolds, Donald O'Connor, Jean Hagen, Cyd Charisse, Rita Moreno
▶ In the late 1920s, Hollywood silent-movie star Kelly adjusts to the coming of sound and romances young actress Reynolds. Kelly's co-star Hagen wants him for herself and schemes against Reynolds. Perhaps the greatest musical of them all is consistently witty, tuneful, and exuberant. Many unforgettable numbers: O'Connor's pratfalls to "Make 'Em Laugh," the justly famous title tune, the lyrical Kelly-Reynolds "You Were Meant for Me" duet in an empty studio. (CC)

SIN OF HAROLD DIDDLEBOCK, THE 1947
★★ NR Comedy 1:30 B&W
Dir: Preston Sturges *Cast:* Harold Lloyd, Frances Ramsden, Rudy Vallee, Jimmy Conlin, Edgar Kennedy, Raymond Walburn
▶ Inventive comedy opens with Lloyd's football heroics from 1925 *The Freshman*, then jumps twenty years to show that he never rose above bookkeeper. After being fired, Lloyd gets first drink from barkeep Kennedy. "Sir, you arouse the artist in me," says Kennedy as he mixes a concoction that sends straitlaced Lloyd on a mad spree that includes purchasing a circus. Underrated Sturges work is just a few shades below his best; sweet Lloyd/Ramsden relationship adds poignance to the humor. Producer Howard Hughes reedited and released the film in 1950 as *Mad Wednesday*, with ten minutes cut from original.

SIROCCO 1951
★★★ NR Mystery-Suspense 1:38 B&W
Dir: Curtis Bernhardt *Cast:* Humphrey Bogart, Marta Toren, Lee J. Cobb, Everett Sloane, Gerald Mohr, Zero Mostel
▶ Downbeat love triangle set in 1920s Syria. Bogart is a black-market gunrunner supplying arms to rebel Arabs; when threatened by Cobb, a French officer, he retaliates by stealing Cobb's girlfriend Toren. But his better instincts take hold when Cobb is kidnapped by the rebels. Effort to recapture the magic of *Casablanca* suffers from gloomy plot and lack of romance.

SISTER KENNY 1946
★★★ NR Biography 1:56 B&W
Dir: Dudley Nichols *Cast:* Rosalind Russell, Alexander Knox, Dean Jagger, Philip Merivale, Beulah Bondi, Charles Dingle

▶ Moving, thoughtful tribute to Elizabeth Kenny, an Australian nurse who fought for decades to have her polio rehabilitation therapy accepted by the medical establishment. Russell received an Oscar nomination for her loving portrayal of Kenny; Knox, who also worked on the screenplay with director Nichols and Mary McCarthy, plays a Scottish doctor who was one of her few allies.

SISTERS 1973
★ R Horror 1:33
☑ Adult situations, explicit language, violence
Dir: Brian De Palma *Cast:* Margot Kidder, Jennifer Salt, Charles Durning, Bill Finley, Lisle Wilson, Barnard Hughes

▶ Staten Island reporter Salt thinks she's witnessed a murder, but police refuse to believe her. She hires detective Durning to tail suspect Kidder while conducting her own dangerous investigation. Film borrows liberally from *Rear Window,* but director De Palma adds unnerving touches. Added benefits are inventive split-screen techniques and an eerie Bernard Herrmann score.

SISTER SISTER 1988
★★ R Mystery-Suspense 1:30
☑ Nudity, adult situations, explicit language, violence
Dir: Bill Condon *Cast:* Eric Stoltz, Jennifer Jason Leigh, Judith Ivey, Dennis Lipscomb, Anne Pitoniak

▶ Dark and chilling Southern gothic mystery/horror about sisters Ivey and Leigh who turn their Louisiana Bayou mansion into a bed and breakfast guest house. Ivey resents the attention her younger sister receives from handsome guest Stoltz. Things turn for the worse when their dog is decapitated, the handyman is sliced up in the swamp, and little sister begins hearing voices from the past. Steamy atmosphere and capable performances; a few notches above its "don't-go-out-alone" competition.

SIX PACK 1982
★★★★ PG Comedy 1:48
☑ Adult situations, explicit language, mild violence
Dir: Daniel Petrie *Cast:* Kenny Rogers,

Diane Lane, Erin Gray, Barry Corbin, Terry Kiser, Anthony Michael Hall

▶ Racer Rogers, attempting to make a comeback after an accident, catches six orphans trying to strip his car. After this rocky start, the kids wear down Rogers's resistance to them and a warm relationship develops. Down-home tale has easy-going charm; Rogers makes a pleasant feature film debut and the kids are cute as a bug. Songs by Rogers, Crystal Gayle, and Merle Haggard.

SIXTEEN CANDLES 1984
★★★★ PG Comedy 1:33
☑ Brief nudity, adult situations, explicit language
Dir: John Hughes *Cast:* Molly Ringwald, Anthony Michael Hall, Paul Dooley, Carlin Glynn, Blanche Baker, Michael Schoeffling

▶ Sweet sixteen turns sour for student Ringwald: parents Dooley and Glynn are so crazed by sister Baker's wedding they forget Molly's birthday; crush on high school hunk Schoeffling appears unrequited; and attention only comes from not-so-meek geek Hall. Good-natured, lowbrow comedy mixes rowdy laughs with sweetly accurate portrayal of puberty blues. Directorial debut for Hughes and launching pad for careers of Ringwald and Hall.

SIX WEEKS 1982
★★★★ PG Drama 1:47
☑ Adult situations, explicit language
Dir: Tony Bill *Cast:* Dudley Moore, Mary Tyler Moore, Katherine Healy, Shannon Wilcox, Joe Regalbuto, John Harkins

▶ Married politician Dudley Moore gets involved with cosmetics mogul Mary Tyler Moore and her dying daughter Healy. Romantic feelings grow between Dudley and Mary as they help Healy make her last weeks meaningful. High-grade tearjerker doesn't insult your intelligence; the leads play off one another with humor and sensitivity and Healy is very appealing.

SKI BUM, THE 1971
☆ R Drama 1:36
☑ Brief nudity, adult situations, explicit language, violence
Dir: Bruce Clark *Cast:* Charlotte Rampling, Zalman King, Joseph Mell, Dimitra Arliss, Lori Shelle, Anna Karen

▶ Married Rampling, having an affair with ski bum King, gets him a job at a lodge. Middle-class owners alienate

King, so he pursues quick riches in a questionable business deal. Loosely based on Romain Gary's novel.

SKIN DEEP 1989
★★★ R Comedy 1:41
☑ Nudity, adult situations, explicit language
Dir: Blake Edwards *Cast:* John Ritter, Vincent Gardenia, Alyson Reed, Joel Brooks, Julianne Phillips, Chelsea Field
▶ Ritter, ostensibly a successful author, tries to cure writer's block with alcohol and obsessive womanizing. His slapstick journey includes encounter with body-building champion Raye Hollit and startling incident with a new brand of condoms. Episodic comedy has overtones of director Edwards's more successful *10*.

SKIN GAME 1971
★★★★ PG Western/Comedy 1:42
☑ Explicit language, mild violence
Dir: Paul Bogart *Cast:* James Garner, Louis Gossett, Jr., Susan Clark, Brenda Sykes, Edward Asner, Andrew Duggan
▶ Two pre–Civil War con men run imaginative scam: "slaveowner" Garner sells "slave" Gossett to dupes and then helps him escape for next sucker. Comfortable ruse runs afoul of con woman Clark, who steals their money and Garner's heart, slave girl Sykes, who wins Gossett's love, suspicious slave trader Asner, and abolitionists who insist on "freeing" Gossett. Amiable comedy with heart makes case for human dignity.

SKIP TRACER 1979 Canadian
★★ NR Mystery-Suspense 1:30
☑ Brief nudity, explicit language
Dir: Zale R. Dalen *Cast:* David Petersen, John Lazarus, Rudy Szabo, Mike Grigg
▶ Driven to win loan agency's "Man of the Year" for fourth time, debt collector Petersen takes his job seriously, callously repossessing the merchandise of those who skip payments. But when his efforts have unforeseen tragic consequences, obsessed Petersen must reassess his life. Low-budget character study can be slow-paced, but is well written and credible.

SKY RIDERS 1976
★★★★ PG Action-Adventure 1:33
☑ Adult situations, violence
Dir: Douglas Hickox *Cast:* James Coburn, Susannah York, Robert Culp, Charles Aznavour, Werner Pochath, Zouzou
▶ When wife York is kidnapped by terrorists, wealthy industrialist Culp turns to her ex-husband Coburn for help. He assembles a team of mercenaries and leads a daring attack by hang-glider on the mountain fortress where York is being held. Shot on location in Greece, film offers marvelous scenery and thrilling aerial sequences.

SKY'S THE LIMIT, THE 1943
★★ NR Musical 1:29 B&W
Dir: Edward H. Griffith *Cast:* Fred Astaire, Joan Leslie, Robert Benchley, Robert Ryan, Elizabeth Patterson
▶ Minor musical about a wartime romance between aviation hero Astaire disguised as an ordinary citizen and journalist Leslie dedicated to the war effort. Undistinguished except for Astaire's brilliant "One for My Baby" and the Oscar-nominated "My Shining Hour."

SLAM DANCE 1987
★ R Mystery-Suspense 1:40
☑ Nudity, adult situations, explicit language, violence
Dir: Wayne Wang *Cast:* Tom Hulce, Virginia Madsen, Mary Elizabeth Mastrantonio, Adam Ant, Harry Dean Stanton, Millie Perkins
▶ Down-on-his-luck Los Angeles cartoonist Hulce, deserted by wife Mastrantonio, is accused of murdering romantic fling Madsen. Pursued by cop Stanton, Hulce finds himself neck-deep in conspiracy as he attempts to exonerate himself. Stylish thriller can be too self-consciously hip, but likable Hulce and subculture setting compensate for many flaws. **(CC)**

SLAMMER GIRLS 1987
☆ R Comedy 1:21
☑ Nudity, adult situations, explicit language, adult humor
Dir: Chuck Vincent *Cast:* Devon Jenkin, Jeff Eagle, Jane Hamilton, Ron Sullivan
▶ Women's prison movie spoof, cheap and tacky, sends up every imaginable cliché. Innocent virgin falsely accused of murder is sent to prison, takes lots of showers, and works the chain gang. She tries to escape, is caught, given shock treatments, put into solitary, and helps a fellow inmate deliver a baby. Bad-taste jokes and poorly acted; strictly late-night fare.

SLAP SHOT 1977
★★★★ R Comedy/Sports 2:03

☑ Brief nudity, adult situations, explicit language, violence
Dir: George Roy Hill *Cast:* Paul Newman, Michael Ontkean, Lindsay Crouse, Jennifer Warren, Melinda Dillon, Strother Martin
▶ Player-coach Newman revives minor-league hockey team's flagging fortunes by turning the players from skaters into fighters. Sensitive Ivy League teammate Ontkean resists the brawling while, off the ice, womanizer Newman pursues Ontkean's wife Crouse and others. Rowdy, unruly, and uproarious; Newman is perfect. The raw language is hilarious but keep the kiddies out of earshot.

SLAPSTICK OF ANOTHER KIND 1984
☆ **PG Comedy 1:24**
☑ Explicit language, adult humor
Dir: Steven Paul *Cast:* Jerry Lewis, Madeline Kahn, Marty Feldman, John Abbott, Jim Backus, Merv Griffin
▶ Rich couple Lewis and Kahn send away embarrassingly ugly twins to be raised by butler Feldman. Fifteen years later, the Chinese (who have solved overcrowding by miniaturizing themselves) announce that the twins, also played by Lewis and Kahn, now eight-foot geniuses, can solve the world's energy crisis. Twins must elude the Chinese and confound efforts of parents to separate them until they're rescued by advanced aliens who are their true parents. Half-baked adaptation of Kurt Vonnegut novel is for Lewis lovers only.

SLATE, WYN & ME 1987 Australian
★ **R Drama 1:30**
☑ Explicit language
Dir: Don McLennan *Cast:* Sigrid Thornton, Simon Burke, Martin Sacks, Tommy Lewis, Lesley Baker, Harold Bigent
▶ Vietnam vet Burke and his brother Sacks kill a cop during a bank robbery and are forced to kidnap Thornton, the only witness, when they flee into Australia's remote Outback. At first fearful for her life, Thornton learns to exploit the brothers for her own ends. Despite beautiful locations, unfocused chase lacks excitement.

SLAUGHTER HIGH 1987
★ **R Horror 1:30**
☑ Nudity, explicit language, violence
Dir: George Dugdale, Mark Ezra, Peter Litten *Cast:* Caroline Munro, Simon Scuddamore, Carmine Iannoccone, Donna Yeager, Sally Cross, Kelly Baker
▶ Cruel high school students tormenting classmate Scuddamore with practical jokes accidentally scar him for life. Years later he returns disguised as a court jester to kill them. Routine horror film filled with gratuitously bloody violence. Also known as *April Fool's Day*.

SLAUGHTERHOUSE 1988
★ **R Horror 1:25**
☑ Explicit language, graphic violence
Dir: Rick Roessler *Cast:* Sherry Bendorf, Don Barrett, William Houch, Joe Barton, Jane Higginson
▶ California radio station sponsoring a "Pig Out" weekend sends a group of teens on a tour of the local pig slaughterhouse. Owner Barrett and his retarded son Barton, angry at losing the slaughterhouse in a tax dispute, respond by murdering the visitors. Uninspired horror exploitation attempts touches of black humor.

SLAUGHTERHOUSE FIVE 1972
★★ **R Sci-Fi 1:44**
☑ Nudity, adult situations, explicit language, violence
Dir: George Roy Hill *Cast:* Michael Sacks, Ron Leibman, Valerie Perrine, Sharon Gans, Roberts Blossom, Kevin Conway
▶ Sacks plays an ordinary guy who finds himself traveling in time and space between three situations: World War II POW during the brutal bombing of Dresden, middle-class husband and father, and caged prisoner kept in captivity with sexy lover Perrine by alien beings. Complex, ambitious adaptation perfectly captures the spirit of Kurt Vonnegut's acclaimed novel.

SLAUGHTER IN SAN FRANCISCO 1981 Hong Kong
☆ **R Martial Arts 1:27**
☑ Adult situations, explicit language, violence
Dir: William Lowe *Cast:* Don Wong, Chuck Norris, Sylvia Channing, Robert Jones, Dan Ivan
▶ When his former partner is murdered, ex-cop Wong relies on his martial arts prowess to track down the killers. Bland kung-fu filler of interest only for an early villainous role by Norris. Set in Daly City (outside San Francisco), shot in 1973, and released here in 1981 to capitalize on Norris's star power.

SLAVE GIRLS FROM BEYOND INFINITY
1987
☆ R Sci-Fi 1:12
☑ Nudity, adult situations, explicit language, violence
Dir: Ken Dixon *Cast:* Elizabeth Cayton, Cindy Beal, Brike Stevens, Don Scribner, Carl Horner, Kirk Graves
▶ Three beautiful escaped convicts crash-land on a jungle planet ruled by the evil Zed. He forces them into a deadly hunt in which they are the prey. Campy, low-budget adventure is primarily an excuse to see the statuesque leads running through woods in lingerie.

SLAYGROUND 1984 British
★ R Action-Adventure 1:29
☑ Explicit language, violence
Dir: Terry Bedford *Cast:* Peter Coyote, Mel Smith, Billie Whitelaw, Philip Sayer, Bill Luhrs
▶ Professional thief Coyote accidentally kills a young girl in upstate New York. Her father hires vicious hit man Sayer for revenge. Coyote flees to England, where amusement park owner Whitelaw involves him in another robbery. Stylish but shallow thriller has a good climax in the amusement park.

SLEEPAWAY CAMP 1983
★★ R Horror 1:25
☑ Explicit language, graphic violence
Dir: Robert Hiltzik *Cast:* Mike Kellin, Felissa Rose, Jonathan Tierston, Karen Fields, Christopher Collet
▶ A young girl witnesses the death of her family in a boating accident near Camp Arawak. Years later teen Rose returns to the camp, which is subsequently plagued by violent murders. Some effective shocks in this low-budget production.

SLEEPER 1973
★★★ PG Comedy 1:28
☑ Adult situations, explicit language
Dir: Woody Allen *Cast:* Woody Allen, Diane Keaton, John Beck, Mary Gregory, Don Keefer, Don McLiam
▶ Health food store owner Allen wakes up after minor ulcer surgery to discover he's been frozen for 200 years. U.S. is now a dictatorship; reluctant Milquetoast Allen is recruited by rebellious underground scientists who defrosted him. To evade capture by police, he pretends to be a robot servant to flaky poet Keaton, eventually drawing her into web of politics and romance. Superb early Allen mixes one-liners with stylish slapstick—

don't miss his wrestling match with future's answer to instant pudding. Bouncy jazz and ragtime score performed by Allen and the Preservation Hall Jazz Band.

SLEEPING BEAUTY 1959
★★★★★ G Animation 1:15
Dir: Clyde Geronimi *Cast:* Voices of Eleanor Audley, Verna Felton, Barbara Jo Allen, Barbara Luddy, Mary Costa, Bill Shirley
▶ Animated version of the Charles Perrault fairy tale, with music from the Tchaikovsky ballet. Evil fairy casts spell on Princess causing eternal sleep. Good fairies must assist Prince's attempt to undo the black magic. Disney spared no expense to make film the pinnacle of animation technology, so movement and detail are remarkable, culminating in Prince's fight with evil dragon. A classic for young and old alike.

SLEEPING CAR MURDERS, THE 1966 French
★ NR Mystery-Suspense 1:31
Dir: Costa-Gavras *Cast:* Simone Signoret, Yves Montand, Pierre Mondy, Catherine Allegret, Michel Piccoli, Jean-Louis Trintignant
▶ A woman is murdered on an overnight train to Paris; as police inspector Montand pursues the chief suspect, a young runaway, the other occupants of the car are killed by an unseen assailant. Directing debut for Costa-Gavras (*Z*) is a fast-paced but often confusing thriller with uniformly good performances. Cat-and-mouse chases build to a first-rate climax.

SLEEPING DOGS 1977 New Zealand
★★ NR Mystery-Suspense 1:47
☑ Nudity, explicit language, violence
Dir: Roger Donaldson *Cast:* Sam Neill, Melissa Donaldson, Bernard Kearns, Ian Mune, Clyde Scott, Warren Oates
▶ New Zealand police state, the future: innocent Neill seeking solitude on offshore island is imprisoned by authorities when framed by Maori revolutionaries. Escaping jail, he is pursued by American mercenary Oates. Politicized by encounter with corrupt government, Neill seeks to join insurgents only to learn they are led by wife's lover Mune (also screenplay author). Plenty of action and intrigue in this paranoid thriller.

SLEUTH 1972
★★★★ PG Mystery-Suspense 2:18

☑ Adult situations, explicit language, violence

Dir: Joseph L. Mankiewicz ***Cast:*** Laurence Olivier, Michael Caine, Alec Cawthorne, Margo Channing, John Matthews, Teddy Martin

▶ Anthony Shaffer's hit play is a dazzling showcase for Olivier and Caine, both Oscar-nominated as ingenious antagonists playing a deadly cat-and-mouse game. Olivier, a detective novelist, tricks Caine (his wife's lover) into committing a crime, but Caine turns the tables on him. Stars are supported by smooth direction and absorbing writing. Red herrings extend to credits as well (including a "performance" by *All About Eve*'s Margo Channing).

SLIPPER AND THE ROSE, THE 1976
British
★★★★ **G Musical/Family 2:08**
Dir: Bryan Forbes ***Cast:*** Richard Chamberlain, Gemma Craven, Annette Crosbie, Kenneth More, Edith Evans, Margaret Lockwood

▶ Musical adaptation of the classic Cinderella fairy tale in which beautiful Craven is made wretched servant to nasty stepmother Lockwood and her daughters. Only when lonely prince Chamberlain announces quest for bride who fits glass slipper does hope enter Craven's life. Lots of singing and dancing, with music and lyrics by the Sherman Brothers of *Mary Poppins* fame. Fun as family fare.

SLOANE 1986
★★ **NR Action-Adventure 1:35**
☑ Nudity, adult situations, explicit language, violence
Dir: Daniel Rosenthal ***Cast:*** Robert Resnik, Debra Blee, Raul Aragon, Victor Ordonez, Carissa Carlos, Ann Milhench

▶ Private investigator Resnik is sent to Manila to locate kidnapped Milhench. There he teams with Milhench's sister Blee, his Filipino pal Aragon, and Aragon's pretty sister Carlos. When not bedding down with Carlos, Resnik busies himself with chases, brawls, and shootouts during search for missing girl. B-grade actioner with no surprises.

SLUGGER'S WIFE, THE 1985
★★★ **PG-13 Comedy 1:44**
☑ Adult situations, explicit language
Dir: Hal Ashby ***Cast:*** Michael O'Keefe, Rebecca De Mornay, Randy Quaid, Martin Ritt, Cleavant Derricks, Lisa Langlois

▶ Slumping baseball player O'Keefe goes on hitting tear when De Mornay, the rock singer he starts dating, attends games. His batting average soars so they marry. Then her career takes off and she stops watching him play. Both marriage and O'Keefe's hitting skills fall apart. Somewhat sluggish comedy written by Neil Simon. **(CC)**

SLUMBER PARTY '57 1977
☆ **R Comedy 1:29**
☑ Nudity, strong sexual content, adult situations, explicit language, adult humor
Dir: William A. Levey ***Cast:*** Noelle North, Bridget Hollman, Debra Winger, Mary Ann Appleseth, Rainbeaux Smith, Janet Wood

▶ Teen girlfriends at a party describe their first sexual encounters. Winger takes on a gang of bikers; another girl is seduced by an older man; a third visits a hayloft with her riding instructor; etc. Flashbacks provide plenty of nudity and raunchy language in this soft-core exploitation. Soundtrack includes Patti Page, Dinah Washington, and Jerry Lee Lewis.

SLUMBER PARTY MASSACRE 1982
★ **R Horror 1:18**
☑ Nudity, explicit language, graphic violence
Dir: Amy Jones ***Cast:*** Michele Michaels, Robin Stille, Michael Villela, Andre Honore, Debra Deliso, Gina Mari

▶ Killer Villela escapes from jail and employs power drill to methodically kill valley girls during slumber party. Attempt at tongue-in-cheek spoof misses mark and instead works as average horror with a few gags. Screenplay by feminist novelist Rita Mae Brown nonetheless provides many opportunities for actresses to disrobe. Popular enough at drive-ins to spawn a sequel.

SLUMBER PARTY MASSACRE PART II 1987
☆ **R Horror 1:15**
☑ Nudity, adult situations, explicit language, graphic violence
Dir: Deborah Brock ***Cast:*** Crystal Bernard, Kimberly McArthur, Juliette Cummins, Patrick Lowe, Heidi Kozak, Atanas Ilitch

▶ On teen getaway weekend Bernard, young sister of victim from original film, suffers nightmare about marauding rocker Ilitch wielding drill-bit guitar. Ilitch suddenly materializes on premises and starts killing Bernard's pals in gory fashion. Sequel abandons humor for straight B-grade horror.

SMALL CHANGE 1976 French
★★ **PG Comedy 1:45**
☑ Brief nudity, explicit language
Dir: François Truffaut *Cast:* Geory Desmouceaux, Philippe Goldman, Claudio Deluca, Frank Deluca, Richard Golfier
► Truffaut's loving, lyrical, and often surprisingly funny tribute to the spirit of childhood and the gift for survival. Not much on plot—the film relates a series of vignettes about the lives of a group of children from the French town of Thiers. Vintage Truffaut ("Life is hard, but it's also wonderful," says a young teacher). Original and insightful but not for all tastes. Ⓢ

SMALL CIRCLE OF FRIENDS, A 1980
★★★ **R Drama 1:52**
☑ Adult situations, explicit language, violence
Dir: Rob Cohen *Cast:* Karen Allen, Brad Davis, Jameson Parker, Shelley Long, John Friedrich
► In the late 1960s, Harvard journalism major Davis meets art student Allen and they live together. They have problems and she moves in with med student Parker. Eventually Allen decides to bed both men at once but before that happens, one of the guys is killed during a student protest. Attractive leads give competent performances but they seldom rise above the clichéd—and now dated—plot.

SMALL TOWN IN TEXAS, A 1976
★★★★ **PG Action-Adventure 1:36**
☑ Explicit language, violence
Dir: Jack Starrett *Cast:* Timothy Bottoms, Susan George, Bo Hopkins, Art Hindle, John Karlen, Buck Fowler
► Texas ex-con Bottoms returns home for revenge on corrupt sheriff Hopkins, who framed him. He and his girlfriend George find evidence that Hopkins is plotting a political assassination, but the knowledge proves deadly as they're involved in a nonstop chase. Highlighted by scores of stunts involving cars, trains, and motorcycles.

SMASH PALACE 1982 New Zealand
★ **NR Drama 1:47**
☑ Nudity, adult situations, explicit language, violence
Dir: Roger Donaldson *Cast:* Bruno

Lawrence, Anna Jemison, Greer Robson, Keith Aberdein, Les Kelly
► Mechanic Lawrence enjoys quiet life running auto junkyard; his wife Jemison grows bored, has an affair, and leaves him. When she gets a court order to keep him away from their daughter Robson, a frustrated Lawrence kidnaps the child. Good acting and production values but predictable story and slow pacing make interest wander.

SMILE 1975
★ **PG Comedy 1:53**
☑ Adult situations, explicit language
Dir: Michael Ritchie *Cast:* Bruce Dern, Barbara Feldon, Michael Kidd, Geoffrey Lewis, Annette O'Toole, Melanie Griffith
► Amusing put-down of beauty contests takes place during the final days of an intense pageant in Santa Rosa, California. Plot switches dizzyingly among contestants, judges, organizers, and bystanders in a series of sight gags that satirize middle-class America with often uncomfortable accuracy. Dern, the head judge and a mobile home salesman, and Kidd, a burnt-out choreographer, stand out in the good cast. Later adapted into a Broadway musical with a score by Marvin Hamlisch.

SMILES OF A SUMMER NIGHT 1957 Swedish
★★ **NR Comedy 1:48 B&W**
Dir: Ingmar Bergman *Cast:* Ulla Jacobsson, Eva Dahlbeck, Margit Carlquist, Harriet Andersson, Gunnar Bjornstrand, Jarl Kulle
► In turn-of-the-century Sweden, a lawyer, his virginal bride, his son, and his old flame gather for a country weekend in which lovers break up and get together in new pairs. Bergman's most enchanting film is wise, amusing, and beautifully mounted without avoiding his usual serious concerns. The basis for the Broadway musical, "A Little Night Music." Ⓢ

SMITHEREENS 1982
★ **R Drama 1:30**
☑ Adult situations, explicit language
Dir: Susan Seidelman *Cast:* Susan Berman, Brad Rinn, Richard Hell, Nada Despotovich
► Oddly realistic punk/teen flick marks the directorial debut of Seidelman. Very low-budget tale of Jersey woman Berman who has little talent but lots of spunk, struggling to make it in the rock world while working in a copy shop. She

loves surly rocker Hell who treats her badly; she abuses the decent Montana boy Rinn who wants to marry her. Credible performances and colorful junkheap locations shot in New York City. Independent film feel will not appeal to some.

SMOKEY AND THE BANDIT 1977
★★★★★ PG
Action-Adventure/Comedy 1:36
☑ Explicit language
Dir: Hal Needham *Cast:* Burt Reynolds, Sally Field, Jackie Gleason, Paul Williams, Jerry Reed, Pat McCormick
▶ Truckers Reynolds and Reed transport bootleg beer across state lines while being pursued by redneck sheriff Gleason. Along the way, Reynolds romances hitchhiking bride-to-be Field. Fast-moving fun, with thrilling car chases and stunts, relaxed electricity generated by Reynolds and Field (a real-life couple at the time), broadly amusing support from Reed and Gleason.

SMOKEY AND THE BANDIT II 1980
★★★★ PG Action-Adventure/Comedy 1:41
☑ Explicit language, adult humor
Dir: Hal Needham *Cast:* Burt Reynolds, Sally Field, Jerry Reed, Jackie Gleason, Dom DeLuise, Paul Williams
▶ The cargo this time for truckers Reynolds and Reed is a pregnant elephant to be delivered to the Republican convention. Reynolds also attempts to win Field back from the sheriff's son and Gleason gives chase in three roles (the sheriff, a patrolman, and a mountie). Knockabout sequel with wild and woolly stunts and racy humor; DeLuise steals the show as a gynecologist who treats the elephant.

SMOKEY AND THE BANDIT—PART 3 1983
★★ PG Action-Adventure/Comedy 1:25
☑ Nudity, explicit language, adult humor
Dir: Dick Lowry *Cast:* Jackie Gleason, Jerry Reed, Paul Williams, Pat McCormick, Colleen Camp, Mike Henry
▶ The wealthy Enoses (Williams, McCormick) bet retiring sheriff Buford T. Justice (Gleason) that he can't make a Miami-Austin trip in twenty-four hours and hire Reed to make Gleason's task difficult. Smutty sex jokes go straight for the groin as third entry fails to compare to its predecessors. Burt Reynolds makes a cameo; the film misses his starring presence.

SMOKEY BITES THE DUST 1981
★★ PG Action-Adventure/Comedy 1:29
☑ Brief nudity, adult situations, explicit language, mild violence, adult humor
Dir: Charles B. Griffith *Cast:* Jimmy McNichol, Janet Julian, Walter Barnes, Patrick Campbell, Kari Lizer, William Forsythe
▶ High school hotshot McNichol kidnaps homecoming queen Julian; her sheriff father Barnes leads the pursuit. Literally one long chase with little in the way of character development or plot. Title recalls the *Smokey and the Bandit* series (of which this is no relation).

SMOOTH TALK 1985
★ PG-13 Drama 1:32
☑ Adult situations, explicit language
Dir: Joyce Chopra *Cast:* Treat Williams, Laura Dern, Mary Kay Place, Levon Helm, Sara Inglis, Margaret Welch
▶ Provocative drama about suburban California teen Dern's initiation into adulthood opens with a realistic look at problems with parents Place and Helm, then veers into an unnerving encounter with edgy drifter Williams. Adaptation of short story "Where Are You Going? Where Have You Been?" by Joyce Carol Oates features knowing performances by Dern and Williams.

SNAKE PIT, THE 1948
★★★★ NR Drama 1:48 B&W
Dir: Anatole Litvak *Cast:* Olivia de Havilland, Mark Stevens, Leo Genn, Celeste Holm, Leif Erickson, Beulah Bondi
▶ Aspiring writer de Havilland marries editorial assistant Stevens but sinks into madness and is institutionalized. Understanding therapist Genn treats her and uncovers past events that led to her breakdown. Honest, disturbing, and ahead of its time; uncompromising performance by de Havilland, strong screenplay and direction giving much insight into mental illness. Six Oscar nominations include Best Picture, Actress (de Havilland), Screenplay; won for Sound.

SNO-LINE 1985
★ R Action-Adventure 1:33
☑ Nudity, adult situations, explicit language, violence
Dir: Douglas F. O'Neons *Cast:* Vince

Edwards, Paul Smith, June Wilkinson, Phil Foster, Louis Guss

▶ Minor action exploitation with Edwards in an uncharacteristic role as a Texas gangster who establishes a cocaine monopoly along the Mexican border. When his drug money is stolen by thugs, he goes on a killing spree. Undistinguished acting undermined by a confusing story line.

SNOOPY COME HOME 1972
★ ★ ★ ★ ★ G Animation 1:21
Dir: Bill Melendez *Cast:* Voices of Chad Webber, Robin Kohn, Stephen Shea, David Carey, Johanna Baer
▶ Second feature based on Charles Schulz's comic-strip characters is a delightful family film concentrating on the headstrong Snoopy. Pooch learns he was originally owned by Lila, and leaves home with Woodstock to visit her in the hospital. Charlie Brown and his friends search frantically for him. Good animation and songs by Richard and Robert Sherman add to the fun. Sequel to *A Boy Named Charlie Brown.* **(CC)**

SNOWBALL EXPRESS, THE 1972
★ ★ ★ ★ G Comedy/Family 2:00
Dir: Norman Tokar *Cast:* Dean Jones, Nancy Olson, Harry Morgan, Keenan Wynn, Johnnie Whitaker
▶ New York accountant Jones inherits a ski resort in the Colorado Rockies. Expecting a glamorous chalet, he heads west with his family to discover a wreck on the verge of ruin. Despite hard work, they encounter disaster after disaster, culminating in an extended chase on snowmobiles. Typical Disney slapstick delivered with polish and flair.

SNOWS OF KILIMANJARO, THE 1952
★ ★ ★ NR Drama 1:57
Dir: Henry King *Cast:* Gregory Peck, Susan Hayward, Ava Gardner, Hildegarde Neff, Leo G. Carroll, Torin Thatcher
▶ Successful author Peck, stricken with fever on an African safari, reviews his past loves with dark beauty Gardner, European countess Neff, and American heiress Hayward. In his delirium he doubts his accomplishments until Hayward courageously defends him. Loosely adapted from a series of Ernest Hemingway stories, although more closely based on the author's own life.

SNOW WHITE AND THE SEVEN DWARFS 1937
★ ★ ★ ★ ★ G Animation 1:23
Dir: David Hand *Cast:* Voices of Adriana Caselotti, Harry Stockwell, Lucille Laverne, Moroni Olsen, Billy Gilbert
▶ Once upon a time an evil queen, jealous of fair Snow White, ordered her huntsman to slay the girl. Instead, he hid her deep in the forest where she moved in with seven eccentric but adorable dwarfs. Enduring classic, a landmark in animation history, still delights young and old, although the smallest children may be frightened by some scary moments. Songs include perennial favorites "Whistle While You Work" and "Heigh-Ho."

S.O.B. 1981
★ ★ R Comedy 2:01
☑ Brief nudity, adult situations, explicit language, violence
Dir: Blake Edwards *Cast:* Julie Andrews, William Holden, Richard Mulligan, Robert Preston, Robert Vaughn, Larry Hagman
▶ Crazed Hollywood producer Mulligan has a nervous breakdown after his big-budget musical starring wife Andrews flops at the box office. He becomes obsessed with recutting the film, adding his wife's nudity, to garner an X rating. Among the vipers in his life: director-in-residence Holden, boozy "Dr. Feelgood" Preston, pushy gossip-monger Loretta Swit, and ruthless studio head Vaughn. Wickedly right-on performances from stellar cast in this offbeat take on Hollywood hustlers.

SO DEAR TO MY HEART 1949
★ ★ ★ ★ NR Family 1:22
Dir: Harold Schuster, Hamilton Luske
Cast: Burl Ives, Beulah Bondi, Bobby Driscoll, Harry Carey, Luana Patten, Raymond Bond
▶ Indiana farmboy Driscoll dreams of winning blue ribbon for his black sheep at the county fair but must find a way to earn the entry fee first. Superb Disney blend of nostalgia, adventure, charming animated sequences, and lively songs will delight children and parents alike.

SO FINE 1981
★ ★ R Comedy 1:29
☑ Adult situations, explicit language
Dir: Andrew Bergman *Cast:* Ryan O'Neal, Jack Warden, Mariangela Melato, Richard Kiel, Fred Gwynne
▶ Fussy English professor O'Neal is kid-

napped by the Mafia to help father Warden revive the family garment business—and pay back a major mob loan. Caught romancing gangster Kiel's wife Melato, O'Neal escapes in her jeans, which split to reveal his backside and instantly create a new fashion sensation. Somewhat shapeless but altogether harmless little comedy with a fine O'Neal. Directorial debut for Bergman, author of the much funnier film, *The In-Laws*.

SOGGY BOTTOM, U.S.A. 1982
★★ PG Comedy 1:30
☑ Adult situations, explicit language
Dir: Theodore J. Flicker *Cast:* Ben Johnson, Ann Wedgeworth, Lois Nettleton, Dub Taylor, Anthony Zerbe, Jack Elam
▶ Broad but agreeable comedy set in Depression-era Louisiana. Johnson, the local sheriff, is determined to win the local coon-dog race, but his plans are upset by the arrival of buxom country-western singer Wedgeworth and her champion mutt. Cast includes Don Johnson, who's surprisingly effective as a scatterbrained inventor.

SOLARBABIES 1986
★★ PG-13 Sci-Fi 1:34
☑ Violence
Dir: Alan Johnson *Cast:* Richard Jordan, Jami Gertz, Jason Patric, Lukas Haas, Sarah Douglas, Charles Durning
▶ Orphans in a futuristic wasteland devoid of water find the Bodhi, a magical sphere that leads them out of their harsh prison. Pursued by Jordan, the chief of the state police, they search for an answer to the planet's crisis. When evil scientist Douglas steals the Bodhi, the children must attack her stronghold. Elaborate fantasy from producer Mel Brooks with an appealing cast of youngsters. **(CC)**

SOLDIER, THE 1982
★★★ R Action-Adventure 1:30
☑ Explicit language, graphic violence
Dir: James Glickenhaus *Cast:* Ken Wahl, Klaus Kinski, William Prince, Alberta Watson, Jeremiah Sullivan
▶ Russian terrorists steal enough plutonium to destroy Saudi Arabia's oil fields, then order Israel to pull back from the West Front. America's only resort is the Soldier (Wahl), a secret agent who battles his way around the world for a solution to the Russian plot. Top-notch stunts (including a breathtaking ski chase) and

rapid pace compensate for confusing plot and thin characters. **(CC)**

SOLDIER BLUE 1974
★★★★ PG Western 1:49
☑ Nudity, adult situations, explicit language, graphic violence
Dir: Ralph Nelson *Cast:* Candice Bergen, Peter Strauss, Donald Pleasence, Bob Carraway, Jorge Rivero, Dana Elcar
▶ Bergen, a white woman kidnapped by the Cheyennes, and cavalry private Strauss are the only survivors of a brutal massacre by the U.S. Army. They encounter further horrifying violence as they struggle to the safety of an Army outpost. Attempt to describe the plight of the Indians in terms of a Vietnam allegory has dated this Western badly.

SOLDIER IN THE RAIN 1963
★★★ NR Drama 1:28 B&W
Dir: Ralph Nelson *Cast:* Jackie Gleason, Steve McQueen, Tuesday Weld, Tony Bill, Tom Poston, Lew Gallo
▶ Supply officer McQueen and career sergeant Gleason share an uneasy relationship on a Southern Army base, especially after McQueen introduces him to a beautiful young Weld. Uneven mixture of slapstick comedy and maudlin sentimentality features an accomplished performance by Gleason and an amusing role by Adam West as a captain. Based on a William Goldman novel. **(CC)**

SOLDIER OF FORTUNE 1955
★★★ NR Action-Adventure 1:36
Dir: Edward Dmytryk *Cast:* Clark Gable, Susan Hayward, Michael Rennie, Gene Barry, Tom Tully, Alex D'Arcy
▶ American housewife Hayward searches Hong Kong for kidnapped husband Barry; hard-bitten smuggler Gable learns he's held captive in Communist China, and organizes rescue mission with local chief of police Rennie. Improbable but smoothly entertaining drama benefits from beautiful Hong Kong locations. Adapted by Ernest K. Gann from his novel.

SOLDIER OF ORANGE 1979 Dutch
★★★ R Drama 2:45
☑ Nudity, violence
Dir: Paul Verhoeven *Cast:* Rutger Hauer, Jeroen Krabbe, Peter Faber, Edward Fox, Susan Penhaligon
▶ In World War II Holland, a group of college pals band together to battle German invaders. One Jewish member is

captured and tortured while another must join the Germans to save his fiancée; a third pursues a traitor. Epic story rouses utmost sympathy for the heroes and antipathy for the Nazi villains. Solid performances and careful period re-creation although story is a bit disjointed. ⑤

SOLDIER'S STORY, A 1984
★ ★ ★ ★ PG Mystery-Suspense 1:41
☑ Explicit language, violence
Dir: Norman Jewison *Cast:* Howard E. Rollins, Jr., Adolph Caesar, Art Evans, Robert Townsend, Denzel Washington, Patti LaBelle
► In 1944, Rollins, a black military attorney from Washington, arrives at segregated Fort Neal, Louisianna, to investigate the murder of Caesar, master sargent to an all-black unit. Series of flashbacks reveal a number of suspects with plenty of motive to kill the hard-nosed sarge. Arresting performances and tightly woven psychological plot adapted from Charles Fuller's Pulitzer prize–winning drama, *A Soldier's Play*. (CC)

SOLDIER'S TALE, A 1988 New Zealand
★ ★ R Romance 1:37
☑ Adult situations, explicit language, violence
Dir: Larry Parr *Cast:* Gabriel Byrne, Marianne Basler, Paul Wyett, Judge Reinhold
► At the end of World War II, British soldier Byrne meets French farm girl Basler, who has run afoul of the Resistance because of her previous involvement with a German soldier. They fall in love and Byrne tries to keep her safe. Reinhold plays a small role as Byrne's American rival for Basler.

SOLOMON AND SHEBA 1959
★ ★ NR Drama 2:19
Dir: King Vidor *Cast:* Yul Brynner, Gina Lollobrigida, George Sanders, David Farrar, Marisa Pavan, Alejandro Rey
► Lavish biblical epic about the famed Israeli king Solomon (Brynner) and his fateful affair with the beautiful Queen of Sheba (Lollobrigida) includes most of the familiar Solomon stories: building the Great Temple, settling a dispute over an infant, challenging the Egyptians and his power-hungry brother Sanders. Sheer spectacle helps overcome historical inaccuracies. Original star Tyrone Power

died during filming and can be glimpsed in some shots.

SOMEBODY UP THERE LIKES ME 1956
★ ★ ★ ★ NR Biography/Sports 1:53
B&W
Dir: Robert Wise *Cast:* Paul Newman, Pier Angeli, Sal Mineo, Eileen Heckart, Everett Sloane, Harold J. Stone
► True story of boxer Rocky Graziano (Newman) who goes through poverty, prison, and troubled army stint. With the support of his devoted wife Angeli, he rises to the middleweight championship. Inspiring and hard-hitting, both in and out of the ring (with the big fight climax especially exciting). Newman is terrific as the tough but vulnerable Graziano. Oscars for Cinematography and Art Direction. (CC)

SOME GIRLS 1988
★ ★ R Romance/Comedy 1:34
☑ Nudity, adult situations, explicit language
Dir: Michael Hoffman *Cast:* Patrick Dempsey, Jennifer Connelly, Andre Gregory, Sheila Kelly, Florinda Bolkan, Lila Kedrova
► American college student Dempsey visits girlfriend Connelly in Quebec City for Christmas. When she dumps him, he turns his romantic attentions to her two sisters. Scenic vehicle for the appealing Dempsey, nicely supported by fetching Connelly and Gregory as her offbeat father.

SOME KIND OF HERO 1982
★ ★ ★ R Comedy 1:37
☑ Adult situations, explicit language, violence
Dir: Michael Pressman *Cast:* Richard Pryor, Margot Kidder, Ray Sharkey, Ronny Cox
► Pryor plays a Vietnam veteran who returns home a national hero after six years in a POW camp to discover his wife's in love with another man, his bookstore is bankrupted, and his mother is in a $1200-a-month nursing home. He meets sympathetic hooker Kidder and turns to a life of crime. Mediocre movie (adapted from James Kirkwood's novel) is redeemed by the ever-entertaining, multi-talented Pryor.

SOME KIND OF WONDERFUL 1987
★ ★ ★ ★ PG-13 Comedy/Drama 1:33
☑ Adult situations, explicit language
Dir: Howard Deutsch *Cast:* Eric Stoltz,

Mary Stuart Masterson, Lea Thompson, Craig Sheffer, John Ashton, Elias Koteas
▶ Stoltz, a sensitive high schooler from wrong side of tracks, pursues gorgeous Thompson, the girlfriend of wealthy brat Sheffer. Tomboyish best pal Masterson helps Stoltz even though she secretly loves him. Warm, funny, and affecting; producer-writer John Hughes explores the universal dilemmas of teens. Masterson's performance is truly some kind of wonderful. **(CC)**

SOME LIKE IT HOT 1959
★★★★ **NR Comedy 2:00 B&W**
Dir: Billy Wilder *Cast:* Marilyn Monroe, Tony Curtis, Jack Lemmon, George Raft, Pat O'Brien, Joe E. Brown
▶ Musicians Curtis and Lemmon are wanted men when they witness gangland rubout in 1920s Chicago, so they don drag and join an all-girl band bound for Florida. Complications arise when Curtis falls for ukelele player Monroe and millionaire Brown pursues Lemmon. Magical and hilarious classic, perhaps one of the funniest films ever, is as fresh today as when it was made. Lemmon and Curtis are incredible in drag and Monroe has never been more disarming. Best scenes: Lemmon's burst of happiness after Brown proposes to him, Curtis's Cary Grant impression.

SOMEONE TO WATCH OVER ME 1987
★★★★ **R Mystery-Suspense 1:46**
☑ Adult situations, explicit language, violence
Dir: Ridley Scott *Cast:* Tom Berenger, Mimi Rogers, Jerry Orbach, Lorraine Bracco, John Rubinstein, Andreas Katsulas
▶ Society beauty Rogers witnesses mob rubout, so happily married, working-class cop Berenger is assigned to protect her. As two fall in love, much to dismay of Berenger's wife Bracco and boss Orbach, hit man Katsulas stalks Rogers. Unable to get near enough to Rogers to kill her, Katsulas abducts Bracco and her kids. Glossy suspense from master imagemaker Scott looks terrific, with fine performances from romantic leads and supporting cast.

SOMETHING FOR EVERYONE 1970
★★ **R Comedy 1:50**
☑ Adult situations
Dir: Harold Prince *Cast:* Angela Lansbury, Michael York, Anthony Corlan,

Heidelinde Weis, Eva-Maria Meineke, Jane Carr
▶ Down-on-her-luck European countess Lansbury hires stranger York as footman. York proceeds to have an affair with Lansbury's son Corlan while also wedding a wealthy young girl, an arrangement that helps restore Lansbury's fortune. Picturesque production, stylishly directed and well-played. However, weird story and perverse characterizations will leave audiences shaking their heads.

SOMETHING OF VALUE 1957
★★★★ **NR Drama 1:53 B&W**
Dir: Richard Brooks *Cast:* Rock Hudson, Sidney Poitier, Dana Wynter, Wendy Hiller, Frederick O'Neal
▶ Hudson and Poitier, childhood pals, work together on Hudson's father's plantation in Kenya. When Poitier is driven away by an act of racial discrimination and joins the radical Mau Mau terrorists, Hudson finds himself at odds with his friend. Exciting story steadily increases tension after slow start. Based on the novel by Robert C. Ruark.

SOMETHING SHORT OF PARADISE 1979
★★★ **PG Romance/Comedy 1:27**
☑ Brief nudity, adult situations, explicit language
Dir: David Helpern, Jr. *Cast:* Susan Sarandon, David Steinberg, Jean-Pierre Aumont, Marilyn Sokol, Joe Grifasi, David Rasche
▶ Magazine writer Sarandon and movie publicist Steinberg become lovers. However, their inability to make a commitment and a misunderstanding involving French actor Aumont jeopardize the relationship. Lightweight fare has thin story but appealing central couple.

SOMETHING SPECIAL 1986
★★ **PG-13 Comedy 1:26**
☑ Adult situations, explicit language
Dir: Paul Schneider *Cast:* Pamela Segall, Eric Gurry, Patty Duke, John Glover, Seth Green, Mary Tanner
▶ Teenage girl Milly (Segall) wishes she could be a boy and wakes up to find wishes do come true. "Willy" must then learn how to fight, talk dirty, and other important skills in a man's world. Farfetched comedy covers familiar territory; pleasant cast does evoke a few smiles.

SOMETHING WICKED THIS WAY COMES 1983
★★ **PG Sci-Fi 1:34**

☑ Adult situations, explicit language
Dir: Jack Clayton *Cast:* Jason Robards, Jonathan Pryce, Diane Ladd, Pam Grier, Vidal Peterson, Shawn Carson

▶ Turn-of-the-century Illinois: teen Peterson has uneasy relationship with elderly dad Robards. Robards helps Peterson and his best pal Carson when mysterious carnival man Pryce comes to town and they discover his dark powers. Wellwrought drama has eerie atmosphere and refreshing human scale despite a few awkward moments. Most chilling scene: Pryce tearing out pages in fiery bursts from a book representing different stages of Robards's life. Adapted by Ray Bradbury from his novel.

SOMETHING WILD 1986
★ ★ R Comedy/Drama 1:53
☑ Nudity, adult situations, explicit language, violence
Dir: Jonathan Demme *Cast:* Jeff Daniels, Melanie Griffith, Ray Liotta, Margaret Colin, Dana Preu
▶ Conservative New York accountant Daniels falls in with unpredictable flirt Griffith, who drives him to her Pennsylvania high school reunion. Offbeat comedy takes an unexpected twist to drama when Griffith introduces Daniels to husband Liotta, a frenzied ex-con. Compelling, beautifully nuanced story ultimately seems too disjointed, but contains many fine vignettes and a knockout soundtrack. Great supporting cast and amusing cameos by directors John Sayles and John Waters.

SOMETIMES A GREAT NOTION 1971
★ ★ ★ PG Drama 1:55
☑ Adult situations, explicit language, violence
Dir: Paul Newman *Cast:* Paul Newman, Henry Fonda, Lee Remick, Michael Sarrazin, Richard Jaeckel, Linda Lawson
▶ Oregon lumbering family is pressured by neighbors to join a strike; crusty patriarch Fonda and his son Newman decide to honor their contract despite escalating violence. Sincere adaptation of Ken Kesey's sprawling novel is noteworthy for Jaeckel's Oscar-nominated performance as Newman's brother. Charlie Pride's rendition of "All His Children" also received an Oscar nomination. Also known as *Never Give an Inch.*

SOMEWHERE IN TIME 1980
★ ★ ★ ★ PG Fantasy/Romance 1:43
☑ Adult situations, explicit language
Dir: Jeannot Szwarc *Cast:* Christopher Reeve, Jane Seymour, Christopher Plummer, Teresa Wright, Bill Erwin, George Voskovec
▶ Playwright Reeve sees picture of 1912 actress Seymour and falls in love. Through self-hypnosis, he travels back in time to be with her but Seymour's jealous manager Plummer tries to sabotage their romance. Entrancing love story with a basic sincerity that touches the heart. Melodic John Barry score, gorgeous cinematography, Oscar-nominated costumes, and beautiful Mackinac Island (Michigan) locations; adapted by Richard Matheson from his novel, *Bid Time Return.*

SOMEWHERE, TOMORROW 1984
★ ★ ★ ★ PG Fantasy 1:31
☑ Explicit language
Dir: Robert Wiemer *Cast:* Sarah Jessica Parker, Nancy Addison, Tom Shea, Rick Weber, Paul Bates, John Evans
▶ Young Parker will lose her beloved horse farm if her mother remarries, and hopes teenaged Shea will help by boarding his horse in her stables. When she discovers Shea is actually a ghost, she enlists him in a different scheme with unexpected results. Overlooked comic fantasy is an understated, charming examination of adolescent love.

SONG IS BORN, A 1948
★ ★ ★ ★ NR Musical 1:53
Dir: Howard Hawks *Cast:* Danny Kaye, Virginia Mayo, Benny Goodman, Hugh Herbert, Steve Cochran, Felix Bressart
▶ Pleasant remake of *Ball of Fire* with Kaye as a professor leading his aged colleagues in a history of jazz. Gangster's moll Mayo, on the run from the police, brings out the hero underneath his bumbling exterior. Remarkable Who's Who list of jazz superstars (Louis Armstrong, Tommy Dorsey, Charlie Barnet, Buck and Bubbles, Mel Powell, Lionel Hampton) provide highlights with versions of "I'm Getting Sentimental Over You," "Redskin Rhumba," "Flyin' Home," more.

SONG OF BERNADETTE, THE 1943
★ ★ ★ ★ ★ NR Biography 2:40 B&W
Dir: Henry King *Cast:* Jennifer Jones, Charles Bickford, Vincent Price, Lee J. Cobb, William Eythe, Gladys Cooper
▶ Nineteenth-century French peasant

girl (Bernadette Soubirous) Jones sees vision of Virgin Mary. Despite skepticism of many, Bernadette persists in her story and soon religious pilgrims flock to her home in Lourdes, seeking the healing waters of a spring miraculously appearing at site of apparition. On advice of priest, she backs out of marriage and joins nunnery where jealous nun Cooper and cold-hearted official Price punish her for perceived blasphemy. Long but well-crafted inspirational film won four Oscars including Best Actress for Jones.

SONG OF NORWAY 1970
★ **G Biography/Music 2:22**
Dir: Andrew L. Stone   *Cast:* Toralv Maurstad, Florence Henderson, Christina Schollin, Frank Porretta, Robert Morley, Edward G. Robinson
▶ Bloated, inaccurate biography of Norwegian classical composer Edvard Grieg (Maurstad) unwisely adds English lyrics to his music and suggests a romantic rivalry between his patron Therese Berg (Schollin) and his first cousin (Henderson, who also sings). Even the beautiful scenery (filmed in Super Panavision) will lose its impact on TV.

SONG OF THE SOUTH 1946
★★★★ **G Musical/Family 1:34**
Dir: Harve Foster, Wilfred Jackson
Cast: James Baskett, Bobby Driscoll, Ruth Warrick, Hattie McDaniel, Luana Patten, Lucile Watson
▶ Driscoll goes to live on grandmother's plantation during the Civil War. Elderly black slave Uncle Remus (Baskett) befriends the lad and entertains him with stories of Brer Rabbit. Vibrant, tender tale of brotherhood from Disney will appeal to young and old alike. Lively mixture of animation (used to illustrate Uncle Remus's stories) and live action. Oscars for Best Song ("Zip-a-dee Doo-Dah") and Baskett (honorary).

SONG OF THE THIN MAN 1947
★★ **NR Mystery-Suspense 1:26 B&W**
Dir: Edward Buzzell   *Cast:* William Powell, Myrna Loy, Keenan Wynn, Dean Stockwell, Gloria Grahame, Jayne Meadows
▶ Musicians, gamblers, and singer Grahame are among the possible suspects when Nick (Powell) and Nora (Loy) Charles investigate the shipboard murder of a bandleader. Final entry in the series is far from peak form although Powell and Loy are still charming.

SONG TO REMEMBER, A 1945
★★★ **NR Biography/Music 1:52**
Dir: Charles Vidor   *Cast:* Cornel Wilde, Merle Oberon, Paul Muni, Stephen Bekassy, Nina Foch, George Coulouris
▶ Nineteenth-century Polish composer Frederic Chopin (Wilde) is taken to Paris by his mentor Joseph Elsner (Muni). There Chopin rises to stardom and has a torrid romance with writer George Sand (Oberon); under her influence, he turns against Elsner. Lavish story of great personal peaks and heartbreaking lows; Wilde and the grand music earned two of six Oscar nominations.

SONGWRITER 1984
★★ **R Musical/Comedy 1:34**
☑ Nudity, adult situations, explicit language
Dir: Alan Rudolph   *Cast:* Willie Nelson, Kris Kristofferson, Melinda Dillon, Rip Torn, Lesley Ann Warren, Richard C. Sarafian
▶ Country-western duo Nelson and Kristofferson part company so that Nelson can become a songwriter. Singer Warren gets a big hit with one of Nelson's songs and tries to seduce him but he's only interested in getting back ex-wife Dillon. Satire of the country music biz is best when the two leads are singing.   (CC)

SON OF DRACULA 1943
★★ **NR Horror 1:20 B&W**
Dir: Robert Siodmak   *Cast:* Lon Chaney, Jr., Robert Paige, Louise Allbritton, Evelyn Ankers, Frank Craven, Samuel S. Hinds
▶ Hungarian Count Alucard (Chaney) journeys to Louisiana, where he steals lovely Allbritton away from boyfriend Paige. She thinks she's entering high society, but Paige unearths disturbing secrets about Alucard's past. Inaccurate title (capitalizing on Universal Studio's string of successful horror films) disguises surprisingly effective vampire tale.

SON OF FRANKENSTEIN 1939
★★★ **NR Horror 1:39 B&W**
Dir: Rowland V. Lee   *Cast:* Basil Rathbone, Boris Karloff, Bela Lugosi, Lionel Atwill, Josephine Hutchinson, Donnie Dunagan
▶ Rathbone, Dr. Frankenstein's son, returns from America to dad's castle. He meets Ygor (Lugosi), the broken-necked survivor of a hanging, who helps Rathbone revive monster Karloff but then uses Karloff for his own sinister purposes. Terrific

third entry in the series, best remembered as the movie that introduced Lugosi's unforgettably creepy Ygor characterization.

SON OF FURY 1942
★★ NR Action-Adventure 1:38 B&W
Dir: John Cromwell *Cast:* Tyrone Power, Gene Tierney, George Sanders, Frances Farmer, Elsa Lanchester, John Carradine
► Nineteenth-century England: nobleman's bastard son Power flees his tyrannical uncle Sanders and goes to the South Seas, where he falls for Polynesian Tierney and finds a fortune in pearls. He returns to England to claim his rightful inheritance. Good-looking cast and production holds interest despite predictable story.

SON OF PALEFACE 1952
★★★ NR Comedy 1:35
Dir: Frank Tashlin *Cast:* Bob Hope, Jane Russell, Roy Rogers, Douglas Dumbrille, Bill Williams
► Harvard grad Hope comes west to claim gold hidden by his legendary Indian-fighter dad. Curvy cafe singer–outlaw Russell and government agent Rogers help him. Sequel to the 1948 *Paleface*; Hope's nifty timing keeps it perking with nice support from Russell, Rogers, and Trigger.

SONS AND LOVERS 1960 British
★★ NR Drama 1:43 B&W
Dir: Jack Cardiff *Cast:* Trevor Howard, Dean Stockwell, Wendy Hiller, Mary Ure, Heather Sears, William Lucas
► In turn-of-the-century England, promising artist Stockwell seeks to escape grimy mining village but is caught between possessive mother Hiller and drunken father Howard. Meanwhile, his heart vacillates between repressed farm girl Sears and married suffragette Ure. Beautifully crafted adaptation of the D. H. Lawrence classic. Seven Oscar nominations include Best Picture, Director, Actor (Howard), Supporting Actress (Ure); won for Cinematography.

SONS OF KATIE ELDER, THE 1965
★★★ NR Western 2:02
Dir: Henry Hathaway *Cast:* John Wayne, Dean Martin, Martha Hyer, Michael Anderson, Jr., Earl Holliman, George Kennedy
► Four brothers reunited by their mother's death learn their father was murdered and put aside their differences to search for the killers. Gunman Wayne, gambler

Martin, silent killer Holliman, and college graduate Anderson are imprisoned and threatened by a lynching party before they uncover the truth. Sprawling Western with an especially physical performance by Wayne.

SONS OF THE DESERT 1933
★★★★ NR Comedy 1:09 B&W
Dir: William A. Seiter *Cast:* Stan Laurel, Oliver Hardy, Charley Chase, Mae Busch, Dorothy Christy, Lucien Littlefield
► The boys are afraid to tell their wives about the Chicago convention of their fraternal order Sons of the Desert, so Ollie fakes a cold and claims he's leaving with Stan for a Hawaiian cure. Their plan naturally backfires with hilarious results in this short, sweet, near-perfect comedy. Fans consider this the best of Laurel and Hardy's feature films.

SOPHIE'S CHOICE 1982
★★★★ R Drama 2:31
☑ Adult situations, explicit language, mild violence
Dir: Alan J. Pakula *Cast:* Meryl Streep, Kevin Klein, Peter MacNicol, Rita Karin, Stephen D. Newman
► Streep's Oscar-winning performance as Sophie dominates this powerful film version of William Styron's best-selling novel. In a Brooklyn boarding house after World War II, southern writer MacNicol meets Sophie, a beautiful Polish Holocaust survivor, and her lover Klein, a Jewish biologist. While the multifaceted plot spirals toward its ultimately tragic conclusion, the characters reveal their long-hidden secrets. Also nominated for Best Screenplay, Cinematography, Score, and Costumes.

SORCERER 1977
★★★ PG Action-Adventure 2:01
☑ Explicit language, violence
Dir: William Friedkin *Cast:* Roy Scheider, Bruno Cremer, Francisco Rabal, Amidou, Ramon Bieri, Karl John
► Four criminals—Arab traitor Amidou, small-time hood Scheider, French embezzler Cremer, and hit man Rabal—agree to transport volatile nitroglycerine to an oil refinery fire. The suicide mission involves a washed-out trail through the South American jungles. Loose remake of the French classic *Wages of Fear* takes a long time to get moving but builds up riveting tension. Highlight is attempt to cross rotting bridge during a thunderstorm. Ⓢ

SORCERESS 1982
☆ R Action-Adventure 1:15
☑ Rape, nudity, explicit language, violence
Dir: Brian Stuart *Cast:* Leigh Harris, Lynette Harris, Bob Nelson, David Millbern, Bruno Rey, Ana De Sade
▶ Inept low-budget medieval fantasy features the Harris sisters as twins marked for sacrifice by their evil wizard father. Aided by warrior Nelson and satyr Rey, the Amazons conquer lascivious monkey men and sex-crazed zombies. High nudity quotient and vulgar jokes almost rate this as a parody.

SORORITY HOUSE MASSACRE 1986
★ R Horror 1:14
☑ Nudity, adult situations, explicit language, graphic violence
Dir: Carol Frank *Cast:* Angela O'Neill, Wendy Martel, Pamela Ross, Nicole Rio, John C. Russell
▶ Vacation weekend empties out Theta Omega sorority house except for psychology major Martel, shy pledge O'Neill, and two friends who fall victim to escaped mental patient Russell. O'Neill learns she is Russell's sister, the only survivor of a mass murder years earlier, before confronting her brother in a bloody climax. Inventive photography helps routine slasher plot.

SORROW AND THE PITY, THE 1970
Swiss
★ PG Documentary 4:20 B&W
☑ Explicit language
Dir: Marcel Ophuls
▶ Incredibly compelling documentary interweaves current-day interviews and extraordinary period footage to create masterful portrait of French collaboration with Nazis during World War II. Chilling revelations as former SS men portray themselves as benevolent conquerors while Frenchmen try to rationalize their behavior. Subtlety and length limit appeal. Dubbed and subtitled versions available. Nominated for Best Documentary. ⑤

SORROWFUL JONES 1949
★★★ NR Comedy 1:28 B&W
Dir: Sidney Lanfield *Cast:* Bob Hope, Lucille Ball, William Demarest, Bruce Cabot, Thomas Gomez, Tom Pedi
▶ Uncredited remake of *Little Miss Marker* with Hope surprisingly restrained as a bookie forced to care for young Mary Jane Saunders when her father skips town. Broadway singer Ball and a collection of typical Damon Runyon eccentrics aid Hope with his new paternal duties. Sentimental rather than snappy. Introduced by Walter Winchell.

SORRY, WRONG NUMBER 1948
★★★★ NR Mystery-Suspense 1:29 B&W
Dir: Anatole Litvak *Cast:* Barbara Stanwyck, Burt Lancaster, Ann Richards, Wendell Corey, Ed Begley, William Conrad
▶ Bedridden, neurotic, and rich Stanwyck overhears phone conversation in which a murder is planned. She soon suspects she is the intended victim, but the police won't believe her paranoid tale. Her only hope is to get through to her hard-to-reach businessman husband Lancaster. Classic suspense earned Oscar nomination for Stanwyck. Adapted from renowned twenty-two-minute radio play written by Lucille Fletcher and starring Agnes Moorehead.

SOUL MAN 1986
★★★ PG-13 Comedy 1:45
☑ Adult situations, explicit language
Dir: Steve Miner *Cast:* C. Thomas Howell, Rae Dawn Chong, James Earl Jones, Arye Gross, James B. Sikking
▶ Along with best friend Gross, rich Southern Californian Howell is accepted to Harvard Law School but father Sikking refuses to pay tuiton and, because of his background, he can't get financial aid. With tanning pills and Afro wig, he wins a minority scholarship—but can he pass as a soul brother? In his "black-like-me" identity, Howell discovers many truths about racial stereotyping and falls for lovely co-ed Chong. Amusing cutting-edge story line, solid performances, and zippy pacing. Jones excels as Howell's intimidating law professor. (CC)

SOUNDER 1972
★★★★ G Family 1:45
Dir: Martin Ritt *Cast:* Cicely Tyson, Paul Winfield, Kevin Hooks, Carmen Mathews, Taj Mahal, James Best
▶ Adaptation of a William Armstrong novel in which Depression-era black sharecropper Winfield steals food to feed family and must serve year sentence at work camp. Wife Tyson is left to run farm and tend younger kids with help of eldest son Hooks. Superior drama distinguished by story of universal appeal and first-rate performances, especially Hooks as youth

on verge of manhood. Top-notch score by Mahal (also in screen debut). Moving family fare nominated for Best Picture, Actor, Actress, and Adaptation. **(CC)**

SOUND OF MUSIC, THE 1965
★ ★ ★ ★ ★ **G Musical 2:54**
Dir: Robert Wise **Cast:** Julie Andrews, Christopher Plummer, Eleanor Parker, Peggy Wood, Angela Cartwright, Richard Haydn
▶ Vibrant musical based on true story of singing Von Trapp family's flight from Austria to Switzerland during World War II. Nun-turned-governess Andrews helps stern widower Plummer guide his flock of kids through good times and bad and eventually softens Plummer for marriage. Songs from Rodgers and Hammerstein's Broadway hit include "My Favorite Things," "Do-Re-Mi," "Climb Every Mountain," and title tune. Memorable music, Alpine scenery, and Andrews's singing made film one of most popular of all time. Winner of five Oscars, including Best Picture. **(CC)**

SOUP FOR ONE 1982
★ **R Comedy 1:24**
☑ Brief nudity, adult situations, explicit language, adult humor
Dir: Jonathan Kaufer **Cast:** Saul Rubinek, Marcia Strassman, Gerrit Graham, Teddy Pendergrass, Richard Libertini, Andrea Martin
▶ Nice Jewish boy Rubinek, tired of Manhattan singles scene, seeks dream mate for wedded bliss. When various dates disappoint him, womanizer friend Graham takes him to singles weekend at Catskills hotel. There he meets Strassman but she rejects him until he bullies his way into her heart. As the altar looms near, however, Rubinek gets cold feet. Erratic satire with likable cast but tired observations.

SOUTHERN COMFORT 1981
★ ★ ★ **R Action-Adventure 1:46**
☑ Explicit language, graphic violence
Dir: Walter Hill **Cast:** Keith Carradine, Powers Boothe, Fred Ward, Franklyn Seales, T. K. Carter, Peter Coyote
▶ Nine National Guardsmen on weekend maneuvers in Louisiana swamp harass Cajun locals and steal some canoes. The Cajuns respond by tracking the interlopers and killing them one by one, often in grisly fashion. Soon only Guardsmen Carradine and Boothe are left, hoping to escape the cat-and-mouse game alive. Well-crafted although somewhat pointless drama with lots of action and fine performances.

SOUTHERNER, THE 1945
★ ★ **NR Drama 1:31 B&W**
Dir: Jean Renoir **Cast:** Zachary Scott, Betty Field, Beulah Bondi, Jean Vanderwilt, Jay Gilpin, J. Carrol Naish
▶ Haunting account of a Texas family's dogged attempts to establish a farm on poor land. Scott, the father, gives up a factory job to work an arid stretch while repairing a rundown shack for his wife Field and children Vanderwilt and Gilpin. Vindictive neighbor Naish refuses to help even when Gilpin falls ill. Director Renoir received an Oscar nomination for his sensitive, uplifting depiction of a heroic battle against poverty.

SOUTH PACIFIC 1958
★ ★ ★ ★ **NR Musical 2:29**
Dir: Joshua Logan **Cast:** Mitzi Gaynor, Rossano Brazzi, Ray Walston, John Kerr, Juanita Hall, France Nuyen
▶ Screen version of the smash Broadway musical, based on the James Michener book, takes place on remote South Pacific island during World War II. Midwestern nurse Gaynor falls in love with widowed plantation owner Brazzi while young Marine Kerr woos native girl Nuyen. Story may be merely serviceable, but with sensational Rodgers and Hammerstein score, who cares? Memorable tunes include "I'm Gonna Wash That Man Right Out of My Hair," "There Is Nothing Like a Dame," "My Girl Back Home," and "Some Enchanted Evening." **(CC)**

SOYLENT GREEN 1973
★ ★ ★ **PG Sci-Fi 1:37**
☑ Adult situations, explicit language
Dir: Richard Fleischer **Cast:** Charlton Heston, Leigh Taylor-Young, Chuck Connors, Joseph Cotten, Brock Peters, Edward G. Robinson
▶ In 2022, overpopulated world is depleted of resources, so most people subsist on a waferlike food known as soylent. Detective Heston investigates assassination of industrialist Cotten who discovered a terrifying secret about the foodstuff. Passable sci-fi noteworthy as legendary Robinson's final movie. Dying of cancer during shoot, he delivered a dignified and poignant performance.

SPACEBALLS 1987
★ ★ **PG Comedy 1:36**
☑ Explicit language
Dir: Mel Brooks **Cast:** Mel Brooks, John

Candy, Rick Moranis, Bill Pullman, Daphne Zuniga, Dick Van Patten
▶ Evil planet Spaceball has run out of air so leader Brooks and underling Dark Helmet (Moranis) conspire to steal atmosphere of neighboring Druidia, ruled by kind king Van Patten. Moranis kidnaps Van Patten's daughter Zuniga as hostage. To the rescue come space maverick Pullman and man-dog sidekick Candy, fresh from training by mini-guru Yogurt (also Brooks). Broad and often erratic parody of *Star Wars* and other sci-fi epics. Best moments come from Moranis's wimpy Napoleonic parody of Darth Vader.

SPACECAMP 1986
★ ★ ★ ★ **PG Action-Adventure 1:47**
☑ Explicit language
Dir: Harry Winer *Cast:* Kate Capshaw, Lea Thompson, Kelly Preston, Larry B. Scott, Leaf Phoenix, Tate Donovan
▶ Teens attend a summer program at the NASA Space Center, where astronaut Capshaw teaches them about the shuttle. Jinx, a friendly but imperfect robot, arranges for them to be launched on an actual mission. When Capshaw is injured, the youngsters must rely on their knowledge and grit to return to Earth safely. Optimistic view of space travel was released just after the *Challenger* disaster.

SPACEHUNTER: ADVENTURES IN THE FORBIDDEN ZONE 1983
★ ★ **PG Sci-Fi 1:29**
☑ Explicit language, violence
Dir: Lamont Johnson *Cast:* Peter Strauss, Molly Ringwald, Ernie Hudson, Michael Ironside, Beeson Carroll, Andrea Marcovicci
▶ Wars and plagues reduce the planet Terra Eleven to a wasteland. Mercenary loner Strauss rockets there to rescue three kidnapped travelers, teaming up with orphaned "Earther" girl Ringwald to battle Bat People, cyborg gladiators, and the evil Overdog. Routine space epic, shot in 3-D, will lose most of its impact on TV. (CC)

SPACE RAGE 1987
★ **R Sci-Fi 1:18**
☑ Explicit language, violence
Dir: Conrad E. Palmisano *Cast:* Richard Farnsworth, Michael Paré, John Laughlin, Lee Purcell, William Windom
▶ Futuristic planet Proxima Centauri 3 provides the backdrop for a sustained battle between bounty hunters and vicious escaped con Paré who's kidnapped warden Windom and his wife Purcell. Farnsworth, leader of the bounty hunters, adds some dignity to this cut-rate sci-fi Western. Subtitle: *Breakout on Prison Planet.*

SPACE RAIDERS 1983
★ ★ **PG Sci-Fi 1:23**
☑ Explicit language, violence
Dir: Howard R. Cohen *Cast:* Vince Edwards, David Mendenhall, Patsy Pease, Thom Christopher, Luca Bercovici, Drew Synder
▶ In authoritarian future, ten-year-old Mendenhall stows away on spaceship stolen by rebels. Mendenhall idolizes outlaws' leader Edwards, who tries unsuccessfully to return kid to home. When evil alien Snyder snatches him for ransom, Edwards and gang come to his rescue. Special effects and score were lifted from producer Roger Corman's previous hit, *Battle Beyond the Stars.* Low-budget entry into the space genre.

SPACE RIDERS 1983
★ **NR Action-Adventure 1:33**
☑ Violence
Dir: Joe Massot *Cast:* Barry Sheene, Gavan O'Herlihy, Toshiya Ito, Stephanie McLean, Sayo Inaba
▶ Daredevils from many nations assemble to compete in a grueling motorcycle race to determine the world's champion. Pounding soundtrack, with songs by Duran Duran and Simple Minds, provides cacophonous backdrop to extensive racing footage.

SPARKLE 1976
★ ★ ★ **PG Drama 1:38**
☑ Adult situations, explicit language
Dir: Sam O'Steen *Cast:* Irene Cara, Lonette McKee, Phillip Michael Thomas, Dwan Smith, Mary Alice, Dorian Harewood
▶ Sisters Cara, McKee, and Smith form a Supremes-like singing group to rise out of the 1950s Harlem ghetto. McKee falls prey to drugs and a gangster boyfriend; Cara reaches stardom with the help of manager-beau Thomas. Underrated drama has gritty direction, and excellent Curtis Mayfield music. McKee's sexy but tragic performance is a revelation.

SPARTACUS 1960
★ ★ ★ ★ **NR Drama 3:05**
Dir: Stanley Kubrick *Cast:* Kirk Douglas, Laurence Olivier, Tony Curtis, Jean Simmons, Charles Laughton, Peter Ustinov

▶ In 73 B.C., gladiator-slave Douglas leads revolt of fellow slaves against tyrannical Roman senator Olivier. Aiding Douglas in his fight: his lover Simmons and his friend Curtis. Exciting, old-fashioned epic with terrific battles and passionate performance by Douglas leading the great cast; more conventional and more accessible than Kubrick's later films.

SPASMS 1983 Canadian
★ R Horror 1:27
☑ Nudity, explicit language, graphic violence
Dir: William Fruet **Cast:** Peter Fonda, Oliver Reed, Kerrie Keane, Al Waxman, Miguel Fernandes, Marilyn Lightstone
▶ Scholar Reed is bitten by a huge snake that kills his brother. When the reptile is captured in New Guinea, Reed realizes he can communicate with it telepathically. Working with ESP expert Fonda, he searches desperately for the snake, aware it is one of the guardians to the gates of hell. Illogical low-budget horror has compelling special effects and a larger-than-life performance by Reed.

SPECIAL DAY, A 1977 Italian/Canadian
★★ NR Drama 1:46
☑ Adult situations, explicit language
Dir: Ettore Scola **Cast:** Sophia Loren, Marcello Mastroianni, John Vernon, Francoise Berd, Nicole Magny, Patrizia Basso
▶ When most of Rome turns out for Hitler and Mussolini's 1938 meeting, harried housewife Loren and tormented homosexual Mastroianni are among few who stay away. Loren seduces Mastroianni before each returns to dreary existence. Fine turns by Italy's two biggest stars, with Oscar nominations for Best Actor and Foreign Film. ⑤

SPECIAL EFFECTS 1984
★★ R Mystery-Suspense 1:33
☑ Nudity, explicit language, violence
Dir: Larry Cohen **Cast:** Eric Bogosian, Zoe Tamerlis, Brad Rijn, Kevin O'Connor, Bill Olland, Richard Greene
▶ Over-the-hill movie director Bogosian attempts career comeback by strangling actress Tamerlis on camera. He finds look-alike actress (also Tamerlis) for rest of film; grieving husband Rijn is consoled by her presence. Cop O'Connor is deterred from his murder investigation by offer of associate producer credit on movie, but soon both Rijn and O'Connor grow suspicious about authenticity of

murder scene. Intriguing suspense premise bogged down by commentary on nature of reality and filmmaking.

SPEEDWAY 1968
★★ G Musical 1:30
Dir: Norman Taurog **Cast:** Elvis Presley, Nancy Sinatra, Bill Bixby, Gale Gordon, William Schallert
▶ Top race-car driver Presley learns his manager Bixby has mishandled his money. IRS agent Sinatra falls for Presley, and helps pay off his debts. Formula wears thin in the King's twenty-seventh film. Sinatra warbles "Your Groovy Self"; other songs include "Who Are You? (Who Am I?)" and "He's Your Uncle, Not Your Dad."

SPELLBINDER 1988
★ R Horror 1:39
☑ Adult situations, explicit language, violence
Dir: Janet Greek **Cast:** Timothy Daly, Kelly Preston, Rick Rossovich, Audra Lindley, Anthony Crivello, Diana Bellamy
▶ Lawyer Daly rescues beautiful Preston from brutal boyfriend Crivello. Daly and Preston become lovers, but she then reveals her past association with satanic cult, which now aims to make her a human sacrifice. Daly battles the evil gang on her behalf.

SPELLBOUND 1945
★★★★ NR Mystery-Suspense 1:52 B&W
Dir: Alfred Hitchcock **Cast:** Ingrid Bergman, Gregory Peck, Jean Acker, Donald Curtis, Rhonda Fleming, Leo G. Carroll
▶ Peck, the new psychiatrist at an asylum, is discovered to be a fraud by staff doctor Bergman; she helps uncover a secret he has been blocking about a murder. Intriguing romance with a psychoanalytic background features a number of good Hitchcock twists and a bizarre dream sequence by Salvador Dali. Received six Oscar nominations, winning for Miklos Rozsa's lush score.

SPETTERS 1980 Dutch
★ R Drama 1:49
☑ Nudity, strong sexual content, explicit language
Dir: Paul Verhoeven **Cast:** Toon Agterberg, Hans Van Tongeren, Rutger Hauer, Maarten Spanjer, Renee Soutendijk, Marianne Boyer
▶ Aimless youths Agterberg, Van Tong-

eren, and Spanjer have little to do in Rotterdam but work and ride motorcycles, aspiring to mimic champ racer Hauer. Enter vampy temptress Soutendijk, hoping to attach herself to the one with best shot for fame and fortune and initiating rivalry between the pals. Sexy study of wayward youth, although heedless hedonism and alienated leads will leave some cold. [S]

SPHINX 1981
★★★ PG Mystery-Suspense 1:57
☑ Adult situations, explicit language, violence
Dir: Franklin J. Schaffner *Cast:* Frank Langella, Lesley-Anne Down, John Gielgud, Maurice Ronet, Martin Benson, Vic Tablian
▶ On research trip to Cairo, Egyptologist Down witnesses murder of crooked antiquities dealer Gielgud. Villains mark her for death while French journalist Ronet and local artifacts authority Langella are curious about her role in the murder. Despite these distractions, Down finds a secret tomb in which she becomes trapped. Striking scenery and exotic Egyptian lore occasionally marred by confusing story line.

SPIES LIKE US 1985
★★★★ PG Comedy 1:43
☑ Explicit language, mild violence, adult humor
Dir: John Landis *Cast:* Dan Aykroyd, Chevy Chase, Steve Forrest, Donna Dixon, Mark Stewart, Sean Daniel
▶ Inept government employees Aykroyd and Chase are recruited and trained as spies for dangerous mission in Afghanistan and USSR. After blundering their way through various crises, they realize they're disposable decoys intended to distract the Soviets. Aykroyd and Chase then team up with Dixon, one of the real agents, to avert end of civilization. Uneven comedy doesn't always fulfill its fine premise, but Aykroyd and Chase fans won't be disappointed. (CC)

SPIKE OF BENSONHURST 1988
★★ R Comedy 1:41
☑ Explicit language, violence
Dir: Paul Morrissey *Cast:* Ernest Borgnine, Sasha Mitchell, Anne De Salvo, Maria Pitillo, Sylvia Miles, Geraldine Smith
▶ Middling Brooklyn prizefighter Mitchell seeks help with career from local Mafia don Borgnine and lands gig as low-level

hood. But when Mitchell seduces Borgnine's daughter Pitillo, the don banishes him to Puerto Rican neighborhood where he is idolized for his mob connections. Mitchell takes on the local drug dealers while trying to get back in Borgnine's good graces. Campy, off-the-wall comedy from Morrissey, director of Andy Warhol films.

SPIKER 1985
★★ R Drama/Sports 1:44
☑ Nudity, adult situations, explicit language
Dir: Roger Tilton *Cast:* Patrick Houser, Kristi Ferrell, Jo McDonnel, Stephen Burns, Christopher Allport, Michael Parks
▶ Pals Houser and Burns try out for Olympic volleyball and discover coach Parks has demeanor of drill sergeant. Houser romances old flame Ferrell, who's writing thesis on the sport, while Burns quits after row with Parks during Japan tour. Meanwhile other player Allport suffers from marital woes due to constant travel. Fine depiction of matches undermined by melodramatic antics.

SPIRAL STAIRCASE, THE 1946
★★★ NR Mystery-Suspense 1:23 B&W
Dir: Robert Siodmak *Cast:* Dorothy McGuire, George Brent, Ethel Barrymore, Kent Smith, Gordon Oliver, Elsa Lanchester
▶ Madman kills deformed women in turn-of-the-century New England village; McGuire, a mute servant in invalid Barrymore's gothic mansion, realizes she may be the next victim. Marvelous thriller exploits every nook and cranny in the spooky setting to provoke terror. Remade with Jacqueline Bisset in 1975.

SPIRAL STAIRCASE, THE 1975 British
★★★ NR Mystery-Suspense 1:29
☑ Explicit language, violence
Dir: Peter Collinson *Cast:* Jacqueline Bisset, Christopher Plummer, Sam Wanamaker, Mildred Dunnock, Gayle Hunnicutt, Elaine Stritch
▶ Attractive young Bisset loses voice as result of severe emotional trauma and moves into old New England house with frail grandmother Dunnock, stern nurse Stritch, psychologist uncle Plummer, and his secretary Hunnicutt. Meanwhile local cop Wanamaker searches for psychopath killer who victimizes the handicapped. A storm traps Bisset and the rest at home as the killer moves in. Remake of

1946 classic suspenser uses gimmick of pursued woman whose screams can't be heard.

SPIRIT OF ST. LOUIS, THE 1957
★★★★ NR Biography 2:17
Dir: Billy Wilder *Cast:* James Stewart, Patricia Smith, Murray Hamilton, Bartlett Robinson, Robert Cornthwaite, Marc Connelly
► Stirring version of Charles Lindbergh's famous 1927 solo flight across the Atlantic, with Stewart delivering a bravura performance as the heroic pilot. Flashbacks during the journey reveal Lindbergh's struggling years as a stunt flier and air-mail pilot. Inspirational, uplifting story was based on the best-selling autobiography.

SPLASH 1984
★★★★ PG Comedy 1:50
☑ Brief nudity, adult situations, explicit language, mild violence, adult humor
Dir: Ron Howard *Cast:* Tom Hanks, Daryl Hannah, John Candy, Eugene Levy, Dody Goodman, Shecky Greene
► Lonely New York bachelor Hanks is saved from drowning off Cape Cod by mermaid Hannah. Sprouting legs, she finds him in the city where, once his shock has worn off, they fall in love. Romance is complicated by Hannah's inability to live out of water more than six days and attempts by zoologist Levy to apprehend and study her. Enormously popular comedy mixes old-fashioned love story with fish-out-of-water jokes. Candy is hilarious as Hanks's lecherous older brother while Goodman steals scenes as a dim-witted secretary.

SPLATTER UNIVERSITY 1984
☆ R Horror 1:20
☑ Adult situations, explicit language, graphic violence
Dir: Richard W. Haines *Cast:* Francine Forbes, Dick Biel, Cathy Lacommare, Ric Randig, Joanna Mihalakis, Denise Texeira
► Forbes, a new professor at a Catholic university, learns her predecessor was stabbed to death in classroom. Murder remains unsolved. Despite assurances of creepy school head Biel, the killer returns to slay others and stalk Forbes. Low-budget horror offers nothing new to genre.

SPLENDOR IN THE GRASS 1961
★★★ NR Drama/Romance 2:04
Dir: Elia Kazan *Cast:* Natalie Wood,

Warren Beatty, Pat Hingle, Audrey Christie, Barbara Loden, Zohra Lampert
► Contrived but effective soap opera set in 1920s Kansas with Wood and Beatty as teenagers indulging in a forbidden love affair despite the objections of their parents. Oscar-winning screenplay by William Inge (who has a cameo as a minister) verges on the maudlin, but breathlessly romantic story is a good showcase for the stars. Film debuts for Beatty and Sandy Dennis.

SPLIT DECISIONS 1988
★★★★ R Drama/Sports 1:35
☑ Adult situations, explicit language, violence
Dir: David Drury *Cast:* Gene Hackman, Jeff Fahey, Jennifer Beals, Craig Sheffer, John McLiam
► When boxer Fahey refuses to throw fight, mobsters beat him up and his opponent-to-be throws him out window to his death. Fahey's brother Sheffer forsakes college to train for grudge match with killer. Father Hackman and grandfather McLiam, both boxing vets, had higher hopes for Sheffer but soon they're in his corner, training him mercilessly. Sheffer romances Fahey's girl Beals before climactic fight for revenge.

SPLIT IMAGE 1982
★★★ R Drama 1:51
☑ Adult situations, explicit language, mild violence
Dir: Ted Kotcheff *Cast:* Michael O'Keefe, Karen Allen, Peter Fonda, Elizabeth Ashley, James Woods, Brian Dennehy
► Bright college jock O'Keefe is lured by dewy-eyed siren Allen to join bizarre cult run by ascetic guru Fonda and soon renounces his family and former life. O'Keefe's well-to-do parents Dennehy and Ashley hire deprogrammer Woods to kidnap son and break him of cult's hold. O'Keefe weakens, however, when Fonda and Allen come looking for him. Thought-provoking topical drama boasts superior cast.

SPLITZ 1984
☆ PG-13 Comedy 1:29
☑ Brief nudity, adult situations, explicit language
Dir: Domonic Paris *Cast:* Robin Johnson, Patti Lee, Barbara M. Bingham, Shirley Stoler, Chuck McQuary
► At Hooter College, female rock band helps nerd sorority win strip basketball

and lingerie wrestling contests, much to the dismay of dictator dean Stoler who wants to replace their house with a sewage plant. *Porky's* clone features surprisingly little nudity and insulting ethnic stereotypes.

SPRING BREAK 1983
★★ R Comedy 1:41
☑ Nudity, adult situations, explicit language, adult humor
Dir: Sean S. Cunningham *Cast:* David Knell, Perry Lang, Steve Bassett, Paul Land, Corinne Alphen, Donald Symington
▶ Virginal college boys Knell and Lang, on spring vacation in Fort Lauderdale, meet experienced party vets Land and Bassett who introduce them to beer, wet T-shirt contests, and willing women. Knell's politician stepfather Symington, leery of bad press, sends henchman to end boys' escapades and close motel housing them, but timely blackmail scheme assures the fun won't stop. Harmless teen comedy is reminiscent of beach-blanket pics of early sixties.

SPRING FEVER 1983 Canadian
★★★ PG Comedy/Sports 1:40
☑ Adult situations, explicit language
Dir: Joseph Scanlan *Cast:* Susan Anton, Frank Converse, Jessica Walter, Stephen Young, Carling Bassett, Shawn Foltz
▶ Las Vegas showgirl Anton escorts daughter Bassett to Junior National Tennis Championships in Florida. Reigning champ Foltz and snobby rich mom Walter lead others to ostracize Anton and Bassett. Anton romances reporter Converse while Bassett casually hustles older males on tennis court. Foltz overcomes snooty background to befriend Bassett prior to finals match between two. Sports real-life tennis stars Bassett and Foltz.

SPRING SYMPHONY 1986 German
☆ PG-13 Biography/Music 1:46
☑ Adult situations
Dir: Peter Schamoni *Cast:* Nastassia Kinski, Herbert Gronemeyer, Rolf Hoppe, Anja-Christine Preussler, Edda Seippel, Andre Heller
▶ Life story of composer Robert Schumann (Gronemeyer) centers on his romance with Kinski, the musically gifted daughter of renowned music teacher Hoppe. Schumann studies under Hoppe and blossoms into major pianist-composer. Teacher and pupil have falling-out

when Hoppe tries to end Gronemeyer's romances with Kinski. ☒

SPY WHO CAME IN FROM THE COLD, THE 1965
★★★★ NR Espionage 1:52 B&W
Dir: Martin Ritt *Cast:* Richard Burton, Claire Bloom, Oskar Werner, Peter Van Eyck, Sam Wanamaker, George Voskovec
▶ Burned-out British spy Burton is recalled from Berlin for mission to eliminate Van Eyck, head of East German counter-espionage. Elaborate ruse in London, during which he romances a librarian with Communist sympathies (Bloom), discredits Burton as drunken foul-up ready to defect. Burton painfully learns he is merely a pawn in larger scheme. Grimly realistic depiction of espionage was adapted from the John le Carré best-seller. (CC)

SPY WHO LOVED ME, THE 1977 British
★★★★ PG
Espionage/Action-Adventure 2:05
☑ Adult situations, violence
Dir: Lewis Gilbert *Cast:* Roger Moore, Barbara Bach, Curt Jurgens, Richard Kiel, Caroline Munro, Walter Gotell
▶ Shipping magnate Jurgens steals both American and Soviet subs, hoping to start World War III and build new underseas civilization in aftermath of destruction. Agent 007 must team with beautiful Russian agent Bach to thwart Jurgens's plan. Tenth Bond epic introduced the toothy Jaws (Kiel). Don't miss the opening ski sequence with breathtaking stunt at climax. Carly Simon's theme song was popular hit.

SQUARE DANCE 1987
★★★ PG-13 Drama 1:52
☑ Adult situations, explicit language
Dir: Daniel Petrie *Cast:* Jane Alexander, Jason Robards, Winona Ryder, Rob Lowe, Deborah Richter, Guich Koock
▶ Texas teenager Ryder, who lives with farmer grandfather Robards, goes to the city to start relationship with trashy mother Alexander, whom she never really knew. Ryder comes of age and gets involved with retarded Lowe. Sensitive and well-crafted. Ryder is winning; Lowe and Alexander are effective in departures from their usual screen personas.

SQUEEZE, THE 1987
★★ PG-13 Comedy 1:42
☑ Adult situations, explicit language
Dir: Roger Young *Cast:* Michael Kea-

ton, Rae Dawn Chong, John Davidson, Meat Loaf, Joe Pantoliano, Danny Aiello
▶ Down-on-his-luck artist Keaton finds a dead body and a mysterious package in his ex-wife's apartment. Thugs pursue him but collection agent Chong helps him uncover a lottery scam. Outlandish but entertaining mixture of laughs and action never takes itself too seriously; appealing performances by Keaton and Chong.

SQUEEZE PLAY 1980
★ R Comedy 1:32
☑ Nudity, adult situations, explicit language
Dir: Samuel Weil *Cast:* Jim Harris, Jenni Hetrick, Rick Getlin, Al Corley
▶ In a New Jersey town, the men are so obsessed with softball that they ignore the women. When one woman is denied a place on the team, the ladies retaliate by forming their own squad to take on the guys. Maintains the noisy atmosphere of a wild party, including a wet T-shirt contest.

SQUIRM 1976
★ PG Horror 1:33
Dir: Jeff Lieberman *Cast:* Don Scardino, Patricia Pearcy, R. A. Dow, Jean Sullivan, Peter MacLean, Fran Higgins
▶ Georgia storm downs power lines over a nest of sandworms, turning them into vicious maneaters. Nearby town succumbs to panic as voracious worms go on an eating spree. Low-budget thriller is scary as well as preposterous; opening credits claim plot is based on a true story.

STACKING 1987
★★★ PG Drama 1:49
☑ Adult situations, explicit language
Dir: Martin Rosen *Cast:* Christine Lahti, Frederic Forrest, Megan Follows, Jason Gedrick, Raymond Baker, Peter Coyote
▶ When her husband is injured, wife Lahti and daughter Follows run the family farm themselves. Hard-drinking hired hand Forrest, Lahti's old flame, helps out and develops feelings for Follows. Homespun and honest; natural performances and lovely Montana scenery, although slow pace poses a problem.

STACY'S KNIGHTS 1983
★★★ PG Drama 1:34
☑ Adult situations, explicit language, mild violence
Dir: Jim Wilson *Cast:* Andra Millian,

Kevin Costner, Eve Lilith, Mike Reynolds, Garth Howard, Ed Semenza
▶ Shy Millian is a born cardsharp. Her lover Costner helps her win big but the casinos resort to cheating and murder to stop the duo. Millian decides to get even. A sleeper; attractive cast will have you pulling for the underdog characters.

STAGECOACH 1939
★★★★ NR Western 1:39 B&W
Dir: John Ford *Cast:* John Wayne, Claire Trevor, Andy Devine, Thomas Mitchell, George Bancroft, John Carradine
▶ Eight people ride a stagecoach through Apache territory to town of Lordsburg and soon are joined by escaped convict Wayne. Lawman Bancroft arrests Wayne, who has plans to avenge his brother's and father's murders, while prostitute Trevor falls in love with the rangy outlaw. When Indians attack, Bancroft frees Wayne to help ward off the savages and later agrees to allow him to confront enemies in Lordsburg. Classic film was director Ford's first Western since silent era and marked beginning of unparalleled work in the genre. Mitchell won Supporting Oscar; Wayne became a star.

STAGE DOOR 1937
★★★★ NR Drama 1:31 B&W
Dir: Gregory La Cava *Cast:* Katharine Hepburn, Ginger Rogers, Adolphe Menjou, Gail Patrick, Andrea Leeds, Constance Collier
▶ Marvelous adaptation of an Edna Ferber–George S. Kaufman play about struggling actresses rooming at the Footlights Club blends drama, comedy, and unbeatable dialogue into a bittersweet tribute to ambition and endurance. Hepburn (with her memorable line "The calla lilies are in bloom again") is a wealthy dilettante whose motives are questioned by earthy Rogers; Leeds won an Oscar nomination as a despairing artist. Excellent cast includes Eve Arden, Franklin Pangborn, Jack Carson, Lucille Ball, and Ann Miller.

STAGE DOOR CANTEEN 1943
★★★ NR Musical 2:12 B&W
Dir: Frank Borzage *Cast:* Cheryl Walker, William Terry, Marjorie Riordan, Lon McCallister, Margaret Early, Michael Harrison
▶ New York's famous World War II club for enlisted men is the setting for flimsy ro-

mance among soldiers on leave and three hostesses, but picture's real asset is its incredible array of over seventy guest stars, ranging from Katharine Hepburn to Harpo Marx to Tallulah Bankhead to Johnny Weissmuller. Katharine Cornell, in her only film appearance, performs from *Romeo and Juliet;* Peggy Lee, Gracie Fields, Count Basie, Benny Goodman, Yehudi Menuhin, and Ray Bolger offer "Why Don't You Do Right," "We Mustn't Say Goodbye," and other songs.

STAGE FRIGHT 1950
★★★ NR Mystery-Suspense 1:50 B&W
Dir: Alfred Hitchcock *Cast:* Jane Wyman, Marlene Dietrich, Michael Wilding, Richard Todd, Alastair Sim, Kay Walsh
▶ Acting student Wyman hides ex-boyfriend Todd, who claims his mistress Dietrich framed him for murder. Playing detective, Wyman takes a job as Dietrich's maid to learn the truth. Arrival of suave but suspicious policeman Wilding complicates the plot. Tricky, underrated mystery falls short of Hitchcock's best work, but offers more than enough humor and suspense. Dietrich is superb singing Cole Porter's "The Laziest Gal in Town."

STAIRWAY TO HEAVEN 1946 British
★★★ NR Fantasy 1:44 C/B&W
Dir: Michael Powell *Cast:* David Niven, Kim Hunter, Roger Livesey, Raymond Massey, Marius Goring, Robert Coote
▶ During World War II, pilot Niven somehow survives seemingly fatal plane battle and falls in love with WAC Hunter. Niven is summoned to heaven because it turns out he was slated for death; there he gets to argue his case before a celestial jury for a second chance at love and life. Extraordinary love story is ultimately very moving, thanks to visually inventive direction by Powell.

STAKEOUT 1987
★★★★ R Comedy/Drama 1:55
☑ Nudity, adult situations, explicit language, violence
Dir: John Badham *Cast:* Richard Dreyfuss, Emilio Estevez, Madeleine Stowe, Aidan Quinn, Dan Lauria, Forest Whitaker
▶ When dangerous killer Quinn escapes prison, detectives Dreyfuss and Estevez stake out home of Quinn's girlfriend Stowe. Surveillance grows complicated when Dreyfuss falls in love with Stowe. Meanwhile, Quinn draws closer to

Stowe's home, where he stashed loot years before. Popular cops-and-robbers comedy rehashes buddy-cop formula with great success due to fine performances and plenty of laughs. **(CC)**

STALAG 17 1953
★★★★★ NR Comedy/Drama 2:00 B&W
Dir: Billy Wilder *Cast:* William Holden, Don Taylor, Otto Preminger, Robert Strauss, Peter Graves, Harvey Lembeck
▶ In World War II POW camp, loner-hustler Holden rejects patriotism and escape plans of cohorts to pursue life of comfort. Camp commandant Preminger repeatedly thwarts escape efforts, so other Americans suspect Holden of spying. But when captured pilot Taylor faces execution for sabotage of German train, Holden turns from heel to hero. Classic war drama mixes laughs with intrigue. Holden won an Oscar in this adaptation of the Broadway play. Real-life producer-director Preminger shines as vicious Nazi.

STAND ALONE 1985
★★★★ R Drama 1:34
☑ Explicit language, violence
Dir: Alan Beattie *Cast:* Charles Durning, Pam Grier, James Keach, Bert Remsen, Barbara Sammeth, Lu Leonard
▶ Decorated World War II veteran Durning witnesses murder by drug dealers and assists police detective Keach. Lawyer Grier advises Durning not to testify against "cocaine cowboys," but Durning, fed up with society's tolerance of crime, fingers the guilty parties and then arms himself with war souvenirs for showdown. Chance to see Durning in a rare leading role.

STAND AND DELIVER 1988
★★★★ PG Biography 1:43
☑ Explicit language
Dir: Ramon Menendez *Cast:* Edward James Olmos, Lou Diamond Phillips, Rosana de Soto, Andy Garcia, Mark Phelan, Virginia Paris
▶ True story of Los Angeles math teacher Jaime Escalante (Olmos) whose charismatic tutelage guided students from poor Hispanic background to record success on advanced math placement exams. Despite authorities who suspect they cheated, Escalante and the kids overcome the odds. An inspirational tale to cherish; powerhouse performance by Oscar-nominated Olmos mixes wry

humor, toughness, and tenderness. (CC)

STAND BY ME 1986
★★★★ R Drama 1:29
☑ Explicit language
Dir: Rob Reiner *Cast:* Wil Wheaton, River Phoenix, Corey Feldman, Jerry O'Connell, Kiefer Sutherland, John Cusack
▶ Twelve-year-old writer-to-be Wheaton joins misunderstood tough Phoenix, daredevil Feldman, and overweight wimp O'Connell in adventurous search for body of boy killed by train. Camping trip provides laughs, thrills, and tears, leading to climactic standoff with town bully Sutherland. Sweetly comic rite-of-passage drama is based on a short story by Stephen King. Narrated by Richard Dreyfuss, who plays the grownup Wheaton. (CC)

STAR CHAMBER, THE 1983
★★★★ R Drama 1:49
☑ Adult situations, explicit language, graphic violence
Dir: Peter Hyams *Cast:* Michael Douglas, Hal Holbrook, Sharon Gless, Yaphet Kotto, James B. Sikking, Joe Regalbuto
▶ Young judge Douglas, disgusted with crooks getting off on technicalities, is recruited by colleague Holbrook for vigilante group of justices. However, Douglas turns against the group when they slate innocent men for death. Exciting and provocative story deals intelligently with serious issues while not stinting on thrilling chases, crisp dialogue, and sharp plot twists.

STARCRASH 1979 Italian
★ PG Sci-Fi 1:36
☑ Mild violence
Dir: Lewis Coates (Luigi Cozzi) *Cast:* Marjoe Gortner, Caroline Munro, Christopher Plummer, David Hasselhoff, Robert Tessier, Joe Spinell
▶ Evil inventor of doom machine sets out to destroy the universe; outer-space pilots Gortner and Munro try to stop him. Moves fast but not convincingly; flat dialogue and acting (save for the dependable Plummer), laughable costumes lead to unintentional comedy.

STAR CRYSTAL 1986
☆ R Sci-Fi 1:34
☑ Explicit language, violence
Dir: Lance Lindsay *Cast:* C. Jutson Campbell, John W. Smith, Faye Bolt, Taylor Kingsley, Marcia Linn
▶ In 2032, scientific expedition to Mars picks up alien who kills most humans on space station. Survivors seek to flee on shuttle to earth but alien tags along for more mayhem and murder. Last survivors Bolt and Campbell learn to communicate with alien and discover killings were in self-defense. Low-budget sci-fi entry suffers from uneven script.

STARDUST MEMORIES 1980
★ PG Comedy 1:31 B&W
☑ Adult situations, explicit language, adult humor
Dir: Woody Allen *Cast:* Woody Allen, Charlotte Rampling, Jessica Harper, Marie-Christine Barrault, Tony Roberts, Daniel Stern
▶ Troubled film director Allen escapes for seminar at resort hotel where he relives old romances in his head while carrying on new ones in the flesh. Meanwhile fans and critics alike complain his recent self-indulgent films aren't as good as earlier comedies. Pseudo-autobiographical effort comically skewers both Allen and his devotees. Many find the laughs are buried under the surrealistic style and somewhat mean-spirited tone.

STAR IS BORN, A 1937
★★★★ NR Drama 1:51
Dir: William Wellman *Cast:* Fredric March, Janet Gaynor, Adolphe Menjou, Lionel Stander, Andy Devine, May Robson
▶ Unknown actress Gaynor marries alcoholic movie star March. She tries to help him as she becomes a star and he goes personally and professionally downhill. Despite two subsequent remakes, this may be the finest of the three; Gaynor's innocence and March's poignance are quite moving. One of the all-time emotional closing lines: "This is Mrs. Norman Maine."

STAR IS BORN, A 1954
★★★★★ PG Musical 2:34
☑ Adult situations
Dir: George Cukor *Cast:* Judy Garland, James Mason, Charles Bickford, Jack Carson, Tom Noonan
▶ Hard-drinking actor Mason on his way down the Hollywood ladder marries ingenue Garland on her way up. Mason deteriorates as Garland watches helplessly. Tearjerker with tunes pulls out all the stops dramatically (Mason's harrowing "I need a job!" speech at the Oscar ceremonies) and musically (Garland's

memorable torch song, "The Man That Got Away"). Reissued version has extra numbers and cut footage reinserted.

STAR IS BORN, A 1976
★★★★★ R Musical 2:20
☑ Brief nudity, adult situations, explicit language
Dir: Frank Pierson *Cast:* Barbra Streisand, Kris Kristofferson, Paul Mazursky, Gary Busey, Oliver Clark, Sally Kirkland
▶ Remake of 1937 and 1954 films changes venue from movies to music. Over-the-hill rock star Kristofferson falls in love with unheralded singer Streisand. As her career skyrockets and his declines, their marriage heads toward a tragic end. Familiar story mishandled in new version, but Streisand's six production numbers will wow fans. Song "Evergreen," by Streisand and Paul Williams, won Oscar.

STARMAN 1984
★★★★ PG Fantasy/Romance 1:55
☑ Adult situations, explicit language, violence
Dir: John Carpenter *Cast:* Jeff Bridges, Karen Allen, Charles Martin Smith, Richard Jaeckel, Robert Phalen, Tony Edwards
▶ Shipwrecked extraterrestrial Bridges, his craft shot down by U.S. missiles, abducts widow Allen for help getting to rendezvous with mother ship. Government agents pursue him and Allen. During cross-country chase Allen loses fear of alien Bridges and falls for him. Charming and uplifting love story in sci-fi wrapping carried by strong turns from fetching Allen and impressively convincing Bridges. **(CC)**

STARS AND BARS 1988
★ R Comedy 1:38
☑ Adult situations, explicit language
Dir: Pat O'Connor *Cast:* Daniel Day-Lewis, Harry Dean Stanton, Spalding Gray, Joan Cusack, Martha Plimpton, Steven Wright
▶ Proper English art dealer Day-Lewis takes job in New York gallery and must fend off advances of owner's fifteen-year-old daughter Plimpton and amorous New Yorker Cusack. First major project is trip to Georgia to purchase rare painting from backwoods Southerner Stanton and his inbred clan. Brit-out-of-water comedy boasts terrific cast but tends to be broad and uneven. **(CC)**

STARS LOOK DOWN, THE 1940 British
★★★ NR Drama 1:50 B&W
Dir: Carol Reed *Cast:* Michael Redgrave, Margaret Lockwood, Emlyn Williams, Nancy Price, Edward Rigby, Cecil Parker
▶ College-educated Redgrave, son of miner Rigby, returns to his hometown and tries to help the miners. A strike and underground disaster make life hard for the men; Redgrave must also deal with unfaithful wife Lockwood. Outstanding adaptation of the A. J. Cronin novel.

STARSTRUCK 1982 Australian
★ PG Musical/Comedy 1:35
☑ Brief nudity, adult situations, explicit language
Dir: Gillian Armstrong *Cast:* Jo Kennedy, Ross O'Donovan, Pat Evison, Margo Lee, Max Cullen, Ned Lander
▶ Fourteen-year-old hustler O'Donovan schemes to make singing star of cousin Kennedy. New punk look and publicity stunt turn Kennedy into a media hit, but to succeed she must compromise her art and abandon O'Donovan. When family business teeters on edge of bankruptcy, O'Donovan and Kennedy reunite to seek grand prize in talent contest. Updated take on old-style "let's put on a show" yarns mixes mild spoof with serious musical numbers.

STARTING OVER 1979
★★★★ R Romance/Comedy 1:45
☑ Adult situations, explicit language
Dir: Alan J. Pakula *Cast:* Burt Reynolds, Jill Clayburgh, Candice Bergen, Mary Kay Place, Frances Sternhagen, Charles Durning
▶ Poignant and clever look at life after marriage from writer James L. Brooks: divorced writer Reynolds, dumped by wife Bergen, tries to start over with teacher Clayburgh. Bergen's reappearance threatens the new relationship. Reynolds's understated performance is one of his best; Clayburgh and Bergen (both Oscar-nominated) are disarming. Funniest scene: Reynolds's nervous breakdown at Bloomingdale's.

STAR TREK—THE MOTION PICTURE 1979
★★★★ G Sci-Fi 2:12
Dir: Robert Wise *Cast:* William Shatner, Leonard Nimoy, DeForest Kelley, James Doohan, Persis Khambatta, Stephen Collins
▶ Mysterious, gigantic cloud heads from

outer space toward earth, so starship Enterprise investigates. Captain Kirk (Shatner), Spock (Nimoy), and crew learn their nemesis is a living machine, superintelligent but without emotions. It takes over body of ship's navigator Khambatta and will wipe out human race until quick thinking by crew and sacrificial gesture by officer Collins save the day. First big-screen outing for characters of cult TV series can be ponderous. Next three sequels are livelier.

STAR TREK II: THE WRATH OF KHAN
1982
★ ★ ★ ★ PG Sci-Fi 1:53
☑ Explicit language, violence
Dir: Nicholas Meyer   *Cast:* William Shatner, Leonard Nimoy, DeForest Kelley, Ricardo Montalban, James Doohan, Kirstie Alley
▶ Evil outlaw Montalban, exiled years before by Kirk (Shatner), escapes in stolen starship and lays trap for nemesis, stealing Genesis technology that can destroy or re-create whole planets. Kirk leaves desk-jockey admiral's job to lead ragtag crew and veteran officers in battle of wits with malevolent Montalban. Sequel has much more life than original. Top-notch effects, hammy turn by Montalban, warm repartee among Kirk and Co., climactic phaser-'em-up, and tearjerker ending add up to engaging trek.

STAR TREK III: THE SEARCH FOR SPOCK 1984
★ ★ ★ ★ PG Sci-Fi 1:45
☑ Violence
Dir: Leonard Nimoy   *Cast:* William Shatner, Leonard Nimoy, DeForest Kelley, James Doohan, Christopher Lloyd, Judith Anderson
▶ Having given his life to save his friends in *Star Trek II*, Spock (Nimoy) is buried on experimental planet Genesis. When it appears the planet may have brought Spock back to life, Captain Kirk (Shatner) and his loyal officers steal their mothballed ship to rescue him. There they find a youth who may be Spock regenerated and an ambitious Klingon (Lloyd) who hopes to steal the power of Genesis. Third offering to Trekkies combines wit and action and shrewdly emphasizes winning characters instead of special effects. (CC)

STAR TREK IV: THE VOYAGE HOME
1986
★ ★ ★ ★ ★ PG Sci-Fi 1:59

☑ Explicit language
Dir: Leonard Nimoy   *Cast:* William Shatner, Leonard Nimoy, DeForest Kelley, James Doohan, Catherine Hicks, Jane Wyatt
▶ Returning home in Klingon vessel to face punishment for theft and destruction of Enterprise and other infractions (from *Star Trek II* and *III*), Kirk (Shatner), Spock (Nimoy), and crew discover unidentified probe is laying waste to Earth. Probe will quit destruction only when answered by call of now-extinct humpback whale, so heroes time-travel to twentieth-century San Francisco to whalenap specimens from biologist Hicks. Generally series lose gas with each outing, but plentiful humor and nifty ecology story make fourth entry arguably the best of the TV spin-offs. (CC)

START THE REVOLUTION WITHOUT ME
1970
★ ★ ★ PG Comedy 1:30
☑ Brief nudity, adult situations, explicit language, violence
Dir: Bud Yorkin   *Cast:* Gene Wilder, Donald Sutherland, Hugh Griffith, Billie Whitelaw, Victor Spinetti, Orson Welles
▶ Peasant twins and their aristocrat counterparts are mixed up at birth; years later, the now-grown mismatched sets (each played by Wilder and Sutherland) find themselves on opposite sides of the French Revolution. Generally amusing if uneven slapstick fun has garnered a cult following since its initial release.

STAR WARS 1977
★ ★ ★ ★ ★ PG Sci-Fi/Action-Adventure 2:01
☑ Adult situations, mild violence
Dir: George Lucas   *Cast:* Harrison Ford, Mark Hamill, Carrie Fisher, Alec Guinness, Peter Cushing, David Prowse
▶ High-tech, action-packed reworking of old Saturday serials portrays efforts of young adventurer Hamill and his mystic mentor Guinness to rescue princess Fisher from clutches of evil despot Cushing and his sinister minion Prowse (with voice of James Earl Jones). They are assisted by mercenary maverick Ford and trio of non-humans, who reluctantly join rebel forces in attempt to defeat Cushing and his menacing Death Star. Fun and funny, box office legend changed Hollywood's approach to filmmaking. Winner of six technical Oscars and Best Score by John Williams. Two sequels *The Empire Strikes*

Back and *Return of the Jedi* completed trilogy. **(CC)**

STAR 80 1983
★ ★ **R Biography 1:43**
☑ Nudity, adult situations, explicit language, graphic violence
Dir: Bob Fosse   *Cast:* Mariel Hemingway, Eric Roberts, Cliff Robertson, Carroll Baker, Roger Rees, David Clennon
▶ Sleazy hustler Paul Snider (Roberts) discovers beautiful teen Dorothy Stratten (Hemingway) hawking ice cream in Vancouver and soon persuades her to pose nude. Photos lead to spread in *Playboy* and marriage of Stratten to Snider despite warnings of publisher Hugh Hefner (Robertson). Stratten's acting career takes off and she leaves Snider to live with filmmaker Rees. Snider seeks revenge in gory fashion. Quality filmmaking from director Fosse and excellent work by two leads, but true story of Stratten is depressing and Roberts's character truly hateful and disturbing to watch.

STATE FAIR 1945
★ ★ ★ ★ **NR Musical 1:40**
Dir: Walter Lang   *Cast:* Jeanne Crain, Dana Andrews, Dick Haymes, Vivian Blaine, Charles Winninger, Fay Bainter
▶ Midwestern family finds adventure and romance at the Iowa State Fair. Dad Winninger and mom Bainter vie for hog and mincemeat honors. Son Haymes falls for married singer Blaine while daughter Crain meets reporter Andrews. Brimming with color and charm; grand Rodgers and Hammerstein score includes the Oscar-winning "It Might as Well Be Spring." Remake of 1933 film, remade again in 1962. **(CC)**

STATE OF SIEGE 1973 French
★ **NR Drama 2:00**
☑ Graphic violence
Dir: Costa-Gavras   *Cast:* Yves Montand, Renato Salvatori, O. E. Hasse, Jacques Weber
▶ U.S. official Montand is kidnapped and interrogated by rebel guerrillas in Uruguay. The incident nearly brings down the government. Challenging but difficult to watch: political slant is controversial (some would say anti-American), the rebels are largely faceless, and Montand's character is clearly unsavory although the acting is excellent. **⑤**

STATE OF THE UNION 1948
★ ★ ★ ★ **NR Drama 1:50 B&W**
Dir: Frank Capra   *Cast:* Spencer Tracy,

Katharine Hepburn, Van Johnson, Angela Lansbury, Adolphe Menjou, Lewis Stone
▶ Idealistic millionaire Tracy, separated from wife Hepburn, is persuaded by lover and newspaper publisher Lansbury to run for Republican Presidential nomination. Hepburn agrees to pose as loving spouse for campaign but cannot tolerate changes in Tracy's values as he succumbs to fevered ambitions of Lansbury, party boss Menjou, and publicity flack Johnson. Nonetheless, Hepburn finds herself falling back in love with Tracy. Some topical commentary is dated, but collision of morals and expediency in politics still remain pertinent subjects. All-star cast shines.

STAY AS YOU ARE 1978 Italian
★ ★ **NR Romance 1:45**
☑ Nudity, adult situations, explicit language
Dir: Alberto Lattuada   *Cast:* Marcello Mastroianni, Nastassia Kinski, Francisco Rabal, Monica Randal
▶ In Florence, middle-aged Mastroianni is pursued by gorgeous young student Kinski. He is reluctant to consummate the relationship because it turns out she might be his daughter by a former lover. Luscious Italian scenery and both Mastroianni and the frequently nude Kinski are perfectly cast; however, slow-moving story never catches fire. **⑤**

STAY HUNGRY 1976
★ ★ **R Comedy/Drama 1:42**
☑ Nudity, adult situations
Dir: Bob Rafelson   *Cast:* Jeff Bridges, Sally Field, Arnold Schwarzenegger, Fannie Flagg, Scatman Crothers
▶ Wealthy Southern scion Bridges invests in local gym, is befriended by bodybuilder Schwarzenegger (his film debut) and blue collar worker Field, and battles corrupt business types who covet the property. Quirky and ambitious plot is a bit too self-consciously eccentric but Bridges, Field, and Schwarzenegger give natural and unassuming performances.

STAYING ALIVE 1983
★ ★ ★ **PG Drama/Dance 1:36**
☑ Adult situations, explicit language
Dir: Sylvester Stallone   *Cast:* John Travolta, Cynthia Rhodes, Finola Hughes, Steve Inwood
▶ *Saturday Night Fever* sequel takes place five years later as Travolta, now a dancer living in Manhattan, auditions for

every musical in town and romances dancers Rhodes and Hughes. Cheerless wisecracks, run-of-the-mill dancing, and a few pleasant new Bee Gees songs (although most of the music is by Frank Stallone, Sly's brother). Travolta looks terrific, though, and that may be enough to draw viewers. **(CC)**

STEALING HEAVEN 1989 British
★ R Romance 1:50
☑ Nudity, adult situations
Dir: Clive Donner   *Cast:* Derek de Lint, Kim Thomson, Denholm Elliott, Bernard Hepton, Kenneth Cranham, Patsy Byrne
▶ Twelfth-century France: philosopher de Lint and pretty scholar Thomson fall in love. He tries to remain true to his vow of chastity but they become lovers, bringing the wrath of the church upon them. Literate screenplay and accomplished acting but very dry story based on life of Abelard and Heloise.

STEALING HOME 1988
★★★ PG-13 Drama 1:38
☑ Adult situations, explicit language
Dir: Steven Kampmann, Will Aldis
Cast: Mark Harmon, Jodie Foster, Blair Brown, Jonathan Silverman, Harold Ramis, John Shea
▶ Baseball player Harmon, whose career has hit the skids, returns home upon learning of childhood friend Foster's suicide. Memories of the unforgettable Foster help Harmon come to terms with his own life. Sentimental story pulls out all the stops; Foster is superb.

STEAMBOAT BILL, JR. 1928
★★★ NR Comedy 1:11 B&W
Dir: Charles Riesner   *Cast:* Buster Keaton, Ernest Torrence, Tom Lewis, Tom McGuire, Marion Byron, Joe Keaton
▶ Steamboat Bill (Torrence), a Mississippi riverboat pilot, is counting on his college-educated son to help stave off bankruptcy, but Junior (Keaton) turns out to be a fop in love with his father's rival. Dazzling silent comedy traces Keaton's progress from wastrel to hero in a series of breathtaking sight gags. Climactic typhoon sequence contains one of the most dangerous stunts ever filmed: entire wall of an actual house collapses on Keaton, who's saved by standing where an upstairs window lands.

STEAMING 1986 British
☆ R Drama 1:35
☑ Nudity, explicit language
Dir: Joseph Losey   *Cast:* Vanessa Redgrave, Sarah Miles, Diana Dors, Patti Love, Brenda Bruce, Felicity Dean
▶ Group of women share confidences and form close relationships in London steambath. When the bath is slated for demolition, they band together to protest. Strong cast with Love and Dors especially shining. However, talkiness, thick accents, and dated feminist slant severely limit appeal. Based on the Nell Dunn play.

STEEL 1980
★★★ PG Action-Adventure 1:41
☑ Explicit language, violence
Dir: Steve Carver   *Cast:* Lee Majors, Jennifer O'Neill, Art Carney, George Kennedy, Harris Yulin, Roger Mosley
▶ After construction chief Kennedy accidentally falls to his death, his daughter O'Neill recruits Majors to finish the building before bank withdraws financing. Majors whips together a wild crew of workers. A sleeper; surprisingly sturdy entertainment with a top-notch cast.

STEEL DAWN 1987
★★ R Action-Adventure 1:40
☑ Brief nudity, violence
Dir: Lance Hool   *Cast:* Patrick Swayze, Lisa Niemi, Christopher Neame, Brion James, Brett Hool, Anthony Zerbe
▶ Post-nuclear war future: wandering swordsman Swayze befriends widow Niemi (Swayze's real-life wife) and her son Hool. Greedy land baron Zerbe wants Niemi's land for its precious water supply and dispatches assassin Neame to kill Swayze. Story derivative of *Mad Max* has impressive swordplay and charismatic Swayze.

STEELE JUSTICE 1987
★★★ R Action-Adventure 1:35
☑ Brief nudity, adult situations, explicit language, violence
Dir: Robert Boris   *Cast:* Martin Kove, Sela Ward, Ronny Cox, Bernie Casey, Joseph Campanella, Soon-Teck Oh
▶ Vietnam vet Kove, having trouble adjusting to civilian life, battles old war enemy Oh, who has come to California to run the Black Tiger, an organization that deals drugs and harasses Vietnamese immigrants. Nonstop action with perfectly cast Kove a sympathetic underdog hero. **(CC)**

STEELYARD BLUES 1973
★★★ PG Comedy 1:32
☑ Explicit language
Dir: Alan Myerson   *Cast:* Jane Fonda,

Donald Sutherland, Peter Boyle, Garry Goodrow, Howard Hesseman, John Savage

▶ Dated, offbeat comedy about hippies who reconstruct a World War II plane to fly them away from conventional society. Sutherland is an ex-con obsessed with demolition derbies; his brother Hesseman, also his parole officer, takes a dim view of the airplane scheme. Zany characters include master of transvestite disguises Boyle, frizzy-haired prostitute Fonda, and mental institution escapee Savage.

STELLA DALLAS 1937
★★★ NR Drama 1:46 B&W
Dir: King Vidor *Cast:* Barbara Stanwyck, John Boles, Alan Hale, Anne Shirley, Marjorie Main, Barbara O'Neil
▶ In a small New England town, social climber Stanwyck uses improvement course to woo upper-class husband Boles. Once married, however, Stanwyck reverts to her loud, somewhat vulgar original self, driving Boles to arms of former sweetheart O'Neil and dismaying their daughter Shirley, who sticks by her mother despite remarks of snobby friends. Stanwyck was nominated as Best Actress for performance as misfit mother in this peerless tearjerker.

ST. ELMO'S FIRE 1985
★★★★ R Comedy/Drama 1:48
☑ Adult situations, explicit language
Dir: Joel Schumacher *Cast:* Emilio Estevez, Rob Lowe, Andrew McCarthy, Judd Nelson, Ally Sheedy, Mare Winningham
▶ Georgetown University grads face a difficult transition to the real world: virginal social worker Winningham yearns for charming but irresponsible Lowe, struggling writer McCarthy battles lawyer Nelson for Sheedy's affections, Estevez madly pursues older woman Andie MacDowell, Demi Moore deals with drug addiction and office romance. Slick story of emerging yuppies has energetic cast (with winsome Winningham faring best) but shallow characterizations. Funniest line: "When I grow up I want to be a bag lady . . . of course, I'd have alligator bags." John Parr title song was a big hit. (CC)

STEPFATHER, THE 1987
★★★ R Mystery-Suspense 1:29
☑ Nudity, adult situations, explicit language, violence

Dir: Joseph Ruben *Cast:* Terry O'Quinn, Jill Schoelen, Shelley Hack, Charles Lanyer, Stephen Shellen
▶ Sensitive teen Schoelen, inexplicably troubled about her new stepfather O'Quinn, checks into his background. Could he be the same man who recently massacred another family? Taut, convincing thriller by Donald Westlake builds to a graphically violent climax. O'Quinn, impressive in a measured, incisive performance, and assured direction place this well above routine slasher films.

STEPFORD WIVES, THE 1974
★★★ PG Mystery-Suspense 1:55
☑ Adult situations, explicit language, violence
Dir: Bryan Forbes *Cast:* Katharine Ross, Paula Prentiss, Patrick O'Neal, Tina Louise, Peter Masterson, Nanette Newman
▶ Ross moves to Connecticut community and finds the other housewives strangely complacent and compliant. She discovers the sinister reason: their husbands have turned them into slave robots. Why? "Because we can," says ringleader O'Neal. Chiller with a satiric feminist slant based on the Ira Levin best-seller.

STERILE CUCKOO, THE 1969
★★★ PG Comedy/Drama 1:47
☑ Adult situations, explicit language
Dir: Alan J. Pakula *Cast:* Liza Minnelli, Wendell Burton, Tim McIntire, Elizabeth Harrower
▶ Minnelli earned her first Oscar nomination in this sensitive story of young love between two college students. As the outspoken Pookie Adams, Minnelli pursues the shy Burton. Their romance hits a snag when she announces she's pregnant. Directorial debut for Pakula, who shows a sure hand with the material. Theme song, "Come Saturday Morning," was also Oscar-nominated.

STEVIE 1978 British
★ PG Biography 1:42
☑ Explicit language
Dir: Robert Enders *Cast:* Glenda Jackson, Mona Washbourne, Alec McCowen, Trevor Howard
▶ Critically acclaimed film adaptation of Hugh Whitemore's play about the profoundly witty English poet, Stevie Smith. In a tour-de-force performance, Jackson plays Stevie in all her glory: funny, fragile, demanding, suicidal, and brave. Washbourne is the dotty aunt with whom Ste-

vie lived, McCowen is her one-time fiancé. Sepia-toned flashbacks and readings of Stevie's poetry (including her most famous and prophetic poem, "Not Waving But Drowning") may slow the pace too much for many viewers. A must for anyone who loves language and/or Glenda.

STEWARDESS SCHOOL 1987
★ R Comedy 1:33
☑ Nudity, adult situations, explicit language
Dir: Ken Blancaro *Cast:* Brett Cullen, Donny Most, Mary Cadorette, Sandahl Bergman, Judy Landers, Sherman Hemsley
► Nearsighted pilot Cullen, his best pal Most, ex-hooker Landers, klutz Cadorette, and wrestler Bergman are among the stewardess school students who complete rigorous training and help a tiny airline pass an FAA inspection. Lackluster romp; cast seems to be having fun but the laughs are few.

ST. HELENS 1981
★★★★ PG Action-Adventure 1:37
☑ Explicit language, violence
Dir: Ernest Pintoff *Cast:* Art Carney, David Huffman, Cassie Yates, Albert Salmi
► Drama about the May 18, 1980, eruption of Mount St. Helen's in southeastern Washington—the greatest explosion ever recorded in the U.S. outside of Alaska. More entertaining than factual, film details the interaction of various residents during the weeks preceding the event. Among the characters: stubborn old coot Carney, who refuses to leave his mountaintop home, hell-bent geologist Huffman, his pushy girl Yates, and greedy local entrepreneur Salmi. Interesting weaving of special effects and real footage.

STICK 1985
★★★ R Action-Adventure 1:49
☑ Adult situations, explicit language, violence
Dir: Burt Reynolds *Cast:* Burt Reynolds, Candice Bergen, George Segal, Charles Durning
► Ex-con Stick (Reynolds) tries to pick up the pieces of his life after seven years in prison but becomes involved in seeking revenge when his pal is murdered by drug king Durning. He takes chauffeur job with Palm Beach millionaire Segal, who does business with Durning. Segal's fi-

nancial advisor Bergen plays Reynolds's love interest. Competent adaptation of Elmore Leonard novel never sizzles, despite star cast and sun-bleached Miami locations. (CC)

STICKY FINGERS 1988
★★ PG-13 Comedy 1:37
☑ Adult situations, explicit language, violence
Dir: Catlin Adams *Cast:* Helen Slater, Melanie Mayron, Carol Kane, Christopher Guest, Danitra Vance, Eileen Brennan
► Flaky East Village musicians Slater and Mayron go on spending spree and land in hot water with cops and assorted thugs when drug-dealer pal leaves them $900,000 in cash. Visually inventive and the two stars are likable. However, frenetic sitcom plot has too many shrill scenes of Slater and Mayron screaming at each other. (CC)

STILETTO 1969
★ R Action-Adventure 1:38
☑ Adult situations, explicit language, violence
Dir: Bernard Kowalski *Cast:* Alex Cord, Britt Ekland, Patrick O'Neal, Joseph Wiseman, Barbara McNair, Roy Scheider
► Hired gun Cord lives the high life working for mob don Wiseman. Cord decides to turn over a new leaf but learns that breaking off is hard to do. Decent cast fails to breathe life into undistinguished adaptation of the Harold Robbins novel.

STILL OF THE NIGHT 1982
★★★★ PG Mystery-Suspense 1:27
☑ Brief nudity, adult situations, explicit language, violence
Dir: Robert Benton *Cast:* Meryl Streep, Roy Scheider, Jessica Tandy, Sandra Botsford, Josef Sommer
► Psychologist Scheider is visited by Streep, the neurotic mistress of his recently murdered patient Sommer. She's the key suspect in the murder but, despite warnings from his psychiatrist mother Tandy, Scheider falls for Streep anyway. Will his attraction prove fatal? Visual tribute to the stylized films of Hitchcock features an attractive, pedigree cast and several suspenseful moments.

STILL SMOKIN' 1983
★★ R Comedy 1:31
☑ Nudity, explicit language, violence
Dir: Thomas Chong *Cast:* Cheech

Marin, Thomas Chong, Carol Van Her-
wijnen, Shirleen Stoker
▶ Cheech & Chong go to Amsterdam in
this random assortment of unrelated skits
aimlessly strung together. The word
"man" is used, at last count, 4,587 times.
Entertaining for die-hard fans only, man.

STING, THE 1973
★★★★★ PG Comedy 2:09
☑ Adult situations, explicit language
Dir: George Roy Hill *Cast:* Paul New-
man, Robert Redford, Robert Shaw,
Charles Durning, Eileen Brennan, Ray
Walston
▶ Chicago, 1930s: after his friend is killed,
Redford teams with con man Newman to
stage elaborate "sting" and bilk gangster Shaw. One of the cleverest and most
intricate plots in movie history will have
you continually guessing and smiling in
this tremendously entertaining comedy.
Gorgeously mounted period settings enhanced by tinkling Scott Joplin piano rag
score, oodles of charm and pizzazz from
Newman and Redford (Oscar-nominated). Seven Oscars include Best Picture, Director, Screenplay, and Music Adaptation (Marvin Hamlisch).

STING II, THE 1983
★★★ PG Comedy 1:42
☑ Adult situations, explicit language,
violence, adult humor
Dir: Jeremy Paul Kagan *Cast:* Jackie
Gleason, Mac Davis, Teri Garr, Karl
Malden, Oliver Reed
▶ In 1940, New York con man Gleason
and boxer Davis stage ring hustle to
"sting" mobster Reed and racketeer
Malden out of big bucks. Garr plays a
co-conspirator whose ultimate loyalty is
uncertain. Good cast and some nice plot
surprises but sophomoric humor lacks the
cleverness of the Oscar-winning original.

STIR CRAZY 1980
★★★★★ R Comedy 1:51
☑ Adult situations, explicit language
Dir: Sidney Poitier *Cast:* Richard Pryor,
Gene Wilder, JoBeth Williams, George
Stanford Brown, Craig T. Nelson, Barry
Corbin
▶ Blockbuster hit about lunatic friends
Wilder and Pryor who leave New York for
an easier life out west and are arrested
for a robbery they didn't commit. Sen-
tenced to 120 years in an Arizona prison,
they attempt to outwit sadistic wardens,
scheming guards, and fellow prisoners.
Explosively funny moments. Chemistry

between leads overcomes somewhat
predictable plot.

STITCHES 1985
★ R Comedy 1:27
☑ Nudity, explicit language, adult
humor
Dir: Alan Smithee *Cast:* Parker Stevenson, Geoffrey Lewis, Eddie Albert, Brian
Tochi, Robin Dearden
▶ Medical school is short on money and
after the partying students wreck the
dean's house, fund-raising seems increasingly unlikely. Other antics for the
rowdy crew include dressing up as
cadavers and watching naked women
through a one-way mirror. Extremely
broad humor is strictly for the undis-
criminating.

ST. IVES 1976
★★★★ PG Action-Adventure 1:34
☑ Violence
Dir: J. Lee Thompson *Cast:* Charles
Bronson, John Houseman, Jacqueline
Bisset, Maximilian Schell, Harry Guardino, Elisha Cook, Jr.
▶ Novelist Bronson, a former crime reporter, is enticed by attorney Houseman
into recovering account books that figure
in a mob trial. He becomes the target of
both sides of a gang war as he deals with
crooked psychiatrist Schell and beautiful
femme fatale Bisset. Above-average
Bronson vehicle is restrained and genuinely perplexing. Look for Daniel J. Travanti and Jeff Goldblum in small roles.

STONE BOY, THE 1984
★★★★ PG Drama 1:28
Dir: Christopher Cain *Cast:* Robert Duvall, Glenn Close, Frederic Forrest, Wilford Brimley, Jason Presson
▶ Young farm boy Presson kills his brother
in a hunting accident and is thrown into
a nearly catatonic state. Unable to communicate with parents Close and Duvall,
he moves in with his grandfather Brimley
but eventually runs away to his aunt in
Reno. Compelling drama of a family's
adjustment to a tragic death is moving
and provocative, although sometimes
slow paced. (CC)

STONE KILLER, THE 1973
★★★ R Action-Adventure 1:35
☑ Adult situations, explicit language,
violence
Dir: Michael Winner *Cast:* Charles
Bronson, Martin Balsam, David Sheiner,
Norman Fell, Ralph Waite, Eddie Fire-
stone

▶ Rapid, hard-edged, extremely violent thriller about ex–New York cop Bronson battling Mafia don Balsam's mass-murder plot. His efforts to combat the scheme are hampered by Balsam's use of Vietnam vets without prison records. Good Bronson vehicle based on John Gardner's *A Complete State of Death.*

STOOGEMANIA 1985
★★ PG Comedy 1:23 C/B&W
☑ Adult humor
Dir: Chuck Workman *Cast:* Josh Mostel, Melanie Chartoff, Mark Holton, Sid Caesar, Victoria Jackson, The Three Stooges
▶ Mostel is engaged to Chartoff but his obsession with the Three Stooges threatens their happiness: he keeps fantasizing about his comic heroes, who appear in clips from their vintage classics. All ends happily for the couple. Stoogemaniacs will enjoy this; others may want to pass.

STOP MAKING SENSE 1984
★★ NR Documentary/Music 1:28
Dir: Jonathan Demme *Cast:* David Byrne, Tina Weymouth, Chris Frantz, Jerry Harrison, Steve Scales, Alex Weir
▶ Concert film from Talking Heads 1983 tour combines iconoclastic lighting and stage design, elements of Japanese kabuki theater, rear projection of thought-poems, riveting presence of lead singer Byrne, and seamless direction by Demme. Byrne and top-notch band perform sixteen songs (three extra on home video version) including "Psycho Killer," "Life During Wartime," and "Burning Down the House." Considered by many the best concert film ever. Byrne's Big Suit shouldn't be missed.

STOPOVER TOKYO 1957
★★ NR Espionage 1:40
Dir: Richard L. Breen *Cast:* Robert Wagner, Joan Collins, Edmond O'Brien, Ken Scott, Reiko Oyama, Larry Keating
▶ Well-crafted espionage thriller concerns American spy Wagner ordered to protect dignitary Keating in Tokyo from Communist assassination plot. Keating refuses to believe anyone intends to kill him while Wagner's romantic interest Collins grows unhappy with his excessive dedication to his job. Scenic tour of Japan and intelligent drama are the strengths of adaptation of John P. Marquand's novel.

STORM 1985 Canadian
☆ NR Action-Adventure 1:21

☑ Adult situations
Dir: David Winning *Cast:* David Palfy, Stan Kane, Tom Schioler, Harry Freedman, Lawrence Elion
▶ Students Palfy and Schioler journey deep into the Alberta woods to play a survival game. There they stumble across three elderly crooks searching for buried loot from a 1946 robbery, leading to extended chase through forest. Ambitious first effort by director Winning suffers from minuscule budget and weak plotting.

STORMY MONDAY 1988 British
★ R Drama 1:33
☑ Nudity, adult situations, explicit language, violence
Dir: Mike Figgis *Cast:* Melanie Griffith, Tommy Lee Jones, Sting, Sean Bean
▶ Young Bean goes to work for Newcastle, England, club owner Sting, whose place is coveted by ruthless American businessman Jones. As Jones uses violence to get what he wants, Bean gets involved with his girlfriend Griffith. Talented cast and Figgis create effective melancholy mood and sense of impending danger; suffers from sketchy plotting and characterizations. **(CC)**

STORMY WEATHER 1943
★★ NR Musical 1:18 B&W
Dir: Andrew L. Stone *Cast:* Lena Horne, Bill "Bojangles" Robinson, Cab Calloway, Katherine Dunham, Fats Waller, Nicholas Brothers
▶ All-star black musical uses song-and-dance numbers to describe turning points in vaudeville dancer Robinson's life from 1911 to 1936, including his troubled relationship with wife Horne. Fats Waller performs "Ain't Misbehavin'," Bojangles Robinson shows off his famous soft shoe routines, and Horne does a stellar version of the title song. Coleman Hawkins and many other jazz stars add specialty numbers. **(CC)**

STORY OF ADELE H., THE 1975 French
★ PG Drama 1:38
☑ Adult situations, explicit language
Dir: François Truffaut *Cast:* Isabelle Adjani, Bruce Robinson, Sylvia Marriott, Reubin Dorey, Joseph Blatchley
▶ Beautiful but often baffling study of Adele H. (Adjani), daughter of the nineteenth-century writer Victor Hugo, and her unrequited passion for callous British officer Robinson. Adele's obsession leads her to the brink of insanity as she follows her lover from Nova Scotia to Barbados.

Complex film received an Oscar nomination for Adjani's controlled acting. S

STORY OF ALEXANDER GRAHAM BELL, THE 1939
★★★ NR Biography 1:38 B&W
Dir: Irving Cummings   *Cast:* Don Ameche, Loretta Young, Henry Fonda, Charles Coburn, Spring Byington, Gene Lockhart
▶ Well-mounted biography gave Ameche one of his most famous roles as Bell, the inventor of the telephone. Originally a pioneer in teaching speech to the deaf, Bell uses money from father of student and girlfriend (Young) to work with assistant Tom Watson (Fonda) on improving telegraph transmissions. Climaxes with stirring defense against Western Union in patent infringement trial.

STORY OF LOUIS PASTEUR, THE 1936
★★★ NR Biography 1:25 B&W
Dir: William Dieterle   *Cast:* Paul Muni, Josephine Hutchinson, Anita Louise, Donald Woods
▶ Nineteenth-century French scientist Louis Pasteur (Muni) defies the scorn of the medical establishment to develop vaccines for anthrax and rabies. Conventional but quite engrossing; Muni won a well-deserved Best Actor Oscar. Best Picture nominee.

STORY OF ROBIN HOOD, THE 1952
★★★ NR Action-Adventure 1:23
Dir: Ken Annakin   *Cast:* Richard Todd, Joan Rice, Peter Finch, James Hayter, James Robertson, Martita Hunt
▶ Exemplary Disney version of the classic adventure casts Todd as the bandit of Sherwood Forest, with Finch suitably villainous as the nefarious Sheriff of Nottingham. Elaborate production with fast pacing and high spirits will entertain parents and children alike.

STORY OF VERNON AND IRENE CASTLE, THE 1939
★★★ NR Biography/Musical 1:33 B&W
Dir: H. C. Potter   *Cast:* Fred Astaire, Ginger Rogers, Edna May Oliver, Walter Brennan, Lew Fields, Etienne Girardot
▶ Enjoyable biography of the Castles, the most popular dancing team of the early twentieth century, with Astaire and Rogers lovingly re-creating their best routines in over thirty real musical numbers ("Row, Row, Row," "The Yama Yama Man," "Rose Room," etc.). Plot describes

their marriage, rigorous training, rise to fame in Europe and America, and Vernon's tragic early death. Last film together for Astaire and Rogers until 1949's *The Barkleys of Broadway*.

STORY OF WILL ROGERS, THE 1952
★★★★ NR Biography 1:49
Dir: Michael Curtiz   *Cast:* Will Rogers, Jr., Jane Wyman, Carl Benton Reid, James Gleason, Eddie Cantor
▶ Life story of the great humorist Will Rogers (played by his son Will Rogers, Jr.) traces his courtship of postmistress–future wife Wyman, his rise from Wild West shows to vaudeville and the movies, and his involvement in politics. Warm, sentimental, and quite enjoyable; Rogers, Jr., and Wyman are ideally cast.

STRAIGHT TIME 1978
★★★ R Crime/Drama 1:54
☑ Nudity, explicit language, violence
Dir: Ulu Grosbard   *Cast:* Dustin Hoffman, Theresa Russell, Harry Dean Stanton, Gary Busey, M. Emmet Walsh
▶ Armed robber Hoffman is paroled after six years in prison. He has an affair with employment agency worker Russell but is unable to stay straight, getting involved with other ex-cons on a robbery spree. Gritty and refreshingly real evocation of the underworld; exceptional performances by Hoffman and first-rate supporting cast.

STRAIGHT TO HELL 1987
☆ R Comedy 1:26
☑ Explicit language, violence
Dir: Alex Cox   *Cast:* Sy Richardson, Joe Strummer, Dick Rude, Grace Jones, Elvis Costello, Dennis Hopper
▶ In Spain, bank robbers bury their money in the desert after their car breaks down. They go into town and battle various types who also want the loot. Strange spoof of spaghetti westerns misfires: self-indulgent humor, repulsive characters, overdone acting.   (CC)

STRAIT-JACKET 1964
★★ NR Horror 1:29 B&W
Dir: William Castle   *Cast:* Joan Crawford, Diane Baker, Leif Erickson, Howard St. John, John Anthony Hayes, George Kennedy
▶ After murdering her husband and his lover with an axe, Crawford spends twenty years in an insane asylum. Upon release she seeks out daughter Baker, a sculptor, but is horrified when axe mur-

ders resume. Mild shocker written by Robert Bloch has a few effective chills.

STRANDED 1987
★ ★ ★ PG-13 Sci-Fi 1:20
☑ Explicit language, violence
Dir: Tex Fuller *Cast:* Ione Skye, Joe Morton, Maureen O'Sullivan, Susan Barnes, Cameron Dye, Michael Greene
▶ Teenager Skye and her grandmother O'Sullivan befriend aliens who are fleeing extraterrestrial assassin. Also involved in the situation: local sheriff Morton and government agent Barnes. Simple but well-rendered tale elicits sympathy for both human and nonhuman characters. O'Sullivan is delightful.

STRANGE BEHAVIOR 1981
Australian/New Zealand
★ R Horror 1:39
☑ Explicit language, violence
Dir: Michael Laughlin *Cast:* Michael Murphy, Louise Fletcher, Dan Shor, Fiona Lewis, Dey Young, Marc McClure
▶ In a midwestern college town, sheriff Murphy battles scientists whose experiments turn students into killers. Standard scare tactics, farfetched plotting; Fletcher and Murphy are fine but deserve better material. Australian locations pass convincingly for America.

STRANGE BREW 1983
★ ★ PG Comedy 1:30
☑ Explicit language, mild violence, adult humor
Dir: Dave Thomas, Rick Moranis *Cast:* Dave Thomas, Rick Moranis, Max Von Sydow, Paul Dooley, Lynne Griffin
▶ SCTV's Moranis and Thomas reprise their beer-guzzling McKenzie Brothers characterizations. The likable "hosers" get the job of their dreams when they are hired to work in a brewery. They uncover evil brewmeister Von Sydow's scheme to conquer the world. Gentle and sweet spirited, even when the gags are less than sophisticated.

STRANGE INVADERS 1983
★ ★ PG Sci-Fi 1:34
☑ Explicit language, violence
Dir: Michael Laughlin *Cast:* Paul LeMat, Nancy Allen, Diana Scarwid, Michael Lerner, Louise Fletcher, Wallace Shawn
▶ Columbia University professor LeMat searches for his missing wife Scarwid in midwestern town taken over by alien beings. Reporter Allen aids LeMat as the aliens also nab his daughter. Stylish di-

rection and acting evoke the classic 1950s sci-fi films; modest special effects, several clever touches.

STRANGER, THE 1946
★ ★ ★ ★ NR Mystery-Suspense 1:31 B&W
Dir: Orson Welles *Cast:* Orson Welles, Loretta Young, Edward G. Robinson, Philip Merivale, Richard Long, Byron Keith
▶ Federal agent Robinson, searching for escaped Nazi criminal, centers in on a small Connecticut town where gentle professor Welles is marrying judge's daughter Young. Robinson doggedly uncovers evidence that places Young's life in jeopardy. Beautifully executed thriller features a strong script, memorable climax, and a chilling performance by Welles. Available in a colorized version. (CC)

STRANGER AND THE GUNFIGHTER, THE 1976 Italian/Hong Kong
★ ★ PG Western/Martial Arts 1:47
☑ Brief nudity, violence
Dir: Anthony M. Dawson (Antonio Margheriti) *Cast:* Lee Van Cleef, Lo Lieh, Patty Shepard, Femi Benussi
▶ Gunslinger Van Cleef and Chinese martial arts expert Lieh team up to find Lieh's family fortune in the Old West. Stiff acting, silly musical score, but fast-paced action combines flying-through-the-air kung-fu with old-fashioned Western shootouts. Good cinematography.

STRANGER IS WATCHING, A 1982
★ ★ ★ R Mystery-Suspense 1:32
☑ Adult situations, explicit language, graphic violence
Dir: Sean S. Cunningham *Cast:* Kate Mulgrew, Rip Torn, James Naughton, Shawn Von Schreiber, Barbara Baxley, Frank Hamilton
▶ Mad killer Torn kidnaps young Von Schreiber, who witnessed his crime, and newscaster Mulgrew, who covered the story. Torn keeps them prisoner under Grand Central Station and demands ransom from Von Schreiber's father Naughton. Effective direction and Lalo Schifrin music generate tension throughout. Based on the Mary Higgins Clark best-seller.

STRANGERS KISS 1984
★ R Drama 1:33 C/B&W
☑ Explicit language
Dir: Matthew Chapman *Cast:* Peter Coyote, Victoria Tennant, Blaine Novak,

Dan Shor, Richard Romanus, Linda Kerridge

▶ On a 1955 Hollywood movie set, actor Novak gets involved with co-star Tennant. As the plot of their movie increasingly reflects real life, the lovers must deal with manipulative director Coyote and Tennant's gangster boyfriend Romanus. Polished production, haunting jazz score, solid acting. However, repetitive scenes of inside moviemaking slow down the pace; the characters and romance fail to hold our interest.

STRANGERS ON A TRAIN 1951
★★★★ NR Mystery-Suspense 1:41
B&W
Dir: Alfred Hitchcock *Cast:* Farley Granger, Ruth Roman, Robert Walker, Leo G. Carroll, Patricia Hitchcock, Marion Lorne

▶ Walker is mesmerizing as a devious psychopath who lures tennis star Granger into a bizarre plan to exchange murders. If Granger refuses to kill Walker's father, he'll be arrested for strangling his wife. Classic thriller improves with each viewing. Dazzling plot and dialogue (adapted by Raymond Chandler from Patricia Highsmith's novel), startling performance by Lorne as Walker's mother, and justly famed sequences in an amusement park and tennis stadium place this at the top of Hitchcock's work. Inspiration for *Throw Mama From the Train.*

STRANGER THAN PARADISE 1984
★ R Comedy 1:29 B&W
☑ Adult situations, explicit language
Dir: Jim Jarmusch *Cast:* John Lurie, Eszter Balint, Richard Edson, Cecillia Stark, Danny Rosen, Rammellzee

▶ Two-bit Newark gambler Lurie plays reluctant host to Hungarian cousin Balint until she moves to Cleveland. A year later, Lurie and pal Edson decide to visit Balint and soon take her to Florida. The Sunshine State turns out to be less than paradise, until Balint accidentally receives a stash of drug profits. Hip road movie using extremely dry humor and static long takes was critical darling, but many felt it simply strange.

STRATEGIC AIR COMMAND 1955
★★★ NR Drama 1:54
Dir: Anthony Mann *Cast:* James Stewart, June Allyson, Frank Lovejoy, Barry Sullivan, Alex Nicol, Bruce Bennett

▶ Due to a critical shortage of pilots, baseball player Stewart is ordered back into the service to fly new jets for the SAC. At first antagonistic over his fate, Stewart learns to appreciate the importance of the unit. Shot with the cooperation of the armed forces, film features outstanding aviation footage but a less-than-inspired earthbound plot.

STRAWBERRY BLONDE, THE 1941
★★★ NR Comedy 1:37 B&W
Dir: Raoul Walsh *Cast:* James Cagney, Olivia de Havilland, Rita Hayworth, Jack Carson, Alan Hale, George Tobias

▶ Dentist Cagney loses strawberry blond Hayworth to dishonest pal Carson, marries wholesome de Havilland instead, and takes prison rap for one of Carson's scams. Years later, Cagney has a chance for revenge but realizes his life turned out for the best after all. Warm and wonderful with marvelous turn-of-the-century period re-creation, robust Cagney, and winning de Havilland.

STRAWBERRY STATEMENT, THE 1970
★ R Drama 1:43
☑ Brief nudity, adult situations, explicit language, violence
Dir: Stuart Hagmann *Cast:* Bruce Davison, Kim Darby, Bud Cort, Murray MacLeod, Danny Goldmann, Bob Balaban

▶ Dated "message" film about the 1968 Columbia University riots shows how uninvolved student Davison becomes a counter-culture leader when he falls for hippie classmate Darby. Muddled adaptation of a novel by James Simon Kunen sacrifices realism for sensationalized portrayals of police brutality. Screenplay by Israel Horovitz; soundtrack includes songs by Crosby, Stills, Nash, and Young; Joni Mitchell; and Thunderclap Newman.

STRAW DOGS 1972
★★ R Drama 1:54
☑ Rape, adult situations, explicit language, graphic violence
Dir: Sam Peckinpah *Cast:* Dustin Hoffman, Susan George, Peter Vaughn, T. P. McKenna, Del Henney, Ken Hutchison

▶ American mathematician Hoffman moves to a remote Cornish village with his wife George to escape violence. When George is raped by local thugs, Hoffman resorts to brutality for revenge. Raw, distasteful film provoked controversy on release for its endorsement of violence, but weak characters and plot lessen its effectiveness.

STREAMERS 1983
★ R Drama 1:58
☑ Brief nudity, adult situations, explicit language, graphic violence, adult humor
Dir: Robert Altman *Cast:* Matthew Modine, Michael Wright, Mitchell Lichtenstein, David Alan Grier, Albert Macklin, Guy Boyd
▶ Wright, a fiery recruit from the black ghetto, serves as catalyst for simmering tensions in a barracks filled with paratroopers awaiting assignment in Vietnam. Adaptation of David Rabe's hard-hitting play suffers from overacting and unconvincing cinematic tricks. George Dzundza delivers the best performance as a boozy sergeant.

STREETCAR NAMED DESIRE, A 1951
★★★★ PG Drama 2:02 B&W
☑ Adult situations
Dir: Elia Kazan *Cast:* Vivien Leigh, Marlon Brando, Kim Hunter, Karl Malden, Rudy Bond
▶ "I've always depended on the kindness of strangers," says fragile Southern belle Blanche DuBois (Leigh), visiting sister Stella (Hunter); but Blanche can't depend on the kindness of Stella's brutal husband, Stanley Kowalski (Brando). His resentment of her presence leads to conflict and a powerful climax. Magnificent adaptation of the Tennessee Williams play with towering Oscar-nominated performance by Brando, Oscar-winning ones by Leigh, Hunter, and Malden. Best Picture nominee. (CC)

STREETCAR NAMED DESIRE, A 1984
★★★★ NR Drama/MFTV 2:04
☑ Adult situations, mild violence
Dir: John Erman *Cast:* Ann-Margret, Treat Williams, Beverly D'Angelo, Randy Quaid
▶ Outstanding cast in an Emmy-winning adaptation of Tennessee Williams's classic. Ann-Margret is the unmarried, desperate Blanche, who invades sister D'Angelo's New Orleans household and battles her husband Williams to a near-tragic conclusion. Not quite in league with 1951 version but still top-notch; Emmy nominations went to D'Angelo, Quaid, and Ann-Margret, who beautifully demonstrates her ever increasing-dramatic range.

STREET HERO 1984 Australian
★ NR Drama 1:40
☑ Adult situations, explicit language, violence
Dir: Michael Pattinson *Cast:* Vincent Colosimo, Sigrid Thornton, Sandy Gore, Bill Hunter, Ray Marshall
▶ Teenage mob courier Colosimo finds refuge from dreary life when girlfriend Thornton and music teacher Gore convince him to join school band as drummer. Colosimo also must deal with mom's abuse by her drunken husband. Teen flick is slickly produced and directed but suffers from cloudy plotting.

STREET SMART 1987
★★★ R Drama 1:36
☑ Brief nudity, adult situations, explicit language, violence
Dir: Jerry Schatzberg *Cast:* Christopher Reeve, Kathy Baker, Morgan Freeman, Mimi Rogers, Andre Gregory, Jay Patterson
▶ Journalist Reeve makes big career move by passing off story about fictitious pimp as truth. He gets more trouble than he bargained for when actual pimp Freeman, accused of murder, attempts to use him as an alibi. Savvy, topical, and taut; Baker is haunting as a prostitute, Oscar-nominated Freeman is mesmerizing, and Reeve is solid as the unsympathetic protagonist. (CC)

STREETS OF FIRE 1984
★★★ PG Action-Adventure 1:34
☑ Adult situations, explicit language, violence
Dir: Walter Hill *Cast:* Michael Paré, Diane Lane, Rick Moranis, Amy Madigan, Willem Dafoe, Deborah Van Valkenburgh
▶ Bikers in a vaguely futuristic ghetto kidnap rock singer Lane; tough loner Paré, aided by an even tougher Madigan, scours the underworld to rescue her. Subtitled "A Rock 'n' Roll Fable," highly stylized drama plays like a feature-length music video. Dafoe is appropriately menacing as the villain. Strong score by Ry Cooder features his band and the Blasters. (CC)

STREETS OF GOLD 1986
★★★★ R Drama/Sports 1:35
☑ Explicit language, violence
Dir: Joe Roth *Cast:* Klaus Maria Brandauer, Adrian Pasdar, Wesley Snipes, Angela Molina, Elya Baksin, Rainbow Harvest

▶ Predictable boxing drama with a commanding performance by Brandauer as a Russian banned from fighting for his Jewish religion. Emigrating to Coney Island, he trains promising youths Pasdar and Snipes for spots on the U.S. team and a chance for revenge against his former coach. Fights are staged realistically, and clash-of-cultures theme works due to Brandauer's conviction.

STREET TRASH 1987
☆ **NR Horror 1:32**
☑ Rape, adult situations, explicit language, graphic violence
Dir: Jim Muro   *Cast:* Bill Chepil, Mike Lackey, Vic Noto, Mark Sferrazza, R. L. Ryan
▶ Bums and winos are found dead in a Brooklyn junkyard ruled by a Vietnam vet. The culprit: a fatal brand of alcohol called Tenafly Viper. Flashily directed but so gross and off-putting that only those looking for cheap thrills need watch.

STREETWALKIN' 1985
★ **R Drama 1:23**
☑ Nudity, strong sexual content, adult situations, explicit language, graphic violence
Dir: Joan Freeman   *Cast:* Melissa Leo, Julie Newmar, Dale Midkiff, Antonio Fargas, Leon Robinson, Annie Golden
▶ Leo supports her little brother by working as a hooker. She flees when pimp Midkiff goes on a murderous rampage but eventually she must take the law into her own hands. Effectively captures the seamier side of New York City and Leo is sympathetic; however, endless brutality toward women and miscast Midkiff (too clean-cut for his role) limit appeal.

STREETWISE 1985
★★ **NR Documentary 1:32**
☑ Brief nudity, adult situations, explicit language
Dir: Martin Bell
▶ Oscar-nominated   no-holds-barred look at true stories of Seattle street kids. They beg, turn tricks, eat from dumpsters, drink, live in deserted buildings, and form close friendships amidst the hardships and depravity. Strong stuff captured with insight and compassion. Depressing but fascinating.

STRIKE UP THE BAND 1940
★★★ **NR Musical 2:00 B&W**
Dir: Busby Berkeley   *Cast:* Mickey Rooney, Judy Garland, Paul Whiteman,

June Preisser, William Tracy, Ann Shoemaker
▶ Rooney's the whole show in this high-spirited musical. As an aspiring drummer desperate to win a new band contest sponsored by Paul Whiteman and His Orchestra, he drums, sings, dances, and plays the xylophone while assembling crackerjack young musicians. Rooney wisely chooses Garland over rich girl Preisser for vocalist. Songs include Oscar-nominated "Our Love Affair" and "Heaven Will Protect the Working Girl."

STRIPES 1981
★★★★ **R Comedy 1:46**
☑ Nudity, adult situations, explicit language, mild violence
Dir: Ivan Reitman   *Cast:* Bill Murray, Harold Ramis, John Candy, Warren Oates, P. J. Soles, Sean Young
▶ After losing his job and girlfriend, down-on-his-luck degenerate Murray and pal Ramis enlist in the army. They clash with stern Sgt. Oates and "borrow" a top-secret mobile weapons center, but prove their mettle by saving the world from nuclear war. Top-rank, low-down tomfoolery will have you laughing from start to finish; Murray's brand of sarcasm has never been funnier, whether urging his fellow soldiers into action with "We're the U.S. Army . . . we're ten and one!" or exhorting overweight recruit Candy to become a "lean, mean fighting machine." (CC)

STRIPPED TO KILL 1987
★★ **R Action-Adventure 1:26**
☑ Nudity, adult situations, explicit language, violence
Dir: Katt Shea Ruben   *Cast:* Kay Lenz, Greg Evigan, Norman Fell, Tracy Crowder, Athena Worthey
▶ Serial killer terrorizes dancers at Los Angeles topless bars; posing as a stripper, undercover cop Lenz offers herself as bait to catch the murderer. Above-average exploitation offers good performances, convincingly tawdry settings, and a puzzling plot.

STRIPPER, THE 1963
★★ **NR Drama 1:35 B&W**
Dir: Franklin J. Schaffner   *Cast:* Joanne Woodward, Richard Beymer, Carol Lynley, Claire Trevor, Robert Webber, Gypsy Rose Lee
▶ Stripper Woodward returns to hometown and has affair with Beymer, the young son of old friend Trevor. However,

her tawdry past and her brutal manager-boyfriend Webber threaten her happiness. Standout performances by Woodward and Trevor enliven a rather flat screenplay.

STRIPPER 1984
★★ R Documentary 1:31
☑ Nudity, adult situations, explicit language, adult humor
Dir: Jerome Gary *Cast:* Janette Boyd, Sara Costa, Kimberly Holcomb, Loree Menton, Lisa Suarez
▶ Offbeat documentary examines six contestants in the first annual Las Vegas Strippers Convention in 1983. Training sessions and interviews alternate with on-stage performances and glimpses of the dancers' home lives. Director Gary (who co-produced *Pumping Iron*) approaches the subject with humor and compassion.

STROKER ACE 1983
★★★ PG Action-Adventure/Comedy 1:34
☑ Adult situations, explicit language, violence
Dir: Hal Needham *Cast:* Burt Reynolds, Loni Anderson, Jim Nabors, Ned Beatty, Parker Stevenson, Bubba Smith
▶ Race-car driver Reynolds signs promotion deal with fast-food chicken mogul Beatty. Soon Reynolds wants out of the contract and into the arms of Beatty's virginal assistant Anderson. Combination of Reynolds's quips, Anderson's looks, and Needham's elaborate car stunts is good-natured and amiable if not terribly sophisticated.

STUCK ON YOU 1983
★ R Comedy 1:30
☑ Nudity, strong sexual content, adult situations, explicit language
Dir: Michael Herz *Cast:* Prof. Irwin Corey, Virginia Penta, Mark Mikulski, Albert Pia, Norma Pratt
▶ Live-in couple Penta and Mikulski break up and go before judge Corey to divide their property. Corey discusses their problems in the context of history (going back to Adam and Eve); the lovers recall happier times and eventually reconcile. Vulgar bathroom humor includes spitting, vomiting, burping, and flatulence. Penta is lovely and she deserves better.

STUD, THE 1978 British
★ R Drama 1:30
☑ Nudity, adult situations, explicit language

Dir: Quentin Masters *Cast:* Joan Collins, Oliver Tobias, Sue Lloyd, Mark Burns, Walter Gotell, Emma Jacobs
▶ Tobias, a waiter in London disco, earns promotion to manager when he he satisfies insatiable sexual appetite of Collins, wife of club owner Gotell. Tobias has ambitions to open own club, but entry into the upper class seems unlikely when he can't keep hands off Gotell's daughter Jacobs. Screenplay by pulp novelist Jackie Collins (sister of Joan) from her book.

STUDENT AFFAIRS 1986
★★ NR Comedy 1:32
☑ Nudity, adult situations, explicit language, adult humor
Dir: Chuck Vincent *Cast:* Louie Bonanno, Jim Abele, Deborah Blaisdell, Beth Broderick, Alan Fisler, Jane Hamilton
▶ Cast and crew of low-budget sex comedy invade New Jersey high school with chaotic results. Ex-centerfold model vainly tries to impress students with her acting talent, secretly homosexual actor searches for new conquests, stand-up comedian infuriates everyone with ill-timed impersonations. Broad, rambling farce with a cast of unknowns is only intermittently funny.

STUDENT BODIES 1981
☆ R Comedy 1:26
☑ Nudity, adult situations, explicit language, violence, adult humor
Dir: Mickey Rose *Cast:* Kristen Riter, Matt Goldsby, Richard Brando, Joe Talarowski, Joe Flood, Mimi Weddell
▶ Texas high school is plagued by series of murders in which young couples are killed just prior to sex. Teen heroes Riter and Goldsby track the killer during senior prom. Spoof of horror pictures flunks out.

STUDENT CONFIDENTIAL 1987
★ R Drama 1:34
☑ Nudity, adult situations, explicit language, violence
Dir: Richard Horian *Cast:* Eric Douglas, Marlon Jackson, Susan Scott, Elizabeth Singer, Ronee Blakley, Richard Horian
▶ Millionaire Horian takes an interest in troubled high school students, successfully counseling Douglas to become a machinist, Scott to cope with a facial scar, Jackson to enter the computer industry, and Singer to battle her promiscuity. The kids join together to help Horian when he considers suicide. Ludicrous

drama is entertaining if viewed as a comedy. Horian also produced, wrote, and edited the film and composed the soundtrack.

STUDENT NURSES 1970
★ R Drama 1:25
☑ Nudity, adult situations, explicit language, violence
Dir: Stephanie Rothman *Cast:* Elaine Giftos, Karen Carlson, Brioni Farrell, Barbara Leigh, Reni Santoni, Richard Rust
▶ Enjoyably trashy exploitation about four beautiful nurses in their last year of school. Giftos falls in love with a dying patient; Carlson breaks off an affair with an abortionist; Leigh is raped by a drug addict; Farrell joins a revolutionary terrorist movement. Low-budget Roger Corman production led to four lesser sequels. Followed by *Private Duty Nurses.*

STUDENT TEACHERS, THE 1973
☆ R Drama 1:19
☑ Nudity, adult situations, explicit language, violence
Dir: Jonathan Kaplan *Cast:* Susan Damante, Brooke Mills, Brenda Sutton, Nora Heflin, Dick Miller, John Kramer
▶ Offshoot of Roger Corman's *Student Nurses* series provides a titillating look at an "alternative learning" high school threatened with closing by a series of rapes. Lively debut for director Kaplan, who would later helm *Project X.* Look quickly for Chuck Norris in a tiny role. Followed by *Summer School Teachers.*

STUDY IN TERROR, A 1965 British
★★ NR Mystery-Suspense 1:35
Dir: James Hill *Cast:* John Neville, Donald Houston, John Fraser, Anthony Quayle, Robert Morley, Barbara Windsor
▶ Overlooked Sherlock Holmes mystery has Neville assaying a younger, more forceful version of the famous detective. Plot pits him against real-life criminal Jack the Ripper, the notorious murderer of prostitutes. Compact, action-filled film features good support by veteran character actors Cecil Parker and Kay Walsh, with Frank Finlay an amusing Inspector Lestrade.

STUFF, THE 1985
☆ R Horror/Comedy 1:33
☑ Explicit language, violence
Dir: Larry Cohen *Cast:* Michael Moriarty, Andrea Marcovicci, Garrett Morris, Paul Sorvino, Scott Bloom, Danny Aiello
▶ New dessert sensation, promoted with slick advertising, threatens ice cream sales. Ice cream industry hires private eye Moriarty and publicist Marcovicci to learn production secret of "the Stuff." Meanwhile, as consumers become addicted to the menacing, mind-controlling Stuff, now-bankrupt cookie king Morris and anti-Communist militia leader Sorvino join fight against the Stuffies. Some laughs but little real horror. **(CC)**

STUNT MAN, THE 1979
★★★ R Drama 2:11
☑ Brief nudity, adult situations, explicit language, violence
Dir: Richard Rush *Cast:* Peter O'Toole, Steve Railsback, Barbara Hershey, Sharon Farrell, Allen Goorwitz, Alex Rocco
▶ Fugitive Railsback, a Vietnam vet, wanders onto movie set and accidentally causes death of a stuntman, so director O'Toole decrees Railsback must replace dead man. Railsback romances film's leading lady Hershey when not learning movie trickery from mentor O'Toole. Soon Railsback suspects O'Toole plans to kill him in a stunt while police draw closer. Delightful movie-about-movies constantly flimflams viewers. O'Toole steals every scene as egomaniacal director.

ST. VALENTINE'S DAY MASSACRE, THE 1967
★★★ NR Crime 1:40
Dir: Roger Corman *Cast:* Jason Robards, Jr., George Segal, Ralph Meeker, Jean Hale, Clint Ritchie, Joseph Campanella
▶ Vivid, unexpectedly accurate version of Chicago gang war between Al Capone (Robards) and Bugs Moran (Meeker) shows their growing hostility in violent flashbacks before meticulously reconstructing the famous 1929 garage killing spree. Cameos include Bruce Dern as a mechanic and Jack Nicholson as a thug who poisons his bullets.

SUBURBIA 1984
☆ R Drama 1:39
☑ Nudity, adult situations, explicit language, graphic violence
Dir: Penelope Spheeris *Cast:* Chris Pederson, Bill Coyne, Jennifer Clay, Tim O'Brien, Michael Bayer
▶ Punk teens rebel against their bad upbringings (alcoholic mothers, homosexual and abusive fathers) and crumbling neighborhood by forming a group called

"The Rejected." They run afoul of local rednecks who blame them for the area's condition.

SUDDEN DEATH 1985
★ ★ R Action-Adventure 1:30
☑ Rape, nudity, adult situations, explicit language, graphic violence
Dir: Sig Shore *Cast:* Denise Coward, Frank Runyeon, Jamie Tirelli, Robert Trumbull, Rebecca Holden, J. Kenneth Campbell
▶ New York businesswoman Coward is raped and beaten. When the cops are unable to catch her attackers, Coward buys a gun, uses herself as bait, and lures rapists to their deaths. Female *Death Wish* pulls few punches in the action department; slickly done but rather exploitative.

SUDDEN IMPACT 1983
★ ★ ★ ★ R Action-Adventure 1:57
☑ Rape, brief nudity, explicit language, graphic violence
Dir: Clint Eastwood *Cast:* Clint Eastwood, Sondra Locke, Pat Hingle, Bradford Dillman, Paul Duke
▶ "Go ahead, make my day," says San Francisco's toughest cop Dirty Harry (Eastwood) to hold-up thugs. After dispatching them in his usual fashion, Harry investigates brutal murders of men who were involved in a rape ten years back and is attracted to artist Locke who may hold a clue. Hard-hitting and pulse-pounding; Eastwood invests the familiar formula with new vitality. Best line: "The three of us: me, Smith, and Wesson." (CC)

SUDDENLY 1954
★ ★ ★ NR Drama 1:15 B&W
Dir: Lewis Allen *Cast:* Frank Sinatra, Sterling Hayden, James Gleason, Nancy Gates, Kim Charney, Paul Frees
▶ Secret Service agents check security for Presidential visit to the small town of Suddenly. Disguised as FBI agents, psychopath Sinatra and two henchmen take hostages in house overlooking the railroad station where the President will stop. Sinatra is riveting as an amoral assassin in this unbearably tense and chillingly prescient drama. Also available in a computer-colorized version, which unfortunately gives Sinatra brown eyes.

SUDDENLY, LAST SUMMER 1959
★ ★ ★ NR Drama 1:54 B&W
Dir: Joseph L. Mankiewicz *Cast:* Elizabeth Taylor, Katharine Hepburn, Montgomery Clift, Albert Dekker, Mercedes McCambridge
▶ Wealthy Hepburn wants brain surgeon Clift to lobotomize her niece Taylor and offers big donation to his hospital. Clift spends time with Taylor and, as family skeletons pour out of the closet, he realizes she isn't nuts. Outrageous, lurid, and fascinating drama whose florid performances (both Taylor and Hepburn nabbed Oscar nominations) perfectly fit writer Tennessee Williams's near-camp style.

SUGARBABY 1985 German
★ NR Comedy/Drama 1:27
☑ Nudity, adult situations
Dir: Percy Adlon *Cast:* Marianne Sägebrecht, Eisi Gulp, Toni Berger, Manuela Denz, Will Spindler
▶ Overweight fraulein Sägebrecht works by day in mortuary and spends lonely nights eating herself silly. Her life changes when she spies handsome subway conductor Gulp, who becomes the object of her pent-up desires. Sägebrecht trails him until finally they meet and enjoy a passionate affair based on shared affection for sweets. Soon enough Gulp's wife gets wind of his adultery. Definitely different, offbeat and stylized comedy is for the discriminating only. Ⓢ

SUGARLAND EXPRESS, THE 1974
★ ★ ★ PG Drama 1:49
☑ Explicit language, violence
Dir: Steven Spielberg *Cast:* Goldie Hawn, Ben Johnson, Michael Sacks, William Atherton, Gregory Walcott, Louise Latham
▶ When Texas authorities threaten to take away her baby, determined mother Hawn springs husband Atherton from jail and leads police and reporters on a fast-paced chase along rural highways and back roads. Consistently engrossing drama, based on a true story, has strong characters as well as technically accomplished action sequences. Spielberg's theatrical directing debut.

SUICIDE CLUB, THE 1988
☆ R Drama 1:30
☑ Explicit language
Dir: James Bruce *Cast:* Mariel Hemingway, Robert Joy, Lenny Henry, Madeleine Potter, Michael O'Donoghue, Alice Drummond
▶ Heiress Hemingway, guilty over her brother's suicide, attends Long Island masquerade party featuring card game

in which the winner is murdered. Intrigued, she returns for another party, despite objections of boyfriend Joy. Dull, preposterous drama was "suggested" by a Robert Louis Stevenson story.

SULLIVAN'S TRAVELS 1941
★★★★ NR Comedy 1:31 B&W
Dir: Preston Sturges *Cast:* Joel McCrea, Veronica Lake, Robert Warwick, William Demarest, Porter Hall, Robert Greig
▶ Tired of making comedies like *Ants in Your Pants of 1939,* Hollywood director McCrea disguises himself as a hobo for a solo journey to discover the real America. His overzealous staff turns the trip into a publicity stunt until McCrea, accompanied by failed actress Lake, gives them the slip. But the heartland turns out to be more dangerous than they anticipated. Unique combination of slapstick, heartbreaking pathos, and devastating satire is among the most perceptive movies ever made about Hollywood. Another masterpiece by writer-producer-director Sturges.

SUMMER CAMP NIGHTMARE 1987
★★ PG-13 Drama 1:25
☑ Rape, adult situations, explicit language, violence
Dir: Bert L. Dragin *Cast:* Chuck Connors, Charles Stratton, Adam Carl, Harold Pruett, Melissa Brennan
▶ Cautionary drama about a boys' camp ruled by strict disciplinarian Connors. Idealistic counselor Stratton organizes a revolt, locking up the adults and taking command of a nearby girls' camp as well. Muddled script based on *The Butterfly Revolution* by William Butler suffers from obvious plotting and overacting. (CC)

SUMMER HEAT 1987
★★ R Drama 1:30
☑ Adult situations, explicit language, violence
Dir: Michie Gleason *Cast:* Lori Singer, Anthony Edwards, Bruce Abbott, Kathy Bates, Clu Gulager, Jessie Kent
▶ Tobacco country of North Carolina, 1937, provides backdrop for torpid love triangle among farmer Edwards, young wife Singer, and hired hand Abbott. Subtle adaptation of Louise Shivers's *Here to Get My Baby Out of Jail* features beautiful production values but suffers from extremely slow pacing.

SUMMER LOVERS 1982
★★ R Romance 1:38
☑ Nudity, strong sexual content, adult situations, explicit language
Dir: Randal Kleiser *Cast:* Peter Gallagher, Daryl Hannah, Valerie Quennessen, Barbara Rush, Carole Cook
▶ Young American couple Gallagher and Hannah vacation in the Aegean. Gallagher starts seeing French girl Quennessen; Hannah responds by finding another guy but then opts for a ménage à trois with Gallagher and Quennessen. Not much of a story, but the stars and the Greek scenery are simply gorgeous.

SUMMER OF '42 1971
★★★ PG Drama 1:44
☑ Adult situations, explicit language
Dir: Robert Mulligan *Cast:* Jennifer O'Neill, Gary Grimes, Jerry Houser, Oliver Conant, Katherine Allentuck, Christopher Norris
▶ Young teenager Grimes summers on New England island and shares growing pains with constantly horny pal Houser and younger, introspective sidekick Conant. Grimes develops crush on beautiful war bride O'Neill, but she thinks he's just a sweet kid. Anxious to lose virginity, Grimes and Houser pore over marriage manual and muster courage to buy condoms. For Grimes, however, sexual initiation must await a tragedy of World War II. Familiar teen territory given sweet and tender presentation. Nominated for four Oscars; winner for Michel Legrand's popular score.

SUMMER PLACE, A 1959
★★★ NR Drama 2:10
Dir: Delmer Daves *Cast:* Robert Egan, Dorothy McGuire, Sandra Dee, Arthur Kennedy, Troy Donahue, Constance Ford
▶ Successful businessman Egan returns to Maine resort where ex-girlfriend McGuire is trapped in an unhappy marriage with alcoholic loser Kennedy. While Egan rekindles his romance with McGuire, daughter Dee falls for McGuire's son Donahue. Plush but superficial adaptation of Sloan Wilson's best-seller was a box office hit, helped immeasurably by Max Steiner's unforgettable theme song.

SUMMER RENTAL 1985
★★★ PG Comedy 1:28
☑ Adult situations, explicit language
Dir: Carl Reiner *Cast:* John Candy,

Richard Crenna, Rip Torn, Karen Austin, Kerri Green

▶ Burnt-out air traffic controller Candy takes his family for a Florida vacation. A series of comic disasters gives Candy little rest and he runs afoul of snobby Crenna. Candy gets a chance for revenge in a boat race against Crenna. Slight but lazily enjoyable; Candy is a quite pleasing everyman hero and Austin gives sturdy support as his understanding wife. **(CC)**

SUMMER SCHOOL 1987
★★★★ **PG-13 Comedy 1:38**
☑ Explicit language, violence
Dir: Carl Reiner *Cast:* Mark Harmon, Kirstie Alley, Robin Thomas, Patrick Labyorteaux, Courtney Thorne Smith, Dean Cameron

▶ Summer-school teacher Harmon has to whip remedial students into shape to pass the big test or face losing his job. Harmon pursues fellow teacher Alley, who initially resists him but then helps him. Jolly, low-brow humor with enough vulgar jokes to give teens a good time. Harmon demonstrates an ingratiating personality. **(CC)**

SUMMER SCHOOL TEACHERS 1977
☆ **R Comedy 1:25**
☑ Nudity, strong sexual content, explicit language
Dir: Barbara Peters *Cast:* Candice Rialson, Pat Anderson, Rhonda Leigh Hopkins, Will Carney, Grainger Hines, Dick Miller

▶ Midwesterners Rialson, Anderson, and Hopkins become teachers in Los Angeles. Rialson tries to form a girls football team and has an affair with another teacher, Anderson teaches chemistry and takes up with one of her students, and Hopkins has two affairs of her own between photography classes. Attractive cast gives performances above genre average although story is predictable.

SUMMER STOCK 1950
★★★★ **NR Musical 1:49**
Dir: Charles Walters *Cast:* Judy Garland, Gene Kelly, Eddie Bracken, Gloria De Haven, Marjorie Main, Phil Silvers

▶ New England farm girl Garland plays reluctant host to Kelly's theatrical troupe when her sister De Haven invites them to use the family barn for the summer production. Despite her initial misgivings, Garland eventually develops the stage

bug herself. High-spirited MGM fun with great stepping and singing from Kelly and Garland. Best number: "Get Happy."

SUMMERTIME 1955
★★★★ **NR Romance 1:39**
Dir: David Lean *Cast:* Katharine Hepburn, Rossano Brazzi, Darren McGavin, Isa Miranda, Mari Aldon, Gaitano Audiero

▶ American spinster Hepburn vacations in Venice, befriends street kid Audiero, and has ill-fated affair with antique-store proprietor Brazzi. Lovely, bittersweet, and scenic; Hepburn and Lean were Oscar-nominated. Based on Arthur Laurents's play *The Time of the Cuckoo*.

SUMMER WISHES, WINTER DREAMS 1973
★★★ **PG Drama 1:35**
☑ Adult situations, explicit language
Dir: Gilbert Cates *Cast:* Joanne Woodward, Martin Balsam, Sylvia Sidney, Dori Brenner, Win Forman, Tresa Hughes

▶ When mother Sidney dies, housewife Woodward realizes she can no longer hide her dissatisfaction with her marriage. European vacation with husband Balsam, reviving his memories of service in World War II, leads to an attempt to confront their problems. Strong performances and earnest tone undermined by frequently tedious plot. Both Woodward and Sidney (returning to film after a sixteen-year hiatus) received Oscar nominations.

SUN ALSO RISES, THE 1957
★★ **NR Drama 2:09**
Dir: Henry King *Cast:* Tyrone Power, Ava Gardner, Mel Ferrer, Errol Flynn, Eddie Albert, Gregory Ratoff

▶ World War I injury cripples Power's romance with beautiful aristocrat Gardner; her attempts to find happiness with other men—including Greek tycoon Ratoff, author Ferrer, and young matador Robert Evans—prove futile. Faithful adaptation of Ernest Hemingway's novel was Power's penultimate film. Flynn offers a knowing self-parody as an alcoholic playboy; Evans later became a noted producer.

SUNBURN 1979
★ **PG Mystery-Suspense/Comedy 1:40**
☑ Adult situations, explicit language, mild violence
Dir: Richard C. Sarafian *Cast:* Farrah Fawcett-Majors, Charles Grodin, Art

Carney, Joan Collins, William Daniels, John Hillerman

▶ In Acapulco, insurance investigator Grodin examines a possible murder which involves $5 million. Grodin enlists Fawcett-Majors to pose as his wife and help him enter city society and also gets help from retired detective Carney. Fawcett-Majors and Acapulco are easy on the eyes but plot and characterizations are rather tired.

SUNDAY, BLOODY SUNDAY 1971 British
★★ R Drama 1:50
☑ Nudity, adult situations, explicit language
Dir: John Schlesinger *Cast:* Glenda Jackson, Peter Finch, Murray Head, Peggy Ashcroft, Tony Britton, Maurice Denham

▶ In London, divorced personnel worker Jackson and prominent physician Finch are both in love with young pop sculptor Head. At first all agree Head will divide attentions between Jackson and Finch, but arrangement falls victim to normal pitfalls of romantic triangles. Shrewd, sophisticated study of hetero- and homosexual relationships and identities written by film critic–novelist Penelope Gilliatt. Jackson, Finch, and director Schlesinger were all Oscar-nominated.

SUNDAYS AND CYBELE 1962 French
★★ NR Drama 1:50 B&W
Dir: Serge Bourguignon *Cast:* Hardy Kruger, Patricia Gozzi, Nicole Courcel, Daniel Ivernel, Michel de Re

▶ War vet Kruger returns home from battle and befriends orphan Gozzi. A warm relationship develops, but the locals misunderstand its innocent nature, leading to a tragic conclusion. Moving and original study of provocative subject won Best Foreign Film Oscar. [S]

SUNDOWNERS, THE 1960
★★★ NR Drama 2:13
Dir: Fred Zinnemann *Cast:* Deborah Kerr, Robert Mitchum, Peter Ustinov, Glynis Johns, Dina Merrill, Chips Rafferty

▶ Excellent family drama, filmed on location in Australia, follows the adventures of headstrong father Mitchum who prefers odd jobs on the open road to the security of a home, despite the pleas of wife Kerr to settle down. Sheep drive, forest fire, and adventures with a race horse provide a strong counterpoint to Kerr's warmly emotional performance. Received five

Oscar nominations, including Johns's role as a spirited hotel owner.

SUNRISE AT CAMPOBELLO 1960
★★★ NR Biography 2:23
Dir: Dore Schary *Cast:* Ralph Bellamy, Greer Garson, Hume Cronyn, Jean Hagen, Ann Shoemaker

▶ In the 1920s, Franklin Delano Roosevelt (Bellamy) is stricken with polio and paralyzed. His wife Eleanor (Garson) and his friend Cronyn give him the courage to attempt to walk again. Inspirational true story features Bellamy's outstanding impersonation of FDR, which is matched by Garson's Oscar-nominated turn. Adapted by Schary from his Broadway hit.

SUNSET 1988
★★★ R Mystery-Suspense 1:47
☑ Adult situations, explicit language, mild violence
Dir: Blake Edwards *Cast:* Bruce Willis, James Garner, Malcolm McDowell, Mariel Hemingway, Kathleen Quinlan, Jennifer Edwards

▶ Real-life lawman Wyatt Earp (Garner) serves as technical advisor on movie starring 1920s screen hero Tom Mix (Willis). The pair team up to solve the murder of a local madam involved with movieland elite. Garner's gallantry, Willis (surprisingly effective playing it straight), and snazzy Roaring Twenties wrapping overcome plot flaws. **(CC)**

SUNSET BOULEVARD 1950
★★★ NR Drama 1:50 B&W
Dir: Billy Wilder *Cast:* William Holden, Gloria Swanson, Erich von Stroheim, Nancy Olson, Jack Webb, Buster Keaton

▶ "I am big—it's the pictures that got small!" claims faded silent screen queen Norma Desmond (Swanson). She hires disillusioned screenwriter Holden to aid her screen comeback. He becomes her lover and gets entrapped in her demented lifestyle. Immortal screen classic, one of Hollywood's sharpest looks at itself, is haunting and poignant all at once (especially in the bridge-game scene). Tremendous performances by Swanson and Holden (both Oscar-nominated, as was the picture, von Stroheim as Swanson's faithful butler, and Olson). Three Oscars include Best Screenplay.

SUNSET STRIP 1986
★★ NR Action-Adventure 1:24

☑ Adult situations, explicit language, violence
Dir: William Webb *Cast:* Tom Eplin, Cheri Cameron Newell, Danny Williams, John Mayall
▶ Photographer gets unwittingly involved in mob plot to take over Sunset Strip club. When the photographer's best pal is murdered, he finds both the police and the mob (who think he has evidence against them) on his trail. Mediocre story and acting.

SUNSHINE BOYS, THE 1975
★★★★ PG Comedy 1:51
☑ Adult situations, explicit language
Dir: Herbert Ross *Cast:* George Burns, Walter Matthau, Richard Benjamin, Lee Meredith, Carol Arthur, Howard Hesseman
▶ Scheming agent Benjamin plans to reunite his irritable comedian uncle Matthau with former partner Burns for TV special. The problem is the two vaudeville vets hate each other, so rehearsals are a running feud. Adaptation of Neil Simon Broadway hit is amusing and heartwarming. Comeback role for Burns (first film since 1939) won Oscar for Best Supporting Actor.

SUPER FLY 1972
★★ R Action-Adventure 1:31
☑ Nudity, adult situations, explicit language, violence
Dir: Gordon Parks, Jr. *Cast:* Ron O'Neal, Sheila Frazier, Carl Lee, Julius W. Harris, Charles McGregor, Sig Shore
▶ Cocaine dealer O'Neal dreams of one big score before retirement with girlfriend Frazier. With partner Lee, O'Neal seeks help from mentor Harris, who directs the two to big drug source: corrupt police inspector Shore. Things heat up for O'Neal when both Lee and Shore double-cross him. Most successful of 70s black exploitation pics boasts hard-hitting depiction of seedy underworld and hit soundtrack from Curtis Mayfield, but story with coke dealer hero seems dated today.

SUPER FUZZ 1981
★★★ PG Comedy 1:37
☑ Explicit language, violence
Dir: Sergio Corbucci *Cast:* Terence Hill, Ernest Borgnine, Joanne Dru, Marc Lawrence
▶ Exposed to radiation due to Everglades nuke test, rookie cop Hill finds himself with extraordinary powers. Hill and partner Borgnine proceed to bust up

mob counterfeiting ring. Modest escapism has interesting premise.

SUPERGIRL 1984
★★ PG Fantasy/Action-Adventure 1:45
☑ Mild violence
Dir: Jeannot Szwarc *Cast:* Helen Slater, Faye Dunaway, Peter O'Toole, Mia Farrow, Peter Cook, Brenda Vaccaro
▶ Superman's teenage cousin Supergirl (Slater) comes to small midwestern town to recover her planet's life-sustaining device. She must battle evil priestess Dunaway, who gets hold of it first. Kids should enjoy this although it's not quite up to the level of the *Superman* series; Dunaway camps it up mercilessly and steals the show, although Slater is perfectly cast.

SUPERMAN 1978
★★★★ PG Fantasy/Action-Adventure 2:23
☑ Explicit language, mild violence
Dir: Richard Donner *Cast:* Christopher Reeve, Marlon Brando, Gene Hackman, Margot Kidder, Glenn Ford, Valerie Perrine
▶ When planet Krypton explodes, scientist Brando sends his only son in a rocket to Earth. After the superpowered being is raised by Pa Kent (Ford) in Kansas, he goes to the city, adopts the identity of mild-mannered reporter Clark Kent, falls for Lois Lane (Kidder), and battles villainous Lex Luthor (Hackman). The original extravaganza impressively combines special effects, comic book heroics, and tongue-in-cheek comedy. Reeve plays Superman/Clark Kent with infectious humor and his aerial romance with Kidder is surprisingly lyrical. Funniest moment: Reeve's phone booth reaction. Spawned three sequels.

SUPERMAN II 1981
★★★★★ PG Fantasy/Action-Adventure 2:07
☑ Adult situations, violence
Dir: Richard Lester *Cast:* Christopher Reeve, Margot Kidder, Gene Hackman, Terence Stamp, Sarah Douglas, Jackie Cooper
▶ Brash, irreverent sequel to *Superman* pits the Man of Steel (Reeve) against three supercriminals from Krypton determined to rule Earth. Reeve's love affair with reporter Lois Lane (Kidder) and the wily schemes of arch-criminal Lex Luthor (Hackman) provide unexpected obsta-

cles to Superman's efforts. Strong direction concentrates on the humor and humanity behind the inspired special effects. Hackman, Stamp, and Douglas are memorable villains in the series's wildest, funniest episode. Followed by *Superman III*.

SUPERMAN III 1983
★ ★ ★ **PG Fantasy/Action-Adventure 2:05**
☑ Adult situations, mild violence
Dir: Richard Lester *Cast:* Christopher Reeve, Richard Pryor, Robert Vaughn, Annette O'Toole, Pamela Stephenson, Jackie Cooper
▶ Man of Steel (Reeve) returns to Smallville for high school reunion. When Superman thwarts plan to control weather satellite, villain Vaughn has computer whiz Pryor make artificial kryptonite to stop him. Third installment in the series is lots of fun with more emphasis on comedy than action. Reeve shines in the sequence where Superman goes bad, drinking, womanizing, and straightening out the Leaning Tower of Pisa. The underrated O'Toole (as Lana Lang) provides a sweet romantic interest as Clark Kent's old sweetheart.

SUPERMAN IV: THE QUEST FOR PEACE 1987
★ ★ **PG Fantasy/Action-Adventure 1:30**
☑ Explicit language, violence
Dir: Sidney J. Furie *Cast:* Christopher Reeve, Gene Hackman, Jackie Cooper, Margot Kidder, Mariel Hemingway, Marc McClure
▶ Superman (Reeve) rids the world of nuclear weapons in response to a child's letter; Lex Luthor (Hackman) takes advantage of the situation to create a nuclear-powered villain to fight the Man of Steel. Fourth in the series is still enjoyable; special effects seem a bit skimpy but Reeve and Hemingway (as the daughter of the *Daily Planet's* new owner, who tries to turn paper into a sensationalist tabloid) are charming. Cleverest scene: Reeve trying to be in two places at once for dates with Hemingway and Lois Lane (Kidder). **(CC)**

SUPERMAN AND THE MOLE MEN 1951
★ **NR Fantasy 0:58 B&W**
Dir: Lee Sholem *Cast:* George Reeves, Phyllis Coates, Jeff Corey, Walter Reed, J. Farrell MacDonald, Stanley Andrews
▶ Pilot episode of the long-running TV series finds *Daily Planet* reporters Clark Kent (Reeves) and Lois Lane (Coates) investigating strange disturbance near an oil-mining town. Talky story skimps on special effects, but Reeves provides an interesting contrast to latter-day Superman Christopher Reeve.

SUPERNATURALS, THE 1986
★ **R Drama 1:20**
☑ Explicit language, violence
Dir: Armand Mastroianni *Cast:* Maxwell Caulfield, Nichelle Nichols, Talia Balsam, Bradford Bancroft, LeVar Burton, Bobby DiCicco
▶ During the Civil War, a group of Confederate soldiers are killed when Union counterparts force them across a minefield. In the present, Sergeant Nichols commands a unit of soldiers in the area. The Confederate zombies come back to life to menace them. **(CC)**

SUPERSTITION 1985
★ ★ **NR Horror 1:24**
☑ Explicit language, graphic violence
Dir: James W. Roberson *Cast:* James Houghton, Albert Salmi, Lynn Carlin, Larry Pennell, Heidi Bohay
▶ In 1692, a demonically possessed woman is drowned for being a witch. The woman's spirit returns in the present to menace residents of an old house. Good production values, decent acting, but routine screenplay lacks suspense and surprises.

SUPPORT YOUR LOCAL SHERIFF! 1969
★ ★ ★ ★ **G Western/Comedy 1:32**
Dir: Burt Kennedy *Cast:* James Garner, Joan Hackett, Walter Brennan, Harry Morgan, Jack Elam, Bruce Dern
▶ Amiable spoof of Westerns, with Garner giving an adroit performance as a peace-loving drifter who becomes the unwilling sheriff of a gold-mining boomtown. Aided by town drunk Elam as his deputy, he arrests immature killer Dern and faces down Dern's father Brennan (lampooning his *My Darling Clementine* role) in a smart parody of shoot-outs. **(CC)**

SURE THING, THE 1985
★ ★ ★ ★ **PG-13 Comedy 1:34**
☑ Adult situations, explicit language
Dir: Rob Reiner *Cast:* John Cusack, Daphne Zuniga, Viveca Lindfors, Tim Robbins, Boyd Gaines, Nicollette Sheridan
▶ College party animal Cusack strikes out with women, including prim and

proper coed Zuniga. Over Christmas break, mismatched duo share ride to California, where Zuniga will visit equally uptight beau Gaines while Cusack has high hopes for gorgeous surfer girl Sheridan, billed as a "sure thing." The two bicker so much their ride abandons them in Midwest. Romantic road comedy with overtones of 1934's *It Happened One Night* was surprise hit. **(CC)**

SURF NAZIS MUST DIE 1987
☆ **R Comedy 1:20**
☑ Nudity, adult situations, explicit language, violence
Dir: Peter George *Cast:* Barry Brenner, Gail Neely, Michael Sonye, Dawn Wildsmith, Tom Shell
▶ Killing and surfing are two of the Surf Nazi gang's favorite activities on California beaches. Victim's mother Neely buys gun, grenades, and motorcycle to get revenge. Overdrawn, cartoonish humor provides some laughs although many will find this racist and repulsive. Neely, however, is wonderful.

SURF II 1984
☆ **R Comedy 1:26**
☑ Nudity, adult situations, explicit language, mild violence, adult humor
Dir: Randall Badat *Cast:* Eddie Deezen, Linda Kerridge, Lyle Waggoner, Ron Paillo, Ruth Buzzi, Eric Stoltz
▶ Wimpy chemist Deezen plots to rid Southern California beaches of surfers by making them drink Buzz Cola, soft drink that literally rots the brain. Healthy bodies, silly humor (including an eating contest and autopsy), and one-note performance by Jerry Lewis clone Deezen in this *Beach Blanket Bingo* update.

SURRENDER 1987
★★★ **PG Romance/Comedy 1:36**
☑ Adult situations, explicit language
Dir: Jerry Belson *Cast:* Sally Field, Michael Caine, Steve Guttenberg, Peter Boyle
▶ Wealthy writer Caine, tired of being taken to the cleaners in divorce proceedings, pretends to be poor. Struggling artist Field falls for Caine but money worries and Field's lawyer beau Guttenberg provide obstacles to the affair. Quite diverting with sparkling chemistry between Field and Caine, funny support from Guttenberg, and the most inventive chance meeting in recent films (Field and Caine are stripped and tied up together when terrorists invade a party). **(CC)**

SURVIVAL GAME 1987
★ **R Action-Adventure 1:32**
☑ Adult situations, explicit language, violence
Dir: Herb Freed *Cast:* Mike Norris, Deborah Goodrich, Seymour Cassel, Arlene Golonka, Ed Bernard
▶ Survival-camp trainee Norris (son of Chuck) meets Goodrich in car crash and falls for her. When Goodrich and her ex-1960s drug guru dad Cassel are kidnapped, Norris battles the abductors. Martial arts master Norris proves himself to be chip-off-the-old-chopping-block and Cassel is hilarious.

SURVIVOR, THE 1980 Australian
★★ **NR Mystery-Suspense 1:24**
☑ Adult situations, explicit language, graphic violence
Dir: David Hemmings *Cast:* Robert Powell, Jenny Agutter, Joseph Cotten, Angela Punch-Mcgregor, Ralph Cotterill, Peter Sumner
▶ When a 747 explodes shortly after takeoff, only pilot Powell survives. He investigates the tragedy and is caught in a web of occult terror and corporate conspiracy. Strong opening will hook viewers, but pacing falls off after rapid start. Intriguing supernatural elements, restrained performances.

SURVIVORS, THE 1983
★★★ **R Comedy 1:43**
☑ Explicit language, violence, adult humor
Dir: Michael Ritchie *Cast:* Robin Williams, Walter Matthau, Jerry Reed, James Wainwright, Kristen Vigard, Annie McEnroe
▶ Executive Williams is fired on the same day Matthau loses his gas station. The luckless pair then witness Reed committing hold-up; they hide in a survivalist camp as Reed pursues them. Mixture of black humor and blunt slapstick is uneven but the two stars generate laughs. **(CC)**

SUSPECT 1987
★★★★★ **R Mystery-Suspense 2:01**
☑ Explicit language, violence
Dir: Peter Yates *Cast:* Cher, Dennis Quaid, Liam Neeson, John Mahoney, Joe Mantegna, Philip Bosco
▶ Cher is a public defender who puts her career in jeopardy when she becomes involved with juror Quaid during the mur-

der trial of homeless Neeson, who is also a deaf-mute. Her case is hindered by tough-as-nails judge Mahoney, macho prosecutor Mantegna, and sleazy, corrupt senator Bosco. Well-done courtroom whodunit features excellent cast and creditable script.

SUSPICION 1941
★★★★ **NR Mystery-Suspense 1:40 B&W**
Dir: Alfred Hitchcock *Cast:* Cary Grant, Joan Fontaine, Cedric Hardwicke, Nigel Bruce, Dame May Whitty, Isabel Jeans
▶ Fontaine, a spinsterish wallflower from a wealthy family, weds flamboyant playboy Grant, disregarding rumors about his past. Soon spendthrift Grant is in financial hot water and Fontaine fears he'll kill her for insurance money. When Grant's best pal Bruce dies, Fontaine's suspicions peak. Fine Hitchcock suspenser will please fans and newcomers alike. Fontaine is memorable in an Oscar-winning turn.

SWAMP THING 1982
★★ **PG Sci-Fi 1:30**
☑ Brief nudity, explicit language, violence
Dir: Wes Craven *Cast:* Louis Jourdan, Adrienne Barbeau, Ray Wise, David Hess, Nicholas Worth, Dick Durack
▶ Scientist Wise tries to combine plant and animal characteristics but formula turns him into monster when villain Jourdan interferes. Jourdan hunts the Swamp Thing; government agent Barbeau battles the bad guy and wins the heart of the creature. Tongue-in-cheek entertainment inspired by the DC Comics character.

SWANN IN LOVE 1984 French
☆ **R Drama 1:50**
☑ Nudity, strong sexual content, adult situations, explicit language
Dir: Volker Schlondorff *Cast:* Jeremy Irons, Ornella Muti, Alain Delon, Fanny Ardant, Marie-Christine Barrault
▶ In the 1880s, aristocrat Irons falls for Muti, an enigmatic Parisian of scandalous reputation. He jeopardizes his social standing to marry her but the relationship slowly deteriorates. Flawless visuals, technically superb production, and knockout performances from Irons, Delon, and Ardant, but film suffers from stately pace, cryptic resolution, and lack of genuine passion, in spite of some graphic sex

scenes. Adapted from Marcel Proust's *Remembrance of Things Past.* Ⓢ

SWAP, THE 1980
★ **R Drama 2:00**
☑ Nudity, adult situations, explicit language
Dir: Jordan Leondopoulos, John C. Broderick *Cast:* Robert De Niro, Jarred Mickey, Jennifer Warren, Terrayne Crawford, Martin Kelley, Viva
▶ New York film editor De Niro, hoping to raise money for a documentary about Richard Nixon, spends a weekend with a crowd of wealthy characters on Long Island. Originally released in 1971 as *Sam's Song;* director Broderick shot new footage for 1980 rerelease in theaters and on video. Flawed and pretentious result is of note only for early performance by De Niro.

SWARM, THE 1978
★★ **PG Horror 1:56**
☑ Adult situations, mild violence
Dir: Irwin Allen *Cast:* Michael Caine, Henry Fonda, Katharine Ross, Richard Widmark, Olivia de Havilland, Fred MacMurray
▶ Scientist Caine and general Widmark lead the effort to stop a swarm of African killer bees who terrorize the Southwest. A military base, a small town flower festival, and the city of Houston are among the bees' targets. Plenty of action and creepy moments; marred by talkiness and stereotyped characters.

SWEET CHARITY 1969
★★★★ **G Musical 2:15**
Dir: Bob Fosse *Cast:* Shirley MacLaine, Sammy Davis, Jr., John McMartin, Ricardo Montalban, Chita Rivera, Paula Kelly
▶ After being literally dumped by boyfriend, dance-hall hostess MacLaine has brief fling with movie star Montalban and tries for relationship with the more stable McMartin. Tuneful good time features energetic direction by Fosse and loads of waifish charm from MacLaine. Exuberant Cy Coleman–Dorothy Fields score includes "If My Friends Could See Me Now" and "Hey, Big Spender." Based on the Broadway musical, in turn adapted from Federico Fellini's *Nights of Cabiria.*

SWEET COUNTRY 1987
★★ **R Drama 2:30**
☑ Nudity, adult situations, explicit language, violence
Dir: Michael Cacoyannis *Cast:* Jane

Alexander, John Cullum, Carole Laure, Franco Nero, Joanna Pettet, Randy Quaid
▶ In 1973, American activist Alexander, her teacher-husband Cullum, and their daughters Laure and Pettet get involved in political intrigue when Chilean Marxist leader Allende is overthrown. Weighty subject matter elicits sympathy but flat dialogue, miscast actors, and dull pacing fail to engage the audience.

SWEET DREAMS 1985
★★★★ **PG-13 Biography/Music 1:55**
☑ Adult situations, explicit language, violence
Dir: Karel Reisz *Cast:* Jessica Lange, Ed Harris, Ann Wedgeworth, David Clennon, James Staley
▶ True story of country singer Patsy Cline (Lange) traces her romance with abusive redneck husband Harris, her rise to stardom, and her tragic plane-crash death. Solid and affecting with meticulous direction by Reisz, tangy down-home dialogue, marvelous soundtrack of Cline's hits (including "Walking After Midnight," "Blue Moon of Kentucky," the title tune), wondrous Oscar-nominated performance by Lange, and superb support from Harris and Wedgeworth as Lange's salt-of-the-earth mom.

SWEET HEARTS DANCE 1988
★★★ **R Drama 1:42**
☑ Brief nudity, adult situations, explicit language
Dir: Robert Greenwald *Cast:* Don Johnson, Susan Sarandon, Jeff Daniels, Elizabeth Perkins, Kate Reid, Justin Henry
▶ Vermont carpenter Johnson suffers thirtysomethingish crisis and walks out on wife Sarandon and three kids; his best pal Daniels, a principal, falls in love with teacher Perkins but she is iffy about marriage. Ernest Thompson screenplay has message as comfy as its New England atmosphere. Neat change-of-pace performance by Johnson, who leads a strong cast, but sluggish script and lack of strong focus detract.

SWEET LIBERTY 1986
★★★ **PG Comedy 1:47**
☑ Brief nudity, adult situations, explicit language
Dir: Alan Alda *Cast:* Alan Alda, Michael Caine, Michelle Pfeiffer, Bob Hoskins, Lillian Gish, Saul Rubinek
▶ Hollywood filmmakers descend on small town to shoot adaptation of Revolutionary War saga written by college professor Alda. Hack screenwriter Hoskins has rewritten Alda's tale with eye on box office and youthful director Rubinek refuses to accommodate Alda's desire for changes. However, Alda quickly learns vain stars Caine and Pfeiffer have real clout and ingratiates himself into their good graces. Amiable comedy tweaks both moviemaking and bed-hopping on campus and film locations. (CC)

SWEET LIES 1988
★★★ **R Romance/Comedy 1:30**
☑ Brief nudity, adult situations, explicit language
Dir: Nathalie Delon *Cast:* Treat Williams, Joanna Pacula, Julianne Phillips
▶ American detective Williams, in Paris to investigate insurance fraud, becomes object of bet between Pacula and Phillips as to who will bed him first. Complications arise when both gals fall for the handsome Williams. Ingratiating farce with appealing performers and picture-postcard views of Paris.

SWEET LORRAINE 1987
★★ **PG-13 Drama 1:31**
☑ Adult situations, explicit language
Dir: Steve Gomer *Cast:* Maureen Stapleton, Trini Alvarado, Lee Richardson, John Bedford Lloyd, Freddie Roman, Giancarlo Esposito
▶ Modest, wistful account of a summer season at a run-down Catskills resort facing bankruptcy. Young Alvarado pitches in to help her grandmother, resort owner Stapleton, and finds herself growing increasingly attached to the staff and guests. Charmingly sentimental and nostalgic despite unfocused plot and subdued style.

SWEET REVENGE 1987
★ **R Action-Adventure 1:19**
☑ Nudity, adult situations, explicit language, violence
Dir: Mark Sobel *Cast:* Nancy Allen, Ted Shackelford, Martin Landau, Sal Landi, Michelle Little
▶ Reporter Allen investigates white slavery ring and is kidnapped and brought before ringleader Landau in the Far East. American smuggler Shackelford helps Allen escape. Low-budget heroics in the vein of *Romancing the Stone* combine drama and comedy.

SWEET SWEETBACK'S BAADASSSSS SONG 1971
☆ R Drama 1:37
☑ Nudity, strong sexual content, adult situations, explicit language
Dir: Melvin Van Peebles *Cast:* Melvin Van Peebles, Rhetta Hughes, Simon Chuckster, John Amos
▶ Nicknamed "Sweetback" by prostitute who seduced him as young boy, sex performer Van Peebles beats two cops who arrest him. Police pursue him as he visits a variety of women. Chase ends in climactic showdown at Mexican border. Sexy and stylish low-budget classic caused great controversy when released. A one-man show from Van Peebles as director, writer, producer, composer, and star. Not for the faint of heart, but daredevils will be amply rewarded.

SWEET 16 1983
★ ★ R Horror 1:25
☑ Adult situations, explicit language, graphic violence
Dir: Jim Sotos *Cast:* Bo Hopkins, Susan Strasberg, Don Stroud, Dana Kimball, Patrick Macnee
▶ Typical teens-in-peril suspenser takes place in small-town Texas. Old Indian is accused of two teen murders and hanged by townsfolk. Plot also involves violating sacred Indian burial ground and a suspect with a bad case of split personality. Climaxes in a rather gory and bloody sweet sixteen party.

SWEPT AWAY . . . 1975 Italian
★ ★ ★ R Comedy 1:56
☑ Nudity, strong sexual content, adult situations, explicit language, adult humor
Dir: Lina Wertmuller *Cast:* Giancarlo Giannini, Mariangela Melato
▶ Shrewish capitalist Melato is rich, haughty, liberated, and miserable. Peasant sailor Giannini on her yacht is a macho Communist continually humiliated by employer. When quirk of fate maroons them on deserted isle, their roles reverse as master becomes slave en route to love. Moral fable with surprise twist at end employs gorgeous cinematography, passionate performances from leads, and laughs rooted in truth. Resulting mix of sex and politics can both outrage and delight. ⑤

SWIMMER, THE 1968
★ PG Drama 1:34
☑ Adult situations

Dir: Frank Perry *Cast:* Burt Lancaster, Janice Rule, Janet Landgard, Tony Bickley, Marge Champion, Nancy Cushman
▶ Based on a short story by John Cheever, episodic drama concerns efforts of middle-aged adman Lancaster to traverse Connecticut suburb by swimming from pool to pool of friends and neighbors. At each stop he encounters someone whose life he's touched, setting off memories and fantasies which gradually reveal the disorder of his life. Intriguing look at upper-class manners and hypocrisy marred by vague and inconclusive ending. Debut score by Marvin Hamlisch.

SWIMMING TO CAMBODIA 1987
★ NR Documentary 1:27
☑ Explicit language
Dir: Jonathan Demme *Cast:* Spalding Gray
▶ Performance artist Gray recounts his experiences in Thailand while playing a small part in *The Killing Fields.* Cleverly understated direction by Demme effectively transfers Gray's stage monologue to the screen, but only the adventurous will warm to his rambling, seriocomic anecdotes.

SWINGING CHEERLEADERS, THE 1974
★ R Comedy 1:31
☑ Nudity, strong sexual content, adult situations, explicit language
Dir: Jack Hill *Cast:* Jo Johnston, Rainbeaux Smith, Colleen Camp, Rosanne Katon, Ian Sanders
▶ College journalist Johnston decides to write exposé on cheerleading to be published by hippie boyfriend Sanders. Johnston joins the squad, discovers Sanders's hypocrisy, and falls in love with the star quarterback. Meanwhile Johnston and new cheerleader pals Camp and Smith thwart point-fixing scheme prior to final game of season. Low-budget sexploitation is dated but boasts more plot than similar efforts.

SWING SHIFT 1984
★ ★ ★ PG Drama 1:40
☑ Adult situations, explicit language
Dir: Jonathan Demme *Cast:* Goldie Hawn, Kurt Russell, Christine Lahti, Ed Harris, Fred Ward, Holly Hunter
▶ When husband Harris enlists in World War II Navy, Hawn takes riveter job at Santa Monica factory. Soon she's romanced by co-worker Russell, who plays

trumpet at dance hall owned by Ward, the former boyfriend of her best pal Lahti. Cozy Hawn-Russell affair pops a seam when Harris gets wind of adultery and Lahti entertains Russell for night. An admirable attempt to portray contributions of working women in preliberation era, but wartime romance doesn't pass muster. Terrific supporting work from underrated Lahti earned Oscar nomination.

SWING TIME 1936
★★★★ NR Musical 1:44 B&W
Dir: George Stevens *Cast:* Fred Astaire, Ginger Rogers, Victor Moore, Helen Broderick, Eric Blore, Betty Furness
► Gambling dancer Astaire goes to New York to earn money for a wedding, but falls in love with dance instructor Rogers instead. One of the best Astaire-Rogers teamings features wonderful comic support from Moore and Broderick, an unforgettable Jerome Kern–Dorothy Fields score (including the Oscar-winning "The Way You Look Tonight"), and unparalleled dancing—particularly Astaire's Oscar-nominated "Bojangles of Harlem" and a dazzling tap duet to "Pick Yourself Up."

SWISS FAMILY ROBINSON 1960
★★★★ G Family 2:06
Dir: Ken Annakin *Cast:* John Mills, Dorothy McGuire, James MacArthur, Janet Munro, Sessue Hayakawa, Tommy Kirk
► Delightful adaptation of Johann Wyss's novel about a nineteenth-century family fleeing Napoleon who are shipwrecked on the tropical paradise of Tobago. Inventive father Mills and sons MacArthur and Kirk construct an ingenious island fortress to repel attacks by pirate Hayakawa. Above-average Disney adventure features lush settings, boisterous humor, and nonstop action.

SWITCHING CHANNELS 1988
★★★ PG Comedy 1:45
☑ Adult situations, explicit language
Dir: Ted Kotcheff *Cast:* Burt Reynolds, Kathleen Turner, Christopher Reeve, Ned Beatty, Henry Gibson
► Fourth (and least successful) remake of the Hecht-MacArthur play *The Front Page*, updated from newspaper room to TV studio. Director Reynolds still loves ex-wife/anchorwoman Turner, who is engaged to business tycoon Reeve. Reynolds tries to delay the wedding by assigning Turner to the story of a con-

victed murderer (Gibson) about to be executed. Some funny bits but no sizzle or chemistry between the leads; lackluster direction. Stick to the Roz Russell–Cary Grant 1940 sparkler, *His Girl Friday*.

SWORD AND THE ROSE, THE 1953
★★★ NR Drama 1:31
Dir: Ken Annakin *Cast:* Richard Todd, Glynis Johns, James Robertson Justice, Michael Gough, Jane Barrett, Peter Copley
► Mary Tudor (Johns), sister of Henry VIII (Justice), loses her heart to commoner Todd but agrees to marry an aged French king to maintain peace. When he dies, Duke of Buckingham (Gough) attempts to usurp Todd's place. Elaborate but historically inaccurate Disney epic is filled with sweeping spectacle and high spirits. Based on Charles Major's *When Knighthood Was in Flower*.

SWORD AND THE SORCERER, THE 1982
★★ R Fantasy 1:40
☑ Brief nudity, adult situations, explicit language, violence
Dir: Albert Pyun *Cast:* Lee Horsley, Kathleen Beller, George Maharis, Simon MacCorkindale, Richard Lynch, Richard Moll
► Evil spirits bring about downfall of a good king. King's son Horsley is aided by a mysterious sword as he fights for the oppressed, wins the heart of Beller, and restores the kingdom to deserving hands. Well paced and well produced; somewhat overplotted, but Horsley exhibits grace and verve.

SWORD IN THE STONE, THE 1963
★★★★ G Animation 1:15
Dir: Wolfgang Reitherman *Cast:* Voices of Rickie Sorenson, Sebastian Cabot, Karl Swenson, Junius Matthews, Alan Napier
► Simplified adaptation of T. H. White's Camelot stories concerns training of Wart, the young lad destined to become King Arthur. Guided by Merlin the Magician, Wart is transformed into various animals to learn how to rely on his intellect rather than his brawn. Blustering Merlin provides most of the fun in this overlooked Disney cartoon. (CC)

SWORDKILL 1986
★★ R Drama 1:20
☑ Adult situations, explicit language, violence
Dir: Larry Carroll *Cast:* Hiroshi Fujioka,

John Calvin, Janet Julian, Charles Lampkin, Frank Schuller, Bill Morey
▶ Fujioka, a sixteenth-century Japanese samurai, is frozen in a glacier while searching for his kidnapped wife. Discovered by present-day skiers, he is brought back to life by Los Angeles scientist Calvin. Aided by Julian, Fujioka escapes from Calvin's hospital to continue his quest. Inventive treatment of engrossing story helps compensate for low budget. Also known as *Ghostwarrior*.

SWORD OF GIDEON 1986
★ ★ ★ ★ NR Action-Adventure/MFTV 2:28
☑ Violence
Dir: Michael Anderson *Cast:* Steven Bauer, Rod Steiger, Colleen Dewhurst, Michael York, Robert Joy, Peter Dvorsky
▶ After the 1972 Munich Olympics massacre, Israeli officer Steiger enlists the aid of captain Bauer in putting together a special team of commandos who will kill terrorists responsible for the deaths of innocent Israelis. Other members include English explosives expert York and veteran soldier of fortune Dvorsky. Thrill-packed mission moves from sands of Jordan desert to the piazzas of Rome and the streets of New York.

SWORD OF THE VALIANT 1984 British
★ ★ PG Action-Adventure 1:42
☑ Violence
Dir: Stephen Weeks *Cast:* Miles O'Keeffe, Sean Connery, Cyrielle Claire, Leigh Lawson, Trevor Howard, Peter Cushing
▶ Knight O'Keeffe decapitates magician Connery, who challenges King Arthur's (Howard) court. Connery resurrects self and gives O'Keeffe one year to solve a riddle or face death. Decent script and showy production; Connery is strong as always but the direction is rather lackluster.

SYBIL 1976
★ ★ ★ ★ NR Biography/MFTV 3:18
Dir: Daniel Petrie *Cast:* Joanne Woodward, Sally Field, Brad Davis, Martine Bartlett, Jane Hoffman, William Prince
▶ Psychiatrist Woodward probes the mind of disturbed Field who, as consequence of childhood trauma, developed seventeen personalities. Emmy-winning miniseries proved so popular with viewers and critics alike it was released on videocassette. Field's memorable performance in a challenging role revitalized her

dormant career. Based on a true story from the book by Flora Rheta Scheiber.

SYLVESTER 1985
★ ★ ★ ★ PG Family 1:43
☑ Explicit language, mild violence
Dir: Tim Hunter *Cast:* Melissa Gilbert, Richard Farnsworth, Michael Schoeffling, Constance Towers
▶ Orphaned tomboy Gilbert trains wild jumping horse Sylvester while protecting her younger brothers from state social workers. Crusty trainer Farnsworth helps Gilbert and Sylvester prepare for big meet. An old-fashioned "feel good" movie: Gilbert is sweet, Farnsworth real and likable, and the story quite satisfying. (CC)

SYLVIA 1985 New Zealand
★ ★ PG Biography 1:38
☑ Adult situations, explicit language
Dir: Michael Firth *Cast:* Eleanor David, Nigel Terry, Tom Wilkinson, Mary Regan, Martyn Sanderson
▶ True story based on the best-sellers *Teacher* and *I Passed This Way* by educator Sylvia Ashton-Warner. Teacher David and headmaster husband Wilkinson come to impoverished New Zealand village. David finds traditional curriculum fails with Maori kids; she reaches them with her own brand of instruction but runs afoul of bureaucrat Terry. Underdog-against-the-system tale has broad appeal. (CC)

SYLVIA SCARLETT 1935
★ ★ NR Drama 1:37
Dir: George Cukor *Cast:* Katharine Hepburn, Cary Grant, Brian Aherne, Edmund Gwenn, Natalie Paley, Dennie Moore
▶ Disguising daughter Hepburn as a man, Gwenn, her ne'er-do-well father wanted by police, sneaks into England. There they are tricked by Cockney charmer Grant who later joins them in a series of money-making schemes culminating in a seaside theater engagement. Odd blend of drama and comedy lacks a consistent tone, but Hepburn (in the first of four films with Grant) is quite impressive in a daring cross-dressing role.

TABLE FOR FIVE 1983
★ ★ ★ ★ PG Drama 1:57
☑ Adult situations, explicit language
Dir: Robert Lieberman *Cast:* Jon Voight, Marie-Christine Barrault, Richard Crenna, Millie Perkins, Roxana Zal
▶ Divorced dad Voight picks up his three

kids from ex-wife Perkins for an ocean cruise to Egypt. On board, he meets pretty blond Barrault. Dad and estranged kids are having trouble adjusting to each other when news comes that mom has been killed in a car accident. Crenna plays the stepfather who fights Voight for custody of the children. Slick tearjerker features exotic locales.

TAFFIN 1988 U.S/British
★ **R Drama 1:32**
☑ Nudity, adult situations, explicit language, violence
Dir: Francis Megahy *Cast:* Pierce Brosnan, Ray McAnally, Alison Doody, Jeremy Child, Dearbhia Molloy
► Debt collector Brosnan rethinks his priorities when he learns athletic field in his Irish home town is the planned site of dangerous chemical plant. He mounts campaign against plant's owners and resorts to violence when hired thugs attack local conservationists. Dreary attempt at socially redeeming drama isn't helped by weak acting.

T.A.G.: THE ASSASSINATION GAME
1982
★★ **PG Mystery-Suspense/Comedy 1:31**
☑ Adult situations, explicit language, violence
Dir: Nick Castle *Cast:* Robert Carradine, Linda Hamilton, Perry Lang, Bruce Abbott, Kristine DeBell, Frazer Smith
► College students unwind with hunter-prey game using harmless dart guns. School paper editor Carradine spies lovely coed Hamilton playing game and follows her under ruse of writing article. Meanwhile Abbott gets shot by player and decides to up the ante: he stalks quarry with lethal ammo. Promising comic start abandoned when picture shifts into standard thriller gear.

TAI-PAN 1986
★★★ **R Action-Adventure 2:07**
☑ Nudity, adult situations, violence
Dir: Daryl Duke *Cast:* Bryan Brown, Joan Chen, John Stanton, Tom Guinee, Bill Leadbitter, Kyra Sedgewick
► Based on James Clavell's best-seller, historical epic depicts life of "Tai-Pan" (Brown), trade leader for European community in nineteenth-century Hong Kong. Principal player in China-Britain opium war, Scotsman Tai-Pan has other woes as well: son Guinee won't forgive father for mistress Chen, while nasty rival Stanton

and his vicious son Leadbitter seek to bankrupt Tai-Pan. Filmed on location, multiplotted potboiler has something for everyone. **(CC)**

TAKE A HARD RIDE 1975
★★ **PG Western 1:43**
☑ Violence
Dir: Anthony M. Dawson (Antonio Margheriti) *Cast:* Jim Brown, Lee Van Cleef, Fred Williamson, Catherine Spaak, Jim Kelly, Dana Andrews
► Honest cowboy Brown treks across Western wilderness to deliver $86,000 from dying rancher boss Andrews to his family. Brown is pursued by happy-go-lucky gambler Williamson who decides to team up with the cowboy when vicious bounty hunter Van Cleef trails them both. Standard spaghetti Western with one new twist: good guys are black while bad dudes are white.

TAKE DOWN 1979
★★★★ **PG Drama/Sports 1:47**
☑ Explicit language
Dir: Kieth Merrill *Cast:* Edward Herrmann, Kathleen Lloyd, Lorenzo Lamas, Maureen McCormick, Nick Beauvy, Kevin Hooks
► Perennial football losers, tiny Utah high school starts wrestling team in hopes of gaining revenge. Shakespeare scholar Herrmann, with no knowledge of sport, is assigned to coach squad. He learns to enjoy the boys and the job when wife Lloyd urges him to stop being such a stiff. His primary challenge: to convince star athlete Lamas to learn to be a winner and not drop out of school. Uplifting and lighthearted Disney effort.

TAKE ME OUT TO THE BALL GAME
1949
★★★ **NR Musical 1:33**
Dir: Busby Berkeley *Cast:* Frank Sinatra, Esther Williams, Gene Kelly, Betty Garrett, Edward Arnold, Jules Munshin
► Pleasant turn-of-the-century musical combines baseball, gambling, and vaudeville into an undemanding trifle. Singers Sinatra and Kelly, teammates on the semipro summer circuit, are pleasantly surprised when their club is purchased by beautiful new manager Williams. Evil gambler Arnold almost leads Kelly astray, but Williams sets him straight. Classic title tune and Kelly's "The Hat My Father Wore on St. Patrick's Day" are highlights; Betty Comden and Adolph Green worked on the rest of the score.

TAKE THE MONEY AND RUN 1969
★★ **PG Comedy 1:25**
☑ Adult situations, explicit language
Dir: Woody Allen *Cast:* Woody Allen, Janet Margolin, Marcel Hillaire, Jacquelyn Hyde, Lonny Chapman
▶ Inept crook Allen tries to support wife Margolin through life of crime, is caught and imprisoned, but later escapes. Very amusing documentary-style satire is Allen's directorial debut. Funniest scenes: Allen attempting to rob bank with illegible stick-up note ("Does this say gun or gub?" the teller wonders) and interracial chain gang posing as "really close family" after escaping.

TAKE THIS JOB AND SHOVE IT 1981
★★★ **PG Comedy 1:40**
☑ Brief nudity, adult situations, explicit language, adult humor
Dir: Gus Trikonis *Cast:* Robert Hays, Art Carney, Barbara Hershey, David Keith, Tim Thomerson, Martin Mull
▶ Johnny Paycheck's hit country-western song provides the inspiration for an appealing comedy about overachiever Hays, who's sent to his hometown of Dubuque to revamp the local brewery. Encounters with old friends and former lover Hershey convince him to reorder his priorities. Good score and cameos by country-western stars Paycheck, Charlie Rich, David Allan Coe, etc., boost predictable plot. **(CC)**

TAKING OF PELHAM ONE TWO THREE, THE 1974
★★★★ **R Action-Adventure 1:44**
☑ Adult situations, explicit language, violence
Dir: Joseph Sargent *Cast:* Walter Matthau, Robert Shaw, Martin Balsam, Hector Elizondo, Jerry Stiller, Kenneth McMillan
▶ Four criminals led by Shaw hijack a Bronx subway and demand one million dollars ransom from transit cop negotiator Matthau. Taut, fast-paced thriller with welcome comic touches features convincing settings, strong action, and first-rate performances by Matthau and Shaw. Based on John Godey's novel.

TALE OF TWO CITIES, A 1935
★★★★ **NR Drama 2:01 B&W**
Dir: Jack Conway *Cast:* Ronald Colman, Elizabeth Allan, Edna May Oliver, Blanche Yurka, Basil Rathbone, Reginald Owen
▶ A far, far better film than any other ad-
aptation of the Charles Dickens French Revolution classic. Solid storytelling given handsome production by David O. Selznick. Yurka is memorable as literature's most evil knitter, Madame DeFarge; Colman's Sydney Carton is heroic and moving, especially in his climactic martyrdom.

TALE OF TWO CITIES, A 1958 British
★★ **NR Drama 1:57 B&W**
Dir: Ralph Thomas *Cast:* Dirk Bogarde, Dorothy Tutin, Cecil Parker, Christopher Lee, Ian Bannen, Donald Pleasence
▶ Paris and London during the French Revolution: English lawyer Bogarde finds purpose in life helping those threatened by French rebels. His resemblance to the husband of the woman he loves leads to a noble act of courage. Adaptation of Charles Dickens classic is well done but the Ronald Colman version still stands apart.

TALES OF ORDINARY MADNESS 1983
Italian/French
☆ **NR Drama 1:47**
☑ Nudity, strong sexual content, adult situations, explicit language, violence
Dir: Marco Ferreri *Cast:* Ben Gazzara, Ornella Muti, Susan Tyrrell, Tanya Lopert, Roy Brocksmith, Katia Berger
▶ Los Angeles skid-row writer Gazzara has unusual sexual encounters with several women: he trails home blond bombshell Tyrrell and rapes her, spars with nymphomaniac ex-wife Lopert, and romances self-destructive prostitute Muti with tragic results. Unblinking look at dregs of society is based on works of poet Charles Bukowski, later the inspiration for Rourke-Dunaway starrer *Barfly*.

TALES OF TERROR 1962
★★ **NR Horror 1:30**
Dir: Roger Corman *Cast:* Vincent Price, Peter Lorre, Basil Rathbone, Maggie Pierce, Joyce Jameson, Debra Paget
▶ Three-part horror omnibus adapted from Edgar Allan Poe stories: in "Morella," grieving widower Price forces a gruesome encounter between daughter Pierce and his mummified wife; in "The Black Cat," Lorre, an alcoholic cuckold, entombs his wife Jameson and lover Price behind a basement wall; "The Case of Mr. Valdemar" concerns evil doctor Rathbone's plot to keep Price comatose while stealing his wife Paget. Uneven an-

thology features a marvelous comic turn by Lorre and unusual color design.

TALK OF THE TOWN, THE 1942
★★★ NR Comedy 1:58 B&W
Dir: George Stevens *Cast:* Cary Grant, Jean Arthur, Ronald Colman, Edgar Buchanan, Glenda Farrell, Rex Ingram
▶ Escaped fugitive Grant hides in schoolteacher Arthur's home, which has just been rented to Supreme Court nominee Colman. Posing as a gardener, Grant engages Colman in a debate over tolerance in the law while wooing Arthur. Stars are extremely appealing in this witty comedy, winner of seven Oscar nominations.

TALK RADIO 1988
★★★ R Drama 1:50
☑ Adult situations, explicit language, violence
Dir: Oliver Stone *Cast:* Eric Bogosian, Ellen Greene, Leslie Hope, Alec Baldwin, John C. McGinley, John Pankow
▶ Dallas talk show host Bogosian rises to nationwide syndication with abrasive style. His insistence on abusing callers provokes crazies in audience and leads to violent conclusion. Bogosian, re-creating his stage role, is dynamic. Stone's moving camera keeps talky but sharpedged script running; however, some may find obnoxiousness of lead character and downbeat ending off-putting. Based on the Bogosian play and the real-life killing of DJ Alan Berg.

TALK TO ME 1984
★★★ NR Drama 1:35
☑ Adult situations, explicit language
Dir: Julius Potocsny *Cast:* Austin Pendleton, Michael Murphy, Barbara Eda Young, Louise Fletcher, Dan Shor, Michael Tolan
▶ Lifelong stutterer Pendleton avoids his problem, preferring to immerse himself in work. Finally tired of his dilemma, Pendleton enrolls in speech therapy institute and meets others who share his disability. With help of tough-but-fair instructor Murphy and new friend Young, he conquers impediment. All profits from inspirational film go to Hollins Communication Research Institute in Virginia, site of Pendleton's cure. **(CC)**

TALL BLOND MAN WITH ONE BLACK SHOE, THE 1972 French
★ PG Mystery-Suspense/Comedy
1:29
☑ Adult humor

Dir: Yves Robert *Cast:* Pierre Richard, Bernard Blier, Jean Rochefort, Mireille Darc, Jean Carmet
▶ Innocent musician Richard becomes pawn of French intelligence director Rochefort in plan to trip up his overly ambitious assistant Blier. Richard also gets involved with gorgeous spy Darc. Understated humor is frequently charming. Spawned a French sequel and American remake (*The Man With One Red Shoe*).
§

TALL IN THE SADDLE 1944
★★★★ NR Western 1:19 B&W
Dir: Edwin L. Marin *Cast:* John Wayne, Ella Raines, Ward Bond, George "Gabby" Hayes, Don Douglas
▶ Cowhand Wayne takes ranch job and discovers his cousin has been killed. The Duke learns that corrupt judge Bond covets the ranch and was responsible for the murder. Wayne falls for owner's niece Raines while battling Bond. Rip-roaring, unpretentious fun with shootouts, fistfights, chases galore.

TALL MEN, THE 1955
★★ NR Western 2:01
Dir: Raoul Walsh *Cast:* Clark Gable, Jane Russell, Robert Ryan, Cameron Mitchell, Juan Garcia, Harry Shannon
▶ Gable and Mitchell play cowpoke brothers and former Confederate raiders who sign up for a Texas-to-Montana cattle drive. Their obstacles include fraud scheme by wealthy businessman Ryan; romantic problems with Russell, the only survivor of an Indian massacre; fierce blizzard; and ambush in a narrow canyon. Elaborate Western fails to deliver enough action.

TAMARIND SEED, THE 1974
★★★★ PG Romance/Espionage
2:03
☑ Mild violence
Dir: Blake Edwards *Cast:* Julie Andrews, Omar Sharif, Anthony Quayle, Dan O'Herlihy, Sylvia Sims, Oscar Homolka
▶ While vacationing in Barbados, English civil servant Andrews and Soviet diplomat Sharif fall in love. Respective governments spy on each when Andrews returns to London and Sharif resumes embassy job in Paris. Lovers can't bear to be apart, so Sharif trades political asylum for info on British politician O'Herlihy, a spy for Russians. Fine romantic drama with star cast is more cloak than dagger as love conquers all, even the Cold War.

TAMING OF THE SHREW, THE 1967
U.S./Italian
★★★★ NR Comedy 2:04
Dir: Franco Zeffirelli *Cast:* Elizabeth Taylor, Richard Burton, Michael York, Cyril Cusack, Michael Hordern, Natasha Pyne
▶ In the sixteenth century, rich Italian merchant Hordern despairs of ever marrying off his tempestuous daughter Taylor, until Burton shows up seeking a wealthy wife. Taylor vows to resist but romantic sparks fly as Burton woos her. Lusty, lavish, and energetic; then-married Taylor and Burton bring charisma and chemistry to Shakespeare. Very entertaining.

TAMMY AND THE BACHELOR 1957
★★★ NR Comedy 1:29
Dir: Joseph Pevney *Cast:* Debbie Reynolds, Leslie Nielsen, Walter Brennan, Mala Powers, Fay Wray, Mildred Natwick
▶ Plane crash brings rich Nielsen and rural Reynolds together. Nielsen takes Reynolds home to meet the family and, despite culture clash, all ends happily. Sweet and likable comedy was first in the series and probably the best. Charming Reynolds sings the theme song with the Ames Brothers.

TAMMY AND THE DOCTOR 1963
★★ NR Comedy 1:28
Dir: Harry Keller *Cast:* Sandra Dee, Peter Fonda, Macdonald Carey, Beulah Bondi, Margaret Lindsay, Adam West
▶ Innocent country girl Dee gets hospital job. Nurse Lindsay befriends Dee and doctor Fonda (in his film debut) falls in love with her. Fonda's boss Carey disapproves of the romance. However, love finds a way in this corny but entertaining third entry in the series.

TAMPOPO 1987 Japanese
★★ NR Comedy 1:54
☑ Nudity, adult situations, adult humor
Dir: Juzo Itami *Cast:* Tsutomu Yamazaki, Nobuko Miyamoto, Koji Yakusho, Ken Watanabe, Rikiya Yasuoka, Kinzo Sakura
▶ Mysterious stranger Yamazaki drives into town and helps sweet widow Miyamoto (director Itami's wife) develop ace recipe for her noodle shop. Delectable concoction combines movie references (if Clint Eastwood were a Japanese chef, he might be the delightfully taciturn Yamazaki), food, and eroticism

(especially in the startling sequence of an egg being passed between mouths). S

TANK 1984
★★★★ PG Action-Adventure/Comedy 1:53
☑ Nudity, adult situations, explicit language, violence
Dir: Marvin J. Chomsky *Cast:* James Garner, Shirley Jones, C. Thomas Howell, G. D. Spradlin, Jenilee Harrison
▶ Army major Garner rescues Howell, his falsely arrested son, by driving a Sherman tank into town, grabbing the boy, and high-tailing it for the state border. Improbable loners-versus-corrupt-system story features Spradlin as the bad sheriff and Jones as Garner's understanding wife. (CC)

TAP 1988
★★★★ PG-13 Drama/Dance 1:50
☑ Explicit language
Dir: Nick Castle *Cast:* Gregory Hines, Sammy Davis, Jr., Suzzanne Douglas, Savion Glover, Joe Morton, Harold Nicholas
▶ Talented tap dancer Hines gets out of jail after serving robbery hitch. He rejoins girlfriend Douglas and retired dancer Davis and fights the lure of a life of crime to develop his art. Occasionally contrived plotting is vehicle for superlative dancing by Hines, who holds his own even when dancing with old-time greats like Nicholas, and teen Glover. A restrained Davis gives one of his best screen performances.

TAPEHEADS 1988
★★ R Comedy 1:37
☑ Brief nudity, adult situations, explicit language
Dir: Bill Fishman *Cast:* John Cusack, Tim Robbins, Mary Crosby, Connie Stevens, Don Cornelius, Clu Gulager
▶ After getting fired, young security guards Cusack and Robbins try their hands at the video business, accidentally coming into possession of a tape damaging to politician Gulager. Thugs search for the tape as the buddies rise to the top. Brash spoof of the music biz has some clever send-ups of rock videos but little to entertain older viewers.

TAPS 1981
★★★★ PG Drama 2:01
☑ Brief nudity, explicit language, violence
Dir: Harold Becker *Cast:* Timothy Hut-

ton, George C. Scott, Ronny Cox, Sean Penn, Tom Cruise
▶ General Scott and cadet major Hutton at a military school beset by financial problems deal with mounting pressures. When the trustees announce plans to close the academy to build condos on the property, the frustrated students seize the campus. Hutton tries to quell the heat, with tragic consequences. Solid cast and well-crafted production, although the ending may seem quite predictable to some viewers. Interesting as early vehicle for Penn and Cruise.

TARAS BULBA 1962
★★ **NR Drama 2:02**
Dir: J. Lee Thompson *Cast:* Tony Curtis, Yul Brynner, Christine Kaufmann, Sam Wanamaker, Brad Dexter, Guy Rolfe
▶ Muddled tale of sixteenth-century Cossack leader Brynner forced into exile; his son Curtis incurs his wrath by romancing beautiful heathen Kaufmann. Large-scale battle sequences add some excitement to this extremely loose adaptation of a Nikolai Gogol story, but Curtis's Bronx accent and clichéd plotting are major drawbacks.

TARGET 1985
★★★★ **R Action-Adventure 1:57**
☑ Brief nudity, adult situations, explicit language, violence
Dir: Arthur Penn *Cast:* Gene Hackman, Matt Dillon, Gayle Hunnicutt, Victoria Fyodorova, Josef Sommer, Guy Boyd
▶ When wife Hunnicutt is kidnapped in Paris, Dallas lumberyard owner Hackman and son Dillon fly there to investigate. When assassins try to kill Hackman, he reveals former life as CIA agent to stunned Dillon. Action scenes are both hair-raising and funny. Hackman turns in usual solid performance while Dillon convincingly portrays slack-jawed kid who can't believe lethargic pop is really ace spy. (CC)

TARGETS 1968
★ **PG Mystery-Suspense 1:30**
☑ explicit violence
Dir: Peter Bogdanovich *Cast:* Boris Karloff, Tim O'Kelly, Nancy Hsueh, James Brown, Sandy Baron, Peter Bogdanovich
▶ Horror-movie star Karloff plans to retire while real-life monster O'Kelly goes on shooting spree that starts with O'Kelly's family, includes innocent bystanders, and eventually targets Karloff in a chilling

drive-in climax. Bogdanovich's directorial debut is timely and ambitious.

TARKA THE OTTER 1979 British
★★★★ **G Family 1:31**
Dir: David Cobham *Cast:* Narrated by Peter Ustinov
▶ Tarka (ancient name meaning Little Wanderer) the otter loses his parents to hunters and their hounds, led by the fearsome Deadlock. Orphaned otter journeys downriver to estuary where he learns to fend for himself. He meets young female White Tip and two return to his river home. There he must fight to death against Deadlock to defend mate and their cubs. Top-notch wildlife footage; superior family fare.

TARNISHED ANGELS, THE 1957
★★ **NR Drama 1:31 B&W**
Dir: Douglas Sirk *Cast:* Rock Hudson, Robert Stack, Dorothy Malone, Jack Carson, Troy Donahue
▶ In 1930s New Orleans, reporter Hudson does story on World War I flyer-turned-barnstorming-pilot Stack, his wife Malone, son, and mechanic Carson. As Hudson gets increasingly involved with the family, Stack's obsession with flying takes a tragic turn. Moody and visually evocative; based on William Faulkner's *Pylon*.

TARZAN, THE APE MAN 1932
★★★ **NR Action-Adventure 1:39 B&W**
Dir: W. S. Van Dyke II *Cast:* Johnny Weissmuller, Maureen O'Sullivan, C. Aubrey Smith, Neil Hamilton, Doris Lloyd, Cheetah the Chimp
▶ First of a long series of jungle adventures starring Olympic swimming star Weissmuller as Edgar Rice Burroughs's hero packs plenty of action and excitement into an enjoyably dated plot about members of an English safari in search of an ivory-filled elephants' graveyard. O'Sullivan, daughter of expedition leader Smith, is a fetching partner to the ape man, who delivers the immortal line "Me Tarzan, you Jane." Amusing, racy classic was remade in 1959 and 1981. Sequel: *Tarzan and His Mate.*

TARZAN, THE APE MAN 1981
★ **R Action-Adventure 1:52**
☑ Nudity, adult situations, explicit language
Dir: John Derek *Cast:* Bo Derek, Richard Harris, Miles O'Keeffe, John Phillip Law, Akushula Selayah
▶ Victorian explorer Harris, his virginal daughter Derek, and handsome photog-

rapher Law fall prey to heathen savages in darkest Africa. O'Keeffe, a mute muscleman raised by apes, saves Derek from a horrible fate. Plot of Edgar Rice Burroughs's classic adventure is largely discarded, as are Derek's clothes, in this campy, inept remake of the 1932 film. Closing credits were the subject of a court battle with the Burroughs estate.

TASTE OF HONEY, A 1962 British
★ NR Drama 1:40 B&W
Dir: Tony Richardson *Cast:* Rita Tushingham, Dora Bryan, Robert Stephens, Murray Melvin, Paul Danquah
▶ Fatherless British teen Tushingham has affair with black sailor Danquah. When her mother Bryan remarries and her lover goes back to sea, Tushingham moves in with gay pal Melvin who takes care of her. Slow beginning, talkiness, and heavy accents may make some restless; however, perfect performances (especially Tushingham) elicit touching moments.

TATTOO 1981
★ R Mystery-Suspense 1:43
☑ Nudity, explicit language, violence
Dir: Bob Brooks *Cast:* Bruce Dern, Maud Adams, Leonard Frey, Rikki Borge, John Getz, Peter Iacangelo
▶ Tattoo artist Dern, hired by fashion magazine to paint temporary tattoos for bathing suit promotion, becomes infatuated with striking model Adams. She at first returns his interest but soon finds his notions of women and dating too old-fashioned for her liberated lifestyle. His passion then becomes dangerously obsessive as he decides to use her body as a canvas for his artwork. Fine premise fizzles after promising start.

TAXI DRIVER 1976
★★★★ R Drama 1:53
☑ Explicit language, graphic violence
Dir: Martin Scorsese *Cast:* Robert De Niro, Jodie Foster, Cybill Shepherd, Harvey Keitel, Peter Boyle, Albert Brooks
▶ Introverted and insomniac ex-Marine De Niro takes job as night shift cab driver in New York that proves a relentless tour of dark side of humanity. De Niro's anxieties become unbearable: rejected by All-American beauty Shepherd and taunted by pimp Keitel about teen prostitute Foster, he vents his tensions in a spree of violence. Frightening look at urban underbelly features superb performances and striking images. Haunting score was the last work by longtime Hitchcock col-

laborator Bernard Herrmann. Nominated for four Oscars.

TEACHERS 1984
★★★★ R Comedy/Drama 1:46
☑ Nudity, adult situations, explicit language, violence
Dir: Arthur Hiller *Cast:* Nick Nolte, Judd Hirsch, JoBeth Williams, Ralph Macchio, Lee Grant, Richard Mulligan
▶ Williams, a lawyer and former student of burnt-out but beloved teacher Nolte, is suing J.F.K. High School because her client graduated but can't read. Fighting the case are conservative vice principal Hirsch and caustic school board advisor Grant. Romancing Williams and caught in between the battle lines, Nolte also deals with rebellious student Macchio. First-rate cast and some fine comic moments in this send-up of public education. You'll cheer Nolte's parting "I'm a teacher!" shot. **(CC)**

TEACHER'S PET 1958
★★ NR Comedy 2:00
Dir: George Seaton *Cast:* Clark Gable, Doris Day, Gig Young, Mamie Van Doren, Nick Adams, Marion Ross
▶ Journalism teacher Day criticizes newspaper editor Gable. He poses as student, becomes her star pupil, then falls for Day and tries to win her away from shrink Young (Oscar-nominated). The three stars are quite winning in this bright and breezy newspaper comedy.

TEEN WOLF 1985
★★★★ PG Comedy 1:32
☑ Adult situations, explicit language
Dir: Rod Daniel *Cast:* Michael J. Fox, James Hampton, Susan Ursitti, Jerry Levine, Matt Adler, Lorie Griffin
▶ Typical teen Fox suffers usual woes: school basketball team is so bad he's on verge of quitting, love for popular beauty Griffin goes unrequited, and perky Ursitti won't leave him alone. Then Fox discovers he's a werewolf. Being mean and hairy does wonders for his basketball game and love life, but sudden success goes to Fox's head until Ursitti tames his ego. Always likable Fox is a howl in good-natured but somewhat predictable comedy. Followed by sequel. **(CC)**

TEEN WOLF TOO 1987
★ PG Comedy 1:35
☑ Adult situations, explicit language
Dir: Chris Leitch *Cast:* Jason Bateman, Kim Darby, John Astin, Paul Sand, James Hampton, Estee Chandler

▶ Bateman, cousin of Michael J. Fox character from *Teen Wolf*, enrolls in college on boxing scholarship despite real interest in veterinary medicine. To satisfy crusty dean Astin and boxing coach Sand and impress girlfriend Chandler, Bateman plays human punching bag to more-talented opponents until genetics bring out his inhuman side and he becomes scourge of the ring and campus hero. Fox-less sequel lacks punch.

TELEFON 1977
★★★★ PG
Espionage/Action-Adventure 1:43
☑ Adult situations, explicit language, violence
Dir: Don Siegel *Cast:* Charles Bronson, Lee Remick, Donald Pleasence, Tyne Daly, Patrick Magee, Sheree North
▶ Conservative KGB renegade Pleasence, upset with softening of superpower hostilities, treks to U.S. to activate Soviet saboteurs planted during Cold War. When they wreak havoc on American military bases to start World War III, crack Russian agent Bronson is dispatched to U.S. to thwart the runaway Red with help of local liaison Remick, who's actually a CIA double agent. First-rate espionage yarn with ever-popular Bronson and timely premise.

TELEPHONE, THE 1988
☆ R Drama 1:22
☑ Adult situations, explicit language
Dir: Rip Torn *Cast:* Whoopi Goldberg, Elliott Gould, John Heard, Severn Darden, Amy Wright, Ronald J. Stallings
▶ Goldberg, an out-of-work actress with a botched love life, unpaid bills, and dumpy apartment, vents frustrations on phone, employing various accents and personas. Her agent Gould offers no hope for future. When macho phone repairman Heard arrives to disconnect line for nonpayment, Goldberg cracks up. Disappointing and claustrophobic one-woman show. Goldberg unsuccessfully sued to prevent film's release. **(CC)**

TELL ME A RIDDLE 1980
★★ PG Drama 1:33
☑ Explicit language
Dir: Lee Grant *Cast:* Melvyn Douglas, Lila Kedrova, Brooke Adams, Dolores Dorn, Bob Elross, Jon Harris
▶ Elderly couple Douglas and Kedrova, immigrants from Russia in 1920s, quarrel over his desire to sell home to move into retirement community and her need to lose herself in novels and scrapbooks of past. When they learn Kedrova suffers from terminal cancer, the couple visits peppy granddaughter Adams in San Francisco. Sincere and restrained look at pitfalls of old age can be slow and downbeat, but Douglas and Kedrova bring depth and credibility to lead roles.

TELL ME THAT YOU LOVE ME 1985
★★ NR Drama 1:31
☑ Adult situations, explicit language
Dir: Tzipi Trope *Cast:* Nick Mancuso, Belinda Montgomery, Ken Walsh, Andre Pelletier, Barbara Williams
▶ Reporter Montgomery, investigating battered wives, suffers marital woes of her own when lawyer husband Mancuso announces plan to work for year in another city. He moves out and she invites abused spouse Williams to move in. Montgomery then copes with amorous advances of Walsh, her best friend's husband, and efforts of Mancuso to woo her to new home. Soap opera examination of contemporary adult situations and emotional traumas.

TELL THEM WILLIE BOY IS HERE 1969
★★★ PG Drama 1:37
☑ Adult situations, explicit language, violence
Dir: Abraham Polonsky *Cast:* Robert Redford, Katharine Ross, Robert Blake, Susan Clark, Barry Sullivan, Mikel Angel
▶ California, 1909: strong-willed Indian Blake woos fellow tribe member Ross against objections of her father Angel; Blake kills Angel in self-defense during quarrel. Lawman Redford, urged on by romantic interest Clark and racist rancher Sullivan, must reluctantly pursue Blake and Ross into the wilderness. Polonksy's first directing assignment after being blacklisted. Tries too hard to capture history of whites versus Indians in a nutshell, but Redford's struggle of conscience and the rugged scenery are nonetheless compelling.

TEMPEST 1982
★★ PG Comedy 2:22
☑ Adult situations, explicit language
Dir: Paul Mazursky *Cast:* John Cassavetes, Gena Rowlands, Susan Sarandon, Molly Ringwald, Raul Julia, Vittorio Gassman
▶ Prosperous New York architect Cassavetes, in mid-life crisis, leaves wife Rowlands and whisks daughter Ringwald away to barren Greek island. With aid of

new girlfriend Sarandon and lecherous goathed Julia, Cassavetes sets up rural housekeeping and seeks peace with un-even results, until Rowlands and casino magnate beau Gassman interrupt the isolation. Offbeat comedy with medita-tions on mortality and human frailty is loosely based on Shakespeare's *The Tempest.*

10 1979
★ ★ ★ **R Comedy 2:03**
☑ Nudity, strong sexual content, adult situations, explicit language
Dir: Blake Edwards   *Cast:* Dudley Moore, Bo Derek, Julie Andrews, Robert Webber, Dee Wallace
► Hollywood songwriter Moore, in throes of male menopause, deserts singer girl-friend Andrews to pursue stunning newly-wed Derek, with whom he's become ob-sessed even though he's never spoken to her. Overcoming all sorts of pitfalls and pratfalls, Moore finally catches up with Derek on honeymoon in Acapulco, only to discover he's not as sexually liberated as he believed. Plenty of physical com-edy, skillfully handled by director Ed-wards. Hugely popular film exposed new-comer Derek to moviegoers.

TENANT, THE 1976 U.S./French
☆ **R Mystery-Suspense 2:05**
☑ Explicit language, graphic violence
Dir: Roman Polanski   *Cast:* Roman Polanski, Isabelle Adjani, Shelley Win-ters, Melvyn Douglas, Jo Van Fleet, Bernard Fresson
► Oddball Parisian loner Polanksi moves into seedy apartment previously occu-pied by woman who committed suicide. He gradually becomes convinced that landlord Douglas, concierge Winters, and previous tenant's friend Adjani are part of conspiracy to drive him to suicide. Eccentric, darkly comic study of burgeon-ing madness will disappoint fans of con-ventional horror.

TEN COMMANDMENTS, THE 1957
★ ★ ★ ★ ★ **G Drama 3:39**
Dir: Cecil B. DeMille   *Cast:* Charlton Heston, Anne Baxter, Yul Brynner, Yvonne De Carlo, Cedric Hardwicke, Edward G. Robinson
► Massive biblical epic, DeMille style, re-tells the Old Testament story of Moses (Heston) from his humble birth to his role as the man who leads the Jewish people out of Egypt and to the Promised Land. Strong cast (especially Brynner as rival King Ramses), magnificent production values (Oscar-winning special effects), and fine dramatic tension. Everyone's fa-vorite scene: the parting of the Red Sea. Grand-scale religious entertainment for the whole family.

TENDER IS THE NIGHT 1962
★ ★ ★ ★ **NR Romance 2:29**
Dir: Henry King   *Cast:* Jennifer Jones, Jason Robards, Jr., Joan Fontaine, Tom Ewell, Jill St. John, Paul Lukas
► In 1920s Europe, neurotic Jones falls for her shrink Robards. They marry, but in-volvements with Jones's domineering sis-ter Fontaine, alcoholic composer Ewell, and movie star St. John put a strain on the marriage. Engrossing soap opera look at the idle rich from the F. Scott Fitz-gerald novel.

TENDER MERCIES 1983
★ ★ ★ ★ **PG Drama 1:29**
☑ Adult situations, explicit language
Dir: Bruce Beresford   *Cast:* Robert Du-vall, Tess Harper, Allan Hubbard, Betty Buckley, Ellen Barkin, Wilford Brimley
► Stark, compelling drama about alco-holic ex–country star Mac Sledge (Duvall) and his struggle for personal redemption with Harper, the widowed owner of a ramshackle Texas motel. Duvall (who wrote and sings his tunes) won an Oscar for his incisive performance, as did Horton Foote for his moving, subdued screen-play. Equally fine are Barkin as Sledge's troubled daughter, and Buckley as his ex-wife and a popular singer.

TENDRES COUSINES 1983 French
★ **R Drama 1:31**
☑ Nudity, strong sexual content, adult situations, explicit language
Dir: David Hamilton   *Cast:* Elisa Cervier, Jean-Yves Chatelais, Pierre Chantepie, Evelyne Dandry, Laure Dechasnel, Val-erie Dumas
► Coming-of-age story set in pre–World War II France presents a sugar-coated view of young Chatelais's introduction to sex at a chateau. Lush, gauzy photogra-phy, attractive cast, and realistically hu-morous look at sexual foibles almost compensate for thin plot. ⑤

TEN FROM YOUR SHOW OF SHOWS 1973
★ ★ ★ ★ **G Comedy/MFTV 1:31 B&W**
Dir: Max Liebman   *Cast:* Sid Caesar, Imogene Coca, Carl Reiner, Howard Morris, Louis Nye, Swen Swanson
► Ten excerpts from "Your Show of

Shows," landmark 1950s TV comedy starring Caesar and Coca in various skits written by then-fledgling talents such as Mel Brooks, Woody Allen, and Larry Gelbart. Best bits are two spoofs: "From Here to Obscurity" with seaside lovers Caesar and Coca doused with buckets of water and "This Is Your Story" in which emcee Reiner is wickedly impervious to humiliation brought upon guest Caesar by review of his life. Only drawback to anthology of classic live comedy: kinescopes from which film is assembled give it crude, grainy look.

TEN LITTLE INDIANS 1966
★★ **NR Mystery-Suspense 1:32 B&W**
Dir: George Pollock *Cast:* Hugh O'Brian, Shirley Eaton, Fabian, Leo Genn, Stanley Holloway, Wilfrid Hyde-White
▶ So-so remake of *And Then There Were None* finds eight guests assembled at an Alpine retreat. They must learn the identity of their host, who plans to kill them one by one. Except for addition of rock star Fabian to cast, a faithful adaptation of Agatha Christie's novel and long-running play. Theatrical release featured two-minute "murder break" for viewers to guess the killer. Remade again in 1975 with Oliver Reed.

TEN LITTLE INDIANS 1975 British
★★★ **PG Mystery-Suspense 1:38**
☑ Violence
Dir: Peter Collinson *Cast:* Oliver Reed, Elke Sommer, Richard Attenborough, Gert Frobe, Herbert Lom, Charles Aznavour
▶ Bland version of the often-filmed Agatha Christie classic. Ten guests are invited to an isolated hotel in Iran where a mysterious murderer bumps them off one by one. Christie's plot struggles to retain its punch under Collinson's flat direction.

TENNESSEE'S PARTNER 1955
★★★ **NR Western 1:27**
Dir: Allan Dwan *Cast:* John Payne, Ronald Reagan, Rhonda Fleming, Coleen Gray, Anthony Caruso, Morris Ankrum
▶ When ranch hand Reagan saves gambler Payne's life during a barroom brawl, Payne proceeds to take over Reagan's life. Offering unwanted advice about women, gambling, and gunfights, he becomes a serious obstacle to Reagan's happiness with girlfriend Gray. Quirky Western loosely based on a Bret Harte short story has a subtle moral. Look

closely for Angie Dickinson as one of madam Fleming's girls.

TEN NORTH FREDERICK 1958
★★★ **NR Drama 1:42 B&W**
Dir: Philip Dunne *Cast:* Gary Cooper, Diane Varsi, Suzy Parker, Geraldine Fitzgerald, Tom Tully, Stuart Whitman
▶ Lawyer Cooper is pushed into politics by ambitious wife Fitzgerald. Fitzgerald ruins daughter Varsi's marriage to Whitman; Cooper tries to reach out to Varsi and falls in love with her roommate Parker, but the age difference dooms the affair. Adaptation of the John O'Hara novel.

10 RILLINGTON PLACE 1971 British
★★★ **PG Drama 1:51**
☑ Adult situations, explicit language, violence
Dir: Richard Fleischer *Cast:* Richard Attenborough, John Hurt, Judy Geeson, Pat Heywood, Isobel Black, Phyllis McMahon
▶ Attenborough is John Reginald Christie, serial rapist/murderer who tells neighbor Hurt he can abort wife Geeson's unwanted baby. Attenborough slays Geeson and couple's other child. Hurt is hanged for the crime because of Attenborough's perjury, leaving the killer free to commit more crimes. Somber and frightening depiction is based on a true story of innocent man's execution, which led to abolition of capital punishment in Britain.

TENTACLES 1977
☆ **PG Horror 1:30**
☑ Violence
Dir: Oliver Hellman *Cast:* Henry Fonda, John Huston, Shelley Winters, Bo Hopkins, Cesare Danova, Alan Boyd
▶ Industrialist Fonda, building marine tunnel off California, employs illegal radio frequencies, causing giant octopus to attack coastal dwellers. Snoopy reporter Huston tries to get to cause of chaos. Marine biologist Hopkins comes to rescue with team of trained killer whales for duel with octopus. Big-name actors deliver squid pro quo performances in *Jaws* rehash.

TENTH VICTIM, THE 1965 Italian
★★ **NR Sci-Fi 1:32**
Dir: Elio Petri *Cast:* Marcello Mastroianni, Ursula Andress, Elsa Martinelli, Salvo Randone, Massimo Serato
▶ In legalized murder game set in the future, hunter Andress seeks her much

coveted "tenth victim"; her chosen quarry, Mastroianni, would also like to kill Andress but things get complicated when the would-be killers fall in love. Charismatic leads and stylish direction illustrate provocative but thin screenplay. Dubbed.

10 TO MIDNIGHT 1983
★ ★ ★ ★ R Action-Adventure 1:42
☑ Nudity, adult situations, explicit language, violence
Dir: J. Lee Thompson *Cast:* Charles Bronson, Lisa Eilbacher, Andrew Stevens, Gene Davis, Wilford Brimley, Geoffrey Lewis
▶ Hard-boiled L.A. cop Bronson trails slasher Davis, whose next victim might be Bronson's daughter Eilbacher. Convinced of Davis's guilt but lacking evidence to convict him, Bronson tries unsuccessfully to frame the killer and is dismissed from the police force. Davis, once again free, stalks Eilbacher, prompting Bronson to take matters into own hands. Vigilante Bronson at his best.

TEQUILA SUNRISE 1988
★ ★ ★ R Drama 1:56
☑ Adult situations, explicit language, violence
Dir: Robert Towne *Cast:* Mel Gibson, Michelle Pfeiffer, Kurt Russell, Raul Julia, J. T. Walsh, Arliss Howard
▶ High school friends Gibson, a retired cocaine dealer, and Russell, a Los Angeles narcotics cop, fall for beautiful Pfeiffer, owner of a trendy restaurant. Or is Russell using Pfeiffer to implicate Gibson in a major drug deal? Attractive stars make the most of director Towne's often confusing screenplay, infusing remarkable romantic chemistry into weak action sequences.

TERMINAL CHOICE 1985 Canadian
★ ★ R Mystery-Suspense 1:39
☑ Brief nudity, adult situations, explicit language, violence
Dir: Sheldon Larry *Cast:* Joe Spano, Diane Venora, David McCallum, Robert Joy, Don Francks, Ellen Barkin
▶ Computer-automated hospital is plagued by a series of fatal mechanical malfunctions. Suspects include alcoholic surgeon Spano, his ex-girlfriend Venora, and sneaky lawyer Francks. Superior cast outweighs farfetched plot in this moderately suspenseful medical drama.

TERMINAL ENTRY 1987
★ R Action-Adventure 1:37
☑ Nudity, adult situations, explicit language, violence
Dir: John Kincaide *Cast:* Eddie Albert, Yaphet Kotto, Paul Smith, Heidi Helmer, Patrick Labyorteaux, Tracy Brooks Swope
▶ Teen computer hackers break into the Terminal Entry program and mistake it for an interactive antiterrorist game. Unfortunately, the program is actually an information source for Middle Eastern killers intent on assassinating the President. Federal security agents Albert and Kotto must find the hackers and the terrorists before an important peace conference begins. Despite good twists, clever premise isn't exploited effectively.

TERMINAL MAN, THE 1974
★ ★ ★ PG Sci-Fi 1:44
☑ Violence
Dir: Mike Hodges *Cast:* George Segal, Joan Hackett, Richard Dysart, Michael C. Gwynne, Donald Moffat, Jill Clayburgh
▶ Computer expert Segal develops murderous impulses after an accident; surgeon Dysart implants a microchip into his brain to control his violent tendencies. But a malfunction turns Segal into a killing machine. Grim adaptation of Michael Crichton's best-seller is often unpleasantly violent.

TERMINATOR, THE 1984
★ ★ ★ ★ R Sci-Fi/Action-Adventure 1:47
☑ Nudity, adult situations, explicit language, graphic violence
Dir: James Cameron *Cast:* Arnold Schwarzenegger, Michael Biehn, Linda Hamilton, Paul Winfield, Lance Henriksen
▶ Schwarzenegger, a twenty-first-century killer cyborg, travels in time to the present to assassinate Hamilton, the future mother of human race's savior; futuristic resistance fighter Biehn follows to save her. Biehn and Hamilton fall in love as they are pursued by Schwarzenegger. Blistering saga has it all: relentless pacing, incredible action, humor, and surprisingly affecting characterizations. A genre movie with guts and brains.

TERMS OF ENDEARMENT 1983
★ ★ ★ ★ ★ PG Comedy/Drama 2:12
☑ Adult situations, explicit language
Dir: James L. Brooks *Cast:* Shirley MacLaine, Debra Winger, Jack Nicholson,

Jeff Daniels, John Lithgow, Danny DeVito

▶ Sweeping Oscar winner—Best Picture, Director, Screenplay (Brooks), Actress (MacLaine), Supporting Actor (Nicholson)—explores the relationship between neurotic MacLaine and her determined daughter Winger, who marries philandering teacher Daniels against her mother's wishes. Endearing, full-bodied character portrayal from extraordinary cast, especially Nicholson as the womanizing, over-the-hill astronaut MacLaine loves. Based on the novel by Larry McMurtry. **(CC)**

TERROR BY NIGHT 1946
★ ★ ★ ★ NR **Mystery-Suspense 1:00 B&W**
Dir: Roy William Neill *Cast:* Basil Rathbone, Nigel Bruce, Alan Mowbray, Dennis Hoey, Renee Godfrey

▶ On a London-Edinburgh train, a diamond is stolen and its owner murdered. Sherlock Holmes (Rathbone) and Watson (Bruce) examine the various suspects and unmask the guilty party. Taut and tense mystery is one of the better Rathbone-Bruce efforts. Available in a colorized version. **(CC)**

TERROR IN THE AISLES 1984
★ ★ R **Horror 1:22 C/B&W**
☑ Nudity, adult situations, explicit language, graphic violence
Dir: Andrew Kuehn *Cast:* Donald Pleasence, Nancy Allen

▶ Exhausting compilation of classic moments from some 75 suspense and horror films (including *Strangers on a Train, Scanners, Carrie, Jaws, Alien, Rosemary's Baby*) feels like a feature-length trailer and unfortunately relies on clips that dissipate rather than build tension. Highlight is a brief interview with Alfred Hitchcock.

TERROR OF TINY TOWN, THE 1938
☆ NR **Western 1:06 B&W**
Dir: Sam Newfield *Cast:* Billy Curtis, Little Billy, Yvonne Moray, Billy Platt

▶ The first (and probably last) all-midget Western in movie history. Bad guy Billy attempts to get his greedy little hands on Tiny Town land by creating feuds between ranchers. Equally diminutive good guy Curtis thwarts him. Literally small in scope and pretty silly.

TERROR TRAIN 1980 Canadian
★ ★ R **Horror 1:37**
☑ Nudity, adult situations, explicit language, graphic violence
Dir: Roger Spottiswoode *Cast:* Ben

Johnson, Jamie Lee Curtis, Hart Bochner, David Copperfield, Derek MacKinnon, Sandee Currie

▶ Practical joke by medical students backfires when their victim goes insane. Three years later he sneaks aboard a chartered train to kill his tormentors during their masquerade party. Presence of veteran actors Curtis and Johnson (playing a friendly conductor) elevate this slightly above other slasher films. Directing debut for Spottiswoode.

TERRORVISION 1986
☆ R **Horror 1:23**
☑ Nudity, adult situations, explicit language, graphic violence
Dir: Ted Nicolaou *Cast:* Jennifer Richards, Diane Franklin, Gerrit Graham, Mary Woronov, Chad Allen, Alejandro Rey

▶ Typical suburban family receives a strange signal from outer space on their new satellite dish. Curiosity turns to horror when a revolting monster suddenly pops out of their TV set. Weak attempt at satire relies heavily on disgusting slime special effects.

TERRY FOX STORY, THE 1983
★ ★ ★ ★ NR **Biography/MFTV 1:37**
☑ Adult situations, explicit language
Dir: Ralph L. Thomas *Cast:* Eric Fryer, Robert Duvall, Michael Zelniker, Chris Makepeace, Rosaline Chao

▶ True story of courage and heroism dramatizes the life of Terry Fox (Fryer), the Canadian who, despite his leg amputation, ran three thousand miles across Canada. His effort raised more than $20 million for cancer research. Duvall plays Bill Vigers, the public relations man who befriends Fox; Makepeace appears as Terry's brother and Chao, his girlfriend. HBO's first original film.

TESS 1980 French/British
★ ★ ★ PG **Drama 2:55**
☑ Adult situations
Dir: Roman Polanski *Cast:* Nastassia Kinski, Peter Firth, Leigh Dawson, John Collin, Tony Church

▶ Thomas Hardy's classic 1891 tale about the enchanting Tess (Kinski), a free spirit who is seduced, impregnated, and abandoned by her cousin Dawson. She finds love with Angel Clair (Firth) but he, too, abandons her when he discovers the secret of her past affair. Old-fashioned, gloriously detailed film won Oscars for

Cinematography, Art Direction, and Costume Design.

TESTAMENT 1983
★★★ **PG Drama 1:30**
☑ Adult situations, explicit language
Dir: Lynne Littman *Cast:* Jane Alexander, William Devane, Ross Harris, Lukas Haas, Roxana Zal, Philip Anglim
► Typical suburban mom Alexander sends commuter hubby Devane off to work in San Francisco and copes with errands and kids Harris, Haas, and Zal on seemingly average day, only to witness drastic changes in wake of nuclear holocaust. Contamination by radioactive fallout, isolation from rest of world, breakdown of law, and shortages of basic supplies become the new norm as death and despair sweep through once-placid community. Restrained, sure-handed look at morbid topic carried by Oscar-nominated Alexander. Rebecca De Mornay and Kevin Costner appear in bit roles. **(CC)**

TEST OF LOVE, A 1985 Australian
★★★★ **PG Drama 1:33**
☑ Adult situations
Dir: Gil Brealey *Cast:* Angela Punch-McGregor, Drew Forsythe, Tina Arhondis, Charles Tingwell, Monica Maughan, Mark Butler
► Young Arhondis, brain-damaged at birth, has lived for years in home for spastics. New doctor McGregor believes Arhondis, although physically incapacitated, is mentally alert and perhaps of above-average intelligence. McGregor teaches Arhondis, who has been treated as a vegetable by uncaring, conservative doctors, to communicate by signs and symbols. Ultimately, McGregor initiates court contest to free girl from institution. Moving drama is based on a true story.

TEX 1982
★★★ **PG Drama 1:43**
☑ Adult situations, explicit language, mild violence
Dir: Tim Hunter *Cast:* Matt Dillon, Jim Metzler, Meg Tilly, Bill McKinney, Ben Johnson, Emilio Estevez
► Left alone for long stints by widower father McKinney, high school senior Metzler struggles to raise younger brother Dillon. Dillon's unsupervised life offers ample opportunities for first tentative experiences with drugs, alcohol, girls, class differences, crime, and death. Best pal Estevez pushes drugs while his tomboy sister Tilly catches Dillon's eye; their rich father Johnson doesn't approve of either hanging out with poor boy Dillon. Adapted from the novel by S. E. Hinton.

TEXAS CHAINSAW MASSACRE, THE 1974
★ **R Horror 1:23**
☑ Graphic violence
Dir: Tobe Hooper *Cast:* Marilyn Burns, Gunnar Hansen, Allen Danziger, Paul A. Partain, William Vail, Edwin Neal
► Five friends travel through Texas and discover a seemingly deserted house that turns out to be not so empty; residents include a crazy father and his two sons who proceed to menace the hapless group with hammers, meat hooks, and chainsaws. Horrifying and suspenseful but also quite violent and repellent. **(CC)**

TEXAS CHAINSAW MASSACRE PART 2 1986
☆ **NR Horror 1:35**
☑ Explicit language, graphic violence
Dir: Tobe Hooper *Cast:* Dennis Hopper, Caroline Williams, Bill Johnson, Jim Siedow, Bill Moseley, Lou Perry
► Sequel to cult horror classic brings back chili chef Siedow and his clan of cannibalistic corpse-robbers. Bible-thumping Texas Ranger Hopper seeks to avenge murder of kin in earlier pic while local DJ Williams, hoping to expose slash-happy family, winds up screaming a lot as captive in underground chamber of horrors. Tongue-in-cheek script offers some laughs, but slice-and-dice exploitation is for diehards only.

THANK GOD IT'S FRIDAY 1978
★★ **PG Musical/Comedy 1:29**
☑ Explicit language
Dir: Robert Klane *Cast:* Donna Summer, Valerie Landsburg, Terri Nunn, Chick Vennera, Ray Vitte, Mark Lonow
► One night in the lives of a crowd at a Los Angeles disco. Ensemble turns include unknown singer Summer in first break en route to stardom, dance-crazy Mexican-American Vennera who wins big boogie contest, underage girls Landsburg and Nunn who get first taste of nightclub life, and disco's manic DJ Vitte. In smaller parts are Jeff Goldblum and Debra Winger; the Commodores appear in finale as themselves. Summer's hit "Last Dance" won an Oscar.

THANK YOUR LUCKY STARS 1943
★★ NR Musical 2:07 B&W
Dir: David Butler *Cast:* Eddie Cantor, Joan Leslie, Dennis Morgan, Dinah Shore, S. Z. Sakall, Edward Everett Horton
▶ Dated but enjoyable concoction about Cantor producing a show with Sakall and Horton was Warner Brothers' contribution to the World War II effort. Their top stars and contract players appear in a variety of song-and-dance numbers to benefit the Hollywood Canteen. Highlights include Bette Davis belting out the Oscar-nominated "They're Either Too Young or Too Old" and Errol Flynn performing the sly "That's What You Jolly Well Get." Shore's film debut.

THAT CHAMPIONSHIP SEASON 1982
★★ R Drama 1:49
☑ Adult situations, explicit language, violence
Dir: Jason Miller *Cast:* Bruce Dern, Robert Mitchum, Stacy Keach, Martin Sheen, Paul Sorvino
▶ Miller adapted his own Pulitzer prize–winning play to the screen. Friends Dern, Keach, Sheen, and Sorvino join their ex-coach Mitchum for the twenty-fourth annual reunion of their high school basketball team, the champs of 1957. The booze flows freely and the talk turns personal. In various ways, each of the men reveals himself as a washout; the only real "winner" is the team member who failed to show up. Excellent cast, especially Mitchum, but the upbeat ending denies everything that has gone on beforehand.

THAT DARN CAT 1965
★★★★ G Family 1:56
Dir: Robert Stevenson *Cast:* Hayley Mills, Dean Jones, Dorothy Provine, Roddy McDowall, Neville Brand, Elsa Lanchester
▶ Amusing Disney romp about a kidnapped banker who hides clue to his whereabouts on the collar of Mills's Siamese cat; FBI agent Jones is dragged through entertaining slapstick situations keeping an eye on the feline. Bright cast includes comic pros William Demarest, Frank Gorshin, and Ed Wynn.

THAT HAMILTON WOMAN 1941
★★★★ NR Biography/Drama 2:05 B&W
Dir: Alexander Korda *Cast:* Vivien Leigh, Laurence Olivier, Alan Mowbray, Gladys Cooper, Henry Wilcoxon, Sara Allgood
▶ Napoleonic Era: beautiful Leigh weds ambassador Mowbray, becomes Lady Hamilton, then falls for Lord Nelson (Olivier), the famous naval commander. Their scandalous romance shocks the world and ends in tragedy. The glamour and magic of then-real-life spouses Leigh and Olivier make this lovingly produced true story one of the most achingly romantic movies of all time. Heart-tugging curtain line: "There was no then, there was no after."

THAT'LL BE THE DAY 1974 British
★ PG Drama 1:26
☑ Explicit language
Dir: Claude Whatham *Cast:* David Essex, Ringo Starr, Rosemary Leach, James Booth, Billy Fury, Keith Moon
▶ Real-life musician Essex brings depth and insight to his role as an alienated youth in late 1950s England who dreams of becoming a rock star. Loosely inspired by the life of John Lennon, film provides accurate look at early music scene in working-class Britain. Sequel: *Stardust*.

THAT OBSCURE OBJECT OF DESIRE 1977 French/Spanish
☆ R Comedy 1:40
☑ Nudity, adult situations, explicit language
Dir: Luis Buñuel *Cast:* Fernando Rey, Angela Molina, Carole Bouquet, Julian Bertheau, Andre Weber, Milena Vukotic
▶ Against a background of terrorist attacks, rich widower Rey falls for younger woman and pursues her obsessively. The object of Rey's desire has a personality so complex that the part is played by two different actresses (the volcanic Molina and the willowy Bouquet). Oscar nominations for Best Foreign Film and Screenplay Adaptation went to Buñuel's last movie.
Ⓢ

THAT'S DANCING! 1985
★★★★ G Dance 1:44
Dir: Jack Haley, Jr. *Cast:* Gene Kelly, Sammy Davis, Jr., Mikhail Baryshnikov, Liza Minnelli, Ray Bolger
▶ Clips trace the history of dance on film, including Depression-era Busby Berkeley, teaming of young Shirley Temple and tap master Bill Robinson, Fred Astaire and Ginger Rogers, and contemporary ballet and rock dancing. Other noteworthy appearances include Jimmy Cagney, Ruby Keeler, Ann Miller, Cyd Charisse, and, in

pitch to younger viewers, John Travolta and Michael Jackson. In an attempt to be all-inclusive, dance jamboree has some slow spots, but highlights can't be beat.

THAT'S ENTERTAINMENT! 1974
★★★★★ G Musical 2:12
Dir: Jack Haley, Jr. *Cast:* Fred Astaire, Liza Minnelli, Frank Sinatra, Bing Crosby, Gene Kelly, Elizabeth Taylor
▶ Compilation of the best numbers from classic MGM musicals may be even more fun than its sources because you don't have to sit through dialogue scenes (writer-director Haley's narration is intelligent and unobtrusive). Among many, many highlights: young Judy Garland singing "Dear Mr. Gable," Esther Williams's lavish water ballets, and Astaire dancing on the ceiling in *Royal Wedding*.

THAT'S ENTERTAINMENT, PART 2 1976
★★★★ G Musical 2:13
Dir: Gene Kelly *Cast:* Fred Astaire, Gene Kelly
▶ Sequel to *That's Entertainment* provides more clips from MGM musical greats as well as material from the studio's non-musical classics (like the Marx Brothers' hilarious stateroom scene from *A Night at the Opera* and William Powell, Myrna Loy, and Asta in *The Thin Man*). In between, Kelly and Astaire narrate and show they can still hoof effectively in new numbers made especially for this film.

THAT'S LIFE! 1986
★★★ PG-13 Comedy/Drama 1:42
☑ Explicit language
Dir: Blake Edwards *Cast:* Julie Andrews, Jack Lemmon, Sally Kellerman, Robert Loggia, Rob Knepper
▶ It's Harvey's sixtieth birthday and he's suffering a bad case of male menopause in this seriously funny Edwards comedy. Harvey (Lemmon) has everything a man could want, but he's throwing tantrums like a childish brat; he's also making everyone miserable, including his wife Gillian (Andrews, a.k.a. Mrs. Edwards), a show biz singer with very real problems of her own. **(CC)**

THAT TOUCH OF MINK 1962
★★★ NR Comedy 1:39
Dir: Delbert Mann *Cast:* Cary Grant, Doris Day, Gig Young, Audrey Meadows, John Astin, Dick Sargent
▶ Out-of-work Day meets rich Grant when his limo goes through a puddle and splashes her. Grant tries to woo the virginal Day with wealth and charm. Will she succumb to his advances? Familiar story works nicely; amusing Oscar-nominated screenplay and pleasant performances. Cameos by Mickey Mantle, Roger Maris, and Yogi Berra.

THAT WAS ROCK (THE T.A.M.I./T.N.T. SHOW) 1984
★★★ NR Music/MFTV 1:32 B&W
Dir: Steve Binder, Larry Peerce *Cast:* Chuck Berry, James Brown, Ray Charles, Marvin Gaye, The Rolling Stones, The Supremes
▶ *The T.A.M.I. Show* (1964) and *The Big T.N.T. Show* (1966) were two of the greatest rock 'n' roll extravaganzas; this compilation features the best of both with a remastered soundtrack. Since both were shot on videotape and transferred to film, picture quality is poor. However, unbeatable stars (also including Bo Diddley, Smokey Robinson and the Miracles, and Ike and Tina Turner) are captured in incredible performances. Also known as *Born to Rock: The T.A.M.I. Show/The T.N.T. Show*.

THAT WAS THEN . . . THIS IS NOW 1985
★★★ R Drama 1:43
☑ Adult situations, explicit language, mild violence
Dir: Christopher Cain *Cast:* Emilio Estevez, Craig Sheffer, Kim Delaney, Jill Schoelen, Barbara Babcock, Morgan Freeman
▶ Disillusioned orphan Estevez has been raised by widow Babcock and her son Sheffer. Sheffer and Estevez take different paths towards adulthood: Sheffer romances cute waitress Delaney and takes on responsibilities while Estevez deals drugs and steals cars. Estevez's deviant behavior puts strain on once-close friendship. Adaptation of S. E. Hinton novel, with screenplay by Estevez, has fine cast but is unrelentingly glum. **(CC)**

THEATRE OF BLOOD 1973 British
★★ R Horror/Comedy 1:44
☑ Explicit language, graphic violence
Dir: Douglas Hickox *Cast:* Vincent Price, Diana Rigg, Ian Hendry, Robert Morley, Coral Browne, Jack Hawkins
▶ Mad ham Price lives out an actor's ultimate revenge fantasy: with the aid of his daughter Rigg, he literally knocks the critics dead in the styles of his favorite

Shakespearean scenes. Ghoulishly funny stuff, deliciously acted by Price and Rigg, has earned cult movie status.

THEM! 1954
★★★ NR Sci-Fi 1:34 B&W
Dir: Gordon Douglas **Cast:** James Whitmore, Edmund Gwenn, Joan Weldon, James Arness, Onslow Stevens, Chris Drake
▶ New Mexico State Troopers Whitmore and Drake find a terrified girl inside the remains of a trailer home; scientist Gwenn and his daughter Weldon discover that nearby radiation tests have spawned a nest of vicious, giant ants. Working with FBI agent Arness, they trace the ants to the storm sewers of Los Angeles. Influential, often terrifying adventure boasts marvelous special effects and a thoughtful script. Look for Fess Parker and Leonard Nimoy in small roles.

THERE'S A GIRL IN MY SOUP 1970
British
★★ R Comedy 1:35
☑ Adult situations, explicit language
Dir: Roy Boulting **Cast:** Peter Sellers, Goldie Hawn, Diana Dors, Nicky Henson, Tony Britton
▶ In London, womanizing English TV host Sellers falls for free-spirited American Hawn, but her unfaithful fiancé Henson creates problems for the relationship. Sellers and Hawn bring chemistry and comic skill to an amusing but thin screenplay.

THERE'S NO BUSINESS LIKE SHOW BUSINESS 1954
★★★★★ NR Musical 1:57
Dir: Walter Lang **Cast:** Ethel Merman, Donald O'Connor, Marilyn Monroe, Dan Dailey, Mitzi Gaynor, Johnny Ray
▶ Vaudeville couple Merman and Dailey and their kids Gaynor, O'Connor, and Ray form a successful act. Ray leaves to become a priest and O'Connor suffers through rocky romance with opening act Monroe but, in the end, all realize there's no business like show business. Very enjoyable; marvelous Irving Berlin score includes "Alexander's Ragtime Band," Monroe singing "Heat Wave," and Merman belting title tune. **(CC)**

THERE WAS A CROOKED MAN . . . 1970
★★★ R Western/Comedy 2:03
☑ Nudity, adult situations, explicit language, mild violence
Dir: Joseph L. Mankiewicz **Cast:** Kirk Douglas, Henry Fonda, Hume Cronyn, Warren Oates, Burgess Meredith, Lee Grant
▶ Outlaw Douglas pulls off big heist but is then arrested. Sheriff Fonda, who nabbed Douglas, becomes prison warden and tries to reform conditions. Douglas cooperates with Fonda but secretly plans to escape and reclaim his loot. Fascinating and outrageous Western is a bit overlong but the cast (especially Douglas and Fonda) is outstanding.

THESE THREE 1936
★★★ NR Drama 1:33 B&W
Dir: William Wyler **Cast:** Miriam Hopkins, Merle Oberon, Joel McCrea, Bonita Granville, Margaret Hamilton, Walter Brennan
▶ Boarding-school brat Granville (Oscar-nominated) spreads lies about officials Hopkins, Oberon, and McCrea, the man they both love, leading to personal and professional trouble for the threesome. Excellent acting and masterful direction highlight this adaptation by Lillian Hellman of her play *The Children's Hour.* Dated but worthwhile.

THEY ALL LAUGHED 1981
★★ PG Romance/Comedy 1:55
☑ Adult situations, explicit language
Dir: Peter Bogdanovich **Cast:** Audrey Hepburn, Ben Gazzara, John Ritter, Colleen Camp, Dorothy Stratten, Patti Hansen
▶ Private eyes Gazzara and Ritter are assigned to tail beautiful wives Hepburn and Stratten and fall in love with their respective quarries. Meanwhile country-western singer Camp and sultry cabbie Hansen provide additional romantic entanglements while others at agency have love complications of their own. Terrific-looking cast and authentic Manhattan setting, but romantic comedy never really takes off. Director Bogdanovich dedicated film to Stratten, killed by her husband after film's completion; her story was filmed as *Star 80.*

THEY CALL ME BRUCE 1982
★★ PG Action-Adventure/Comedy 1:27
☑ Brief nudity, explicit language, violence
Dir: Elliot Hong **Cast:** Johnny Yune, Margaux Hemingway, Ralph Mauro, Pam Huntington
▶ Named for the famed karate champ Bruce Lee, Yune plays a totally inept

Mafia cook. He drops out of karate school but accidentally becomes a hero when he foils a robbery. Chop-socky spoof also known as a *A Fistful of Chopsticks*. Sequel: *They Still Call Me Bruce*.

THEY CALL ME MISTER TIBBS! 1970
★ ★ ★ PG Mystery-Suspense 1:48
☑ Adult situations, explicit language, violence
Dir: Gordon Douglas *Cast:* Sidney Poitier, Martin Landau, Barbara McNair, Anthony Zerbe, Jeff Corey, David Sheiner
▶ Tough cop Poitier investigates prostitute's murder; his close friend, activist priest Landau, is chief suspect. Poitier's aggressive pursuit of all likely killers leads to several threats on his life. Poitier recreated his enormously popular *In the Heat of the Night* character Virgil Tibbs and made his uncredited directorial debut by helming a number of scenes. Third (and last) in series of Tibbs films was *The Organization*.

THEY CALL ME TRINITY 1971 Italian
★ ★ G Western 1:49
Dir: E. B. Clucher (Enzo Barboni) *Cast:* Terence Hill, Bud Spencer, Farley Granger, Steffen Zacharias, Dan Sturkie, Gisela Hahn
▶ Lighthearted spoof of spaghetti Westerns about amoral sheriff Hill and his dopey half-brother Spencer, who are unexpectedly forced to defend a Mormon family from Mexican bandits. Surprise international success led to sequel *They Still Call Me Trinity*.

THEY CAME FROM WITHIN 1975 Canadian
☆ R Horror 1:27
☑ Nudity, adult situations, explicit language, graphic violence
Dir: David Cronenberg *Cast:* Paul Hampton, Joe Silver, Lynn Lowry, Allen Magicovsky, Susan Petrie, Barbara Steele
▶ Scientist specializing in parasites infects his mistress with a mutant bug that turns her into a sexually voracious maniac. She subsequently spreads the parasite to most of the occupants of a Canadian high rise. Intriguing allegory on venereal disease features incredibly disgusting special effects. Also known as *Shivers* and *The Parasite Murders*.

THEY CAME TO CORDURA 1959
★ ★ NR Western 2:03
Dir: Robert Rossen *Cast:* Gary Cooper,

Rita Hayworth, Van Heflin, Tab Hunter, Richard Conte, Dick York
▶ In 1916, accused coward Cooper and alleged traitor Hayworth accompany five American army heroes on a forced march through the Mexican desert. During the arduous journey, Cooper proves his actual worth and the others demonstrate their darker natures. Gritty and tough; Cooper and Hayworth are quite affecting.

THEY DIED WITH THEIR BOOTS ON 1941
★ ★ ★ NR Western 2:18 B&W
Dir: Raoul Walsh *Cast:* Errol Flynn, Olivia de Havilland, Arthur Kennedy, Charley Grapewin, Anthony Quinn
▶ True story of General George Custer (Flynn) traces his early days at West Point, his courtship and marriage to de Havilland, his military triumphs, and the Little Big Horn massacre. As a history lesson, the movie is distorted; as large-scale entertainment, amazingly exciting. Flynn is outstanding. Available in a colorized version.

THEY DRIVE BY NIGHT 1940
★ ★ NR Drama 1:33 B&W
Dir: Raoul Walsh *Cast:* George Raft, Ann Sheridan, Ida Lupino, Humphrey Bogart, Alan Hale, Roscoe Karns
▶ Trucker brothers Raft and Bogart encounter dangers in life on the road; Bogart is crippled after a crash while Raft gets involved with Lupino, the scheming wife of boss Hale. Gripping and realistic with hard-nosed acting and direction. Available in a colorized version.

THEY GOT ME COVERED 1943
★ ★ NR Comedy 1:34 B&W
Dir: David Butler *Cast:* Bob Hope, Dorothy Lamour, Otto Preminger, Lenore Aubert, Donald Meek
▶ Reporter Hope, canned for making wrong prediction about World War II, gets redemption by uncovering Nazi bigwig Preminger's plot to destroy Washington. Fast-paced and enormously funny comedy with Hope at his peak, wisecracking his way out of tight spots with clever one-liners, ably supported by lovely Lamour and a hairy Preminger.

THEY LIVE 1988
★ ★ R Sci-Fi 1:37
☑ Nudity, explicit language, violence
Dir: John Carpenter *Cast:* Roddy Piper, Keith David, Meg Foster, George

"Buck" Flower, Peter Jason, Raymond St. Jacques
▶ Construction worker Piper acquires special pair of sunglasses that reveal seemingly normal folk as aliens. Piper becomes a hunted man as he teams with co-worker David to stop the invaders. Intriguing paranoid premise provides vehicle for breathlessly paced stunts and escapes.

THEY LIVE BY NIGHT 1949
★★ NR Drama 1:35 B&W
Dir: Nicholas Ray   *Cast:* Farley Granger, Cathy O'Donnell, Howard da Silva, Jay C. Flippen, Helen Craig, Will Wright
▶ Naive convict Granger joins hardened criminals da Silva and Flippen in an escape attempt. Wounded in an accident, he's nursed to health by equally naive teen O'Donnell, who quickly falls in love. Although desperate to elude his past, the two are hounded by police until they meet a tragic fate. A classic example of film noir, Ray's directing debut is a moody, tense study of implacable destiny. Based on Edward Anderson's novel *Thieves Like Us*, and remade under that title in 1974.

THEY MADE ME A CRIMINAL 1939
★★ NR Drama 1:32 B&W
Dir: Busby Berkeley   *Cast:* John Garfield, Gloria Dickson, Claude Rains, Ann Sheridan, May Robson, Billy Halop
▶ Boxing champ Garfield, told he has murdered a reporter, flees to Arizona under an assumed name. Pursued by detective Rains, he finds a measure of self-respect on a farm for juvenile delinquents. Will he sacrifice his freedom to help the boys in a prize fight? The Dead End Kids (Halop, Leo Gorcey, Bobby Jordan, Huntz Hall, Gabriel Dell) provide some humor in this dated but sincere drama.

THEY MIGHT BE GIANTS 1971
★★ G Comedy/Drama 1:38
Dir: Anthony Harvey   *Cast:* George C. Scott, Joanne Woodward, Jack Gilford, Rue McClanahan, Lester Rawlins, Kitty Winn
▶ New York psychiatrist Dr. Watson (Woodward) examines patient Scott, who believes he is Sherlock Holmes. This unusual Holmes-Watson team gets involved in a mystery as Scott's relative Rawlins schemes to get his hands on the family fortune. Unusual and interesting;

Scott has a grand time with his role and Woodward plays off him skillfully. Adapted by James Goldman from his play.

THEY'RE PLAYING WITH FIRE 1984
★★ R Mystery-Suspense 1:36
☑ Strong sexual content, violence
Dir: Howard Avedis   *Cast:* Sybil Danning, Eric Brown, Andrew Prine, Paul Clemens, Gene Bicknell, K. T. Stevens
▶ College student Brown is seduced by sexy professor Danning. Danning and her husband Prine then blackmail Brown into scaring his grandmother to death. Tasteless and pedestrian, with stomach-turning violence and explicit sex scenes.

THEY SAVED HITLER'S BRAIN 1964
☆ NR Sci-Fi 1:14
Dir: David Bradley   *Cast:* Walter Stocker, Audrey Caire, Carlos Rivas, John Holland
▶ Caire and husband Stocker, looking for missing relatives, encounter group of unrepentant Nazis instead. The boys have indeed saved the Führer's cranium and plot to take over the world. Campy and so inept that it provides unintentional laughs.

THEY SHOOT HORSES, DON'T THEY? 1969
★★ PG-13 Drama 2:01
☑ Adult situations, explicit language, violence
Dir: Sydney Pollack   *Cast:* Jane Fonda, Michael Sarrazin, Susannah York, Gig Young, Red Buttons, Bonnie Bedelia
▶ Chicago dance marathon of 1930s serves as microcosm of life. Disagreeable loner Fonda, pregnant farm girl Bedelia, sultry aspiring actress York, and sailor Buttons are among the marathoners goaded toward self-destruction by sadistic emcee Young over period of weeks for $1500 prize. Fonda established herself as a serious actress, standing out among many splendid performances. Nominated for nine Oscars; Young won Supporting Actor.

THEY WERE EXPENDABLE 1945
★★★★ NR War 2:15 B&W
Dir: John Ford   *Cast:* Robert Montgomery, John Wayne, Donna Reed, Jack Holt, Ward Bond, Leon Ames
▶ Classic World War II adventure about the doomed battle for the Philippines concentrates on Montgomery, the leader of a squad of PT boats, and his second-in-command Wayne, an officer

impatient with the squad's minor duties until his men fall victim to overpowering Japanese. Despite story's tragic outcome, director Ford emphasizes the heroic in inspiring vignettes of fighting. Montgomery's role was based on PT captain John Bulkeley, who won the Congressional Medal of Honor.

THEY WON'T BELIEVE ME 1947
★★ NR Drama 1:35 B&W
Dir: Irving Pichel *Cast:* Robert Young, Susan Hayward, Jane Greer, Rita Johnson, Tom Powers, George Tyne
▶ Grim tale of amoral rake Young who marries Johnson for her money, then starts affairs with writer Greer and secretary Hayward. Murder and blackmail force him to flee to Jamaica, but in an unexpected twist he is arrested in a suicide case. Strong drama features a great trick ending. Young is impressive in a rare villainous role.

THEY WON'T FORGET 1937
★★ NR Drama 1:35 B&W
Dir: Mervyn LeRoy *Cast:* Claude Rains, Gloria Dickson, Edward Norris, Otto Kruger, Allyn Joslyn, Lana Turner
▶ When sexpot student Turner is slain during a Confederate Day parade, ambitious district attorney Rains accuses Yankee teacher Norris of the crime and railroads a conviction. Shocking drama of justice gone awry was based on the 1915 events that initiated the revival of the Ku Klux Klan. Turner and her soon-famous sweater were only on screen for the opening minutes, but her striking appearance and the legend of her discovery at Schwab's soda fountain made her an overnight sensation.

THIEF 1981
★★★★ R Crime 1:58
☑ Adult situations, explicit language, violence
Dir: Michael Mann *Cast:* James Caan, Tuesday Weld, Willie Nelson, James Belushi, Robert Prosky
▶ Character portrait examines diamond thief Caan's struggle to remain independent of mob influence. Caught between the middle class values of his wife Weld and the criminal ambitions of vicious mob boss Prosky, Caan decides to pull one last diamond heist to get enough money to live straight. Nelson plays Caan's jailhouse mentor. Gripping and meticulously crafted drama was first theatrical film for Mann.

THIEF OF BAGDAD, THE 1940 British
★★★★ NR Fantasy/Action-Adventure 1:46
Dir: Michael Powell, Ludwig Berger, Tim Whelan *Cast:* Sabu, Conrad Veidt, John Justin, June Duprez, Rex Ingram
▶ Thief Sabu is aided by genie Ingram and magic carpet in his quest to help prince Justin regain his kingdom from evil magician Veidt. The ultimate Arabian Nights movie is a treat for the eye and ear with wondrous special effects (including a giant spider and a flying toy horse), perfect casting (especially the rascally Sabu), exceptional music score, and larger-than-life storytelling. Three Oscars (Special Effects, Color Cinematography, Art Direction).

THIEF OF HEARTS 1984
★★★ R Drama 1:40
☑ Nudity, strong sexual content, explicit language, violence
Dir: Douglas Day Stewart *Cast:* Steven Bauer, Barbara Williams, John Getz, David Caruso, Christine Ebersole, George Wendt
▶ San Francisco thief Bauer robs house with help from buddy Caruso. They take money and private journals belonging to the beautiful Williams. Bauer becomes obsessed with the fantasies Williams has written in her journal, spies on her and eventually, they meet and fall into bed. Complications arise with her husband and Bauer's partner, who kills a cop on their next job. Beautifully shot, well acted and edited; weak dialogue but, on the whole, delivers. Video features more explicit sex than the theatrically released version. **(CC)**

THIEF WHO CAME TO DINNER, THE 1973
★★★ PG Comedy 1:45
☑ Adult situations, explicit language
Dir: Bud Yorkin *Cast:* Ryan O'Neal, Jacqueline Bisset, Warren Oates, Jill Clayburgh, Ned Beatty
▶ Bored computer programmer O'Neal chucks the straight life to become Houston's most successful jewel thief. He falls for bemused society girl Bisset, befriends insurance investigator Oates, and is seduced by his ex-wife Clayburgh. Caper comedy is harmless enough but rather short on laughs.

THIN BLUE LINE, THE 1988
★★★★ NR Documentary 1:46
☑ Explicit language, violence

Dir: Errol Morris **Cast:** Randall Adams, David Harris, Edith James, Dennis White, Sam Kittrell
▶ Unnerving study of the chance encounter in 1976 between hitchhiker Randall Adams and runaway David Harris that led to the murder of a Texas policeman. Although proclaiming his innocence, Adams was sentenced to death on Harris's testimony. But through adroit re-creations and interviews, director Morris reveals the possibility of a horrible miscarriage of justice. Ominous Philip Glass score adds to the tension in this first-rate documentary, which helped convince Texas Court of Criminal Appeals to overturn Adams's conviction.

THING, THE 1951
★★★★ **NR Sci-Fi 1:20 B&W**
Dir: Christian Nyby **Cast:** Kenneth Tobey, Margaret Sheridan, Robert Cornthwaite, Douglas Spencer, James Young, James Arness
▶ Arctic scientists uncover a frozen alien that, when thawed, runs amok through their isolated outpost. Influential, thrilling study of a peer group's grace under pressure is among the best of all sci-fi films. Rich characters, rapid dialogue, exotic Dimitri Tiomkin score, and streamlined direction (often credited to producer Howard Hawks) add up to immensely exciting entertainment. Full title: *The Thing From Another Planet.* Remade in 1982.

THING, THE 1982
★★★ **R Sci-Fi 1:49**
☑ Explicit language, graphic violence
Dir: John Carpenter **Cast:** Kurt Russell, A. Wilford Brimley, T. K. Carter, David Clennon, Keith David, Richard Dysart
▶ American scientists at remote Antarctic research center stumble across a buried spaceship and unleash a fierce alien capable of transforming into any shape. Technically accomplished remake of the 1951 film remains truer to John W. Campbell, Jr.'s novella *Who Goes There?,* but tension and characterizations take a back seat to gruesome special effects.

THINGS ARE TOUGH ALL OVER 1982
★★ **R Comedy 1:30**
☑ Nudity, adult situations, explicit language, adult humor
Dir: Thomas K. Avildsen **Cast:** Cheech Marin, Thomas Chong, Shelby Fiddis, Rikki Marin, Evelyn Guerrero, Rip Taylor
▶ Popular comedians Cheech and Chong play dual roles: their usual buffoonish selves and the rich Arabs who hire them in Chicago to drive a limo carrying secret stash of $5 million. High jinks revolve around loss of the money and attempts to recover the loot before meeting employers in Las Vegas. Fans will be delighted by comics' customary clowning.

THINGS CHANGE 1988
★★ **PG Comedy 1:40**
☑ Brief nudity, adult situations, explicit language
Dir: David Mamet **Cast:** Don Ameche, Joe Mantegna, Robert Prosky, J. J. Johnston, Ricky Jay, Mike Nussbaum
▶ Italian shoeshine man Ameche, bearing uncanny resemblance to mobster facing jail term, agrees to take the rap and enter prison; guard Mantegna decides to give him final whirl at Lake Tahoe. Bittersweet fable written by director Mamet and Shel Silverstein has glowing performance by Ameche and intermittently sharp dialogue, but leaden pacing and trick ending are drawbacks.

THINGS TO COME 1936 British
★★ **NR Sci-Fi 1:32 B&W**
Dir: William Cameron Menzies **Cast:** Raymond Massey, Ralph Richardson, Edward Chapman, Margaret Scott, Cedric Hardwicke, Maurice Bradell
▶ In a war-ravaged, plague-ridden future, despot Richardson rules over the remains of Everytown until Massey and a team of scientists bring peace and build a new world. Years later, artist Hardwicke leads a rebellion against the soulless, high-tech society. Visually stunning science fiction epic, with screenplay by H. G. Wells from his essay *The Shape of Things to Come,* suffers somewhat from stilted dialogue and lack of drama.

THING WITH TWO HEADS, THE 1979
☆ **PG Horror/Comedy 1:33**
☑ Adult humor
Dir: Lee Frost **Cast:** Ray Milland, Rosey Grier, Don Marshall, Chelsea Brown, Roger Perry
▶ Bigot Milland conducts head-transplant experiments to beat terminal cancer, but in a mix-up he finds himself stitched onto the body of Grier, a black convicted killer. The two disparate, hate-filled heads make for some interesting arguments and silly gags. An insane premise done with enough energy to elicit some chuckles.

THIN MAN, THE 1934
★★★★ NR Mystery-Suspense 1:33 B&W
Dir: W. S. Van Dyke II *Cast:* William Powell, Myrna Loy, Maureen O'Sullivan, Nat Pendleton, Cesar Romero, Edward Ellis
▶ Wealthy heiress O'Sullivan contacts retired detective Nick Charles (Powell) to find her missing father Ellis. Nick's wife Nora (Loy) and dog Asta provide invaluable assistance in cracking the case. Sparkling adaptation of Dashiell Hammett's novel introduced one of film's best-loved duos. The tipsy, wisecracking, and happily married Charleses inspired five lesser sequels, a TV series, and countless imitators—although the "Thin Man" sobriquet actually refers to Ellis, not Powell.

THIN MAN GOES HOME, THE 1944
★★ NR Mystery-Suspense 1:40 B&W
Dir: Richard Thorpe *Cast:* William Powell, Myrna Loy, Gloria De Haven, Anne Revere, Lucile Watson, Harry Davenport
▶ Nick and Nora Charles (Powell, Loy) return to his hometown to see parents Davenport and Watson, but their vacation is cut short when they investigate the murder of a local painter. Fifth installment in the series is okay but not one of their better efforts.

THIRD MAN, THE 1949 British
★★★ NR Mystery-Suspense 1:45 B&W
Dir: Carol Reed *Cast:* Orson Welles, Joseph Cotten, Valli, Trevor Howard, Paul Hoerbiger, Ernst Deutsch
▶ Haunting, superbly directed classic improves with each viewing. Cotten is marvelous as a writer of pulp Westerns searching the ruins of post–World War II Vienna for his friend Harry Lime (Welles), and he's matched by Howard's effortless performance as a British major. Justifiably famed for its intriguing Graham Greene script, Oscar-winning photography (by Robert Krasker), and unforgettable Anton Karas zither score. Also available in an edition containing film's original trailer.

THIRD MAN ON THE MOUNTAIN 1959
★★★★ NR Action-Adventure/Family 1:47
Dir: Ken Annakin *Cast:* James MacArthur, Michael Rennie, Janet Munro, James Donald, Herbert Lom, Laurence Naismith
▶ When his father is killed trying to climb the Matterhorn, young MacArthur vows to complete the ascent. First he must learn the fundamentals of mountain climbing from Rennie. Excellent Disney drama has excitement, breathtaking scenery, and worthwhile themes for younger viewers. Based on *Banner in the Sky* by James Ramsey Ullmann (who appears in a cameo with MacArthur's real-life mother Helen Hayes).

13 GHOSTS 1960
★ NR Horror 1:28 B&W
Dir: William Castle *Cast:* Charles Herbert, Jo Morrow, Martin Milner, Rosemary DeCamp, Margaret Hamilton, Donald Woods
▶ Struggling paleontologist Woods and his family inherit an old house from their late uncle. The good news is there's a fortune hidden inside; the bad news is the place is haunted by thirteen ghosts who terrorize the clan. Tacky chiller with slipshod production values; does have a few laughs. Hamilton is a treat as the housekeeper.

13 RUE MADELEINE 1947
★★★ NR Mystery-Suspense 1:35 B&W
Dir: Henry Hathaway *Cast:* James Cagney, Annabella, Richard Conte, Frank Latimore, Walter Abel, Sam Jaffe
▶ Adventurer Cagney trains crack unit of agents to discover German rocket site in France before the Allied invasion. The mission is threatened by the presence of a German agent within Cagney's group. Documentary-style classic, based on a true story, delivers maximum tension; Cagney is first-rate.

30 FOOT BRIDE OF CANDY ROCK, THE 1959
★★★ NR Fantasy/Comedy 1:13
Dir: Sidney Miller *Cast:* Lou Costello, Dorothy Provine, Gale Gordon, Jimmy Conlin, Charles Lane
▶ When his girlfriend Provine mysteriously grows into a thirty-foot giant, garbage man–amateur scientist Costello marries her and tries to correct the condition with one of his inventions. Amusing spoof should please the kids; Costello generates chuckles in his last film.

30 IS A DANGEROUS AGE, CYNTHIA 1968 British
★ NR Comedy 1:24
Dir: Joseph McGrath *Cast:* Dudley Moore, Eddie Foy, Jr., Suzy Kendall, Patricia Routledge, Duncan MacRae, Michael MacLiammoir
▶ Shy pianist Moore, feeling pressured by his impending thirtieth birthday, vows to

write a hit musical and get married within six weeks. Boyish charm and dry wit from Moore (who cowrote the screenplay), but uneven plotting goes off on too many tangents with offbeat humor of limited appeal.

39 STEPS, THE 1935
★ ★ ★ ★ NR Mystery-Suspense 1:26 B&W
Dir: Alfred Hitchcock *Cast:* Robert Donat, Madeleine Carroll, Lucie Mannheim, Godfrey Tearle, Peggy Ashcroft, John Laurie
► Donat, a Canadian vacationing in London, learns of a foreign spy ring from British agent Mannheim. When dying Mannheim turns up in Donat's room and delivers a map of Scotland, police pursue Donat for murder as villains chase him for the map. Flight to Scotland involves reluctant ally Carroll and encounter with master spy Tearle. Breakthrough film for Hitchcock, loosely based on the John Buchan novel, established him as master of suspense.

THIRTY-NINE STEPS, THE 1980 British
★ ★ ★ ★ PG Mystery-Suspense 1:42
☑ Adult situations, explicit language, mild violence
Dir: Don Sharp *Cast:* Robert Powell, David Warner, John Mills, Eric Porter, Karen Dotrice, George Baker
► In 1914, British colonel Mills, with info on Prussian plot to start World War I, seeks refuge in home of stranger Powell. Villain Warner and his assassins slay Mills and pursue Powell, believing he has conspiracy plan, while police suspect Powell is Mills's killer. Fleeing for his life, Powell finds ally Dotrice, who believes him innocent. Chase through trains and Scottish moors leads to climax atop Big Ben. Contemporary version sticks closer to John Buchan's novel than Hitchcock's renowned 1935 adaptation.

THIRTY SECONDS OVER TOKYO 1944
★ ★ ★ NR War 2:18 B&W
Dir: Mervyn LeRoy *Cast:* Van Johnson, Spencer Tracy, Robert Walker, Phyllis Thaxter, Robert Mitchum, Don DeFore
► World War II American pilot Johnson participates in General Doolittle's (Tracy) inaugural bombing raid on Japan. When his plane crashes near China, Johnson faces hardship and injury. Fact-based and first-rate; strong performances from Johnson, Tracy, and Thaxter (as Johnson's

understanding wife). Oscar-winning special effects.

THIS GUN FOR HIRE 1942
★ ★ ★ NR Mystery-Suspense 1:21 B&W
Dir: Frank Tuttle *Cast:* Alan Ladd, Veronica Lake, Robert Preston, Laird Cregar, Tully Marshall, Marc Lawrence
► Taut but bleak melodrama about hired killer Ladd, double-crossed by Nazi double agent Cregar and pursued through a hostile urban landscape by police. Nightclub singer Lake becomes an unwilling accomplice as he seeks revenge. Adaptation of a Graham Greene novel made Ladd a star, and led to three further teamings with Lake.

THIS IS ELVIS 1981
★ ★ ★ ★ PG Documentary/Biography 1:44 C/B&W
☑ Adult situations, explicit language
Dir: Malcolm Leo, Andrew Solt *Cast:* Elvis Presley, David Scott, Paul Boensch III, Johnny Harra, Rhonda Lyn, Dana MacKay
► Controversial biography of Elvis Presley combines documentary footage, home movies, film and concert clips, and staged reconstructions for a definitive look at the King's career. Opening with his death at age forty-two, film uses flashbacks to trace his rise from truck driver to international star. Cooperation of Col. Tom Parker (Presley's manager) and inclusion of thirty-eight songs add to authenticity, although his late decline receives glossy treatment.

THIS ISLAND EARTH 1955
★ NR Sci-Fi 1:27
Dir: Joseph Newman *Cast:* Jeff Morrow, Faith Domergue, Rex Reason, Lance Fuller, Russell Johnson
► When his planet faces destruction in an outer-space war, alien Morrow recruits Earth scientists Reason and Domergue for help. Will they reach Morrow's world in time to save it? Imaginative special effects and story but laughable dialogue. Although dated, has cult following among genre fans.

THIS IS SPINAL TAP 1984
★ R Comedy 1:22
☑ Adult situations, explicit language
Dir: Rob Reiner *Cast:* Rob Reiner, Michael McKean, Christopher Guest, Harry Shearer, Tony Hendra
► Vastly underrated cult film is a breathtakingly scathing satire about the rock music business where "there's such a fine

line between clever and stupid." Reiner casts himself as a documentary film-maker covering the fictional rock group Spinal Tap, in the U.S. to promote their newest album, "Smell the Glove." Hilarious, good-natured spoof recounts the group's rise from obscurity to "one of England's loudest bands." Original Spinal Tap songs include "Listen to the Flower People" and their current hit, "Big Bottom," extolling the virtues of a lover's rear end.

THIS IS THE ARMY 1943
★★ NR Musical 2:01
Dir: Michael Curtiz *Cast:* George Murphy, Ronald Reagan, Joan Leslie, Alan Hale, Dolores Costello, Kate Smith
▶ During World War II, lieutenant Reagan, son of producer Murphy, gets the assignment of putting together a morale-boosting revue for the troops. Irving Berlin wrote the score (and appears in the "Oh, How I Hate to Get Up in the Morning" number) for this patriotic tribute. Sentimental and endearing songs include "God Bless America" and "This Is the Army, Mr. Jones."

THIS PROPERTY IS CONDEMNED 1966
★★★★ NR Drama/Romance 1:50
☑ Adult situations, mild violence
Dir: Sydney Pollack *Cast:* Natalie Wood, Robert Redford, Charles Bronson, Mary Badham, Kate Reid, Robert Blake
▶ Adaptation of a Tennessee Williams one-act play concerns beautiful Wood stifled by life in mother Reid's boarding house for railway workers. Wood falls madly in love with newcomer Redford, who arrives to lay off railroad men. When he's driven out of town, Wood plans to flee with him, but circumstances and her own pride lead to a tragic conclusion. Fine performances from all, with Wood especially affecting. Francis Ford Coppola cowrote screenplay.

THIS SPORTING LIFE 1963 British
★★ NR Drama/Sports 2:14 B&W
Dir: Lindsay Anderson *Cast:* Richard Harris, Rachel Roberts, Alan Badel, William Hartnell, Colin Blakely, Vanda Godsell
▶ "You see something you want and you go out and get it. It's as simple as that." Armed with this credo, Harris leaves life as miner to win fame and fortune as aggressive rugby player. All that eludes him is Roberts, the widow with whom he lodges.

She eventually yields to his persistent efforts, but their affair fails due to his insensitivity. Scathing portrayal of man-as-beast also boasts powerful rugby footage. Harris and Roberts were both Oscar nominees.

THOMAS CROWN AFFAIR, THE 1968
★★★ R Mystery-Suspense 1:42
☑ Brief nudity, adult situations, explicit language, violence
Dir: Norman Jewison *Cast:* Steve McQueen, Faye Dunaway, Paul Burke, Jack Weston, Biff McGuire, Yaphet Kotto
▶ Insurance investigator Dunaway matches wits with McQueen, a wealthy Boston crook who has pulled off daring bank heist. They fall in love playing cat and mouse. Exciting caper features jazzy Jewison direction and sizzling McQueen/Dunaway chemistry (especially in the sexiest chess game scene in film history). Oscar for Best Song, "The Windmills of Your Mind."

THOROUGHLY MODERN MILLIE 1967
★★ NR Musical 2:18
Dir: George Roy Hill *Cast:* Julie Andrews, Mary Tyler Moore, Carol Channing, John Gavin, James Fox, Beatrice Lillie
▶ Flapper Andrews arrives in Roaring Twenties New York with thoroughly modern notion of marrying her boss Gavin. However, love rears its head in the form of Fox and adventure follows when white slavery ring kidnaps Andrews's roommate Moore. Crammed with music, fun, production values, and nifty performances (Channing was Oscar-nominated but don't overlook the delightful Fox). Received seven Oscar nominations, winning for Best Original Score.

THOSE LIPS, THOSE EYES 1980
★★ R Drama 1:46
☑ Nudity, adult situations, explicit language
Dir: Michael Pressman *Cast:* Frank Langella, Tom Hulce, Glynnis O'Connor, Kevin McCarthy, Jerry Stiller
▶ In 1950s Cleveland, stagestruck premed student Hulce gets job with summer theater, finds romance with chorus girl O'Connor and is taken under wing of leading man Langella, who gives him lessons in life. Sweet and simple but a bit tepid and slow; Langella is terrific.

THOSE MAGNIFICENT MEN IN THEIR FLYING MACHINES 1965
★ ★ ★ G Comedy 2:13
Dir: Ken Annakin *Cast:* Stuart Whitman, Sarah Miles, James Fox, Alberto Sordi, Robert Morley, Benny Hill
▶ Morley, a 1910 British press baron, offers prize for air race from London to Paris, hoping to prove Commonwealth reigns over skies as well as seas. Competitors include Royal Navy airman Fox with stiff upper lip, Italian count Sordi, and barnstorming American Whitman. Fox and Whitman also vie for attentions of Morley's lovely daughter Miles. Well-meaning and lighthearted comedy makes fine family fare, despite occasional lapses. Kids will walk away singing, "They go up-pity-up-up, they go downditty-down-down . . ."

THOUSAND CLOWNS, A 1965
★ ★ NR Comedy 1:58 B&W
Dir: Fred Coe *Cast:* Jason Robards, Barbara Harris, Martin Balsam, Barry Gordon, Gene Saks, William Daniels
▶ Delightful, often hysterically funny adaptation by Herb Gardner of his Broadway play depicts unemployed TV writer Robards living with twelve-year-old nephew Gordon. They share nonconformist philosophy, as one morning uncle advises boy: "You're about to see the scariest thing on earth—people on their way to work." Social worker Daniels insists Robards get a job or lose custody of boy; Daniels's co-worker Harris falls in love with Robards. Title song by saxophonist Gerry Mulligan and wife, actress Judy Holliday.

THOUSANDS CHEER 1944
★ ★ ★ NR Musical 2:06
Dir: George Sidney *Cast:* Gene Kelly, Kathryn Grayson, Mary Astor, Jose Iturbi, John Boles
▶ During World War II, circus performer Kelly finds army life intolerable; he woos colonel's daughter Grayson in hopes of winning a transfer but then actually falls in love. Wartime rouser crammed to the brim with tunes climaxes with a big show featuring zillions of MGM stars (Mickey Rooney, Judy Garland, Lucille Ball, Eleanor Powell, Red Skelton, Donna Reed, Lena Horne, Frank Morgan, June Allyson, Gloria De Haven, and others).

THRASHIN' 1986
★ ★ PG-13 Drama 1:32
☑ Adult situations, mild violence
Dir: David Winters *Cast:* Josh Brolin, Robert Rusler, Pamela Gilday, Brooke McCarter, Brett Marx
▶ *West Side Story* on skateboards. Ace skateboarder Brolin meets Gilday, sister of rival team leader Rusler. Gang war breaks out, culiminating in final battle during the Twenty-Mile Downhill Massacre Race. Airhead entertainment for teens only. Rated PG-13 because of one brief and discreet pubescent love scene.

THREE AMIGOS! 1986
★ ★ PG Comedy 1:43
☑ Explicit language, mild violence
Dir: John Landis *Cast:* Steve Martin, Chevy Chase, Martin Short, Patrice Martinez, Joe Mantegna, Alfonso Arau
▶ Silent-screen heroes Martin, Chase, and Short, mistaken for the real article by Martinez, are summoned to Mexican village to fight bandito Arau. The bumbling trio are in for a rude awakening as they think they've been signed for a personal appearance. Nutty and amiable if not sidesplitting. Best laughs: Randy Newman's songs (including one with singing horses), Martin's rousing "Everyone has an El Guapo in his life" speech.

THREE COINS IN THE FOUNTAIN 1954
★ ★ ★ ★ NR Drama 1:41
Dir: Jean Negulesco *Cast:* Clifton Webb, Dorothy McGuire, Jean Peters, Louis Jourdan, Maggie McNamara, Rossano Brazzi
▶ Three single Americans—secretary McNamara, executive Peters, and writer's assistant McGuire—pin their hopes for romance on Rome's Fountain of Trevi. McNamara snares Italian prince Jourdan, Peters reforms gigolo Brazzi, and McGuire finds true love with her boss Webb. Slight, predictable drama given a tremendous boost by Milton Krasner's Oscar-winning location photography and Frank Sinatra's beautiful version of the title song (also an Oscar winner for Jule Styne and Sammy Cahn).

THREE DAYS OF THE CONDOR 1975
★ ★ ★ ★ ★ R Mystery-Suspense 1:57
☑ Adult situations, explicit language, violence
Dir: Sydney Pollack *Cast:* Robert Redford, Faye Dunaway, Cliff Robertson, Max Von Sydow, John Houseman
▶ In New York, CIA researcher Redford has seemingly innocuous job of reading novels until his entire office is wiped out and he's targeted for death by his superiors. He kidnaps innocent bystander

Dunaway to help him and a wary love affair ensues. Riveting story enhanced by evocative direction by Pollack, top-notch performances (Von Sydow shines as a gentlemanly hit man), and intelligent plotting with a haunting climax.

THREE FACES OF EVE, THE 1957
★ ★ ★ ★ **NR Biography/Drama 1:31**
B&W
Dir: Nunnally Johnson *Cast:* Joanne Woodward, Lee J. Cobb, David Wayne, Vince Edwards, Nancy Kulp
▶ Georgia housewife Woodward is brought to shrink Cobb after attacking her own child. Cobb examines Woodward and attempts to cure a case of multiple personality. Brilliant true story has lean pacing and uplifting conclusion. Dominated by Woodward's Oscar-winning tour-de-force performance.

3:15—MOMENT OF TRUTH 1986
★ **R Drama 1:35**
☑ Nudity, adult situations, explicit language
Dir: Larry Gross *Cast:* Adam Baldwin, Deborah Foreman, René Auberjonois, Ed Lauter, Joseph Brutsman, Scott McGinnis
▶ Gang-rumble film stars Baldwin as a former member of East L.A. leather and chain gang, the Cobras. After a drug bust, Baldwin is branded a traitor and must contend with gang leader De La Paz, wicked principal Auberjonois, frightened girlfriend Foreman, and nerdy friend Brutsman. Final confrontation is set for 3:15, the moment of truth after school.

THREE FOR THE ROAD 1987
★ ★ ★ **PG Comedy 1:30**
☑ Adult situations
Dir: B.W.L. Norton *Cast:* Charlie Sheen, Kerri Green, Alan Ruck, Sally Kellerman, Blair Tefkin
▶ Sheen, an ambitious senator's aide, agrees to escort boss's troubled daughter Green to a reform school and brings his obnoxious roommate Ruck along for the ride. Sheen handcuffs himself to Green to prevent her from escaping to visit divorced mom Kellerman, which she manages to do anyway. In the end, Sheen discovers the senator has feet of clay and he saves the woman he loves from the looney bin. Plot offers few surprises.

THREE FUGITIVES 1989
★ ★ ★ ★ **PG-13 Comedy 1:36**
☑ Explicit language, violence
Dir: Francis Veber *Cast:* Nick Nolte, Martin Short, Sarah Rowland Doroff, James Earl Jones, Kenneth McMillan, Alan Ruck
▶ Criminal Nolte gets out of jail, enters bank to open account, and is taken hostage by novice bank robber Short. The cops figure Nolte is involved, and he is forced on the lam with Short and his little daughter Doroff. Frisky formula filmmaking longer on energy than inspiration. Nolte and Short work well together, and the Nolte/Doroff relationship is very sweet. Funniest scene: Short in drag. Director Veber's remake of his own French film, *Les Fugitifs.*

THREE GODFATHERS 1948
★ ★ ★ ★ **NR Western 1:45**
Dir: John Ford *Cast:* John Wayne, Pedro Armendariz, Harry Carey, Jr., Ward Bond, Mildred Natwick, Jane Darwell
▶ Sentimental version of an oft-filmed story about Wayne, Armendariz, and Carey, outlaws chased into the desert by a posse. They find pregnant Natwick who dies giving birth, and vow to bring the child to New Jerusalem, Arizona. Oddly touching and not without moments of humor. Director Ford's first color film was dedicated to Carey's father, Harry Carey, Sr., a Western veteran who appeared in a 1916 version of the story.

THREE IN THE ATTIC 1968
★ ★ **R Comedy 1:30**
☑ Nudity, strong sexual content, adult situations, explicit language
Dir: Richard Wilson *Cast:* Christopher Jones, Yvette Mimieux, Judy Pace, Maggie Thrett, Nan Martin, John Beck
▶ College womanizer Jones seduces Mimieux but can't settle down with one girl; Pace becomes yet another conquest. Mimieux, Pace, and Thrett, Jones's third lover, get revenge by trapping him in an attic and wearing him out sexually. Strong on sex but lacking in subtlety.

THREE KINDS OF HEAT 1987
★ ★ **R Action-Adventure 1:27**
☑ Adult situations, explicit language, violence
Dir: Leslie Stevens *Cast:* Robert Ginty, Victoria Barrett, Shakti, Sylvester McCoy, Barry Foster, Jeannie Brown
▶ Secret agent Ginty tracks down nefarious Chinese mobster McCoy with the help of beautiful New York police officer

Barrett and exotic Hong Kong cop Shakti. Trail leads from Big Apple to London warehouse filled with explosives. Routine mayhem presented with little flair. (CC)

THREE LITTLE WORDS 1950
★ ★ ★ ★ **NR Musical 1:42**
Dir: Richard Thorpe *Cast:* Fred Astaire, Red Skelton, Vera-Ellen, Arlene Dahl, Keenan Wynn, Gale Robbins
▶ Biography of 1920s songwriting team Bert Kalmar and Harry Ruby features fourteen of their best songs: "Who's Sorry Now," "Hooray for Captain Spaulding," "She's Mine, All Mine," more. Plot sticks to the facts, following the unlikely friendship of vaudeville dancer Kalmar (Astaire) and aspiring baseball player Ruby (Skelton) through their split-up and reconciliation. Debbie Reynolds sparked her career with "I Wanna Be Loved by You," but highlight is Astaire's surrealistic duet with Vera-Ellen to "Mr. and Mrs. Hoofer at Home."

THREE LIVES OF THOMASINA, THE 1963
★ ★ ★ ★ **NR Fantasy/Family 1:35**
Dir: Don Chaffey *Cast:* Patrick McGoohan, Susan Hampshire, Karen Dotrice, Laurence Naismith, Jean Anderson, Finlay Currie
▶ Scottish veterinarian McGoohan decides his daughter Dotrice's sick cat Thomasina must be put to sleep, but the pet escapes and hides with Hampshire, a recluse with mysterious powers. She later uses the feline to mend rift between McGoohan and Dotrice. Heartwarming Disney adaptation of a Paul Gallico story will thrill children.

THREE MEN AND A CRADLE 1985
French
★ ★ ★ **PG-13 Comedy 1:46**
☑ Brief nudity, adult situations, explicit language
Dir: Coline Serreau *Cast:* Roland Giraud, Michel Boujenah, Andre Dussolier, Philippe Leroy Beaulieu
▶ Warm and winning comedy about three Parisian bachelors who suddenly find themselves in charge of the infant girl one of them has unknowingly fathered. Grappling with diapers, formulas, and all-night crying jags, the men eventually fall hopelessly in love with the tiny baby. One of France's all-time top grossing films was nominated for a foreign language Oscar and remade in the U.S. as *Three Men and a Baby.* ⓢ

THREE MEN AND A BABY 1987
★ ★ ★ ★ ★ **PG Comedy 1:39**
☑ Explicit language
Dir: Leonard Nimoy *Cast:* Tom Selleck, Steve Guttenberg, Ted Danson, Nancy Travis, Margaret Colin, Philip Bosco
▶ New York bachelors Selleck, Guttenberg, and Danson fall into fatherhood when infant girl is left on their doorstep. The guys make hilarious transition from party boys to proud papas. Frothy, foolproof entertainment was major box office smash. Selleck demonstrates deft comic touch, and the baby is adorable. Confident direction by Nimoy leaves no diaper joke unturned. Based on the French *Three Men and a Cradle.*

THREE MUSKETEERS, THE 1948
★ ★ ★ **NR Action-Adventure 2:05**
Dir: George Sidney *Cast:* Lana Turner, Gene Kelly, Van Heflin, Angela Lansbury, June Allyson, Vincent Price
▶ Country boy D'Artagnan (Kelly) arrives in seventeenth-century Paris and joins the fabled musketeers led by Heflin. The swordsmen thwart a plot against the throne by evil prime minister Price and countess co-conspirator Turner. Adaptation of the Alexandre Dumas classic is frisky fun, thanks to Kelly's fast footwork and stylish production.

THREE MUSKETEERS, THE 1974 British
★ ★ ★ ★ **PG Action-Adventure 1:45**
☑ Adult situations, violence
Dir: Richard Lester *Cast:* Oliver Reed, Michael York, Richard Chamberlain, Raquel Welch, Frank Finlay, Geraldine Chaplin
▶ In eighteenth-century France, bumpkin York befriends more worldly Reed, Chamberlain, and Finlay, leaders of the king's guard known as the Musketeers. His new pals are only interested in brawling, boozing, and wenching until York romances queen Chaplin's lady-in-waiting Welch. She reveals a plan to besmirch milady's honor and wrest power from the weak-willed king, sending the quartet into action. Rollicking, often slapstick version of the oft-filmed Dumas tale also stars Charlton Heston and Faye Dunaway.

THREE O'CLOCK HIGH 1987
★ ★ **PG-13 Comedy 1:41**
☑ Explicit language, violence
Dir: Phil Joanou *Cast:* Casey Sie-

maszko, Anne Ryan, Richard Tyson, Jeffrey Tambor, Philip Baker Hall, John P. Ryan

▶ Nerdy teen Siemaszko upsets the new school bully Tyson, a hulking transfer student who challenges him to a fight after class. Siemaszko spends the rest of the day dreading the confrontation. Capable cast and amusing directorial flourishes rank this slightly above similar adolescent comedies.

THREEPENNY OPERA, THE 1931
German
★ NR Musical 1:52 B&W
Dir: G. W. Pabst *Cast:* Rudolf Forster, Carola Neher, Reinhold Schunzel, Lotte Lenya, Fritz Rasp, Valeska Gert
▶ Infamous outlaw Mackie Messer (Forster) announces his engagement to Neher, daughter of the king of the beggars (Rasp). Rasp threatens to disrupt upcoming coronation ceremonies if the wedding goes through. Prostitute Lenya, who sings a dazzling "Pirate Jenny," betrays Mack the Knife to the police. Technically dated version of the Bertolt Brecht/Kurt Weill play, itself based on John Gay's eighteenth-century classic *The Beggar's Opera*, effectively captures atmosphere of pre-Nazi Germany. Remade with Sammy Davis, Jr., in 1963.
⑤

THREE STOOGES MEET HERCULES, THE 1962
★★★ NR Comedy 1:20 B&W
Dir: Edward Bernds *Cast:* Moe Howard, Larry Fine, "Curly" Joe De Rita, Vicki Trickett, George N. Neise, Samson Burke
▶ Predictable family-oriented slapstick as the latter-day edition of the Stooges travel in a time machine to ancient Greece. Dressed in togas and sandals, the boys form a conga line on a slave galley, encounter a Siamese twin cyclops, and add pie-fighting to a chariot race.

THREE STRANGERS 1946
★★★ NR Drama 1:32 B&W
Dir: Jean Negulesco *Cast:* Sydney Greenstreet, Geraldine Fitzgerald, Peter Lorre, Joan Lorring, Robert Shayne, Marjorie Riordan
▶ After a chance meeting, unscrupulous lawyer Greenstreet, alcoholic thief Lorre, and Fitzgerald, a woman abandoned by her lover, impetuously agree to share a sweepstakes ticket. Greenstreet hopes

to enter a prestigious club, Lorre wants to open a tavern, and Fitzgerald wishes for her lover's return—but an unexpected twist of fate alters all of their plans. Stylish melodrama features wonderful stars and an unusual script by John Huston and Howard Koch.

3:10 TO YUMA 1957
★ NR Western 1:32 B&W
Dir: Delmer Daves *Cast:* Van Heflin, Glenn Ford, Felicia Farr, Richard Jaeckel, Leora Dana, Henry Jones
▶ Family man Heflin takes job escorting killer Ford on 3:10 train to Yuma prison. Ford's gang shows up to help him escape as respect grows between between outlaw and guard. Enormously suspenseful western with impressive performances and unusual psychological insight; based on a story by Elmore Leonard.

3 WOMEN 1977
★ PG Drama 2:04
☑ Adult situations
Dir: Robert Altman *Cast:* Shelley Duvall, Sissy Spacek, Janice Rule, Robert Fortier, John Cromwell, Ruth Nelson
▶ Self-deluded Duvall takes in new roommate Spacek. Spacek assumes Duvall's psychological traits and personality transference takes place. Lurking in the background is a third woman: mysterious painter Rule. Stunning performances by Duvall and Spacek and eerie visuals from director Altman; however, arty story line and ambiguous ending limit accessibility.

THREE WORLDS OF GULLIVER, THE 1960
★★ NR Fantasy/Family 1:39
Dir: Jack Sher *Cast:* Kerwin Mathews, June Thorburn, Jo Morrow, Lee Patterson
▶ Eighteenth-century English doctor Mathews joins ship's crew and is swept overboard for adventures among the tiny inhabitants of Lilliput and the giants of Brobdingnag. Ray Harryhausen special effects and Bernard Herrmann score highlight this worthwhile adaptation of Jonathan Swift's *Gulliver's Travels*. Ideal for the younger set.

THRESHOLD 1983
★★★ PG Drama 1:37
☑ Nudity, explicit language
Dir: Richard Pearce *Cast:* Donald Sutherland, Mare Winningham, Jeff Goldblum, John Marley, Sharon Acker
▶ Reknowned surgeon Sutherland and

biologist Goldblum team up to develop artificial heart. When patient Winningham suffers irreparable damage, Sutherland implants the experimental device in her. Low-key and quite credible, with noteworthy Sutherland and Goldblum, winning Winningham. One caveat: surgery scenes are quite graphic.

THRILL OF IT ALL, THE 1963
★★★ NR Comedy 1:47
Dir: Norman Jewison *Cast:* Doris Day, James Garner, Arlene Francis, Edward Andrews, ZaSu Pitts, Reginald Owen
▶ Ordinary housewife Day forsakes home and hearth to become a big hit as TV commercial spokeswoman. Her neglected hubby Garner has trouble dealing with her success and schemes to restore things to normal. Bright and clever vehicle for the stars.

THROUGH A GLASS DARKLY 1960
Swedish
★ NR Drama 1:31 B&W
Dir: Ingmar Bergman *Cast:* Harriet Andersson, Gunnar Bjornstrand, Max Von Sydow, Lars Passgard
▶ Mentally unstable Andersson leaves institution and spends summer with family on island. Her father Bjornstrand, husband Von Sydow, and brother Passgard are unable to help as she descends into madness once more. Dark but involving psychodrama won Best Foreign Film Oscar. Ⓢ

THROW MOMMA FROM THE TRAIN 1987
★★★★ PG-13 Comedy 1:28
☑ Adult situations, explicit language, mild violence
Dir: Danny DeVito *Cast:* Billy Crystal, Danny DeVito, Anne Ramsey, Kim Greist, Rob Reiner, Kate Mulgrew
▶ Teacher Crystal suffers writer's block because ex-wife Mulgrew stole his manuscript and turned it into a best-seller. One of Crystal's students, DeVito, endures bullying, grotesque mother Ramsey. When Crystal advises DeVito to see Hitchcock's *Strangers on a Train*, student thinks teacher means to suggest they kill each other's nemesis, just as in the movie. Trouble breaks loose when DeVito keeps his end of bargain. Best are hilarious writer's block gags and diabolical but childlike DeVito. **(CC)**

THUNDER ALLEY 1985
★★★ R Drama 1:41

☑ Nudity, adult situations, explicit language
Dir: J. S. Cardone *Cast:* Roger Wilson, Jill Schoelen, Scott McGinnis, Cynthia Eilbacher, Leif Garrett, Clancy Brown
▶ Tucson keyboardist McGinnis forms rock 'n' roll band, but hostility of lead singer Garrett deters ace guitarist Wilson from joining. Wilson eventually signs on and group's success seems assured; he and McGinnis romance Schoelen and Eilbacher, who work at ice cream parlor. When McGinnis gets involved with drugs, band's fortunes take turn for worse.

THUNDER AND LIGHTNING 1977
★★ PG Action-Adventure/Comedy 1:34
☑ Brief nudity, explicit language
Dir: Corey Allen *Cast:* David Carradine, Kate Jackson, Roger C. Carmel, Sterling Holloway, Ed Barth, Ron Feinberg
▶ Independent Florida bootlegger Carradine destroys still run by mob-backed moonshiner Carmel and must ward off revenge attempts. Carmel's daughter Jackson is also Carradine's girlfriend; she can't believe daddy's up to no good until bullets begin flying and cars start crashing at high speeds. Real stars on this nonstop actioner are the stunt men. **(CC)**

THUNDERBALL 1965 British
★★★★ PG
Espionage/Action-Adventure 2:12
☑ Adult situations, violence
Dir: Terence Young *Cast:* Sean Connery, Claudine Auger, Adolfo Celi, Luciana Paluzzi, Rick Van Nutter
▶ Fourth outing for 007 (Connery) has him battling evil SPECTRE, led by eye-patched villain Celi and his seductive sidekick Paluzzi. Celi has hijacked two NATO atom bombs and demands multi-million-dollar ransom. Search for bombs leads Bond to Bahamas for encounters with bikini-clad women (including skin-diving dish Auger) and underwater shoot-'em-up finale. Droll Connery, eye-catching scenery, and spectacular underwater footage are highlights.

THUNDER BAY 1953
★★★ NR Action-Adventure 1:42
Dir: Anthony Mann *Cast:* James Stewart, Joanne Dru, Gilbert Roland, Dan Duryea, Harry Morgan, Marcia Henderson
▶ Stewart and Duryea team up to drill for "black gold" in Gulf of Mexico, construct-

ing stormproof oil-rig platform. Local shrimp fishermen, already suffering tough times, aren't keen about newcomers. Tensions peak when Stewart and Duryea romance local Louisiana girls Dru and Henderson. Wildcatters must then battle elements, financial crisis, and angry mob. Plenty of action and fine cast make for entertaining yarn.

THUNDERBOLT AND LIGHTFOOT 1974
★★★ R Action-Adventure 1:54
☑ Adult situations, explicit language, violence
Dir: Michael Cimino *Cast:* Clint Eastwood, Jeff Bridges, George Kennedy, Geoffrey Lewis, Catherine Bach, Gary Busey
▶ Amiable drifter Bridges hooks up with ex-thief Eastwood on the lam from cohorts Kennedy and Lewis, who believe Eastwood set them up and took loot in robbery of years past. When Kennedy and Lewis apprehend the duo, a truce is struck: they'll rob the same bank the same way. Engrossing caper features fully realized characters and commendable acting, especially from Bridges. First feature outing for writer/director Cimino.

THUNDER ROAD 1958
★★ NR Action-Adventure 1:32 B&W
Dir: Arthur Ripley *Cast:* Robert Mitchum, Gene Barry, Jacques Aubuchon, Keely Smith, Trevor Bardette, Jim Mitchum
▶ Korean vet Robert Mitchum reestablishes his Tennessee moonshine business, fighting off Aubuchon's mob hit men and antibootlegging Fed Barry while dissuading his brother (his real-life son Jim Mitchum) from a life of crime. Mitchum produced, wrote the story and theme song "Whippoorwill" (which he later made a hit song), and gave one of his most enjoyable performances in this influential cult film. Good car chases and pop star Smith's offbeat role add to the fun.

THUNDER RUN 1986
★★ PG-13 Action-Adventure 1:31
☑ Explicit language, violence
Dir: Gary Hudson *Cast:* Forrest Tucker, John Ireland, John Shepherd, Jill Whitlow, Wally Ward, Cheryl M. Lynn
▶ Retired trucker Tucker agrees to transport shipment of plutonium across Nevada despite presence of heavily armed terrorists who need the ore to build nuclear weapons. Tucker's last film

is half dull chase, half teenage high jinks from Sheperd and his adolescent friends.

THX 1138 1971
★★ PG Sci-Fi 1:28
☑ Brief nudity, adult situations, violence
Dir: George Lucas *Cast:* Robert Duvall, Donald Pleasence, Don Pedro Colley, Maggie McOmie, Ian Wolfe, Sid Haig
▶ Computers run a futuristic subterranean society where love and sex are outlawed while daily drug dose represses free will. Young rebels Duvall and McOmie cease taking drug and discover romance. Imprisoned for insubordination, they team with fellow convict Pleasence and attempt escape to above-ground world. Feature debut for director Lucas.

TICKET TO HEAVEN 1981 Canadian
★★★ PG Drama 1:48
☑ Explicit language
Dir: Ralph L. Thomas *Cast:* Nick Mancuso, Meg Foster, Saul Rubinek, Kim Cattrall, R. H. Thomson, Jennifer Dale
▶ In wake of break-up with girlfriend, young Canadian Mancuso vacations in San Francisco and is seduced into joining religious cult by group's spooky cheerleaders Foster and Cattrall. Soon thoroughly brainwashed by propaganda and spartan regimen, Mancuso rejects family and past. Best friend Rubinek and pro deprogrammer Thomson set out to liberate Mancuso from cult's clutches. Chilling and realistic look at exploitation of vulnerable minds by fraudulent, profit-hungry religions.

TICKLE ME 1965
★★ NR Musical 1:30
Dir: Norman Taurog *Cast:* Elvis Presley, Julie Adams, Jocelyn Lane, Jack Mullaney, Merry Anders, Bill Williams
▶ Singing rodeo star Presley forsakes hard riding for a handyman's job at Adams's all-girl dude ranch and beauty spa. He romances beautiful Lane and rescues her from kidnappers determined to steal her gold mine, while singing "Dirty, Dirty Feeling," "Night Rider," "It Feels So Right," and other tunes. More gags than usual in this middling Presley vehicle.

TIGER BAY 1959 British
★★ NR Drama 1:45 B&W
Dir: J. Lee Thompson *Cast:* John Mills, Horst Buchholz, Hayley Mills, Yvonne Mitchell, Megs Jenkins, Anthony Dawson
▶ Smashing film debut for Hayley Mills,

who plays a young girl of the Cardiff slums who witnesses sailor Buchholz killing his girlfriend. Stealing the murder weapon, she is pursued by Buchholz, who gradually develops a grudging respect for her. John Mills (Hayley's real-life father) is a police detective who forces her to choose between her new friend and justice. Unusual material receives a fresh, absorbing treatment.

TIGERS IN LIPSTICK 1979 Italian
★ R Sex/Comedy 1:23
☑ Nudity, strong sexual content, explicit language
Dir: Luigi Zampa *Cast:* Ursula Andress, Laura Antonelli, Sylvia Kristel, Monica Vitti, Michele Placido, Roberto Benigni
▶ Omnibus of sketches starring four of Europe's most beautiful sexpots. Andress exposes herself to startled drivers who crash into each other, then takes her cut from the auto mechanic who arranged the scheme; Kristel frames an ardent admirer for murder; Antonelli teases an aroused orchestra conductor. Leering skits are dated and surprisingly soft.

TIGER'S TALE, A 1988
★ ★ R Comedy 1:37
☑ Nudity, adult situations, explicit language
Dir: Peter Douglas *Cast:* Ann-Margret, C. Thomas Howell, Charles Durning, Kelly Preston, Ann Wedgeworth, William Zabka
▶ Texas teen Howell falls for ex-girlfriend Preston's divorced mother Ann-Margret. Unexpected pregnancy (courtesy of Preston punching hole in mom's diaphragm) complicates the relationship. Adolescent wish-fulfillment plot has tangy small-town atmosphere and luscious Ann-Margret investing her role with shading and wit.

TIGER WARSAW 1988
★ ★ ★ R Drama 1:32
☑ Adult situations, explicit language
Dir: Amin Chandrini *Cast:* Patrick Swayze, Piper Laurie, Barbara Williams, Bobby DiCicco, Lee Richardson, Mary McDonnell
▶ When McDonnell plans marriage, black sheep brother Swayze returns home after fifteen years. Mother Laurie is glad to see him, but father Richardson doesn't want him around due to rift from years ago. While coping with family woes, Swayze chums with old pal DiCicco and rediscovers magic with former girlfriend Williams. Competently crafted working-class melodrama.

TIGHTROPE 1984
★ ★ ★ ★ R Mystery-Suspense 1:54
☑ Nudity, adult situations, explicit language, violence
Dir: Richard Tuggle *Cast:* Clint Eastwood, Genevieve Bujold, Dan Hedaya, Alison Eastwood, Jennifer Beck, Marco St. John
▶ Eastwood adds new depth to his macho persona in this twisty, satisfying thriller. A New Orleans vice cop separated from his wife and caring for two daughters, he searches for a serial killer whose victims are the same prostitutes he frequently visits. Intelligent script and direction effectively exploit French Quarter settings without sensationalizing story's seedier aspects. That's Eastwood's real-life daughter Alison playing his older girl. **(CC)**

TILL DEATH DO US PART 1972
☆ PG Mystery-Suspense 1:26
☑ Adult situations, explicit language, adult humor
Dir: Timothy Bond *Cast:* James Keach, Claude Jutra, Helen Hughes, Jack Creley, Matt Craven, Candace O'Connor
▶ Reporter Keach attends weekend therapy session at mansion of unorthodox marriage counselor Jutra. When someone starts murdering the patients, Keach investigates. B-movie attempt at black comedy has skimpy plot and overly broad performances.

TILL MARRIAGE DO US PART 1974 Italian
★ ★ R Comedy 1:37
☑ Nudity, adult situations, explicit language
Dir: Luigi Comencini *Cast:* Laura Antonelli, Alberto Lionello, Michele Placido, Jean Rochefort, Karin Schubert
▶ On her wedding night, virginal Antonelli learns groom Lionello is actually her stepbrother. He runs off to war, forcing her to ease her frustrations with ardent Rochefort and chauffeur Placido. Glossy showcase for voluptuous Antonelli has beautiful turn-of-the-century settings.

TILL THE CLOUDS ROLL BY 1947
★ ★ ★ NR Biography/Musical 2:17
Dir: Richard Whorf *Cast:* Robert Walker, Judy Garland, Lucille Bremer, Van Heflin, Van Johnson, Angela Lansbury
▶ Composer Jerome Kern (Walker) rises

to the top of the Broadway and London stages. Along the way, he gets married, suffers the death of his producer, and deals with other backstage problems. Thin story line provides vehicle for MGM stars (Frank Sinatra, Lena Horne, Cyd Charisse, Dinah Shore, and others) to perform Kern's classic music (like "I Won't Dance," "Smoke Gets in Your Eyes," and "A Fine Romance").

TILT 1979
★★ **PG Drama 1:51**
☑ Explicit language
Dir: Rudy Durand *Cast:* Brooke Shields, Ken Marshall, Charles Durning, Johnny Crawford, Geoffrey Lewis
▶ Teenage pinball champ Shields falls for rocker Marshall and uses her talent to finance his budding music career. She then takes on veteran ace Durning for a big-bucks showdown. Shields's natural sweetness and Durning's believability rise above aimless plotting and inconsistent characterizations.

TIM 1979 Australian
★★★★ **NR Drama 1:30**
☑ Adult situations
Dir: Michael Pate *Cast:* Mel Gibson, Piper Laurie, Alwyn Kurts, Pat Evison, Peter Gwynne, Deborah Kennedy
▶ Fortyish Laurie falls for mentally retarded gardener Gibson and helps him through some personal crises. Gibson's sister Kennedy objects to the relationship. Tender and compassionate, with lovely low-key performances by Gibson and Laurie. Based on the novel by Colleen McCullough.

TIME AFTER TIME 1979
★★★★ **PG Sci-Fi 1:52**
☑ Adult situations, explicit language, violence
Dir: Nicholas Meyer *Cast:* Malcolm McDowell, Mary Steenburgen, David Warner, Charles Cioffi, Joseph Maher, Patti D'Arbanville
▶ Victorian English writer H. G. Wells (McDowell) thinks he's unleashed a madman on Utopia when Jack the Ripper (Warner) steals his time machine and goes to present-day San Francisco. McDowell pursues Warner and finds romance with bank employee Steenburgen. Imaginative and literate adventure features engaging performances by McDowell and Steenburgen (husband and wife in real life), clever plotting, and amusing moments (McDowell at McDon-

ald's) intelligently mixed with a thought-provoking message.

TIME BANDITS 1981 British
★★ **PG Fantasy/Comedy 1:55**
☑ Explicit language, violence, adult humor
Dir: Terry Gilliam *Cast:* Craig Warnock, David Rappaport, Kenny Baker, Sean Connery, David Warner, Ralph Richardson
▶ Bored English schoolboy Warnock is whisked away by ragtag group of midget bandits, former employees of the Supreme Being (Richardson), who have stolen map of creation to travel through time and space in search of riches. Many adventures lead to battle with Evil (Warner), who wants map for own nefarious purposes. Antics of boy and "little people" include cameos by Sean Connery as Agamemnon and John Cleese as Robin Hood. Inventive, witty fun for young and old alike. Baker was R2D2 in *Star Wars*.

TIME GUARDIAN 1987 Australian
★ **PG Sci-Fi 1:39**
☑ Brief nudity, violence, explicit language
Dir: Brian Hannant *Cast:* Tom Burlinson, Carrie Fisher, Dean Stockwell
▶ A battle in a another dimension sends futuristic good guys (including Fisher) into present-day Australia, but bad guys from their century also show up in pursuit. Silly script and cheesy special effects; Fisher is fine and kids may enjoy the hectic action scenes.

TIME MACHINE, THE 1960
★★★ **G Sci-Fi 1:43**
Dir: George Pal *Cast:* Rod Taylor, Yvette Mimieux, Alan Young, Sebastian Cabot, Tom Helmore, Whit Bissell
▶ Victorian inventor Taylor develops time machine and travels ahead into the twentieth century. After encountering world wars, he goes to the year 802,701 and helps a peaceful blond race battle apelike predators. Terrific adaptation of the H. G. Wells novel features marvelous Oscar-winning special effects, solid Taylor, and an intelligent screenplay.

TIME OF DESTINY, A 1988
★★ **PG-13 Drama 1:58**
☑ Explicit language, violence
Dir: Gregory Nava *Cast:* William Hurt, Timothy Hutton, Melissa Leo, Francisco Rabal, Stockard Channing, Megan Follows

▶ Basque-American Hurt vows revenge when his dad dies the night Hutton elopes with his sister Leo. In World War II, Hurt gets sent to Hutton's unit and tries to kill him. Old-fashioned soap opera has excellent acting (Hurt does nicely in his unsympathetic role). Vivid plot with plenty of twists and turns overcomes some sappy melodramatics.

TIME OF TEARS 1988
★ NR Drama 1:35
☑ Adult situations, explicit language
Dir: Costa Mantis *Cast:* Frank Urso, Angelo Madrigale, Sharon Westley, Lou Liotta
▶ After the death of his grandfather, young Madrigale is befriended by elderly long-lost relative Urso who helps him cope with the loss. Sincere and unassuming; heart in the right place but low budget and slow pacing lead to lack of real punch.

TIMERIDER 1983
★★★ PG Fantasy/Action-Adventure 1:33
☑ Adult situations, explicit language, violence
Dir: William Dear *Cast:* Fred Ward, Belinda Bauer, Peter Coyote, Richard Masur, Ed Lauter
▶ Motorcyclist Ward gets lost during desert race and finds himself in the midst of time-travel experiment. Ward is transported back to 1877 California, where he gets involved with outlaws and beautiful gunslinger Bauer. Easygoing entertainment with intriguing premise and surprising sense of humor.

TIMES OF HARVEY MILK, THE 1984
★★★★ NR Documentary 1:28
☑ Adult situations, explicit language
Dir: Robert Epstein *Cast:* Harvey Milk, Dan White, George Moscone
▶ Oscar-winning documentary follows career of Harvey Milk, the first openly gay person elected to San Francisco's City Council. The homosexual community is outraged when Council member Dan White murders Milk and Mayor George Moscone. Compelling film examines White's trial (based on the infamous Twinkies defense) and release as well as Milk's influence on San Francisco politics. Narrated by Harvey Fierstein.

TIMES SQUARE 1980
★ R Drama 1:51
☑ Brief nudity, explicit language
Dir: Alan Moyle *Cast:* Tim Curry, Trini Alvarado, Robin Johnson, Peter Coffield, Herbert Berghof
▶ Wealthy teenager Alvarado, neglected by her politician father, runs away with rebellious mental patient Johnson to New York's Times Square. Alvarado becomes a stripper and Johnson a punk-rock star; sinister radio DJ Curry turns them into media celebrities. Ambitious soundtrack can't salvage this highly contrived and sanitized look at runaways.

TIME TRAVELERS, THE 1964
★★ NR Sci-Fi 1:22
Dir: Ib Melchior *Cast:* Preston Foster, Phil Carey, Merry Anders, John Hoyt, Steve Franken
▶ Scientists develop a time machine and travel to 2071. They find the world devastated by a nuclear war; the few remaining humans are fighting a race of mutants while using androids to build a spaceship for escape to another planet. A neglected genre treat makes up for moderate budget with clever story and brisk pace.

TIME WALKER 1982
★★ PG Horror 1:23
☑ Explicit language, violence
Dir: Tom Kennedy *Cast:* Ben Murphy, Nina Axelrod, Kevin Brophy, James Karen, Austin Stoker, Shari Belafonte-Harper
▶ American archaeologist Murphy transports Egyptian mummy to California campus. When valuable jewels are stolen from the mummy's sarcophagus, it comes to rampaging life. Some spookiness and genuine jolts although plot gets increasingly farfetched as it goes along.

TIN DRUM, THE 1980 German
★ R Drama 2:22
☑ Rape, nudity, strong sexual content, adult situations, explicit language, violence
Dir: Volker Schlondorff *Cast:* David Bennent, Angela Winkler, Mario Adorf, Daniel Olbrychski, Katharina Thalbach, Heinz Bennent
▶ Adaptation of world-renowned novel by Günter Grass tells of young Bennent, who rebels against bleak world of Nazi Germany in unusual ways: he becomes obsessed with banging on toy tin drum, develops glass-shattering scream, and refuses to grow bigger. With these bizarre talents, tiny Bennent survives World War II as entertainer for Nazis even as he

staunchly opposes them; rest of family suffers horrors of dictatorship and war. Haunting performance by Bennent in unusual, surreal winner of Oscar for Best Foreign film. [S]

TIN MAN 1987
★★★ NR Drama 1:35
☑ Nudity, adult situations, explicit language
Dir: John G. Thomas *Cast:* Timothy Bottoms, Deana Jurgens, John Phillip Law, Troy Donahue, Gerry Black
▶ Genius deaf boy Bottoms develops computer through which he can hear and speak. Jurgens, a teacher for deaf, finds work for Bottoms with a computer outfit. Operation restores Bottoms's hearing and love bloom between him and Jurgens. Their subsequent love affair suffers when Bottoms falls under the spell of evil corporate executive Donahue. Often melodramatic treatment of original premise.

TIN MEN 1987
★★★ R Comedy 1:52
☑ Adult situations, explicit language
Dir: Barry Levinson *Cast:* Richard Dreyfuss, Danny DeVito, Barbara Hershey, John Mahoney, Jackie Gayle, J. T. Walsh
▶ Baltimore aluminum siding salesmen Dreyfuss and DeVito feud when their Cadillacs collide. Battle between "tin men" escalates until Dreyfuss seduces DeVito's wife Hershey. Meanwhile, a state commission investigates scams used by Dreyfuss, DeVito, and cohorts Mahoney, Gayle, and Walsh to sucker prospective customers. Leads are fine as macho, pigheaded foes, but real stars are ensemble of supporting tin men and comic dialogue by writer-director Levinson. **(CC)**

TIN STAR, THE 1957
★★★★ NR Western 1:33 B&W
Dir: Anthony Mann *Cast:* Henry Fonda, Anthony Perkins, Betsy Palmer, Michael Ray, Neville Brand, John McIntire
▶ Former sheriff/bounty hunter Fonda rides into town and teaches rookie lawman Perkins the tricks of the trade. Together the tough guy and the tenderfoot battle vigilante gunman Brand. Fine Western concentrates on character rather than action.

TOAST OF NEW YORK, THE 1937
★★★ NR Biography 1:49 B&W
Dir: Rowland V. Lee *Cast:* Edward Arnold, Cary Grant, Frances Farmer, Jack Oakie, Donald Meek, Clarence Kolb
▶ Lively, entertaining biography of robber baron Jim Fisk, who amassed post–Civil War fortune by defrauding Cornelius Vanderbilt, only to lose everything in a scheme to corner the gold market. Arnold approaches his role as "Jubilee Jim" with relish, while Grant brings touch of elegance to character based on Jay Gould. Farmer is charming as Josie Mansfield, center of a tragic love triangle.

TO BE OR NOT TO BE 1942
★★★★ NR Comedy 1:42 B&W
Dir: Ernst Lubitsch *Cast:* Carole Lombard, Jack Benny, Robert Stack, Felix Bressart, Lionel Atwill, Sig Rumann
▶ In this black comedy classic, Benny is quite droll as the Polish actor trying to outwit the Nazis and, in her last film, Lombard exudes glamour as his flirtatious wife. Lubitsch's direction subtly interweaves comedy and more serious themes as writer Edwin Justis Mayer provides some darkly funny lines: "So they call me Concentration Camp Erhardt!" and "What he did to Shakespeare, we're doing to Poland." Inspired the Mel Brooks 1983 remake.

TO BE OR NOT TO BE 1983
★★ PG Comedy 1:47
☑ Explicit language, mild violence
Dir: Alan Johnson *Cast:* Mel Brooks, Anne Bancroft, Tim Matheson, Charles Durning, Jose Ferrer, Christopher Lloyd
▶ Warsaw, 1939: hammy theatre troupe leader Brooks, being cuckolded by co-star wife Bancroft with soldier Matheson, must impersonate top-ranking Nazis to get his company out of German-occupied Poland. Remake of 1942 classic is broad but good-natured. Bancroft shines. Funniest scene: Bancroft and Brooks dueting "Sweet Georgia Brown" in Polish! **(CC)**

TOBRUK 1967
★★★ NR War 1:50
Dir: Arthur Hill *Cast:* Rock Hudson, George Peppard, Nigel Green, Guy Stockwell, Jack Watson, Norman Rossington
▶ Competent World War II drama about a daring mission across the African desert to destroy Nazi supplies at Tobruk. German Jews posing as Axis troops and commandos disguised as POWs undertake the trek. Hudson and Green, the respective American and British leaders,

suspect a traitor when they are unexpectedly ambushed. Large-scale action scenes boost familiar plot.

TOBY TYLER, OR TEN WEEKS WITH A CIRCUS 1960
★★★ NR Family 1:36
Dir: Charles Barton *Cast:* Kevin Corcoran, Henry Calvin, Gene Sheldon, Bob Sweeney, Mr. Stubbs, James Drury
▶ At the turn of the century, young Corcoran runs away from his family and joins the circus, where he is befriended by concessioner Sweeney and chimp Mr. Stubbs. The boy gets to perform and learn about life, but he eventually discovers there's no place like home. Entertaining Disney adaptation of the James Otis Kaler novel.

TO CATCH A KING 1983
★★★ NR Action-Adventure/MFTV 1:53
☑ Adult situations, mild violence
Dir: Clive Donner *Cast:* Robert Wagner, Teri Garr, Barbara Parkins, Horst Janson, Marcel Bozzuffi
▶ In World War II Lisbon, American nightclub owner Wagner teams with beautiful cabaret singer Garr to thwart Nazi plan to kidnap the Duke and Duchess of Windsor. Race-against-time tension blends with foreign intrigue and romance in this adaptation of the Jack Higgins best-seller.

TO CATCH A THIEF 1955
★★★★ NR Drama 1:46
Dir: Alfred Hitchcock *Cast:* Cary Grant, Grace Kelly, Jessie Royce Landis, John Williams, Charles Vanel, Brigitte Auber
▶ Lightweight but elegant drama about dashing, retired cat burglar Grant, the chief suspect when daring burglaries plague hotels along the French Riviera. Grant must catch the culprit to exonerate himself; alluring heiress Kelly offers herself as bait. Suspense is downplayed for frequently audacious double entendres, gorgeous Edith Head costumes, and scenic, Oscar-winning photography by Robert Burks.

TO HAVE AND HAVE NOT 1944
★★★★ NR Drama 1:40 B&W
Dir: Howard Hawks *Cast:* Humphrey Bogart, Walter Brennan, Lauren Bacall, Dolores Moran, Hoagy Carmichael, Marcel Dalio
▶ Fishing charter captain Bogart agrees to run guns for Free French forces to help sultry saloon singer Bacall escape the Nazis. Intensely romantic World War II drama is famous as the film that brought Bogey and Bacall together, but other aspects of this loose adaptation of Ernest Hemingway's best-seller hold up equally well. Bacall's film debut includes her unforgettable "whistling" sequence as well as two charming songs with Carmichael; Brennan offers solid comic support as an addle-brained rummy. Screenplay by Jules Furthman and William Faulkner.

TO HELL AND BACK 1955
★★★ NR Biography 1:46
Dir: Jesse Hibbs *Cast:* Audie Murphy, Marshall Thompson, Jack Kelly, Susan Kohner, Charles Drake, David Janssen
▶ Murphy gives a disarming performance as himself in this drama based on his best-selling autobiography. His childhood as son of Texas sharecroppers and rejection by Marines and Navy in World War II are tastefully depicted, but film's highlights are strong battle scenes as the Army private rises through the ranks to win the Congressional Medal of Honor.

TO KILL A MOCKINGBIRD 1962
★★★★ NR Drama 2:09 B&W
Dir: Robert Mulligan *Cast:* Gregory Peck, Mary Badham, Phillip Alford, John Megna, Brock Peters, Robert Duvall
▶ In a prejudice-filled 1930s Alabama town, widowed lawyer Peck tries to raise children Badham and Alford while defending Peters, a black unjustly accused of rape. A masterpiece in which director Mulligan creates a portrait of time and place that is at once haunting, nostalgic, and clear-eyed. Magnificent performance by Peck nabbed one of film's three Oscars (Screenplay Adaptation, Art Direction/Set Decoration); also nominated for Best Picture and Supporting Actress for Badham, who gave one of the most natural child performances ever. Based on Harper Lee's Pulitzer prize–winning novel.

TOKYO OLYMPIAD 1966 Japanese
★★ NR Documentary/Sports 2:34
Dir: Kon Ichikawa
▶ Dazzling documentary on the 1964 Tokyo Olympics is one of the greatest testimonials to athletics ever filmed. Working with hundreds of technicians, director Ichikawa fashioned a breathtaking mosaic of gymnasts, swimmers, racers, and onlookers. Among the highlights are future heavyweight champ Joe Frazier's gold-winning performance and his room-

mate Bob Hayes's hundred-yard dash. An hour cut from the original U.S. release has recently been restored. [S]

TOKYO POP 1988
★★ R Drama 1:37
☑ Adult situations, explicit language
Dir: Fran Kuzui *Cast:* Carrie Hamilton, Yutako Tadokoro, Taiji Tonoyoma, Tetsura Tanba, Masumi Harukawa, Toki Shiozawa
► Young American rock singer Hamilton travels to Tokyo on a whim. She soon attracts the attentions of Tadokoro, who feels a tall blond vocalist will give his struggling rock band an edge over the competition. East-meets-West romance combined with rising star saga is an extended music video primarily for teens. Hamilton is comedienne Carol Burnett's daughter.

TO LIVE AND DIE IN L.A. 1985
★★★ R Mystery-Suspense 1:56
☑ Nudity, explicit language, graphic violence
Dir: William Friedkin *Cast:* William L. Petersen, Willem Dafoe, John Pankow, John Turturro, Darlanne Fluegel, Dean Stockwell
► When counterfeiter Dafoe causes the death of a Secret Service agent, Petersen, the dead man's partner, relentlessly seeks revenge. Petersen's new cohort Pankow intially objects to his methods but becomes caught up in his obsession. Cynical but riveting thriller features complex (although unsympathetic) characters, twisty story, and exciting action with the best chase scene (Petersen driving against the L.A. traffic) since Friedkin's *The French Connection*. Hit theme song by Wang Chung. **(CC)**

TOMB OF LIGEIA, THE 1965 British
☆ NR Horror 1:20
Dir: Roger Corman *Cast:* Vincent Price, Elizabeth Shephard, John Westbrook, Oliver Johnston
► Final entry in Roger Corman's series of Edgar Allan Poe adaptations stars Price as a widower obsessed with the memory of his wife. He marries Shephard, who resembles the late Ligeia, whose menacing spirit causes trouble for the newlyweds. Screenplay by Robert Towne.

TOMBOY 1985
★★ R Romance/Comedy 1:30
☑ Nudity, adult situations, explicit language, mild violence
Dir: Herb Freed *Cast:* Betsy Russell,

Jerry Dinome, Kristi Somers, Richard Erdman, Phillip Sterling, Eric Douglas
► Female mechanic Russell shows little interest in men until she meets handsome racer Dinome. When their romance hits the rocks, she makes a bet that climaxes in a car race between them. Delivers nudity and soft-core sex but avoids offending; Russell and Somers are pleasant company.

TOM BROWN'S SCHOOLDAYS 1951 British
★★ NR Drama/Family 1:33 B&W
Dir: Gordon Parry *Cast:* John Howard Davies, Robert Newton, Diana Wynyard, Hermione Baddeley, Kathleen Byron, John Forrest
► Well-mounted version of Thomas Hughes's 1857 novel about the adventures of young Brown (Davies) at Rugby, an exclusive English boys' school dominated by bullies. Forrest portrays Brown's nemesis Flashman (later the hero of a series of comic novels by George MacDonald Fraser); Newton is the novice headmaster who treats his students with unprecedented respect.

TOM HORN 1980
★★★★ R Western 1:37
☑ Adult situations, explicit language, violence
Dir: William Wiard *Cast:* Steve McQueen, Linda Evans, Richard Farnsworth, Slim Pickens, Billy Green Bush, Elisha Cook, Jr.
► In 1901, legendary bounty-hunter Tom Horn (McQueen) is hired by Wyoming cattlemen to kill rustlers. The hunter does his job but, when he no longer fits into his employers' schemes, is framed for murder. Cynical and timely; McQueen, in one of his last performances, is quite sympathetic as the real-life martyr. Nice support from Farnsworth.

TOM JONES 1963 British
★★★ NR Comedy 2:08
Dir: Tony Richardson *Cast:* Albert Finney, Susannah York, Hugh Griffith, Edith Evans, Joyce Redman, Diane Cilento
► In nineteenth-century England, rakish young orphan Finney makes time with the ladies while making his way in the world; a rival plots against him for the affections of virginal heiress York. Stunning adaptation of Henry Fielding's classic novel works like a charm, thanks to Richardson's wonderfully playful direction. Among many standout scenes: the eat-

ing orgy between Finney and Redman. Oscars for Best Picture, Director, Score, and Screenplay Adaptation. Acting nominations went to Finney, Redman, Evans, Cilento, and Griffith.

TOMMY 1975 British
★ PG Musical 1:51
☑ Adult situations
Dir: Ken Russell   *Cast:* Ann-Margret, Oliver Reed, Roger Daltrey, Elton John, Eric Clapton, Keith Moon
▶ Abused by his parents Reed and Ann-Margret, Tommy (Daltrey) grows up a deaf, dumb, and blind pinball wizard and the leader of a bizarre religious cult. Flamboyant adaptation of Pete Townshend's famous rock opera contains some startling cameos (notably Tina Turner as the Acid Queen and Jack Nicholson as a doctor), but some viewers may not swallow the sight of Ann-Margret dancing in baked beans. The Who (Townshend and Daltrey's rock group) appear briefly.

TOMORROW 1972
★★★★ NR Drama 1:42 B&W
Dir: Joseph Anthony   *Cast:* Robert Duvall, Olga Bellin, Sudie Bond, Richard McConnell, Peter Masterson, William Hawley
▶ Meticulous, slowly paced adaptation of a William Faulkner short story about poor Mississippi farmer Duvall who cares for pregnant Bellin after she's abandoned by her husband and family. When she dies giving birth, he raises her son as his own—only to lose him in a cruel twist. Duvall is magnificent in a stark, unpolished drama that captures the atmosphere of Faulkner's work. Screenplay by Horton Foote.

TOM SAWYER 1973
★★★★ G Musical/Family 1:39
Dir: Don Taylor   *Cast:* Johnnie Whitaker, Celeste Holm, Jeff East, Warren Oates, Jodie Foster, Lucille Benson
▶ Musical adaptation of Mark Twain's classic story of boy's adventures in 1830s Midwest features Whitaker as Tom Sawyer, Holm as warm but impatient Aunt Polly, East as dropout Huck Finn, Oates as town drunk Muff Potter, and young, scene-stealing Foster as Becky Thatcher. First-rate family entertainment with screenplay and music by Richard and Robert Sherman, composers of *Mary Poppins*. Picture earned Oscar nominations for Set Decoration, Costume Design,

and Score. Best tunes: "Freebootin'," sung by Whitaker and Oates, and "A Man's Gotta Be What He's Born to Be," from Oates and East. **(CC)**

TOM THUMB 1958
★★ G Fantasy 1:32
Dir: George Pal   *Cast:* Russ Tamblyn, Alan Young, Peter Sellers, Terry-Thomas, Jessie Matthews, June Thorburn
▶ Thumb-sized lad Tamblyn is beloved by townsfolk for his high spirits; evil Sellers and Terry-Thomas want to use Tamblyn for no good but are foiled. Oscar-winning special effects from technical master George Pal highlight adaptation of the Charles Perrault fairy tale; kids of all ages should have a good time.

TONY ROME 1967
★★ NR Mystery-Suspense 1:51
Dir: Gordon Douglas   *Cast:* Frank Sinatra, Jill St. John, Richard Conte, Sue Lyon, Gena Rowlands, Simon Oakland
▶ Miami private eye Sinatra gets involved with blackmailers, junkies, and killers when he rescues alcoholic heiress Lyon from a seedy motel. Sinatra's comfortable performance and frequent action boost extremely confusing plot. Followed by *Lady in Cement*.

TOO LATE THE HERO 1970
★★★ PG War 2:13
☑ Explicit language, violence
Dir: Robert Aldrich   *Cast:* Michael Caine, Cliff Robertson, Henry Fonda, Ian Bannen, Harry Andrews, Denholm Elliott
▶ During World War II, American Robertson and Brit Caine are chosen for dangerous mission to destroy Japanese encampment on Pacific island. Although they don't get along, they prove their heroism. Macho derring-do is familiar but fast-paced in the patented Aldrich fashion. Also known as *Suicide Run*.

TOO SCARED TO SCREAM 1985
★★ R Drama 1:39
☑ Nudity, adult situations, explicit language, violence
Dir: Tony Lo Bianco   *Cast:* Mike Connors, Anne Archer, Leon Isaac Kennedy, Ian McShane, Ruth Ford, John Heard
▶ When a woman is stabbed to death in a posh Manhattan high rise, tough cop Connors convinces his partner Archer to pose as a tenant to lure the killer out of hiding. Chief suspect is Shakespeare-quoting doorman McShane, who lives in

a luxurious brownstone with his invalid mother, Maureen O'Sullivan. Although graphic at times, unpretentious drama follows a comfortable formula.

TOOTSIE 1982
★ ★ ★ ★ ★ **PG Comedy 1:56**
☑ Adult situations, explicit language
Dir: Sydney Pollack *Cast:* Dustin Hoffman, Jessica Lange, Teri Garr, Dabney Coleman, Bill Murray, Charles Durning
▶ Bona fide blockbuster features Hoffman as Michael Dorsey, a New York actor who has become, in his agent's (director Pollack) words, "a cult failure." He can't earn enough money to mount roommate Murray's play, *Return to Love Canal*, so he dresses as a woman and lands a role on a popular soap opera. Complications arise when he falls for co-star Lange and then almost becomes engaged to her father Durning. Remarkably funny comedy offers many astute observations about sexual roles; one of the few movies that can be recommended without reservation. Nominated for ten Oscars; Lange won for Best Supporting Actress. (CC)

TOPAZ 1969
★ ★ **PG Mystery-Suspense 2:07**
☑ Violence
Dir: Alfred Hitchcock *Cast:* John Forsythe, Frederick Stafford, Dany Robin, Karin Dor, John Vernon, Michel Piccoli
▶ CIA agent Forsythe and French counterpart Stafford find themselves up to their necks in intrigue involving the 1962 Cuban Missile Crisis. The trail leads Stafford to corruption and double crosses within his own organization. Adaptation of the Leon Uris best-seller evokes some tension, but overall one of Hitchcock's lesser efforts.

TOP GUN 1986
★ ★ ★ ★ ★ **PG Action-Adventure 1:50**
☑ Adult situations, explicit language
Dir: Tony Scott *Cast:* Tom Cruise, Kelly McGillis, Anthony Edwards, Tom Skerritt, Val Kilmer, John Stockwell
▶ Hotshot, rule-breaking Navy fighter pilot Maverick (Cruise) and his partner Goose (Edwards) are sent to Top Gun school where one percent of fighter pilots learn the 1980s high-tech style of dogfighting. Cruise's attitude problem gets him in trouble with leader Viper (Skerritt), rival pilot Iceman (Kilmer), and instructor-love interest McGillis. He triumphs to save the day, shoot down a few Commie MIGs

and get the girl. Eye-popping flying footage, smugly macho Cruise, relentless rock music soundtrack (including the Oscar-winning "Take My Breath Away" by Berlin), and superslick production values turned this into a major blockbuster hit.

TOP HAT 1935
★ ★ ★ ★ **NR Musical 1:39 B&W**
Dir: Mark Sandrich *Cast:* Fred Astaire, Ginger Rogers, Edward Everett Horton, Helen Broderick, Erik Rhodes, Eric Blore
▶ In London, song-and-dance man Astaire falls for his downstairs neighbor Rogers, but true love runs a rocky course when she mistakenly assumes he is married to her friend Broderick. Absolutely divine; Astaire and Rogers have never been more perfect. Many romantic moments: Astaire spreading sand on the floor so as not to disturb Rogers during a tap routine, the duo getting caught in the rain to the strains of "Isn't This a Lovely Day," and their "Cheek to Cheek" duet. Best Picture nominee also features able comic support from Horton, Rhodes, and Blore.

TOPKAPI 1964
★ ★ ★ **NR Comedy 2:00**
Dir: Jules Dassin *Cast:* Melina Mercouri, Peter Ustinov, Maximilian Schell, Robert Morley, Akim Tamiroff, Gilles Segal
▶ Dazzling caper movie about an attempt by a disparate band of inventors, con artists, and acrobats to steal a priceless dagger from a heavily guarded Turkish museum. Mercouri (director Dassin's real-life wife) assembles the team, unaware that the paunchy final member (Ustinov) is a police informer. Funny, unpredictable, and highlighted by a bravura sequence detailing the break-in. Ustinov won a Supporting Actor Oscar for his perfect comic timing. Based on an Eric Ambler novel.

TOPPER 1937
★ ★ ★ ★ **NR Fantasy/Comedy 1:36 B&W**
Dir: Norman Z. McLeod *Cast:* Cary Grant, Constance Bennett, Roland Young, Billie Burke, Eugene Pallette, Arthur Lake
▶ Freewheeling couple Grant and Bennett are killed in a drunk-driving accident and become ghosts. Needing to accomplish a good deed to reach heaven, Grant and Bennett teach stuffy banker

Young the lighter side of life. Whimsical fun with three top performances and terrific effects. Spawned two sequels, a TV series, and made-for-TV remake; available in a colorized version.

TOP SECRET 1984
★★ PG Comedy 1:30
☑ Mild violence, adult humor
Dir: Jim Abrahams, David Zucker, Jerry Zucker *Cast:* Val Kilmer, Lucy Gutteridge, Omar Sharif, Jeremy Kemp, Peter Cushing, Michael Gough
▶ American rock star Kilmer performs in East Germany and gets involved in intrigue involving beautiful Gutteridge, whose father has been kidnapped by Nazi organization. Painless lunacy mixes scattered hits with many misses. Funniest moments: the musical numbers, Sharif's bout with a trash compactor, and Kilmer's introduction to French spy "Deja Vu" ("Haven't we met somewhere before, monsieur?"). **(CC)**

TORA! TORA! TORA! 1970
U.S./Japanese
★★★ G War 2:23
Dir: Richard Fleischer, Toshio Masuda, Kinji Fukasaku *Cast:* Martin Balsam, Soh Yamamura, Jason Robards, Joseph Cotten, Tatsuya Mihashi, E. G. Marshall
▶ Lavish and accurate re-creation of events leading up to Japanese sneak attack on Pearl Harbor in 1941. Japanese plan to further expansionist goals despite reservations of admiral Yamamura assigned to lead assault. Meanwhile, American military men go about peacetime business, ignoring warnings of suspicious intelligence officer Marshall. Talky first half redeemed by impressive action sequences in climax. Two versions of film were shot, each showing one nation's side: U.S. version bombed, but Japanese was huge hit.

TORCHLIGHT 1985
★ R Drama 1:32
☑ Adult situations, explicit language
Dir: Tom Wright *Cast:* Pamela Sue Martin, Steve Railsback, Ian McShane, Al Corley
▶ Lackluster cautionary tale about cocaine addiction was co-written and associate produced by Martin. She stars as a successful artist who falls in love with architect Railsback. They marry and are happy but by their first anniversary, he has begun free-basing cocaine with evil drug dealer McShane. Some pulp vitality

but, overall, a predictable soap opera with about as much subtlety as a sledgehammer.

TORCH SONG TRILOGY 1988
★★★ R Comedy/Drama 2:06
☑ Adult situations, explicit language
Dir: Paul Bogart *Cast:* Harvey Fierstein, Anne Bancroft, Matthew Broderick, Brian Kerwin, Karen Young, Eddie Castrodad
▶ Gay female impersonator finds search for Mr. Right rocky, until he meets and falls in love with bisexual teacher Kerwin. Fierstein's fiery mom Bancroft still won't accept her son's homosexuality and keeps trying to find him a nice Jewish girl. He finds greater purpose in life when he adopts troubled gay teen Castrodad as his son. Frank adaptation of Fierstein's Tony-winning play will merit kudos from the discerning, although humorous moments work better than the dramatic ones.

TORMENT 1986
★★ R Mystery-Suspense 1:23
☑ Explicit language, violence
Dir: Samson Aslanian, John Hopkins *Cast:* Taylor Gilbert, William Witt, Eve Brenner, Warren Lincoln, Najean Cherry, Stan Weston
▶ Moody thriller about psychotic killer Witt preying on single women in San Francisco. He singles out detective's fiancée Gilbert as his next victim, and traps her in the remote house of her crippled future mother-in-law, Brenner. Despite budget constraints, inventive directing provides some effective shocks.

TORN CURTAIN 1966
★★★ PG Espionage 2:05
☑ Violence
Dir: Alfred Hitchcock *Cast:* Paul Newman, Julie Andrews, Lila Kedrova, Hansjorg Felmy, Tamara Toumanova, Ludwig Donath
▶ Nuclear physicist Newman defects from West to East, taking puzzled girlfriend/assistant Andrews with him. Soon she understands his plan: he dupes East German scientist Donath into revelations about Soviet missile program. Can they escape to the free world with the info? Not one of Hitchcock's better outings.

TORTURE GARDEN 1968 British
★ NR Horror 1:33
Dir: Freddie Francis *Cast:* Jack Palance, Burgess Meredith, Beverly Adams, Peter Cushing, Barbara Ewing

▶ Uneven horror compendium tied together by sideshow seer Meredith, who can predict the future: "Enoch" concerns a cat with an insatiable appetite for human heads; "Terror Over Hollywood" reveals a famous star to be a robot; "Mr. Steinway" is a curious romantic triangle involving a concert pianist, his fiancée, and a jealous piano; "The Man Who Collected Poe" learns that he's also acquired the author's ghost. Written by Robert Bloch.

TO SIR, WITH LOVE 1967 British
★★★★ NR Drama 1:45
Dir: James Clavell *Cast:* Sidney Poitier, Judy Geeson, Lulu, Suzy Kendall, Christian Roberts, Faith Brook
▶ Black teacher Poitier takes job in London's toughest slum. The kids resist him at first but he wins their respect through unorthodox lessons and treating them as equals. Heartfelt and very moving; Poitier is terrific, interacting beautifully with his young charges. Lulu co-stars as one of the students and sings the hit title song.

TOUCH AND GO 1986
★★★★ R Drama 1:41
☑ Brief nudity, adult situations, explicit language, violence
Dir: Robert Mandel *Cast:* Michael Keaton, Maria Conchita Alonso, Ajay Naidu, Maria Tucci, Max Wright
▶ Hotshot hockey jock Keaton is attacked by gang and captures Naidu, one of the punks. Tough-talking kid charms Keaton and takes him home where he meets and falls for the kid's mom, Alonso. Their budding relationship hits many snags but this stand-up-and-cheer sleeper delivers in the end. Both Keaton and Alonso are charming.

TOUCHED 1982
★★★ R Drama 1:29
☑ Adult situations, explicit language
Dir: John Flynn *Cast:* Robert Hays, Kathleen Beller, Ned Beatty, Gilbert Lewis, Lyle Kessler
▶ Mental patient Hays escapes from an institution and finds job at boardwalk amusement park. He returns to the asylum to free his schizophrenic girlfriend, Beller, hoping to establish an independent life. Sincere, uplifting drama is a bit too predictable, despite fine performances by Hays and Beller.

TOUCHED BY LOVE 1980
★★★★★ PG Drama 1:34
☑ Explicit language
Dir: Gus Trikonis *Cast:* Deborah Raffin, Diane Lane, Michael Learned, John Amos, Cristina Raines, Mary Wickes
▶ Nursing trainee Lena Canada (Raffin) develops friendship with a young cerebral palsy victim (Lane) and encourages her to write to her idol, Elvis Presley. Responsive to the girl's plight, Presley becomes a supportive pen pal. Earnest, sentimental drama, based on a true story by Canada, features effectively restrained performances and an uplifting theme.

TOUCH OF CLASS, A 1973
★★★ PG Romance/Comedy 1:45
☑ Adult situations, explicit language
Dir: Melvin Frank *Cast:* Glenda Jackson, George Segal, Paul Sorvino, Hildegard Neil, Cec Linder, K. Callan
▶ In London, married American insurance man Segal meets divorced Englishwoman Jackson during Hyde Park baseball game. They embark on initially casual affair, but true love rears its difficult head. Brightly funny and breezily whimsical, with bubbling chemistry between Segal and Oscar-winning Jackson.

TOUCH OF EVIL 1958
★★★ NR Mystery-Suspense 1:35 B&W
Dir: Orson Welles *Cast:* Charlton Heston, Janet Leigh, Orson Welles, Joseph Calleia, Akim Tamiroff, Valentin de Vargas
▶ In U.S-Mexican border town, Mexican cop Heston and corrupt gringo detective Welles lock horns while investigating murder of local bigwig. When Welles frames an innocent man for the crime, Heston tries unsuccessfully to blow the whistle. Welles and drug dealer Tamiroff retaliate by framing Heston's wife Leigh for sordid crimes. Compelling portrayal of decadence and deception opens with spectacular three-minute shot that ranks among best in film history. Look for unbilled cameos by Marlene Dietrich, Mercedes McCambridge, Zsa Zsa Gabor, and Joseph Cotten.

TOUGH ENOUGH 1983
★★★ PG Drama 1:46
☑ Nudity, adult situations, explicit language, violence
Dir: Richard Fleischer *Cast:* Dennis Quaid, Carlene Watkins, Stan Shaw, Pam Grier, Warren Oates, Wilford Brimley
▶ Aspiring country-western singer Quaid enters a local "Toughman" boxing com-

petition, and catches the eye of shady promoter Oates, who promises him a chance to sing on national TV if he will throw a prizefight. Oates gives a delicately shaded performance in his last film role; Quaid is appealing both in the ring and with a guitar.

TOUGH GUYS 1986
★ ★ ★ ★ PG Comedy 1:42
☑ Adult situations, explicit language
Dir: Jeff Kanew *Cast:* Burt Lancaster, Kirk Douglas, Charles Durning, Alexis Smith, Dana Carvey, Darlanne Fluegel
▶ In their seventh film teaming, Lancaster and Douglas play two elderly convicts, the last successful train robbers in America, who find it hard to cope with a strange new Los Angeles after thirty years in jail. Lancaster, suffering in a nursing home, and Douglas, offered a series of demeaning jobs, join up for one last robbery. Wonderful stars provide all the luster in this slight comedy.

TOUGH GUYS DON'T DANCE 1987
★ ★ R Mystery-Suspense 1:48
☑ Nudity, adult situations, explicit language
Dir: Norman Mailer *Cast:* Ryan O'Neal, Isabella Rossellini, Debra Sandlund, Wings Hauser, Lawrence Tierney, John Bedford Lloyd
▶ Adaptation by Norman Mailer of his novel about booze, drugs, murder, and sex in Provincetown, Cape Cod. Occasional writer O'Neal wakes up after drunken binge caused by departure of unfaithful wife Sandlund to find blood in his car and severed head buried under dope stash. Local police chief Hauser fingers O'Neal for crimes, leading O'Neal to uncover wholesale cocaine deal and sexual intrigue in attempt to prove innocence. Convoluted plot plagued by frequent flashbacks and heavy-handed narration.

TOURIST TRAP 1979
★ PG Horror 1:26
☑ Explicit language, graphic violence
Dir: David Schmoeller *Cast:* Chuck Connors, Jon Van Ness, Jocelyn Jones, Robin Sherwood, Tanya Roberts
▶ When their friend disappears after an auto mishap, a group of teens trace him to Slausen's Lost Oasis, a museum filled with life-size mannequins. Imprisoned by caretaker Connors, the youngsters are terrified to learn that the dummies are alive and deadly. Routine slasher exercise done in by bad special effects.

TOWERING INFERNO, THE 1974
★ ★ ★ ★ PG Action-Adventure 2:45
☑ Explicit language, violence
Dir: John Guillermin, Irwin Allen *Cast:* Paul Newman, Steve McQueen, William Holden, Faye Dunaway, Fred Astaire, Susan Blakely
▶ During dedication party, San Francisco skyscraper goes up in flames, trapping celebrants on top floors. Newman the stunned architect, Holden the greedy developer who cost-cut architect's safety features, and McQueen the heroic fire chief who seeks to minimize loss of life and douse the flames. First-rate visual spectacle overcomes sometimes silly personal drama. Grand disaster epic started the trend and earned seven Oscar nominations, including Best Picture and Supporting Actor (for Astaire); winner for Cinematography and Editing. **(CC)**

TOWN THAT DREADED SUNDOWN, THE 1976
★ ★ ★ R Mystery-Suspense 1:30
☑ Violence
Dir: Charles B. Pierce *Cast:* Ben Johnson, Andrew Prine, Dawn Wells, Jimmy Clem, Charles B. Pierce, Cindy Butler
▶ Unsolved murder spree in Texarkana during the summer of 1946 is the basis of an effective, low-budget thriller. Documentary approach shows town's growing panic and the inability of local law officers to pinpoint the killer, identified only by his hooded mask. Texas Ranger Johnson, brought in to help, is also stymied by lack of evidence.

TOXIC AVENGER, THE 1985
★ R Comedy 1:25
☑ Explicit language, graphic violence
Dir: Michael Herz, Samuel Weil *Cast:* Andree Maranda, Mitchell Cohen, Jennifer Baptist, Cindy Manion, Robert Prichard
▶ Skinny nerd falls into a vat of toxic waste and emerges as the Toxic Avenger (Cohen), a liberal monster determined to clean up his corrupt hometown. While dispatching his enemies, he falls for a beautiful blind girl (Maranda) who fixes him Drano sandwiches. Tongue-in-cheek tone and pro-environment stance don't atone for film's tawdry style. Followed by *Toxic Avenger II*.

TOY, THE 1982
★ ★ ★ ★ PG Comedy 1:42

☑ Explicit language
Dir: Richard Donner *Cast:* Richard Pryor, Jackie Gleason, Ned Beatty, Scott Schwartz, Teresa Ganzel
▶ Business tycoon Gleason tells bratty son Schwartz he can have anything in the store for Christmas. The kid selects the janitor Pryor, an out-of-work writer who can be bought. Eventually, Pryor teaches Schwartz about love, hope, politics, racial tolerance, and nuclear physics—but not before they share many very funny adventures. Excellent cast will delight kids. Remake of a French comedy by Francis Veber.

TOY SOLDIERS 1984
★ **R Action-Adventure 1:31**
☑ Nudity, adult situations, explicit language, violence
Dir: David Fisher *Cast:* Jason Miller, Cleavon Little, Terri Garber, Rodolfo De Anda, Douglas Warhit
▶ When her friends are taken hostage by Central American guerrillas, feisty coed Garber forms a rescue mission with grizzled captain Miller and neighborhood tough Little. Mindless adventure is often unintentionally funny.

TRACK 29 1988 British
☆ **R Drama 1:30**
☑ Rape, adult situations, explicit language
Dir: Nicolas Roeg *Cast:* Theresa Russell, Gary Oldman, Christopher Lloyd, Sandra Bernhard, Colleen Camp, Seymour Cassel
▶ Bored Texas housewife Russell, whose doctor husband Lloyd is more interested in model trains and nurse Bernhard than in her, meets mysterious Englishman Oldman. Is he the son she abandoned years ago or a figment of her imagination? Oddball story given dash by Roeg's direction and performances by Russell and Oldman, but many viewers will be left scratching heads in bewilderment. Written by Dennis Potter.

TRADING HEARTS 1988
★★★ **PG Drama 1:30**
☑ Adult situations, explicit language
Dir: Neil Leifer *Cast:* Raul Julia, Beverly D'Angelo, Jenny Lewis, Parris Buckner, Robert Gwaltney, Mark Harris
▶ Cut by his team, Red Sox pitcher Julia is pounced on by Lewis, a cute tomboy desperate for a new dad. But her lounge-singing mom D'Angelo can't stand Julia, a problem that doesn't deter young

Lewis. Nostalgic drama by sportswriter Frank Deford captures 1957 Miami effectively, but low-key plot offers few surprises.

TRADING PLACES 1983
★★★★★ **R Comedy 1:56**
☑ Nudity, adult situations, explicit language, adult humor
Dir: John Landis *Cast:* Dan Aykroyd, Eddie Murphy, Ralph Bellamy, Don Ameche, Denholm Elliott, Jamie Lee Curtis
▶ Powerhouse casting sparks this hit comedy about role reversals. How will black con artist Murphy and stuffy Main Line financier Aykroyd react to switching professions? Millionaire brothers Bellamy and Ameche engineer the plot on a whim. Feisty hooker Curtis teaches Aykroyd how to survive on the streets while Murphy adjusts to a new world of wealth and privilege. Excellent script and brilliant performance by Murphy highlight an enjoyably shrewd film. **(CC)**

TRAIL OF THE PINK PANTHER 1982
★★★ **PG Comedy 1:37**
☑ Brief nudity, explicit language, adult humor
Dir: Blake Edwards *Cast:* Peter Sellers, David Niven, Herbert Lom, Richard Mulligan, Joanna Lumley, Robert Loggia
▶ Once again the Pink Panther diamond is stolen from mythical city of Lugash and Inspector Clouseau (Sellers) is sent to investigate the theft. Sellers's plane disappears so he's presumed dead. French TV reporter Lumley then interviews detective's colleagues and family, setting up flashbacks to previous movies. Attempt to continue popular series despite death of star is strange brew of new footage and old outtakes, but worthy for previously unreleased Sellers gags. Followed by *The Curse of the Pink Panther*.

TRAIN ROBBERS, THE 1973
★★★ **PG Western 1:28**
☑ Explicit language
Dir: Burt Kennedy *Cast:* John Wayne, Ann-Margret, Rod Taylor, Ben Johnson, Christopher George, Ricardo Montalban
▶ Outlaw's widow Ann-Margret proposes deal to aging Civil War vet Wayne: help her return $500,000 in stolen bank funds hidden by hubby so family honor is restored and Wayne can keep $50,000 reward. Widow, war vet, and hired hands set off for Mexican badlands, site of buried loot; in pursuit are enigmatic loner

Montalban and gunmen hired by out-law's former partners. Fine, old-style horse opera, Wayne's 149th screen appearance, features surprise ending.

TRANCERS 1985
★★ **PG-13 Sci-Fi 1:17**
☑ Explicit language, violence
Dir: Charles Band *Cast:* Tim Thomerson, Helen Hunt, Michael Stefani, Art La Fleur, Biff Manard
▶ Stefani, the sinister ruler of future Los Angeles, returns to the present-day city to kill the ancestors of his enemies. He's followed by Trooper Jack Deth (Thomerson), who teams up with beautiful guide Hunt to stop Stefani's scheme. Low-budget variation on *The Terminator* offers enough clever touches to remain intriguing. Also known as *Future Cop.*

TRANSMUTATIONS 1987 British
☆ **R Horror 1:43**
☑ Adult situations, violence
Dir: George Pavlou *Cast:* Denholm Elliott, Steven Berkoff, Larry Lamb, Miranda Richardson, Art Malik, Nicola Cowper
▶ Drug experiments by mad doctor Elliott turn people into underground mutants. When prostitute Cowper is kidnapped by these beings, gangster Berkoff hires detective Lamb to rescue her. Mesmerizing visuals but muddled storytelling and torpid pacing. Also known as *Underworld.*

TRANSYLVANIA 6-5000 1985
★★ **PG Horror/Comedy 1:30**
☑ Mild violence
Dir: Rudy DeLuca *Cast:* Jeff Goldblum, Joseph Bologna, Ed Begley, Jr., Carol Kane, Geena Davis, Jeffrey Jones
▶ Sensational tabloid sends reporters Goldblum and Begley to investigate rumors of modern-day ghouls. Begley loses his heart to village vampire Davis, while Goldblum grapples with servile mayor Jones, mad doctor Bologna, and Kane, the sex-starved wife of incompetent butler John Byner. Frantic horror spoof features talented cast but few real laughs. (CC)

TRAPEZE 1956
★★★ **NR Drama 1:45**
Dir: Carol Reed *Cast:* Burt Lancaster, Tony Curtis, Gina Lollobrigida, Katy Jurado, Thomas Gomez, Johnny Puleo
▶ Lancaster, a former trapeze acrobat famous for performing triple somersault prior to injury, works as rigger for Parisian circus. Newcomer Curtis persuades him to return to trapeze as "catcher" to help

younger man perfect famed triple. Two aerialists become close until scheming tumbler Lollobrigida, hoping to move up to more prestigious trapeze act, turns her feminine charms on both men. Spectacular trapeze footage and colorful three-ring atmosphere.

TRASH 1970
☆ **NR Drama 1:43**
☑ Nudity, strong sexual content, adult situations, explicit language, violence
Dir: Paul Morrissey *Cast:* Joe Dallesandro, Holly Woodlawn, Jane Forth, Michael Sklar, Geri Miller, Andrea Feldman
▶ Junkie hustler Dallesandro is made impotent by frequent drug abuse, causing problems with girlfriend Woodlawn and customers. Semblance of plot and Morrissey's controlled direction make this one of the more accessible of Andy Warhol's Factory films, but trademark assault on decorum will still prove rough going for most.

TRAVELLING NORTH 1988 Australian
★ **PG-13 Drama 1:35**
☑ Explicit language
Dir: Carl Schultz *Cast:* Leo McKern, Julia Blake, Graham Kennedy, Henri Szeps, Michele Fawdon, Diane Craig
▶ Cantankerous Melbourne civil engineer McKern retires at age seventy and coaxes widow Blake to start new life in subtropical northern Australia. Spectacular scenery, new friends Kennedy and Szeps, and sexual reawakening make their domestic arrangement a success until McKern's health deteriorates. Crotchety but endearing McKern and luminous Blake excel in often humorous and always touching down-under drama.

TRAXX 1988
★ **R Comedy 1:25**
☑ Brief nudity, adult situations, explicit language, violence
Dir: Jerome Gary *Cast:* Shadoe Stevens, Priscilla Barnes, Willard E. Pugh, Robert Davi, John Hancock
▶ Ex-cop-turned-mercenary Stevens returns to Texas town to start cookie business. Hoping for reward money from sexy mayor Barnes, he teams with black sidekick Pugh to clean up crime-ridden neighborhood and take on local mafia. Impish crime comedy aided and abetted by Stevens's droll spirit.

TREASURE ISLAND 1934
★ ★ ★ NR Action-Adventure 1:45 B&W
Dir: Victor Fleming *Cast:* Wallace
Beery, Jackie Cooper, Lionel Barrymore,
Otto Kruger, Lewis Stone, Nigel Bruce
▶ Dying sailor passes a treasure map to
young English lad Cooper, who takes a
job as cabin boy on a ship bound for the
secret island. Long John Silver (Beery), a
treacherous pirate, leads a rebellion that
endangers Cooper and captain Stone.
Large-scale adaptation of Robert Louis
Stevenson's classic adventure is first-rate
on all levels, with Beery particularly boisterous in one of his best roles. Remade in
1950 and 1972.

TREASURE ISLAND 1950
★ ★ ★ ★ G Family 1:36
Dir: Byron Haskin *Cast:* Bobby Driscoll,
Robert Newton, Basil Sydney, Walter
Fitzgerald, Denis O'Dea, Ralph Truman
▶ Young Driscoll inherits treasure map
from aged captain; accompanied by
lawyer Fitzgerald and doctor O'Dea, he
sets out for the remote island, unaware
that his ship's crew is made up of bloodthirsty pirates. Superb Disney adventure is
the best version of Robert Louis Stevenson's classic, with an especially strong
performance by Newton (who repeated
his role in 1954's *Long John Silver*).
Bloodier moments were trimmed from
the original to gain a G rating.

TREASURE ISLAND 1972 British
★ ★ ★ G Family 1:35
Dir: John Hough *Cast:* Orson Welles,
Kim Burfield, Walter Slezak, Lionel
Stander, Paul Muller, Maria Rohm
▶ Colorful adaptation of Robert Louis
Stevenson's classic adventure features
Welles in a broad portrayal of the peg-
legged pirate Long John Silver and Bur-
field as young cabin boy Jim Hawkins.
Antiseptic approach downplays vio-
lence, making this more suitable for chil-
dren than 1934 and 1950 versions. Welles
also worked on the screenplay under the
pseudonym O. W. Jeeves.

TREASURE OF THE AMAZONS, THE
1985 Mexican
☆ NR Action-Adventure 1:44
☑ Nudity, adult situations, explicit lan-
guage, graphic violence
Dir: Rene Cardona, Jr. *Cast:* Stuart
Whitman, Emilio Fernandez, Donald
Pleasence, Bradford Dillman, John Ire-
land
▶ Low-rent hokum set in South America

about an Amazonian expedition searching for lost gold. Whitman plays an irascible guide; Pleasence is an ex-Nazi whose
native wife helps him through the jungle.
Inept plot features plenty of violence.

TREASURE OF THE FOUR CROWNS
1983 U.S./Spanish
★ PG Action-Adventure 1:40
☑ Explicit language, graphic violence
Dir: Ferdinando Baldi *Cast:* Tony Anthony, Ana Obregon, Gene Quintano,
Francisco Rabal, Jerry Lazarus
▶ Daring adventurer Anthony dodges
booby traps in a castle to snatch the key
to jeweled crowns, then assembles a
team of mercenaries to wrest the treasure from an evil leader of a religious cult.
Action-packed adventure filmed in 3-D
will lose many of its best effects on TV.

TREASURE OF THE SIERRA MADRE, THE
1948
★ ★ ★ ★ NR Action-Adventure 2:06
B&W
Dir: John Huston *Cast:* Humphrey Bogart, Walter Huston, Tim Holt, Bruce
Bennett, Barton MacLane, Alfonso Be-
doya
▶ Down-and-out Americans Bogart and
Holt seek to change their luck by teaming with veteran prospector Huston to
mine for gold in Mexican mountains. Trio
strikes paydirt and accumulates riches,
causing Bogart and Holt to grow paranoid about being robbed by comrades.
Timeless masterpiece employs action
and intrigue to examine corruption of
human spirit. Film won Oscars for father-
son team John Huston (Director and
Screenplay) and Walter Huston (Supporting Actor), an Academy first.

TREASURE OF THE YANKEE ZEPHYR
1983 Australian/New Zealand
★ ★ ★ PG Action-Adventure 1:38
☑ Adult situations, explicit language,
violence
Dir: David Hemmings *Cast:* Ken Wahl,
George Peppard, Lesley Ann Warren,
Donald Pleasence
▶ Elderly Pleasence discovers wreck of
World War II plane filled with gold bars
and is kidnapped by wealthy villain Peppard. Pleasence's daughter Warren and
partner Wahl team up to rescue him and
beat Peppard to the treasure. Above-average genre effort with plenty of action.

TREE GROWS IN BROOKLYN, A 1945
★ ★ ★ ★ NR Drama 2:08 B&W
Dir: Elia Kazan *Cast:* Dorothy McGuire,

Joan Blondell, James Dunn, Peggy Ann Garner, Lloyd Nolan, Ted Donaldson
▶ Classic, endearing tale of bright young Garner's coming of age in a Brooklyn tenement. She's a dreamer who idolizes her alcoholic, ne'er-do-well father, Dunn, and resents her down-to-earth mother, McGuire. Blondell plays a beloved aunt. Oscars for Dunn and Garner. Kazan's directorial debut. Based on the popular novel by Betty Smith. **(CC)**

TRENCHCOAT 1983
★★ PG Comedy 1:31
☑ Explicit language, violence
Dir: Michael Tuchner *Cast:* Margot Kidder, Robert Hays, David Suchet, Gila von Weitershausen, Daniel Faraldo, Ronald Lacey
▶ Court stenographer Kidder travels to Malta to write a mystery novel, then finds herself in the middle of an international plot to steal plutonium. Hays, a handsome stranger with uncertain motives, offers help when Kidder is kidnapped by Arabs. Attempt by Disney Studio to broaden its image offers engaging performances and beautiful scenery along with a farfetched plot.

TRIAL OF BILLY JACK, THE 1974
★★ PG Drama 2:50
☑ Explicit language, violence
Dir: Tom Laughlin *Cast:* Tom Laughlin, Delores Taylor, Victor Izay, Teresa Laughlin, Riley Hill, Sparky Watt
▶ Navajo half-breed/karate expert Laughlin, free after prison sentence, retreats to the Southwest to find inner peace but soon must defend Taylor and her progressive Freedom School from attack by reactionaries. Lengthy and erratic effort preaches unusual peace-through-violence message. Sequel to *Billy Jack;* followed by *Billy Jack Goes to Washington.*

TRIAL OF THE CANTONSVILLE NINE, THE 1972
★★ PG Drama 1:25
☑ Explicit language
Dir: Gordon Davidson *Cast:* Ed Flanders, Barton Heyman, Mary Jackson, Richard Jordan, Donald Moffat, Douglass Watson
▶ The trial of nine antiwar protestors who burned their draft cards is retold in a straightforward version, emphasizing defendants' personal reasons for breaking the law. Heavy-handed adaptation of a play by Father Daniel Berrigan, one of the participants in the trial. Produced by Gregory Peck.

TRIBUTE 1981 Canadian
★★★★ PG Comedy/Drama 1:59
☑ Nudity, adult situations, explicit language
Dir: Bob Clark *Cast:* Jack Lemmon, Robby Benson, Lee Remick, Kim Cattrall, Colleen Dewhurst, John Marley
▶ Intellectual Benson is estranged from Lemmon, his frenetic, extroverted dad, a New York press agent who has just been diagnosed with terminal cancer. Aided by ex-wife/mom Remick, the two are reconciled and Benson arranges a testimonial for Lemmon in a Broadway theater. Moving family drama, powered by Lemmon's bravura performance. Based on the Broadway play by Bernard Slade, which starred the Tony-winning Lemmon.

TRICK OR TREAT 1986
★ R Horror 1:37
☑ Brief nudity, explicit language, violence
Dir: Charles Martin Smith *Cast:* Marc Price, Tony Fields, Lisa Orgolin, Gene Simmons, Ozzy Osbourne
▶ Well-made teen revenge/horror film. Satanic rock star Fields, killed in a hotel fire, comes back to life to seek revenge on his most ardent critics (including real-life rock star Osborne as a minister). Fields is aided by geeky high school kid Price who idolizes the rocker. Genial, not terribly frightening, with superb technical credits. **(CC)**

TRICK OR TREATS 1982
★ R Horror/Comedy 1:31
☑ Explicit language, violence
Dir: Gary Graver *Cast:* Jackelyn Giroux, Peter Jason, Carrie Snodgress, David Carradine, Chris Graver
▶ Terrified babysitter horror spoof. Parents Snodgress and Carradine leave practical-joker son Graver with pretty blond sitter Giroux on Halloween eve. They are unknowingly stalked by Snodgress's first husband Jason, who has just escaped from the local insane asylum. Amiable tone, a few chuckles, and minor gore.

TRIP, THE 1967
★★ NR Drama 1:25
☑ Nudity, adult situations, explicit language, violence
Dir: Roger Corman *Cast:* Peter Fonda, Susan Strasberg, Bruce Dern, Dennis Hopper, Dick Miller, Peter Bogdanovich

▶ Dated psychedelia from the era when folks didn't "just say no." Troubled TV director Fonda hooks up with guru Dern and decides to take LSD. The drug inspires a series of fantasies and unusual situations. Screenplay by Jack Nicholson.

TRIP TO BOUNTIFUL, THE 1985
★★★★ PG Drama 1:46
☑ Adult situations
Dir: Peter Masterson *Cast:* Geraldine Page, John Heard, Carlin Glynn, Richard Bradford, Rebecca De Mornay, Kevin Cooney
▶ In 1947, elderly widow Page lives in Houston with son Heard and daughter-in-law Glynn, but longs for one last visit to her hometown, Bountiful. One day she runs away, boarding a bus where she meets De Mornay, the young wife of a soldier. Seeing her old, tumbled-down home brings back a flood of memories. Richly detailed but rather slow moving. Page won Best Actress Oscar; Horton Foote's screenplay was nominated. (CC)

TRISTANA 1970 Spanish/French
★★ PG Drama 1:35
☑ Adult situations, explicit language
Dir: Luis Buñuel *Cast:* Catherine Deneuve, Fernando Rey, Franco Nero, Lola Gaos, Antonio Casas, Jesus Fernandez
▶ Young Deneuve is seduced by her hypocritical guardian Rey, who has warned others not to take advantage of her. She leaves Rey to pursue passion with artist Nero, but illness tempts her to return to her benefactor's support. Allegorical drama about Spain's inability to overcome stifling traditional values is seamlessly directed by master Buñuel, but is not for mainstream tastes. Oscar-nominated for Best Foreign Film. Ⓢ

TRIUMPH OF THE WILL 1935 German
★ NR Documentary 1:50 B&W
Dir: Leni Riefenstahl
▶ Chilling documentary of Nazi rallies in Nuremberg, 1934, is among the most influential pieces of propaganda ever filmed. Shot with cooperation of armed forces, this powerful record remains fascinating despite distasteful subject matter. Opening sequence depicting Hitler's descent from majestic clouds is often cited as a perfect montage.

TRIUMPHS OF A MAN CALLED HORSE
1983 U.S./Mexican
★★★★ PG Western 1:26

☑ Explicit language, violence
Dir: John Hough *Cast:* Richard Harris, Michael Beck, Ana De Sade, Anne Seymour, Vaughn Armstrong, Buck Taylor
▶ In 1875, English nobleman Harris, captured by Sioux and inducted into tribe thirty years previous, is now an aged warrior determined to halt invasion of Indian territory by gold prospectors. Gunmen, hoping to rile Sioux onto warpath, kill Harris. His son Beck, aided by feisty Crow girl De Sade, must fill father's moccasins in battle against outsiders. Preceded by *A Man Called Horse* and *Return of a Man Called Horse*.

TROLL 1986
★★ PG-13 Horror 1:23
☑ Explicit language, violence
Dir: John Buechler *Cast:* Michael Moriarty, Shelley Hack, Nan Hathaway, Jennifer Beck, June Lockhart, Phil Fondacaro
▶ Book reviewer Moriarty, wife Hack, and kids Hathaway and Beck move into new San Francisco apartment. Soon evil troll possesses Beck, causing havoc at home and trouble in other apartments. Good witch Lockhart enlists aid of Hathaway to defeat troll.

TRON 1982
★★★ PG Animation/Sci-Fi 1:36
☑ Mild violence
Dir: Steven Lisberger *Cast:* Jeff Bridges, David Warner, Cindy Morgan, Bruce Boxleitner, Barnard Hughes, Dan Shor
▶ In the future, most lives are controlled by the Master Computer. Evil executive Warner secretly plots to control the computer. Free-thinking computer whiz Bridges, seeking to prove Warner stole programs he created, is transformed into miniaturized prisoner of Master Computer's microcircuits. There Bridges, Morgan, Boxleitner, and Hughes must engage Warner and Master Computer in video game warfare. Dazzling adventure combines live action with animation. Breathtaking video game action compensates for confusing plot.

TROUBLE IN MIND 1985
★★ R Drama 1:52
☑ Nudity, adult situations, explicit language, violence
Dir: Alan Rudolph *Cast:* Kris Kristofferson, Genevieve Bujold, Lori Singer, Keith Carradine, Joe Morton, Divine
▶ Former detective Kristofferson returns

home after serving prison sentence for slaying mobster and moves into apartment over seedy diner run by former lover Bujold. Small-time hood Carradine and girlfriend Singer park camper next to Bujold's diner. While Carradine grows more ambitious and arrogant, Kristofferson falls for Singer. When crime kingpin Divine orders hit on Carradine, Kristofferson intervenes for Singer's sake. Moody, atmospheric, and often meandering yarn spells trouble for many; fans of director Rudolph and adventurous may find rewards. **(CC)**

TROUBLE IN PARADISE 1932
★★ NR Comedy 1:23 B&W
Dir: Ernst Lubitsch   *Cast:* Herbert Marshall, Miriam Hopkins, Kay Francis, Charles Ruggles, Edward Everett Horton, C. Aubrey Smith
▶ Suave jewel thief Marshall worms his way into the household of rich Parisian widow Francis, only to find that his rival and ex-lover Hopkins also has designs on the widow's fortune. Sly, elegant trifle may be the most sophisticated and enjoyable of director Lubitsch's comedies. Horton is hilarious as one of the thieves' former victims.

TROUBLE WITH ANGELS, THE 1966
★★★ NR Comedy/Family 1:52
Dir: Ida Lupino   *Cast:* Rosalind Russell, Hayley Mills, June Harding, Binnie Barnes, Camilla Sparv, Gypsy Rose Lee
▶ Mother Superior Russell has heavenly hands full with mischievous convent students Mills and Harding, whose pranks scandalize the nuns. Russell manages to tame Mills and bring out her more serious instincts. Genial comedy spawned sequel *Where Angels Go—Trouble Follows.*

TROUBLE WITH DICK, THE 1987
★★ NR Comedy 1:26
☑ Adult situations, explicit language, violence
Dir: Gary Walkow   *Cast:* Tom Villard, Susan Dey, Elaine Giftos, Elizabeth Gorcey, David Clennon, Jack Carter
▶ Villard, a sci-fi author suffering from writer's block, moves into Los Angeles boarding house where ex-girlfriend Dey lives. Amorous affairs with landlady Giftos and her daughter Gorcey lead to a nervous breakdown. Modest, low-key film suffers from minuscule budget and awkward sci-fi interludes.

TROUBLE WITH HARRY, THE 1955
★★★ PG Comedy 1:39

Dir: Alfred Hitchcock   *Cast:* Shirley MacLaine, John Forsythe, Edmund Gwenn, Mildred Natwick, Mildred Dunnock, Jerry Mathers
▶ Vermont hunter Gwenn stumbles across corpse and, believing he's the accidental killer, buries the body. But dead man "Harry" refuses to stay buried: repeated discovery of corpse sets about romance between Gwenn and middle-aged spinster Natwick and between local artist Forsythe and Harry's widow MacLaine. Offbeat black comedy sports fine cast, saucy dialogue, and striking shots of New England in autumn. Screen debut for MacLaine; catchy score by Bernard Herrmann was first in famed collaboration with director Hitchcock.

TROUBLE WITH SPIES, THE 1987
★ PG Comedy 1:29
☑ Brief nudity, explicit language, mild violence
Dir: Burt Kennedy   *Cast:* Donald Sutherland, Ruth Gordon, Ned Beatty, Robert Morley, Lucy Gutteridge, Michael Hordern
▶ Bumbling British agent Sutherland is sent by superior Morley to Mediterranean isle of Ibiza to ferret out Soviet spies who perfected truth serum. Sutherland takes room at hotel and romances proprietor Gutteridge. When unknown assailants attempt but fail to kill Sutherland, he suspects other guests Beatty, Gordon, and Hordern. Inspector Clouseau–style shenanigans don't quite work in this unfunny, unsatisfying spy concoction.

TRUCK STOP WOMEN 1974
★ R Action-Adventure 1:28
☑ Nudity, adult situations, explicit language, violence
Dir: Mark L. Lester   *Cast:* Claudia Jennings, Lieux Dressler, John Martino, Dennis Fimple, Dolores Dorn
▶ Restaurant fronting for prostitution ring is so successful that the Mafia muscles in for a cut. Good-natured but badly dated sleaze features plenty of truck chases and nudity. Dressler stands out as a cynical madam.

TRUE CONFESSIONS 1981
★★★ R Drama 1:48
☑ Nudity, adult situations, explicit language, violence
Dir: Ulu Grosbard   *Cast:* Robert De Niro, Robert Duvall, Charles Durning, Ed Flanders, Burgess Meredith, Rose Gregorio

▶ In 1930s Los Angeles, shabby police detective Duvall, investigating brutal slaying of girl, follows the trail to building contractor Durning, a major contributor to the wealthy parish run by ambitious priest De Niro, Duvall's brother. Brothers clash as Duvall, formerly corrupt and now in pursuit of justice no matter the cost, exhorts worldly De Niro to assist in arrest of Durning. Slow but sure-handed character study mixes the disparate views of a sleazy crime underworld and the church. Adapted by John Gregory Dunne and wife Joan Didion from his novel.

TRUE GRIT 1969
★★★★★ G Western 2:08 B&W
Dir: Henry Hathaway *Cast:* John Wayne, Glen Campbell, Kim Darby, Jeff Corey, Robert Duvall, Dennis Hopper
▶ Feisty young Darby hires hard-drinking, over-the-hill U.S. Marshall Wayne to pursue Corey, her father's killer, into Indian territory. Straight-arrow Texas Ranger Campbell joins them in chase leading to shootouts with outlaws Duvall and Hopper and brushes with Indians. Immensely popular adaptation of the Charles Portis best-seller offers much to admire: sure-handed direction from veteran Hathaway (seventy-one years old at time), romantic cinematography, and charming interaction of Wayne and Darby. Wayne won first Oscar in forty years on screen, and reprised his role in 1975's *Rooster Cogburn*.

TRUE STORIES 1986
★ PG Musical/Comedy 1:51
☑ Adult situations
Dir: David Byrne *Cast:* David Byrne, John Goodman, Swoosie Kurtz, Spalding Gray, Annie McEnroe, Joe Harvey Allen
▶ Narrator Byrne leads tour of small town Virgil, Texas, on state's 150th anniversary. Musical encounters with eccentric citizens include lovable bachelor Goodman advertising for wife; Kurtz, who hasn't left bed in years; and lying Allen who claims to have written "Billie Jean" and be pals with Rambo. Much-ballyhooed film foray by director Byrne, lead singer of rock group Talking Heads, has charming bits and lively tunes by Byrne and band, but patronizing tone and frequent flat spots sabotage effort. **(CC)**

TUCKER: THE MAN AND HIS DREAM 1988
★★★★ PG Biography 1:51

☑ Explicit language
Dir: Francis Ford Coppola *Cast:* Jeff Bridges, Joan Allen, Martin Landau, Frederic Forrest, Mako, Dean Stockwell
▶ True story of 1940s inventor Preston Tucker (Bridges). Although his plan to make a luxurious, safe, and affordable automobile was destroyed by big-business conspiracy, his essential optimism remained unvanquished. Coppola directs with a technical exuberance and Bridges performs with an upbeat energy perfectly reflecting their visionary subject in this irresistible biography. Dazzling production design, bouncy Joe Jackson score, and an Oscar-nominated supporting performance by Landau as Bridges's business partner.

TUCK EVERLASTING 1980
★★★ NR Family 1:40
Dir: Frederick King Keller *Cast:* Margaret Chamberlain, James McGuire, Paul Flessa, Fred A. Keller, Sonia Raimi, Bruce D'Auria
▶ Young girl is introduced to the Tuck family, wealthy New Yorkers whose estate contains a mysterious spring. The Tucks reveal the secret of their drinking water, only to fall victim to an unscrupulous stranger who greedily attempts to steal their land. Despite budget restrictions, an intelligent, rewarding family film adapted from Natalie Babbitt's absorbing novel.

TUFF TURF 1985
★★★ R Drama 1:52
☑ Nudity, adult situations, explicit language, graphic violence
Dir: Fritz Kiersch *Cast:* James Spader, Kim Richards, Robert Downey, Jr., Paul Mones, Matt Clark, Claudette Nevins
▶ Spader, a Connecticut youth transferred to tough Los Angeles high school, becomes the target of a gang of thugs when he pursues beautiful moll Richards. Visually stylish drama features a strong soundtrack (including Marianne Faithfull and Jim Carroll) and a good performance by Downey as Spader's only friend. **(CC)**

TUNES OF GLORY 1960 British
★★★ NR Drama 1:47
Dir: Ronald Neame *Cast:* Alec Guinness, John Mills, Dennis Price, Susannah York, John Fraser
▶ Scottish colonel Guinness drinks too much and maintains loose discipline; his men adore him. When by-the-book Mills

arrives to replace Guinness, intraregiment conflict is created. Masterful drama, with towering performances by Guinness and Mills. Oscar-nominated screenplay by James Kennaway, adapted from his novel.

TUNNELVISION 1976
★ R Comedy 1:08
☑ Nudity, explicit language, adult humor
Dir: Brad Swirnoff, Neil Israel *Cast:* Phil Proctor, Rich Hurst, Laraine Newman, Howard Hesseman, Roger Bower, Ernie Anderson
▶ Collection of irreverent skits purporting to show how TV had advanced by 1985 is a tasteless and uneven hodgepodge of parodies and one-liners that are often extremely dated. Frequent cameos by future stars (Chevy Chase, Ron Silver, Tom Davis, Al Franken, etc.) can't salvage the endless Richard Nixon jokes.

TURK 182! 1985
★★★ PG-13 Drama 1:36
☑ Adult situations, explicit language
Dir: Bob Clark *Cast:* Timothy Hutton, Robert Urich, Kim Cattrall, Robert Culp, Darren McGavin, Peter Boyle
▶ Renegade graffiti artist Hutton avenges the injustices done to his firefighter brother Urich, disabled in the line of duty. His acts of rebellion catch the attention of the entire city, culiminating in a climatic scheme to disrupt the lighting of the Queensboro Bridge during a celebration. Cattrall plays a social worker romantically involved with Hutton. Street-smart script will have viewers rooting for the underdog. **(CC)**

TURNING POINT, THE 1977
★★★★ PG Drama/Dance 1:59
Dir: Herbert Ross *Cast:* Shirley MacLaine, Anne Bancroft, Mikhail Baryshnikov, Tom Skerritt, Leslie Browne, Martha Scott
▶ Longterm friendship between Bancroft, a famous ballerina, and MacLaine, a former dancer who gave up her career to be a wife and mother in Oklahoma, is threatened when MacLaine's daughter Browne, a promising ballerina, has a shot at the kind of career her mother gave up. Baryshnikov, in his film debut, co-stars as Browne's partner on stage and in the bedroom; Skerritt plays MacLaine's husband. High-quality soap opera enlivened by extraordinary dancing. Eleven Oscar nominations.

TURTLE DIARY 1986 British
★★★ PG Drama 1:36
☑ Adult situations, explicit language
Dir: John Irvin *Cast:* Glenda Jackson, Ben Kingsley, Michael Gambon, Richard Johnson, Harriet Walter, Jeroen Krabbe
▶ Lonely Londoners Kingsley and Jackson share a passion for sea turtles. With the help of surprisingly sympathetic zookeeper Gambon, they devise a plan to free turtles from the zoo and bring them to sea. Slyly intelligent and touchingly humane. Harold Pinter's screenplay refreshingly avoids clichés. Subtle performances by the leads, but slow pace and film's narrow scope may not appeal to mainstream audiences.

TWELVE ANGRY MEN 1957
★★★ NR Drama 1:35 B&W
Dir: Sidney Lumet *Cast:* Henry Fonda, Lee J. Cobb, Martin Balsam, Jack Klugman, Ed Begley, Jack Warden
▶ Jurors convene to decide on a seemingly cut-and-dried murder case. Eleven vote guilty but holdout Fonda gradually convinces others of his views, although Cobb (the angriest of the angry men) fights him all the way. One-set movie in incredibly engrossing; co-producer Fonda leads an outstanding ensemble. Oscar nominations for Picture, Director, Screenplay (Reginald Rose, who adapted his television play). **(CC)**

TWELVE CHAIRS, THE 1970
★★ G Comedy 1:33
Dir: Mel Brooks *Cast:* Ron Moody, Frank Langella, Dom DeLuise, Mel Brooks, Bridget Brice
▶ Russia, 1927: fallen aristocrat Moody is informed by dying mama that ten years ago she hid a cache of jewels in one of twelve matching chairs. His search for the chairs takes him across Russia and into Siberia, aided by beggar Langella and priest DeLuise, who heard mama's dying confession. Commie-comedy features Brooks's theme song, "Hope for the Best (Expect the Worst)."

TWELVE O'CLOCK HIGH 1949
★★★★★ NR War 2:12 B&W
Dir: Henry King *Cast:* Gregory Peck, Hugh Marlowe, Gary Merrill, Dean Jagger, Millard Mitchell, Paul Stewart
▶ Compelling World War II drama examines how the burdens of leadership affect Peck, commander of a B-17 bomber squadron stationed in England. At first a

strict disciplinarian, he loses objectivity when he starts to identify with his men. Influential film highlighted by adroit use of combat footage and Oscar-winning support by Jagger. Loosely based on the experiences of Maj. Gen. Frank Armstrong.

TWENTIETH CENTURY 1934
★ ★ ★ ★ **NR Comedy 1:31 B&W**
Dir: Howard Hawks *Cast:* John Barrymore, Carole Lombard, Roscoe Karns, Walter Connolly, Ralph Forbes, Etienne Girardot
▶ Delightful screwball farce about egomaniacal director Barrymore who pins his fading fortunes on former protégé Lombard, now a Hollywood goddess engaged to lunkhead football player Forbes. Barrymore's zany schemes to win back Lombard during a train journey from Chicago to New York range from dazzling insults to camel imitations. Brilliant script by Ben Hecht and Charles MacArthur inspired the Broadway musical *On the Twentieth Century*.

20,000 LEAGUES UNDER THE SEA 1954
★ ★ ★ ★ **G Sci-Fi 2:07**
Dir: Richard Fleischer *Cast:* Kirk Douglas, James Mason, Paul Lukas, Peter Lorre, Robert J. Wilke, Carleton Young
▶ Walt Disney classic based on the novel by Jules Verne. In 1868, professor Lukas, his aide Lorre, and harpoonist Douglas are taken prisoner by visionary scientist Captain Nemo (Mason) on his advanced submarine, the *Nautilus*. Nemo plans to use his craft to enforce world peace; Douglas tries to stop him. Beautifully crafted and acted (Mason and Lorre shine). Oscars for Special Effects and Art/Set Decoration.

23 PACES TO BAKER STREET 1956
★ ★ ★ **NR Mystery-Suspense 1:43**
Dir: Henry Hathaway *Cast:* Van Johnson, Vera Miles, Cecil Parker, Patricia Laffan, Maurice Denham, Estelle Winwood
▶ Blind London playwright Johnson overhears a conversation that reveals a kidnapping plot, but the police and friends refuse to believe him. With the help of sidekick Miles and secretary Parker, he seeks to thwart the criminals on his own. Fine suspenser with unusual premise.

TWICE IN A LIFETIME 1985
★ ★ ★ **R Drama 1:45**
☑ Adult situations, explicit language
Dir: Bud Yorkin *Cast:* Gene Hackman,

Ellen Burstyn, Ann-Margret, Ally Sheedy, Amy Madigan, Brian Dennehy
▶ Powerhouse cast enhances familiar story of middle-aged Hackman, who leaves wife Burstyn for barmaid Ann-Margret. The breakup causes havoc for the couple's daughters Madigan and Sheedy. Madigan cannot forgive her father but, despite her objections, Sheedy invites her to her wedding. Emotionally charged domestic drama will strike a responsive chord in many viewers. **(CC)**

TWILIGHT'S LAST GLEAMING 1977
U.S./German
★ ★ ★ ★ **R Drama 2:24**
☑ Adult situations, explicit language, violence
Dir: Robert Aldrich *Cast:* Burt Lancaster, Richard Widmark, Charles Durning, Melvyn Douglas, Paul Winfield, Burt Young
▶ Vietnam vet Lancaster takes over Strategic Air Command base and attempts to blackmail President Durning into revealing the true reasons for our country's involvement in the war. Despite predictable plotting, ambitious, high-powered thriller offers a convincing indictment of military arrogance.

TWILIGHT ZONE—THE MOVIE 1983
★ ★ ★ **PG Sci-Fi 1:41**
☑ Explicit language, graphic violence
Dir: John Landis, Steven Spielberg, Joe Dante, George Miller *Cast:* Dan Aykroyd, Albert Brooks, Vic Morrow, Scatman Crothers, Kathleen Quinlan, John Lithgow
▶ Anthology of four supernatural tales, three based on old "Twilight Zone" episodes, gained considerable notoriety for the death of Morrow during a Vietnam battle sequence. Other stories include a saccharine fantasy about an old-age home, a chilling version of "It's a Good Life" in which a child's magical powers turn his home into a terrifying cartoon, and a breathtaking "Nightmare at 20,000 Feet," with Lithgow as a paranoid airplane passenger who sees a monster lurking on the wing. Narrated by Burgess Meredith.

TWINS 1988
★ ★ ★ ★ **PG Comedy 1:43**
☑ Adult situations, explicit language, violence
Dir: Ivan Reitman *Cast:* Danny DeVito, Arnold Schwarzenegger, Kelly Preston,

Chloe Webb, Bonnie Bartlett, Marshall Bell

▶ Schwarzenegger and DeVito are fraternal twins, spawned by a scientific experiment and separated at birth. Schwarzenegger, raised by a scientist on a remote island, is now an intellectual straight-shooter. DeVito, kicked out of convent school for corrupting a nun, is a womanizing, thieving hustler. Reunited twins search for their long-lost mom while evading hit man who's after DeVito's hide. Broad, outlandish comic fare, with DeVito carrying most of the comic muscle.

TWIST AND SHOUT 1986 Danish
★ R Drama 1:47
☑ Nudity, strong sexual content, adult situations
Dir: Billie August *Cast:* Adam Tonsberg, Lars Simonsen, Camilla Soeberg, Ulrikke Juul Bondo, Thomas Nielsen, Lone Lindorff
▶ Round-robin of teen love in Denmark: straitlaced blond Bondo dotes on handsome drummer Tonsberg; Tonsberg and voluptuous beauty Soeberg are madly in love; Tonsberg's best pal Simonsen has unrequited crush on Bondo. When Soeberg gets pregnant and rejects Tonsberg after abortion, he reevaluates Bondo's romantic overtures. Sequel to director August's *Zappa*. Ⓢ

TWO FOR THE ROAD 1967 British
★★ NR Drama 1:53
Dir: Stanley Donen *Cast:* Audrey Hepburn, Albert Finney, Eleanor Bron, William Daniels, Claude Dauphin, Jacqueline Bisset
▶ Trip to France by an unhappily married couple—architect Finney and disillusioned wife Hepburn—prompts a series of flashbacks showing their earlier relationship. Despite irritatingly trendy direction, a generally satisfying romance highlighted by Bron's amusing turn as an American tourist and Henry Mancini's lush score. Oscar-nominated screenplay by Frederic Raphael.

TWO HUNDRED MOTELS 1971
☆ R Musical 1:38
☑ Nudity, explicit language, adult humor
Dir: Frank Zappa, Tony Palmer *Cast:* Ringo Starr, Theodore Bikel, Keith Moon, Jimmy Carl Black, The Mothers of Invention, Frank Zappa
▶ Ostensibly about exploits of rock band

on tour, with the Mothers of Invention as themselves and bewigged, goateed Starr as bandleader Zappa, film is more a hodepodge of visual effects and music laced with Zappa's trademark subversive wit. Predecessor to music videos was first color feature to be shot on tape and transferred to film. Result is uneven and often unsettling, but some moments are truly inspired. Historical curio is probably for Zappa fans and film buffs only.

TWO-MINUTE WARNING 1976
★★★★★ R Mystery-Suspense 1:55
☑ Brief nudity, violence
Dir: Larry Peerce *Cast:* Charlton Heston, John Cassavetes, Martin Balsam, Beau Bridges, David Janssen, Marilyn Hassett
▶ Lone sniper holds packed L.A. football stadium under siege during Super Bowl. Heston plays a police captain and Cassavetes is the cynical SWAT leader. Balsam, Bridges, and Hassett are potential targets. Tense thriller comes to climax during two-minute warning of football game. All-star cast also includes Jack Klugman, Gena Rowlands, and veteran Walter Pidgeon. Appearing as themselves are Howard Cosell, Frank Gifford, Dick Enberg, and Merv Griffin (singing the national anthem).

TWO MULES FOR SISTER SARA 1970
★★★★ PG Western 1:45
☑ Adult situations, explicit language, violence
Dir: Don Siegel *Cast:* Clint Eastwood, Shirley MacLaine, Monolo Fabregas, Alberto Morin, Armando Silvestre, John Kelly
▶ During the Mexican Revolution, taciturn drifter Eastwood rescues nun MacLaine from rapists, then reluctantly agrees to help her attack a French fortress. Eastwood is troubled by his unnatural attraction to MacLaine, who eventually reveals a surprising background. Apart from the bloody climax, a lighthearted Western showcasing the stars' natural charm.

TWO OF A KIND 1983
★★★ PG Fantasy 1:27
☑ Adult situations, explicit language, violence
Dir: John Herzfeld *Cast:* Olivia Newton-John, John Travolta, Charles Durning, Beatrice Straight, Scatman Crothers, Oliver Reed
▶ Angels Durning, Straight, and Crothers

convince God (voice of Gene Hackman) to put the Apocalypse on hold, claiming they can prove the existence of selflessness on earth by following the lives of two star-crossed lovers: New York inventor Travolta, in debt to the Mob, and aspiring actress Newton-John, working as a bank teller. He tries to rob her bank, she steals his loot. Satan (Reed) himself appears to thwart them but love—and salvation—triumph. **(CC)**

TWO RODE TOGETHER 1961
★★★ NR Western 1:49
Dir: John Ford   *Cast:* James Stewart, Richard Widmark, Shirley Jones, Linda Cristal, Andy Devine, John McIntire
▶ Cavalry lieutenant Widmark agrees to pay corrupt sheriff Stewart five hundred dollars for each hostage taken from the Commanche tribe who kidnapped them years earlier, but their mission leads to bloodshed and tragedy. Somber, thoughtful Western features a convincing performance by Stewart in an atypical role.

2001: A SPACE ODYSSEY 1968
U.S./British
★★★ G Sci-Fi 2:18
Dir: Stanley Kubrick   *Cast:* Keir Dullea, Gary Lockwood, William Sylvester, Daniel Richter, Leonard Rossiter
▶ In 2001, the discovery of a mysterious monolith beneath moon's surface initiates voyage to Jupiter. In deep space, computer HAL (voice of Douglas Rain) goes berserk; astronauts Dullea and Lockwood seek to turn off the machine that runs the ship. Landmark special effects movie with ape-to-astronaut theme evokes widespread opinions, with minimal dialogue and ambiguous ending leaving many unmoved. Virtuoso visuals (Oscar winner for special effects), filmed in wide-screen Cinerama, lack impact on video.

2010 1984
★★★★ PG Sci-Fi 1:56
☑ Explicit language, mild violence
Dir: Peter Hyams   *Cast:* Roy Scheider, John Lithgow, Helen Mirren, Bob Balaban, Keir Dullea
▶ Sequel to *2001: A Space Odyssey* finds U.S. and Russia on brink of war, but scientists unite to locate missing spaceship from *2001*. American leader Scheider, guilt-ridden by role in original mission, brings along colleagues Lithgow and Balaban for journey to Jupiter on Soviet craft skippered by Mirren. Scientists reactivate computer HAL (voice of Douglas Rain), encounter lone survivor of *2001* launch (Dullea), and discover truth of mystic monolith. High-tech sequel has more drama and humanity than original.

TWO WOMEN 1961 Italian
★ NR Drama 1:39 B&W
Dir: Vittorio De Sica   *Cast:* Sophia Loren, Jean-Paul Belmondo, Eleonora Brown, Raf Vallone, Renato Salvatori
▶ During World War II, Italian mother Loren and adolescent daughter Brown attempt to survive as the Allies invade and the Germans retreat. Both fall for farmer's son Belmondo but hardships ensue after the women are raped by Allied soldiers. Their efforts to deal with the attack and Brown's burgeoning womanhood make for an emotion-packed, immensely moving film. Staggering performance by Loren nabbed Best Actress Oscar. **(CC)** Ⓢ

TYCOON 1947
★★★ NR Drama 2:08
Dir: Richard Wallace   *Cast:* John Wayne, Laraine Day, Cedric Hardwicke, Judith Anderson, James Gleason, Anthony Quinn
▶ Mining magnate Hardwicke hires engineer Wayne to build a railroad over the Andes but balks at Wayne's plan for an expensive bridge instead of a hazardous tunnel. Wayne further complicates matters by falling for Hardwicke's daughter Day. Lengthy but engrossing drama with the Duke performing smartly in an atypical role.

UFORIA 1980
☆ PG Sci-Fi 1:34
☑ Adult situations, explicit language, mild violence
Dir: John Binder   *Cast:* Cindy Williams, Harry Dean Stanton, Fred Ward, Beverly Hope Atkinson, Harry Carey, Jr., Diane Deifendorf
▶ Drifter Ward falls for Williams, a born-again supermarket checkout clerk who believes she's been chosen as a Noah for an imminent UFO expedition. Bogus faith healer Stanton publicizes her mission in an effort to earn money. Eccentric but good-natured blend of comedy, romance, and science fiction may please fans of the offbeat.

UGLY AMERICAN, THE 1963
★★ NR Drama 2:00
Dir: George Englund   *Cast:* Marlon

Brando, Eiji Okada, Sandra Church, Pat Hingle, Arthur Hill, Jocelyn Brando
► Former journalist Brando is appointed ambassador to Vietnam-like country. Although he is friendly with rebel leader Okada, Brando finds himself caught between government and Communist factions. Cautionary tale of political intrigue highlighted by Brando's change-of-pace performance.

UGLY DACHSHUND, THE 1966
★★★★ NR Comedy/Family 1:33
Dir: Norman Tokar *Cast:* Dean Jones, Suzanne Pleshette, Charles Ruggles, Kelly Thordsen, Mako
► The ugly dachshund is actually a Great Dane who grows up with the smaller breed and adopts their mannerisms. Husband Jones enters the big beast against one of his wife Pleshette's dachshunds in a dog show. Friendly Disney antics stolen by the four-legged thespians.

ULTIMATE WARRIOR, THE 1975
★★ R Sci-Fi 1:34
☑ Adult situations, explicit language, violence
Dir: Robert Clouse *Cast:* Yul Brynner, Max Von Sydow, Joanna Miles, William Smith, Richard Kelton
► Twenty-first-century New York City decimated by plagues provides the battleground for fight to the finish between commune headed by Von Sydow and deadly rivals led by Smith. Brynner, a hero known as Knife Fighter, arrives to lead Von Sydow's sister Miles to safety in New Jersey. Routine adventure marred by cheap special effects.

ULYSSES 1955 Italian
★★ NR Action-Adventure 1:44
Dir: Mario Camerini *Cast:* Kirk Douglas, Anthony Quinn, Silvana Mangano, Rossana Podesta
► Adventurer Douglas suffers amnesia after fighting in the Trojan War. As he recovers on an island in the care of princess Podesta, his wife Mangano is pursued by his rival Quinn. Douglas's brawny heroics highlight this exciting adaptation of Homer's *The Odyssey*. Dubbed.

ULYSSES 1967
★★ NR Drama 2:20 B&W
Dir: Joseph Strick *Cast:* Barbara Jefford, Milo O'Shea, Maurice Roeves, T. P. McKenna, Martin Dempsey, Sheila O'-Sullivan
► Ambitious adaptation of one of this century's greatest works of literature.

O'Shea is impotent Irish Jew Leopold Bloom, walking the streets of Dublin, hooking up with poet Roeves and reflecting on wife Jefford's infidelity and on tragedies in his past. Uneven but captures some of author James Joyce's spirit.

ULZANA'S RAID 1972
★★ R Western 1:43
☑ Brief nudity, adult situations, explicit language, graphic violence
Dir: Robert Aldrich *Cast:* Burt Lancaster, Bruce Davison, Jorge Luke, Richard Jaeckel, Joaquin Martinez, Lloyd Bochner
► Liberal lieutenant Davison, on the trail of renegade Apaches, comes into conflict with scout Lancaster, a hardened veteran who shows no mercy for the savages. Tough, extremely violent Western can be viewed as a provocative allegory on the Vietnam War. Third teaming of Lancaster and director Aldrich (after *Apache* and *Vera Cruz*).

UMBRELLAS OF CHERBOURG, THE 1964 French
★ NR Musical 1:31
Dir: Jacques Demy *Cast:* Catherine Deneuve, Nino Castelnuovo, Anne Vernon, Marc Michel, Ellen Farner, Mireille Perrey
► Young lovers Deneuve and Castelnuovo are separated when he's drafted into the army for two years; her pregnancy forces a hard decision steeped in sorrow. Cinematic operetta, in which all dialogue is sung, features haunting music by Michel Legrand and stunning young Deneuve. However, mainstream audiences will be put off by this stylized experiment. Oscar-nominated for Best Foreign Film, Story and Screenplay, Song: ("I Will Wait For You"), and Score. Available dubbed. Ⓢ

UNBEARABLE LIGHTNESS OF BEING, THE 1988
★★★ R Drama/Romance 2:52
☑ Nudity, strong sexual content, adult situations, explicit language
Dir: Philip Kaufman *Cast:* Daniel Day-Lewis, Juliette Binoche, Erland Josephson, Lina Olin, Derek de Lint, Pavel Landowsky
► In Prague, 1966, just before Russian invasion of Czechoslovakia, promiscuous young surgeon Day-Lewis, dedicated to privacy and loneliness, enjoys unfettered life—a "lightness of being." Then he meets romantic waitress Binoche; she

and the arrival of Russian tanks prompt Day-Lewis to reconsider philosophy of life. Day-Lewis, Binoche, and his on-again, off-again lover, Olin, all flee to safety of Geneva for further explorations of fidelity, eroticism, and politics. Fine young cast in a sensuous and provocative adaptation of the novel by Czech author Milan Kundera. **(CC)**

UNCOMMON VALOR 1983
★★★★ R Action-Adventure 1:45
☑ Explicit language, violence
Dir: Ted Kotcheff *Cast:* Gene Hackman, Patrick Swayze, Robert Stack, Randall "Tex" Cobb, Fred Ward, Reb Brown
▶ Grieving Hackman, convinced son is still alive ten years after he was reported missing in action in Vietnam, traces him to a prison camp in Laos. Financed by oil tycoon Stack, whose boy is also missing, Hackman assembles Cobb, Ward, and Brown, former members of son's Marine outfit, for rescue mission. After extensive training program by younger Marine Swayze and attempt by CIA to derail raid, Hackman and crew sneak into Laos. Plenty of gut-busting action, rough-and-ready heroes, and impressive stunts in upbeat film. **(CC)**

UNDEFEATED, THE 1969
★★★ G Western 1:59
Dir: Andrew V. McLaglen *Cast:* John Wayne, Rock Hudson, Roman Gabriel, Tony Aguilar, Lee Meriwether, Merlin Olsen
▶ In post–Civil War Mexico, Union officer Wayne, on mission to deliver horse herd, meets up with Southern counterpart Hudson. The two former foes team up when they run afoul of Mexican general Aguilar. The Duke, Hudson, and football stars Gabriel and Olsen add up to lots of beefy macho in an otherwise middling vehicle. **(CC)**

UNDERACHIEVERS, THE 1987
★ R Comedy 1:27
☑ Nudity, adult situations, explicit language
Dir: Jackie Kong *Cast:* Edward Albert, Barbara Carrera, Michael Pataki, Susan Tyrrell, Mark Blankfield, Vic Tayback
▶ Failed shortstop Albert becomes narc at a combination reformatory–high school specializing in remedial education. Albert's arrest rate plummets when he falls for beautiful counselor Carrera, an unwilling accomplice in her col-league Tyrrell's dope ring. Low-budget, lowbrow high jinks climax in an extended catfight between Carrera and Tyrrell.

UNDER CAPRICORN 1949
★★★★ NR Drama 1:57
Dir: Alfred Hitchcock *Cast:* Ingrid Bergman, Joseph Cotten, Michael Wilding, Margaret Leighton, Cecil Parker
▶ Bergman, a seemingly frail alcoholic, is tormented by husband Cotten in nineteenth-century Australia. Wilding, a visitor from Ireland, upsets the household when he tries to free Bergman from her bondage. Leighton plays an evil housekeeper in love with Cotten. Obscure, unusual, slowly paced, and with little suspense; may disappoint Hitchcock fans.

UNDER COVER 1987
★★★ R Action-Adventure 1:34
☑ Adult situations, explicit language, violence
Dir: John Stockwell *Cast:* David Neidorf, Jennifer Jason Leigh, Barry Corbin, David Harris, Kathleen Wilhoite, John Philbin
▶ When his fellow cop is killed, Baltimore plainclothes expert Neidorf infiltrates South Carolina high school to break up drug ring. Helped by his beautiful new partner Leigh, Neidorf gathers evidence which is inexplicably ignored by his boss, Corbin. Overaged stars are too implausible for this routine tale. Stockwell's directing debut. **(CC)**

UNDER FIRE 1983
★★★★ R Drama 2:08
☑ Brief nudity, adult situations, explicit language, graphic violence
Dir: Roger Spottiswoode *Cast:* Nick Nolte, Gene Hackman, Joanna Cassidy, Ed Harris, Jean-Louis Trintignant, Richard Masur
▶ Explosive tale of journalists covering Nicaraguan conflict combines complex politics, gritty action, and a convincing love triangle into engrossing entertainment. Hardened photo-journalist Nolte tests his objectivity when asked to stage a pro-terrorist picture that could contribute to the fall of Somoza's regime. Superb performances by Hackman, as a cynical editor, and Harris, as a gung-ho mercenary, add to picture's depth.

UNDER MILK WOOD 1973 British
☆ PG Drama 1:30
☑ Adult situations, explicit language
Dir: Andrew Sinclair *Cast:* Richard Bur-

ton, Elizabeth Taylor, Peter O'Toole, Glynis Johns, Vivien Merchant, Sian Phillips
▶ Episodic look at the people of Llaregubb, a Welsh fishing village, cuts among a variety of characters: blind sea captain O'Toole, shrewish butcher Merchant, local prostitute Taylor, etc. Based on a Dylan Thomas radio play, film offers engaging dialogue and settings but very little drama. Burton provides voice-over and appears briefly in transitions.

UNDER THE BOARDWALK 1988
★★ R Drama 1:40
☑ Adult situations, explicit language, violence
Dir: Fritz Kiersch *Cast:* Keith Coogan, Danielle von Zerneck, Corky Carroll, Sonny Bono, Roxana Zal, Richard Joseph Paul
▶ *Romeo and Juliet* meets the California surf scene. Local girl von Zerneck falls for Valley guy Paul, her brother's rival in upcoming competition, while Paul's nerdy cousin Coogan romances wave whiz Zal. In climactic meet Paul must either win the title for the honor of the Valley or give up the $5,000 prize for von Zerneck's love. Stale surfer saga with plenty of pecs and bikinis.

UNDER THE CHERRY MOON 1986
★ PG-13 Drama 1:40 B&W
☑ Adult situations, explicit language, violence
Dir: Prince *Cast:* Prince, Jerome Benton, Kristin Scott-Thomas, Steven Berkoff, Francesca Annis, Emmanuelle Sallet
▶ Bronx expatriate Prince searches for love on the French Riviera, settling on Scott-Thomas, an heiress to a shipping fortune. Romance hits a snag when Prince's best friend Benton questions his motives. Extravagant throwback to 1940s glamour musicals suffers from terminally silly plot. Although "Kiss" and other tunes from Prince's platinum album *Parade* are featured on soundtrack, film lacks musical scenes. **(CC)**

UNDER THE RAINBOW 1981
★★ PG Comedy 1:38
☑ Brief nudity, adult situations, explicit language, violence
Dir: Steve Rash *Cast:* Chevy Chase, Carrie Fisher, Eve Arden, Joseph Maher, Robert Donner, Billy Barty
▶ Scores of little people gather at a Hollywood hotel hoping for parts as Munchkins in *The Wizard of Oz;* talent scout Fisher, babysitting them, faces additional

chaos from Secret Service agent Chase, a Japanese spy, visiting royalty, and midget assassins. Bright premise wears out quickly in this labored comedy.

UNDER THE VOLCANO 1984
★★ R Drama 1:52
☑ Nudity, adult situations, explicit language
Dir: John Huston *Cast:* Albert Finney, Jacqueline Bisset, Anthony Andrews, Ignacio Lopez Tarso, Katy Jurado, James Villiers
▶ In 1938, crises overwhelm alcoholic ex-British consul Finney on the Day of the Dead (November 1) in Mexico, despite the efforts of his estranged wife Bisset and half-brother Andrews to help. Ambitious attempt to adapt Malcolm Lowry's novel fails to capture book's dense symbolism, but offers strong performances, beautiful Gabriel Figueroa photography, and assured direction. Finney and soundtrack composer Alex North received Oscar nominations.

UNDERWORLD U.S.A. 1961
★★ NR Crime 1:38 B&W
Dir: Samuel Fuller *Cast:* Cliff Robertson, Dolores Dorn, Beatrice Coll, Larry Gates, Paul Dubov
▶ A child witnesses his dad's murder by four syndicate leaders. The kid grows up into hoodlum Robertson and proceeds to get revenge against the killers. Explosive and uncomplicated; fast pace, moody direction, and top-notch performances deliver excitement.

UNFAITHFULLY YOURS 1948
★★★ NR Comedy 1:45 B&W
Dir: Preston Sturges *Cast:* Rex Harrison, Linda Darnell, Barbara Lawrence, Rudy Vallee, Kurt Krueger, Lionel Stander
▶ Famed British conductor Harrison suspects hanky-panky between sexy young wife Darnell and his handsome personal secretary Krueger. That night Harrison leads orchestra in three symphonies; mood of each causes him to imagine trio of different resolutions to romantic dilemma, including murder. Splendid Harrison carries fanciful farce by writer-director Sturges. Some flat moments in music-inspired fantasies; brilliant comic bits are compensation.

UNFAITHFULLY YOURS 1984
★★★ PG Comedy 1:36
☑ Brief nudity, adult situations, explicit language, mild violence, adult humor

Dir: Howard Zieff   *Cast:* Dudley Moore, Nastassja Kinski, Albert Brooks, Armand Assante, Richard Libertini, Cassie Yates
▶ Stylish remake of the 1948 Preston Sturges film about famous conductor Moore who learns agent Brooks has assigned private eye to tail Moore's gorgeous young wife Kinski. Circumstantial evidence suggests Kinski has been having affair with violinist Assante, leading Moore to imagine murdering Kinksi and framing Assante for crime. When Moore tries to turn fantasy into fact, scheme goes comically awry. **(CC)**

UNFORGIVEN, THE 1960
★★★ NR Western 2:05
Dir: John Huston   *Cast:* Burt Lancaster, Audrey Hepburn, Audie Murphy, John Saxon, Charles Bickford, Lillian Gish
▶ Sprawling Western about a Texas cattle family battling Kiowa Indians over Hepburn, an Indian orphan adopted by matriarch Gish. Uneven plot forsakes genuinely interesting racial themes and suggestions of incest (between Hepburn and Lancaster, playing Gish's blood son) for rousing attacks and fights.

UNHOLY, THE 1988
★★ R Horror 1:40
☑ Nudity, adult situations, explicit language, violence
Dir: Camilo Vila   *Cast:* Ben Cross, Hal Holbrook, Jill Carroll, Trevor Howard, Ned Beatty, Nicole Fortier
▶ Archbishop Holbrook assigns previously invincible priest Cross to rid a New Orleans parish of the devil. Satanic cult prepares to sacrifice virgin waitress Carroll, while Cross battles Fortier, an incredibly erotic demon. Powerful stars lift this above similar horror vehicles

UNHOLY ROLLERS, THE 1972
★★ R Action-Adventure 1:28
☑ Nudity, adult situations, explicit language, violence
Dir: Vernon Zimmerman   *Cast:* Claudia Jennings, Louis Quinn, Betty Anne Rees, Roberta Collins, Alan Vint, Candice Roman
▶ Factory worker Jennings enters the roller derby circuit determined to become a star. Her teammates are dismayed when she rejects staged brawls and phony fights for real violence. Low-budget Roger Corman production may be the best film ever about roller derbies.

UNIDENTIFIED FLYING ODDBALL, THE 1979
★★★ G Fantasy/Comedy 1:33
Dir: Russ Mayberry   *Cast:* Dennis Dugan, Ron Moody, Jim Dale, Kenneth More, John Le Mesurier
▶ Modern American scientist Dugan and his robot duplicate are transported into England during the reign of King Arthur (More). There Dugan runs afoul of the sorcerer Merlin (Moody). Disney high jinks adapted from Mark Twain's *A Connecticut Yankee in King Arthur's Court*.

UNION CITY 1980
☆ PG Drama 1:25
☑ Explicit language, violence
Dir: Mark Reichert   *Cast:* Dennis Lipscomb, Deborah Harry, Irina Maleeva, Everett McGill, Sam McMurray, Pat Benatar
▶ Insecure husband Lipscomb, suspicious of slatternly wife Harry, murders an innocent drifter before succumbing to madness. Gloomy film noir set in 1953 was based on Cornell Woolrich's "The Corpse Next Door." Acting debut for Harry, former singer for rock group Blondie.

UNION PACIFIC 1939
★★★ NR Western 2:15 B&W
Dir: Cecil B. DeMille   *Cast:* Barbara Stanwyck, Joel McCrea, Robert Preston, Akim Tamiroff, Brian Donlevy, Anthony Quinn
▶ Railroad executive McCrea builds the Union Pacific across the post–Civil War West, although bad guys, including his old war buddy Preston, try to stop him. Stanwyck, the woman involved with both men, reforms Preston. History-based tale provides larger-than-life excitement.

UNMARRIED WOMAN, AN 1978
★★★★ R Drama 2:04
☑ Nudity, adult situations, explicit language
Dir: Paul Mazursky   *Cast:* Jill Clayburgh, Alan Bates, Michael Murphy, Cliff Gorman, Lisa Lucas, Kelly Bishop
▶ New Yorker Clayburgh faces difficult adjustment to single life when husband Murphy walks out for younger woman. After one-night stand with heel Gorman, she finds new love with passionate artist Bates, but maintains her hard-won independence. A winning drama whose sensitive script and direction convey contemporary humor, razor-sharp insight, and bright New York City atmosphere.

Oscar-nominated Clayburgh is fabulous. A Best Picture nominee.

UNSEEN, THE 1980
★ R Horror 1:31
☑ Rape, nudity, explicit language, graphic violence
Dir: Peter Foleg *Cast:* Barbara Bach, Sydney Lassick, Stephen Furst, Lelia Goldoni, Karen Lamm, Doug Barr
▶ TV reporter Bach and two colleagues covering a Danish heritage festival in California are forced to stay in a remote mansion where Lassick and his sister Goldoni are hiding a dark family secret in the basement. Unimaginative horror film fails to exploit its incest premise with conviction.

UNSINKABLE MOLLY BROWN, THE 1964
★★ NR Biography/Musical 2:08
Dir: Charles Walters *Cast:* Debbie Reynolds, Harve Presnell, Ed Begley, Jack Kruschen, Hermione Baddeley, Harvey Lembeck
▶ True story of title character (Reynolds) who rises from poverty when her husband Presnell becomes rich. Acceptance in posh society eludes her until she achieves fame surviving the wreck of the *Titanic.* Oscar-nominated Reynolds is the prime attraction here. Based on the Broadway hit; hummable score by Meredith Wilson (*The Music Man*).

UNTIL SEPTEMBER 1984
★★★ R Romance 1:35
☑ Nudity, adult situations, explicit language
Dir: Richard Marquand *Cast:* Karen Allen, Thierry Lhermitte, Christopher Cazenove, Marie-Catherine Conti, Nitzi Saul
▶ Star-crossed romance between Allen, an American stranded in Paris, and Lhermitte, a well-to-do banker whose wife and children are in the country until September. The couple spend three idyllic weeks together exploring Paris and the surrounding countryside. Will their summer love end? City of Lights never looked better; neither have the very attractive leads. (CC)

UNTOUCHABLES, THE 1987
★★★★★ R Action-Adventure 2:00
☑ Explicit language, violence
Dir: Brian De Palma *Cast:* Kevin Costner, Sean Connery, Charles Martin Smith, Andy Garcia, Robert De Niro, Billy Drago
▶ Smashing account of Federal agent Elliot Ness's (Costner) efforts to nab crimelord Al Capone (De Niro) is nonstop entertainment in the best Hollywood manner. Loosely inspired by the famous TV series, David Mamet's script offers excellent roles for Garcia (an Italian sharpshooter) and Drago (Capone's psychotic hitman Frank Nitti), but Connery steals the film in his Oscar-winning turn as an honest street cop who lends a guiding hand to Ness. Bravura shootout in Chicago's Union Station is only one of many highlights.

UP FROM THE DEPTHS 1979
★ R Horror 1:25
☑ Brief nudity, adult situations, explicit language, graphic violence
Dir: Charles B. Griffith *Cast:* Sam Bottoms, Suzanne Reed, Virgil Frye, Kedric Wolf, Charles Howerton
▶ Monstrous fish attacks visitors at a Hawaiian tourist resort, prompting locals to stage contest to capture it. Many lives are lost as the fish proves smarter than anticipated. Low-rent *Jaws* rip-off filmed in the Philippines makes a few stabs at humor, but its satire is as weak as the bloody action.

UPHILL ALL THE WAY 1986
★★★ PG Comedy 1:26
☑ Brief nudity, explicit language, violence
Dir: Frank Dobbs *Cast:* Roy Clark, Mel Tillis, Burl Ives, Glen Campbell, Trish Van Devere, Elaine Joyce
▶ Country-western stars Clark and Tillis team up as bumbling con men mistaken for bank robbers in the Wild West. Comedy of errors includes encounters with the Army, Mexican bandits, and beautiful widow Van Devere. Amiably slapdash spoof of Westerns features appearances by Burt Reynolds, Frank Gorshin, and Sheb Wooley, and songs by Clark, Tillis, Campbell, and Waylon Jennings.

UP IN SMOKE 1978
★★★ R Comedy 1:27
☑ Nudity, adult situations, explicit language
Dir: Lou Adler *Cast:* Cheech Marin, Thomas Chong, Stacy Keach, Edie Adams, Tom Skerritt, Zane Buzby
▶ Genial, irreverent comedy about barrio hustler and rich hippie searching for dynamite pot introduced comedy team Cheech and Chong to feature films. Bawdy, drug-oriented humor is

broad and juvenile, but duo's good spirits are infectious. Keach mugs shamelessly as a redneck cop in pursuit of the pair; Buzby as a crazed hitchhiker has the most bizarre gags. Sequel: *Cheech & Chong's Next Movie.*

UP THE ACADEMY 1980
★★ R Comedy 1:27
☑ Explicit language, adult humor
Dir: Robert Downey *Cast:* Ron Leibman, Wendell Brown, Tom Citera, J. Hutchinson, Ralph Macchio, Tom Poston
▶ Raunchy teen comedy set in a military academy ruled by a sadistic major (Leibman, who had his name removed from film's publicity) is alternately tasteless, crude, and surprisingly funny. Poston is amusing as a swishy dance instructor; Barbara Bach has a cameo as a weapons instructor. Presented by *Mad* magazine.

UP THE CREEK 1984
★★ R Comedy 1:35
☑ Nudity, adult situations, explicit language, violence
Dir: Robert Butler *Cast:* Tim Matheson, Jennifer Runyon, Stephen Furst, Dan Monahan, Jeff East, Blaine Novak
▶ Four college misfits led by Matheson must win white-water raft race to graduate; they're opposed by East's cruel preppies and Novak's vicious military academy rejects. Fitfully inspired comedy stretches thin; Chuck the Wonder Dog steals film in a hilarious charades sequence.

UP THE DOWN STAIRCASE 1967
★★★ NR Drama 2:04
Dir: Robert Mulligan *Cast:* Sandy Dennis, Patrick Bedford, Eileen Heckart, Jean Stapleton, Ruth White, Sorrell Booke
▶ Young teacher Dennis starts a job at New York City school. Her ideals quickly run up against the realities of an incompetent faculty and disinterested students. However, Dennis manages to get through to the kids. Generally sincere and well-crafted; based on the Bel Kaufman best-seller.

UP THE SANDBOX 1972
★★ R Comedy/Drama 1:38
☑ Adult situations, explicit language, violence
Dir: Irvin Kershner *Cast:* Barbra Streisand, David Selby, Barbara Rhodes,

Jane Hoffman, Jacobo Morales, Ariane Heller
▶ New York housewife Streisand, mother of two with a third on the way, is unappreciated by professor husband Selby. She finds solace in fantasies about Africa, Fidel Castro, abortion, and other subjects. Uneven but challenging change-of-pace for Streisand. Based on the novel by Anne Richardson Roiphe.

UPTOWN SATURDAY NIGHT 1974
★★★ PG Comedy 1:44
☑ Adult situations, explicit language, violence
Dir: Sidney Poitier *Cast:* Sidney Poitier, Bill Cosby, Harry Belafonte, Flip Wilson, Richard Pryor, Rosalind Cash
▶ Pals Poitier and Cosby sneak away from their wives and go to a gambling house. When the joint is robbed, the guys lose a wallet containing a winning lottery ticket. In their attempt to recover the item, they encounter gangster Belafonte, preacher Wilson, and others. Uproarious comedy led to sequel *Let's Do It Again.* Poitier holds his own among the all-star comic cast.

URBAN COWBOY 1980
★★★★ PG Romance 2:15
☑ Adult situations, explicit language, violence
Dir: James Bridges *Cast:* John Travolta, Debra Winger, Scott Glenn, Madolyn Smith, Barry Corbin
▶ Tough-talking but soft-hearted honky-tonk romance between refinery worker Travolta and Winger, the girl he picks up at the world-famous Gilley's bar. They marry and then split without much thought. While Travolta wrestles both Gilley's mechanical bull and debutante Smith, bad guy Glenn catches Winger on the rebound. Classic boy-meets-girl tale enlivened by down-home Texas flavor, sassy soundtrack, first-rate production values, and electrifying chemistry between leads. Sexiest scene: Winger rides the bull.

USED CARS 1980
★★★ R Comedy 1:52
☑ Brief nudity, explicit language, adult humor
Dir: Robert Zemeckis *Cast:* Kurt Russell, Jack Warden, Gerrit Graham, Frank McRae, Deborah Harmon, Joe Flaherty
▶ The Fuchs brothers (Warden, in a dual role) compete viciously with rival car dealerships. When the kindly Fuchs dies,

aspiring politician and master salesman Russell disregards ethics in an epic battle of wits with the nasty Fuchs brother. Breathless, tasteless, insulting, genuinely inventive comedy is remarkably funny until the forced climax. Kudos to Peanuts, a brilliant pooch. Produced by Steven Spielberg and John Milius.

U2: RATTLE AND HUM 1988
★★★ PG-13 Documentary/Music
1:39 C/B&W
☑ Explicit language
Dir: Phil Joanou *Cast:* Bono Vox, The Edge, Larry Mullen, Jr., Adam Clayton, B. B. King
▶ American odyssey of U2, one of the hottest rock groups of the eighties, alternates concert footage with scenes of four band members discovering their stateside musical roots. Quartet re-records hit "I Still Haven't Found What I'm Looking For" with Harlem gospel singers and cuts "Love Comes to Town" with bluesmaster King. Concert tunes include cover versions of Beatles' "Helter Skelter" and Bob Dylan's "All Along the Watchtower."

VAGABOND 1986 French
☆ NR Drama 1:45
☑ Nudity, adult situations, explicit language
Dir: Agnes Varda *Cast:* Sandrine Bonnaire, Macha Meril, Stephane Freiss, Laurence Cortadellas, Marthe Jarnias, Yolande Moreau
▶ In the south of France, eighteen-year-old Bonnaire hitchhikes, does odd jobs, lives in a tent through the winter, forms fleeting relationships with those she encounters, and meets a tragic fate. Melancholy and finely detailed; Bonnaire's performance is haunting, although the vivid and ultimately depressing depiction of her vagabond lifestyle is not for everyone. Ⓢ

VALACHI PAPERS, THE 1972 Italian
★★★ PG Crime/Drama 2:05
☑ Adult situations, explicit language, violence
Dir: Terence Young *Cast:* Charles Bronson, Lino Ventura, Joseph Wiseman, Jill Ireland, Gerald S. O'Loughlin, Walter Chiari
▶ Imprisoned mafioso Bronson, marked for death by gang boss Ventura, decides to cooperate with FBI man O'Loughlin. In flashbacks, Bronson's life and crimes among mobsters unfolds. *Godfather*-like

saga from the fact-based Peter Maas best-seller. One of Bronson's more serious performances although Wiseman is the cast's standout as a mob chief.

VALET GIRLS 1987
★ R Comedy 1:23
☑ Nudity, adult situations, explicit language
Dir: Rafal Zielinski *Cast:* Meri D. Marshall, April Stewart, Mary Kohnert, Christopher Weeks, Patricia Scott Michel
▶ Aspiring singer Marshall, psychology major Stewart, and Southern belle Kohnert displace three jealous male carhops at a slimy agent's endless parties. The boys respond with a series of practical jokes, hoping to get the girls fired. Brainless comedy fails to deliver enough gags.

VALLEY GIRL 1983
★★ R Romance/Comedy 1:39
☑ Nudity, explicit language
Dir: Martha Coolidge *Cast:* Nicolas Cage, Deborah Foreman, Colleen Camp, Frederic Forrest, Michael Bowen
▶ Foreman is like totally a valley girl and must choose between surfer boyfriend Bowen and Cage, the punkish Hollywood dude she meets at a party. Meanwhile, she has to work in the totally gross health food store run by Forrest and Camp, her hippie parents. Slightly better-than-average teen flick was inspired by pop song.

VALLEY OF THE DOLLS 1967
★★ PG Drama 2:03
☑ Adult situations, explicit language
Dir: Mark Robson *Cast:* Barbara Parkins, Patty Duke, Susan Hayward, Sharon Tate, Martin Milner, Lee Grant
▶ Parkins, Duke, and Tate seek show business fame and fortune but soon run into professional problems, drugs, bad affairs, and disease. Trashy and vulgar with little redeeming social value; nevertheless, kind of fun. Based on Jacqueline Susann's best-seller.

VALS, THE 1983
★ R Comedy 1:37
☑ Nudity, adult situations, explicit language
Dir: James Polakof *Cast:* Jill Carroll, Elena Stratheros, Michelle Laurita, Gina Calabrase, Chuck Connors, Sonny Bono
▶ Valley girls Carroll, Stratheros, Laurita, and Calabrase attempt to raise money for a struggling orphanage by bilking coke dealers. Good-looking cast struts its stuff against a surprising antidrug mes-

sage; simplistic story makes this strictly drive-in fare.

VAMP 1986
★ R Horror 1:34

☑ Nudity, adult situations, explicit language, violence

Dir: Richard Wenk *Cast:* Chris Makepeace, Grace Jones, Robert Rusler, Gedde Watanabe, Sandy Baron, Dedee Pfeiffer

▶ Fraternity pledges Makepeace and Rusler agree to provide stripper for upcoming party. With Watanabe, they journey to nightclub that's actually den of vampires. Dazzling stripper Jones sinks her teeth into Rusler while Makepeace, Watanabe, and cute waitress Pfeiffer try to flee from monsters. Uneven genre hybrid emphasizes dark terrors lurking beneath swinging nightlife. **(CC)**

VAMPING 1984
★★ R Drama 1:30

☑ Brief nudity, adult situations, explicit language, violence

Dir: Frederick King Keller *Cast:* Patrick Duffy, Catherine Hyland, Rod Arrants, Fred A. Keller, David Booze

▶ Down-on-his-luck saxophonist Duffy robs widow Hyland's mansion, making off with valuable ring and love letters from her late husband. Letters inspire both Duffy's sax playing and heart: he winds up in bed with Hyland, only to be tailed by mysterious man who may or may not be a cop. Duffy is soon involved in murder, double crosses, and blackmail. Wildly convoluted plot, passive role for Duffy, and downbeat ending derail promising start.

VAMPIRE AT MIDNIGHT 1988
★★ R Horror 1:33

☑ Nudity, explicit language, violence

Dir: Gregory McClatchy *Cast:* Jason Williams, Gustav Vintas, Lesley Milne, Esther Alise, Jeanie Moore, Robert Random

▶ L.A. police detective Williams pursues vampire Vintas, who's leaving a trail of bodies. Vintas is a hypnotherapist whose gaze mesmerizes women; they become either victims or servant drones. Williams's pianist girlfriend Milne falls under Vintas's spell: he must battle to save her life and end threat to city. Bloodsucking thrills and bevy of undraped beauties should please fans of genre. **(CC)**

VAMPIRE'S KISS 1988
★ R Horror 1:43

☑ Nudity, adult situations, explicit language, violence

Dir: Robert Bierman *Cast:* Nicolas Cage, Maria Conchita Alonso, Jennifer Beals, Elizabeth Ashley, Kasi Lemmons, Bob Lujan

▶ Swinging Manhattan yuppie Cage picks up beautiful Beals in singles bar. One catch: she's a vampire and her kiss turns him wild. Cage grows increasingly manic at work, abusing his suffering secretary Alonso. He then completely cracks up, going on psychotic killing spree while begging for someone to end his misery. Fine cast wasted as seriocomic start degenerates into unanticipated mayhem made worse by Cage's frantic overacting.

VAMPYR 1932 French/German
★ NR Horror 1:10 B&W

Dir: Carl Theodor Dreyer *Cast:* Julian West, Henriette Gerard, Jan Hieronimko, Maurice Schutz, Rena Mandel, Sybille Schmitz

▶ While exploring a remote village, naturalist West learns that a vampire is slowly destroying the inhabitants. Demanding, slowly paced adaptation of Sheridan le Fanu's *In a Glass Darkly* is historically significant for its subtly eerie tone and Rudolph Maté's extraordinary photography. Evocative score by Wolfgang Zeller and almost complete absence of dialogue add to unnerving atmosphere. ⓢ

VANISHING POINT 1971
★★★ PG Drama 1:38

☑ Explicit language, violence

Dir: Richard C. Sarafian *Cast:* Barry Newman, Cleavon Little, Dean Jagger, Victoria Medlin, Robert Donner, Severn Darden

▶ Driver Newman takes impossible bet that he can zip from Colorado to California in fifteen hours. Blind disc jockey Little learns of his quest and advises him over the air how to avoid the pursuing cops. Bizarre but compelling chase movie. Busy musical score includes numbers by Kim Carnes, Jerry Reed, and Delaney and Bonnie.

VANISHING WILDERNESS 1974
★★★★★ G Documentary 1:26

Dir: Arthur Dubs, Heinz Seilmann

▶ Scenic documentary travels 32,000 miles from Alaska to Florida, examining plight of wildlife from polar bears to pelicans. Outstanding family fare with a message features breathtaking photography and narration by cowboy actor Rex Allen.

VELVET VAMPIRE, THE 1971
☆ **R Horror 1:21**
☑ Nudity, adult situations, explicit language, graphic violence
Dir: Stephanie Rothman *Cast:* Michael Blodgett, Sherry Miles, Celeste Yarnall, Jerry Daniels, Gene Shane
▶ Newlyweds Blodgett and Miles fall under the spell of sexy art patron Yarnall, who reveals an unhealthy thirst for blood at her desert hideaway. Stylish but ultimately far-fetched horror marred by weak acting.

VENDETTA 1986
★★ **R Action-Adventure 1:29**
☑ Rape, nudity, adult situations, explicit language, graphic violence
Dir: Bruce Logan *Cast:* Karen Chase, Lisa Clarson, Lisa Hullana, Linda Lightfoot, Sandy Martin, Michelle Newkirk
▶ Innocent Newkirk, serving prison sentence for slaying would-be rapist, is killed by gang of lesbian toughs. Newkirk's sister Chase, a professional stunt woman and kung-fu expert, intentionally gets herself incarcerated to seek revenge. Series of vendetta murders leads to showdown with gang leader Martin. Violent and sensationalist women-behind-bars pic lacks usual tongue-in-cheek humor of genre.

VENOM 1982 British
★★ **R Mystery-Suspense 1:32**
☑ Explicit language, violence
Dir: Piers Haggard *Cast:* Klaus Kinski, Oliver Reed, Nicol Williamson, Sarah Miles, Sterling Hayden, Lance Holcomb
▶ German criminal Kinski, aided by butler Reed, attempts to kidnap rich boy Holcomb from London townhouse. Unbeknownst to hoodlums, Holcomb has inadvertently acquired deadly black mamba snake. Reptile escapes, threatening all in home, including boy's protective grandfather Hayden. Superior cast in average suspense thriller.

VERA CRUZ 1954
★★★ **NR Western 1:34**
Dir: Robert Aldrich *Cast:* Gary Cooper, Burt Lancaster, Denise Darcel, Cesar Romero, Sarita Montiel, Ernest Borgnine
▶ American mercenaries Cooper and Lancaster form a wary alliance while guiding a gold shipment to Emperor Maximilian's Vera Cruz fortress. Beautiful aristocrat Darcel convinces Cooper to hand the loot over to Juarez's rebels, but Lancaster has his own plans for the gold. Solid, action-packed Western has a small role by Charles Bronson under his Buchinski surname.

VERDICT, THE 1982
★★★★★ **R Drama 2:09**
☑ Adult situations, explicit language, mild violence
Dir: Sidney Lumet *Cast:* Paul Newman, Charlotte Rampling, Jack Warden, James Mason, Milo O'Shea, Lindsay Crouse
▶ Alcoholic Boston lawyer Newman gets one last stab at redemption when he takes on the medical establishment and the church in a malpractice suit against a Catholic hospital. Complicating his task: big-time opposing attorney Mason, unsympathetic judge O'Shea, and mystery woman Rampling. Superlative courtroom drama works up maximum empathy for the underdog. Immaculate direction by Lumet, performance by Newman that's both daring and subtle, and incisive David Mamet script. Oscar nominations: Best Picture, Director, Screenplay, Actor (Newman), Supporting Actor (Mason).

VERTIGO 1958
★★★★★ **PG Mystery-Suspense 2:00**
☑ Adult situations
Dir: Alfred Hitchcock *Cast:* James Stewart, Kim Novak, Barbara Bel Geddes, Tom Helmore, Henry Jones, Ellen Corby
▶ Retired detective Stewart is hired by old friend Helmore to tail his unstable wife Novak. Stewart becomes obsessed with his quarry, but his fear of heights leads to tragedy. A masterpiece whose hypnotic direction conveys emotion and meaning with every shot, leading to a climax of almost unbearable intensity. Stewart's complex performance and Bernard Herrmann's score add to the haunting mood.

VERY CLOSE QUARTERS 1984
☆ **R Comedy 1:41**
☑ Explicit language, adult humor
Dir: Vladimir Riff *Cast:* Paul Sorvino, Shelley Winters, Theodore Bikel, Farley Granger, Lee Taylor Allen, Ellen Barber
▶ Thirty-one Russians share one crowded Moscow apartment, leading to long waits for the bathroom as well as other problems. Against this stifling back-

ground, Winters tries to fix up daughter Allen with rich Sorvino. Simply atrocious; some good actors fail to breathe life into an awful screenplay.

VERY PRIVATE AFFAIR, A 1962
French/Italian
★★ NR Drama 1:35
Dir: Louis Malle   *Cast:* Brigitte Bardot, Marcello Mastroianni, Gregor von Ressori, Eleonore Hirt, Ursula Kubler, Dirk Sanders
▶ Unconvincing depiction of the rise to fame of Swiss model (Bardot) and her subsequent withdrawal from public life when the pressures of stardom grow too strong. Theatrical director Mastroianni tries to protect her privacy in this moody drama based on several incidents in Bardot's life. Ⓢ

VIBES 1988
★★ PG Comedy 1:39
☑ Explicit language, violence
Dir: Ken Kwapis   *Cast:* Cyndi Lauper, Jeff Goldblum, Peter Falk, Julian Sands, Googy Gress, Michael Lerner
▶ Psychics Lauper and Goldblum meet at seminar conducted by ESP expert Sands and are soon recruited by Falk to find his missing son in the mountains of Ecuador. Once in the Andes, they learn Falk has a more nefarious purpose. Singer Lauper's screen debut is fluffy fare mainly for teens.

VICE SQUAD 1982
★★★ R Action-Adventure 1:37
☑ Nudity, strong sexual content, adult situations, explicit language, graphic violence
Dir: Gary A. Sherman   *Cast:* Season Hubley, Gary Swanson, Wings Hauser, Pepe Serna, Beverly Todd, Joseph DiGiroloma
▶ Young mother Hubley reluctantly works as prostitute to support child. When vicious pimp Hauser slays another hooker, vice squad cop Swanson persuades Hubley to work undercover to capture the killer. Average sleazy crime drama offers few surprises.

VICE VERSA 1988
★★★ PG Comedy 1:37
☑ Adult situations, explicit language
Dir: Brian Gilbert   *Cast:* Judge Reinhold, Fred Savage, Corinne Bohrer, Swoosie Kurtz, Jane Kaczmarek, David Proval
▶ Father-son role reversal comedy boasts memorable performances from

both Reinhold and Savage. Reinhold brings vigor and freshness to his role as an eleven-year-old interested in heavy metal and his pet frog. Savage also excels as kid with the brain of a yuppie executive. More clever and a lot more fun than similarly plotted *Like Father, Like Son.* (CC)

VICTIM 1961 British
★★★★ NR Drama 1:40 B&W
Dir: Basil Dearden   *Cast:* Dirk Bogarde, Sylvia Sims, Dennis Price, Anthony Nichols, Nigel Stock, Peter McEnery
▶ Homosexual lawyer Bogarde finds his marriage and career endangered when his young lover McEnery kills himself. Bogarde pursues the blackmailers responsible for McEnery's death. Powerful statement approaches subject matter with tact and dignity. Crisply directed and well played by all.

VICTOR/VICTORIA 1982
★★★★ PG Musical/Comedy 2:14
☑ Adult situations, explicit language
Dir: Blake Edwards   *Cast:* Julie Andrews, Robert Preston, James Garner, Lesley Ann Warren, Alex Karras
▶ Down-on-her-luck actress Andrews is starving in 1930s Paris when she meets Preston, a similarly unemployed entertainer. Together, they create a nightclub act by passing Andrews off as a guy who impersonates women. She/he is an overnight sensation but complications arise when American tycoon Garner falls in love and sets out to prove Andrews is all woman. Meanwhile, Garner's obnoxious girlfriend Warren spreads the rumor that he's in love with a man. Screamingly funny, classic comedy of errors.

VICTORY 1981
★★★★ PG War/Drama 1:56
☑ Explicit language, violence
Dir: John Huston   *Cast:* Michael Caine, Sylvester Stallone, Max Von Sydow, Pelé, Werner Roth, Carole Laure
▶ Nazi propaganda officer Von Sydow organizes soccer match in Paris between Allied POW all-stars and German national squad. Caine, head of POW squad, plans escape for team during game, so tough American Stallone breaks out of camp to notify French Resistance and then returns to play goalie. During game Allies must choose between escape and victory. Rousing drama from veteran director Huston boasts unusual premise and world-fa-

mous soccer stars, including legendary Pelé and former New York Cosmos player Roth.

VIDEO DEAD, THE 1987
★★ R Horror 1:30
☑ Explicit language, violence
Dir: Robert Scott *Cast:* Roxanna Augesen, Rocky Duvall, Vickie Bastel, Sam David McClelland, Michael St. Michaels, Jennifer Miro
▶ TV set is accidentally delivered to writer St. Michaels. Even when unplugged, it plays same black-and-white zombie movie. Zombies walk out of set and kill St. Michaels. Months later siblings Augesen and Duvall move into house; they and neighbors are threatened by zombies.

VIDEODROME 1983 Canadian
★ R Horror 1:27
☑ Nudity, strong sexual content, adult situations, explicit language, graphic violence
Dir: David Cronenberg *Cast:* James Woods, Deborah Harry, Sonja Smits, Peter Dvorsky, Les Carlson, Jack Creley
▶ In the near future, Woods, unsavory head of sleazy Toronto cable TV station, becomes obsessed with torture-mutilation program called "Videodrome." Woods learns images have irreversible effect on viewers; he and kinky girlfriend Harry succumb to dire effects of Videodrome. Intriguing premise of TV displacing reality is overwhelmed by confusing techno-speak and grandiose plot.

VIEW TO A KILL, A 1985 British
★★★★ PG
Espionage/Action-Adventure 2:11
☑ Adult situations, explicit language, violence
Dir: John Glen *Cast:* Roger Moore, Christopher Walken, Tanya Roberts, Grace Jones, Patrick Macnee, Patrick Bauchau
▶ Investigating murder of fellow British agent in Alps, James Bond (Moore) narrowly escapes on one ski from Soviet assassins. Trail leads to Russian spy Walken with a plan to destroy Silicon Valley, home of U.S. computer industry, by inducing an earthquake. Jones is Walken's evil assistant; Roberts is at first his unwitting dupe, then Moore's ally and romantic interest. Moore's efforts to thwart Walken lead to two climaxes: one below ground, the other on top of Golden Gate Bridge. (CC)

VIGILANTE 1982
★★ R Action-Adventure 1:30
☑ Rape, nudity, adult situations, explicit language, graphic violence
Dir: William Lustig *Cast:* Robert Forster, Fred Williamson, Richard Bright, Rutanya Alda, Don Blakely, Joseph Carberry
▶ When thugs attack his wife and murder their young son, New York blue-collar worker Forster seeks justice in court, but simpleton judge and crooked lawyer spring hoods. Forster then joins neighborhood vigilantes, led by co-worker Williamson, for spree of retribution killings. Hard-hitting action yarn, in tradition of *Death Wish* pictures, is only for those with stomach for extreme violence.

VIKINGS, THE 1958
★★★ NR Action-Adventure 1:54
Dir: Richard Fleischer *Cast:* Kirk Douglas, Tony Curtis, Ernest Borgnine, Janet Leigh, James Donald, Alexander Knox
▶ Viking prince Douglas and slave Curtis, half-brothers (although they don't know it) and rivals for the love of princess Leigh, fight each other but later team up when their father Borgnine is killed. Brawny and muscular. Curtis and Douglas provide plenty of heroics; Leigh contributes sex appeal.

VILLAGE OF THE DAMNED 1960 British
★★ NR Sci-Fi 1:18 B&W
Dir: Wolf Rilla *Cast:* George Sanders, Barbara Shelley, Michael Gwynn, Laurence Naismith, Martin Stephens
▶ In an English village, the women become mysteriously pregnant and give birth to a race of superpowered kids. When the children evince evil intent, scientist-father Sanders tries to stop them. Spooky and unusual, with moody direction and chilling child actors. Based on the novel *The Midwich Cuckoos* by John Wyndham; spawned sequel *Children of the Damned*.

VILLAGE OF THE GIANTS 1965
★★ NR Sci-Fi 1:22
Dir: Bert I. Gordon *Cast:* Tommy Kirk, Beau Bridges, Ron Howard, Johnny Crawford, Joy Harmon, Toni Basil
▶ Teens go on a rampage after being turned into giants by young scientist Howard's new type of food. Low-rent shenanigans with a rather inane screenplay inspired by H. G. Wells novel *The Food of the Gods*; unfaithful to the source.

VILLAIN, THE 1979
★★★★ PG Western/Comedy 1:33
☑ Explicit language, adult humor
Dir: Hal Needham *Cast:* Kirk Douglas, Ann-Margret, Arnold Schwarzenegger, Paul Lynde, Foster Brooks, Ruth Buzzi
▶ Villainous Douglas tries to steal money from lovely Ann-Margret and her bodyguard Schwarzenegger in what is an admitted live action counterpart to the Road Runner cartoons. Plotless result has Douglas repeatedly foiled in his attempts to rob the chesty duo. Silly, broad Western comedy packed with pratfalls is best suited to adults who still need their Saturday morning cartoon fix.

VINDICATOR, THE 1986 Canadian
★★ R Horror 1:2
☑ Brief nudity, explicit language, violence
Dir: Jean-Claude Lord *Cast:* Terri Austin, Richard Cox, Pam Grier, Maury Chaykin, David McIlwraith
▶ Brilliant scientist Cox develops indestructible cyborg killer and is slain by jealous colleague McIlwraith. McIlwraith then installs Cox's brain in cyborg prototype, but creature escapes before installation of control mechanism and goes on rampage. Also released as *Frankenstein '88*, low-budget updating of Mary Shelley classic works best as camp. **(CC)**

VIOLATED 1984
★ R Action-Adventure 1:28
☑ Nudity, adult situations, violence
Dir: Richard Cannistraro *Cast:* J. C. Quinn, April Daisy White, John Heard, Lisanne Falk, Samantha Fox, Jonathan Ward
▶ Actress White, raped by gangsters at a party, gets involved with policeman Quinn. In a twist of fate, the same thugs run afoul of the mob, and killer Heard hires Quinn, who is also a hired gun, to rub out one of White's tormentors. Exploitation item is short on logic and talent save for the dependable Heard.

VIOLETS ARE BLUE 1986
★★★ PG-13 Romance 1:26
☑ Brief nudity, adult situations
Dir: Jack Fisk *Cast:* Sissy Spacek, Kevin Kline, Bonnie Bedelia, John Kellogg, Jim Standiford, Augusta Dabney
▶ Spacek, a successful photojournalist, and Kline, a married newspaper editor, are former high school sweethearts reunited fifteen years after they were romantically involved. They try to fight their feelings for each other but their old passion is rekindled. They collaborate on a local story and then have the opportunity to work together on a Paris assignment. Will Kline give up wife Bedelia and his teenage son? Tender and touching love story tapestry directed by Spacek's husband. **(CC)**

VIRGINIA CITY 1940
★★ NR Western 2:01 B&W
Dir: Michael Curtiz *Cast:* Errol Flynn, Miriam Hopkins, Randolph Scott, Humphrey Bogart, Frank McHugh, Alan Hale
▶ During the Civil War, Union officer Flynn tries to stop multimillion-dollar Confederate gold shipment. Opposing him are his old nemesis Scott, bandit Bogart, and Hopkins, a beautiful Southerner who eventually falls for Flynn. Lively genre fare.

VIRGIN QUEEN, THE 1955
★★ NR Biography 1:32
Dir: Henry Koster *Cast:* Bette Davis, Richard Todd, Joan Collins, Herbert Marshall, Dan O'Herlihy, Rod Taylor
▶ In sixteenth-century England, explorer Walter Raleigh (Todd) wins the heart of elderly Queen Elizabeth (Davis, who played the same role in 1939's *The Private Lives of Elizabeth and Essex*). She is willing to finance his expeditions but becomes jealous when he rebuffs her in favor of lady-in-waiting Collins. Well made and well cast; Davis is first-rate. **(CC)**

VIRGIN QUEEN OF ST. FRANCIS HIGH, THE 1987 Canadian
☆ PG Comedy 1:34
☑ Adult situations
Dir: Francesco Lucente *Cast:* Joseph R. Straface, Stacy Christensen, J. T. Wotton, Anna-Lisa Iapaolo, Lee Barringer, Bev Wotton
▶ Socially inept high schooler Straface bets tough guy Barringer he can lure stuck-up virgin Christensen to no-tell motel for hanky panky by summer's end. Christensen accepts Straface's invite to bungalow but insists he act like a gentleman. He does just that and two develop chaste friendship. Low-budget teen comedy (beware bottom-of-the barrel production values) resists usual descent into sexploitation.

VIRGIN SPRING, THE 1960 Swedish
★ NR Drama 1:28 B&W
Dir: Ingmar Bergman *Cast:* Max Von Sydow, Brigitta Valberg, Gunnel Lindblom, Brigitta Pettersson, Axel Duberg

▶ When his virginal daughter Pettersson is raped and killed in medieval Sweden, Von Sydow takes violent revenge on the perpetrators. His faith in God is shaken until a miracle occurs. Grim but gripping tale nabbed Foreign Film Oscar. Available dubbed. ⑤

VIRIDIANA 1961 Spanish
★ NR Drama 1:30 B&W
Dir: Luis Buñuel **Cast:** Silvia Pinal, Francisco Rabal, Fernando Rey, Margarita Lozano, Victoria Zinny, Teresa Rabal
▶ Pinal, raised in a sheltered convent, is ordered to visit her wealthy uncle Rey before taking vows. When he commits suicide, she turns his estate into a refuge for beggars. Director Buñuel's first film in his native Spain after a twenty-five-year exile was immediately banned by authorities for its political implications. Haunting mixture of blasphemy and surrealism will reward discriminating viewers. ⑤

VIRUS 1982 Japanese
★★ PG Sci-Fi 1:42
☑ Explicit language, violence
Dir: Kinji Fukasaku **Cast:** Sonny Chiba, Chuck Connors, Stephanie Faulkner, Glenn Ford, Olivia Hussey, Robert Vaughn
▶ Virus released in plane crash kills most of humanity; nuclear explosions wipe out the rest, except for a few hardy survivors in the Antarctic. Large-scale disaster epic with an international cast of stars contains beautiful South Pole sequences.

VISION QUEST 1985
★★★★ R Drama/Sports 1:47
☑ Adult situations, explicit language, violence
Dir: Harold Becker **Cast:** Matthew Modine, Linda Fiorentino, Michael Schoeffling, Ronny Cox, Harold Sylvester, Charles Hallahan
▶ Coming-of-age story set in Spokane focuses on high school wrestler Modine, who embarks on a personal mission to lose weight for an important match. Beautiful older Fiorentino, boarding in his house, becomes a tempting distraction. Predictable plot enhanced by convincing, attractive stars. Madonna appears briefly in a nightclub performance. (CC)

VISITING HOURS 1982 Canadian
★★ R Horror 1:45
☑ Brief nudity, adult situations, explicit language, graphic violence

Dir: Jean-Claude Lord **Cast:** Michael Ironside, Lee Grant, Linda Purl, William Shatner, Harvey Atkin
▶ Psychotic killer Ironside, who likes to photograph his victims, fails in his first attempt to murder TV reporter Grant. He stalks her through a hospital in this crude but undeniably effective shocker. Purl is appealing as Grant's nurse.

VISITOR, THE 1979 U.S./Italian
★★ R Horror 1:30
☑ Adult situations, explicit language, graphic violence
Dir: Michael J. Paradise (Giulio Paradisi) **Cast:** Mel Ferrer, Glenn Ford, Lance Henriksen, John Huston, Joanne Nail, Shelley Winters
▶ Atlanta millionaire Ferrer wants his wife to deliver another demonic child like their daughter; when she refuses, his satanic cult tortures her. Detective Ford, investigating the group, meets a gruesome end. Visually stylish but predictable effort features Hitchcockian bird attacks and a cameo by director Sam Peckinpah as an abortionist.

VIVACIOUS LADY 1938
★★★ NR Comedy 1:30 B&W
Dir: George Stevens **Cast:** Ginger Rogers, James Stewart, Charles Coburn, James Ellison, Beulah Bondi, Frances Mercer
▶ Small-town professor Stewart goes to New York and falls in love with nightclub singer Rogers. After they marry, Stewart takes Rogers to his hometown but worries about how his disapproving parents Coburn and Bondi will react. Sparkling fun with a nifty cast, but contrived plot keeps Stewart and Rogers apart for too long.

VIVA KNIEVEL! 1977
★★ PG Drama 1:44
☑ Explicit language, violence
Dir: Gordon Douglas **Cast:** Evel Knievel, Gene Kelly, Lauren Hutton, Red Buttons, Leslie Nielsen, Frank Gifford
▶ Showcase for formerly notorious daredevil Knievel finds him visiting orphanages, performing motorcycle stunts, falling for glamorous reporter Hutton, rescuing alcoholic mechanic Kelly from despair, and stopping evil drug lord Nielsen from smuggling a fortune in cocaine into the country. Scary stunts add some bite.

VIVA LAS VEGAS 1964
★★★ NR Musical 1:26
Dir: George Sidney **Cast:** Elvis Presley,

Ann-Margret, Cesare Danova, William Demarest, Nicky Blair, Jack Carter
▶ Desperate to beat wealthy rival Danova in the Las Vegas Grand Prix, singing race-car driver Presley becomes a hotel waiter to buy a new engine. The King romances the hotel's swimming instructor Ann-Margret with "What'd I Say," "The Yellow Rose of Texas," and other tunes before competing in the race. Silly but satisfying fluff enhanced by Ann-Margret's considerable skills.

VIVA ZAPATA! 1952
★★★ NR Biography 1:53 B&W
Dir: Elia Kazan *Cast:* Marlon Brando, Jean Peters, Anthony Quinn, Joseph Wiseman, Arnold Moss, Alan Reed
▶ Meticulous biography of Emiliano Zapata (Brando), an illiterate Mexican peasant who helped unseat the corrupt President Diaz in 1911 and then briefly led the country. Downbeat John Steinbeck screenplay describes Zapata's courtship of merchant's daughter Peters and troubles with his alcoholic brother Eufemio (Quinn, who won Supporting Oscar), as well as the labrynthine politics that thwarted the popular revolution. Impressive production is brooding and slowly paced.

VOICES 1979
★★★★ PG Drama 1:46
☑ Nudity, adult situations, explicit language
Dir: Robert Markowitz *Cast:* Michael Ontkean, Amy Irving, Barry Miller, Alex Rocco, Viveca Lindfors
▶ Hoboken truck driver/aspiring singer Ontkean falls in love with deaf aspiring dancer Irving. Among the obstacles to love's triumph: her protective mom Lindfors, his gambling dad Rocco and delinquent brother Miller. Sweet and sensitive story of love overcoming the odds; Irving gives a marvelously realistic and winning performance.

VOICES OF SARAFINA! 1988
★★★ NR Documentary 1:44
Dir: Nigel Noble *Cast:* Mbongeni Ngema, Miriam Makeba; cast of *Sarafina!*
▶ Stirring documentary mixes excerpts from the hit Broadway musical *Sarafina!* and interviews with the young black South African cast about racial strife in their homeland. Writer/director Ngema advises the energetic performers to tone down their comments lest they be targeted for reprisal back home. Later, the youngsters enjoy a moving meeting with their idol Makeba, the singer banned from South Africa for her politics. Hardhitting and entertaining.

VOLUNTEERS 1985
★★★ R Comedy 1:47
☑ Adult situations, explicit language, adult humor
Dir: Nicholas Meyer *Cast:* Tom Hanks, John Candy, Rita Wilson, Tim Thomerson, Gedde Watanabe, George Plimpton
▶ Insolent preppie playboy Hanks, on the run from mob loansharks, finds himself shanghaied into a Peace Corps project to build a bridge for poor Thai peasants. His partners include beautiful Long Island idealist Wilson and inept American patriot Candy, who's later brainwashed by Communists. Broad, genial satire takes a scattershot approach to its 1962 targets.

VON RYAN'S EXPRESS 1965
★★★ NR War 1:57
Dir: Mark Robson *Cast:* Frank Sinatra, Trevor Howard, Raffaela Carra, Brad Dexter, Sergio Fantoni, James Brolin
▶ American flier Sinatra, newly imprisoned in Italy, is scorned by his fellow POWs until he proves his courage in a daring jailbreak. Italians aid the escape attempt, but the Nazis mount an all-out assault on the prisoners as they flee to Switzerland. Straightforward, no-frills adventure boasts strong cast and impressive action sequences.

VOYAGE OF THE DAMNED 1976
British/Spanish
★★★★ PG Drama 2:14
☑ Adult situations, explicit language
Dir: Stuart Rosenberg *Cast:* Faye Dunaway, Max Von Sydow, Oskar Werner, Malcolm McDowell, Orson Welles, James Mason
▶ True story of ill-fated 1939 voyage of German liner *St. Louis* is the basis for an often heartbreaking drama. Nazi propagandists filled the ship with Jewish passengers who hoped to emigrate to Cuba but were subsequently denied entry permits. Von Sydow makes a strong impression as the boat's captain. All-star cast includes Oscar-nominated Lee Grant, Ben Gazzara, Julie Harris, Wendy Hiller, and Denholm Elliott.

VOYAGE OF THE ROCK ALIENS 1985
☆ PG Comedy 1:32
☑ Explicit language

Dir: James Fargo *Cast:* Pia Zadora, Tom Nolan, Craig Sheffer, Alison Lapiaca, Ruth Gordon, Jermaine Jackson
▶ Oddball combination of sci-fi, musical, and beach party genres concerns hip aliens on the lookout for a groovy planet with rock 'n' roll music. Landing in California, they stumble across aspiring singer and beach bunny Zadora. Series of second-rate rock videos grows tiresome. Opening "When the Rain Begins to Fall" sequence featuring Jackson was directed by Bob Giraldi.

VOYAGE TO THE BOTTOM OF THE SEA
1961
★★★ NR Sci-Fi 1:45
Dir: Irwin Allen *Cast:* Walter Pidgeon, Joan Fontaine, Barbara Eden, Peter Lorre, Robert Sterling, Michael Ansara
▶ Admiral Pidgeon commands crew of ultra-advanced nuclear submarine. He attempts to save the world from radiation-induced destruction by shooting missiles into space. Oddly mixed cast, decent effects, middling screenplay; spawned the television series of the same name. (CC)

WACKIEST SHIP IN THE ARMY, THE
1961
★★ NR Comedy 1:39
Dir: Richard Murphy *Cast:* Jack Lemmon, Ricky Nelson, John Lund, Chips Rafferty, Tom Tully, Warren Berlinger
▶ During World War II, lieutenant Lemmon must lead a motley crew on a run-down vessel for a mission inside Japanese territory. Lemmon clowns, Nelson sings, and the antics are appropriately wacky. Pleasant but far from memorable. Inspired the television series of the same name.

WACKO 1983
★ R Comedy 1:24
☑ Explicit language, violence
Dir: Greydon Clark *Cast:* Joe Don Baker, Stella Stevens, George Kennedy, Julia Duffy, Scott McGinnis, Jeff Altman
▶ Limp spoof of horror movies parodies everything from *Psycho* to *Halloween*, but fails to connect with solid gags. Baker plays a sheriff on the trail of a "lawnmower killer" tormenting the teenagers at Hitchcock High during their annual Pumpkin Dance; subsequent mayhem includes mad scientists, a football game, and an elephant.

WAGES OF FEAR, THE 1955
French/Italian
★ NR Action-Adventure 2:20
Dir: Henri-Georges Clouzot *Cast:* Yves Montand, Charles Vanel, Vera Clouzot, Folco Lulli, Peter Van Eyck, William Tubbs
▶ When an oil fire breaks out in a South American country, Montand, Vanel, Lulli, and Van Eyck are hired to drive trucks containing nitroglycerine through dangerous mountains. One wrong move means instant death. One of the most hair-raising cinematic journeys ever; blistering direction and incredible physical production combine for suspense with an existential edge. Remade in America as 1977's *Sorcerer*. ⑤

WAGONMASTER 1950
★★★ NR Western 1:26 B&W
Dir: John Ford *Cast:* Ward Bond, Ben Johnson, Harry Carey, Jr., Joanne Dru, Jane Darwell, Alan Mowbray
▶ Bond leads a Mormon wagon train to Utah in search of religious freedom. Outlaws and Indians are encountered along the way but cowboys Johnson and Carey help them make the perilous journey. One of John Ford's more overlooked efforts is marvelously crafted and very involving.

WAITING FOR THE MOON 1987
☆ PG Drama 1:28
☑ Adult situations, explicit language
Dir: Jill Godmilow *Cast:* Linda Hunt, Linda Bassett, Bernadette Lafont, Bruce McGill, Andrew McCarthy, Jacques Boudet
▶ Fictionalized version of the relationship between Alice B. Toklas (Hunt) and Gertrude Stein (Bassett) presents hypothetical episodes from their lives in 1936. Slow, muddled, and pretentious drama offers some pretty images but almost no insight into their characters. Produced for PBS's "American Playhouse." (CC)

WAITRESS! 1982
★ R Comedy 1:28
☑ Nudity, adult situations, explicit language, adult humor
Dir: Samuel Weil, Michael Herz *Cast:* Carol Drake, Jim Harris, Carol Bevar, Renata Majer, David Hunt
▶ Lowbrow comedy about three New York City waitresses: Drake is desperate to break into show biz; Bevar, a secret journalist, is working on a "how to date men" article; prep school dropout Majer

wrecks her dad's restaurant during a temper tantrum. Episodic, juvenile slapstick from the makers of *Squeeze Play*.

WAIT UNTIL DARK 1967
★★★★ NR Mystery-Suspense 1:48
Dir: Terence Young *Cast:* Audrey Hepburn, Alan Arkin, Richard Crenna, Efrem Zimbalist, Jr., Jack Weston, Samantha Jones
▶ New York commercial artist Zimbalist unwittingly brings home doll stuffed with heroin to blind wife Hepburn. Psychotic criminal Arkin and henchmen Crenna and Weston lure Zimbalist away from apartment and try to retrieve drugs. In climactic nighttime showdown with crazed Arkin, Hepburn turns off all the lights to even odds. Edge-of-your-seat thriller, based on Broadway play, is carried by Hepburn, who spent weeks wearing eye shades to prepare for role.

WALKABOUT 1971 Australian
★ PG Drama 1:35
☑ Brief nudity, violence
Dir: Nicolas Roeg *Cast:* Jenny Agutter, Lucien John, David Gulpilil, John Meillon, Peter Carver, John Illingsworth
▶ Stranded in Australian Outback by suicidal father, city-bred children Agutter and John wander through desert with little hope for survival. Then young aborigine Gulpilil on his "walkabout," an ancient rite of passage in which teens survive solo in wasteland, shows them how to fend for themselves. Sexual attraction between Agutter and Gulpilil ends in tragedy. Sometimes uneven and heavy-handed, powerful film nonetheless succeeds due to mesmerizing visuals and haunting score.

WALK, DON'T RUN 1966
★★★★ NR Comedy 1:56
Dir: Charles Walters *Cast:* Cary Grant, Samantha Eggar, Jim Hutton, John Standing, Miiko Taka, Ted Hartley
▶ Pleasant remake of *The More the Merrier* updates the story to 1964 Tokyo, where hotel rooms are at a premium due to the Olympics. Industrialist Grant (playing the old Charles Coburn role) rents room from embassy secretary Eggar, then gives half his share to Hutton, a member of the U.S. walking team. Subsequent romance is predictable but amusing. Grant's last film.

WALKER 1987
☆ R Biography/Action-Adventure
1:35

☑ Nudity, explicit language, violence
Dir: Alex Cox *Cast:* Ed Harris, Richard Masur, René Auberjonois, Keith Szarabajka, Sy Richardson, Peter Boyle
▶ Based on the true story of American soldier of fortune William Walker (Harris), who proclaimed himself president of Nicaragua in 1855. Hired by robber baron Cornelius Vanderbilt (Boyle), mercenary Harris leads invasion force into Central America and displaces existing government. Director Cox intended to satirize modern American interference in Nicaragua, using moments such as Harris reading about himself in *Newsweek* to drive home his point, but result misfires.

WALKING TALL 1973
★★★ R Action-Adventure 2:05
☑ Adult situations, explicit language, violence
Dir: Phil Karlson *Cast:* Joe Don Baker, Elizabeth Hartman, Gene Evans, Noah Beery, Jr., Brenda Benet, John Brascia
▶ Tennessee sheriff Baker, fed up with gambling, moonshining, and prostitution in his county, wields baseball bat to clean out hoods. Criminal kingpins retaliate, severely beating Baker and killing his wife Hartman. Now really mad, sheriff goes on rampage to end problem once and for all. Based on true-life story of legendary sheriff Buford Pusser, runaway hit inspired two sequels, *Walking Tall, Part 2* and *Final Chapter—Walking Tall*, a TV movie, *A Real American Hero*, and a short-lived network series.

WALKING TALL, PART 2 1975
★★★ PG Action-Adventure 2:09
☑ Adult situations, explicit language, violence
Dir: Earl Bellamy *Cast:* Bo Svenson, Luke Askew, Noah Beery, Jr., Robert DoQui, John Chandler, Bruce Glover
▶ In sequel to *Walking Tall*, Svenson plays Tennessee sheriff Buford Pusser. Angered by events related in first film, local crime conglomerate tries repeatedly to slay Svenson. Patched-up sheriff then uses favorite baseball bat to bash a few heads. Pusser was supposed to play himself, but legendary hero died in a mysterious car crash just prior to film's shooting.

WALKING THE EDGE 1985
★★ R Action-Adventure 1:33
☑ Nudity, explicit language, graphic violence
Dir: Norbert Meisel *Cast:* Robert Forster, Nancy Kwan, Joe Spinell,

A. Martinez, Aarika Wells, Wayne Woodson

▶ Cab driver–part-time numbers runner Forster gets involved with vigilante Kwan seeking to avenge murder of husband and son by nasty hoodlum Spinell and his thugs. Kwan slays some of her kin's murderers and hides out at Forster's home. When Spinell's men kill Forster's buddy Martinez, Forster catches revenge bug himself. Average actioner will appeal to genre fans.

WALK IN THE SPRING RAIN, A 1970
★★ PG Romance 1:38
☑ Adult situations
Dir: Guy Green *Cast:* Ingrid Bergman, Anthony Quinn, Fritz Weaver, Katherine Crawford, Tom Fielding
▶ On a trip to the South, Bergman, wife of urban academic Weaver, finds romance with rural married man Quinn. Obstacles to their happiness include his son Fielding and her daughter Crawford. Love story features good performances from the dependable Bergman and Quinn.

WALK IN THE SUN, A 1945
★★★ NR War 1:57 B&W
Dir: Lewis Milestone *Cast:* Dana Andrews, Richard Conte, John Ireland, George Tyne, Lloyd Bridges, Sterling Holloway
▶ The story of an infantry platoon's attack on a Nazi hideout in Italy, from their beach landing in Salerno to their final objective, a farmhouse six miles inland. Early fatalities put sergeant Andrews in command of a mixed bag of personalities. Adaptation of Robert Rossen's novel concentrates as much on depicting men under stress as on action.

WALK LIKE A MAN 1987
★★★ PG Comedy 1:26
☑ Explicit language
Dir: Melvin Frank *Cast:* Howie Mandel, Christopher Lloyd, Cloris Leachman, Colleen Camp, Amy Steel
▶ Lost in wilderness as child and raised by wolves for twenty-nine years, Mandel is discovered by biologist Steel and returned to civilization. Scurrying around on all fours, Mandel is reunited with debt-ridden brother Lloyd, his alcoholic wife Camp, and his eccentric rich mother Leachman. Steel teaches Mandel human behavior and falls in love with him, while Lloyd tries to swindle his brother out of inheritance.

WALK ON THE WILD SIDE 1962
★★★★ NR Drama 1:54 B&W
Dir: Edward Dmytryk *Cast:* Laurence Harvey, Jane Fonda, Capucine, Anne Baxter, Barbara Stanwyck
▶ Texan Harvey searches for his long-lost love Capucine and finds her in a New Orleans whorehouse. Unfortunately, tough madam Stanwyck won't give her up without a fight. Spicy soap opera has wisecracking Fonda and terrific credit sequence (featuring a black cat and Elmer Bernstein's distinctive title tune). Drawbacks are an uneven story and draggy pacing.

WALL STREET 1987
★★★★ R Drama 2:08
☑ Nudity, adult situations, explicit language
Dir: Oliver Stone *Cast:* Michael Douglas, Charlie Sheen, Daryl Hannah, Martin Sheen, Terence Stamp, Hal Holbrook
▶ Ambitious stock broker Charlie Sheen is lured into insider trading scheme by unscrupulous bigwig financier Douglas. Soon Sheen is living the good life, buying a luxury apartment and squiring around beautiful decorator Hannah. But when Douglas schemes to buy and dismantle the airline employing Sheen's dad Martin Sheen, the corrupt broker has a change of heart and seeks to thwart his mentor with the aid of Douglas's arch-rival Stamp. Director Stone's morality tale is slick and entertaining. Douglas won Best Actor Oscar with lines like: "Lunch is for wimps, pal." (CC)

WALTZ ACROSS TEXAS 1983
★★★ PG Romance 1:39
☑ Brief nudity, adult situations, explicit language
Dir: Ernest Day *Cast:* Anne Archer, Terry Jastrow, Noah Beery, Jr., Mary Kay Place, Richard Farnsworth, Josh Taylor
▶ Ivy League geologist Archer clashes with down-home Texas wildcatter Jastrow until they team up to drill for oil together. Workers dislike having a woman boss and the well turns up dry, but Jastrow and Archer fall in love. They decide to give oil biz one more shot. Romance of opposites carried by fine supporting cast. An uplifting celebration of independent underdog.

WALTZ OF THE TOREADORS 1962 British
★ NR Comedy 1:45
Dir: John Guillermin *Cast:* Peter Sellers,

Dany Robin, Margaret Leighton, John Fraser, Cyril Cusack, Prunella Scales

▶ Retired army officer Sellers, unhappily married to Leighton, seeks to resume relationship with old flame Robin but is beaten to the punch by his young assistant, Fraser. Okay adaptation of the play by Jean Anouilh features good work from Sellers and the supporting cast.

WANDERERS, THE 1979
★★★ R Drama 1:53
☑ Adult situations, explicit language, violence
Dir: Philip Kaufman *Cast:* Ken Wahl, John Friedrich, Karen Allen, Toni Kalem, Alan Rosenberg, Jim Youngs
▶ The Bronx, 1963: high schoolers Wahl and Friedrich in Italian gang called the Wanderers have run-ins, both verbal and physical, with ethnic counterparts. Encounters with ethnic counterparts end mostly in harmless bluster, but brushes with shaved-headed Baldies and vicious Duck Boys result in violence. Meanwhile boys pursue Allen and Kalem, using ploys like strip poker. Despite unevenness of plot and tone, adaptation of Richard Price's novel is a cult favorite due to spirited cast and director Kaufman's fresh approach to familiar material.

WANTED: DEAD OR ALIVE 1987
★★★★ R Action-Adventure 1:44
☑ Explicit language, graphic violence
Dir: Gary A. Sherman *Cast:* Rutger Hauer, Robert Guillaume, Gene Simmons, Mel Harris, William Russ, Susan McDonald
▶ Bounty hunter Hauer, an ex-CIA agent, is hired by former boss Guillaume to capture terrorist Simmons. Deal is Hauer gets $250,00 to bring in Simmons within a week, with $50,000 bonus if killer happens to be alive. When Simmons slays Hauer's buddy Russ and girlfriend McDonald, bonus incentive becomes incidental. Action fans will be enthralled, but squeamish should stay away. Loosely based on fifties TV series of same name starring Steve McQueen; tight-lipped Hauer plays McQueen's grandson. **(CC)**

WAR AND LOVE 1985
★★ PG-13 War/Drama 1:52
☑ Adult situations, violence
Dir: Moshe Mizrahi *Cast:* Sebastian Keneas, Kyra Sedgewick, David Spielberg, Cheryl Gianini, Eda Reiss-Merin, Brita Youngblood
▶ In 1939, young Jew Keneas flees the Warsaw ghetto by posing as Christian after the Nazi invasion. He falls in love with Jewish woman Sedgewick who's using same ruse to survive and together they dodge Nazis to smuggle food to friends and family. Separated when captured by Germans, the two vow to be reunited some day. Based on the true story of Jack Eisner, film's producer. Powerful material given uninspired treatment by director Mizrahi.

WAR AND PEACE 1956 U.S./Italian
★★ NR Action-Adventure 3:28
Dir: King Vidor *Cast:* Audrey Hepburn, Henry Fonda, Mel Ferrer, Vittorio Gassman, John Mills, Anita Ekberg
▶ Sprawling melodrama centered on a romantic triangle between prince Ferrer, his good friend Fonda, and young beauty Hepburn prior to and during Napoleon's invasion of Russia. Old-fashioned Hollywood spectacle, based on Tolstoy's epic novel, has first-rate cast, sweeping story, and terrific battle scenes. However, length and erratic script are drawbacks.

WAR AND PEACE 1968 Russian
★ PG Action-Adventure 6:10
☑ Adult situations, explicit language, violence
Dir: Sergei Bondarchuk *Cast:* Lyudmila Savelyeva, Sergei Bondarchuk, Vyacheslav Tikhonov, Viktor Stanitsyn, Kira Golovko, Oleg Tabakov
▶ Elaborate, extremely long production by his countrymen of Tolstoy's epic novel may be the most expensive movie ever made, as the Soviets claim it cost $100 million. Authentic battle scenes and sequences featuring Russian aristocracy in genuine settings are impressive, but the drama and emotion get lost in the fuss. Stick with the 1956 Audrey Hepburn and Henry Fonda version. Dubbed into English; original uncut version ran 8:27.

WARGAMES 1983
★★★★ PG Drama 1:52
☑ Explicit language, mild violence
Dir: John Badham *Cast:* Matthew Broderick, Ally Sheedy, Dabney Coleman, John Wood, Barry Corbin, Juanin Clay
▶ Brilliant teen Broderick, bored with school, spends most of his time fooling with computer at home. He and girlfriend Sheedy accidentally tap into a Pentagon computer and, thinking they're playing a game, put U.S. defense network on

full alert against presumed Soviet attack. Government bigwig Coleman and his men search for Broderick; he seeks out Wood, the computer's programmer, before nuclear war breaks out. Blockbuster hit entertains with thrilling end-of-the-world scenario and engaging Broderick. **(CC)**

WARLOCK 1959
★★★ NR Western 2:01
Dir: Edward Dmytryk *Cast:* Richard Widmark, Henry Fonda, Anthony Quinn, Dorothy Malone, Dolores Michaels, Wallace Ford
▶ Unusually complex Western about a frontier town terrorized by bandits that hires gunslinger Fonda as sheriff. With the help of club-footed sidekick Quinn, he imposes a measure of security, but at a stiff price. Widmark is the deputy who must stand up to Fonda. Dark psychological twists enhance frequent gunfights. **(CC)**

WARLORDS OF THE 21ST CENTURY 1982
☆ PG Action-Adventure 1:31
☑ Adult situations, explicit language, violence
Dir: Harley Corkliss *Cast:* Michael Beck, Annie McEnroe, James Wainwright, John Ratzenberger, Randolph Powell, Bruno Lawrence
▶ In the future, "oil wars" have depleted most of world's fuel, leaving vehicles useless and civilization in ruins. Marauding pirate Wainwright, with secret gasoline supply and a band of thugs, loots and kills all in his path. His daughter McEnroe, appalled by dad, runs away to peace-loving commune, aided by motorcycle-riding loner Beck. When Wainwright seeks daughter, Beck must fight for her independence. Cheap rip-off of *The Road Warrior* will disappoint all but diehard genre fans.

WAR LOVER, THE 1962
★★ NR War 1:45 B&W
Dir: Phillip Leacock *Cast:* Steve McQueen, Robert Wagner, Shirley Anne Field, Gary Cockrell, Michael Crawford
▶ World War II England: daredevil bomber pilot McQueen and his more cautious colleague Wagner fall in love with Englishwoman Field. The fliers' lives are endangered during a large-scale mission. Adaptation of the John Hersey novel features fine flying sequences but spends too much time on the ground.

WARNING SIGN 1985
★★★ R Sci-Fi 1:39
☑ Explicit language, violence
Dir: Hal Barwood *Cast:* Sam Waterston, Kathleen Quinlan, Yaphet Kotto, Jeffrey DeMunn, Richard Dysart, G. W. Bailey
▶ At a secret germ warfare laboratory in Utah run by fanatical scientist Dysart, gene-splicing experiment goes awry and turns all workers into homicidal zombies. Local sheriff Waterston seeks to control zombies and rescue researcher wife Quinlan before she succumbs. Army major Kotto arrives with troops to assist Waterston while microbiologist DeMunn seeks cure. Intriguing "it could happen here" premise and blood-chilling action. **(CC)**

WAR OF THE WORLDS, THE 1953
★★★ G Sci-Fi 1:25
Dir: Byron Haskin *Cast:* Gene Barry, Ann Robinson, Les Tremayne, Robert Cornthwaite, Lewis Martin, Cedric Hardwicke
▶ Martians invade the Earth, sending ordinary Americans fleeing in terror from their heat rays. Caught in the crossfire: Pacific Tech scientist Barry and his girlfriend Robinson. The excitement and thrills are virtually nonstop, thanks to amazing Oscar-winning special effects and breathless pacing. Scariest moments: the Martians zapping preacher who tries to reason with them and Robinson's encounter with an alien.

WAR PARTY 1988
★★★ NR Action-Adventure 1:39
☑ Explicit language, graphic violence
Dir: Franc Roddam *Cast:* Kevin Dillon, Jimmie Ray Weeks, M. Emmet Walsh, Tim Sampson, Tantoo Cardinal
▶ Young Blackfoot Indians Dillon, Weeks, and Sampson eagerly prepare for 100th anniversary reenactment of the Milk River Battle in Montana. During staged battle, a white-trash youth uses real bullets and kills another Blackfoot teen. Dillon and Weeks slay white boy in revenge and flee with Sampson into mountains. Police, racist posse, and bounty hunter Walsh pursue the youths as national media descend on local town. Gripping and thought-provoking drama both entertains and moves.

WARRIOR AND THE SORCERESS, THE 1984
★ R Action-Adventure 1:21

☑ Nudity, violence
Dir: John Broderick   *Cast:* David Carradine, Luke Askew, Maria Socas, Anthony DeLongis, Harry Townes
▶ Holy warrior Carradine arrives in village where rival clans vie for control of water well while oppressing peasants. Mercenary Carradine plays each side against the other. Then, with gift of magic sword from beautiful, bare-chested sorceress Socas, he fights to free hapless villagers. Low-budget remake of plots from *Yojimbo* and *A Fistful Of Dollars* has sufficient swordplay and kung-fu to satisfy action fans.

WARRIOR OF THE LOST WORLD 1985
Italian
☆ R Sci-Fi 1:30
☑ Violence
Dir: David Worth   *Cast:* Robert Ginty, Donald Pleasence, Fred Williamson, Persis Khambatta, Harrison Muller, Janna Ryan
▶ In the future, nuclear war has destroyed civilzation and left remnants of humanity under sway of ruthless dictator Pleasence and his terrorizing troops. Nameless warrior Ginty on supersonic motorcycle helps rebel leader Muller and feisty daughter Khambatta attempt overthrow of despot. Second-rate spaghetti sci-fi strikes out.

WARRIOR QUEEN 1986
★ R Drama 1:20
☑ Rape, nudity, adult situations, explicit language, violence
Dir: Chuck Vincent   *Cast:* Sybil Danning, Donald Pleasence, Richard Hill, J. J. Jones, Tally Chanel, Samantha Fox
▶ Cheesy exploitation filmed in Italy purports to offer an inside look at decadent aristocrats cavorting under the shadow of Vesuvius. Danning, the well-endowed queen, bids on a few slaves, but her role is almost as brief as Pleasence's (playing Pompeii's Mayor Clodius). Climactic eruption was lifted from other films. Cassette version, unrated by MPAA, contains additional sex scenes.

WARRIORS, THE 1955
★ NR Action-Adventure 1:25
Dir: Henry Levin   *Cast:* Errol Flynn, Joanne Dru, Peter Finch, Yvonne Furneaux, Michael Hordern
▶ After the British defeat the French during the Hundred Years War, French count Finch kidnaps English lady Dru to entrap British prince Flynn. Flynn infiltrates Finch's troops incognito. Outstanding production values and dependable Flynn combine for above-average genre fare.

WARRIORS, THE 1979
★★★ R Action-Adventure 1:29
☑ Explicit language, violence
Dir: Walter Hill   *Cast:* Michael Beck, James Remar, Thomas Waites, Dorsey Wright, Brian Tyler, David Harris
▶ During delegate rally of two hundred street gangs in the Bronx, one gang leader is assassinated by a lunatic. Angry delegates wrongfully accuse the Warriors and seek violent retribution. Flight back to Warriors' Coney Island turf is filled with fights against vicious rivals and encounters with bizarre denizens of the night. Nonstop pace, stark but hypnotic images, and unusual gang motifs distinguish actioner tinted with fantasy.

WARRIORS OF THE WASTELAND 1984
Italian
☆ R Sci-Fi 1:27
☑ Rape, nudity, adult situations, explicit language, graphic violence
Dir: Enzo Castellari   *Cast:* Timothy Brent, Fred Williamson, Anna Kanakis, Vennatino Venantini, George Eastman, Andrea Coppola
▶ In the wake of nuclear holocaust, lone heroes Brent and Williamson protect religious leader Venantini and flock from violent marauders in souped-up cars. Thugs abduct and rape Brent, causing crisis of confidence, but pep talk from Williamson restores fighting spirit. Venantini's murder leads to final confrontation. Low-budget schlock with some truly distasteful scenes is yet another retread of *The Road Warrior.*

WAR WAGON, THE 1967
★★★ NR Western 1:41
Dir: Burt Kennedy   *Cast:* John Wayne, Kirk Douglas, Howard Keel, Robert Walker, Jr., Keenan Wynn, Bruce Dern
▶ Framed by a greedy mine owner, Wayne sets out for revenge upon release from jail. The target: an armor-plated wagon holding a fortune in gold dust. Douglas, originally hired to kill the Duke, joins forces with Wayne's men in the daring heist. Sharp-tongued Indian Keel and irascible codger Wynn offer strong comic support in this fast-paced, funny Western.

WATCHER IN THE WOODS, THE 1981
★★★ PG Family 1:24
☑ Mild violence
Dir: John Hough   *Cast:* Bette Davis,

Carroll Baker, David McCallum, Lynn-Holly Johnson, Kyle Richards, Ian Bannen

► McCallum and Baker with kids Johnson and Richards, in England for the summer, rent a secluded mansion from eccentric recluse Davis. Ghost of blindfolded girl and other specters haunt the family. Johnson learns Davis's daughter disappeared during seance thirty years prior—could the phantom be the long-lost girl? First-rate family fare from Disney offers creepy supernatural story, teen sleuth for kids, and immortal Davis for older crowd.

WATCHERS 1988
★★ R Sci-Fi 1:32
☑ Adult situations, explicit language, graphic violence
Dir: Jon Hess *Cast:* Corey Haim, Barbara Williams, Michael Ironside, Lala, Duncan Fraser, Blu Mankuma

► Secret government project develops a brainy dog that can type and play Scrabble and an unearthly monster called Oxcom that hates the brilliant canine. The dog escapes to hide in a small town with Haim and his mom Williams. Oxcom pursues its nemesis, killing those in its way, while ruthless government agent Ironside tracks both runaways. Adapted from the Dean R. Koontz novel.

WATCH ON THE RHINE 1943
★★★ NR Drama 1:54 B&W
Dir: Herman Shumlin *Cast:* Bette Davis, Paul Lukas, Geraldine Fitzgerald, Lucile Watson, Beulah Bondi, George Coulouris

► Respectful adaptation of Lillian Hellman's ground-breaking antifascist play concerns European family visiting relatives in Washington on the eve of World War II. Father Lukas (in an Oscar-winning performance) is threatened with blackmail by a German informer, but doesn't lose faith in his ideals. Screenplay by Dashiell Hammett.

WATER 1986 British
★ PG-13 Comedy 1:35
☑ Adult situations, explicit language
Dir: Dick Clement *Cast:* Michael Caine, Valerie Perrine, Brenda Vaccaro, Billy Connolly, Leonard Rossiter, Jimmie C. Walker

► Economically depressed British island in Caribbean, run by pot-smoking governor Caine with bird-brained wife Vaccaro, is ignored by the world. Then an abandoned oil rig spews forth Perrier

water, causing Cuba, England, and France to compete for control of the valuable well. Meanwhile wealthy environmentalist Perrine makes pitch of her own to Caine. Uneven comedy has few effervescent moments.

WATER BABIES, THE 1979 British
★★★★ NR Animation 1:33
Dir: Lionel Jeffries *Cast:* James Mason, Billie Whitelaw, Bernard Cribbins, Tommy Pender, Joan Greenwood, David Tomlinson

► In combination of live action and animation, young chimney sweep Pender in 1850 England is wrongfully accused of theft by bosses Mason and Cribbins. To escape from pursuers, Pender dives into a pond. Trapped underwater, he encounters animated world populated by pond dwellers with human traits. With aid of fairy godmother, Pender helps "water babies" in battle against bad fish. Appealing diversion for youngsters, but adults may get restless. Based on Charles Kingsley's classic children's tale.

WATERHOLE #3 1967
★★★ NR Western 1:35
Dir: William Graham *Cast:* James Coburn, Carroll O'Connor, Margaret Blye, Claude Akins, Timothy Carey, Bruce Dern

► Broad, racy spoof of Westerns finds crooked cavalry sergeant Akins, apoplectic sheriff O'Connor, his nubile daughter Blye, and charming con man Coburn all racing for a fortune in gold hidden in the desert. Good bits by Joan Blondell and James Whitmore, bawdy situations (notably Coburn's "assault with a friendly weapon"), and smart dialogue add up to amusing entertainment.

WATERLOO BRIDGE 1940
★★★ NR Romance 1:43 B&W
Dir: Mervyn LeRoy *Cast:* Vivien Leigh, Robert Taylor, Lucile Watson, C. Aubrey Smith, Maria Ouspenskaya, Virginia Field

► During World War I air raid, dancer Leigh and army officer Taylor meet on London's Waterloo Bridge. They fall in love but, when he is presumed dead, she falls into prostitution to support herself. He turns out to be alive but her past haunts their renewed chance at happiness. Highly emotional heartbreaker with lovely Leigh-Taylor chemistry and an ending that will have you reaching for the Kleenex. Based on the Robert Sherwood play. **(CC)**

WATERMELON MAN 1970
★★ R Comedy 1:40
☑ Adult situations, explicit language
Dir: Melvin Van Peebles *Cast:* Godfrey Cambridge, Estelle Parsons, Howard Caine, Mantan Moreland, Erin Moran, D'Urville Martin
▶ White conservative Cambridge must eat his own bigoted words when he wakes up one morning to find himself a black man. His wife Parsons and business associates have a tough time adjusting to his new state. Racy satire of racism scores salient social points although some of it is a bit obvious.

WATERSHIP DOWN 1978 British
★★★★ PG Animation 1:32
☑ Violence
Dir: Martin Rosen *Cast:* Voices of John Hurt, Ralph Richardson, Denholm Elliott, Zero Mostel, Richard Briers, Harry Andrews
▶ In a rabbit warren, prophet Hazel warns of impending destruction of home and leads group of male believers on a perilous search for a new place to live. Surviving dogs, owls, foxes, and men, they reach a hill called Watership Down. There they must lure women away from neighboring clan of hostile rabbits. Well-handled adaptation of Richard Adams's allegorical novel offers thoughtful entertainment for all ages.

WAVELENGTH 1983
★★★ PG Sci-Fi 1:27
☑ Nudity, explicit language, violence
Dir: Mike Gray *Cast:* Robert Carradine, Cherie Currie, Keenan Wynn, Cal Bowman, James Hess, Terry Burns
▶ In an underground Hollywood Hills facility, the Air Force conducts medical experiments on three extraterrestrials. Rock musician Carradine and girlfriend Currie discover apparently abandoned site and investigate with help of grizzled prospector Wynn. Soon trio is also held captive by military and must befriend somewhat intimidating aliens. Reasonably diverting sci-fi fare boasts inventive soundtrack by rock group Tangerine Dream.

WAXWORK 1988
★★ R Horror 1:37
☑ Adult situations, explicit language, graphic violence
Dir: Anthony Hickox *Cast:* Zach Galligan, Deborah Foreman, Michelle Johnson, David Warner, Patrick Macnee, John Rhys-Davies
▶ Galligan and Foreman are among six college kids invited to wax museum owner Warner's midnight opening. The kids should have stayed in bed—the relics come to murderous life. Polished surface but lackluster direction; young cast plays it strictly tongue-in-cheek. Goriest scene: the vampire done in by the wine rack.

WAY OUT WEST 1937
★★★★★ G Comedy 1:05 B&W
Dir: James W. Horne *Cast:* Stan Laurel, Oliver Hardy, James Finlayson, Sharon Lynne, Stanley Fields, Rosina Lawrence
▶ Laurel and Hardy head for the frontier town of Brushwood Gulch to hand over a gold mine deed to their friend's daughter; bartender Mickey Finn (Finlayson) learns of the deed and sets out to steal it from the boys. Genial Western spoof may be the duo's best feature: marvelous gags, perfect timing, and charming soft-shoe versions of "Trail of the Lonesome Pine" and "Commence Dancing" add up to sheer delight. Available in a colorized version.

WAY WEST, THE 1967
★★★ NR Western 2:02
Dir: Andrew V. McLaglen *Cast:* Kirk Douglas, Robert Mitchum, Richard Widmark, Lola Albright, Michael Witney, Stubby Kaye
▶ Limp adaptation of A. B. Guthrie's Pulitzer prize–winning novel concerns wagon train led by widowed senator Douglas and aging scout Mitchum across the Oregon Trail. Newlywed Witney leaves wife for tramp Sally Field (in her film debut), then provokes war with the Sioux. Mitchum's brooding performance can't salvage meandering plot.

WAY WE WERE, THE 1973
★★★★★ PG Romance 1:58
☑ Adult situations, explicit language
Dir: Sydney Pollack *Cast:* Barbra Streisand, Robert Redford, Bradford Dillman, Murray Hamilton, Viveca Lindfors, Lois Chiles
▶ Hugely popular romance about the unlikely courtship and marriage of political activist Streisand and WASPy Ivy League writer Redford. After World War II they move to California, where she reads scripts and turns his novel into a movie. Hollywood blacklisting makes their politi-

cal differences even harder to live with. One of the great screen romances, with true chemistry between the leads, was adapted by Arthur Laurents from his novel. Nominated for five Oscars, including Streisand as Best Actress; won for score and for hit title song.

W.C. FIELDS AND ME 1976
★ ★ ★ ★ **PG Biography 1:51**
☑ Explicit language
Dir: Arthur Hiller *Cast:* Rod Steiger, Valerie Perrine, John Marley, Jack Cassidy, Bernadette Peters, Billy Barty
▶ Bittersweet biography of W. C. Fields (Steiger) focuses on bulbous-nosed comic's relationship with mistress Carlotta Monti (Perrine), friendship with John Barrymore (Cassidy), rise to stardom, and bouts with the bottle. Steiger's performance perfectly captures Fields's contradictory nature. Most memorable moment: Fields propping up Barrymore's corpse for round of toasts. Based on Monti's memoir.

WEDDING, A 1978
★ **PG Comedy 2:00**
☑ Brief nudity, adult situations, explicit language
Dir: Robert Altman *Cast:* Carol Burnett, Mia Farrow, Lillian Gish, Geraldine Chaplin, Howard Duff, Lauren Hutton
▶ Forty-eight-character extravaganza explores traumas of disastrous wedding between offspring of nouveau riche Southerners and old Midwestern money. Director Altman's satire of the wealthy suffers from meanness of spirit; his use of multiple plots and ensemble cast works much better in *Nashville*.

WEDDING PARTY, THE 1969
★ **NR Comedy 1:30 B&W**
Dir: Brian De Palma, Cynthia Munroe *Cast:* Jill Clayburgh, Charles Pfluger, Jennifer Salt, Valda Satterfield, Robert De Niro
▶ De Palma's first feature and the film debut of both Clayburgh and De Niro is a talky, not-too-funny comedy of errors. Clayburgh and Pfluger are about to be married but he begins to have serious doubts after meeting her family and ex-boyfriends and sampling her cooking. Mainly of interest to film buffs and De Palma fans.

WEEDS 1987
★ ★ ★ **R Drama 1:59**
☑ Nudity, adult situations, explicit language, violence

Dir: John Hancock *Cast:* Nick Nolte, Lane Smith, Rita Taggart, John Toles-Bey, Joe Mantegna, William Forsythe
▶ Sentenced for life, prisoner Nolte forms a theater company to perform his play about life behind bars. Drama critic Smith writes a favorable review and works to get him released. On the outside, he continues his theatrical work and romances Smith. When the troupe has financial problems, Nolte considers committing another robbery to pay expenses. Nolte showcase is talky but the characters are well drawn. Based on a true story.

WEEKEND PASS 1984
★ **R Comedy 1:29**
☑ Nudity, adult situations, explicit language, violence
Dir: Lawrence Bassoff *Cast:* D. W. Brown, Peter Ellenstein, Patrick Hauser, Chip McAllister, Pamela G. Kay, Hilary Shapiro
▶ Sailors Brown, Ellenstein, Hauser, and McAllister finish basic training in San Diego and celebrate with a weekend pass to L.A. Among their adventures: a strip joint, an aerobics class, a visit to Watts, and a comeuppance for one sailor who looks up his old (and now snobby) girlfriend. Standard fare doesn't really pay off.

WEEKEND WARRIORS 1986
★ ★ **R Comedy 1:29**
☑ Nudity, adult situations, explicit language, adult humor
Dir: Bert Convy *Cast:* Chris Lemmon, Vic Tayback, Lloyd Bridges, Graham Jarvis, Daniel Greene, Marty Cohen
▶ In 1961, a group of show biz types spends weekends in the Air Force Reserve but prefer high jinks to soldiering. When the men are slated for inspection, they must get their act together or be sent off to fight. More profanity and flatulence than real wit; however, the young cast is appealing and some of the tasteless humor hits home. Also known as *Hollywood Air Force Base*.

WEE WILLIE WINKIE 1937
★ ★ **NR Family 1:15 B&W**
Dir: John Ford *Cast:* Shirley Temple, Victor McLaglen, C. Aubrey Smith, June Lang, Michael Whalen, Cesar Romero
▶ Rudyard Kipling story becomes a charming vehicle for Temple, who stops a rebel uprising in colonial India by bringing irascible British colonel Smith and insurgent leader Romero to the negotiat-

ing table. Unlikely pairing of Temple and McLaglen is surprisingly successful.

WEIRD SCIENCE 1985
★★★★ PG-13 Fantasy/Comedy 1:33
☑ Brief nudity, explicit language, adult humor
Dir: John Hughes *Cast:* Anthony Michael Hall, Kelly LeBrock, Ilan Mitchell-Smith, Bill Paxton, Suzanne Snyder, Robert Downey, Jr.
▶ Nerdy teens Hall and Mitchell-Smith create fantasy woman LeBrock with a computer. LeBrock teaches them to fight bullies, solve family problems, and win girls their own age. Frisky, wild, and woolly; cute premise has Hall showing nice comic timing. Best scene: LeBrock meets the parents. **(CC)**

WELCOME TO BLOOD CITY 1977
British/Canadian
☆ NR Sci-Fi 1:36
☑ Adult situations, explicit language, graphic violence
Dir: Peter Sasdy *Cast:* Jack Palance, Keir Dullea, Samantha Eggar, Barry Morse, Hollis McLaren, Chris Wiggins
▶ In the future, a computer-controlled dictatorship transports Dullea to a fantasy Western setting. There he must battle for survival against Palance, the town's killer and master. Cheap rip-off of *Westworld*.

WELCOME TO 18 1986
★★ PG-13 Comedy/Drama 1:31
☑ Brief nudity, adult situations, explicit language
Dir: Terry Carr *Cast:* Courtney Thorne-Smith, Mariska Hargitay, Jo Ann Willette, Cristen Kauffman, John Putch, Erich Anderson
▶ After high school graduation, California girls Thorne-Smith, Hargitay, and Willette take jobs at a Nevada resort. There they help new friend Kauffman escape the clutches of gangster Anderson. Teen flick has thoughtful aspirations above the run-of-the-mill; nicely cast and shot, although transvestite comic relief is pretty weak.

WELCOME TO L.A. 1976
★ R Drama 1:46
☑ Nudity, adult situations, explicit language
Dir: Alan Rudolph *Cast:* Keith Carradine, Geraldine Chaplin, Sally Kellerman, Lauren Hutton, Harvey Keitel, Sissy Spacek
▶ Songwriter Carradine arrives in Los Angeles and gets involved with a variety of women, including his dad's girlfriend Hutton, married Chaplin, realtor Kellerman, and maid Spacek. Director Rudolph shows talent but an excess of self-consciousness; moody movie lacks the humor he brought to his later (and superior) *Choose Me*.

WE'RE NO ANGELS 1955
★★★ NR Comedy 1:46
Dir: Michael Curtiz *Cast:* Humphrey Bogart, Aldo Ray, Peter Ustinov, Joan Bennett, Basil Rathbone, Leo G. Carroll
▶ Criminals Bogart, Ray, and Ustinov escape from Devil's Island. They intend to rob struggling couple Bennett and Carroll but instead decide to help them fight their evil relative Rathbone. Amusing trifle with nifty comic performances by Bogart and company.

WESTERNER, THE 1940
★★★★ NR Western 1:40 B&W
Dir: William Wyler *Cast:* Gary Cooper, Walter Brennan, Doris Davenport, Fred Stone, Chill Wills, Forrest Tucker
▶ Drifter Cooper, sentenced to hang by the infamous Judge Roy Bean (Brennan), postpones his execution by promising to introduce Bean to his idol, Lily Langtry. Sly, unpredictable Western is a consistent delight. Brennan won his third Oscar (the first actor to do so) for his wily performance. Film debuts for Tucker and Dana Andrews.

WESTERN UNION 1941
★★★★ NR Western 1:31
Dir: Fritz Lang *Cast:* Randolph Scott, Robert Young, Dean Jagger, Virginia Gilmore, John Carradine, Barton MacLane
▶ Spirited account of the building of the first telegraph across the Wild West, with an appealing Scott as a reformed outlaw and scout. Obstacles include storms, Indians, and Scott's former gang of bandits. Gilmore provides the love interest as a telegraph operator torn between the outlaw and Eastern dandy Young.

WEST SIDE STORY 1961
★★★★ NR Musical 2:35
Dir: Robert Wise, Jerome Robbins
Cast: Natalie Wood, Richard Beymer, Russ Tamblyn, Rita Moreno, George Chakiris, John Astin
▶ Shakespeare's *Romeo and Juliet* updated to a New York ghetto: Puerto Rican Wood falls in love with white Beymer, but their respective warring

gangs make the romance ill-fated. Smashing adaptation of the Broadway hit with magnetic Jerome Robbins choreography, glorious Sondheim-Bernstein score ("Tonight," "Maria," "I Feel Pretty"), outstanding performances, and authentic New York City locations. Ten Oscars include Best Picture, Director, Supporting Actor (Chakiris), Supporting Actress (Moreno), and a special award for Robbins. **(CC)**

WESTWORLD 1973
★★★ **PG Sci-Fi 1:29**
☑ Adult situations, graphic violence
Dir: Michael Crichton *Cast:* Yul Brynner, Richard Benjamin, James Brolin, Alan Oppenheimer, Victoria Shaw, Dick Van Patten
▶ Vacationers Benjamin and Brolin take time off at ultra-futuristic resort where amazingly lifelike robots simulate Old West characters. Fun and games come to a rude end when gunslinger Brynner malfunctions and starts stalking guests. Inventive and stylish action spiced with ironic humor. Brynner is perfectly cast as the implacable menace.

WETHERBY 1985 British
☆ **R Drama 1:37**
☑ Brief nudity, adult situations, explicit language, violence
Dir: David Hare *Cast:* Vanessa Redgrave, Ian Holm, Judi Dench, Marjorie Yates, Tom Wilkinson, Joely Richardson
▶ In a small English village, a stranger kills himself at the house of schoolteacher Redgrave. Secrets in Redgrave's past emerge as the police investigate. Interesting performances (with Redgrave's real-life daughter Richardson playing her in flashbacks), but many will find slack pacing and bewildering plot off-putting. **(CC)**

WE THINK THE WORLD OF YOU 1988 British
★★ **PG Drama 1:34**
☑ Adult situations, explicit language
Dir: Colin Gregg *Cast:* Alan Bates, Gary Oldman, Frances Barber, Liz Smith, Max Wall, Kerry Wise
▶ Nineteen-fifties London provides the setting for offbeat struggle over German shepherd Evie by wealthy Bates and his jailed lover, Oldman. Bates, concerned about dog's welfare, must also contend with Oldman's wife Barber and parents' desire for the pet. Low-key, emotionally detached adaptation of Joseph R. Ack-

erley's novel may please pet fanciers. Amusing cameo by Ryan Batt, perhaps the world's ugliest infant.

WHALES OF AUGUST, THE 1987
★★ **NR Drama 1:30**
☑ Explicit language
Dir: Lindsay Anderson *Cast:* Bette Davis, Lillian Gish, Ann Sothern, Vincent Price, Harry Carey, Jr.
▶ Davis and Gish are elderly sisters living on the coast of Maine. Davis is going blind and, possibly, senile. Sothern is a family friend who tries to convince them to sell the house. Neighbor Price is forced to look for a place to live after his landlady dies. Not much plot but old-timer cast works hard to generate emotion. First-rate production and gorgeous views of Maine. Sothern was Oscar-nominated.

WHAT COMES AROUND 1985
★★ **PG Comedy 1:28**
☑ Explicit language, mild violence
Dir: Jerry Reed *Cast:* Jerry Reed, Bo Hopkins, Barry Corbin, Arte Johnson
▶ Shaggy-dog mixture of comedy, car chases, and country music. Band leader Corbin manages Reed, a country-western singer with a drinking problem. Reed is kidnapped by his brother Hopkins and delivered to a rehab to dry out. While there, the guys discover Reed has been stealing millions from Reed, and plot a revenge involving several diesel trucks. Relatively harmless but doesn't really cook. **(CC)**

WHAT DO YOU SAY TO A NAKED LADY? 1970
★ **R Comedy 1:30**
☑ Nudity, adult situations, explicit language
Dir: Alan Funt
▶ Leering version of Funt's popular TV show "Candid Camera," with a heavy emphasis on salacious situations. Hidden cameras record innocent bystanders' reactions to naked hitchhikers, naked elevator occupants, etc.; also includes interviews about sexual preferences. Quickly grows tedious.

WHAT EVER HAPPENED TO AUNT ALICE? 1969
★★ **PG Mystery-Suspense 1:41**
☑ Violence
Dir: Lee H. Katzin *Cast:* Geraldine Page, Ruth Gordon, Rosemary Forsyth, Robert Fuller, Mildred Dunnock, Peter Bonerz
▶ Mad Page hires maids, then kills and

robs them. Aunt Alice (Gordon) goes undercover as Page's next employee when her pal becomes a victim; Gordon's nephew Fuller provides support. More chills from producer Robert Aldrich in the vein of his *What Ever Happened to Baby Jane?* and *Hush Hush...Sweet Charlotte.*

WHAT EVER HAPPENED TO BABY JANE? 1962
★★★ NR Horror 2:12 B&W
Dir: Robert Aldrich *Cast:* Bette Davis, Joan Crawford, Victor Buono, Anna Lee, Marjorie Bennett
▶ In a rotting Los Angeles mansion, former child star Davis terrorizes her wheelchair-bound sister Crawford in revenge for Crawford's greater success in movies. First teaming of the screen superstars inspired a rash of grisly horror films featuring older actresses. Powerful and unsettling story received Oscar nominations for Davis and Buono, her unbalanced piano accompanist; won for Norma Koch's costume design.

WHAT PRICE GLORY? 1952
★★★★ NR Comedy 1:50
Dir: John Ford *Cast:* James Cagney, Dan Dailey, Robert Wagner, Corinne Calvet, William Demarest, James Gleason
▶ Soldiers Cagney and Dailey have a love/hate relationship in France during World War I. When they are not fighting the enemy, they fight each other and vie for the affections of Frenchwoman Calvet. Genial remake of the 1926 silent classic works best as a vehicle for Cagney's comic carousing and sparring with Dailey.

WHAT'S NEW, PUSSYCAT? 1965
★★ NR Comedy 1:48
Dir: Clive Donner *Cast:* Peter O'Toole, Peter Sellers, Woody Allen, Romy Schneider, Paula Prentiss, Ursula Andress
▶ Womanizer O'Toole visits neurotic shrink Sellers for help but is unable to thwart gorgeous gals (including Schneider and Andress) from pursuing him. Allen wrote the screenplay and costars, stealing scenes as an extremely frustrated strippers' assistant. Freewheeling, uneven, but often very funny. Tom Jones sings the Bacharach-David title tune.

WHAT'S UP, DOC? 1972
★★★★ G Comedy 1:30
Dir: Peter Bogdanovich *Cast:* Barbra

Streisand, Ryan O'Neal, Kenneth Mars, Madeline Kahn, Austin Pendleton
▶ Zany Streisand and eccentric professor O'Neal become involved in a wild chase to recover four identical flight bags containing top-secret information, a wealth of jewels, Ryan's musical rocks, and Streisand's clothes. Great cast of clowns and a marvelous Kahn as O'Neal's uptight fiancée.

WHAT'S UP, TIGER LILY? 1966
★ PG Comedy 1:19
☑ Explicit language, violence
Dir: Woody Allen *Cast:* Tatsuya Mihashi, Miya Hana, Eiko Wakabayashi, Tadao Nakamura, Woody Allen
▶ Japanese imitation James Bond movie about a devious plot to steal the world's best egg-salad recipe. Allen took a third-rate Japanese spy movie and redubbed it using the voices of his friends, including then-wife Louise Lasser. Cute idea, goofy dialogue, and outlandish plot deliver a fair amount of laughs but eventually wear thin.

WHEN A STRANGER CALLS 1979
★★★★ R Mystery-Suspense 1:40
☑ Explicit language, violence
Dir: Fred Walton *Cast:* Carol Kane, Charles Durning, Rachel Roberts, Ron O'Neal, Colleen Dewhurst, Tony Beckley
▶ Exciting woman-in-jeopardy thriller about babysitter Kane who is tormented by threatening phone calls. Tracing the calls, police officer Durning discovers caller Beckley is in her house. Beckley murders the children and is sent to an asylum where, seven years later, he escapes to find Kane, who has young children of her own. Durning, now a private investigator, returns to track him down. Genuinely scary and suspenseful, good use of ominous music, well paced, and fine performances by pro cast.

WHEN THE LEGENDS DIE 1972
★★ PG Drama 1:45
☑ Adult situations, explicit language
Dir: Stuart Millar *Cast:* Richard Widmark, Frederic Forrest, Luana Anders, Vito Scotti, Herbert Nelson, John War Eagle
▶ Indian Forrest leaves the reservation, joins the rodeo, and becomes star rider under hard-drinking old pro Widmark's guidance. A close relationship develops between the two although Widmark tries to exploit his protégé. Widmark and Forrest give fine performances.

WHEN THE WIND BLOWS 1988 British
☆ NR Animation/Adult 1:25
Dir: Jimmy T. Murakami *Cast:* Voices
of Peggy Ashcroft, John Mills
▶ Ordinary couple reminisce about the
past and worry about the future when
nuclear war breaks out. Their fallout shelter ultimately offers little protection as the
effects of radiation become apparent.
Cartoon overstates commendable message; dry British humor and one-dimen-
sional animation quickly grow tiresome.
Raymond Briggs adapted from his best-
seller; title song by David Bowie.

WHEN TIME RAN OUT 1980
★★★★ PG Drama 2:01
☑ Adult situations, explicit language
Dir: James Goldstone *Cast:* Paul Newman, Jacqueline Bisset, William Holden,
Red Buttons, Ernest Borgnine, James
Franciscus
▶ Hawaiian hotel and oil field owned by
Holden are endangered when nearby
volcano erupts. Wildcatter Newman attempts to lead girlfriend Bisset and others
to safety on high ground. Tremendous
cast, workmanlike dialogue, lots of lava
in standard disaster genre brew from the
master, Irwin Allen.

WHEN WORLDS COLLIDE 1951
☆ G Sci-Fi 1:22
Dir: Rudolph Maté *Cast:* Barbara
Rush, Richard Derr, John Hoyt, Larry
Keating, Peter Hanson, Frank Cady
▶ Scientists predict the impending destruction of Earth as runaway planet and
star head our way. Wealthy businessmen
finance spaceship to start human race
again on another planet but must face
the wrath of those left behind. Classic
genre movie combines emphasis on
human aspect with Oscar-winning special effects.

WHERE ARE THE CHILDREN? 1986
★★★★ R Mystery-Suspense 1:37
☑ Adult situations, explicit language,
violence
Dir: Bruce Malmuth *Cast:* Jill Clay-
burgh, Max Gail, Harley Cross, Elisabeth
Harnois, Barnard Hughes, Frederic For-
rest
▶ When her two children are kidnapped,
Clayburgh is forced to confront a similar
tragedy in her past. Contrived but effec-
tive thriller about a sensitive issue builds
to a shocking climax. Beautiful Cape
Cod locations and strong performances

by Hughes and Forrest are bonuses.
(CC)

WHERE EAGLES DARE 1968
★★★★ PG War 2:38
☑ Adult situations, explicit language,
mild violence
Dir: Brian G. Hutton *Cast:* Richard Bur-
ton, Clint Eastwood, Mary Ure, Patrick
Wymark, Michael Hordern, Donald
Houston
▶ Crack commandos led by Burton and
Eastwood attack a Nazi fortress in the
Alps to free an Allied general, but their
mission is endangered by a double
agent. Thrilling World War II drama has
relentless pacing and extraordinary
stunts. Alistair MacLean later turned his
screenplay into a novel.

WHERE'S POPPA? 1970
★★★ R Comedy 1:23
☑ Adult humor
Dir: Carl Reiner *Cast:* George Segal,
Ruth Gordon, Ron Leibman, Trish Van
Devere, Barnard Hughes, Vincent Gar-
denia
▶ Because his senile old mom Gordon
makes relationships impossible for him,
New York City attorney Segal, who's
vowed never to put her in a nursing
home, considers scaring mom to death.
Irreverent and outrageous black comedy
features inspired teamwork by Segal and
Gordon, ably supported by Van Devere
as the nurse who falls for Segal and Leib-
man as his gorilla suit-wearing brother.
(CC)

WHERE THE BOYS ARE 1960
★★★ NR Comedy 1:39
Dir: Henry Levin *Cast:* Dolores Hart,
George Hamilton, Yvette Mimieux, Jim
Hutton, Paula Prentiss, Connie Francis
▶ College girls Hart, Mimieux, Prentiss,
and Francis head for Fort Lauderdale dur-
ing spring break. Hart loses her heart to
Ivy Leaguer Hamilton while Mimieux gets
involved with a womanizer. Awkward
Prentiss has clumsy romance with Hutton
while Francis gets to sing title song on her
way to love. Entertaining smash period
hit is now a nostalgic cult item.

WHERE THE BOYS ARE '84 1984
★★ R Comedy 1:35
☑ Nudity, adult situations, explicit lan-
guage
Dir: Hy Averback *Cast:* Lisa Hartman,
Russell Todd, Lorna Luft, Wendy Schall,
Howard McGillin, Lynn-Holly Johnson
▶ Remake of the 1960 original. Hartman,

Luft, Schall, and Johnson are the college foursome who find love on the Fort Lauderdale beach. Among their adventures: a drunk-driving charge, a Hot Bod contest, and Hartman's romance with a musician. Deep it's not, but has toe-tapping music and acres of bared tanned skin from a good-looking cast. Luft, although a bit long in the tooth for her role, steals her scenes. **(CC)**

WHERE THE BUFFALO ROAM 1980
★ **R Comedy 1:36**
☑ Adult situations, explicit language, adult humor
Dir: Art Linson **Cast:** Bill Murray, Peter Boyle, Bruno Kirby, René Auberjonois, R. G. Armstrong, Danny Goldman
▶ Uneven comedy loosely based on "gonzo" journalist Dr. Hunter S. Thompson (Murray) takes a scattershot, often confusing approach to the writer's coverage of marijuana trials, political campaigns, and Las Vegas. Episodic structure undermines the gags, although Boyle is excellent as Thompson's attorney friend. Music by Neil Young.

WHERE THE RIVER RUNS BLACK 1986
★★★ **PG Action-Adventure 1:36**
☑ Brief nudity, mild violence
Dir: Christopher Cain **Cast:** Charles Durning, Alessandro Rabelo, Ajay Naidu, Peter Horton, Conchata Ferrell, Dana Delany
▶ Rabelo is raised by dolphins after his parents are killed. After being placed in an orphanage and looked after by priest Durning, the boy must adjust to civilization and get revenge against his mom's killer. Lively and lovely; authentic Brazilian locations, stunning camerawork and music create an unusual fable that will appeal to families. **(CC)**

WHICH WAY IS UP? 1977
★★★ **R Comedy 1:34**
☑ Explicit language, adult humor
Dir: Michael Schultz **Cast:** Richard Pryor, Morgan Woodward, Lonette McKee, Margaret Avery, Marilyn Coleman, Bebe Drake-Hooks
▶ Through a quirk of fate, California citrus picker Pryor becomes union hero. New notoriety leads to career opportunities, so Pryor leaves wife Avery and moves to Los Angeles for fast-lane lifestyle, including urban beauty McKee and sell-out to corporate cash. Based on Italian director Lina Wertmuller's *The Seduction of Mimi*, tale of man's corruption and self-re-demption never quite works, but Pryor's antics provide continual laughs.

WHICH WAY TO THE FRONT? 1970
★★ **G Comedy 1:36**
Dir: Jerry Lewis **Cast:** Jerry Lewis, John Wood, Jan Murray, Steve Franken, Willie Davis, Dack Rambo
▶ During World War II, wealthy Lewis, rejected for the military, raises his own private army and stages European invasion. Subsequent high jinks include an encounter with Hitler. Low-brow humor hits occasional targets.

WHISKY GALORE! 1949 British
★★ **NR Comedy 1:23 B&W**
Dir: Alexander Mackendrick **Cast:** Basil Radford, Catherine Lacey, Bruce Seton, Joan Greenwood, Gordon Jackson, Wylie Watson
▶ Wartime shortages cut off remote Scottish island's whisky supply; the islanders are overjoyed when a ship filled with liquor sinks just offshore. However, strict Home Guard officer Radford wants to turn the cargo over to authorities, prompting ingenious schemes to liberate it. Delightful comedy based on a true incident is a genuine treat for fans of British humor. American title: *Tight Little Island*.

WHISTLE BLOWER, THE 1987 British
★ **PG Mystery-Suspense 1:50**
☑ Explicit language, violence
Dir: Simon Langton **Cast:** Michael Caine, James Fox, Nigel Havers, Felicity Dean, John Gielgud, Kenneth Colley
▶ When a colleague is arrested for spying, British intelligence agent Havers complains to his father, salesman Caine. As the unfolding spy scandal results in a number of suspicious deaths, Caine finds his faith in social values undermined. Suspenseful intrigue eschews action for cogent critique of English class system. **(CC)**

WHISTLE DOWN THE WIND 1961 British
★★ **NR Family 1:39 B&W**
Dir: Bryan Forbes **Cast:** Hayley Mills, Alan Bates, Bernard Lee, Diane Holgate, Alan Barnes, Norman Bird
▶ English children Mills, Holgate, and Barnes find fugitive Bates in family barn and believe he is Jesus returned to earth. As events increasingly parallel Christ's life, they care for Bates and hide him from their elders. Fascinating tale of childhood innocence moves swiftly to a memorable conclusion. Poignant performances by the kids; Bates is equally excellent.

WHITE CHRISTMAS 1954
★★★★ NR Musical 2:00
Dir: Michael Curtiz *Cast:* Bing Crosby, Danny Kaye, Rosemary Clooney, Vera-Ellen, Dean Jagger
▶ Army pals Crosby and Kaye learn that their old general Jagger's ski resort is facing bankruptcy; they stage a musical benefit that climaxes with Crosby's rendition of the classic title tune. Irving Berlin score includes "Blue Skies," "Snow," and the Oscar-nominated "Count Your Blessings Instead of Sheep." Borrows heavily from the superior *Holiday Inn.* (CC)

WHITE DAWN, THE 1974
★★ PG Action-Adventure 1:50
☑ Adult situations, violence
Dir: Philip Kaufman *Cast:* Warren Oates, Timothy Bottoms, Louis Gossett, Jr., Simonie Kopapik, Joanasie Salamonie, Pilitak
▶ In 1896, whalers Oates, Bottoms, and Gossett are rescued in the Arctic by Eskimo tribe. Their Western values soon conflict with the ethics of their hosts. Beautiful cinematography and startlingly authentic production values enliven this off-beat adventure.

WHITE DOG 1982
★★ PG Drama 1:30
☑ Explicit language, graphic violence
Dir: Samuel Fuller *Cast:* Kristy McNichol, Jameson Parker, Paul Winfield, Burl Ives
▶ Struggling L.A. actress McNichol adopts stray dog and discovers it's been trained by previous owner to attack blacks. She takes perilous pet to black trainer Winfield, who attempts to reverse canine's bigoted upbringing. Disturbing antiracism parable from the Romain Gary story. Briskly paced and absorbing, but marred by an unsatisfying ending.

WHITE HEAT 1949
★★★★ NR Crime/Drama 1:54 B&W
Dir: Raoul Walsh *Cast:* James Cagney, Edmond O'Brien, Virginia Mayo, Margaret Wycherly, Steve Cochran
▶ Criminal Cagney has an obsessive soft spot for his ma (Wycherly), but a hard edge and quick gun for everyone else. Lawman O'Brien goes undercover and befriends Cagney in an effort to get the goods on him. One of Cagney's most riveting performances. Walsh grabs you by the throat and doesn't let go until the literally explosive ending. Most memorable scene: jailed Cagney learning ma's fate. (CC)

WHITE LIGHTNING 1973
★★★★ PG Action-Adventure 1:41
☑ Adult situations, explicit language
Dir: Joseph Sargent *Cast:* Burt Reynolds, Jennifer Billingsley, Ned Beatty, Bo Hopkins, Matt Clark, Louise Latham
▶ Framed bootlegger Reynolds is offered freedom if he informs on his moonshine cohorts. Reynolds agrees for ulterior motives: he wants to find his brother's killers. Top-notch car chases and hard-edged action lift this above typical redneck melodramas. Reynolds repeated his role in 1976's *Gator.*

WHITE LINE FEVER 1975
★★★★ PG Action-Adventure 1:30
☑ Adult situations, explicit language, violence
Dir: Jonathan Kaplan *Cast:* Jan-Michael Vincent, Kay Lenz, Slim Pickens, L. Q. Jones, Don Porter, Sam Laws
▶ Sturdy B-movie about Air Force vet Vincent who discovers firsthand that the produce trucking industry is corrupt. Despite bribes, beatings, and blackmail, he maintains his integrity and exposes the villains with the help of supportive wife Lenz. Assured direction and knockout truck stunts have made this a cult favorite.

WHITE NIGHTS 1985
★★★★ PG-13 Drama 2:15
☑ Explicit language, violence
Dir: Taylor Hackford *Cast:* Mikhail Baryshnikov, Gregory Hines, Isabella Rossellini, Helen Mirren, Jerzy Skolimowski, Geraldine Page
▶ Former Soviet ballet star Baryshnikov, a defector to West, survives plane crash in Russia but is captured by the government he fled years before. Soviets put Baryshnikov in care of American tap dancer Hines and Russian wife Rossellini. Hostility erupts as Hines must convince Baryshnikov to dance with Kirov Ballet again, but shared interest in dance and freedom soon leads to friendship and plans for escape. Gripping drama mixes thrills and sensational dancing. (CC)

WHITE OF THE EYE 1987 British
★★ R Mystery-Suspense 1:50
☑ Adult situations, explicit language, violence
Dir: Donald Cammell *Cast:* David Keith, Cathy Moriarty, Alan Rosenberg,

Art Evans, Michael Greene, Danielle Smith

▶ Arizona audio expert Keith, unfaithful to wife Moriarty, becomes cop Evans's number one suspect in series of local housewife murders. Moriarty and daughter Smith are menaced by the killer. Glitzy-looking production with style to burn gives new life to old formula. Good performances, especially the earthy Moriarty, and interesting script twists; however, fractured narrative and weird ending will leave some with bad taste. (CC)

WHITE ROSE, THE 1983 German
★ NR Drama 1:48
☑ Brief nudity, explicit language, violence
Dir: Michael Verhoeven *Cast:* Lena Stolze, Martin Benrath, Wulf Kessler, Werner Stocker, Oliver Siebert, Ulrich Tucker
▶ In Munich, 1942, student underground group the White Rose rebels against Nazis. True story of suppressed uprising centers on Benrath and Stolze, the siblings who are tried and executed as leaders of insurrection. Historically interesting subject gets flat, uninspired treatment. ⑤

WHITE WATER SUMMER 1987
★★★ PG Action-Adventure 1:30
☑ Explicit language, mild violence
Dir: Jeff Bleckner *Cast:* Kevin Bacon, Sean Astin, Jonathan Ward, K. C. Martel, Matt Adler, Caroline McWilliams
▶ Wealthy youngster Astin joins three other boys at summer camp. Counselor Bacon proves demanding and unyielding during a tough wilderness expedition up a fast-moving river and a frightening rock climb. Beautiful nature photography and realistic coming-of-age theme should please teen viewers.

WHO AM I THIS TIME? 1982
★★★★ NR Romance/MFTV 1:00
Dir: Jonathan Demme *Cast:* Susan Sarandon, Christopher Walken, Robert Ridgely
▶ Sarandon, new girl in a small town, wins role in local theater group and falls for co-star Walken. The problem is, shy Walken only comes to romantic life when on stage. Sarandon arrives at an ingenious solution in this delightful love story. Direction by Demme is simple yet wonderful; Sarandon and Walken act to-

gether with moving delicacy. Based on a Kurt Vonnegut short story.

WHO FRAMED ROGER RABBIT 1988
★★★★★ PG Animation/Comedy 1:36
☑ Explicit language, violence
Dir: Robert Zemeckis *Cast:* Bob Hoskins, Christopher Lloyd, Joanna Cassidy, Stubby Kaye, Alan Tilvern, Richard Le Parmentier
▶ Top-grossing film of 1988, an amazing blend of live action and animation, takes place in a 1947 Hollywood where cartoon characters are second-class citizens relegated to the Toon Town ghetto. Private eye Hoskins reluctantly agrees to help slapstick star Rabbit, prime suspect in producer's murder. Hilarious, fast-paced, technically breathtaking, and filled with many cartoon cameos. Stolen by Rabbit's sultry wife Jessica and her booby trap (Kathleen Turner does her speaking voice, Amy Irving her song).

WHO HAS SEEN THE WIND? 1977 Canadian
★★ NR Family 1:40
☑ Explicit language
Dir: Allan King *Cast:* Gordon Pinsent, Jose Ferrer, Brian Painchaud, Douglas Junor, Chapelle Jaffe, Helen Shaver
▶ In depression-era Saskatchewan, strong-willed and mischievous farm boy Painchaud must grow up fast when father dies, while buddy Junor may be sent to reform school for behavioral problems. Based on a novel assigned for decades as standard reading in Canadian classrooms, familiar story is carried by credible performances from young stars and beautiful photography of wind-swept northern plains. (CC)

WHO IS KILLING THE GREAT CHEFS OF EUROPE? 1978
★★★ PG Mystery-Suspense 1:52
☑ Adult situations, explicit language
Dir: Ted Kotcheff *Cast:* George Segal, Jacqueline Bisset, Robert Morley, Jean-Pierre Cassel, Philippe Noiret, Jean Rochefort
▶ International gourmet magazine runs articles on world's greatest meal, featuring six courses by six world-class chefs. One by one the chefs are murdered in the manner of their featured dish. (Pity the poor cook who prepared the pressed duck!) Dessert chef Bisset fears for her life as police investigate. Suspects include magazine's publisher Morley and Bisset's

jealous ex-husband Segal, a fast-food franchiser. Laughs and intrigue abound in diverting romp with fine cast and scenes in the world's finest restaurants.

WHO'LL STOP THE RAIN? 1978
★★★★ R Drama 2:06
☑ Brief nudity, adult situations, explicit language, violence
Dir: Karel Reisz   *Cast:* Nick Nolte, Tuesday Weld, Michael Moriarty, Anthony Zerbe, Richard Masur, Ray Sharkey
▶ Vietnam vet Nolte agrees to smuggle two pounds of heroin to California for his best friend Moriarty, then is forced on the run by double-crossing narcotics agent Zerbe. Somewhat sanitized adaptation of Robert Stone's *Dog Soldiers* is still a gripping, powerful study of corruption and heroism.

WHOLLY MOSES! 1980
★★ PG Comedy 1:43
☑ Adult situations, explicit language, adult humor
Dir: Gary Weis   *Cast:* Dudley Moore, Laraine Newman, James Coco, Paul Sand, Jack Gilford, Dom DeLuise
▶ Moore, a slave in ancient Egypt, overhears God's instructions to Moses and, thinking the words are for him, sets out to lead the Jews from Pharoah's tyranny to the promised land. Naturally, Moses beats him to the punch at every turn. Fine cast and cameos by Richard Pryor, John Houseman, Madeline Kahn, and John Ritter wasted in second-rate comedy.

WHOOPEE BOYS, THE 1986
★★ R Comedy 1:28
☑ Brief nudity, adult situations, explicit language, adult humor
Dir: John Byrum   *Cast:* Michael O'Keefe, Paul Rodriguez, Denholm Elliott, Carole Shelley, Andy Bumatai, Eddie Deezen
▶ Con artist O'Keefe enters Elliott's etiquette school to win Shelley away from her snob fiancé. His friend Rodriguez indulges in frequent practical jokes while O'Keefe learns the secrets of becoming a perfect gentleman. Tasteless comedy feels unfocused due to improvisational style.

WHO'S AFRAID OF VIRGINIA WOOLF? 1966
★★★ NR Drama 2:09 B&W
Dir: Mike Nichols   *Cast:* Elizabeth Taylor, Richard Burton, George Segal, Sandy Dennis
▶ New England English professor Burton and wife Taylor invite younger faculty couple Segal and Dennis to their home for drinks. Drunken arguments and mind games between Burton and Taylor reveal their suppressed frustrations and disappointments. Searing drama features Burton and Taylor at pinnacle of their marriage and acting talents. Nominated for fourteen Academy Awards, film won five Oscars for Best Actress (Taylor), Supporting Actress (Dennis), Cinematography, Art Direction, and Costume Design. Adaptation of Edward Albee's Broadway hit was feature debut for director Nichols.

WHOSE LIFE IS IT, ANYWAY? 1981
★★★★ R Drama 1:58
☑ Nudity, adult situations, explicit language
Dir: John Badham   *Cast:* Richard Dreyfuss, John Cassavetes, Christine Lahti, Bob Balaban, Kenneth McMillan, Kaki Hunter
▶ Dreyfuss's rising career as a sculptor is terminated when auto crash leaves him paralyzed. His depression grows so profound he hires attorney Balaban to argue for his right to die. Hospital head Cassavetes and sympathetic doctor Lahti seek to convince Dreyfuss to live. Surehanded direction by Badham and convincing performance from Dreyfuss elevate potentially sentimental subject into effective drama. Based on the hit Broadway play by Brian Clark.

WHO'S HARRY CRUMB? 1989
★★★ PG-13 Comedy 1:27
☑ Adult situations, explicit language, adult humor
Dir: Paul Flaherty   *Cast:* John Candy, Jeffrey Jones, Annie Potts, Barry Corbin, Tim Thomerson, Shawnee Smith
▶ Candy is Harry Crumb, a detective so inept that kidnapper Jones enlists him to solve his crime, figuring the case won't be cracked. The joke's on Jones, as Candy, with help from the victim's sister Smith, stumbles his way to a solution. Broad slapstick fun with ingenious sight gags anchored by surprisingly affecting Candy/Smith relationship. Comic highlights: Candy's impersonation of an Indian and bout with a ceiling fan.

WHO SLEW AUNTIE ROO? 1971
★★ PG Horror 1:29
☑ Adult situations, violence
Dir: Curtis Harrington   *Cast:* Shelley Winters, Ralph Richardson, Mark Lester,

Lionel Jeffries, Hugh Griffith, Chloe Franks

▶ In England, American widow Winters remains obsessed with the memory of her late daughter. She takes in orphan Franks, who reminds her of the child, but Franks's brother Lester becomes suspicious of Winters's ultimate intent. Bizarre and not quite satisfying although the cast is strong.

WHO'S MINDING THE MINT? 1967
★★★★ NR Comedy 1:38
Dir: Howard Morris *Cast:* Jim Hutton, Dorothy Provine, Milton Berle, Joey Bishop, Bob Denver, Walter Brennan
▶ Hapless Hutton, a worker at the U.S. Mint, accidentally destroys $50,000. To keep his job, he enlists a motley crew—ice cream man Denver, pawnbroker Berle, retiree Brennan, and sewer man Bishop—in a scheme to replace the loot. Hilarious gem evokes freshly minted laughs.

WHO'S THAT GIRL 1987
★ PG Comedy 1:34
☑ Explicit language
Dir: James Foley *Cast:* Madonna, Griffin Dunne, John Mills, Haviland Morris, John McMartin, Bibi Besch
▶ On the day before his wedding to an heiress, lawyer Dunne is asked to escort feisty ex-con Madonna from New York to Philadelphia. Supposedly easy trip turns to chaos with the introduction of a cheetah, gun-runners, cops, and romance. Throwback to 1930s screwball comedies borrows heavily from *Bringing Up Baby*. Madonna's version of the title tune became a pop hit. **(CC)**

WHO'S THAT KNOCKING AT MY DOOR? 1967
☆ R Drama 1:30 B&W
☑ Rape, nudity, adult situations, explicit language, violence
Dir: Martin Scorsese *Cast:* Harvey Keitel, Zina Bethune, Anne Collette, Lennard Kuras, Michael Scala, Harry Northrup
▶ Young Italian-American Keitel, sexually confused by rigid Catholic upbringing, dates non-Catholic Bethune, but relationship sours when he learns she was once raped. Overly stylized and autobiographical first feature from director Scorsese was also film debut for Keitel.

WHY SHOOT THE TEACHER? 1982
Canadian
★★ NR Drama 1:40

☑ Adult situations, explicit language
Dir: Silvio Narizzano *Cast:* Bud Cort, Samantha Eggar, Chris Wiggins, Gary Reineke, John Friesen, Michael J. Reynolds
▶ In 1930s Saskatchewan, immature Cort travels to prairies to teach in one-room school. Hardships such as the severe winter and social isolation are balanced by occasional joys of hard-working farm life and delights of innocent young minds introduced to knowledge. Wryly humorous and wistful, small-scale drama delivers on all counts.

WICKED LADY, THE 1983 British
★ R Action-Adventure 1:39
☑ Nudity, adult situations, explicit language, violence
Dir: Michael Winner *Cast:* Faye Dunaway, Alan Bates, John Gielgud, Denholm Elliott, Prunella Scales, Oliver Tobias
▶ Dunaway, a fetching seventeenth-century aristocrat, turns to highway robbery to relieve her boredom, helped in more ways than one by randy bandit Bates. Lively remake of a 1945 film spoofs costume dramas by concentrating on nudity and sex. Dunaway cracks a mean bullwhip in the funniest scene.

WICKED STEPMOTHER 1989
★ PG-13 Horror/Comedy 1:32
☑ Explicit language, violence, adult humor
Dir: Larry Cohen *Cast:* Bette Davis, Barbara Carrera, Colleen Camp, David Rasche, Lionel Stander, Tom Bosley
▶ Rasche and wife Camp return home after a vacation and discover Camp's widowed dad Stander has married Davis, a horrible woman who turns out to be a witch. Later, Davis's equally evil daughter Carrera makes trouble for the family. Promising premise gets lost in the ineffective telling; Davis left the set after dispute with writer/director Cohen and her character was written out of the movie's second half.

WICKER MAN, THE 1975 British
★ R Horror 1:43
☑ Nudity, adult situations, explicit language, violence
Dir: Robin Hardy *Cast:* Edward Woodward, Christopher Lee, Diane Cilento, Britt Ekland, Ingrid Pitt, Lindsay Kemp
▶ Woodward, a policeman searching for lost young girl, travels to Summerisle, a remote Scottish island whose inhabitants

have an unusual fondness for heathen rituals. Obscure, slowly paced drama has a small cult reputation for its Anthony Shaffer script and tongue-in-cheek performance by Lee.

WIFEMISTRESS 1979 Italian
★★ R Drama 1:38
☑ Nudity, adult situations
Dir: Marco Vicario *Cast:* Laura Antonelli, Marcello Mastroianni, Leonard Mann, Olga Karlatos, Anne Belle, Gastone Moschin
▶ In turn-of-the-century Italy, Mastroianni disappears after getting involved in murder. His sickly wife Antonelli investigates his affairs, discovers his infidelities, and develops new vitality as she takes a lover of her own. Secretly spying on his wife, Mastroianni falls in love all over again. Lusty and sumptuously filmed. ⑤

WILBY CONSPIRACY, THE 1975
★★★ PG Action-Adventure 1:41
☑ Adult situations, explicit language, violence
Dir: Ralph Nelson *Cast:* Sidney Poitier, Michael Caine, Nicol Williamson, Prunella Gee, Persis Khambatta, Saeed Jaffrey
▶ In South Africa, black antiapartheid leader Poitier goes on the lam with white fugitive Caine while racist policeman Williamson chases them both. Fast-paced and slick mayhem with a message and a terrific cast. (CC)

WILD ANGELS, THE 1966
★ PG Action-Adventure 1:33
☑ Adult situations, explicit language, violence
Dir: Roger Corman *Cast:* Peter Fonda, Nancy Sinatra, Bruce Dern, Lou Procopio, Michael J. Pollard, Diane Ladd
▶ Fonda, leader of leather-clad biker gang, kidnaps injured buddy Dern from hospital while cohorts wreak mayhem on staff and patients. When Dern dies, gang takes over church for drunken, orgiastic funeral ceremony, causing retaliation by local townspeople. First in wave of biker movies released in late sixties was panned by critics but earned $25 million on budget of $350,000. Actual Hell's Angels play bit parts.

WILD BUNCH, THE 1969
★★★ R Western 2:23
☑ Brief nudity, adult situations, explicit language, graphic violence
Dir: Sam Peckinpah *Cast:* William Holden, Ernest Borgnine, Robert Ryan,

Edmond O'Brien, Warren Oates, Ben Johnson
▶ Western bank robbers, unable to adapt to 1913's automobiles and machine guns, flee to Mexico, where they become unwilling accomplices in a revolutionary movement. Magisterial Western, once controversial for its unprecedented violence, now has all the earmarks of a genuine classic. Editing, photography, directing, and performances, including memorable roles by Bo Hopkins and Strother Martin, are all extraordinary. Cassette version contains additional sequences cut from original release.

WILDCATS 1986
★★★★ R Comedy 1:46
☑ Brief nudity, adult situations, explicit language
Dir: Michael Ritchie *Cast:* Goldie Hawn, Swoosie Kurtz, Robyn Lively, Brandy Gold, James Keach, Nipsey Russell
▶ Divorcée Hawn, determined to coach high school football, takes tough assignment at an inner-city ghetto school. She wins over her athletes through perseverance and wit, then battles her ex-husband for custody of her daughters. Winning comedy makes expert use of Hawn's charm. (CC)

WILD CHILD, THE 1969 French
★ G Drama 1:25 B&W
Dir: François Truffaut *Cast:* François Truffaut, Jean-Pierre Cargol, Jean Daste, Paul Ville
▶ True story concerns young boy Cargol discovered running wild and unclothed in the forests of eighteenth-century France. Unable to speak or walk erect, he is exhibited as a freak until enlightened physician Truffaut takes on task of educating the lad. Cargol develops a genuine bond with Truffaut, but longs for the freedom of his former life. Modest, well-acted story will be too restrained for some. ⑤

WILD COUNTRY, THE 1971
★★★ G Family 1:32
Dir: Robert Totten *Cast:* Steve Forrest, Vera Miles, Jack Elam, Ron Howard, Frank De Kova, Morgan Woodward
▶ In the 1880s, aspiring rancher Forrest moves wife Miles and family from Pittsburgh to Wyoming, only to discover the land he's purchased is inhabited by mountain man Elam and his Indian side-

kick De Kova. Others woes include fire, tornado, and refusal of nasty neighbor Woodward to share water rights. Superior family fare centers on rite-of-passage for teen son Howard.

WILD DUCK, THE 1983 Australian
★★ PG Drama 1:36
☑ Explicit language
Dir: Henri Safran *Cast:* Liv Ullmann, Jeremy Irons, Lucinda Jones, John Meillon, Arthur Dignam, Michael Pate
▶ In the course of two days and nights, the lives of married couple Irons and Ullmann and their teen daughter Jones are destroyed by the reappearance of Irons's boyhood friend Dignam, a stern moralist who corrects the lies which previously allowed the family to peacefully coexist. Well-cast adaptation of classic Ibsen play moves slowly.

WILDERNESS FAMILY, PART 2, THE 1978
★★★★ G Family 1:45
Dir: Frank Zuniga *Cast:* Robert Logan, Susan Dimante Shaw, Heather Rattray, Ham Larsen, George "Buck" Flower, Brian Cutler
▶ Sequel to popular *Adventures of the Wilderness Family* portrays further Rocky Mountain exploits of former city-dwellers living in remote log cabin. Parents Logan and Shaw savor life away from the rat race while kids Rattray and Larsen enjoy company of animals, both tamed and wild. Sole human visitors are crusty old trapper Flower and mail pilot Cutler. The real stars in this wholesome adventure are the animals and stunning mountain landscapes.

WILDFIRE 1989
★★ PG Drama 1:38
☑ Adult situations, explicit language, violence
Dir: Zalman King *Cast:* Steven Bauer, Linda Fiorentino, Will Patton, Marshall Bell, Sandra Seacat, Richard Bradford
▶ Orphans Bauer and Fiorentino dream of raising a family, but Bauer is jailed after unsuccessful bank robbery. Fiorentino moves to small California town, where she marries hardworking Patton. When Bauer is released eight years later, he attempts reconciliation with his lost love. Improbable soap opera plot bolstered by attractive cast.

WILD GEESE, THE 1978 British
★★★★ R Action-Adventure 2:14
☑ Explicit language, violence

Dir: Andrew V. McLaglen *Cast:* Richard Burton, Roger Moore, Richard Harris, Stewart Granger, Hardy Kruger, Jack Watson
▶ British industrialist Granger hires veteran warrior Burton to organize rescue of democratic African leader deposed by dictator. With help of old fighting chums Moore and Harris, Burton leads successful mission. Granger then strikes a deal with the new dictator to resume his old business, so he cancels the air evacuation and leaves the gaggle of mercenaries to their fate. First-rate action boasts sturdy cast and well-staged derring-do. A sequel followed.

WILD GEESE II 1985 British
★★★ R Action-Adventure 2:05
☑ Adult situations, explicit language, violence
Dir: Peter Hunt *Cast:* Scott Glenn, Laurence Olivier, Barbara Carrera, Edward Fox, Robert Webber, Robert Freitag
▶ Sequel to *The Wild Geese*. American TV network commissions mercenary Glenn and debonair sidekick Fox to bust Nazi war criminal Rudolf Hess (Olivier) out of impregnable Spandau prison. Ambushes, double-crosses, and kidnapping of journalist Carrera ensue as soldiers of fortune encounter hostile Germans, Soviets, and Palestinians. Premise is far-fetched, but action fans will not be disappointed. Dedicated to Richard Burton, who died before reprising role from hit original.

WILD IN THE COUNTRY 1961
★★ NR Drama/Musical 1:54
Dir: Philip Dunne *Cast:* Elvis Presley, Hope Lange, Tuesday Weld, Millie Perkins, Rafer Johnson, John Ireland
▶ Presley is a backwoods delinquent groomed by widowed psychiatrist Lange for a literary career. The King also must decide between overconfident Weld and her shy rival Perkins. Unexpectedly sincere drama was written by Clifford Odets. Songs include "I Slipped, I Stumbled, I Fell," and "In My Way."

WILD IN THE STREETS 1968
★ PG Drama 1:37
☑ Adult situations, explicit language, violence
Dir: Barry Shear *Cast:* Shelley Winters, Christopher Jones, Diane Varsi, Ed Begley, Hal Holbrook, Richard Pryor
▶ Rebellious teen Jones runs away from home and within years becomes world's

most idolized entertainer, living million-aire's life in Beverly Hills with flower child mistress Varsi and fawning entourage (including Pryor). Next challenge for Jones: by doping Congress with LSD, he persuades the legislators to lower the minimum age for voting and holding office to fourteen. Jones soon is elected President and sends anyone over thirty-five-years old to compulsory "retirement camps." Sixties satire, critics' favorite when released, may seem dated.

WILD LIFE, THE 1984
★ R Comedy 1:36
☑ Nudity, adult situations, explicit language, adult humor
Dir: Art Linson *Cast:* Christopher Penn, Eric Stoltz, Rick Moranis, Lea Thompson, Jenny Wright, Hart Bochner
▶ Responsible teen Stoltz graduates from high school, moves into own apartment, and takes in bowling alley co-worker Penn as roommate to make ends meet. Swinging singles they're not: Penn's girl Wright leaves while Stoltz's former steady Thompson has fling with older policeman Bochner. Their answer is to party hearty. Uneven and episodic teen comedy mostly misfires. **(CC)**

WILD ONE, THE 1954
★★★ NR Drama 1:19 B&W
Dir: Laslo Benedek *Cast:* Marlon Brando, Mary Murphy, Robert Keith, Lee Marvin, Jay C. Flippen, Peggy Maley
▶ Biker Brando and his gang, the Black Rebels, disrupt life in a small town while he romances Murphy, daughter of the sheriff. Second gang of bikers, headed by Brando's former riding buddy Marvin, rides into town, causing angry townsfolk to take matters into their own hands. Original biker movie was also one of the first films to deal with alienated youth. Somewhat dated by its successors, but worthy for Brando's performance, one of his best. **(CC)**

WILD PAIR, THE 1987
★★ R Action-Adventure 1:28
☑ Nudity, adult situations, explicit language, violence
Dir: Beau Bridges *Cast:* Beau Bridges, Bubba Smith, Lloyd Bridges, Gary Lockwood, Raymond St. Jacques, Danny De La Paz
▶ Black L.A. cop Smith and white FBI agent Beau Bridges form grudging friendship, investigating ghetto drug ring run by bar owner St. Jacques. Trail leads to group of white supremacists led by ex-colonel Lloyd Bridges, aided by corrupt police captain Lockwood. When racists kidnap and torture Smith, Beau Bridges turns into a one-man army. Uninspired *Lethal Weapon* clone is for hard-core action fans.

WILD PARTY, THE 1975
★ R Drama 1:35
☑ Nudity, adult situations, explicit language, violence
Dir: James Ivory *Cast:* James Coco, Raquel Welch, Perry King, Tiffany Boiling, David Dukes, Royal Dano
▶ In the 1920s, fading silent movie comic Coco throws huge bash. He gets drunk as his girlfriend Welch falls for younger man King, a triangle that leads to tragedy. Ivory lays on the gloomy atmosphere and wall-to-wall music way too thick in this ambitious failure. Welch and Coco struggle dutifully with ludicrous dialogue. Story loosely resembles the Fatty Arbuckle scandal.

WILD RIVER 1960
★★★ NR Drama 1:45
Dir: Elia Kazan *Cast:* Montgomery Clift, Lee Remick, Jo Van Fleet, Albert Salmi, Jay C. Flippen, James Westerfield
▶ Clift, an agent for the Tennessee Valley Authority in the 1930s, tries to remove widow Van Fleet from her home so a dam can be built. The locals side with Van Fleet against the liberal, racially tolerant Clift, except for Van Fleet's granddaughter Remick, who falls in love with the Yankee. Issue-oriented drama pits tradition against progress; Van Fleet was Oscar-nominated.

WILDROSE 1984
★ NR Drama/Romance 1:35
☑ Brief nudity, adult situations, explicit language, violence
Dir: John Hanson *Cast:* Lisa Eichhorn, Tom Bower, James Cada, Cinda Jackson, Dan Nemanick, Lydia Olson
▶ Divorced Eichhorn, a truck driver in a Minnesota strip mine, is demoted to all-male pit crew due to recession. At first she resists advances of co-worker Bower but soon succumbs to his charms. When both are laid off, she must consider his offer to move to Lake Superior shore to operate fishing business. Modest romantic drama best for small moments of blue-collar life.

WILD ROVERS 1971
★★★★ PG Western 1:49
☑ Explicit language, violence

Dir: Blake Edwards **Cast:** William Holden, Ryan O'Neal, Karl Malden, Tom Skerritt, Lynn Carlin, Joe Don Baker
▶ Older ranch worker Holden and his young sidekick O'Neal embark on bank holdup but soon find themselves on the lam from the law and heading for Mexico. Rare foray into western territory for writer/director/producer Edwards who elicits outstanding performances from the two stars.

WILD STRAWBERRIES 1959 Swedish
★★ **NR Drama 1:30**
Dir: Ingmar Bergman **Cast:** Victor Sjostrom, Bibi Andersson, Ingrid Thulin, Gunnar Bjornstrand, Jullan Kindahl, Folke Sundquist
▶ En route to receive honorary degree, elderly medical professor Sjostrom reviews his life while coping with difficult car passengers, including disenchanted daughter-in-law Thulin and Andersson, who resembles the sweetheart of his youth. Flashbacks and dream sequences provide the film's most memorable moments. Generally considered director Bergman's finest work, touching drama is a must for film buffs; others will find it too symbolic and intellectual. ⑤

WILD THING 1987
★ **PG-13 Action-Adventure 1:32**
☑ Adult situations, explicit language, violence
Dir: Max Reid **Cast:** Rob Knepper, Kathleen Quinlan, Robert Davi, Betty Buckley, Maury Chaykin
▶ Knepper, orphaned at age three in Montreal, learns to survive on his own into adulthood, becoming legend as "the wild thing" in the inner-city jungle known as the Zone. Leaping from rooftops and materializing out of alleys, he protects the ghetto's street people from villains. Intriguing premise gets confused and uninteresting treatment; best part of film is title song, the sixties hit by Chip Baker and the Troggs.

WILLARD 1971
★★ **PG Horror 1:35**
☑ Explicit language, violence
Dir: Daniel Mann **Cast:** Bruce Davison, Ernest Borgnine, Elsa Lanchester, Sondra Locke, Michael Dante
▶ Mild-mannered young Davison, mistreated by cruel boss Borgnine and others, discovers he can communicate with rats and train them to follow his orders. Davison gets revenge but eventually

finds drawbacks to rats as man's best friends. Diabolically clever genre flick is alternately creepy and poignant. Best line: "Tear him up." Spawned sequel *Ben*.

WILLIE AND PHIL 1980
★ **R Romance/Comedy 1:56**
☑ Brief nudity, adult situations, explicit language
Dir: Paul Mazursky **Cast:** Margot Kidder, Ray Sharkey, Michael Ontkean, Jan Miner, Tom Brennan, Julie Bovasso
▶ During the seventies, Sharkey and Ontkean become friends and alternately romance free-spirited Kidder. Sunny romantic triangle fails when it apes its inspiration, François Truffaut's *Jules and Jim*, but evokes knowing chuckles when satirizing fads of the decades. Best among the actors is Kidder, who convincingly controls the romantic triangle in understated fashion.

WILLOW 1988
★★★★ **PG Fantasy 2:04**
☑ Violence
Dir: Ron Howard **Cast:** Val Kilmer, Jean Marsh, Joanne Whalley, Warwick Davis, Patricia Hayes, Ruth and Kate Greenfield
▶ Evil queen Marsh casts infant into river lest the child fulfill prophecy of unseating the villainous ruler. Amiable dwarf Davis rescues child and, with help of valiant mercenary Kilmer, sets out to defeat Marsh. Sprawling fantasy created by George Lucas with plenty of action and derring-do featuring dragons, fairies, sorcerers, wicked witches, heroes, and damsels in distress. A feast for eyes and imagination, though some effects will lose impact on video. **(CC)**

WILL PENNY 1968
★★★ **NR Western 1:49**
Dir: Tom Gries **Cast:** Charlton Heston, Joan Hackett, Donald Pleasence, Bruce Dern, Lee Majors, Ben Johnson
▶ After running afoul of evil preacher Pleasence, grizzled cowboy Heston befriends widow Hackett and her son. Heston falls for Hackett and protects her from Pleasence's wrath. Overlooked on first release but reputation has deservedly grown over the years; features one of Heston's subtlest performances and gritty Gries direction.

WILL SUCCESS SPOIL ROCK HUNTER? 1957
★★ **NR Comedy 1:34**
Dir: Frank Tashlin **Cast:** Tony Randall,

Jayne Mansfield, Betsy Drake, Joan Blondell, John Williams, Mickey Hargitay
▶ Ad executive Randall persuades pouty-mouthed movie star Mansfield to endorse agency's biggest client, Stay-Put Lipstick. Mansfield quickly pulls Randall into her whirlwind life, much to the annoyance of his girlfriend Drake and her beau Hargitay. Spoof of ad-TV world of fifties can be dated, but many gags still click. Cameo by Groucho Marx.

WILLY WONKA AND THE CHOCOLATE FACTORY 1971
★★★★ G Musical/Family 1:38
Dir: Mel Stuart   *Cast:* Gene Wilder, Jack Albertson, Peter Ostrum, Michael Bollner, Ursula Reit, Denise Nickerson
▶ Wilder, the mysterious owner of a fantastical chocolate factory, holds a contest in which five winners are awarded tour of plant and lifetime supply of sweets. His real motive: to find an honest child to be his heir. Young lad Ostrum wins coveted tour and takes along bed-ridden grandfather Albertson, but Wilder's tests may prove too tempting for any child. Musical adaptation of Roald Dahl's popular children's book will please the young.

WIMPS 1987
★ R Comedy 1:34
☑ Nudity, adult situations, explicit language
Dir: Chuck Vincent   *Cast:* Louie Bonanno, Deborah Blaisdell, Jim Abele, Jane Hamilton, Eddie Prevot, Derrick Roberts
▶ Brainy nerd freshman Bonanno helps college jocks with homework. Soon he's persuaded to help star quarterback Abele woo fetching librarian Blaisdell, who has been turned off by Abele's rah-rah demeanor. Bonanno writes love letters to Blaisdell in Abele's name while falling for her himself. Updating of classic tale *Cyrano de Bergerac* lacks muscle; stick with superior Steve Martin vehicle *Roxanne.*

WINCHESTER '73 1950
★★★ NR Western 1:32 B&W
Dir: Anthony Mann   *Cast:* James Stewart, Shelley Winters, Dan Duryea, Stephen McNally, Millard Mitchell, Charles Drake
▶ Stewart delivers a brooding, magnetic performance as a drifter obsessed with recovering a rifle stolen from him during a sharpshooting contest. After encounters

in grim trading posts, Indian ambushes, and attacks on homesteaders, his odyssey forces him to confront a dark secret in his past. First teaming of Stewart and director Mann greatly influenced subsequent Westerns for its disturbing psychological themes. Look for Will Geer, Rock Hudson, and Tony Curtis in small roles.

WIND, THE 1987
☆ NR Mystery-Suspense 1:32
☑ Explicit language, violence
Dir: Nico Mastorakis   *Cast:* Meg Foster, Wings Hauser, Robert Morley, Steve Railsback, David McCallum, John Michaels
▶ Mystery writer Foster rents house on Greek island from eccentric owner Morley, despite his warnings of dangerous wind in region and presence of creepy caretaker Hauser. Foster begins to write mystery based on Morley and Hauser's characters which is soon mimicked by real life. Predictable suspenser has few scares.

WIND AND THE LION, THE 1975
★★★★ PG Action-Adventure 1:59
☑ Adult situations, explicit language, violence
Dir: John Milius   *Cast:* Sean Connery, Candice Bergen, Brian Keith, John Huston, Geoffrey Lewis, Steve Kanaly
▶ When rebellious Arab chieftain Connery kidnaps beautiful American Bergen in 1904, President Teddy Roosevelt (Keith) threatens to send Marines to rescue her. Meanwhile Germany sends troops to northern Africa, hoping to turn delicate situation to its advantage. Splendid performance by Connery as strong-willed, full-of-life rogue carries this colorful adventure. Keith as Connery's respected adversary is also fine. Nominated for two technical Oscars.

WINDOW, THE 1949
★★★ NR Mystery-Suspense 1:13 B&W
Dir: Ted Tetzlaff   *Cast:* Bobby Driscoll, Barbara Hale, Arthur Kennedy, Ruth Roman, Paul Stewart, Anthony Ross
▶ Imaginative little boy Driscoll tells tall tales. When he actually sees a murder, no one believes him and he becomes the killer's next target. Not a wasted moment in this extremely gripping thriller. Driscoll won a special Oscar for his performance. Remade as 1984's *Cloak & Dagger.*

WINDWALKER 1981
★★★★ PG Drama 1:47
☑ Violence

Dir: Kieth Merrill **Cast:** Trevor Howard, Nick Ramus, James Remar, Serene Hedin, Dusty Iron Wing McCrea, Silvana Gallardo

► In the late eighteenth century, dying Cheyenne warrior Howard tells two grandsons of murder of his wife Hedin and abduction of his son Ramus by rival Crows years before. Howard dies but is brought back to life to complete his mission of finding his lost son and punishing the Crow. Unusual and extremely effective drama uses Indian languages and English subtitles for authentic treatment of Native American culture set against striking backdrop of Utah's Wasatch Mountains. ⑤

WINDY CITY 1984
★ R Drama 1:42
☑ Adult situations, explicit language
Dir: Armyan Bernstein **Cast:** John Shea, Kate Capshaw, Josh Mostel, Jim Borelli, Jeffrey DeMunn, Eric Pierpoint

► Lifelong Chicago friends, now in their thirties, struggle with fast-fading dreams. Mailman Shea still hopes to be a writer while Capshaw, the woman he loves, plans to wed another. Shea's comedian pal Mostel has tasted success, but he's dying of leukemia. Shea assembles the old gang for final cruise with Mostel. Well-intentioned drama is soft and melodramatic. (CC)

WINGS 1927
★★ NR War 2:19 B&W
Dir: William Wellman **Cast:** Clara Bow, Gary Cooper, Richard Arlen, Buddy Rogers, El Brendel, Jobyna Ralston

► Silent classic soars in the air (amazing footage from pilot Wellman) and on the ground with stirring story of World War I fliers Arlen and Rogers, pals but rivals for the same gal, who discover the excitement, romance, and horrors of battle. Winner of the first Best Picture Oscar.

WINGS OF DESIRE 1988
German/French
☆ PG-13 Drama 2:10 C/B&W
☑ Explicit language
Dir: Wim Wenders **Cast:** Bruno Ganz, Solveig Dommartin, Otto Sander, Curt Bois, Peter Falk

► Intensely lyrical fantasy about guardian angels watching over the citizens of West Berlin became an art-house favorite for its exquisite Henri Alékan photography and romantic screenplay (by director Wenders and Peter Handke). Ganz is unexpectedly moving as an angel who yearns to become human; Falk adds an amusing cameo as an American movie star with a surprising secret. ⑤

WINNERS TAKE ALL 1987
★★ PG-13 Drama/Sports 1:42
☑ Brief nudity, adult situations, explicit language
Dir: Fritz Kiersch **Cast:** Don Michael Paul, Kathleen York, Robert Krantz, Deborah Richter, Courtney Gains, Paul Hampton

► Dirt-track motorcycle superstar Krantz returns home for race and romances Richter, girlfriend of talented also-ran Paul. Paul challenges Krantz on dirt track and loses badly. Spunky trainer York helps Paul regain confidence for big showdown in Dallas. Plenty of romance and even more motorcycle action in amiable *Rocky* on wheels. (CC)

WINNING 1969
★★★ PG Drama/Sports 2:03
☑ Adult situations, explicit language, mild violence
Dir: James Goldstone **Cast:** Paul Newman, Joanne Woodward, Robert Wagner, Richard Thomas, David Sheiner, Clu Gulager

► Car racer Newman marries divorcée Woodward and adopts her teen son Thomas. Couple are apart during racing season but reunite for Indianapolis 500. There Newman spends so much time with his car that Woodward succumbs to the amorous advances of rival driver Wagner. Above-average drama about man obsessed with winning sports spectacular racing footage and strong turns from Newman and Woodward.

WINTER FLIGHT 1986 British
★★ NR Drama/Romance 1:43
☑ Adult situations, explicit language
Dir: Roy Battersby **Cast:** Reece Dinsdale, Nicola Cowper, Gary Olsen, Sean Benn, Beverly Hewitt, Shelagh Stephenson

► Bittersweet romance portrays sometimes rocky development of relationship between innocent airman Dinsdale, in charge of keeping birds off runway at RAF base, and more worldly barmaid Cowper. When Cowper reveals she's pregnant by Dinsdale's predecessor, he nonetheless offers to marry her and can't understand her hesitancy. Simple drama with message ending convinces, but strong English accents could cause some problems.

WINTER KILLS 1979
★ ★ ★ ★ R Comedy/Drama 1:37
☑ Nudity, adult situations, explicit language, violence
Dir: William Richert *Cast:* Jeff Bridges, John Huston, Anthony Perkins, Richard Boone, Anthony Perkins, Sterling Hayden
▶ Seriocomic adaptation of Richard Condon novel, loosely based on the Kennedy family. Nineteen years after the assassination of a President, his half-brother Bridges pursues new conspiracy evidence which may implicate their father Huston, the country's richest man. Farfetched cult favorite has many loose screws but always outrages and delights. All-star cast also includes Eli Wallach, Toshiro Mifune, Dorothy Malone, and cameo by Elizabeth Taylor. Stunningly shot by Vilmos Zsigmond.

WINTER OF OUR DREAMS 1982 Australian
★ NR Drama 1:29
☑ Adult situations, explicit language
Dir: John Duigan *Cast:* Judy Davis, Bryan Brown, Cathy Downes, Baz Luhrman, Peter Mochrie, Mervyn Drake
▶ Upscale Sydney bookseller Brown ventures into red light district to learn why ex-girlfriend committed suicide. There he meets waifish prostitute/junkie Davis. Despite sexual attraction, two remain just friends as he helps her kick heroin while she reveals life's underbelly to him. Well-acted drama gets mired in relentless earnestness and gloom.

WIRED TO KILL 1986
★ ★ R Sci-Fi 1:36
☑ Explicit language, graphic violence
Dir: Franky Schaeffer *Cast:* Emily Longstreth, Matt Hoelscher, Merritt Butrick, Frank Collison, Garth Gardner, Kristina David
▶ Los Angeles, 1998: after massive plague, normal humans in quarantine zone are on defensive from marauding renegades. One such gang slays Hoelscher's family and beats him so badly he loses use of his legs. With help of girlfriend Longstreth, techno-wizard seeks revenge from his wheelchair. B-grade action with explicit violence is for hard-core thrillseekers.

WISDOM 1986
★ ★ R Drama 1:49

☑ Brief nudity, adult situations, explicit language, violence
Dir: Emilio Estevez *Cast:* Emilio Estevez, Demi Moore, Tom Skerritt, Veronica Cartwright, William Allen Young, Richard Minchenberg
▶ Pegged for life as a criminal because of teen car theft, Estevez can't find a steady job despite sympathies of parents Skerritt and Cartwright and girlfriend Moore. He decides to become a latter-day Robin Hood, torching bank mortgages of those threatened with foreclosure. After initial reluctance, Moore joins Estevez for traveling crime spree. Directing and writing debut for twenty-three-year-old star Estevez. **(CC)**

WISE BLOOD 1979
★ PG Drama 1:48
☑ Adult situations, explicit language
Dir: John Huston *Cast:* Brad Dourif, Ned Beatty, Harry Dean Stanton, Dan Shor, Amy Wright, Mary Nell Santacroce
▶ Obsessed with religion, Army veteran Dourif forms the Church of Christ Without Christ in rural Georgia, but finds unexpected competition from fraudulent managers and preachers. One-of-a-kind film adapted from Flannery O'Connor's novel is astonishly bleak, haunting, and funny. Quirky drama's light-hearted blasphemy and vivid violence will reward discriminating viewers. Huston, directing his thirty-third feature, has an amusing cameo as a preacher.

WISE GUYS 1986
★ ★ ★ R Comedy 1:32
☑ Explicit language, violence, adult humor
Dir: Brian De Palma *Cast:* Danny DeVito, Joe Piscopo, Harvey Keitel, Ray Sharkey, Dan Hedaya, Captain Lou Albano
▶ Mafia gofers DeVito and Piscopo lose $10,000 belonging to boss Hedaya at race track; Hedaya tells each separately to kill the other. The two flee to Atlantic City, hoping to win back missing money, with hit man Albano in pursuit. Slight, padded excursion into humor by director De Palma doesn't click. **(CC)**

WISH YOU WERE HERE 1987 British
★ ★ R Drama 1:30
☑ Adult situations, explicit language
Dir: David Leland *Cast:* Emily Lloyd, Tom Bell, Clare Clifford, Barbara Durkin, Geoffrey Hutchings, Charlotte Barker

▶ Spunky but troubled teen Lloyd suffers growing pains in British seaside resort during the 1950s. Still aching from death of her mom years before, Lloyd rebels against her father, Bell; ill-fated sexual encounters ensue, including one with her father's sleazy friend Hutchings. Familiar drama delivers taunting performance by Lloyd as a precocious free spirit.

WITCHBOARD 1987
★★ R Horror 1:38
☑ Nudity, explicit language, violence
Dir: Kevin S. Tenney *Cast:* Todd Allen, Tawny Kitaen, Stephen Nichols, Kathleen Wilhoite, Burke Byrnes
▶ Evil spirit of drowned boy uses ouija board with mysterious qualities as a bridge to the real world, endangering Kitaen, who's unaware of the board's powers. Low-budget horror works up some good chills when the spirit reveals its true identity. Extremely brief cameo by comedienne Rose Marie.

WITCHES OF EASTWICK, THE 1987
★★★ R Fantasy/Comedy 1:58
☑ Adult situations, explicit language
Dir: George Miller *Cast:* Jack Nicholson, Michelle Pfeiffer, Susan Sarandon, Cher, Veronica Cartwright, Richard Jenkins
▶ Pfeiffer, Sarandon, and Cher, independent women stifled by small-town New England life and frustrated by lack of eligible men, dream of a "tall dark prince traveling under a curse." Soon the "witches" see their wish fulfilled: lecherous millionaire Nicholson moves into town and quickly seduces all three. But when the witches realize Nicholson is a woman-hating devil, they cast a spell to get rid of him. Hamming Nicholson carries uneven but fun romp, loosely based on the John Updike novel. **(CC)**

WITCHFIRE 1986
★ R Mystery-Suspense 1:32
☑ Nudity, adult situations, explicit language, violence
Dir: Vincent J. Primitera *Cast:* Shelley Winters, Frances De Sapio, Corrine Chateau, Gary Swanson
▶ Mental patient Winters, distraught over death of beloved psychiatrist, leads fellow inmates De Sapio and Chateau in an escape from the hospital. Convinced they're witches, trio tries to raise the dead doctor in an abandoned mansion. When Swanson stumbles onto property, the madwomen believe he's the resurrected

shrink and abduct him. Little real suspense, although Winters gets some laughs. Best line: "I may be insane, but I'm not stupid."

WITHNAIL AND I 1987 British
☆ R Comedy 1:48
☑ Adult situations, explicit language
Dir: Bruce Robinson *Cast:* Richard E. Grant, Paul McGann, Richard Griffiths, Ralph Brown, Michael Elphick, Daragh O'Mallery
▶ In 1969 London, roommates Grant and McGann, fed up with the hedonistic excesses of the decade, trek to country for soul-cleansing weekend in a cottage owned by Griffiths, Grant's homosexual uncle. Restorative holiday doesn't turn out as expected, especially when Griffiths makes a play for McGann. Writer-director Robinson offers some funny dialogue, but heavy accents, British idioms, and excessive talk make this offbeat comedy rough going for many American viewers.

WITHOUT A CLUE 1988
★★★★ PG Mystery-Suspense 1:47
☑ Mild violence
Dir: Thom Eberhardt *Cast:* Michael Caine, Ben Kingsley, Jeffrey Jones, Lysette Anthony, Paul Freeman, Nigel Davenport
▶ New take on oft-filmed Sherlock Holmes/Dr. Watson sleuthing team makes Watson (Kingsley) the brilliant detective. Wishing to remain anonymous, he hires drunken actor Caine to play the role of Holmes, master deducer. When they investigate sudden influx of counterfeit five-pound notes, Caine's degeneracy offsets his public relations value. Kingsley meanwhile begins to long for the praise he deserves. Plenty of dry and bawdy wit.

WITHOUT A TRACE 1983
★★★★★ PG Drama 1:59
☑ Adult situations, explicit language
Dir: Stanley Jaffe *Cast:* Kate Nelligan, Judd Hirsch, David Dukes, Stockard Channing, Jacqueline Brookes, Daniel Corkill
▶ New York professor Nelligan and ex-husband Dukes learn their six-year-old son Corkill has disappeared on way to school. Police detective Hirsch doggedly pursues case as initial press furor fades over course of months. Nelligan bears up admirably under stress of child loss and continuing marital strife, but Hirsch suspects she's losing her grip on reality when

she consults a psychic for help finding Corkill. Nelligan shines in a drama taken in part from a true story.

WITHOUT WARNING 1980
★ R Sci-Fi 1:29
☑ Adult situations, explicit language, violence
Dir: Greydon Clark   *Cast:* Jack Palance, Martin Landau, Cameron Mitchell, Ralph Meeker, Sue Ane Langdon, Larry Storch
▶ Four teens are warned by gas station owner Palance not to go near the lake. The kids do so anyway and encounter killer alien on the loose. Complicating their slim chances for survival: trigger-happy veteran Landau, who mistakes the teens for extraterrestrials.

WITH SIX YOU GET EGGROLL 1968
★★★ G Comedy 1:35
Dir: Howard Morris   *Cast:* Doris Day, Brian Keith, Barbara Hershey, Pat Carroll, George Carlin, Alice Ghostley
▶ Day, widowed mom with three sons, falls for Hershey's widowed dad Keith. They marry but must deal with their feuding offspring. After some comic shenanigans, the kids see the family light. Friendly and pleasant. Most heartwarming scene: Day gives Hershey tomorrow's chores.

WITNESS 1985
★★★★★ R Drama 1:52
☑ Nudity, adult situations, explicit language, violence
Dir: Peter Weir   *Cast:* Harrison Ford, Kelly McGillis, Alexander Godunov, Josef Sommer, Lukas Haas, Jan Rubes
▶ Amish boy Haas, on trip to Philadelphia with widowed mother McGillis, witnesses murder. Streetwise cop Ford soon learns killer was narcotics cop and reports finding to superior Sommer. When a cop tries to kill Ford, he flees with Haas and McGillis to Amish farm run by Rubes, her father-in-law. Cross-cultural romance blooms between Ford and McGillis, to chagrin of her Amish suitor Godunov. Top-notch yarn combines star-crossed love story and suspenseful action. Film received eight Oscar nominations, including Ford as Best Actor; won two including Original Screenplay.

WITNESS FOR THE PROSECUTION 1957
★★★★ NR Mystery-Suspense 1:54 B&W
Dir: Billy Wilder   *Cast:* Marlene Dietrich, Tyrone Power, Charles Laughton, Elsa Lanchester, John Williams, Henry Daniell
▶ Movie version of hit play by Agatha Christie returns retired attorney Laughton to court to defend drifter Power, accused of murdering rich widow for money. Power's wife Dietrich offers his only alibi but she isn't allowed to testify in his behalf. Classy drama with surprise ending was nominated for six Oscars, including Best Picture, Director, Actor (Laughton), and Supporting Actress (Lanchester).

WIZ, THE 1978
★★★ G Musical 2:14
Dir: Sidney Lumet   *Cast:* Diana Ross, Michael Jackson, Richard Pryor, Lena Horne, Nipsey Russell, Ted Ross
▶ Movie version of all-black Broadway musical, based on L. Frank Baum's novel and the 1939 Judy Garland movie, casts Ross as Harlem-dwelling twenty-four-year-old Dorothy. From the ghetto she's transported to Oz where scarecrow Jackson, tin man Russell, and lion Ted Ross escort her to wizard Pryor, who may help her return to New York. Expensive song-and-dance extravaganza has terrific cast and creative sets, but musical numbers fall flat.

WIZARD OF LONELINESS, THE 1988
★★★ PG-13 Drama 1:50
☑ Adult situations, explicit language, violence
Dir: Jenny Bowen   *Cast:* Lukas Haas, Lea Thompson, Lance Guest, John Randolph
▶ Small-scale family melodrama set in Vermont during World War II. Haas, a spoiled L.A. brat, is sent to small town to live with his grandparents after his mother dies and his father is shipped off to fight. His life is greatly affected by his disabled uncle (Guest) and aunt (Thompson) who gives birth to an illegitimate child. Good cast and excellent production values compensate for rather disparate story.

WIZARD OF OZ, THE 1939
★★★★★ G Fantasy 1:42 C/B&W
Dir: Victor Fleming   *Cast:* Judy Garland, Ray Bolger, Bert Lahr, Jack Haley, Margaret Hamilton, Frank Morgan
▶ Hollywood's most enduring fantasy has delighted generations of viewers with its Harold Arlen–E. Y. Harburg songs, remarkable cast, and marvelous plot. Free adaptation of L. Frank Baum's classic about

a Kansas girl's adventures in a magical kingdom has become a rite of passage for children, who are unfailingly moved by the special effects and music. Won Oscars for "Over the Rainbow," Herbert Stothart's score, and a special award for Garland. Remade in 1978 as *The Wiz*; sequels include the animated *Journey Back to Oz* and Disney's *Return to Oz*.

WIZARDS OF THE LOST KINGDOM
1985
★ ★ PG Fantasy/Action-Adventure
1:16
☑ Mild violence
Dir: Hector Olivera   *Cast:* Bo Svenson, Vidal Peterson, Thom Christopher, Barbara Stock, Maria Socas, Dolores Michaels
▶ Wandering warrior Svenson decides to help young prince Peterson, whose father has been murdered and his kingdom overrun by evil magician Christopher. Tacky, low-budget sword-and-sorcery may appeal to kids.

WOLF AT THE DOOR 1987
French/Danish
☆ R Biography 1:32
☑ Nudity, adult situations, explicit language
Dir: Henning Carlsen   *Cast:* Donald Sutherland, Max Von Sydow, Valerie Morea, Merete Voldstedlund, Fanny Bastien
▶ Paris, 1843: forty-five-year-old Paul Gauguin (Sutherland) is living a bohemian life after Polynesian sojourn. His post-Impressionist work is laughed at and he's debt-ridden. Private life is muddled by wife Voldstedlund and four kids he deserted, former mistress Bastien, and Javanese slave girl Morea. He discusses art with playwright and art critic August Strindberg (Von Sydow). Tame retelling of artist's life although Sutherland delivers a compelling performance. **(CC)**

WOLFEN 1981
★ ★ R Horror 1:55
☑ Nudity, adult situations, explicit language, graphic violence
Dir: Michael Wadleigh   *Cast:* Albert Finney, Diane Venora, Gregory Hines, Edward James Olmos, Tom Noonan, Dick O'Neill
▶ New York City detective Finney and psychologist Venora team up to solve a series of murders. The trail leads to a group of American Indians and a race of supernaturally powered wolves. Astonish-ing camerawork and special effects, droll black humor from Finney and Hines (as the coroner), and appealing Venora compensate for ambitious but uneven screenplay. Some real scares although violence is a bit excessive.

WOLF MAN, THE 1941
★ ★ ★ NR Horror 1:10 B&W
Dir: George Waggner   *Cast:* Claude Rains, Lon Chaney, Jr., Evelyn Ankers, Ralph Bellamy, Maria Ouspenskaya, Bela Lugosi
▶ While out on the English moors, Chaney is bitten by a werewolf. When a full moon rises, the helpless Chaney is transformed into a murderous wolf man. Bone-chilling genre classic delivers deliciously ominous atmosphere. Ouspenskaya as a gypsy seer and Rains as Chaney's concerned dad stand out in the top-drawer cast. Spawned sequel (*Frankenstein Meets the Wolf Man*) and many variations.

WOLFMAN 1978
★ NR Horror 1:41
☑ Graphic violence
Dir: Worth Keeter   *Cast:* Earl Owensby, Kristina Reynolds, Richard Dedmon, Ed L. Grady, Maggie Lauterer
▶ Owensby returns to family estate upon his father's death and discovers he has inherited the family curse: when the full moon rises, he becomes a werewolf. He battles the evil reverend Grady, who is the keeper of the curse. Predictable reworking of a familiar story; the acting is atrocious.

WOMAN IN GREEN, THE 1945
★ ★ NR Mystery-Suspense 1:08 B&W
Dir: Roy William Neill   *Cast:* Basil Rathbone, Nigel Bruce, Hillary Brooke, Henry Daniell, Paul Cavanagh, Matthew Boulton
▶ Famed Baker Street sleuth Sherlock Holmes (Rathbone) investigates a series of mutilation murders that leave Scotland Yard puzzled. Holmes follows the trail to a confrontation with Moriarty (Daniell), his arch-enemy, long presumed dead. Fatigue of long-running series reveals itself in lackluster performances (save for villainous Daniell) and uninspired script.

WOMAN IN RED, THE 1984
★ ★ ★ PG-13 Comedy 1:26
☑ Brief nudity, adult situations, explicit language
Dir: Gene Wilder   *Cast:* Gene Wilder,

Charles Grodin, Joseph Bologna, Judith Ivey, Kelly LeBrock, Gilda Radner
► Wilder, an advertising executive married to Ivey, suffers a mid-life crisis when he falls for leggy model LeBrock. His friends Bologna and Grodin have their own romantic problems. Best running gag: spurned co-worker Radner takes her revenge on Wilder's car. Remake of French farce *Pardon Mon Affaire* is paper-thin but sweetly amusing. Won Best Original Song Oscar for Stevie Wonder's "I Just Called to Say I Love You."

WOMAN OF DISTINCTION, A 1950
★★ NR Comedy 1:25 B&W
Dir: Edward Buzzell *Cast:* Rosalind Russell, Ray Milland, Edmund Gwenn, Janis Carter, Mary Jane Saunders, Francis Lederer
► Russell, a stuffy women's college dean, knows nothing of relaxation or romance. Then gossip columnist Carter spreads scandalous rumors about Russell and visiting professor Milland. Russell holds the baffled Milland responsible, but soon succumbs to his charms. Classic romantic comedy boasts slapstick energy and top-notch Russell. Lucille Ball makes cameo appearance as herself in opening sequence.

WOMAN OF THE YEAR 1942
★★★★ NR Comedy 1:52 B&W
Dir: George Stevens *Cast:* Spencer Tracy, Katharine Hepburn, Fay Bainter, Reginald Owen, William Bendix, Minor Watson
► Down-to-earth sportswriter Tracy and sophisticated columnist Hepburn wed in an attraction of opposites. Marriage hits the rocks as Hepburn fails to balance love and work. Delightful Tracy-Hepburn vehicle (their first together) with the stars in top form. Feminists may blanch at the notorious scene in which Hepburn struggles in the kitchen. Witty screenplay nabbed Oscar.

WOMAN'S FACE, A 1941
★★ NR Drama 1:45 B&W
Dir: George Cukor *Cast:* Joan Crawford, Melvyn Douglas, Conrad Veidt, Reginald Owen, Albert Basserman, Marjorie Main
► Remake of a 1937 Ingrid Bergman Swedish film depicts Crawford as woman disfigured during her youth and bitterly seeking revenge on the world. Penniless aristocrat Veidt uses his wiles to enlist her in a murder plot, but when physician

Douglas performs successful plastic surgery on her face, Crawford changes her outlook on life. Well-crafted drama with Crawford at the peak of her powers.

WOMAN TIMES SEVEN 1967
★★ NR Comedy 1:39
Dir: Vittorio De Sica *Cast:* Shirley MacLaine, Peter Sellers, Rossano Brazzi, Alan Arkin, Vittorio Gassman, Michael Caine
► MacLaine fans will enjoy seeing her play seven different parts in this episodic movie. Among the roles: a widow wooed by suitor Sellers at her husband's funeral, a wife upset with her writer husband's obsession with fictional creations, and an adulterous lover whose suicide pact with beau Arkin goes awry.

WOMEN, THE 1939
★★★★ NR Comedy 2:13 C/B&W
Dir: George Cukor *Cast:* Norma Shearer, Joan Crawford, Rosalind Russell, Mary Boland, Paulette Goddard, Joan Fontaine
► Unique behind-the-scenes look at society women gossiping, catfighting, and stealing husbands is superb entertainment thanks to its all-female cast, superior dialogue (adapted by Anita Loos and Jane Murfin from Claire Boothe Luce's Broadway hit), and smooth direction. Amoral sales clerk Crawford and Russell, who has an amazing nervous breakdown, are standouts among the many stars. Brief Adrian fashion show was filmed in Technicolor.

WOMEN IN LOVE 1970 British
★ R Drama 2:10
☑ Nudity, strong sexual content, adult situations, adult humor
Dir: Ken Russell *Cast:* Alan Bates, Oliver Reed, Glenda Jackson, Jennie Linden, Eleanor Bron, Alan Webb
► Lushly sensual adaptation of D. H. Lawrence novel explores romantic-sexual interplay between sisters Jackson and Linden and Bates and Reed, the close friends the women love. Visually stunning battle-of-the-sexes was nominated for four Academy Awards, with Jackson getting nod for Best Actress. Challenging and provocative film will not suit all tastes.

WOMEN ON THE VERGE OF A NERVOUS BREAKDOWN 1988 Spanish
★★ R Comedy 1:28
☑ Adult situations, explicit language
Dir: Pedro Almodovar *Cast:* Carmen

Maura, Antonio Banderas, Julieta Serrano, Maria Barranco, Rossy De Palma, Fernando Guillen

▶ Actress Maura is on the verge of a nervous breakdown after break-up with womanizing lover Guillen. While attempting to reach him, she gets involved in wild plot involving Guillen's wife, his new lover, his son, his son's girlfriend, an eccentric taxi driver, cops, terrorists, and a bowl of spiked gazpacho. Stylishly vibrant direction by Almodovar and marvelous cast (led by magnificent Maura and the striking De Palma) combine to create outrageous lunacy. Nominated for Best Foreign Film Oscar. ⑤

WOMEN'S CLUB, THE 1987
★ R Comedy 1:26
☑ Strong sexual content, explicit language, adult humor
Dir: Sandra Weintraub *Cast:* Michael Paré, Maud Adams, Eddie Velez, Dotty Coloroso
▶ Low-rent version of *American Gigolo* about struggling L.A. scriptwriter Paré who loses both his waitering job and girlfriend Coloroso. Adams offers him work in a posh women's health club where he's supposed to have sex with wealthy L.A. ladies. Shoddy production showcases a hunky Paré but generates no real excitement.

WOMEN'S PRISON MASSACRE 1985
Italian/French
★ NR Action-Adventure 1:29
☑ Rape, nudity, adult situations, explicit language, graphic violence
Dir: Gilbert Roussel *Cast:* Laura Gemser, Gabriele Tinti, Lorraine de Selle, Ursula Flores, Maria Romano
▶ Sentenced to depraved prison, framed sexpot Gemser becomes a pawn in her lesbian cellmates' war against the warden. Relentlessly lurid exploitation was filmed under the title *Emanuelle's Escape from Hell* as a companion piece to *Caged Women*. Unintentionally funny drama features grotesque overacting, poor dubbing, and a budget so small the producers could only afford a dozen prisoners.

WONDERFUL WORLD OF THE BROTHERS GRIMM, THE 1962
★★★ G Musical 2:09
Dir: Henry Levin *Cast:* Laurence Harvey, Carl Boehm, Claire Bloom, Walter Slezak, Barbara Eden, Oscar Homolka
▶ Fictionalized account of the lives of the Grimm brothers (Harvey, Boehm) frames three of their fairy tales: in "The Dancing Princess" a woodsman wins the king's daughter; "The Cobbler and the Elves" finds an overworked shoemaker saved by friendly sprites; "The Singing Bone" is an amusing struggle between a servant and his master over credit for killing a dragon. Disappointing whimsy despite George Pal special effects and star-filled cast, including Yvette Mimieux, Russ Tamblyn, Buddy Hackett, Terry-Thomas.

WON TON TON, THE DOG WHO SAVED HOLLYWOOD 1976
★★★ PG Comedy 1:32
☑ Explicit language
Dir: Michael Winner *Cast:* Madeline Kahn, Bruce Dern, Art Carney, Phil Silvers, Ron Leibman, Teri Garr
▶ Canine star rises to top in movieland, later hits hard times, but eventually all ends happily. Affectionate Hollywood satire with winning Kahn, amusing Dern (whose idea for a movie about killer shark is frowned on in silent era), and host of cameos (Morey Amsterdam, Edgar Bergen, Cyd Charisse, and many others). Cleverest bit: prison movie parody with dog receiving priestly last rites before "reprieve from the governor."

WOODEN HORSE, THE 1950 British
★★ NR War 1:41 B&W
Dir: Jack Lee *Cast:* Leo Genn, David Tomlinson, Anthony Steel, David Greene, Peter Burton, Patrick Waddington
▶ POW drama has British prisoners using a vaulting horse in the camp's exercise yard to cover their tunneling operations. Genn, Tomlinson, and Steel then escape and attempt to reach friendly territory. Suspenseful drama based on an actual World War II escape by Brits from Stalag Luft III.

WOODSTOCK 1970
★★ R Documentary/Music 3:00
☑ Nudity, explicit language
Dir: Michael Wadleigh *Cast:* Jefferson Airplane, Joe Cocker, Crosby, Stills, and Nash, Jimi Hendrix, Santana, The Who
▶ Oscar-winning documentary records communal, three-day 1969 outdoor rock concert in the Summer of Love. Historic behind-the-scenes footage is mixed with classic performances by era's rock greats. Highlights: Joe Cocker's "With a Little Help from My Friends," the Who's "Summertime Blues," Airplane's "Volun-

teers," and Jimi Hendrix's acid-rock "The Star-Spangled Banner." Future director Martin Scorsese apprenticed as an editor on project. Rock and nostalgia buffs will be delighted, but video lessens impact. Available on two tapes, each running 1:30.

WORDS AND MUSIC 1948
★ ★ ★ NR Biography/Musical 1:59
Dir: Norman Taurog   *Cast:* Mickey Rooney, Tom Drake, Ann Sothern, Perry Como, Janet Leigh, Betty Garrett
▶ Life story of the composers Richard Rodgers (Drake) and Lorenz Hart (Rooney). Rodgers finds true love with Leigh; Hart suffers romantic setbacks. Far from factual but still fun, thanks to MGM stars (including Gene Kelly and Judy Garland) making appearances to belt out team's classic tunes. Lena Horne's "The Lady Is a Tramp" and June Allyson's "Thou Swell" stand out among over thirty songs.

WORKING GIRL 1988
★ ★ ★ ★ R Romance/Comedy 1:55
☑ Nudity, adult situations, explicit language
Dir: Mike Nichols   *Cast:* Harrison Ford, Sigourney Weaver, Melanie Griffith, Alec Baldwin, Joan Cusack, Philip Bosco
▶ Wall Street secretary Griffith is long on brains but short on luck. When scheming boss Weaver tries to steal her idea, Griffith finds success is best revenge; she impersonates a bigwig and puts together big money deal with broker Ford. Fabulous corporate fairy tale for the eighties. Star-making performance by Griffith mixes tenderness and grit; Cusack shines as her best friend from Staten Island. Best line: "I sing and dance in my underwear sometimes but that doesn't make me Madonna." Nominated for six Oscars, including Best Picture, Director, Actress (Griffith), Supporting Actress (Weaver and Cusack), it won for Carly Simon's song "Let the River Run."

WORKING GIRLS 1987
★ NR Drama 1:33
☑ Nudity, strong sexual content, explicit language
Dir: Lizzie Borden   *Cast:* Louise Smith, Ellen McElduff, Amanda Goodwin, Marusia Zach, Janne Peters, Helen Nicholas
▶ Unvarnished study of typical day at a Manhattan brothel shows the mechanics of prostitution without condemning or praising the "work." Intellectually intriguing subject marred by stiff acting and tiny budget; feminist director Borden's anti-erotic approach is worthwhile but predictable.

WORLD ACCORDING TO GARP, THE 1982
★ ★ ★ R Comedy/Drama 2:16
☑ Nudity, adult situations, explicit language, violence
Dir: George Roy Hill   *Cast:* Robin Williams, Mary Beth Hurt, Glenn Close, John Lithgow, Jessica Tandy, Swoosie Kurtz
▶ Williams gives his gentlest screen performance as T. S. Garp, writer, family man, husband to winsome Hurt, and bastard son of feminist Close. Life's absurdities, tragedies, and joys provide fuel for Garp's art. Screenwriter Steve Tesich's adaptation transforms John Irving's brilliant but sprawling best-seller into a concise script. An original that is alternately lyrical (Williams writing "Magic Gloves") and hysterically funny (Lithgow's reaction to an accident involving Hurt's lover). Oscar-nominated performances by Close and Lithgow as a transsexual ex-football star.

WORLD APART, A 1988 British
★ ★ ★ ★ PG Drama 1:53
☑ Adult situations, explicit language, violence
Dir: Chris Menges   *Cast:* Barbara Hershey, Jodhi May, Jeroen Krabbe, Carolyn Clayton-Cragg, Merav Gruer, Yvonne Bryceland
▶ In 1963, a crackdown on antiapartheid protests causes dissident Krabbe to flee South Africa, leaving behind wife Hershey and daughters May, Clayton-Cragg, and Gruer. Eldest, thirteen-year-old May, seeks affection from mother, but dedicated Hershey is too wrapped up in politics. May's resentment grows as Hershey takes greater risks on behalf of oppressed blacks. Heartbreaking, sensitive tale of motherhood and apartheid as seen through teen's eyes is based on screenwriter Shawn Slovo's own life.

WORLD GONE WILD 1988
★ R Sci-Fi 1:34
☑ Rape, nudity, adult situations, explicit language, graphic violence
Dir: Lee H. Katzin   *Cast:* Bruce Dern, Michael Paré, Catherine Mary Stewart, Adam Ant, Anthony James, Rick Podell
▶ Postapocalyptic survivors jealously guarding their precious water are at-

tacked by vicious thugs led by the androgynous Ant, who quotes the writings of Charles Manson as inspiration. Elder statesman Dern hires mercenary Paré to help in the battle. Low-budget *Mad Max* clone has appealing tongue-in-cheek humor. **(CC)**

WORLD OF HENRY ORIENT, THE 1964
★★★ NR Comedy 1:55
Dir: George Roy Hill *Cast:* Peter Sellers, Angela Lansbury, Paula Prentiss, Tippy Walker, Merrie Spaeth, Phyllis Thaxter
▶ The world of Henry Orient (Sellers) features piano concerts (in which he's fair to middling) and womanizing (at which he's a pro). Teenagers Walker and Spaeth worship Orient and obsessively follow him around New York; Orient makes Walker's mom Lansbury his next conquest. Exceptional performances by the kids and adults highlight this bewitching comedy. **(CC)**

WORLD'S GREATEST ATHLETE, THE 1973
★★★★ G Comedy/Family 1:29
Dir: Robert Scheerer *Cast:* Jan-Michael Vincent, John Amos, Roscoe Lee Browne, Tim Conway, Dayle Haddon, Nancy Walker
▶ After Tarzan-like upbringing in Africa, Vincent comes to America. There his athletic prowess helps beleaguered college coach Amos revive his long-suffering team. Never less than playful and amusing Disney fare. Howard Cosell appears in a cameo.

WORLD'S GREATEST LOVER, THE 1977
★★ PG Comedy 1:29
☑ Explicit language
Dir: Gene Wilder *Cast:* Gene Wilder, Carol Kane, Dom DeLuise, Fritz Feld, Cousin Buddy, Matt Collins
▶ In the 1920s, Milwaukee baker Wilder answers the call when a Hollywood studio holds nationwide talent hunt to find the next Valentino. Wilder's wife Kane has a crush on the real Valentino (Collins) which threatens their marriage. Collins helps Wilder win back Kane. Beguiling and handsomely produced; Wilder and Kane evince sweet comic chemistry although the fun wears thin.

WRAITH, THE 1986
★★ PG-13 Horror 1:32
☑ Adult situations, explicit language, violence
Dir: Mike Marvin *Cast:* Charlie Sheen,
Nick Cassavetes, Sherilyn Fenn, Randy Quaid, Griffin O'Neal, Clint Howard
▶ In an Arizona town, mysterious driver Sheen appears to battle gang leader Cassavetes and his cohorts in a series of deadly drag races. Is Sheen one of Cassavetes's victims, back from the beyond? Ideal drive-in fare: far-out story, original touches, and sense of humor compensate for unbelievable villains. Quaid steals the show as the sheriff.

WRITTEN ON THE WIND 1957
★★★ NR Drama 1:39
Dir: Douglas Sirk *Cast:* Rock Hudson, Lauren Bacall, Robert Stack, Dorothy Malone, Robert Keith, Grant Williams
▶ Hard-drinking Texas oil scion Stack marries Bacall; Stack's best pal Hudson also falls for Bacall, although Stack's trampy sister Malone adores Hudson. Combustible combination leads to impotence, suspicions of infidelity, a miscarriage, and a shooting. Lurid, overwrought, yet enthralling and emotion-packed. Oscar for Best Supporting Actress (Malone).

WRONG BOX, THE 1966 British
★★ NR Comedy 1:47
☑ Adult situations, mild violence
Dir: Bryan Forbes *Cast:* John Mills, Ralph Richardson, Michael Caine, Peter Cook, Dudley Moore, Nanette Newman
▶ Irreverent adaptation of the Robert Louis Stevenson–Lloyd Osbourne novel concerns Victorian-era brothers Mills and Richardson, who must outlive each other to inherit trust fund. Neither codger seems likely to die, so offsprings Moore and Cook conspire to speed the process. Antics include unscrupulous doctor Sellers and hot-blooded lovers Caine and Newman, constrained by morals of era. Plot and gags sometimes stumble, but madcap yarn of sex, greed, bodysnatching, and homicide offers more than enough laughs.

WRONG GUYS, THE 1988
★★ PG Comedy 1:26
☑ Adult situations, mild violence
Dir: Danny Bilson *Cast:* Louie Anderson, Richard Lewis, Richard Belzer, Franklyn Ajaye, Tim Thomerson, John Goodman
▶ Former Cub Scout Anderson calls together his old troupe, including neurotic Lewis, earnest DJ Ajaye, horny dress designer Belzer, and dumb surfer Thomer-

son, for adult reunion. Escaped killer Goodman stalks the overgrown campers. Silly but kind of sweet; oversized Anderson in Scout uniform is hard to resist. Funniest moment: Goodman humming "Tammy" while loading his machine gun. (CC)

WRONG IS RIGHT 1982
★ ★ R Action-Adventure/Comedy
1:57
☑ Adult situations, explicit language, violence
Dir: Richard Brooks *Cast:* Sean Connery, Katharine Ross, Robert Conrad, George Grizzard, Leslie Nielsen, Ron Moody
► Network anchorman Connery finds himself up to his neck in intrigue when U.S. politicians, the CIA, an Arab king, and a Khaddafi-like madman vie for possession of a pair of A-bombs. Ambitious, fast-paced combination of satire and action; jumbled story sometimes too clever for its own good, but Connery and company do well.

WRONG MAN, THE 1957
★ ★ ★ NR Biography/Mystery-Suspense
1:45 B&W
Dir: Alfred Hitchcock *Cast:* Henry Fonda, Vera Miles, Anthony Quayle, Harold J. Stone, Nehemiah Persoff, Esther Minciotti
► New York jazz musician Fonda, wrongly accused of robbery, is arrested and tried. When the case against Fonda looks convincing, his wife Miles cracks up and is institutionalized. Based on a true story, documentary-style drama depicts case of musician Manny Balestrero through actual events and sites. Result is Hitchcock's bleakest and, to many, most tedious film, foregoing even the usual cameo by the director.

WUTHERING HEIGHTS 1939
★ ★ ★ ★ ★ NR Drama/Romance **1:44 B&W**
Dir: William Wyler *Cast:* Laurence Olivier, Merle Oberon, David Niven, Geraldine Fitzgerald, Flora Robson, Donald Crisp
► In nineteenth-century England, orphan stable-boy Olivier is taken in by Yorkshire family and falls in love with daughter Oberon. Oberon marries wealthy Niven but her ill-fated involvement with Olivier continues. Grandly passionate adaptation of the Emily Brontë classic boasts superlative direction and performances.

One of the most romantic movies of all time. Seven Oscar nominations include Best Picture, Actor (Olivier), Supporting Actress (Fitzgerald); won for Cinematography.

WUTHERING HEIGHTS 1971 British
★ ★ ★ G Drama/Romance **1:45**
Dir: Robert Fuest *Cast:* Anna Calder-Marshall, Timothy Dalton, Harry Andrews, Pamela Brown, Ian Ogilvy
► Remake of the 1939 classic is actually more faithful to the Emily Brontë novel than its predecessor. Calder-Marshall and Dalton are spirited as the doomed lovers; Ogilvy essays the David Niven role as the wealthy husband. The authentic locations help but the end result lacks the power of the original and the Oberon-Olivier chemistry. Michel Legrand contributes a syrupy score.

W.W. AND THE DIXIE DANCEKINGS 1975
★ ★ ★ ★ PG Action-Adventure/Comedy
1:31
☑ Adult situations, explicit language, violence
Dir: John G. Avildsen *Cast:* Burt Reynolds, Conny Van Dyke, Art Carney, Jerry Reed, Ned Beatty, James Hampton
► In the 1950s, con artist Reynolds preys on a corporation's gas stations in the deep South, splitting proceeds with the underpaid workers. Life of crime finances a more legit pursuit: country singer Van Dyke's struggling band. Perky country music score and one of Reynolds's most charming turns make this a gentle, sweet, and quite winning treat.

XANADU 1980
★ ★ PG Musical **1:36**
☑ Explicit language
Dir: Robert Greenwald *Cast:* Olivia Newton-John, Gene Kelly, Michael Beck, James Sloyan, Dimitra Arliss, Katie Hanley
► Mythological muse Newton-John comes to life and inspires artist Beck to build roller disco. Man and muse fall in love but can the mixed relationship work? Agreeably silly story embellished with top-ten soundtrack. Highlights: Newton-John singing "Magic" and dueting with Kelly on old-fashioned "Whenever You're Away from Me."

X—THE MAN WITH X-RAY EYES 1963
★ NR Sci-Fi **1:20**
Dir: Roger Corman *Cast:* Ray Milland,

Diana Van Der Vlis, Harold J. Stone, Don Rickles, John Hoyt
▶ Doctor Milland discovers the ability to see through things. The power proves a double-edged gift: he loses his job, is reduced to carnival attraction managed by Rickles, and descends into physical pain and madness. Minor visionary classic builds to a shattering conclusion; striking Floyd Crosby cinematography and top Milland performance.

XTRO 1983 British
★ R Sci-Fi 1:22
☑ Nudity, adult situations, explicit language, graphic violence
Dir: Harry Bromley Davenport   *Cast:* Philip Sayer, Bernice Stegers, Danny Brainin, Simon Nash, Maryam d'Abo
▶ Sayer returns to family after three-year absence due to alien kidnapping. In interim, he has become killer monster and he soon turns his son Nash into a similar aberration. Low-budget hodgepodge of familiar genre elements; acting and special effects leave a lot to be desired.

X, Y AND ZEE 1972 British
☆ PG Drama 1:50
☑ Brief nudity, adult situations, explicit language
Dir: Brian G. Hutton   *Cast:* Elizabeth Taylor, Michael Caine, Susannah York, Margaret Leighton, John Standing
▶ Widow York wins heart of married architect Caine. Caine's rejected wife Taylor wages war to break up lovers; at one point she even resorts to seduction of the bisexual York. Charismatic star trio deserves better material.

YAKUZA, THE 1975
★★★ R Action-Adventure 1:52
☑ Adult situations, explicit language, violence
Dir: Sydney Pollack   *Cast:* Robert Mitchum, Takakura Ken, Brian Keith, Herb Edelman, Richard Jordan, Kishi Keiko
▶ Daughter of U.S. shipping magnate Keith is kidnapped by the Yakuza, Japan's answer to the Mafia, to force him to deliver a cache of arms. Keith dispatches old Army buddy Mitchum to retrieve her, despite Mitchum's painful memories of star-crossed love affair with Keiko, sister of Yakuza gangster Ken. Clash-of-cultures yarn mixes action, romance, intrigue, and an ancient code of honor. Screenplay by Paul Schrader and Robert Towne.

YANKEE DOODLE DANDY 1942
★★★★★ NR Biography/Musical
2:06 B&W
Dir: Michael Curtiz   *Cast:* James Cagney, Joan Leslie, Walter Huston, Irene Manning, Rosemary DeCamp, Richard Whorf
▶ Classic portrait of show biz legend George M. Cohan (Cagney), the playwright, songwriter, singer, dancer, and actor. Born on the Fourth of July, Cohan started off in vaudeville and rose to become one of Broadway's brightest stars. Patriotic numbers include "You're a Grand Old Flag," "Over There," and the sing-along title tune. Nominated for seven Academy Awards and winner of three, including Best Actor for Cagney. Available in a colorized version.

YANKS 1979
★★★★ R Drama/Romance 2:22
☑ Nudity, adult situations, explicit language, violence
Dir: John Schlesinger   *Cast:* Richard Gere, Lisa Eichhorn, Vanessa Redgrave, William Devane, Chick Vennera, Wendy Morgan
▶ During World War II, American troops are stationed in an English town prior to fighting the Nazis. Three international romances ensue: U.S. army cook Gere with British lass Eichhorn (whose beau is away at war), Gere's pal Vennera with Morgan, and American lieutenant Devane with married Englishwoman Redgrave. Beautifully mounted and quite passionate. Gere gives a performance of surprising innocence, well matched by the underrated Eichhorn.

YEARLING, THE 1946
★★★★ G Family 2:14
Dir: Clarence Brown   *Cast:* Gregory Peck, Jane Wyman, Claude Jarman, Jr., Chill Wills, Clem Bevans, Margaret Wycherly
▶ Moving adaptation of Marjorie Kinnan Rawlings's classic novel about a poor Florida boy whose attachment to an orphaned fawn endangers his father Peck's small farm. Oscar-winning photography, set designs, and beautifully nuanced performances contribute to the story's superb moral. Jarman received a special Oscar for his role as Peck's son.

YEAR MY VOICE BROKE, THE 1988 Australian
★★ PG-13 Drama 1:43
☑ Adult situations

Dir: John Duigan   *Cast:* Noah Taylor, Leone Carmen, Ben Mendelsohn, Graeme Blundell, Lynette Curran, Malcolm Robertson
▶ Fourteen-year-old Taylor watches in dismay as childhood friend/sweetheart Carmen, a year older and maturing faster, falls for older jock Mendelsohn. Taylor tries in vain to help Carmen when first encounters with adulthood lead to tragedy. Sensitive, well-handled coming-of-age drama won Australian Oscar-equivalent for Best Picture.

YEAR OF LIVING DANGEROUSLY, THE
1983 Australian
★★★ PG Drama 1:55
☑ Adult situations, explicit language, violence
Dir: Peter Weir   *Cast:* Mel Gibson, Sigourney Weaver, Linda Hunt, Michael Murphy, Bill Kerr, Noel Ferrer
▶ In 1965, Indonesia stands on brink of civil war. Novice Australian journalist Gibson befriends savvy, mystical photographer Hunt (playing the role of a man). Hunt shows him the ropes and introduces him to beautiful British embassy employee Weaver. When Weaver tips Gibson to secret report of Communist arms delivery, he must choose between betraying sources and breaking exclusive scoop. Ambitious drama made Gibson's reputation as a serious actor; Hunt won Supporting Oscar.

YEAR OF THE DRAGON 1985
★★★ R Action-Adventure 2:16
☑ Nudity, adult situations, explicit language, graphic violence
Dir: Michael Cimino   *Cast:* Mickey Rourke, John Lone, Ariane, Leonard Termo, Raymond J. Barry, Caroline Kava
▶ Ambitious police captain Rourke seeks to clean up gangland violence in New York's Chinatown, putting him at odds with violent new crime boss Lone. Rourke enlists aid of Ariane, a pretty Chinese TV reporter, to publicize his crusade and soon romances her, much to the dismay of his estranged wife Kava. Self-important script, but fast-paced yarn should delight action fans.

YELLOWBEARD 1983
★★ PG Comedy 1:37
☑ Nudity, explicit language, violence, adult humor
Dir: Mel Damski   *Cast:* Graham Chapman, Peter Boyle, Cheech Marin, Thomas Chong, Peter Cook, Madeline Kahn
▶ Pirate Chapman busts out of jail and tries to recover fortune in buried treasure. Also looking for the loot: Chapman's son Hewitt, the pirate's old flame Kahn, and evil navy man Boyle. All-star cast of comic cut-ups generates laughs out of sheer energy and talent, although the script has too many uninspired stretches.

YELLOW HAIR AND THE FORTRESS OF GOLD 1984
★ R Action-Adventure 1:42
☑ Explicit language, violence
Dir: Matt Cimber   *Cast:* Laurene Landon, Ken Roberson, Luis Lorento, John Ghaffari, Aldo Sambrel, Isabella Gravi
▶ Blond Landon, raised by Apaches, teams with adventurer Roberson to find fabled fortress of gold guarded by torture-minded tribe. Evil colonel Lorento also covets the treasure. Campy adventure has okay action sequences, scenic Spanish backgrounds, but atrocious dubbed dialogue and ridiculous plot. Also known as *Yellow Hair and the Pecos Kid.*

YELLOW SKY 1948
★★★★ NR Western 1:39 B&W
Dir: William Wellman   *Cast:* Gregory Peck, Anne Baxter, Richard Widmark, Robert Arthur, John Russell, Harry Morgan
▶ Peck and his gang of outlaws are chased onto desolate salt flats after robbing a bank. They stumble across a ghost town inhabited by a rascally gold prospector and his granddaughter Baxter. Peck's efforts to go straight are countered by his sinister underling Widmark. Stark, brutal Western is first-rate on all levels.

YELLOW SUBMARINE 1968 British
★★★★ G Animation 1:25
Dir: George Dunning   *Cast:* Voices of John Clive, Geoffrey Hughes, Peter Batten, Dick Emery, Paul Angelus
▶ The Beatles travel by yellow submarine to a fantasy land where their music and love triumph over the evil Blue Meanies. Richly imaginative and clever, with eye-popping pop art animation. Actors provide the speaking voices of the Beatle characters but the group itself supplies the wonderful soundtrack ("Lucy in the Sky With Diamonds," "Nowhere Man," "Eleanor Rigby," "All You Need Is Love," "Only a Northern Song," more).

YENTL 1983
★★★★ PG Musical 2:13
☑ Adult situations, mild violence, adult humor
Dir: Barbra Streisand *Cast:* Barbra Streisand, Mandy Patinkin, Amy Irving, Nehemiah Persoff, Steven Hill, Ruth Goring
▶ Eastern Europe, circa 1904: after the death of her father Persoff, headstrong Yentl (Streisand) disguises herself as a boy to study at the all-male yeshiva. Befriended by fellow student Patinkin and his fiancée Irving, Yentl finds her disguise has serio-comic results. Sterling performances, masterfully shot and lovingly adapted from Isaac Bashevis Singer's short story; a joy for Streisand fans but may seem overly long to others. Five nominations, including Oscar-winning score.

YOJIMBO 1962 Japanese
★★ NR Action-Adventure 1:50 B&W
Dir: Akira Kurosawa *Cast:* Toshiro Mifune, Eijiro Tono, Seizaburo Kawazu, Isuzu Yamada, Hiroshi Tachikawa, Kyu Sazanka
▶ Engrossing, action-packed "samurai Western" about nineteenth-century professional killer Mifune, who gains control of a warring village by playing both sides against each other. Unexpectedly tough and funny, with a commanding performance by Mifune and first-rate direction. Prime inspiration for *A Fistful of Dollars.*
Ⓢ

YOL 1982 Turkish
☆ PG Drama 1:54
☑ Adult situations, violence
Dir: Serif Goren *Cast:* Tarik Akan, Serif Sezer, Halil Ergun, Meral Orhonsoy, Necmettin Cobanoglu, Semra Ucar
▶ Five Turkish prisoners, given temporary leaves of absence, find unhappy family situations and death waiting for them on the outside. Exotic glimpse into a harsh world where fear and hardship are a way of life. Emotionally sincere but technically crude. Screenwriter-editor Yimez Guney supervised production while still in prison himself. Shared Cannes Film Festival Best Film with *Missing.* Ⓢ

YOLANDA AND THE THIEF 1945
★★ NR Musical 1:48
Dir: Vincente Minnelli *Cast:* Fred Astaire, Lucille Bremer, Frank Morgan, Mildred Natwick, Mary Nash, Leon Ames
▶ Astaire pretends to be an angel to bilk innocent convent-educated Bremer out of her fortune. However, he falls in love with his quarry. Offbeat but rewarding: Astaire and Bremer work together charmingly and Minnelli provides his usual skillful use of color and production design.

YOR, THE HUNTER FROM THE FUTURE 1983 Italian
★ PG Sci-Fi 1:29
☑ Violence
Dir: Anthony M. Dawson (Antonio Margheriti) *Cast:* Reb Brown, Corinne Clery, John Steiner, Carole Andre, Alan Collins, Syshe Gul
▶ In a post-holocaust future, caveman Brown battles dinosaurs and other prehistoric monsters. Next he takes on evil overlord Steiner and destructive robots to save Clery's tribe. Brown's discovery of his secret past evens the odds against Steiner. B-grade sci-fi, shot in Italy and Turkey, is mainly for genre fans.

YOU CAN'T CHEAT AN HONEST MAN 1939
★★ NR Comedy 1:16 B&W
Dir: George Marshall *Cast:* W. C. Fields, Edgar Bergen, Constance Moore, Mary Forbes, Thurston Hall, Eddie "Rochester" Anderson
▶ Struggling circus owner Fields feuds with featured act Bergen; Bergen falls in love with Fields's daughter Moore, but she considers marrying a rich guy to aid dad. The combination of Fields and ventriloquist Bergen (along with dummies Charlie McCarthy and Mortimer Snerd) adds up to a consistently frisky and funny vehicle.

YOU CAN'T HURRY LOVE 1988
★ R Comedy 1:32
☑ Nudity, adult situations, explicit language
Dir: Richard Martini *Cast:* David Packer, David Leisure, Scott McGinnis, Bridget Fonda, Anthony Geary, Frank Bonner
▶ Dumped by his fiancée, young Ohioan Packer moves to L.A. to pursue swinging lifestyle with hipster cousin McGinnis, who's housesitting Beverly Hills mansion for ad exec Leisure. Packer has nothing but trouble with the opposite sex—until he meets dream date Fonda. Lightweight but likable comedy with cameos by Charles Grodin, Kristy McNichol, and Sally Kellerman. Leisure is recognizable as Joe Izuzu, lying pitchman of TV fame.

YOU CAN'T TAKE IT WITH YOU 1938
★ ★ ★ ★ ★ **NR Comedy 2:06 B&W**
Dir: Frank Capra   *Cast:* James Stewart,
Jean Arthur, Edward Arnold, Ann Miller,
Lionel Barrymore, Spring Byington
▶ Screen version of Moss Hart–George S.
Kaufman Broadway hit chronicles the
lives of an eccentric family. When eligible
daughter Arthur falls in love with charming Stewart, son of stuffed-shirt conserva-
tives, comic conflict results. Motto uttered
by patriarch Barrymore: "You can't take it
with you! The only thing you can take with
you is the love of your friends." Hollywood
classic was nominated for seven Oscars;
won for Best Picture and Director.

YOU LIGHT UP MY LIFE 1977
★ ★ ★ **PG Drama/Romance 1:31**
☑ Adult situations
Dir: Joseph Brooks   *Cast:* Didi Conn,
Joe Silver, Michael Zaslow, Stephen
Nathan, Melanie Mayron, Jerry Keller
▶ Young woman aspires to be pop
singer-songwriter, but her father, a sec-
ond-rate Borscht Belt comic, insists she
follow in his footsteps. To further her ambi-
tions, she breaks engagement to sweet
tennis instructor Nathan for casting-
couch affair with movie director Zaslow.
Written, produced, and directed by
Brooks, meandering drama examines
difficulty of romance in show biz. Brooks-
composed title track won Oscar and
Grammy.

YOU'LL NEVER GET RICH 1941
★ ★ ★ ★ **NR Musical 1:29 B&W**
Dir: Sidney Lanfield   *Cast:* Fred Astaire,
Rita Hayworth, Robert Benchley, John
Hubbard, Osa Massen, Frieda Inescort
▶ Choreographer Astaire loves dancer
Hayworth but hurts her by participating in
producer Benchley's scheme to fool his
wife. Drafted into the army, Astaire gets a
second chance when Hayworth visits sol-
dier-beau Hubbard. One of Astaire's best
non-Rogers films has surprising chemistry
between him and sexy Hayworth (a swell
dancer). Benchley provides snappy
comic support. Oscar-nominated Cole
Porter score and song, "Since I Kissed My
Baby Goodbye."

YOUNG AND INNOCENT 1937 British
★ ★ **NR Mystery-Suspense 1:23 B&W**
Dir: Alfred Hitchcock   *Cast:* Nova Pil-
beam, Derrick de Marney, Percy Mar-
mont, Edward Rigby, Mary Clare, John
Longden
▶ Policeman's daughter Pilbeam be-

friends de Marney, a suspect in a murder
case, and embarks on a mad dash for
the real killer while a manhunt closes in.
Buoyant, light-hearted thriller, one of
Hitchcock's most-overlooked films, contains some of his best sequences: a dazzling game of blind man's bluff, frightening coal mine accident, more.

YOUNG AT HEART 1954
★ ★ ★ ★ **NR Musical 1:57**
Dir: Gordon Douglas   *Cast:* Doris Day,
Frank Sinatra, Gig Young, Ethel Bar-
rymore, Dorothy Malone, Alan Hale, Jr.
▶ Day falls for composer Young, unaware
that her sister Malone also loves him.
Sinatra, Young's cynical partner, then
tries to win Day's heart. Glossy musical
remake of the 1938 soap opera *Four
Daughters* includes "Just One of Those
Things," "One for My Baby," and "Some-
one to Watch Over Me."

YOUNGBLOOD 1986
★ ★ ★ ★ **R Drama/Sports 1:50**
☑ Nudity, adult situations, explicit language, violence
Dir: Peter Markle   *Cast:* Rob Lowe, Patrick Swayze, Cynthia Gibb, Ed Lauter,
Jim Youngs, George Finn
▶ Canadian farm boy Lowe leaves
home to pursue hockey career with semipro team; coach Lauter tries to mold talented Lowe into a star. Romance with
Lauter's daughter Gibb leads to bench-
ing while rivalry erupts with Finn, a goon
from another squad. When Finn cracks a
teammate's skull, Lowe wants to quit the
violent sport. Swayze plays his best friend
on team.

YOUNG DOCTORS IN LOVE 1982
★ ★ **R Comedy 1:31**
☑ Brief nudity, adult situations, explicit
language, adult humor
Dir: Garry Marshall   *Cast:* Michael
McKean, Sean Young, Harry Dean
Stanton, Patrick Macnee, Hector Elizondo, Pamela Reed
▶ Soapy send-up of the medical profession features doctor McKean, who hates
blood, sexy intern Young with a strange
disorder, Mafia lieutenant Elizondo who
dresses in drag, deranged surgeon Dabney Coleman, prune-faced head nurse
Reed, lab worker Stanton who confuses
urine specimens—and lots of jokes about
bodily fluids and functions. Silly but occasionally savvy.

YOUNG EINSTEIN 1989 Australian
☆ **PG Comedy 1:32**

☑ Adult situations, explicit language
Dir: Yahoo Serious *Cast:* Yahoo Serious, Odile Le Clezio, John Howard, Pee Wee Wilson, Su Cruickshank
▶ Revisionist look at the life of scientist Albert Einstein (Serious) plunks character down in 1906 Australia, where he not only comes up with the theory of relativity but discovers rock 'n' roll and surfing to boot. Daffy comic antics are often funny, but off-beat humor may not please everyone; Serious is definitely not for the serious.

YOUNG FRANKENSTEIN 1974
★★★★ PG Comedy 1:46 B&W
☑ Adult humor
Dir: Mel Brooks *Cast:* Gene Wilder, Peter Boyle, Madeline Kahn, Teri Garr, Marty Feldman, Cloris Leachman
▶ Mad takeoff on the monster genre with Wilder as Frankenstein's grandson who returns to Transylvania, reworks his ancestor's experiment, and, this time, gets it right. As the man-made monster, Boyle is hysterical and touching, especially in top hat and tails singing "Puttin' on the Ritz." Memorable performances from Feldman as Wilder's hunchback assistant, lab assistant Garr, and Kahn as the monster's girl. Marvelous, moody, and fun.

YOUNG GUNS 1988
★★★ R Western 1:37
☑ Adult situations, explicit language, violence
Dir: Christopher Cain *Cast:* Emilio Estevez, Kiefer Sutherland, Lou Diamond Phillips, Charlie Sheen, Dermot Mulroney, Casey Siemaszko
▶ Disappointing Western recasts Billy the Kid myth with Hollywood's hot male stars to little effect. Estevez essays the famous killer who finds himself and five followers on the wrong side of the law during 1878 New Mexico range wars. Terence Stamp (his foster father) and villain Jack Palance bring some dignity to loud, violent, but routine plot; hard rock soundtrack proves major drawback.

YOUNG LIONS, THE 1958
★★★★ NR Drama 2:51 B&W
Dir: Edward Dmytryk *Cast:* Marlon Brando, Montgomery Clift, Dean Martin, Hope Lange, Maximilian Schell, Barbara Rush
▶ Adaptation of the Irwin Shaw novel depicts the effects of World War II upon three very different men. Brando, an idealistic young German officer, embraces

Hitler as cure for nation's ills, but war turns him against the Nazis. American soldiers Clift and Martin becomes pals as they struggle with personal problems: Jewish Clift fights anti-Semitism in American ranks as entertainer Martin struggles with cowardice. Nominated for three technical Oscars.

YOUNG MAN WITH A HORN 1950
★★★★ NR Drama/Musical 1:52 B&W
Dir: Michael Curtiz *Cast:* Kirk Douglas, Lauren Bacall, Doris Day, Hoagy Carmichael, Juano Hernandez, Mary Beth Hughes
▶ Douglas, inspired by jazz trumpeter Hernandez, takes up horn playing to escape ghetto. His talent leads to New York gigs, friendship with vocalist Day, and marriage to socialite Bacall, but marital discord and an untimely death result in alcoholism. Classic drama with topnotch cast and terrific music (jazz great Harry James dubs for Douglas) was inspired by life of trumpeter Bix Beiderbecke.

YOUNG MR. LINCOLN 1939
★★★★★ NR Biography 1:40 B&W
Dir: John Ford *Cast:* Henry Fonda, Alice Brady, Marjorie Weaver, Arleen Whelan, Eddie Collins, Pauline Moore
▶ Early years in the life of Abraham Lincoln are shown with insight and humor. Fonda gives an uncanny impression of the President, haunted by his lost love Ann Rutledge (Moore) and struggling as a backwoods lawyer in the early 1800s. Second half is devoted to an engrossing trial, which displays Lincoln's subtle wit. Lamar Trotti's story received an Oscar nomination.

YOUNG NURSES, THE 1973
★ R Drama 1:15
☑ Nudity, strong sexual content, explicit language, mild violence
Dir: Clinton Kimbro *Cast:* Jean Manson, Ashley Porter, Angela Gibbs, Zack Taylor, Richard Miller
▶ Adventures of three beautiful nurses prove moderately entertaining in this low-budget exploitation. Manson falls in love with a sailor; Porter must choose between rich boyfriend and work at a medical clinic; Gibbs uncovers a hospital drug ring run by an unethical doctor (director Sam Fuller in a brief cameo). Fourth entry in Roger Corman's "Nurses" series has a heavy emphasis on sex; followed by *Candy Stripe Nurses*.

YOUNG PHILADELPHIANS, THE 1959
★ ★ ★ NR Drama 2:16 B&W
Dir: Vincent Sherman *Cast:* Paul Newman, Barbara Rush, Alexis Smith, Brian
Keith, Robert Vaughn, Diane Brewster
▶ Newman plays a Philadelphia lawyer
of dubious heritage who passes up marriage to society girl Rush in order to further his ambitions. Later, Newman defends army buddy Vaughn on a murder
charge; in the process, he gets in touch
with his more idealistic side and wins
back Rush. Newman and a solid supporting cast make this engrossing drama
work.

YOUNG SHERLOCK HOLMES 1985
★ ★ ★ ★ PG-13 Action-Adventure 1:50
☑ Violence
Dir: Barry Levinson *Cast:* Nicholas
Rowe, Alan Cox, Sophie Ward, Anthony
Higgins, Susan Fleetwood, Freddie
Jones
▶ Entertaining romp from producer
Steven Spielberg asks what might have
happened if Sherlock Holmes and Dr.
John Watson first met as teenage stu-
dents. The answer is elementary: adven-
tures on a par with the later exploits of
the Arthur Conan Doyle hero. Young de-
tective Rowe and sidekick Cox, along
with romantic interest Ward, investigate
a series of murders. Best bits: roots of
Holmes's trademark pipe, deerstalker
cap, violin playing, and bachelorhood.

YOUNG WARRIORS 1983
★ R Action-Adventure 1:45
☑ Rape, nudity, strong sexual content,
explicit language, graphic violence
Dir: Lawrence D. Foldes *Cast:* Richard
Roundtree, James Van Patten, Ernest
Borgnine, Anne Lockhart, Linda Day
Shawn, Dick Shawn
▶ When violent thugs gang-rape and
murder a young woman, her cop father
Borgnine follows normal procedures with
partner Roundtree in pursuit of goons.
Van Patten, anguished brother of the vic-
tim, grows impatient; he and fraternity
mates assemble arsenal for vigilante ac-
tion. Revenge drama lacks subtlety.

YOUNG WINSTON 1972 British
★ ★ PG Biography 2:25
☑ Explicit language, violence
Dir: Richard Attenborough *Cast:*
Simon Ward, Anne Bancroft, Robert
Shaw, John Mills, Jack Hawkins, Edward
Woodward
▶ True story of Winston Churchill (Ward)

traces his early years, including adventures as war correspondent in India and
South Africa, the death of his father
(Shaw), first political defeat, and first
election to Parliament. Large-scale and
exciting. Ward is fine; Bancroft holds her
own in the great English cast.

YOU ONLY LIVE ONCE 1937
★ ★ ★ ★ NR Drama 1:26 B&W
Dir: Fritz Lang *Cast:* Henry Fonda,
Sylvia Sidney, Barton MacLane, Jean
Dixon, William Gargan
▶ Ex-con Fonda tries to reform with wife
Sidney but is sentenced to prison for a
crime he didn't commit. After killing a
man during a jailbreak; he and Sidney go
on the lam but find the law closing in on
them. Haunting variation on the Bonnie
and Clyde story with superlative performances and direction.

YOU ONLY LIVE TWICE 1967 British
★ ★ ★ ★ PG
Espionage/Action-Adventure 1:55
☑ Adult situations, violence
Dir: Lewis Gilbert *Cast:* Sean Connery,
Donald Pleasence, Akiko Wakabayashi,
Mie Hama, Teru Shimada, Karin Dor
▶ From his Japanese volcano headquar-
ters, archvillain Blofeld (Pleasence) nabs
Russian and American space capsules in
hopes of starting a world conflict; agent
James Bond (Connery) tries to stop him.
One of the best of the series features to-
tally in-stride Connery, exotic Japanese
locations, zippy pacing, great gadgets
(especially a miniature flying machine)
and chases. Nancy Sinatra sings the
haunting title tune.

YOUR CHEATIN' HEART 1964
★ ★ ★ NR Biography/Music 1:38 B&W
Dir: Gene Nelson *Cast:* George Hamilton, Susan Oliver, Red Buttons, Arthur
O'Connell, Shary Marshall, Rex Ingram
▶ Heavily sanitized biography of country-
western legend Hank Williams still provides a good overview of his career on
the Louisiana Hayride, unprecedented
success with the Grand Ole Opry, and
tragic early death. Hamilton is surprisingly
good in what may be his best performance. Hank Williams, Jr. (himself the subject of TV biopic *Living Proof*) dubbed his
father's singing voice on eleven of his
songs.

YOU'RE A BIG BOY NOW 1967
★ NR Comedy 1:36
Dir: Francis Ford Coppola *Cast:* Eliza-
beth Hartman, Geraldine Page, Julie

Harris, Peter Kastner, Rip Torn, Karen Black

▶ Lighthearted coming-of-age comedy describes Kastner's introduction to sex, drugs, and love after fleeing his doting Long Island parents for a position as Manhattan librarian. His futile obsession with dancer Hartman eventually leads to romance with shy Black. Strong performances and bouncy Lovin' Spoonful soundtrack help episodic, occasionally arch plot.

YOU TALKIN' TO ME? 1987
★ R Drama 1:37
☑ Explicit language, violence
Dir: Charles Winkler *Cast:* Jim Youngs, James Noble, Faith Ford, Mykel T. Williamson, Bess Motta, Rex Ryon
▶ Aspiring actor Youngs fancies himself another Robert De Niro and moves to Los Angeles, only to discover his dark, brooding type is no longer in fashion. Dyeing his hair blond and adopting a laid-back surfer manner, he quickly lands dishy girlfriend Ford. She gets him work on dad Noble's racist TV show, much to the dismay of black pal Williamson. Uneven effort switches midway from comedy to social drama.

YOU WERE NEVER LOVELIER 1942
★★ NR Musical 1:37 B&W
Dir: William A. Seiter *Cast:* Fred Astaire, Rita Hayworth, Adolphe Menjou, Xavier Cugat, Leslie Brooks, Adele Mara
▶ South American hotel magnate Menjou, concerned about daughter Hayworth's lack of interest in romance, creates a phantom lover with flowers and fake letters to stir her up. Hayworth mistakes down-on-his-luck entertainer Astaire for the phony suitor. Classic escapist fare uses first-class score by famed Johnny Mercer–Jerome Kern duo for delightful song-and-dance numbers like "Dearly Beloved," "I'm Old-Fashioned," and the title tune. Nominated for three Oscars.

YURI NOSENKO, KGB 1986
★★ NR Espionage/MFTV 1:29
☑ Explicit language
Dir: Mick Jackson *Cast:* Tommy Lee Jones, Oleg Rudnick, Josef Sommer, Ed Lauter, Stephen Newman, Alexandra O'Karma
▶ True story of KGB defector Yuri Nosenko (Rudnick), who agreed to provide information about Lee Harvey Oswald in the 1960s. CIA agent Jones is assigned the task of learning whether Nosenko is a true defector or a KGB plant. Gripping drama re-creates grueling interrogations and baffling clues; acclaimed performances by Jones and Rudnick.

Z 1969 French
★★★ PG Drama 2:07
☑ Violence
Dir: Costa-Gavras *Cast:* Yves Montand, Jean-Louis Trintignant, Irene Papas, Jacques Perrin, Charles Denner, François Périer
▶ Powerful drama turns 1963 assassination of Greek liberal Gregorios Lambrakis into a hard-hitting, often dazzling thriller. Montand plays the murdered leader; Trintignant is appointed investigating magistrate in what the government hopes will be a whitewash of the facts. But he uncovers corruption that ultimately leads to a coup. Oscar winner for Best Foreign Film and Editing.

ZABRISKIE POINT 1970
☆ R Drama 1:52
☑ Nudity, adult situations, explicit language, violence
Dir: Michelangelo Antonioni *Cast:* Mark Frechette, Daria Halprin, Rod Taylor, Paul Fix, G. D. Spradlin, Bill Garaway
▶ Frechette, a student radical framed for murder, steals an airplane and flies to Death Valley, where secretary Halprin introduces him to drugs and orgies. Dated counterculture epic seemed confusing and self-indulgent when released, but now provides a visually interesting time capsule of the hippie movement. Soundtrack includes songs by Pink Floyd, Grateful Dead, and Rolling Stones; Sam Shepard and Clare Peploe worked on the screenplay.

ZACHARIAH 1970
★★ PG Western/Musical 1:33
☑ Explicit language
Dir: George Englund *Cast:* John Rubinstein, Don Johnson, Pat Quinn, Elvin Jones, Country Joe and the Fish, Doug Kershaw
▶ In the 1870s, restless youth Rubinstein embarks on gunslinger career with best pal Johnson. Encounters with gang of outlaws (played by Country Joe and the Fish), fast-drawing Jones, and legendary tomboy Quinn lead duo to divergent lives. Hailed as first rock Western, uneven yarn mixes performances by rock bands

in cowboy garb, spoofs of genre, and hip pacifist ending. Comedy troupe The Firesign Theater cowrote script but asked to be removed from credits.

ZAPPED! 1982
★ ★ ★ R Comedy 1:38
☑ Nudity, adult situations, explicit language
Dir: Robert J. Rosenthal *Cast:* Scott Baio, Willie Aames, Heather Thomas, Scatman Crothers, Felice Schacter
▶ Shy teen genius Baio dabbles in botany experiment and accidentally gives himself telekinetic powers. Outgoing buddy Aames wants him to use psychic prowess to beat the odds in Las Vegas, but Baio's more interested in employing mind-over-matter to disrobe high school girls. Sex comedy climaxes in parody of *Carrie,* as Baio's libido and powers run amok at senior prom.

ZARDOZ 1974 British
☆ R Sci-Fi 1:44
☑ Nudity, adult situations, explicit language, violence
Dir: John Boorman *Cast:* Sean Connery, Charlotte Rampling, Sara Kestelman, John Alderton, Niall Buggy
▶ In the twenty-third century, society is divided into barbarians and an elite group of intelligent but sterile immortals. Brainy barbarian Connery invades the enclave of the latter, gets involved with Rampling and Kestelman, and turns the society upside down. Visually extravagant (watch out for that flying head) and wildly ambitious but not always in control. Best moments: Connery being tested for potency, the revelation of what the title means.

ZELIG 1983
★ ★ PG Comedy 1:19 C/B&W
☑ Adult situations, explicit language, adult humor
Dir: Woody Allen *Cast:* Woody Allen, Mia Farrow, Garrett Brown, Stephanie Farrow, Will Holt, Sol Lomita
▶ Documentary-style comedy follows the fictional life of Leonard Zelig (Allen) who has the chameleonlike power to transform himself into almost anyone: Indian, rabbi, Chinaman. Dedicated shrink Farrow works to give Zelig a single personality. Clever editing of actual newsreel footage from the thirties and forties places Zelig next to Pope Pius XI, Fanny Brice, Herbert Hoover, even Hitler. Technical masterpiece with some truly inspired

sight gags and poignant moments unfortunately wears thin and may be best appreciated by sophisticated viewers.

ZELLY AND ME 1988
★ ★ ★ PG Drama 1:27
☑ Adult situations
Dir: Tina Rathborne *Cast:* Isabella Rossellini, Glynis Johns, Alexandra Johnes, Kaiulani Lee, David Lynch, Joe Morton
▶ In 1958, young orphan Johnes lives in a Virginia mansion with cold, overbearing grandmother Johns; only loving relationship is with her governess Rossellini. When Johnes's fixation on Joan of Arc leads the girl to self-mutilation, Rossellini looks to her suitor Lynch for help moving the child to a healthier environment. Pyschological drama stars real-life couple Rossellini and noted film director Lynch. (CC)

ZERO BOYS, THE 1986
★ ★ NR Action-Adventure 1:29
☑ Adult situations, explicit language, graphic violence
Dir: Nico Mastorakis *Cast:* Dan Hirsch, Kelli Maroney, Tom Shell, Jared Moses, Crystal Carson, John Michaels
▶ Buddies Hirsch, Shell, Moses, and Michaels take part in weekend survivalist games. The fun takes a deadly turn when they encounter a deserted house and a brutal killer. Professionally crafted but somewhat unsavory; Moses is excellent. Best line: "Freud, he's the dude who changed it all."

ZIEGFELD FOLLIES 1946
★ ★ ★ NR Musical 1:50
Dir: Vincente Minnelli *Cast:* William Powell, Fred Astaire, Gene Kelly, Judy Garland, Lena Horne, Fanny Brice
▶ Powell, reprising his *Great Ziegfeld* role, imagines a star-studded review from his new home in heaven. Following routines include first Astaire/Kelly teaming in "The Babbit and the Bromide," amusing Garland sketch about an audition, Red Skelton's idea of a TV liquor commercial, elaborate "Limehouse Blues" with Astaire and Lucille Bremer. Extravagant fun in the MGM style.

ZOMBIE ISLAND MASSACRE 1984
☆ R Horror 1:35
☑ Nudity, adult situations, explicit language, violence
Dir: John N. Carter *Cast:* David Broadnax, Rita Jenrette, Tom Cantrell, Diane Clayre Holub
▶ American tourists in Caribbean sign up for special trip to remote island to witness

voodoo rites. There they get more than they bargained for, as cannibal zombies knock them off, one by one. Drive-in fare stars Jenrette, ex-wife of the Congressman indicted in the Abscam sting and later subject of a *Playboy* spread.

ZONE TROOPERS 1985
★★ **PG Sci-Fi 1:28**
☑ Explicit language, violence
Dir: Danny Bilson *Cast:* Timothy Van Patten, Tim Thomerson, Biff Manard, Art La Fleur, William Paulson
▶ During World War II, a platoon of American soldiers, including tough sarge Thomerson, greenhorn private Van Patten, dumb-but-lovable corporal La Fleur, and obnoxious journalist Manard, gets caught behind enemy lines. While trying to escape, they encounter a wrecked spacecraft and rescue the surviving alien from Nazis. Unusual sci-fi premise renders competent war saga.

ZOO GANG, THE 1986
★★ **PG-13 Comedy/Drama 1:37**
☑ Explicit language, violence
Dir: Pen Densham, John Watson *Cast:* Jackie Earle Haley, Eric Gurry, Tiffany Helm, Jason Gedrick, Ben Vereen
▶ Scruffy teens Haley, Gurry, Helm, and Gedrick turn an abandoned building into a nightclub. Neighborhood toughs prey on the club, so, with help of alcoholic ex-wrestler Vereen, the kids must fight for their right to party. Teen turf war should appeal to peer group.

ZOOT SUIT 1981
☆ **R Musical 1:43**
☑ Adult situations, explicit language, violence
Dir: Luis Valdez *Cast:* Edward James Olmos, Daniel Valdez, Charles Aidman, Tyne Daly, John Anderson, Abel Franco
▶ Adaptation of a stage musical is based on a true 1942 story of four Chicano gang members, led by idealistic youth Valdez, who were unjustly jailed in San Quentin for murder. Dedicated Communist lawyer Daly seeks to have them freed. Well-intended musical drama is sabotaged by fractured narrative, intrusive direction, and stylized appearances of Olmos as Valdez's zoot-suited alter ego.

ZORBA THE GREEK 1964
★★★ **NR Drama 2:26 B&W**
Dir: Michael Cacoyannis *Cast:* Anthony Quinn, Alan Bates, Irene Papas, Lila Kedrova, George Foundas, Eleni Anousaki
▶ Life-embracing Greek peasant Quinn befriends uptight Englishman Bates. Although their involvements with widow Papas and elderly prostitute Kedrova are ultimately tragic, Bates loosens up under Quinn's tutelage. Highly emotional and strongly recommended experience; Quinn's Oscar-nominated turn is absolutely magnificent. Best Picture nominee won Best Supporting Actress (Kedrova), Cinematography, and Art Direction.

ZORRO, THE GAY BLADE 1981
★★ **PG Comedy 1:34**
☑ Explicit language, adult humor
Dir: Peter Medak *Cast:* George Hamilton, Lauren Hutton, Brenda Vaccaro, Ron Leibman, Donovan Scott, James Booth
▶ Hamilton, the son of legendary masked rider Zorro, must continue family tradition of aiding the oppressed. When a busy social life takes up too much of his time, he enlists the aid of his homosexual brother (also Hamilton). Their cause: pretty newcomer Hutton, who seeks to organize peasant revolt against local tyrant Leibman. Broad spoof is inconsistent.

ZULU 1964 British
★★★ **NR Action-Adventure 2:15**
Dir: Cy Endfield *Cast:* Stanley Baker, Jack Hawkins, Michael Caine, Ulla Jacobsson, James Booth, Nigel Green
▶ True story of 1879 Zulu attack on the British. Co-producer Baker plays the brave commander who rallied the outnumbered English forces to an inspiring victory. Caine, in his first major role, is outstanding as an upper-crust officer. Well-crafted storytelling with enthralling battle scenes.

ZULU DAWN 1980 U.S./Dutch
★★★ **PG Action-Adventure 1:57**
☑ Violence
Dir: Douglas Hickox *Cast:* Burt Lancaster, Peter O'Toole, Simon Ward, John Mills, Denholm Elliott
▶ True story of the 1879 Battle of Islandhlwana in which the British Army's inferior numbers and inappropriate fighting methods led to defeat by the Zulu nation. Old-fashioned epic has impressive location shooting and vividly staged battle scenes, but the human drama suffers from stereotyped characters and uninspired script.

CAST INDEX

DIRECTOR INDEX

DEEP IN THE HEART
DEFIANCE
DEFIANT ONES, THE
DELIVERANCE
DELTA FORCE, THE
DETROIT 9000
DEVIL AT 4 O'CLOCK, THE
DIAMONDS
DIAMONDS ARE FOREVER
DIE HARD
DIRTY HARRY
DIRTY MARY, CRAZY LARRY
DOC SAVAGE: THE MAN OF BRONZE
DOGS OF WAR, THE
$ (DOLLARS)
DRIVER, THE
DR. NO
DRUMS
DUDES
EACH DAWN I DIE
EARTHQUAKE
EAT MY DUST
EDDIE MACON'S RUN
EIGER SANCTION, THE
EL CID
ELIMINATORS, THE
EMERALD FOREST, THE
EMPEROR OF THE NORTH, THE
EMPIRE STRIKES BACK, THE
ENEMY TERRITORY
ENFORCER, THE
ESCAPE TO ATHENA
EVIL THAT MEN DO, THE
EXCALIBUR
EXECUTIONER, THE
EXTERMINATOR, THE
EXTERMINATOR 2
EXTREME PREJUDICE
EYE OF THE TIGER
FAMILY, THE
FAST COMPANY
FATAL BEAUTY
FEAR CITY
FIFTH MUSKETEER, THE
55 DAYS AT PEKING
FIGHTING BACK
FIGHTING PRINCE OF DONEGAL, THE
FINAL CHAPTER: WALKING TALL
FINAL MISSION
FIRE DOWN BELOW
FIREFOX
FIREPOWER
FIREWALKER
FIRST BLOOD
FIRST DEADLY SIN, THE
FITZCARRALDO
FIVE WEEKS IN A BALLOON
FLAME AND THE ARROW, THE
FLASHPOINT
FLESH + BLOOD
FLIGHT OF THE PHOENIX
FLORIDA STRAITS
48 HRS.
FOR YOUR EYES ONLY
FOUR FEATHERS, THE
FOUR MUSKETEERS, THE
FOXY BROWN
FRAMED
FREEBIE AND THE BEAN
FROM RUSSIA, WITH LOVE
FUZZ
F/X
GAMBIT
GATOR
GAUNTLET, THE
GETAWAY, THE
GLORIA
GLOVE, THE
G-MEN
GOLDEN CHILD, THE
GOLDEN NEEDLES
GOLDEN SEAL, THE
GOLDFINGER
GRAND THEFT AUTO

GREAT TEXAS DYNAMITE CHASE, THE
GREEN ICE
GRISSOM GANG, THE
GRIZZLY
GUMBALL RALLY, THE
GUNGA DIN
HANDS OF STEEL
HATARI!
HAWK THE SLAYER
HEARTS AND ARMOUR
HEAT
HEATED VENGEANCE
HELLFIGHTERS
HELL'S ANGELS ON WHEELS
HERCULES (1959)
HERCULES (1983)
HERO AND THE TERROR
HIDDEN FORTRESS, THE
HIGHLANDER
HIGHPOINT
HIGH RISK
HIGH ROAD TO CHINA
HOOPER
HORSEMEN, THE
HORSE WITHOUT A HEAD, THE
HOSTAGE
HOTEL COLONIAL
HUNDRA
HUNTER, THE
HUNTER'S BLOOD
HURRICANE, THE
HURRICANE
ICEMAN
ICE STATION ZEBRA
INDIANA JONES AND THE TEMPLE OF DOOM
INSTANT JUSTICE
INVASION U.S.A.
IRON EAGLE
IRON EAGLE II
IRON WARRIOR
I, THE JURY
IVANHOE
JACKSON COUNTY JAIL
JAKE SPEED
JANE AND THE LOST CITY
JAWS
JAWS 2
JAWS 3
JAWS THE REVENGE
JEWEL OF THE NILE, THE
JOURNEY OF NATTY GANN, THE
JUGGERNAUT
JUNGLE RAIDERS
JUNGLE WARRIORS
KAGEMUSHA
KHARTOUM
KIDNAPPED (1960)
KIDNAPPED (1986)
KILLER ELITE, THE
KILLER FISH
KILLER FORCE
KILLPOINT
KIM
KING SOLOMON'S MINES
KINJITE—FORBIDDEN SUBJECTS
KLONDIKE FEVER
KNIGHTRIDERS
KNIGHTS OF THE ROUND TABLE
LASSITER
LAST DAYS OF POMPEII, THE
LAST DRAGON, THE
LAST PLANE OUT
LAWRENCE OF ARABIA
LEFT HAND OF GOD, THE
LETHAL WEAPON
LET'S GET HARRY
LIONHEART
LION OF AFRICA, THE
LITTLE TREASURE
LIVE AND LET DIE
LIVES OF A BENGAL LANCER, THE
LIVING DAYLIGHTS, THE
LONE RUNNER
LONE WOLF McQUADE

LOST HORIZON
LOVE AND BULLETS
MACON COUNTY LINE
MADIGAN
MAD MAX
MAD MAX BEYOND THUNDERDOME
MAGNUM FORCE
MALONE
MAN FROM SNOWY RIVER, THE
MANHUNTER
MAN WHO WOULD BE KING, THE
MAN WITH THE GOLDEN GUN, THE
MARK OF ZORRO, THE
McQ
MEAN DOG BLUES
MECHANIC, THE
MEGAFORCE
MERCENARY FIGHTERS
MESSENGER OF DEATH
METEOR
MIDNIGHT RUN
MISSING IN ACTION
MISSING IN ACTION 2—THE BEGINNING
MISSION, THE
MISSION KILL
MOBY DICK
MOGAMBO
MOONRAKER
MOONSHINE COUNTY EXPRESS
MOSQUITO COAST, THE
MOTHER LODE
MR. BILLION
MR. MAJESTYK
MURDERERS' ROW
MURPHY'S LAW
MUTINY ON THE BOUNTY
MYSTERIOUS ISLAND
NAKED CAGE, THE
NAKED JUNGLE, THE
NAKED PREY, THE
NAPOLEON AND SAMANTHA
NATE AND HAYES
NEVER CRY WOLF
NEVER SAY NEVER AGAIN
NEVER TOO YOUNG TO DIE
NIGHT CROSSING
NIGHTFORCE
NIGHTHAWKS
NIGHT OF THE JUGGLER
NIGHTSTICK
NOMADS
NO MERCY
NUMBER ONE WITH A BULLET
OCTOPUSSY
ODESSA FILE, THE
OMEGA SYNDROME
ONE MILLION YEARS B.C.
ON HER MAJESTY'S SECRET SERVICE
OPERATION THUNDERBOLT
OPPOSING FORCE
OUTLAW BLUES
OUT OF CONTROL
OVER THE EDGE
PAPILLON
PASSAGE TO MARSEILLES
PATRIOT, THE
PENITENTIARY
PENITENTIARY II
PENITENTIARY III
PERILS OF GWENDOLINE, THE
PIRATES
POINT BLANK
POSEIDON ADVENTURE, THE
POWER PLAY
PREDATOR
PRIDE AND THE PASSION, THE
PRIME CUT
PRINCE AND THE PAUPER, THE
PRISONER OF ZENDA, THE (1952)
PROTECTOR, THE
PURSUIT OF D.B. COOPER, THE
QUEST FOR FIRE
QUIET COOL
QUO VADIS

RAGE
RAIDERS OF THE LOST ARK
RAISE THE TITANIC
RAMBO: FIRST BLOOD, PART II
RAMBO III
RAW DEAL
REAP THE WILD WIND
REBEL ROUSERS
RED DAWN
RED HEAT
RED SONJA
RED TENT, THE
REFORM SCHOOL GIRLS
REMO WILLIAMS: THE ADVENTURE BEGINS
RENT-A-COP
REPO MAN
REPORT TO THE COMMISSIONER
RESCUE, THE
RETALIATOR, THE
RETURN FROM WITCH MOUNTAIN
RETURN OF THE JEDI
RETURN TO MACON COUNTY
RIDDLE OF THE SANDS, THE
RIGHT STUFF, THE
ROADHOUSE 66
ROAD WARRIOR, THE
ROBIN AND MARIAN
ROLLERBALL
ROLLERCOASTER
ROLLING THUNDER
ROLLING VENGEANCE
ROMANCING THE STONE
ROPE OF SAND
ROYAL FLASH
RUCKUS
RUNAWAY TRAIN
RUNNING MAN, THE
RUNNING SCARED
SAFARI 3000
SAHARA (1984)
SALVADOR
SAND PEBBLES, THE
SAVAGE DAWN
SAVAGE STREETS
SCARAMOUCHE
SCARLET PIMPERNEL, THE
SCAVENGERS
SCORPION
SEA HAWK, THE
SEARCH AND DESTROY
SEA WOLVES, THE
SEVEN-PER-CENT SOLUTION, THE
SEVEN SAMURAI, THE
SEVEN-UPS, THE
SHAFT
SHAKEDOWN
SHAKER RUN
SHAMUS
SHANGHAI SURPRISE
SHARKS' TREASURE
SHARKY'S MACHINE
SHEENA
SHOGUN
SHOOT TO KILL
SHOUT AT THE DEVIL
SICILIAN, THE
SILENCERS, THE
SILENT RAGE
SINBAD THE SAILOR
SKY RIDERS
SLAYGROUND
SLOANE
SMALL TOWN IN TEXAS, A
SMOKEY AND THE BANDIT
SMOKEY AND THE BANDIT II
SMOKEY AND THE BANDIT—PART 3
SMOKEY BITES THE DUST
SNO-LINE
SOLDIER, THE
SOLDIER OF FORTUNE
SON OF FURY
SORCERER
SORCERESS
SOUTHERN COMFORT

SPACECAMP
SPACE RIDERS
SPY WHO LOVED ME, THE
STAR WARS
STEEL
STEEL DAWN
STEELE JUSTICE
ST. HELENS
STICK
STILETTO
ST. IVES
STONE KILLER, THE
STORM
STORY OF ROBIN HOOD, THE
STREETS OF FIRE
STRIPPED TO KILL
STROKER ACE
SUDDEN DEATH
SUDDEN IMPACT
SUNSET STRIP
SUPER FLY
SUPERGIRL
SUPERMAN
SUPERMAN II
SUPERMAN III
SUPERMAN IV: THE QUEST FOR PEACE
SURVIVAL GAME
SWEET REVENGE
SWORD OF GIDEON
SWORD OF THE VALIANT
TAI-PAN
TAKING OF PELHAM ONE TWO THREE, THE
TANK
TARGET
TARZAN, THE APE MAN (1932)
TARZAN, THE APE MAN (1981)
TELEFON
10 TO MIDNIGHT
TERMINAL ENTRY
TERMINATOR, THE
THEY CALL ME BRUCE
THIEF OF BAGDAD, THE
THIRD MAN ON THE MOUNTAIN
THREE KINDS OF HEAT
THREE MUSKETEERS, THE (1948)
THREE MUSKETEERS, THE (1974)
THUNDER AND LIGHTNING
THUNDERBALL
THUNDER BAY
THUNDERBOLT AND LIGHTFOOT
THUNDER ROAD
THUNDER RUN
TIMERIDER
TO CATCH A KING
TOP GUN
TOWERING INFERNO, THE
TOY SOLDIERS
TREASURE ISLAND (1934)
TREASURE OF THE AMAZONS, THE
TREASURE OF THE FOUR CROWNS
TREASURE OF THE SIERRA MADRE, THE
TREASURE OF THE YANKEE ZEPHYR
TRUCK STOP WOMEN
ULYSSES (1955)
UNCOMMON VALOR
UNDER COVER
UNHOLY ROLLERS, THE
UNTOUCHABLES, THE
VENDETTA
VICE SQUAD
VIEW TO A KILL, A
VIGILANTE
VIKINGS, THE
VIOLATED
WAGES OF FEAR, THE
WALKER
WALKING TALL
WALKING TALL, PART 2
WALKING THE EDGE
WANTED: DEAD OR ALIVE
WAR AND PEACE (1956)
WAR AND PEACE (1968)
WARLORDS OF THE 21ST CENTURY

WAR PARTY
WARRIOR AND THE SORCERESS, THE
WARRIORS, THE (1955)
WARRIORS, THE (1979)
WHERE THE RIVER RUNS BLACK
WHITE DAWN, THE
WHITE LIGHTNING
WHITE LINE FEVER
WHITE WATER SUMMER
WICKED LADY, THE
WILBY CONSPIRACY, THE
WILD ANGELS, THE
WILD GEESE, THE
WILD GEESE II
WILD PAIR, THE
WILD THING
WIND AND THE LION, THE
WIZARDS OF THE LOST KINGDOM
WOMEN'S PRISON MASSACRE
WRONG IS RIGHT
W.W. AND THE DIXIE DANCEKINGS
YAKUZA, THE
YEAR OF THE DRAGON
YELLOW HAIR AND THE FORTRESS OF GOLD
YOJIMBO
YOUNG SHERLOCK HOLMES
YOUNG WARRIORS
YOU ONLY LIVE TWICE
ZERO BOYS, THE
ZULU
ZULU DAWN

ANIMATION
ALICE IN WONDERLAND (1951)
AMERICAN POP
AMERICAN TAIL, AN
ANIMALYMPICS
BLACK CAULDRON, THE
BON VOYAGE, CHARLIE BROWN (AND DON'T COME
   BACK!)
BOY NAMED CHARLIE BROWN, A
BUGS BUNNY/ROAD RUNNER MOVIE, THE
BUGS BUNNY'S 3RD MOVIE: 1001 RABBIT TALES
CARE BEARS MOVIE, THE
CARE BEARS MOVIE II: A NEW GENERATION
CARE BEARS ADVENTURE IN WONDERLAND, THE
CHARLOTTE'S WEB
CINDERELLA
DAFFY DUCK'S MOVIE: FANTASTIC ISLAND
DUMBO
FIRE AND ICE (1983)
FRITZ THE CAT
GREAT MOUSE DETECTIVE, THE
HEAVY TRAFFIC
HEY GOOD LOOKIN'
LADY AND THE TRAMP
LAND BEFORE TIME, THE
LION, THE WITCH & THE WARDROBE, THE
LOONEY LOONEY LOONEY BUGS BUNNY MOVIE
LORD OF THE RINGS, THE
MISSING LINK, THE
MY LITTLE PONY, THE MOVIE
OLIVER & COMPANY
101 DALMATIONS
1001 ARABIAN NIGHTS
PHANTOM TOLLBOOTH, THE
PINOCCHIO
PLAGUE DOGS, THE
RACE FOR YOUR LIFE, CHARLIE BROWN
RAGGEDY ANN AND ANDY
RAINBOW BRITE AND THE STAR STEALER
ROCK & RULE
SECRET OF NIMH, THE
SLEEPING BEAUTY
SNOOPY COME HOME
SNOW WHITE AND THE SEVEN DWARFS
SWORD IN THE STONE, THE
TRON
WATER BABIES, THE
WATERSHIP DOWN
WHEN THE WIND BLOWS
WHO FRAMED ROGER RABBIT
YELLOW SUBMARINE

BIOGRAPHY

ABE LINCOLN IN ILLINOIS
ACT OF VENGEANCE
ADVENTURES OF MARK TWAIN, THE
AGONY AND THE ECSTASY, THE
AL CAPONE
ALEXANDER THE GREAT
ALL THE KING'S MEN
AMERICAN HOT WAX
AUTOBIOGRAPHY OF MISS JANE PITTMAN, THE
BARBARIAN AND THE GEISHA, THE
BEAR, THE
BENNY GOODMAN STORY, THE
BILL
BILL ON HIS OWN
BIRD
BIRDMAN OF ALCATRAZ
BIRTH OF THE BEATLES
BONNIE AND CLYDE
BOUND FOR GLORY
BRIAN'S SONG
BUDDY HOLLY STORY, THE
CAPONE
CARBINE WILLIAMS
CAST A GIANT SHADOW
CHAMPIONS
CHANEL SOLITAIRE
COAL MINER'S DAUGHTER
CROMWELL
CROSS CREEK
CRY FREEDOM
CRY IN THE DARK, A
DEATH OF A CENTERFOLD: THE DOROTHY STRATTEN STORY
DEEP IN MY HEART
DESERT FOX, THE
DIARY OF ANNE FRANK, THE
DILLINGER
ELENI
ELVIS
EVEL KNIEVEL
EXECUTIONER'S SONG, THE
FABULOUS DORSEYS, THE
FALCON AND THE SNOWMAN, THE
FEAR STRIKES OUT
FIVE PENNIES, THE
FRANCES
FUNNY GIRL
FUNNY LADY
GABY—A TRUE STORY
GALLANT HOURS, THE
GANDHI
GENE KRUPA STORY, THE
GENTLEMAN JIM
GLENN MILLER STORY, THE
GORILLAS IN THE MIST
GREASED LIGHTNING
GREAT CARUSO, THE
GREATEST, THE
GREAT IMPOSTOR, THE
GREAT ZIEGFELD, THE
GYPSY
HANNA'S WAR
HANS CHRISTIAN ANDERSEN
HARLOW
HEART LIKE A WHEEL
IF YOU COULD SEE WHAT I HEAR
IMAGINE: JOHN LENNON
INN OF THE SIXTH HAPPINESS, THE
IN THE MOOD
ISADORA
I WANT TO LIVE!
JANIS
JIM THORPE—ALL-AMERICAN
JOKER IS WILD, THE
JOLSON SINGS AGAIN
JOLSON STORY, THE
JUAREZ
KNUTE ROCKNE—ALL AMERICAN
LA BAMBA
LADY IN RED, THE
LADY JANE
LADY SINGS THE BLUES

LAST AMERICAN HERO, THE
LAST EMPEROR, THE
LAWRENCE OF ARABIA
LENNY
LEPKE
LIFE OF EMILE ZOLA, THE
LISZTOMANIA
LOVE ME OR LEAVE ME
LUST FOR LIFE
MACARTHUR
MAHLER
MANDELA
MAN WHO BROKE 1,000 CHAINS, THE
MARIE
MARY OF SCOTLAND
McVICAR
MIRACLE WORKER, THE (1962)
MIRACLE WORKER, THE (1979)
MUSSOLINI: THE DECLINE AND FALL OF IL DUCE
NAPOLEON
NIGHT AND DAY
OTHER SIDE OF THE MOUNTAIN, THE
OTHER SIDE OF THE MOUNTAIN PART II, THE
PAPILLON
PATTON
PATTY HEARST
PRESIDENT'S LADY, THE
PRIDE OF THE YANKEES, THE
PRIEST OF LOVE
PRISONER OF SHARK ISLAND, THE
PRIVATE FILES OF J. EDGAR HOOVER, THE
PRIVATE LIFE OF HENRY VIII, THE
PT 109
RAGING BULL
REDS
REMBRANDT
RUNNING BRAVE
SAKHAROV
SERGEANT YORK
SERPICO
SEVEN LITTLE FOYS, THE
SID AND NANCY
SILKWOOD
SISTER KENNY
SOMEBODY UP THERE LIKES ME
SONG OF BERNADETTE, THE
SONG OF NORWAY
SONG TO REMEMBER, A
SPIRIT OF ST. LOUIS, THE
SPRING SYMPHONY
STAND AND DELIVER
STAR 80
STEVIE
STORY OF ALEXANDER GRAHAM BELL, THE
STORY OF LOUIS PASTEUR, THE
STORY OF VERNON AND IRENE CASTLE, THE
STORY OF WILL ROGERS, THE
SUNRISE AT CAMPOBELLO
SWEET DREAMS
SYBIL
SYLVIA
TERRY FOX STORY, THE
THAT HAMILTON WOMAN
THIS IS ELVIS
THREE FACES OF EVE, THE
TILL THE CLOUDS ROLL BY
TOAST OF NEW YORK, THE
TO HELL AND BACK
TUCKER: THE MAN AND HIS DREAM
UNSINKABLE MOLLY BROWN, THE
VIRGIN QUEEN, THE
VIVA ZAPATA!
WALKER
W.C. FIELDS AND ME
WOLF AT THE DOOR
WORDS AND MUSIC
WRONG MAN, THE
YANKEE DOODLE DANDY
YOUNG MR. LINCOLN
YOUNG WINSTON
YOUR CHEATIN' HEART

COMEDY

ABBOTT AND COSTELLO MEET FRANKENSTEIN
ABSENT MINDED PROFESSOR, THE
ADAM'S RIB
ADVENTURE OF SHERLOCK HOLMES' SMARTER BROTHER, THE
ADVENTURES IN BABYSITTING
AFTER HOURS
AFTER THE FOX
AIRPLANE!
AIRPLANE II: THE SEQUEL
ALEX IN WONDERLAND
ALL IN A NIGHT'S WORK
ALL NIGHT LONG
ALL OF ME
ALL THROUGH THE NIGHT
ALMOST YOU
ALONG CAME JONES
ALWAYS
AMARCORD
AMAZON WOMEN ON THE MOON
AMERICAN GRAFFITI
AMERICANIZATION OF EMILY, THE
AMERICAN SUCCESS COMPANY, THE
AND NOW FOR SOMETHING COMPLETELY
  DIFFERENT
ANDROCLES AND THE LION
ANDY WARHOL'S BAD
ANDY WARHOL'S DRACULA
ANDY WARHOL'S FRANKENSTEIN
ANGEL ON MY SHOULDER
ANIMAL CRACKERS
ANIMAL HOUSE
ANNIE HALL
ANY WEDNESDAY
ANY WHICH WAY YOU CAN
APARTMENT, THE
APPLE DUMPLING GANG, THE
APPLE DUMPLING GANG RIDES AGAIN, THE
APPRENTICESHIP OF DUDDY KRAVITZ, THE
APRIL FOOLS, THE
ARMED AND DANGEROUS
ARNOLD
ARSENIC AND OLD LACE
ARTHUR
ARTHUR 2 ON THE ROCKS
ASSAULT OF THE KILLER BIMBOS
AS YOU LIKE IT
ATTACK OF THE KILLER TOMATOES
AT THE CIRCUS
AUNTIE MAME
AUTHOR! AUTHOR!
AVANTI!
AWFUL TRUTH, THE
BABY BOOM
BACHELOR AND THE BOBBYSOXER, THE
BACHELOR MOTHER
BACHELOR PARTY
BACK ROADS
BACK TO SCHOOL
BACK TO THE BEACH
BACK TO THE FUTURE
BAD MANNERS
BAD MEDICINE
BAD NEWS BEARS, THE
BAD NEWS BEARS GO TO JAPAN, THE
BAD NEWS BEARS IN BREAKING TRAINING, THE
BAGDAD CAFE
BALLAD OF CABLE HOGUE, THE
BALL OF FIRE
BANANAS
BANK DICK, THE
BANK SHOT
BAREFOOT IN THE PARK
BASIC TRAINING
BAWDY ADVENTURES OF TOM JONES, THE
BEACHBALLS
BEACH BLANKET BINGO
BEACHES
BEACH GIRLS
BEAT THE DEVIL
BEDAZZLED
BEDTIME FOR BONZO
BEER

BEER DRINKER'S GUIDE TO FITNESS AND FILM MAKING,
  THE
BEETLEJUICE
BEGINNER'S LUCK
BEING THERE
BELL, BOOK AND CANDLE
BELLBOY, THE
BELLES OF ST. TRINIAN'S, THE
BEST DEFENSE
BEST FRIENDS
BEST OF TIMES, THE
BETTER LATE THAN NEVER
BETTER OFF DEAD
BETWEEN THE LINES
BEVERLY HILLS COP II
BEYOND THERAPY
BIG
BIG BUS, THE
BIG BUSINESS
BIG DEAL ON MADONNA STREET
BIG MOUTH, THE
BIG PICTURE, THE
BIG STORE, THE
BIG TOP PEE-WEE
BIG TROUBLE
BIKINI BEACH
BILL & TED'S EXCELLENT ADVENTURE
BILL COSBY—"HIMSELF"
BILLION DOLLAR HOBO, THE
BILLY LIAR
BILOXI BLUES
BLACK AND WHITE IN COLOR
BLACKBEARD'S GHOST
BLACK BIRD, THE
BLAME IT ON RIO
BLAST OFF
BLAZING SADDLES
BLIND DATE (1987)
BLITHE SPIRIT
BLOCKHEADS
BLOOD BATH AT THE HOUSE OF DEATH
BLUE IGUANA, THE
BLUES BROTHERS, THE
BLUE SKIES AGAIN
BLUME IN LOVE
BOARDING SCHOOL
BOATNIKS, THE
BOB AND CAROL AND TED AND ALICE
BOBO, THE
BODY SLAM
BONNIE SCOTLAND
BORN IN EAST L.A.
BORN YESTERDAY
BOSS'S WIFE, THE
BREAD AND CHOCOLATE
BREAKING ALL THE RULES
BREAKING AWAY
BREWSTER McCLOUD
BREWSTER'S MILLIONS (1945)
BREWSTER'S MILLIONS (1985)
BRIGHTON BEACH MEMOIRS
BRINGING UP BABY
BRINK'S JOB, THE
BRITANNIA HOSPITAL
BROADCAST NEWS
BROADWAY DANNY ROSE
BRONCO BILLY
BROTHER FROM ANOTHER PLANET, THE
BROTHER JOHN
BUCK PRIVATES
BUDDY BUDDY
BUDDY SYSTEM, THE
BUGSY MALONE
BULL DURHAM
BULLFIGHTERS, THE
BULLSHOT
BUNNY O'HARE
'BURBS, THE
BUS STOP
BUSTIN' LOOSE
BUTTERFLIES ARE FREE
BUY AND CELL
CACTUS FLOWER
CADDY, THE

CADDYSHACK
CADDYSHACK II
CALIFORNIA DREAMING
CALIFORNIA SPLIT
CALIFORNIA SUITE
CAMPUS MAN
CANDY
CANNONBALL RUN, THE
CANNONBALL RUN II
CAN SHE BAKE A CHERRY PIE?
CAN'T BUY ME LOVE
CAPTAIN NEWMAN, M.D.
CAPTAIN'S PARADISE, THE
CARBON COPY
CARLTON-BROWNE OF THE F.O.
CARS THAT ATE PARIS, THE
CAR WASH
CASANOVA'S BIG NIGHT
CASINO ROYALE
CASTAWAY COWBOY, THE
CASUAL SEX?
CAT AND THE CANARY, THE
CAT BALLOU
CATCH-22
CAT FROM OUTER SPACE, THE
CAVEMAN
CHANCES ARE
CHANGE OF SEASONS, A
CHAPTER TWO
CHARLEY AND THE ANGEL
CHARLIE CHAN AND THE CURSE OF THE DRAGON
  QUEEN
CHATTANOOGA CHOO CHOO
CHEAP DETECTIVE, THE
CHEAPER TO KEEP HER
CHECK IS IN THE MAIL, THE
CHEECH & CHONG'S NEXT MOVIE
CHEECH & CHONG'S NICE DREAMS
CHEECH & CHONG'S THE CORSICAN BROTHERS
CHLOE IN THE AFTERNOON
C.H.O.M.P.S.
CHRISTMAS IN CONNECTICUT
CHRISTMAS IN JULY
CHRISTMAS STORY, A
CHU CHU AND THE PHILLY FLASH
C.H.U.D. II
CITY LIGHTS
CLAIRE'S KNEE
CLARA'S HEART
CLASS
CLOCKWISE
CLOSELY WATCHED TRAINS
CLUB PARADISE
CLUE
CLUNY BROWN
COAST TO COAST
COCA-COLA KID, THE
COCOANUTS
COLD FEET
COMEDY OF TERRORS, THE
COMFORT AND JOY
COMIC, THE
COMING TO AMERICA
COMPUTER WORE TENNIS SHOES, THE
CONDORMAN
CONSUMING PASSIONS
COOLEY HIGH
COUCH TRIP, THE
COUP DE TETE
COUP DE TORCHON
COURT JESTER, THE
COUSIN, COUSINE
COUSINS
CRACKERS
CRACKING UP
CREATOR
CRIME AND PASSION
CRIMES OF THE HEART
CRIMEWAVE
CRITICAL CONDITION
CROSSING DELANCEY
CROSS MY HEART
CURSE OF THE PINK PANTHER
DARK EYES

DAY AT THE RACES, A
DAY FOR NIGHT
D.C. CAB
DEAD HEAT
DEAD MEN DON'T WEAR PLAID
DEAL OF THE CENTURY
DEAR BRIGITTE
DECLINE OF THE AMERICAN EMPIRE, THE
DELIVERY BOYS
DESIGN FOR LIVING
DESIGNING WOMAN
DESIRE
DESK SET
DESPERATELY SEEKING SUSAN
DETECTIVE SCHOOL DROPOUTS
DEVIL AND MAX DEVLIN, THE
DEVIL AND MISS JONES, THE
DIE LAUGHING
DIM SUM: A LITTLE BIT OF HEART
DINER
DINNER AT EIGHT
DIRT BIKE KID, THE
DIRTY ROTTEN SCOUNDRELS
DIRTY TRICKS
DISCREET CHARM OF THE BOURGEOISIE, THE
DISORDERLIES
DISORDERLY ORDERLY, THE
DIVORCE OF LADY X, THE
DOCTOR AT SEA
DOCTOR DETROIT
DOCTOR TAKES A WIFE, THE
DOIN' TIME ON PLANET EARTH
DONA FLOR AND HER TWO HUSBANDS
DONOVAN'S REEF
DON'S PARTY
DON'T DRINK THE WATER
DON'T GIVE UP THE SHIP
DON'T RAISE THE BRIDGE, LOWER THE RIVER
DOOR TO DOOR
DOWN AND OUT IN BEVERLY HILLS
DRAGNET (1987)
DR. STRANGELOVE OR: HOW I LEARNED TO STOP
  WORRYING AND LOVE THE BOMB
DUCHESS AND THE DIRTWATER FOX, THE
DUCK SOUP
EASY LIVING (1937)
EASY MONEY
EATING RAOUL
EAT THE RICH
ECHO PARK
EDDIE MURPHY RAW
EGG AND I, THE
18 AGAIN
11 HARROWHOUSE
ELVIRA, MISTRESS OF THE DARK
END, THE
ENSIGN PULVER
ERNEST GOES TO CAMP
ERNEST SAVES CHRISTMAS
ERRAND BOY, THE
EVERY WHICH WAY BUT LOOSE
FAMILY JEWELS, THE
FANCY PANTS
FANDANGO
FARMER'S DAUGHTER, THE
FAR NORTH
FAST BREAK
FATHER GOOSE
FATHER OF THE BRIDE
FATHER'S LITTLE DIVIDEND
FATSO
FEARLESS VAMPIRE KILLERS, THE, OR PARDON ME, BUT
  YOUR TEETH ARE IN MY NECK
FEDS
FERRIS BUELLER'S DAY OFF
FIENDISH PLOT OF DR. FU MANCHU, THE
FINDERS KEEPERS
FINE MADNESS, A
FINE MESS, A
FINIAN'S RAINBOW
FIREMAN'S BALL, THE
FIRST FAMILY
FIRST MONDAY IN OCTOBER
FIRST NUDIE MUSICAL, THE

FIRST TIME, THE
FISH CALLED WANDA, A
FISH THAT SAVED PITTSBURGH, THE
FLAMINGO KID, THE
FLETCH
FLIM FLAM MAN, THE
FM
FOOLIN' AROUND
FOREIGN AFFAIR, A
FOREIGN BODY
FOREVER, LULU
FOR KEEPS?
FOR LOVE OF IVY
FOR PETE'S SAKE
FOR THE LOVE OF BENJI
FORTUNE, THE
FORTUNE COOKIE, THE
FORTY CARATS
FOUL PLAY
FOUR SEASONS, THE
FRANCIS
FRATERNITY VACATION
FREAKY FRIDAY
FREEBIE AND THE BEAN
FRENCH POSTCARDS
FRISCO KID, THE
FROM THE HIP
FRONT PAGE, THE (1931)
FRONT PAGE, THE (1974)
FULLER BRUSH MAN, THE
FULL MOON HIGH
FULL MOON IN PARIS
FUNNY FARM, THE
FUNNY FARM
FUNNY MONEY
FUNNY THING HAPPENED ON THE WAY ON THE WAY TO
   THE FORUM, A
FUN WITH DICK AND JANE
GABRIELA
GALAXINA
GANG THAT COULDN'T SHOOT STRAIGHT, THE
GARBO TALKS
GAS
GAS-S-S-S!
GENERAL, THE
GENEVIEVE
GEORGY GIRL
GET CRAZY
GET OUT YOUR HANDKERCHIEFS
GET TO KNOW YOUR RABBIT
GHOSTBUSTERS
GHOST FEVER
GHOST GOES WEST, THE
GIDGET
GIDGET GOES HAWAIIAN
GIDGET GOES TO ROME
GIFT, THE
GIG, THE
GILDA LIVE
GIRL CAN'T HELP IT, THE
GIRLFRIENDS
GIRL FROM PETROVKA, THE
GIRL IN EVERY PORT, A
GIRL IN THE PICTURE, THE
GNOME-MOBILE, THE
GODS MUST BE CRAZY, THE
GOIN' ALL THE WAY
GOING BANANAS
GOING IN STYLE
GOING PLACES
GOIN' SOUTH
GOLD RUSH, THE
GOODBYE, COLUMBUS
GOODBYE GIRL, THE
GOODBYE, NEW YORK
GOOD MORNING, VIETNAM
GOOD NEIGHBOR SAM
GORP
GOSPEL ACCORDING TO VIC
GOTCHA!
GO WEST
GRACE QUIGLEY
GRADUATE, THE
GRASS IS GREENER, THE

GREAT DICTATOR, THE
GREAT LOVER, THE
GREAT McGINTY, THE
GREAT MUPPET CAPER, THE
GREAT OUTDOORS, THE
GREAT RACE, THE
GREAT SCOUT AND CATHOUSE THURSDAY, THE
GREAT WALL, A
GREGORY'S GIRL
GREMLINS
GROOVE TUBE, THE
GUIDE FOR THE MARRIED MAN, A
GUMSHOE
GUNG HO
GUS
HAIL THE CONQUERING HERO
HAIRSPRAY
HAMBURGER . . . THE MOTION PICTURE
HANDLE WITH CARE
HANKY PANKY
HANNAH AND HER SISTERS
HAPPY HOOKER, THE
HAPPY NEW YEAR (1973)
HAPPY NEW YEAR (1987)
HARDBODIES
HARDBODIES 2
HARD DAY'S NIGHT, A
HARDLY WORKING
HARD ROCK ZOMBIES
HAROLD AND MAUDE
HARPER VALLEY P.T.A.
HARRY AND THE HENDERSONS
HARRY AND TONTO
HARRY AND WALTER GO TO NEW YORK
HARVEY
HAUNTED HONEYMOON
HEAD
HEAD OFFICE
HEARTBREAK HOTEL
HEARTBREAK KID, THE
HEARTBURN
HEARTS OF THE WEST
HEATHERS
HEAT OF DESIRE
HEAVEN CAN WAIT (1943)
HEAVEN CAN WAIT (1978)
HEAVEN HELP US
HEAVENLY KID, THE
HEAVENS ABOVE!
HELLO AGAIN
HELP!
HER ALIBI
HERBIE RIDES AGAIN
HERE COMES MR. JORDAN
HERE COME THE TIGERS
HERO AT LARGE
HEROES
HE'S MY GIRL
HIDING OUT
HIGH ANXIETY
HIGH SEASON
HIGH SPIRITS
HIS GIRL FRIDAY
HISTORY OF THE WORLD—PART I
HOBSON'S CHOICE
HOLD THAT GHOST
HOLIDAY
HOLLYWOOD BOULEVARD
HOLLYWOOD HIGH
HOLLYWOOD HIGH II
HOLLYWOOD HOT TUBS
HOLLYWOOD OR BUST
HOLLYWOOD SHUFFLE
HOMEWORK
HONKY TONK FREEWAY
HOPSCOTCH
HORSE FEATHERS
HORSE IN THE GRAY FLANNEL SUIT, THE
HOSPITAL, THE
HOT DOG . . . THE MOVIE
HOTEL NEW HAMPSHIRE, THE
HOT LEAD AND COLD FEET
HOT MOVES
HOT PURSUIT

HOT RESORT
HOT ROCK, THE
HOT STUFF
HOT TO TROT
HOT T-SHIRTS
HOUSEBOAT
HOUSE CALLS
HOW I WON THE WAR
HOW TO BEAT THE HIGH COST OF LIVING
HOW TO MARRY A MILLIONAIRE
HOW TO STEAL A MILLION
HOW TO STUFF A WILD BIKINI
HUNK
IDIOT'S DELIGHT
ILLEGALLY YOURS
I LOVE MY WIFE
I LOVE YOU, ALICE B. TOKLAS
I'M ALL RIGHT, JACK
I MARRIED A WITCH
I'M GONNA GIT YOU SUCKA
IMPORTANCE OF BEING EARNEST, THE
IMPROPER CHANNELS
INCREDIBLE SHRINKING WOMAN, THE
IN-LAWS, THE
INNERSPACE
INSPECTOR GENERAL, THE
INTERNATIONAL HOUSE
INVISIBLE KID, THE
INVITATION TO A WEDDING
I OUGHT TO BE IN PICTURES
IRMA LA DOUCE
IRRECONCILABLE DIFFERENCES
I SAILED TO TAHITI WITH AN ALL-GIRL CREW
ISHTAR
IT CAME FROM HOLLYWOOD
IT HAPPENED ONE NIGHT
IT'S A GIFT
IT'S A MAD, MAD, MAD, MAD WORLD
IT SHOULD HAPPEN TO YOU
IT'S MY TURN
IT TAKES TWO
I WANNA HOLD YOUR HAND
I WILL, I WILL . . . FOR NOW
I WONDER WHO'S KILLING HER NOW
JABBERWOCKY
JEKYLL AND HYDE . . . TOGETHER AGAIN
JERK, THE
JINXED!
JOCKS
JOHNNY BE GOOD
JOHNNY DANGEROUSLY
JO JO DANCER, YOUR LIFE IS CALLING
JOSEPH ANDREWS
JOSHUA THEN AND NOW
JOY OF SEX
JOYSTICKS
JUDGE PRIEST
JUMPIN' JACK FLASH
JUST ONE OF THE GUYS
JUST TELL ME WHAT YOU WANT
KENTUCKY FRIED MOVIE, THE
KEY EXCHANGE
KID, THE
KIDCO
KID FROM BROOKLYN, THE
KIND HEARTS AND CORONETS
KING OF COMEDY, THE
KING OF HEARTS
KISS ME GOODBYE
KNOCK ON WOOD
KOTCH
LA CAGE AUX FOLLES
LA CAGE AUX FOLLES II
LA CAGE AUX FOLLES 3: THE WEDDING
LADY EVE, THE
LADYKILLERS, THE
LADY ON THE BUS
LAST AMERICAN VIRGIN, THE
LAST MARRIED COUPLE IN AMERICA, THE
LAST OF THE RED HOT LOVERS
LAST REMAKE OF BEAU GESTE, THE
LAST RESORT
LAVENDER HILL MOB, THE
LEADER OF THE BAND

LEAGUE OF GENTLEMEN, THE
LEMON DROP KID, THE
LEONARD PART VI
LES COMPERES
LET'S DO IT AGAIN
LET'S MAKE LOVE
LIBELED LADY
LICENSE TO DRIVE
LIFE WITH FATHER
LIKE FATHER LIKE SON
LILY IN LOVE
LIMELIGHT
LITTLE DARLINGS
LITTLE MISS MARKER
LITTLE ROMANCE, A
LITTLE SEX, A
LITTLE SHOP OF HORRORS, THE
LITTLEST HORSE THIEVES, THE
LOCAL HERO
LOLITA
LONELY GUY, THE
LONGEST YARD, THE
LONG GONE
LONGSHOT, THE
LOOSE SCREWS
LOOSE SHOES
LOSIN' IT
LOST AND FOUND
LOST EMPIRE, THE
LOST IN AMERICA
LOVE AND DEATH
LOVE AT FIRST BITE
LOVE AT STAKE
LOVE IN THE AFTERNOON
LOVELINES
LOVE OR MONEY
LOVER COME BACK
LOVERS AND LIARS
LOVERS AND OTHER STRANGERS
LOVESICK
LOVING COUPLES
LUCAS
LUCKY JIM
LUNCH WAGON GIRLS
LUST IN THE DUST
LUV
MACARONI
MAGIC CHRISTIAN, THE
MAID TO ORDER
MAIN EVENT, THE
MAJOR BARBARA
MAKING MR. RIGHT
MAKING THE GRADE
MALCOLM
MALIBU BIKINI SHOP, THE
MAN, A WOMAN AND A BANK, A
MANHATTAN
MAN IN THE WHITE SUIT, THE
MANNEQUIN
MAN'S FAVORITE SPORT?
MAN WHO LOVED WOMEN, THE (1977)
MAN WHO LOVED WOMEN, THE (1983)
MAN WITH BOGART'S FACE, THE
MAN WITH ONE RED SHOE, THE
MAN WITH TWO BRAINS, THE
MARRIED TO THE MOB
M*A*S*H
M*A*S*H: GOODBYE, FAREWELL & AMEN
MASS APPEAL
MAX DUGAN RETURNS
MAXIE
MEATBALLS
MEATBALLS PART II
MEATBALLS III
MELVIN AND HOWARD
MEMORIES OF ME
MEN
MICKI & MAUDE
MIDNIGHT MADNESS
MIDSUMMER NIGHT'S DREAM, A
MIDSUMMER NIGHT'S SEX COMEDY, A
MILLION DOLLAR MYSTERY
MIRACLE OF MORGAN'S CREEK, THE
MIRACLE ON 34TH STREET

MIRACLES
MISCHIEF
MISSIONARY, THE
MISTER ROBERTS
MODEL BEHAVIOR
MODERN PROBLEMS
MODERN ROMANCE
MODERN TIMES
MONEY PIT, THE
MONKEY BUSINESS (1931)
MONKEY BUSINESS (1952)
MON ONCLE
MONSIEUR VERDOUX
MONSTER IN THE CLOSET
MONSTER SQUAD, THE
MONTENEGRO
MONTY PYTHON AND THE HOLY GRAIL
MONTY PYTHON LIVE AT THE HOLLYWOOD BOWL
MONTY PYTHON'S LIFE OF BRIAN
MONTY PYTHON'S THE MEANING OF LIFE
MOON IS BLUE, THE
MOON OVER PARADOR
MOONSTRUCK
MORE THE MERRIER, THE
MORGAN: A SUITABLE CASE FOR TREATMENT
MORGAN STEWART'S COMING HOME
MORONS FROM OUTER SPACE
MOSCOW ON THE HUDSON
MOUSE THAT ROARED, THE
MOVE OVER, DARLING
MOVERS & SHAKERS
MOVIE MOVIE
MOVING
MOVING VIOLATIONS
MR. & MRS. SMITH
MR. BLANDINGS BUILDS HIS DREAM HOUSE
MR. DEEDS GOES TO TOWN
MR. HOBBS TAKES A VACATION
MR. HULOT'S HOLIDAY
MR. LOVE
MR. LUCKY
MR. MOM
MR. NICE GUY
MR. NORTH
MR. PEABODY AND THE MERMAID
MUGSY'S GIRLS
MUNCHIES
MUPPET MOVIE, THE
MUPPETS TAKE MANHATTAN, THE
MURDER BY DEATH
MURPHY'S ROMANCE
MUSCLE BEACH PARTY
MY BEAUTIFUL LAUNDRETTE
MY BEST FRIEND IS A VAMPIRE
MY BODYGUARD
MY CHAUFFEUR
MY DEMON LOVER
MY FAVORITE BRUNETTE
MY FAVORITE WIFE
MY FAVORITE YEAR
MY LIFE AS A DOG
MY LITTLE CHICKADEE
MY MAN ADAM
MY MAN GODFREY
MYRA BRECKENRIDGE
MY SCIENCE PROJECT
MY STEPMOTHER IS AN ALIEN
MY TUTOR
NADINE
NAKED GUN, THE: FROM THE FILES OF POLICE SQUAD
NASHVILLE
NASTY HABITS
NATIONAL LAMPOON'S CLASS REUNION
NATIONAL LAMPOON'S EUROPEAN VACATION
NATIONAL LAMPOON'S VACATION
NAVIGATOR, THE
NEIGHBORS
NETWORK
NEVER GIVE A SUCKER AN EVEN BREAK
NEVER ON SUNDAY
NEW LEAF, A
NEW LIFE, A
NEW YORK STORIES
NEXT STOP, GREENWICH VILLAGE

NICE GIRLS DON'T EXPLODE
NIGHT AT THE OPERA, A
NIGHT BEFORE, THE
NIGHT IN CASABLANCA, A
NIGHT IN THE LIFE OF JIMMY REARDON, A
NIGHT OF THE CREEPS
NIGHT PATROL
NIGHT SHIFT
NIGHT THEY RAIDED MINSKY'S, THE
1941
NINE TO FIVE
90 DAYS
99 AND 44/100% DEAD
NINOTCHKA
NOBODY'S FOOL
NOBODY'S PERFEKT
NO DEPOSIT, NO RETURN
NORTH DALLAS FORTY
NO SMALL AFFAIR
NOT FOR PUBLICATION
NOTHING IN COMMON
NOTHING SACRED
NO TIME FOR SERGEANTS
NUTTY PROFESSOR, THE
O.C. AND STIGGS
OCEAN'S ELEVEN
ODD COUPLE, THE
ODD JOBS
OFF BEAT
OFF LIMITS (1953)
OH, GOD!
OH, GOD! BOOK II
OH, GOD! YOU DEVIL
OH HEAVENLY DOG!
OLD ENOUGH
ONCE BITTEN
ONCE UPON A HONEYMOON
ONE AND ONLY, THE
ONE CRAZY SUMMER
ONE FLEW OVER THE CUCKOO'S NEST
ONE FROM THE HEART
ONE MORE SATURDAY NIGHT
ONE OF OUR DINOSAURS IS MISSING
ONE, TWO, THREE
ONE WOMAN OR TWO
ONLY WHEN I LAUGH
ON THE RIGHT TRACK
OPERATION PETTICOAT
OUR MAN FLINT
OUT COLD
OUT OF TOWNERS, THE
OUTRAGEOUS!
OUTRAGEOUS FORTUNE
OVERBOARD
OVER THE BROOKLYN BRIDGE
OWL AND THE PUSSYCAT, THE
OXFORD BLUES
PALEFACE, THE
PALM BEACH STORY, THE
PANDEMONIUM
PAPA'S DELICATE CONDITION
PAPER MOON
PARADISE MOTEL
PARAMEDICS
PARENT TRAP, THE
PARIS WHEN IT SIZZLES
PARTNERS
PARTY CAMP
PASSPORT TO PIMLICO
PASS THE AMMO
PAT AND MIKE
PATERNITY
PATTI ROCKS
PAULINE AT THE BEACH
PEE-WEE'S BIG ADVENTURE
PEOPLE WILL TALK
PERSONALS, THE
PERSONAL SERVICES
PHILADELPHIA STORY, THE
PICK-UP ARTIST, THE
PIECE OF THE ACTION, A
PILLOW TALK
PINK FLAMINGOS
PINK PANTHER, THE

PINK PANTHER STRIKES AGAIN, THE
PIRATES
PLANES, TRAINS & AUTOMOBILES
PLAYING FOR KEEPS
PLAY IT AGAIN, SAM
PLAZA SUITE
POCKETFUL OF MIRACLES
POCKET MONEY
POLICE ACADEMY
POLICE ACADEMY 2: THEIR FIRST ASSIGNMENT
POLICE ACADEMY 3: BACK IN TRAINING
POLICE ACADEMY 4: CITIZENS ON PATROL
POLICE ACADEMY 5: ASSIGNMENT MIAMI BEACH
POLICE SQUAD! HELP WANTED
POLYESTER
POM POM GIRLS, THE
PORKY'S
PORKY'S II: THE NEXT DAY
PORKY'S REVENGE
POT O' GOLD
PREPPIES
PRESIDENT'S ANALYST, THE
PRETTY IN PINK
PRETTY SMART
PRIDE AND PREJUDICE
PRINCE AND THE SHOWGIRL, THE
PRINCESS ACADEMY, THE
PRINCESS AND THE PIRATE, THE
PRINCESS BRIDE, THE
PRISONER OF SECOND AVENUE, THE
PRISONER OF ZENDA, THE (1979)
PRIVATE BENJAMIN
PRIVATE EYES, THE
PRIVATE FUNCTION, A
PRIVATE LESSONS
PRIVATE RESORT
PRIVATE SCHOOL
PRIVATES ON PARADE
PRIZE FIGHTER, THE
PRIZZI'S HONOR
PRODUCERS, THE
PROTOCOL
PUBERTY BLUES
PURPLE ROSE OF CAIRO, THE
PUTNEY SWOPE
PYGMALION
QUACKSER FORTUNE HAS A COUSIN IN THE BRONX
QUARTET
RABBIT TEST
RADIO DAYS
RAFFERTY AND THE GOLD DUST TWINS
RAINMAKER, THE
RAISING ARIZONA
RANCHO DELUXE
REAL GENIUS
REAL LIFE
REAL MEN
RECRUITS
REIVERS, THE
RENTED LIPS
REPO MAN
RETURN OF THE LIVING DEAD, THE
RETURN OF THE LIVING DEAD II, THE
RETURN OF THE PINK PANTHER, THE
RETURN OF THE SECAUCUS 7
REUBEN, REUBEN
REVENGE OF THE NERDS
REVENGE OF THE NERDS II: NERDS IN PARADISE
REVENGE OF THE PINK PANTHER
RHINESTONE
RICHARD PRYOR HERE AND NOW
RICHARD PRYOR—LIVE IN CONCERT
RICHARD PRYOR LIVE ON THE SUNSET STRIP
RIDERS ON THE STORM
RIKKY AND PETE
RISKY BUSINESS
RITA, SUE AND BOB TOO
RITZ, THE
ROAD TO RIO
ROAD TO UTOPIA
ROCKIN' ROAD TRIP
ROLLER BOOGIE
ROMANTIC COMEDY
ROOM SERVICE

ROSEBUD BEACH HOTEL, THE
ROXANNE
ROYAL FLASH
RUGGLES OF RED GAP
RULES OF THE GAME
RULING CLASS, THE
RUSSIANS ARE COMING, THE RUSSIANS ARE COMING,
  THE
RUSTLERS' RHAPSODY
RUTHLESS PEOPLE
SABRINA
SAD SACK, THE
SAFETY LAST
SALTY
SALVATION!
SAME TIME, NEXT YEAR
SAMMY AND ROSIE GET LAID
SATURDAY THE 14TH
SAY YES
SCANDALOUS
SCAVENGER HUNT
SCHLOCK
SCHOOL DAZE
SCREEN TEST
SCREWBALL ACADEMY
SCREWBALLS
SCROOGED
SECOND THOUGHTS
SECRET ADMIRER
SECRET DIARY OF SIGMUND FREUD, THE
SECRET LIFE OF AN AMERICAN WIFE, THE
SECRET LIFE OF WALTER MITTY, THE
SECRET OF MY SUCCESS, THE
SECRET WAR OF HARRY FRIGG, THE
SEDUCTION OF MIMI, THE
SEEMS LIKE OLD TIMES
SEMI-TOUGH
SENATOR WAS INDISCREET, THE
SEND ME NO FLOWERS
SENIORS
SEPARATE VACATIONS
SERIAL
SEVEN BEAUTIES
SEVEN MINUTES IN HEAVEN
SEVEN YEAR ITCH, THE
SEXTETTE
SHADEY
SHAG
SHAGGY D.A., THE
SHAGGY DOG, THE
SHAMPOO
SHE DONE HIM WRONG
SHEILA LEVINE IS DEAD AND LIVING IN NEW YORK
SHE'S GOTTA HAVE IT
SHE'S HAVING A BABY
SHOP AROUND THE CORNER, THE
SHORT CIRCUIT
SHORT CIRCUIT II
SHOT IN THE DARK, A
SIDEWALKS OF LONDON
SILENT MOVIE
SILVER STREAK
SIMON
SIN OF HAROLD DIDDLEBOCK, THE
SIX PACK
SIXTEEN CANDLES
SKIN DEEP
SKIN GAME
SLAMMER GIRLS
SLAP SHOT
SLAPSTICK OF ANOTHER KIND
SLEEPER
SLUGGER'S WIFE, THE
SLUMBER PARTY '57
SMALL CHANGE
SMILE
SMILES OF A SUMMER NIGHT
SMOKEY AND THE BANDIT
SMOKEY AND THE BANDIT II
SMOKEY AND THE BANDIT—PART 3
SMOKEY BITES THE DUST
SNOWBALL EXPRESS, THE
S.O.B.
SO FINE

SOGGY BOTTOM, U.S.A.
SOME GIRLS
SOME KIND OF HERO
SOME KIND OF WONDERFUL
SOME LIKE IT HOT
SOMETHING FOR EVERYONE
SOMETHING SHORT OF PARADISE
SOMETHING SPECIAL
SOMETHING WILD
SONGWRITER
SON OF PALEFACE
SONS OF THE DESERT
SORROWFUL JONES
SOUL MAN
SOUP FOR ONE
SPACEBALLS
SPIES LIKE US
SPIKE OF BENSONHURST
SPLASH
SPLITZ
SPRING BREAK
SPRING FEVER
SQUEEZE, THE
SQUEEZE PLAY
STAKEOUT
STALAG 17
STARDUST MEMORIES
STARS AND BARS
STARSTRUCK
STARTING OVER
START THE REVOLUTION WITHOUT ME
STAY HUNGRY
STEAMBOAT BILL, JR.
STEELYARD BLUES
ST. ELMO'S FIRE
STERILE CUCKOO, THE
STEWARDESS SCHOOL
STICKY FINGERS
STILL SMOKIN'
STING, THE
STING II, THE
STIR CRAZY
STITCHES
STOOGEMANIA
STRAIGHT TO HELL
STRANGE BREW
STRANGER THAN PARADISE
STRAWBERRY BLONDE, THE
STRIPES
STROKER ACE
STUCK ON YOU
STUDENT AFFAIRS
STUDENT BODIES
STUFF, THE
SUGARBABY
SULLIVAN'S TRAVELS
SUMMER RENTAL
SUMMER SCHOOL
SUMMER SCHOOL TEACHERS
SUNBURN
SUNSHINE BOYS, THE
SUPER FUZZ
SUPPORT YOUR LOCAL SHERIFF!
SURE THING, THE
SURF NAZIS MUST DIE
SURF II
SURRENDER
SURVIVORS, THE
SWEET LIBERTY
SWEET LIES
SWEPT AWAY . . .
SWINGING CHEERLEADERS, THE
SWITCHING CHANNELS
T.A.G.: THE ASSASSINATION GAME
TAKE THE MONEY AND RUN
TAKE THIS JOB AND SHOVE IT
TALK OF THE TOWN, THE
TALL BLOND MAN WITH ONE BLACK SHOE, THE
TAMING OF THE SHREW, THE
TAMMY AND THE BACHELOR
TAMMY AND THE DOCTOR
TAMPOPO
TANK
TAPEHEADS

TEACHERS
TEACHER'S PET
TEEN WOLF
TEEN WOLF TOO
TEMPEST
10
TEN FROM YOUR SHOW OF SHOWS
TERMS OF ENDEARMENT
THANK GOD IT'S FRIDAY
THAT OBSCURE OBJECT OF DESIRE
THAT'S LIFE!
THAT TOUCH OF MINK
THEATRE OF BLOOD
THERE'S A GIRL IN MY SOUP
THERE WAS A CROOKED MAN . . .
THEY ALL LAUGHED
THEY CALL ME BRUCE
THEY GOT ME COVERED
THEY MIGHT BE GIANTS
THIEF WHO CAME TO DINNER, THE
THINGS ARE TOUGH ALL OVER
THINGS CHANGE
THING WITH TWO HEADS, THE
30 FOOT BRIDE OF CANDY ROCK, THE
30 IS A DANGEROUS AGE, CYNTHIA
THIS IS SPINAL TAP
THOSE MAGNIFICENT MEN IN THEIR FLYING MACHINES
THOUSAND CLOWNS, A
THREE AMIGOS!
THREE FOR THE ROAD
THREE FUGITIVES
THREE IN THE ATTIC
THREE MEN AND A CRADLE
THREE MEN AND A BABY
THREE O'CLOCK HIGH
THREE STOOGES MEET HERCULES, THE
THRILL OF IT ALL, THE
THROW MOMMA FROM THE TRAIN
THUNDER AND LIGHTNING
TIGERS IN LIPSTICK
TIGER'S TALE, A
TILL MARRIAGE DO US PART
TIME BANDITS
TIN MEN
TO BE OR NOT TO BE (1942)
TO BE OR NOT TO BE (1983)
TOMBOY
TOM JONES
TOOTSIE
TOPKAPI
TOPPER
TOP SECRET
TORCH SONG TRILOGY
TOUCH OF CLASS, A
TOUGH GUYS
TOXIC AVENGER, THE
TOY, THE
TRADING PLACES
TRAIL OF THE PINK PANTHER
TRANSYLVANIA 6-5000
TRAXX
TRENCHCOAT
TRIBUTE
TRICK OR TREATS
TROUBLE IN PARADISE
TROUBLE WITH ANGELS, THE
TROUBLE WITH DICK, THE
TROUBLE WITH HARRY, THE
TROUBLE WITH SPIES, THE
TRUE STORIES
TUNNELVISION
TWELVE CHAIRS, THE
TWENTIETH CENTURY
TWINS
UGLY DACHSHUND, THE
UNDERACHIEVERS, THE
UNDER THE RAINBOW
UNFAITHFULLY YOURS (1948)
UNFAITHFULLY YOURS (1984)
UNIDENTIFIED FLYING ODDBALL, THE
UPHILL ALL THE WAY
UP IN SMOKE
UP THE ACADEMY
UP THE CREEK

UP THE SANDBOX
UPTOWN SATURDAY NIGHT
USED CARS
VALET GIRLS
VALLEY GIRL
VALS, THE
VERY CLOSE QUARTERS
VIBES
VICE VERSA
VICTOR/VICTORIA
VILLAIN, THE
VIRGIN QUEEN OF ST. FRANCIS HIGH, THE
VIVACIOUS LADY
VOLUNTEERS
VOYAGE OF THE ROCK ALIENS
WACKIEST SHIP IN THE ARMY, THE
WACKO
WAITRESS!
WALK, DON'T RUN
WALK LIKE A MAN
WALTZ OF THE TOREADORS
WATER
WATERMELON MAN
WAY OUT WEST
WEDDING, A
WEDDING PARTY, THE
WEEKEND PASS
WEEKEND WARRIORS
WEIRD SCIENCE
WELCOME TO 18
WE'RE NO ANGELS
WHAT COMES AROUND
WHAT DO YOU SAY TO A NAKED LADY?
WHAT PRICE GLORY?
WHAT'S NEW, PUSSYCAT?
WHAT'S UP, DOC?
WHAT'S UP, TIGER LILY?
WHERE'S POPPA?
WHERE THE BOYS ARE
WHERE THE BOYS ARE '84
WHERE THE BUFFALO ROAM
WHICH WAY IS UP?
WHICH WAY TO THE FRONT?
WHISKY GALORE!
WHO FRAMED ROGER RABBIT
WHOLLY MOSES!
WHOOPEE BOYS, THE
WHO'S HARRY CRUMB?
WHO'S MINDING THE MINT?
WHO'S THAT GIRL
WICKED STEPMOTHER
WILDCATS
WILD LIFE, THE
WILLIE AND PHIL
WILL SUCCESS SPOIL ROCK HUNTER?
WIMPS
WINTER KILLS
WISE GUYS
WITCHES OF EASTWICK, THE
WITHNAIL AND I
WITH SIX YOU GET EGGROLL
WOMAN IN RED, THE
WOMAN OF DISTINCTION, A
WOMAN OF THE YEAR
WOMAN TIMES SEVEN
WOMEN, THE
WOMEN ON THE VERGE OF A NERVOUS
  BREAKDOWN
WOMEN'S CLUB, THE
WON TON TON, THE DOG WHO SAVED HOLLYWOOD
WORKING GIRL
WORLD ACCORDING TO GARP, THE
WORLD OF HENRY ORIENT, THE
WORLD'S GREATEST ATHLETE, THE
WORLD'S GREATEST LOVER, THE
WRONG BOX, THE
WRONG GUYS, THE
WRONG IS RIGHT
W.W. AND THE DIXIE DANCEKINGS
YELLOWBEARD
YOU CAN'T CHEAT AN HONEST MAN
YOU CAN'T HURRY LOVE
YOU CAN'T TAKE IT WITH YOU
YOUNG DOCTORS IN LOVE

YOUNG EINSTEIN
YOUNG FRANKENSTEIN
YOU'RE A BIG BOY NOW
ZAPPED!
ZELIG
ZOO GANG, THE
ZORRO, THE GAY BLADE

CRIME

AL CAPONE
ASPHALT JUNGLE, THE
BANK SHOT
BONNIE AND CLYDE
BOSTON STRANGLER, THE
CAPONE
CRISS CROSS
CROSSFIRE
D.I., THE
DILLINGER
DRAGNET (1954)
11 HARROWHOUSE
FBI STORY, THE
FRENCH CONNECTION, THE
FRENCH CONNECTION II, THE
GLITTER DOME, THE
GUARDIAN, THE
GUN CRAZY
HOT ROCK, THE
IN COLD BLOOD
KISS OF DEATH
LADY IN RED, THE
LAVENDER HILL MOB, THE
LEPKE
LITTLE CAESAR
LONG GOOD FRIDAY, THE
McVICAR
MURDER ONE
NAKED CITY, THE
NEW CENTURIONS, THE
ONCE UPON A TIME IN AMERICA
PUBLIC ENEMY
RACKET, THE
ROARING TWENTIES, THE
SCARFACE (1932)
SCARFACE (1983)
SERPICO
STRAIGHT TIME
ST. VALENTINE'S DAY MASSACRE, THE
THIEF
UNDERWORLD U.S.A.
VALACHI PAPERS, THE
WHITE HEAT

DANCE

CARMEN (1983)
DANCERS
DIRTY DANCING
FAST FORWARD
FLASHDANCE
INVITATION TO THE DANCE
ISADORA
NUTCRACKER: THE MOTION PICTURE
RED SHOES, THE
SALSA
SATURDAY NIGHT FEVER
STAYING ALIVE
TAP
THAT'S DANCING!
TURNING POINT, THE

DOCUMENTARY

ANIMALS ARE BEAUTIFUL PEOPLE
ATOMIC CAFE, THE
BEER DRINKER'S GUIDE TO FITNESS AND FILM MAKING,
  THE
BEST BOY
BETTE MIDLER: DIVINE MADNESS
BILL COSBY—"HIMSELF"
BRING ON THE NIGHT
BROKEN RAINBOW
BROTHER, CAN YOU SPARE A DIME?
CATASTROPHE
COMPLEAT BEATLES, THE
CONCERT FOR BANGLADESH, THE
DEAR AMERICA: LETTERS HOME FROM VIETNAM

DECLINE OF WESTERN CIVILIZATION, THE
DECLINE OF WESTERN CIVILIZATION PART II, THE: THE
  METAL YEARS
EDDIE MURPHY RAW
ELVIS: THAT'S THE WAY IT IS
FROM MAO TO MOZART: ISAAC STERN IN CHINA
GILDA LIVE
GIMME SHELTER
GIZMO!
GOSPEL
HAIL! HAIL! ROCK 'N' ROLL
HEARTS AND MINDS
HEAVEN
HELLSTROM CHRONICLE, THE
HOLLYWOOD GHOST STORIES
IMAGINE: JOHN LENNON
JANIS
JUST ANOTHER MISSING KID
KIDS ARE ALRIGHT, THE
KOYAANISQATSI
LAST WALTZ, THE
LET IT BE
LET'S SPEND THE NIGHT TOGETHER
LIVING DESERT, THE
MAN WHO SAW TOMORROW, THE
MARLENE
MONDO CANE
MONDO NEW YORK
MONTEREY POP
MONTY PYTHON LIVE AT THE HOLLYWOOD BOWL
OLYMPIA
POWAQQATSI
PUMPING IRON
PUMPING IRON II: THE WOMEN
RICHARD PRYOR HERE AND NOW
RICHARD PRYOR—LIVE IN CONCERT
RICHARD PRYOR LIVE ON THE SUNSET STRIP
SAY AMEN, SOMEBODY
SECRET POLICEMAN'S OTHER BALL, THE
SIGN O' THE TIMES
SORROW AND THE PITY, THE
STOP MAKING SENSE
STREETWISE
STRIPPER
SWIMMING TO CAMBODIA
THIN BLUE LINE, THE
THIS IS ELVIS
TIMES OF HARVEY MILK, THE
TOKYO OLYMPIAD
TRIUMPH OF THE WILL
U2: RATTLE AND HUM
VANISHING WILDERNESS
VOICES OF SARAFINA!
WOODSTOCK

DRAMA

ABOUT LAST NIGHT
ABSENCE OF MALICE
ACCIDENT
ACCIDENTAL TOURIST, THE
ACCUSED, THE
ADAM
ADVISE AND CONSENT
AGATHA
AGNES OF GOD
ALAMO BAY
ALEX IN WONDERLAND
ALFIE
ALICE ADAMS
ALICE DOESN'T LIVE HERE ANYMORE
ALL ABOUT EVE
ALL MY SONS
ALLNIGHTER, THE
ALL THAT HEAVEN ALLOWS
ALL THAT JAZZ
. . . ALL THE MARBLES
ALL THE PRESIDENT'S MEN
ALL THE RIGHT MOVES
ALMOST ANGELS
ALOHA, BOBBY AND ROSE
ALOHA SUMMER
ALPHABET CITY
AMADEUS
AMARCORD

AMAZING GRACE AND CHUCK
AMERICAN ANTHEM
AMERICAN FLYERS
AMERICAN FRIEND, THE
AMERICAN GRAFFITI
AMY
ANATOMY OF A MURDER
. . . AND GOD CREATED WOMAN
AND GOD CREATED WOMAN
. . . AND JUSTICE FOR ALL
AND THE SHIP SAILS ON
ANGEL
ANGELO, MY LOVE
ANGELS OVER BROADWAY
ANGELS WITH DIRTY FACES
ANNA
ANNA AND THE KING OF SIAM
ANNA CHRISTIE
ANNA KARENINA
ANNE OF GREEN GABLES (1934)
ANNE OF GREEN GABLES (1985)
ANNE OF THE THOUSAND DAYS
ANOTHER COUNTRY
ANOTHER MAN, ANOTHER CHANCE
ANOTHER WOMAN
ANTHONY ADVERSE
ANTONY AND CLEOPATRA
APPRENTICE TO MURDER
ARCH OF TRIUMPH
ARRANGEMENT, THE
ASPHALT JUNGLE, THE
ASSAULT, THE
ASSISI UNDERGROUND, THE
AS SUMMERS DIE
AT CLOSE RANGE
ATLANTIC CITY
AU REVOIR, LES ENFANTS
AUTUMN LEAVES
AUTUMN SONATA
BABETTE'S FEAST
BABY DOLL
BABY, THE RAIN MUST FALL
BACHELOR PARTY, THE
BACK STREET
BAD AND THE BEAUTIFUL, THE
BAD BOYS
BAD DAY AT BLACK ROCK
BADGE 373
BADLANDS
BAD SEED, THE
BAD TIMING: A SENSUAL OBSESSION
BAJA OKLAHOMA
BALTIMORE BULLET, THE
BANG THE DRUM SLOWLY
BARABBAS
BARBARY COAST
BAREFOOT CONTESSA, THE
BARFLY
BARRY LYNDON
BATTLE OF ALGIERS, THE
BATTLESHIP POTEMKIN
BAY BOY, THE
BEACHES
BEAU PERE
BECKET
BEDFORD INCIDENT, THE
BEGUILED, THE
BEHOLD A PALE HORSE
BELIZAIRE THE CAJUN
BELLE DE JOUR
BELL JAR, THE
BELLMAN AND TRUE
BELLS OF ST. MARY'S, THE
BELOW THE BELT
BERLIN ALEXANDERPLATZ
BERLIN EXPRESS
BEST MAN, THE
BEST SELLER
BEST YEARS OF OUR LIVES, THE
BETRAYAL
BETRAYED
BETSY, THE
BETTY BLUE
BETWEEN FRIENDS

BEYOND THE FOREST
BEYOND THE LIMIT
BEYOND THE VALLEY OF THE DOLLS
BIBLE, THE
BICYCLE THIEF, THE
BIG CARNIVAL, THE
BIG CHILL, THE
BIG COMBO, THE
BIG MO
BIG STREET, THE
BIG TOWN, THE
BIG WEDNESDAY
BILLY BUDD
BILLY GALVIN
BINGO LONG TRAVELING ALL-STARS AND MOTOR
  KINGS, THE
BIRCH INTERVAL
BIRDY
BITCH, THE
BITTERSWEET LOVE
BLACKBOARD JUNGLE, THE
BLACK FURY
BLACK LEGION
BLACK LIKE ME
BLACK MAGIC
BLACK MARBLE, THE
BLACK NARCISSUS
BLACK ORPHEUS
BLAME IT ON THE NIGHT
BLESS THE BEASTS AND CHILDREN
BLONDE VENUS
BLOOD AND SAND
BLOODBROTHERS
BLOOD FEUD
BLOOD OF OTHERS, THE
BLUE ANGEL, THE
BLUEBEARD
BLUEBERRY HILL
BLUE COLLAR
BLUE LAGOON, THE
BOBBY DEERFIELD
BOB LE FLAMBEUR
BODY AND SOUL (1947)
BODY AND SOUL (1981)
BOLERO
BONJOUR TRISTESSE
BOOM!
BOOMERANG
BOOST, THE
BORDER, THE
BORN FREE
BORN TO KILL
BORN TO RACE
BOSTONIANS, THE
BOUNTY, THE
BOXCAR BERTHA
BOY IN BLUE, THE
BOY ON A DOLPHIN
BOYS IN THE BAND, THE
BOYS NEXT DOOR, THE
BOYS TOWN
BOY WITH GREEN HAIR, THE
BREAKER MORANT
BREAKFAST CLUB, THE
BREAK OF HEARTS
BREATHLESS (1961)
BREATHLESS (1983)
BRIDGE OF SAN LUIS REY, THE
BRIDGE ON THE RIVER KWAI, THE
BRIGHT LIGHTS, BIG CITY
BRIMSTONE AND TREACLE
BROADCAST NEWS
BROTHERHOOD, THE
BROTHER JOHN
BROTHERS KARAMAZOV, THE
BROTHER SUN, SISTER MOON
BROWNING VERSION, THE
BRUBAKER
BULLFIGHTER AND THE LADY
BURN!
BURNING BED, THE
BURNING SECRET
BUSINESS AS USUAL
BUS RILEY'S BACK IN TOWN

BUTTERFIELD 8
BUTTERFLIES ARE FREE
BUTTERFLY
BY DESIGN
CABOBLANCO
CADDIE
CAESAR AND CLEOPATRA
CAINE MUTINY, THE
CAL
CALIFORNIA SPLIT
CALIGULA
CAMILLE
CANDIDATE, THE
CANDLESHOE
CANNERY ROW
CAPE FEAR
CAPTAIN NEWMAN, M.D.
CAPTAINS COURAGEOUS
CAPTIVE
CAPTIVE HEARTS
CARDINAL, THE
CAREFUL, HE MIGHT HEAR YOU
CARNAL KNOWLEDGE
CARNY
CARPETBAGGERS, THE
CASABLANCA
CASTAWAY
CAT ON A HOT TIN ROOF
CEASE FIRE
CHALK GARDEN, THE
CHAMP, THE
CHAMPION
CHANGE OF HABIT
CHAN IS MISSING
CHAPTER TWO
CHARIOTS OF FIRE
CHARLY
CHASE, THE
CHEERS FOR MISS BISHOP
CHILDREN OF A LESSER GOD
CHILDREN OF PARADISE
CHILLY SCENES OF WINTER
CHINA GIRL
CHINA SEAS
CHINA SYNDROME, THE
CHINATOWN
CHOCOLATE WAR, THE
CHOOSE ME
CHOSEN, THE (1982)
CHRISTMAS CAROL, A
CINCINNATI KID, THE
CINDERELLA LIBERTY
CIRCLE OF POWER
CIRCLE OF TWO
CIRCUS WORLD
CITADEL, THE
CITIZEN KANE
CITY GIRL, THE
CLARA'S HEART
CLASH BY NIGHT
CLASS
CLASS OF '44
CLAUDINE
CLEAN AND SOBER
CLEOPATRA
CLOCKWORK ORANGE, A
CLOSE TO MY HEART
CLOUD DANCER
CLOWN, THE
COCKTAIL
COLDITZ STORY, THE
COLOR OF MONEY, THE
COLOR PURPLE, THE
COME AND GET IT
COME BACK, LITTLE SHEBA
COME BACK TO THE FIVE AND DIME, JIMMY DEAN,
  JIMMY DEAN
COMES A HORSEMAN
COMING HOME
COMPETITION, THE
COMPULSION
CONFORMIST, THE
CONRACK
CONSPIRACY: THE TRIAL OF THE CHICAGO 8

CONTEMPT
CONTROL
CONVERSATION, THE
CONVERSATION PIECE
COOL HAND LUKE
CORNBREAD, EARL AND ME
CORN IS GREEN, THE
CORRUPT
COTTON CLUB, THE
COUNTRY
COUNTRY GIRL, THE
COUP DE TORCHON
COVERGIRL
CRAIG'S WIFE
CRAZY MOON
CRIES AND WHISPERS
CRIMES OF PASSION
CRIMES OF THE HEART
CROSS COUNTRY
CROSSOVER
CROSSOVER DREAMS
CROSSROADS
CRUISING
CRY FREEDOM
CRY IN THE DARK, A
CRYSTAL HEART
CRY, THE BELOVED COUNTRY
CUBA
CYRANO DE BERGERAC
DA
DAISY MILLER
DAMNED, THE
DANCERS
DANCE WITH A STRANGER
DANGEROUS
DANGEROUS LIAISONS
DANGEROUSLY CLOSE
DANGEROUS MOVES
DANIEL
DANTON
DARK EYES
DARK MIRROR, THE
DARK PAST, THE
DARK VICTORY
DARLING
DAS BOOT (THE BOAT)
DAVID AND LISA
DAVID COPPERFIELD
DAY AFTER, THE
DAY FOR NIGHT
DAY OF THE LOCUST, THE
DAYS OF HEAVEN
DAYS OF WINE AND ROSES
DEAD, THE
DEAD END
DEADLINE
DEADLINE U.S.A.
DEADLY AFFAIR, THE
DEAD RINGERS
DEATH IN VENICE
DEATH OF AN ANGEL
DEATH OF A SALESMAN (1951)
DEATH OF A SALESMAN (1985)
DEATH OF A SOLDIER
DEATHWATCH
DECEPTION
DECLINE OF THE AMERICAN EMPIRE, THE
DEER HUNTER, THE
DEJA VU
DERSU UZALA
DESERT BLOOM
DESERT HEARTS
DESIREE
DESIRE UNDER THE ELMS
DESPAIR
DESTRUCTORS, THE
DETECTIVE STORY
DETOUR
DEVIL IN THE FLESH
DEVILS, THE
DEVIL'S PLAYGROUND, THE
DIAMOND HEAD
DIARY OF A MAD HOUSEWIFE
DIFFERENT STORY, A

DINER
DISTANT THUNDER
DOBERMAN GANG, THE
DOCTORS' WIVES
DOCTOR ZHIVAGO
DODES'KA-DEN
DODSWORTH
DOG DAY AFTERNOON
DOMINICK AND EUGENE
DON IS DEAD, THE
DON'T CRY, IT'S ONLY THUNDER
DON'T LOOK NOW
DOUBLE LIFE, A
DOWN BY LAW
DOWNHILL RACER
DRAGON SEED
DREAMCHILD
DREAMER
DREAM LOVER
DRIVER'S SEAT, THE
DRUM
DRUMS ALONG THE MOHAWK
DUEL
DUELLISTS, THE
DUET FOR ONE
DUSTY
EARLY FROST, AN
EARTHLING, THE
EAST OF EDEN
EASY LIVING (1949)
EASY RIDER
ECHOES
ECHO PARK
EDDIE AND THE CRUISERS
EDUCATION OF SONNY CARSON, THE
EGYPTIAN, THE
8½
EIGHT MEN OUT
8 MILLION WAYS TO DIE
84 CHARING CROSS ROAD
ELECTRA GLIDE IN BLUE
ELECTRIC HORSEMAN, THE
ELENI
ELEPHANT BOY
ELEPHANT CALLED SLOWLY, AN
ELEPHANT MAN, THE
ELMER GANTRY
EL NORTE
EMIGRANTS, THE
EMPEROR JONES, THE
EMPIRE OF THE SUN
ENCORE
ENDANGERED SPECIES
END OF THE LINE
END OF THE ROAD
ENIGMA
ENTERTAINER, THE
ENTRE NOUS
EQUUS
ESCAPE ARTIST, THE
EUREKA
EVERYBODY'S ALL-AMERICAN
EXECUTIVE ACTION
EXODUS
EXPERIENCE PREFERRED . . . BUT NOT ESSENTIAL
EXTREMITIES
FACE IN THE CROWD, A
FAIL-SAFE
FAKE OUT
FALCON AND THE SNOWMAN, THE
FALLEN IDOL, THE
FALLING IN LOVE AGAIN
FALL OF THE ROMAN EMPIRE, THE
FAME
FANNY
FANNY AND ALEXANDER
FAREWELL TO THE KING
FAST FORWARD
FAST TIMES AT RIDGEMONT HIGH
FAST-WALKING
FATAL ATTRACTION
FAT CITY
FELLINI'S SATYRICON
FEVER PITCH

FIFTH FLOOR, THE
FINAL ASSIGNMENT
FINAL OPTION, THE
FINGERS
FINNEGAN BEGIN AGAIN
FIRE AND ICE (1987)
FIRE OVER ENGLAND
FIRE WITH FIRE
FIRSTBORN
FIRST MONDAY IN OCTOBER
F.I.S.T.
FIVE CORNERS
FIVE DAYS ONE SUMMER
FIVE EASY PIECES
FLANAGAN
FLASHDANCE
FLASH OF GREEN, A
FLIGHT OF THE EAGLE, THE
FOOL FOR LOVE
FOOTLOOSE
FORBIDDEN
FORBIDDEN GAMES
FORMULA, THE
FORT APACHE, THE BRONX
FORTRESS
FOUNTAINHEAD, THE
FOUR FRIENDS
FOUR HORSEMEN OF THE APOCALYPSE, THE
400 BLOWS, THE
FOUR SEASONS, THE
4TH MAN, THE
FOURTH PROTOCOL, THE
FOXES
FREEWAY
FRENCH LIEUTENANT'S WOMAN, THE
FRESH HORSES
FRIENDLY PERSUASION
FRIENDS OF EDDIE COYLE, THE
FROM HERE TO ETERNITY
FROM THE TERRACE
FRONT, THE
FUGITIVE, THE
FUGITIVE KIND, THE
FULL MOON IN BLUE WATER
FURY
GABY—A TRUE STORY
GAMBLER, THE
GARBO TALKS
GARDEN OF THE FINZI-CONTINIS, THE
GARDENS OF STONE
GATE OF HELL
GATHERING, THE
GATHERING OF EAGLES, A
GENTLEMAN'S AGREEMENT
GETTING OF WISDOM, THE
GIANT
GIG, THE
GILDA
GINGER AND FRED
GIRLFRIENDS
GIVE 'EM HELL, HARRY!
GLASS MENAGERIE, THE (1950)
GLASS MENAGERIE, THE (1973)
GLASS MENAGERIE, THE (1987)
GLEAMING THE CUBE
GLEN OR GLENDA
GO-BETWEEN, THE
GODDESS, THE
GODFATHER, THE
GODFATHER, PART II, THE
GODFATHER SAGA, THE
GOD'S LITTLE ACRE
GOING MY WAY
GOLDEN BOY
GOLDENGIRL
GONE WITH THE WIND
GOODBYE, MR. CHIPS
GOODBYE, NORMA JEAN
GOODBYE PEOPLE, THE
GOOD EARTH, THE
GOOD FATHER, THE
GOOD MORNING, BABYLON
GOOD MORNING, VIETNAM
GOOD MOTHER, THE

GOOD WIFE, THE
GOSPEL ACCORDING TO VIC
GOTHIC
GRAND HOTEL
GRAND ILLUSION
GRAND PRIX
GRANDVIEW, U.S.A.
GRAPES OF WRATH, THE
GREATEST SHOW ON EARTH, THE
GREATEST STORY EVER TOLD, THE
GREAT EXPECTATIONS
GREAT GATSBY, THE (1949)
GREAT GATSBY, THE (1974)
GREAT SANTINI, THE
GREAT TRAIN ROBBERY, THE
GREAT WALDO PEPPER, THE
GREEK TYCOON, THE
GREYSTOKE: THE LEGEND OF TARZAN, LORD OF THE
  APES
GROUP, THE
GUESS WHO'S COMING TO DINNER
GULAG
GUN CRAZY
HADLEY'S REBELLION
HAIL MARY
HALF A LIFETIME
HALF MOON STREET
HAMLET (1948)
HAMLET (1969)
HANDFUL OF DUST, A
HANNA K
HARD CHOICES
HARDCORE
HARD COUNTRY
HARDER THEY COME, THE
HARDER THEY FALL, THE
HARD TIMES
HAREM
HARRAD EXPERIMENT, THE
HARRY AND SON
HARRY AND TONTO
HATFUL OF RAIN, A
HAWAII
HAWKS
HEART
HEARTACHES
HEART BEAT
HEARTBREAKERS
HEART IS A LONELY HUNTER, THE
HEARTLAND
HEARTS OF FIRE
HEAT AND DUST
HEATWAVE
HEAVEN KNOWS, MR. ALLISON
HEDDA
HEIRESS, THE
HELTER SKELTER
HENNESSY
HENRY V
HERO AIN'T NOTHIN' BUT A SANDWICH, A
HESTER STREET
HIDE IN PLAIN SIGHT
HIGH COUNTRY, THE
HIGH SCHOOL CONFIDENTIAL
HIGH SIERRA
HIGH TIDE
HIGH WIND IN JAMAICA, A
HIROSHIMA, MON AMOUR
HISTORY IS MADE AT NIGHT
HITLER: THE LAST TEN DAYS
HOMECOMING, THE
HONEYSUCKLE ROSE
HONKYTONK MAN
HOOSIERS
HOPE AND GLORY
HOTEL
HOT TOUCH
HOUSEKEEPING
HOWARDS OF VIRGINIA, THE
HOW GREEN WAS MY VALLEY
HUD
HUMAN COMEDY, THE
HUMAN FACTOR, THE
HUNCHBACK OF NOTRE DAME, THE

HUSTLER, THE
I AM A CAMERA
I AM A FUGITIVE FROM A CHAIN GANG
I AM THE CHEESE
ICE CASTLES
ICE PALACE
I COVER THE WATERFRONT
IDOLMAKER, THE
IF . . .
IMAGEMAKER, THE
I'M DANCING AS FAST AS I CAN
IMITATION OF LIFE
IN CROWD, THE
INDEPENDENCE DAY
I NEVER PROMISED YOU A ROSE GARDEN
I NEVER SANG FOR MY FATHER
INFORMER, THE
INHERIT THE WIND
IN NAME ONLY
INNOCENT, THE
INNOCENTS, THE
IN OLD CHICAGO
IN PRAISE OF OLDER WOMEN
INQUIRY, THE
INSERTS
INSIDE MOVES
INSIDE OUT
INSIGNIFICANCE
INTERIORS
INTERMEZZO
INTERNATIONAL VELVET
INTERNS, THE
IN THE REALM OF THE SENSES
INTIMATE CONTACT
INTO THE HOMELAND
I REMEMBER MAMA
IRONWEED
I SENT A LETTER TO MY LOVE
ISLANDS IN THE STREAM
IT'S A WONDERFUL LIFE
JACKNIFE
JANE EYRE
JAZZ SINGER, THE (1980)
JEAN DE FLORETTE
JESUS
JEZEBEL
JOAN OF ARC
JOE
JOEY
JOHNNY BELINDA
JOHNNY TREMAIN
JO JO DANCER, YOUR LIFE IS CALLING
JONATHAN LIVINGSTON SEAGULL
JOYRIDE
JUDGMENT AT NUREMBERG
JUDGMENT IN BERLIN
JULES AND JIM
JULIA
JUNGLE BOOK, THE
JUNIOR BONNER
JUST BETWEEN FRIENDS
JUSTINE
JUST THE WAY YOU ARE
KANDYLAND
KANGAROO
KANSAS
KARATE KID, THE
KARATE KID, PART II, THE
KENTUCKY
KEY LARGO
KEYS OF THE KINGDOM, THE
KIDNAPPING OF THE PRESIDENT, THE
KILLER INSIDE ME, THE
KILLERS, THE
KILLING AFFAIR, A
KILLING FIELDS, THE
KILLING OF SISTER GEORGE, THE
KIND OF LOVING, A
KING DAVID
KING LEAR
KING OF COMEDY, THE
KING OF KINGS
KING OF MARVIN GARDENS, THE
KING OF THE GYPSIES

KING OF THE MOUNTAIN
KISS OF THE SPIDER WOMAN
KITCHEN TOTO, THE
KITTY FOYLE
KNIGHTS OF THE CITY
KNOCK ON ANY DOOR
KRAMER VS. KRAMER
LA DOLCE VITA
LADY CHATTERLEY'S LOVER
LA RONDE
LAST DETAIL, THE
LAST FIGHT, THE
LAST HOLIDAY
LAST HURRAH, THE
LAST METRO, THE
LA STRADA
LAST SUMMER
LAST TANGO IN PARIS
LAST TEMPTATION OF CHRIST, THE
LAST TYCOON, THE
LAST WORD, THE
LAUGHING POLICEMAN, THE
LEARNING TREE, THE
LEGEND OF BILLIE JEAN, THE
LES MISERABLES
LESS THAN ZERO
LETTER, THE
LETTER TO THREE WIVES, A
LIANNA
LIAR'S MOON
LIBERATION OF L.B. JONES, THE
LIES MY FATHER TOLD ME
LIFE AND DEATH OF COLONEL BLIMP, THE
LIFEBOAT
LIFEGUARD
LIGHT OF DAY
LIGHTSHIP, THE
LILIES OF THE FIELD
LILITH
LIMELIGHT
LION IN WINTER, THE
LION OF THE DESERT
LIPSTICK
LITTLE FOXES, THE
LITTLE LORD FAUNTLEROY
LITTLE WOMEN
LIVING FREE
LLOYDS OF LONDON
LOLA MONTES
LONELINESS OF THE LONG DISTANCE RUNNER, THE
LONELYHEARTS
LONELY LADY, THE
LONELY PASSION OF JUDITH HEARNE, THE
LONG DAY'S JOURNEY INTO NIGHT
LONG GOOD FRIDAY, THE
LONG, HOT SUMMER, THE
LONG VOYAGE HOME, THE
LOOK BACK IN ANGER
LOOKING FOR MR. GOODBAR
LOOKIN' TO GET OUT
LORD JIM
LORDS OF DISCIPLINE, THE
LORDS OF FLATBUSH, THE
LOST WEEKEND, THE
LOUISIANA
LOVE CHILD
LOVE IS A DOG FROM HELL
LOVELESS, THE
LOVE MACHINE, THE
LOVERS AND LIARS
LOVES OF CARMEN, THE
LOVE STORY
LOVE STREAMS
LUCAS
LUCKY LUCIANO
M
MACARONI
MACBETH
MACK, THE
MADAME BOVARY
MADAME ROSA
MADAME SOUSATZKA
MADAME X
MADE FOR EACH OTHER

MADE IN THE U.S.A.
MAGNIFICENT AMBERSONS, THE
MAGNIFICENT OBSESSION
MAHOGANY
MAKING LOVE
MANDINGO
MAN FOR ALL SEASONS, A
MAN FRIDAY
MANHATTAN PROJECT, THE
MANON OF THE SPRING
MAN OUTSIDE
MAN WITH THE GOLDEN ARM, THE
MAN, WOMAN AND CHILD
MARIA'S LOVERS
MARKED WOMAN
MARNIE
MARRIAGE OF MARIA BRAUN, THE
MARTIN'S DAY
MARTY
MARVIN AND TIGE
MARY OF SCOTLAND
MASK
MASSACRE AT CENTRAL HIGH
MASS APPEAL
MASSIVE RETALIATION
MATA HARI
MATEWAN
MATTER OF TIME, A
MAURICE
MEAN SEASON, THE
MEAN STREETS
MEDIUM COOL
MEET JOHN DOE
MELVIN AND HOWARD
MEMBER OF THE WEDDING, THE
MEMORIES OF ME
MEN, THE
MEN'S CLUB, THE
MEPHISTO
MERRY CHRISTMAS, MR. LAWRENCE
MIDNIGHT COWBOY
MIDNIGHT EXPRESS
MIKE'S MURDER
MIKEY AND NICKY
MILAGRO BEANFIELD WAR, THE
MILDRED PIERCE
MILES FROM HOME
MIRACLES
MISFITS, THE
MISHIMA
MISSING
MISSISSIPPI BURNING
MISUNDERSTOOD
MODERNS, THE
MOLLY MAGUIRES, THE
MOMMIE DEAREST
MONA LISA
MON ONCLE D'AMERIQUE
MONSIGNOR
MONTH IN THE COUNTRY, A
MOON IN THE GUTTER, THE
MOONLIGHTING
MORE AMERICAN GRAFFITI
MORNING GLORY
MOROCCO
MOSCOW DOES NOT BELIEVE IN TEARS
MR. SKEFFINGTON
MR. SMITH GOES TO WASHINGTON
MRS. SOFFEL
MY AMERICAN COUSIN
MY BEAUTIFUL LAUNDRETTE
MY BRILLIANT CAREER
MY DINNER WITH ANDRE
MY LIFE AS A DOG
NAKED FACE, THE
NASHVILLE
NASHVILLE GIRL
NATIONAL VELVET
NATIVE SON
NATURAL, THE
NEW LAND, THE
NEW LIFE, A
NEWSFRONT
NEW YORK STORIES

NICHOLAS AND ALEXANDRA
NICHOLAS NICKLEBY
NICKEL MOUNTAIN
NIGHTCOMERS, THE
NIGHT GAMES
NIGHT IN HEAVEN, A
'NIGHT, MOTHER
NIGHT OF THE HUNTER, THE
NIGHT OF THE IGUANA, THE
NIGHT PORTER, THE
NIGHTS OF CABIRIA
NIGHT THE LIGHTS WENT OUT IN GEORGIA, THE
NIGHT TO REMEMBER, A
NIGHT WATCH
9½ WEEKS
1918
1984
1900
1969
92 IN THE SHADE
NINTH CONFIGURATION, THE
NO MAN'S LAND
NONE BUT THE LONELY HEART
NORMA RAE
NORTH SHORE
NOTHING IN COMMON
NOT QUITE PARADISE
NUN'S STORY, THE
NUTS
ODE TO BILLY JOE
OFFICER AND A GENTLEMAN, AN
OFFICIAL STORY, THE
OF HUMAN BONDAGE (1934)
OF HUMAN BONDAGE (1964)
O'HARA'S WIFE
OKLAHOMA CRUDE
OLD BOYFRIENDS
OLD MAID, THE
OLD MAN AND THE SEA, THE
OLIVER TWIST
O LUCKY MAN!
ONCE IS NOT ENOUGH
ONCE UPON A TIME IN AMERICA
ONCE WE WERE DREAMERS
ONE FLEW OVER THE CUCKOO'S NEST
ONE MAGIC CHRISTMAS
ONE ON ONE
ONE SUMMER LOVE
ONE TRICK PONY
ON GOLDEN POND
ONION FIELD, THE
ONLY ANGELS HAVE WINGS
ONLY GAME IN TOWN, THE
ONLY WHEN I LAUGH
ON THE BEACH
ON THE EDGE
ON THE WATERFRONT
ON THE YARD
ON VALENTINE'S DAY
ORDINARY PEOPLE
ORGANIZATION, THE
ORPHANS
OSCAR, THE
OTHER SIDE OF MIDNIGHT, THE
OUR TOWN
OUT OF AFRICA
OUT OF THE BLUE
OUTRAGEOUS!
OUTSIDERS, THE
OVER THE SUMMER
OVER THE TOP
PANIC IN NEEDLE PARK
PAPER CHASE, THE
PAPER LION
PARADINE CASE, THE
PARADISE
PARADISE ALLEY
PARIS BLUES
PARIS, TEXAS
PARK IS MINE, THE
PARTING GLANCES
PASCALI'S ISLAND
PASSAGE TO INDIA, A
PASSENGER, THE

PASSION OF JOAN OF ARC, THE
PATCH OF BLUE, A
PATHS OF GLORY
PAWNBROKER, THE
PAYDAY
PELLE THE CONQUEROR
PENDULUM
PENITENT, THE
PENNY SERENADE
PEOPLE NEXT DOOR, THE
PERFECT
PERFORMANCE
PERMANENT RECORD
PERSONA
PERSONAL BEST
PERSONAL SERVICES
PETE KELLY'S BLUES
PETE 'N' TILLIE
PETRIFIED FOREST, THE
PETULIA
PHAR LAP
PHONE CALL FROM A STRANGER
PICK-UP ARTIST, THE
PICNIC
PICNIC AT HANGING ROCK
PICTURE OF DORIAN GRAY, THE
PINKY
PIXOTE
PLACE IN THE SUN, A
PLACES IN THE HEART
PLAYERS
PLAYING FOR TIME
PLENTY
PLOUGHMAN'S LUNCH, THE
POPE OF GREENWICH VILLAGE, THE
PORTNOY'S COMPLAINT
POSTMAN ALWAYS RINGS TWICE, THE (1946)
POSTMAN ALWAYS RINGS TWICE, THE (1981)
POWER
PRAYER FOR THE DYING, A
PRETTY BABY
PRICK UP YOUR EARS
PRIME RISK
PRINCE OF THE CITY
PRINCIPAL, THE
PRIVATE INVESTIGATIONS
PRIVATE LIVES OF ELIZABETH AND ESSEX, THE
PRIVATE ROAD
PRIVILEGE
PRIZZI'S HONOR
PROJECT X
PROMISED LAND
PROMISES IN THE DARK
PROVIDENCE
PSYCH-OUT
PULSEBEAT
PURPLE HEARTS
PURPLE TAXI, THE
PURSUIT OF HAPPINESS, THE
QUADROPHENIA
QUARTET
QUEEN CHRISTINA
QUEEN OF THE ROAD
QUERELLE
QUESTION OF SILENCE, A
QUICKSILVER
QUIET EARTH, THE
QUIET MAN, THE
QUINTET
RACE WITH THE DEVIL
RACHEL, RACHEL
RACING WITH THE MOON
RAD
RAGGEDY MAN
RAGTIME
RAID ON ENTEBBE
RAIN
RAINMAKER, THE
RAIN MAN
RAIN PEOPLE, THE
RAINTREE COUNTY
RAINY DAY FRIENDS
RAISIN IN THE SUN, A
RAMPAGE

RAN
RANDOM HARVEST
RAPPIN'
RARE BREED, A
RASHOMON
RATBOY
RAZOR'S EDGE, THE (1946)
RAZOR'S EDGE, THE (1984)
REBECCA
REBEL
REBEL LOVE
REBEL WITHOUT A CAUSE
RECKLESS
RED BADGE OF COURAGE, THE
RED SHOES, THE
REEFER MADNESS
REFLECTIONS IN A GOLDEN EYE
REQUIEM FOR A HEAVYWEIGHT
RESURRECTION
RETURN OF MARTIN GUERRE, THE
RETURN OF THE SECAUCUS 7
RETURN OF THE SOLDIER, THE
REUBEN, REUBEN
REVOLUTION
RICH AND FAMOUS
RICHARD III
RICH KIDS
RIGHT HAND MAN, THE
RIGHT OF WAY
RIVER, THE
RIVER RAT, THE
RIVER'S EDGE
ROBE, THE
ROCKET GIBRALTAR
ROCKY
ROCKY II
ROCKY III
ROCKY IV
ROLLOVER
ROMAN SPRING OF MRS. STONE, THE
ROMANTIC ENGLISHWOMAN, THE
ROOM AT THE TOP
ROOM WITH A VIEW, A
ROOTS
ROSELAND
ROSE TATTOO, THE
'ROUND MIDNIGHT
R.P.M.
RUBY GENTRY
RULES OF THE GAME
RULING CLASS, THE
RUMBLE FISH
RUNNER STUMBLES, THE
RUNNING
RUNNING ON EMPTY
RUNNING WILD
RUSSKIES
RYAN'S DAUGHTER
SAILOR WHO FELL FROM GRACE WITH THE SEA, THE
SAINT JACK
SAINT JOAN
SALAAM BOMBAY!
SALAMANDER
SALOME
SALOME'S LAST DANCE
SALSA
SALZBURG CONNECTION, THE
SAMMY AND ROSIE GET LAID
SAMSON AND DELILAH
SAN FRANCISCO
SATISFACTION
SATURDAY NIGHT FEVER
SAVE THE TIGER
SAVING GRACE
SAYONARA
SCARECROW
SCARFACE (1932)
SCARFACE (1983)
SCARRED
SCENE OF THE CRIME
SCENES FROM A MARRIAGE
SCENES FROM THE GOLDMINE
SCRUBBERS
SEA WOLF, THE

SECOND CHANCE
SECRET CEREMONY
SECRET HONOR
SECRET PLACES
SEDUCTION OF JOE TYNAN, THE
SEIZE THE DAY
SEPARATE PEACE, A
SEPARATE TABLES
SEPARATE WAYS
SEPTEMBER
SERPENT'S EGG, THE
SERVANT, THE
SET-UP, THE
SEVEN BEAUTIES
SEVENTH SEAL, THE
SEVENTH VEIL, THE
SEX THROUGH A WINDOW
SHADOW PLAY
SHAME
SHIP OF FOOLS
SHOES OF THE FISHERMAN, THE
SHOOTING PARTY, THE
SHOOT THE MOON
SHOOT THE PIANO PLAYER
SHOP ON MAIN STREET, THE
SHORT EYES
SHY PEOPLE
SIESTA
SILENCE OF THE NORTH
SILKWOOD
SILVER BEARS
SILVER CHALICE, THE
SILVER DREAM RACER
SINCERELY YOURS
SINCE YOU WENT AWAY
SIX WEEKS
SKI BUM, THE
SLATE, WYN & ME
SMALL CIRCLE OF FRIENDS, A
SMASH PALACE
SMITHEREENS
SMOOTH TALK
SNAKE PIT, THE
SNOWS OF KILIMANJARO, THE
SOLDIER IN THE RAIN
SOLDIER OF ORANGE
SOLOMON AND SHEBA
SOME KIND OF WONDERFUL
SOMETHING OF VALUE
SOMETHING WILD
SOMETIMES A GREAT NOTION
SONS AND LOVERS
SOPHIE'S CHOICE
SOUTHERNER, THE
SPARKLE
SPARTACUS
SPECIAL DAY, A
SPETTERS
SPIKER
SPLENDOR IN THE GRASS
SPLIT DECISIONS
SPLIT IMAGE
SQUARE DANCE
STACKING
STACY'S KNIGHTS
STAGE DOOR
STAKEOUT
STALAG 17
STAND ALONE
STAND BY ME
STAR CHAMBER, THE
STAR IS BORN, A (1937)
STARS LOOK DOWN, THE
STATE OF SIEGE
STATE OF THE UNION
STAY HUNGRY
STAYING ALIVE
STEALING HOME
STEAMING
STELLA DALLAS
ST. ELMO'S FIRE
STERILE CUCKOO, THE
STONE BOY, THE
STORMY MONDAY

STORY OF ADELE H., THE
STRAIGHT TIME
STRANGERS KISS
STRATEGIC AIR COMMAND
STRAWBERRY STATEMENT, THE
STRAW DOGS
STREAMERS
STREETCAR NAMED DESIRE, A (1951)
STREETCAR NAMED DESIRE, A (1984)
STREET HERO
STREET SMART
STREETS OF GOLD
STREETWALKIN'
STRIPPER, THE
STUD, THE
STUDENT CONFIDENTIAL
STUDENT NURSES
STUDENT TEACHERS, THE
STUNT MAN, THE
SUBURBIA
SUDDENLY
SUDDENLY, LAST SUMMER
SUGARBABY
SUGARLAND EXPRESS, THE
SUICIDE CLUB, THE
SUMMER CAMP NIGHTMARE
SUMMER HEAT
SUMMER OF '42
SUMMER PLACE, A
SUMMER WISHES, WINTER DREAMS
SUN ALSO RISES, THE
SUNDAY, BLOODY SUNDAY
SUNDAYS AND CYBELE
SUNDOWNERS, THE
SUNSET BOULEVARD
SUPERNATURALS, THE
SWANN IN LOVE
SWAP, THE
SWEET COUNTRY
SWEET HEARTS DANCE
SWEET LORRAINE
SWEET SWEETBACK'S BAADASSSSS SONG
SWIMMER, THE
SWING SHIFT
SWORD AND THE ROSE, THE
SWORDKILL
SYLVIA SCARLETT
TABLE FOR FIVE
TAFFIN
TAKE DOWN
TALE OF TWO CITIES, A (1935)
TALE OF TWO CITIES, A (1958)
TALES OF ORDINARY MADNESS
TALK RADIO
TALK TO ME
TAP
TAPS
TARAS BULBA
TARNISHED ANGELS, THE
TASTE OF HONEY, A
TAXI DRIVER
TEACHERS
TELEPHONE, THE
TELL ME A RIDDLE
TELL ME THAT YOU LOVE ME
TELL THEM WILLIE BOY IS HERE
TEN COMMANDMENTS, THE
TENDER MERCIES
TENDRES COUSINES
TEN NORTH FREDERICK
10 RILLINGTON PLACE
TEQUILA SUNRISE
TERMS OF ENDEARMENT
TESS
TESTAMENT
TEST OF LOVE, A
TEX
THAT CHAMPIONSHIP SEASON
THAT HAMILTON WOMAN
THAT'LL BE THE DAY
THAT'S LIFE!
THAT WAS THEN . . . THIS IS NOW
THESE THREE
THEY DRIVE BY NIGHT

THEY LIVE BY NIGHT
THEY MADE ME A CRIMINAL
THEY MIGHT BE GIANTS
THEY SHOOT HORSES, DON'T THEY?
THEY WON'T BELIEVE ME
THEY WON'T FORGET
THIEF OF HEARTS
THIS PROPERTY IS CONDEMNED
THIS SPORTING LIFE
THOSE LIPS, THOSE EYES
THRASHIN'
THREE COINS IN THE FOUNTAIN
THREE FACES OF EVE, THE
3:15—MOMENT OF TRUTH
THREE STRANGERS
3 WOMEN
THRESHOLD
THROUGH A GLASS DARKLY
THUNDER ALLEY
TICKET TO HEAVEN
TIGER BAY
TIGER WARSAW
TILT
TIM
TIME OF DESTINY, A
TIME OF TEARS
TIMES SQUARE
TIN DRUM, THE
TIN MAN
TO CATCH A THIEF
TO HAVE AND HAVE NOT
TO KILL A MOCKINGBIRD
TOKYO POP
TOM BROWN'S SCHOOLDAYS
TOMORROW
TOO SCARED TO SCREAM
TORCHLIGHT
TORCH SONG TRILOGY
TO SIR, WITH LOVE
TOUCH AND GO
TOUCHED
TOUCHED BY LOVE
TOUGH ENOUGH
TRACK 29
TRADING HEARTS
TRAPEZE
TRASH
TRAVELLING NORTH
TREE GROWS IN BROOKLYN, A
TRIAL OF BILLY JACK, THE
TRIAL OF THE CANTONSVILLE NINE, THE
TRIBUTE
TRIP, THE
TRIP TO BOUNTIFUL, THE
TRISTANA
TROUBLE IN MIND
TRUE CONFESSIONS
TUFF TURF
TUNES OF GLORY
TURK 182!
TURNING POINT, THE
TURTLE DIARY
TWELVE ANGRY MEN
TWICE IN A LIFETIME
TWILIGHT'S LAST GLEAMING
TWIST AND SHOUT
TWO FOR THE ROAD
TWO WOMEN
TYCOON
UGLY AMERICAN, THE
ULYSSES (1967)
UNBEARABLE LIGHTNESS OF BEING, THE
UNDER CAPRICORN
UNDER FIRE
UNDER MILK WOOD
UNDER THE BOARDWALK
UNDER THE CHERRY MOON
UNDER THE VOLCANO
UNION CITY
UNMARRIED WOMAN, AN
UP THE DOWN STAIRCASE
UP THE SANDBOX
VAGABOND
VALACHI PAPERS, THE

VALLEY OF THE DOLLS
VAMPING
VANISHING POINT
VERDICT, THE
VERY PRIVATE AFFAIR, A
VICTIM
VICTORY
VIRGIN SPRING, THE
VIRIDIANA
VISION QUEST
VIVA KNIEVEL!
VOICES
VOYAGE OF THE DAMNED
WAITING FOR THE MOON
WALKABOUT
WALK ON THE WILD SIDE
WALL STREET
WANDERERS, THE
WAR AND LOVE
WARGAMES
WARRIOR QUEEN
WATCH ON THE RHINE
WEEDS
WELCOME TO 18
WELCOME TO L.A.
WETHERBY
WE THINK THE WORLD OF YOU
WHALES OF AUGUST, THE
WHEN THE LEGENDS DIE
WHEN TIME RAN OUT
WHITE DOG
WHITE HEAT
WHITE NIGHTS
WHITE ROSE, THE
WHO'LL STOP THE RAIN?
WHO'S AFRAID OF VIRGINIA WOOLF?
WHOSE LIFE IS IT, ANYWAY?
WHO'S THAT KNOCKING AT MY DOOR?
WHY SHOOT THE TEACHER?
WIFEMISTRESS
WILD CHILD, THE
WILD DUCK, THE
WILDFIRE
WILD IN THE COUNTRY
WILD IN THE STREETS
WILD ONE, THE
WILD PARTY, THE
WILD RIVER
WILDROSE
WILD STRAWBERRIES
WINDWALKER
WINDY CITY
WINGS OF DESIRE
WINNERS TAKE ALL
WINNING
WINTER FLIGHT
WINTER KILLS
WINTER OF OUR DREAMS
WISDOM
WISE BLOOD
WISH YOU WERE HERE
WITHOUT A TRACE
WITNESS
WIZARD OF LONELINESS, THE
WOMAN'S FACE, A
WOMEN IN LOVE
WORKING GIRLS
WORLD ACCORDING TO GARP, THE
WORLD APART, A
WRITTEN ON THE WIND
WUTHERING HEIGHTS (1939)
WUTHERING HEIGHTS (1971)
X, Y AND ZEE
YANKS
YEAR MY VOICE BROKE, THE
YEAR OF LIVING DANGEROUSLY, THE
YOL
YOU LIGHT UP MY LIFE
YOUNGBLOOD
YOUNG LIONS, THE
YOUNG MAN WITH A HORN
YOUNG NURSES, THE
YOUNG PHILADELPHIANS, THE
YOU ONLY LIVE ONCE

YOU TALKIN' TO ME?
Z
ZABRISKIE POINT
ZELLY AND ME
ZOO GANG, THE
ZORBA THE GREEK

ESPIONAGE

AMBUSHERS, THE
BILLION DOLLAR BRAIN
BLACK WINDMILL, THE
DIAMONDS ARE FOREVER
DR. NO
EIGER SANCTION, THE
FOR YOUR EYES ONLY
FROM RUSSIA, WITH LOVE
FUNERAL IN BERLIN
GOLDFINGER
IMPOSSIBLE SPY, THE
IPCRESS FILE, THE
JIGSAW MAN, THE
LITTLE DRUMMER GIRL, THE
LIVE AND LET DIE
LIVING DAYLIGHTS, THE
LOOKING GLASS WAR, THE
MACKINTOSH MAN, THE
MAN WITH THE GOLDEN GUN, THE
MOONRAKER
MURDERERS' ROW
NEVER SAY NEVER AGAIN
OCTOPUSSY
ON HER MAJESTY'S SECRET SERVICE
OUR MAN FLINT
QUILLER MEMORANDUM, THE
SILENCERS, THE
SPY WHO CAME IN FROM THE COLD, THE
SPY WHO LOVED ME, THE
STOPOVER TOKYO
TAMARIND SEED, THE
TELEFON
THUNDERBALL
TORN CURTAIN
VIEW TO A KILL, A
YOU ONLY LIVE TWICE
YURI NOSENKO, KGB

FAMILY

ADVENTURES OF HUCKLEBERRY FINN, THE (1985)
ADVENTURES OF THE WILDERNESS FAMILY, THE
AMAZING DOBERMANS, THE
AMERICAN CHRISTMAS CAROL, AN
BABES IN TOYLAND
BAD NEWS BEARS, THE
BAD NEWS BEARS GO TO JAPAN, THE
BAD NEWS BEARS IN BREAKING TRAINING, THE
BEDKNOBS AND BROOMSTICKS
BENIKER GANG, THE
BENJI
BENJI THE HUNTED
BIG RED
BILLION DOLLAR HOBO, THE
BLACK BEAUTY
BLACK STALLION, THE
BLACK STALLION RETURNS, THE
BOATNIKS, THE
BORN FREE
CAPTAINS COURAGEOUS
CASEY'S SHADOW
CHARLIE, THE LONESOME COUGAR
CHITTY CHITTY BANG BANG
CHRISTMAS CAROL, A
CHRISTMAS THAT ALMOST WASN'T, THE
CHRISTMAS TO REMEMBER, A
CURLY TOP
DARBY O'GILL AND THE LITTLE PEOPLE
DIMPLES
DOBERMAN GANG, THE
DOCTOR DOLITTLE
DOG OF FLANDERS, A
ELEPHANT BOY
ELEPHANT CALLED SLOWLY, AN
E.T. THE EXTRA-TERRESTRIAL
FISH HAWK
FLIPPER
FOLLOW ME, BOYS

FOR THE LOVE OF BENJI
GENTLE GIANT
GREAT MUPPET CAPER, THE
HAMBONE AND HILLIE
HANS BRINKER AND THE SILVER SKATES
HAPPIEST MILLIONAIRE, THE
HEIDI (1937)
HEIDI (1968)
HERE COMES SANTA CLAUS
HORSE IN THE GRAY FLANNEL SUIT, THE
HORSE WITHOUT A HEAD, THE
HUCKLEBERRY FINN (1974)
HUCKLEBERRY FINN (1975)
INCREDIBLE JOURNEY, THE
IN SEARCH OF A GOLDEN SKY
IN SEARCH OF THE CASTAWAYS
INTERNATIONAL VELVET
ISLAND OF THE BLUE DOLPHINS
JIMMY THE KID
JOHN AND JULIE
JOURNEY OF NATTY GANN, THE
JUNGLE BOOK, THE
KIDCO
LABYRINTH
LIGHT IN THE FOREST, THE
LITTLE COLONEL, THE
LITTLE PRINCESS, THE
LITTLEST HORSE THIEVES, THE
LITTLEST REBEL, THE
LIVING FREE
LOVE BUG, THE
MAC AND ME
MAGIC OF LASSIE, THE
MARY POPPINS
MISTY
MOUNTAIN FAMILY ROBINSON
MUPPET MOVIE, THE
MUPPETS TAKE MANHATTAN, THE
MY FRIEND FLICKA
MYSTERY MANSION
NAPOLEON AND SAMANTHA
NATIONAL VELVET
NEVERENDING STORY, THE
NEW ADVENTURES OF PIPPI LONGSTOCKING, THE
NIGHT CROSSING
NO DEPOSIT, NO RETURN
NUTCRACKER: THE MOTION PICTURE
OH HEAVENLY DOG!
OLD YELLER
OLLY, OLLY, OXEN FREE
ONE MAGIC CHRISTMAS
PARENT TRAP, THE
PEANUT BUTTER SOLUTION, THE
PETE'S DRAGON
POLLYANNA
POOR LITTLE RICH GIRL
PRIVATE EYES, THE
PROUD REBEL, THE
RAILWAY CHILDREN, THE
REBECCA OF SUNNYBROOK FARM
RED PONY, THE
RETURN FROM WITCH MOUNTAIN
RETURN TO OZ
RING OF BRIGHT WATER
RUMPELSTILTSKIN
SALTY
SANTA CLAUS
SAVANNAH SMILES
SEA GYPSIES, THE
SESAME STREET PRESENTS: FOLLOW THAT BIRD
SHAGGY D.A., THE
SHAGGY DOG, THE
SINBAD AND THE EYE OF THE TIGER
SLIPPER AND THE ROSE, THE
SNOWBALL EXPRESS, THE
SO DEAR TO MY HEART
SONG OF THE SOUTH
SOUNDER
SWISS FAMILY ROBINSON
SYLVESTER
TARKA THE OTTER
THAT DARN CAT
THIRD MAN ON THE MOUNTAIN
THREE LIVES OF THOMASINA, THE

THREE WORLDS OF GULLIVER, THE
TOBY TYLER, OR TEN WEEKS WITH A CIRCUS
TOM BROWN'S SCHOOLDAYS
TOM SAWYER
TREASURE ISLAND (1950)
TREASURE ISLAND (1972)
TROUBLE WITH ANGELS, THE
TUCK EVERLASTING
UGLY DACHSHUND, THE
WATCHER IN THE WOODS, THE
WEE WILLIE WINKIE
WHISTLE DOWN THE WIND
WHO HAS SEEN THE WIND?
WILD COUNTRY, THE
WILDERNESS FAMILY, PART 2, THE
WILLY WONKA AND THE CHOCOLATE FACTORY
WORLD'S GREATEST ATHLETE, THE
YEARLING, THE

FANTASY

ALICE IN WONDERLAND (1933)
ANGEL ON MY SHOULDER
BABES IN TOYLAND
BEASTMASTER, THE
BEAUTY AND THE BEAST
BEETLEJUICE
BISHOP'S WIFE, THE
BLACKBEARD'S GHOST
BLUE BIRD, THE
BOY WHO COULD FLY, THE
CHERRY 2000
CLASH OF THE TITANS
COCOON
COCOON: THE RETURN
CONNECTICUT YANKEE IN KING ARTHUR'S COURT, A
DARBY O'GILL AND THE LITTLE PEOPLE
DARK CRYSTAL, THE
DATE WITH AN ANGEL
DEATH TAKES A HOLIDAY
DEVIL AND DANIEL WEBSTER, THE
DONA FLOR AND HER TWO HUSBANDS
DRAGONSLAYER
ENCHANTED COTTAGE, THE
ESCAPE TO WITCH MOUNTAIN
E.T. THE EXTRA-TERRESTRIAL
GHOST AND MRS. MUIR, THE
GOLDEN VOYAGE OF SINBAD, THE
GOONIES, THE
GREMLINS
GUY NAMED JOE, A
HEARTBEEPS
HEAVEN CAN WAIT (1943)
HEAVEN CAN WAIT (1978)
HEAVENLY KID, THE
HERE COMES MR. JORDAN
HIGH SPIRITS
HOWARD THE DUCK
I MARRIED A WITCH
INNERSPACE
IN SEARCH OF THE CASTAWAYS
INVISIBLE KID, THE
IT HAPPENED TOMORROW
JASON AND THE ARGONAUTS
KISS ME GOODBYE
KRULL
LABYRINTH
LADYHAWKE
LEGEND
MAC AND ME
MADE IN HEAVEN
MAKING CONTACT
MASTER OF THE WORLD
MASTERS OF THE UNIVERSE
MAXIE
MIRACLE ON 34TH STREET
MR. PEABODY AND THE MERMAID
MYSTERIOUS ISLAND
NEVERENDING STORY, THE
PEGGY SUE GOT MARRIED
PRINCESS BRIDE, THE
QUEEN OF SPADES, THE
RETURN TO OZ
7 FACES OF DR. LAO
SEVEN MAGNIFICENT GLADIATORS, THE

7TH VOYAGE OF SINBAD, THE
SHE
SINBAD AND THE EYE OF THE TIGER
SOMEWHERE IN TIME
SOMEWHERE, TOMORROW
STAIRWAY TO HEAVEN
STARMAN
SUPERGIRL
SUPERMAN
SUPERMAN II
SUPERMAN III
SUPERMAN IV: THE QUEST FOR PEACE
SUPERMAN AND THE MOLE MEN
SWORD AND THE SORCERER, THE
THIEF OF BAGDAD, THE
30 FOOT BRIDE OF CANDY ROCK, THE
THREE LIVES OF THOMASINA, THE
THREE WORLDS OF GULLIVER, THE
TIME BANDITS
TIMERIDER
TOM THUMB
TOPPER
TWO OF A KIND
UNIDENTIFIED FLYING ODDBALL, THE
WEIRD SCIENCE
WILLOW
WITCHES OF EASTWICK, THE
WIZARD OF OZ, THE
WIZARDS OF THE LOST KINGDOM

HORROR

ALCHEMIST, THE
ALLIGATOR
AMERICAN GOTHIC
AMERICAN WEREWOLF IN LONDON, AN
AMITYVILLE HORROR, THE
AMITYVILLE II: THE POSSESSION
AMITYVILLE 3-D
ANDY WARHOL'S DRACULA
ANDY WARHOL'S FRANKENSTEIN
ANGUISH
APRIL FOOL'S DAY
AUDREY ROSE
AWAKENING, THE
BAD DREAMS
BARON BLOOD
BARRACUDA
BASKET CASE
BAT PEOPLE, THE
BEAST WITHIN, THE
BEDLAM
BEES, THE
BEING, THE
BELIEVERS, THE
BEN
BERSERK
BLACK CAT, THE
BLACK ROOM, THE
BLACK SABBATH
BLACK SUNDAY (1961)
BLACULA
BLOOD BATH AT THE HOUSE OF DEATH
BLOOD BEACH
BLUE MONKEY
BLUE SUNSHINE
BODY SNATCHER, THE
BOOGENS, THE
BRAIN, THE
BRIDE, THE
BRIDE OF FRANKENSTEIN, THE
BROOD, THE
BROTHERHOOD OF SATAN, THE
BUG
BURNING, THE
BURNT OFFERINGS
CAR, THE
CARRIE
CAT PEOPLE (1942)
CAT PEOPLE (1982)
CAT'S EYE
CELLAR DWELLER
CHANGELING, THE
CHILDREN, THE
CHILDREN OF THE CORN

CHILDREN OF THE DAMNED
CHILD'S PLAY
CHOPPING MALL
CHOSEN, THE (1978)
CHRISTINE
C.H.U.D.
C.H.U.D. II
CIRCUS OF HORRORS
CLASS OF NUKE 'EM HIGH
CLOWNHOUSE
COMEDY OF TERRORS, THE
COMING SOON
COMPANY OF WOLVES, THE
COUNT YORGA, VAMPIRE
CRAWLSPACE
CREATURE FROM THE BLACK LAGOON
CREEPERS
CREEPING FLESH, THE
CREEPSHOW
CREEPSHOW 2
CRIMSON CULT, THE
CRITTERS
CRITTERS 2: THE MAIN COURSE
CROCODILE
CRY OF THE BANSHEE
CUJO
CURSE, THE
CURSE OF FRANKENSTEIN, THE
CURSE OF THE CAT PEOPLE, THE
CURSE OF THE DEMON
CURTAINS
DAMIEN—OMEN II
DARK OF THE NIGHT
DARK PLACES
DAWN OF THE DEAD
DAWN OF THE MUMMY
DAY OF THE ANIMALS
DAY OF THE DEAD
DEAD AND BURIED
DEADLY BLESSING
DEADLY EYES
DEADLY FRIEND
DEADLY INTRUDER, THE
DEAD OF NIGHT
DEADTIME STORIES
DEATH SHIP
DEEP RED
DEEPSTAR SIX
DEMON, THE
DEMONS OF THE MIND
DEVIL DOLL, THE
DIE, DIE MY DARLING
DIE, MONSTER, DIE!
DOCTOR AND THE DEVILS, THE
DOLLS
DRACULA (1931)
DRACULA (1979)
DRACULA'S WIDOW
DR. JEKYLL AND MR. HYDE (1932)
DR. JEKYLL AND MR. HYDE (1941)
DR. PHIBES RISES AGAIN
ERASERHEAD
EVIL, THE
EVIL DEAD, THE
EVIL DEAD II
EXORCIST, THE
EXORCIST II: THE HERETIC
FADE TO BLACK
FINAL CONFLICT, THE
FINAL TERROR, THE
FIRESTARTER
FLY, THE (1958)
FLY, THE (1986)
FLY II, THE
FOG, THE
FOOD OF THE GODS
FRANKENSTEIN
FRANKENSTEIN MEETS THE WOLF MAN
FREAKS
FRIDAY THE 13TH
FRIDAY THE 13TH, PART 2
FRIDAY THE 13TH, PART 3
FRIDAY THE 13TH—THE FINAL CHAPTER
FRIDAY THE 13TH PART V: A NEW BEGINNING

FRIDAY THE 13TH PART 6: JASON LIVES
FRIDAY THE 13TH PART VII—THE NEW BLOOD
FRIGHT NIGHT
FRIGHT NIGHT II
FROGS
FROM BEYOND
FROM BEYOND THE GRAVE
FULL MOON HIGH
FUNERAL HOME
FUNHOUSE, THE
GATE, THE
GHOST STORY
GHOULIES
GHOULIES II
GIRLS NIGHT OUT
GOD TOLD ME TO
GRADUATION DAY
HALLOWEEN
HALLOWEEN II
HALLOWEEN III: SEASON OF THE WITCH
HALLOWEEN IV: THE RETURN OF MICHAEL MYERS
HAND, THE
HAPPY BIRTHDAY TO ME
HAUNTED PALACE, THE
HAUNTING, THE
HAUNTING OF JULIA, THE
HEARSE, THE
HE KNOWS YOU'RE ALONE
HELLBOUND: HELLRAISER II
HELL COMES TO FROGTOWN
HELL NIGHT
HELLO MARY LOU: PROM NIGHT II
HELLRAISER
HILLS HAVE EYES, THE
HILLS HAVE EYES PART II, THE
HORROR OF DRACULA
HORROR OF FRANKENSTEIN, THE
HOUSE
HOUSE II: THE SECOND STORY
HOUSE OF THE LONG SHADOWS
HOUSE OF WAX
HOUSE ON HAUNTED HILL
HOUSE ON SORORITY ROW, THE
HOUSE THAT DRIPPED BLOOD, THE
HOUSE WHERE EVIL DWELLS, THE
HOWLING, THE
HOWLING II: YOUR SISTER IS A WEREWOLF
HOWLING III: THE MARSUPIALS
HUMANOIDS FROM THE DEEP
HUMONGOUS
HUNGER, THE
HUSH . . . HUSH, SWEET CHARLOTTE
IGOR AND THE LUNATICS
INCUBUS, THE
INITIATION, THE
INVASION OF THE FLESH HUNTERS
INVISIBLE MAN, THE
ISLAND OF DR. MOREAU, THE
ISLE OF THE DEAD
IT LIVES AGAIN
IT'S ALIVE
IT'S ALIVE III: ISLAND OF THE ALIVE
I WALKED WITH A ZOMBIE
I WAS A TEENAGE ZOMBIE
JESSE JAMES MEETS FRANKENSTEIN'S DAUGHTER
KEEP, THE
KILLER PARTY
KINDRED, THE
KISS, THE
LAIR OF THE WHITE WORM, THE
LAST HOUSE ON THE LEFT, THE
LEGACY, THE
LEGEND OF BOGGY CREEK, THE
LEGEND OF HELL HOUSE, THE
LINK
LITTLE SHOP OF HORRORS, THE
LOST BOYS, THE
MADHOUSE
MANIAC COP
MANITOU, THE
MASQUE OF THE RED DEATH, THE
MAXIMUM OVERDRIVE
MEPHISTO WALTZ, THE
MIND KILLER

MONKEY SHINES: AN EXPERIMENT IN FEAR
MONSTER IN THE CLOSET
MONSTER SQUAD, THE
MORTUARY
MOTEL HELL
MUMMY, THE (1932)
MUMMY, THE (1959)
MUTANT
MUTILATOR, THE
MY BLOODY VALENTINE
NATIONAL LAMPOON'S CLASS REUNION
NEAR DARK
NECROPOLIS
NEON MANIACS
NIGHTMARE ON ELM STREET, A
NIGHTMARE ON ELM STREET, PART 2, A: FREDDY'S
  REVENGE
NIGHTMARE ON ELM STREET 3: DREAM WARRIORS, A
NIGHTMARE ON ELM STREET 4, A: THE DREAM MASTER
NIGHTMARES
NIGHT OF THE CREEPS
NIGHT OF THE LIVING DEAD
NIGHT SCHOOL
NIGHTWING
NOSFERATU, THE VAMPYRE
OBLONG BOX, THE
OF UNKNOWN ORIGIN
OMEN, THE
ONE DARK NIGHT
OTHER, THE
PAPERHOUSE
PARASITE
PARENTS
PHANTASM
PHANTASM II
PHANTOM OF THE OPERA
PIECES
PIRANHA
PIRANHA II: THE SPAWNING
PIT AND THE PENDULUM, THE
POLTERGEIST
POLTERGEIST II: THE OTHER SIDE
POLTERGEIST III
POWER, THE
PREMATURE BURIAL, THE
PREY, THE
PRINCE OF DARKNESS
PRISON
PROM NIGHT
PROPHECY
PROWLER, THE
PSYCHO II
PSYCHO III
PSYCHO GIRLS
PUMPKINHEAD
Q
RABID
RAVEN, THE (1935)
RAVEN, THE (1963)
RAWHEAD REX
RAZORBACK
RE-ANIMATOR
RETURN OF THE FLY
RETURN OF THE LIVING DEAD, THE
RETURN OF THE LIVING DEAD II, THE
RETURN TO HORROR HIGH
RETURN TO SALEM'S LOT
ROSEMARY'S BABY
SALEM'S LOT: THE MOVIE
SATURDAY THE 14TH
SCALPEL
SCANNERS
SCARED STIFF
SCARS OF DRACULA
SCREAM AND SCREAM AGAIN
SENTINEL, THE
SEVENTH SIGN, THE
SHADOWS RUN BLACK
SHINING, THE
SILENT MADNESS
SILENT NIGHT, DEADLY NIGHT
SILENT NIGHT, DEADLY NIGHT PART 2
SILENT SCREAM
SILVER BULLET

SISTERS
SLAUGHTER HIGH
SLAUGHTERHOUSE
SLEEPAWAY CAMP
SLUMBER PARTY MASSACRE
SLUMBER PARTY MASSACRE PART II
SON OF DRACULA
SON OF FRANKENSTEIN
SORORITY HOUSE MASSACRE
SPASMS
SPELLBINDER
SPLATTER UNIVERSITY
SQUIRM
STRAIT-JACKET
STRANGE BEHAVIOR
STREET TRASH
STUFF, THE
SUPERSTITION
SWARM, THE
SWEET 16
TALES OF TERROR
TENTACLES
TERROR IN THE AISLES
TERROR TRAIN
TERRORVISION
TEXAS CHAINSAW MASSACRE, THE
TEXAS CHAINSAW MASSACRE PART 2
THEATRE OF BLOOD
THEY CAME FROM WITHIN
THING WITH TWO HEADS, THE
13 GHOSTS
TIME WALKER
TOMB OF LIGEIA, THE
TORTURE GARDEN
TOURIST TRAP
TRANSMUTATIONS
TRANSYLVANIA 6-5000
TRICK OR TREAT
TRICK OR TREATS
TROLL
UNHOLY, THE
UNSEEN, THE
UP FROM THE DEPTHS
VAMP
VAMPIRE AT MIDNIGHT
VAMPIRE'S KISS
VAMPYR
VELVET VAMPIRE, THE
VIDEO DEAD, THE
VIDEODROME
VINDICATOR, THE
VISITING HOURS
VISITOR, THE
WAXWORK
WHAT EVER HAPPENED TO BABY JANE?
WHO SLEW AUNTIE ROO?
WICKED STEPMOTHER
WICKER MAN, THE
WILLARD
WITCHBOARD
WOLFEN
WOLF MAN, THE
WOLFMAN
WRAITH, THE
ZOMBIE ISLAND MASSACRE

MARTIAL ARTS

AMERICAN NINJA
AMERICAN NINJA 2: THE CONFRONTATION
BIG BRAWL, THE
BLACK BELT JONES
BLOODSPORT
BUSHIDO BLADE, THE
CHINESE CONNECTION, THE
CIRCLE OF IRON
ENTER THE DRAGON
ENTER THE NINJA
EYE FOR AN EYE, AN
FISTS OF FURY
FORCED VENGEANCE
FORCE OF ONE, A
GAME OF DEATH
GOOD GUYS WEAR BLACK
GYMKATA

KILL AND KILL AGAIN
KILL OR BE KILLED
LIGHTNING SWORDS OF DEATH
9 DEATHS OF THE NINJA
NINJA III—THE DOMINATION
NINJA TURF
NO RETREAT, NO SURRENDER
OCTAGON, THE
PRAY FOR DEATH
RAGE OF HONOR
RETURN OF THE DRAGON
REVENGE OF THE NINJA
SHOGUN ASSASSIN
SLAUGHTER IN SAN FRANCISCO
STRANGER AND THE GUNFIGHTER, THE

MUSIC

AMERICAN HOT WAX
BETTE MIDLER: DIVINE MADNESS
BIRD
BRING ON THE NIGHT
BUDDY HOLLY STORY, THE
CARMEN (1984)
COAL MINER'S DAUGHTER
COMPLEAT BEATLES, THE
CONCERT FOR BANGLADESH, THE
DECLINE OF WESTERN CIVILIZATION, THE
DECLINE OF WESTERN CIVILIZATION PART II, THE: THE
  METAL YEARS
ELVIS: THAT'S THE WAY IT IS
FROM MAO TO MOZART: ISAAC STERN IN CHINA
GENE KRUPA STORY, THE
GIMME SHELTER
GOSPEL
GREAT CARUSO, THE
HAIL! HAIL! ROCK 'N' ROLL
KIDS ARE ALRIGHT, THE
KNIGHTS OF THE CITY
LA BAMBA
LAST WALTZ, THE
LA TRAVIATA
LET IT BE
LET'S SPEND THE NIGHT TOGETHER
LISZTOMANIA
MAGIC FLUTE, THE
MAHLER
MONTEREY POP
OTELLO
PINK FLOYD: THE WALL
QUADROPHENIA
'ROUND MIDNIGHT
SAY AMEN, SOMEBODY
SECRET POLICEMAN'S OTHER BALL, THE
SID AND NANCY
SIGN O' THE TIMES
SONG OF NORWAY
SONG TO REMEMBER, A
SPRING SYMPHONY
STOP MAKING SENSE
SWEET DREAMS
THAT WAS ROCK (THE T.A.M.I./T.N.T. SHOW)
U2: RATTLE AND HUM
WOODSTOCK
YOUR CHEATIN' HEART

MUSICAL

ABSOLUTE BEGINNERS
ALICE'S RESTAURANT
ALL THAT JAZZ
AMERICAN IN PARIS, AN
AMERICAN TAIL, AN
ANCHORS AWEIGH
ANNIE
ANNIE GET YOUR GUN
ARIA
BABES IN ARMS
BACK TO THE BEACH
BAND WAGON, THE
BARKLEYS OF BROADWAY, THE
BEACH PARTY
BEATLEMANIA
BEAT STREET
BELLE OF NEW YORK, THE
BELLS ARE RINGING
BENNY GOODMAN STORY, THE

BEST FOOT FORWARD
BEST LITTLE WHOREHOUSE IN TEXAS, THE
BILLY ROSE'S JUMBO
BLUE HAWAII
BLUE SKIES
BODY ROCK
BOY FRIEND, THE
BREAKIN'
BREAKING GLASS
BREAKIN' 2: ELECTRIC BOOGALOO
BRIGADOON
BROADWAY MELODY OF 1938
BROADWAY MELODY OF 1940
BYE BYE BIRDIE
CABARET
CABIN IN THE SKY
CALAMITY JANE
CAMELOT
CAN-CAN
CAN'T STOP THE MUSIC
CAREFREE
CARMEN JONES
CAROUSEL
CHITTY CHITTY BANG BANG
CHORUS LINE, A
CHRISTMAS THAT ALMOST WASN'T, THE
CLAMBAKE
CURLY TOP
DADDY LONG LEGS
DAMES
DAMN YANKEES
DAMSEL IN DISTRESS, A
DANCING LADY
DANGEROUS WHEN WET
DARLING LILI
DEEP IN MY HEART
DIAMOND HORSESHOE
DIMPLES
DOCTOR DOLITTLE
DOUBLE TROUBLE
DU BARRY WAS A LADY
EASTER PARADE
EASY COME, EASY GO
FABULOUS DORSEYS, THE
FAME
FIDDLER ON THE ROOF
FINIAN'S RAINBOW
FIVE PENNIES, THE
FLOWER DRUM SONG
FLYING DOWN TO RIO
FOLLOW THAT DREAM
FOLLOW THE FLEET
FOOTLIGHT PARADE
FOR ME AND MY GAL
FORTY-SECOND STREET
FRANKIE AND JOHNNY
FUN IN ACAPULCO
FUNNY FACE
FUNNY GIRL
FUNNY LADY
GAY DIVORCEE, THE
GENTLEMEN PREFER BLONDES
G.I. BLUES
GIGI
GIRL CRAZY
GIRL HAPPY
GIRLS! GIRLS! GIRLS!
GIRLS JUST WANT TO HAVE FUN
GIVE MY REGARDS TO BROAD STREET
GLENN MILLER STORY, THE
GOLD DIGGERS OF 1933
GOOD NEWS
GREASE
GREASE 2
GREAT ZIEGFELD, THE
GUYS AND DOLLS
GYPSY
HAIR
HANS CHRISTIAN ANDERSEN
HAPPIEST MILLIONAIRE, THE
HARD DAY'S NIGHT, A
HARDER THEY COME, THE
HARUM SCARUM
HARVEY GIRLS, THE

HEAVENLY BODIES
HELLO, DOLLY
HELP!
HIGH SOCIETY
HOLIDAY INN
HUCKLEBERRY FINN (1974)
IN THE GOOD OLD SUMMERTIME
IT HAPPENED AT THE WORLD'S FAIR
IT'S ALWAYS FAIR WEATHER
JAILHOUSE ROCK
JAZZ SINGER, THE (1927)
JAZZ SINGER, THE (1980)
JESUS CHRIST SUPERSTAR
JOLSON SINGS AGAIN
JOLSON STORY, THE
KID FROM BROOKLYN, THE
KID GALAHAD
KID MILLIONS
KING AND I, THE
KING CREOLE
KISMET
KISSIN' COUSINS
KISS ME, KATE
KNOCK ON WOOD
KRUSH GROOVE
LADY SINGS THE BLUES
LES GIRLS
LET'S MAKE LOVE
LILI
LITTLE NIGHT MUSIC, A
LITTLE PRINCE, THE
LITTLE SHOP OF HORRORS
LITTLEST REBEL, THE
LOVE ME OR LEAVE ME
LOVING YOU
MAME
MAN OF LA MANCHA
MARY POPPINS
MEET ME IN ST. LOUIS
MUSIC MAN, THE
MY FAIR LADY
NEW YORK, NEW YORK
NIGHT AND DAY
NIGHTS IN WHITE SATIN
OKLAHOMA!
OLD CURIOSITY SHOP, THE
OLIVER!
ON A CLEAR DAY YOU CAN SEE FOREVER
ON THE TOWN
PAINT YOUR WAGON
PAJAMA GAME, THE
PAL JOEY
PARADISE, HAWAIIAN STYLE
PENNIES FROM HEAVEN
PETE'S DRAGON
PHANTOM OF THE PARADISE
PIRATE, THE
PIRATE MOVIE, THE
PIRATES OF PENZANCE, THE
POOR LITTLE RICH GIRL
POPEYE
PRESENTING LILY MARS
PRODUCERS, THE
PURPLE RAIN
RAPPIN'
REBECCA OF SUNNYBROOK FARM
RHINESTONE
ROBERTA
ROBIN AND THE SEVEN HOODS
ROCK AND ROLL HIGH SCHOOL
ROCK AROUND THE CLOCK
ROCK, ROCK, ROCK
ROCKY HORROR PICTURE SHOW, THE
ROMAN SCANDALS
ROSE, THE
ROSE MARIE
ROUSTABOUT
ROYAL WEDDING
RUDE BOY
RUMPELSTILTSKIN
SCENES FROM THE GOLDMINE
SCHOOL DAZE
SCROOGE
SEVEN BRIDES FOR SEVEN BROTHERS

SEVEN LITTLE FOYS, THE
1776
SGT. PEPPER'S LONELY HEARTS CLUB BAND
SHALL WE DANCE
SHOCK TREATMENT
SHOW BOAT (1936)
SHOW BOAT (1951)
SILK STOCKINGS
SINGIN' IN THE RAIN
SKY'S THE LIMIT, THE
SLIPPER AND THE ROSE, THE
SONG IS BORN, A
SONG OF THE SOUTH
SONGWRITER
SOUND OF MUSIC, THE
SOUTH PACIFIC
SPEEDWAY
STAGE DOOR CANTEEN
STAR IS BORN, A (1954)
STAR IS BORN, A (1976)
STARSTRUCK
STATE FAIR
STORMY WEATHER
STORY OF VERNON AND IRENE CASTLE, THE
STRIKE UP THE BAND
SUMMER STOCK
SWEET CHARITY
SWING TIME
TAKE ME OUT TO THE BALL GAME
THANK GOD IT'S FRIDAY
THANK YOUR LUCKY STARS
THAT'S ENTERTAINMENT!
THAT'S ENTERTAINMENT, PART 2
THERE'S NO BUSINESS LIKE SHOW BUSINESS
THIS IS THE ARMY
THOROUGHLY MODERN MILLIE
THOUSANDS CHEER
THREE LITTLE WORDS
THREEPENNY OPERA, THE
TICKLE ME
TILL THE CLOUDS ROLL BY
TOMMY
TOM SAWYER
TOP HAT
TRUE STORIES
TWO HUNDRED MOTELS
UMBRELLAS OF CHERBOURG, THE
UNSINKABLE MOLLY BROWN, THE
VICTOR/VICTORIA
VIVA LAS VEGAS
WEST SIDE STORY
WHITE CHRISTMAS
WILD IN THE COUNTRY
WILLY WONKA AND THE CHOCOLATE FACTORY
WIZ, THE
WONDERFUL WORLD OF THE BROTHERS GRIMM, THE
WORDS AND MUSIC
XANADU
YANKEE DOODLE DANDY
YENTL
YOLANDA AND THE THIEF
YOU'LL NEVER GET RICH
YOUNG AT HEART
YOUNG MAN WITH A HORN
YOU WERE NEVER LOVELIER
ZACHARIAH
ZIEGFELD FOLLIES
ZOOT SUIT

MYSTERY-SUSPENSE
ADVENTURES OF SHERLOCK HOLMES, THE
AFTER THE THIN MAN
AGAINST ALL ODDS
AGENCY
AMATEUR, THE
AMBASSADOR, THE
AMERICAN GIGOLO
ANDERSON TAPES, THE
AND SOON THE DARKNESS
AND THEN THERE WERE NONE
ANGEL HEART
ANOTHER THIN MAN
APOLOGY
APPOINTMENT WITH DEATH

ARABESQUE
AROUSERS, THE
BACKFIRE
BEDROOM WINDOW, THE
BIG CLOCK, THE
BIG EASY, THE
BIG FIX, THE
BIG HEAT, THE
BIG SLEEP, THE (1946)
BIG SLEEP, THE (1978)
BIG STEAL, THE
BIRDS, THE
BLACK SUNDAY (1977)
BLACK WIDOW
BLIND ALLEY
BLIND DATE (1984)
BLINDSIDE
BLOODLINE
BLOOD LINK
BLOOD SIMPLE
BLOW OUT
BLOW-UP
BLUE CITY
BLUE VELVET
BODY DOUBLE
BODY HEAT
BOYS FROM BRAZIL, THE
BRAINWAVES
BRASS TARGET
BUNNY LAKE IS MISSING
CALL ME
CAT AND MOUSE
CAT AND THE CANARY, THE
CHARADE
CLAIRVOYANT, THE
CLUE
COLD ROOM, THE
COLLECTOR, THE
COMA
COMPROMISING POSITIONS
COP
CRIMINAL LAW
CUTTER'S WAY
DARK CORNER, THE
DARK PASSAGE
DEADLY ILLUSION
DEADLY STRANGERS
DEAD OF WINTER
DEAD RECKONING
DEAD ZONE, THE
DEATH ON THE NILE
DEATHTRAP
DEATH VALLEY
DEFENCE OF THE REALM
DESPERATE HOURS, THE
DETECTIVE, THE
DIABOLIQUE
DIAL M FOR MURDER
DIVA
D.O.A. (1949)
D.O.A. (1988)
DOMINO PRINCIPLE, THE
DOUBLE INDEMNITY
DRESSED TO KILL (1946)
DRESSED TO KILL (1980)
DROWNING POOL, THE
EAGLE HAS LANDED, THE
EMIL AND THE DETECTIVES
ESCAPE FROM ALCATRAZ
EVIL UNDER THE SUN
EXPOSED
EYE OF THE NEEDLE
EYES OF A STRANGER
EYES OF LAURA MARS, THE
EYEWITNESS
FALCON'S BROTHER, THE
FALCON TAKES OVER, THE
FAMILY PLOT
FAN, THE
FAREWELL, MY LOVELY
FEAR
FEAR IN THE NIGHT
FFOLKES
52 PICK-UP

FLOWERS IN THE ATTIC
FOREIGN CORRESPONDENT
FRANTIC
FRENZY
FURY, THE
GASLIGHT
GETTING EVEN
GOLDEN RENDEZVOUS
GORKY PARK
GRAY LADY DOWN
GREEN FOR DANGER
GROUNDSTAR CONSPIRACY, THE
GROUND ZERO
HAMMETT
HARD WAY, THE
HARPER
HELLHOLE
HINDENBURG, THE
HIT, THE
HITCHER, THE
HOLCROFT COVENANT, THE
HONEYMOON KILLERS, THE
HOT CHILD IN THE CITY
HOUND OF THE BASKERVILLES, THE (1939)
HOUND OF THE BASKERVILLES, THE (1959)
HOUSEKEEPER, THE
HOUSE OF FEAR, THE
HOUSE OF GAMES
HOUSE OF THE RISING SUN
HOUSE ON CARROLL STREET, THE
HUSTLE
I CONFESS
IN THE HEAT OF THE NIGHT
INTO THE NIGHT
I SEE A DARK STRANGER
ISLAND, THE
JACK'S BACK
JAGGED EDGE
JANUARY MAN, THE
JOHNNY ANGEL
JOURNEY INTO FEAR
JULIA AND JULIA
JUMPIN' JACK FLASH
KEEPING TRACK
KILLING TIME, THE
KISS ME DEADLY
KLUTE
LADY BEWARE
LADY FROM SHANGHAI, THE
LADY IN A CAGE
LADY IN THE LAKE
LADY IN WHITE
LADY VANISHES, THE
LAGUNA HEAT
LAST EMBRACE
LAST INNOCENT MAN, THE
LAST OF SHEILA, THE
LAST WAVE, THE
LATE SHOW, THE
LAURA
LEGAL EAGLES
LEOPARD MAN, THE
LIST OF ADRIAN MESSENGER, THE
LITTLE GIRL WHO LIVES DOWN THE LANE, THE
LITTLE NIKITA
LONG DARK NIGHT, THE
LOOKER
MAGIC
MALTESE FALCON, THE
MANCHURIAN CANDIDATE, THE
MANIAC
MAN WHO KNEW TOO MUCH, THE (1934)
MAN WHO KNEW TOO MUCH, THE (1956)
MARATHON MAN
MARLOWE
MAROONED
MASQUERADE
MEDUSA TOUCH, THE
MIDNIGHT CROSSING
MIDNIGHT LACE
MIRROR CRACK'D, THE
MOON-SPINNERS, THE
MORNING AFTER, THE
MOST DANGEROUS GAME, THE

MURDER BY DECREE
MURDER, MY SWEET
NAME OF THE ROSE, THE
NEW KIDS, THE
NIAGARA
NIGHT MOVES
NIGHT OF THE GENERALS
NIGHT STALKER, THE
NIGHT TRAIN TO MUNICH
NORTH BY NORTHWEST
NOTORIOUS
NO WAY OUT
NO WAY TO TREAT A LADY
NOWHERE TO HIDE
OBSESSION
ODD MAN OUT
OFF LIMITS (1988)
ONE DEADLY SUMMER
ORCA
ORDEAL BY INNOCENCE
OSTERMAN WEEKEND, THE
OUT OF BOUNDS
OUT OF THE PAST
PANIC IN THE STREETS
PARALLAX VIEW, THE
PEARL OF DEATH, THE
PEEPING TOM
PHYSICAL EVIDENCE
PLAIN CLOTHES
PLAY MISTY FOR ME
POSITIVE I.D.
PRESIDIO, THE
PRETTYKILL
PRETTY POISON
PRIVATE LIFE OF SHERLOCK HOLMES, THE
PSYCHIC KILLER
PSYCHO
PURSUIT TO ALGIERS
REAR WINDOW
REFLECTION OF FEAR, A
REINCARNATION OF PETER PROUD, THE
REPULSION
RETURN TO BOGGY CREEK
RIDER ON THE RAIN
ROAD GAMES
ROPE
ROSARY MURDERS, THE
ROUGH CUT
RUSSIAN ROULETTE
SABOTAGE
SABOTEUR
SAPPHIRE
SCARLET CLAW, THE
SCARLET STREET
SCHIZOID
SCREAM FOR HELP
SEANCE ON A WET AFTERNOON
SECRET AGENT
SEDUCTION, THE
SEE NO EVIL
SENDER, THE
SERPENT AND THE RAINBOW, THE
SEVEN DAYS IN MAY
SEVEN HOURS TO JUDGMENT
SHADOW OF A DOUBT
SHADOW OF THE THIN MAN
SHERLOCK HOLMES AND THE SECRET WEAPON
SHERLOCK HOLMES AND THE SPIDER WOMAN
SHERLOCK HOLMES AND THE VOICE OF TERROR
SHERLOCK HOLMES FACES DEATH
SHERLOCK HOLMES IN WASHINGTON
SILENT PARTNER, THE
SIROCCO
SISTER SISTER
SKIP TRACER
SLAM DANCE
SLEEPING CAR MURDERS, THE
SLEEPING DOGS
SLEUTH
SOLDIER'S STORY, A
SOMEONE TO WATCH OVER ME
SONG OF THE THIN MAN
SORRY, WRONG NUMBER
SPECIAL EFFECTS

SPELLBOUND
SPHINX
SPIRAL STAIRCASE, THE (1946)
SPIRAL STAIRCASE, THE (1975)
STAGE FRIGHT
STEPFATHER, THE
STEPFORD WIVES, THE
STILL OF THE NIGHT
STRANGER, THE
STRANGER IS WATCHING, A
STRANGERS ON A TRAIN
STUDY IN TERROR, A
SUNBURN
SUNSET
SURVIVOR, THE
SUSPECT
SUSPICION
T.A.G.: THE ASSASSINATION GAME
TALL BLOND MAN WITH ONE BLACK SHOE, THE
TARGETS
TATTOO
TENANT, THE
TEN LITTLE INDIANS (1966)
TEN LITTLE INDIANS (1975)
TERMINAL CHOICE
TERROR BY NIGHT
THEY CALL ME MISTER TIBBS!
THEY'RE PLAYING WITH FIRE
THIN MAN, THE
THIN MAN GOES HOME, THE
THIRD MAN, THE
13 RUE MADELEINE
39 STEPS, THE
THIRTY-NINE STEPS, THE
THIS GUN FOR HIRE
THOMAS CROWN AFFAIR, THE
THREE DAYS OF THE CONDOR
TIGHTROPE
TILL DEATH DO US PART
TO LIVE AND DIE IN L.A.
TONY ROME
TOPAZ
TORMENT
TOUCH OF EVIL
TOUGH GUYS DON'T DANCE
TOWN THAT DREADED SUNDOWN, THE
23 PACES TO BAKER STREET
TWO-MINUTE WARNING
VENOM
VERTIGO
WAIT UNTIL DARK
WHAT EVER HAPPENED TO AUNT ALICE?
WHEN A STRANGER CALLS
WHERE ARE THE CHILDREN?
WHISTLE BLOWER, THE
WHITE OF THE EYE
WHO IS KILLING THE GREAT CHEFS OF EUROPE?
WIND, THE
WINDOW, THE
WITCHFIRE
WITHOUT A CLUE
WITNESS FOR THE PROSECUTION
WOMAN IN GREEN, THE
WRONG MAN, THE
YOUNG AND INNOCENT

MFTV (MADE FOR TELEVISION)
ACT OF VENGEANCE
ADAM
ALL THE RIVERS RUN
AMERICAN CHRISTMAS CAROL, AN
ANNE OF GREEN GABLES (1985)
APOLOGY
AS SUMMERS DIE
AUTOBIOGRAPHY OF MISS JANE PITTMAN, THE
BAJA OKLAHOMA
BERLIN ALEXANDERPLATZ
BETWEEN FRIENDS
BILL
BILL ON HIS OWN
BIRTH OF THE BEATLES
BLOOD OF OTHERS, THE
BRIAN'S SONG
BURNING BED, THE

CHRISTMAS TO REMEMBER, A
COLD ROOM, THE
CONSPIRACY: THE TRIAL OF THE CHICAGO 8
CONTROL
DAY AFTER, THE
DEAR AMERICA: LETTERS HOME FROM VIETNAM
DEATH OF A CENTERFOLD: THE DOROTHY STRATTEN
  STORY
DEATH OF A SALESMAN (1985)
DRAW!
DUEL
EARLY FROST, AN
ELVIS
EXECUTIONER'S SONG, THE
FAR PAVILIONS, THE
FINNEGAN BEGIN AGAIN
FLORIDA STRAITS
FORBIDDEN
FORTRESS
GATHERING, THE
GLASS MENAGERIE, THE (1973)
GLITTER DOME, THE
GUARDIAN, THE
GULAG
HALF A LIFETIME
HELTER SKELTER
HOMECOMING, THE
HUCKLEBERRY FINN (1975)
IMPOSSIBLE SPY, THE
INTIMATE CONTACT
INTO THE HOMELAND
JUST ANOTHER MISSING KID
LAGUNA HEAT
LAST INNOCENT MAN, THE
LION OF AFRICA, THE
LONG GONE
LOUISIANA
MANDELA
MAN WHO BROKE 1,000 CHAINS, THE
M*A*S*H: GOODBYE, FAREWELL & AMEN
MIRACLE WORKER, THE (1979)
MUSSOLINI: THE DECLINE AND FALL OF IL DUCE
PARK IS MINE, THE
PLAYING FOR TIME
POLICE SQUAD! HELP WANTED
QUICK AND THE DEAD, THE
RAID ON ENTEBBE
RIGHT OF WAY
ROOTS
SAKHAROV
SEIZE THE DAY
SHOGUN
STREETCAR NAMED DESIRE, A (1984)
SWORD OF GIDEON
SYBIL
TEN FROM YOUR SHOW OF SHOWS
TERRY FOX STORY, THE
THAT WAS ROCK (THE T.A.M.I./T.N.T. SHOW)
TO CATCH A KING
WHO AM I THIS TIME?
YURI NOSENKO, KGB

ROMANCE

AFFAIR TO REMEMBER, AN
ALL THE RIVERS RUN
ALL THIS AND HEAVEN TOO
ALMOST PERFECT AFFAIR, AN
BABY, IT'S YOU
BREAKFAST AT TIFFANY'S
BRIEF ENCOUNTER
BUS STOP
BUSTER AND BILLIE
CAPTIVE HEARTS
CINDERELLA LIBERTY
CONTINENTAL DIVIDE
COUSIN, COUSINE
COUSINS
CROSSING DELANCEY
DIANE
DIRTY DANCING
ELECTRIC DREAMS
ELVIRA MADIGAN
ENDLESS LOVE
FALLING IN LOVE

FAREWELL TO ARMS, A
FAR PAVILIONS, THE
FIRE WITH FIRE
FIRST LOVE
FORTY CARATS
GARDEN OF ALLAH, THE
GHOST AND MRS. MUIR, THE
GIRL IN THE PICTURE, THE
HANOVER STREET
HARD TO HOLD
IF EVER I SEE YOU AGAIN
INDISCREET
INTERMEZZO
IT'S MY TURN
JOHN AND MARY
KENTUCKY
KEY EXCHANGE
LAST TIME I SAW PARIS, THE
LETTER TO BREZHNEV
LITTLE ROMANCE, A
LITTLE SEX, A
LOVE IS A MANY SPLENDORED THING
LOVE LETTERS
LOVE OR MONEY
LOVER COME BACK
LOVESICK
MADE IN HEAVEN
MAN AND A WOMAN, A
MAN AND A WOMAN, A: 20 YEARS LATER
MAN IN LOVE, A
MAYERLING
MOONSTRUCK
MURPHY'S ROMANCE
MYSTIC PIZZA
9½ WEEKS
NOW AND FOREVER
NOW, VOYAGER
OFFICER AND A GENTLEMAN, AN
OLIVER'S STORY
ONCE IN PARIS
ONE FROM THE HEART
ONE WOMAN OR TWO
OVERBOARD
OVER THE BROOKLYN BRIDGE
PILLOW TALK
PRETTY IN PINK
QUIET MAN, THE
RACHEL AND THE STRANGER
ROBIN AND MARIAN
ROMAN HOLIDAY
ROMANTIC COMEDY
ROMEO AND JULIET
ROXANNE
SABRINA
SAME TIME, NEXT YEAR
SANDPIPER, THE
SHOP AROUND THE CORNER, THE
SOLDIER'S TALE, A
SOME GIRLS
SOMETHING SHORT OF PARADISE
SOMEWHERE IN TIME
SPLENDOR IN THE GRASS
STARMAN
STARTING OVER
STAY AS YOU ARE
STEALING HEAVEN
SUMMER LOVERS
SUMMERTIME
SURRENDER
SWEET LIES
TENDER IS THE NIGHT
THEY ALL LAUGHED
THIS PROPERTY IS CONDEMNED
TOMBOY
TOUCH OF CLASS, A
UNBEARABLE LIGHTNESS OF BEING, THE
UNTIL SEPTEMBER
URBAN COWBOY
VALLEY GIRL
VIOLETS ARE BLUE
WALK IN THE SPRING RAIN, A
WALTZ ACROSS TEXAS
WATERLOO BRIDGE
WAY WE WERE, THE

WHO AM I THIS TIME?
WILDROSE
WILLIE AND PHIL
WINTER FLIGHT
WORKING GIRL
WUTHERING HEIGHTS (1939)
WUTHERING HEIGHTS (1971)
YANKS
YOU LIGHT UP MY LIFE

SCI-FI

ADVENTURES OF BUCKAROO BANZAI, THE: ACROSS THE 8TH DIMENSION
ALIEN
ALIEN NATION
ALIEN PREDATOR
ALIENS
ALTERED STATES
ANDROID
ANDROMEDA STRAIN, THE
ANGRY RED PLANET, THE
ANNA TO THE INFINITE POWER
ATTACK OF THE 50-FOOT WOMAN
AURORA ENCOUNTER, THE
BACK TO THE FUTURE
BARBARELLA
BATTERIES NOT INCLUDED
BATTLE BEYOND THE STARS
BATTLE FOR THE PLANET OF THE APES
BATTLESTAR GALACTICA
BENEATH THE PLANET OF THE APES
BLACK HOLE, THE
BLADE RUNNER
BLAST OFF
BLOB, THE (1958)
BLOB, THE (1988)
BOY AND HIS DOG, A
BRAINSTORM
BRAIN THAT WOULDN'T DIE, THE
BRAZIL
BROTHER FROM ANOTHER PLANET, THE
CAPRICORN ONE
CITY LIMITS
CLOSE ENCOUNTERS OF THE THIRD KIND
CONQUEST OF THE PLANET OF THE APES
COUNTDOWN
CREATURE
DALEKS—INVASION EARTH 2150 A.D.
DAMNATION ALLEY
DARK STAR
D.A.R.Y.L.
DAY THE EARTH CAUGHT FIRE, THE
DAY THE EARTH STOOD STILL, THE
DEATHSPORT
DEF-CON 4
DEMON SEED
DESTINATION MOON
DONOVAN'S BRAIN
DREAMSCAPE
DUNE
DUNGEONMASTER, THE
EARTH VS. THE FLYING SAUCERS
EMBRYO
EMPIRE OF THE ANTS
EMPIRE STRIKES BACK, THE
ENEMY MINE
ESCAPE FROM NEW YORK
ESCAPE FROM THE PLANET OF THE APES
EXPLORERS
FAHRENHEIT 451
FANTASTIC VOYAGE
FINAL COUNTDOWN, THE
FIRST MAN INTO SPACE
FIRST MEN IN THE MOON
FIVE MILLION YEARS TO EARTH
FLASH GORDON
FLIGHT OF THE NAVIGATOR, THE
FLY, THE (1958)
FLY, THE (1986)
FORBIDDEN PLANET
FUTURE-KILL
FUTUREWORLD
GALAXINA
GALAXY OF TERROR

GODZILLA, KING OF THE MONSTERS
GODZILLA VS. MOTHRA
GODZILLA 1985
HIDDEN, THE
ICE PIRATES, THE
ILLUSTRATED MAN, THE
I MARRIED A MONSTER FROM OUTER SPACE
IMPULSE
INCREDIBLE SHRINKING MAN, THE
INVADERS FROM MARS (1953)
INVADERS FROM MARS (1986)
INVASION OF THE BEE GIRLS
INVASION OF THE BODY SNATCHERS (1956)
INVASION OF THE BODY SNATCHERS (1978)
IT CAME FROM BENEATH THE SEA
IT CAME FROM OUTER SPACE
JOURNEY TO THE CENTER OF THE EARTH
JOURNEY TO THE FAR SIDE OF THE SUN
JOURNEY TO THE 7TH PLANET
KING KONG (1933)
KING KONG (1976)
KING KONG LIVES
LAST STARFIGHTER, THE
LIFEFORCE
LIQUID SKY
LOGAN'S RUN
LOST EMPIRE, THE
LOST WORLD, THE
MAN WHO FELL TO EARTH, THE
METALSTORM: THE DESTRUCTION OF JARED-SYN
METROPOLIS
MIGHTY JOE YOUNG
MIRACLE MILE
MOON PILOT
MOTHRA
MY SCIENCE PROJECT
MY STEPMOTHER IS AN ALIEN
NIGHT FLYERS
NIGHT OF THE COMET
OMEGA MAN, THE
OUTLAND
PHASE IV
PHILADELPHIA EXPERIMENT, THE
PLANET OF BLOOD
PLANET OF THE APES
PLANET OF THE VAMPIRES
PLAN 9 FROM OUTER SPACE
PREDATOR
QUATERMASS CONCLUSION, THE
RADIOACTIVE DREAMS
REMOTE CONTROL
RETURN, THE
RETURN OF THE JEDI
ROBINSON CRUSOE ON MARS
ROBOCOP
ROBOT MONSTER
ROCKY HORROR PICTURE SHOW, THE
RODAN
RUNAWAY
RUNNING MAN, THE
SANTA CLAUS CONQUERS THE MARTIANS
SATURN 3
SHORT CIRCUIT
SHORT CIRCUIT II
SILENT RUNNING
SLAUGHTERHOUSE FIVE
SLAVE GIRLS FROM BEYOND INFINITY
SOLARBABIES
SOMETHING WICKED THIS WAY COMES
SOYLENT GREEN
SPACEHUNTER: ADVENTURES IN THE FORBIDDEN ZONE
SPACE RAGE
SPACE RAIDERS
STARCRASH
STAR CRYSTAL
STAR TREK—THE MOTION PICTURE
STAR TREK II: THE WRATH OF KHAN
STAR TREK III: THE SEARCH FOR SPOCK
STAR TREK IV: THE VOYAGE HOME
STAR WARS
STRANDED
STRANGE INVADERS
SWAMP THING
TENTH VICTIM, THE

TERMINAL MAN, THE
TERMINATOR, THE
THEM!
THEY LIVE
THEY SAVED HITLER'S BRAIN
THING, THE (1951)
THING, THE (1982)
THINGS TO COME
THIS ISLAND EARTH
THX 1138
TIME AFTER TIME
TIME GUARDIAN
TIME MACHINE, THE
TIME TRAVELERS, THE
TRANCERS
TRON
20,000 LEAGUES UNDER THE SEA
TWILIGHT ZONE—THE MOVIE
2001: A SPACE ODYSSEY
2010
UFORIA
ULTIMATE WARRIOR, THE
VILLAGE OF THE DAMNED
VILLAGE OF THE GIANTS
VIRUS
VOYAGE TO THE BOTTOM OF THE SEA
WARNING SIGN
WAR OF THE WORLDS, THE
WARRIOR OF THE LOST WORLD
WARRIORS OF THE WASTELAND
WATCHERS
WAVELENGTH
WELCOME TO BLOOD CITY
WESTWORLD
WHEN WORLDS COLLIDE
WIRED TO KILL
WITHOUT WARNING
WORLD GONE WILD
X—THE MAN WITH X-RAY EYES
XTRO
YOR, THE HUNTER FROM THE FUTURE
ZARDOZ
ZONE TROOPERS

SEX

ANGEL OF H.E.A.T.
BLACK EMANUELLE
BOARDING SCHOOL
CALIGULA
CATHERINE & CO.
EMMANUELLE
GOODBYE EMMANUELLE
HAPPY HOOKER, THE
MALIBU EXPRESS
NEW YORK NIGHTS
PREPPIES
R.S.V.P.
SCREEN TEST
SENSUOUS NURSE, THE
SEX THROUGH A WINDOW
TIGERS IN LIPSTICK

SPORTS

AMERICAN ANTHEM
BALTIMORE BULLET, THE
BANG THE DRUM SLOWLY
BEAR, THE
BELOW THE BELT
BODY AND SOUL (1947)
BODY AND SOUL (1981)
BORN TO RACE
BULL DURHAM
CHAMPION
CHAMPIONS
CHARIOTS OF FIRE
DOWNHILL RACER
DREAMER
EIGHT MEN OUT
FEAR STRIKES OUT
FIRE AND ICE (1987)
GENTLEMAN JIM
GOLDEN BOY
GREASED LIGHTNING
GREATEST, THE
HEART LIKE A WHEEL

JIM THORPE—ALL-AMERICAN
KNUTE ROCKNE—ALL AMERICAN
LAST AMERICAN HERO, THE
LAST FIGHT, THE
LONGEST YARD, THE
NATURAL, THE
NORTH DALLAS FORTY
OLYMPIA
OVER THE TOP
PAPER LION
PERSONAL BEST
PHAR LAP
PRIDE OF THE YANKEES, THE
RAGING BULL
REQUIEM FOR A HEAVYWEIGHT
ROCKY
ROCKY II
ROCKY III
ROCKY IV
RUNNING BRAVE
SEMI-TOUGH
SET-UP, THE
SILVER DREAM RACER
SLAP SHOT
SOMEBODY UP THERE LIKES ME
SPIKER
SPLIT DECISIONS
SPRING FEVER
STREETS OF GOLD
TAKE DOWN
THIS SPORTING LIFE
TOKYO OLYMPIAD
VISION QUEST
WINNERS TAKE ALL
WINNING
YOUNGBLOOD

WAR

AIR FORCE
ALL QUIET ON THE WESTERN FRONT
ANZIO
ATTACK FORCE Z
BACK TO BATAAN
BATAAN
BATTLE CRY
BATTLE OF BRITAIN
BATTLE OF THE BULGE
BAT 21
BEAST, THE
BELL FOR ADANO, A
BIG RED ONE, THE
BITTER VICTORY
BLUE MAX, THE
BOYS IN COMPANY C, THE
BREAKTHROUGH
BRIDGE ON THE RIVER KWAI, THE
BRIDGE TOO FAR, A
CATCH-22
COMMANDOS STRIKE AT DAWN, THE
CRUEL SEA, THE
DAM BUSTERS, THE
DAMN THE DEFIANT!
DAS BOOT (THE BOAT)
DAWN PATROL, THE
DESERT FOX, THE
DESTINATION TOKYO
DIRTY DOZEN, THE
EDGE OF DARKNESS
ENEMY BELOW, THE
FLYING LEATHERNECKS
FLYING TIGERS
FORCE 10 FROM NAVARONE
FROM HERE TO ETERNITY
FULL METAL JACKET
GALLIPOLI
GO TELL THE SPARTANS
GREAT ESCAPE, THE
GREATEST BATTLE, THE
GREEN BERETS, THE
GUADALCANAL DIARY
GUNS OF NAVARONE, THE
HAMBURGER HILL
HANOI HILTON, THE
HEARTBREAK RIDGE

HELLCATS OF THE NAVY
HELL IN THE PACIFIC
HIGHEST HONOR, THE
HOME OF THE BRAVE
IN WHICH WE SERVE
IRON TRIANGLE, THE
JOHNNY GOT HIS GUN
KELLY'S HEROES
KING RAT
LIGHTHORSEMEN, THE
LONGEST DAY, THE
LOST PATROL, THE
M*A*S*H
MIDWAY
NAKED AND THE DEAD, THE
NIGHT OF THE GENERALS
NORTHERN PURSUIT
OBJECTIVE, BURMA!
PATHS OF GLORY
PLATOON
PLATOON LEADER
PORK CHOP HILL
P.O.W. THE ESCAPE
RAID ON ROMMEL
RED BADGE OF COURAGE, THE
RETURN FROM THE RIVER KWAI
RUN SILENT, RUN DEEP
SAHARA (1943)
SANDS OF IWO JIMA, THE
SECRET WAR OF HARRY FRIGG, THE
THEY WERE EXPENDABLE
THIRTY SECONDS OVER TOKYO
TOBRUK
TOO LATE THE HERO
TORA! TORA! TORA!
TWELVE O'CLOCK HIGH
VICTORY
VON RYAN'S EXPRESS
WALK IN THE SUN, A
WAR AND LOVE
WAR LOVER, THE
WHERE EAGLES DARE
WINGS
WOODEN HORSE, THE

WESTERN

ALAMO, THE
ALONG CAME JONES
ALONG THE GREAT DIVIDE
ALVAREZ KELLY
ANGEL AND THE BADMAN
ANNIE OAKLEY
APACHE
APPALOOSA, THE
BAD COMPANY
BALLAD OF CABLE HOGUE, THE
BALLAD OF GREGORIO CORTEZ, THE
BANDOLERO!
BARBAROSA
BEND OF THE RIVER
BIG COUNTRY, THE
BIG JAKE
BIG SKY, THE
BITE THE BULLET
BLOOD ON THE MOON
BRAVADOS, THE
BREAKHEART PASS
BROKEN ARROW
BROKEN LANCE
BUCK AND THE PREACHER
BUFFALO BILL AND THE INDIANS, OR SITTING BULL'S
  HISTORY LESSON
BUTCH AND SUNDANCE: THE EARLY DAYS
BUTCH CASSIDY AND THE SUNDANCE KID
CAHILL—U.S. MARSHALL
CARSON CITY
CAT BALLOU
CATTLE ANNIE AND LITTLE BRITCHES
CATTLE QUEEN OF MONTANA
CHEYENNE AUTUMN
CHINO
CHISUM
COMANCHEROS, THE
COMES A HORSEMAN

COWBOYS, THE
CULPEPPER CATTLE COMPANY, THE
DESTRY RIDES AGAIN
DODGE CITY
DRAW!
DUCK, YOU SUCKER!
DUEL AT DIABLO
DUEL IN THE SUN
EL CONDOR
EL DORADO
ESCAPE FROM FORT BRAVO
FAR COUNTRY, THE
FASTEST GUN ALIVE, THE
FIGHTING KENTUCKIAN, THE
FIRECREEK
FISTFUL OF DOLLARS, A
FIVE CARD STUD
FLAMING STAR
FOR A FEW DOLLARS MORE
FORT APACHE
FOUR FOR TEXAS
FRISCO KID, THE
FROM NOON TILL THREE
GOOD, THE BAD, AND THE UGLY, THE
GREAT NORTHFIELD, MINNESOTA RAID, THE
GREY FOX, THE
GUNFIGHT, A
GUNFIGHT AT THE O.K. CORRAL
GUNFIGHTER, THE
GUN FURY
HANG 'EM HIGH
HEAVEN'S GATE
HIGH NOON
HIGH PLAINS DRIFTER
HOMBRE
HORSE SOLDIERS, THE
HOT LEAD AND COLD FEET
HOUR OF THE GUN
HOW THE WEST WAS WON
JEREMIAH JOHNSON
JESSE JAMES
JESSE JAMES MEETS FRANKENSTEIN'S
  DAUGHTER
JOE KIDD
JOHNNY GUITAR
JUBAL
KENTUCKIAN, THE
LAST TRAIN FROM GUN HILL
LEFT-HANDED GUN, THE
LEGEND OF THE LONE RANGER, THE
LIFE AND TIMES OF JUDGE ROY BEAN, THE
LIGHT IN THE FOREST, THE
LITTLE BIG MAN
LONELY ARE THE BRAVE
LONG RIDERS, THE
LOVE ME TENDER
LUST IN THE DUST
MACKENNA'S GOLD
MAD DOG MORGAN
MAGNIFICENT SEVEN, THE
MAJOR DUNDEE
MAN AND BOY
MAN CALLED HORSE, A
MAN FROM LARAMIE, THE
MANHUNT, THE
MAN WHO LOVED CAT DANCING, THE
MAN WHO SHOT LIBERTY VALANCE, THE
MAN WITHOUT A STAR
McCABE & MRS. MILLER
MISSOURI BREAKS, THE
MONTE WALSH
MOUNTAIN MEN, THE
MY DARLING CLEMENTINE
NAKED SPUR, THE
NEVADA SMITH
NORTH TO ALASKA
OKLAHOMA KID, THE
ONCE UPON A TIME IN THE WEST
ONE-EYED JACKS
100 RIFLES
OUTLAW, THE
OUTLAW JOSEY WALES, THE
OX-BOW INCIDENT, THE
PALEFACE, THE

PALE RIDER
PAT GARRETT AND BILLY THE KID
PLAINSMAN, THE
POCKET MONEY
PROFESSIONALS, THE
PROUD REBEL, THE
QUICK AND THE DEAD, THE
RANCHO DELUXE
RANCHO NOTORIOUS
RARE BREED, THE
RED-HEADED STRANGER
RED RIVER
RETURN OF A MAN CALLED HORSE
RETURN OF FRANK JAMES, THE
RETURN TO SNOWY RIVER
RIDE IN THE WHIRLWIND
RIDE THE HIGH COUNTRY
RIO BRAVO
RIO CONCHOS
RIO GRANDE
RIO LOBO
RIVER OF NO RETURN
ROOSTER COGBURN
RUSTLERS' RHAPSODY
SAN ANTONIO
SANTA FE TRAIL
SEARCHERS, THE
SERGEANT RUTLEDGE
SERGEANTS 3
SHALAKO
SHANE
SHENANDOAH
SHE WORE A YELLOW RIBBON
SHOOTING, THE
SHOOTIST, THE
SHOOT THE SUN DOWN
SILVERADO
SKIN GAME
SOLDIER BLUE
SONS OF KATIE ELDER, THE
STAGECOACH

STRANGER AND THE GUNFIGHTER, THE
SUPPORT YOUR LOCAL SHERIFF!
TAKE A HARD RIDE
TALL IN THE SADDLE
TALL MEN, THE
TENNESSEE'S PARTNER
TERROR OF TINY TOWN, THE
THERE WAS A CROOKED MAN . . .
THEY CALL ME TRINITY
THEY CAME TO CORDURA
THEY DIED WITH THEIR BOOTS ON
THREE GODFATHERS
3:10 TO YUMA
TIN STAR, THE
TOM HORN
TRAIN ROBBERS, THE
TRIUMPHS OF A MAN CALLED HORSE
TRUE GRIT
TWO MULES FOR SISTER SARA
TWO RODE TOGETHER
ULZANA'S RAID
UNDEFEATED, THE
UNFORGIVEN, THE
UNION PACIFIC
VERA CRUZ
VILLAIN, THE
VIRGINIA CITY
WAGONMASTER
WARLOCK
WAR WAGON, THE
WATERHOLE #3
WAY WEST, THE
WESTERNER, THE
WESTERN UNION
WILD BUNCH, THE
WILD ROVERS
WILL PENNY
WINCHESTER '73
YELLOW SKY
YOUNG GUNS
ZACHARIAH